AMERICAN
DEMOCRACY
NOW

AMERICAN DEMOCRACY NOW

FOURTH EDITION

BRIGID CALLAHAN HARRISON
Montclair State University

JEAN WAHL HARRIS
University of Scranton

MICHELLE D. DEARDORFF
University of Tennessee at Chattanooga

Reinforced Binding

What does it mean?

Since high schools frequently adopt for several years, it is important that a textbook can withstand the wear and tear of usage by multiple students. To ensure durability, McGraw-Hill has elected to manufacture this textbook with a reinforced binding.

McGraw Hill Education

AMERICAN DEMOCRACY NOW, FOURTH EDITION

Published by McGraw-Hill Education, 2 Penn Plaza, New York, NY 10121. Copyright © 2015 by McGraw-Hill Education. All rights reserved. Printed in the United States of America. Previous editions © 2013, 2011, and 2009. No part of this publication may be reproduced or distributed in any form or by any means, or stored in a database or retrieval system, without the prior written consent of McGraw-Hill Education, including, but not limited to, in any network or other electronic storage or transmission, or broadcast for distance learning.

Some ancillaries, including electronic and print components, may not be available to customers outside the United States.

This book is printed on acid-free paper.

1 2 3 4 5 6 7 8 9 0 DOR/DOR 1 0 9 8 7 6 5 4

ISBN 978-0-07-676297-2
MHID 0-07-676297-1

Senior Vice President, Products & Markets: *Kurt L. Strand*
Vice President, General Manager, Products & Markets: Michael Ryan
Vice President, Content Design & Delivery: *Kimberly Meriwether David*
Managing Director: *Gina Boedeker*
Brand Manager: *Laura Wilk*
Director, Product Development: *Meghan Campbell*
Senior Marketing Manager: *April Cole*
Lead Product Developer: *Dawn Groundwater*
Senior Product Developer: *Cara Labell*
Director, Content Design & Delivery: *Terri Schiesl*
Program Manager: *Marianne Musni*
Content Project Managers: *Susan Trentacosti, Katie Klochan, Judi David*
Buyer: *Debra R. Sylvester*
Design: *Debra Kubiak*
Content Licensing Specialists: *John C. Leland, Beth Thole*
Cover Illustration: *McCutcheon Design*
Compositor: *Laserwords Private Limited*
Typeface: *10/12 Times LT Std Roman*
Printer: *R. R. Donnelley*

All credits appearing on page or at the end of the book are considered to be an extension of the copyright page.

Library of Congress Cataloging-in-Publication Data
Harrison, Brigid C., author.
   American democracy now / Brigid Callahan Harrison, Jean Wahl Harris, Michelle D. Deardorff. — Fourth edition.
      pages cm
   Includes bibliographical references and index.
   ISBN 978-0-07-676297-2 (alk. paper)
   1. United States—Politics and government—Textbooks. 2. Political participation—United States—Textbooks.
I. Harris, Jean (Jean Wahl), 1960- author. II. Deardorff, Michelle D. III. Title.
   JK276.H36 2015
   320.473—dc23

2014032197

The Internet addresses listed in the text were accurate at the time of publication. The inclusion of a website does not indicate an endorsement by the authors or McGraw-Hill Education, and McGraw-Hill Education does not guarantee the accuracy of the information presented at these sites.

www.mhhe.com

McGraw-Hill
ONboard™
AP* U.S. GOVERNMENT & POLITICS

AP* Course Prep

ONBoard™ for AP United States Government and Politics is a series of self-paced, online, interactive modules that help students master the skills and content necessary to be successful in AP U.S. Government and Politics coursework and on the AP Exam. Research-based and developed with AP teaching experts, *ONBoard™* features animations, videos, and interactive activities. The content strikes a balance between skills, including analyzing data and political bias, and background knowledge, such as civics and essential AP government vocabulary. Students self-check to ensure comprehension while the pre-test and comprehensive final assessment helps teachers identify skill and knowledge gaps.

connect® plus+

AP* Course Support

Connect Plus is a robust, web-based assignment and assessment platform that helps students to better connect with coursework, teachers, and important concepts they will need to know for success now and in the future. It houses AP Multiple Choice and Free Response test banks that give students additional practice answering AP-style questions. Connect Plus also houses LearnSmart's adaptive study tool and SmartBook's adaptive reading experience for this new edition of *American Democracy Now*.

McGraw-Hill
SCOREboard
AP* U.S. GOVERNMENT & POLITICS

AP* Test Prep

SCOREboard™ AP United States Government and Politics is the first Advanced Placement Exam Preparation solution that truly adapts to each student's learning needs, delivering personalized learning and mini-lessons to ensure student comprehension as they prepare in the weeks and months leading up to the AP Exam. *SCOREBoard™* is an online, personalized learning plan with an adaptive, focused content review and four complete AP Practice Exams. Students learn at their own pace and set their study schedules. A comprehensive reporting system provides feedback to both students and teachers.

*AP and Advanced Placement Program are registered trademarks of the College Board, which was not involved in the production of and does not endorse these products.

MHEonline.com

Contents

Part I Foundations of American Democracy

Part II Fundamental Principles

Part III
Linkages Between the People and Government

6 POLITICAL SOCIALIZATION AND PUBLIC OPINION   188

7 INTEREST GROUPS   216

10 THE MEDIA 308

11 POLITICS AND TECHNOLOGY 332

Part V · Public Policy

16 ECONOMIC POLICY 486

Economic Health and the American Dream **488**

The American Economy **489**

Economic Theories That Shape Economic Policy **490**
  Laissez-Faire Economics: An Unrealized Policy **490**
  Keynesian Economics **491**
  Supply-Side Economics **492**
  Monetarism **492**
  Should One Economic Theory Predominate? **493**

Measuring Economic Health **493**
  Traditional Measures of Economic Health **493**
  ■ ANALYZING THE SOURCES: *How Is the U.S. Economy Doing?* **494**
  Other Measures of Economic Health **494**

Fiscal Policy and Economic Health **496**
  Tax Policy **496**
  ■ GLOBAL CONTEXT: *A New Tax in Mexico: 16 Percent Sales Tax on Pet Food* **497**
  Spending Policy **498**
  Creating Fiscal Policy Through the National Budget Process **498**
  Deficit Spending and Debt **501**

Monetary Policy and the Federal Reserve System **502**
  ■ THINKING CRITICALLY ABOUT DEMOCRACY: *Should We Demand a Balanced National Budget?* **503**

Regulatory Policy **504**
  Business Regulation **504**
  Social Regulation **505**
  The Costs of Regulation **506**

Trade Policy in the Global Economy **507**
  Trade Policy: Protectionist or Free Trade? **507**
  International Trade Agreements **507**

The U.S. Economy and the American Dream Today **509**

17 DOMESTIC POLICY 516

Citizen Engagement and Domestic Policy **518**
  ■ ANALYZING THE SOURCES: *Differences in Top Policy Priorities of U.S. Citizens Yield Policy Debates* **519**

Tools of Domestic Policy **520**
  Laws and Regulations **520**
  Direct Provision of Public Goods **521**
  Cash Transfers **521**
  Loans, Loan Guarantees, and Insurance **522**
  Grants-in-Aid and Contracting Out **523**

Environmental Policy **523**
  Environmental Degradation **523**
  Environmental Protection **524**

Energy Policy **526**
  Evolution of U.S. Energy Policy **526**
  Energy Policy Today **527**

Income Security Programs **529**
  Social Security **529**
  Unemployment Compensation **530**
  Minimum Wage **530**
  Earned Income Tax Credit **531**
  Temporary Assistance for Needy Families **531**
  ■ THINKING CRITICALLY ABOUT DEMOCRACY: *Should There Be a Federal Minimum Wage?* **532**
  Government Definitions of Poverty **533**

Health Care Policy **534**
  Medicaid **534**
  Medicare **535**
  The Patient Protection and Affordable Care Act **535**

Homeland Security **536**

Immigration Policy **537**
  Authorized and Unauthorized Immigration **537**
  ■ GLOBAL CONTEXT: *Americans Immigrate Too!* **539**
  Proposed Immigration Policy Reforms **540**

18 FOREIGN POLICY AND NATIONAL SECURITY 546

The Tools of U.S. Foreign Policy **548**
  Diplomacy **548**
  Trade and Economic Policies **548**
  ■ GLOBAL CONTEXT: *The United States and Iran—A Complex History* **550**
  The Military Option **551**

American Democracy Now—cutting

Since its inception, *American Democracy Now* was built by master teachers intent on giving today's students the critical thinking skills needed to actively and critically engage in the American government course. Now, guided by student data, the fourth edition focuses more than ever on helping students interact more with material, perform better during the course, and become more active, engaged citizens in the world.

AP Students Have the Advantage with ConnectPlus

Study smarter, not harder! **McGraw-Hill ConnectPlus** is a digital teaching and learning environment that strengthens the link between teachers, students and coursework, helping everyone accomplish more in less time. ConnectPlus works with the AP course prep and practice of ONboard and the AP exam prep and practice of SCOREboard to offer a comprehensive method to promote online learning. Cutting-edge technology engages students in the course content so they are better prepared, are more active in discussion, and achieve better results.

- ConnectPlus can generate a number of powerful reports and charts
- Dynamic eBooks allow students to highlight, take notes, and access assignments
- **AP Suggested Assignments** include AP-style multiple choice and free-response test bank questions and scoring rubrics for AP Exam practice

The Instructor Resources website that accompanies *American Democracy Now* houses a wealth of valuable AP resources including the **AP Teacher Manual,** presentations, and tools for the teacher. This website is available through ConnectPlus.

- The **AP Teacher's Manual** includes a chapter overview and suggested pacing, learning objectives, key terms and people, suggested lecture topics and activities for the AP classroom, practice free-response questions, and additional online resources. This Teacher's Manual helps guide the AP teacher through the essentials that must be covered to help students succeed on the AP exam.
- The **AP Correlation** helps teachers target specific AP Topics to better prepare students for the AP Exam.

SMARTBOOK™ Students Study More Effectively with SmartBook

LearnSmart is an adaptive learning program designed to help students learn faster, study smarter, and retain more knowledge for greater success. Distinguishing what students know from what they don't, and focusing on concepts they are most likely to forget, LearnSmart continuously adapts to each student's needs by building an individual learning path. Millions of students have answered over a billion questions in LearnSmart since 2009, making it the most widely used and intelligent adaptive study tool that's proven to strengthen memory recall, keep students in class, and boost grades.

edge resources and AP teacher support

Fueled by LearnSmart, SmartBook is the first and only adaptive reading experience currently available.

■ **Make It Effective.** SmartBook creates a personalized reading experience by highlighting the most impactful concepts a student needs to learn at that moment in time. This ensures that every minute spent with SmartBook is returned to the student as the most value-added minute possible.

■ **Make It Informed.** The reading experience continuously adapts by highlighting content based on what the student knows and doesn't know. Real-time reports quickly identify the concepts that require more attention from individual students—or the entire class. SmartBook detects the content a student is most likely to forget and brings it back to improve long-term knowledge retention.

Student Performance Reports Show You Their Progress

The first and only analytics tool of its kind, Connect Insight is a series of visual data displays—each framed by an intuitive question—to provide at-a-glance information regarding how your class is doing.

■ **Make It Intuitive.** You receive an instant, at-a-glance view of student performance matched with each student activity.

■ **Make It Dynamic.** Connect Insight puts real-time analytics in your hands so you can take action early and keep struggling students from falling behind.

■ **Make It Mobile.** Connect Insight travels from office to classroom, available on demand wherever and whenever it's needed.

The **ConnectED eBook** is a downloadable, digital version of *American Democracy Now* that offers powerful and instant search capability and helps students manage notes, highlights, and bookmarks all in one place.

Critical Thinking

At the heart of *American Democracy Now* is a rich set of instructional tools that move students along the path to critical thinking.

CHAPTER 12

Congress

THEN
The framers granted to Congress both explicit powers and implied powers, by which the national government strengthened and broadened its authority.

NOW
A much more demographically diverse but ideologically polarized Congress exercises wide powers, its decision making influenced by shifting constituencies in a changing nation.

NEXT
Will increased polarization of Republicans and Democrats in Congress continue to define the congressional agenda?

Will the composition and policy making of Congress more broadly reflect the changing face of the United States?

Will technology significantly affect the ability of "average" citizens to influence Congress?

361

Then Now Next

Partisanship in Congress

Then (1980s)

	Now
Congress was divided; Democrats controlled the House of Representatives, and Republicans controlled the Senate.	Republicans control both the House and Senate.
Although incumbents enjoyed a considerable advantage, many congressional districts were a mix of constituents of both major parties.	Fewer congressional districts are competitive. Many districts are more homogeneous because district boundaries can be drawn with sophisticated computer programs.
Partisan voting was evident, but legislators were often forced to base their positions on constituent preferences in addition to their own party loyalty.	With the advent of less competitive districts, legislators are more partisan than their predecessors.

WHAT'S NEXT?

> Has the outcome of the 2014 elections increased or decreased party tensions, in your view? Why?

> In recent years, partisanship has increased when there has been a president of one party and a Congress of another. Does such a scenario exist today? What implications does that have for the future of partisanship in Congress for the next several years?

> Increases in technological sophistication could make redistricting an even more exact science. What effect would this change have on partisanship in Congress?

A "Then, Now, Next" framework encourages students to understand historical contexts and precedents, so that they can weigh them against current political events and actions, begin to formulate an informed judgment about politics, and consider how the past and present might shape the future.

Analyzing the Sources

POSTING AND TWEETING ABOUT POLITICS

The graph shows the proportion within each age group who engage in different civic or political behaviors.

Percentage of social networking site and Twitter users who engage in these activities

■ Ages 18–29   ■ Ages 30–49   ■ Ages 50–64   ■ Ages 65+

(bar graph showing percentages for activities: Like/promote political material 44, 32, 36, 24; Encourage others to vote 34, 36, 34, 32; Post thoughts on issues 42, 34, 28, 20; Repost political content 36, 32, 29, 31; Encourage others to act 36, 27, 27, 21; Post links to political stories 33, 28, 25, 18; Belong to political group on SNS 26, 21, 14, 8; Follow officials/candidates on social media 25, 20, 15, 10)

Percentage (y-axis 0–50)

SOURCE: Pew Research Center's Internet & American Life Project Civic Engagement Survey, conducted July 16–August 7, 2012, on landline and cell phones and in English and Spanish. N for social media users ages 18–29=323. N for social media users ages 30–49=388. N for social media users ages 50–64=323. N for social media users ages 65+=167.

Evaluating the Evidence

1. What is the most common way in which each age group participates in politics online?

2. Generally, describe the trend with regard to age and political activities online. What is the implication of this trend?

3. Are there any political activities in which Millennials are not the most likely group to participate? Why do you think this might be the case?

"Analyzing the Sources" guides students in thinking through original resources in American politics.

Thinking Critically About Democracy

Should Super PACs Enjoy Unlimited Free Speech?

The Issue: Super PACs emerged as an important factor in the 2012 elections, and remained so in the 2014 midterm congressional races. Super PACs are a special, relatively new form of PAC that raise unlimited amounts of money from individuals and then spend unlimited amounts in political races. Unlike traditional PACs, they may not contribute directly to the candidates they are supporting, and they must report their independent expenditures to the Federal Election Commission (FEC). The legal path for the creation of Super PACs was paved in the 2010 D.C. District Court of Appeals decision SpeechNow. org v. Federal Election Commission. The question has thus become whether Super PACs represent an important tool of free speech or whether they constitute merely another avenue for the wealthy to dominate the electoral process.

Yes: Some free speech proponents argue that the ruling has increased the amount of information available to voters. Under previous regulations, free speech advocates argue, limitations to PACs restricted "the individuals' freedom of speech by limiting the amount that an individual can contribute to Speech-Now and thus the amount the organization may spend." Brad Smith, former chairman of the FEC and chair of the Center for Competitive Politics, argued in favor of the decision: "The rise of independent expenditure groups made possible by the SpeechNow ruling has increased the information available to voters and increased the number of competitive races." Many conservatives also argue that organizations consist of individuals who form associations and that the Constitution protects not only free speech but also freedom of association.

No: Critics of the decision argue that it facilitates unmitigated corporate influence in political campaigns. Giving organizations protected rights that individuals enjoy, like free speech, detracts from the protection of individual human rights. Some critics argue that enabling these organizations to spend freely to influence campaigns has a detrimental effect on campaigns, because the wealthy have a disproportionate say in campaigns through their ability to spend unlimited sums.

Other Approaches: In light of the SpeechNow ruling, voters need to be increasingly skeptical of claims made by organizations about political candidates. In effect, these Super PACs are only as powerful as average Americans enable them to be, and their influence can be countered through the formation of opposing groups comprising individuals who share a viewpoint. The availability of technology provides a medium for average citizens both to get information and to form groups with like-minded people, thus potentially mitigating the effect of the influence of Super PACs.

Federal Election Commission, "Speechnow.org v. FEC Case Summary," 2010, www.fec.gov/law/litigation/speechnow.shtml#summary.

Center for Competitive Politics, "SpeechNow.org v. FEC—Protecting Free Speech for the Last 2 Years," 2012, www.campaignfreedom.org/2012/03/23/speechnow-org-v-fec-protecting-free-speech-for-the-last-2-years/.

What do you think?

1. Do you believe that enabling Super PACs to purchase unlimited independent expenditure ads is a protected right?

2. What will be the effect of this decision, in your view?

3. How can average Americans get their opinions about candidates heard? How can they find out whether allegations made by Super PACs are accurate?

"Thinking Critically About Democracy" gives students a comprehensive appreciation of the many sides of a political issue and an opportunity to formulate well-reasoned opinions.

Political Inquiry

FIGURE 4.2 ■ TECHNOLOGY MOVING FROM FIGHTING TERROR TO CRIME CONTROL What message is the cartoonist trying to convey? What challenges might the government find in using technologies initially deployed for the war against terror in domestic criminal investigations? How does this revise the debate over liberty versus security? Are the constitutional due process provisions robust enough to protect citizens against abuses in the use of this technology?

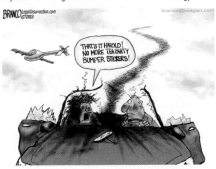

Students continue to build skills through additional tools, such as "Political Inquiry," which prompts them to analyze data and images presented in the program.

INSTRUCTOR RESOURCES CENTER

The password-protected online Instructor Resources Center (available through the Library tab in ConnectPlus) contains a wealth of materials: an AP Teacher Manual; AP correlations; an Instructor's Manual that ties all text features to individual and group projects in and out of class; a full Test Bank tied to Bloom's taxonomy; PowerPoint slides; and an Image Gallery.

■ The Instructor's Manual includes chapter summaries, chapter outlines, lecture outlines with integrated PowerPoints, and abundant class activities.

■ The Test Bank includes more than 1,000 multiple-choice and short-answer questions to accompany the chapters in *American Democracy Now,* along with questions to be used in class (with PowerPoints) and student self-check questions.

About the AP United States Government

Course Themes and Structure

The AP United States Government and Politics course is designed to mirror undergraduate courses in United States government and politics, which are typically a semester long. But in high schools across the country AP United States Government and Politics courses may be taught on a semester, trimester, or a yearlong basis. Additionally, the course is offered at many levels in high schools: tenth grade AP United States Government and Politics is not unusual, but seniors often take the course as well sometimes instead of a required civics class.

There are no prerequisites for the class, but a background in United States history is especially useful for a student of AP United States Government and Politics. Though the AP United States Government and Politics course contains a great deal of data and analysis not found in United States history classes, the United States history class takes up some of the same material that may be found on the AP United States Government and Politics Exam: the founding of the Republic; the framing of the Constitution and the writing of the Bill of Rights; many important Supreme Court decisions as well as presidencies; important legislation; and the history of political parties. Students certainly can do well on the AP United States Government and Politics Exam without a United States history background, but a recent United States history course provides an advantage.

ABOUT THE EXAM

The two-hour and twenty-five minute AP United States Government and Politics Exam has two sections. Section I is multiple choice. Students have 45 minutes to complete 60 multiple-choice questions. Section II is the free-response section. In this section, students have 100 minutes to answer four free-response questions.

What is covered

Breakdown of the AP US Government Exam

Percentage of Questions	Topics
5–15%	Constitutional Underpinnings of United States Government
10–20%	Political Beliefs and Behaviors
10–20%	Political Parties, Interest Groups, and Mass Media
35–45%	Institutions of National Government: The Congress, the Presidency, the Bureaucracy, and the Federal Courts
5–15%	Public Policy
5–15%	Civil Rights and Civil Liberties

TABLE 1

Understanding the Format

As explained earlier, the AP United States Government and Politics Exam is a two-hour and twenty-five-minute exam. The College Board administers this exam in May. The multiple-choice section accounts for one-half of the score, and a free-response section provides the other half of the score.

Multiple-Choice Questions

The first portion of the exam consists of sixty multiple-choice questions, which are to be answered within forty-five minutes. The multiple-choice questions can include a wide range of information, including: important facts, concepts, and theories pertaining to U.S. government and politics; understanding of typical patterns of political processes and behavior and their consequences; and the ability to analyze and interpret basic data relevant to U.S. government and politics.

Since students have less than a minute for each question, working rapidly is critical. Generally the best strategy might be described as "eliminate, eliminate, eliminate choose the better of the two remaining answers and move on." Going back and forth is usually a bad idea. If a student does not know the answer when he or she first reads the question, the answer is not likely to come to later. It is easy, however, for a student to read too much into questions and change correct answers into incorrect answers. So the best advice is to quickly, but methodically, move through the questions. Students are advised to pay close attention to charts, tables, and even political cartoons as they move through their text. There are always some multiple-choice questions that call for analysis of these sorts of items, and once a student is familiar with how to interpret such items it makes tackling these types of questions much less daunting since the answer does not require extensive content recall, but rather interpretation skills.

Free-Response Questions

The second portion of the exam consists of four free-response questions and students are given one hundred minutes to answer these questions. The College Board suggests that students spend approximately twenty-five minutes writing each answer. This section stresses the same areas as the multiple-choice section, but tends to stress the "linkage" between institutions, ideas, and concepts rather than the recall of information. Students sometimes think they have not studied "linkages," but they have. "Linkages" are the interactions between the various elements of civil society and government—how the media interact with Congress; how polling affects Congressional voting; how the courts impact public policy; and how lobbying impacts the federal bureaucracy. Students need to pay close attention to these sorts of interactions as the course progresses, and to be aware that making connections between chapters of their text is critical. Additionally, many of the concepts studied in this course and assessed on the exam will become clearer when students apply them to current events.

TABLE 3

Overall Grade Distribution

Grade Distribution	
Multiple Choice:	50%
Free Response:	50%

Multiple-Choice Questions

Each question has five potential answers labeled A-E. Each correct answer is worth one point, while questions left blank earn no points. The total points available for this section is 60, one half of the total 120 points available on the whole exam.

TABLE 2

Breakdown of the AP United States Government and Politics Exam Format

Summary of Exam Format

Section I:	Multiple Choice	No penalty for incorrect answers.
	60 questions	
	Time: 45 minutes	
	_____[10-minute break]_____	
Section II:	Free Response	
	Four free-response questions	
	Time: 100 minutes	
	(recommended 25 minutes per question)	

To guess or not to guess?

Beginning with the May 2011 AP United States Government and Politics Exam, total scores on the multiple-choice section will be based on the number of questions answered correctly. Points will no longer be deducted for incorrect answers The obvious strategy for students is to make to make an educated guess on every question, There is a 20% chance of being correct under any circumstances, and guessing on every question reduces the possibility of "mislineation," the bubbling in of the right answer into the wrong space on the answer sheet.

Free-Response Questions

The free-response questions are graded with rubrics. The rubrics are developed by table-leaders who use actual student answers in the rubrics formulation. Readers are often "back-read" by a table-leader to ensure that the rubric has been adhered to during the grading process.

Grading of the AP Exam

The multiple-choice section of the AP United States Government and Politics Exam is scored electronically and readers grade the free-response section, using core scoring. The College Board then applies a weighted formula and combines the raw multiple-choice and free-response scores to create a composite score. Finally, a conversion factor is used to award the student one of five final scores with a 5 being extremely well qualified and a 1 being no recommendation.

Colleges and universities often grant credits equivalent to that which is offered for their introductory United States government and politics course to those students who successfully complete the AP exam. The exam scores accepted, usually a score of 3, 4, or 5, vary by institution.

In the free-response section, students need not concern themselves with a thesis statement providing background or rhetorical flourishes. But, what they should keep in mind is that the readers who give out those scores are looking for analysis of the question in the answer. So it is worth taking time to write a precise answer. Students should realize is that though the answers to these questions do not require a great deal of writing, answers should be precisely thought out, and show a clear understanding of the question(s) being asked.

Also, it is a safe policy to guess as well on the free-response section. Suppose part of question asked the student to give an example of a lobbying group. The student debates between describing the NRA and KFC, and decides on KFC. Clearly KFC is a fried chicken franchise, not a lobby group as such, and the student gets no points, but neither are points deducted. So, nothing was lost on the part of the student. In fact, depending on the details given in the free-response answer, it is possible for a student to receive some points for an answer even if it does not answer the question completely.

A few pointers on Free-Response Questions:

■ Vocabulary matters. A word that makes perfect sense in context may throw a student who encounters it on an exam question, so students are advised to keep a running list of the vocabulary specific to the course as they read.

■ Keep in mind that an essay asking about "federalism" may be looking at the era of the founding of the Republic, or it may be asking about the relationship between the state and the federal government.

■ Questions on the exam sometimes ask about the ways that political culture affect political participation, so it's important to pay attention to the effect that demographics—economic, religious, ethnic, minority, gender, locality—have on citizens' beliefs about government and leaders.

■ Review campaign finance laws and the role of PACs in elections and the role played by lobbying groups in all aspects of government—especially the legislature and the bureaucracy.

■ Be sure to develop a sense of the connections between the branches of national government and political parties, interest groups, the media, and state and local governments, as these are typical of FRQ "linkages." Issue networks, iron triangles, and various policy "subgovernments" are frequent topics on the AP exam.

■ When FRQs about policy are asked, usually some other areas of the course are involved as well (Congress, lobbying. . .) and sometimes there is a choice regarding policy areas. In other words, the process is usually more important than the specific policy, though it's a good idea to review fiscal, environmental, civil rights, and health care policies.

■ AP United States Government and Politics students need to know a number of judicial interpretations of various civil rights and liberties including freedom of speech, assembly, and expression; the rights of the accused, and the rights of minority groups and women. Especially important is the impact of the Fourteenth Amendment on the constitutional development of rights and liberties. Students are advised to keep track of the names of court cases as they come up in the reading. It's not unusual for a question to contain a case name that's critical to answering the question. So students are advised to keep a running list or to keep flashcards.

One final note:

Because the AP United States Government and Politics course is often a semester course, it can present a unique challenge to students. Students taking AP United States Government and Politics during the first semester or trimester must plan to put in some time for review because the exam is not given until the first week of May. So holding and attending review sessions is critical! Students may also want to consider the order in which they go about reviewing. There is always the temptation to "begin at the beginning", but using Table 1 as the basis for allocating review time is a wiser strategy. It probably makes more sense to begin with the core chapters on political processes, institutions, and major court decisions.

AP Correlation
American Democracy Now, Fourth Edition

TOPICS	CHAPTERS | PAGES
I. CONSTITUTIONAL UNDERPINNINGS OF UNITED STATES GOVERNMENT (5–15%)	**CHAPTERS 1–3**
Considerations that influenced the formulation and adoption of the Constitution	11–14, 36–41, 42–48, 61
Separation of powers	61, 407. Appendix B, Appendix C
Checks and balances	61, 369–372, 446–447, 471–472, Appendix B, Appendix C
Federalism	86–108
Theories of democratic government	219–220
II. POLITICAL BELIEFS AND BEHAVIORS (10–20%)	**CHAPTERS 1, 6, 9, 11**
Beliefs that citizens hold about their government and its leaders	14–16, 17–19
Processes by which citizens learn about politics	190–196
The nature, sources, and consequences of public opinion	196–201
The ways in which citizens vote and otherwise participate in public life	276, 281–299
Factors that influence citizens to differ from one another in terms of political beliefs and behaviors	194–201, 295–298
III. POLITICAL PARTIES, INTEREST GROUPS, AND MASS MEDIA (10–20%)	**CHAPTERS 7, 8, 10, 11**
Political parties and elections:	
Functions	247–251
Organization	251–253, 258–269
Development	254–258
Effects on the political process	260–262
Electoral laws and systems	261, 362–367, 394–395
Interest groups, including political action committees (PACs):	
The range of interests represented	219, 228–230
The activities of interest groups	226, 233
The effects of interest groups on the political process	219
The unique characteristics and roles of PACs in the political process	237–238
The mass media:	
The functions and structures of the news media	310–311
The impacts of the news media on politics	315–320, 323–324
The news media industry and its consequences	315–319
IV. Institutions of National Government: The Congress, the Presidency, the Bureaucracy, and the Federal Courts (35–45%)	**Chapters 11–15**
The major formal and informal institutional arrangements of power	367–384, 395–421, 428–451, 458–477

(continued)

AP Correlation
American Democracy Now, Fourth Edition

TOPICS	CHAPTERS | PAGES
Relationships among these four institutions and varying balances of power	371, 377, 383, 409, 417–418, 444–447, 461–462, 477–478
Linkages between institutions and the following:	
Public opinion and voters	201–209
Interest groups	Chapter 7, 216–243
Political parties	Chapter 8, 244–273
The media	Chapter 10, 308–331
State and local governments	
V. PUBLIC POLICY (5–15%)	**CHAPTERS 16–18**
Policymaking in a federal system	88–100
The formation of policy agendas	380–384, 395–400, 439–443, 475
The role of institutions in the enactment of policy	439–448
The role of the bureaucracy and the courts in policy implementation and interpretation	439–448, 472–477
Linkages between policy processes and the following:	
Political institutions and federalism	435
Political parties	253–254
Interest groups	226, 233–235
Public opinion	207–209
Elections	300
Policy networks	233, 439–443, 554
VI. CIVIL RIGHTS AND CIVIL LIBERTIES (5–15%)	**CHAPTERS 4–5**
The development of civil liberties and civil rights by judicial interpretation	118–125
Knowledge of substantive rights and liberties	125–146
The impact of the Fourteenth Amendment on the constitutional development of rights and liberties	101–102, 121–123, 161, 163, 173, 181–182

From the Authors

Welcome to the fourth edition of *American Democracy Now!* In this program, we share our passion for politics while providing students with the foundation they need to become informed citizens in a rapidly changing democracy.

In creating the first edition of *American Democracy Now,* we sought to merge our years of experience as classroom instructors and our desire to captivate students with the compelling story of their democracy into a student-centered program. We refined those goals with an integrated learning program for American government to maximize student performance in the second edition. The third edition revolutionized how we think about American democracy by incorporating for the first time a chapter on Politics and Technology, demonstrating the extent to which technology has become integral to how citizens participate in their democracy and how governments serve their citizenry.

The fourth edition of *American Democracy Now* continues our tradition. Relying on data garnered from thousands of students who have used our Connect and LearnSmart platforms, we have revised our program to ensure greater clarity in areas that have proven complex for past student readers. We have continued to integrate an examination of the increasing role that technology is playing in politics. And we have continued our quest to create a student-centered program that increases students' sense of political efficacy by exciting them about the political conversations of the day and by integrating a critical thinking framework that not only explains the past and present of politics, but also asks them to think critically about the future: What's next for their democracy? In *American Democracy Now,* fourth edition, students learn how the fundamental principles of American democracy inform their understanding of the politics and policies of today, so that they can think about the policies they would like to see take shape tomorrow. In short, they learn to inquire: How does *then* and *now* shape what's going to happen *next?* This "Then, Now, Next" approach to critical thinking serves as the basis for student participation.

American Democracy Now, fourth edition, takes a broader view of participation than other programs. To us, participation encompasses a variety of activities from the modest, creative, local, or even personal actions students can take to the larger career choices they can make. And today, technology plays an enormous role in shaping political participation—particularly the participation of young people. By recognizing the legitimacy of new forms of political participation, we are giving students the tools needed to define what participation means to them and to make active choices about where, when, and how to participate. And choosing how to participate makes American government matter.

Today's partisan politics and ever-changing technology provide challenges for those seeking to ensure that the rights guaranteed by the Constitution are protected, and they present opportunities for those striving to fulfill the responsibilities that come with living in a constitutional democracy. *American Democracy Now,* fourth edition, enables students to garner a solid understanding of the essential elements, institutions, and dynamics of national government and politics, while fostering critical thinking skills that are essential to meeting these novel challenges and realizing these new opportunities.

Facilitating success—as students, but also as citizens and participants—means honing their critical thinking skills, harnessing their energy, and creating tools that foster success in the American government course and in our polity. We know we have succeeded when students apply their knowledge and sharpened skills to consider the outcomes they—as students, citizens, and participants—would like to see.

Creating this success means joining increasingly diverse students where they are so they can see the relevance of politics in their everyday lives. The fourth edition of *American Democracy Now* further integrates technology into our students' study of politics, so that their engagement with content is seamless. Facebook, YouTube, Twitter, and Instagram are not only powerful social networking tools, but also powerful political and educational tools. New technologies help politicians to communicate with citizens, citizens to communicate with each other, and you to communicate with your students.

We are excited to present you with this revised edition of *American Democracy Now,* and we wish you and your students success.

BRIGID CALLAHAN HARRISON
JEAN WAHL HARRIS
MICHELLE D. DEARDORFF

BRIGID CALLAHAN HARRISON specializes in the civic engagement and political participation of Americans, especially the Millennial Generation, the U.S. Congress, and the Presidency. Brigid has taught American government for 20 years at Montclair State University in New Jersey. She takes particular pride in creating a learning experience in the classroom that shapes students' lifelong understanding of American politics, sharpens their critical thinking about American government, and encourages their participation in civic life. She enjoys supervising student internships in political campaigns and government and is a frequent commentator in print and electronic media on national and New Jersey politics. She currently serves as president of the New Jersey Political Science Association, and is past president of the National Women's Caucus for Political Science. She received her B.A. from The Richard Stockton College, her M.A. from Rutgers, The State University of New Jersey, and her Ph.D. from Temple University. Harrison lives in Longport, New Jersey, and has three children: Caroline (20), Alexandra (14), and John (11). She is engaged to be married to Paul Meilak, a retired New York City police detective. Born and raised in New Jersey, Harrison is a fan of Bruce Springsteen and in her spare time, she enjoys reading on the beach, traveling, and cycling.

JEAN WAHL HARRIS'S research interests include political socialization and engagement, federalism, and the gendered nature and effects of U.S. politics. She teaches introductory courses in local, state, and national government and upper-level courses in public administration, public policy, and judicial politics. As a faculty member in the Political Science Department and the Women's Studies Program at the University of Scranton, Jean seeks to cultivate students' sense of political efficacy, empowering and inspiring them to engage in local, state, national, and/or international politics. She earned her B.A., M.A., and Ph.D. from the State University of New York at Binghamton. In 1994, the University of Scranton named her its CASE (Council for Advancement and Support of Education) professor of the year. She was an American Council on Education (ACE) Fellow during the 2007–2008 academic year. Jean lives in Nicholson, Pennsylvania, with her husband, Michael. She enjoys reading on her deck overlooking the Endless Mountains of Northeast Pennsylvania.

MICHELLE D. DEARDORFF'S teaching and research focus on the constitutional and statutory protections surrounding gender, race, and religion. She particularly enjoys developing classes that allow students to apply their understandings of law, politics, and political theory to current events; she seeks to foster critical citizens prepared to participate in governing our communities and nation. Deardorff is currently head of Political Science, Public Administration, and Nonprofit Management at the University of Tennessee at Chattanooga. Before coming to UTC, she spent 10 years teaching at Jackson State, an historically black university in Mississippi, and another decade at Millikin University, a small private college in Illinois. She recently chaired the American Political Science Association's standing Committee on Teaching and Learning and is a founding faculty member of the Fannie Lou Hamer National Institute on Citizenship and Democracy, a coalition of academics who promote civic engagement and popular sovereignty through the study of the struggle for civil rights in the United States. She lives in Chattanooga with her husband, David, where they enjoy kayaking, hiking, live music, and reading in beautiful places.

AMERICAN
DEMOCRACY
NOW

CHAPTER 1

People, Politics, and Participation

THEN

Cynicism, distrust, and apathy characterized Americans' relationship with their government for the past generation.

NOW

New information technologies, generational politics, and a diversifying population give cause for optimism as the nation responds to the challenges of a new millennium.

NEXT

Will the present generation break the cycle of cynicism that has pervaded the politics of the recent past?

Will new information technologies facilitate and energize political participation?

Will the face of American politics change as the nation's population grows and shifts?

This chapter of *American Democracy Now* provides a framework for your study of American government.

FIRST, we delve into the basic question, why should you study American democracy now?

SECOND, we explore what government does.

THIRD, we explain how political scientists categorize the various types of government.

FOURTH, we consider the origins of American democracy, including the ideas of natural law, a social contract, and representative democracy.

FIFTH, we examine political culture and American values, which centrally include liberty; equality; consent of the governed; capitalism; and the importance of the individual, the family, and the community.

SIXTH, we look at ideology as a prism through which American politics can be viewed.

SEVENTH, we focus on the changing face of American democracy as the population grows and diversifies.

The United States was founded

by individuals who believed in the power of democracy to respond to the will of citizens. Historically, citizen activists have come from all walks of life, but they have shared one common attribute: the belief that, in the ongoing conversation of democracy, their government listens to *people like them*. This idea is vital if individuals are to have an impact on their government; people who don't believe they can have any influence rarely try. From the Pilgrims' flight from religious persecution, to the War for Independence, to the Civil War, to the Great Depression, to World War II, and to the great movements for social justice—civil rights, women's liberation, gay rights, and more—the story of the United States is the story of people who are involved with their government, who know what they want their government to do, and who have confidence in their ability to influence its policies.[1] *American Democracy Now* tells the story of how today's citizen activists are participating in the conversation of democracy—in the politics, governance, and civic life of their communities and their nation during a time of technological revolution and unprecedented global change. This story is the next chapter in America's larger story.

The history of democracy in the United States is rife with examples of ordinary people who have made and are making a difference.[2] Throughout this book, we describe the effects that individuals and groups have had, and continue to have, in creating and changing the country's institutions of government. We also explore how individuals have influenced the ways in which our governments—national, state, and local—create policy.[3] These stories are important not only in and of themselves but also as motivators for all of us who want to live in a democracy that responds to all its citizens.

A fundamental principle underlying this book is that your beliefs and your voice—and ultimately how you use those beliefs and that voice—matter. Whatever your beliefs, it is important that you come to them thoughtfully, by employing introspection and critical thinking. Similarly, however you choose to participate, it is crucial that you take part in the civic life of your community. This book seeks both to inform and to inspire your participation. A sentiment voiced by American anthropologist Margaret Mead expresses a powerful truth: "Never doubt that a small group of thoughtful, committed citizens can change the world. Indeed, it's the only thing that ever has."

y shd u stdy am dem now? Or, Why Should You Study American Democracy Now?

politics
the process of deciding who benefits in society and who does not

Politics as practiced today is not your parents' brand of politics. **Politics**—the process of deciding who benefits in society and who does not—is a much different process today than it was even a decade ago. Advances in technology have altered the political landscape in many ways. In some countries, these advances have facilitated the overthrow of governments. In other countries, they are changing how voters and candidates communicate with each other, how governments provide information to individuals, how people get their news about events, and how governments administer laws. The political landscape has also changed because of world events. In the past several years, a slow recovery from a global recession has placed demands on governments and propelled policy makers to reconsider issues of income inequality in the domestic policy sphere. Meanwhile, the federal government has had to contend with the instability of regimes in the Middle East and Asia. These realities take place within a political context built on the foundation of the terrorist attacks of September 11, 2001, and the wars in Afghanistan and Iraq, which markedly changed many aspects of American life. These shifts in how Americans interact with government and in what issues concern them represent distinct changes that make the study of politics today interesting, exciting, and important.

How Technology Has Changed Politics

It would be difficult to overstate the influence of the technological revolution on politics as it is practiced today. In electoral politics, faster computers, the Internet, micro-targeting, and social media have revolutionized a process that, until the advent of the personal computer, the Internet, and cellular technology, was not very different in 1990 from the way it was carried out in 1890. Today, many voters get much of their information from Facebook, Twitter, and Internet-based news sites and blogs. Campaigns rely on e-mail and instant and text messaging, and they use websites and social networking sites such as Facebook and Twitter to communicate with and organize supporters. State governments rely on computers to conduct elections, and cities use computers to provide services to their residents.

Because of these unprecedented shifts in the ways politics happens and government is administered, Americans today face both new opportunities and new challenges. How might we use technology to ensure that elections are conducted fairly? How might the abundance and reach of media technology be directed toward informing and enriching us rather than overwhelming us or perpetuating the citizen cynicism of recent years? What privacy rights can we be sure of in the present digital age? Whatever your age, as a student, you are a member of one of the most tech-savvy groups in the country, and your input, expertise, and participation are vital to sorting out the opportunities and obstacles of this next stage of American democracy. Throughout this text, we examine the many ways in which people are using technology to link with each other and with the branches of government in an effort to influence those branches.

The Political Context Now

The political context today centers on a debate taking place in Washington, D.C., and throughout the nation about the appropriate size and role of government, particularly as it relates to health care. In the 2014 midterm elections, campaign battles in many U.S. congressional districts focused on whether a candidate had supported the health care reform act passed by Congress in 2010. But policy makers and private citizens also have placed the issue of economic equality—and the government's responsibility to create more equitable conditions—on the national political agenda. These issues have sparked great passion, primarily because of the tenuous economic

Then Now Next

Technology and Political Participation

Then (1970s)	Now
47 percent of 18- to 20-year-olds voted in the 1976 presidential election.	About 50 percent of 18- to 20-year-olds voted in the 2012 presidential election.
People got their national news from one half-hour-long nightly news broadcast.	People get their news from an array of sources, including Twitter feeds, Internet news services, and 24-hour news networks available on demand via computers and cell phones.
Many people participated in civic life primarily through demonstrations, protests, and voting.	Voting remains the pinnacle of political participation. While some people still participate through demonstrations and protests, Internet activism is now mainstream. Online protests and petitions are commonplace and Facebook groups designed to express viewpoints and mobilize activists have replaced many in-real-life (IRL) groups.

WHAT'S NEXT?

> Will the upswing of voter participation by 18- to 20-year-olds continue?

> How might advancing media technologies further transform the ways that people "consume" their news?

> What new forms of civic participation will emerge?

situation many Americans find themselves in as a result of the nation's slow economic recovery from the global recession of 2007–2009. Government officials today seek to walk a fine line between placating those demanding action on the economy to create more equitable conditions and those who fear that increased government spending and regulations on business will overburden a fragile recovery process.

Also part of the U.S. political context is a global environment, which is characterized by violence and instability. In 2014, the Unites States initiated air strikes in Iraq targeting the insurgent group ISIS, or the Islamic State, which had taken control of parts of Iraq and Syria. In the meantime, Syria was embroiled in a civil war, and tensions flared between Israel and Palestine, as Israel launched rocket strikes against Palestinians in retaliation for mortar shelling launched into Israel by Palestine. Instability also reigned in Ukraine, where pro-Russian separatists sought to carve out a section of eastern Ukraine as part of Russia.

These domestic and foreign policy debates take place within the context of a post–September 11 world. Though we are removed from the terror attacks of that day by more than a dozen years, that watershed event inexorably changed both our national consciousness and the global political environment. The United States' international image was altered in light of the nation's decision to engage in a multi-front war on terror that began in 2002 and lasted for over a dozen years. But Americans themselves changed, too. Their attitudes about their government and their priorities shifted in light of the attacks. Some of these changes were temporary, but others remain a deeply ingrained part of Americans' national identity.

The events of September 11, 2001, jolted American politics and the nation, and the altered political context provoked changes in popular views—notably, young people's opinions. "The attacks of 9/11 . . . changed the way the Millennial Generation [people born between 1981 and 2000—the first generation to come of age in the new millennium] thinks about politics. Overnight, their attitudes were more like [those of] the Greatest Generation [the generation of Americans who lived through the Great Depression and World War II]," observed John Della Volpe, a pollster who helped Harvard University students construct a national poll of young people's views.[4]

As patriotic spirits soared, suddenly 60 percent of college students trusted government to do the right thing. Ninety-two percent considered themselves patriotic. Some 77 percent thought that politics was relevant to their lives.[5] In the immediate aftermath of the September 11, 2001, attacks, then-president George W. Bush and Congress enjoyed record-high approval ratings. Roughly 80 percent of young people and nearly that same percentage of all Americans supported U.S. military actions in Afghanistan. Beyond opinions, actions changed as well:

- More than 70 percent of college students gave blood, donated money, or volunteered in relief efforts.
- Nearly 70 percent volunteered in their communities (up from 60 percent in 2000).
- Eighty-six percent believed their generation was ready to lead the United States into the future.[6]

Then the political context changed again, over months and then years, as the wars in Afghanistan and Iraq wore on, as casualties mounted, and as military spending skyrocketed. Trust in government, particularly of the president, plummeted. The changes after September 11 continued to affect how Americans, particularly young Americans, participate in politics.

These transformations in attitude are remarkable, particularly given the recent history of Americans' views of their government. Since the early 1970s—a decade blemished by the intense unpopularity of the Vietnam War and by scandals that ushered in the resignation of President Richard Nixon in 1974—Americans' attitudes about government have been dismal.[7] Numerous surveys of the American public, including an ongoing Gallup poll, have demonstrated low levels of trust in government and of confidence in government's ability to solve problems.[8] Young people's views have mirrored those of the nation as a whole. In 2000, one study of undergraduate college students, for example, showed that nearly two-thirds (64 percent) did not trust the federal government to do the right thing most of the time, an attitude that reflected the views of the larger population.[9] Distrust; lack of **efficacy**, which is a person's belief that he or she has the ability to achieve something desirable and that the government genuinely listens to individuals; and apathy are prevalent among young people.

efficacy
citizens' belief that they have the ability to achieve something desirable and that the government listens to people like them

These attitudes are expressed through one of the most easily measured contexts: voter turnout. Figure 1.1 shows the jump in participation by young voters in the 2004 presidential election. (In contrast, for voters aged 66–74, participation actually decreased in 2004.) Among voters aged 18–21, the largest increases in turnout occurred among 19-year-olds, whose turnout rivaled that of voters in their 30s. (See "Thinking Critically About Democracy.") In 2008, that trend continued, with estimates indicating that voters aged 18–20 increased by 2.2 million, surpassing the young voter turnout since 18-year-olds voted for the first time in 1972. In 2012, the youth vote dipped. But because Millennials now constitute over 25 percent of the electorate, their vote is important, particularly in presidential races.

As these statistics demonstrate, lingering media characterizations of a cynical young electorate are off the mark. Evidence indicates that many young people are enthusiastic participants in civic and political life.[10] Others are taking part in ways that have not traditionally been thought of, and measured as, participation, including Internet activism and using one's power as a consumer to send political messages. For many students, that foundation of political participation, volunteerism, or community action has already provided them with a rationale for increasing their knowledge of, and participation in, their communities.

Individuals who engage in politics and civic life experience many benefits. Engaged citizens are knowledgeable about public issues; actively communicate with policy makers and others; press government officials to carry out the people's will; advocate for their own self-interest and the interests of others; and hold public officials accountable for their decisions and actions. You will find that advocating for your own interests or working with others in similar situations sometimes (perhaps to your surprise) leads to desired outcomes. This is efficacy in action. And you will discover that with experience you will become more effective at advocacy—the more you do, the better you get. Furthermore, you will derive social and psychological benefits from being civically engaged.

In addition, and equally important, local communities, states, and the nation benefit from an engaged populace. Governments are more effective when people voice their views. As we will see as we explore *American Democracy Now,* today's citizens and others have more opportunities to influence governmental action than at any other time in history. If you have the knowledge and tools, you should be able to make the most of these opportunities.

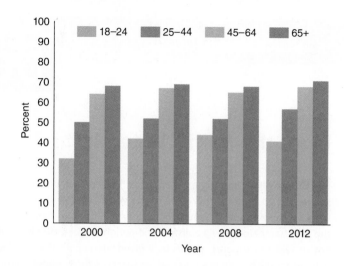

FIGURE 1.1

Voter Turnout in Presidential Elections (2000–2012) by Voter Age How has the turnout rate changed over time for voters aged 18–24? For other age groups?

SOURCE: U.S. Census Bureau, www.census.gov/hhes/www/socdemo/voting/publications/historical/index.html.

Civic Engagement: Acting on Your Views

One vitally important goal of this book is to encourage you to engage in a respectful, continuing conversation about your views and to make the connection between having ideas and opinions and acting on them. Political scientist Michael Delli Carpini has defined **civic engagement** as

> individual and collective actions designed to identify and address issues of public concern. Civic engagement can take many forms, from individual voluntarism to organizational involvement to electoral participation. It can include efforts to directly address an issue, work with others in a community to solve a problem or interact with the institutions of representative democracy.[11]

The possibilities for citizen involvement are so broad and numerous that the idea of civic engagement encompasses a range of activities. Civic engagement might include everything from tutoring an underprivileged child to volunteering at a conservative think tank. In this book, we focus in particular on civic engagement that takes the form of **political engagement**—that is, citizen actions that are intended to solve public problems through political means. As you read this book, you will find that a variety of political actions are possible, from boycotting and *buycotting* (buying goods produced by companies whose policies you agree with) to running for office.

civic engagement
individual and collective actions designed to identify and address issues of public concern

political engagement
citizen actions that are intended to solve public problems through political means

Democracy

Does the Youth Vote Matter?

The Issue: During the 2012 presidential election, much emphasis was placed on the importance of the youth vote. After President Barack Obama received resounding support from young Americans in the 2008 campaign, many pollsters and pundits argued that he could not sustain this support, particularly given the impact that a struggling economy had on the financial prospects of the youngest voters, who were hardest hit by the recession. In 2012, many political scientists believed that turnout among young voters had the potential to determine the outcome of that year's presidential race.

To that end, we saw a multitude of individuals, from politicians to rappers to clothing designers, urging young people to come out and vote. The national political parties took notice, too: Because Americans aged 18–29, drawn exclusively from the vast Millennial generation, constitute a larger cohort than similar age brackets, both parties sought to tap the potential of this huge voting bloc in 2012.

Yes: The youth vote did matter in 2012, and it will continue to play an important role in future elections. The 2012 presidential election saw strong participation by young Americans: About 50 percent of those aged 18–29 voted, though participation did dip for the younger members of that cohort. Only 41 percent of those under age 25 voted. Although that turnout rate is not comparable to that of older segments of the population (whose turnout rates ranged from 52 percent to 68 percent, depending on age), the overall trend among young people indicates that they are increasingly involved in political issues. In 2008, a near record turnout rate was magnified by the large proportion of young Americans who voted for Barack Obama. Fully 66 percent of those aged 18–29 voted for Obama that year, and although his support was not as strong among young voters in 2012, a generational divide in candidate preference was evident nonetheless. This breakdown was the first sign of a new era of generational politics, and those who came of age politically in the era of Obama will be loyal to the Democratic Party for years to come. Because of the size of this generation, the impact of their participation is likely to be influential in future campaigns. In 2012, voters under age 30 constituted 25 percent of the electorate; by 2020, nearly 37 percent of American voters will be members of the Millennial generation.

No: The turnout of young Americans, though increasing historically, will not be the determining factor in future federal elections. The low participation rate by young Americans in 2010 and the decline in their 2012 participation indicates that the 2008 Obama phenomenon was a flash-in-the-pan occurrence and that Democrats cannot count young Americans among their loyal party supporters. As a candidate in 2008, Obama relied on a message and an electronic medium that were attractive to young Americans. But those tactics proved difficult to replicate in the complicated process of governing, and the 2010 and 2012 turnouts among young people are indicative of young voters' disenchantment with both President Obama in particular and politics in general.

Other Approaches: Younger voters were attracted to Obama's brand of politics, and they will remain loyal to Democrats nationally in years to come. But as the 2010 and 2014 turnout indicated, that support does not translate into support for other Democratic candidates who are running in non-national contests such as congressional races. In smaller-scale elections, there is little chance of developing the momentum generated by a national movement that relies on technology to mobilize a broad-based constituency. Nonetheless, today's younger voters—Millennial voters—will become the determining constituency in federal elections in years to come, because of the size of their generation and because of the unique set of political viewpoints they bring to the political table as a result of being socialized in a post–September 11 world.

What do you think?

1. How did the significance of the youth vote in 2012 compare with that of 2008?

2. What issues motivate young voters to vote? What kinds of candidates motivate younger voters?

3. Do the positions of Millennial voters differ from those of older voters?

We hope that this book not only empowers you by teaching you about the institutions, policies, and processes of government but also inspires you to become civically and politically engaged. Today, many students choose to stick their toes into the waters of political activism by using the Internet—by following an elected official on Twitter, for example. You can take part in your democracy by joining a Facebook group advocating for an issue you care about, organizing a fund-raising event, signing an e-petition, joining a volunteer group, volunteering for a campaign, or even participating in a protest march, to name just a few of the many options available to you.

Consider which potential volunteer activities pique your interest. Think about what might best suit your schedule, lifestyle, and personal and professional goals. By taking part, you will ensure that your voice is heard, and you will derive the satisfaction of knowing that your community and the nation benefit from your actions as well.

What Government Does

In this section, we look at the nature of government and the functions a government performs. **Government** is an institution that creates and implements the policy and laws that guide the conduct of a nation and its citizens. **Citizens** are those members of a political community—town, city, state, or country—who, through birth or naturalization, enjoy the rights, privileges, and responsibilities attached to membership in a given nation. **Naturalization** is the process of becoming a citizen by means other than birth, as in the case of immigrants. Although governments vary widely in how well they perform, most national governments share some common functions.

> One way in which individuals articulate their political views is through the products they choose to purchase. In 2014, Nabisco created a stir when it featured gay, lesbian, and mixed-race families in advertisements for their Honey Maid Graham Crackers using the slogan "this is wholesome." The ads prompted some protests, but also generated much support. Have you ever boycotted or buycotted a manufacturer based on your political view?

To get a clear sense of the business of government, consider the following key functions performed by government in the United States and many other national governments:

- **To protect their sovereign territory and their citizenry and to provide national defense.** Governments protect their *sovereign territory* (that is, the territory over which they have the ultimate governing authority) and their citizens at home and abroad. Usually they carry out this responsibility by maintaining one or more types of armed services, but governments also provide for the national defense through counterterrorism efforts.

   In the United States, the armed services include the Army, Navy, Marines, Air Force, and Coast Guard. For the year 2015, the U.S. Department of Defense budget was approximately $525 billion. Governments also preserve order domestically. In the United States, domestic order is preserved through the National Guard and federal, state, and local law enforcement agencies.

- **To preserve order and stability.** Governments also preserve order by providing emergency services and security in the wake of disasters. Governments also maintain stability by providing a political structure that has **legitimacy:** a quality conferred on government by citizens who believe that its exercise of power is right and proper.[12]

- **To establish and maintain a legal system.** Governments create legal structures by enacting and enforcing laws that restrict or ban certain behaviors. In the United States, the foundation of this legal structure is the federal Constitution.[13] Governments also provide the means to implement laws through the actions of local police and other state and national law enforcement agencies. By means of the court system, governments administer justice and impose penalties.

- **To provide services.** Governments distribute a wide variety of services to their citizens. In the United States, government agencies provide services ranging from inspecting the meat we consume to ensuring the safety of our workplaces. Federal, state, and local governments provide roads, bridges, transportation, education, and health services. They facilitate communication, commerce, air travel, and entertainment.

Many of the services governments provide are called **public goods** because their benefits, by their nature, cannot be limited to specific groups or individuals. For example, everyone enjoys national defense, equal access to clean air and clean water, airport security, highways, and other similar services. Because the value and the benefits of these goods are extended to everyone, government makes them available through revenue collected by taxes. Not all goods that government provides are public goods, however; some goods, such as access to subsidized housing, are available only to the poor.

government
the institution that creates and implements policies and laws that guide the conduct of the nation and its citizens

citizens
members of the polity who, through birth or naturalization, enjoy the rights, privileges, and responsibilities attached to membership in a given nation

naturalization
the process of becoming a citizen by means other than birth, as in the case of immigrants

legitimacy
a quality conferred on government by citizens who believe that its exercise of power is right and proper

public goods
goods whose benefits cannot be limited and that are available to all

> Children are socialized to the dominant political culture from a very early age. When children emulate police officers, for example, they begin the process of learning about the functions governments perform.

- **To raise and spend money.** All the services that governments provide, from national protection and defense to health care, cost money.[14] Governments at all levels spend money collected through taxes. Depending on personal income, between 25 and 35 cents of every dollar earned by those working in the United States and earning above a certain level goes toward federal, state, and local income taxes. Governments also tax *commodities* (commercially exchanged goods and services) in various ways—through sales taxes, property taxes, "sin" taxes, and luxury taxes.
- **To socialize new generations.** Governments play a role in *socialization,* the process by which individuals develop their political values and opinions. Governments perform this function, for example, by providing funding for schools, by establishing standards for curriculum, by introducing young people to the various "faces" of government (perhaps through a police officer's visiting a school or a mayor's bestowing an honor on a student), and by facilitating participation in civic life through institutions such as libraries, museums, and public parks. In these ways, governments transmit cultural norms and values such as patriotism and build commitment to fundamental values such as those we explore later in this chapter. For a detailed discussion of political socialization, see Chapter 6.

Types of Government

When social scientists categorize the different systems of government operating in the world today, two factors influence their classifications. The first factor is *who participates in governing or in selecting those who govern.* These participants vary as follows, depending on whether the government is a monarchy, an oligarchy, or a democracy:

monarchy
government in which a member of a royal family, usually a king or a queen, has absolute authority over a territory and its government

- In a **monarchy,** a member of a royal family, usually a king or a queen, has absolute authority over a territory and its government. Monarchies typically are inherited—they pass down from generation to generation. Most modern monarchies, such as those in Great Britain and Spain, are *constitutional monarchies,* in which the monarch plays a ceremonial role but has little say in governance, which is carried out by elected leaders. In contrast, in traditional monarchies, such as the Kingdom of Saudi Arabia, the monarch is both the ceremonial and the governmental head of state.

oligarchy
government in which an elite few hold power

- In an **oligarchy,** an elite few hold power. Some oligarchies are *dictatorships,* in which a small group, such as a political party or a military junta, supports a dictator. North Korea is a present-day example of an oligarchy.

democracy
government in which supreme power of governance lies in the hands of its citizens

- In a **democracy,** the supreme power of governance lies in the hands of citizens. The United States and most other modern democracies are *republics,* sometimes called *representative democracies,* in which citizens elect leaders to represent their views. We discuss the republican form of government in Chapter 2.

When classifying governments, social scientists also consider *how governments function* and *how they are structured:*

totalitarianism
system of government in which the government essentially controls every aspect of people's lives

- Governments that rule according to the principles of **totalitarianism** essentially control every aspect of their citizens' lives. In these tyrannical governments, citizens enjoy neither rights nor freedoms, and the state is the tool of the dictator. Totalitarian regimes tend to center on a particular ideology, religion, or personality. North Korea is a contemporary example of a totalitarian regime, as was Afghanistan under the Islamic fundamentalist regime of the Taliban.

authoritarianism
system of government in which the government holds strong powers but is checked by some forces

- When a government rules by the principles of **authoritarianism,** it holds strong powers, but they are checked by other forces within the society. China and Cuba are examples of authoritarian states, because their leaders are restrained in their exercise of power by political parties, constitutions, and the military. Individuals living under an authoritarian regime may enjoy some rights, but often those rights are not protected by the government. (See "Global Context.")

Context

LEGITIMACY AND INSTABILITY IN EGYPT

Order and stability are linked directly to citizens' perceptions of the legitimacy of the government. When citizens believe that government's exercise of power is right and proper, they recognize the government's right to exist and to create policy—even if they don't agree with the policies chosen.

But when governments are not perceived as legitimate—particularly when they do not largely have consent of the governed—instability often ensues. The graph shows the responses of Egyptian citizens when asked about the confidence they had in the honesty of the country's elections.

In early 2011, citizens in Egypt rebelled as part of the larger Arab Spring movement that spread throughout the Middle East. Until that time, there was widespread lack of confidence in the honesty of Egypt's election process—for years, only 28 percent of the country believed that the electoral process was honest. After former president Hosni Mubarak was ousted in 2011, the public experienced a sudden hike in confidence that illustrated the hope Egyptians felt that democracy would take hold. Quickly, a large majority—69 percent—believed in the honesty of elections, a figure that climbed to 89 percent.

In this country, do you have confidence in each of the following, or not? How about the honesty of elections?

Asked of Egyptian adults

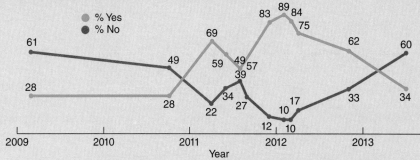

SOURCE: Mohamed Younis, "Egyptians' Views of Government Crashed Before Overthrow," Gallup World, www.gallup.com/poll/163796/egyptian-views-government-crashed-overthrow.aspx.

But throughout 2012, Egyptians' confidence in the honesty of elections eroded, presaging the issuance of a decree by then-president Mohamed Morsi, which greatly expanded the president's power and stripped away the judiciary's power to check the president's authority. Even though Morsi rescinded the decree, confidence in elections continued to erode, and in July 2013, Morsi was deposed as president in a military coup.

- **Constitutionalism,** a form of government structured by law, provides for **limited government**— a government that is restricted in what it can do so that the rights of the people are protected. Constitutional governments can be democracies or monarchies. In the United States, the federal Constitution created the governmental structure, and this system of government reflects both the historical experiences and the norms and values of the founders.

The Constitution's framers (authors) structured American government as a *constitutional democracy*. In this type of government, a constitution creates a representative democracy in which the rights of the people are protected. We can trace the roots of this modern constitutional democracy back to ancient times.

constitutionalism
government that is structured by law, and in which the power of government is limited

limited government
government that is restricted in what it can do so that the rights of the people are protected

The Origins of American Democracy

The ancient Greeks first developed the concept of a democracy. The Greeks used the term *demokratia* (literally, "people power") to describe some of the 1,500 *poleis* ("city-states"; also the root of *politics*) on the Black and the Mediterranean Seas. These city-states were not democracies in the modern sense of the term, but the way they were governed provided the philosophical origins of American democracy. For example, citizens decided public issues using majority rule in many of the city-states. However, in contrast to modern democracies, the Greek city-states did not

In Congress, July 4, 1776.

The unanimous Declaration of the thirteen united States of America.

[facsimile of the Declaration of Independence]

count women as citizens. The Greeks also did not count slaves as citizens. American democracy also traces some of its roots to the Judeo-Christian tradition and the English common law, particularly the ideas that thrived during the Protestant Reformation.[15]

Democracy's Origins in Popular Protest: The Influence of the Reformation and the Enlightenment

We can trace the seeds of the idea of modern democracy almost as far back as the concept of monarchy—back to several centuries ago, when the kings and emperors who ruled in Europe claimed that they reigned by divine sanction, or God's will. The monarchs' claims reflected the political theory of the **divine right of kings,** articulated by Jacques-Benigne Bossuet (1627–1704), who argued that monarchies, as a manifestation of God's will, could rule absolutely without regard to the will or well-being of their subjects. Challenging the right of a monarch to govern or questioning one of his or her decisions thus represented a challenge to the will of God.

At odds with the theory of the divine right of kings was the idea that people could challenge the Crown and the church—institutions that seemed all-powerful. This idea took hold during the Protestant Reformation, a movement to reform the Catholic Church. In October 1517, Martin Luther, a German monk who would later found the Lutheran Church, posted his *95 Theses,* criticizing the harmful practices of the Catholic Church, to the door of the church at Wittenberg Castle. The Reformation continued throughout the sixteenth century, during which time reform-minded Protestants (whose name is derived from *protest*) challenged basic tenets of Catholicism and sought to *purify* the church.

In England, some extreme Protestants, known as Puritans, thought that the Reformation had not gone far enough in reforming the church. Puritans asserted their right to communicate directly with God through prayer rather than through an intermediary such as a priest. This idea that an individual could speak directly with God lent support to the notion that the people could govern themselves. Faced with persecution in England, congregations of Puritans, known to us today as the Pilgrims, fled to America, where they established self-governing colonies, a radical notion at the time. Before the Pilgrims reached shore in 1620, they drew up the Mayflower Compact, an example of a **social contract**—an agreement between people and their leaders, whereby the people give up some liberties so that their other liberties will be protected. In the Mayflower Compact, the Pilgrims agreed to be governed by the structure of government they formed, thereby establishing the idea of consent of the governed.

In the late seventeenth century came the early beginnings of the Enlightenment, a philosophical movement that stressed the importance of individuality, reason, and scientific endeavor. Enlightenment scientists such as Sir Isaac Newton (1642–1727) drastically changed how people thought about the universe and the world around them, including government. Newton's work in physics, astronomy, math, and mechanics demonstrated the power of science and repudiated prevalent ideas based on magic and superstition. Newton's ideas about **natural law,** the assertion that the laws that govern human behavior are derived from the nature of humans themselves and can be applied universally, laid the foundation for the ideas of the political philosophers of the Enlightenment.

divine right of kings
the assertion that monarchies, as a manifestation of God's will, could rule absolutely without regard to the will or well-being of their subjects

social contract
an agreement between people and their leaders in which the people agree to give up some liberties so that their other liberties are protected

natural law
the assertion that standards that govern human behavior are derived from the nature of humans themselves and can be applied universally

>In his scientific work, Sir Isaac Newton demonstrated the power of science to explain phenomena in the natural world and discredited prevalent ideas based on magic and superstition. Newton's ideas laid the foundation for the political philosophers of the Enlightenment.

The Modern Political Philosophy of Hobbes and Locke

The difficulty of individual survival under the rule of an absolute monarch is portrayed in British philosopher Thomas Hobbes's book *Leviathan* (1651). Hobbes (1588–1679), who believed in the righteousness of absolute monarchies, argued that the strong naturally prey on the weak and that through a social contract, individuals who relinquish their rights can enjoy the protection offered by a sovereign. Without such a social contract and without an absolute monarch, Hobbes asserted, anarchy prevails, describing this state as one lived in "continuall feare, and danger of violent death; And the life of man, solitary, poore, nasty, brutish, and short."[16]

John Locke (1632–1704) took Hobbes's reasoning concerning a social contract one step further. In the first of his *Two Treatises on Civil Government* (1689), Locke systematically rejected the notion that the rationale for the divine right of kings is based on scripture. By providing a theoretical basis for discarding the idea of a monarch's divine right to rule, Locke paved the way for more radical notions about the rights of individuals and the role of government. In the second *Treatise,* Locke argued that individuals possess certain unalienable (or natural) rights, which he identified as the rights to life, liberty, and property, ideas that would prove pivotal in shaping Thomas Jefferson's articulation of the role of government and the rights of individuals found in the Declaration of Independence. Locke, and later Jefferson, stressed that these rights are inherent in people as individuals; that is, government can neither bestow them nor take them away. When people enter into a social contract, Locke said, they do so with the understanding that the government will protect their natural rights. At the same time, according to Locke, they agree to accept the government's authority; but if the government fails to protect the inherent rights of individuals, the people have the right to rebel.

The French philosopher Jean-Jacques Rousseau (1712–1778) took Locke's notion further, stating that governments formed by social contract rely on **popular sovereignty,** the theory that government is created by the people and depends on the people for the authority to rule. **Social contract theory,** which assumes that individuals possess free will and that every individual possesses the God-given right of self-determination and the ability to consent to be governed, would eventually form the theoretical framework of the Declaration of Independence.

> ⟩Thomas Jefferson's ideas about the role of government shaped the United States for generations to come. In 1999, descendants of Thomas Jefferson, including those he fathered with his slave, Sally Hemings, who was also his wife's half-sister, posed for a group photo at his plantation, Monticello, in Charlottesville, Virginia.

popular sovereignty
the theory that government is created by the people and depends on the people for the authority to rule

social contract theory
the idea that individuals possess free will and that every individual is equally endowed with the God-given right of self-determination and the ability to consent to be governed

The Creation of the United States as an Experiment in Representative Democracy

The American colonists who eventually rebelled against Great Britain and who became the citizens of the first 13 states were shaped by their experiences of living under European monarchies. Many rejected the ideas of absolute rule and the divine right of kings, which had been central to rationalizing the monarchs' authority. The logic behind the rejection of the divine right of kings—the idea that monarchs were not chosen by God—was that people could govern themselves.

In New England, where many colonists settled after fleeing England to escape religious persecution, a form of **direct democracy,** a structure of government in which citizens discuss and decide policy through majority rule, emerged in *town meetings* (which still take place today). In every colony, the colonists themselves decided who was eligible to participate in government, and so in some localities, women and people of color who owned property participated in government well before they were granted formal voting rights under amendments to the federal Constitution.

Beyond the forms of direct democracy prevalent in the New England colonies, nearly all the American colonies had councils structured according to the principle of representative democracy, sometimes called **indirect democracy,** in which citizens elect representatives who decide policies on their behalf. These representative democracies foreshadow important political values that founders such as Thomas Jefferson and James Madison would incorporate into key founding documents, including the Declaration of Independence and the Constitution.

Political Culture and American Values

On September 11, 2002, the first anniversary of the terrorist attacks on the United States, *The New York Times* ran an editorial, "America Enduring," that described how the United States and its residents had weathered the difficult year after the terrorist attacks of September 11, 2001. "America isn't bound together by emotion. It's bound together by things that transcend emotion, by principles and laws, by ideals of freedom and justice that need constant articulation."[17] These ideals are part of American **political culture**—the people's collective beliefs and attitudes about government and the political process. These ideals include liberty, equality, capitalism, consent of the governed, and the importance of the individual (as well as family and community).

Liberty

The most essential quality of American democracy, **liberty** is both freedom from government interference in our lives and freedom to pursue happiness. Many of the colonies that eventually became the United States were founded by people who were interested in one notion of liberty: religious freedom. Those who fought in the War of Independence were intent on obtaining economic and political freedom. The framers of the Constitution added to the structure of the U.S. government many other liberties,[18] including freedom of speech, freedom of the press, and freedom of association.[19]

There is evidence all around us of ongoing tensions between people attempting to assert their individual liberty on the one hand and the government's efforts to exert control on the other. For example, in February 2012, President Obama faced opposition from religious groups and Catholic lawmakers in both parties over his decision to mandate that employers with health care plans provide free birth control coverage (which was reclassified as "preventative care")—even when the employers, including the Catholic Church, object to the use of birth control. Although churches, synagogues, and mosques are exempt from the mandate, religious nonprofits, including church-based organizations that do charity work, are not. In the wake of continued pressure, President Obama offered a compromise: Insurance companies, not the religious employers paying for the insurance plans, would bear the responsibility for the change.

Throughout history and to the present day, liberties have often conflicted with efforts by the government to ensure a secure and stable society by exerting restraints on liberties. When

---

direct democracy
a structure of government in which citizens discuss and decide policy through majority rule

indirect democracy
sometimes called a *representative democracy,* a system in which citizens elect representatives who decide policies on behalf of their constituents

political culture
the people's collective beliefs and attitudes about government and political processes

liberty
the most essential quality of American democracy; it is both the freedom from governmental interference in citizens' lives and the freedom to pursue happiness

government officials infringe on personal liberties, they often do so in the name of security, arguing that such measures are necessary to protect the rights of other individuals, institutions (including the government itself), or society as a whole. Such was the case when it was revealed that the National Security Agency had recorded information about 125 million cell phone communications in a 30-day period, including 3 million communications originating in the United States.

The meaning of liberty—how we define our freedoms—is constantly evolving. Today, technological innovation prompts new questions about individual privacy, including what information the government should be privy to. Should the government be permitted to collect metadata—data about communications data (the length of calls, for example)—of members of suspected terror cells? Should they be able to monitor phone calls and text messages to individuals in these cells? What if that person is suspected of plotting a terrorist attack—should officers be required to obtain a warrant first

> The terror attacks of September 11, 2001, profoundly changed many Americans' perception of government. For many, it also solidified their belief in core American political values. Here, the child of a victim of the terror attacks participates in a memorial observance.

in that situation? Similarly, just a decade ago, Americans were forced to evaluate how far the government should go in curtailing liberties to provide security after September 11. Should law enforcement officers be allowed to track a person's movements using GPS (Global Positioning System) if that person is suspected of a crime? Or should they be required to get a warrant first? What if one of the suspected plotters is not a U.S. citizen?

Equality

The Declaration of Independence states that "all men are created equal. . . ." But the founders' notions of equality were vastly different from those that prevail today. Their ideas of equality evolved from the emphasis the ancient Greeks placed on equality of opportunity. The Greeks envisioned a merit-based system in which educated freemen could participate in democratic government rather than inheriting their positions as a birthright. The Judeo-Christian religions also emphasize the idea of equality. All three major world religions—Christianity, Judaism, and Islam—stress that all people are equal in the eyes of God. These notions of equality informed both Jefferson's assertion about equality in the Declaration of Independence and, later, the framers' structuring of the U.S. government in the Constitution.[20]

The idea of equality evolved during the 19th and 20th centuries. In the early American republic, all women, as well as all men of color, were denied fundamental rights, including the right to vote. Through long, painful struggles—including the abolition movement to free the slaves; the suffrage movement to gain women the right to vote; various immigrants' rights movements; and later the civil rights, Native American rights, and women's rights movements of the 1960s and 1970s (Chapter 5)—members of these disenfranchised groups won the rights previously denied to them.

Several groups are still engaged in the struggle for legal equality today, notably gay and lesbian rights organizations and groups that advocate for fathers', children's, and immigrants' rights. And historic questions about the nature of equality have very modern implications: Do children enjoy the same rights that adult citizens do? And should they be afforded special protections by the government? Are the advantages of U.S. democracy reserved only for citizens, or should immigrants living legally in the United States also enjoy these advantages?

Beyond these questions of legal equality, today many arguments over equality focus on issues of economic equality, a concept about which there is substantial disagreement. As we saw from the Occupy movements that formed across the United States in fall 2011, some people in the United States believe that the government should do more to eliminate disparities in wealth—by taxing wealthy people more heavily than others, for example, or by providing more subsidies and services to the poor. Others disagree, however, and argue that although people should have equal opportunities for economic achievement, their attainment of that success should depend on factors such as education and hard work, and that success should be determined in the marketplace rather than through government intervention.

Capitalism

Although the founders valued the notion of equality, capitalism was enormously important to them. **Capitalism** is an economic system in which the means of producing wealth are privately owned and operated to produce profits. In a pure capitalist economy, the marketplace determines the regulation of production, the distribution of goods and services, wages, and prices. In this type of economy, for example, businesses pay employees the wage that they are willing to work for, without the government's setting a minimum wage by law. Although capitalism is an important value in American democracy, the U.S. government imposes certain regulations on the economy. For example, it mandates a minimum wage, regulates and inspects goods and services, and imposes tariffs on imports and taxes on domestically produced goods that have an impact on pricing.

One key component of capitalism is **property**—anything that can be owned. There are various kinds of property: businesses, homes, farms, the material items we use every day, and even ideas are considered property. Property holds such a prominent position in American culture that it is considered a natural right, and the Constitution protects some aspects of property ownership.

Consent of the Governed

The idea that, in a democracy, the government's power derives from the consent of the people is called the **consent of the governed.** As we have seen, this concept, a focal point of the rebellious American colonists and eloquently expressed in Jefferson's Declaration of Independence, is based on John Locke's idea of a social contract. Implicit in Locke's social contract is the principle that the people agree to the government's authority, and if the government no longer has the consent of the governed, the people have the right to revolt.

The concept of consent of the governed also implies **majority rule**—the principle that, in a democracy, only policies with 50 percent plus one vote are enacted. Governments based on majority rule include the idea that the majority has the right of self-governance and typically also protect the rights of people in the minority. A particular question about this ideal of governing by the consent of the governed has important implications for the United States in the early 21st century: Can a democracy remain stable and legitimate if less than a majority of its citizens participate in elections?

Individual, Family, and Community

Emphasis on the individual is a preeminent feature of American democratic thought. In the Constitution, rights are bestowed on, and exercised by, the individual. The importance of the individual—an independent, hearty entity exercising self-determination—has powerfully shaped the development of the United States, both geographically and politically.

Family and community have also played central roles in the U.S. political culture, both historically and in the present day. A child first learns political behavior from his or her family, and in this way the family serves to perpetuate the political culture. From the earliest colonial settlements to Instagram today, communities have channeled individuals' political participation. Indeed, the intimate relationship between individualism and community life is reflected in the First Amendment of the Constitution, which ensures individuals' freedom of assembly—one component of which is their right to form or join any type of organization, political party, or club without penalty.

Ideology: A Prism for Viewing American Democracy

Besides focusing on the demographic characteristics of the U.S. population, we can also analyze political events and trends by looking at them through the prism of ideology. **Political ideology** is an integrated system of ideas or beliefs about political values in general and the role of government in particular (see "Analyzing the Sources"). Political ideology provides a framework for thinking about politics, about policy issues, and about the role of government in society. In the United States, one key component of various ideologies is the *extent* to which adherents believe that the government should have a role in people's everyday lives. Table 1.1 summarizes the key ideologies we consider in this section.

political ideology

integrated system of ideas or beliefs about political values in general and the role of government in particular.

Liberalism

Modern **liberalism** in the United States is associated with the ideas of liberty and political equality; its advocates favor change in the social, political, and economic realms to better protect the well-being of individuals and to produce equality within society. They emphasize the importance of civil liberties, including freedom of speech, assembly, and the press, as outlined in the Bill of Rights. Modern liberals also advocate the separation of church and state, often opposing measures that bring religion into the public realm, such as prayer in the public schools. In addition, they support political equality, advocating contemporary movements that promote the political rights of gay and lesbian couples and voting rights for the disenfranchised.

liberalism

an ideology that advocates change in the social, political, and economic realms to better protect the well-being of individuals and to produce equality within society

The historical roots of modern liberalism reach back to the ideals of classical liberalism: freedom of thought and the free exchange of ideas, limited governmental authority, the consent of the governed, the rule of law in society, the importance of an unfettered market economy, individual initiative as a determinant of success, and access to free public education. These also were some of the founding ideals that shaped American democracy as articulated in the Declaration of Independence and the Constitution.

Modern liberalism, which emerged in the early 20th century, diverged from its classical roots in a number of ways. Most important, modern liberals expect the government to play a more active role in ensuring political equality and economic opportunity. Whereas classical liberals emphasized the virtues of a free market economy, modern liberals, particularly after the Great Depression that began in 1929, advocated government involvement in economic affairs. Today, we see this expectation in action when liberals call for prioritizing economic policies that benefit

The Traditional Ideological Spectrum

TABLE 1.1

	SOCIALISM	LIBERALISM	MIDDLE OF ROAD (MODERATE)	CONSERVATISM	LIBERTARIANISM
GOAL OF GOVERNMENT	Equality	Equality of opportunity; protection of fundamental liberties	Nondiscrimination in opportunity; protection of some economic freedoms; security; stability	Traditional values; order; stability; economic freedom	Absolute economic and social freedom
ROLE OF GOVERNMENT	Strong government control of economy	Government action to promote opportunity	Government action to balance the wants of workers and businesses; government fosters stability	Government action to protect and bolster capitalist system; few limitations on fundamental rights	No governmental regulations of economy; no limitations on fundamental rights

the poor and middle class, including job creation and tax policies, as well as their support for the health care reform act, sometimes called Obamacare, which was rolled out in 2013. In modern times, liberals also are likely to advocate for affirmative action; increases in social welfare programs such as Social Security, Medicare, and Medicaid; and government regulation of business and workplace conditions.

Conservatism

conservatism
an ideology that emphasizes preserving tradition and relying on community and family as mechanisms of continuity in society

Advocates of **conservatism** recognize the importance of preserving tradition—of maintaining the status quo, or keeping things the way they are. Conservatives emphasize community and family as mechanisms of continuity in society. Ironically, some modern conservative ideals are consistent with the views of classical liberalism. In particular, the emphasis on individual initiative, the rule of law, limited governmental authority, and an unfettered market economy are key components of both classical liberalism and contemporary conservatism.

Traditionally, one of the key differences between modern liberals and conservatives has been their view of the role of government. In fact, one of the best ways of determining your own ideology is to ask yourself, "To what extent should the government be involved in people's everyday lives?" Modern liberals believe that the government should play a role in ensuring the public's well-being, whether through the regulation of industry or the economy, through antidiscrimination laws, or by providing an economic "safety net" for the neediest members of society. By contrast, conservatives believe that government should play a more limited role in people's everyday lives. They think that government should have a smaller role in regulating business and industry and that market forces, rather than the government, should largely determine economic policy. Conservatives believe that families, faith-based groups, and private charities should be more responsible for protecting the neediest and the government less so. When governments must act, conservatives prefer decentralized action by state governments rather than a nationwide federal policy. Conservatives also believe in the importance of individual initiative as a key determinant of success. Conservative ideas are the fundamental basis of policies such as the Welfare Reform Act of 1996, which placed the development and administration of welfare (Temporary Aid to Needy Families, or TANF) in the hands of the states rather than the federal government.

In recent years, several core groups within the conservative ideology have exerted strong influence in the U.S. political arena. In particular, evangelical Christians, who on the whole tend to hold very traditional social values while deemphasizing fiscal matters, and Tea Party activists, who often advocate for lower taxes and less federal government interference in people's lives, have held sway. The Tea Party first flexed its muscles during the 2010 congressional elections, in which several Tea Party candidates challenged traditional Republican candidates (and, in some cases, won). In the 2012 presidential primary process, Republican Rick Santorum's campaign gained traction in the early primary season against rival Mitt Romney because of the support Santorum received from Evangelical Christians in several states. In 2014, the Tea Party succeeded again in successfully challenging several moderate Republican incumbents in primary elections.

Other Ideologies on a Traditional Spectrum: Socialism and Libertarianism

Although liberals and conservatives dominate the U.S. political landscape, other ideologies reflect the views of some Americans. In general, those ideologies tend to be more extreme than liberalism or conservatism. Advocates of certain of these ideologies call for *more* governmental intervention than modern liberalism does, and supporters of other views favor even *less* governmental interference than conservatism does.

socialism
an ideology that advocates economic equality, theoretically achieved by having the government or workers own the means of production (businesses and industry)

For example, **socialism**—an ideology that stresses economic equality, theoretically achieved by having the government or workers own the means of production (businesses and industry)—lies to the left of liberalism on the political spectrum.[21] Although socialists play a very limited role in modern American politics, this was not always the case.[22] In the early part of the 20th century, socialists had a good deal of electoral success. Two members of Congress (Representative Meyer London of New York and Representative Victor Berger of Wisconsin), more than 70 mayors of cities of various sizes, and numerous state legislators (including 5 in the New York

IDEOLOGY BY AGE

The figures below show the results of a Gallup poll that measures ideology by age. Note that there are significant differences in political ideology between age groups. There is a trend of increasing conservatism among all Americans since 2002, but this is seen primarily among adults aged 30 and older. Although those aged 18–29 grew more conservative for a brief period from 2002 through 2005, this shift was temporary and declined to less than 30 percent by 2011.

Evaluating the Evidence

1. Describe the ideology of the Millennial generation. Are they more likely to identify with either ideology? Why do you think this is the case?

2. Which generation is likely to have nearly equal proportions of liberals and conservatives?

3. Which voters are the most conservative? Which are the most liberal?

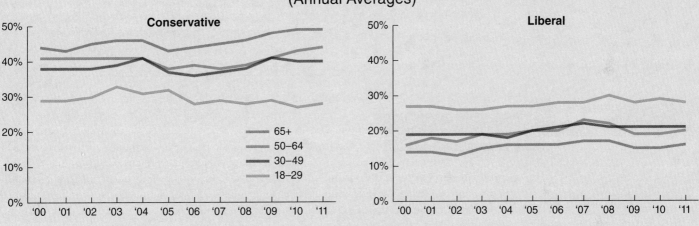

U.S. Political Ideology by Age (Annual Averages)

SOURCE: Lydia Saad, "Conservatives Remain Largest Ideological Group in U.S," Gallup Politics, www.gallup.com/poll/152021/Conservatives-Remain-Largest-Ideological-Group.aspx.

General Assembly and many municipal council members throughout the country) were socialists. In 1912, Socialist Party presidential candidate Eugene Debs garnered 6 percent of the presidential vote—six times what Green Party candidate Ralph Nader netted in 2004.

According to **libertarianism,** in contrast, government should take a "hands-off" approach in most matters. This ideology can be found to the right of conservatism on a traditional ideological spectrum. Libertarians believe that the less government intervention, the better. They chafe at attempts by the government to foster economic equality or to promote a social agenda, whether that agenda is the equality espoused by liberals or the traditional values espoused by conservatives. Libertarians strongly support the rights of property owners and a *laissez-faire* (French for "let it be") capitalist economy.

libertarianism

an ideology whose advocates believe that government should take a "hands-off" approach in most matters

A Three-Dimensional Political Model

A one-dimensional ideological continuum is limited, however, because it sometimes fails to reflect the complexity of many individuals' views. For example, although an individual may believe that government should play a strong role in regulating the economy, he or she may also believe that the government should allow citizens a high degree of personal freedom of speech or religion. Even the traditional ideologies do not always fit easily into a single continuum that

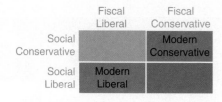

	Fiscal Liberal	Fiscal Conservative
Social Conservative		Modern Conservative
Social Liberal	Modern Liberal	

FIGURE 1.2

Multidimensional Ideological Grid Where would you place yourself on this grid? How has your socialization formed your ideology? Can you imagine future circumstances that might cause your views to change?

measures the extent to which the government should play a role in citizens' lives. Liberals supposedly advocate a larger role for the government. But although this may be the case in matters related to economic equality, liberals generally take a more laissez-faire approach when it comes to personal liberties, advocating strongly for privacy and free speech. And although conservatives support less governmental intervention in the economy, they sometimes advocate government action to promote traditional values, such as constitutional amendments to ban flag burning and abortion and laws that mandate prayer in public schools.

Scholars have developed various *multidimensional scales* that attempt to represent peoples' ideologies more accurately.[23] Many of these scales measure people's opinions on the proper role of government in the economy—whether the government should act aggressively to ensure economic equality (fiscal liberalism) or prioritize a hands-off approach to the economy (social conservatism) on one axis and their beliefs about personal freedom on social issues on a second axis. As shown in Figure 1.2, these scales demonstrate that traditional liberals (lower-left quadrant) and traditional conservatives (upper-right quadrant) believe in social liberty and economic equality, and economic liberty and social conservatism, respectively. But the scale also acknowledges that some people prioritize economic equality and social order, whereas others embrace economic liberty and social order.

Ideology is one of the most important factors influencing people's belief structure about the types of issues they prioritize and the solutions they see to various policy challenges. But ideology alone does not explain priorities and preferred solutions. Also important are the characteristics of who we are, as these characteristics often make us more likely to identify certain issues as important, or render us more likely to favor one policy solution over another.

The Changing Face of American Democracy

Figure 1.3 shows how the U.S. population has grown since the first census in 1790. At that point, there were fewer than 4 million Americans. By 2015, the U.S. population had reached nearly 320 million.

Immigrants have always been part of the country's population growth, and over the centuries they have made innumerable contributions to American life and culture.[24] Immigrants from lands all around the world have faced the kinds of struggles that today's undocumented immigrants encounter. And efforts to improve the lot of immigrant populations are not new either: Chinese Americans, for example, were instrumental in pioneering the West and completing the construction of the transcontinental railroad in the mid-19th century, but the Chinese Exclusion Act of 1881 prevented them from becoming U.S. citizens. Faced with the kinds of persecution that today would be considered hate crimes, Chinese Americans used civil disobedience to fight against the so-called Dog Tag Laws that required them to carry registration cards. In one incident, in 1885, they fought back against unruly mobs that drove them out of the town of Eureka, California, by suing the city for reparations and compensation.[25]

POLITICAL Inquiry

FIGURE 1.3 ▪ GROWTH OF THE U.S. POPULATION From 1790 to 1900, the U.S. population increased gradually, and it did not reach 100 million until the second decade of the 20th century. What factors caused the steep rise during the 20th century? How will these forces continue to affect the size of the U.S. population during this century?

SOURCE: U.S. Census Bureau, www.census.gov/population/censusdata/table-4.pdf, www.census.gov/popclock/, and www.census.gov/population/projections/data/national/2012.html.

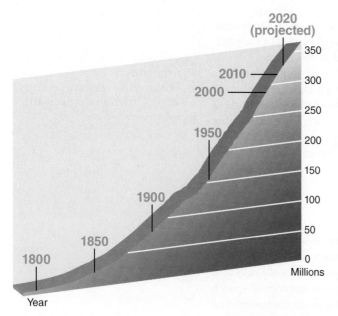

A Population That Is Growing—and on the Move

Between the 1960 census and the last census taken in 2010, the population of the United States increased by more than 50 percent. As the population increases, measures of who the American people are and what percentage of each demographic group makes up the population have significant implications for the policies, priorities, values, and preferred forms of civic and political participation of the people. All the factors contributing to U.S. population growth—including

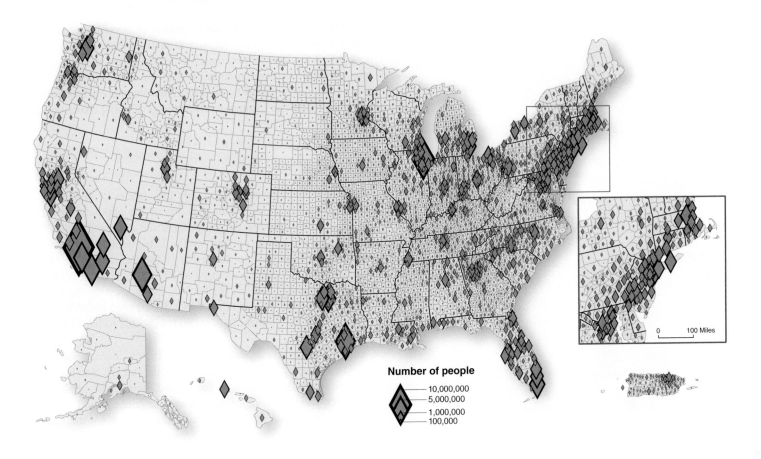

FIGURE 1.4

Population Distribution by County The area of each diamond symbol is proportioned by the number of people in a county. The legend presents example symbol sizes from the many symbols shown on the map. Where are the largest population centers in the United States? What areas have comparatively sparse population?

SOURCE: U.S. Census Bureau, "Population Distribution and Change: 2000 to 2010," 2011, www.census.gov/2010census/popmap/.

Number of people

10,000,000
5,000,000
1,000,000
100,000

immigration, the birth rate, falling infant mortality rates, and longer life spans—influence both politics and policy, as the ongoing debate about immigration reform shows. Generational differences in preferred methods of participation are yet another, as is the national conversation about the future of Social Security.

Accompanying the increase in population over the years has been a shift in the places where people live. Figure 1.4 shows that much of the population in the United States is concentrated in just a few densely populated areas: the Northeast, the Great Lake states, the Carolinas, Florida, Texas, and California. Between 2000 and 2010, the South and West accounted for 84 percent of the country's increase in population. Though not shown in Figure 1.4, census data indicates that many of the

> The Chinese Exclusion Act of 1881 prevented Chinese from becoming U.S. citizens, and local laws, including one in Brooklyn depicted here, banned them from employment. Faced with the kinds of persecution that today would be considered hate crimes, Chinese Americans used civil disobedience to fight against the so-called Dog Tag Laws that required them to carry registration cards. Are there groups in the United States who are persecuted in similar ways today?

KNOW-NOTHINGISM IN BROOKLYN.

"None but citizens of the United States can be licensed to engage in any employment in this city."
Brooklyn Board of Aldemen.

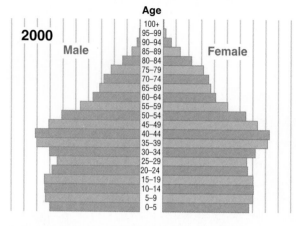

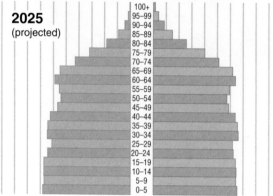

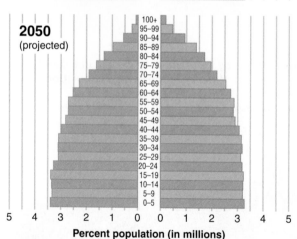

Age

2000

Male   Female

100+
95–99
90–94
85–89
80–84
75–79
70–74
65–69
60–64
55–59
50–54
45–49
40–44
35–39
30–34
25–29
20–24
15–19
10–14
5–9
0–5

2025
(projected)

100+
95–99
90–94
85–89
80–84
75–79
70–74
65–69
60–64
55–59
50–54
45–49
40–44
35–39
30–34
25–29
20–24
15–19
10–14
5–9
0–5

2050
(projected)

100+
95–99
90–94
85–89
80–84
75–79
70–74
65–69
60–64
55–59
50–54
45–49
40–44
35–39
30–34
25–29
20–24
15–19
10–14
5–9
0–5

5   4   3   2   1   0   0   1   2   3   4   5

Percent population (in millions)

FIGURE 1.5

The Aging U.S. Population, 2000–2050

SOURCE: U.S. Census Bureau, National Population Projections, www.census.gov/population/projections/data/national/.

states in the Midwest are facing an out-migration of population, particularly of younger residents who are moving to metropolitan areas seeking employment. All of the 10 most populous metro areas grew, as did 9 of the 10 most populous cities. In rural areas of the Midwest, though, some of this out-migration is counterbalanced by migration into these areas by families and retirees attracted by the comparatively low cost of living characteristic of these areas.

An Aging Population

As the U.S. population increases and favors new places of residence, it is also aging. Figure 1.5 shows the distribution of the population by age and by sex as a series of three pyramids for three different years. The 2000 pyramid shows the "muffin top" of the baby boomers, who were 36–55 years old in that year. A quarter century later, the echo boom of the Millennials, who will be between the ages of 30 and 55 in 2025, is clearly visible. The pyramid evens out and thickens by 2050, showing the effects of increased population growth and the impact of extended longevity, with a large number of people (women, in particular) expected to live to the age of 85 and older.

Some areas of the United States are well-known meccas for older Americans. For example, the reputation of Florida and the Southwest as the premier retirement destinations in the United States is highlighted in Figure 1.6, which shows that older Americans are concentrated in those areas, as well as in a broad north-south band that runs down the United States' midsection. Older people are concentrated in the Midwest and Plains states because of the high levels of out-migration from these areas by younger Americans, who are leaving their parents behind to look for opportunity elsewhere.

A Changing Complexion: Race and Ethnicity in the United States Today

The population of the United States is becoming not only older but also more racially and ethnically diverse. Figure 1.7 shows the racial and ethnic composition of the U.S. population according to the last census conducted in 2010. Notice that Hispanics* now make up a greater proportion of the U.S. population than do blacks. As Figure 1.7 also shows, this trend has been continuous over the past several decades. Figure 1.7 also indicates that the percentage of Asian Americans has more than doubled in recent decades, from just over 2 percent of the U.S. population in 1980 to 5 percent today. The Native American population has increased marginally but still constitutes less than 1 percent of the whole population. Figure 1.7 also shows the proportion of people reporting that they belonged to two or more racial groups—3 percent of the population today. This category was not an option on the census questionnaire until 2000, and the population proportion of this group has doubled since that time.

---

*A note about terminology: When discussing data for various races and ethnicities for the purpose of making comparisons, we use the terms *black* and *Hispanic,* because these labels are typically used in measuring demographics by the U.S. Census Bureau and other organizations that collect this type of data. In more descriptive writing that is not comparative, we use the terms *African American* and *Latino* and *Latina,* which are the preferred terms at this time. Although the terms *Latino* and *Latina* exclude Americans who came from Spain (or whose ancestors did), these people compose a very small proportion of this population in the United States.

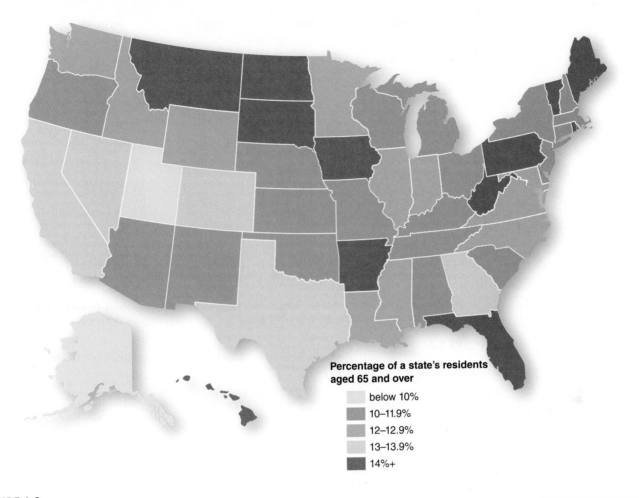

Percentage of a state's residents aged 65 and over

- below 10%
- 10–11.9%
- 12–12.9%
- 13–13.9%
- 14%+

FIGURE 1.6

Where the Older Americans Are

SOURCE: U.S. Department of Health and Human Services, Administration on Aging, *A Profile of Older Americans: 2010*, www.aoa.gov/aoaroot/aging_statistics/Profile/2010/docs/2010profile.pdf.

As Figures 1.8 and 1.9 show, minority populations tend to be concentrated in different areas of the United States. Figure 1.8 shows the concentration of non-Hispanic African Americans. At 13 percent of the population, African Americans are the largest racial minority in the United States. (Hispanics are an ethnic minority.) As the map illustrates, the African American population tends to be centered in urban areas and in the South, where, in some counties, African Americans constitute a majority of the population.

Hispanics, in contrast, historically have tended to cluster in Texas, Arizona, and California along the border between the United States and Mexico and in the urban centers of New Mexico (as shown in Figure 1.9), but the decade between 2000 and 2010 saw significant growth in the number of Hispanics living in the South. In that decade, Hispanic populations also

> Hispanics are the fastest-growing ethnic group in the United States, with 16 percent of the U.S. population identifying themselves as Hispanic in the latest census, an increase of nearly 10 percent since 1980. Lobbying for the rights of immigrants is a cause of paramount importance to many Hispanics today.

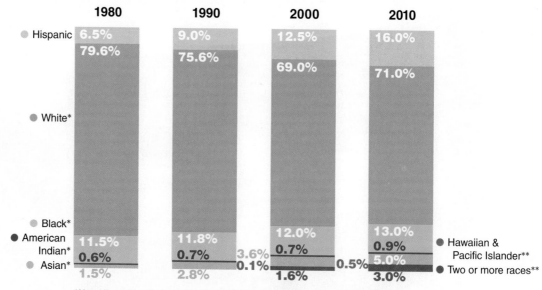

	1980	**1990**	**2000**	**2010**
Hispanic	6.5%	9.0%	12.5%	16.0%
White*	79.6%	75.6%	69.0%	71.0%
Black*	11.5%	11.8%	12.0%	13.0%
American Indian*	0.6%	0.7%	0.7%	0.9%
Asian*	1.5%	2.8%	1.6%	5.0%

3.6% 0.1% 0.5%

● Hawaiian & Pacific Islander**

● Two or more races**

3.0%

*Non-Hispanic only; in 1980 and 1990 "Asians" included Hawaiians and Pacific Islanders.
**Option available for the first time in 2000 census.

FIGURE 1.7

Population by Race Since 1990

SOURCES: www.censusscope.org; Social Science Data Analysis Network, University of Michigan, www.ssdan.net; and U.S. Census Bureau, "Population: Estimates and Projections by Age, Sex, Race/Ethnicity," www.census.gov/compendia/statab/cats/population/estimates_and_projections_by_age_sex_raceethnicity.html.

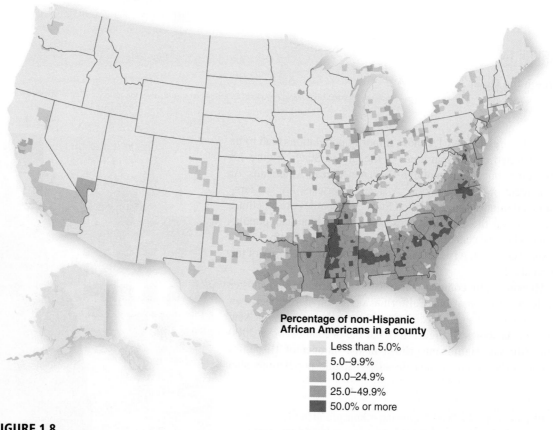

Percentage of non-Hispanic African Americans in a county

- Less than 5.0%
- 5.0–9.9%
- 10.0–24.9%
- 25.0–49.9%
- 50.0% or more

FIGURE 1.8

Where African Americans Live

SOURCE: U.S. Census Bureau, Census Data Mapper, http://tigerweb.geo.census.gov/datamapper/map.html.

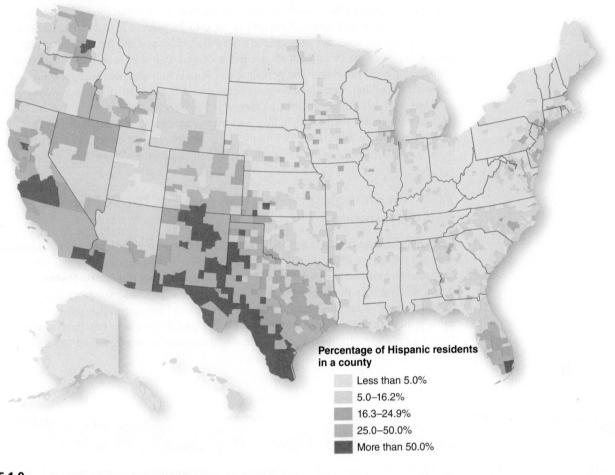

FIGURE 1.9

Where Hispanics Live

Percentage of Hispanic residents in a county

- Less than 5.0%
- 5.0–16.2%
- 16.3–24.9%
- 25.0–50.0%
- More than 50.0%

SOURCE: U.S. Census Bureau, Census Data Mapper, http://tigerweb.geo.census.gov/datamapper/map.html.

increased in Florida and the Northeast. Hispanics are the fastest-growing ethnic group in the United States, with 16 percent of the U.S. population identifying themselves as Hispanic in 2010, an increase of nearly 10 percent since 1980. Among people of Hispanic ethnicity, Mexicans make up the largest number (about 7 percent of the total U.S. population), followed by Puerto Ricans (1 percent in 2000) and Cubans (0.4 percent).

Changing Households: American Families Today

The types of families that are counted by the U.S. census are also becoming more diverse. The traditional nuclear family, consisting of a stay-at-home mother, a breadwinning father, and their children, was at one time the stereotypical "ideal family" in the United States. Many—though hardly all—American families were able to achieve that cultural ideal during the prosperous 1950s and early 1960s. But since the women's liberation movement of the 1970s, in which women sought equal rights with men, the American family has changed drastically. In recent years, the economic downturn has also affected family living arrangements. For example, between 2005 and 2013, the proportions of young adults living in their parents' homes increased, growing from 14 percent of 25- to 34-year-old men in 2005 to 18 percent in 2013 and from 8 percent to 11 percent for women. During those years, most 18- to 24-year-olds also lived in their parents' homes (those living in a college dorm are considered to be living at home for census purposes)—59 percent of men (up from 53 percent in 2005) and 50 percent of women (up from 46 percent). The primary factor for this shift is economic: Young people have higher unemployment rates than older workers, but the sour economy also meant that parents might receive help from the contributions of grown children to the household. Also on the rise is the proportion of single-person households (which increased from 13 percent in 1960 to 28 percent in 2011). Explanations for these trends include the tendency of people to marry at an older age and the fact that, as the population ages, rising numbers of individuals are left widowed. A bad economy also may have led some couples to put off marriage. The percentage of female householders without spouses (both with and without children) remained constant between 2000 and 2010 after experiencing a significant increase from 1970 through 1990, as shown in Figure 1.10. The proportion of male householders without spouses increased slightly, and men without a spouse are more likely to be raising children than they were in 1980. Finally, the proportion of the population living in nonfamily households, both those living alone and those living with others, rose slightly.

Why the Changing Population Matters for Politics and Government

Each of the changes to the U.S. population described here has implications for American democracy. As the nature of the electorate shifts, a majority of the nation's people may have different priorities, and various policies may become more or less important. For example, in recent years, we have seen increased demands for comprehensive immigration reform, often propelled by immigrants or families of immigrants with a vested interest in this reform. In addition, the swift growth in U.S. population means that demand for the services government provides—from schools, to highways, to health care—will continue to increase. The aging population will

FIGURE 1.10 ■ U.S. HOUSEHOLD TRENDS What factors might explain the increase in male householders without spouses between 1990 and 2012? What factors might explain the increase in nonfamily households? What impact, if any, might these trends have on policy in the future?

SOURCES: CensusScope, "Household and Family Structure," www.censusscope.org/us/chart_house.html; Social Science Data Analysis Network, University of Michigan, www.ssdan.net; and U.S. Census Bureau, "America's Families and Living Arrangements: 2008," www.census.gov/population/www/socdemo/hh-fam/cps2008.html.

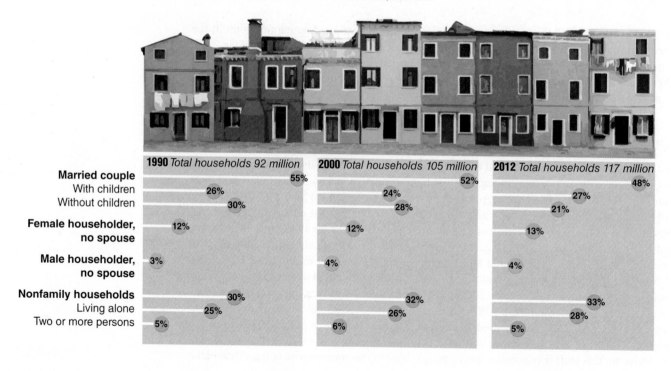

	1990 Total households 92 million	2000 Total households 105 million	2012 Total households 117 million
Married couple	55%	52%	48%
With children	26%	24%	27%
Without children	30%	28%	21%
Female householder, no spouse	12%	12%	13%
Male householder, no spouse	3%	4%	4%
Nonfamily households			
Living alone	30%	32%	33%
Two or more persons	25%	26%	28%
	5%	6%	5%

inevitably increase the burden on the nation's Social Security and government-supported health care system, which will be forced to support the needs of that rising population.

Changes in the population's racial and ethnic composition also matter, as does the concentration of racial minorities in specific geographic areas. The racial and ethnic makeup of the population (along with other influences) can significantly affect the nation's political culture and people's political attitudes. It has implications too for who will govern, as more and more representatives of the country's various racial and ethnic groups become candidates for political office and as *all* political candidates must reach out to increasingly diverse groups of voters—or possibly pay the price at the ballot box for failing to do so.

Conclusion Thinking Critically About What's Next in American Democracy

Now is an exciting time to study American democracy. The fast-paced changes in American society today make participation in government and civic life more vitally important than ever. The effects of participating in the continuing conversation of American democracy through both words and actions are unequivocally positive—for you, for others, and for the government—and can have large ripple effects.

Will the present generation break the cycle of cynicism that has pervaded the politics of the recent past? Today, it is clear that generational changes, particularly the distinctive political opinions of the Millennial generation, underscore why it is essential for members of that generation to voice their views. Millennials are participating in the civic life of their communities and the nation through unprecedented—and efficacious—new forms of political participation and community activism. Technology will continue to play a significant role in how they and the population at large communicate and participate in politics and how government creates and administers policy. Major transformations have come to pass in the political realm, and there is no end to them in sight.

Demographic changes in American society—particularly the aging and growing diversity of the U.S. population—are giving rise to new public policy demands and creating new challenges. Challenges mean opportunities for those who are ready for them, and citizens who respond to those challenges will have an impact on the future of the nation.

Summary

1. y shd u stdy am dem now? Or, Why Should You Study American Democracy Now?

American democracy is at a crossroads with respect to the effects of technology and a rapidly changing global political environment on politics. The young Americans of today differ from earlier generations in notable ways, and their fresh opinions and means of organizing and communicating with one another make them a significant political force.

2. What Government Does

Governments perform a variety of essential functions. They provide for the national defense, preserve order and stability, establish and maintain a legal system, distribute services, raise and spend money, and socialize new generations of citizens.

3. Types of Government

In categorizing governmental systems, political scientists evaluate two factors. One factor is who participates in governing or in selecting those who govern. In a monarchy, a king or a queen has absolute authority over a territory and its government (although most of today's monarchies are constitutional), whereas in an oligarchy, an elite few hold power. In a democracy, the people hold and exercise supreme power. Scholars also categorize governmental systems according to how governments function and are structured. Totalitarian governments effectively control every aspect of their citizens' lives. Authoritarian governments have strong powers but are checked by other forces within the society. In democracies, the people have a say in their governance either by voting directly or, as in the United States, by electing representatives to carry out their will.

4. The Origins of American Democracy

American democracy was shaped by individuals who believed in the right of citizens to have a voice in their government. Through principles developed by Enlightenment philosophers such as Thomas Hobbes, John Locke, and Jean-Jacques Rousseau, the key tenets of American democracy emerged, including the idea of a social contract creating a representative democracy.

5. Political Culture and American Values

Political culture refers to the people's collective beliefs and attitudes about the government and the political process. Though aspects of political culture change over time, certain fundamental values have remained constant in American democracy. These include liberty, which is both freedom *from* government interference in daily life and freedom *to* pursue happiness; and equality, the meaning of which has fluctuated significantly over the course of U.S. history. Capitalism—an economic system in which the means of producing wealth are privately owned and operated to produce profits—is also a core value of American political culture, as is consent of the governed, with its key components of popular sovereignty and majority rule. Finally, the American political system values the importance of the individual, the family, and the community.

6. Ideology: A Prism for Viewing American Democracy

Liberals emphasize civil liberties, separation of church and state, and political equality. Conservatives prefer small government, individual initiative, and an unfettered market economy. Socialists advocate government intervention in the economy to promote economic equality, whereas libertarians argue that government should take a hands-off approach to most matters. Some social scientists prefer to use a three-dimensional framework rather than a two-dimensional continuum for understanding and analyzing political ideology. Regardless of their ideology, citizens can and should act upon their views through civic and political engagement.

7. The Changing Face of American Democracy

The population of the United States is growing, aging, and becoming increasingly diverse. Hispanics now make up the country's largest ethnic minority. U.S. families have undergone fundamental structural alterations as the numbers of nonfamily households and of households headed by single people have increased. These changes have already had an impact on communities, and their effect on government policies will intensify. The demographic shifts may create demand for changes in current policies, or they may indicate that the nature of the electorate has shifted and that different priorities are favored by a majority of the people.

Key Terms

authoritarianism 10

capitalism 16

citizens 9

civic engagement 7

consent of the governed 16

conservatism 18

constitutionalism 11

democracy 10

direct democracy 14

divine right of kings 12

efficacy 6

government 9

indirect democracy 14

legitimacy 9

liberalism 17

libertarianism 19

liberty 14

limited government 11

majority rule 16

monarchy 10

natural law 12

naturalization 9

oligarchy 10

political culture 14

political engagement 7

political ideology 17

politics 4

popular sovereignty 13

property 16

public goods 9

social contract 12

social contract theory 13

socialism 18

totalitarianism 10

For Review

1. In what ways has technology changed how politics happens and how government works? What impact did September 11, 2001, and the subsequent war on terrorism have on how Americans thought—and think—about their government?

2. Explain the functions that governments perform.

3. Describe how social scientists categorize governments.

4. How did the ideas of the Enlightenment shape people's views on the proper role of government?

5. Explain the fundamental values of American democracy.

6. Contrast liberals' and conservatives' views on government.

7. Describe the general trends with regard to population change in the United States.

For Critical Thinking and Discussion

1. In what ways do you use technology in your daily life? Do you use technology to get information about politics or to access government services? How? If not, what information and services may be obtained using technological tools?

2. Do you believe there are differences between your political views and those held by members of other generations? Explain. Have the wars in Afghanistan and Iraq changed how you view government? Describe.

3. Why do governments perform the functions they do? Can you think of any private entities that provide public goods?

4. Think of the advantages and disadvantages of direct versus indirect democracies. Do you participate in any form of direct decision making? If you do, how well, or poorly, does it work?

5. Examine the demographic maps of the United States in this chapter, and describe what they reveal about the population in your home state.

MULTIPLE CHOICE: Choose the lettered item that answers the question correctly.

1. The institution that creates and implements policies and laws that guide the conduct of the nation and its citizens is called
   a. a democracy.
   c. government.
   b. efficacy.
   d. citizenry.

2. Public goods include
   a. clean air.
   b. clean water.
   c. highways.
   d. all of these.

3. The economic system in which the means of producing wealth are privately owned and operated to produce profits is
   a. capitalism.
   b. monetarism.
   c. socialism.
   d. communism.

4. Emphasizing the importance of conserving tradition and of relying on community and family as mechanisms of continuity in society is known as
   a. communism.
   b. conservatism.
   c. liberalism.
   d. libertarianism.

5. Citizens' belief that they have the ability to achieve something desirable and that the government listens to them is called
   a. popular sovereignty.
   b. democracy.
   c. civic engagement.
   d. efficacy.

6. A system in which citizens elect representatives who decide policies on behalf of their constituents is referred to as
   a. an indirect democracy.
   b. a representative democracy.
   c. consent of the governed.
   d. both (a) and (b).

7. A belief by the people that a government's exercise of power is right and proper is
   a. authoritarianism.
   b. democracy.
   c. popular sovereignty.
   d. legitimacy.

8. The principle that the standards that govern human behavior are derived from the nature of humans themselves and can be applied universally is called
   a. the social contract.
   b. legitimacy.
   c. natural law.
   d. representative democracy.

9. An agreement between the people and their leaders in which the people agree to give up some liberties so that other liberties are protected is called
   a. a Mayflower Compact.
   b. a social contract.
   c. republicanism.
   d. natural law.

10. A form of government that essentially controls every aspect of people's lives is
    a. socialism.
    b. neoconservatism.
    c. liberalism.
    d. totalitarianism.

FILL IN THE BLANKS

11. _____ is individual and collective actions designed to identify and address issues of public concern.

12. _____ is the institution that creates and implements policy and laws that guide the conduct of the nation and its citizens.

13. _____ is the idea that in a democracy, only policies with 50 percent plus one vote are enacted.

14. _____ are services governments provide that are available to everyone, such as clean air, clean water, airport security, and highways.

15. A form of government that is structured by law, and in which the power of government is limited, is called _____.

Answers: 1. c, 2. d, 3. a, 4. b, 5. d, 6. d, 7. d, 8. c, 9. b, 10. d, 11. Civic engagement, 12. Government, 13. Majority rule, 14. Public goods, 15. constitutionalism.

Resources for Research AND Action

Internet Resources

CIRCLE: The Center for Information & Research on Civic Learning & Engagement
www.civicyouth.org Circle is the premier clearinghouse for research and analysis on civic engagement.

Association of American Colleges and Universities
www.aacu.org/resources/civicengagement/index.cfm The AACU's website offers a clearinghouse of Internet resources on civic engagement.

American Political Science Association
www.apsanet.org The professional association for political scientists offers many resources on research about civic engagement, education, and participation.

The 2010 Census
www.census.gov/2010census/ The U.S. Census Bureau's 2010 census website is a clearinghouse for information about the census, including information on why the census is important, data, and how you can get involved in the census.

Recommended Readings

Howe, Neil, and William Strauss. *Millennials Rising: The Next Great Generation*. New York: Vintage, 2000. A pre–September 11, 2001, examination of the unique characteristics of the Millennial generation.

Levine, Peter. *The Future of Democracy: Developing the Next Generation of American Citizens*. Medford, MA: Tufts University Press (UPNE), 2007. An examination of how today's youth are participating in politics differently than previous generations did and how they lack the skills necessary to facilitate some forms of civic participation. The author proposes educational, political, and institutional changes to correct this problem.

Putnam, Robert D. *Bowling Alone: The Collapse and Revival of American Community*. New York: Touchstone, 2000. A classic volume demonstrating the decline in traditional forms of civic participation.

Verba, Sidney, Kay Lehman Schlozman, and Henry E. Brady. *Voice and Equality: Civic Voluntarism in American Politics*. Cambridge, MA: Harvard University Press, 1995. An analysis of how people come to be activists in their communities, what issues they raise when they participate, and how activists from various demographic groups differ.

Winograd, Morley, and Michael D. Hais. *Millennial Makeover: MySpace, YouTube, and the Future of American Politics*. New Brunswick, NJ: Rutgers University Press, 2008. A study of the impact of Millennials' use of changing technology on political life.

Zukin, Cliff, Scott Keeter, Molly Andolina, Krista Jenkins, and Michael X. Delli Carpini. *A New Engagement? Political Participation, Civic Life and the Changing American Citizen*. Oxford: Oxford University Press, 2006. A study of participation and political viewpoints across generations.

Movies of Interest

The Messenger (2009)
This film, starring Ben Foster and Woody Harrelson, depicts one side of the ravages of war through the experiences of the U.S. Army's Casualty Notification officers. Through their experiences, viewers explore the values of the families of fallen soldiers, as well as those of society at large.

V for Vendetta (2005)
Actress Natalie Portman becomes a revolutionary in this thriller, which depicts an uprising against an authoritarian government.

Blind Shaft (2003)
This Chinese thriller explores the interaction between free market incentives and aspects of political culture, including traditional communal values and human decency, in the context of an increasingly globalized economy.

Blue Collar (1978)
This classic film tracing the experience of three autoworkers in the late 1970s explores racial and economic strife in the United States.

CHAPTER 2

The Constitution

THEN

The Constitution's framers divided governmental power between the federal and the state governments and created checks and balances among the three separate branches of the national government to ensure a representative democracy that protected individual liberties.

NOW

The courts continue to probe and interpret the Constitution's meaning, and members of Congress introduce proposed constitutional amendments annually.

NEXT

Will Congress heed the states' calls for a constitutional convention?

Will the Constitution's third century witness a greater volume of ratified constitutional amendments as the people's calls for "a more perfect union" intensify?

Will the Supreme Court resolve conflicting interpretations of constitutional amendment processes?

We trace various constitutional conflicts throughout this textbook. So that you can understand these conflicts, this chapter concentrates on the roots of the U.S. Constitution and the basic governing principles, structures, and procedures it establishes.

FIRST, we probe the question, what is a constitution? by considering the three main components of constitutional documents: descriptions of mission, foundational structures, and essential operating procedures.

SECOND, we explore the political, economic, and social factors that were the catalysts for the creation of the United States of America.

THIRD, we survey the crafting of the Constitution and the processes of compromise, ratification, and quick amendment.

FOURTH, we focus on the Constitution as a living, evolving document—a vitality that derives from the alteration (formal amendment) of its written words and from the Supreme Court's (re)interpretation of its existing language to create new meaning.

The Constitution of the United

States is the oldest written constitution in the world. The fact that it has been in effect since 1789 is amazing, because most countries replace their constitutions on average every 19 years.[1] Scholars attribute its long life to several factors. One factor is the basic governmental structures created by the Constitution: a federal system with two levels of sovereignty (national and state) and three branches of government in the national government. A second factor is the fundamental principles on which the framers built the government (popular sovereignty and protection of life, liberty, and the pursuit of happiness), principles that address the vision of the colonists who declared their independence from the British Crown in 1776. Finally, scholars attribute the Constitution's longevity to the vague and ambiguous language found throughout the document, which allows each generation to debate, deliberate, and interpret it in order to meet the needs and demands of an ever-changing nation in an ever-changing world.

The delegates at the convention that crafted the Constitution of the United States deliberated, negotiated, compromised, and then patched together a document that began an experiment in governance. Learning from their unsatisfactory experiences as colonists subject to the rule of the British Crown and the less-than-perfect alliance of independent states (the confederation created by the Articles of Confederation), the convention delegates attempted to create a representative democracy that would protect individual liberties while ensuring a healthy economy and a strong nation. Because they needed the approval of the already existing, independent state governments to establish a new central (national) government, they had to accommodate state sovereignty as they created national sovereignty—a difficult and still ongoing balancing act.

This chapter explores the colonists' experiences under British rule and their subsequent efforts to create the structures and operating procedures of a democratic government that protects the people's life, liberty, and pursuit of happiness. In the process of replacing the problematic confederation with a more perfect union, the architects of the Constitution resolved major conflicts over principles and structures of government through compromise and agreement on frequently ambiguous language. Today, the debates over the vision of the Declaration and the meaning of constitutional language that began even before the states ratified the Constitution continue (see "Thinking Critically About Democracy").

What Is a Constitution?

constitution
the fundamental principles of a government and the basic structures and procedures by which the government operates to fulfill those principles; may be written or unwritten

A **constitution** presents the fundamental principles of a government and establishes the basic structures and procedures by which the government operates to fulfill those principles. Constitutions may be written or unwritten. An *unwritten constitution,* such as the constitution of Great Britain, is a collection of written laws approved by a legislative body and unwritten common laws established by judges, based on custom, culture, habit, and previous judicial decisions. A *written constitution,* such as the Constitution of the United States, is one specific document supplemented by judicial interpretations that clarify its meaning.

If you read a government's written constitution, or even your school's student government constitution, you will find three essential pieces of information about the government. First, you will find a statement of the government's mission or the long-term goals of the government as envisioned by its framers. Second, you will discover a description of how the government is organized into foundational structures, core government bodies that accomplish its mission. Finally, you will uncover the details of the government's essential operating procedures.

Democracy

Is It Time for a Second Constitutional Convention?

The Issue: Thomas Jefferson and James Madison both believed that the Constitution would need to be reviewed critically and revised over time to keep up with human development, technological advances, and changes in opinions and values as society evolved. Believing that every generation should make the Constitution its own, Thomas Jefferson wrote in a 1789 letter to James Madison that "Every constitution . . . naturally expires at the end of 19 years. If it be enforced longer, it is an act of force and not of right."* In fact, on average, countries replace their constitutions every 19 years! Today, more than 225 years after the U.S. Constitution went into effect, many citizens believe that parts of the Constitution are not working. Is it time for a second constitutional convention to fix the problems in the U.S. Constitution?

Yes: Look at the signs of our times: A government shutdown caused by partisan battles. Major national economic problems. Excessive influence of special interest groups to the detriment of majority preferences. A presidential election decided by the U.S. Supreme Court. Perpetual questions about the balance between civil rights and liberties and national security. Growing tensions between the national government and state governments and citizens' calls for secession. All of these signs indicate that we need a major overhaul of our governmental institutions and governing procedures. A constitutional amendment here or there is not sufficient, and even if it were, Congress has been a "graveyard" for constitutional revision.** Thousands of proposals have been introduced in Congress in the past half century, with just one submitted to the states for ratification. The framers, concerned that Congress might not propose amendments when it was part of the problem, established in Article V the power of states to request a constitutional convention. It is time.

No: The last time a constitutional convention occurred, the existing constitution was replaced by a new constitution through a ratification process that violated the existing constitution. What is to prevent such a constitutional violation from occurring again? The current process to amend the Constitution requires three-quarters of the states to agree. Given today's partisan divide among the states, the chance of getting three-quarters of state legislatures or conventions to agree to anything is pretty slim. Either the convention would be a waste of time, ending with no agreement for any change, or the delegates would do as the delegates at the first constitutional convention did: change the amendment process to make it easier to amend, or even replace, the Constitution. Is the Constitution so problematic that we want to risk replacing it? No. The nation cannot afford a constitutional convention and the battles it would engender.

Other Approaches: Article V delegates to the states the power to demand a "Convention for proposing amendments," not a demand for a full-blown constitutional convention. Since 1789, 49 states have submitted to Congress over 700 applications for a convention call. This exceeds the constitutional hurdle of 34 states (two-thirds of the states) requesting a convention. Article V states "Congress *shall* call a convention" when two-thirds of the states request one. It seems that Congress has no choice but to call a convention for proposing amendments to the Constitution.

What do you think?

1. Although 49 states have submitted over 700 applications for a convention, concerns raised in many of these applications have been addressed by the first through the twenty-seventh constitutional amendments. Should the states review their previous applications and then report to Congress on whether or not the applications are still valid? How do you think Congress would react to that?

2. Do you think the states have grounds to sue Congress for violation of Article V? Explain.

3. Opponents of a convention fear a run-away convention that goes beyond amending the Constitution. Some proponents argue that Article V limits a convention to the consideration of amendments proposed by the state governments. Which do you think is the proper interpretation of Article V? Explain your answer.

---

*Quoted in Larry Sabato. 2007. *A More Perfect Union: Why the Constitution Must Be Revised: Ideas to Inspire a Generation* (New York: Walker), 7–8.
**Ibid., 8.

Typically, constitutions begin with a description of the mission. For example, the first sentence in the Constitution of the United States, known as the Preamble, states:

> *We the People of the United States, in Order to form a more perfect Union, establish Justice, insure domestic Tranquility, provide for the common defence, promote the general Welfare, and secure the Blessings of Liberty to ourselves and our Posterity, do ordain and establish this Constitution for the United States of America.*

After the Preamble, the first three articles (main sections) of the U.S. Constitution describe the structure of the national government. Specifically the articles describe three foundational government bodies—the legislative, executive, and judicial branches—and articulate the responsibilities of each body as well as the relationships among those bodies. The Constitution also details essential operating procedures, including those used to select national government officials, to make laws, and to amend the Constitution, as well as the process by which the Constitution itself was to be ratified.

In addition to finding the mission statement, descriptions of foundational structures, and details of essential operating procedures in a constitution, you will typically find some vague and ambiguous language. For example, reread the Constitution's Preamble. What do you think "promote the general welfare" means? Does it mean that the government is responsible for ensuring that all people living in the nation have decent health care so that people do not pass their illnesses to others? Does it mean that the government needs to ensure that all people have sufficient and nutritious food and safe housing? What liberties did the framers expect the government to secure to themselves and their posterity (future generations)?

Debates over the meaning of constitutional language were taking place in living rooms, in bars, in government offices and courtrooms, and on the streets even before the states ratified the Constitution. Ultimately, the U.S. Supreme Court has the final word on the meaning of constitutional language. You will learn as you read the chapters in this book that members of the Supreme Court do not always agree on what constitutional language means. Moreover, throughout U.S. history, as the members of the Supreme Court changed and the nation's economy, technology, and culture evolved, societal understanding of constitutional language changed, as has citizen and judicial interpretation.

To comprehend today's debates about constitutional language, we need to first develop an understanding of what the framers of the Constitution and the citizens who debated it were hoping to achieve. What was their vision of a more perfect union?

The Creation of the United States of America

In the 1600s, waves of Europeans made the dangerous sea voyage to America to start new lives. Some people with connections to the king of England received large grants of land and the authority to govern. Many more voyagers came as *indentured servants,* who would work for a number of years for a master who paid for their passage. Others came to create communities with people of the same religion so that they could practice their faith without government interference. Countless others—Africans brought to the colonies as slaves—came against their will. In short, a diversity of people and a mix of economic classes migrated to the colonies, joining the Native American peoples who already inhabited North America.

By the early 18th century, a two-tier system of governing the British colonies in America had evolved, with governance split between the colonies and Britain. The colonists elected local officials to colonial assemblies that had the authority to rule on day-to-day matters (including criminal law and civil law) and to set and collect taxes to implement laws regarding day-to-day matters. Back in England, Parliament, with no representatives from the colonies, enacted laws with which the colonists had to comply. Governors appointed by the king oversaw the enforcement of British law in the colonies.

In the latter half of the 18th century, Parliament tried to raise additional revenue to pay for its growing debt (due to war expenses in Europe and America) and to confirm its sovereignty over its colonists. To accomplish these goals, Parliament approved legislation that put more and more restrictions on the colonists' freedoms and their pursuit of economic well-being. Eventually, the colonists' conversations about the British government's damaging treatment of them coalesced around the principles of government by the people (popular sovereignty) and for the people (government established to protect the people's liberties). Criticism turned into rebellion, which became a revolution. In the process, a new country was born.

British Policies Incite Revolution in the Colonies

Between 1756 and 1763, Britain and France were engaged in the Seven Years' War, a military conflict that involved all the major European powers of the era. At the same time, British and French forces (and France's Native American allies) were battling in North America, in a conflict known as the French and Indian War. To help pay the costs of waging those wars and the postwar costs of maintaining peace in America, the British Parliament turned to the colonies for increased revenues. As colonists criticized and then protested new tax laws, Parliament enacted laws to affirm its power to tax the colonists and force them to share the costs of British troops in America. Eventually protests turned to revolution.

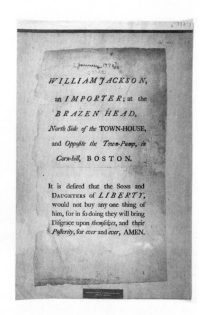

TAXES AND BOYCOTTS   The first new tariff imposed after the Treaty of Paris (1763) ended the Seven Years' War and the French and Indian War was the Sugar Act (1764). The Sugar Act increased taxes on such imported goods as molasses, coffee, and textiles. In addition, the act directed that all the taxes thus collected be sent directly to Britain instead of to the colonial assemblies, as had been the practice.[2] Almost immediately, the colonists condemned the law, saying that because they had no representatives in Parliament, they had no obligation to pay taxes imposed by that body. Then in 1765 Parliament passed the Stamp Act, which taxed the paper used for all legal documents, bills of sale, deeds, advertisements, newspapers, and even playing cards.[3] The Stamp Act introduced a new level of British involvement (some thought interference) in the day-to-day matters of the colonies.

> Participation by women, as supported by the Daughters of Liberty, was essential to the success of the boycotts. What explains why women's participation was essential to the success of boycotts?

After passage of the Stamp Act, the colonists began to organize acts of resistance and protest. For example, they began by boycotting goods imported from Great Britain. Women, including groups of upper-class women known as Daughters of Liberty, substituted homegrown or homespun goods for the banned items. Although the boycotts were largely peaceful, other acts of resistance were not. The Sons of Liberty, founded by Boston brewer Samuel Adams in 1765, opposed the Stamp Act by intimidating British stamp commissioners and sometimes engaging in acts of violence.

Parliament, looking to support the growing number of British troops in the colonies, fueled the colonists growing rebellion with passage of the Quartering Act in 1765. The Quartering Act directed each colonial assembly to provide supplies to meet the basic needs of the British soldiers stationed within the colonies. Parliament expanded this law in 1766 to require the colonial assemblies to ensure housing for the soldiers.[4] Throughout the colonies, violent reactions to the quartering law erupted as many viewed this act as an indirect tax forcing the colonists to pay some of the costs of the troops, which the colonists saw as a threat.[5]

In addition to the boycotts, the colonists called for the repeal of the Stamp Act. British merchants, feeling a financial effect from the boycotts, also called for repeal of the Stamp Act. In 1766, Parliament repealed the hated Stamp Act, but it paired that repeal with passage of the Declaratory Act. This new law gave Parliament the blanket power to make laws over any matters it saw fit, laws that the colonists were legally obligated to follow.[6] The next year, the colonists understood how momentous this law was, when Parliament used the Declaratory Act as the basis for the Townshend Revenue Act of 1767, which expanded the list of imported goods that would be taxed. The act also confirmed that Parliament had unilateral power to impose taxes as a way of raising revenue and that the colonists had no right to object.[7] Clearly, the two-tier system of colonial government, in which the colonies exerted some local governing authority through the colonial assemblies, was beginning to dissolve.

In 1768, the Massachusetts colonial legislature, led by activist Samuel Adams, petitioned King George III to repeal the Townshend Revenue Act, condemning it as taxation without representation. The Massachusetts legislature also called on other colonial legislatures to do the same. In 1770, Parliament repealed the Townshend duties, except for the duty on tea. At the same time, Parliament again reaffirmed its right to tax the colonists.

A "MASSACRE" AND A TEA PARTY   By 1770, more than 4,000 British soldiers were quartered in the homes of the 16,000 civilians living in Boston. To make matters worse, the British soldiers, who were financially supported by the colonists due to the Quartering Act, sought additional work, competing with the colonists for those jobs. Growing tensions came to a head in Boston on March 5, 1770, when an angry mob of nearly 1,800 struggling colonists clashed with the British soldiers. The soldiers shot into the crowd, leaving five dead and six wounded.[8] The Sons of Liberty and Samuel Adams—an expert at "spinning" a news story—condemned the event as "the Boston Massacre." Calls for resistance and protests grew.

Continuing with his rebellious acts, in 1772, Samuel Adams created the Massachusetts Committee of Correspondence, a group dedicated to encouraging and maintaining the free flow of information and the spread of calls for rebellion among the Massachusetts colonists. Radicals in

Then Now

> The Boston Tea Party (1773) was a rebellious act of colonists angered by Parliament's string of new tax laws, including a tax on imported tea, which gave the East India Tea Company a monopoly on importing tea to the American colonies. Without representation in Parliament, the rebellious colonists did not believe they were obligated to comply with the laws. In 2009, the Tea Party movement was founded, demanding fewer and lower taxes, cuts in government spending, greater protection of individual liberties, and less government regulation of the economy, demands similar to those of rebellious colonists of the 1770s and 1780s. How successful has the Tea Party movement been in influencing the policies and actions of the national government?

other colonies followed his lead.[9] These communication networks served as a kind of colonial-era Internet, facilitating the sharing of news among the colonists. But in this case, the swift transmission of information occurred by way of riders on horseback and printers at their presses rather than by the keystrokes of citizens typing on computers and cell phones—today's vital communication network for rallying people behind a cause and mobilizing political activism.

Adding fuel to the fire of rebellion, in 1773 Parliament passed the Tea Act, which gave the East India Tea Company a monopoly on tea imported into the colonies. The Sons of Liberty questioned the act's legitimacy, vowed they would block the Company's ships from docking in ports, and called for renewed boycotts of British goods. The Sons of Liberty successfully swayed public opinion and became the catalyst for the Boston Tea Party. In November 1773, the first post–Tea Act shipment of tea arrived in Boston Harbor on three East India ships. Under cover of darkness on the night of December 16, 1773, more than 100 colonists, dressed as Mohawk Indians, boarded the three ships, broke open hundreds of crates, and dumped thousands of pounds of tea into the harbor.[10] The Boston Tea Party had a cataclysmic effect, not only on the relationship between Britain and the colonies but also on relationships among the colonists themselves.

Parliament responded to the Boston Tea Party with the Coercive Acts (Intolerable Acts) in 1774, which closed the port of Boston and kept it closed until the colonists paid for the lost tea. In addition, the new laws imposed martial law, shut down the colonial assembly, and banned virtually all town meetings, thus curtailing legal opportunities for colonists in Massachusetts to engage in politics.[11] At the same time, Parliament stepped up enforcement of the Quartering Act. King George III and Parliament thought these actions would coerce the colonists into obedience, but instead they stiffened the colonists' resolve to work together to protect their rights.

THE FIRST CONTINENTAL CONGRESS: A DECLARATION OF RIGHTS   Sympathy among the colonies for Massachusetts's plight, along with rising concerns about how the British government was generally abusing its powers (at least in the eyes of colonists), reinforced the colonists' growing sense of community and their shared consciousness of the need for collective action. The Massachusetts and Virginia colonial assemblies requested a meeting of delegates from all the colonies to develop a joint statement of concern they would send to the king. In September 1774, every colony but Georgia sent delegates to Philadelphia for what became known as the First Continental Congress.

The Continental Congress (the assembled delegates) adopted and sent to King George the Declaration of Rights and Grievances. This declaration listed numerous rights to which the delegates argued the colonists were entitled. Some of the rights included in the list were life, liberty, and property; representation in Parliament; and consideration of their grievances and petitions to the king.[12] The Congress also adopted the Articles of Association, which put forth a plan to create a parliament for the colonies.[13] Finally, the Congress scheduled a second meeting of delegates—the Second Continental Congress—to discuss the anticipated king's response to their declaration of rights and list of grievances.

King George III refused to respond to the First Continental Congress's declaration. Colonists' talk about pursuing independence grew louder. On April 19, 1775, before the Second Continental Congress met, shots rang out at Lexington and Concord, Massachusetts, as British troops moved to seize the colonists' store of guns and ammunition. On May 10, 1775, the Second Continental Congress convened. The assembled delegates authorized the Congress to function as an independent government and to prepare for war with Britain, appointing George Washington to command the to-be-created Continental Army. The rebellion sparked by Parliament's policies was now a military conflict that would last for eight years (1775–1783).

The Common Sense of Declaring Independence

In July 1775, the Second Continental Congress made one last effort to avert a full-blown war. The Congress petitioned King George III to end hostile actions against the colonists. The king refused and sent even more troops to the colonies to put down the growing rebellion. Yet even as the Congress prepared for war, many colonists remained unsure about cutting their ties with Britain. A pamphlet written by Thomas Paine, a recently arrived radical from Britain, and published in January 1776 transformed many such wavering colonists into revolutionary patriots. Paine's *Common Sense* argued that war with Great Britain was not only necessary but also unavoidable. Only through independence would Americans attain civil and religious liberty.[14]

In May 1776, Richard Henry Lee, Virginia delegate to the Congress, asserted "that these united Colonies are, and of right ought to be free and independent States, [and] that they are absolved from all allegiance to the British crown."[15] Lee's resolution also called for the drafting of a plan of union for the colonies that would be sent to all the colonies for approval. This "declaration of independence," which congressional delegates from other colonies subsequently echoed, led the Second Continental Congress to establish a committee to write down, in formal language, a collective declaration of independence. The committee selected Virginia delegate Thomas Jefferson, a wealthy plantation owner, to draft the declaration.

Unanimously endorsed by the Second Continental Congress on July 4, 1776, Jefferson's Declaration of Independence drew on the work of John Locke and Jean-Jacques Rousseau, as "Analyzing the Sources" highlights. Jefferson's Declaration was groundbreaking. It put forth three principles that at the time were radical. First, he held that all men are equal, with **natural rights** (also called *unalienable rights*), which are rights possessed by all humans as a gift from nature, or God, not from government. Jefferson stated that the natural rights that all men have are the rights to life, liberty, and the pursuit of happiness. Second, he proposed that all governments must be based on the consent of the people they govern. Finally, he stated that if a government is not protecting the rights of the people, then the people have the duty to abolish it and to create a new government.

natural rights
the rights possessed by all humans as a gift from nature, or God, including the rights to life, liberty, and the pursuit of happiness (also called *unalienable rights*)

After establishing those three radical principles, the Declaration spelled out a list of grievances against King George in an attempt to convince the colonists and the European powers that the break with Great Britain was necessary and justified. The Declaration won the hearts and minds of people in the colonies and abroad. Until this point, the patriots were united in their hatred toward Britain but lacked a rallying point. The Declaration provided that rallying point by promising a new government that would be based on the consent of the people, with liberty and equality as its central goals.

The War for Independence (the American Revolutionary War), which began at Lexington and Concord in 1775, would end eight years later with the signing of a peace treaty in Paris in 1783. However, the colonists could not wait until the end of the war to establish a new government. Even before the colonial delegates at the Second Continental Congress endorsed the Declaration of Independence, they encouraged the legislative assembly of each colony to write a constitution establishing a government independent of Great Britain. In addition, by 1777, the Second Continental Congress drafted and submitted to the states a constitution, the Articles of Confederation, which designed a collaborative governing alliance among the states.

THE THEORIES OF LOCKE AND ROUSSEAU AS APPLIED BY JEFFERSON

John Locke's Theories: *Two Treatises of Government* (1689)

All people are born free and equal.

All people are born into a "state of nature" and choose to enter into government for protection against being harmed.

Every person has the right to "life, liberty and property," and government may not interfere with this right.

Jean-Jacques Rousseau's Theories: *The Social Contract* (1762)

All power ultimately resides in the people.

People enter into a "social contract" with the government to ensure protection of their lives, liberties, and property.

If government abuses its powers and interferes with the people's exercise of their civil liberties, then the people have both the right and the duty to create a new government.

Thomas Jefferson drew on the work of John Locke and Jean-Jacques Rousseau when writing the Declaration of Independence. In the first of his *Two Treatises of Government* (1689), Locke systematically rejected the commonly held notion that the rationale for the divine right of kings to rule was based on scripture. In his second *Treatise,* Locke discussed the rights men have that precede the establishment of government, and that are superior to the rule of kings and governments. Jean-Jacques Rousseau's *The Social Contract* (1762) took Locke's theories further, stating that government is created by the people and depends on the people for the authority to rule and that governments must rely on popular sovereignty.

Evaluating the Evidence

1. Read the Declaration of Independence (Appendix A). Where can you see Jefferson's application of Locke's theories in the Declaration of Independence?

2. Where can you see Jefferson's application of Rousseau's theories in the Declaration of Independence?

3. How would you summarize the views of Locke, Rousseau, and Jefferson on the purposes of government and the source of government power?

4. What justifications does Jefferson present to support the right of the colonists to create a new government?

The State Constitutions

By the end of 1776, eight colonies had ratified state constitutions. New York, Georgia, and Vermont followed suit in 1777. After four years of intense deliberation, Massachusetts adopted a state constitution in 1780. Connecticut and Rhode Island continued to operate under revised royal charters (governing documents from the British government with references to the king removed) until they enacted new constitutions in 1818 and 1843, respectively.[16]

The new state constitutions were revolutionary for three primary reasons. First, they were each a single, written document that specified the principles, structures, and operating procedures of the government established by the consent of the people. Second, they were adopted at a specific moment in time, unlike constitutions before them, which were accumulations of disparate laws written over time or created by judges through the years, based on customs and traditions.[17] So, the state constitutions were the first written constitutions in the world. Third, they transformed "subjects" under the rule of a king into citizens sharing in popular sovereignty.

The framers of the first state constitutions attempted to implement the principles of popular sovereignty and natural rights presented in the Declaration of Independence. Each state constitution established a **republic,** better known today as representative democracy. Moreover, most state constitutions asserted explicitly that the people held the power—government was by consent of the people. Whereas the Articles of Confederation would create one national governing body, state governments included three governing bodies—the legislative, executive, and judicial branches. **Bicameral legislatures,** which are legislatures comprising two parts (or

republic
a government that derives its authority from the people and in which citizens elect government officials to represent them in the processes by which laws are made; a representative democracy

bicameral legislature
legislature comprising two parts, called *chambers*

chambers), were the norm in the states. State legislators, who were elected directly by voters in most states, were delegated more governing powers than members of the other two branches, who were not typically elected by voters. The prevailing view of people of the time was that the legislature offered the best prospects for representative government that would ensure popular sovereignty.

The mission of all the state governments was to ensure natural rights. This is evident in their bills of rights. State bills of rights affirmed that all government's power derives from the people; endorsed rights such as trial by jury and religious freedom; and included protections for free speech and press, protection from excessive fines and bail, and protection from unreasonable search and seizure. Authors of the first state constitutions wrote into them limits to prevent state governments from infringing on individuals' liberties and pursuit of happiness, infringements the colonists experienced under British rule. Hence, the inclusion of a written list of citizens' liberties, a *bill of rights,* limited government by ensuring that both the people and the government knew what freedoms the government could not violate.

The states of the new American republic used their new constitutions to guide them in handling day-to-day domestic matters. Meanwhile, members of the Second Continental Congress turned their attention to developing a plan for a confederation that would allow the states to engage collectively in international affairs.

The Articles of Confederation (1781–1789)

Because of the colonists' bitter experience under the British Crown, the people and their delegates to the Second Continental Congress distrusted a strong, distant central government; they preferred limited local government, which they established in their state constitutions. The delegates nevertheless recognized the need for a unified authority to engage in international trade, foreign affairs, and defense.

The Congress drafted and submitted to the states the Articles of Confederation in 1777. The Articles established a **confederation:** a union of independent states in which each state retains its sovereignty—that is, its ultimate power to govern—and agrees to work collaboratively on matters the states expressly agree to delegate to a central governing body. Through the Articles of Confederation, the states created an alliance for mutual well-being in the international realm yet continued to pursue independently their own self-interests, within their own borders. In 1781, after 13 states ratified it, the Articles of Confederation went into effect, as the War for Independence continued for another two years.

confederation
a union of independent states in which each state retains its sovereignty—that is, its ultimate power to govern—and agrees to work collaboratively on matters the states expressly agree to delegate to a central governing body

unicameral legislature
a legislative body with a single chamber

STRUCTURE AND AUTHORITY OF THE CONFEDERATION Structurally the Articles created only one governing body, a Congress. The Congress was a **unicameral legislature,** meaning that it had only one chamber. Every state had from two to seven delegates in Congress, but only one vote. Each state determined how its congressional delegates would be selected. Approving policies and ratifying treaties required affirmative votes from nine of the state delegations in Congress. The Articles did not create a judicial branch, an executive branch, or a president. Congressional delegates would select one of their members to serve as president, to preside over the meetings of Congress. State courts would resolve legal conflicts, unless the dispute was between states, in which case Congress would resolve it. State governments would implement and pay for congressionally approved policies. Finally, and important to remember, amending the Articles of Confederation required unanimous agreement among all 13 state congressional delegations.

The Congress had very limited authority. Although it could approve policies relevant to foreign affairs, defense, and the coining of money, it was not authorized to raise revenue through taxation. Only state governments could levy and collect taxes. Therefore, to pay the national government's bills, Congress had to request money from each state.

❯On June 14, 1777, the Continental Congress adopted the following resolution: "Resolved that the flag of the 13 United States be thirteen stripes, alternate red and white: that the union be thirteen stars, white, in a blue field, representing a new constellation." Several configurations of the 13 stars were used, including the stars in a circle, the signature of the Betsy Ross flag.

WEAKNESSES OF THE CONFEDERATION The Articles of Confederation emphasized the sovereignty of individual, independent states at the expense of a powerful national government and national identity. Citizens' allegiance was to their states; there was no mass national conscience. Under the Articles of Confederation, the states retained ultimate authority in matters of commerce and currency, there was no centralized economic policy. As a result, other nations were not willing to negotiate trade policies with Congress. In addition, each state taxed all goods coming into the state from foreign nations and from other states. Moreover, the states issued their own money and required the use of that currency for all business within the state. The cumulative effect of each state's having its own economic policies was that interstate and international commerce was hampered, putting the nation's economic health in jeopardy.[18] The poor economy and its effects on citizens led to uprisings.

In Massachusetts, economic pressures reached a head in 1786 when small farmers, many of whom had fought in the War for Independence, could not pay their legal debts and faced bankruptcy and the loss of their land. Farmer and war veteran Daniel Shays led an uprising, today known as Shays's Rebellion, of those debt-burdened farmers. The rebels first broke into county courthouses and burned all records of their debts, then proceeded to the federal arsenal. Massachusetts asked Congress for assistance in putting down the rebellion. Congress appealed to each state for money to fulfill that request, but only Virginia complied. The weaknesses of the national confederacy—including its lack of authority to develop national economic policies and its inability to defend against domestic uprising—were becoming apparent.

CALLS TO REMEDY DEFECTS OF THE ARTICLES OF CONFEDERATION As the Congress faced bankruptcy and as violent rebellions threatened peace and security in the states, five states sent delegates to Annapolis, Maryland, in 1786, to "remedy defects of the Federal Government," as the government created by the Articles of Confederation was known at that time. The states charged their Annapolis delegates with considering the trade and commerce problems of the United States. However, in the report of their proceedings, the delegates noted that the "embarrassments which characterize the present State of our national affairs, foreign and domestic" suggested that trade and commerce were not the only problems of the federal government. Therefore, the delegates called for a future convention, to be attended by representatives from all 13 states, to devise amendments to the Articles of Confederation that would fix its weaknesses and to submit its proposals to "the United States in Congress assembled."[19]

Crafting the Constitution: Compromise, Ratification, and Quick Amendment

The convention called to address the defects of the Articles of Confederation was held in Philadelphia from May 25 through September 17, 1787. All states except Rhode Island sent delegates. The delegates to this Constitutional Convention were among the most elite Americans. Some 80 percent had served as members of the Continental Congress, and most were lawyers, businessmen, or plantation owners. Many were engaged in highly lucrative international trade, and all were wealthy. These elites contrasted sharply with the masses, who included the country's hard-pressed farmers, struggling local merchants, and those engaged in trade. In fact, historian Charles Beard contended in 1913 that the Constitution's framers succeeded in forging a government that protected their elite status.[20] (See "Global Context" about a recent constitutional process driven by popular, mass participation.)

Although very early in the convention the delegates agreed on the need for a stronger national government than the Articles had created, there was conflict over how best to structure a stronger national government while incorporating principles of representative democracy and protecting liberties. There was also conflict over the issue of slavery. In working through those conflicts to create compromises they could support, the delegates were pragmatic. They had to balance their preference for a strong central government with the citizens' distrust of a strong central government. Ultimately, the delegates framed a new constitution, establishing new foundational

THE "POTS AND PANS" REVOLUTION LEADS TO CROWDSOURCING A PROPOSED CONSTITUTION

Iceland's financial crash of 2008 sparked the "Pots and Pans" revolution, with citizens crowding into Parliament Square in Reykjavik (Iceland's capital city) banging pots and pans and calling for major changes, including a new constitution. The revolution forced the entire government to resign and the new government moved to formulate a new constitution.

The post-revolution government opened up the constitutional formulation process to the people. Parliament approved the establishment of a national assembly that would decide the need for a new constitution and the major concerns such a document should address. The National Assembly was comprised of 950 people *drawn at random* from the national registry of citizens, 18 years of age and older.

The National Assembly, after one day of deliberation, passed a resolution stating that a new constitution was needed and indicating what provisions in the existing constitution raised concerns. While the National Assembly was doing its work, the citizens elected 25 individuals (from a pool of 522 candidates) to a constituent assembly that was responsible for converting the National Assembly's resolution into a proposed constitution. The Supreme Court ruled the election null and void as the result of a successful court challenge by opponents of a new constitution. In response, Parliament appointed the 25 citizens who won the election to the Constitutional Council.

The Constitutional Council opened the process to popular participation via *crowdsourcing,* by seeking input through its interactive website. In addition to the thousands of communications received on its website, the Constitutional Council also received more than 300 unsolicited reports from the public. In four months and in full view of the public, the Council formulated and then unanimously approved a proposed constitution that it submitted to Parliament for consideration.

Parliament voted to hold a consultative (nonbinding) referendum on the document, allowing the citizens to vote their support or rejection of the Council's proposal as the basis for a new constitution. In October 2012, Icelandic voters overwhelming voted to support the Constitutional Council's proposed constitution. The next step was for Parliament to draft the bill that would be the proposed new constitution.

Unfortunately, opponents of the new constitution used questionable procedures to prevent parliament from voting on it before parliament recessed. Thus, the popular participation in creating the constitution, and the majority support (among the people and Parliament) for ratifying it, were thwarted. Today, Iceland's 1944 constitution remains in effect.

SOURCES: Thorvaldur Gylfason, "Iceland: Direct Democracy in Action," November 12, 2012, www.opendemocracy.net/thorvaldur-gylfason/iceland-direct-democracy-in-action; Thorvaldur Gylfason. "Democracy on Ice: A Post-Mortem of the Icelandic Constitution," June 19, 2013, www.opendemocracy.net/can-europe-make-it/thorvaldur-gylfason/democracy-on-ice-post-mortem-of-icelandic-constitution; Liz Farmer, "Tweet, the People," *Governing,* February 2013, 9.

government structures and operating procedures to achieve the principles laid out in the Declaration of Independence. Thereafter, proponents of the proposed new constitution would win its ratification only after acknowledging the need to amend it quickly by adding a bill of rights to limit the power of the national government it created.

Areas of Consensus

According to the congressional charge, the convention delegates had to send their final proposal to the existing Congress for action. Remember that the Congress, as structured by the constitution in effect at the time of the Constitutional Convention (the Articles of Confederation), was made up of representatives of the state governments. The framers recognized that these representatives, selected by the states, were not likely to ratify a document that created a strong central government at the expense of the existing state governments. Therefore, the framers had to balance a strong central government, national sovereignty, and existing state sovereignty. That balance would hinge on delegating governing powers to the national government in the policy areas that were problematic under the Articles of Confederation—interstate and international trade, foreign affairs, and defense—and leaving the remaining domestic matters with the states.

dual sovereignty
a system of government in which ultimate governing authority is divided between two levels of government, a central government and regional governments, with each level having ultimate authority over different policy matters

DUAL SOVEREIGNTY The framers created an innovative system of government with **dual sovereignty**—a system of government in which ultimate governing authority is divided between two levels of government—a central government and regional governments—with each level having ultimate authority over different policy matters. Today, we call this a *federal system* of government. Article I of the Constitution lists the matters over which the national legislature (Congress) has lawmaking authority, such as regulating interstate and foreign commerce, coining money, raising and funding an army, and declaring war. Article I also prohibits state governments from engaging in several specific activities, such as negotiating treaties. (Chapter 3 focuses on dual sovereignty and the constitutional distribution of power between the national and the state governments.)

supremacy clause
a clause in Article VI of the Constitution that states that the Constitution and the treaties and laws created by the national government in compliance with the Constitution are the supreme law of the land

NATIONAL SUPREMACY The framers anticipated that this system of dual sovereignty would cause tension between the national government and the state governments. Therefore, they included in Article VI of the Constitution a **supremacy clause,** which states that the Constitution and the treaties and laws created by the national government in compliance with the Constitution are the supreme law of the land.

The framers did not include a list or even a vague outline of the matters over which the states had sovereignty. Citizens apprehensive of a strong central government would argue that this vacuum of information on state sovereignty was a major fault in the Constitution, because it would allow the national government to infringe on state sovereignty. The lack of a list of individual liberties to limit the power of the national government, a bill of rights such as each state constitution had, was also a major concern for citizens afraid of a strong central government.

separation of powers
the Constitution's delegation of authority for the primary governing functions among three branches of government so that no one group of government officials controls all the governing functions

SEPARATION OF POWERS WITH INTEGRATED CHECKS AND BALANCES Another area where there was convergence of opinion among the framers was that of the foundational structures of the new government they were creating. Borrowing from the states, the framers separated the primary governing functions among three branches of government—referred to as the **separation of powers**—so that no one group of government officials controlled all the governing functions. Under the terms of the separation of powers, each branch of the government has specific powers and responsibilities that allow it to operate independently of the other branches: the legislative branch has authority to formulate policy; the executive branch has authority to implement policy; and the judicial branch has authority to resolve conflicts over the law.

checks and balances
a system in which each branch of government can monitor and limit the functions of the other branches

Once the framers separated the primary functions, they established various mechanisms by which each branch can monitor and limit the functions of the other branches to ensure that no branch acts to the detriment of citizens' natural rights. These mechanisms collectively form a system of **checks and balances.** If one branch tries to move beyond its own sphere or to behave tyrannically, this arrangement ensures that the other branches can take action to stop it. For example, Congress formulates and approves legislation; However, before legislation becomes law, the president has the opportunity to approve or reject it (through the veto process). Although the president has authority to nominate top executive branch officials and federal judges, the Senate has the authority to accept (confirm) or reject the nominees. Figure 2.1 shows how specific checks and balances contribute to the separation of powers.

The delegates spent most of the first two months of the Constitutional Convention arguing about the national legislature and focused primarily on the question of state representation in Congress. They devoted less than a month to the other issues before them, including the

Separation of Powers with Checks and Balances

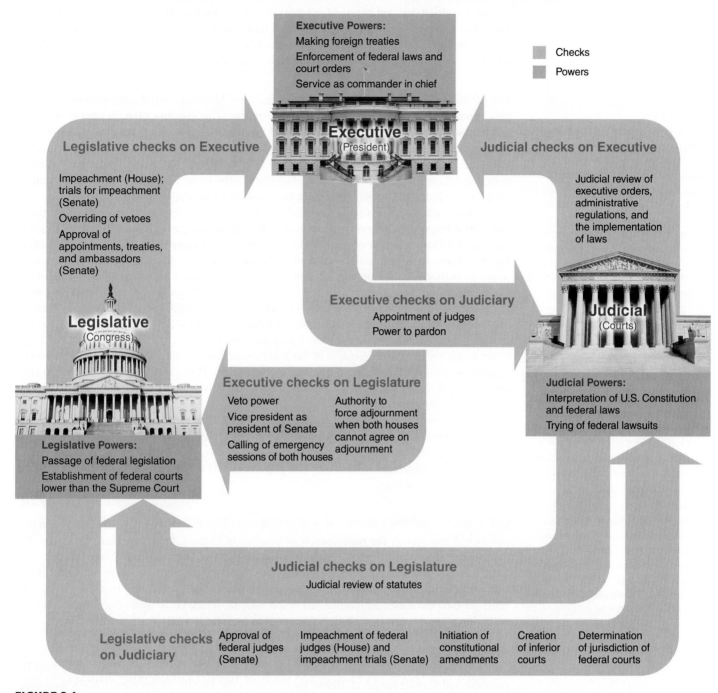

FIGURE 2.1

Why did the Constitution's framers separate powers among the three branches of the national government? What specific powers does each branch have? What is the purpose of the Constitution's checks and balances? For each branch of the government—legislative, executive, judicial—name a specific check that it can exert on each of the other two.

structure of the executive and judicial branches; the relationship between the federal and the state governments; the process for amending the new constitution, should the need arise to do so; the procedures for the Constitution's ratification; and a series of compromises over the slave trade.[21]

Conflict and Compromise Over Representative Democracy

Among the delegates' top points of contention was representation in the national government. There was disagreement about two elements of representation. First, how should the government officials in each of the three branches of this newly formed republican national government be selected? Second, how would the states be represented in the national government?

THE CONNECTICUT COMPROMISE Virginian James Madison arrived at the convention with a plan in hand for restructuring the national government. The **Virginia Plan,** drafted by Madison and proposed by the Virginia delegation, called for a radically revamped government, consisting of three branches: a bicameral legislature (Congress), an executive elected by the legislature, and a separate national judiciary. State representation in Congress would be proportional, based on state population. The people would elect members to the lower house, and members elected by the people to the lower house would elect the members of the upper house.

The states with smaller populations quickly and aggressively responded to Madison's Virginia Plan with a proposal of their own. Their concerns about the Virginia Plan were obvious. Because the Virginia Plan called for proportional representation in Congress based on state population, the small states stood to lose significant power because under the Articles of Confederation, each state, no matter what its population and no matter how many representatives it had in the Congress, had one vote. Under the Virginia Plan, states with larger populations would have more representatives and therefore more votes. On behalf of the less populous states, William Paterson of New Jersey presented a series of resolutions known as the **New Jersey Plan,** which essentially reworked the Articles of Confederation. Under the New Jersey Plan, a unicameral national legislature would remain the centerpiece of the government, and all states would have an equal voice (equal representation) in this government. The New Jersey Plan also called for Congress to elect several people to form an executive office, and the executive office had the authority to appoint members to a Supreme Court.

The disagreement and negotiation over the Virginia and the New Jersey Plans resulted in several compromises, most notably the **Connecticut Compromise** (also known as the *Great Compromise*). This compromise created today's bicameral Congress, with state representation in the House of Representatives based on state population and equal state representation in the Senate (two senators per state).

THE CONSTITUTION'S LIMITS ON REPRESENTATIVE DEMOCRACY At the heart of representative democracy is the participation of citizens in electing their government officials. Yet the framers allowed citizens to elect directly only the members of the House of Representatives, thereby placing tremendous limits on representative democracy. Until the Constitution was amended in 1913, by the Seventeenth Amendment, state legislators (not the voting citizens) selected the state's representatives in the national senate (U.S. senators). The Seventeenth Amendment gave voters in each state the power to elect their representatives in the Senate.

The process that the framers devised for the election of the president and the vice president prevents citizens from directly selecting them. The Constitution delegates to states the authority to appoint individuals (*electors*), using a process determined by the state legislature, to elect the president and the vice president. Before ratification of the Twelfth Amendment (1804), these electors would cast two votes for president. The candidate receiving the largest majority of electors' votes would become president and the candidate receiving the second largest number of votes would become vice president. Since ratification of the Twelfth Amendment, each elector casts one vote for president and one vote for vice president. Today, in nearly every state, your presidential vote, combined with the votes of other citizens from your state, determines which political party's slate of representatives (*electors*) will participate on behalf of your state in the **Electoral College,** the name given to the body of electors that actually selects the president and the vice president.

In addition to limiting the national government officials directly elected by citizens to just their representative in the House of Representatives, the framers effectively limited voting rights to a minority of citizens. The framers left to the states the authority to determine eligibility to vote. Existing state constitutions allowed only property-owning white men to vote. The one exception was New Jersey, where property-owning white women could also vote until 1807, when the state constitution was amended to deny women the right to the vote. Hence, all women (except in New Jersey from 1776 to 1807) and many men, including Native Americans and slaves, were denied the right to vote under the new Constitution. Therefore, representative democracy in the national government was very limited under the Constitution as ratified in 1788. Most inhabitants could not vote, and those who could voted to elect representatives to only one chamber of Congress.

Conflict and Compromise Over Slavery

Delegates to the Constitutional Convention also disagreed on the "peculiar institution" (as Thomas Jefferson called it) of slavery. In 1790, slaves made up 18 percent of the U.S. population, and most slaves resided in the southern states.[22] Delegates from the southern states, whose economy relied on slave labor, feared that a strong central government would abolish slavery. Meanwhile, northern delegates, who were widely concerned that a weak national government would limit the United States' ability to engage in commerce and international trade, believed that the nation needed a more powerful

> Before the Constitution was amended formally, it did not guarantee any citizen the right to vote. Rather, state governments determined voting rights. Today the Constitution guarantees the right to vote to citizens who are at least 18 years old (Twenty-Sixth Amendment), regardless of their race (Fifteenth Amendment) or sex (Nineteenth Amendment). State and local governments must comply with the voting rights established in the U.S. Constitution; however, compliance does not prevent them from offering additional rights. Therefore, state and local governments can allow their citizens to vote in state and local elections at an age younger than 18 years. Takoma Park, Maryland, is an example of a local government that allows its citizens 16 years of age and older to vote in municipal elections.

central government than had existed under the Articles of Confederation. Ultimately, to get the southern states to agree to a stronger central government, the northern states compromised on the slavery issue.

A provision in Article I, Section 9, of the Constitution postponed debate on the legality of slavery—and consequently kept it legal—by prohibiting Congress from addressing the importation of new slaves into the United States until January 1, 1808. Moreover, Article IV, which deals with interstate relations, established the states' obligation to deliver all fugitive slaves back to their owners. This measure aimed to ensure that people in nonslaveholding states would continue to respect the property rights of slaveholders—including the right to own slaves, who were legally property, not people with natural rights guaranteed by government.

Although enslaved African and African American people were legally property, Article I, Section 2, established a formula for "counting" slaves for purposes of representation in the House of Representatives, apportionment of electors for the Electoral College, and the allocation of tax burdens among the states. This **Three-Fifths Compromise** counted each enslaved person as three-fifths of a free man. The southern states benefited from this compromise: They gained greater representation in the House and in the Electoral College than they would have if only nonslaves were counted. The benefit to the northern states was that if the national government imposed a direct tax on the states based on their populations, southern states would pay more than they would if only nonslaves were counted. (The national government has never imposed such a direct tax on the states.)

James Madison, while deploring slavery, argued that the delegates' "compromise" over slavery was "in the spirit of accommodation which governed the Convention." He insisted that without the Three-Fifths Compromise, the Constitution would never have been signed.

So at the Constitutional Convention, delegates resolved some disagreements, such as the large state–small state conflict over congressional representation. They put on hold other differences,

Three-Fifths Compromise
the negotiated agreement by the delegates to the Constitutional Convention to count each slave as three-fifths of a free man for the purpose of representation and taxes

such as their divisions over slavery. In the end, the document that the framers sent to the states for ratification described a government structure that aimed to fulfill the principles of the Declaration of Independence, for a select group of people. Foremost among those principles was the idea that it is up to the people to create a government that protects their natural rights to life, liberty, and the pursuit of happiness. To ensure those rights, which were initially meant only for white, property-owning men, the framers devised two key arrangements: the separation of powers with an integrated system of checks and balances, and a federal system in which the national and state governments had distinct, ultimate authorities. Although there was consensus on the mission of the new government, the conflict and arguments over the appropriate structure of government and government processes (including the processes for selecting government officials) resulted in compromises and often vague language that the framers anticipated would be clarified in the future.

What About a Bill of Rights?

While the Declaration of Independence argued that governments were created by the people to protect their natural rights to life, liberty, and the pursuit of happiness, unlike state constitutions, the Constitution as drafted by the framers did not provide protections for these rights. On September 12, 1787, George Mason, a delegate from Virginia, called for a bill of rights such as those found in state constitutions, which listed fundamental freedoms that the federal government could not infringe. Roger Sherman, a delegate from Connecticut, argued that there was no need for one, because state constitutions included bills of rights. With hardly any discussion, the delegates decided not to add a bill of rights to the proposed constitution.[23] The lack of a bill of rights would become a main target for critics.

>In February 2014, Senator Martin Heinrich (D-N.M.) introduced a bill to make Puerto Rico the 51st state, as long as Puerto Ricans living on the island support statehood in a referendum (a policy proposal on an Election Day ballot for voters to approve or reject). Heinrich's bill is similar to a bill introduced in the House of Representatives by Puerto Rico's nonvoting House delegate, Pedro Pierluisi (seen here). Puerto Rico has been a U.S. territory since 1889, and since 1917, Puerto Ricans (both those living in one of the 50 states and those living on the island of Puerto Rico) have been U.S. citizens. However, Puerto Ricans living on the island do not have the right to vote for president or for congressional members with voting rights in Congress, even though Congress and the president enact legislation with which Puerto Ricans must comply. At the same time, Puerto Ricans living in the states do have voting rights guaranteed to U.S. citizens.

Congress Sends the Constitution to the States for Ratification

On September 17, 1787, thirty-nine convention delegates signed the Constitution. Following the Articles of Confederation, the delegates delivered their proposed constitution to the standing Congress. However, fearful that the document would not garner the approval of all 13 state legislatures as mandated by the Articles' amendment process, the framers included in the Constitution a new ratification process that required the approval of conventions of just 9 states.

The framers requested that Congress send the proposed constitution to the states and that the state legislatures each establish a special, popularly elected convention to review and ratify the Constitution. One argument made to support this ratification process, which violated the Articles of Confederation, was that ratification by popularly elected conventions would validate the Constitution as the supreme law of the land, legitimized by the consent of the people. Congress acquiesced to the framers' request, and sent the proposed constitution to the states for ratification votes in special conventions.

The proposed constitution sent to the states was a product of conflict, deliberation, compromise, and pragmatism. In seven articles, the framers established a new national government with structures modeled after the state governments—distributing the basic governing functions among three branches and giving each branch a means to check the others—and a radical new system of government, a federal system, with dual sovereignty. Before exploring the states' debate and ratification of the Constitution, we review the blueprint of government embodied in the constitution sent to the states. To explore the entire Constitution, as amended since 1791, turn to the annotated Constitution that follows this chapter on pages 61–83.

ARTICLE I: THE LEGISLATIVE BRANCH   Article I of the Constitution delegates lawmaking authority to Congress, describes the structure of the legislative branch, and outlines the legislative process. Article I specifies that the legislature is bicameral, comprising the House of Representatives and the Senate. Each state is represented in the House based on its population. In contrast, state representation in the Senate is equal, with each state having two senators.

According to Article I, a proposed piece of legislation—a *bill*—requires simple majority votes (50 percent plus one vote) in both the House and the Senate to become a law. This requirement means that the House and the Senate can check each other in the legislative process, because even if one chamber garners a majority vote, the other chamber can kill the bill if its majority does not support it. Because all pieces of legislation supported by the majority of the House and the majority of the Senate go to the president for approval or rejection, the president has a check on the legislative authority of Congress.

ARTICLE II: THE EXECUTIVE BRANCH   Article II of the Constitution describes the authority of the president. This article gives the president authority to ensure that the laws are faithfully executed, to appoint people to assist in administering the laws, to negotiate treaties, and to command the military. In addition to those executive functions, Article II allows the president several checks on the power of the other two branches of government.

All pieces of legislation approved by the House and the Senate must be forwarded to the president's desk. The president has 10 days to act on a bill, or it will automatically become law. Within those 10 days, the president can either sign the bill into law or **veto** it—that is, reject it, sending it back to Congress with his objections noted. Because Congress has primary responsibility for the legislative function, it can set aside the president's veto—that is, override the veto—with two-thirds of House members and two-thirds of the senators voting to approve the vetoed bill.

With respect to the legislature's checks on the executive, the Constitution gives the Senate the power of **advice and consent**—the power to approve or reject—for treaties and presidential appointments. The Senate's advice and consent authority extends to the president's judicial nominees, as well.

ARTICLE III: THE JUDICIAL BRANCH   Article III describes the judicial branch. More specifically, Article III establishes the U.S. Supreme Court, and it delegates to Congress the authority to establish other, inferior (lower) courts. The Supreme Court and the other federal courts established by Congress have the authority to resolve lawsuits arising under the Constitution, national laws, and international treaties. In 1803, in the case of **Marbury v. Madison,**[24] the Supreme Court interpreted Article III to mean that the Court has the authority to determine whether an action taken by any government official or governing body violates the Constitution; this is the power of **judicial review.**

ARTICLE IV: STATE-TO-STATE RELATIONS   The Constitution does not include a list of state powers, rights, or responsibilities as it does for the national government. However, in Article IV, the Constitution does describe how the states must respect the rights and liberties of the citizens of all states as well as the legal proceedings and decisions of the other states. Article IV also establishes the means by which Congress can add new states to the union at the same time it prohibits Congress from changing state borders without consent of the affected states. This article also obligates the national government to ensure that all states are representative democracies.

veto
the president's rejection of a bill, which is sent back to Congress with the president's objections noted

advice and consent
the Senate's authority to approve or reject the president's appointments and negotiated treaties

Marbury v. Madison
the 1803 Supreme Court case that established the power of judicial review, which allows courts to determine that an action taken by any government official or governing body violates the Constitution

judicial review
court authority to determine that an action taken by any government official or governing body violates the Constitution; established by the Supreme Court in the 1803 *Marbury v. Madison* case

Amending the Constitution

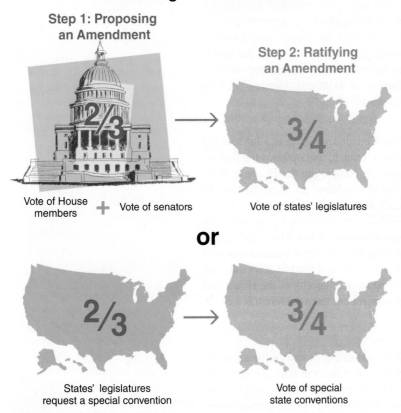

Step 1: Proposing an Amendment

2/3

Vote of House members **+** Vote of senators

or

2/3

States' legislatures request a special convention

Step 2: Ratifying an Amendment

3/4

Vote of states' legislatures

3/4

Vote of special state conventions

FIGURE 2.2

What steps are involved in proposing a constitutional amendment? In what two ways can an amendment be ratified? Who has the authority to ratify amendments to the Constitution? Why is the designation of this authority important to the balance of power between the national and state governments? Explain.

ARTICLE V: THE AMENDMENT PROCESS The framers recognized that the Constitution was a compromise born of their attempts to resolve existing problems, and therefore future generations would want to, and need to, revise the document in light of their own experiences and circumstances. Therefore, the framers provided processes to amend the Constitution.

The Constitution's framers wanted to ensure that widespread deliberation among the American people would precede any and all changes in the written Constitution. Thus, they made it no easy matter to amend the U.S. Constitution—that is, to change its written language. Amendment is a two-step process, entailing, first, the proposal of the amendment and, second, the ratification of the proposed amendment. Article V describes two different procedures for *proposing* an amendment (see Figure 2.2). The first method requires a two-thirds majority vote in both the House and the Senate, after which Congress sends the approved proposal to the states for ratification. The second method (which has never been used) requires a special constitutional convention. If two-thirds of the state legislatures petition Congress to consider an amendment, such a convention, where state delegates vote on the possible amendment, takes place; an approved proposal then goes to the states for ratification.

Article V also outlines two avenues by which the second step, ratifying a proposed amendment, may occur. An amendment is ratified by a vote of approval in either three-quarters of the state legislatures or three-quarters of special state conventions. Citizens have no vote in the process by which the U.S. Constitution is amended, nor did they have a vote in the original Constitution's ratification. In contrast, 49 of the 50 states in the United States mandate that their citizens approve amendments to their state constitutions as well as new state constitutions.

ARTICLE VI: SUPREMACY OF THE CONSTITUTION Article VI proclaims that the new national government will be legally responsible for all debts incurred by the Congress of the United States established by the Articles of Confederation. In addition, the article states that the Constitution, and laws and treaties made in compliance with it by the national government, are the supreme law of the land. Moreover, all national and state government officials must uphold the Constitution of the United States.

ARTICLE VII: THE CONSTITUTIONAL RATIFICATION PROCESS According to Article VII of the Constitution, ratification of the Constitution required the affirmative vote of special conventions in 9 of the 13 original states. After the delegates signed the Constitution, the standing Congress forwarded it to the states, directing them to hold ratification conventions.

The Federalist–Anti-Federalist Debate

Two days after 39 delegates signed the Constitution, it was published in a special issue of a newspaper called the *Pennsylvania Packet*. Almost immediately, opponents of the proposed Constitution began to write letters, issue pamphlets, and make stirring speeches urging the state legislatures to reject the document. The debate developed as one between the Federalists and the

Federalists
individuals who supported the new Constitution as presented by the Constitutional Convention in 1787

Anti-Federalists
individuals who opposed ratification of the Constitution because they were deeply suspicious of the powers it gave to the national government and of the impact those powers would have on states' authority and individual freedoms

Anti-Federalists. The **Federalists** supported the Constitution as presented by the convention delegates. The **Anti-Federalists** opposed the Constitution because it gave the national government too much power—power that would erode states' authority, which was left undefined in the document, and endanger individual freedoms because it was not limited by a bill of rights.

The weak national government created by the Articles of Confederation was a federal government, as Americans understood the term before the ratification battle. Indeed, the critics of the Articles who called for the Constitutional Convention called for remedying the "defects of the *federal government*." However, those supporting ratification of the Constitution called themselves Federalists in an effort to persuade citizens that the states retained considerable powers under the Constitution and that the federal government was a limited government (as it was under the Articles of Confederation).

It was in the Pennsylvania debate between the Federalists and the Anti-Federalists that the public call for the inclusion of a bill of rights to limit the powers of the federal government clearly emerged. Geared toward addressing the main Anti-Federalist complaints about the Constitution, the proposal for a bill of rights became the dominant point of contention in the ratification campaign. In the end, the success or failure of the ratification process would hinge on the debate over a bill of rights.

THE FEDERALIST PAPERS: IN SUPPORT OF A STRONG NATIONAL GOVERNMENT The Federalists made their most famous arguments in a series of essays known as ***The Federalist Papers.*** The authors of *The Federalist Papers,* James Madison, Alexander Hamilton, and John Jay, knew that achieving ratification depended on convincing the public and state legislators that the Constitution would empower the new nation to succeed. They also understood that many of the Anti-Federalists' concerns centered on how much power the national government would have under the Constitution and how that authority would affect the states and individual freedoms. Consequently, they approached the ratification debate strategically, penning eloquently reasoned essays (in the form of letters) to consider those specific issues.

Addressing fears of lost state power, in *Federalist* No. 51 (see Appendix C), Madison explains how the Constitution's provision of both a separation of powers and a system of checks and balances would prevent the national government from usurping the powers of the states and also ensure that no one branch of the federal government would dominate the other two. With regard to protecting individual rights, in *Federalist* No. 10 (see Appendix B), Madison reassuringly details how the republican government created by the Constitution would ensure that many views would be heard and that a majority of the population would not be permitted to trample the rights of the numerical minority. Writing in *Federalist* No. 84, Hamilton argues that because "the people surrender nothing, and as they retain every thing" by way of the Constitution, there was no danger that the new government would usurp individual rights and liberties.[25]

THE ANTI-FEDERALIST RESPONSE: CONCERN FOR THE RIGHTS OF CITIZENS AND STATES On the other side of the debate, Anti-Federalists penned countless letters, speeches, and essays warning of the dangers of the new government and urging Americans to reject it. Anti-Federalists argued that the Constitution ceded much too much power to the national government, at the expense of both the states and the people. Without a bill of rights, they reasoned, there was no way of truly limiting the actions the new government might take to achieve its goals.

Articulating Anti-Federalist views, Thomas Jefferson, author of the Declaration of Independence, insisted that the inclusion of a bill of rights in the Constitution was essential to protecting citizens' rights. Federalist Alexander Hamilton countered that listing those rights might endanger the very kind of individual freedoms and rights they sought to safeguard. It was possible, Hamilton reasoned, that the list would be incomplete and that at some future time people might legitimately argue that because a given right was not specifically enumerated, it did not exist. Jefferson's response was that "half a loaf is better than no bread" and that "if we cannot secure all our rights, let us secure what we can."[26]

Along with Jefferson, Mercy Otis Warren was among the most influential Anti-Federalists. Through her political writings and personal relationships with many of the leading politicians of her time, Warren affected public debate first over declaring independence from Great Britain,

The Federalist Papers
a series of essays, written by James Madison, Alexander Hamilton, and John Jay, that argued for the ratification of the Constitution

MERCY WARREN

>Mercy Otis Warren was a politically engaged woman of the 18th century who influenced many of the framers of the new nation, including Thomas Jefferson, George Washington, and Alexander Hamilton. Her letters, plays, poems, and pamphlets influenced the debates over declaring independence from Britain, ratification of the Articles of Confederation, ratification of the Constitution, and proposing and ratifying the Bill of Rights. Have you heard of her? One reason you may not know about Mercy Otis Warren is that she was an Anti-Federalist (on the losing side of the ratification debate). Another reason you might not have heard about her is she was a politically engaged woman at a time when society believed women should not be involved in politics. What are some signs that today most U.S. citizens accept women's political participation?

then over ratifying the Articles of Confederation, and finally over ratifying the Constitution. Under the pen name "A Columbian Patriot," Warren wrote a pamphlet "Observations on the New Constitution, and on the Federal and State Conventions" (1788), which presented a comprehensive argument against the proposed Constitution. The circulation of her pamphlet was larger than that of Hamilton, Madison, and Jay's *Federalist Papers.* Political scientist James McGregor Burns cited the "Columbian Patriot"—that is, Warren—as the spokesperson for the Anti-Federalist position.[27]

Ratification (1788) and Amendment with the Bill of Rights (1791)

In the end, Jefferson's and Warren's views and the larger public conversation about states' rights and individuals' liberties placed significant pressure on the Federalists to reconsider the need for inclusion of a bill of rights. With the proviso that a bill of rights would be the first order of business for the new Congress, Massachusetts, Maryland, South Carolina, and New Hampshire—the last four states of the nine needed for ratification—ratified the Constitution in 1788. In 1790, Rhode Island was the last of the original 13 states to ratify the Constitution.

In the opening days of the first session of the newly constituted Congress in March 1789, Virginia congressman James Madison introduced a bill of rights. Comprising 12 amendments, this proposed addition to the Constitution powerfully reflected the public concerns voiced during the ratification debates by enumerating limits on the national government's right to infringe on the natural rights of life, liberty, and the pursuit of happiness and by preserving the states' sovereignty. Congress passed all 12 proposed amendments and sent them to the states for approval. By 1791, the required number of states had quickly ratified 10 of the 12 amendments, which we refer to today as the **Bill of Rights.**

Bill of Rights
the first 10 amendments to the Constitution, which were ratified in 1791, constituting an enumeration of the individual liberties with which the government is forbidden to interfere

The first eight amendments in the Bill of Rights establish the government's legal obligation to protect several specific liberties to which the Declaration of Independence referred when it stated that men were "endowed by their creator with certain unalienable rights." These natural rights became government-protected liberties, *civil liberties,* through the ratification process. With the Jefferson and Hamilton debate over the pros and cons of listing citizens' rights in mind, the Ninth Amendment indicates that the list of liberties in the first eight amendments is not exhaustive and therefore "shall not be construed to deny or disparage others retained by the people." (Chapter 4 discusses in depth the civil liberties established in the Bill of Rights.) The tenth and last amendment in the Bill of Rights, preserves the states' rights. The Tenth Amendment states that the powers not delegated to the national government by the Constitution "nor prohibited by it to the states, are reserved to the states respectively, or to the people." By listing rights of citizens and the states, the Bill of Rights addressed the core concerns raised by the Anti-Federalists by imposing limits on the national government.

The Constitution as a Living, Evolving Document

The authors of the Constitution were pragmatic men who were willing to compromise to resolve the problems confronting the new nation and to get a new constitution ratified.[28] To win the votes needed to move the document from first draft through ratification, the framers had to negotiate and compromise over constitutional language. As a result of this give-and-take, the Constitution is replete with vague and ambiguous phrases, which the framers expected would be reviewed and revised through both formal amendment of the Constitution and judicial interpretation. According to James Madison's convention notes on the discussion of Article V, the formal amendment process, delegate "Elbridge Gerry noted that 'the novelty and difficulty of the experiment requires periodical revisions.'"[29] Thomas Jefferson even proposed during the discussion of Article V that a constitutional convention be called at the beginning of each new century.[30] At the time of his retirement, President George Washington (1789–1797) stated that he thought "the People (for it is with them to Judge) can as they will have the advantage of experience on their Side, decide with as much propriety on the alterations and amendments which are necessary [as] ourselves. I do not think we are more inspired, have more wisdom, or posses more virtue, than those who will come after us."[31]

The framers also expected judges to interpret the Constitution, and laws made under its provisions, in light of the realities of their own time. Alexander Hamilton wrote, "A constitution is in fact, and must be, regarded by judges as a fundamental law. It therefore belongs to them to ascertain its meaning as well as the meaning of any particular act proceeding from the legislative body. . . . The courts must declare the sense of the law. . . ."[32] As Supreme Court justice Charles Evans Hughes (1862–1948) observed more recently, "The Constitution is what the Judges say it is."[33]

Judges—and principally the justices sitting on the U.S. Supreme Court, which has the final authority to rule on what the Constitution means—have reinterpreted constitutional clauses many times. The Constitution has been *formally amended,* meaning the states have approved changes to the words in the document, only 27 times, however. The reason for the relatively low number of constitutional amendments is that the framers established a difficult amendment process, requiring supermajority votes: two-thirds of the members in each chamber in Congress and three-quarters approval among the states. They did so to ensure that nationwide public discourse would take place before the written words in the Constitution, the supreme law of the land, could be changed.

The alteration of this document—through both the passage of formal amendments and judicial reinterpretation of key clauses—derives from a continuing conversation among citizens about the core beliefs and principles of the framers and the generations that have followed them, including Americans today, and what those beliefs mean for today's realities.

In this concluding section, we consider the amendments that the states have approved to date as the American people have undertaken efforts to perfect the union established by the Constitution. We also highlight the recurring issues addressed by the U.S. Supreme Court as it interprets constitutional language in the process of solving conflicts over the law.

Formal Amendment of the Constitution

Every term, members of Congress introduce between 100 and 200 proposals for new constitutional amendments. That amounts to more than 10,000 proposals since 1789! Members of Congress who oppose a ruling by the U.S. Supreme Court or a law that engenders a great deal of public debate may propose an amendment to supersede the Court ruling or the law. Often, members of Congress introduce amendments

Then Now Next

Evolution of the Union and Its Constitutional Structures

	Then (1814)	Now
Numbers of states	18	50
Population	7.2 million*	309 million*
Number of representatives in the U.S. House	182**	435
Number of U.S. senators	36	100
Number of cabinet departments	2	15
Voting rights	Determined by the states	U.S. Constitution guarantees to citizens 18 years and older
Electoral College	Candidate with the most electoral votes wins the presidency; candidate with the second most votes wins the vice presidency	Electors each have one vote for president and one vote for vice president
Number of constitutional amendments	12	27

WHAT'S NEXT?

> Will the number of seats in the U.S. House of Representatives be increased so that the number of constituents per House member decreases to improve voters' ability to influence their representatives? Or is new technology sufficient to amplify voters' voices and secure representation?

> Congress last submitted to the states a proposed constitutional amendment for ratification in 1978. The Twenty-Seventh Amendment, ratified in 1992, had been sent to the states in 1791. Will Congress acknowledge the framers' notion that each generation should review and revise the Constitution by sending to the states for ratification amendments to perfect the union within the next 19 years?

> Will Congress heed the state applications for a convention to amend the Constitution by calling a convention sometime within the next 19 years?

*1810 and 2010 Census data, respectively.

**U.S. House of Representatives, *Congress Profiles,* http://history.house.gov/Congressional-Overview/Profiles/13th/.

knowing that they will never be ratified but wanting to appease their core constituencies by at least instigating public conversation about how our government should function and what rights and freedoms individuals possess.

Only a tiny fraction of the thousands of proposed amendments have cleared Congress—in fact, only 33 have achieved the two-thirds vote necessary in both the House and the Senate—and, as noted, the states have ratified only 27. The amendments that the states have ratified fit into one of three categories: They have (1) extended civil liberties and civil rights (equal protection of laws for citizens), (2) altered the selection of officials or operation of the branches of the national government, or (3) dealt with important policy issues. Table 2.1 summarizes the eleventh through the twenty-seventh constitutional amendments.

The Eleventh Through Twenty-Seventh Amendments to the Federal Constitution

AMENDMENTS THAT PROTECT CIVIL LIBERTIES AND CIVIL RIGHTS

Thirteenth	1865	Banned slavery
Fourteenth	1868	Established that all people have the right to equal protection and due process before the law, and that all citizens are guaranteed the same privileges and immunities
Fifteenth	1870	Guaranteed that the right to vote could not be abridged on the basis of race or color
Nineteenth	1920	Guaranteed that the right to vote could not be abridged on the basis of sex
Twenty-third	1961	Defined how the District of Columbia would be represented in the Electoral College
Twenty-fourth	1964	Outlawed the use of a poll tax, which prevented poor people from exercising their right to vote
Twenty-sixth	1971	Lowered the voting age to 18 years

AMENDMENTS THAT RELATE TO THE SELECTION OF GOVERNMENT OFFICIALS OR THE OPERATION OF THE BRANCHES OF GOVERNMENT

Eleventh	1795	Limited federal court jurisdiction by barring citizens of one state from suing another state in federal court
Twelfth	1804	Required the electors in the Electoral College to vote twice: once for president and once for vice president
Seventeenth	1913	Mandated the direct election of senators by citizens
Twentieth	1933	Set a date for the convening of Congress and the inauguration of the president
Twenty-second	1951	Limited to two the number of terms the president can serve
Twenty-fifth	1967	Established the procedure for presidential succession in the event of the disability or death of the president; established the procedure for vice-presidential replacement when the position becomes vacant before the end of the term
Twenty-seventh	1992	Required that there be an intervening election between the time when Congress votes itself a raise and when that raise can be implemented

AMENDMENTS THAT ADDRESS SPECIFIC PUBLIC POLICIES

Sixteenth	1913	Empowered Congress to establish an income tax
Eighteenth	1919	Banned the manufacture, sale, and transportation of liquor
Twenty-first	1933	Repealed the ban on the manufacture, sale, and transportation of liquor

TABLE 2.1

Interpretation by the U.S. Supreme Court

Beyond the addition of formal amendments, the Constitution has changed over time through reinterpretation by the courts. This reinterpretation began with the U.S. Supreme Court's landmark *Marbury v. Madison* decision in 1803, in which the Court established the important power of judicial review—the authority of the courts to rule on whether acts of government officials and governing bodies violate the Constitution. Although the U.S. Supreme Court's interpretation is final, if the Supreme Court does not review constitutional interpretations made by lower federal courts, then the interpretations of those lower courts are the final word.

How do judges decide what the Constitution means? To interpret its words, they may look at how courts have ruled in past cases on the phrasing in question or what the custom or usage of the words has generally been. They may try to ascertain what the authors of the Constitution meant. Alternatively, the judges may consider the policy implications of differing interpretations, gauging them against the mission presented in the Constitution's Preamble. In any given case, the deciding court must determine which of those points of reference it will use and how it will apply them to interpret the constitutional principles under consideration.

The power of judicial review has allowed the courts to continue to breathe life into the Constitution. Richard Beeman, a widely respected constitutional scholar, identifies three recurring themes evident in Supreme Court rulings: (1) the nature of the Constitution as a document that continues evolving as the courts interpret changing social norms, (2) the tensions created by the separation of powers and the dual sovereignty of our federal system, and (3) the clarification of fundamental rights guaranteed by the Bill of Rights.[34] With regard to changing societal norms, Court decisions reflect an expansion in the interpretation of the principle of equality as well as of the liberties and rights granted by the Bill of Rights and subsequent amendments (see Table 2.1). For example, in 1896 the Supreme Court decreed that the Fourteenth Amendment allowed laws requiring the segregation of white and black citizens.[35] By 1954, however, in the case of *Brown v. the Board of Education of Topeka, Kansas,*[36] the Supreme Court declared such segregation to be an unconstitutional violation of the Fourteenth Amendment. The right to privacy also represents an expansion of civil liberties through the Court's interpretations of the First, Third, Fourth, and Ninth Amendments of the Constitution.

Although controversial, Court decisions often capture significant media attention. In most cases, the Court's rulings are in step with public opinion. Analysts note that the Court does not often lead public opinion—in fact, it more often follows it.[37] And even if the justices wanted to take some very controversial and unpopular action, the system of checks and balances forces them to consider how the other branches would react. Recall that the Court has the power to interpret the law; it does not have the power to implement or to enforce the law and must be concerned about how the other branches might retaliate against it for highly unpopular decisions. Therefore, for the most part, changes to the Constitution, both formal (constitutional amendment) and informal (court reinterpretation), are incremental and further the will of the people because they are the product of widespread public discourse—an ongoing conversation of democracy.

Conclusion Thinking Critically About What's Next for the Constitution

The governing principles proclaimed in the Declaration of Independence successfully unified American colonists to fight the War for Independence. Government created by the consent of the people with the mission of protecting the people's natural rights to life, liberty, and the pursuit of happiness has proven difficult. Economic upheaval experienced under the Articles of Confederation sparked the call for a convention to amend the constitution. The product of the convention to amend the Articles was a proposed new constitution replete with compromises over major issues (such as how to implement representative government and the right to enslave people) and vague language. Formally amended only 27 times since 1789, the vague language in the Constitution has been interpreted and reinterpreted over the past 225 years.

The framers believed that each generation should review and revise the Constitution based on its experiences living under it, allowing the Constitution to evolve with society and technology. Today, many Americans believe that parts of the Constitution are not working. Some observers argue that the government is not serving the people well, that the government is infringing on individual liberties and the pursuit of happiness. Others focus on the foundational structures and operating procedures established by the Constitution, claiming that the government is not implementing them properly. Many argue that the more perfect union envisioned by the framers of the Constitution is not being fulfilled. To address these contemporary governing defects, some people have proposed constitutional amendments while others are calling for a constitutional convention. However, the amendment ratification process established in 1789 continues to make ratification of constitutional amendments very difficult. In addition, the vague constitutional language regarding when Congress must call a constitutional convention and how a convention would proceed remains a hurdle for those calling for a convention. The creation of a more perfect union is still a work in progress.

Summary

1. What Is a Constitution?

Constitutions may be written or unwritten. A written constitution presents the fundamental principles of a government, establishes the basic structures of the government, and outlines the procedures by which the government operates to fulfill the fundamental principles.

2. The Creation of the United States of America

By the mid-18th century, the American colonists were protesting the effect of British policies on their lives and livelihoods. Pamphlets, newspaper articles, public discourse, and eloquent revolutionaries persuaded the colonists that it was common sense, as well as their obligation, to declare their independence from Britain and to create a new government. Yet the weak national government established by the country's first constitution, the Articles of Confederation, did not serve the economic, diplomatic, or safety needs of the people well.

3. Crafting the Constitution: Compromise, Ratification, and Quick Amendment

In response to a growing desire for a more perfect union of the states, representatives from the states met in Philadelphia in 1787 to remedy the defects of the Articles of Confederation. Debate and deliberation led to compromise and a new constitution replete with vague language, supported by the Federalists and opposed by the Anti-Federalists. The addition of the Bill of Rights two years after the states ratified the Constitution addressed the primary Anti-Federalist concerns about individual liberties and states' authority.

4. The Constitution as a Living, Evolving Document

The words in the Constitution of the United States have been changed through formal amendment a mere 27 times over its 225-plus years of life. This rare occurrence of formal change to the Constitution's written words belies the reality of its perpetual revision through the process of judicial review and interpretation. The U.S. Supreme Court ultimately decides what the written words in the Constitution mean, and through that authority, the Court clarifies and modifies (hence, revises) the Constitution regularly.

Key Terms

advice and consent 49

Anti-Federalists 51

bicameral legislature 40

Bill of Rights 52

checks and balances 44

confederation 41

Connecticut Compromise
(Great Compromise) 46

constitution 34

dual sovereignty 44

Electoral College 46

The Federalist Papers 51

Federalists 51

judicial review 49

Marbury v. Madison 49

natural rights
(unalienable rights) 39

New Jersey Plan 46

republic 40

separation of powers 44

supremacy clause 44

Three-Fifths
Compromise 47

unicameral legislature 41

veto 49

Virginia Plan 46

For Review

1. Describe the three essential pieces of information contained in a written constitution.

2. How did the events leading up to the War for Independence shape the core principles of the U.S. Constitution, including representative democracy and protection of life, liberty, and the pursuit of happiness?

3. How did conflict and compromise influence the drafting and ratification of the Constitution? What specific issues caused conflict and required compromise for their resolution? On what matters was there early consensus among the framers?

4. What are the formal and informal mechanisms for changing the Constitution?

For Critical Thinking and Discussion

1. What similarities are there in the first state constitutions and the U.S. Constitution, which was written more than a decade later, with regard to mission, foundational structures, and essential operating procedures?

2. Think about important debates in American society today. Describe one that you think is linked in some way to the compromises upon which the Constitution is based and its often vague and ambiguous language.

3. Imagine that you are living during the Revolutionary era and writing an article for a newspaper in England. You are trying to explain why the colonists have destroyed thousands of pounds of British tea at the Boston Tea Party. How might you, as an English citizen living in England, characterize the colonists' motives? How might you, as an English citizen living in the colonies, characterize the colonists' motives?

4. What do you think would have happened had the Anti-Federalists, rather than the Federalists, prevailed in the ratification process of the Constitution? What kind of government would they have shaped? How would that government have dealt with the difficult issues facing the new republic—slavery, concerns about mob rule, and continuing hostility in the international community?

MULTIPLE CHOICE: Choose the lettered item that answers the question correctly.

1. According to the Declaration of Independence, the natural, unalienable rights include all of the following except
   a. liberty.
   b. life.
   c. property.
   d. the pursuit of happiness.

2. The existence of three branches of government, each responsible for a different primary governing function, is the implementation of the foundational organizational structure called
   a. judicial review.
   b. the federal system.
   c. representative democracy.
   d. separation of powers.

3. *Marbury v. Madison* (1803) is a landmark case because it
   a. clarified the Electoral College system.
   b. clarified congressional legislative authority.
   c. clarified the courts' judicial review authority.
   d. clarified presidential appointment authority.

4. Ratification of an amendment to the U.S. Constitution requires
   a. approval of the majority of citizens voting in a referendum.
   b. approval of three-quarters of the members of Congress.
   c. approval of three-quarters of either the House or the Senate.
   d. approval of three-quarters of the state legislatures or special conventions.

5. All of the following were authors of *The Federalist Papers* except the Anti-Federalist
   a. John Jay.
   b. Thomas Jefferson.
   c. Alexander Hamilton.
   d. James Madison.

6. The document (or set of documents), grounded in social contract theory and stating that citizens have an obligation to replace their government if it is not serving them and protecting their unalienable rights, is
   a. the Articles of Confederation.
   b. the Constitution of the United States of America.
   c. the Declaration of Independence.
   d. *The Federalist Papers.*

7. At the Constitutional Convention, the delegates devoted the bulk of their time to resolving the issue of
   a. procedures for electing the president and the vice president.
   b. representation in the national legislature.
   c. the necessity for a bill of rights.
   d. slavery.

8. The ultimate authority to interpret the meaning of constitutional language, and hence to decide what is the supreme law of the land, is held by
   a. the majority of members of Congress.
   b. the majority of members of state legislatures.
   c. the majority of justices on the U.S. Supreme Court.
   d. the president of the United States.

9. The required nine states ratified the Constitution of the United States in
   a. 1776.
   b. 1781.
   c. 1788.
   d. 1791.

10. One check that the Senate has on both the executive branch and the judicial branch is its power of
    a. advice and consent.
    b. impeachment.
    c. ratification of treaties.
    d. veto override.

FILL IN THE BLANKS

11. Currently there are _____ amendments to the U.S. Constitution, and the last amendment was added in the year _____, 203 years after it was sent to the states for ratification.

12. The United States' first constitution was the _____.

13. _____ wrote a pamphlet that summarized the Anti-Federalist position in the debate leading to ratification of the Constitution.

14. The Virginia delegate to the Second Continental Congress who wrote the Declaration of Independence, and later became an Anti-Federalist, was _____.

15. Many of the Anti-Federalist criticisms of the Constitution were addressed in 1791 with the ratification of the _____.

Answers: 1. c, 2. d, 3. c, 4. d, 5. b, 6. c, 7. b, 8. c, 9. c, 10. a, 11. 27 and 1992, 12. Articles of Confederation, 13. Mercy Otis Warren (the Columbian Patriot), 14. Thomas Jefferson, 15. Bill of Rights (first 10 amendments to the Constitution).

Internet Resources

FindLaw
www.findlaw.com This site offers links to news regarding current cases before the U.S. Supreme Court as well as access to decisions of all federal and state appellate courts.

Library of Congress Memory Project
www.ourdocuments.gov/content.php?page=milestone This comprehensive website provides links to 100 milestone documents, compiled by the National Archives and Records Administration, that chronicle U.S. history, from Lee's Resolution calling for independence in 1776 through the Voting Rights Act of 1965.

The U.S. Constitution Online
www.USConstitution.net This interesting site helps to place the U.S. Constitution in a contemporary context. Its current events section discusses how the pending issues are affected by constitutional principles.

Recommended Readings

Beeman, Richard. *The Penguin Guide to the United States Constitution*. New York: Penguin Books, 2010. This book has a fully annotated Declaration of Independence, a fully annotated U.S. Constitution, selections from *The Federalist Papers,* chapters presenting the history of the making and the initial enactment of the Constitution, and brief overviews of several landmark Supreme Court decisions.

Hamilton, Alexander, James Madison, and John Jay. *The Federalist Papers*. Cutchogue, NY: Buccaneer Books, 1992. A compilation of the 85 newspaper articles written by the authors to persuade the voters of New York to ratify the proposed Constitution of the United States, featuring a comprehensive introduction that puts the articles in context and outlines their principal themes—and hence, the underlying principles of the Constitution.

Roberts, Cokie. *Founding Mothers: The Women Who Raised Our Nation*. New York: Perennial Press, 2004. An examination of the Revolution and its aftermath, focusing on how women contributed to the war effort and to wider discussions about how the new government should be structured and what goals it should advance.

Sabato, Larry. *A More Perfect Constitution: 23 Proposals to Revitalize Our Constitution and Make America a Fairer Country*. New York: Walker Publishing, 2007. An exploration by political scientist Larry Sabato into why a constitutional convention is needed. The book includes proposals for 23 amendments—many of which citizens support, according to a poll commissioned by the author—that Sabato argues will perfect the Constitution. His real goal in writing the book was to kindle a national conversation on what he perceives as the deficiencies in U.S. representative democracy.

Movies of Interest

Return to the Land of Wonder (2004)
This documentary follows Adnan Pachachi's return to Iraq in 2003, after 37 years in exile, to head a committee charged with drafting a new constitution and bill of rights. The movie focuses on the torturous process of trying to resolve conflicts created by the demands of the United States and the expectations of Iraqis, as well as the realities of everyday life in Iraq in 2003.

An Empire of Reason (1998)
A thought-provoking answer to an intriguing "what if?" question: What if the ratification debates were held using the media tools of the 21st century, specifically, television?

Amistad (1997)
This film depicts the mutiny and subsequent trial of Africans aboard the ship *Amistad* in 1839–1840. Viewers get a glimpse of the intense civic discourse over slavery in the period leading up to the Civil War.

The Constitution of the United States of America

Preamble

We the People of the United States, in Order to form a more perfect Union, establish Justice, insure domestic Tranquility, provide for the common defence, promote the general Welfare, and secure the Blessings of Liberty to ourselves and our Posterity, do ordain and establish this Constitution for the United States of America.

> The Preamble states that "the People" are creating a new government, which is described in the Constitution. The Preamble also decrees that it is the mission of this new government to serve the people better than did the government established by the Articles of Confederation, which had been in effect since before the end of the War for Independence.

POLITICAL INQUIRY:

1. *What did the people of the United States in the late 18th century mean by "promote the general Welfare"?*

2. *What are some of the debates among people of the United States today related to the goal of promoting the general welfare?*

ARTICLE I. (Legislative Branch)

> Article I presents the organization, procedures, and authority of the lawmaking branch, the Congress, a bicameral (two-chamber) legislature comprising the House of Representatives and the Senate.

Section 1. (Bicameral Legislative Branch)

All legislative Powers herein granted shall be vested in a Congress of the United States, which shall consist of a Senate and House of Representatives.

Section 2. (The House of Representatives)

Clause 1: The House of Representatives shall be composed of Members chosen every second Year by the People of the several States, and the Electors in each State shall have the Qualifications requisite for Electors of the most numerous Branch of the State Legislature.

> House members are elected to serve a two-year term.

Clause 2: No Person shall be a Representative who shall not have attained to the age of twenty five Years, and been seven Years a Citizen of the United States, and who shall not, when elected, be an Inhabitant of that State in which he shall be chosen.

Clause 3: Representatives and direct Taxes shall be apportioned among the several States which may be included within this Union, according to their respective Numbers, which shall be determined by adding to the whole Number of free Persons, including those bound to Service for a Term of Years, and excluding Indians not taxed, three fifths of all other Persons. The actual Enumeration shall be made within three Years after the first Meeting of the Congress of the United States, and within every subsequent Term of ten Years, in such Manner as they shall by Law direct. The Number of Representatives shall not exceed one for every thirty Thousand, but

> The Constitution specifies only three qualifications to be elected to the House: You must be at least 25 years old; you must be a U.S. citizen for at least seven years (so a foreign-born, naturalized citizen can be a House member); and you must be a resident of the state you will represent. By tradition, House members live in the district that they represent.

each State shall have at Least one Representative; and until such enumeration shall be made, the State of New Hampshire shall be entitled to chuse three, Massachusetts eight, Rhode-Island and Providence Plantations one, Connecticut five, New-York six, New Jersey four, Pennsylvania eight, Delaware one, Maryland six, Virginia ten, North Carolina five, South Carolina five, and Georgia three.

Clause 4: When vacancies happen in the Representation from any State, the Executive Authority thereof shall issue Writs of Election to fill such Vacancies.

Clause 5: The House of Representatives shall chuse their Speaker and other Officers; and shall have the sole Power of Impeachment.

Section 3. (The Senate)

Clause 1: The Senate of the United States shall be composed of two Senators from each State, chosen by the Legislature thereof, for six Years; and each Senator shall have one Vote.

POLITICAL INQUIRY: *The Great (Connecticut) Compromise at the Constitutional Convention created the bicameral legislature, with the House seats apportioned among the states based on population and each state having two senators. Today, Vermont's 625,000 residents are represented by two U.S. senators, and so are New York's 19 million residents. In the 1960s, the Supreme Court ruled that the proper implementation of representative democracy must follow the principle of one person, one vote in state legislative bodies, which means each elected representative in a state House should represent about the same number of constituents, and each elected representative in a state Senate should represent about the same number of constituents.*

1. *Because of the Great Compromise, the U.S. Senate is not in incompliance with the principle of one person, one vote. Do you support the Great Compromise, or do you think that the principle of one person, one vote should be upheld, which would mean amending the Constitution? Justify your answer.*

2. *What are the chances that states with small populations would support an amendment that would apportion senators based on state population, as is done for the House of Representatives? Explain.*

Clause 2: Immediately after they shall be assembled in Consequence of the first Election, they shall be divided as equally as may be into three Classes. The Seats of the Senators of the first Class shall be vacated at the Expiration of the second Year, of the second Class at the Expiration of the fourth Year, and of the third Class at the Expiration of the sixth Year, so that one third may be chosen every second Year; and if Vacancies happen by Resignation, or otherwise, during the Recess of the Legislature of any State, the Executive thereof may make temporary Appointments until the next Meeting of the Legislature, which shall then fill such Vacancies.

Clause 3: No Person shall be a Senator who shall not have attained to the Age of thirty Years, and been nine Years a Citizen of the United States, and who shall not, when elected, be an Inhabitant of that State for which he shall be chosen.

Clause 4: The Vice President of the United States shall be President of the Senate but shall have no Vote, unless they be equally divided.

> Governors have the authority to call for a special election to fill any of their states' House seats that become vacant.

> House members select their presiding officer, the Speaker of the House. The Speaker is in line to succeed the president if both the president and the vice president are unable to serve. The Constitution gives the House a check on officials of the executive and judicial branches through its power of impeachment: the power to accuse such officials formally of offenses such as treason, bribery, and abuse of power. If the officials are subsequently found guilty in a trial held by the Senate, they are removed from office.

> Every even-numbered year, congressional elections are held in which one-third of the Senate's 100 seats and all 435 House seats are up for election. Every state elects two senators, who serve six-year terms.

> Initially, senators were selected by the members of their state's legislature, not by their state's voters. The Seventeenth Amendment (1913) changed this election process; today, senators are elected by the voters in their states. This amendment also authorized each state's governor to call for elections to fill vacancies as well as authorizing the state's legislature to determine how its state's vacant Senate seats would be temporarily filled until the election of a new senator.

> Senators must be at least 30 years old, either natural-born citizens or immigrants who have been citizens for at least nine years, and—like members of the House—residents of the state they are elected to represent.

> The vice president serves as the president of the Senate, with the authority to preside over meetings of the Senate and to vote when there is a tie.

> Although the first few vice presidents did preside over daily meetings of the Senate, the vice president rarely does so today.

Clause 5: The Senate shall chuse their other Officers, and also a President pro tempore, in the Absence of the Vice President, or when he shall exercise the Office of President of the United States.

Clause 6: The Senate shall have the sole Power to try all Impeachments. When sitting for that Purpose, they shall be on Oath or Affirmation. When the President of the United States is tried the Chief Justice shall preside: And no Person shall be convicted without the Concurrence of two thirds of the Members present.

> The Senate exercises a check on officials of the executive and judicial branches of the federal government by trying them once they have been impeached by the House of Representatives.

Clause 7: Judgment in Cases of Impeachment shall not extend further than to removal from Office, and disqualification to hold and enjoy any Office of honor, Trust or Profit under the United States: but the Party convicted shall nevertheless be liable and subject to Indictment, Trial, Judgment and Punishment, according to Law.

> If the Senate convicts an impeached official, he or she is removed from office and may be subject to prosecution in the criminal courts.

Section 4. (Congressional Elections)

Clause 1: The Times, Places and Manner of holding Elections for Senators and Representatives, shall be prescribed in each State by the Legislature thereof; but the Congress may at any time by Law make or alter such Regulations, except as to the Places of chusing Senators.

> Though states have the authority to organize and conduct elections, today they rely heavily on local governments to assist them. Congress has passed numerous laws to ensure constitutionally guaranteed voting rights. The first such law was passed shortly after ratification of the Fifteenth Amendment to criminalize attempts to deny black men their newly won right to vote. Congress has also enacted laws to make voter registration easier. For example, a 1996 federal law requires states to allow citizens to register to vote through the mail.

POLITICAL INQUIRY: *To increase voter turnout (the percentage of eligible voters that vote on Election Day), states have enacted laws allowing voters to vote by mail, to register to vote on Election Day, and even to vote during a two-week window instead of only on Election Day.*

1. *What are some advantages of and some concerns raised by allowing voters to vote by Internet?*

2. *What are some advantages of and some concerns raised by allowing voters to vote during a two-week window?*

Clause 2: The Congress shall assemble at least once in every Year, and such Meeting shall be on the first Monday in December, unless they shall by Law appoint a different Day.

Section 5. (Powers and Responsibilities of the House)

Clause 1: Each House shall be the Judge of the Elections, Returns and Qualifications of its own Members, and a Majority of each shall constitute a Quorum to do Business; but a smaller Number may adjourn from day to day, and may be authorized to compel the Attendance of absent Members, in such Manner, and under such Penalties as each House may provide.

> Each chamber decides whether the election of each of its members is legitimate. A majority of the members of each chamber must be present to conduct business: at least 218 members for the House and 51 senators for the Senate.

Clause 2: Each House may determine the Rules of its Proceedings, punish its Members for disorderly Behaviour, and, with the Concurrence of two thirds, expel a Member.

> After each congressional election, both the House and the Senate determine how they will conduct their business, and each chamber selects from among its members a presiding officer. Moreover, the members of each chamber establish codes of behavior, which they use to judge and—if necessary—punish members' misconduct.

Clause 3: Each House shall keep a Journal of its Proceedings, and from time to time publish the same, excepting such Parts as may in their Judgment require Secrecy; and the Yeas and Nays of the Members of either House on any question shall, at the Desire of one fifth of those Present, be entered on the Journal.

> The House and the Senate must keep and publish records of their proceedings, including a record of all votes for and against proposals, except those that they decide require secrecy. However, if one-fifth of the members of a chamber demand that a vote be recorded, it must be recorded. Congress publishes a record of its debates, called the Congressional Record.

Clause 4: Neither House, during the Session of Congress, shall, without the Consent of the other, adjourn for more than three days, nor to any other Place than that in which the two Houses shall be sitting.

> To close down business for more than three days during a session, or to conduct business at another location, each chamber needs to get approval from the other one. This ensures that one chamber cannot stop the legislative process by refusing to meet.

> Today, each member of Congress earns at least $174,000 per year, paid by taxes collected by the national government. Members of Congress are protected from civil lawsuits and criminal prosecution for the work they do as legislators. They are also protected from arrest while Congress is in session except for a charge of treason, of committing a felony, or of committing a breach of the peace.

> To ensure the separation of basic governing functions, no member of Congress can hold another federal position while serving in the House or the Senate. Moreover, members of Congress cannot be appointed to a position in the executive or judicial branch that was created during their term of office.

> This section details the legislative process.

> Although all revenue-raising bills, such as tax bills, must originate in the House, the Senate reviews them and has the authority to make modifications; ultimately the House and the Senate must approve the identical bill for it to become law.

> After the House and the Senate approve the identical bill by a simple majority vote in each chamber, it is sent to the president for approval or rejection. The president has 10 days in which to act, or the bill will automatically become law (unless Congress has adjourned, in which case the bill dies—a pocket veto). If the president signs the bill within 10 days, it becomes law. If the president rejects—vetoes—the bill, he or she sends it back to the chamber of its origin with objections. Congress can then rewrite the vetoed bill and send the revised bill through the legislative process. Or Congress can attempt to override the veto by garnering a supermajority vote of approval (two-thirds majority) in each chamber.

> The president must approve or veto everything that Congress approves, except its vote to adjourn or any resolutions that do not have the force of law.

> This section specifies the constitutionally established congressional powers. These powers are limited to those listed and any other powers that Congress believes are "necessary and proper" for Congress to fulfill its listed powers. Congress has used the "necessary and proper" clause (Clause 18) to justify laws that expand its listed powers. Laws that appear to go beyond the listed powers can be challenged in the courts, with the Supreme Court ultimately deciding their constitutionality.

> The power to raise money and to authorize spending it for common defense and the general welfare is one of the most essential powers of Congress. The Sixteenth Amendment (1913) authorizes a national income tax, which was not previously possible given the "uniformity" requirement in Clause 1.

> Today, after years of borrowing money to pay current bills, the national government has a debt of over $17 trillion.

Section 6. (Rights of Congressional Members)

Clause 1: The Senators and Representatives shall receive a Compensation for their Services, to be ascertained by Law, and paid out of the Treasury of the United States. They shall in all Cases, except Treason, Felony and Breach of the Peace, be privileged from Arrest during their Attendance at the Session of their respective Houses, and in going to and returning from the same; and for any Speech or Debate in either House, they shall not be questioned in any other Place.

Clause 2: No Senator or Representative shall, during the Time for which he was elected, be appointed to any civil Office under the Authority of the United States, which shall have been created, or the Emoluments whereof shall have been encreased during such time; and no Person holding any Office under the United States, shall be a Member of either House during his Continuance in Office.

Section 7. (The Legislative Process)

Clause 1: All Bills for raising Revenue shall originate in the House of Representatives; but the Senate may propose or concur with amendments as on other Bills.

Clause 2: Every Bill which shall have passed the House of Representatives and the Senate, shall, before it become a law, be presented to the President of the United States: If he approve he shall sign it, but if not he shall return it, with his Objections to that House in which it shall have originated, who shall enter the Objections at large on their Journal, and proceed to reconsider it. If after such Reconsideration two thirds of that House shall agree to pass the Bill, it shall be sent, together with the Objections, to the other House, by which it shall likewise be reconsidered, and if approved by two thirds of that House, it shall become a Law. But in all such Cases the Votes of both Houses shall be determined by Yeas and Nays, and the Names of the Persons voting for and against the Bill shall be entered on the Journal of each House respectively. If any Bill shall not be returned by the President within ten Days (Sundays excepted) after it shall have been presented to him, the Same shall be a Law, in like Manner as if he had signed it, unless the Congress by their Adjournment prevent its Return, in which Case it shall not be a Law.

Clause 3: Every Order, Resolution, or Vote to which the Concurrence of the Senate and House of Representatives may be necessary (except on a question of Adjournment) shall be presented to the President of the United States; and before the Same shall take Effect, shall be approved by him, or being disapproved by him, shall be repassed by two thirds of the Senate and House of Representatives, according to the Rules and Limitations prescribed in the Case of a Bill.

Section 8. (The Lawmaking Authority of Congress)

Clause 1: The Congress shall have Power To lay and collect Taxes, Duties, Imposts and Excises, to pay the Debts and provide for the common Defence and general Welfare of the United States; but all Duties, Imposts and Excises shall be uniform throughout the United States;

Clause 2: To borrow Money on the credit of the United States;

POLITICAL INQUIRY: *Some economists, politicians, and citizens fear that the national debt harms the United States by limiting the amount of money available to invest in growing the economy. Moreover, citizens worry that their children and grandchildren, saddled with the obligation* of paying back this debt, may face limited government services. Therefore, there have been repeated calls for a balanced budget amendment, which would force Congress to spend no more than the money it raises in each budget year.

1. What arguments might the members of Congress, elected officials who want to be reelected, put forth against ratification of a balanced budget amendment?

2. What national situations might require spending more money than is raised in a budget year?

Clause 3: To regulate Commerce with foreign Nations, and among the several States, and with the Indian Tribes;

Clause 4: To establish an uniform Rule of Naturalization, and uniform Laws on the subject of Bankruptcies throughout the United States;

Clause 5: To coin Money, regulate the Value thereof, and of foreign Coin, and fix the Standard of Weights and Measures;

Clause 6: To provide for the Punishment of counterfeiting the Securities and current Coin of the United States;

Clause 7: To establish Post Offices and post Roads;

Clause 8: To promote the Progress of Science and useful Arts, by securing for limited Times to Authors and Inventors the exclusive Right to their respective Writings and Discoveries;

Clause 9: To constitute Tribunals inferior to the supreme Court;

Clause 10: To define and punish Piracies and Felonies committed on the high Seas, and Offences against the Law of Nations;

Clause 11: To declare War, grant Letters of Marque and Reprisal, and make Rules concerning Captures on Land and Water;

Clause 12: To raise and support Armies, but no Appropriation of Money to that Use shall be for a longer Term than two Years;

Clause 13: To provide and maintain a Navy;

Clause 14: To make Rules for the Government and Regulation of the land and naval Forces;

Clause 15: To provide for calling forth the Militia to execute the Laws of the Union, suppress Insurrections and repel Invasions;

Clause 16: To provide for organizing, arming, and disciplining, the Militia, and for governing such Part of them as may be employed in the Service of the United States, reserving to the States respectively, the Appointment of the Officers, and the Authority of training the Militia according to the discipline prescribed by Congress;

Clause 17: To exercise exclusive Legislation in all Cases whatsoever, over such District (not exceeding ten Miles square) as may, by Cession of Particular States, and the Acceptance of Congress, become the Seat of the Government of the United States, and to exercise like Authority over all Places purchased by the Consent of the Legislature of the State in which the Same shall be, for the Erection of Forts, Magazines, Arsenals, dock-Yards and other needful Buildings;—And

> With the Supreme Court's support, Congress has interpreted Clause 3 in a way that has allowed it to expand its involvement in the economy and the daily lives of U.S. citizens, using this clause to regulate business as well as to outlaw racial segregation. However, state governments have frequently challenged Congress's expansion of power by way of the commerce clause when they believe that Congress is infringing on their constitutional authority.

> Congress has the authority to establish the process by which foreigners become citizens (Clause 4). Recently, national legislation has made it more difficult for individuals to file for bankruptcy.

> The authority to make and regulate money as well as to standardize weights and measures is essential to the regulation of commerce (Clause 5).

> Congress exercised its authority under Clause 9 to create the federal court system other than the Supreme Court, which was established under Article III of the Constitution.

> Every nation in the world possesses the authority to establish its own laws regarding crimes outside its borders and violations of international law (Clause 10).

> Clauses 11 through 15 collectively delegate to Congress the authority to raise and support military troops, to enact rules to regulate the troops, to call the troops to action, and to declare war. However, the president as commander in chief (Article II) has the authority to wage war. Presidents have committed armed troops without a declaration of war, leading to disputes over congressional and presidential war powers. Clause 11 also provides Congress with the authority to hire an individual for the purpose of retaliating against another nation for some harm it has caused the United States—that is, to provide a letter of Marque, an outdated practice.

> Clauses 15 and 16 guarantee the states the right to maintain and train a militia (today's National Guard), but state control of the militia is subordinate to national control when the national government needs the support of these militias to ensure that laws are executed, to suppress domestic uprisings, and to repel invasion.

POLITICAL INQUIRY: Article IV of the Constitution delegates to Congress the authority to admit new states to the union. The citizens of Washington, D.C., the seat of national government over which Congress has legislative power, have petitioned Congress to become a state.

> Congress has the authority to govern Washington, D.C., which is the seat of the national government. Today, citizens living in Washington, D.C., elect local government officials to govern the city with congressional oversight. The national government also governs federal lands throughout the states that are used for federal purposes, such as military installations.

> Clause 18 grants Congress authority to make all laws it deems necessary and proper to fulfill its responsibilities under the Constitution, including those listed in Section 8. This clause also authorizes Congress to pass laws it deems necessary to ensure that the other two branches are able to fulfill their responsibilities. Congress has also used this clause to expand its powers.

> Article I, Section 9 limits Congress's lawmaking authority and mandates that Congress be accountable to the people in how it spends the public's money.

> Clause 1 barred Congress from passing laws to prohibit the slave trade until 1808 at the earliest. The Thirteenth Amendment (1865) made slavery illegal.

> Clauses 2 and 3 guarantee protections to those accused of crimes. Clause 2 establishes the right of imprisoned persons to challenge their imprisonment in court (through a writ of habeas corpus). It notes that Congress can deny the right to a writ of habeas corpus during times of a rebellion or invasion if public safety is at risk.

> Clause 3 prohibits Congress from passing laws that declare a person or a group of people guilty of an offense (bills of attainder). Only courts have the authority to determine guilt. Congress is also prohibited from passing laws that punish a person tomorrow for an action he or she took that was legal today (ex post facto laws).

> Clause 4 prohibits Congress from directly taxing individual people, such as imposing an income tax. The Sixteenth Amendment (1913) authorized congressional enactment of a direct income tax on individual people.

> Congress is prohibited from taxing goods that are exported from any state, either those sent to foreign lands or to other states (Clause 5).

> Congress cannot favor any state over another in its regulation of trade (Clause 6).

> The national government can spend money only as authorized by Congress through enacted laws (no more than authorized and only for the purpose authorized) and must present a public accounting of revenues and expenditures.

> Congress cannot grant individuals special rights, privileges, or a position in government based on their heredity (birth into a family designated as nobility), which is how kings, queens, and other officials were granted their positions in the British monarchy. In addition, federal officials cannot accept gifts from foreign nations except those Congress allows (which today are gifts of minimal value).

> Clause 1 specifically prohibits states from engaging in several activities that the Constitution delegates to the national government, including engaging in foreign affairs and creating currency. In addition, it extends several of the prohibitions on Congress to the states.

1. *What would be the benefits of making Washington, D.C., a state?*

2. *What problems might arise if Washington, D.C., were to become a state?*

Clause 18: To make all Laws which shall be necessary and proper for carrying into Execution the foregoing Powers and all other Powers vested by this Constitution in the Government of the United States, or in any Department or Officer thereof.

Section 9. (Prohibitions on Congress)

Clause 1: The Migration or Importation of such Persons as any of the States now existing shall think proper to admit, shall not be prohibited by the Congress prior to the Year one thousand eight hundred and eight, but a Tax or duty may be imposed on such Importation, not exceeding ten dollars for each Person.

Clause 2: The Privilege of the Writ of Habeas Corpus shall not be suspended, unless when in Cases of Rebellion or Invasion the public Safety may require it.

Clause 3: No Bill of Attainder or ex post facto Law shall be passed.

Clause 4: No Capitation, or other direct, Tax shall be laid, unless in Proportion to the Census of Enumeration herein before directed to be taken.

Clause 5: No Tax or Duty shall be laid on Articles exported from any State.

Clause 6: No Preference shall be given by any Regulation of Commerce or Revenue to the Ports of one State over those of another: nor shall Vessels bound to, or from, one State, be obliged to enter, clear or pay Duties in another.

Clause 7: No Money shall be drawn from the Treasury, but in Consequence of Appropriations made by Law; and a regular Statement and Account of the Receipts and Expenditures of all public Money shall be published from time to time.

POLITICAL INQUIRY: *Today there exists a secret budget (black budget) for some military operations, intelligence operations, and counterterrorism operations. Some argue that the existence of the black budget violates the Constitution's requirement for "a regular Statement and Account of the Receipts and Expenditures of all public Money"?*

1. *What justification does the federal government use for the black budget?*

2. *Are you comfortable with the existence of a black budget? Explain your answer.*

Clause 8: No Title of Nobility shall be granted by the United States: And no Person holding any Office of Profit or Trust under them, shall, without the Consent of the Congress, accept of any present, Emolument, Office, or Title, of any kind whatever, from any King, Prince or foreign State.

Section 10. (Prohibitions on the States)

Clause 1: No State shall enter into any Treaty, Alliance, or Confederation; grant Letters of Marque and Reprisal; coin Money; emit Bills of Credit; make any Thing but gold and silver Coin a Tender in Payment of Debts; pass any Bill of Attainder, ex post facto Law, or Law impairing the Obligation of Contracts, or grant any Title of Nobility.

Clause 2: No State shall, without the Consent of the Congress, lay any Imposts or Duties on Imports or Exports, except what may be absolutely necessary for executing its inspection Laws: and the net Produce of all Duties and Imposts, laid by any State on Imports or Exports, shall be for the Use of the Treasury of the United States; and all such Laws shall be subject to the Revision and Control of the Congress.

Clause 3: No State shall, without the Consent of Congress, lay any Duty of Tonnage, keep Troops, or Ships of War in time of Peace, enter into any Agreement or Compact with another State, or with a foreign Power, or engage in War, unless actually invaded, or in such imminent Danger as will not admit of delay.

ARTICLE II. (Executive Branch)

Section 1. (Executive Powers of the President)

Clause 1: The executive Power shall be vested in a President of the United States of America. He shall hold his Office during the Term of four Years, and, together with the Vice President, chosen for the same Term, be elected, as follows:

Clause 2: Each State shall appoint, in such Manner as the Legislature thereof may direct, a Number of Electors, equal to the whole Number of Senators and Representatives to which the State may be entitled in the Congress: but no Senator or Representative, or Person holding an Office of Trust or Profit under the United States, shall be appointed an Elector.

Clause 3: The Electors shall meet in their respective States, and vote by Ballot for two Persons, of whom one at least shall not be an Inhabitant of the same State with themselves. And they shall make a List of all the Persons voted for, and of the Number of Votes for each; which List they shall sign and certify, and transmit sealed to the Seat of the Government of the United States, directed to the President of the Senate. The President of the Senate shall, in the Presence of the Senate and House of Representatives, open all the Certificates, and the Votes shall then be counted. The Person having the greatest Number of Votes shall be the President, if such Number be a Majority of the whole Number of Electors appointed; and if there be more than one who have such Majority, and have an equal Number of Votes, then the House of Representatives shall immediately chuse by Ballot one of them for President; and if no Person have a Majority, then from the five highest on the List the said House shall in like Manner chuse the President. But in chusing the President, the Votes shall be taken by States, the Representatives from each State having one Vote; a quorum for this Purpose shall consist of a Member or Members from two thirds of the States, and a Majority of all the States shall be necessary to a Choice. In every Case, after the Choice of the President, the Person having the greatest Number of Votes of the Electors shall be the Vice President. But if there should remain two or more who have equal Votes, the Senate shall chuse from them by Ballot the Vice President.

> States cannot, without congressional approval, levy import taxes, sign agreements or treaties with foreign nations, or enter into compacts (agreements) with other states.

> Clause 2 prevents states from interfering in foreign trade without congressional approval.

> Article II outlines the authority of the president and the vice president and the process of their selection.

> The Constitution delegates to the president the authority to administer the executive branch of the national government. The term of office for the president and his vice president is four years. No term limit was specified; until President Franklin D. Roosevelt (1933–1945), there was a tradition of a two-term limit. President Roosevelt served four terms.

> The Electoral College system was established as a compromise between those who wanted citizens to elect the president directly and others who wanted Congress to elect the president. Each state government has the authority to determine how their state's electors will be selected.

> Electors, who are selected through processes established by the legislatures of each state, have the authority to select the president and the vice president. Citizens' votes determine who their state's electors will be. Electors are individuals selected by officials of the state's political parties to participate in the Electoral College if the party wins the presidential vote in the state. Before passage of the Twelfth Amendment (1804), each elector had two votes. The candidate receiving the majority of votes won the presidency, and the candidate with the second highest number of votes won the vice presidency. Today, when the electors meet as the Electoral College, each elector casts one vote for the presidency and one vote for the vice presidency. If no presidential candidate wins a majority of the electoral votes, the House selects the president. If no vice-presidential candidate wins a majority of the electoral votes, the Senate selects the vice president.

POLITICAL INQUIRY: *The Electoral College system is criticized for many reasons. Some critics argue that deciding the presidential election by any vote other than that of the citizens is undemocratic. Others complain that in 2000 the system allowed George W. Bush to become president, even though he had not won the popular vote. Many argue that the Electoral College system should be eliminated and replaced by direct popular election of the president and the vice president.*

1. *What might be the benefits of eliminating the Electoral College?*
2. *What might be the potential harm to the nation of eliminating the Electoral College?*

> Today, by law, national elections are held on the Tuesday following the first Monday in November, in even-numbered years. During presidential election years, the electors gather in their state capitals on the Monday after the second Wednesday in December to vote for the president and the vice president. When Congress convenes in January after the presidential election, its members count the electoral ballots and formally announce the newly elected president and vice president.

> The president (and the vice president) must be at least 35 years old and must have lived within the United States for at least 14 years. Unlike the citizenship qualification for members of the House and the Senate, the president and the vice president must be natural-born citizens; they cannot be immigrants who have become citizens after arriving in the United States. Therefore, prominent public figures such as former California governor Arnold Schwarzenegger, who was born in Austria; Madeleine Albright, secretary of state under President Bill Clinton (1993–2001), who was born in what is now the Czech Republic; and Senator Mel Martinez (R-Fla.), who was born in Cuba, could never be elected president.

> Clause 6 states that the powers and duties of the presidency are transferred to the vice president when the president is no longer able to fulfill them. It also states that Congress can pass legislation to indicate who shall act as president if both the president and the vice president are unable to fulfill the president's powers and duties. The "acting" president would serve until the disability is removed or a new president is elected. The Twenty-Fifth Amendment (1967) clarifies when the vice president acts as president temporarily—such as when the president undergoes surgery—and when the vice president actually becomes president.

> Currently the president's salary is $400,000 per year plus numerous benefits, including a nontaxable expense account.

> Under the Constitution, the authority to ensure that laws are carried out is delegated to the president. The president and the vice president are elected to serve concurrent four-year terms. The call for a term limit followed President Franklin Roosevelt's election to a fourth term. The Twenty-Second Amendment (1951) established a two-term limit for presidents.

> The president is the commander of the military and of the National Guard (militia of the several states) when it is called to service by the president. When they are not called to service by the president, the state divisions of the National Guard are commanded by their governors. The president is authorized to establish the cabinet, the presidential advisory body comprising the top officials (secretaries) of each department of the executive branch. As the chief executive officer, the president can exercise a check on the judicial branch by decreasing or eliminating sentences and even pardoning (eliminating guilty verdicts of) federal prisoners.

Clause 4: The Congress may determine the Time of chusing the Electors, and the Day on which they shall give their Votes; which Day shall be the same throughout the United States.

Clause 5: No Person except a natural born Citizen, or a Citizen of the United States, at the time of the Adoption of this Constitution, shall be eligible to the Office of President; neither shall any person be eligible to that Office who shall not have attained to the Age of thirty five Years, and been fourteen Years a Resident within the United States.

Clause 6: In Case of the Removal of the President from Office, or of his Death, Resignation, or Inability to discharge the Powers and Duties of the said Office, the Same shall devolve on the Vice President, and the Congress may by Law provide for the Case of Removal, Death, Resignation or Inability, both of the President and Vice President, declaring what Officer shall then act as President, and such Officer shall act accordingly, until the Disability be removed, or a President shall be elected.

POLITICAL INQUIRY: *Other than being a heartbeat away from the presidency, the vice president has no responsibilities or obligations defined by the Constitution. The framers created the vice presidency to address concerns of succession, but they did not expect the vice president to do much and indeed, until the late 20th century, vice presidents traditionally did not have much of a job. Since Vice President Walter Mondale (1977–1981), vice presidents have been important, active members of presidential administrations. Yet, citizens do not get to vote for the vice president. Presidential candidates choose the person who will be their running mate but citizens have one vote with which they select a president. They do not have a second vote to select a vice president.*

1. *Should voters be concerned about the increased responsibilities of the vice president? Explain your answer.*
2. *What responsibilities do you think are appropriate for the vice president?*
3. *Should the Constitution be amended to include an enumeration of vice-presidential responsibilities and constraints? Why or why not?*

Clause 7: The President shall, at stated Times, receive for his Services, a Compensation, which shall neither be increased nor diminished during the Period for which he shall have been elected, and he shall not receive within that Period any other Emolument from the United States, or any of them.

Clause 8: Before he enter on the Execution of his Office, he shall take the following Oath or Affirmation:—"I do solemnly swear (or affirm) that I will faithfully execute the Office of President of the United States, and will to the best of my Ability, preserve, protect and defend the Constitution of the United States."

Section 2. (Powers of the President)

Clause 1: The President shall be Commander in Chief of the Army and Navy of the United States, and of the Militia of the several States, when called into the actual Service of the United States; he may require the Opinion, in writing, of the principal Officer in each of the executive Departments, upon any Subject relating to the Duties of their respective Offices, and he shall have Power to Grant Reprieves and Pardons for Offences against the United States, except in Cases of Impeachment.

Clause 2: He shall have Power, by and with the Advice and Consent of the Senate, to make Treaties, provided two thirds of the Senators present concur; and he shall nominate, and by and with the Advice and Consent of the Senate, shall appoint Ambassadors, other public Ministers and Consuls, Judges of the supreme Court, and all other Officers of the United States, whose Appointments are not herein otherwise provided for, and which shall be established by Law: but the Congress may by Law vest the Appointment of such inferior Officers, as they think proper, in the President alone, in the Courts of Law, or in the Heads of Departments.

> The Constitution provides a check on the president's authority to negotiate treaties and appoint foreign ambassadors, top officials in the executive branch, and Supreme Court justices by requiring that treaties be ratified or appointments confirmed by the Senate. Congress can create additional executive branch positions and federal courts and can decree how these legislatively created positions will be filled.

Clause 3: The President shall have Power to fill up all Vacancies that may happen during the Recess of the Senate, by granting Commissions which shall expire at the End of their next Session.

> If vacancies occur when the Senate is not in session and is therefore not available to confirm presidential appointees, the president can fill the vacancies. The appointees serve through the end of the congressional session.

POLITICAL INQUIRY: *Although the president can fill vacancies when the Senate is in recess, the Constitution does not define recess. Indeed, we have witnessed the Senate claim it is in session, not recess, when only one senator is present for weeks, coming to the Senate chambers to gavel the "session" to order and then a minute later gaveling adjournment for the day.*

1. *Why do you think the Senate goes through the exercise of having one senator gavel it in session and then a minute later gavel the session adjourned for the day?*

2. *How did the U.S. Supreme Court define recess in its 2014 decision (National Labor Relations Board v. Noel Canning)?*

Section 3. (Responsibilities of the President)

He shall from time to time give to the Congress Information on the State of the Union, and recommend to their Consideration such Measures as he shall judge necessary and expedient; he may, on extraordinary Occasions, convene both Houses, or either of them, and in Case of Disagreement between them, with Respect to the Time of Adjournment, he may adjourn them to such Time as he shall think proper; he shall receive Ambassadors and other public Ministers; he shall take Care that the Laws be faithfully executed, and shall Commission all the Officers of the United States.

> As chief executive officer of the nation, the president is required to ensure that laws are properly implemented by overseeing the executive branch agencies to be sure they are doing the work of government as established in law. The president is also required from time to time to give an assessment of the status of the nation to Congress and to make recommendations for the good of the country. This has evolved into the annual televised State of the Union Address, which is followed within days by the presentation of the president's budget proposal to Congress. The president can also call special sessions of Congress.

Section 4. (Impeachment)

The President, Vice President and all Civil Officers of the United States, shall be removed from Office on Impeachment for and Conviction of, Treason, Bribery, or other high Crimes and Misdemeanors.

> Presidents, vice presidents, and other federal officials can be removed from office if the members of the House of Representatives formally accuse them of treason (giving assistance to the nation's enemies), bribery, or other vaguely defined abuses of power ("high Crimes and Misdemeanors") and two-thirds of the Senate members find them guilty of these charges.

ARTICLE III. (Judicial Branch)

Section 1. (Federal Courts and Rights of Judges)

The judicial Power of the United States, shall be vested in one supreme Court, and in such inferior Courts as the Congress may from time to time ordain and establish. The Judges, both of the supreme and inferior Courts, shall hold their Offices during good Behaviour, and shall, at stated Times, receive for their Services, a Compensation, which shall not be diminished during their Continuance in Office.

> Article III presents the organization and authority of the U.S. Supreme Court and delegates to Congress the authority to create other courts as its members deem necessary.

> To ensure that judges make neutral and objective decisions, and are protected from political influences, federal judges serve until they retire, die, or are impeached by the House and convicted by the Senate. In addition, Congress cannot decrease a judge's pay.

> Federal courts have the authority to hear all lawsuits pertaining to national laws, the Constitution of the United States, and treaties. They also have jurisdiction over cases involving citizens of different states and citizens of foreign nations. Note that the power of judicial review, that is, the power to declare acts of government officials or bodies unconstitutional, is not enumerated in the Constitution.

Section 2. (Jurisdiction of Federal Courts)

Clause 1: The judicial Power shall extend to all Cases, in Law and Equity, arising under this Constitution, the Laws of the United States, and Treaties made, or which shall be made, under their Authority;—to all Cases affecting Ambassadors, other public ministers and Consuls;—to all Cases of admiralty and maritime Jurisdiction;—to Controversies to which the United States shall be a Party;—to Controversies between two or more States;—between a State and Citizens of another State;—between Citizens of different States;—between Citizens of the same State claiming Lands under Grants of different States, and between a State, or the Citizens thereof, and foreign States, Citizens or Subjects.

> The Supreme Court hears cases involving foreign diplomats and cases in which states are a party. Today, such cases are rare. For the most part, the Supreme Court hears cases on appeal from lower federal courts.

Clause 2: In all Cases affecting Ambassadors, other public Ministers and Consuls, and those in which a State shall be Party, the supreme Court shall have original Jurisdiction. In all the other Cases before mentioned, the supreme Court shall have appellate Jurisdiction, both as to Law and Fact, with such Exceptions, and under such Regulations as the Congress shall make.

> Defendants accused of federal crimes have the right to a jury trial in a federal court located in the state in which the crime was committed.

Clause 3: The Trial of all Crimes, except in Cases of Impeachment, shall be by Jury; and such Trial shall be held in the State where the said Crimes shall have been committed; but when not committed within any State, the Trial shall be at such Place or Places as the Congress may by Law have directed.

Section 3. (Treason)

> This clause defines treason as making war against the United States or helping its enemies. At least two witnesses to the crime are required for a conviction.

Clause 1: Treason against the United States, shall consist only in levying War against them, or in adhering to their Enemies, giving them Aid and Comfort. No Person shall be convicted of Treason unless on the Testimony of two Witnesses to the same overt Act, or on Confession in open Court.

> This clause prevents Congress from redefining treason. Those found guilty of treason can be punished, but their family members cannot be (no "Corruption of Blood").

Clause 2: The Congress shall have Power to declare the Punishment of Treason, but no Attainder of Treason shall work Corruption of Blood, or Forfeiture except during the Life of the Person attainted.

ARTICLE IV. (State-to-State Relations)

> Article IV establishes the obligations states have to each other and to the citizens of other states.

> States must respect one another's legal judgments and records, and a contract agreed to in one state is binding in the other states.

Section 1. (Full Faith and Credit of Legal Proceedings and Decisions)

Full Faith and Credit shall be given in each State to the public Acts, Records, and judicial Proceedings of every other State. And the Congress may by general Laws prescribe the Manner in which such Acts, Records and Proceedings shall be proved, and the Effect thereof.

Court found that the national government must recognize all marriages defined as legal by each state and provide spousal benefits to all legally married couples. Today, one of the many issues being debated is whether states with laws defining marriage as a contract between one man and one woman need to give full faith and credit to a same-sex marriage contract from a state where such marriages are legal, such as Massachusetts.

1. Does the full faith and credit clause require states that deny marriage contracts to same-sex couples to recognize legal same-sex marriage contracts from other states and thereby provide all spousal rights to same-sex couples legally married in other states?

2. Can you identify a compelling public interest that you believe can be achieved only by the government's denying marriage contracts to same-sex couples?

Section 2. (Privileges and Immunities of Citizens)

Clause 1: The Citizens of each State shall be entitled to all Privileges and Immunities of Citizens in the several States.

> No matter what state they find themselves in, all U.S. citizens are entitled to the same privileges and rights as the citizens of that state.

Clause 2: A Person charged in any State with Treason, Felony, or other Crime, who shall flee from Justice, and be found in another State, shall on Demand of the executive Authority of the State from which he fled, be delivered up, to be removed to the State having Jurisdiction of the Crime.

> If requested by a governor of another state, a state is obligated to return an accused felon to the state from which he or she fled.

Clause 3: No Person held to Service or Labour in one State, under the Laws thereof, escaping into another, shall, in Consequence of any Law or Regulation therein, be discharged from such Service or Labour, but shall be delivered up on Claim of the Party to whom such Service or Labour may be due.

> The Thirteenth Amendment (1865) eliminated a state's obligation to return slaves fleeing from their enslavement in another state.

Section 3. (Admission of New States)

Clause 1: New States may be admitted by the Congress into this Union; but no new State shall be formed or erected within the Jurisdiction of any other State; nor any State be formed by the Junction of two or more States, or Parts of States, without the Consent of the Legislatures of the States concerned as well as of the Congress.

> Congress can admit new states to the union, but it cannot alter established state borders without the approval of the states that would be affected by the change.

Clause 2: The Congress shall have Power to dispose of and make all needful Rules and Regulations respecting the Territory or other Property belonging to the United States; and nothing in this Constitution shall be so construed as to Prejudice any Claims of the United States, or of any particular State.

> The federal government has authority to administer all federal lands, wherever they are located, including national parks and historic sites as well as military installations.

Section 4. (National Government Obligations to the States)

The United States shall guarantee to every State in this Union a Republican Form of Government, and shall protect each of them against Invasion; and on Application of the Legislature, or of the Executive (when the Legislature cannot be convened) against domestic Violence.

> The national government must ensure that every state has a representative democracy, protect each state from foreign invasion, and assist states in addressing mass breaches of domestic tranquility. Under this section, Congress has authorized the president to send in federal troops to protect public safety. During the civil rights movement, for example, federal troops ensured the safety of black students attending newly desegregated high schools and colleges.

ARTICLE V. (Formal Constitutional Amendment Process)

> Article V details the process by which the Constitution can be amended.

The Congress, whenever two thirds of both Houses shall deem it necessary, shall propose Amendments to this Constitution, or, on the Application of the Legislatures of two thirds of the several States, shall call a Convention for proposing Amendments, which, in either Case, shall be valid to all Intents and Purposes, as Part of this Constitution, when ratified by the Legislatures of three fourths of the several States, or by Conventions in three fourths thereof, as the one or the other Mode of Ratification may be

> Amendments can be proposed either by Congress or by a special convention called at the request of the states. States have the authority to ratify amendments to the Constitution; three-fourths of the state legislatures must ratify an amendment for it to become part of the Constitution. Every year dozens of constitutional amendments are proposed in Congress, yet only 27 have been ratified since 1789.

proposed by the Congress; Provided that no Amendment which may be made prior to the Year One thousand eight hundred and eight shall in any Manner affect the first and fourth Clauses in the Ninth Section of the first Article; and that no State, without its Consent, shall be deprived of its equal Suffrage in the Senate.

POLITICAL INQUIRY: *The framers of the constitution indicated that they believed each generation should make the Constitution its own. Since ratification of the Constitution, each of the 50 states has applied for a constitutional convention at least once. However, Congress has never called for a constitutional convention and has sent only 33 proposed constitutional amendments to the states for ratification.*

1. *What is a potential benefit of calling a constitutional convention at regular intervals, as is done in several states?*

2. *What is a potential problem of calling a constitutional convention at regular intervals?*

> Article VI decrees that the Constitution is the supreme law of the land.

> This provision states that the new federal government created by the Constitution was responsible for the financial obligations of the national government created by the Articles of Confederation.

> The Constitution, and all laws made to fulfill its mission that are in compliance with it, is the supreme law of the land; no one is above the supreme law of the land.

> All national and state officials must take an oath promising to uphold the Constitution. This article also prohibits the government from requiring officeholders to submit to a religious test or swear a religious oath, hence supporting a separation of government and religion.

> Article VII outlines the process by which the Constitution will be ratified.

> When the Constitutional Convention presented the proposed second constitution, the Constitution of the United States, to the states for ratification, the Articles of Confederation (the first constitution) were still in effect. The Articles required agreement from all thirteen states to amend it, which some argued meant that all thirteen states had to agree to replace the Articles of Confederation with the Constitution. Yet the proposed second constitution decreed that it would replace the Articles when nine states had ratified it. The first Congress met under the Constitution of the United States in 1789.

A R T I C L E V I. (Supremacy of the Constitution)

Clause 1: All Debts contracted and Engagements entered into, before the Adoption of this Constitution, shall be as valid against the United States under this Constitution, as under the Confederation.

Clause 2: This Constitution, and the Laws of the United States which shall be made in Pursuance thereof; and all Treaties made, or which shall be made, under the Authority of the United States, shall be the supreme Law of the Land; and the Judges in every State shall be bound thereby, any Thing in the Constitution or Laws of any state to the Contrary notwithstanding.

Clause 3: The Senators and Representatives before mentioned, and the Members of the several State Legislatures, and all executive and judicial Officers, both of the United States and of the several States, shall be bound by Oath or Affirmation, to support this Constitution; but no religious Test shall ever be required as a Qualification to any Office or public Trust under the United States.

A R T I C L E V I I. (Constitutional Ratification Process)

Clause 1: The Ratification of the Conventions of nine States, shall be sufficient for the Establishment of this Constitution between the States so ratifying the same.

POLITICAL INQUIRY: *The framers of the Constitution developed a ratification process that violated the process of constitutional amendment established in the Articles of Confederation. Not only did their process allow for the new constitution to replace the constitution in effect since 1781 with 9 votes of approval instead of an unanimous vote of approval, but they also suggested that special state conventions, not the state legislatures, vote to ratify the new constitution.*

1. *Do you think ratification of the Constitution would have occurred in just two years if ratification required approval by the existing state legislatures instead of special conventions? Explain your answer.*

2. *With the fact that no delegates from Rhode Island signed the proposed constitution, do you think ratification would have occurred in just two years (or at all) if the vote had to be unanimous (as called for in the Article of Confederation)? Explain your answer.*

Clause 2: Done in Convention by the Unanimous Consent of the States present the Seventeenth Day of September in the Year of our Lord one thousand seven hundred and Eighty seven and of the Independence of the United States of America the Twelfth. In witness whereof We have hereunto subscribed our Names,

G. Washington—Presid't. and deputy from Virginia

Delaware	George Read
	Gunning Bedford, Jr.
	John Dickinson
	Richard Bassett
	Jacob Broom
Maryland	James McHenry
	Daniel of St. Thomas Jenifer
	Daniel Carroll
Virginia	John Blair
	James Madison, Jr.
North Carolina	William Blount
	Richard Dobbs Spaight
	Hugh Williamson
South Carolina	John Rutledge
	Charles Cotesworth Pinckney
	Charles Pinckney
	Pierce Butler
Georgia	William Few
	Abraham Baldwin
New Hampshire	John Langdon
	Nicholas Gilman
Massachusetts	Nathaniel Gorham
	Rufus King
Connecticut	William Samuel Johnson
	Roger Sherman
New York	Alexander Hamilton
New Jersey	William Livingston
	David Brearley
	William Patterson
	Jonathan Dayton
Pennsylvania	Benjamin Franklin
	Thomas Mifflin
	Robert Morris
	George Clymer
	Thomas FitzSimons
	Jared Ingersoll
	James Wilson
	Gouverneur Morris

Amendments to the Constitution of the United States of America
THE BILL OF RIGHTS: AMENDMENTS I–X (ratified in 1791)

> Government cannot make laws that limit freedom of expression, which includes freedom of religion, speech, and the press, as well as the freedom to assemble and to petition the government to address grievances. None of these individual freedoms is absolute, however; courts balance the protection of individual freedoms (as provided for in this Constitution) with the protection of public safety, including national security.

Amendment I (1791)

Congress shall make no law respecting an establishment of religion, or prohibiting the free exercise thereof; or abridging the freedom of speech, or of the press; or the right of the people peaceably to assemble, and to petition the Government for a redress of grievances.

> Today, states and the federal government balance the right of the people to own guns with the need to protect the public.

Amendment II (1791)

A well regulated Militia, being necessary to the security of a free State, the right of the people to keep and bear Arms, shall not be infringed.

POLITICAL INQUIRY: *Some people interpret the phrase "well regulated Militia" as imposing limits on the right to bear arms. Typically, those same people note that no rights in the Constitution are absolute. Indeed, the government must balance individual rights with the general welfare and public safety.*

1. *What do you think the phrase "a well regulated Militia" means?*

2. *How has the Supreme Court answered this question?*

> Military troops cannot take control of private homes during peacetime.

Amendment III (1791)

No Soldier shall, in time of peace be quartered in any house, without the consent of the Owner, nor in time of war, but in a manner to be prescribed by law.

> Government officials must obtain approval before they search or seize a person's property. The approval must come either from the person whose private property they are searching or seizing or from a judge who determines that the government is justified in taking this action to protect public safety and therefore signs a search warrant.

Amendment IV (1791)

The right of the people to be secure in their persons, houses, papers, and effects, against unreasonable searches and seizures, shall not be violated, and no Warrants shall issue, but upon probable cause, supported by Oath or affirmation, and particularly describing the place to be searched, and the persons or things to be seized.

POLITICAL INQUIRY: *Since the terrorist attacks on September 11, 2001, the national government has tried to balance the right of people to be secure in their person and property with public safety and national security.*

1. *What reasons have the president and members of Congress offered in defense of allowing intelligence agencies to bypass the requirement that they obtain judicial permission to conduct searches or seizures of phone records of suspected terrorists?*

2. *How valid are those reasons? In your opinion, can they be reconciled with constitutional protections?*

Amendment V (1791)

No person shall be held to answer for a capital, or otherwise infamous crime, unless on a presentment or indictment of a Grand Jury, except in cases arising in the land or naval forces, or in the Militia, when in actual service in time of War or public danger; nor shall any person be subject for the same offence to be twice put in jeopardy of life or limb; nor shall be compelled in any criminal case to be a witness against himself, nor be deprived of life, liberty, or property, without due process of law; nor shall private property be taken for public use, without just compensation.

Amendment VI (1791)

In all criminal prosecutions, the accused shall enjoy the right to a speedy and public trial, by an impartial jury of the State and district wherein the crime shall have been committed, which district shall have been previously ascertained by law, and to be informed of the nature and cause of the accusation; to be confronted with the witnesses against him; to have compulsory process for obtaining witnesses in his favor, and to have the Assistance of Counsel for his defence.

Amendment VII (1791)

In Suits at common law, where the value in controversy shall exceed twenty dollars, the right of trial by jury shall be preserved, and no fact tried by a jury, shall be otherwise re-examined in any Court of the United States, than according to the rules of the common law.

Amendment VIII (1791)

Excessive bail shall not be required, nor excessive fines imposed, nor cruel and unusual punishments inflicted.

Amendment IX (1791)

The enumeration in the Constitution, of certain rights, shall not be construed to deny or disparage others retained by the people.

POLITICAL INQUIRY: *Thomas Jefferson and Alexander Hamilton debated the need for a bill of rights. Hamilton argued that a list of rights would be incomplete and therefore, people might argue that because a given right was not listed, it did not exist.*

1. *How well do you think the Ninth Amendment addresses Hamilton's argument against a bill of rights? Explain.*

2. *What rights, not enumerated, do you think citizens retain?*

3. *What rights has the Supreme Court identified that are not enumerated in the Constitution?*

Amendment X (1791)

The powers not delegated to the United States by the Constitution, nor prohibited by it to the States, are reserved to the States respectively, or to the people.

Amendment XI (1795)

The Judicial power of the United States shall not be construed to extend to any suit in law or equity, commenced or prosecuted against one of the United States by Citizens of another State, or by Citizens or Subjects of any Foreign State.

> The Fifth Amendment provides much more than the familiar protection against self-incrimination that we hear people who are testifying before Congress and the courts claim by "taking the Fifth." For example, before the government can punish a person for a crime (take away a person's life, liberty, or pursuit of happiness), it must follow certain procedures specified in law; it must follow due process of the law. The federal government guarantees those accused of federal crimes a grand jury hearing in which the government presents its evidence to a selected group of citizens who determine whether there is sufficient evidence to go to trial. If a defendant is found not guilty of a specific criminal offense, he or she cannot be brought to trial again by the same government for the same offense. If the government determines it needs private property for a public use, the owner is compelled to sell the land, and the government must pay a fair price based on the market value of the property.

> The Sixth Amendment outlines additional procedures that the government must follow before taking away a person's life, liberty, or pursuit of happiness. People accused of crimes have the right to know what they are accused of doing, to hear from witnesses against them, and to defend themselves in a trial that is open to the public within a reasonable amount of time after the accusations are made. An indigent (very poor) person is guaranteed a government-provided lawyer in serious criminal cases. It is assumed all others can afford to hire a lawyer.

> Either party (the complainant or the person accused of causing harm or violating a contract) in a federal civil lawsuit involving more than $20 can demand a jury trial.

> The Eighth Amendment protects those accused of crimes as well as those found guilty from overly punitive decisions. Bail, a payment to the government that can be required to avoid incarceration before and during trial, cannot be set at an excessively high amount, unless the judge determines that freedom for the accused would jeopardize public safety or that he or she might flee. The punishment imposed on those convicted of crimes is expected to "fit" the crime: It is to be reasonable given the severity of the crime. Punishment cannot be excessive or cruel.

> The Ninth Amendment acknowledges that there are additional rights, not listed in the preceding eight amendments, that the government cannot deny to citizens. The Supreme Court has interpreted the First, Fourth, Fifth, and Ninth Amendments collectively to provide individuals with a right to privacy.

> The Tenth Amendment acknowledges that state governments retain all authority they had before ratification of the Constitution that has not been delegated to the national government by the Constitution. This amendment was demanded by the Anti-Federalists, who opposed ratification of this Constitution. The Anti-Federalists feared that the national government would infringe on people's freedoms and on the authority of the state governments. The vagueness of the rights retained by the states continues to cause tensions and disputes between the state governments and the national government.

> The courts have interpreted this amendment to mean that federal courts do not have the authority to hear lawsuits brought by citizens against their own state or against another state, or brought by foreigners against a state.

> The presidential election in 1800 ended with a tie in Electoral College votes between Thomas Jefferson and Aaron Burr. Because the candidate with the most votes was to become president and the candidate with the second highest number of votes was to become vice president, the tie meant that the job of selecting the president was turned over to the House of Representatives. The House selected Jefferson. Calls to change the procedure were answered by the enactment of this amendment. Today, each elector has two votes: one for a presidential candidate and one for a vice-presidential candidate. The presidential candidate who wins the majority of electoral votes wins the presidency, and the same is true for the vice-presidential candidate. If no presidential candidate wins a majority of the votes, the House selects the president. If no vice-presidential candidate wins a majority of the votes, the Senate selects the vice president.

Amendment XII (1804)

The Electors shall meet in their respective states and vote by ballot for President and Vice-President, one of whom, at least, shall not be an inhabitant of the same state with themselves; they shall name in their ballots the person voted for as President, and in distinct ballots the person voted for as Vice-President, and they shall make distinct lists of all persons voted for as President, and of all persons voted for as Vice-President, and of the number of votes for each, which lists they shall sign and certify, and transmit sealed to the seat of the government of the United States, directed to the President of the Senate;—The President of the Senate shall, in the presence of the Senate and House of Representatives, open all the certificates and the votes shall then be counted;—The person having the greatest Number of votes for President, shall be the President, if such number be a majority of the whole number of Electors appointed; and if no person have such majority, then from the persons having the highest numbers not exceeding three on the list of those voted for as President, the House of Representatives shall choose immediately, by ballot, the President. But in choosing the President, the votes shall be taken by states, the representation from each state having one vote; a quorum for this purpose shall consist of a member or members from two-thirds of the states, and a majority of all the states shall be necessary to a choice. And if the House of Representatives shall not choose a President whenever the right of choice shall devolve upon them, before the fourth day of March next following, then the Vice-President shall act as President, as in the case of the death or other constitutional disability of the President—The person having the greatest number of votes as Vice-President, shall be the Vice-President, if such number be a majority of the whole number of Electors appointed, and if no person have a majority, then from the two highest numbers on the list, the Senate shall choose the Vice-President; a quorum for the purpose shall consist of two-thirds of the whole number of Senators, and a majority of the whole number shall be necessary to a choice. But no person constitutionally ineligible to the office of President shall be eligible to that of Vice-President of the United States.

POLITICAL INQUIRY: *Electors in the Electoral College have two votes: one vote for a presidential candidate and one vote for a vice-presidential candidate. Citizens have just one vote; citizens vote for a ticket that includes both a presidential candidate and the vice-presidential candidate selected by the presidential candidate.*

1. *What effect might each citizen having two votes as do the electors—one vote for a presidential candidate and one vote for a vice-presidential candidate—have on presidential campaigns?*

2. *What effect might it have on the ability of the president to govern?*

> This amendment abolished slavery.

Amendment XIII (1865)

Section 1. Neither slavery nor involuntary servitude, except as a punishment for crime whereof the party shall have been duly convicted, shall exist within the United States, or any place subject to their jurisdiction.

Section 2. Congress shall have power to enforce this article by appropriate legislation.

Amendment XIV (1868)

Section 1. All persons born or naturalized in the United States and subject to the jurisdiction thereof, are citizens of the United States and of the State wherein they reside. No State shall make or enforce any law which shall abridge the privileges or immunities of citizens of the United States; nor shall any State deprive any person of life, liberty, or property, without due process of law; nor deny to any person within its jurisdiction the equal protection of the laws.

> This amendment extends the rights of citizenship to all those born in the United States and those who have become citizens through naturalization. States are prohibited from denying U.S. citizens their rights and privileges and must provide all people with due process before taking away their life, liberty, or pursuit of happiness. States must also treat all people equally and fairly. The courts have also used this section of the Fourteenth Amendment to require that states ensure citizens their protections under the Bill of Rights.

POLITICAL INQUIRY: *Recently some citizens and politicians have claimed that undocumented immigrants and their children, who are citizens if they were born in the United States, cost the nation's taxpayers a great deal of money in public services guaranteed to all citizens, including public education.*

1. *Make an argument for amending the Constitution to deny citizenship to those born in the United States to parents who are in the country without required documentation.*

2. *Make an argument against amending the Constitution to deny citizenship to those born in the United States to parents who are in the country without required documentation.*

Section 2. Representatives shall be apportioned among the several States according to their respective numbers, counting the whole number of persons in each State, excluding Indians not taxed. But when the right to vote at any election for the choice of electors for President and Vice President of the United States, Representatives in Congress, the Executive and Judicial officers of a State, or the members of the Legislature thereof, is denied to any of the male inhabitants of such State, being twenty-one years of age, and citizens of the United States, or in any way abridged, except for participation in rebellion, or other crime, the basis of representation therein shall be reduced in the proportion which the number of such male citizens shall bear to the whole number of male citizens twenty-one years of age in such State.

> This section of the Fourteenth Amendment is the first use of the term *male* in the Constitution. This section requires that if a state denies men over the age of 21 the right to vote, its representation in the House will be diminished accordingly. The Fifteenth Amendment makes this section unnecessary.

Section 3. No person shall be a Senator or Representative in Congress, or elector of President and Vice President, or hold any office, civil or military, under the United States, or under any State, who, having previously taken an oath, as a member of Congress, or as an officer of the United States, or as a member of any State legislature, or as an executive or judicial officer of any State, to support the Constitution of the United States, shall have engaged in insurrection or rebellion against the same, or given aid or comfort to the enemies thereof. But Congress may by a vote of two-thirds of each House, remove such disability.

Section 4. The validity of the public debt of the United States, authorized by law, including debts incurred for payment of pensions and bounties for services in suppressing insurrection or rebellion, shall not be questioned. But neither the United States nor any State shall assume or pay any debt or obligation incurred in aid of insurrection or rebellion against the United States, or any claim for the loss or emancipation of any slave; but all such debts, obligations and claims shall be held illegal and void.

> The intent of this section was to prevent government officials who supported the Confederacy during the Civil War from serving in government. Congress voted in 1898 to eliminate this prohibition.

Section 5. The Congress shall have power to enforce, by appropriate legislation, the provisions of this article.

> All male citizens meeting their state's minimum age requirement are guaranteed the right to vote.

> This amendment authorizes the national government to establish taxes on personal and corporate income.

> Since the ratification of the Seventeenth Amendment in 1913, senators are elected by the citizens in each state rather than by state legislatures. The amendment also allows each state legislature to establish the process by which vacancies in the Senate will be filled, either through special election or by gubernatorial appointment.

> The "Prohibition" amendment—making it illegal to manufacture, sell, or transport alcoholic beverages in the United States—was widely disobeyed during the years it was in effect. The Twenty-First amendment repealed this amendment.

Amendment XV (1870)

Section 1. The right of citizens of the United States to vote shall not be denied or abridged by the United States or by any State on account of race, color, or previous condition of servitude.

Section 2. The Congress shall have power to enforce this article by appropriate legislation.

Amendment XVI (1913)

The Congress shall have power to lay and collect taxes on incomes, from whatever source derived, without apportionment among the several States, and without regard to any census or enumeration.

Amendment XVII (1913)

The Senate of the United States shall be composed of two Senators from each State, elected by the people thereof, for six years; and each Senator shall have one vote. The electors in each State shall have the qualifications requisite for electors of the most numerous branch of the State legislatures.

When vacancies happen in the representation of any State in the Senate, the executive authority of such State shall issue writs of election to fill such vacancies: Provided, That the legislature of any State may empower the executive thereof to make temporary appointments until the people fill the vacancies by election as the legislature may direct.

This amendment shall not be so construed as to affect the election or term of any Senator chosen before it becomes valid as part of the Constitution.

Amendment XVIII (1919)

Section 1. After one year from the ratification of this article the manufacture, sale, or transportation of intoxicating liquors within, the importation thereof into, or the exportation thereof from the United States and all territory subject to the jurisdiction thereof for beverage purposes is hereby prohibited.

Section 2. The Congress and the several States shall have concurrent power to enforce this article by appropriate legislation.

Section 3. This article shall be inoperative unless it shall have been ratified as an amendment to the Constitution by the legislatures of the several

States, as provided in the Constitution, within seven years from the date of the submission hereof to the States by the Congress.

POLITICAL INQUIRY: *Today, alcohol is legally manufactured, transported, and sold in the United States.*

> **1.** *What happened to this amendment so that alcohol can be legally manufactured, transported and sold today?*
>
> **2.** *Does the Eighteenth Amendment provide for fundamental law—as part of the basic legal and political document that puts forth the foundational principles, structures, and rules of operation for a government—or does it sound more like a public policy? Explain your answer.*

Amendment XIX (1920)

The right of citizens of the United States to vote shall not be denied or abridged by the United States or by any State on account of sex. Congress shall have power to enforce this article by appropriate legislation.

> All female citizens meeting their state's minimum age requirement are guaranteed the right to vote.

POLITICAL INQUIRY: *All male citizens gained the right to vote with the Fifteenth Amendment in 1870, 50 years before all women citizens did. Today, women's voter turnout is typically higher than is men's voter turnout and women voters lean more Democratic than men voters.*

> **1.** *What does the fact that women did not win the vote until 1920 suggest about the status of women in the United States during the 19th and early 20th centuries?*
>
> **2.** *What effect do you think women's voter turnout patterns have had on presidential campaigns and public policy debates in the 21st century?*

Amendment XX (1933)

Section 1. The terms of the President and Vice President shall end at noon on the 20th day of January, and the terms of Senators and Representatives at noon on the 3d day of January, of the years in which such terms would have ended if this article had not been ratified; and the terms of their successors shall then begin.

Section 2. The Congress shall assemble at least once in every year, and such meeting shall begin at noon on the 3d day of January, unless they shall by law appoint a different day.

> The first two sections of the Twentieth Amendment establish new starting dates for the president's and vice president's terms of office (January 20) as well as for members of Congress (January 3). Section 2 also decrees that the annual meeting of Congress will begin on January 3 unless Congress specifies a different date.

Section 3. If, at the time fixed for the beginning of the term of the President, the President elect shall have died, the Vice President elect shall become President. If a President shall not have been chosen before the time fixed for the beginning of his term, or if the President elect shall have failed to qualify, then the Vice President elect shall act as President until a President shall have qualified; and the Congress may by law provide for the case wherein neither a President elect nor a Vice President elect shall have qualified, declaring who shall then act as President, or the manner in which one who is to act shall be selected, and such person shall act accordingly until a President or Vice President shall have qualified.

> Sections 3 and 4 of this amendment establish that if the president elect dies before his or her term of office begins, the vice president elect becomes president. If the president elect has not been selected or is unable to begin the term, the vice president elect serves as acting president until the president is selected or is able to serve.

Section 4. The Congress may by law provide for the case of the death of any of the persons from whom the House of Representatives may choose a President whenever the right of choice shall have devolved upon them, and for the case of the death of any of the persons from whom the Senate may choose a Vice President whenever the right of choice shall have devolved upon them.

Section 5. Sections 1 and 2 shall take effect on the 15th day of October following the ratification of this article.

Section 6. This article shall be inoperative unless it shall have been ratified as an amendment to the Constitution by the legislatures of three-fourths of the several States within seven years from the date of its submission.

Amendment XXI (1933)

Section 1. The eighteenth article of amendment to the Constitution of the United States is hereby repealed.

Section 2. The transportation or importation into any State, Territory, or possession of the United States for delivery or use therein of intoxicating liquors, in violation of the laws thereof, is hereby prohibited.

Section 3. This article shall be inoperative unless it shall have been ratified as an amendment to the Constitution by conventions in the several States, as provided in the Constitution, within seven years from the date of the submission hereof to the States by the Congress.

POLITICAL INQUIRY: *Congress has sent only 33 proposed amendments to the states, and the states have ratified only 27 of the amendments. The Eighteenth Amendment is the only amendment repealed.*

1. *What led to the repeal of the Eighteenth Amendment 14 years after its passage?*
2. *What does the fact that the amendment was repealed so quickly say about the nature of fundamental law and principles versus public policy and the fluidity of public opinion on public policies?*

Amendment XXII (1951)

Section 1. No person shall be elected to the office of the President more than twice, and no person who has held the office of President, or acted as President, for more than two years of a term to which some other person was elected President shall be elected to the office of the President more than once. But this Article shall not apply to any person holding the office of President, when this Article was proposed by the Congress, and shall not prevent any person who may be holding the office of President, or acting as President, during the term within which this Article becomes operative from holding the office of President or acting as President during the remainder of such term.

Section 2. This article shall be inoperative unless it shall have been ratified as an amendment to the Constitution by the legislatures of three-fourths of the several States within seven years from the date of its submission to the States by the Congress.

Amendment XXIII (1961)

Section 1. The District constituting the seat of Government of the United States shall appoint in such manner as the Congress may direct: A number of electors of President and Vice President equal to the whole number of Senators and Representatives in Congress to which the District would be entitled if it were a State, but in no event more than the least populous State; they shall be in addition to those appointed by the States, but they shall be considered, for the purposes of the election of President and Vice President, to be electors appointed by a State; and they shall meet in the District and perform such duties as provided by the twelfth article of amendment.

Section 2. The Congress shall have power to enforce this article by appropriate legislation.

> Citizens living in Washington, D.C., are given the right to elect three voting members to the Electoral College. Before this amendment, these citizens were not represented in the Electoral College.

Amendment XXIV (1964)

Section 1. The right of citizens of the United States to vote in any primary or other election for President or Vice President, for electors for President or Vice President, or for Senator or Representative in Congress, shall not be denied or abridged by the United States or any State by reason of failure to pay any poll tax or other tax.

Section 2. The Congress shall have power to enforce this article by appropriate legislation.

> Governments are prohibited from requiring a person to pay a tax in order to vote.

POLITICAL INQUIRY: *Several states have enacted laws requiring voters to show a government-issued photo ID to vote. However, many elderly, poor, and urban residents do not have a government-issued photo ID and therefore would have to pay for one, or would be prevented from voting.*

1. *Is this a modern poll tax? Why or why not?*

2. *What is the explanation states provide for enacting laws requiring a government-issued photo ID to vote?*

> The vice president becomes president if the president resigns or dies.

> The president can nominate a person to fill a vice-presidential vacancy. Congress must approve the nominee. President Richard Nixon appointed and Congress confirmed Gerald Ford to the vice presidency when Vice President Spiro Agnew resigned. When President Nixon resigned, Vice President Ford, who had not been elected, became president. He subsequently appointed and Congress confirmed Nelson Rockefeller to be vice president.

> If the president indicates in writing to Congress that he or she cannot carry out the duties of office, the vice president becomes acting president until the president informs Congress that he or she is again fit to resume the responsibilities of the presidency.

> If the vice president in concert with a majority of cabinet officials (or some other body designated by Congress) declares to Congress in writing that the president is unable to fulfill the duties of office, the vice president becomes acting president until the president claims he or she is again fit for duty. However, if the vice president and a majority of cabinet officials challenge the president's claim, then Congress must decide within three weeks if the president can resume office.

Amendment XXV (1967)

Section 1. In case of the removal of the President from office or of his death or resignation, the Vice President shall become President.

Section 2. Whenever there is a vacancy in the office of the Vice President, the President shall nominate a Vice President who shall take office upon confirmation by a majority vote of both Houses of Congress.

Section 3. Whenever the President transmits to the President pro tempore of the Senate and the Speaker of the House of Representatives his written declaration that he is unable to discharge the powers and duties of his office, and until he transmits to them a written declaration to the contrary, such powers and duties shall be discharged by the Vice President as Acting President.

Section 4. Whenever the Vice President and a majority of either the principal officers of the executive departments or of such other body as Congress may by law provide, transmit to the President pro tempore of the Senate and the Speaker of the House of Representatives their written declaration that the President is unable to discharge the powers and duties of his office, the Vice President shall immediately assume the powers and duties of the office as Acting President.

Thereafter, when the President transmits to the President pro tempore of the Senate and the Speaker of the House of Representatives his written declaration that no inability exists, he shall resume the powers and duties of his office unless the Vice President and a majority of either the principal officers of the executive department or of such other body as Congress may by law provide, transmit within four days to the President pro tempore of the Senate and the Speaker of the House of Representatives their written declaration that the President is unable to discharge the powers and duties of his office. Thereupon Congress shall decide the issue, assembling within forty-eight hours for that purpose if not in session. If the Congress, within twenty-one days after receipt of the latter written declaration, or, if Congress is not in session, within twenty-one days after Congress is required to assemble, determines by two-thirds vote of both Houses that the President is unable to discharge the powers and duties of his office, the Vice President shall continue to discharge the same as Acting President; otherwise, the President shall resume the powers and duties of his office.

Amendment XXVI (1971)

Section 1. The right of citizens of the United States, who are eighteen years of age or older, to vote shall not be denied or abridged by the United States or by any State on account of age.

Section 2. The Congress shall have power to enforce this article by appropriate legislation.

> Citizens 18 years of age and older are guaranteed the right to vote.

Amendment XXVII (1992)

No law varying the compensation for the services of the Senators and Representatives shall take effect, until an election of Representatives shall have intervened.

> Proposed in 1789, this amendment prevents members of Congress from raising their own salaries. Approved salary increases cannot take effect until after the next congressional election.

POLITICAL INQUIRY: *Now that you have read the Constitution, do you think three-quarters of state legislatures would ratify this document—even as amended—today? Why or why not?*

CHAPTER 3

Federalism

THEN

The newly created national government and the preexisting state governments acted independently as they implemented the innovative federal system of government established in 1789.

NOW

National, state, and local governments challenge one another regularly over the proper interpretation of the Constitution's distribution of power in the federal system.

NEXT

Will Supreme Court justices continue to issue conflicting interpretations of federalism?

Will state and local governments continue their efforts to be laboratories for the creation of effective domestic policies?

Will the growing states' rights movement lead to the development of a new form of federalism?

This chapter examines the nature and evolution of the constitutional distribution of authority between the national and state governments in the U.S. federal system of government.

FIRST, we take an overview of the U.S. federal system and its distinct dual sovereignty.

SECOND, we explore the details of dual sovereignty by considering the constitutional distribution of authority between the national and the state governments.

THIRD, we focus on the evolution of the federal system and see how the relationship between the national and the state governments has changed over time.

FOURTH, we survey the complex intergovernmental relations that dominate U.S. federalism now.

FIFTH, we assess the advantages and disadvantages of today's federal system.

Wherever you live in the United

States, at least five governments (the national, a state, and several local governments) collect taxes from you, provide services to you, and establish your civil rights and liberties and your civil responsibilities. With so many governments in action, citizens who are interested in influencing public policies have many access points. Yet it may not be clear which government has the authority to address your concerns. It may not even be clear to your government officials. Ultimately, the Constitution of the United States, as interpreted by the U.S. Supreme Court justices, determines which government is responsible for which matters.

The framers of the U.S. Constitution balanced their preference for a strong central government with the people's preference for close-to-home governments (state and local) by creating the federal system of government with dual sovereignty. The Constitution provides the national government with ultimate authority (sovereignty) over some policy matters and the state governments with ultimate authority (sovereignty) over different policy matters. However, the constitutional language is not always clear. Debates to clarify the policies for which the national government is sovereign and the policies for which the state governments are sovereign have been ongoing since before ratification of the Constitution, and they continue today.

Since ratification of the U.S. Constitution, which created the federal system, the number of governments in the United States has grown, as Congresses admitted new states to the union and as each state government created a variety of local governments to help it serve its citizens better. Today, there are more than 89,500 distinct units of government in the United States—one national, 50 state, and over 89,400 local governments. Not only has the number of governments in the United States grown tremendously since 1789, so has the number and complexity of matters for which citizens turn to their governments for assistance.

The federal system's dual sovereignty is still the defining characteristic of the United States' system of government. However, intergovernmental relations (the ways in which the national, state, and local governments deal with one another) and the relative roles, responsibilities, and levels of influence of each type of government[1] have evolved over the centuries as societal problems became more diverse and complex. An understanding of the intergovernmental relations of today's federal system is essential to the study of and participation in American democracy now.

An Overview of the U.S. Federal System

federal system

a governmental structure with two levels of government in which each level has sovereignty over different policy matters and geographic areas; a system of government with dual sovereignty

The U.S. Constitution established an unprecedented government structure, a federal system. A **federal system** has two constitutionally recognized levels of government, each with sovereignty—that is, ultimate governing authority, with no legal superior—over different policy matters and geographic areas. According to the Constitution, the national government has ultimate authority over some matters, and the state governments hold ultimate authority over different matters. In addition, the national government's jurisdiction covers the entire geographic area of the nation, and each state government's jurisdiction covers the geographic area within the state's borders. The existence of two governments, each with ultimate authority over different matters and geographic areas—an arrangement called *dual sovereignty*—is what distinguishes the federal system of government from the two other most common systems of government worldwide, known as unitary and confederal. The American colonists' experience with a unitary system, and subsequently the early U.S. citizens' life under a confederal system (1781–1788), led to the creation of the innovative federal system.

Unitary System

Colonial Americans lived under Great Britain's unitary system of government. Today, the majority of the countries in the world have unitary governments. In a **unitary system,** the central government is *the* sovereign government. It can create other governments (regional governments) and delegate governing powers and responsibilities to them. In addition, the sovereign central government in a unitary system can unilaterally take away any governing powers and responsibilities it delegated to the regional governments it created. Ultimately, the sovereign central government can even eliminate the regional governments it created.

Indeed, under Britain's unitary system of government during the American colonial period, the British Crown (the sovereign central government) created colonial governments (regional governments) and gave them authority to handle day-to-day matters such as regulating marriages, resolving business conflicts, providing for public safety, and maintaining roads. As the central government in Britain approved tax and trade policies that harmed the colonists' quality of life, growing public discourse and dissension spurred the colonists to protest. It was the colonists' failed attempts to influence the central government's policies that eventually sparked more radical acts such as the Boston Tea Party and the colonists' declaration of independence from Great Britain.

unitary system
a governmental structure in which one central government is *the* sovereign government and it creates other, regional governments to which it delegates some governing powers and responsibilities; however, the central government retains ultimate authority (sovereignty)

Confederal System

When the colonies declared their independence from Great Britain in 1776, each became an independent sovereign state and adopted its own constitution. As a result, no state had a legal superior; each was *the* sovereign government for its geographic area. In 1777, delegates from every state except Rhode Island met in a convention and agreed to a proposed alliance of the 13 sovereign state governments. In 1781, the thirteen independent state governments ratified the Articles of Confederation, the first U.S. constitution, which created a confederal system of government.

In a **confederal system,** several independent sovereign governments (such as the first 13 state governments in the American case) agree to cooperate on specified policy matters while each sovereign state retains ultimate authority over all other governmental matters within its borders. The cooperating sovereign state governments delegate some governing responsibilities to a central governing body. Each sovereign government selects its own representatives to the central governing body. However, in a confederal system, the sovereign state governments retain ultimate authority and can modify or even eliminate governing responsibilities they agreed to delegate to the central government.

confederal system
a governmental structure in which several independent sovereign states agree to cooperate on specified policy matters by creating a central governing body; each sovereign state retains ultimate authority over other governmental matters within its borders, so the central governing body is not a sovereign government

As detailed in Chapter 2, the effectiveness of the confederal government created by the Articles of Confederation increasingly came into question. In February 1787, the national Congress (the central governing body created by the sovereign states) passed a resolution calling for a constitutional convention "for the sole and express purpose of revising the Articles of Confederation" in order to preserve the union. Clear-eyed about the failures of the unitary system they experienced as British colonies, and the confederal system, the citizens of the United States decided to experiment with a unique government system—a federal system. The federal system created by the Constitution of the United States has succeeded in strengthening and preserving the union first established by the Articles of Confederation.

Federal System

The state delegates who met in Philadelphia in 1787 drafted a new constitution that created the innovative federal system of government with dual sovereignty. The Constitution's framers established dual sovereignty by detailing a new, sovereign national government for the United States and modifying the sovereignty of the existing state governments. The sovereign national government thus created has no legal superior on matters over which the Constitution gives it

FIGURE 3.1 ■ THREE GOVERNING SYSTEMS What does it mean to be a sovereign government? Distinguish between the three systems of government by explaining what level, or levels, of government holds sovereignty in each system.

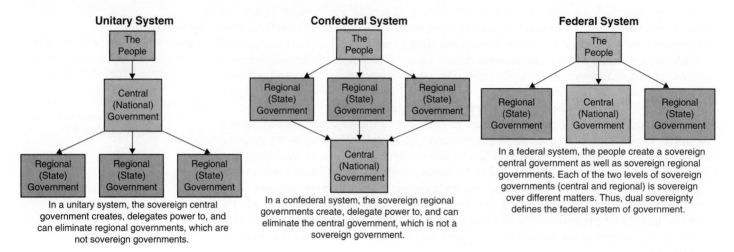

In a unitary system, the sovereign central government creates, delegates power to, and can eliminate regional governments, which are not sovereign governments.

In a confederal system, the sovereign regional governments create, delegate power to, and can eliminate the central government, which is not a sovereign government.

In a federal system, the people create a sovereign central government as well as sovereign regional governments. Each of the two levels of sovereign governments (central and regional) is sovereign over different matters. Thus, dual sovereignty defines the federal system of government.

authority, and the sovereign state governments have no legal superior on the matters which the Constitution grants to them.

Such dual sovereignty does not exist in unitary and confederal systems, where sovereignty is held by one level of government (the central government in a unitary system and the regional governments in a confederal system). Figure 3.1 compares the three types of governing systems.

The federal system, as it works in the United States today, can be confusing—not only to citizens but also to elected officials and even Supreme Court justices. The confusion is a product of at least three factors. First, vague constitutional language that distributes sovereignty between two levels of government, the national government and the state governments, fuels questions about which government is sovereign over specific matters. Second, state governments have established tens of thousands of local governments—a third level of government—delegating some governing powers and responsibilities to them, to assist the state in serving its citizens. The relationship between a state government and the local governments it creates follows the *unitary system* of government; the sovereign state government retains ultimate authority over all the matters it delegates to its local governments, can remove power and responsibilities it delegates to its local governments, and ultimately can eliminate any local government it creates. Today there are more than 89,400 local governments governing in the United States. (See Figure 3.2 for the number of local governments in each state.)

Adding to the confusion of the federal system is the fact that today most services and benefits citizens receive are a product of collaborative efforts by two or more governments. The national government works with governments at the state and local levels to serve the public. Political scientists label the collaborative efforts of two or more governments within the federal system working to serve the public **intergovernmental relations (IGR).**

intergovernmental relations (IGR) collaborative efforts of two or more levels of government working to serve the public

What a Federal System Means for Citizens

For citizens, living in a federal system of government means that their legal rights and liberties and their civic responsibilities vary depending on where they live. The majority of U.S. citizens live under the jurisdiction of at least five governments: national, state, county (called *borough* in Alaska and *parish* in Louisiana), municipal or township, and school district. Each of these governments can impose responsibilities on the people living in its jurisdiction. The most obvious

FIGURE 3.2 ■ NUMBER OF LOCAL GOVERNMENTS IN EACH STATE What might explain the range in the number of local governments that exist in the 50 states? Do the states with the largest geographic area have the largest number of local governments? Are there regional patterns? Do states with smaller populations have fewer local governments?

SOURCE: American Fact Finder. "Local Governments by Type and State 2012," http://factfinder2.census.gov/faces/tableservices/jsf/pages/productview. xhtml?pid=COG_2012_ORG02.US01&prodType=table.

Number of Local Governments in Each State

responsibility is to pay taxes. These taxes can include the national personal income tax; state sales and personal income taxes; and county, municipal, township, and school district property taxes. Each government can also guarantee personal liberties and rights. The Constitution lists individual liberties in the Bill of Rights. In addition, every state constitution has its own bill of rights, and some local governments offer further protections to their citizens. For example, some cities and counties prohibit discrimination in employment and public accommodations based on an individual's sexual orientation, yet most states do not, nor does the national government. A growing number of states provide marriage contracts to same-sex couples, yet the majority of states do not. While some states have tight gun control laws, other states do not, and some local governments even require citizens to have a gun in their home.[2] Clearly, people's rights and responsibilities vary depending on where they live in the United States (as discussed further in Chapter 4).

Thus, the federal system can be confusing for citizens. It can also be confusing for the many governments created to serve the people. Which government is responsible for what services and policies? Because the Constitution of the United States is the supreme law of the land, it is to the Constitution that we must turn to answer that question. Yet constitutional language is not always clear. As we saw in Chapter 2, the framers hammered out the Constitution through intensive bargaining and compromise that produced a text that is often vague and ambiguous.

Then Now Next

Number of Governments in the United States

	Then (1942)	Now
Sovereign governments		
National	1	1
State	48	50
Local governments		
County	3,050	3,031
Municipal	16,220	19,519
Town/township	18,919	16,360
School district	108,579	12,880
Special purpose	8,299	38,266
Total	155,116	90,107

WHAT'S NEXT?

> Will the number of school districts continue to decrease?

> Will Congress vote on a bill, such as the New Columbia Admissions Act, to admit Washington, D.C., as the 51st state of the union?

> Will Congress vote on a bill that would authorize a ratification vote in Puerto Rico on its admission to the union as a state if a majority of voters ratify Puerto Rico's desire for statehood?

SOURCE: Carma Hogue, "Government Organization Summary Report: 2012," U.S. Census Bureau, www.census.gov/govs/cog/.

Also as discussed in Chapter 2, the U.S. Supreme Court has the authority to determine what the Constitution means and hence what is constitutional. This authority came from the Court's decision in the *Marbury v. Madison* case (1803), in which the justices established the principle of *judicial review:* the Court's authority to determine whether an action of any government operating within the United States violates the Constitution.[3]

Although the Supreme Court is the final interpreter of the Constitution, the Court's interpretations have changed over time. For example, it is true that dual sovereignty—and therefore a federal system—still exists in the United States today, but the courts have interpreted the Constitution in such a way that the authority of the national government has expanded significantly over the past 225-plus years (although, as discussed later, we are now witnessing a movement to expand the authority of state governments). In addition, the determination of which government has ultimate authority over specific matters has become even less clear because of the evolution of intergovernmental relations among the levels of government working together to meet the various responsibilities that the Constitution delegates, implies, or reserves to them.

Later in this chapter, we consider this evolution of the U.S. federal system. Before we do, it is useful to examine the constitutional distribution of authority to the national and state governments.

Constitutional Distribution of Authority

By distributing some authority to the national government and different authority to the state governments, the Constitution creates the dual sovereignty that defines the U.S. federal system. The Constitution specifically lists the several matters over which the national government has ultimate authority, and it implies additional national authority. The Constitution spells out just a few matters over which the state governments have authority. The Constitution lacks detail on state authority in part because, at the time of the Constitution's drafting, the states expected to retain their authority, except for matters that, by way of the Constitution, they agreed to turn over to the newly created national government.

To fulfill their responsibilities to their citizens, both the national and the state governments have the authority to engage in basic governing functions inherent to all sovereign governments. These concurrent powers held by the national and state governments are the first topic in this section.

Concurrent Powers

To function, sovereign governments need basic governing powers such as the authority to make policy, raise money, implement policies, and establish courts to interpret policy when a conflict arises about its meaning. In the U.S. federal system, these basic governing powers are

concurrent powers because the national government and all state governments exercise them, independently and at the same time. For example, national and state governments make their own public policies, raise their own revenues, and spend those revenues to implement their policies. In addition, the national court system resolves conflicts over the interpretation of national laws and each state has its own court system to resolve conflicts over its state laws. State governments delegate some concurrent powers to the local governments they create so that the local governments can govern. Table 3.1 lists concurrent powers of the national and the state governments.

In addition to the basic governing powers that the national and state governments hold concurrently, in the federal system of dual sovereignty, the national government and the state governments have sovereignty over different matters. We now consider the distinct sovereign powers of the national and state governments.

National Sovereignty

The Constitution distributes powers that are (1) enumerated, or specifically listed, and (2) implied for the national government's three branches—legislative, executive, and judicial. For example, Article I of the Constitution enumerates the matters over which Congress holds the authority to make laws, including interstate and foreign commerce, the system of money, general welfare, and national defense. These matters are **enumerated powers** of the national government. The Constitution also gives Congress **implied powers**—that is, powers that are not described explicitly but that may be interpreted to be necessary to fulfill the enumerated powers. Congress specifically receives implied powers through the Constitution's **necessary and proper clause,** sometimes called the **elastic clause** because the national government uses this passage to stretch its enumerated authority. The necessary and proper clause in Article I, Section 8, of the Constitution states that Congress has the power to "make all Laws which shall be necessary and proper" for carrying out its enumerated powers.

Articles II and III of the Constitution also enumerate powers of the national government. Article II delegates to the president the responsibility to ensure the proper implementation of national laws and, with the advice and consent of the U.S. Senate, the authority to make treaties with foreign nations and to appoint foreign ambassadors. With respect to the U.S. Supreme Court and the lower federal courts, Article III enumerates jurisdiction over legal cases involving U.S. constitutional issues, national legislation, and treaties. The jurisdiction of the Supreme Court also extends to disagreements between two or more state governments, as well as to conflicts between citizens from different states. Figure 3.3 lists national powers enumerated in Articles I, II, and III of the Constitution.

THE SUPREMACY CLAUSE   The country's founders obviously anticipated disagreements over the interpretation of constitutional language and prepared for them by creating the Supreme Court. The Court has mostly supported the national government when states, citizens, or interest groups have challenged Congress's use of the necessary and proper clause to take on new responsibilities beyond its enumerated powers. Unless the Supreme Court finds a national law to be outside of the enumerated or implied powers, that law is constitutional and hence the **supreme law of the land,** as defined by the supremacy clause in Article VI of the Constitution: "This Constitution, and the Laws of the United States which shall be made in Pursuance thereof; and all Treaties made, or which shall be made, under the Authority of the United States, shall be the supreme Law of the Land." State and local governments are thereby obligated to comply with national laws that implement national enumerated and implied powers, as well as with treaties— including treaties with Native American nations.

NATIONAL TREATIES WITH INDIAN NATIONS   Throughout U.S. history, the national government has signed treaties with Native American nations, which are legally viewed as sovereign foreign nations. As with all treaties, treaties with Native American nations are supreme law with

concurrent powers
basic governing functions that are exercised by the national and state governments independently, and at the same time, including the power to make policy, raise revenue, implement policies, and establish courts

TABLE 3.1

Concurrent Powers of National and State Governments

Make policy

Raise revenue

Borrow money

Implement policy

Charter banks and corporations

Establish courts

Take private property for public use (eminent domain)

enumerated powers
powers of the national government that are listed in the Constitution

implied powers
powers of the national government that are not enumerated in the Constitution but that Congress claims are necessary and proper for the national government to fulfill its enumerated powers in accordance with the necessary and proper clause of the Constitution

necessary and proper clause (elastic clause)
a clause in Article I, Section 8, of the Constitution that gives Congress the power to do whatever it deems necessary and constitutional to meet its enumerated obligations; the basis for the implied powers

supreme law of the land
the Constitution's description of its own authority, meaning that all laws made by governments within the United States must be in compliance with the Constitution

NATIONAL POWERS

- Punish offenses against the laws of the nation
- Lay and collect taxes for the common defense and the general welfare
- Coin and regulate money
- Establish courts inferior to the U.S. Supreme Court
- Raise and support armies
- Administer the Capitol district and military bases
- Declare war
- Organize, arm, and discipline state militias when called to suppress insurrections and invasions
- Provide for copyrights for authors and inventors
- Regulate interstate and foreign commerce
- Provide, organize, and maintain armed forces
- Establish standard weights and measures
- Create naturalization laws
- Punish the counterfeiting of money
- Punish piracies and felonies on the seas
- Develop roads and postal service
- Admit new states to the union
- Make treaties

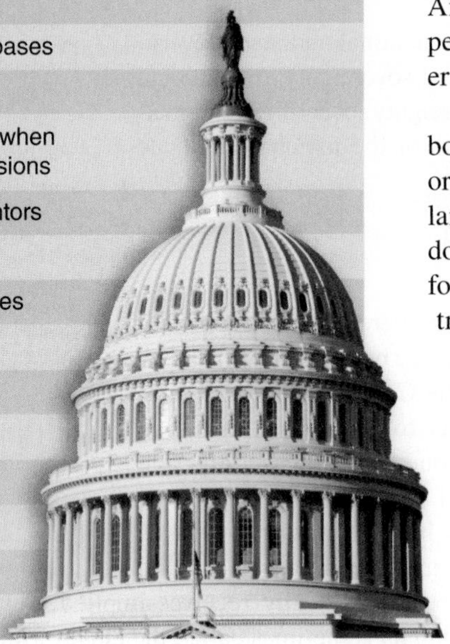

FIGURE 3.3

Enumerated Powers of National Government Can you locate each enumerated power in the Constitution that precedes this chapter (by section and clause)?

which the national government and state and local governments must comply. The core issue in the majority of these treaties is the provision of land (reservations) on which the native peoples would resettle after non-Indians took their lands during the 18th and 19th centuries. Today, the federal government recognizes more than 550 Indian tribes. Although most Native Americans no longer live on reservations—most native peoples have moved to cities—approximately 300 reservations remain, in 34 states.[4]

Even though Indian reservations lie within state borders, national treaties and national laws, not state or local laws, apply to the reservation populations and lands. State and local laws, including laws having to do with taxes, crime, and the environment, are unenforceable on reservations. Moreover, Native American treaty rights to hunt, fish, and gather on reservations and on public lands supersede national, state, and local environmental regulations.[5]

With the exception of Native American reservations, state governments are sovereign within their state borders over matters the Constitution distributes to them. What are the matters that fall within state sovereignty?

State Sovereignty

The Constitution specifies only a few state powers. It provides the states with a role in national politics and gives them the final say on formally amending the U.S. Constitution. One reason for the lack of constitutional specificity regarding the matters over which state governments are sovereign is because, unlike the newly created national government, the state governments were already functioning when the states ratified the Constitution. Other than those responsibilities that the states agreed to delegate to the newly created national government through their ratification of the Constitution, the states expected to retain their sovereignty over all the day-to-day matters internal to their borders that they were already handling. Yet the original Constitution did not speak of this sovereignty explicitly.

POWERS RESERVED TO THE STATES The Constitution's limited attention to state authority caused concern among citizens of the early American republic. Many people feared that the new national government would meddle in matters for which states had been responsible, in that way compromising state sovereignty. Citizens were also deeply concerned about their own freedoms. As described in Chapter 2, within two years of the states' ratification of the Constitution, they ratified the Bill of Rights (1791), the first 10 amendments to the U.S. Constitution, in response to those concerns.

The Tenth Amendment asserts that the "powers not delegated to the United States by the Constitution, nor prohibited by it to the States, are *reserved to the States* respectively, or to the people." This **reserved powers** clause of the Tenth Amendment acknowledged the domestic matters over which the states had exercised authority since the ratification of their own constitutions. These matters included the handling of the daily affairs of the people—laws regarding birth, death, marriage, intrastate business, commerce, crime, health, morals, and safety. The states' reserved powers to protect the health, safety, lives, and property of their citizens are their **police powers.** It was over these domestic matters, internal to each state, that the states retained sovereignty according to the Tenth Amendment. Figure 3.4 summarizes the constitutionally reserved powers of the states at the time of the Tenth Amendment's ratification.

reserved powers
the matters referred to in the Tenth Amendment over which states retain sovereignty

police powers
the states' reserved powers to protect the health, safety, lives, and properties of residents in a state

POWERS DELEGATED TO THE STATES Although the Constitution does not list all the specific powers reserved to the states, it does assign, or delegate, several powers to the states. These powers provide the states with a distinct voice in the composition and priorities of the national government. Members of Congress are elected by voters in their home states (in the case of senators) or their home districts (in the case of representatives in the House). Therefore, members of Congress are accountable to the voters in the state that elected them. State governments also have the authority to redraw the boundaries of the U.S. House districts within the state after each decennial census. In addition, each state government determines the procedure by which the state's Electoral College electors will be selected to participate in the state's vote for the president and the vice president, as we saw in Chapter 2. Overall, state voters expect that the officials whom they elect to the national government will carefully consider their concerns when creating national policy. This is representative government in action.

In addition to establishing the various electoral procedures that give voice to state interests in the national policy-making process, the Constitution creates a formal means by which the states can ensure that the language in the Constitution is not changed in such a way that their sovereignty is threatened. Specifically, the Constitution stipulates that three-fourths of the states (through votes in either their legislatures or special conventions, as discussed in Chapter 2) must ratify amendments to the Constitution. By having the final say in whether the supreme law of the land will be changed formally through the passage of amendments to the U.S. Constitution, the states can protect their constitutional powers. Indeed, they did just that when they ratified the Tenth Amendment.

STATE POWERS

- Conduct local, state, and national elections
- Build and maintain infrastructure (roads, bridges, canals, ports)
- Administer family laws (e.g., marriage and divorce)
- Ratify amendments to the U.S. Constitution
- Establish criminal laws (except on the high seas)
- Provide education
- Redistrict U.S. House districts
- Protect public health and safety
- Regulate occupations and professions
- Regulate intrastate commerce
- Protect property rights
- Regulate banks and credit
- Establish insurance laws
- Regulate charities
- Regulate land use

FIGURE 3.4

Constitutionally Delegated and Reserved Powers Few of these powers are specified in the Constitution. Which of these state powers are listed in the Constitution? Where do the other powers come from?

Supreme Court Interpretation of the Constitution's Distribution of Authority

Vague language in the U.S. Constitution continues to spark disputes over what are the constitutional powers of the national government versus what are the constitutional powers of the state governments. Some constitutional clauses that the Courts have had to interpret repeatedly include the *necessary and proper* powers of Congress and the powers of Congress to provide for the *general welfare* and to regulate *commerce among the several states.* In addition, the Courts are continually interpreting and reinterpreting the meaning of the *reserved powers clause* of the Tenth Amendment. The U.S. Supreme Court has the final say over what constitutional language means. Since as early as 1819, the Court has resolved legal conflicts by distinguishing among national enumerated and implied powers and the powers reserved for the states.

THE POWER TO REGULATE COMMERCE The landmark case of **McCulloch v. Maryland** (1819) exemplifies a Supreme Court ruling that established the use of the implied powers to expand the national government's enumerated authority.[6] The case stemmed from Congress's establishment of a national bank, and in particular a branch of that bank located in the state of Maryland, which the Maryland state authorities tried to tax. Attorneys for the state of Maryland argued that Congress did not have the constitutional authority to establish a national bank, noting that doing so was not an enumerated power. Maryland's legal counsel also argued that if the Court interpreted the Constitution such that the national government did have the implied power to establish a national bank, then Maryland had the concurrent power to tax the bank. Lawyers for the national government in turn argued that the Constitution did indeed imply federal

McCulloch v. Maryland
established that the necessary and proper clause justifies broad understandings of enumerated powers

authority to establish a national bank and that Maryland's levying a tax on the bank was unconstitutional, for it impinged on the national government's ability to fulfill its constitutional responsibilities by taking some of its financial resources.

The Supreme Court decided in favor of the national government. The justices based their ruling on their interpretation of the Constitution's necessary and proper clause and the enumerated powers of Congress to "lay and collect taxes, to borrow money . . . and to regulate commerce among the several states." The Court said that, combined, these enumerated powers implied that the national government had the authority to charter a bank and to locate a branch in Maryland. Moreover, the Court found that Maryland did not have the right to tax that bank, because taxation by the state would interfere with the exercise of national authority.

In the *McCulloch* case, the Supreme Court established that the necessary and proper clause allows Congress to broadly interpret the enumerated powers of the national government. Moreover, the Court interpreted the national supremacy clause to mean that in the event of a conflict between national legislation (the law chartering the national bank) and state legislation (Maryland's tax law), the national law is supreme *as long as* it falls under the enumerated and implied powers that the Constitution distributes to the national government.

A few years later, in the case of *Gibbons v. Ogden* (1824), the Supreme Court again justified a particular national action on the basis of the implications of an enumerated power.[7] The *Gibbons* case was the first suit brought to the Supreme Court seeking clarification on the constitutional meaning of *commerce* in the Constitution's clause on the regulation of interstate commerce. The Court established a broad definition of commerce: "all commercial intercourse—meaning all business dealings." The conflict in this case concerned which government, New York State or the national government, had authority to regulate the operation of boats on the waterways between New York and New Jersey. The Court ruled that regulation of commerce implied regulation of navigation and that therefore the national government had authority to regulate it, not New York State.

Following the *Gibbons* decision, the national government frequently justified many of its actions by arguing that they were necessary to fulfill its enumerated powers to regulate interstate commerce. The Court typically agreed with Congress's broad understanding of what its enumerated powers implied it could do through legislation. The case of *United States v. Lopez* (1995) is an example, however, of the Court's recent trend of being more critical of Congress's attempts to use broad implications of the commerce clause to justify a national law.[8] At issue in this case was the constitutionality of the national Gun-Free School Zones Act of 1990, which mandated gun-free zones within a specified area surrounding schools. The lawyers for Alfonso Lopez, a 12th grader charged with violating this national law by bringing a .38-caliber handgun to school, argued successfully that the law was unconstitutional. The Court rejected the national government's claim that the 1990 law was a necessary and proper means to regulate interstate commerce. Instead, the Court found that the law was a criminal statute, for which the state governments, not the national government, have authority. The Court upheld reserved powers of the states and denied a broad implication of the national government's enumerated power to regulate interstate commerce.[9]

> In *United States v. Lopez* (1995), the U.S. Supreme Court ruled the national Gun-Free School Zones Act unconstitutional and affirmed that state governments have the right to establish gun-free school zones. What constitutional clauses did the Court have to interpret to resolve the *United States v. Lopez* case?

THE POWER TO PROVIDE FOR THE GENERAL WELFARE
Another enumerated power that has expanded through Court interpretation of what the Constitution implies is the power of the national government to provide for the general welfare. The national government's landmark Social Security Act of 1935 was a response to the Great Depression's devastating impact on the financial security of countless Americans. The congressional vote to establish Social Security was overwhelmingly favorable. Yet the constitutionality of this expansive program, which has become the most expensive national program each budget year, was challenged in the courts shortly after its passage. In 1937, the Supreme Court had to decide: Was Social Security indeed a matter of general welfare for which Congress is delegated the authority to raise

and spend money? Or was Social Security a matter for the state governments to address? The Court found the national policy to be constitutional—a reasonable congressional interpretation, the justices wrote, of the enumerated and implied powers of the national government.[10]

The Supreme Court's decisions in the *McCulloch, Gibbons,* and Social Security cases set the stage for the expansion of national power in domestic policy matters by combining the necessary and proper clause with such enumerated powers as the regulation of commerce and providing for the general welfare. Although throughout U.S. history the Court has typically supported Congress's enactment of laws dealing with matters implied by—but not specifically discussed in—the Constitution, Congress does not always get its way. The Court's decision in the *Lopez* case is one example of states' rights winning over national power.

In addition to establishing dual sovereignty and creating two independently operating levels of government, the Constitution enumerates some obligations that the national government has to the states (see Table 3.2) and obligations that states have to one another.

State-to-State Obligations: Horizontal Federalism

In Article IV, the Constitution sets forth obligations that the states have to one another and to each other's citizens. Collectively, these state-to-state obligations and the relationships they mandate are forms of **horizontal federalism.** For example, state governments have the right to forge agreements with other states, known as **interstate compacts.** Congress must review and approve interstate compacts to ensure that they do not harm the states that are not party to them and the nation as a whole. States enter into cooperative agreements to provide services and benefits for one another, such as monitoring paroled inmates from other states; sharing and conserving natural resources that spill over state borders, such as water; and decreasing pollution that crosses state borders.

TABLE 3.2

National Obligations to the States

The federal government:

- must treat states equally in matters of the regulation of commerce and the imposition of taxes
- cannot approve the creation of a new state from the property of an existing state without the consent of the legislatures of the states concerned
- cannot change state boundaries without the consent of the states concerned
- must guarantee a republican form of government
- must protect states from foreign invasion
- must, at their request, protect states against domestic violence

horizontal federalism
the state-to-state relationships created by the U.S. Constitution

interstate compacts
agreements between states that Congress has the authority to review and reject

> In 1921, Congress approved an interstate compact creating the Port Authority of New York and New Jersey to improve commerce and trade. The Port Authority, created to develop and modernize the New York Harbor area (covering approximately 1,500 square miles from both states) continues to build, maintain, and operate bridges, tunnels, terminals, and airports. What are some policy matters for which interstate compacts are common?

extradition
the return of individuals accused of a crime to the state in which the crime was committed, upon the request of that state's governor

privileges and immunities clause
the Constitution's requirement that a state extend to other states' citizens the privileges and immunities it provides for its own citizens

full faith and credit clause
the constitutional clause that requires states to comply with and uphold the public acts, records, and judicial decisions of other states

States also cooperate through a procedure called **extradition,** the legal process of sending individuals back to a state that accuses them of having committed a crime, and from which they have fled. The Constitution establishes a state governor's right to request the extradition of an accused criminal. Yet the courts have also supported governors' refusals to extradite individuals.

The Constitution asserts, too, that each state must guarantee the same **privileges and immunities** it provides to its citizens to all U.S. citizens, including citizens from other states who visit or move into the state. This guarantee does not prohibit states from imposing reasonable requirements before extending rights to visiting or new state residents. For example, states can and do charge higher tuition costs to out-of-state college students. In addition, in many states, new state residents must wait 30 days before they can register to vote. Yet no state can deny new state residents who are U.S. citizens the right to register to vote once they meet a reasonable state residency requirement.

Today, one controversial state-to-state obligation stems from the full faith and credit clause of Article IV, Section 1, of the Constitution. The **full faith and credit clause** asserts that each state must recognize as legally binding (that is, valid and enforceable) the public acts, records, and judicial proceedings of every other state. For example, states must recognize the validity of out-of-state driver's licenses. But, do states have to recognize the validity of out-of-state same-sex marriage contracts? In the summer of 2013, Adrian Shanker and Brandon Pariser were married in Darien, Connecticut, where same-sex marriage is legal. As they traveled home to Pennsylvania, their driver's licenses remained legal from Connecticut through New York and New Jersey to Pennsylvania. However, the legal status of their marriage changed. Their marriage remained legal in New York State. In New Jersey, a state that recognizes same-sex civil unions but not marriages, their marriage contract took on a different legal meaning. When they crossed into Pennsylvania, they were no longer legally married because at that time, Pennsylvania law recognized only marriages between a man and a woman.[11]

The debates over same-sex marriage and civil unions raise several challenging constitutional questions. Because the Constitution is the supreme law of the land, answers to those questions will eventually come from the Supreme Court's interpretation of the Constitution. In the summer of 2013, the Court acknowledged that states have long had the power to define and regulate marriage (a reserved power of the states). Based on this reality, the Court ruled the 1996 national Defense of Marriage Act unconstitutional, finding that the national government must recognize legal state marriage contracts, including same-sex marriage contracts. Therefore, the national government must extend rights and benefits provided by national law based on marital status to same-sex spouses.[12] A question the Court has not yet answered is, can a state define marriage as only between a man and a woman? Does a state law that bans same-sex marriage violate the constitutional guarantees of equal protection of the law?

It is important to note that the rights and privileges guaranteed by the U.S. Constitution are the minimum rights and privileges that all governments in the United States (national, state, and local governments) must uphold. However, the U.S. Supreme Court has ruled that state and local governments can guarantee additional rights and privileges to their citizens.

Judicial Federalism

Today, state and local governments throughout the country have passed laws (legislation and constitutional clauses and amendments) that provide their citizens with rights and privileges that the U.S. Constitution does not guarantee. For example, the Pennsylvania constitution states: "The people have a right to clean air, pure water, and to the preservation of the natural, scenic, historic and esthetic values of the environment." The U.S. Constitution does not guarantee such a right. The California state constitution protects freedom of speech and expression in privately owned properties, such as shopping centers. The U.S. Constitution's guaranteed freedom of expression does not extend to privately owned properties.[13] In Takoma Park, Maryland, citizens as young as 16 have the right to vote in municipal elections (the voting age for state and federal elections is still 18 in Takoma Park).[14] In numerous municipalities and counties across the country, laws prohibit discrimination due to a person's sexual orientation. The U.S. Constitution does not prohibit such discrimination.

Historically, state courts turned to the U.S. Constitution when deciding civil rights and liberties cases. However, beginning in the 1970s, state courts increasingly based these decisions on their own state constitutions, which guaranteed more extensive rights to their citizens than did the U.S. Constitution. For example, after the U.S. Supreme Court 1973 ruling that the equal protection clause of the Fourteenth Amendment did not require equal funding of schools in Texas,[15] state courts in 15 states ruled that their state constitutions required equal funding of schools in their states.[16] The state courts interpreted clauses in their state constitutions that guaranteed "efficient" and "effective" public education to mean equal opportunity supported by equal school funding. Political scientists refer to the reliance of state courts on their state constitutions as **judicial federalism.**

judicial federalism
state courts' use of their state constitutions to determine citizens' rights, particularly when state constitutions guarantee greater protections than does the U.S. Constitution

The federal system in the United States can be confusing to citizens and government officials. In the U.S. federal system, governments at three levels (national, state, and local) have concurrent powers necessary to governing and serving the people. The U.S. Constitution distributes sovereignty between the national government (enumerated and ambiguous implied powers) and state governments (vague reserved powers and limited delegated powers). However, courts continue to resolve conflicts over what the concurrent, enumerated, implied, and reserved powers mean for the day-to-day operations of governments. In addition, governments at all three levels protect the rights established in the U.S. Constitution. At the same time, state and local governments often guarantee additional rights and liberties that they establish through their own laws.

To complicate matters further, over the course of U.S. history, national, state, and local governments have moved from functioning independently to meet their constitutional responsibilities to working together on many policy matters to serve their citizens better. The national, state, and local governments often collaborate in the creation, financing, and implementation of a given public policy. These collaborative efforts are known as intergovernmental relations. We now explore the evolution of intergovernmental relations in the U.S. federal system.

>Oregon allows assisted suicide (euthanasia). Colorado and Washington legalized recreational pot use. Fifteen states have made undocumented immigrant students, brought to the country by their undocumented parents when they were young, eligible for lower in-state tuition at state colleges. These are just a few examples of rights provided by state governments that go beyond rights protected by the national government. Does your state protect more civil liberties or rights than what the national government protects?

Evolution of Intergovernmental Relations in the Federal System

In all systems of government (unitary, confederal, and federal), when there is more than one level of government (such as the three levels in the United States—local, state, and national), the governments will interact. Political scientists study these interactions, or intergovernmental relations.

Evolution is a slow and continuous change, often from the simple to the complex. The federal system established by the Constitution has evolved from a simple system of *dual federalism* to a complex system of intergovernmental relations characterized by *conflicted federalism*.

Evolution has occurred in the relationships between the national government and the states, the state governments and their local governments, and the national government and local governments. However, our focus here is on the evolution of the dual sovereignty established by the U.S. federal system of government. We first survey four types of federalism, characterized by four different relationships (intergovernmental relations) between the national and the state governments, all of which continue to this day. Political scientists have identified these four models of intergovernmental relations, also known as four models of federalism, as dual federalism, cooperative federalism, centralized federalism, and conflicted federalism. We then explore various means by which the national government has altered the relationship between itself and the state governments.

Dual Federalism

dual federalism
the initial model of national and state relations in which the national government takes care of its enumerated powers while the state governments independently take care of their reserved powers

Initially, the dual sovereignty of the U.S. federal system was implemented in such a way that the national and state governments acted independently of each other. Political scientists give the name **dual federalism** to this pattern of implementation of the federal system, whereby the national government takes care of its enumerated powers and the states independently take care of their reserved powers. From 1789 through 1932, dual federalism was the dominant pattern of national-state relations. Congresses and presidents did enact some laws that states argued infringed on their powers, and the U.S. Supreme Court typically found in favor of the states in those cases. Yet, as the 1819 *McCulloch* case shows, sometimes the Supreme Court ruled in favor of the national government.

Cooperative Federalism

grant-in-aid
transfer of money, from one government to another government, that does not need to be paid back

cooperative federalism
intergovernmental relations in which the national government supports state governments' efforts to address the domestic matters reserved to them

A crippling economic depression that reached global proportions, known as the Great Depression, began in 1929. To help state governments deal with the domestic problems spawned by the economic collapse, Congress and President Franklin D. Roosevelt (1933–1945) approved numerous policies, collectively called the New Deal. **Grants-in-aid**—transfers of money from one government (the national government) to another government (state and local governments) that need not be paid back—became a main mechanism of President Roosevelt's New Deal programs. State and local governments welcomed the national grants-in-aid, which assisted them in addressing the domestic matters that fell within their sovereignty while allowing them to make most of the specific program decisions to implement the policy. Through grants-in-aid, dual federalism was replaced by **cooperative federalism** in numerous policy matters. Collaborative intergovernmental relations was a product of cooperative federalism, which dominated national and state government relations from the New Deal era to the early 1960s.

Centralized Federalism

centralized federalism
intergovernmental relations in which the national government imposes its policy preferences on state and local governments

By the time of Lyndon Johnson's presidency (1963–1969), a new kind of federalism was developing. In this new form of federalism, the national government imposed its own policy preferences on state and local governments. Specifically, in **centralized federalism,** directives in national legislation, including grant-in-aid programs with ever-increasing conditions or strings attached to the money, force state and local governments to implement a particular national policy. Therefore, in centralized federalism, the national government dominates intergovernmental relations, imposing its policy preferences on state and local governments.

devolution
the process whereby the national government returns policy responsibilities to state and/or local governments

Presidents since Richard Nixon (1969–1974) have fought against this centralizing tendency by proposing to return policy responsibilities (policy making, policy financing, and policy implementation) to state and local governments. Presidents Nixon and Ronald Reagan (1981–1989) gave the name *new federalism* to these efforts, and today we use the term **devolution** to refer to the return of power to state and local governments.

Today, Republicans and Democrats (including presidents, members of Congress, and state and local lawmakers) broadly support devolution, but they debate *which elements of the policy-making process* should be devolved: policy creation, financing, and/or implementation. They also butt heads over *which policies* to devolve. The legislation and court decisions that result from these debates make for a complicated coexistence of dual federalism, cooperative federalism, and centralized federalism.

Conflicted Federalism

David B. Walker, a preeminent scholar of federalism and intergovernmental relations, argues that the term **conflicted federalism** best describes the intergovernmental relations of the federal system today because conflicting elements of dual federalism, cooperative federalism, and centralized federalism are evident in domestic policies implemented by state and local governments.[17] For some policy matters, the national and state governments operate independently of each other, and hence dual federalism is at work. For most policies, however, intergovernmental efforts are the norm. These efforts may be a means to advance state policy priorities (cooperative federalism), or they may be compelled by national legislation (centralized federalism) to advance national policy priorities.

The era of conflicted federalism has seen an increase in the number of legal challenges to national legislation that mandates state and local action. In the various cases that the Supreme Court has heard, the justices have ruled inconsistently, sometimes upholding or even expanding state sovereignty and at other times protecting or expanding national sovereignty. For example, in 1976 the Supreme Court ruled in *National League of Cities v. Usery* that state and local governments were not legally required to comply with the national minimum wage law—hence protecting state authority.[18] Then nine years later, in the *Garcia v. San Antonio Transportation Authority* (1985) case, the Court ruled that national minimum wage laws did apply to state and local government employees—thus expanding national authority.[19]

Another policy matter that has been subject to conflicting Court decisions is the medical use of marijuana. California has fought an up-and-down battle with the national government over medical uses of marijuana. In 1996, California voters approved the Compassionate Use Act, allowing people to grow, obtain, or smoke marijuana for medical needs, with a doctor's recommendation. Then in 2001, the U.S. Supreme Court ruled that the national government could charge people who distributed marijuana for medical use with a crime, even in California, where the state law allowed such activity.[20] The Court interpreted the national supremacy clause to mean that national narcotics laws took precedence over California's law, which California had argued was grounded in the reserved powers of the states. But in 2003, the U.S. Supreme Court refused to review a case challenging a California law allowing doctors to recommend marijuana use to their patients. As a consequence of the Court's refusal to take on the case, the decision from the California court prevailed. The California court's ruling had been that doctors could *not* be charged with a crime for recommending marijuana to patients. To add to the confused legal status of medicinal marijuana in California, the U.S. Supreme Court in 2005 upheld the

conflicted federalism
intergovernmental relations in which elements of dual federalism, cooperative federalism, and centralized federalism are evident in the domestic policies implemented by state and local governments

> Between 1789 and the Great Depression, the model of federalism implemented in the United States was dual federalism. Dual federalism is often depicted as a slice of layer cake, with three distinct layers—three levels of government with clear distinctions among their responsibilities and powers. Today, conflicted federalism rules the day. In this model of federalism, which is depicted as a slice of marble cake with swirls of colors that flow into each other, the responsibilities and powers of the three levels of government are not clear and distinct. A confusion of conflicting intergovernmental relations dominates most domestic policies.

Context

A WORLDWIDE INTERGOVERNMENTAL PROBLEM: CONFLICTING NATIONAL AND REGIONAL POT POLICIES

In the United States, 18 states have legalized marijuana for medical use. The states of Colorado and Washington have also legalized the sale, cultivation, and use of marijuana for recreational purposes. Those state laws are in conflict with national law that classifies marijuana as a Schedule I narcotic. For the most part, the national government, under President Obama, has not pushed for prosecution of people using marijuana in violation of national law if they are complying with the state law that legalizes and regulates its use. At the same time, some local governments have enacted land-use laws (zoning laws) to limit where (or even if) marijuana can be sold legally in their communities.

This pattern of conflicting national and regional (state and local) marijuana laws and confusion over their implementation and enforcement is also evident in the Czech Republic, Portugal, Switzerland, and the Netherlands. Amsterdam, in the Netherlands, offers a good case study of conflicting national and local laws, as well as confusion over their enforcement.

The Netherlands (Dutch) government has a unitary structure, including a central government, 12 provincial governments, and 3 special municipal governments (governing three islands in the Caribbean). According to Dutch law, people can legally purchase and smoke pot in "coffee" shops. Amsterdam has hundreds of coffee shops that draw tourists to the city. Dutch "tourist officials estimate that 35 percent of all visitors to Amsterdam stop by a coffee shop."

In May 2012, the Dutch government enacted a new law requiring membership in a coffee shop as a condition for legally purchasing pot. By law, coffee shop memberships are available only to residents; tourists cannot purchase a coffee shop membership and therefore cannot legally purchase pot. According to Prime Minister Mark Rutte, the law's goal was "to combat the nuisance and crime associated with coffee shops and the trade in drugs." The mayor of Amsterdam argued that the new law would actually increase crime rates in the city. Tourists and others without coffee shop memberships would "swarm all over the city looking for drugs." The sale of marijuana would move out of the shops into the streets and back alleys where the regulations controlling the quality of the drugs would not be enforceable. The mayor predicted more robberies and fights in the streets.

In response to the complaints sparked by the 2012 law, the Dutch government decided to leave its enforcement to local officials. In Amsterdam, local officials are not enforcing the national law. In states in the United States where marijuana sales and use is legal (for either recreational or medicinal purposes), some local officials enforce national drug laws and others enforce state and local laws. National officials, for the most part, leave enforcement to state and local officials.

SOURCE: Donald Kettl, "Tokin' Times: Worldwide, Local Pot Laws Are Increasingly at Odds With National Policies," *Governing* (February 2013): 16–17.

right of the national government to prosecute people who smoke the drug at the recommendation of their doctors, as well as those who grow it for medical purposes.[21]

The confusion caused by conflicting state and national laws as well as Court decisions regarding medical marijuana has become even more problematic since October 2009, when President Obama's attorney general announced that the federal government will not prosecute individuals who are dispensing marijuana or who are using it in compliance with state law in one of the states that has legalized such activities. Then, in 2011, federal attorneys raided and seized property from California medical marijuana growers and dispensaries. In 2012, voters in Colorado and Washington approved state laws legalizing the sale and possession of small amounts of marijuana for recreational use (the same day that voters in Arkansas defeated a law legalizing medicinal marijuana).[22] Therefore, although national law makes the sale, cultivation, and possession of marijuana a crime, 18 states plus the District of Columbia have laws that legalize the sale, cultivation, and possession of marijuana for medical use (when prescribed by a physician) and two states have legalized the sale and possession of small amounts of marijuana for recreational use. In August 2013, the U.S. Department of Justice announced that while marijuana was still illegal under federal law, it expects states that have legalized it to enforce tightly their state laws that regulate its use. In addition, the department reserves the right to challenge state actions and laws as it deems necessary.[23] Conflict between the national (central government) and state (regional governments) marijuana laws is not unique to the United States (see the "Global Context" feature).

How did the U.S. federal system evolve from dual federalism to today's conflicted and quite confusing federalism? Constitutional amendments, legislation, grants-in-aid, and court interpretations of laws are all pieces of the puzzle.

Constitutional Amendments and the Evolution of Federalism

Understanding the U.S. federal system's evolution from dual federalism to conflicted federalism requires a brief review of several constitutional amendments that fostered changes in the relationship between the national government and state governments. Although the formal language of the Constitution that established the federal system's dual sovereignty remains essentially as it was in 1791, three amendments—the Fourteenth, Sixteenth, and Seventeenth—have had a tremendous impact on the relationship between national and state government. The Civil War, which was a catalyst for ratification of the Fourteenth Amendment, also influenced the national-state power relationship.

THE CIVIL WAR AND THE POSTWAR AMENDMENTS   The military success of the northern states in the Civil War (1861–1865) meant the preservation of the union—the United States of America. The ratification of the Thirteenth Amendment (1865) brought the legal end of slavery in every state. In addition, the Fourteenth Amendment (1868), which extended the rights of citizenship to individuals who were previously enslaved, also placed certain limits and obligations on state governments.

The Fourteenth Amendment authorizes the national government to ensure that the state governments follow fair procedures (due process) before taking away a person's life, liberties, or pursuit of happiness and that the states guarantee all people the same rights (equal protection of the laws) to life, liberties, and the pursuit of happiness, without discrimination. In addition, the amendment guarantees the privileges and immunities of U.S. citizenship to all citizens in all states. Accordingly, since the Fourteenth Amendment's ratification, Congresses and presidents have approved national laws that direct the states to ensure due process and equal protection. This legislation includes, for example, laws mandating that all government buildings, including state and local edifices, provide access to all persons, including individuals with physical disabilities. In addition, the Supreme Court has used the Fourteenth Amendment to justify extending the Bill of Rights' limits on national government to state and local governments (under incorporation theory, which Chapter 4 considers). And in *Bush v. Gore* (2000), the Supreme Court used the amendment's equal protection clause to end a controversial Florida ballot recount in the 2000 presidential election.[24]

Conducting elections is a power reserved for the states. Therefore, state laws detail how citizens will cast their votes and how the state will count them to determine the winners. In the 2000 presidential election, Democratic candidate Al Gore successfully challenged, through Florida's court system, the vote count in that state. The Florida state Supreme Court interpreted Florida election law to require the state to count ballots that it initially did not count. In response, Republican candidate George W. Bush challenged the Florida Supreme Court's finding by appealing to the U.S. Supreme Court. Lawyers for candidate Bush argued that Florida's election law violated the Fourteenth Amendment's equal protection clause by not ensuring that the state would treat each person's vote equally. The U.S. Supreme Court found in favor of candidate Bush, putting an end to the vote recount called for by the Florida Supreme Court. Candidate Bush became President Bush.

THE SIXTEENTH AMENDMENT   Passage of the Sixteenth Amendment (1913) powerfully enhanced the ability of the national government to raise money. It granted Congress the authority to collect income taxes from workers and corporations without apportioning those taxes among the states on the basis of population (which had been mandated by the Constitution before this amendment).

The national government uses these resources to meet its constitutional responsibilities and to assist state governments in meeting their constitutional responsibilities. Moreover, the national

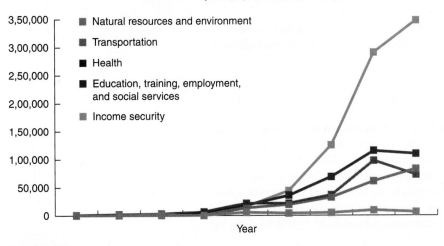

Federal Grants-in-Aid to State and Local Governments in Select Policy Areas (in millions of dollars)

- ■ Natural resources and environment
- ■ Transportation
- ■ Health
- ■ Education, training, employment, and social services
- ■ Income security

Year

FIGURE 3.5

Federal Grants-in-Aid to State and Local Governments for Selected Policy Areas (in millions of dollars) Through grants-in-aid, the federal government provides state and local governments with close to 25 percent of the revenue they spend annually to provide services and benefits. Over the years, state and local governments have come to depend on federal grants-in-aid.

SOURCE: White House Office of Management and Budget. "Total Outlays for Grants to State and Local Governments by Function and Fund Groups: 1940–2019," Table 12.2, http://www.whitehouse.gov/omb/budget/Historicals.

government also uses these resources as leverage over state and local governments, encouraging or coercing them to pursue and implement policies that the national government thinks best. Specifically, by offering state and local governments grants-in-aid, national officials have gained the power to determine many of the policies these governments approve, finance, and implement. For example, by offering grants to the states for highways, the federal government encouraged each state to establish a legal drinking age of 21 years (which we explore later in the chapter). Figure 3.5 presents historical information on federal grants-in-aid to states in selected policy areas. In 2011, federal grants to state and local governments made up 25 percent of all state and local expenditures.[25]

THE SEVENTEENTH AMENDMENT Before ratification of the Seventeenth Amendment in 1913, the Constitution called for state legislatures to select U.S. senators. By that arrangement, the framers strove to ensure that Congress and the president would take the concerns of state governments into account in national policy making. Essentially, the original arrangement provided the state legislatures with lobbyists in the national policy-making process who would be accountable to the states. Once ratified, the Seventeenth Amendment shifted the election of U.S. senators to a system of popular vote by the citizens in a state.

With that change, senators were no longer directly accountable to the state legislatures, because the latter no longer selected the senators. Consequently, state governments lost their direct access to national policy makers. Some scholars of federalism and intergovernmental relations argue that this loss has decreased the influence of state governments in national policy making.[26]

Tools of Intergovernmental Relations: Grants, Mandates, and Preemption

In 1837, the national government shared its revenue surplus with the states in the form of grants-in-aid. However, the national government did not make a habit of offering grants-in-aid to state and local governments until the Great Depression of the 1930s. Today, federal grants-in-aid amount to close to 20 percent of the national government's annual spending, and they pay for about 25 percent of the annual spending by state and local governments.[27] The pervasiveness of intergovernmental transfers of money has led political scientists to the study of **fiscal federalism**—the intergovernmental relationship between the national government and state and local governments that grows out of the grants of money that the national government provides to state and local governments. (See the "Thinking Critically About Democracy" feature for a debate about the need to limit fiscal federalism.)

fiscal federalism

the relationship between the national government and state and local governments whereby the national government provides grant money to state and local governments

categorical formula grant

a grant-in-aid for a narrowly defined purpose, whose dollar value is based on a formula

CATEGORICAL GRANTS Historically, the most common type of grant-in-aid has been the **categorical formula grant**—a grant of money from the federal government to state and local governments for a narrow purpose, as defined by the federal government. The legislation that creates such a grant includes a formula determining how much money is available to each grant recipient. The formula is typically based on factors related to the purpose of the grant, such as the number of people in the state in need of the program's benefits. Categorical grants come with strings attached—that is, rules and regulations with which the recipient government must comply.

Thinking Critically About
Democracy

Should Fiscal Federalism Be Limited?

The Issue: Today's federalism, replete with intergovernmental relations, is confusing. Some observers argue that it also makes all levels of government less efficient and effective. With the national government debt at more than $17 trillion and climbing, should the national government stop providing grants-in-aid to state and local governments? Should the national government stick to its enumerated powers and force state governments to act independently to implement their reserved powers and get out of the business of fiscal federalism?

Yes: The architects of the U.S. federal system expected the national and state governments to function independently of each other. They argued that state governments, working with their local governments, were in the best position to understand and address local problems. Today, federal grants undermine the effectiveness and efficiency of state governments by encouraging them to act on federal government priorities, instead of local priorities, and to implement policies established by federal officials who do not understand local problems. Ultimately, the national government would need to spend a lot less money, eventually eliminating its huge debt.

No: Citizens today expect a great deal from their state and local governments. Their great expectations have been encouraged by fiscal federalism. If the federal government stops providing grants, states will not be able to continue many of the programs people depend on, because the states do not have adequate financial resources. Since the Great Recession (2007–2009), state governments have cut spending in numerous policy areas, including education, social services, and

infrastructure (such as roads and bridges). Federal grants are vital to state governments' abilities to fulfill their responsibilities.

Other Approaches: If the revenue-raising capacity of state governments were increased, then these governments could survive incremental decreases in federal grants-in-aid. For example, in 2013 the House and the Senate each approved the same version of the Marketplace Fairness Act, a proposed federal law that would allow states to compel online and catalog retailers to collect state sales tax at the time of a transaction. Since a 1993 Supreme Court ruling, retailers have not had to collect sales tax when they are shipping an item to another state. States would collect billions of dollars in additional taxes if this law were enacted.

What do you think?

1. State governments have been fighting for a law like the Marketplace Fairness Act for decades. What powerful interests might oppose this law? Explain.

2. Can national politicians get beyond the gridlock of today's policy making and enact the Marketplace Fairness Act, or are they too concerned with national issues to worry about state government finances?

3. Would elimination of federal grants-in-aid, and the strings attached to them, make state and local governments as well as the national government more efficient and effective? Explain.

One typical string is a **matching funds requirement,** which obligates the government receiving the grant to spend some of its own money to match a specified percentage of the grant money provided. Matching funds requirements allow the national government to influence the budget decisions of state and local governments by forcing them to spend some of their own money on a national priority, which may or may not also be a state priority, in order to receive national funding.

Since the 1960s, the national government has also offered categorical project grants. Like the categorical formula grant, a **categorical project grant** covers a narrow purpose (program area), but unlike the formula grant, a project grant does not include a formula specifying how much money a recipient will receive. Instead, state and local governments interested in receiving such a grant must compete for it by writing proposals detailing what programs they wish to implement and what level of funding they need. A categorical project grant has strings attached to it and typically offers much less funding than a categorical formula grant.

BLOCK GRANTS Another type of formula-based intergovernmental transfer of money, the **block grant,** differs from categorical formula and categorical project grants in that the matters for which state and local governments can use the money is not narrowly defined, allowing state

matching funds requirement
a grant requirement that obligates the government receiving the grant to spend some of its own money to match a specified percentage of the grant money provided

categorical project grant
a grant-in-aid for a narrowly defined purpose for which governments compete with each other by proposing specific projects

block grant
a grant-in-aid for a broadly defined policy area, whose funding amount is typically based on a formula

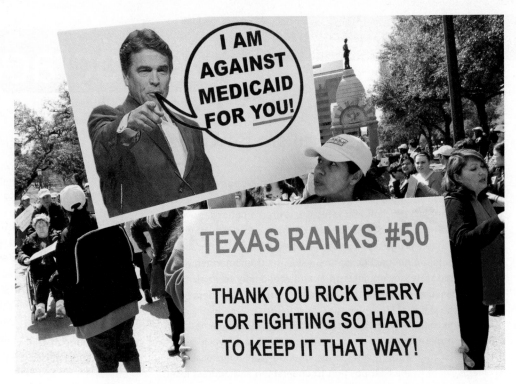

> The 2010 Affordable Care Act's (ACA) mandate for states to expand Medicaid to more of their citizens (paid for with grants-in-aid from the national government) highlights the conflicts and complexities of today's federalism. In a 2012 lawsuit challenging the mandated expansion, the U.S. Supreme Court agreed with state governments that claimed the national government did not have the authority to require states to expand Medicaid coverage even if it provided grants-in-aid to cover the cost. Some states decided to accept the federal grants to expand Medicaid while other states chose not to expand coverage. Many Texans were not pleased with Governor Rick Perry's decision to maintain the status quo with regard to Medicaid coverage in Texas after the 2012 Supreme Court decision. Did your state expand Medicaid coverage as a result of the ACA grants-in-aid?

and local governments more discretion to decide how to spend the money. Whereas a categorical grant might specify that the money is to be used for a child care program, a block grant gives the recipient government more discretion to determine what program it will be used for within a broad policy area such as assistance to economically needy families with children. When first introduced by the Nixon administration in the 1970s, the block grant also had fewer strings attached to it than the categorical grants. Today, however, the number and the specificity of conditions included in block grants are increasing.

State and local governments have grown dependent on national financial assistance, and so grants are an essential tool of national power to direct state and local government activity. Although the states welcome federal grant money, they do not welcome the strings attached to the funds, or *mandates*.

mandates
clauses in legislation that direct state and local governments to comply with national legislation and national standards

MANDATES National **mandates** are statements in national laws, including grants-in-aid, that require state and local governments to do something specified by the national government. Many national mandates relate to ensuring citizens' constitutional rights. For example, the mandate in the Rehabilitation Act of 1973 requires all government buildings, including state government and local government buildings, to be accessible to persons with disabilities to ensure equal protection of the law. In this case, the national government enacted the law to fulfill its constitutional responsibilities and imposes it on state and local governments.

When the national government assumes the entire cost of a mandate it imposes on a state or local government, it is a *funded mandate*. However, more often than not the national government does not cover the entire cost of its mandates. When the state or local government must cover all or some of the cost, it is an *unfunded mandate*. Because grants-in-aid are voluntary—that is, state and local governments can decide to accept a grant-in-aid or to reject it—state and local governments can determine whether or not they can afford to accept the grant and hence its mandate. Although state and local governments have always opposed the strings attached to grants, the attaching of mandates to grant money has come under increasing fire. The recent recession forced state and local governments to rely more heavily on national grants-in-aid and the attached conditions inspired resentment.

In the 1923 case *Massachusetts v. Mellon*,[28] one of the first cases in which state governments questioned the national government's right to attach mandates to grant money, the Supreme Court found the mandates in national grants-in-aid to be constitutional, arguing that grants-in-aid are voluntary cooperative arrangements. By voluntarily accepting the national grant, the justices ruled, the state government agrees to the grant conditions. The Court's decision did not end states' challenges to grant mandates.

In 1987, South Dakota challenged a 1984 national transportation law that penalized states whose legal drinking age was lower than 21 years. The intent of the national law was to decrease "drinking while intoxicated" (DWI) car accidents. States with legal drinking ages lower than 21 years would lose 10 percent of their national grant money for transportation. South Dakota argued that Congress was using grant conditions to put a law into effect that Congress could not achieve through national legislation because the law dealt with a power reserved to the states—determining the legal age for drinking alcoholic beverages.

In its decision in *South Dakota v. Dole*, the Court confirmed that the national government could not impose a national drinking age because setting a drinking age is indeed a reserved power of the states.[29] However, the Court found that the national government could *encourage* states to set a drinking age of 21 years by threatening to decrease their grants-in-aid for highway construction. In other words, conditions attached to voluntarily accepted grants-in-aid are constitutional. Ultimately, the

> Although in 1987 the Supreme Court found the drinking age mandate to be constitutional because it was attached to a grant, in 2012 the Court found unconstitutional a grant mandate attached to the national Affordable Care Act of 2010. What did the Affordable Care Act mandate require of states? What model of federalism do these two divergent Court decisions support?

national policy goal of a drinking age of 21 was indeed accomplished by 1988—not through a national law but through a condition attached to national highway funds offered to state governments, funds on which the states are dependent.

In the summer of 2012, the U.S. Supreme Court ruled on the constitutionality of the Affordable Care Act of 2010.[30] In its decision, the Court found unconstitutional the act's mandate requiring states that accepted Medicaid grants to extend Medicaid coverage to additional lower-income citizens. The act made the national government responsible for 100 percent of the cost to each state for its new Medicaid enrollees for the next three years, after which state governments would pay for no more than 10 percent of the cost for their new enrollees. Therefore, although state governments "voluntarily" participate in the Medicaid program by accepting Medicaid categorical grants (which have a matching fund requirement), this ruling challenges the ability of the national government to attach strings to its grant money. As a result of the Court's ruling, some states (particularly those with Republican governors) have decided not to expand Medicaid coverage whereas other states (particularly those with Democratic governors) have.

PREEMPTION   Another means by which the national government can direct the actions of state and local governments is through preemption. **Preemption** means that a national policy supersedes a state or local policy because it deals with an enumerated or implied national power. Therefore, people must obey, and states must enforce, the national law even if the state or local government has its own law on the matter. We see preemption in immigration policies particularly when state governments have passed laws limiting the ability of undocumented immigrants to rent properties. However, states can enact laws that offer people more rights and liberties than national law does. For example, at least 15 states allow undocumented students brought to the United States as children by their parents to be eligible for lower, in-state tuition at public colleges.

preemption
a constitutionally based principle that allows a national law to supersede state or local laws

The United States' experiment with a federal system of government has lasted more than 225 years. (See the "Analyzing the Sources" feature to assess how the experiment is going.) What began as a system of government with dual sovereignty implemented through a model of dual federalism has evolved into a system of government with dual sovereignty implemented through a model of confused federalism. Although the national government works independently on some policy matters (such as national defense and foreign policy) and state governments work independently on others (such as land use and the regulation of occupations and professions), most domestic matters are addressed through mutual efforts of at least two, if not three, levels of government, through intergovernmental relations.

MADISON'S VISION OF THE U.S. FEDERAL SYSTEM COMPARED TO THE FEDERAL SYSTEM TODAY

In *Federalist* No. 45, James Madison argued that under the proposed Constitution, the states will retain "a very extensive portion of active sovereignty." More specifically, he noted that

> the powers delegated by the proposed Constitution to the federal government are few and defined. Those which are to remain in the State governments are numerous and indefinite. The former will be exercised principally on external objects, as war, peace, negotiation, and foreign commerce; with which last the power of taxation will, for the most part, be connected. The powers reserved to the several States will extend to all the objects which, in the ordinary course of affairs, concern the lives, liberties, and properties of people, and the internal order, improvement, and prosperity of the State.

Based on the information in this chapter, address the following questions about how well today's federalism matches Madison's description of the federal system the Constitution would create.

Evaluating the Evidence

1. Have the powers delegated to the national government in the Constitution proven to be few and defined? Explain your answer.

2. Does the national government principally exercise its powers, and spend its money, on the "external objects" of war, peace, negotiation, and foreign commerce? Explain your answer.

3. Do the state governments operate independently of the national government in matters that "concern the lives, liberties, and properties of people, and the internal order, improvement, and prosperity of the State"? Explain.

4. Neither the Constitution nor Madison mentioned local governments, even though local governments existed in 1789. How important are local governments to the fulfillment of state responsibilities today? Give some examples.

5. Can Madison's claim that under the Constitution the states will retain "a very extensive portion of active sovereignty" be supported today? Explain.

IGR: U.S. Federalism Now

To govern, a government must have the authority to formulate and approve a plan of action, to raise and spend money to finance the plan, and to hire workers to put the plan into action. Therefore, there are three elements to all public policies: the policy *statement,* the policy *financing,* and the policy *implementation.* In the U.S. federal system today, the responsibility for these three elements of any given public policy may rest entirely with one level of government (national, state, or local), or may be shared in a collaborative effort by two or more of these levels. As noted earlier, political scientists label the collaborative efforts of two or more levels of government working to serve the public as *intergovernmental relations (IGR).* The provision of elementary and secondary public education is a good example of IGR today.

Educational Policy Statements

The U.S. Constitution does not mention education; it does not enumerate education as a national responsibility. Therefore, education is a policy matter reserved for the states. In all but four states, the state governments have created school districts—which are local-level governments—to provide elementary and secondary education. However, all three levels of government—national, state, and local school districts—have enacted educational policies. Therefore, in providing education, the school districts implement national and state policy, as well as their own policy statements. For example, Titles VI and IX of the national Civil Rights Act require that educational institutions receiving federal funding provide equal educational opportunities for all children no matter their race, religion, ethnicity, color, or sex. The national Individuals With Disabilities Education Act mandates equal educational opportunity for all children, no matter their disabilities, in educational institutions receiving federal funds. Among other policies, state laws determine what requirements an individual must meet to earn state certification to teach in public schools. State compulsory education laws determine for how many years, or until what grade, children must attend school. At the local level of government, school districts determine policies for the day-to-day operations of elementary and secondary schools, including school dress codes, the hours of the school day, and discipline procedures.

In 2002, President George Bush signed into law the No Child Left Behind (NCLB) Act. NCLB (a grant program) required schools to test students annually in grades three through eight in reading and math. The law delegated to state governments responsibilities for creating statewide tests and establishing annual achievement targets for the proportion of students who needed to pass state-created exams. Therefore, NCLB was a national policy that called on state governments to create state policies. School districts would also need to establish policies to guide teachers in preparing students for the annual tests. As the 2014 deadline for 100 percent of all students to meet the NCLB-established competencies approached, many state governments requested and received waivers from the law, eliminating their responsibility for meeting the law's competency standards, which many claimed were unrealistic.

Still concerned with the quality of education in the United States, state government officials took the lead in formulating a common set of academic standards by which they would measure their states' and school districts' education policies. By 2013, 45 states had committed to the Common Core State Standards, with testing on the standards beginning during the 2014–2015 school year.

Educational Policy Financing

All three levels of government provide some funding for elementary and secondary education. School districts collect property taxes from those who own property within the geographic area served by the district. State governments provide grants-in-aid to each school district to supplement its property tax revenue. On average, state grants to school districts cover about 50 percent of the total cost of elementary and secondary education. Historically, the federal government provided grants to ensure equal educational opportunities, which covered less than 10 percent of the cost of elementary and secondary education. Federal grants for elementary and secondary education increased as states and school districts began to implement NCLB, although the increase in grant money did not cover all of the increased costs to school districts trying to comply with NCLB (which was therefore an unfunded mandate).

In 2009, the national government established the Race to the Top project, designating $4 billion for education reform grants for which state governments could compete (a categorical project grant). To win a Race to the Top grant, states had to propose innovative plans to improve student outcomes, student assessment, teacher effectiveness, and data collection. Here we see the federal government using money as an incentive to foster educational policy reform, with specific strings attached, by state governments.

In February 2012, President Barack Obama included the Recognizing Educational Success, Professional Excellence, and Collaborative Teaching (RESPECT) project in his budget proposal for 2013. The RESPECT project calls for $5 billion in competitive grant money. Like Race to the Top, states can compete for RESPECT money (a categorical project grant with strings attached) by proposing innovative programs that bring together state and school district officials and teachers with the goal of keeping good teachers in the schools and rewarding the best teachers. Arne Duncan, the national secretary of education, stated that the goal of RESPECT "is to work with teachers in rebuilding their profession and to elevate the teacher voice in federal, state, and local educational policy."[31]

> President Barack Obama and Congress included $100 billion for education grants to states in the American Recovery and Reinvestment Act enacted in 2009. The act does not specify how the states should spend the money. In addition, states competed for $4 billion of these education funds through the Race to the Top grant program. In his budget proposal for 2013, President Obama included $5 billion for the Recognizing Educational Success, Professional Excellence, and Collaborative Teaching (RESPECT) project. What type of grants are these, categorical formula or categorical project?

Educational Policy Implementation

No matter which government establishes elementary and secondary public educational policies, or helps to finance their implementation, local government employees put these policies into action. School districts hire the personnel—teachers, custodians, coaches, librarians, cafeteria workers, principals, superintendents, and others—who implement national, state, and school district educational policies. The United States thus delivers the public good of elementary and secondary education through a complex network of intergovernmental relations wherein the three levels of government share education-policy-making responsibility and the funding of educational policy, and where government employees hired by school districts put the policy into action on a daily basis (policy implementation). Although education policy is a reserved power of the states, today's reality is that education policy, like most domestic policies, is a product of IGR.

An Assessment of the Advantages and Disadvantages of Today's Federal System

In the Preamble to the U.S. Constitution, the framers stated that their goal in establishing the federal system was to form a more perfect union. How is it working?

When political scientists discuss the advantages and disadvantages of the federal system, often what one person argues is an advantage another person argues is a disadvantage. For example, a frequently stated advantage of the federal system is the numerous access points for citizens to participate in their governments. Citizens can engage with national, state, county, municipal, and school district governments. They elect representatives to multiple governments and they "hire" all those elected officials to be responsive to their needs and to protect their rights.

For citizens, however, the availability of so many access points might be confusing and time consuming. Which government is the one with the legal responsibility to solve the problem you want addressed? Which elected official or government has the authority and the resources to solve a specific problem? Vague constitutional language does not make these easy questions for citizens, government officials, including judges, to answer.

Moreover, each election requires citizens to research candidates running for office. Who has the time? Some political scientists argue that voter turnout would be higher if there were fewer elections.

Another proclaimed advantage of the federal system is that it offers flexibility that makes for more efficient, effective, and responsive government. For example, because of their proximity, local and state governments can respond more quickly, and with a better understanding, to regional problems and needs than can the national government. In addition, what is a problem in one location may not be a problem elsewhere in the nation. Therefore, a national policy may not be appropriate. Moreover, the solution (program) supported by citizens in one area may not be supported by citizens in a different area. One-size-fits-all national policies are not necessarily effective for all or supported by all. The federal system accommodates state-to-state differences in needs and policy preferences.

Yet, there are problems and needs that cross state borders and affect the entire nation. As a result, we need national policies for some matters, state policies for other matters, and local policies for still other matters. A federal system provides for policies at all three levels of government.

However, this flexibility may lead to duplication of effort as multiple governments enact policies to address the same concern of their overlapping citizens. Duplication of effort is costly to taxpayers and inefficient, wasting taxpayer money and human resources. At the same time, multiple governments' enacting of different policies to address the same problem allows for experimentation and innovation in the search for the best solution. Governments observing other governments' efforts to solve a problem can then adopt the policy they deem best for their citizens.

One clear disadvantage to the federal system is that it creates inequalities in services and policies; some state or local governments provide their citizens with better public services or more rights than other citizens. Today, legal rights and privileges (such as the right to same-sex marriage, abortion, gun ownership, voting, and lower in-state college tuition) depend on the state in which you live. Such inequalities may satisfy those who support state laws on given matters, but dissatisfy those who do not support the laws and want the same rights as citizens in other states. Vague constitutional language also allows states to enact policies that may infringe on national sovereignty and the national government to enact policies that may infringe on state sovereignty. Conflicts over sovereignty can disrupt domestic tranquility (via protests and demonstrations) and lead to costly lawsuits. They may also fuel distrust and dissatisfaction with government.

Today, we see hostility and tension between state governments and the national government over numerous issues, including immigration reform, the right to bear arms and gun control, the right to abortion, the right to same-sex marriage, the expansion of Medicaid eligibility, and the proper implementation of the Affordable Care Act. Some observers of government have begun to discuss a new states' rights movement[32] as state governments that do not agree with a national policy enact their own laws that may conflict with national laws (consider the previously discussed movement to legalize medicinal and recreational marijuana in a growing number of states).

Polarization of partisans in Congress, which leads to gridlock, is fueling the states' rights movement. When Congress cannot agree on policy to solve problems, state governments pass their own policies. The result can be conflicting state policies and state policies that infringe on national sovereignty. Ultimately, the courts may have to resolve these conflicts.

Conclusion Thinking Critically About What's Next for Federalism

Until recent decades, the pattern of Supreme Court interpretation of the distribution of constitutional power between the national and the state governments favored an expansion of the national government's enumerated and implied powers in domestic policy matters. However, the past few decades have witnessed inconsistency in the Court's interpretations. The Court protects and even expands national powers in some cases while protecting states' powers in other cases.

Traditionally, state and local governments have been laboratories for domestic policies. Addressing long-term problems, such as poverty, and confronting new problems, such as global climate change, state and local governments have experimented regularly with innovative policies and programs. Federal grants-in-aid have supported state and local governments to develop solutions to domestic problems. Often, the mandates attached to federal grants specified the direction and details of state solutions, as evidenced by the Race to the Top and the proposed RESPECT competitive federal grant programs for educational reform. Citizens as well as the federal government rely on state and local governments as laboratories for new domestic policies.

The federal system with three levels of government relies on intergovernmental relations, which can be cooperative or contentious, as well as ineffective and inefficient. Governments can disagree on which government, if any, is responsible for addressing a problem. They may also disagree on what action needs to occur. Moreover, two or more levels of government may decide to act independently of each other, causing overlap in efforts and waste of resources. Although intergovernmental relations are confusing and sometimes cause conflicts, they evolved out of dual federalism as a means to address the growing complexity and overlap of societal problems that all three levels of government are called upon, by their citizens, to address. The growing states' rights movement could foster new interpretations of the Constitution, and give rise to a new form of federalism.

Summary

1. An Overview of the U.S. Federal System

Dual sovereignty is the defining characteristic of the United States' federal system of government. Under a federal system, the national government is sovereign over specific matters, and state governments are sovereign over different matters.

2. Constitutional Distribution of Authority

The vagueness of the U.S. Constitution's language providing for enumerated and implied national powers, reserved state powers, concurrent powers, and national supremacy has provoked ongoing conflict between the federal government and the states over the proper distribution of sovereignty. The U.S. Supreme Court has the final word on the interpretation of the Constitution—and hence the final say on national and state sovereignty.

3. Evolution of Intergovernmental Relations in the Federal System

The Supreme Court's interpretations of the Constitution's distribution of authority have reinforced the ability of national officials to compel state and local governments to implement national policy preferences. Mandates and preemption, as well as conditions placed on voluntarily accepted national grants-in-aid, require states to assist in financing and implementing national policies. As a result, relations between the national government and the states have evolved from a simple arrangement of dual federalism to a complex system of intergovernmental relations.

4. IGR: U.S. Federalism Now

Today, intergovernmental relations dominate domestic policy implementation. As we see in public education policy, most domestic matters are addressed by policies enacted at all three levels of government, financed by all three levels of government, and implemented predominantly by local government employees.

5. An Assessment of the Advantages and Disadvantages of Today's Federal System

The federal system of government offers efficiency, effectiveness, and responsiveness to citizens. At the same time, it is confusing, allows for duplication of effort and therefore wasted resources, and results in inequalities in rights, services, and benefits. Today, partisan gridlock at the national level sparks state policy actions that differ across the states and often conflict with national sovereignty and policy.

Key Terms

block grant 103
categorical formula
  grant 102
categorical project grant 103
centralized federalism 98
concurrent powers 91
confederal system 87
conflicted federalism 99
cooperative federalism 98
devolution 98
dual federalism 98
enumerated powers 91

extradition 96
federal system 86
fiscal federalism 102
full faith and credit clause 96
grants-in-aid 98
horizontal federalism 95
implied powers 91
intergovernmental
  relations (IGR) 88
interstate compacts 95
judicial federalism 97
mandates 104

matching funds
  requirement 103
McCulloch v. Maryland 93
necessary and proper clause
  (elastic clause) 91
police powers 92
preemption 105
privileges and immunities
  clause 96
reserved powers 92
supreme law of the land 91
unitary system 87

For Review

1. In terms of which government is sovereign, differentiate among a unitary system, a confederal system, and a federal system of government.

2. To which level of government does the Constitution distribute the enumerated powers? Implied powers? Concurrent powers? Reserved powers? Provide several examples of each power.

3. What matters fall within the scope of state sovereignty?

4. Differentiate among dual federalism, cooperative federalism, centralized federalism, and conflicted federalism.

5. How does the national government use grants-in-aid, mandates, and preemption to direct the policy of state and local governments?

6. What do we mean by intergovernmental relations? Why is the term a good description of U.S. federalism today?

7. List several advantages and several disadvantages of a federal system.

For Critical Thinking and Discussion

1. Is the federal system of government that provides citizens with the opportunity to elect a large number of officials each year a benefit or a burden for citizens? Explain your answer.

2. Would the amount of money citizens pay for their governments through taxes and fees decrease if there were fewer governments serving them? Defend your answer.

3. Would the quality or quantity of government services decrease if there were fewer governments in the United States? Why or why not?

4. Note at least three societal problems you believe the national government can address best (more effectively and efficiently than state or local governments). Discuss why you believe the national government is best suited to address these problems. Do these problems fit in the category of enumerated national powers? Explain your answer.

5. Note at least three societal problems you believe state or local governments can address best (more effectively and efficiently than the national government). Discuss why you believe state or local governments are best suited to address these problems. Do these problems fit in the category of powers reserved to the states? Explain your answer.

6. Which level of government do you believe James Madison expected would have the greatest effect on your daily life? Which level of government do you believe has the greatest effect on your daily life? Explain your answer.

Practice Quiz

MULTIPLE CHOICE: Choose the lettered item that answers the question correctly.

1. The characteristic that distinguishes a federal system of government from both a unitary and a confederal system is
   a. dual sovereignty.
   b. the existence of three levels of government.
   c. sovereignty held by only the central government.
   d. sovereignty held by only the regional governments.

2. The power to make policy, raise money, establish courts, and implement policy, which are basic functions of government, are examples of
   a. concurrent powers.
   b. enumerated powers.
   c. implied powers.
   d. reserved powers.

3. The necessary and proper clause of the Constitution establishes the
   a. enumerated powers of the national government.
   b. implied powers of the national government.
   c. implied powers of the state governments.
   d. reserved powers of the state governments.

4. The authority to coin and regulate money, to regulate interstate and foreign commerce, and to make treaties with foreign nations (including Native American nations) are examples of
   a. concurrent powers.
   b. enumerated powers.
   c. implied powers.
   d. reserved powers.

5. The Supreme Court used implied powers to confirm the national government's authority to establish a national bank, and applied the national supremacy clause to deny state authority to tax branches of the national bank, in the case of
   a. *Gibbons v. Ogden.*
   b. *United States v. Lopez.*
   c. *Marbury v. Madison.*
   d. *McCulloch v. Maryland.*

6. The state-to-state obligations detailed in the Constitution create state-to-state relationships known as
   a. centralized federalism.
   b. cooperative federalism.
   c. dual federalism.
   d. horizontal federalism.

7. The current debate over states' recognizing same-sex marriage contracts from other states may eventually force the Supreme Court to interpret the Article IV clause that concerns
   a. extradition.
   b. full faith and credit.
   c. interstate compacts.
   d. privileges and immunities.

8. The powers that the Tenth Amendment to the Constitution establishes are the
   a. enumerated powers.
   b. concurrent powers.
   c. implied powers.
   d. reserved powers.

9. Political scientists label today's federalism
   a. centralized federalism.
   b. conflicted federalism.
   c. dual federalism.
   d. horizontal federalism.

10. _____ provide(s) state governments with the most discretion over their policy actions (including policy formulation, policy financing, and policy implementation).
    a. National block grants
    b. National categorical grants
    c. National mandates
    d. National preemption

FILL IN THE BLANKS

11. _____ is the name political scientists give to the collaborative efforts of two or more levels of government working to serve the public.

12. All national, state, and local laws must comply with the Constitution of the United States, for the Constitution is the _____.

13. The practice whereby state judges base decisions regarding civil rights and liberties on their state constitutions, rather than on the U.S. Constitution, when their state constitution guarantees more than the minimum rights, is labeled _____.

14. The national government has used the _____ clause of the Constitution, also known as the elastic clause, to stretch its enumerated powers.

15. Beginning in the 1970s, state governments and presidents began to respond to centralized federalism by calling for _____, which is the return of policy creation, financing, and/or implementation to the state governments.

Answers: 1. a, 2. a, 3. b, 4. b, 5. d, 6. d, 7. b, 8. d, 9. b, 10. a, 11. Intergovernmental relations, 12. supreme law of the land, 13. judicial federalism, 14. necessary and proper, 15. devolution.

Resources for Research AND Action

Internet Resources

Bureau of the Census
www.census.gov Access multiple sources of data about national and state governments at this site.

Catalog of Federal Domestic Assistance
www.cfda.gov On this site you will find a full listing of all federal programs available to state and local governments; federally recognized tribal governments; public and private organizations and institutions; specialized groups; and individuals.

Council of State Governments
www.csg.org At this site, state officials can share information on common problems and possible solutions.

National Conference of State Legislatures
www.ncsl.org This site provides resources to state legislatures to fulfill the NCSL's goals of ensuring positive intergovernmental relations, by fostering a strong cohesive voice for state legislatures in the federal system and promoting policy innovation and communication among the states.

National Governors Association (NGA)
www.nga.org The NGA lobbies the national government on behalf of governors and also provides the governors with opportunities to share information on policies.

Publius
www.publius.oxfordjournals.org This is the website of *Publius,* a scholarly journal for the study of federalism.

Recommended Readings

Edwards, Chris. *Downsizing the Federal Government.* Washington, D.C.: CATO Institute, 2005. With an eye toward balancing the federal budget, budget expert Chris Edwards identifies more than 100 federal programs that he argues should be terminated, devolved to state governments, or handed over to private sector organizations.

O'Toole, Laurence J. *American Intergovernmental Relations: Foundations, Perspectives, and Issues,* 3rd ed. Washington, D.C.: CQ Press, 2000. A collection of readings giving a comprehensive overview of U.S. federalism and intergovernmental relations, covering historical, theoretical, and political perspectives as well as fiscal and administrative views.

Rehnquist, William H. *The Supreme Court: Revised and Updated.* New York: Vintage Books, 2001. A history of the Supreme Court by then–chief justice Rehnquist, probing the inner workings of the Court, key Court decisions in the evolution of federalism, and insights into the debates among the justices.

Robertson, David Brian. *Federalism and the Making of America.* New York: Routledge, 2012. A comprehensive review of the evolution of federalism in the United States, with a focus on the effect of intergovernmental relations on major policy battles in U.S history.

Walker, David B. *The Rebirth of Federalism: Slouching Toward Washington,* 2nd ed. Washington, D.C.: CQ Press, 2000. Both a history of U.S. federalism and an assessment of the status of U.S. federalism today.

Movies of Interest

When the Levees Broke: A Requiem in Four Acts (2006)
This Spike Lee documentary critically examines the responses of federal, state, and local governments to Hurricane Katrina. Through images of the disaster, interviews with Katrina's victims, and clips of government officials' media interviews, Lee focuses on racial issues and intergovernmental ineptitude—from the poor construction of the levees to the delayed and inadequate federal, state, and local response.

Hoxie: The First Stand (2003)
This documentary presents one of the first integration battles in the South post–*Brown v. Board of Education of Topeka, Kansas.* The opponents are the Hoxie Board of Education, which in the summer of 1955 decided to integrate its schools, and grassroots citizens' organizations that resisted integration through petitions, harassment, and threats of violence against the school board members, their families, and the school superintendent.

Dances With Wolves (1990)
Sent to command the U.S. Army's westernmost outpost in the 1860s, Lieutenant John Dunbar witnesses, as an observer and a participant, the conflicts created in the Dakota Territory as white settlers encroach on territory of the Sioux Indians. Movie critics and historians praised Kevin Costner (the movie's director and lead actor) for correcting the erroneous image of Native Americans presented in classic Hollywood Westerns.

CHAPTER 4

Civil Liberties

 ## THEN

The Bill of Rights was designed to protect citizens' rights to speak and act without undue monitoring by or interference from the national government; however, Congress soon legislated exceptions to those protections.

 ## NOW

The national government monitors the words and actions of citizens and others to combat terrorism, while questions emerge regarding the rights of journalists and citizens.

 ## NEXT

Will the Court uphold laws that require Internet providers to secretly share personal information about their clients with the FBI?

Will the use of drones be expanded for crime control purposes in the United States?

Will the nation find ways to balance the Second Amendment's guarantee of a protected individual right to bear arms with concerns about security and the increased visibility of mass shootings?

The subject of this chapter is civil liberties, the personal freedoms that protect citizens from government interference and allow them to participate fully in social and political life.

FIRST, we discuss the protection of civil liberties in the American legal system—including the freedoms protected by the Bill of Rights, the application of those protections to state governments, and the tensions inherent within the Bill of Rights.

SECOND, we consider freedoms in practice by looking at the controversy over the Second Amendment and the right to bear arms.

THIRD, we explore the freedoms of speech, assembly, and the press: First Amendment freedoms in support of civic engagement.

FOURTH, we examine how the freedoms of religion, privacy, and criminal due process strengthen civil society by encouraging inclusiveness and community engagement.

FIFTH, we consider the changing nature of civil liberties in post–September 11 America.

civil liberties
constitutionally established guarantees that protect citizens, opinions, and property against arbitrary government interference

A strong belief in civil liberties

is deeply embedded in our understanding of what it means to be an American. Civil liberties protect people from government intrusion and allow them to follow their own belief systems. Civil liberties also empower people to speak out against the government, as long as they do not harm others.

Since the nation's founding, political discourse among the people has often focused on the ideals of liberty and freedom. The colonists took up arms against Britain because the king and Parliament refused to recognize their liberties as English citizens—freedoms their counterparts in Great Britain took for granted: freedom of speech and assembly and the right to be free from unrestrained governmental power, especially in the investigation and prosecution of crimes. As scholar Stephen L. Carter noted, by declaring their independence, the colonists engaged in the ultimate act of dissent.[1] Withdrawing their consent to be governed by the king, they created a new government that would tolerate political discourse and disagreement and that could not legally disregard the collective or individual will of citizens.

Ideologies of liberty and freedom inspired the War for Independence and the founding of the new nation.[2] Those rights, though guaranteed, were never absolute. In fact, one of the early acts passed by Congress after the Bill of Rights was the Alien and Sedition Acts (1789), which not only limited immigration but also prohibited certain criticisms of the government. From its origins, the Constitution guaranteed basic liberties, but those protections were tempered by other goals and values, perhaps most importantly by the goal of order and the need to protect people and their property. Following the terrorist attacks of September 11, 2001, the national government enacted laws aimed at protecting American citizens and property from further attacks, such as the Boston Marathon bombing of 2013. But those laws, in some cases, overturned decades of legal precedents that protected civil liberties. As technology evolves, the government's ability to engage in surveillance activities that escape public awareness increases, as does the capacity of private individuals and anonymous groups to expose these activities. Is such public exposure a way of holding the government accountable or an act of treason?

Civil Liberties in the American Legal System

Civil liberties are individual liberties established in the Constitution and safeguarded by state and federal courts. We also refer to civil liberties as *personal freedoms* and often use the concepts of "liberty" and "freedom" interchangeably.

Civil liberties differ from civil rights. **Civil liberties** are constitutionally established guarantees that protect citizens, opinions, and property *against* arbitrary government interference. In contrast, civil rights (the focus of Chapter 5) reflect positive acts of government (in the form of constitutional provisions or statutes) *for* the purpose of protecting individuals against arbitrary or discriminatory actions. For example, the freedom of speech, a liberty established in the First Amendment to the U.S. Constitution, protects citizens against the government's censorship of their words, in particular when those words are politically charged. In contrast, the constitutionally protected right to vote requires the government to step in to ensure that all citizens be allowed to vote, without restriction by individuals, groups, or governmental officials.

The Freedoms Protected in the American System

The U.S. Constitution, through the Bill of Rights, and state constitutions explicitly recognize and protect civil liberties. As Table 4.1 summarizes, the first 10 amendments to the Constitution explicitly limited the power of the legislative, executive, and judicial branches of the national government.

The Bill of Rights established the freedoms that are essential to individuals' and groups' free and effective participation in the larger community. Consider how the absence of freedom to speak one's mind or the absence of protection against the arbitrary exercise of police powers might affect the nature and the extent of people's engagement in political and community debates and discussions. Without these protections, citizens could not freely express their opinions through rallies, speeches, protests, letters, pamphlets, tweets, blogs, e-mail, and other forms of civic engagement. The Constitution's framers, who had been denied these liberties under British rule, saw them as indispensable to forming a new democratic republic.

The meanings of these precious freedoms have shifted over the course of U.S. history, as presidents, legislators, judges, and ordinary citizens have changed their minds about how much freedom the people should have. When Americans have not perceived themselves as being under some external threat, they generally have adopted an expansive interpretation of civil liberties. At those times, citizens tend to believe that the government should interfere as little as necessary in individuals' lives. Accordingly, they strongly support people's right to gather with others and to speak their minds, even when the content of that speech is controversial. When the nation has been under some perceived threat, citizens have often allowed the government to limit protected freedoms.[3] (See "Analyzing the Sources" on page 120.) Limits have also extended to many **due process** protections—legal safeguards that prevent the government from arbitrarily depriving people of life, liberty, or property without adhering to strict legal procedures. In this chapter, we consider not only the historical context of our civil liberties but also recent changes in how Congress, the president, and the courts interpret these liberties.

due process
legal safeguards that prevent the government from arbitrarily depriving citizens of life, liberty, or property; guaranteed by the Fifth and Fourteenth Amendments

TABLE 4.1

The Bill of Rights: Limiting Government Power

Amendment I: Limits on Congress	Congress cannot make any law establishing a religion or abridging the freedom of religious exercise, speech, assembly, or petition.
Amendments II, III, IV: Limits on the Executive	The executive branch cannot infringe on the right of the people to bear arms (II), cannot house soldiers in citizens' houses (III), and cannot search for or seize evidence without a legal warrant from a court of law (IV).
Amendments V, VI, VII, VIII: Limits on the Judiciary	The courts cannot hold trials for serious offenses without providing for a grand jury (V), a trial jury (VII), a fair trial (VI), and legal counsel (VI). The accused also have the right to hear the charges against them (VI), to confront hostile witnesses (VI), and to refrain from giving testimony against themselves (V); and they cannot be tried more than once for the same crime (V). In addition, neither bail nor punishment can be excessive (VIII), and no property can be taken from private citizens without "just compensation" (V).
Amendments IX, X: Limits on the Federal Government	Any rights not listed specifically in the Constitution for the national government are reserved to the states or to the people (X), and the enumeration of certain rights in the Constitution should not be interpreted to mean that those are the only rights the people have (IX).

BALANCING THE CONSTITUTIONAL TENSION

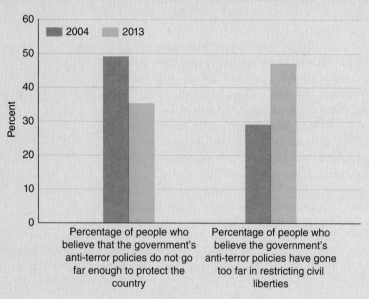

1. The September 11 attack occurred in 2001. No major terrorist attack has been carried out on American soil since that time. How has opinion about balancing civil liberties and security changed?

2. If another major terrorist attack were to occur on American soil, how do you think public opinion on this issue would shift?

3. How could Congress better hold the government accountable for protecting civil liberties, while pursuing national security?

The Historical Basis for American Civil Liberties: The Bill of Rights

The framers vividly remembered the censorship and suppression of speech that they had suffered under British rule. Colonists had been harshly punished, often by imprisonment and confiscation of their property and even death, if they criticized the British government, through both speech and the publication of pamphlets. The framers understandably viewed liberty as a central principle guiding the creation of a new democratic republic. Federalists such as Alexander Hamilton saw the Constitution itself as a bill of rights because it delegated specific powers to the national government and contained specific provisions designed to protect citizens against an abusive government.

The protections listed in Table 4.2 were designed to protect people from being punished, imprisoned, or executed for expressing political beliefs or opposition. However, the Anti-Federalists still stressed the need for a written bill of rights. As we saw in Chapter 2, the ratification of the Constitution stalled because citizens feared that the government might use its expanded powers to limit individual freedoms, particularly those associated with political speech and engagement. The First Amendment, which ensures freedom of religion, the press, assembly, and speech, was essential to political speech and to discourse in the larger society.

The freedoms embodied in the Bill of Rights are broad principles rather than specific prohibitions

TABLE 4.2

Citizens' Protections in the Original Constitution

CLAUSE	PROTECTION
Article I, Sec. 9	Guarantee of *habeas corpus*—a court order requiring that an individual in custody be brought into court and told the cause for detention
Article I, Sec. 9	Prohibition of *bills of attainder*—laws that declare a person guilty of a crime without a trial
Article I, Sec. 9	Prohibition of *ex post facto laws*—retroactive laws that punish people for committing an act that was legal when the act was committed
Article III	Guarantee of a trial by jury in the state where the crime was committed

against governmental action. From the nation's beginnings, the vagueness of the Bill of Rights led to serious disagreement about how to interpret its amendments. For example, the First Amendment's establishment clause states simply that "Congress shall make no law respecting an establishment of religion." Some commentators, most notably Thomas Jefferson, argued that the clause mandated a "wall of separation between church and state" and barred any federal support of religion. Others interpreted the clause more narrowly as barring only the establishment of a national religion or the requirement that all public officials swear an oath to some particular religion. This disagreement about the breadth of the establishment clause is ongoing today, as courts and lawyers continue to try to determine what the proper relationship should be between church and state.

Other freedoms, too, have been subject to differing interpretations, including the First Amendment guarantees of freedom of speech, assembly, and the press. These conflicting interpretations often arise in response to public crises or security concerns. Security concerns also affect the protections offered to those accused of threatening the safety of the nation. For example, the USA PATRIOT Act, passed by Congress almost immediately after the September 11 attacks and amended in 2002, allows law enforcement a good deal of legal leeway. It permits agents to sidestep well-established rules that govern how searches and seizures may be conducted and to restrict criminal due process protections severely, particularly for persons suspected of involvement in organizations thought to have ties to suspected terrorists. Civil liberties advocates worry that fear is causing Americans to give up their most precious freedoms.

Incorporation of the Bill of Rights to Apply to the States

The framers intended the Bill of Rights to restrict the powers of only the *national government*. They did not see the Bill of Rights as applicable to the state governments. In general, there was little public worry that the states would curtail civil liberties, because most state constitutions included a bill of rights that protected the individual against abuses of state power. Further, it was generally believed that because the state governments were geographically closer to the people than the national government, they would be less likely to encroach upon individual rights and liberties.

Through most of early U.S. history, the Bill of Rights applied to the national government, but not to the states. That assumption is illustrated by the case of *Barron v. Baltimore* (1833), in which a wharf owner named Barron sued the city of Baltimore. Barron claimed that the city

> Three years after the Supreme Court incorporated the Second Amendment, declaring gun bans unconstitutional, a young man walked into Sandy Hook Elementary School, in Newtown, Connecticut, and shot and killed 20 children and 6 adults. This and similar incidents have resulted in calls for stricter gun laws, highlighting the tension between security and civil liberties. How might current events like the Newtown shooting impact people's position on negotiating the tension between security and personal liberty?

had violated the "takings clause" of the Fifth Amendment, which bars the taking of private property for public use without just compensation. *Barron* argued that by paving its streets, the city of Baltimore had changed the natural course of certain streams; the resulting buildup of silt and gravel in the harbor made his wharf unusable. The question before the Supreme Court was whether or not the Fifth Amendment protects individuals from actions taken by both the federal and state or local governments. The Court determined that the Fifth Amendment applies only to actions taken by the federal government.[4]

In 1868, three years after the Civil War ended, the Fourteenth Amendment was added to the U.S. Constitution. The Fourteenth Amendment reads as if it were meant to extend the protections of the Bill of Rights to citizens' interactions with *state governments:*

> No State shall make or enforce any law which shall abridge the privileges or immunities of citizens of the United States; nor shall any State deprive any person of life, liberty, or property, without due process of law; nor deny to any person within its jurisdiction the equal protection of the laws.

Although this language sounds like an effort to protect citizens' rights and liberties from arbitrary interference by state governments, the Supreme Court rejected the doctrine of **total incorporation:** that is, the application of *all* the protections contained in the Bill of Rights to the states. Instead, beginning with a series of cases decided by the Court in the 1880s, the justices formulated a narrower approach, known as **selective incorporation.**[5] This approach considered each protection individually, one case at a time, for possible incorporation into the Fourteenth Amendment and application to the states. In each case, the justices rejected the plaintiff's specific claims of protection against the state. But the Court held that due process mandates the incorporation of those rights that serve the fundamental principles of liberty and justice, those that were at the core of the "very idea of free government" and that were unalienable rights of citizenship.

Despite those early cases, the Supreme Court continued to embrace the idea that although citizenship meant being a citizen of a state and of the nation as a whole, the Bill of Rights protected citizens only against the national government. As Table 4.3 shows, not until 1925 did the Court gradually begin the process of incorporation, starting with the First Amendment protections most central to democratic government and civic engagement. That year, in the case of *Gitlow v. New York,* the Court held that freedom of speech is "among the fundamental personal rights and 'liberties' protected by the due process clause of the Fourteenth Amendment from impairment by the states."[6] This was the first time the Supreme Court applied the protections found in the Bill of Rights to actions by states or local governments. In 1931, in its decision in *Near v. Minnesota,* the Court added freedom of the press, and in 1937 it added freedom of assembly to the list of incorporated protections.[7]

Incorporation progressed further with the landmark case of *Palko v. Connecticut* (1937), in which the Court laid out a formula for defining fundamental rights that later courts have used time and time again in incorporation cases, as well as in due process cases more generally. The justices found that fundamental rights were rooted in the traditions and conscience of the American people. Moreover, if those rights were eliminated, the justices argued, neither liberty nor justice could exist.[8] Judges in subsequent cases have used this formula to determine which Bill of Rights protections should be applied to the states. In case after case, the justices have considered whether such a right is fundamental—that is, rooted in the American tradition and conscience and essential for liberty and justice—and they have been guided by the principle that citizen participation in government and society is necessary for democracy in gauging the importance of each constitutionally protected right.

Over time, the Supreme Court has incorporated most Bill of Rights protections, as Table 4.3 summarizes, requiring the states to provide these guarantees to their citizens. Among the few notable exceptions to the trend of incorporation are the Third Amendment's prohibition against the quartering of soldiers in citizens' homes, which has not been an issue since colonial times. The Fifth Amendment's provision for a grand jury indictment, whereby a panel of citizens determines whether or not there is enough evidence for prosecutors to bring a criminal case, runs counter to a trend in state criminal cases away from a reliance on grand juries; a grand jury is not required to guarantee that states adhere to Fifth and Sixth Amendment protections during the arrest, interrogation, and trial of criminal defendants. Similarly, the Seventh Amendment's provision of a jury in a civil trial is widely viewed as less important than the Sixth Amendment's guarantee of a jury trial in criminal cases in which life and liberty may be at stake.

total incorporation
the theory that the Fourteenth Amendment's due process clause requires the states to uphold *all* freedoms in the Bill of Rights; rejected by the Supreme Court in favor of selective incorporation

selective incorporation
the process by which, over time, the Supreme Court applied those freedoms that served *some* fundamental principle of liberty or justice to the states, thus rejecting total incorporation

Selective Incorporation of the Bill of Rights

TABLE 4.3

AMENDMENT	LIBERTY	DATE	KEY CASE
I	Freedom of speech	1925	*Gitlow v. New York*
	Freedom of the press	1931	*Near v. Minnesota*
	Freedom of assembly and petition	1937	*DeJonge v. Oregon*
	Freedom to practice religion	1940	*Cantwell v. Connecticut*
	Freedom from government-established religion	1947	*Everson v. Board of Education*
II	Right to bear arms	2010	*McDonald v. City of Chicago*
III	No quartering of soldiers		Not incorporated
IV	No unreasonable searches and seizures	1949	*Wolf v. Colorado*
	Exclusionary rule	1961	*Mapp v. Ohio*
V	Right to just compensation (for property taken by government)	1897	*Chicago, B&Q RR Co. v. Chicago*
	No compulsory self-incrimination	1964	*Malloy v. Hogan*
	No double jeopardy	1969	*Benton v. Maryland*
	Right to grand jury indictment		Not incorporated
VI	Right to a public trial	1948	*In re Oliver*
	Right to counsel in criminal cases	1963	*Gideon v. Wainwright*
	Right to confront witnesses	1965	*Pointer v. Texas*
	Right to an impartial jury	1966	*Parker v. Gladden*
	Right to a speedy trial	1967	*Klopfer v. North Carolina*
	Right to a jury in criminal trials	1968	*Duncan v. Louisiana*
VII	Right to a jury in civil trials		Not incorporated
VIII	No cruel and unusual punishments	1962	*Robinson v. California*
	No excessive fines or bail		Not incorporated

Freedoms in Practice: Controversy Over the Second Amendment and the Right to Bear Arms

The fierce debate today over gun control illustrates much about the conflicts surrounding the civil liberties protected in the United States. Americans disagree about how to interpret the Second Amendment of the Constitution, but they do agree to have their disputes settled through laws and court rulings rather than armed conflict. Private citizens and political interest groups use their First Amendment freedoms of speech and assembly to voice their opinions about the place of guns in society. They also work behind the scenes to influence elected officials through campaign contributions and lobbying (see Chapter 7). At the heart of this debate is the question of the role of guns in creating a safe and free society and negotiating the tension between personal liberty and community security.

Changing Interpretations of the Second Amendment

Recently, the Supreme Court has changed its interpretation of the Second Amendment, which reads

> A well-regulated Militia, being necessary to the security of a free State, the right of the people to keep and bear Arms, shall not be infringed.

The Second Amendment was initially interpreted by the Supreme Court as ensuring that state militias could support the government in maintaining public order; under this interpretation the right to bear arms is a group right subject to regulation by Congress and the states.[9]

In 2008, the Supreme Court ruled in the *District of Columbia v. Heller* that the Second Amendment confers an individual right to possess a firearm for lawful purposes, such as self-defense.[10] In the 2010 case of *McDonald v. Chicago,* the Court incorporated the Second Amendment to the states, requiring states to respect this new individual constitutional right when they regulated citizen access to guns.[11] This forced many states to change their laws to allow individuals to carry concealed weapons, though there remains a great deal of variation in how these laws are implemented (see Figure 4.1).

Citizens Engaged: Fighting for a Safer Nation

While the gun homicide rate in the United States has decreased by 49 percent between 1993 and 2010,[12] the increased visibility of mass shootings—such as Columbine High School; Virginia Tech; Sandy Hook Elementary School; the Aurora, Colorado, movie theater; and Fort Hood, in Texas—has kept the question of domestic security visible. Some activists, like the interest group Connecticut Against Gun Violence (organized after the Sandy Hook shooting), argue that stricter weapons laws are necessary for a safe society.

Other groups, like the National Rifle Association, believe that if more law-abiding citizens can carry weapons, fewer violent crimes will be committed. Both groups have joined vocally in

POLITICAL

Inquiry

FIGURE 4.1 ■ GUN LAWS All 50 states allow individuals the right to carry a concealed weapon. Only the District of Columbia prohibits it. In addition, some states have adopted "Stand Your Ground" laws that affirm a person's right to stand his or her ground against an imminent threat, with no duty to retreat, as long as the person has a right to be where he or she is. Other states have enacted the "Castle Doctrine," allowing a person the right to stand his or her ground in a home or an office. Still other states have passed "Duty to Retreat" laws, which do not allow people to resort to deadly force in self-defense if it is possible to safely avoid the risk of harm or death by running away or by other means. What regional variations do you see regarding these laws? How do you think we can resolve this highly contested issue? How does your home state currently address gun ownership?

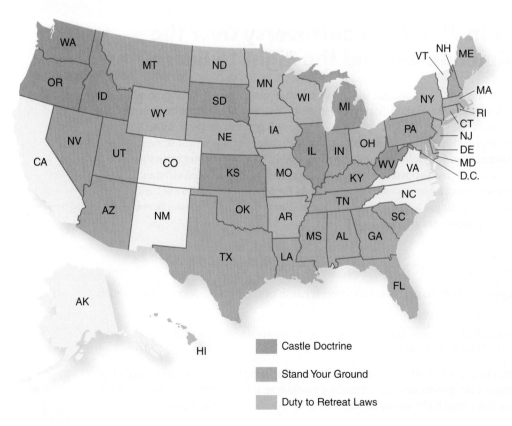

■ Castle Doctrine

■ Stand Your Ground

■ Duty to Retreat Laws

the public debate, exercising their freedom of speech and assembly to influence opinions about guns in the United States.

By 2014, every state allowed for some form of concealed-carry protection, permitting citizens to have weapons on them or in close proximity. In addition, the nation has been debating the wisdom of "Stand Your Ground" laws, allowing individuals who feel threatened to fire their weapons in self-defense. The shooting death of Trayvon Martin, a 17-year-old African American high school student in February 2012 in Stanford, Florida, galvanized many critics of Stand Your Ground laws. George Zimmerman, a 28-year-old neighborhood watch coordinator, claimed that he felt threatened by the unarmed Martin. Later that year, the shooting of Jordan Davis, another unarmed 17-year-old high school student at a Florida convenience store, by Michael David Dunn, sparked protests against liberal gun laws. Dunn objected to the volume of the music playing in the car in which Davis was riding. Unlike Zimmerman, Dunn was convicted of murder and sentenced to life in prison and another 90 years for three counts of attempted murder. Critics argued that the mere perception of a threat does not constitute one, while many civil rights groups contend that Stand Your Ground laws ultimately result in the deaths of innocent, young African American men, like Martin and Davis, who are more likely to be unfairly stereotyped as a threat.

> Nicole Oulson viewed a photo of her husband, Chad, and their daughter, Alexis, at a memorial service for him.

Stand your ground was again called into question in Florida in 2014 when Curtis Reeves, a 71-year-old retired police captain, shot 43-year-old Chad W. Oulson, 43, a Navy veteran who was white. Reeves objected when Oulson used his cell phone in a movie theater to text his babysitter to check on his daughter, who wasn't feeling well. An altercation ensued, and when something—perhaps popcorn—struck Reeves's face, he perceived a threat and used his .380 caliber gun to shoot and kill Oulson. Shootings like these have prompted lawmakers to consider "Duty to Retreat" laws, requiring those who feel threatened to back down, unless they are secure in their own homes. Advocates on each side of this issue believe their proposed policies maximize the personal liberty of individuals, while maintaining domestic security.

Freedoms of Speech, Assembly, and the Press: First Amendment Freedoms Supporting Civic Discourse

Civic discourse and free participation in the political process have certain requirements. As we consider in this section, an individual must be able to express his or her political views through speech, assembly, and petition. The person must also live in a society with a press that is independent of government censorship. Freedom of speech, assembly, petition, and the press is essential to an open society and to democratic rule. These freedoms ensure that individuals can discuss the important issues facing the nation and try to agree about how to address these matters. Scholars have referred to this sharing of contrasting opinions as the **marketplace of ideas.** It is through the competition of ideas—some of them radical, some even loathsome—that solutions emerge. Freedom of the press allows for the dissemination and discussion of these varying ideas and encourages consensus building.

The marketplace of ideas enables people to voice their concerns and views freely and allows individuals to reconsider their ideas on important national and local issues. The centrality of the freedom of political expression to the First Amendment reflects the founders' belief that democracy would flourish only through robust discussion and candid debate.

marketplace of ideas
a concept at the core of the freedoms of expression and press, based on the belief that true and free political discourse depends on a free and unrestrained discussion of ideas

The First Amendment and Political Instability

Over time, the Supreme Court has distinguished between political expression that the First Amendment protects and expression that the government may limit or even prohibit. The government has tried to limit speech, assembly, and the press during times of national emergency, when it has viewed that expression as more threatening than it would be in normal times.

> With the multiple releases of classified government documents by the international activist group WikiLeaks, the public became more aware of secret activities by governments around the world. The group claimed it provided public accountability by releasing these materials to the global media; governments claimed these were acts of terrorism. How can we balance these competing understandings of liberty?

habeus corpus
an ancient right that protects an individual in custody from being held without the right to be heard in a court of law

THE TENSION BETWEEN FREEDOM AND ORDER   A fundamental tension exists between the Bill of Rights, with its goal of protecting individual freedoms, and the government's central goal of ensuring order. Not even a decade had gone by after the Constitution's ratification when Congress passed the Alien and Sedition Acts (1798). These laws placed the competing goals of freedom and order directly in conflict. The Sedition Act criminalized all speech and writings judged to be critical of the government, Congress, or the president. This was just the first of many times in U.S. history that lawmakers sacrificed free speech and freedom of the press in an effort to ensure national security and order. For example, President Abraham Lincoln (1861–1865) attempted to silence political dissidents during the Civil War by mandating that they be tried in military courts, without the due process protections afforded in a civilian court. Lincoln also suspended the writ of ***habeus corpus*** (Latin, meaning "you have the body"), an ancient right and constitutional guarantee that protects an individual in custody from being held without the right to be heard in a court of law.[13] Again, political dissidents were targeted for indefinite detention without trial. Whenever the nation has perceived itself under attack or threat, pressure has been placed on the government by some citizens to limit individual freedom to ensure societal order, and other citizens have pressured the government to maintain freedom while securing order.

The struggle for a balance between freedom and order continues today as the United States fights a global war on terrorism. Part of the 1789 Alien and Sedition Acts, known as the Alien Enemies Act, empowered the president to deport aliens suspected of threatening the nation's security or to imprison them indefinitely.[14] After the September 11 terrorist attacks on U.S. soil, President George W. Bush (2001–2009) invoked those same powers for enemy combatants, insurgents, and suspected terrorists captured in the United States or abroad. Like President Lincoln, President Bush also argued that military combatants and suspected terrorists should be tried in military tribunals and denied the protections of civilian courts, including the right to a speedy and public trial.[15] While the Obama adminstration moved to try some detainees in civilian criminal courts,[16] Guantánamo Bay remained open. With the passage of the National Defense Authorization Act of 2012,[17] there has been much debate over whether this law ensures the continued military detention of civilians.[18] President Barack H. Obama, however, in a statement made when signing the act, noted that his administration would not allow the indefinite detaining of citizens without a trial.[19]

clear and present danger test
a standard established in the 1919 Supreme Court case *Schenck v. U.S.* whereby the government may silence speech or expression when there is a clear and present danger that such speech will bring about some harm that the government has the power to prevent

THE HISTORICAL CONTEXT FOR FREE SPEECH LAWS   The Supreme Court's willingness to suppress or punish political speech has changed over time in response to perceived internal and external threats to the nation. During World War I, the Court upheld the conviction of socialist and war protester Charles Schenck for distributing a pamphlet to recently drafted men urging them to resist the draft.[20] For the first time, the Court created through its ruling a test to evaluate such government actions, called the **clear and present danger test.** Under this standard, the government may silence speech or expression only when there is a clear and present danger that such speech will bring about some harm that the government has the power to prevent. In the *Schenck* case, the Court noted that the circumstances of war permit greater restrictions on the freedom of

Context

CIVIL LIBERTIES IN THE POST–ARAB SPRING EGYPT

In 1922, Egypt gained independence establishing a constitutional monarchy. The government held elections for its bicameral parliament until a military coup in 1952 brought Gamal Nasser to head a strong presidential government. He established a one-party socialist regime. Upon his death in 1970, Anwar al-Sadat assumed the office. Following the assassination of Sadat by Islamic extremists, Vice President Hosni Mubarak became president. During the presidencies of Nasser, Sadat, and Mubarak, multiparty parliamentary elections were held. However, civil liberties, such as freedom of the press, were limited. The government frequently cracked down on dissident groups, such as the Muslim Brotherhood. The government was allowed to tap phones, read mail, engage in warrantless searches, and detain suspects indefinitely. There was clear gender inequality under the law. In response to international pressure, Mubarak's administration held the first multiparty presidential elections in 2005. Mubarak won readily, but many observers accused the regime of election fraud.

How does a nation make the transition from providing order and security to uniformly protecting civil liberties?

In December 2010, a wave of protests called the Arab Spring spread across the Middle East, bringing much attention to youth frustration with the economy and political repression. In response to the uprising in Egypt, Hosni Mubarak stepped down and the interim government created a new constitution.

In 2012, the Muslim Brotherhood's Freedom and Justice Party and their leader Mohamed Morsi won elections that were widely regarded as free. The new government wrote a new constitution which was ratified with the overwhelming support of the voters. After a popular uprising against the Morsi government for granting itself unlimited presidential authority, confrontations between pro-Morsi and anti-Morsi supporters resulted in violent clashes over the next 7 months. By July 2013, a coup d'état removed President Morsi and the military installed its own regime. Morsi and his supporters were detained and civilian protests resulted in government violence against dissenters in which hundreds of police, citizens, insurgents, and military personnel have died. The military has blocked the public media and banned specific news outlets from reporting, including the international Arabic media network al-Jazeera. Neither the Morsi nor the military administration has protected the rights of dissidents or limited their own authority. Instead police abuses have been unchecked, dissenters persecuted, a group of young female protestors sentenced to a decade of imprisonment, and civil liberties continue to be diminished.

However, the Egyptian people remain optimistic about the potential for change. A September 2013 survey found that 66 percent of Egyptians valued a government that provided security and order, hoping for "a more inclusive democracy" with civilian leadership. They want to see a national reconciliation including the Muslim Brotherhood and the military. For many Egyptians, the immediate priority is job creation through a strengthened economy. For these citizens, continuous violence and unrest is only limiting progress toward this goal.

SOURCE: Arab American Institute, Zogby Research Services poll, "Egyptian Attitudes: September 2013."

speech than would be allowable during peacetime. The justices ruled that Schenck's actions could endanger the nation's ability to carry out the draft and prosecute the war.

Soon after the *Schenck* case, a majority of the justices adopted a far more restrictive test that made it easier to punish citizens for the content of their speech. This test, known as the **bad tendency test,** was extended in the case of Benjamin Gitlow, who was convicted of violating a New York State criminal anarchy law by publishing pamphlets calling for a revolutionary mass action to create a socialist government.[21] The political context of Gitlow's conviction is revealing: A so-called red scare—fears that the socialist revolution in the Soviet Union would spread to other nations with large populations of workers—was sweeping the nation. Gitlow's lawyer contended that there was no proof that Gitlow's pamphlet created a clear and present danger of a violent uprising. The Court disagreed, however, ruling that any speech that had the tendency to incite crime or disturb the public peace could be silenced.

bad tendency test
a standard extended in the 1925 case *Gitlow v. New York* whereby any speech that has the tendency to incite crime or disturb the public peace can be silenced

This highly restrictive test required only that the government demonstrate that some speech may at some time help to bring about harm. The threat did not need to be immediate or even direct. The test sacrificed the freedoms of speech and the press to concerns about public safety and protection of the existing order. The bad tendency test lasted only a short while; by the late 1930s, the Court had reverted to the clear and present danger test, which the justices interpreted more broadly to protect speech and participation. The relative peace and stability of the period between the two world wars is apparent in the Court's handling of speech and press cases, as the justices required government officials to demonstrate that the speech clearly posed a danger to public safety.

Even after the Court reverted to the clear and present danger test, however, it still allowed concerns about national security to control its handling of First Amendment cases. In the wake of World War II, a war of conflicting ideologies emerged between the United States and the Soviet Union. Termed the *Cold War* because it did not culminate in a direct military confrontation between the countries, this development nevertheless created a climate of fear and insecurity in both nations. Concerns about the spread of communism in the United States led to prosecutions of individuals deemed to be sympathetic to communism and socialism under the Smith Act of 1940. This federal law barred individuals from advocating or teaching about "the duty, necessity, desirability, or propriety of overthrowing or destroying any government in the United States by force or violence."

In the most important case of this period, the Supreme Court upheld the conviction of several individuals who were using the writings of German philosophers Karl Marx and Friedrich Engels, along with those of Soviet leaders Vladimir Lenin and Josef Stalin, to teach about socialism and communism.[22] In upholding the convictions, the justices found that although the use of these writings did not pose a risk of imminent danger to the government, it created the *probability* that such harm would result. The seriousness of the evil was key to the test that came out of this ruling, known as the **clear and probable danger test.** Because the government was suppressing speech to avoid the gravest danger, an armed takeover of the United States, the Supreme Court majority ruled that it was justified in its actions—even if the risk or probability of this result was relatively remote.

As the Cold War subsided and concerns diminished about a potential communist takeover of the United States, the Court shifted to a broader interpretation of the First Amendment speech and press protections. Beginning with *Brandenburg v. Ohio* (1969), the Court signaled that it would give more weight to First Amendment claims and less to government concerns about security and order. In this case, the Court considered the convictions of the leaders of an Ohio Ku Klux Klan group who were arrested after they made a speech at a televised rally, during which they uttered racist and anti-Semitic comments and showed guns and rifles. Local officials charged them with violating a state law that banned speech that disturbed the public peace and threatened armed overthrow. In overturning the convictions, the Court reverted to a strict reading of the clear and present danger test. The justices held that government officials had to demonstrate that the speech they sought to silence went beyond mere advocacy, or words, and that it created the risk of imminent disorder or lawlessness.[23]

THE STANDARD TODAY: THE IMMINENT LAWLESS ACTION TEST   The *Brandenburg* test, known as both the **imminent lawless action test** and the **incitement test,** altered the clear and present danger test by making it even more stringent. Specifically, after the *Brandenburg* decision, any government in the United States—national, state, or local—trying to silence speech would need to show that the risk of harm from the speech was highly likely and that the harm was imminent or immediate. The imminent lawless action test is the standard the courts use today to determine whether speech is protected from government interference.

Even though the *Brandenburg* test is well established, the issue of whether speech is protected continues to be debated. For example, since the September 11 attacks, public attention has increasingly focused on websites operated by terrorists and terrorist sympathizers, especially members of militant Islamic groups. Some of these sites carry radical messages; for example, one site urges viewers to eliminate all "enemies of Allah" by any necessary means and gives instructions on loading weapons. Do First Amendment guarantees protect such sites? What about websites that encouraged property damage against offices of the Democratic Party

clear and probable danger test
a standard established in the 1951 case *Dennis v. U.S.,* whereby the government could suppress speech to avoid grave danger, even if the probability of the dangerous result was relatively remote; replaced by the imminent lawless action (incitement) test in 1969

imminent lawless action test (incitement test)
a standard established in the 1969 *Brandenburg v. Ohio* case, whereby speech is restricted only if it goes beyond mere advocacy, or words, to create a high likelihood of imminent disorder or lawlessness

after the health care reform bill passed? Courts examining this question must determine not only whether the speech intends to bring about a bad result—most would agree that intent exists—but also whether the speech incites lawless action that is imminent.

Freedom of Speech

The freedom to speak publicly, even critically, about government and politics is central to the democratic process. Citizens cannot participate fully in a political system if they are unable to share information, opinions, advice, and calls to action. Citizens cannot hold government accountable if they cannot criticize government actions or demand change.

> Freedom of speech includes the right to speak critically about government policies. Here, a group seeking changes to the country's immigration policy exercises those rights by sponsoring a billboard in Florida. While U.S. population will increase by 50 percent by 2050, only 30 percent of current growth comes from new immigrants. What current issues are hot button topics for those exercising free speech rights today?

PURE SPEECH VERSUS SYMBOLIC SPEECH The Supreme Court has made a distinction between pure speech that is "just words" and advocacy that couples words with actions. With respect to civic discourse, both are important. When speech moves beyond words into the realm of action, it is considered to be **symbolic speech,** nonverbal "speech" in the form of an action such as picketing or wearing an armband to signify a protest.

symbolic speech
nonverbal "speech" in the form of an action such as picketing, flag burning, or wearing an armband to signify a protest

Unless words threaten imminent lawless action, the First Amendment will likely protect the speaker. But in civic discourse, words are often combined with action. For example, in the 1960s, antiwar protesters were arrested for burning their draft cards to demonstrate their refusal to serve in Vietnam, and public high school students were suspended from school for wearing black armbands to protest the war. When the two groups brought their cases to the Supreme Court, the justices had to determine whether their conduct rose to the level of political expression and merited First Amendment protection. Together, these cases help to define the parameters for symbolic speech.

In the first of these cases, *U.S. v. O'Brien,* the justices considered whether the government could punish several Vietnam War protesters for burning their draft cards in violation of the Selective Service Act, which made it a crime to "destroy or mutilate" those cards. The Court balanced the free expression guarantee against the government's need to prevent the destruction of the cards. Because the cards were critical to the nation's ability to raise an army, the Court ruled that the government had a compelling interest in preventing their destruction. Moreover, because the government had passed the Selective Service Act to facilitate the draft and not to suppress speech, the impact of the law on speech was incidental. When the justices balanced the government's interest in making it easy to raise an army against the incidental impact that this law had on speech, they found that the government's interest overrode that of the political protesters.[24]

In contrast, when the Court considered the other symbolic speech case of this era, *Tinker v. Des Moines,* they found that the First Amendment did protect the speech in question. In this case, the justices ruled that the political expression in the form of the students' wearing black armbands to school to protest the Vietnam War was protected.[25] On what basis did the justices distinguish the armbands in the *Tinker* case from the draft cards in the *O'Brien* case? They cited legitimate reasons for the government to ban the burning of draft cards in a time of war; but there were no comparable reasons to ban the wearing of armbands, apart from the school district's desire to curb or suppress political expression on school grounds. School officials could not show that the armbands had disrupted normal school activities.[26] For that reason, the Court argued, the symbolic speech in *Tinker* warranted more protection than that in *O'Brien.*

The highly controversial case of *Texas v. Johnson* (1989) tested the Court's commitment to protecting symbolic speech of a highly unpopular nature. At issue was a man's conviction under

> In 2011, the Supreme Court ruled in *Snyder v. Phelps* (131 S. Ct. 1207, 2011) that the First Amendment's guarantee of free speech protects Rev. Fred Phelps and his congregation's protests at military funerals and other visible events. The Kansas-based group typically carries signs stating "God Hates Fags" and "You're Going to Hell" to protest America's growing acceptance of homosexuality. The Court determined that the speech is protected as a matter of "public concern," as opposed to unprotected speech regarding matters of "purely private" interest.

commercial speech
advertising statements that describe products

libel
false written statements about others that harm their reputation

slander
false verbal statements about others that harm their reputation

obscenity
indecent or offensive speech or expression

state law for burning the American flag during the Republican National Convention in 1984 to emphasize his disagreement with the policies of the administration of President Ronald Reagan (1981–1989). The Supreme Court overturned the man's conviction, finding that the flag burning was political speech worthy of protection under the First Amendment.[27] After the *Johnson* decision, Congress quickly passed the Flag Protection Act in an attempt to reverse the Court's ruling. Subsequently, however, in the case of *U.S. v. Eichman* (1990), the Court struck down the new law by the same 5–4 majority as in the *Johnson* ruling.[28]

The decisions in these flag-burning cases were very controversial and prompted Congress to pursue the only remaining legal avenue to enact flag protection statutes—a constitutional amendment. Every other year from 1995 to 2006, the proposed amendment has received the two-thirds majority necessary for approval in the U.S. House of Representatives, but failed to achieve the same constitutionally required supermajority vote in the U.S. Senate.

NOT ALL SPEECH IS CREATED EQUAL: UNPROTECTED SPEECH The Supreme Court long ago rejected the extreme view that all speech should be free in the United States. Whereas *political speech* tends to be protected against government suppression, other forms of speech can be limited or prohibited.

The courts afford **commercial speech,** that is, advertising statements, limited protection under the First Amendment. According to the Supreme Court, commercial speech may be restricted as long as the restriction "seeks to implement a substantial government interest, directly advances that interest, and goes no further than necessary to accomplish its objective." Restrictions on tobacco advertising, for example, limit free speech in the interest of protecting the health of society. In 2010, the Supreme Court, in the controversial *Citizens United v. Federal Elections Commission* decision, revised its previous rulings and determined that the First Amendment also protected corporate spending during elections as a form of free speech. Legislation that limits such spending was an unconstitutional banning of political speech.[29]

Other forms of speech, including libel and slander, receive no protection under the First Amendment. **Libel** (written statements) and **slander** (verbal statements) are false statements that harm the reputation of another person. To qualify as libel or slander, the defamatory statement must be made publicly and with fault, meaning that reporters, for example, must undertake reasonable efforts to verify allegations. The statement must extend beyond mere name-calling or insults that cannot be proven true or false. Those who take a legal action on the grounds that they are victims of libel or slander, such as government officials, celebrities, and people involved with specific public controversies, are required to prove that the defendant acted with malice—with knowledge that the statement was false or recklessly disregarded the truth or falsity of the statement.

Obscenity, indecent or offensive speech or expression, is another form of speech that is not protected under the First Amendment. After many unsuccessful attempts to define obscenity, in 1973 the Supreme Court developed a three-part test in *Miller v. California*.[30] The Court ruled that a book, a film, or another form of expression is legally obscene if

- the average person applying contemporary standards finds that the work taken as a whole appeals to the prurient interest—that is, tends to excite unwholesome sexual desire;
- the work depicts or describes, in a patently offensive way, a form of sexual conduct specifically prohibited by an antiobscenity law;
- the work taken as a whole lacks serious literary, artistic, political, or scientific value.

Of course, these standards do not guarantee that people will agree on what materials are obscene. What is obscene to some may be acceptable to others. For that reason, the Court has been reluctant to limit free speech, even in the most controversial cases.

The Court may also ban speech known as **fighting words**—speech that inflicts injury or results in public disorder. The Court first articulated the fighting-words doctrine in *Chaplinsky v. New Hampshire* (1942). Walter Chaplinsky was convicted of violating a New Hampshire statute that prohibited the use of offensive, insulting language toward persons in public places after he made several inflammatory comments to a city official. The Court, in upholding the statute as constitutional, explained the limits of free speech: "These include the lewd and obscene, the profane, the libelous, and the insulting or fighting words—those which by their very utterance inflict injury or tend to incite an immediate breach of the peace."[31] Thus the Court ruled that, like slander, libel, and obscenity, "fighting words" do not advance the democratic goals of free speech. Cross burning, for example, has been a form of symbolic speech that in the United States has come to represent racial violence and intimidation against African Americans and other vulnerable groups. In 2005, the Supreme Court in *Virginia v. Black* found that a state could ban cross burning when it was used to threaten or attempt to silence other individuals, but that the state law could not assume all cross burnings attempt to communicate that message.[32]

fighting words
speech that is likely to bring about public disorder or chaos; the Supreme Court has held that such speech may be banned in public places to ensure the preservation of public order

Even the types of "unprotected speech" we have considered enjoy broad protection under the law. Although cigarette ads are banned from television, many products are sold through every media outlet imaginable. Though a tabloid such as the *National Inquirer* sometimes faces lawsuits for the false stories it prints, most celebrities do not pursue legal action because of the high burden of proving that the paper knew the story was false, intended to damage the subject's reputation, and in fact caused real harm. Even though network television is censored for broadcasting objectionable material, the Supreme Court has ruled that the government cannot ban (adult) pornography on the Internet or on paid cable television channels.[33] The Court even struck down a ban on the transmission of "virtual" child pornography, arguing that no real children were harmed in the creation of these photographic or computer-generated images.[34] And, despite continued reaffirmation of the fighting-words doctrine, the Supreme Court has declined to uphold any convictions for fighting words since *Chaplinsky*. In short, the Court is reluctant to do anything that might limit the content of adults' free speech and expression, even when that speech is unpopular or offensive.

Freedom of Assembly and Redress of Grievances

The First Amendment says that people have the freedom to assemble peaceably and to seek redress of (compensation for) grievances against the government; yet, there are limits placed on assembly. As the Supreme Court has considered free assembly cases, it has been most concerned about ensuring that individuals and groups can get together to discuss their concerns and that they can take action in the public arena that advances their political goals.

The Court's stance in free speech cases provides insight into its leanings in cases concerning freedom of assembly. The Court is keenly aware of the need for order in public forums and will clamp down on speech that is intended and likely to incite public unrest and anger. That is one reason the Court has reaffirmed the fighting-words doctrine. Although officials cannot censor speech before it occurs, they can take action to limit speech once it becomes apparent that public disorder is going to erupt. In its rulings, the Court has also allowed content-neutral **time, place, and manner restrictions**—regulations regarding when, where, or how expression may occur. Such restrictions do not target speech based on content, and to stand up in court, they must be applied in a content-neutral manner. For example, people have the right to march in protest, but not while chanting into bullhorns at four o'clock in the morning in a residential neighborhood.

time, place, and manner restrictions
regulations regarding when, where, or how expression may occur; must be content neutral

The Court's rulings in these various cases illustrate how the government is balancing the freedom of public assembly against other concerns, notably public safety and the right of an individual to be left alone. The Court is carefully weighing the freedoms of one group of individuals against another and attempting to ensure the protection of free public expression.

Freedom of the Press

Throughout American history, the press has played a crucial role in the larger debate about political expression. Before the War for Independence, when the British monarchy sought to clamp down on political dissent in the colonies, the king and Parliament quickly recognized the urgency of silencing the press. A free press is essential to democratic ideals, and democracy cannot survive when a government controls the press. The First Amendment's guarantees of a free press ensure not only that American government remains accountable to its constituents but also that the people hear competing ideas about how to deal with matters of public concern. Increasingly, the Internet has become the place where ordinary citizens share their views on important political issues.

Ensuring a free press can complicate the work of government. Consider the challenge presented to the George W. Bush administration when the *New York Times* broke a story in late 2005 that the National Security Agency (NSA) had been using futuristic spy technology against thousands of individuals inside the United States.[35,36] The NSA is responsible for monitoring the communications of foreigners outside U.S. borders and does not have authority to engage in surveillance of Americans in the United States. Moreover, the Fourth Amendment protects American citizens against searches without either a warrant or a court order. Despite claims to the contrary during his campaign, President Obama has allowed the NSA to expand its surveillance activities (see "Thinking Critically About Democracy").

Certain well-established principles govern freedom of the press in the United States. First and foremost, the courts almost never allow the government to engage in prior restraint. **Prior restraint** means censorship—the attempt to block the publication of material that is considered to be harmful. The Supreme Court established this rule against censorship in 1931 in the landmark case of *Near v. Minnesota*. After editor Jay Near wrote a story in the *Saturday Press* alleging that Jews were responsible for corruption, bribery, and prostitution in Minneapolis, a state judge barred all future sales of the newspaper. The Court overturned the state judge's ruling, finding that the sole purpose of the order was to suppress speech. Because freedom of the press has strong historical foundations, the Court concluded, censorship is clearly prohibited.

In the *Near* ruling, the Court recognized, however, that there might be times when governmental officials could limit the publication of certain stories. Specifically, such censorship might be justified under extraordinary circumstances related to ensuring public safety or national security or in cases involving obscenity. In reality, though, the Court has disallowed prior restraint in the vast majority of cases. For example, in the most important case examining the national security exception, *New York Times v. U.S.* (1971), the Court rejected the government's attempt to prevent publication of documents that detailed the history of the United States' involvement in Vietnam. In this case, also known as the *Pentagon Papers* case, the government argued that censorship was necessary to prevent "irreparable injury" to national security. But the Court dismissed that argument, asserting that full disclosure was in the interest of all Americans and that publication of the documents could contribute to the ongoing debate about the U.S. role in the Vietnam War.[37] In their ruling, the justices recognized that some materials are clearly necessary for full and fair discussion of issues facing the nation, whereas others are far less important to political discourse.

The Court is far more willing to allow the government to impose constraints on broadcast media than on print media. Why should a distinction be made between print and broadcast media? Probably the most important justification is that only a limited number of channels can be broadcast, and the government is responsible for parceling out those channels. Because the public owns the airwaves, the people may also impose reasonable regulations on those who are awarded licenses to operate broadcast channels.

The Court views the Internet to be more like print media than like broadcast media. Thus far, the Court has signaled its interpretation that the Internet is an enormous resource for democratic forums, one that allows users access to virtually unlimited sites at very low cost (*Reno v. ACLU,* 1997). The Court's assumption is that print media and the Internet provide relatively cheap and virtually unlimited access and enable people to tap easily into discussions about issues facing the nation. In contrast, broadcast media, with much scarcer channels, represent a much more limited arena for dialogue and thus can reasonably be regulated.

Was Edward Snowden's Release of Classified Security Documents the Act of a Patriot?

The Issue: Edward Snowden was an IT contractor with the National Security Agency (NSA) who downloaded approximately 200,000 classified documents revealing that the NSA is engaged in large-scale surveillance of both American citizens and residents of other countries. The NSA's meta-data collection includes most of the phone calls made in the United States (the numbers involved and length of call, not the conversation itself), e-mail, Facebook posts, text messages (with the cooperation of many social media platforms such as Google and Facebook), raw Internet traffic, and an unknown number of phone conversations. Snowden also had information on the surveillance activities of other countries. He fled the United States to Hong Kong and has been slowly sharing this information with *The Guardian* and *The Washington Post.* When the United States announced its plan to prosecute him for espionage, he escaped to Russia, a country that does not have an extradition agreement with the United States.

Yes: Western governments and intelligence agencies have been expanding the scope of their own power, eroding privacy rights, civil liberties, and public control of policy. For years, people have feared wholesale surveillance of entire populations, militarization of the Internet, and an end of privacy. The government has taken these actions under the guise of "national security," a justification that limits debate and guarantees governments cannot be held accountable because their actions must be kept secret. There are secret laws, secret interpretations of secret laws by secret courts, and no effective congressional oversight. The media have ignored the unprecedented persecution of whistleblowers, initiated by the Bush administration and severely accelerated by the Obama administration, while record numbers of well-meaning people are charged with serious felonies simply for letting their fellow citizens know what is happening. Blowing the whistle on powerful entities comes at a high personal price, but it remains the last avenue for truth, balanced debate, and the protection of civil liberties. Since the summer of 2013, the public has witnessed a shift in debate over these matters due to Edward Snowden's actions. He not only blew the whistle on the litany of government abuses, but made sure to supply a multitude of supporting documents to a few trustworthy journalists. The echoes of his actions are still heard around the world—and there are still many revelations to come.[*]

No: Edward Snowden is a spy. The damage he is doing is similar to that done by Cold War government officials who sold information to the Soviet Union and revealed the names of American agents.

Snowden is not dealing in human information but electronic intelligence, which is now more important, but the results are the same, compromising American security interests. Snowden was able to claim the moral high ground when spilling out the inner workings and policies of the U.S. and British security agencies to the world. However, he lost the right to be called a whistleblower when he fled to negotiate first with the Chinese and then the Russians for political asylum, taking with him all the information. Whistleblowers stand up and face the consequences; Snowden crawled out and ran away. Accessing secret information and downloading it to be shared with the press is treason. Snowden justified his actions saying: "I don't want to live in a society that does these sort of things [surveillance on its citizens]. . . . My sole motive is to inform the public as to that which is done in their name and that which is done against them." Presumably that is why he is now living in Russia, that Mecca of human rights.[**]

Other Approaches: Even if Snowden was wrong to disclose this material, the media had a responsibility to make this information public, after carefully evaluating and redacting any material that could be explicitly detrimental to national security. The current debate has ignored the measures put in place to secure privacy as these data are collected. In light of the 100 billion e-mails sent daily, security agencies are only interested in information that will address the next security threat, not private conversations of law-abiding citizens.

What do you think?

1. What questions regarding the boundaries between liberty and security do the revelations made by Edward Snowden raise?

2. Do you believe anyone is ever justified in releasing classified information to the general public? If so, under what circumstances? If not, how can the government be held accountable for its covert activities?

3. How do you draw the line between a whistleblower and a spy?

[*]Drake, Thomas, Daniel Ellsberg, Katharine Gun, Peter Kofod, Ray McGovern, Jesselyn Radack, and Coleen Rowley. 2013. "Former whistleblowers: open letter to intelligence employees after Snowden," *The Guardian,* December 11, www.theguardian.com/commentisfree/2013/dec/11/whistleblowers-open-letter-after-snowden-revelations.

[**]Boffey, Chris. 2013. "Why Edward Snowden is not a patriot, whistleblower or hero—but a spy," *The Drum,* September 3, www.thedrum.com/opinion/2013/09/03/why-edward-snowden-not-patriot-whistleblower-or-hero-spy.

Freedoms of Religion, Privacy, and Criminal Due Process: Encouraging Community and Civic Engagement

The Constitution's framers understood that the government they were creating could use its powers to single out certain groups for either favorable or unfavorable treatment and in that way could interfere with the creation of community—and with citizens' engagement within that community. The founders' commitment to community building and citizens' engagement lies at the heart of several constitutional amendments in the Bill of Rights. Specifically these are the amendments establishing the freedom of religion, the right to privacy, and the right to due process for individuals in the criminal justice system.

The First Amendment and the Freedom of Religion

The religion clauses of the First Amendment—the establishment clause and the free exercise clause—essentially do two things. First, they bar the government from establishing or supporting any one religious sect over another, and second, they ensure that individuals are not hindered in the exercise of their religion. Whereas the establishment clause requires that the government be neutral toward religious institutions, favoring neither one specific religion over others nor all religious groups over nonreligious groups, the free exercise clause prohibits the government from taking action that is hostile toward individuals' practice of their religion. As we now consider, there is tension between these two clauses.

establishment clause
First Amendment clause that bars the government from passing any law "respecting an establishment of religion"; often interpreted as a separation of church and state but increasingly questioned

THE ESTABLISHMENT CLAUSE   Stating only that "Congress shall make no law respecting an establishment of religion," the **establishment clause** does little to clarify what the relationship between church and state should be. The Constitution's authors wanted to ensure that Congress could not create a national religion, as a number of European powers (notably France and Spain) had done; the framers sought to avoid that level of government entanglement in religious matters. Further, many colonists had immigrated to America to escape religious persecution in Europe, and although many were deeply religious, uncertainty prevailed about the role that government should play in the practice of religion. That uncertainty, too, is reflected in the brevity of the establishment clause. The question arises, does the clause prohibit the government from simply preferring one sect over another, or is it broader, encompassing any kind of support of religion?

This is a crucial question because religious institutions have always been important forums for community building and engagement in the United States. Americans continue to be a very religious people. In 2009, over 81 percent of Americans surveyed said religion was fairly or very important in their lives.[38] But even given their strong religious affiliations, most Americans believe in some degree of separation between religious organizations and the government. The actual debate has been about how much separation the establishment clause requires.

Over time, scholars and lawyers have considered three possible interpretations of the establishment clause. One interpretation, called separationism, is that the establishment clause requires a *strict separation of church and state* and bars most or all government support for religious sects. Supporters of the strict separationist view invoke the writings of Thomas Jefferson, James Madison, and others that call for a "wall of separation" between church and state.[39] They also point to societies outside the United States in which religious leaders dictate how citizens may dress, act, and pray as examples of what can happen without strict separation.

A second, and more flexible, interpretation allows the government to offer support to religious sects as long as that support is neutral and not biased toward one sect. This interpretation, known as *neutrality* or the *preferential treatment standard,* would permit government support provided that this support extended to all religious groups. The third interpretation is the most flexible and reads the establishment clause as barring only establishment of a state religion. This interpretation, known as *accommodationism,* allows the government to offer support to any or all religious groups provided that this support does not rise to the level of recognizing an official religion.[40]

> Throughout the first decades of the 21st century, the Supreme Court wrestled with protecting student-initiated prayer and study, as demonstrated by this picture of a "Rally Round the Flagpole" prayer. Now the Court is wrestling with new issues, such as whether or not religious memorials from the mid-20th century are unlawful establishments of religion or traditional historical expressions of belief now devoid of religious content. The constitutionality of Southern California's Mt. Soledad Memorial, which honors Korean War veterans, is under challenge. What is the difference between traditions of belief and religious endorsement?

Which of these three vastly different interpretations of the establishment clause is correct? Over time, the Supreme Court has shifted back and forth in its opinions, usually depending on the kind of government support in question. Overall, the courts have rejected the strictest interpretation of the establishment clause, which would ban virtually any form of aid to religion. Instead, they have allowed government support for religious schools, programs, and institutions if the support advances a secular (nonreligious) goal and does not specifically endorse a particular religious belief.

For example, in 1974, the Court upheld a New Jersey program that provided funds to the parents of parochial school students to pay for bus transportation to and from school.[41] The Court reasoned that the program was necessary to help students to get to school safely and concluded that if the state withdrew funding for any of these programs for parochial school students, it would be impossible to operate these schools. The impact would be the hindrance of the free exercise of religion for students and their parents.

In another landmark case, *Lemon v. Kurtzman* (1971), however, the Court struck down a state program that used cigarette taxes to reimburse parochial schools for the costs of teachers' salaries and textbooks. The Court found that subsidizing parochial schools furthered a process of religious teaching and that the "continuing state surveillance" that would be necessary to enforce the specific provisions of the laws would inevitably entangle the state in religious affairs.[42]

In the *Lemon* case ruling, the Court refined the establishment clause standard to include three considerations.

- Does the state program have a secular, as opposed to a religious, purpose?
- Does it have as its principal effect the advancement of religion?
- Does the program create an excessive entanglement between church and state?

This three-part test is known as the ***Lemon* test.** The programs most likely to withstand scrutiny under the establishment clause are those that have a secular purpose, have only an incidental effect on the advancement of religion, and do not excessively entangle church and state.

More recently, the Court upheld an Ohio program that gave vouchers to parents to offset the cost of parochial schooling.[43] The justices ruled that the purpose of the program was secular, not religious, because it was intended to provide parents with an alternative to the Cleveland public schools. Any aid to religious institutions—in this case, mostly Catholic schools—was indirect, because the primary beneficiaries were the students themselves. Finally, there was little entanglement between the church and state, because the parents received the vouchers based on financial need and then were free to use these vouchers as they pleased. There was no direct relationship between the religious schools and the state.

Lemon test
a three-part test established by the Supreme Court in the 1971 case *Lemon v. Kurtzman* to determine whether government aid to parochial schools is constitutional; the test is also applied to other cases involving the establishment clause

If a government program offers financial support, the Court has tended to evaluate the program by using either the preferential treatment standard or the accommodationist standard. If a program or policy involves prayer in the schools or issues related to the curriculum, however, the Court has adopted a standard that looks more like strict separationism. Table 4.4 summarizes the Court's decisions in a variety of school-related free exercise and establishment clause cases.

As Table 4.4 illustrates, a series of cases beginning with *Engel v. Vitale* (1962) has barred formalized prayer in the schools, finding that such prayer has a purely religious purpose and that prayer is intended to advance religious, as opposed to secular, ideals.[44] For that reason, the Court has barred school-organized prayer in public elementary and secondary schools on the grounds that it constitutes a state endorsement of religion. Student-organized prayer is constitutional because the state is not engaging in any coercion by mandating or encouraging student participation.

Recently, courts have begun to grapple with the decision of some school boards to mandate the inclusion of intelligent design in the curriculum.[45] **Intelligent design** is the assertion that the apparent design in the universe and in living things is the product of an intelligent cause rather than of an undirected process such as natural selection. Though not stated by its primary proponents, many supporters believe that the designer is God, and they seek to redefine science to accept supernatural explanations.

Advocates of intelligent design claim that unlike **creationism,** which defends a literal interpretation of the biblical story of Genesis, intelligent design is a scientific theory. For that reason, they say, school boards should be permitted to include it in the curriculum, alongside evolution. Opponents claim that intelligent design is just another form of creationism, because it is based upon a

intelligent design
theory that the apparent design in the universe and in living things is the product of an intelligent cause rather than of an undirected process such as natural selection; its primary proponents believe that the designer is God and seek to redefine science to accept supernatural explanations

creationism
theory of the creation of the earth and humankind based on a literal interpretation of the biblical story of Genesis

TABLE 4.4

Religion and Schools: Permissible and Impermissible Activities

PUBLIC FUNDING NOT PERMITTED	SUPREME COURT CASE	YEAR
Parochial school salaries	*Lemon v. Kurtzman*	1971
Parochial school textbooks	*Lemon v. Kurtzman*	1971

PUBLIC FUNDING PERMITTED	SUPREME COURT CASE	YEAR
Parochial school busing	*Everson v. Board of Education*	1947
Parochial/private school computers	*Mitchell v. Helms*	2000
Public/private school vouchers	*Zelman v. Simmons-Harris*	2002

PUBLIC SCHOOL ACTIVITIES NOT PERMITTED	SUPREME COURT CASE	YEAR
Requiring all students to say the Pledge	*W. Virginia Board of Ed. v. Barnette*	1943
Teacher-led nondenominational prayer	*Engel v. Vitale*	1962
Banning the teaching of evolution	*Epperson v. Arkansas*	1968
Requiring Ten Commandments posting	*Stone v. Graham*	1980
Moment of silence for voluntary prayer	*Wallace v. Jaffree*	1985
Requiring teaching of creationism	*Edward v. Aguillard*	1987
Official graduation ceremony prayers	*Lee v. Weisman*	1992
Student-led prayers using PA system	*Santa Fe School District v. Doe*	2000

PUBLIC SCHOOL ACTIVITIES PERMITTED	SUPREME COURT CASE	YEAR
Off-campus release-time religion classes	*Zorach v. Clauson*	1952
After-school student-led religion club	*Board of Education of Westside Community Schools v. Mergens*	1990
Use of public school building by religious groups (after hours)	*Lamb's Chapel v. Center Moriches School District*	1993
Public school teachers teaching in parochial schools	*Agostini v. Felton*	1997
Voluntary after-school Bible study	*Good News Club v. Milford Central School*	2001

belief in a divine being, does not generate any predictions, and cannot be tested by experiment. Mandating that schools teach intelligent design, critics argue, constitutes an endorsement of religion by the state.

THE FREE EXERCISE CLAUSE The tension between the establishment and free exercise clauses arises because the establishment clause bars the state from helping religious institutions, whereas the **free exercise clause** makes it illegal for the government to enact laws prohibiting the free practice of religion by individuals. Establishment clause cases often raise free exercise claims, and so courts must frequently consider whether, by banning state aid, they are interfering with the free exercise of religion.

Although free exercise and establishment cases raise many of the same concerns, they are different kinds of cases, whose resolution depends on distinct legal tests. Establishment clause cases typically involve well-established and well-known religious institutions. Because establishment clause cases often center on state aid to religious schools, many involve the Roman Catholic Church, which administers the largest number of private elementary and secondary schools in the country. In contrast, free exercise clause cases tend to involve less mainstream religious groups, among them Mormons, Jehovah's Witnesses, Christian Scientists, and Amish. These groups' practices tend to be less well known—or more controversial. For example, free exercise clause cases have involved the right to practice polygamy, to use hallucinogens, to refuse conventional medical care for a child, and to refuse to salute the flag.

The Supreme Court has refused to accept that the government is barred from *ever* interfering with religious exercise. Free exercise claims are difficult to settle because they require that courts balance the individual's right to free practice of religion against the government's need to adopt some policy or program. First and foremost, the Court has always distinguished between religious beliefs, which government may not interfere with, and religious actions, which government is permitted to regulate. For example, although adults may refuse lifesaving medical care on the basis of their own religious beliefs, they may not refuse medical procedures required to save the lives of their children.[46]

In assessing those laws that interfere with religiously motivated action, the Court has distinguished between laws that are neutral and generally applicable to all religious sects and laws that single out one sect for unfavorable treatment. In *Employment Division, Department of Human Resources v. Smith* (1990), the Court allowed the state of Oregon to deny unemployment benefits to two substance-abuse counselors who were fired from their jobs after using peyote as part of their religious practice. Oregon refused to provide benefits because the two men had been fired for engaging in an illegal activity. The Court concluded that there was no free exercise challenge, because Oregon had good reason for denying benefits to lawbreakers who had been fired from their jobs. The justices concluded that the state was simply applying a neutral and generally applicable law to the men as opposed to singling them out for bad treatment.[47] One consequence of this case was that several states, including Oregon, passed laws excluding members of the Native American Church, who smoke peyote as part of traditional religious rites, from being covered by their controlled-substance laws.

Then Now Next

How Does the Changing Religious Affiliation of Americans Affect the First Amendment?

	Then (2000)	Now
Protestant	54%	51%
Catholic	24	24
Jewish	2	2
Other faith	5	4
None	14	20

WHAT'S NEXT?

> As Americans' religious affiliations continue to slowly decline, what might be the implications for the First Amendment? Will the battles around the free exercise clause and the establishment clause become more intense or less relevant?

> The Millennial generation has the highest levels of nonaffiliation of any generation previously. What might the consequences be for debates surrounding the First Amendment?

SOURCES: All data derived from the General Social Survey: The Association of Religion Data Archives, www.thearda.com/quickstats/qs_101_t.asp; and "More Americans Have No Religious Preference: Key Findings from the 2012 General Social Survey," The Institute for the Study of Societal Issues, 2013, http://issi.berkeley.edu/sites/default/files/shared/docs/Hout%20et%20al_No%20Relig%20Pref%202012_Release%20Mar%202013.pdf.

free exercise clause
First Amendment clause prohibiting the government from enacting laws prohibiting an individual's practice of his or her religion; often in contention with the establishment clause

In summary, people are free to hold and profess their own beliefs, to build and actively participate in religious communities, and to allow their religious beliefs to inform their participation in politics and civil society. However, individual *actions* based on religious beliefs may be limited if those actions conflict with existing laws that are neutrally applied in a nondiscriminatory fashion.

The Right to Privacy

So far in this section, we have explored the relationship between civil liberties and some key themes of this book: civic participation, inclusiveness, community building, and community engagement. We now shift our focus somewhat to consider the **right to privacy,** the right of an individual to be left alone and to make decisions freely, without the interference of others. Privacy is a core principle for most Americans, and the right to make decisions, especially about intimate or personal matters, is at the heart of this right. Yet the right to privacy is also necessary for genuine inclusiveness and community engagement, because it ensures that each individual is able to act autonomously and to make decisions about how he or she will interact with others.

The right to privacy is highly controversial and the subject of much public debate. In large part, the reason is that this right is tied to some of the most divisive issues of our day, including abortion, aid in dying, and sexual orientation. The right to privacy is also controversial because, unlike the freedoms of speech, the press, assembly, and religion, it is not mentioned explicitly anywhere in the Constitution. A further reason for the debate surrounding the right to privacy is that the Supreme Court has only recently recognized it.

THE EMERGENT RIGHT TO PRIVACY For more than 100 years, Supreme Court justices and lower-court judges have concluded that the right to privacy is implied in all the other liberties spelled out in the Bill of Rights. Not until the landmark Supreme Court case *Griswold v. Connecticut* (1965) did the courts firmly establish the right to privacy. The issue in this case may seem strange to us today: whether the state of Connecticut had the power to prohibit married couples from using birth control. In their decision, the justices concluded that the state law violated the privacy right of married couples by preventing them from seeking to access birth control, and the Court struck down the Connecticut prohibition. The Court argued that the right to privacy was inherent in many of the other constitutional guarantees, most importantly the First Amendment freedom of association, the Third Amendment right to be free from the quartering of soldiers, the Fourth Amendment right to be free from unreasonable searches and seizures, the Fifth Amendment protection against self-incrimination, and the Ninth Amendment assurance of rights not explicitly listed in the Bill of Rights. Justice William O. Douglas and his colleagues effectively argued that a zone of privacy surrounded every person in the United States and that government could not pass laws that encroached upon this zone.[48]

In its ruling, the Court asserted that the right to privacy existed quite apart from the law. It was implicit in the Bill of Rights and fundamental to the American system of law and justice. The right to privacy hinged in large part on the right of individuals to associate with one another, and specifically the right of marital partners to engage in intimate association.

In a 1984 case, the Supreme Court ruled that the Constitution protects two kinds of freedom of association: (1) intimate associations and (2) expressive associations.[49] The protection of intimate associations allows Americans to maintain private human relationships as part of their personal liberty. The protection of expressive associations allows people to form associations with others and to practice their First Amendment freedoms of speech, assembly, petition, and religion.

THE RIGHT TO PRIVACY APPLIED TO OTHER ACTIVITIES The challenge for the Court since *Griswold* has been to determine which activities fall within the scope of the privacy right, and that question has placed the justices at the center of some of the most controversial issues of the day. For example, the first attempt to extend the privacy right, which raised the question of whether the right protected abortion, remains at least as controversial today as it was in 1973 when the Court decided the first abortion rights case, *Roe v. Wade*.[50] In *Roe* and the many abortion cases the Court has heard since, the justices have tried to establish whether a woman's right to abortion takes precedence over any interests the state may have in either the woman's health or the fetus's life. Over time, the Court has adopted a compromise position by rejecting the view

right to privacy
the right of an individual to be left alone and to make decisions freely, without the interference of others

that the right to abortion is absolute and by attempting to determine when states can regulate, or even prohibit, access to abortion. In 1992, the Court established the "undue burden" test, which asks whether a state abortion law places a "substantial obstacle in the path of a woman seeking an abortion before the fetus attains viability."[51] Although the Court used this standard to strike down spousal notification requirements, it has upheld other requirements imposed by some states, including waiting periods, mandatory counseling, and parental consent.

After the citizens of Colorado and Mississippi rejected state constitutional amendments designed to ensure that legal personhood begins at conception or fertilization, 11 states rejected similar referendums on the 2012 ballot. North Dakota voters stand to vote on a personhood amendment in 2014. Advocates emphasize that such state constitutional amendments will effectively ban abortion and expand fetal rights; challengers note the vagueness of the language, the unknown consequences of expanding the legal definition of personhood, and the potential of indirectly banning some forms of birth control and in vitro fertilization, plus the potential of criminal charges being filed against pregnant women engaging in behavior that is perceived as risky.

The Court has also stepped gingerly around other privacy rights, such as the right to choose one's sexual partners and the right to terminate medical treatment or engage in physician-assisted suicide. Both of these rights have been presented to the Court as hinging on the much broader right to privacy. With respect to the right to terminate medical treatment, the Court has been fairly clear. Various Court decisions have confirmed that as long as an individual is competent to terminate treatment, the state may not stop him or her from taking this action, even if stopping treatment will lead to the person's death.[52]

>Public debate over abortion was not settled by the Supreme Court's 1973 decision in *Roe v. Wade*. In these photos taken more than three decades later, pro-life and pro-choice activists in Washington, D.C., hold signs supporting their differing viewpoints. Abortion rights advocates frame the issue in terms of a woman's right to privacy and to control her own body without interference from the government. Abortion rights opponents view abortion as murder and frame the issue in terms of the rights of an unborn child. Where do you believe the privacy line should be drawn in the question of abortion?

The Court has been less clear in its rulings when an incompetent person's right is advanced by another individual, such as a spouse, a parent, or a child. In these circumstances, the Court has accepted the state's argument that before treatment may be terminated, the state may require that the person seeking to end life show that his or her loved one would have wanted that course of action.[53] When a person's wishes are not clear, loved ones may wage legal battles over whether to discontinue life support.

In cases involving the right to engage in consensual sexual activities with a partner of one's choosing, the Supreme Court has also employed a less than absolute approach. For many years, the Court allowed states to criminalize homosexual activity, finding that the right to engage in consensual sexual activity did not extend to same-sex partners.[54] In a 2003 case, *Lawrence v. Texas,* the Court changed course by ruling that the right to engage in intimate sexual activity was protected as a liberty right, especially when the activity occurred inside one's home, and that states could not criminalize this activity.[55] Since that decision, rights activists have worked through the courts and state and federal legislatures to secure for same-sex partners the same rights that heterosexual couples enjoy, including benefits provided by group health insurance and marriage. Marriage is regulated by the states, and there is a wide range of state laws pertaining to marriage; many of these laws were passed only recently. The *Lawrence* decision aside, states are still free to prohibit a range of sexual activities, including prostitution, child sexual abuse, and sex in public places.[56] In the Court's view, these activities can be prohibited primarily because they are not consensual or do not take place in the home, a place that accords special protection by the privacy right.

The right to privacy remains very controversial. Cases brought under the right to privacy tend to link this right with some other civil liberty, such as the protection against unreasonable search and seizure, the right to free speech, or the protection against self-incrimination. In other words, the privacy right, which the justices themselves created, seems to need buttressing by other rights that the Bill of Rights *explicitly* establishes. The explanation for this development may be the contentiousness of Americans' civic discourse about abortion, aid in dying, and other privacy issues. In short, continuing civic disagreement may have forced the Court to fall back on rights that are well established and more widely accepted.

GOVERNMENT USE OF SOCIAL MEDIA IN INVESTIGATIONS Public discourse about privacy is constantly evolving as people voluntarily share more and more information about themselves through online networking sites such as Facebook, MySpace, Twitter, LinkedIn, and now Google+. Users of such sites and bloggers share stories, photos, and videos of themselves—as well as of others, who may be unaware that they are the subject of a posting, a blog, or a video. Civil libertarians worry about the misuse and theft of personal information in a high-tech society where people's financial, employment, consumer, legal, and personal histories are so easily accessible.

In 2013, global media organizations disclosed evidence that the National Security Agency had tracked and reviewed international and domestic phone calls, texts messages, and e-mails of an unknown number of Americans without first obtaining a warrant.[57] Social media platforms operated by such entities as Facebook, Apple, Microsoft, LinkedIn, Twitter, Google, and Yahoo are seeking to provide greater transparency as to their cooperation with governmental requests for user information.[58] However, governmental requests for personal data continue to increase. Without legislation to determine when and if social media organizations may deny warrantless requests and without legislation that mandates public disclosure of the scope of inquiries, no clear limits exist on the government.

The Fourth, Fifth, Sixth, and Eighth Amendments: Ensuring Criminal Due Process

The last category of civil liberties that bear directly on civic engagement consists of the criminal due process protections established in the Fourth, Fifth, Sixth, and Eighth Amendments. Does it surprise you that so many of the Bill of Rights amendments focus on the rights of individuals accused of crimes? The context for this emphasis is the founders' concern with how the British monarchy had abused its power and used criminal law to impose its will on the American colonists. The British government had used repeated trials, charges of treason, and imprisonment without bail to stifle political dissent. The founders therefore wanted to ensure that there were effective checks on the power of the federal government, especially in the creation and enforcement of criminal law. As we have seen, the Bill of Rights amendments were incorporated to apply to the states and to their criminal codes through the process of selective incorporation. Thus, criminal due process protections are the constitutional limits imposed on law enforcement personnel.

These four amendments together are known as the **criminal due process rights** because they establish the guidelines that the government must follow in investigating, bringing to trial, and punishing individuals who violate criminal law. Each amendment guides the government in administering some facet of law enforcement, and all are intended to ensure justice and fairness in the administration of the law. Criminal due process is essential to guarantee that individuals can participate in the larger society and that no one person is singled out for better or worse treatment under the law. Like the First Amendment, due process protects political speech and freedom. Without these liberties, government officials could selectively target those who disagree with the laws and policies they advocate.

Moreover, without these rights, there would be little to stop the government from using criminal law to punish those who want to take action that is protected by the other amendments we have examined in this chapter. For example, what good would it do to talk about the freedom of speech if the government could isolate or punish someone who spoke out critically against it without having to prove in a public venue that the speech threatened public safety or national security? The criminal due process protections are essential to ensuring meaningful participation and engagement in the larger community and to safeguarding justice and fairness.

criminal due process rights
safeguards for those accused of crime; these rights constrain government conduct in investigating crimes, trying cases, and punishing offenders

THE FOURTH AMENDMENT AND THE PROTECTION AGAINST UNREASONABLE SEARCHES AND SEIZURES
The Fourth Amendment requires police to get a warrant before engaging in a search and guides law enforcement personnel in conducting criminal investigations and in searching an individual's body or property. It has its roots in colonial history—specifically, in the British government's abuse of its law enforcement powers to prosecute and punish American colonists suspected of being disloyal.

The Fourth Amendment imposes significant limits on law enforcement. In barring police from conducting any unreasonable searches and seizures, it requires that they show probable cause that a crime has been committed before they can obtain a search warrant. The warrant ensures that police officers can gather evidence only when they have probable cause. Further, a judicially created ruling known as the **exclusionary rule** compels law enforcers to carry out searches properly. Established for federal prosecutions in 1914, the exclusionary rule forbids the courts to admit illegally seized evidence during trial.[59] This rule was extended to state court proceedings in the Supreme Court decision *Mapp v. Ohio* (1961).[60] In this case, the Court overturned an Ohio court's conviction of Dollree Mapp for the possession of obscene materials. Police had found pornographic books in Mapp's apartment after searching it without a search warrant and despite the defendant's refusal to let them in. Critics of the exclusionary rule note that securing a warrant is not always necessary or feasible and that guilty people sometimes go free because of procedural technicalities. They argue that reasonable searches should not be defined solely by the presence of a court-ordered search warrant.[61]

What are "reasonable" and "unreasonable" searches under the Fourth Amendment? Over time, the U.S. Supreme Court has established criteria to guide both police officers and judges hearing cases. In the strictest definition of reasonableness, there is a warrant: where there is no warrant, the search is considered to be unreasonable. However, the Supreme Court has ruled that even without a warrant, some searches would still be reasonable. In 1984, for example, the Court held that illegally obtained evidence could be admitted at trial if law enforcers could prove that they would have obtained the evidence legally anyway.[62] In another case the same year, the Court created a "good faith" exception to the exclusionary rule by upholding the use of evidence obtained with a technically incorrect warrant, because the police officer had acted in good faith.[63]

More broadly, a warrantless search is valid if the person subjected to it has no reasonable expectation of privacy in the place or thing being searched. From colonial times to the

exclusionary rule
criminal procedural rule stating that evidence obtained illegally cannot be used in a trial

> Jonathan Fleming, who had already served 24 years in prison for a crime he didn't commit, hugging his mother. Disregarding the constitutional rights of the accused can lead to wrongful convictions, like the 50 cases currently under review by the Brooklyn district attorney. Do you believe that ensuring that innocent people are not wrongfully convicted is worth the societal cost of allowing some guilty people to go free?

present, the assumption has been that individuals have a reasonable expectation of privacy in their homes. Where there is no reasonable expectation of privacy, however, there can be no unreasonable search, and so the police are not required to get a warrant before conducting the search or surveillance. Since the 1990s, the Court has expanded the situations in which there is no reasonable expectation of privacy and hence no need for a warrant. For example, there is no reasonable expectation of privacy in one's car, at least in those areas that are in plain view, such as the front and back seats. There is also no expectation of privacy in public places such as parks and stores, because it is reasonable to assume that a person knowingly exposes his or her activities to public view in those places. The same is true of one's trash: because there is no reasonable expectation of privacy in the things that one discards, police may search this material without a warrant.[64]

In instances when there is a reasonable expectation of privacy, individuals or their property may be searched if law enforcement personnel acquire a warrant from a judge. To obtain a warrant, the police must provide the judge with evidence that establishes probable cause that a crime has been committed. Also, the warrant must be specific about the place to be searched and the materials that the agents are seeking. These requirements limit the ability of police simply to go on a "fishing expedition" to find some bit of incriminating evidence.

As society changes, expectations of privacy change as well. For example, technological innovation has given us new technology, such as e-mail and the Internet, and Fourth Amendment law has had to adapt to these inventions. As an example, in 2012, the Supreme Court ruled in *United States v. Jones* that the warrantless placement of a GPS tracking device on a suspect's car in order to track its movements is an unlawful search and violation of the Fourth Amendment.[65] Is there a reasonable expectation of privacy in our communications on the Internet? This is an important question, especially in light of citizens' heightened concerns about terrorism and white-collar crime.

THE FIFTH AND SIXTH AMENDMENTS: THE RIGHT TO A FAIR TRIAL AND THE RIGHT TO COUNSEL The Fifth and Sixth Amendments establish the rules for conducting a trial. These two amendments ensure that criminal defendants are protected at the formal stages of legal proceedings. Although less than 10 percent of all charges result in trials, these protections have significant symbolic and practical importance, because they hold the state to a high standard whenever it attempts to use its significant power to prosecute a case against an individual.

The Fifth Amendment bars **double jeopardy** and compelled self-incrimination. These safeguards mean, respectively, that a person may not be tried twice for the same crime or forced to testify against himself or herself when accused of a crime. These safeguards are meant to protect people from persecution, harassment, and forced confessions. A single criminal action, however, can lead to multiple trials if each trial is based on a separate offense.

The Sixth Amendment establishes the rights to a speedy and public trial, to a trial by a jury of one's peers, to information about the charges against oneself, to the confrontation of witnesses testifying against oneself, and to legal counsel. The protection of these Fifth and Sixth Amendment liberties is promoted by the *Miranda* **rights,** based on the Supreme Court decision in *Miranda v. Arizona* (1966).[66] In the *Miranda* case, the Court outlined the requirement that "prior to questioning, the person must be warned that he has a right to remain silent, that any statement

double jeopardy
the trying of a person again for the same crime that he or she has been cleared of in court; barred by the Fifth Amendment

***Miranda* rights**
criminal procedural rule, established in the 1966 case *Miranda v. Arizona,* requiring police to inform criminal suspects, on their arrest, of their legal rights, such as the right to remain silent and the right to counsel; these warnings must be read to suspects before interrogation

he does make may be used against him, and that he has a right to the presence of an attorney, either retained or appointed." Later cases have created some exceptions to *Miranda* (see Table 4.5).

Together, the Fourth, Fifth, and Sixth Amendments ensure the protection of individuals against abuses of power by the state, and in so doing they promote a view of justice that the community widely embraces. Because these rights extend to individuals charged with violating the community's standards of right and wrong, they promote a broad sense of inclusiveness—a respect even for persons who allegedly have committed serious offenses, and a desire to ensure that the justice system treats all people fairly.

The Court has considered the community's views in reaching its decisions in cases brought before it. For example, through a series of Supreme Court cases culminating with *Gideon v. Wainwright* (1963), the justices interpreted the right to counsel to mean that the government must provide lawyers to individuals who are too poor to hire their own.[67]

TABLE 4.5

Cases Weakening Protection Against Self-Incrimination

YEAR	CASE	RULING
1986	*Moran v. Burbine*	Confession is not inadmissible because police failed to inform suspect of attorney's attempted contacts.
1991	*Arizona v. Fulminante*	Conviction is not automatically overturned in cases of coerced confession if other evidence is strong enough to justify conviction.
1994	*Davis v. U.S.*	Suspect must unequivocally and assertively state his right to counsel to stop police questioning.
2013	*Salina v. Texas*	Accused must explicitly invoke the Fifth Amendment for it to apply.

The justices adopted this standard because they came to believe that the community's views of fundamental fairness dictated this result. Before this decision, states had to provide attorneys only in cases that could result in capital punishment.

THE EIGHTH AMENDMENT: PROTECTION AGAINST CRUEL AND UNUSUAL PUNISHMENT

The meaning of *cruel* and *unusual* has changed radically since the Eighth Amendment was ratified, especially with regard to the imposition of capital punishment—the death penalty. Moreover, Americans have always disagreed among themselves about the death penalty itself. Throughout the country's history, citizens and lawmakers have debated the morality of capital punishment as well as the circumstances under which the death penalty should be used. Central to the public debate have been the questions of which crimes should be punished by death and how capital punishment should be carried out.

Generally, the Court has supported the constitutionality of the death penalty. An exception was the landmark case *Furman v. Georgia* (1972), in which, in a 5–4 decision, the Court suspended the use of the death penalty.[68] Justices Brennan and Marshall believed the death penalty to be "incompatible with evolving standards of decency in contemporary society." The dissenting justices argued in turn that capital punishment had always been regarded as appropriate under the Anglo-American legal tradition for serious crimes and that the Constitution implicitly authorized death penalty laws because of the Fourteenth Amendment's reference to the taking of "life." The majority decision came about as a result of concurring opinions by Justices Stewart, White, and Douglas, who focused on the arbitrary nature with which death sentences had been imposed. The Court's decision forced the states and the national legislature to rethink their statutes for capital offenses to ensure that the death penalty would not be administered in a capricious or discriminatory manner.[69] Over time, the courts have also interpreted the Eighth Amendment as requiring that executions be carried out in the most humane and least painful manner. Public discourse and debate have strongly influenced thinking about which methods of execution are appropriate.

Recent studies, however, suggest that states' administration of the sedative sodium pentothal has left individuals conscious and in agony but paralyzed and thus unable to cry out while they are dying. But in 2008, the Supreme Court ruled in a 7–2 decision that lethal injection does not constitute cruel and unusual punishment,[70] paving the way for 10 states, which had halted lethal injections pending the case's outcome, to resume executions. The 2008 decision of *Baze v. Rees* marked the first time the Supreme Court reviewed the constitutionality of a method of execution since 1878, when the Court upheld Utah's use of a firing squad.[71]

In that early ruling, the Court said the Constitution prohibits executions that involve torture, such as burning alive or drawing and quartering an individual, as well as other infliction of "unnecessary cruelty" that the justices did not define. States have greatly differed in their interpretation of a constitutionally legitimate means of execution. In *Baze v. Rees,* lawyers for the Kentucky inmates argued that the state is violating that standard by using drugs that pose a risk of extreme pain if something goes wrong and by failing to provide adequate safeguards. But the Court ruled that there is no Eighth Amendment requirement that a government-sanctioned execution be pain free, only that it does not involve a "substantial" or "objectively intolerable" risk of serious harm—a risk greater than possible alternatives.

Civil Liberties in Post–September 11 America

Public discussion about the proper balance of individual freedom with public action extends from First Amendment freedoms to gun laws to the rights of the accused. Debate has intensified as the nation struggles with the threat of terrorism and a growing protest culture at home. Citizens and government leaders are rethinking their beliefs about the proper scope of governmental power.

Over the course of U.S. history, liberty and security have coexisted in a state of tension. In the wake of September 11, 2001, this tension has become more acute as the federal, state, and local governments have taken certain actions that directly intrude on individual freedoms. New technologies have increased the government's capacity to invade citizens' privacy, and a heightened fear of internal and external threats has been used to justify such invasions. The government argues that these actions are necessary to protect life and property. But civil libertarians shudder at what they see as unprecedented violations of individual freedoms and rights.

Perceived Intrusions on Free Speech and Assembly

Although the tension between liberty and order has been clear since the origins of our republic, this conflict has become more intense in recent years. For instance, the Foreign Intelligence Surveillance Act (FISA) of 1978, which empowers the government to conduct secret searches where necessary to protect national security, significantly broadened the powers of law enforcement agencies to engage in investigation. Agencies must go before a designated court, the Foreign Intelligence Surveillance Act Court, to justify a secret search. Civil libertarians are concerned about the FISA court's concealed location and sealed records, as well as its judicial proceedings, in which the suspect is never told about the investigation and probable cause is not required to approve surveillance or searches of any person suspected of having some link to terrorism.

Following September 11, 2001, a number of government agencies engaged in the surveillance of political groups in the United States. In late 2005, the media exposed a program by the Bush administration and the National Security Agency (NSA) to target U.S. civilians for electronic surveillance without judicial oversight. Members of the Bush administration claimed that they had monitored only communications where one party was suspected of links to terrorism and was currently overseas. Beginning in 2005, however, the American Civil Liberties Union (ACLU) issued a series of reports demonstrating that the Federal Bureau of Investigation (FBI) spied not only on people suspected of taking part in terrorist plots but also on individuals involved in peaceful political activities.[72] In one instance, the FBI monitored the organizers of an antiwar protest who had gathered at a Denver bookstore, and agents compiled a list with the descriptions and license plates of cars in the store's vicinity. In 2009, the ACLU filed a lawsuit challenging the constitutionality of the 2008 FISA Amendment Act, which increased the ability of the federal government to engage in the warrantless surveillance of American citizens.[73] Despite governmental challenges, this lawsuit is ongoing.[74] The ACLU has released similar reports describing the Pentagon's database of peaceful war protesters.[75]

The ACLU and other critics of the domestic surveillance program have argued that the federal government is targeting political protest, not domestic terrorism plots. Opponents of the policy warn that the FBI and other agencies are infringing upon free speech, assembly, and expression. But employees of the NSA and the Department of Justice have defended the government's expanded investigation and enforcement activities, claiming that the threats to national security are grave and that the government must be given the power it needs to protect against these dangers.[76]

Perceived Intrusions on Criminal Due Process

Even though several years have passed since September 11, 2001, concern lingers about another terrorist attack on U.S. soil, and many Americans are willing to accept some infringement on their freedoms if it makes them safer. These citizens assume that criminal activity may be afoot and that the surveillance is not being used to target groups that are politically unpopular or critical of the administration. Much of the debate about the surveillance activities of the FBI and other groups centers on the distinction between criminally active groups and politically unpopular groups. How do we know which groups the federal government is using its powers to investigate?

To what extent must administration officials provide evidence of criminal intent before placing a suspect under surveillance? Since September 11, 2001, the laws that govern domestic spying have been modified in such a way that the government has much more leeway in conducting searches and investigations, even where there is no proof of criminal activity.

The terrorism of September 11 led to important shifts in U.S. policy. One example is the USA PATRIOT Act, which Congress passed six weeks after the attacks with little debate in either the House or the Senate.[77] This law, reauthorized in 2005 and 2011, allows the FBI and other intelligence agencies to access personal information and records without getting permission from, or even informing, targeted individuals. Much of the data come from private sources, which are often ordered to hand over their records. For example, the USA PATRIOT Act authorized the FBI to order Internet service providers to give information about their clients to the FBI. The USA PATRIOT Act also empowered intelligence agencies to order public libraries to hand over records of materials that the targeted individuals borrowed or viewed.

On July 28, 2007, President Bush called on Congress to pass legislation to reform the FISA in order to ease restrictions on the surveillance of terrorist suspects in cases where one party or both parties to the communication are located overseas. The Protect America Act of 2007, signed into law on August 5, 2007, essentially legalized ongoing NSA practices.[78] Under the act, the U.S. government may wiretap without FISA court supervision any communications that begin or end in a foreign country. The act removes from the definition of "electronic surveillance" in FISA any surveillance directed at a person reasonably believed to be located outside the United States. This means that the government may listen to conversations without a court order as long as the U.S. attorney general approves the surveillance. Supporters stress that flexibility is needed to monitor the communications of suspected terrorists and their networks. Critics, however, worry that the law is too vague and provides the government with the ability to monitor any group or individual it opposes, regardless of whether it has links to terrorism. In 2009, the Inspectors General of the Department of Defense, the Department of Justice, the CIA, the NSA, and the Office of the Director of National Intelligence revealed that the surveillance program had a much larger scope than previously believed. The report also demonstrated conflict within the Obama and Bush administrations as to how helpful the information obtained through these measures was in combating terrorism.[79]

Although many Americans are concerned about domestic surveillance, especially in situations where it targets political speech and expression, these laws remain on the books, and this surveillance likely will continue. For the time being, the line between suspected criminal activity and purely political expression remains blurred. Civic discourse about how to balance liberty and national security continues to evolve as Americans consider how much freedom they should sacrifice to protect public safety.

In addition to conversations about search and surveillance procedures, the nation is struggling with larger questions about the rights of detainees accused of conducting or supporting terrorist activities. Some political commentators argue that the torture of these individuals is appropriate in specific situations.[80] They point to a "ticking time bomb" scenario, in which the torture of a single suspect known to have information about the location of a nuclear bomb would be justified in order to save thousands or millions of innocent lives. Critics of this logic note that information obtained through torture is unreliable and not worth the price of violating our moral codes. Further, they argue that if the United States legalizes torture, Americans will lose their standing as a moral society and alienate potential allies in the war against terror.[81]

In response to the criticism of torture, Congress and the president passed the Detainee Treatment Act of 2005, which bans cruel, inhuman, or degrading treatment of detainees in U.S. custody, but provides significant exceptions to the definition of torture, such as waterboarding (the practice of pouring water over the nose and mouth while the victim is strapped to an inclined board to induce the sensation of drowning).[82] Despite this legislation, questions remain. For example, in 2006 various media outlets reported the practice of **rendition,** which involves the transfer of custody of suspected terrorists to other nations for imprisonment and interrogation. Critics saw the practice as an attempt to circumvent U.S. law, which requires due process and prohibits torture. Former secretary of state Condoleezza Rice denied that U.S. officials transfer suspects to places where they know these individuals will be tortured.[83] But according to a February 2007 European Parliament report, the CIA conducted 1,245 flights over European territory between 2001 and April 2006, many of them to destinations where suspects could face torture.[84] The Obama adminstration continued the policy of rendition but pledged to closely monitor the treatment of the incarcerated to ensure that they were not tortured.[85] Unquestionably, the global war on terror has caused U.S. citizens and public officials to reconsider the boundaries of acceptable behavior as they balance the need to protect the civil liberties of the accused with the desire to prevent terrorist attacks. The implementation of new technologies such as full-body scanners used in airports and the portable biometric scanners that provide instant facial recognition and iris identification for patrol officers increases the tension between liberty and order.

rendition
transfer of suspected terrorists to other nations for imprisonment and interrogation; this practice circumvents U.S. law, which requires due process and prohibits torture

Drones and Privacy Rights

The development of the unmanned combat air vehicle, also known as combat drone, has changed the nature of modern warfare. Operated remotely, drones have been used by the United States since the Gulf War. The Obama administration has greatly expanded their use in the War on Terror in Pakistan, Yemen, and Somalia. However, reports of casualties among civilian populations have led to rising criticism, including challenges by the Yemeni parliament. The debate has centered on the ability of drones to accurately distinguish between civilian and military personnel. Drone strikes do result in civilian casualties. The Bureau of Investigative Journalism has estimated that between 400 and 890 civilians have been reported as killed in Pakistan by drones since 2004, between 14 and 48 civilians in Yemen since 2002, and between 0 and 15 since 2007 in Somalia.[86] In response to growing criticism, President Obama has noted that these civilian deaths "will haunt us for as long as we live," but in discussing the members of terrorist cells who are targeted, he also stated that "the death toll from their acts of terrorism against Muslims dwarfs any estimate of civilian casualties from drone strikes."[87]

The growing reliance on drones in the military and potential commercial applications of drones (for example, Amazon has suggested that it will be able to deliver orders via drones within the next several years) has led to heightened concerns regarding the domestic use of drones for surveillance and crime control purposes. In 2013, 42 states considered 96 bills related to the use of domestic drones, with most of the laws addressing privacy concerns. Most of the laws passed have focused on the requirement of a probable cause warrant for a drone to be used in a criminal investigation to gain evidence; others have focused on limiting governmental use of data obtained by third-party drones or limits on the time span that data can be retained.[88] As the private and public use of domestic drones expands, questions of civil liberties implications will continue to be raised.

FIGURE 4.2 ■ TECHNOLOGY MOVING FROM FIGHTING TERROR TO CRIME CONTROL What message is the cartoonist trying to convey? What challenges might the government find in using technologies initially deployed for the war against terror in domestic criminal investigations? How does this revise the debate over liberty versus security? Are the constitutional due process provisions robust enough to protect citizens against abuses in the use of this technology?

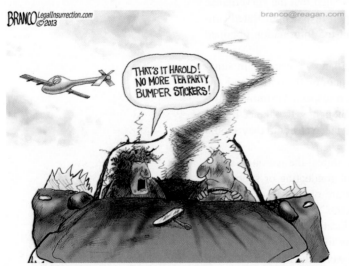

Conclusion

Thinking Critically About What's Next for Civil Liberties

At the core of the U.S. political and legal system lies a strong belief in individual liberties and rights. This belief is reflected in the Bill of Rights, the first 10 amendments to the Constitution. The freedoms therein are at the heart of civic engagement and ensure that individuals can freely participate in the political and social life of their communities. But these freedoms are also malleable, and at times the government has starkly limited them, as when officials perceive a threat to national security.

The inevitable tension between freedom and order is heightened in a post–September 11 world. Americans and their government struggle to protect essential liberties while guarding the nation against future terrorist attacks. Debates over state Stand Your Ground and Duty to Retreat laws remain unresolved and continue to mobilize groups to protest and campaign. Privacy continues to be a concern of citizens as Internet providers create new services that consumers both demand and desire. Tension between national security and personal freedom is reflected in contemporary debates over free speech and the right to privacy.

Meanwhile, governmental mining of private information through warrantless surveillance of social media sites and cell phone usage, as well as the increased reliance on drones, raises new questions regarding the limits of liberty. The issues we confront will continue to evolve as we struggle to maintain the commitment to liberty that defines our nation while preserving the country itself.

Summary

1. Civil Liberties in the American Legal System

The U.S. Constitution—and more specifically, the Bill of Rights, the first 10 amendments—protects individuals against the unrestrained exercise of power by the federal government. The framers intended the Bill of Rights to ensure that individuals could engage freely in political speech and civic discourse in the larger society. Although the Bill of Rights was initially interpreted as imposing limits only on the national government, over time the Supreme Court has interpreted most of its protections as applying to the state governments as well.

2. Freedoms in Practice: Controversy Over the Second Amendment and the Right to Bear Arms

Historical context is crucial to our understanding of the freedoms protected by the Bill of Rights. Americans actively disagree about the proper interpretation of the Second Amendment and about the role of guns in maintaining a free and safe society.

3. Freedoms of Speech, Assembly, and the Press: First Amendment Freedoms Supporting Civic Discourse

Civic engagement is possible only in a society that fully protects civil liberties. Some of the civil liberties guaranteed in the Bill of Rights relate specifically to political participation and discourse. Most important, the freedoms of speech, assembly, petition, and the press empower individuals to engage actively and freely in politics and public life. These freedoms have always existed in a state of tension with the goal of national security; in times of crisis or instability, the judicial system has interpreted them narrowly.

4. Freedoms of Religion, Privacy, and Criminal Due Process: Encouraging Community and Civic Engagement

Other Bill of Rights freedoms encourage inclusiveness and community building, ensuring that individuals can be fully engaged in the social life of the nation. The freedom of religion, right to privacy, and criminal due process protections ensure that no one individual or group may be singled out for either favorable or unfavorable treatment.

5. Civil Liberties in Post–September 11 America

The tension between liberty and security, always present in U.S. political culture, has become more acute since the terrorist attacks of September 11, 2001. In the wake of those attacks, federal and state law enforcement officials have limited the speech, assembly, petition, and due process rights of some American citizens. Recent protests have also raised the issue of where the line between freedom and order should be drawn.

Key Terms

bad tendency test 127
civil liberties 118
clear and present danger test 126
clear and probable danger test 128
commercial speech 130
creationism 136
criminal due process rights 141
double jeopardy 142
due process 119

establishment clause 134
exclusionary rule 141
fighting words 131
free exercise clause 137
habeus corpus 126
imminent lawless action test (incitement test) 128
intelligent design 136
Lemon test 135
libel 130
marketplace of ideas 125

Miranda rights 142
obscenity 130
prior restraint 132
rendition 146
right to privacy 138
selective incorporation 122
slander 130
symbolic speech 129
time, place, and manner restrictions 131
total incorporation 122

For Review

1. What are civil liberties? How do civil liberties differ from civil rights? Why do we protect civil liberties?

2. How does the First Amendment support civic discourse?

3. What protections does the Bill of Rights provide to those accused of committing a crime?

4. What are the two sides of the issue of Second Amendment rights? How has the Supreme Court interpreted this right?

5. How have the terrorist attacks of September 11, 2001, affected civil liberties in the United States?

For Critical Thinking and Discussion

1. Under what circumstances should the government be allowed to regulate or punish speech?

2. Under what circumstances should the government be able to punish people for practicing their religious beliefs?

3. Should the government be allowed to search people and property without a warrant based on probable cause that a crime was committed? Explain.

4. Do you believe that the USA PATRIOT Act and the NSA domestic surveillance program make the nation safer? Why or why not?

5. Will giving up liberty to enhance security protect the nation against terrorists, or will it destroy the fundamental values on which the nation was founded? Defend your position.

6. Are you concerned that technologies developed to fight wars against terrorism could be used to control the behavior of citizens in the United States? Where do you believe the line should be drawn?

MULTIPLE CHOICE: Choose the lettered item that answers the question correctly.

1. Civil liberties
   a. are protected only in Article III of the U.S. Constitution.
   b. entitle all citizens to equal protection of the laws.
   c. protect individuals against an abuse of government power.
   d. did not exist until the 21st century.

2. Which of the following is protected by the U.S. Constitution and the courts?
   a. slander
   b. libel
   c. fighting words
   d. symbolic speech

3. Teacher-led prayer in public schools is prohibited by
   a. the establishment clause.
   b. the free exercise clause.
   c. the due process clause.
   d. the equal protection clause.

4. The right to privacy was first established in the case
   a. *Griswold v. Connecticut.*
   b. *Roe v. Wade.*
   c. *Lemon v. Kurtzman.*
   d. *Miller v. California.*

5. Criminal defendants' rights to legal counsel and a jury trial are protected by the
   a. First Amendment.
   b. Second Amendment.
   c. Fourth Amendment.
   d. Sixth Amendment.

6. Critics of the USA PATRIOT Act charge that the law violates the
   a. Second Amendment.
   b. Fourth Amendment.
   c. Eighth Amendment.
   d. Tenth Amendment.

7. Police would most likely be required to use a warrant if they wanted to collect evidence from
   a. a house.
   b. the back seat of a car.
   c. a school locker.
   d. a prison cell.

8. According to the Supreme Court, burning the U.S. flag is a form of
   a. hate speech.
   b. libel.
   c. symbolic speech.
   d. treason.

9. Citizens' disagreement about how to interpret the Eighth Amendment is reflected in the current debate over
   a. school vouchers.
   b. intelligent design.
   c. "virtual" child pornography.
   d. lethal injection.

10. The Second Amendment protects U.S. citizens'
    a. free speech.
    b. freedom from self-incrimination.
    c. freedom of religion.
    d. freedom to bear arms.

FILL IN THE BLANKS

11. _____ refers to the process by which the Supreme Court has applied to the states those provisions in the Bill of Rights that serve some fundamental principle of liberty or justice.

12. _____ set guidelines that the government must follow in investigating, bringing to trial, and punishing those accused of committing a crime.

13. Under the _____, evidence obtained illegally cannot be used in a trial.

14. The Fifth Amendment protection against _____ ensures that criminal defendants cannot be tried again for the same crime when a court has already found them not guilty of committing that crime.

15. Speech that is likely to bring about public disorder or chaos and that may be banned in public places to ensure the preservation of public order is called _____.

Answers: 1. c, 2. d, 3. a, 4. a, 5. d, 6. b, 7. a, 8. c, 9. d, 10. d, 11. Selective incorporation, 12. Criminal due process rights, 13. exclusionary rule, 14. double jeopardy, 15. fighting words.

Resources for Research AND Action

Internet Resources

Center for Democracy and Technology
www.cdt.org The effect of new computer and communications technologies on American civil liberties is the subject of this site.

National Rifle Association-Institute for Legislative Action
www.nraila.org The lobbying arm of the National Rifle Association, focuses on guaranteeing safe access to guns for law-abiding individuals.

American Civil Liberties Union
www.aclu.org With the tagline "Because Freedom Can't Protect Itself," this national organization with state branches prioritizes liberty over all other priorities.

Recommended Readings

Carroll, Jamuna, ed. *Privacy.* Detroit, MI: Greenhaven Press, 2006. An edited volume of point-counterpoint articles exploring a wide variety of issues, including counterterrorism measures, Internet privacy, video surveillance, and employee monitoring.

Denvir, John. *Freeing Speech: The Constitutional War Over National Security.* New York: New York University Press, 2010. Argues that a broad definition of presidential power and a weak interpretation of the First Amendment by Congress and the judiciary has changed American democracy for the worse.

Fisher, Louis. *The Constitution and 9/11: Recurring Threats to America's Freedoms.* Lawrence, KS: University Press of Kansas, 2008. This book, written by one of the nation's foremost experts on separation of powers, surveys the historic responses to threats to national security by the branches of the federal government and then evaluates the current challenges to the constitutional law of national security after 9/11.

Rosen, Jeffrey, and Benjamin Wittes, eds. *Constitution 3.0: Freedom and Technological Change.* Washington, D.C.: Brookings Institution Press, 2011. Considers the way in which future and current technology may affect current constitutional doctrine, evolving into new constitutional challenges and tensions with citizens' right to individual freedom.

Spitzer, Robert J. *The Politics of Gun Control,* 4th ed. Washington, D.C.: CQ Press, 2007. Analysis of the gun control debate in the United States, including its history, the constitutional right to bear arms, the criminological consequences of guns, citizen political action, and the role and impact of American governing institutions.

Movies of Interest

The Fifth Estate (2013)
A popular portrayal of the evolution of the WikiLeaks organization and its global impact when it reveals many governments' secrets relative to security, surveillance, and corruption, focusing on WikiLeaks's founder, Julian Assange.

J. Edgar (2011)
A biographic picture of the life and career of J. Edgar Hoover, the head of the FBI from 1924 to when he died in 1972. The film explores the ways in which the government, with Hoover's leadership, criminalized and investigated the activities of dissidents in the United States.

Rendition (2007)
When an Egyptian terrorism suspect "disappears" on a flight from Africa to Washington, D.C., his American wife and a CIA analyst struggle to secure his release from a secret detention (and torture) facility somewhere outside the United States.

Good Night and Good Luck (2005)
This film examines the conflict between veteran journalist Edward R. Murrow and Senator Joseph McCarthy as Murrow attempts to investigate and discredit McCarthy's tactics in investigating and destroying communist elements in the federal government and larger society.

The People versus Larry Flynt (1996)
This film documents the economic success, courtroom battles, and personal challenges of *Hustler* magazine publisher Larry Flynt. Flynt is obnoxious and hedonistic in ways that offend and anger "decent people," even as he fights to protect freedom of speech for all.

CHAPTER 5

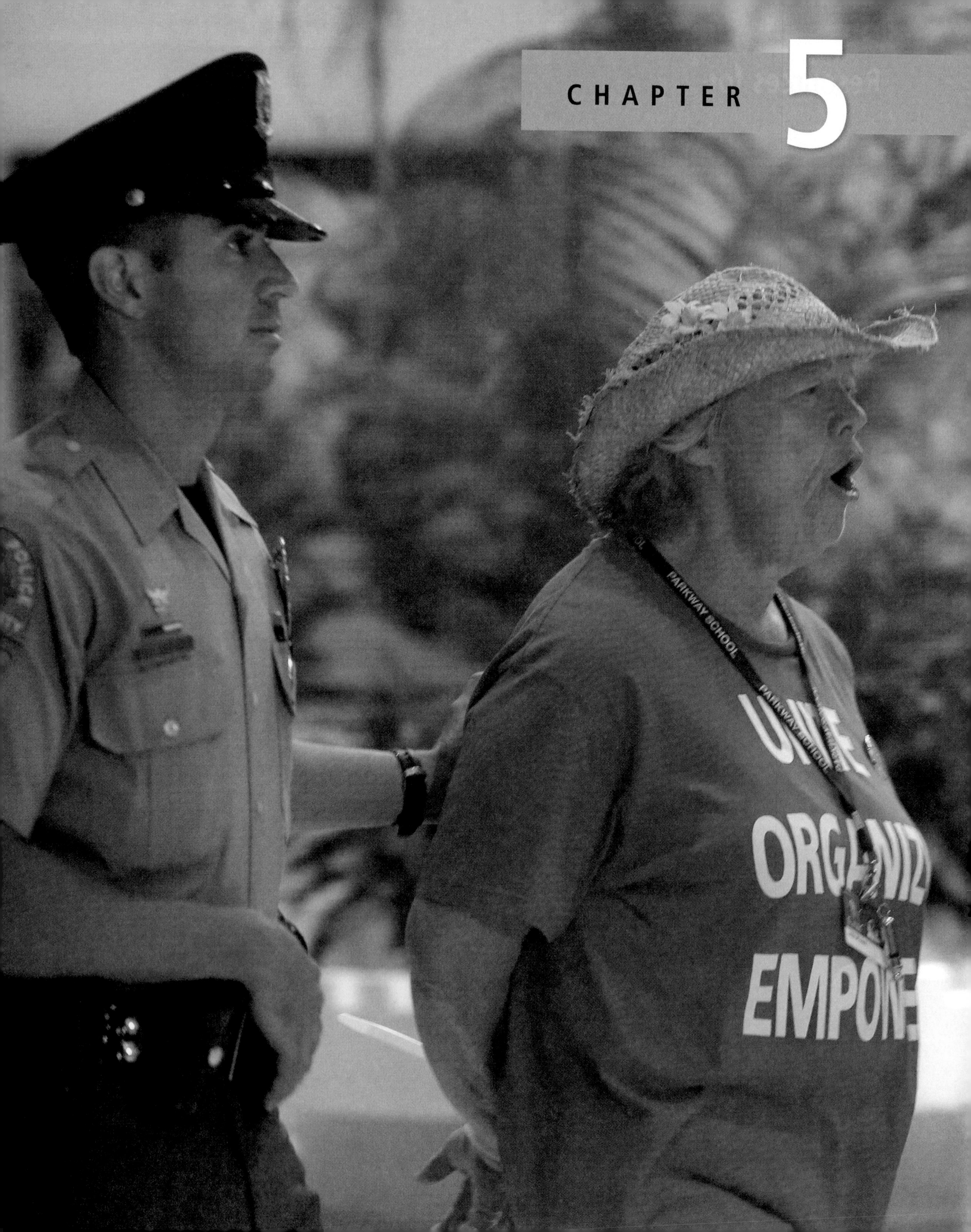

Civil Rights

THEN

African Americans, women, Native Americans, Latinos, and other groups struggled to achieve equality in the United States.

NOW

Rapid changes in state laws relative to marriage equality for same-sex couples has led to some states legislating protections for individuals who disagree with the new policies.

NEXT

How will changing understandings of gender identity impact our protection of civil rights?

How will we ensure that equality is available to all women regardless of race, ethnicity, class, religion, or sexual identity?

What protections will the nation be willing to extend to undocumented immigrants and their children?

civil rights
the rights and privileges guaranteed under the equal protection and due process clauses of the Fifth and Fourteenth Amendments; the idea that individuals are protected from discrimination based on characteristics such as race, national origin, religion, and sex

inherent characteristics
individual attributes such as race, national origin, religion, and gender

Although the Declaration of

Independence claims that all men are created equal and are endowed with the natural rights of life, liberty, and the pursuit of happiness, neither the Articles of Confederation nor the Constitution as initially ratified guaranteed that the government would treat or protect all men equally. Indeed, those constitutions did *not* guarantee nonwhite men or women of all races and colors the same legal rights that they guaranteed to white men. For example, African American men and women had no legal rights and were bought and sold as property until 1865, when the Thirteenth Amendment to the Constitution made such enslavement illegal. The Constitution did not guarantee American women the right to sue, nor did it protect married women's right to own property, until well into the 19th century. Many Americans experienced unequal treatment under the law throughout U.S. history.

Fast-forward to today. When asked what principles or ideals they hold most dear, many Americans will mention equality. Yet, even today, not all people in the United States are treated equally under the law. Moreover, people disagree strongly on the meaning of "equal protection of the law," which has been a stated constitutional guarantee since 1868, when the states ratified the Fourteenth Amendment to the U.S. Constitution.

Disagreement about what constitutes "equal treatment" is at the heart of many past and current struggles for equality. Does equal treatment mean that the government must ensure that all people have equal opportunities to pursue their happiness? Does it bar all differential treatment by the government and its officials, or are there certain situations in which it is acceptable for the government to treat people differently to fulfill its mission (establish justice, ensure domestic tranquility, provide for the common defense, promote the general welfare, and secure the blessings of liberty)?

In this chapter, we examine the concept of equality under the law. We focus on how groups of citizens who were originally deprived of equal protection of their liberties and pursuit of happiness have been able to expand their rights in numerous areas, including voting rights and equal access to educational and employment opportunities, to housing, and to public accommodations.

The Meaning of Equality Under the Law

Although the issue of protecting civil liberties was in the forefront at the nation's founding, as we discussed in Chapter 4, the issue of guaranteeing civil rights reached the national agenda much later.[1] When we talk about **civil rights** in the United States, we mean the rights and privileges guaranteed by the government under the equal protection and due process clauses of the Fifth and Fourteenth Amendments and the privileges and immunities clause of the Fourteenth Amendment. These rights are based on the idea that the government should protect individuals from discrimination that results from inherent characteristics. **Inherent characteristics** are individual characteristics that are part of a person's nature, such as race, religion, national origin, and sex. Some of these rights are extended only to citizens (such as the right to vote), but there is a significant debate around what protections are extended to other individuals.[2]

The Constitution imposes constraints (civil liberties) and responsibilities (civil rights) on governments, which includes government officials and employees, but *not* on private individuals or organizations. However, governments can write laws that prohibit private individuals and organizations from infringing on civil liberties and civil rights. For example, the national government

Same-Sex Marriage

The issue of marriage rights has been a focal point for LGBT rights activists in recent years. With the right to marry comes a host of advantages, including inheritance rights, rights to governmental benefits, and hospital visitation rights. Like other struggles for civil rights, the movement for marriage equality has relied on court action, bills in state legislatures, public referenda, and other strategies.

The issue of same-sex marriage gained considerable momentum in 2012 when President Barack Obama noted during a television interview that he was supportive of same-sex marriages, although he believed that states should make this determination individually. The change in President Obama's position reflected the shifting views of many Americans, who are more supportive of same-sex marriage than in previous decades. The 2013 Supreme Court case of *United States v. Windsor* paved the way for many states to change their laws when it determined that the federal Defense of Marriage Act (DOMA) defining marriage as inherently heterosexual was unconstitutional under the equal protection clause of the Fifth Amendment.[4]

DOMA, an act passed by Congress and signed by President Clinton in 1996, stated that the federal government did not recognize same-sex marriages or civil unions, legalized by any state. DOMA also released states from recognizing same-sex marriages allowed by other states. In addition to the federal act, many states passed their own DOMA laws. By 2014, 13 of the 33 states with DOMA laws had been overturned by the federal courts as unconstitutional. When the Supreme Court was requested to hear state appeals of these decision, the Court decided not to intervene leaving the lower courts' determinations allowing same-sex couples to marry in these states. But later that year, when the 6th circuit federal appeals court panel upheld gay marriage bans in Michigan, Ohio, Tennessee, and Kentucky, it became nearly certain that the U.S. Supreme Court would take up the matter in 2015.

Nonetheless, the *Windsor* decision spawned significant changes in many states. By mid-November 2014, 34 states and the District of Columbia allowed same-sex couples to marry. In addition, several states respected marriages and civil union/domestic partnership statuses that same-sex couples entered into in the other states that allow them. Thus, laws relative to same-sex marriage remain in flux in many states. Despite this flux, the struggle for securing rights for LGBT individuals has made significant strides since its early origins.

> On the presidential campaign trail in 2008, Barack Obama promised to work for advances in the civil rights of gay and lesbian citizens. In May 2012, the president announced that he was personally in support of same-sex marriages.

Gay Pride Movement

Several LGBT civil rights organizations were founded after the Stonewall Rebellion. In June 1969, groups of gay men and lesbians clashed violently with police in New York City, in a protest over the routine harassment by law enforcement of members of the lesbian and gay community. This influential conflict, which started at the Stonewall bar, marked the first time that members of this community acted collectively and in large numbers to assert their rights. Shortly after this event, in 1970, Lambda Legal, a national organization fighting for full recognition of the civil rights of LGBT citizens, was founded. Within a few years, gays and lesbians began to hold gay pride marches throughout the country, and many new groups, such as the Human Rights Campaign and the National Gay and Lesbian Task Force, began advocating for LGBT rights.

As a result of organized educational and lobbying efforts by the gay community, during the 1980s a number of state and local governments adopted laws prohibiting discrimination in employment, housing, public accommodations, and employee benefits—that is, guaranteeing equal protection of some laws—for LGBT persons. In 1982, Wisconsin was the first state to prohibit such discrimination. Yet during the same decade, numerous states had laws on the books prohibiting sex between mutually consenting adults of the same sex, typically in the form of anti-sodomy laws. In the 1986 case of *Bowers v. Hardwick,* the U.S. Supreme Court upheld Georgia's antisodomy law.[5] In 2003, another lawsuit challenging the constitutionality of a state antisodomy law came before the Supreme Court in the case of *Lawrence v. Texas*.[6] This time, the Court overturned the 1986 *Bowers* decision, finding that the Fourteenth Amendment provides due process and equal protection for sexual privacy and therefore the Texas law was unconstitutional.

Advocates for the rights of LGBT persons hoped this 2003 ruling would lead to federal protections of LGBT citizens' civil rights. But there is still no federal law prohibiting LGBT-based discrimination or any protecting against discrimination based on gender identity. In contrast to the lack of federal legislation, by mid-2014, 33 states and the District of Columbia had antidiscrimination laws guaranteeing equal access to employment, housing, or public accommodations regardless of sexual orientation. Sixteen states and Washington, D.C., also prohibit gender identity discrimination.[7]

Backlash Against LGBT Civil Rights

Though the LGBT community is winning some of its civil rights battles in a growing number of states, in many areas the battle has just begun. For example, in the area of family law, issues involving adoption rights and child custody as well as divorce and property rights are now battlegrounds. While states and municipalities have begun to address discrimination based on gender identity, this form of discrimination has not been incorporated in most legal protections.

In 2014, Arizona, Mississippi, and Kansas considered legislation that affirmed the religious liberty of business owners to choose to refuse service to lesbians, gay men, and other individuals, but neither measure became law. Eighteen states have laws banning such discrimination, but the remaining states have not addressed this new form of discrimination.

hate crime
a crime committed against a person, property, or society, in which the offender is motivated, in part or in whole, by his or her bias against the victim because of the victim's race, religion, disability, sexual orientation, or ethnicity

In addition, hate crimes continue to be a problem for members of the LGBT community as well as for citizens (and noncitizens) with nonwhite ancestry. The national government enacted its first hate crime law in 1969. Since then, it has expanded the inherent characteristics for which the law guarantees protection. Today, under federal law, a **hate crime** is a crime in which the offender is motivated in part or entirely by her or his bias against the victim because of the victim's actual or perceived race, color, religion, nationality, ethnicity, gender, sexual orientation, gender identity, or disability. Forty-five states and the District of Columbia also have hate crime laws, but the inherent characteristics covered by those laws vary. Although all the state laws cover race, religion, and ethnicity, and most cover gender, sexual orientation, and disability, only a handful also cover gender identity.[8] The Matthew Shepard and James Byrd, Jr., Hate Crimes Prevention Act of 2009 was designed to allow the federal government to help tribal, local, and state jurisdictions investigate and prosecute hate crimes. This law was passed to commemorate the 1998 murders of Matthew Shepard, a college student in Wyoming, who was tortured and killed because he was believed to be gay, and James Byrd, Jr., an African American man in Texas who was tied to the back of a truck by two white supremacists and dragged until he was decapitated.

Slavery and Its Aftermath

Probably the most blatant example of discrimination in U.S. history is slavery. This practice was protected under the law, and enslaved people were considered to be the property of their owners. When it was first written, the Constitution implicitly endorsed the unequal and discriminatory treatment of African Americans.[9] Some of the most important provisions of the new constitution treated people of African descent as property, allowing states to continue to permit them to be enslaved and to be sold in open markets. Although the movement to abolish slavery was in its early stages in 1787, the year the Constitution was completed, by the early to mid-1800s, it had gained significant momentum in the North, largely because of the activism of various religious and humanitarian groups.[10]

Slavery in the United States

Most African Americans today are the descendants of Africans who were forcibly brought to the New World. In 1619, twenty Africans arrived in Jamestown as *indentured servants,* workers with a fixed term of service. But by the mid-1600s, slavery began to replace indentured servitude.

OPPOSITION TO SLAVERY Many chafed at the hypocrisy of those who sought freedom and equality but kept slaves. Among the first to challenge slavery were former slaves, who staged both peaceful protests and armed insurrections throughout the late 1700s and early 1800s. These activists successfully rallied support in the North for the gradual abolition of slavery by 1804. They argued forcefully against the injustice of the slave system, moving the opponents of slavery to action by their horrifying firsthand accounts of the treatment of slaves. By 1860, many northern states had abolished slavery (Figure 5.1).

Despite those arguments, the U.S. Congress, wary of the divisiveness caused by the slavery issue, sought to balance the antislavery position of the abolitionist states with the proslavery sentiments of the slaveholding states. One such attempt was the Missouri Compromise, passed by Congress in 1820. The compromise regulated slavery in the newly acquired western territories: slavery was prohibited north of the 36° 30′ north parallel, except within the state of Missouri.

The abolitionists, including organizations such as the American Anti-Slavery Society, objected to the efforts of Congress to accommodate the slaveholding states and called for the emancipation of all slaves. Members of the American Anti-Slavery Society were actively engaged in **civil disobedience,** which is nonviolent refusal to comply with laws or government policies that are morally objectionable. Specifically, American Anti-Slavery Society members actively supported the Underground Railroad, a series of safe houses that allowed escaping slaves to flee to the northern states and Canada. Between 1810 and 1850, an estimated 100,000 people escaped slavery through the Underground Railroad. But in 1850, the U.S. Congress—in an attempt to stall or prevent the secession, or separation, of southern states from the Union—passed the Fugitive Slave Act. The law required federal marshals to return runaway slaves or risk a $1,000 fine (over $20,000 in today's dollars); private citizens who harbored or abetted runaway slaves could be imprisoned for six months and fined $1,000. Passage of this law meant that "conductors" on the Underground Railroad operated in clear violation of the statute, risking their own livelihoods and property.

civil disobedience
active, but nonviolent, refusal to comply with laws or governmental policies that are morally objectionable

THE CIVIL WAR ERA Abolitionists were bolstered in their efforts when Harriet Beecher Stowe's popular book *Uncle Tom's Cabin* was published in 1852. Vividly depicting the harsh reality of slavery in the United States, this work inspired many to actively challenge slavery. By the late 1850s, the widespread distribution of *Uncle Tom's Cabin,* as well as the trial and execution of John Brown, a white abolitionist who tried to ignite a slave insurrection in Harpers Ferry, in what was then Virginia and is now West Virginia, had convinced many northerners that slavery was immoral.

Yet the U.S. Supreme Court ruled otherwise. In 1857, Dred Scott, an African American enslaved by a surgeon in the U.S. Army, sued for his freedom, arguing that because he had lived in both a free state (Illinois) and a free territory (the Wisconsin Territory, now Minnesota), he had become a free man and as such he could not be re-enslaved when he moved to Missouri. The Supreme Court rejected Scott's claim and in *Dred Scott v. Sandford* ruled that the Missouri Compromise of 1820 was unconstitutional because the U.S. Congress lacked the authority to ban slavery in the territories.[11] It also ruled that Scott was not a U.S. citizen, asserting that because of their race, African Americans were not citizens with **standing to sue,** or the legal right to bring lawsuits in court. Although the *Dred Scott* decision appeared to be a victory for slaveholding states, it was also pivotal in mobilizing the abolitionist movement and swaying public opinion in favor of a war to prevent secession and to bring about emancipation.

standing to sue
the legal right to bring lawsuits in court

Certain that their way of life was under siege and alarmed by the election of Abraham Lincoln as president in 1860, the southern states decided that they should secede from the union. By May 1861, eleven southern states had declared their independence and created the Confederate States of America. A long and bloody civil war followed as the North fought to bring the southern states back into the union.

One of the most important turning points of the Civil War was the Emancipation Proclamation, issued by Abraham Lincoln in April 1862. This order abolished slavery in the states that had seceded from the Union. The Union army and navy were charged with implementing the order. The proclamation had several purposes: It decreed that the abolition of slavery was a goal of the war, and by doing so it effectively prevented Britain and France from intervening in the war on the southern side, because those countries had both renounced the institution of slavery.

FIGURE 5.1 ■ CHANGING NATURE OF SLAVERY IN THE UNITED STATES When we think of slavery in the United States, we often consider only the South. Look at the two maps below showing the population of enslaved people in 1800 and 1860. By 1860, many northern states had abolished slavery and had no enslaved population. Consider how the nature of slavery changed over 100 years. What surprises you about these maps? What trends do you observe in terms of the changing demographics? These data come from the federal census; what liabilities might result from relying on these data? Why might there be so many states with unknown enslaved populations in 1860?

SOURCE: The United States Historical Census Data Browser, http://mapserver.lib.virginia.edu/.

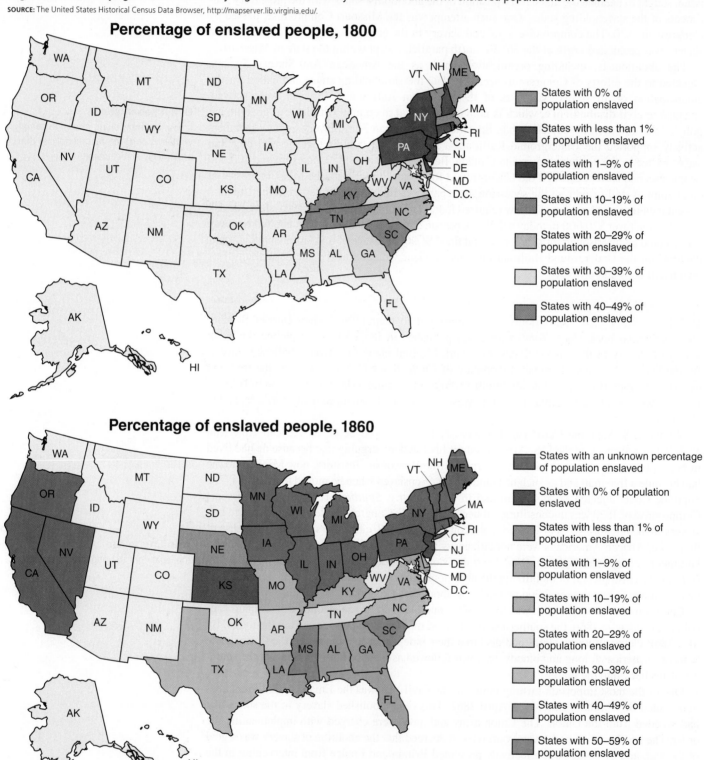

Percentage of enslaved people, 1800

- States with 0% of population enslaved
- States with less than 1% of population enslaved
- States with 1–9% of population enslaved
- States with 10–19% of population enslaved
- States with 20–29% of population enslaved
- States with 30–39% of population enslaved
- States with 40–49% of population enslaved

Percentage of enslaved people, 1860

- States with an unknown percentage of population enslaved
- States with 0% of population enslaved
- States with less than 1% of population enslaved
- States with 1–9% of population enslaved
- States with 10–19% of population enslaved
- States with 20–29% of population enslaved
- States with 30–39% of population enslaved
- States with 40–49% of population enslaved
- States with 50–59% of population enslaved

When the South finally surrendered in April 1865, it did so knowing that its economic way of life, which depended on slave-based plantation farming, was over. At the end of the war, nearly 4 million slaves in the United States were freed. The states then ratified three constitutional amendments to codify the victories won on the battlefield:

- the Thirteenth Amendment (1865), which ended slavery throughout the United States and prohibited it in the future;
- the Fourteenth Amendment (1868), which defines *citizens* as "all persons born or naturalized in the United States" and mandates the same privileges and immunities for all citizens and due process and equal protection for all people;
- the Fifteenth Amendment (1870), which decrees that every man has the right to vote, regardless of color.

Reconstruction and the First Civil Rights Acts

After the North won the war and Lincoln was assassinated in April 1865, members of Congress and others in government disagreed about the best way to proceed in the South. Many Republicans thought that the South should be stabilized and quickly brought back into the political fold. Like Lincoln, these moderates endorsed a plan that would enable the southern states to be quickly represented in Congress. Others, however, took a more radical view and argued that all those who had ever supported the Confederacy should be kept out of national and state politics. As the 1860s drew to a close, many of these more radical Republicans had come to power and had strictly limited the people in southern states who could participate in politics. As a result of their activities, during the **Reconstruction era** between 1866 and 1877—when the institutions and the infrastructure of the South were rebuilt—freed slaves, who could easily say they had never supported the Confederacy, made up a sizeable portion of both the electorate and the candidate pool in the southern states. Federal troops provided protection that facilitated their participation. During this decade, African American voters made the most of their position in the South and elected a substantial number of other African Americans to legislative offices in the local, state, and federal governments. In some places, such as South Carolina, African American legislators outnumbered whites, giving them a majority during the Reconstruction years.

Between 1865 and 1875, Congress passed a series of laws designed to solidify the rights and protections outlined in the Thirteenth, Fourteenth, and Fifteenth Amendments. Congress needed to spell out the rights of African Americans because of the pervasiveness of **Black Codes,** laws passed immediately after the Civil War by the confederate states that limited the rights of "freemen," or former slaves. These codes prevented freemen from voting, owning property, or bringing suit. To remedy that situation, Congress passed laws that sought to negate the Black Codes. One law, the Civil Rights Act of 1866, extended the definition of *citizen* to anyone born in the United States (including freemen) and granted all citizens the right to sue, own property, bear witness in a court of law, and enter into legal contracts. The Enforcement Act of 1870 bolstered the Fifteenth Amendment by establishing penalties for interfering with the right to vote. The Civil Rights Act of 1872, also known as the Anti–Ku Klux Klan Act, made it a federal crime to deprive individuals of their rights, privileges, or immunities protected by the Constitution. Although the Reconstruction-era Congress sought to remedy the new forms of inequality that emerged after the Civil War, its efforts would be short-lived.

Backlash: Jim Crow Laws

In 1877, the inauguration of President Rutherford Hayes (1877–1881) brought the Reconstruction era to a decisive end, almost immediately rolling back the gains African Americans had achieved in education and political participation. Under Hayes, the federal troops that had protected African Americans from physical reprisals were withdrawn. State and local governments throughout the South mandated racial segregation by enacting what came to be known as **Jim Crow laws.** These laws required the strict separation of racial groups, with whites and "nonwhites" going to separate schools, being employed in different jobs, and using segregated public accommodations, such as transportation and restaurants. **De jure segregation,** legally mandated separation of the races, became the norm in much of the South.

Reconstruction era
the time after the Civil War between 1866 and 1877 when the institutions and infrastructure of the South were rebuilt

Black Codes
laws passed immediately after the Civil War by the confederate states that limited the rights of "freemen" (people formerly enslaved)

Jim Crow laws
laws requiring strict separation of racial groups, with whites and "nonwhites" required to attend separate schools, work in different jobs, and use segregated public accommodations, such as transportation and restaurants

de jure segregation
segregation mandated by law

HUMAN TRAFFICKING

The United Nations has defined human trafficking as recruiting, transporting, harboring, or receiving people using fraud or coercion for the purpose of exploitation. Typical purposes for trafficking include prostitution and other forms of sexual exploitation, forced labor, slavery, or the removal of organs. When Americans think of slavery, they think of our nation's own historical experience with the institution of slavery: slave ships, race-based enslavement, and public auctions. It surprises many that in the 21st century, slavery still exists.

Women and children, particularly in Asia and Eastern Europe, are sometimes forced to be part of prostitution rings that operate in those countries as well as in Western democracies. Often traffickers advertise in local newspapers, offering high-paying jobs as models, domestic servants, hotel maids, nannies, or shop clerks in Western nations and promising to help secure the required visa applications and work permits. To lure people, traffickers rely on people's desire for a better life. Once victims are out of their homelands, they may be raped and forced into prostitution. Frequently, traffickers confiscate the victim's identification and travel permits (often forgeries), withhold food or shelter unless the victim complies, and use the threat of imprisonment by authorities or the threat of harm to the victim's family at home as means of ensuring compliance.

According to a 2013 study of 162 countries by the Walk Free Foundation, an estimated 29.8 million people worldwide are victimized by sex trafficking, debt bondage, forced labor, and other forms of modern slavery. The United Nations has found that sexual exploitation is the most typical type of slavery (79 percent), followed by forced labor (18 percent), which is the most difficult kind of human trafficking to trace.

By 2013, information companies like Google and Thomson Reuters were becoming involved in order to use global data sets to help identify and stop human traffickers. Because these organized crime networks are now understood to be transnational organizations, the battle to stop global slavery requires cooperation between nations, the public and private sectors, nongovernmental organizations, and law enforcement. The use of these data allows for prosecution without relying solely on the testimony of victims, who may not want to relive their experiences or may be vulnerable to threats, encouraging them not to participate in the prosecution of traffickers. As S. E. M. Vuk Jeremić, president of the General Assembly of the United Nations noted in 2013, "[There is] real need for increased cooperation, partnerships and technical assistance to better implement the Global Plan of Action and relevant legal instruments. In addition to bilateral and multilateral exchanges and better coordination among UN entities . . . there is a dire need to develop partnerships with the media and private sector, and to focus on a 'bottom up' approach where appropriate. This will ensure that our prevention work focuses on the villages and towns where sophisticated trafficking routes often start."*

*Closing Remarks to the High-Level Meeting on the Appraisal of the Global Plan of Action to Combat Trafficking in Persons, May 14, 2013.

The idea behind the Jim Crow laws was that whites and nonwhites should occupy separate societies and have little to do with each other. Many whites feared that racial mixing would result in interracial dating and marriage, which would inevitably lead to the decline of their superior position in society; thus in many southern states, miscegenation laws, which banned interracial marriage, cohabitation, or sex, were passed and severe penalties imposed for those who violated them. Interracial couples who married risked losing their property and even their liberty, since heavy fines and jail sentences were among the penalties for breaking those laws.

State and local governments in the South also found creative ways to prevent African Americans from exercising their right to vote. They relied on several tactics:

white primary

a primary election in which a party's nominees for general election were chosen but in which only white people were allowed to vote

- The **white primary** was a primary election in which only white people were allowed to vote. Because Democrats dominated politics so heavily in the post–Civil War South, the only races that really mattered were the primary races that determined the Democratic nominees. But southern states restricted voting in these primaries to whites only.

- The **literacy test** determined eligibility to vote. Literacy tests were designed so that few voters would stand a chance of passing the exam administered to African American voters, whereas the test for white voters was easy to pass. Typically, white voters were exempt from literacy tests because of a grandfather clause.
- A **poll tax,** a fee levied for voting, often presented an insurmountable obstacle to poor African Americans. White voters were often exempt from poll taxes because of a grandfather clause.
- The **grandfather clause** exempted individuals from conditions on voting (such as poll taxes or literacy tests) if they or their ancestors had been eligible to vote before 1870. Because African Americans did not have the right to vote in southern states before the Civil War, the grandfather clause was a mechanism to protect the voting rights of whites.

These laws were enforced not only by government agents, particularly police, but by nongovernmental groups as well. Among the most powerful of these groups was the Ku Klux Klan (KKK). During the late 1800s and into the 1900s, the Klan was dreaded and hated throughout the southern states, and it used violence to threaten and intimidate those African Americans and whites who dared to question its core principle: that whites are in every way superior to African Americans. The Klan's particular brand of intimidation, the burning cross and the lynching noose, was reviled throughout the southern and border states, but few could dispute the power the Klan wielded in those areas.

Governmental Acceptance of Discrimination

The federal government too had seemingly abandoned African Americans and the quest for equality under the law. In the *Civil Rights Cases* of 1883, the Supreme Court ruled that Congress lacked the authority to prevent discrimination by private individuals and organizations. Rather, Congress's jurisdiction, the Court claimed, was limited to banning discrimination in official acts of state or local governments. The Court also declared that the Civil Rights Act of 1875, which had sought to mandate "full and equal enjoyment" of a wide variety of facilities and accommodations, was unconstitutional.

In 1896, the Court struck what seemed to be the final blow against racial equality. In 1890, Louisiana passed a law that required separate accommodations for blacks and whites on railroad trains. Several citizens of New Orleans sought to test the constitutionality of the law and enlisted Homer Plessy, who was one-eighth African American (but still considered "black" by Louisiana state law) to serve as plaintiff. The choice of Plessy, who could pass for white, was intended to show the arbitrary nature of the statute. On June 7, 1892, Plessy boarded a railroad car designated for whites only. Plessy was asked to leave the whites-only car, and he refused. He was then arrested and jailed, charged with violating the state law. In 1896, the U.S. Supreme Court heard ***Plessy v. Ferguson,*** in which Plessy's attorneys argued that the Louisiana state law violated the **equal protection clause** of the Fourteenth Amendment, which states that no state shall "deny to any person within its jurisdiction the equal protection of the laws."

In a 7–1 decision, the Court rejected Plessy's arguments, claiming that segregation based on race was not a violation of the equal protection clause. Rather, the court made this argument:

> We consider the underlying fallacy of the plaintiff's argument to consist in the assumption that the enforced separation of the two races stamps the colored race with a badge of inferiority. If this be so, it is not by reason of anything found in the act, but solely because the colored race chooses to put that construction upon it.[12]

In its decision, the Court created the **separate but equal doctrine,** declaring that separate but equal facilities do not violate the Fourteenth Amendment's equal protection clause. Under this doctrine, the Court upheld state laws mandating separation of the races in schools and all public accommodations such as businesses, public transportation, restaurants, hotels, swimming pools, and recreational facilities. The only condition the Court placed on these segregated facilities was that the state had to provide public facilities for both whites and nonwhites. The Court paid little attention to whether the school systems or public accommodations were comparable in quality. As long as the state had some kind of facilities in place for both whites and nonwhites, the segregation was permitted. This doctrine would become the legal backbone of segregationist policies for more than five decades to come.

The Civil Rights Movement

In the early decades of the 20th century, African Americans continued their struggle for equal protection of the laws. Though the movement for civil rights enjoyed some early successes, the century was nearly half over before momentous victories by civil rights activists finally began to change the status of African Americans in revolutionary ways. These victories were the result of strong leadership at the helm of the movement, the effective strategies used by activists, and a national government that was finally ready to fulfill the promise of equality embodied in the Declaration of Independence.

Fighting Back: Early Civil Rights Organizations

In the early years of the 20th century, the political climate was open to reform, with activists in the Progressive and Black Women's Club movements calling for an end to government corruption, reforms to labor laws, the protection of children from abusive labor practices, and an expansion of rights, including the right of women to vote and the civil rights of African Americans (see Chapter 8 for more on the Progressive movement). In 1909, W. E. B. Du Bois (an influential African American writer and scholar, who is today acknowledged as the father of social science) joined many other prominent African American and white male and female activists to form the National Association for the Advancement of Colored People (NAACP). One of the targets of the NAACP for the next several decades was the separate but equal doctrine, which remained in place through the first half of the 20th century.

Citing the lack of graduate schools, law schools, and medical schools for African Americans, the NAACP argued that the states had violated the equal protection clause by failing to make such schools available to African Americans. During the 1930s, lawsuits brought by the NAACP in several states ended discriminatory admissions practices in professional schools.[13] Momentum in the movement for equality continued to grow, fueled in part by the growing political activism of African American soldiers returning home after fighting against fascism abroad during World War II. Many of these soldiers began to question why they were denied freedom and equality in their own country, and they mobilized for civil rights in their communities. Though the Court had not yet overturned the separate but equal doctrine, by 1950 the U.S. Supreme Court had ruled that segregating classrooms, dining rooms, or library facilities in colleges, universities, and professional schools was unconstitutional.

Taking cues from those court decisions, by the 1950s the NAACP and other groups had changed their tactics. Instead of arguing that states had to provide equivalent schools and programs for African Americans and whites, these groups began to argue that segregation itself was a violation of the equal protection clause. But it was not until 1954 that the U.S. Supreme Court struck down the separate but equal doctrine, finding it inherently unequal and therefore unconstitutional.

The End of Separate but Equal

In the fall of 1951, Oliver Brown, a welder at the Santa Fe Railroad yard in Topeka, Kansas, sought to have his daughter Linda enrolled in the third grade in an all-white public school seven blocks from their home. The act was not accidental; it was the calculated first step in an NAACP legal strategy that would result in sweeping changes to the nation's public school system, effectively shattering the segregated school system dominant in the South.[14] The Browns lived in an integrated neighborhood in Topeka, and Topeka schools were segregated, as allowed (but not required) under Kansas state law. Oliver Brown spoke with a Topeka attorney and with the Topeka NAACP, which persuaded him to join a lawsuit against the Topeka Board of Education. Brown agreed and was directed to attempt to register Linda at the all-white public school. Linda was denied admission.

Brown v. Board of Education of Topeka
the 1954 Supreme Court decision that ruled that segregated schools violated the equal protection clause of the Fourteenth Amendment

The stand taken by Oliver Brown and the other plaintiffs was not in vain. Thurgood Marshall, who would go on to become the first African American to sit on the U.S. Supreme Court, argued the case, and in a unanimous decision in 1954 the Supreme Court ruled in *Brown v. Board of Education of Topeka* that segregated schools violate the equal protection clause of the

Fourteenth Amendment. In one stroke, the Court concluded that "separate but equal" schools were inherently unequal, because they stamped African American children with a "badge of racial inferiority" that stayed with them throughout their lives.

The Movement Gains National Visibility

In 1955, a 14-year-old African American Chicago teen who was visiting his uncle in Mississippi was kidnapped, tortured, and killed because of alleged comments he made to a white female shopkeeper. His mother ensured the nation saw his mutilated corpse by allowing a photograph to run in *Jet* magazine. His white killers, who later confessed in another national magazine, *Life,* were quickly acquitted. The young people who were Emmett Till's age in 1955 would be the generation who engaged in political resistance to racial injustice in the 1960s.

>The 1955 Chicago funeral of Emmett Till, a teenager who was tortured and killed in Mississippi, attracted national attention. His mother insisted on an open casket funeral because she "wanted the whole world to see" what racism had done to her son. Many scholars believe the national attention on this murder helped mobilize a generation of young people to push for radical social change in the 1960s.

Although African Americans had boycotted segregated public transportation throughout the South since the late 19th century, it would not be until 1955 that this protest would help to spark a national movement. In Montgomery, Alabama, and throughout the South, buses were segregated, with white riders boarding in the front and sitting front to back and African American riders sitting in the rear of the bus.[15] In December, Rosa Parks was on a bus returning home from work. The bus driver asked the 43-year-old African American woman to give up her seat for a white man; Parks refused and was arrested for violating a local segregation law.

The Montgomery chapter of the NAACP, which Parks helped lead, had sought a test case to challenge the constitutionality of the state's Jim Crow laws. Parks agreed to participate in the case, and her arrest came at a pivotal time in the civil rights movement. Civil rights activists were buoyed by the *Brown* decision, but white supremacists were mobilized.[16] Momentum favored the civil rights activists in the South, and their cause was bolstered when civil rights and religious leaders in Montgomery chose a 27-year-old minister relatively new to the city to lead a bus boycott to protest Parks's arrest and segregated public facilities. The name of this preacher was Martin Luther King, Jr.[17]

Local Organizing and the Strategies of Civil Disobedience

The year-long bus boycott garnered national media attention, and King became a national symbol for the civil rights movement. King's leadership skills were put to the test during the battle: He was arrested. His home was bombed. Death threats were made against him. But for 381 days, the buses of Montgomery remained virtually empty, representing a serious loss in revenue to the city and causing the NAACP to be banned in the state of Alabama. African Americans walked to and from work, day in and day out, for over a year. White employers drove some domestic servants to and from work. Finally, in December 1956, the U.S. Supreme Court ruled that segregated buses were unconstitutional.[18] The bus boycott was a success on many fronts: its justness was confirmed by the Supreme Court, the protests garnered national media attention and evoked public sympathy, and the civil rights movement had gained an articulate leader who was capable of unifying and motivating masses and who had an effective strategy for challenging racism within American society. King advocated protesting government-sanctioned discrimination through civil disobedience and peaceful demonstrations, boycotts, and marches. African American students, as well as white students and other civil rights activists from across the country, adopted these tactics to challenge the policies of segregation.

Other groups, including the Student Nonviolent Coordinating Committee (SNCC) and the Congress of Racial Equality (CORE), advocated the use of more direct action nonviolent strategies—voter registration drives and sit-ins—in the most violent of the southern states, Mississippi and Georgia. In 1961, SNCC and CORE joined the NAACP and Martin Luther King's Southern

Analyzing the Sources

A FAMOUS IMAGE FROM THE CIVIL RIGHTS ERA

In this photograph, Fannie Lou Hamer, a former sharecropper from Mississippi who became an activist with the Student Nonviolent Coordinating Committee, gives testimony before the Democratic National Convention held in Atlantic City in 1964. Local Mississippians and civil rights activists joined together in the interracial Mississippi Freedom Democratic Party (MFDP) to challenge the all-white Democratic Party in Mississippi. Mrs. Hamer told the nation of her attempts to register to vote and how, as a result, she and other women were severely beaten in a Winona Mississippi jail, and she was thrown off the plantation where she and her husband had worked for many years. She asked that the Mississippi Freedom Democratic

Party be seated and that the all-white Mississippi delegation be sent home. President Lyndon Johnson, who was running for reelection, offered to seat two of the MFDP delegates and determined that beginning in 1968 all national convention state delegations had to be reflective of the demographics of their state, including race, gender, and age. In 1972, the Republican Party made the same ruling.

Evaluating the Evidence

1. What makes this picture unusual in terms of how we see official governmental actions? Would most Americans have heard stories like Mrs. Hamer's from the people who experienced them? What does this picture tell us about the power of the media to make change in a democratic society?

2. In 1964, there were only three television stations, so when a national event like the Democratic National Convention aired, all stations would cover it. When Mrs. Hamer spoke, it was during the prime evening hours when the viewing audience was the largest. President Johnson was so concerned about this talk that he attempted to interrupt it with a national address of his own. Why do you think this testimony has been seen as having such an important impact?

Christian Leadership Conference (SCLC) under the umbrella organization of COFO (Coalition of Federated Organizations) to focus on common goals. SNCC, CORE, and the NAACP emphasized building leadership skills of local African American citizens in southern communities based on the groundwork laid by WWII veterans. Emphasizing voter registration and education, one of COFO's most nationally visible endeavors was the 1964 Summer Project in which northern college students came down to work with local communities in Freedom Schools and voter registration drives. One outcome of this work was the establishment of the racially integrated Mississippi Freedom Democratic Party at the 1964 Democratic Convention, which forced presidential candidate Lyndon Johnson and the Democratic Party to refuse to seat all-white delegations in the future.[19]

Besides political protest, activists from all these groups engaged in mass marches to draw public attention to their challenge to Jim Crow segregation and racial inequality. The violence in such places as Birmingham and Montgomery (Alabama), Jackson (Mississippi), and Albany (Georgia) televised on the evening news kept white America aware of the aims of the protestors. One famous series of marches occurred in early March 1965 from Selma to Montgomery, Alabama. On Sunday, March 7, about 600 civil rights activists began a march out of Selma, protesting the policies of intimidation and violence that prevented African Americans from registering to vote. The demonstrators walked only six blocks to the Edmund Pettus bridge, where law enforcement officials were waiting.[20] When the protesters peacefully attempted to cross the bridge, law enforcement officers brutally attacked them, using tear gas, bull whips, and nightsticks. Dubbed Bloody Sunday, the march and the beatings were televised nationally and were instrumental in swaying public opinion in favor of civil rights. The marches sparked a renewed focus on the lack of voting rights for African Americans and ultimately helped to pressure Congress to pass the Voting Rights Act in 1965.[21]

Although the violence used against protesters generated positive opinions of the civil rights movement, another form of violence, urban riots, eroded feelings of white goodwill toward the movement. For five days in 1965, rioting in the Watts neighborhood of Los Angeles resulted in 34 deaths, more than 1,000 injuries, and over 4,000 arrests. Although the immediate cause of the violence was an altercation between white police officers and an African American man who had been arrested for drunk driving, the frustration and anger that spilled over had long been brewing in this poor, predominantly African American neighborhood.

On April 4, 1968, Martin Luther King was in Memphis, Tennessee, in support of African American sanitation workers who were striking for equal treatment and pay with white workers. Standing on a balcony at the Lorraine Motel, King was killed by an assassin's bullet. Heartbreak, hopelessness, and despair followed King's assassination—a feeling manifested in part by further rioting in over 100 cities. Many Americans, both black and white, objected to the looting depicted in nightly news broadcasts. But some noted that because of the accumulated injustices against African Americans, the government and the rule of law had lost legitimacy in the eyes of those who were rioting.[22]

>African American sanitation workers in Memphis, Tennessee, went on strike in 1968 to protest dangerous working conditions and better pay. They organized under the slogan "I Am a Man." Martin Luther King, Jr., was in Memphis supporting the strike as part of his Poor People's Campaign when he was assassinated.

The Government's Response to the Civil Rights Movement

The civil rights movement is credited not only with ending segregation in public schools but also with the desegregation of public accommodations such as buses, restaurants, and hotels and with promoting universal suffrage. As a result of the movement, Congress passed the 1965 Voting Rights Act, which aggressively sought to counter nearly 100 years of disenfranchisement, as well as the 1964 Civil Rights Act, which bars racial discrimination in accommodations and private employment, and the 1968 Civil Rights Act, which prohibits racial discrimination in housing.

The Civil Rights Act of 1964

Simultaneously expanding the rights of many Americans and providing them with important protections from discrimination, the Civil Rights Act of 1964 includes provisions that mandate equality on numerous fronts:

- It outlaws arbitrary discrimination in voter registration practices within the states.
- It bans discrimination in public accommodations, including hotels, restaurants, and theaters.
- It prohibits state and local governments from banning access to public facilities on the basis of race, religion, or ethnicity.
- It empowers the U.S. attorney general to sue to desegregate public schools.
- It bars government agencies from discrimination, and imposes the threat of the loss of federal funding if an agency violates the ban.
- It establishes a standard of equality in employment opportunity.

The last part of the act, Title VII, which establishes the equality standard in employment opportunity, provides the legal foundation for a body of law that regulates fair employment practices. Specifically, Title VII bans discrimination in employment based on inherent characteristics—race, national origin, religion, and sex. Title VII also established the Equal Employment Opportunity Commission (EEOC), a government body that still administers Title VII today.

> Two young college students help a Mississippi woman register to vote during the Freedom Summer of 1964. In that summer, thousands of civil rights activists encouraged and assisted African Americans in the Deep South to register to vote. During the Freedom Summer more than 1,000 civil rights volunteers were arrested, close to 100 were beaten by angry mobs and police officers, and at least one white volunteer, one white civil rights worker and one black civil rights worker were murdered in response to their efforts to register African American voters.

The Voting Rights Act of 1965

Although the Civil Rights Act of 1964 sought to address discrimination in access to public accommodations, employment, and education, many civil rights leaders believed that further legislation was necessary to protect the voting rights of African Americans in the South because they had been so systematically intimidated and prevented from participating.[23] In some southern counties, less than a third of all eligible African Americans were registered to vote, whereas nearly two-thirds of eligible white voters were registered in the same counties.

During the summer of 1964, thousands of civil rights activists, including many college students, worked to register black voters in southern states where black voter registration was dismal. Within months, a quarter of a million new voters had been added to the voting rolls. However, because of violent attacks on civil rights activists and citizens, and the murders of activists in Mississippi in the summer of 1964, Congress determined that it needed to enact a federal law to eliminate discriminatory local and state government registration and voting practices. The Voting Rights Act of 1965 (VRA) banned voter registration practices, such as literacy tests. Moreover, the VRA mandated federal intervention in any county in which less than 50 percent of eligible voters were registered.

An element of this requirement forced nine states, and many other counties and communities, to receive preclearance from the Justice Department before implementing any laws that would impact voting procedures, such as redrawing districts. In 2013, the Supreme Court in *Shelby County v. Alabama* found this portion of the law to be unconstitutional. Disagreement on the Court, and in the nation as a whole, centered around whether racial minorities continue to confront barriers to exercising the ballot in states with a history of racial animus. The majority argued that voter turnout of African Americans was higher in some of the protected states than in states that were not covered by this provision. Those who disagreed with the decision pointed to the number of claims that continue to come before the Justice Department claiming disenfranchisement through governmental policies and actions.[24]

Impact of the Civil Rights Movement

The culmination of many acts of resistance by individuals and groups, the civil rights movement has had a momentous impact on society by working for the laws and rulings that bar discrimination in employment, public accommodations, education, and housing. The movement has also had a profound impact on voting rights by establishing the principle that the laws governing voter registration and participation should ensure that individuals are permitted to vote regardless of their race. As a result of the Voting Rights Act, in Mississippi, for example, the percentage of African Americans registered to vote jumped from 7 percent in 1965 to 72 percent in 2006, and then to 90 percent in 2012. Today, in some states, including Georgia, Mississippi, and South Carolina, a greater percentage of African Americans are registered than whites. In addition, all states, especially those in the South, have seen an increase in the number of African Americans elected to serve in offices at the state, county, and municipal levels and in school districts. Indeed, more African Americans serve in local elected office in Mississippi than in any other state, and all southern states are among those with the highest numbers of African American local elected officials.[25] However, Mississippi has not elected an African American official to a state wide office since Reconstruction.

In addition to having a profound effect on race relations and civil rights law, the civil rights movement soon came to be regarded by other groups as a model of political engagement. Women, ethnic minorities, and persons with disabilities have adopted many tactics of the movement in their own quest to secure their civil rights.

The Movement for Women's Civil Rights

FIGURE 5.2 ▇ THE WAGE GAP, BY GENDER AND RACE If white, non-Hispanic men are at 100 percent, then white non-Hispanic women are at 78 percent, African American men at 73 percent, African American women at 64 percent, Hispanic men at 64 percent, and Hispanic women at 54 percent. How is the intersectionality discussed by Third Wave Feminists (page 174) demonstrated by this data? What hypotheses can you generate to explain the differences in earning—across education levels and types of jobs—based on race and gender? Why might civil rights legislation not have remedied this issue? Are these disparities something the government should be concerned about? why or why not?

SOURCE: National Women's Law Center, "Closing the Wage Gap Is Crucial for Women of Color and Their Families," November 2013, www.nwlc.org/sites/default/files/pdfs/2013.11.13_closing_the_wage_gap_is_crucial_for_woc_and_their_families.pdf.

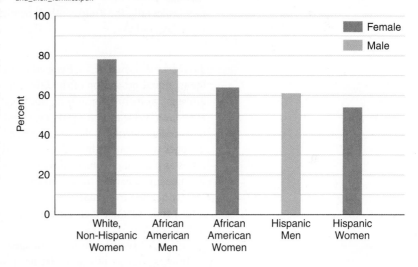

As already noted, the pronouncement in the Declaration of Independence that "all men are created equal" initially applied only to white men, and usually only to those who owned property. Not only did the concept of equal protection of the laws not apply to nonwhite male citizens, until the Civil War amendments to the Constitution and subsequent pieces of national legislation such as the Voting Rights and Civil Rights Acts, it also did not apply to female citizens—white or nonwhite. Like African American men, women had to wait until the Constitution was amended and civil rights legislation was adopted, in response to the women's rights movement, for equal protection of the laws.

Advocates for women's civil rights began their efforts in the mid-1800s, initially focusing on gaining the right to vote for women citizens. That endeavor, the first of three waves of the women's rights movement, won suffrage for women in 1920.

The First Wave of the Women's Rights Movement

The segregation of the women delegates at the 1840 World Anti-Slavery Conference in London was a defining moment for the first wave of the U.S. women's rights movement. Forced to sit in the balcony behind a drawn curtain, Lucretia Mott and Elizabeth Cady Stanton recognized that without improving their own legal and political status, women were not going to be successful in fighting for the legal rights of other groups of people.

In 1848, Mott and Stanton organized a meeting at Seneca Falls, New York, to talk about the lack of legal rights of U.S. citizens who happened to be born female. At the end of the convention, the participants signed the Declaration of Sentiments. This Declaration, modeled after the Declaration of Independence, listed many rights and opportunities that the law did not guarantee women, including the right to vote, educational and employment opportunities equal to those of white men, and married women's rights to own property as well as legal standing to sue. At the end of the convention, the participants signed the Declaration of Sentiments (see Appendix D).

Clearly, John Adams and the other architects of the Constitution had ignored Abigail Adams's request to her husband and his colleagues to "remember the ladies" when they created the new system of government. Adams warned her husband that not only would women not feel bound to obey laws in which they had no say but also the ladies would "foment a rebellion" if they were not provided a voice in government.

The signatories of the Declaration of Sentiments began Adams's forecasted rebellion. The document they signed insisted "that [women] have immediate admission to all rights and privileges which belong to them as citizens of these United States." For those women and men who joined this new movement for women's civil rights, the right to vote became the focal point. They recognized that this right was the foundational right that would enable women to win the other rights and privileges of citizenship.

Because the Constitution initially reserved for the states the authority to determine who had the right to vote as well as to be employed and obtain the best possible education, many of the initial battles for women's rights took place at the state level of government. Eventually, as the national government's responsibilities expanded through court interpretations of the Constitution, especially the Fourteenth Amendment, the federal government's role in guaranteeing civil rights expanded.

STATE-LEVEL RIGHTS Even after ratification of the Fourteenth Amendment (1868) guaranteeing equal protection of the laws for all people and the same privileges and immunities to all citizens, women's educational and work opportunities were limited by social norms as well as state laws. Education for girls prepared them to be good wives and mothers, not to be economically independent. By the late 1800s, a few colleges began to admit women, and several women's colleges were established. Yet most colleges did not offer women the same educational opportunities as men, and women who graduated and aspired to a career were limited in two ways. First, by choosing a career, these educated women gave up the possibility of marriage. They were not legally banned from marriage, but societal norms prevented them from having both a career and a husband. Second, their career choices were limited: teaching, the developing professions of nursing and social work, or missionary work.

In 1873, Myra Bradwell challenged women's limited career choices when she sued the state of Illinois over its refusal to let her practice law.[26] In this case, the Supreme Court found that women's God-given destiny was to "fulfill the noble and benign offices of wife and mother" and that allowing women to practice law would impinge on that destiny. The *Bradwell* case established the precedent for the Court to justify allowing women to be treated differently than men are (sex-based discrimination) if the different treatment was deemed a *rational* means by which the government could fulfill a *legitimate* public interest. In the *Bradwell* case, the Court applied the *ordinary scrutiny* test, deeming it legitimate for the government to protect the role of women as wives and mothers, and, to accomplish that protection, it was rational to deny them equal employment opportunities.

In 1875, Virginia Minor of Missouri (actually her husband, because she, like all married women, did not have standing to sue) challenged the constitutionality of the Missouri law that guaranteed the right to vote only to male U.S. citizens. In this case, *Minor v. Happersett,* the Supreme Court acknowledged that women were citizens, yet it also decreed that state governments established voting rights, not the U.S. Constitution.[27] Therefore, the justices argued that the Fourteenth Amendment's privileges and immunities clause did not give women rights not established in the Constitution, hence it did not extend to women the right to vote. Although by 1875 some local governments (school districts specifically) had extended voting rights to women, no state other than New Jersey had ever given women the right to vote. Women who owned property in New Jersey had the right to vote for a brief period between the end of the War for Independence and 1807, when it was taken away in response to the lobbying of politicians and professional men.

THE NINETEENTH AMENDMENT TO THE CONSTITUTION The American Women's Suffrage Association (AWSA), directed by Lucy Stone, had been leading the battle to extend the right to vote to women in the states since 1869. Simultaneously, the National Women's

Suffrage Association (NWSA), directed by Susan B. Anthony and Elizabeth Cady Stanton, had been fighting to extend to women all rights of citizenship, including but not limited to the right to vote. In 1890, frustrated by their lack of success in the battle to extend suffrage to women, the AWSA and the NWSA joined forces, creating the National American Women's Suffrage Association (NAWSA). The NAWSA focused its efforts on amending the U.S. Constitution.

In 1916, Alice Paul founded the National Women's Party, which adopted more radical tactics than the NAWSA had been willing to use in its fight for suffrage. Noting the lack of support on the part of national officials for suffrage, Paul's organization called on voters in the 1916 election not to vote for candidates who opposed women's suffrage, including President Woodrow Wilson (1913–1921), who was running for reelection. In 1917, after President Wilson was reelected, Paul and other suffragists chained themselves to the White House fence and called on Wilson to support the suffrage amendment. Arrested, jailed, and force-fed when they engaged in a hunger strike, the women gained media attention, which in turn brought national attention to their struggle for suffrage and the president's opposition. After several months and persistent media pressure, President Wilson called on the House and the Senate to approve the women's suffrage amendment.

Congress approved this amendment in June 1919, and by the following year 36 states had ratified it. The Nineteenth Amendment prohibited the national and state governments from abridging or denying citizens the right to vote on account of sex. The right to vote was extended to another group of citizens in 1971 when the states ratified the Twenty-sixth Amendment. This amendment guarantees citizens 18 years of age and older the right to vote. However, college students and civil rights advocates have raised concerns about lack of equal protection of voting rights for college students living away from their parents.

The Second Wave of the Women's Rights Movement

After the Nineteenth Amendment was added to the Constitution, the push for women's rights ceased to be a mass movement. Women were still organized in groups and lobbied the government for women's civil rights, but the many women's organizations were no longer working collectively toward a single goal, such as the right to vote. Another mass women's movement did not arise until the 1960s. Several factors account for the mobilization of the second wave of the women's movement in the 1960s, which focused this time on the plethora of rights related to the social, economic, and political status of women, many of the same rights originally demanded in the Declaration of Sentiments.

By the 1960s, large numbers of women were working outside the home in the paid labor force. Working women talked with one another about their work and family lives and came to recognize common concerns and problems, including discrimination in educational opportunities, employment opportunities, and pay; lack of child care; domestic violence; the problem of rape, for which *they* were often blamed; and their inability to obtain credit (borrow money) without having a male cosign on the loan. Women recognized that as a class of citizens they did not have equal protection of the laws.

In 1961, at the prodding of Esther Peterson, the director of the Women's Bureau in the Department of Labor, President John F. Kennedy (1961–1963) established a Commission on the Status of Women, chaired by Eleanor Roosevelt. In 1963, the commission reported that women in the United States were discriminated against in many areas of life, including education and employment. In its report, the commission argued that women needed to pursue lawsuits that would allow the Supreme Court to interpret properly the Fourteenth Amendment's equal protection clause, hence prohibiting discrimination against women.

By the mid-1960s, the women's rights movement was rejuvenated with a second wave of mass activity. The goal of this second wave was equal legal rights for women. The means to achieve that goal included public demonstrations, legislation, litigation, and an as yet unsuccessful attempt to enact the Equal Rights Amendment (ERA), which had been written by Alice Paul and first introduced in Congress in 1923.

FEDERAL LEGISLATION AND WOMEN'S RIGHTS In 1955, Edith Green (D-Oreg.) introduced into Congress the first piece of national legislation written specifically to protect women, the Equal Pay Act. Enacted into law in 1963, the Equal Pay Act prohibited employers from paying women less than men were paid for the same job, which was the standard employment practice at the time.

The 1964 Civil Rights Act as initially drafted prohibited discrimination in education, employment, and public accommodations based on race, ethnicity, and religion. Yet because of congressional women's efforts, Title VII of the proposed act was rewritten to prohibit discrimination in all personnel decisions based on *sex* as well as the other inherent characteristics. Initially, the

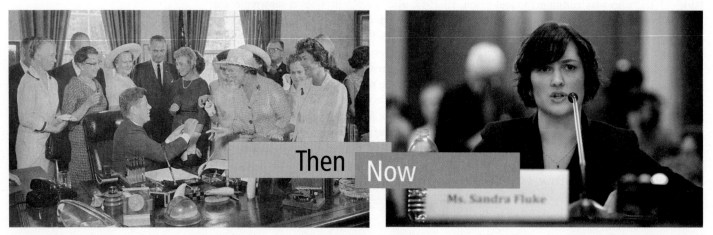

Then Now

Ms. Sandra Fluke

> Members of the Business and Professional Women (an advocacy and educational organization that has promoted women's equity since 1919) and Representative Catherine May (R-Wash.), one of the 13 women serving in Congress at the time, surround President John Kennedy as he signs the Equal Pay Act in 1963. Fifty years later, Sandra Fluke came to national attention when she was denied the opportunity to testify before Congress regarding her belief that insurance plans should cover contraception. Rush Limbaugh, on his national talk show, referred to her as a "slut" who wanted the American people to pay for her sexual activity. Her responses to this characterization of the role of contraception impacted the national debate. In 2014, she announced her intention to run for Congress. How might generational differences in culture and the issues faced change the strategies that women use to advocate for equality?

EEOC, the federal agency responsible for monitoring Title VII implementation, did not take sex-based discrimination complaints seriously. Women serving on state committees on the status of women responded by establishing the National Organization for Women (NOW) in 1966. NOW's initial statement of purpose is modeled on the requests of the 1848 Seneca Falls Declaration of Sentiments, demonstrating the continued lack of progress toward the goal of women's equality under the law.[28]

To take advantage of Title VII's promise of equal employment opportunities, women needed to pursue educational opportunities on an equal basis with men. Yet Title VI of the 1964 Civil Rights Act does not prohibit sex-based discrimination in institutions that receive federal funds, including educational institutions. By 1972, women's rights advocates won an amendment to the 1964 Civil Rights Act, Title IX, which prohibits sex-based discrimination in educational institutions receiving federal funds.

The Equal Pay Act, Title VII, and Title IX are landmark pieces of national legislation that provide equal protection of the law for women. At the same time that Congress was enacting laws prohibiting sex-based discrimination, the courts were reinterpreting the equal protection clause of the Fourteenth Amendment.

WOMEN'S RIGHTS AND THE EQUAL PROTECTION CLAUSE In 1971, in the case of *Reed v. Reed,* the Supreme Court for the first time in history used the equal protection clause of the Fourteenth Amendment to find a law that discriminated against women unconstitutional.[29] In the *Reed* case, the Supreme Court found that an Idaho state law giving automatic preference to men to administer the estate of a deceased person who had not named an administrator was not a rational means to fulfill a legitimate government interest. Hence, using the ordinary scrutiny test established in the 1873 *Bradwell* case, the court ruled this discriminatory treatment of women was unconstitutional.

Then, in 1976, the Supreme Court developed a new test for the legality of sex-based discrimination. Oklahoma law allowed women 18 years of age to buy beer with 3.2% alcohol content. Yet men in Oklahoma had to be 21 years of age to purchase 3.2% beer. Men challenged the law, asking the Court to decide if this sex-based discrimination was constitutional. In this case, *Craig v. Boren,* the Court established the heightened scrutiny test for sex-based discrimination cases: Different treatment is legal if it is substantially related to an important government interest.[30] The Court used this test in the *Craig* case to find the Oklahoma law unconstitutional. The Court also used the heightened scrutiny test in the 1996 *United States v. Virginia* case.[31] In this case, the Court found the male-only admissions policy of the Virginia Military Institute unconstitutional. Justice Ruth Bader Ginsburg noted in her opinion that the state of Virginia had not shown that this discriminatory admissions policy was substantially related to the important government objective of training soldiers.

Today, courts sometimes use the ordinary scrutiny test and other times the heightened scrutiny test when deciding sex-based discrimination cases as well as other non-race-based discrimination cases. Proponents of an ERA argue that the strict scrutiny test, which is used in race-, religion-, and ethnic-based discrimination cases, should also be used in sex-based discrimination cases and that this will not happen until the Constitution is amended to explicitly guarantee equality of rights under the law whether a person is a man or a woman.

THE PROPOSED EQUAL RIGHTS AMENDMENT During the 1970s, as the Supreme Court was reinterpreting the implications of the Fourteenth Amendment for sex-based discrimination, lobbying for the Equal Rights Amendment increased. In 1972, Congress approved the ERA, which states that "equality of rights under the law shall not be denied or abridged by the United States or by any State on account of sex." Finally, 49 years after it was first introduced in Congress, the ERA was sent to the states for ratification.

Opponents of the ERA argued it was a duplication of the Fourteenth Amendment and therefore was not needed. Opponents also claimed that passage of the amendment would make women subject to the military draft; would lead to the integration of all single-sex institutions, including schools and public bathrooms; and would result in the legalization of and public funding for all abortions. Moreover, they argued that the ERA was not needed because Congress was passing laws that guaranteed women equal protection in employment and education. Whether or not the claims of its opponents were accurate, they were successful in defeating the ERA, which had not been ratified by enough states by the deadline of 1982.

The Third Wave of the Women's Rights Movement

Although the first two waves of the women's movement advocated for formal equality or identical legal treatment with men, by the 1990s, feminists realized that a good deal still needed to be done to realize these goals in practice. Despite legal and constitutional change, women still battle inequities, including unequal pay, sexual harassment, and the glass ceiling (aspiring to higher-level jobs but being unable to win them). Moreover, although the situation for women has greatly improved, not all women have benefited equally from gains in women's rights. Third-wave feminism recognizes that women have unequal access to legal rights owing to differences in race, class, ethnicity, and religion. For example, although *Roe v. Wade* secured a woman's right to an abortion, many women cannot afford one. (Abortions can cost anywhere from a few hundred dollars to many thousands of dollars.) Third-wave organizations, such as the Chicago Abortion Fund, seek to overcome economic barriers to reproductive rights by helping women fund abortions. Another key issue has been the ending of sexual violence, particularly that against women; groups such as V-Day have worked to mobilize women globally on political, economic, and cultural fronts to help to make the lives of women safer. Women of color face the intertwined challenges of race and gender, which civil rights laws do not recognize, particularly in the area of employment discrimination. For instance, under the Civil Rights Act of 1964, women of color must challenge employment discrimination as being based on either their gender or their race; there is no legal recognition of the ways in which perceptions of their race and gender could create difficulties in the workplace. If the white women in the workplace are not similarly mistreated, then it is not gender discrimination, and if the men of color are not similarly mistreated, then it is not considered racial discrimination. Third-wave feminists refer to this as **intersectionality,** the experience of multiple forms of oppression simultaneously. Low-income and working-class women of all ethnicities seek solutions to such problems as affordable child and health care. Lesbian, bisexual, and transgendered women are examining the intersection between gender discrimination and oppression based on their sexual identity.

Third-wave feminists also struggle to overcome cultural or sexual identity barriers to equality. Their organizations aim to change norms, spread awareness, and build leadership skills among specific ethnic groups. For example, programs such as the Khmer Girls in Action reach out to Southeast Asian women and girls to help them to set career goals and develop skills for college. And third-wave online communities such as Jezebel provide a feminist critique of the popular culture; riot grrls groups and guerrilla street theater troupes such as the Radical Cheerleaders challenge popular stereotypes of what it means to be female in order to encourage the public to rethink our assumptions concerning gender.

These types of challenges to the portrayal of women in the popular culture have led some people to characterize third-wave feminists as "Lipstick Feminists," rebelling against second-wave feminism. This interpretation has been rejected by third-wave feminists as mistaken; instead, this movement has focused on expanding the political and economic gains made for women in the 1970s and 1980s to all women.[32] Third-wave feminism is a broader movement seeking redress on multiple fronts—not merely legal and political, but cultural and economic as well.

Other Civil Rights Movements

Today, discriminatory treatment is still a reality for many groups of citizens. The civil rights acts notwithstanding, discrimination in employment, education, housing, and due process still occurs. Moreover, battles for civil rights continue. Unfortunately, we cannot discuss all the civil rights movements that have occurred or are ongoing in the United States. Therefore, we will explore the civil rights battles of just a few groups of citizens: Native Americans, Hispanic

intersectionality
the experience of multiple forms of oppression (based on race, gender, class, and/or sexuality) simultaneously

Americans, Asian Americans, and citizens with disabilities. The hard-fought victories and aspirations of these groups offer an overview of both the history and the breadth of contemporary civil rights movements.

Native Americans' Rights

At first, the fledgling nation recognized the native residents of the land that became the United States as members of sovereign and independent nations with inherent rights. The federal government entered into more than 370 treaties with Native American tribes between 1778 and 1870.[33] Most of those treaties promised land to tribes that agreed to move, and almost all those promises were empty, with the government reneging on most of the agreements. In addition, in 1830, Congress passed the Indian Removal Act, which called for the forced relocation of all native peoples to lands west of the Mississippi. In the end, most Native Americans were dispossessed of their lands and wound up living on reservations. The federal government treated Indians as subhumans, relegating them to second-class status, as they had African Americans.

Until Congress passed the Indian Citizenship Act in 1924, Native Americans had virtually no rights to U.S. citizenship, and even the laws that allowed immigrants to become citizens did not apply to Native Americans. The Indian Rights Association, founded in 1882 and active in lobbying Congress and the state

> Elouise Cobell watches Deputy Secretary of the Interior David Hayes testify during a Dec. 17, 2009, Senate Indian Affairs Committee hearing in Washington, D.C., on a multi-billion-dollar lawsuit in which Cobell, a member of the Blackfeet Nation of Montana, was the lead plaintiff. In the suit, which took 13 years to make its way through the courts, Cobell accused the federal government of mismanaging funds held in trust for Native Americans since 1887. The settlement reached in 2009 awarded Native Americans $3.4 billion in reparations, but distribution of the settlement began in 2014.

legislatures until the 1930s, was one of the most important of the early groups that actively campaigned for full suffrage for native peoples, in the belief that enfranchisement would help to "civilize" them. The early 1900s also saw the founding of the Society of American Indians and the American Indian Defense Association, both of which fought for citizenship for Native Americans and then for their civil rights. However, for more than 40 years after passage of the Indian Citizenship Act, the basic rights enumerated in the Bill of Rights were not granted to Native Americans. In the 1960s, Indian activists became more radical, occupying government buildings, picketing, and conducting protests. In 1968, the American Indian Movement (AIM) was founded. In the same year, Congress passed the Indian Civil Rights Act, which ensured that Native Americans would have the full protection of the Bill of Rights both on and off their reservations. Although this law had significant symbolic impact, it lacked an enforcement mechanism, and so native peoples continued to be deprived of basic due process protections and equal education and employment opportunities. The National Indian Education Association (NIEA), founded in 1969, continues to confront the lack of quality educational opportunities for Native Americans and the loss of native culture and values.

During the 1970s, Native American organizations began a new effort to force the federal government to honor treaties granting Indians fishing and hunting rights as well as rights to the natural resources buried in their lands. Indians in New York, Maine, and elsewhere sued for land taken from them decades or even a century ago in violation of treaties. Starting with the 1975 Indian Self-Determination and Education Assistance Act, the national government has enacted laws that support greater autonomy for Indian tribes and give them more control of their assets.

The 1988 Indian Gaming Regulatory Act is the best known of the federal laws enacted to support Indian self-determination. This law authorizes Indian tribes to establish gaming operations on their property and requires them to negotiate compacts with the states in which their lands are located. The compacts typically include a profit-sharing understanding that requires the Indian tribe to give a proportion of its profits to the state government and possibly to contiguous local governments. The act mandates that the money made through gaming operations be used for education, economic development, infrastructure (for example, roads and utilities), law enforcement, and courts. By 2013, the National Indian Gaming Commission, the independent agency that regulates Indian gaming, reported that more than 240 of the federally recognized 562 Indian tribes operate more than 400 casinos and bingo halls in 28 states. The gross revenues for these gaming activities totaled $27.9 billion in 2012.[34] Clearly, one goal of the Gaming Act was to generate resources that would increase the educational and employment opportunities on Indian reservations.

Even with gaming profits, however, the prospects for many Native Americans today remain bleak. According to race and ethnic relations scholars Joe R. Feagin and Clairece Booher Feagin, "Native Americans have endured the longest Depression-like economic situation of any U.S. racial or ethnic group."[35] They are among the poorest, least educated U.S. citizens. Moreover, congressional testimony and materials submitted to support reauthorization of the Voting Rights Act in 2005 documented a pattern of continued discrimination against Native Americans in their right to vote in several states, including Arizona and South Dakota.[36] Like many other groups of U.S. citizens, Native Americans continue to fight in the halls of government, in the courtrooms, and in the public arena for their constitutionally guaranteed rights and privileges.

Citizens of Latin American Descent

U.S. citizens of Latin American descent (Latinos) include those whose families hail from Central America, South America, or the Caribbean. Latinos are the largest minority group in the United States, making up 17 percent of the total U.S. population. Sixty-four percent of this Latino population is composed of natural-born U.S. citizens.[37] Latinos make up a large percentage of the population of several states, including New Mexico, California, Texas, Arizona, and Florida.

In the 2012 presidential election, 48 percent of eligible Hispanic voters voted, constituting almost 8 percent of the voters. In contrast, the voter turnout for blacks was 66.6 percent and for whites was 64.1 percent.[38] So far, the elections that have occurred in the 21st century have been followed by numerous lawsuits claiming that individual citizens, organized groups, and local governments have prevented eligible Latino voters from voting. For example, in 2006 the national government sued Philadelphia's city government for failing to assist voters effectively—specifically Spanish-speaking voters—who had limited English proficiency. Limited English proficiency continues to cause problems with access to voting and equal educational and employment opportunities for many U.S. citizens, including Latino citizens. We focus here on U.S. citizens of Mexican origin—the largest Latino population in the United States today.

EARLY STRUGGLES OF MEXICAN AMERICANS   In 1846, because of land disputes sparked by white immigrants from the United States encroaching on Mexican territory, the United States declared war on Mexico. By the terms of the 1848 Treaty of Guadalupe Hidalgo, which ended the war, Mexico ceded territory to the United States for $15 million. The Mexican landowners living within this ceded territory had the choice of staying on their land and remaining in what was now the United States or relocating to Mexico. According to the treaty, those Mexicans who stayed on their land would become U.S. citizens, and their civil rights would be protected. Although nearly 77,000 Mexicans chose to do so, and became U.S. citizens, their civil rights were *not* protected.[39] Thus began a long and continuing history of discrimination against U.S. citizens of Mexican descent.

At the turn of the 20th century, Mexican Americans organized to protest the various forms of discrimination they were experiencing, which included segregated schools, inequities in employment opportunities and wages, discrimination by law enforcement officers, and barriers to their voting rights such as poll taxes and English-only literacy tests. In 1929, several Mexican American organizations combined to create the League of United Latin American Citizens (LULAC).[40]

In 1945, LULAC successfully challenged the segregated school systems in California, which provided separate schools for Mexican children that were of poorer quality than the schools for white children. In this case, *Mendez v. Westminister,* the federal court set an important precedent by using the Fourteenth Amendment to guarantee equal educational opportunities.[41]

In 1954, the U.S. Supreme Court followed this lower court's precedent when it ended legal race-based segregation in public schools throughout the nation in the *Brown v. Board of Education of Topeka* case.

THE CHICANO MOVEMENT   In addition to the women's rights movement and the civil rights movement for African American rights, the 1960s witnessed the birth of the Chicano Movement, the mass movement for Mexican American civil rights. The Chicano Movement was composed of numerous Latino organizations focusing on a variety of issues, including rights to equal employment and educational opportunities. One of the most widely recognized leaders in the Chicano Movement was Cesar Chavez.

Cesar Chavez began his civil rights work as a community organizer in 1952, encouraging Mexican Americans to vote and educating them about their civil rights. In the early 1960s, Chavez, along with Jessie Lopez and Dolores Huerta, founded the Agricultural Workers Organizing Committee (AWOC) and the National Farm Worker Association (NFWA). Under Chavez's leadership, the AWOC and the NFWA merged to form the United Farm Workers (UFW) in 1966. The UFW organized successful protests and boycotts to improve working conditions and pay for farmworkers.[42]

The activism of Mexican American workers inspired others to call for additional civil rights protections, including access to equal educational opportunity. In 1968, Mexican American high school students in East Los Angeles staged a walkout to protest high dropout rates of Latino students and the lack of bilingual education, Mexican American history classes, and Mexican American teachers. Though the student walkout did not lead to many immediate changes in the school system, it drew national attention, empowered the students, and inspired other protests.

> Cesar Chavez began his civil rights work as a community organizer in 1952 by encouraging Mexican Americans to vote and use their civil rights. Together with Dolores Huerta, he founded the United Farm Workers. From the early 1960s until his death in 1993, Chavez was the leading voice for and organizer of migrant farmworkers in the United States. Huerta was a prominent Chicana labor leader in the country, developing leaders and advocating for the rights of immigrant workers, women, and children.

Until 1971, Latinos were not legally considered a racial minority group, and therefore antidiscrimination laws, such as the 1964 Civil Rights Act, did not apply to them. In the landmark case *Corpus Christi Independent School District v. Cisneros*[43] (1971), the Supreme Court upheld a lower court's ruling that Latinos are a racial minority group; therefore, they are covered by laws protecting the rights of minority groups.[44]

EMPLOYMENT DISCRIMINATION AND OTHER CIVIL RIGHTS ISSUES   Since the 1986 Immigration Reform and Control Act went into effect, organizations that work to protect the rights of Latinos and other minority citizens have been receiving increasing numbers of complaints about employment discrimination. Under this act, employers who hire undocumented immigrant workers are subject to sanctions. To comply with this law, some employers refuse to hire—and thus discriminate against—any applicants for whom English is a second language and any who look Latino, under the assumption that all such people could be undocumented immigrants. This means that employers are violating the equal employment rights of Latino citizens in many cases, for they are mistakenly assuming they are undocumented immigrants.

In response to heightened pressure from the states concerned about an increased presence of illegal immigrants from Mexico and Central America, both the Bush and Obama administrations have enhanced worksite enforcement.

Several state legislators and governors, concerned about growing numbers of illegal immigrants and the lack of a strong federal policy, began passing state laws designed to increase state authority to regulate immigration. For instance, Arizona's 2010 laws added state sanctions related to federal immigration law enforcement. For example, it became a state crime for aliens not to carry their registration documents with them, and state law enforcement officers were required to determine a suspect's immigration status during any lawful stop. The Supreme Court upheld much of the law in *Arizona v. United States* (2012), indicating that evidence of racial profiling would call the law into question.[45] Civil rights activists remain concerned that the law will be used to target the Latino community.

Citizens of Asian Descent

Asian American citizens come from, or have ancestors from, a number of different countries with diverse cultures, religions, histories, and languages. Today, the largest percentage of Asian Americans have Chinese origins, followed by those of Filipino, Asian Indian, Vietnamese, Korean, and Japanese ancestry. Large numbers of immigrants from Japan came to the United States around the turn of the 20th century, but it was not until the 1940s that the flow of immigrants from other Asian countries began to increase, beginning with the Philippines. In the 1960s, the number of immigrants from Korea and India began to increase significantly, and in the 1970s—as the Vietnam War ended—immigrants from Vietnam began to arrive in large numbers. Today, nearly 6 percent of the U.S. population is of Asian descent. The largest Asian American populations live in California, New York, Hawaii, Texas, New Jersey, and Illinois.[46]

Like other U.S. citizens with significant nonwhite ancestry, Asian Americans have had to fight continually for their civil rights, specifically for equal protection under the law and particularly for equal access to educational and employment opportunities as well as citizenship. Asian immigrants and Asian Americans created organizations to fight for citizenship and equal protection of the law, such as the Japanese American Citizens League (JACL; founded in the 1930s). One successful result of those efforts was the 1952 Immigration and Nationality Act, which allowed Asian immigrants to become citizens for the first time. Before passage of this law, only U.S.-born children of Asian immigrants could be citizens.

INTERNMENT OF JAPANESE AMERICANS DURING WORLD WAR II As noted previously, one of the most egregious violations of the civil rights of tens of thousands of Asian American citizens occurred during World War II when Americans of Japanese ancestry were forced to move to government-established camps. Under President Franklin Roosevelt's Executive Order 9066, over 120,000 Japanese Americans, two-thirds of whom were native-born U.S. citizens, were relocated from the West Coast of the United States after Japan's attack on Pearl Harbor. During that same period, the federal government also restricted the travel of Americans of German and Italian ancestry who were living on the West Coast (the United States was also fighting against Germany and Italy), but those citizens were not relocated. Many relocated Japanese Americans lost their homes and businesses.

The JACL fought for decades to obtain reparations for the citizens who were interned and for the repeal of a section of the 1950 Internal Security Act that allowed the government to imprison citizens deemed enemy collaborators during a crisis. Congress repealed the section of the 1950 law targeted by the JACL, and in 1987 President Ronald Reagan signed a bill providing $1.2 billion in reparations.

CONTEMPORARY ISSUES FOR ASIAN AMERICANS During the 1960s and 1980s, the number of organizations and coalitions pressing for the civil rights of Asian Americans grew as large numbers of new immigrants from Asian countries arrived in the United States in response to changes in U.S. immigration laws. During the 1960s, Asian Americans on college campuses organized and fostered a group consciousness about the need to protect their civil rights. During the 1980s, Asian American organizations began to pay more attention to voting rights as well as to hate crimes and employment discrimination. Then in 1996, numerous organizations, each representing Asian Americans with ancestry from one country, joined to form the National Council of Asian Pacific Americans (NCAPA), which presses for equal protection of the law for all Asians.

With the exception of Korean Americans and Vietnamese Americans, Asian Americans have the highest median income compared with the population as a whole.[47] Asian Americans are also twice as likely as the population as a whole to earn a bachelor's degree or higher.[48] Moreover, Asian Americans are better represented in professional and managerial positions than any other racial or ethnic group, including white Americans. Yet like women, Asian American citizens appear to hit a glass ceiling, for they are not represented in the very top positions in the numbers that their high levels of educational achievement would seem to predict. Therefore, those advocating for Asian American civil rights are increasingly concentrating their efforts on discrimination in employment. Professor Don T. Nakanishi, an expert on Asian Americans, points out that Asian Americans are becoming "more organized, more visible and more effective as participants and leaders in order to advance—as well as to protect—their individual and group interests, and to contribute to our nation's democratic processes and institutions."[49] Today, more than 3,000 Asian Americans serve as elected or appointed officials in all levels of government throughout the nation.

>Asian Americans have become more organized as voters and consequently have seen a record number of elected officials from the Asian American community. Why do you think concerted efforts to "get out the vote" have been so important in African American and Asian American communities?

Citizens with Disabilities

The civil rights movements of the 1960s and 1970s made society more aware of the lack of equal protection of the laws for diverse groups of citizens, including people with disabilities. The first law to mandate equal protection for people with physical and mental disabilities was the 1973 Rehabilitation Act, which prohibited discrimination against people with disabilities in federally funded programs. In 1990, people with disabilities achieved a significant enhancement of this earlier victory in their fight to obtain protection of their civil rights. The Americans with Disabilities Act (ADA), enacted in that year, extends the ban on discrimination against people with disabilities in education, employment, health care, housing, and transportation to all programs and organizations, not just those receiving federal funds. The ADA defines a disability as any "physical or mental impairment that substantially limits one or more of the major life activities of the individual." The ADA does not enumerate every disability that it covers, resulting in much confusion over which conditions it covers and which it excludes.

A series of U.S. Supreme Court rulings in the late 1990s and early 2000s narrowed the interpretation of "disability," which decreased the number of people benefiting from the ADA. For example, the Court determined that if an individual can take an action to mitigate an impairment (such as taking medication to prevent seizures), then the impairment is not a disability protected by the ADA. In response, disability advocates, including the National Coalition of Disability Rights and the ADA Watch, successfully lobbied Congress to propose an act restoring the broader interpretation of the term "disability" and, hence, increasing the number of people benefiting from the ADA. The Americans with Disabilities Act Amendments of 2008 went into effect in January 2009. The act applies to the equal protection

>Access to public transportation is key to education and employment opportunities, independence, and full community engagement for people with disabilities. The 1990 Americans with Disabilities Act prohibits discrimination against and sets specific requirements to accommodate transportation for people with disabilities on publicly and privately funded transportation systems.

guaranteed in the Rehabilitation Act (1973) and the ADA (1990). It does not change the written definition of "disability" that is in the ADA, but it does broaden what "substantially limits" and "major life activities" mean, and no longer considers actions taken to mitigate impairments as relevant to determining if employers and educational institutions must accommodate a person's mental or physical disability in public facilities and housing.[50]

There is no question that the ADA has enhanced the civil rights of citizens with disabilities. Before the ADA was enacted, people with disabilities who were fired from their jobs or denied access to schools, office buildings, or other public places had no recourse. Cities were under no obligation to provide even the most reasonable accommodations to people with disabilities who sought employment or the use of public transportation systems. And employers were under no obligation to make even the most minor modifications to their workplaces for employees with disabilities. For example, if a qualified job applicant was wheelchair bound, an employer did not have to consider installing ramps or raising desks to accommodate the wheelchair but could simply refuse to hire the individual. The ADA changed that situation by requiring employers and governmental organizations to make it possible for people with disabilities to participate meaningfully in their communities through reasonable accommodations.

Affirmative Action: Is It Constitutional?

Laws reinforcing constitutional guarantees by prohibiting discriminatory treatment are the most common objectives of civil rights battles. Nevertheless, in the 1960s the federal government also began implementing policies aimed at reinforcing equal access to employment by mandating recruitment procedures that actively sought to identify qualified minority men for government positions. This policy of **affirmative action** was extended to women in employment and then to educational opportunities. However, affirmative action policies have been and continue to be very controversial.

affirmative action
in the employment arena, intentional efforts to recruit, hire, train, and promote underutilized categories of workers (women and minority men); in higher education, intentional efforts to diversify the student body

How Affirmative Action Works

In 1961, President John F. Kennedy used the term *affirmative action* in an executive order regarding the hiring and employment practices of projects performed by private contractors that were financed with federal funds. The order did more than prohibit race-based discrimination. It required that employers receiving federal funds take affirmative action to ensure that their hiring and employment practices were free of racial discrimination. In 1965, President Lyndon B. Johnson extended Kennedy's affirmative action order to include the inherent characteristics of race, color, religion, and national origin. Then in 1967, Johnson again extended affirmative action to include women.

Today, affirmative action policies cover such processes as hiring, training, and promoting. Private companies, nonprofit organizations, and government agencies that receive federal government contracts worth at least $50,000 are required by law to have an affirmative action plan for their workers and job candidates.

Affirmative action does not require organizations to hire unqualified candidates, nor does it require the hiring of a qualified minority candidate over a qualified nonminority candidate. Affirmative action does require that an organization make intentional efforts to diversify its workforce by providing equal opportunity to classes of people that have been historically, and in many cases are still today, subject to discrimination. It focuses attention on an employer's history of personnel decisions. If over the years an employer with an affirmative action plan does not hire qualified underutilized workers (women and minority men), it will appear to many that the employer is discriminating and is violating Title VII of the Civil Rights Act. However, critics of affirmative action argue that it discriminates against Caucasians, and they have questioned whether the way it is applied to personnel policies as well as to college admissions policies is constitutional.

In the 1970s, institutions of higher education began to adopt intentional efforts to expand educational opportunities for both men and women from various minority groups. In addition, colleges and universities use affirmative action to ensure a student body that is diverse in race,

Democracy

Should We Offer Paths to Citizenship for Undocumented Workers?

The Issue: There are approximately 11 million illegal immigrants in the United States. The Department of Homeland Security estimates that a significant number arrived with legal, temporary visas but overstayed past the visa closure date. Fears that "undocumented" workers hold down wages for Americans workers, cost millions of dollars a year for services like health care and education, and present a security risk post–September 11 have led to calls for stronger responses to illegal immigration. Others note that we are a nation of immigrants and that these undocumented workers serve a key economic role in filling low-wage jobs. Do we need to find ways to integrate these families into productive citizenship?

Yes: These individuals form the backbone of many small businesses throughout the United States and, without them, our slowly recovering economy would falter. Workers come here for opportunity, but we force them to live with uncertainty and the constant risk of deportation, limiting their ability to contribute to our economy. We have created a dangerous situation in which workers fear for their lives and livelihoods without any protection of laws or basic human dignity. We should offer these aspiring Americans the chance to integrate fully into our society and not live in fear of deportation. A path to earned citizenship is the only reasonable way to fix this problem and now is time for action.

No: Providing a path to citizenship will allow millions of illegal immigrants to work immediately when 21 million Americans and legal workers are unemployed or underemployed. The fact that we have too many workers for the jobs currently available is the most serious issue facing middle-class and low-wage Americans. Increasing immigration means lower earnings for middle-class and working-class citizens. If we reward illegal immigrants with the possibility of citizenship, we are also condoning illegal behavior, inviting more illegal immigration, and losing control over our borders.

Other Approaches: In order for us to sustain a process in which we provide ways by which currently illegal aliens become citizens, we must simultaneously increase spending on border security, improve our systems for verifying the eligibility of new employees, and focus on increasing the immigration rates of high-skilled workers. Many of these individuals just want to cease living in fear of deportation. They are less interested in citizenship. What they—and our economy—need is to find a means of legalization, not paths to citizenship.

What do you think?

1. Do you find compelling reasons to protect the rights and interests of illegal immigrants and their children? If so, what are they?

2. Some opponents of immigration reform argue that there should be no protection of undocumented workers because they violated the law in coming to the United States or in staying beyond what their visas allow. How do you respond to this argument?

3. If you had to choose, do you think providing pathways to citizenship or the legalization of undocumented workers would be the best way to address the nation's immigration issues?

---

color, economic status, and other characteristics. These institutions believe that having students on campus from a wide variety of backgrounds enhances all students' educational experience and best prepares them to function successfully in a nation that is increasingly diverse. Yet like affirmative action in personnel policies, affirmative action in college admission policies has been controversial.

Opposition to Affirmative Action

In the important *Bakke* decision in 1978, the U.S. Supreme Court found unconstitutional the University of California at Davis's affirmative action plan for admission to its medical school.[51] The UC Davis plan set aside 16 of the 100 seats in its first-year medical school class for racial minorities (specifically, African Americans, Latinos, Asian Americans, and Native Americans).

Justice Powell noted in his opinion that schools can take race into consideration as one of several factors for admission but cannot use it as the sole consideration.

Opponents have challenged affirmative action in the courts as well as through legislative processes and statewide ballot measures. In two cases involving the University of Michigan in 2003, the U.S. Supreme Court upheld the *Bakke* decision that universities can use race as a factor in admissions decisions, but not as the overriding factor. Using the strict scrutiny test, the Court said in the *Grutter v. Bollinger* case that the school's goal of creating a diverse student body serves a *compelling public interest:* a diverse student body enhances "cross-racial understanding . . . breaks down racial stereotypes . . . and helps students better understand persons of different races."[52]

In 2007, however, the Supreme Court found unconstitutional two school districts' policies of assigning students to elementary schools based on race to ensure a diverse student body.[53] The majority of justices argued that those policies violated the equal protection clause of the Fourteenth Amendment. Chief Justice Roberts, writing for the majority, argued that governments should not use laws to remedy racial imbalances caused by economic inequalities, individual choices, and historical biases (de facto imbalances). He stated that such laws put in place discrimination that the Court found unconstitutional in the *Brown* case back in 1954. The justices who dissented from the majority opinion noted that today's policies are trying to ensure inclusion of minorities, not create segregation of, and hence cause harm to, minorities. The dissenters view policies that take race into account to ensure inclusion and balance as necessary means to achieving the compelling public good gained by a diverse student body.

Are affirmative action policies aimed at ensuring equal educational and employment opportunities for women and minority men constitutional, or do they violate the equal protection clause of the Fourteenth Amendment? When the Supreme Court revisited this issue in the 2013 decision of *Fisher v. the University of Texas,* despite great public speculation, the Court remanded the decision to the lower court, instructing the judges to apply a strict scrutiny test as required by *Bakke* and *Grutter,* to ensure that the university's use of race in admissions was constitutional.[54]

POLITICAL

Inquiry

FIGURE 5.3 ■ COLLEGE ADMISSION This cartoon suggests a number of the factors that colleges consider when making admissions decisions. Why is membership in a minority group controversial, whereas other factors—such as the ability to play a certain sport or being the son or daughter of a graduate—are not? In the future, how can colleges achieve the goals of a diverse campus and a fair admissions process?

Conclusion
Thinking Critically About What's Next in Civil Rights

For most of U.S. history, the law allowed, and in some cases even required, discrimination against people based on inherent characteristics such as race, ethnicity, and sex. This discriminatory treatment meant that the U.S. government did not guarantee all citizens equal protection of their civil rights. The long and continuing battles for civil rights of African Americans, Native Americans, and women are only part of the story. Latinos, Asian Americans, citizens with disabilities, and LGBT citizens are all currently engaged in political, legal, and civic activities aimed at guaranteeing equal protection of their civil rights. Numerous other groups are working to gain their civil rights as well. These include older Americans, poor Americans, and children born in the United States to parents who are in the country illegally. (The Fourteenth Amendment extends citizenship, and hence civil rights, to these children.)

Building on the legal gains of previous activists for gender equality, the current movement has expanded its focus to ensure that the concerns of all women, regardless of race, ethnicity, class, religion, or sexual identity, are heard. While legal and political battles are still fought, this movement has expanded to consider cultural and economic challenges to women, and it capitalizes on new techniques provided by social media. Although the goals of the women's movement remain the same, third-wave feminism's aims are more diffuse than in the past and are being pursued through myriad organizations focusing on a wide variety of cultural and policy objectives.

As individuals whose interests were not previously considered in discussions of civil rights intensify their challenges to oppression, the nation will continue to struggle with the scope and meaning of civil rights.

Summary

1. The Meaning of Equality Under the Law

The Fourteenth Amendment guarantees all people equal protection of the laws. However, courts use one of three tests—ordinary scrutiny, heightened scrutiny, or strict scrutiny—to determine when discriminatory treatment is a legal means by which the government can fulfill its responsibility to a public interest.

2. Lesbian, Gay, Bisexual, and Transgendered Citizens

Rapid changes in housing, employment, and family protections, as well as marital rights to lesbian, gay, bisexual, and transgendered citizens, are happening in both the legislative and judicial realms and in states and the federal government. However, while more states are extending rights, other states are seeking legislative approaches to limiting them.

3. Slavery and Its Aftermath

One legacy of slavery in the United States was a system of racial segregation. Under that system, both the states and the federal government condoned and accepted a structure of inherent inequality for African Americans in nearly all aspects of life, and they were forced to use separate facilities, from water fountains to educational institutions.

4. The Civil Rights Movement

Through the efforts of the early and modern civil rights organizations such as the NAACP, chinks appeared in the armor of the segregationists. The strategy of using the justice system to right previous wrongs proved instrumental in radically changing the nation's educational system, especially with the key *Brown v. Board of Education* decision in 1954, in which the Supreme Court ruled against segregation. In other arenas, such as public accommodations and housing, Dr. Martin Luther King's leadership and strategy of nonviolent civil disobedience proved instrumental in winning victories in both legislatures and the court of public opinion. The government responded to the demands for equal rights for African Americans with an important series of laws that attempted to secure fundamental rights, including voting rights and rights to employment, public accommodations, housing, and equal pay.

5. The Movement for Women's Civil Rights

The 1848 Seneca Falls Convention, which produced the Declaration of Sentiments, was the beginning of the first wave of the women's rights movement in the United States. This first wave focused on winning for women the right to vote, which was accomplished by the ratification of the Nineteenth Amendment in 1920. The second wave of the women's rights movement began in the 1960s with women organizing and lobbying for laws guaranteeing them equality of rights. Today, a third wave of feminists seeks to make gains achieved by earlier generations accessible to all women regardless of race, ethnicity, class, religion, nationality, or sexual identity.

6. Other Civil Rights Movements

In addition to African Americans and women, numerous other groups of U.S. citizens have battled for, and continue to fight for, equal treatment under the law. These groups include Native Americans, Latino and Asian American citizens, and citizens with disabilities. They seek equal employment opportunities, educational opportunities, housing, voting rights, and marriage rights, among others.

7. Affirmative Action: Is It Constitutional?

Since 1866, the national government has enacted civil rights laws that have prohibited discrimination. In a 1961 executive order, President John F. Kennedy introduced the nation to a proactive policy of intentional actions to recruit minority male workers, which he labeled *affirmative action*. President Lyndon B. Johnson extended affirmative action to women. Institutions of higher education also adopted the concept of affirmative action in their admissions policies. Affirmative action has been controversial, however, and a review of recent Supreme Court cases indicates that the constitutionality of affirmative action is in question.

Key Terms

affirmative action 180

Black Codes 161

Brown v. Board of Education of Topeka 164

civil disobedience 159

civil rights 154

de jure segregation 161

equal protection clause 163

grandfather clause 163

hate crime 158

heightened scrutiny test (intermediate scrutiny test) 155

inherent characteristics 154

intersectionality 174

Jim Crow laws 161

literacy test 163

ordinary scrutiny test (rational basis test) 156

Plessy v. Ferguson 163

poll tax 163

Reconstruction era 161

separate but equal doctrine 163

standing to sue 159

strict scrutiny test 155

suspect classifications 155

white primary 162

For Review

1. What is meant by *suspect classification?*

2. What tactics did whites in the South use to prevent African Americans from achieving equality before the civil rights era?

3. What strategy did the early civil rights movements employ to end discrimination?

4. What civil rights did the 1964 Civil Rights Act protect for minority, male citizens but not for female citizens?

5. Why did those fighting for women's civil rights begin their work by concentrating their efforts on state governments rather than on the national government?

6. Other than color and sex, what inherent (immutable) characteristics have been used as a basis for discriminatory treatment of citizens?

7. Explain how an approach to improving access to employment and educational opportunity based on affirmative action differs from an approach based on civil rights legislation.

For Critical Thinking and Discussion

1. Is it constitutional to deny any citizen the equal protection of marriage laws; is denying gay men and lesbians the right to marry a necessary means to a compelling public interest? Explain.

2. Today, more women than men are in college pursuing their bachelor's degrees. Is it legal for schools to give preference to male applicants by accepting men with lower SAT scores and high school grade-point averages than women, to maintain sex balance in the student body? Explain.

3. Many organizations fighting for civil rights protections include in their name the phrase "legal defense and education fund." What do you think explains the common two-pronged focus of these organizations?

4. What would be the effect of using the strict scrutiny test to determine the legality of sex-based discrimination? Would sex-based affirmative action pass the test? Explain.

MULTIPLE CHOICE: Choose the lettered item that answers the question correctly.

1. The idea that individuals are protected from discrimination on the basis of race, national origin, religion, and sex is called
   a. civil liberties.
   b. civil rights.
   c. natural rights.
   d. unalienable rights.

2. Individual attributes such as race, national origin, religion, and sex are called
   a. unalienable rights.
   b. inherent characteristics.
   c. indiscriminatory qualities.
   d. civil rights categories.

3. Laws that required the strict separation of racial groups, with whites and "nonwhites" attending separate schools, working in different jobs, and using segregated public accommodations such as transportation and restaurants are called
   a. Fred Samuels laws.
   b. Sally Hemmings laws.
   c. Jim Crow laws.
   d. Abraham Lincoln laws.

4. An election in which a party's nominees were chosen but in which only white people were allowed to vote is called
   a. a general election.
   b. a run-off primary.
   c. an uncontested primary.
   d. a white primary.

5. A mechanism that exempted individuals from conditions on voting (such as poll taxes or literacy tests) if they or their ancestors had been eligible to vote before 1870 is called
   a. a poll tax.
   b. a white primary.
   c. the grandfather clause.
   d. a literacy test.

6. Unlike sex-based discrimination, race-based discrimination must pass the
   a. heightened scrutiny test.
   b. ordinary scrutiny test.
   c. strict scrutiny test.
   d. ultimate scrutiny test.

7. Initially the courts interpreted which amendment in such a way that women were told they were citizens but that they had no constitutional right to vote?
   a. Thirteenth Amendment
   b. Fourteenth Amendment
   c. Fifteenth Amendment
   d. Nineteenth Amendment

8. What right does Title IX protect for women?
   a. equal access to credit
   b. equal access to educational opportunities
   c. equal access to employment opportunities
   d. suffrage

9. In what decade was the ERA ratified and added to the U.S. Constitution?
   a. 1920s
   b. 1970s
   c. 1980s
   d. It has not been ratified and added to the U.S. Constitution.

10. Today, citizens of what descent experience the highest educational and income level compared with the nation as a whole?
    a. African
    b. Asian
    c. Mexican
    d. Native American

FILL IN THE BLANKS

11. _____ was the period between 1866 and 1877 when the institutions and infrastructure of the South were rebuilt after the Civil War.

12. The legal right to bring lawsuits in court is called _____.

13. To pass the strict scrutiny test, differential treatment must be _____ for the government to achieve a _____ public interest.

14. During World War II, the federal government relocated citizens of _____ descent to internment camps.

15. The ADA is the _____.

Answers: 1. b, **2.** b, **3.** c, **4.** d, **5.** c, **6.** c, **7.** b, **8.** b, **9.** d, **10.** b, **11.** Reconstruction, **12.** standing to sue, **13.** necessary, compelling, **14.** Japanese, **15.** Americans with Disabilities Act.

Resources for Research AND Action

Internet Resources

Equal Employment Opportunity Commission
www.eeoc.gov/facts/qanda.html This federal government site offers a list of federal laws relevant to equal employment opportunities and includes answers to the most frequently asked questions regarding equal employment laws.

Lambda Legal
www.lambdalegal.org Lambda Legal is a national organization committed to achieving full recognition of the civil rights of lesbians, gay men, transgendered people, and people with HIV through litigation, education, and public policy work.

Leadership Conference on Civil Rights/Leadership Conference on Civil Rights Education Fund
www.civilrights.org Founded by the LCCR and the LCCREF, this site seeks to serve as the "online nerve center" for the fight against discrimination in all its forms.

The Southern Poverty Law Center
www.splcenter.org The Southern Poverty Law Center is a nonprofit civil rights organization dedicated to fighting hate and bigotry and is known internationally for tracking and exposing the activities of hate groups.

The United States Department of Justice, Civil Rights Division
www.justice.gov/crt/index.php This site is maintained by the law enforcement arm of the federal government, which researches, investigates, and prosecutes violations of constitutional protections of civil rights.

Recommended Readings

Fleischer, Doris, and Frieda Zames. *The Disability Rights Movement: From Charity to Confrontation.* Philadelphia, PA: Temple University Press, 2011. A history of the disability rights movement drawn from interviewing over 100 activists, the book highlights the strategies adapted to make political change and the changing perceptions of disability.

Harrison, Brigid. *Women in American Politics: An Introduction.* Belmont, CA: Wadsworth, 2003. *American Democracy Now* coauthor Brigid Harrison introduces the study of women's participation in American politics, including their historical and contemporary participation in political groups, as voters, and in government.

Klarman, Michael. *From the Closet to the Altar: Courts, Backlash, and the Struggle for Same-Sex Marriage.* New York: Oxford University Press, 2014. A revised version of a book tracing the conflicts among legislatures and courts, state and federal governments, and interest groups over the rapidly changing legal status of same-sex marriage.

Lawson, Steven F., Charles Payne, and James T. Patterson. *Debating the Civil Rights Movement, 1945–1968.* Lanham, MD: Rowman & Littlefield Publishers, 2006. Integrates primary documents with essays comparing visions of the civil rights movement as being "bottom up" with a focus on local people or "top down" with a focus on the national leaders and statutory changes.

Rosenberg, Gerald. *The Hollow Hope: Can Courts Bring About Social Change?* 2nd ed. Chicago: The University of Chicago Press, 2008. Rosenberg supports his argument that Congress, the White House, and civil rights activists—not the courts—bring about social change by reviewing the evolution of federal policy in the areas of desegregation, abortion, and the struggle for LGBT rights.

Movies of Interest

Milk (2008)
The story of California's first openly gay elected official, San Fransisco Board of Supervisor member Harvey Milk. The movie examines his involvement in local politics, his fight to expand gay rights, and the opposition he faced until his assassination in 1978.

Bury My Heart at Wounded Knee (2007)
Based on Dee Brown's book of the same name, this HBO made-for-television movie chronicles ordeals of Sioux and Lakota tribes as the U.S. government displaces them from their lands.

Iron Jawed Angels (2004)
The little-known story of the tensions between the young, militant women's suffrage advocates, led by Alice Paul, and the older, more conservative advocates, such as Carrie Chapman Catt. The details of the suffrage battle during wartime, with a popular president opposed to women's suffrage, are well presented in this made-for-television movie.

Freedom Song (2000)
Supported by civil rights movement veterans, this movie tells the story of the movement through the eyes of the Student Nonviolent Coordinating Committee (SNCC). Danny Glover is a concerned Mississippi father who watches his son become increasingly involved in the civil rights movement and begin agitating for racial equality and social change.

CHAPTER 6

Political Socialization and Public Opinion

 # THEN

Families and schools were the most important influences on children as they developed their political views.

 # NOW

Families and schools remain influential, but the media have been enormously important in developing the political views of the Millennial generation.

 # NEXT

How will technology affect the socialization of new generations of Americans?

How will polling organizations find ways to harness the power of the Internet to predict political behavior accurately?

How can pollsters measure opinions of potential respondents who own only cell phones?

PREVIEW

In this chapter, we consider the ways in which people become socialized to politics and explain the influence of various agents of socialization. We consider how public opinion is measured and take a look at how Americans currently view their governmental institutions.

FIRST, we examine the process of political socialization and how it can lead to civic participation.

SECOND, we consider the different agents of socialization, including family, the media, schools, churches, peers, community and political leaders, and demographic characteristics.

THIRD, we look at ways of measuring public opinion.

FOURTH, we focus on what Americans think about politics.

The process of developing

informed opinions about issues begins with the process of political socialization. Through socialization, we acquire our basic political beliefs and values. Through political socialization, we come to value the attributes of our own political culture. We also develop our ideological outlook and perhaps even begin to identify with a particular political party. Although the process of political socialization begins in early childhood, throughout our lives, institutions, peers, and the media continue to influence our views.

Through the process of socialization, individuals acquire the ideology and the perspective that shape their political opinions. Though seemingly simple, public opinion is a fundamental building block on which American democracy rests. When we discuss public opinion, we often do so in the context of various public opinion polls that ask respondents everything from whether they approve of the president's job performance to how many sugars they take in their skim milk lattes. Political scientist V. O. Key, Jr., wrote: "To speak with precision of public opinion is a task not unlike coming to grips with the Holy Ghost."[1] Key was referring to the nebulous nature of public opinion, which changes from day to day, is sometimes difficult to pinpoint, and is open to subjective interpretation. The glut in the number of "latest polls" has perhaps made us forget that the act of voting is simply the act of expressing one's opinion. Indeed, the word *poll* means to gauge public opinion as well as the location where one casts a ballot.

Public opinion is one of the ways citizens interact with their government. Through public opinion surveys, people express their policy priorities ("What do you think is the country's most important problem?") and their approval or disapproval of both government officials ("Do you approve or disapprove of the way the president is handling his job?") and the policies they create ("Do you agree or disagree with President Obama's position on wage equality?"). Much of the literature bemoaning the decline of civic involvement is based on public opinion research. But studies of civic involvement reveal that public opinion is the starting point for many forms of informed participation—participation that begins when individuals learn about an issue and choose to express their views on it using a variety of media.

Political Socialization and Civic Participation

How do we acquire our political views? Although an infant would be hard pressed to evaluate the president's job performance, children begin to acquire political opinions at an early age, and this process continues throughout adulthood. As noted earlier, the process by which we develop our political values and opinions is called **political socialization.** As we develop our political values, we form the bedrock of what will become our political ideology, our integrated system of general political values. As this ideology emerges, it shapes how we view most political subjects: what side we take on public issues, how we evaluate candidates for office, and what our opinions on policies will be.

Although many people tend to think that political socialization occurs only as they approach voting age, in reality this process begins at home in very early childhood. Core tenets of our belief system—including our political ideology, our beliefs about people of different races and sexes, even our party identification—are often firmly embedded before we have completed elementary school.

political socialization
the process by which we develop our political values and opinions throughout our lives

A key aspect of political socialization is whether children are socialized to participate in politics. Simply put, civically engaged parents often have civically engaged children. Parents who engage in active forms of participation, such as volunteering on a campaign, and passive forms, such as staying informed and discussing important events, watching the nightly news, or reading a newspaper, demonstrate to children what matters to them. Parents who change the channel to a *Modern Family* rerun during an important presidential news conference are also socializing their children to their values. Children absorb the political views of their parents as well: A parent's subtle (or sometimes not so subtle!) comments about the president, a political news story, or a policy debate contribute to a child's political socialization by shaping that child's views.

The Process of Political Socialization

The beliefs and values we learn early in life also help shape how we view new information. Although events may change our views, we often choose to perceive events in a way that is consistent with our earlier beliefs. For example, people's evaluation of which candidate "won" a debate often coincides strongly with their party identification. Thus, the process of political socialization tends to be cumulative.

Historically, most social scientists have agreed that family and school have the strongest influence on political socialization. Our families teach us that it is—or is not—valuable to be an informed citizen and coach us in the ways in which we should participate in the civic life of our communities. For example, if your mother is active in Republican Party politics in your town, you are more likely to be active in that party than someone whose parents are not involved. Is your father active in charitable organizations such as the local food bank? He might ask you to run in a 5K race to raise money to buy food for the upcoming holiday season. Schools also influence our political socialization by teaching us shared cultural values. And in recent times, the omnipresent role that the media play in everyday life warrants their inclusion as one of the prime agents of political socialization.

> Children are socialized to the views of their parents at a very early age. What opinions were you socialized to as a young child?

Participating in Civic Life

Does the process of socialization matter in determining whether individuals are active in civic life? Studies indicate that socialization does matter in a number of ways. First, children whose parents are active in politics or in their community are more likely to be active themselves. Schools also play an important role in socializing young people to become active in civic life—high school and college students are more likely to participate than young people of the same age who are not attending school, and the longer a person continues their education, the more likely they will be active in their communities.[2] Research also indicates that socialization actually *generates* participation. People who have been socialized to participate in civic life are more likely to volunteer for a charitable or a political organization in their communities when they are invited to do so.

From our families and schools we also learn the value of becoming informed. Parents and schools, along with the media and the other agents of socialization that are discussed in the next section, provide us with important information that we can use to make decisions about our political actions. People who lack political knowledge, by contrast, tend not to be actively involved in their communities.[3] In fact, research indicates that when young people use any source of information regularly, including newspapers, radio, television, magazines, and the Internet,

> Young white people are more likely to be members of a community or political group than other racial and ethnic groups. Christina Benton, from Duquesne University in Pittsburgh, Pennsylvania, and other students from the Crossroads Christian Fellowship spent their spring breaks in Florida landscaping and painting Habitat for Humanity homes.

agents of socialization
the individuals, organizations, and institutions that facilitate the acquisition of political views

they are more likely to engage in all forms of civic participation. There is also a strong link between being informed and voting behavior. According to the results of one survey that measured civic engagement among young people, "youth who are registered to vote are more informed than their nonregistered peers. Eighty-six percent of young registered voters answered at least one of the knowledge questions (measuring political knowledge) correctly as opposed to 78 percent of youth who are not registered to vote."[4]

Agents of Socialization

Learning, culture, and socialization occur through **agents of socialization,** the individuals, organizations, and institutions that facilitate the acquisition of political views. Among the most important agents of socialization are the family, the media, schools, churches, peers, and political and community leaders. Our political views are also shaped by who we are; our race, ethnicity, gender, and age all influence how we become socialized to political and community life.

Family Influences on Activism and Attitudes

Family takes one of the most active roles in socializing us to politics and influencing our political views and behaviors. We learn whether our family members value civic activism by observing their actions and listening to their views. By example, parents show children whether community matters. The children of political activists are taught to be engaged citizens. They may see their parents attend city council meetings, host Democratic or Republican club meetings in their home, or help local candidates for office by volunteering to campaign door to door on a weekend afternoon. Other parents may teach different forms of political engagement—some young children might attend protests or demonstrations with their parents. Others might learn to boycott a particular product for political reasons. When political activists discuss their own involvement, they often observe that "politics is in my blood." In reality, political activism is passed from one generation to the next *through example.*

In other homes, however, parents are not involved in politics or their communities. They may lack the time to participate in political activities, or they may fail to see the value of doing so. They may have a negative opinion of people who participate in politics, constantly making such comments as "all politicians are corrupt," "they're just in it for themselves," or "it's all about ego." Such opinions convey to children that politics is not valued and may in fact be frowned on. A parent's political apathy need not necessarily sour a son or a daughter on politics or civic engagement permanently, however. Instead, first-generation activists often point to external influences such as school, the media, friends, and public policies, any of which can cause someone to become involved in civic life, regardless of family attitudes.

Our families influence not only whether or not we are civically active participants in the political process but also what we believe. While parents or older siblings may discuss specific issues or policies, their attitudes and outlook also shape children's general political attitudes and ideology. Children absorb their parents' beliefs—whether their parents think the government should have a larger or smaller role in people's lives, whether they value equality between the sexes and the races, whether they consider people in government to be trustworthy, and even specific opinions they have about political leaders. In fact, we can see evidence of how strongly parents' views are transmitted to their children in one of the best predictors of the results of presidential elections: Each election year, the *Weekly Reader,* a current events magazine that many school districts subscribe to, conducts a nonrandomized poll of its readers. Since 1956, the first- through twelfth-grade student poll has correctly predicted the outcome of every presidential election. Children know for whom their parents will vote and mimic that behavior in their responses to the poll.

The Media's Ever-Increasing Role in Socialization

An almost ever-present fixture in the lives of young Americans today, the media contribute to the political socialization of Americans in many ways. Television, radio, social media, the Internet, and various forms of electronic entertainment and print media help shape Americans' political perspectives. First, the media help shape societal norms. In our early lives, the media impart norms and values on children's shows such as *Sesame Street, Barney,* and *Dora the Explorer,* which teach about racial diversity and tolerance. For example, Barney's friends include children with and without disabilities. These shows and others reflect changing societal standards and values. The media also reinforce core democratic values. Television programs such as *Dancing with the Stars, American Idol,* and *The Biggest Loser* incorporate the principle of voting: through telephone, online, or texted votes, viewers decide which contestant stays or goes.

Second, the media also help determine the national agenda. Whether they are covering the civil war in Syria, the latest economic news, or congressional policy debates, the media focus the attention of the American public. This attention may then have spillover effects as people demand action on a policy issue.

Third, the media educate the public about policy issues. Local and national news programs, newsmagazine shows, and even comedies such as *The Daily Show with Jon Stewart* or *Saturday Night Live*'s "Weekend Update" inform viewers about current events, the actions of policy makers, and public policy challenges in communities, states, and the nation.

Finally, the media, particularly television, can skew people's perception of public policy priorities and challenges. The oft-quoted saying "if it bleeds, it leads" demonstrates the attention that most local news stations focus on violence. Although crime rates have dropped since the 1970s, the reporting of crime, particularly violent crime, on nightly news broadcasts has increased. Even national news broadcasts and talk shows fall prey to the tendency to emphasize "visual" news—fires, floods, auto accidents, and plane crashes. Although these stories are important to those involved, they have very little long-term effect on society as a whole. But because they pique viewer interest more effectively than, say, a debate in Washington or in a state capital, news programs devote more time to them. Internet news sources also cover these dramatic events, but the sheer number of Internet news sites and blogs makes it more likely that at least some of them will also cover more important news, and people interested in political events and debates can find Internet news sources that cover such events and issues.

>In the movie *How to Train Your Dragon 2,* Gobber the Belch (voiced by Craig Ferguson) subtly alluded to being homosexual. While watching a heterosexual couple argue, Gobber says, "this is why I never got married," and in an unscripted ad-lib, Ferguson added, "Yup, Gobber is coming out of the closet," a line that stayed in the movie. In today's society, the media play an ever-increasing role in socializing us to changing societal standards.

Schools, Patriotism, and Civic Participation

As early as preschool, children in the United States are socialized to believe in democracy and express patriotism. Schools socialize children to the concept of democracy by making the idea tangible for them. On Election Day, children might vote for their favorite snack and wait for the results at the end of the day. Or they might compare different kinds of apples or grapes, or different books, and then vote for a favorite. Lessons such as these introduce children to processes associated with democracy at its most basic level: They learn about comparing attributes, choosing a favorite, voting, and winning and losing.

Children also are taught patriotism as they recite the Pledge of Allegiance every day, sing patriotic songs, and learn to venerate the "founding fathers," especially George Washington, and other American heroes, including Abraham Lincoln, Dr. Martin Luther King, Jr., and John F. Kennedy. Traditionally, elementary and high schools in the United States emphasized the "great men in great moments" form of history, a history that traditionally concentrated solely on the contributions of men in formal governmental or military settings. Today, however, the curriculum often includes contributions by women and racial and ethnic minorities, including African Americans and Latinos.

Education also plays a pivotal role in determining *who* will participate in the political affairs of the community. Research indicates that higher levels of education are associated with higher levels of political activism, which is passed through generations. In a book on civic voluntarism, Sidney Verba, Kay Schlozman, and Henry Brady wrote: "Well-educated parents are more likely to also be politically active and to discuss politics at home and to produce children who are active in high school. Growing up in a politicized household and being active in high school are associated with political engagement."[5]

Churches: The Role of Religion

The influence of church and religion in general on one's political socialization varies a great deal from individual to individual. For some people, religion plays a key, defining role in the development of their political beliefs. For others, it is irrelevant.

For many years, political scientists have examined the effect that religious affiliation—whether one is Catholic or Jewish, Protestant or Muslim—has on political preferences. For example, religion is related to how people view various issues, especially the issue of abortion. (See "Thinking Critically About Democracy.") But more recent analysis shows that a better predictor of the impact of religion on voting is not so much the religion an individual practices but how regularly he or she practices it. In general, it seems that those who regularly attend religious services are more likely to share conservative values—and support Republican candidates in general elections. For example, in the 2012 presidential election, very religious voters supported Republican Mitt Romney over Barack Obama, 54–37, but the nonreligious supported Obama over Romney, 61–30.[6]

Research also shows that this relationship between frequency of church attendance and identification with the Republican Party is particularly strong among white Protestants but less so among Catholics, who are generally more Democratic, and among African Americans. African American voters are even more likely than Catholics to vote for a Democratic candidate but are also likely to have high levels of religiosity, as measured by frequency of attending services.

Figure 6.1 shows the breakdown in party affiliation by religiosity. The results are based on respondents' assessment of the importance of religion in their lives and their frequency of church attendance. Note in this figure that a large proportion of highly religious people (41 percent of Americans, not shown in the figure) are Republicans or lean Republican in voting. Among the moderately religious (29 percent of Americans), Democrats held sway with 44 percent leaning Democrat and 38 percent leaning Republican. Among the nonreligious (30 percent of the U.S. population), 43 percent identify themselves as Democratic leaners, while 30 percent of the nonreligious identify as leaning Republican. Though there is a strong link between religiosity and political party, the differences between the proclivities of religious and nonreligious voters are applicable only to white voters—as discussed later in this chapter. African Americans are likely to be Democrats no matter how religious they are—only 10 percent of very religious African Americans identify themselves as Republican. And although religious Latinos and Asian Americans are more likely to be Republican, by and large, majorities of both groups identify as Democrats. Nonetheless, the relationship between religiosity and party identification is an important factor in American politics, particularly to the extent that religiosity shapes political views on social issues—abortion or gay marriage, say—and renders them moral imperatives for voters, rather than mere opinions.

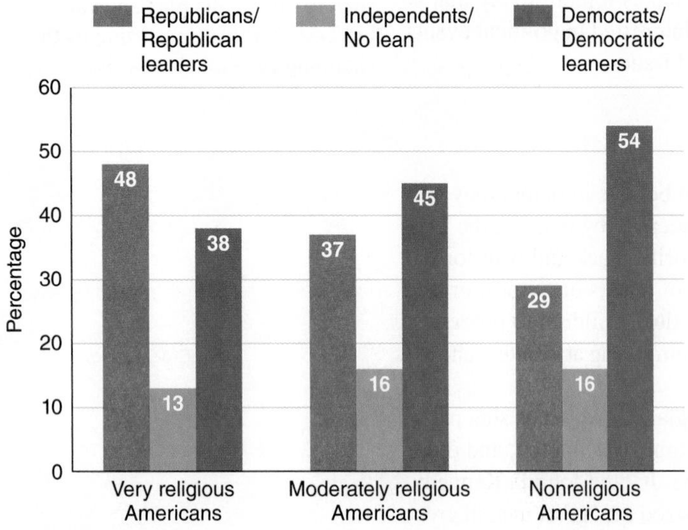

Peers and Group Norms

Friends, neighbors, coworkers, and other peers influence political socialization. Through peers, we learn about community and the political climate and values of the area in which we live. For example, your neighbors might inform you that a particular member of the city council is a strong advocate for your neighborhood on the council, securing funds for recreational facilities or increased police protection in your area. Or a coworker might let you know what your member of Congress is doing to help save jobs in the industry in which you work. Keep in mind, however,

FIGURE 6.1

Political Party Affiliation by Religiosity

SOURCE: Frank Newport, "In U.S., Very Religious Americans Still Align More With GOP," June 27, 2011, www.gallup.com/poll/148274/religious-americans-align-gop.aspx.

Democracy

Should Abortion Be Legal?

The Issue: In the 1973 decision *Roe v. Wade*, the Supreme Court legalized abortion, essentially ruling that abortion would be legal in the first trimester of pregnancy, that states could regulate it in the second trimester (for example, by requiring that abortions be performed in a hospital), and that states had the power to ban abortion in the third trimester. Since that time, several other cases have influenced public policy on this issue, with the Court granting states more powers to regulate the circumstances surrounding abortion. Many states now require a mandatory waiting period before obtaining an abortion and/or parental consent for minors who wish to have an abortion. The Court has also struck down some proposed regulations, including a requirement that women notify their spouses before having an abortion.

Abortion is one of the most divisive issues in the United States, and public opinion on this issue has changed very little since the decision in *Roe v. Wade* was announced in 1973. Over a quarter of Americans believe that abortion should be legal under any circumstances (28 percent), 50 percent believe that it should be legal under certain circumstances, and 21 percent think it should be illegal in all circumstances.* And nearly equal percentages of Americans identify as either "pro-choice" (47 percent in 2014) or "pro-life" (46 percent in 2014). Although individuals tend to hold very strong views on the abortion issue, very few people base their vote for a candidate solely on that candidate's position on this issue. The divisiveness is heightened because those who hold different positions on the abortion issue also differ on other issues as well. Consider the stances articulated below, which typify the views people express on this issue.

Yes: Women are the ones affected by a pregnancy, and they should be able to make decisions about their own bodies, without interference from the government—the pro-choice stance. Therefore, abortion should be legal under all circumstances until the point of viability. Women should be able to choose abortion, in consultation with their doctors, up to the time when the fetus can survive outside the womb, and there should be no restrictions on a woman's options.

No: Life begins at the moment of conception, and a fetus is another human life, as worthy of protection from the law as any other human being—the pro-life stance. We need to value life at every stage. Abortion should be illegal except to save the life of the mother; no other exceptions should be allowed. Doctors and others who perform abortions should be subject to criminal prosecution.

Other Approaches: Abortion should be legal, but states should be allowed to place various restrictions on abortion. Parents should be notified when their underage daughters are seeking the procedure, for example, and states can require providers to inform women about alternatives such as adoption or make them wait 24 hours before having the procedure. In other words, the goal should be to make abortion "legal but rare."

What do you think?

1. Do you consider your view to be pro-choice or pro-life, or do you favor another approach? Do you think that abortion should be legal or illegal under all circumstances, or legal but with restrictions?

2. Have you ever based, or would you ever base, your vote solely on a candidate's position on abortion? Why or why not?

3. Think about your own socialization process—how did family, church, peers, and events shape your views on this issue?

With respect to the abortion issue, would you consider yourself to be pro-choice or pro-life?

Trend from polls where pro-life/pro-choice was asked after question on legality of abortion

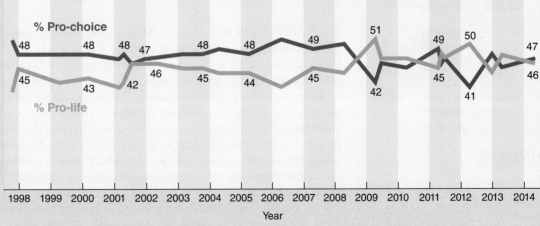

*Gallup poll, "Historical Trends: Abortion," www.gallup.com/poll/1576/Abortion.aspx.

> One-quarter of Latinos (more than twice the proportion of any other group) have protested, primarily in immigration rights demonstrations. In Phoenix, high school and college students took to the streets to voice their outrage at the treatment of immigrants in Arizona. The march was organized by Movimiento Estudiantil Chicano de Aztlán (MEChA), Chicano Student Movement of Aztlán.

that much research indicates that the primary function of peers is to reinforce our already-held beliefs and values. Typically, the people with whom you are acquainted are quite similar to you. Although diversity exists in many settings, the norms and values of the people you know tend to be remarkably similar to your own.

Political and Community Leaders: Opinion Shapers

Political and community leaders also help to socialize people and influence public opinion. Positions advocated by highly regarded government leaders hold particular sway, and the president plays an especially important role in shaping Americans' views. For example, President Obama's prioritization on wage equality propelled it to become a higher priority for many average Americans. Other national leaders can also propel issues to the forefront of our national consciousness. Consider, for example, the heightened awareness of the issue of the childhood obesity that has resulted from first lady Michelle Obama's advocacy on this topic. But the role of political leaders in influencing public opinion is not limited to the national stage. In your city, chances are that the views of community leaders—elected and not—influence the way the public perceives local policies. Perhaps the fire or police chief endorses a candidate for city council, or the popular football coach for the Police Athletic League makes the funding of a new football field a policy priority in your town. Often we rely on the recommendations and priorities of well-respected leaders who have earned our trust.

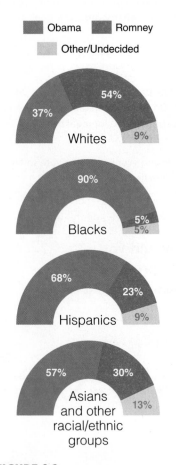

Obama ■ Romney

Other/Undecided

54%
37%
9%
Whites

90%
5%
5%
Blacks

68%
23%
9%
Hispanics

57%
30%
13%
Asians and other racial/ethnic groups

FIGURE 6.2

Candidate Support by Racial and Ethnic Group

SOURCE: Frank Newport, Jeffrey M. Jones, and Lydia Saad, "In Tight Race, Both Obama, Romney Have Core Support Groups," May 10, 2012, www.gallup.com/poll/154568/Tight-Race-Obama-Romney-Core-Support-Groups.aspx.

Demographic Characteristics: Our Politics Are a Reflection of Us

Who we are often influences our life experiences, which shape our political socialization and therefore what we think. The racial and ethnic groups to which we belong, our gender, our age and the events that have shaped our lives, and where we live all play a role in how we are socialized to political and community life, our values and priorities, and even whom we vote for. Demographic characteristics also shape our levels of civic involvement and may even help determine the ways in which we contribute to the civic life of our communities and our nation.

RACE AND ETHNICITY   Whites, African Americans, Latinos, and Asian Americans prefer different candidates, hold different political views, and have different levels of civic involvement. Among the most salient of these differences are the candidate preferences, which are reflective of party affiliation and ideology.

When analyzing candidate support by various racial and ethnic groups in the 2012 election, we can see that there are significant differences in the levels of support given to the Democratic and Republican candidates for president among African Americans and non-Hispanic whites, though of course there is variation within these groups. As shown in Figure 6.2, a majority of whites (54 percent) supported Republican Mitt Romney, whereas an overwhelming proportion of African Americans (90 percent) supported Democrat Barack Obama. President Obama also enjoyed strong support from Hispanics (at 68 percent) and Asian Americans (at 57 percent).

This breakdown of 2012 voter preferences is not unique; rather, it reflects well-established differences in party affiliation and ideology between racial and ethnic minorities and whites. But there are also significant differences even within racial and ethnic groups.[7] Table 6.1 shows how the various categories of Latinos differ in terms of party identification. As the table shows,

TABLE 6.1

Latino Party Identification by National Origin

NATIONAL ORIGIN	PARTY IDENTIFICATION		
	REPUBLICAN	DEMOCRATIC	INDEPENDENT
Puerto Rican	17%	58%	25%
Mexican	11	41	47
Cuban	41	29	30
Dominican	6	58	36
Salvadoran	9	43	47
Other	15	41	44

SOURCE: Author's calculations based on data provided in Luis R. Fraga, John A. Garcia, Rodney E. Hero, Michael Jones-Correa, Valerie Martinez-Ebers, Gary M. Sebure, *Latinos in the New Millennium: An Almanac of Opinion, Behavior, and Policy* (New York: Cambridge, 2012): 281; "Changing Faiths: Latinos and the Transformation of American Religion," © 2006 Pew Hispanic Center, a Pew Research Center project, www.pewhispanic.org>www.pewhispanic.org.

majorities of Latinos who identify themselves as Puerto Rican and Dominican identify as Democrats, and Latinos of almost all other national origins (including Mexican Americans, which constitute the largest nationality of all Hispanic Americans) are more likely to be Democrats than Republicans. Cubans, however, identify more strongly as Republicans.

Party affiliation among ethnic groups within the Asian American community also varies somewhat, as Figure 6.3 shows. In general, about 60 percent of all Asian Americans are registered Democrats. South Asians are most likely to be Democrats, and majorities of Chinese and Koreans are Democrats as well. A quarter to a third of all Korean, Southeast Asian, Filipino, and Chinese Americans are unaffiliated with either party.

White, African American, Latino, and Asian American youth also differ significantly in their levels of civic engagement as well as in how they connect with their communities. Trends reported in *The Civic and Political Health of the Nation: A Detailed Look at How Youth Participate in Politics and Communities* include the following:

- African American youth are the most politically engaged racial or ethnic group. They are the most likely to vote, belong to political groups, make political contributions, display buttons or signs, canvass voters, and contact the media about political issues.
- Asian Americans are more likely to have been active in their communities. They are more apt to work to solve community problems, volunteer, engage in boycotts, sign petitions, and raise charitable contributions.
- Young Latinos are the least likely to be active in politics or their communities, but they are most likely to have engaged in political protests. One-quarter of Latinos (more than twice the proportion of any other group) have protested, primarily in immigration rights demonstrations. The lack of civic involvement may arise from barriers to participation—including the fact that many Latino youths in the United States are not citizens, which would bar them from voting. The slogan of many immigration reform marches, *Hoy marchamos! Mañana votamos!* ("Today we march! Tomorrow we vote!") may be a promise of increased political participation among young Latinos in the future.

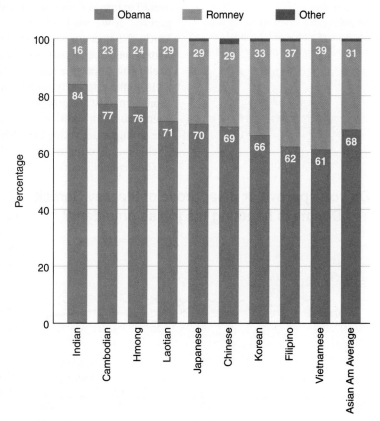

FIGURE 6.3

Asian Americans' Support of Presidential Candidates by National Origin

SOURCE: National Asian American Survey, Post Election Survey of Asian Americans and Pacific Island Voters in 2012, www.naasurvey.com/resources/Presentations/2012-aapipes-national.pdf.

> **Eleanor Smeal, president of the Feminist Majority and a former president of the National Organization for Women, coined the term "gender gap" after the 1980 presidential election. Smeal noticed that in poll after poll women favored Democratic incumbent Jimmy Carter over Republican challenger Ronald Reagan. Was there a gender gap in the 2012 presidential election?**

gender gap

the measurable difference in the way women and men vote for candidates and in the way they view political issues

• Young white people are moderately likely to engage in many community and political activities. They are more likely than other groups to run, walk, or bike for charity, and they are also more likely to be members of a community or political group. Of the groups of young people considered here, they are the least likely to protest, the least likely to contribute money to a political cause, and the least likely to persuade others to vote.[8]

GENDER Public opinion polls and voting behavior indicate that men and women have very different views on issues, have different priorities when it comes to public issues, and often favor different candidates, particularly in national elections. This difference in men's and women's views and voting preferences is called the **gender gap,** the measurable difference in the way women and men vote for candidates and in the way they view political issues. Eleanor Smeal, who at the time was president of the National Organization for Women, first noticed the gender gap. In the 1980 presidential election, Democrat incumbent Jimmy Carter lost to Republican challenger Ronald Reagan, but Smeal noticed that in poll after poll, women favored Carter.

Since that watershed 1980 election, the gender gap has been a factor in every subsequent presidential election, and in every presidential election, women are more likely than men to favor Democratic candidates. In the 2012 election, the United States saw the largest gender gap in history: Women favored President Barack Obama by 12 points (56 percent, to Republican challenger Mitt Romney's 44 percent). Romney won among men by an 8-point margin (54 percent, to Obama's 46 percent). Thus, the total gap of 20 points is the largest since pollsters started measuring the gender gap in 1952.

Women's support of President Obama has continued throughout his administration, as shown in Figure 6.4. From this figure, we see that a gender gap existed in terms of presidential approval, with women consistently assessing the Obama administration more favorably. While Obama's overall approval rating has varied from a low of 41 percent to a high of 66 percent, greater proportions of women have always approved, on average by about 5 or 6 percent more than men. Much of the gender gap illustrated in the varying presidential approval ratings can be attributed to the gender gap in party affiliation: Democrats are more likely to assess President Obama positively, and women are more likely to be Democrats.

In addition to party affiliation, voting turnout patterns increase the effect of the gender gap. Women in most age groups—except those under age 25—are more likely to vote than their male counterparts. In addition, on average women also live longer than men, so older women constitute an important voting bloc. The difference in women's candidate preferences and their higher likelihood of voting mean that the gender gap is a political reality that any candidate seeking election cannot ignore.

Do you approve or disapprove of the way Barack Obama is handling his job as president?

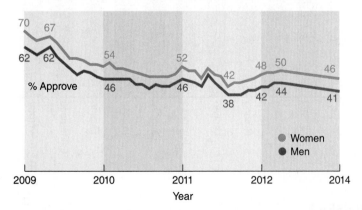

FIGURE 6.4

The Gender Gap in President Obama's Approval Ratings

SOURCE: Gallup Presidential Job Approval Center, www.gallup.com/poll/124922/Presidential-Approval-Center.aspx.

Young men and women also differ in their level of civic engagement, in the ways in which they are involved with their communities, and in their perspectives on the government. While majorities of young men and women believe it is their *responsibility* (rather than their choice) to get involved to make things better for society, how they choose to get involved varies by gender. As Figure 6.5 shows, women in particular are more likely to participate in certain forms of community activism, such as volunteering and running, walking, biking, or engaging in other fund-raising activities for charity. Men and women are about equally likely to work on solving a community problem, such as volunteering for a nonprofit mediation service that helps negotiate disputes between neighbors. Men are more likely than women to choose formal political forms of activism, such as voting, persuading others to vote, and contributing money to political campaigns.

Women's and men's opinions also differ on public policy issues, although often in unexpected ways. On the one hand, there is very little difference of opinion between men and women on the issue of abortion. On the other hand, men are about 10 percent more likely than women to favor the death penalty.[9] And men's and women's views on the optimal role of government vary greatly: 66 percent of young women believe that government should do more to solve problems (versus 60 percent of young men), whereas only 27 percent of women believe that government does too many things better left to businesses and individuals, as opposed to 35 percent of men.[10]

AGE AND EVENTS Differences in the candidates voters prefer—party, gender, the age of the candidates themselves—are one reflection of age and political opinions. People's opinions are also influenced by the events they have lived through and by their political socialization; an epic event may lead to a widespread change in political views. The **generational effect** (sometimes called the *age-cohort effect*) is the influence of a significant external event in shaping the views of a generation. Typically, generational effects are felt most strongly by young people. As a result of the attacks that occurred on

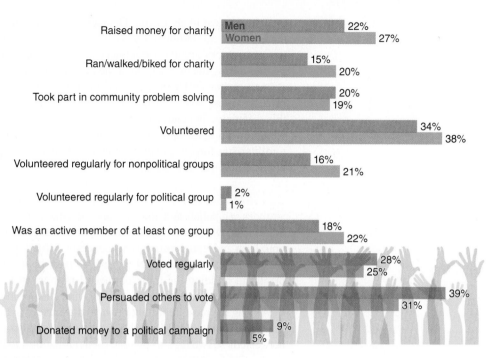

	Men	Women
Raised money for charity	22%	27%
Ran/walked/biked for charity	15%	20%
Took part in community problem solving	20%	19%
Volunteered	34%	38%
Volunteered regularly for nonpolitical groups	16%	21%
Volunteered regularly for political group	2%	1%
Was an active member of at least one group	18%	22%
Voted regularly	28%	25%
Persuaded others to vote	39%	31%
Donated money to a political campaign	9%	5%

FIGURE 6.5

Participation in Civic Activities Among Young Men and Women

SOURCE: Karlo Barrios Marcelo, Mark Hugo Lopez, and Emily Hoban Kirby, *Civic Engagement among Young Men and Women* (College Park, MD: Circle: The Center for Information and Research on Civic Learning and Engagement, 2007).

September 11, 2001, people who were under age 30 on that day might place a heightened priority on keeping the United States safe in the face of a new kind of threat, for instance. Other key events that have shaped the socialization of a generation include World War II for the oldest Americans and the war in Vietnam and the changes in society that occurred during the 1960s for the Baby Boom generation born between 1946 and 1964. The major events that occur while we grow up affect our socialization by shaping our viewpoints and our policy priorities.

One of the strongest examples of the generational effect is the Great Depression, the deep economic depression that lasted from 1929 through 1939. Those who came of age during the era of Democratic president Franklin D. Roosevelt's New Deal social programs, were, throughout

generational effect
the influence of an important external event in shaping the views of a generation

Then   Now

> Generational effects are felt most strongly by young people. The defining event of the Millennial generation was the terror attacks of September 11, 2001. In the immediate aftermath of the attacks, Americans shared the fear, uncertainty, and terror of those who lost loved ones. People who were under age 30 on that day might place a heightened priority on keeping the United States safe in the face of a new kind of threat, a burden placed squarely on the shoulders of those who serve as president.

their lives, most likely to vote Democratic. But often the consequences of events are not imme- diately apparent. Political scientists continue to measure the effects of the September 11, 2001, terrorist attacks and the subsequent war on terror on the views of the generation socialized to politics during the first decade of the 21st century. In the 2008 presidential election, young voters strongly preferred Democratic senator Barack Obama over Republican senator John McCain; in 2012, young voters continued to favor Obama over Republican rival Mitt Romney. But was this difference in candidate preference a result of the generational effect? Will the Americans who grew up in the wake of those attacks be more patriotic than their parents? Will they resist a militaristic foreign policy throughout their lifetimes? These types of questions will interest public opinion researchers in the decades to come.

GEOGRAPHIC REGION   Since the nation's founding, Americans have varied in their political attitudes and beliefs and how they are socialized to politics, depending on the region of the United States from which they come. These differences stem in part from historical patterns of immigra- tion: Irish and Italian immigrants generally settled on the northeastern seaboard, influencing the political culture of Boston, New York, Philadelphia, and Baltimore. Chinese immigrants, instru- mental in building the transcontinental railroad in the 19th century, settled in California and areas of the Pacific Northwest and have had a major influence on the political life of those areas.

Among the most important regional differences in the United States is the difference in politi- cal outlook between those who live in the Northeast and those in the South. The differences between these two regions predate even our nation's founding. During the Constitutional Conven- tion in 1787, northern and southern states disagreed as to the method that should be used to count slaves for the purposes of taxation and representation. The differences between these two regions were intensified in the aftermath of the Civil War—the quintessential manifestation of regional differences in the United States. Since the Republican Party was the party of Lincoln and the North, the South became essentially a one-party region, with all political competition occurring *within* the Democratic Party. The Democratic Party dominated the South until the later part of the 20th century, when many Democrats embraced the civil rights movement (as described in Chapter 5). Differences in regional culture and political viewpoints between North and South remain. Today, in national elections, Republicans tend to carry the South, the West, and most of the Midwest, except for large cities in these regions. Democrats are favored in the Northeast, on the West Coast, and in most major cities.

Figure 6.6 illustrates one factor that contributes to these differences in regional political cli- mate: religiosity. As discussed earlier in this chapter, religiosity affects political viewpoints, and the regional differences in levels of religiosity mean that those differences are manifested as regional differences as well. From Figure 6.6, we can see that the most religious states are found primarily in the South (Mississippi, Alabama, Louisiana, Arkansas, South Carolina, Tennessee, North Carolina, and Georgia), and none of the most religious states are in the Northeast or on the West Coast. Contrast that with where we find the least religious states: Nearly all are found in the Northeast (Vermont, New Hampshire, Maine, Massachusetts, Connecticut, New York, and Rhode Island), and four are in the West (Alaska, Oregon, Nevada, and Washington).

The regional differences in levels of religiosity are compounded by the differences in the domi- nant religious denominations in each area. The South is much more Protestant than other regions of the United States. Not surprisingly, Republicans dominate in this area, particularly among the most religious Protestants, born-again Christians and Evangelicals. Catholics and Jews tend to dominate in the Northeast along the East Coast; both groups are more frequently supporters of the Democratic

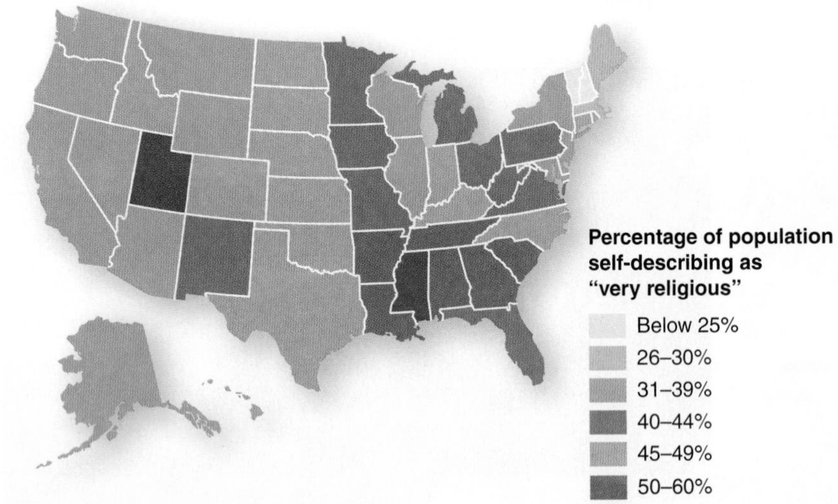

FIGURE 6.6

Levels of Religiosity in the United States

Percentage of population self-describing as "very religious"

- Below 25%
- 26–30%
- 31–39%
- 40–44%
- 45–49%
- 50–60%
- 60%+

SOURCE: Frank J. Newport, "Mississippi Most Religious State, Vermont Least Religious," February 3, 2014, www.gallup. com/poll/167267/mississippi-religious-vermont-least-religious-state.aspx.

Party, which is underscored by their lower levels of religiosity. People without a religious affiliation, who tend to value independence and have negative views of governmental activism, tend to live in the West and vote Republican. We can discern many of the similarities and differences between the political beliefs of members of these various demographic groups because of the increasingly sophisticated and accurate ways in which we can measure public opinion.

Measuring Public Opinion

Public opinion consists of the public's expressed views about an issue at a specific point in time. Public opinion and ideology are inextricably linked because ideology is the prism through which people view all political issues; hence their ideology informs their opinions on a full range of political issues. Indeed, the growing importance of public opinion has even led some political scientists, such as Elizabeth Noelle-Neumann, to argue that public opinion itself is a socializing agent in that it provides an independent context that affects political behavior.[11] Though we are inundated every day with the latest public opinion polls on television, on the Internet, in magazines, and even on Twitter, the importance of public opinion is not a new phenomenon in American politics.

As early as the War for Independence, leaders of the Continental Congress were concerned with what the people thought. Popular opinion mattered because support was critical to the success of the volunteer revolutionary army. The dissatisfaction of ordinary people troubled by debt precipitated Shays's Rebellion in Massachusetts and the adoption of the new Constitution. And once the Constitution was drafted, *The Federalist Papers* were used as a tool to influence public opinion and generate support for the new form of government.

Public opinion is manifested in various ways: demonstrators protesting on the steps of the state capitol; bloggers posting their opinions; citizens communicating directly with government officials, perhaps by telling their local city council members what they think of the town's plan to develop a recreation center or by calling their members of Congress to indicate their opinion on a current piece of legislation. One of the most important ways public opinion is measured is through the act of voting, discussed in Chapter 9. But another important tool that policy makers, researchers, and the public rely on as an indicator of public opinion is the **public opinion poll,** a survey of a given population's opinion on an issue at a particular time. Policy makers, particularly elected officials, care about public opinion because they want to develop and implement policies that reflect the public's views.[12] Such policies are more likely to attract support from other government leaders, who are also relying on public opinion as a gauge, but they also help ensure that elected leaders will be reelected, because they are representing their constituents' views.[13]

public opinion
the public's expressed views about an issue at a specific point in time

public opinion poll
a survey of a given population's opinion on an issue or a candidate at a particular time

The Origins of Public Opinion Polls

In his book *Public Opinion,* published in 1922, political writer Walter Lippmann stressed both the importance of public opinion for policy makers and the value of measuring it accurately. Lippmann's thought informed a generation of public opinion researchers, who in turn shaped two divergent areas of opinion research: marketing research, used by businesses to increase sales, and public opinion research, used to measure people's opinions on political issues.

Among the first efforts to gauge public opinion were attempts to predict the outcomes of presidential elections. In 1916, the *Literary Digest,* a popular magazine similar in format to today's *Reader's Digest,* conducted its first successful **straw poll,** a poll conducted in an unscientific manner to predict the outcome of an election. (The term comes from the use of natural straw to determine which way the wind is blowing; so, too, does a straw poll indicate how the winds of public opinion are blowing.) Between 1920 and 1932, *Literary Digest* correctly predicted the winner of every presidential race by relying on its subscribers to mail in postcards indicating their vote choice. The 1936 presidential election between Democrat Franklin D. Roosevelt and Republican governor Alfred M. "Alf" Landon of Kansas centered on one issue, however: the government's role in responding to the Great Depression. In effect, the election was a mandate on Roosevelt's New Deal policies. The *Literary Digest* poll predicted that Landon would defeat Roosevelt, 57 percent to 43 percent, but Roosevelt won that election by a landslide, receiving nearly 63 percent of the popular vote.

straw poll
a poll conducted in an unscientific manner, used to predict election outcomes

Where did the *Literary Digest* go wrong? The greatest error the magazine committed was to use an unrepresentative sample to draw conclusions about the wider voting public. The straw poll respondents were selected from a list of subscribers to the magazine, automobile owners, and people listed in telephone directories. At the height of the Great Depression, this sample excluded most members of the working and middle classes. And class mattered in the 1936 election, with Roosevelt deriving his support primarily from poor, working-class, and middle-class voters. *Literary Digest* had committed what Lippmann termed an error of the casual mind: "to pick out or stumble upon a sample which supports or defies its prejudices, and then to make it the representative of a whole class."[14] Note the similarity between *Literary Digest*'s faulty straw poll and many of today's voluntary Internet polls: self-selected respondents often differ dramatically in their views from those of the broader public, thus resulting in poll results that may not accurately reflect public opinion.

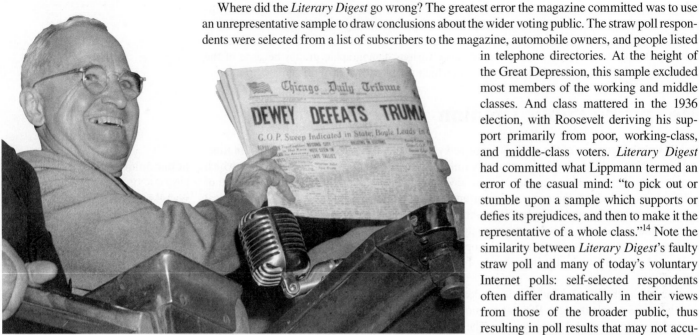

> President Truman holds a copy of the *Chicago Daily Tribune* that mistakenly announced his Republican rival's electoral victory. Because the three largest polling organizations concluded their polls too soon, all three mistakenly predicted that Dewey would beat Truman in 1948.

Although the 1936 election destroyed the credibility of the *Literary Digest* poll, it was also the watershed year for a young Princeton-based public opinion researcher named George Gallup. Gallup's entry in political public opinion research was driven in part by a desire to help his mother-in-law, Ola Babcock Miller, win election as Iowa's secretary of state, the first woman elected to that position. In 1935, Gallup founded the American Institute of Public Opinion, which would later become the Gallup Organization. Gallup gained national recognition when he correctly predicted the outcome of the 1936 election, and so scientific opinion polls, which rely on the random selection of participants rather than their own self-selection, gained enormous credibility during this era.

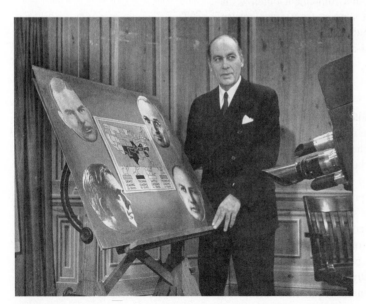

> Pollsters, including Dr. George Gallup, used the latest technology of the times to measure public opinion. Here, Gallup discusses Americans' political views on a CBS Television series called *America Speaks* in 1948. Today's technologies are again revolutionizing how public opinion is measured. Internet polling is one facet of this revolution.

Gallup's credibility suffered a substantial setback, however, after the presidential election of 1948 between Democrat Harry S Truman and Republican Thomas E. Dewey. That year, the "big three" polling organizations, Gallup, Roper, and Crossley, all concluded their polls in October, and all predicted a Dewey victory. By ending their efforts early, the polls missed the swing of third-party voters back to Truman's camp in the final days of the campaign. The organizations didn't anticipate that many voters would switch back to the Democratic nominee, who wound up winning the presidency. During his administration, Truman would sometimes offer a good-natured barb at the pollsters who had prematurely predicted his demise, and George Gallup responded in kind: "I have the greatest admiration for President Truman, because he fights for what he believes. I propose to do the same thing. As long as public opinion is important in this country, and until someone finds a better way of appraising it, I intend to go right ahead with the task of reporting the opinions of the people on issues vital to their welfare."[15] Today, the Gallup Organization and other polling organizations conduct public opinion polls regularly not only in the United States, but internationally as well (see "Global Context").

How Public Opinion Polls Are Conducted

In politics, public opinion polls are used for many reasons.[16] Political scientist Herbert Asher noted: "Polling plays an integral role in

INTERNATIONAL OPINION OF WOMEN'S EQUALITY

In 2014, members of the militant sect Boko Haram kidnapped 276 Nigerian schoolgirls, held them hostage, and threatened to sell them as sex slaves. Later that year, a pregnant 25-year-old Pakistani woman, Farzana Parveen, was stoned to death by her own family members in an "honor killing" because she married a man without her family's consent. Parveen was one of an estimated 1,000 Pakistani women murdered in such a way each year, a practice that 40 percent of Pakistanis described as "justified in some circumstances."

To many Americans of the Millennial generation, equality between the sexes may be a given. Those who were born and came of age after the women's rights movement of the 1970s largely accept that men and women should have equal rights. But this is not the case universally. Indeed, there is some variation throughout the world in people's opinions concerning the importance of equality between the sexes. The British Broadcasting Company (BBC) regularly conducts polls gauging public opinion throughout the world. In one poll, respondents were asked to evaluate how important it is for women to have full equality of rights compared to men. Large majorities indicated that it is important for "women to have full equality of rights compared to men," ranging from 60 percent in India to 98 percent in Mexico and Britain. On average, 86 percent of the respondents said women's equality is important, with 59 percent saying it is very important.

Defying the Western stereotypes, vast majorities in predominantly Muslim nations said equality is important: 83 percent in the Palestinian territories, 91 percent in Indonesia and Turkey, 90 percent in Egypt, 85 percent in Azerbaijan, 83 percent in Jordan, and 78 percent in Iran.

Interestingly, there was little difference between men's and women's views on the question of equality. Overall, 84 percent of men as well as 89 percent of women said equality is important, though women were more likely to say equality is very important (65 percent), compared to men (53 percent).

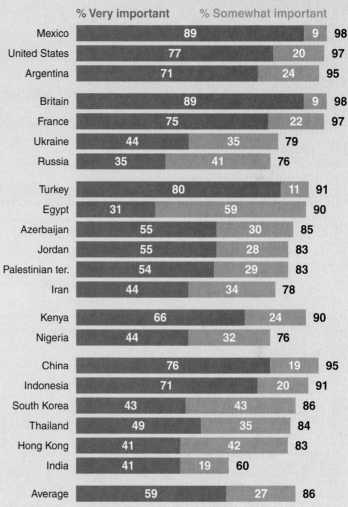

Importance of Women's Rights

How important do you think it is for women to have full equality of rights compared to men?

	% Very important	% Somewhat important	
Mexico	89	9	98
United States	77	20	97
Argentina	71	24	95
Britain	89	9	98
France	75	22	97
Ukraine	44	35	79
Russia	35	41	76
Turkey	80	11	91
Egypt	31	59	90
Azerbaijan	55	30	85
Jordan	55	28	83
Palestinian ter.	54	29	83
Iran	44	34	78
Kenya	66	24	90
Nigeria	44	32	76
China	76	19	95
Indonesia	71	20	91
South Korea	43	43	86
Thailand	49	35	84
Hong Kong	41	42	83
India	41	19	60
Average	59	27	86

SOURCE: WorldPublicOpinion.org, "International Poll Finds Large Majorities in All Countries Favor Equal Rights for Women," www.worldpublicopinion.org/pipa/pdf/mar08/WPO_Women_Mar09_rpt.pdf.

political events at the national, state, and local levels. In any major event or decision, poll results are sure to be a part of the news media's coverage and the decision makers' deliberations."[17] In addition, public opinion polls help determine who those decision makers will be: Candidates for public office use polls to determine their initial name recognition, the effectiveness of their campaign strategy, their opponents' weaknesses, and how potential voters are responding to their message. Once elected to office, policy makers often rely on public opinion polls to gauge their constituents' opinions and to measure how well they are performing on the job.

The process of conducting a public opinion poll consists of several steps. Those conducting the poll first need to determine the **population** they are targeting for the survey—the group of

population
in a poll, the group of people whose opinions are of interest and/or about whom information is desired

people whose opinions are of interest and about whom information is desired. For example, if your neighbor were considering running for the U.S. House of Representatives, she would want to know how many people recognize her name. But she would be interested only in those people who live in your congressional district. Furthermore, she would probably narrow this population by looking only at those people in the district who are registered to vote. She might even want to narrow her target population further by limiting her survey to likely voters, perhaps those who have voted in past congressional elections.

SAMPLING   Once the target population is determined and the survey measurement instrument, or poll, is designed, pollsters then must select a sample that will represent the views of this population. Because it is nearly impossible to measure all the opinions of any given population, pollsters frequently rely on **random sampling,** a scientific method of selection in which each member of the population has an equal chance of being included in the sample. Relying on random sampling helps to ensure that the sample is not skewed so that one component of the population is overrepresented.

To demonstrate this point, suppose the dean of students asks your class to conduct a public opinion survey that will measure whether students believe that parking facilities are adequate at your school. In this case, the population you need to measure is the entire student body. But clearly how you conduct the sampling will affect the responses. If you ask only students in your 8:00 a.m. American government class, you might find that they have little trouble parking, because the campus is not crowded at that hour. If you ask students who attend classes only during peak hours, you might get different, yet not necessarily representative, views as well, since these students may have more difficulty parking than average. How then would you obtain a random sample? The best way would be to ask the registrar for a list of all students, determine your sample size, randomly select every nth student from the list, contact each nth student, and ask for his or her views.

Researchers have noted, however, that one problem with polls is that even those conducted using random samples may not provide the accurate data needed to illuminate political opinions and behaviors. Part of the problem is that randomization can go only so far. One standard method for conducting telephone surveys is to use random-digit dialing of telephones.[18] Some polling organizations still exclude cellular lines from their population,[19] although most major polling organizations now include cell phone users in order to create an accurate sample of Americans. Today, 40 percent of the U.S. population relies exclusively on cell phones and has no landline phone.[20] People who rely exclusively on landlines are likely to be older than those who rely exclusively on cell phones. Indeed, a study by the National Institutes of Health found that two-thirds (66 percent) of adults aged 25–29 years lived in cell-only households.[21] And some individuals who eliminate landlines from their homes do so to save money. In fact, in 2014, adults living in poverty were one and a half times as likely to rely on cell phones exclusively, compared with those with higher incomes.[22] But even those polling organizations that include cell phone subscribers face a high rate of nonresponse because of the nearly universal use of caller ID, and the transportable nature of cell phones that makes their owners less likely to answer calls when involved in other activities.[23] In fact, one study found that those who are willing to respond to pollsters' questions are more politically engaged than those who hit "ignore." (See "Analyzing the Sources" to consider how these and other factors might impact polling results.)

One way pollsters attempt to address these types of concerns is through the use of a **quota sample,** a more scientifically sophisticated method of sampling than random sampling. A pollster using this method structures the sample so that it is representative of the characteristics of the target population. Let's say that your mother is running for mayor of your town, and you would like to conduct a poll that measures opinions of her among various constituencies. From census data, you learn that your town is 40 percent white, 35 percent African American, 20 percent Latino, and 5 percent Asian. Therefore, at a citywide event you structure your sample so that it reflects the proportions of the population. With a sample of 200 voters, you would seek to include 80 white respondents, 70 African Americans, 40 Latinos, and 10 Asians. Pollsters routinely rely on quota sampling, though often they may not ask participants about their demographic characteristics until the end of the poll.

Another method used to address problems in sampling is **stratified sampling,** in which the national population is divided into fourths and certain areas within these regions are selected as representative of the national population. Although some organizations still rely on quota

random sampling
a scientific method of selection in which each member of the population has an equal chance of being included in the sample

quota sample
a method by which pollsters structure a sample so that it is representative of the characteristics of the target population

stratified sampling
a process of random sampling in which the national population is divided into fourths and certain areas within these regions are selected as representative of the national population

EXAMINING AMERICANS' IDEOLOGY

This graph shows the trend over time regarding Americans' self-described ideology. In all the surveys, respondents were asked to describe their political views as very conservative, conservative, moderate, liberal, or very liberal. Very conservative/conservative and very liberal/liberal responses have been consolidated.

How would you describe your political views?

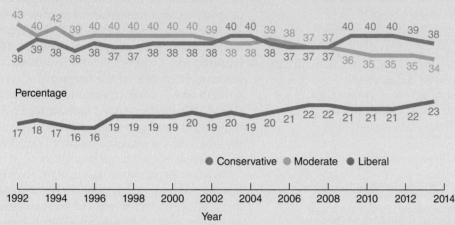

● Conservative ● Moderate ● Liberal

Year

SOURCE: Jeffrey M. Jones," Liberal Self-Identification Edges Up to New High in 2013," January 10, 2014, www.gallup.com/poll/166787/liberal-self-identification-edges-new-high-2013.aspx.

Evaluating the Evidence

1. What does the graph indicate about how most people identify themselves now? What has been the trend in recent years? Why do you think this is the case?

2. Why do the 2009 data stand out? Are the 2009 data consistent with those of previous years?

3. Based on what you've learned about demographics and ideology, how might a polling process that does not reach out to cell-phone-only users affect the results of polls taken in recent years?

---

sampling, larger organizations and media polls now use stratified sampling, the most reliable form of random sample. Today, nearly every major polling organization relies on U.S. census data as the basis of their four sampling regions. Stratified sampling is the basis for much of the public opinion data used by political scientists and other social scientists, in particular the General Social Survey (GSS) and the American National Election Study.

SAMPLING ERROR   As we have seen, to accurately gauge public opinion, pollsters must obtain an accurate sample from the population they are polling. A sample need not be large to reflect the population's views. In fact, most national polling organizations rarely sample more than 1,500 respondents; most national samples range from 1,000 to 1,500. To poll smaller populations (states or congressional districts, for example), polling organizations routinely use samples of between 300 and 500 respondents.

The key is having a sample that accurately reflects the population. Let's say that your political science instructor offers extra credit if you attend a weekly study group. The group initially convenes immediately after your regular class session. At the conclusion of the study group, the leader asks if this is a convenient time for everyone to meet. Since everyone present has attended the study group, chances are that the time is more convenient for them than it is for those students who did not attend—perhaps because they have another class immediately after your political science class, or they work during that time period, or they have child care responsibilities. In other words, the composition of the sample—in this case, the students in the study group—will skew the responses to this question. Similarly, if a poll is administered to a nonrepresentative sample of a population, the responses will not accurately reflect the population's views.

Public Opinion Polling

Then (1970s)	Now
Telephone polls replaced mail-in and door-to-door polling, because most American households had landlines.	Internet polls are at the cutting edge of public opinion research, but anonymity and multiple responses from the same person can damage a poll's accuracy.
Early telephone polls over-represented the views of homemakers and retirees, who were more likely to answer the phone during the day.	The accuracy of telephone polls is affected by the difficulty of reaching people who use only cell phones or who screen calls using caller ID.
Pollsters remedied nonrepresentative sampling through quota sampling.	Pollsters rely on stratified sampling to ensure the most representative sample of the population they are targeting.

WHAT'S NEXT?

> How will technologies such as YouTube and social networking sites shape polling in the future?

> How might pollsters overcome the obstacles associated with Internet polls, in particular, the problem of anonymous respondents giving false answers or responding to the same poll multiple times?

> How will cell phones and text messaging change the way in which public opinion is measured in the future?

In selecting a representative sample, pollsters need to pay particular attention to the time of day a poll is administered: Afternoons yield a disproportionate number of mothers with small children and retirees, and evenings may yield more affluent individuals who do not do shift work. Today's telephone technology presents pollsters with even more obstacles. As we have seen, many potential respondents, particularly young people, have opted out of telephone landlines in favor of cell phones, making them a subset of the population that is more difficult for pollsters to reach. People with caller ID on both cell phones and landlines frequently screen out unknown numbers and those of survey research companies.

Internet polls present their own set of obstacles, including the ability of some individuals to complete surveys (or vote for their favorite reality show contestant) repeatedly.[24] Nonetheless, market research firms, public opinion polling organizations, and even political candidates are increasingly relying on the Internet as a survey research tool.[25] Some organizations, such as the Harris Poll Online, offer "memberships": Poll respondents can earn rewards for completing surveys that help the organization create a representative sample of their target population.

To adjust for problems with sampling, every poll that relies on a sample has a **sampling error** (sometimes called a margin of error), which is a statistical calculation of the difference in results between a poll of a randomly drawn sample and a poll of the entire population. Most polls have a sampling error of ± 3 percentage points ("plus or minus 3 percentage points"). This means that 3 percentage points should be added and subtracted from the poll results to find the range for the population.

---

sampling error
also called *margin of error;* a statistical calculation of the difference in results between a poll of a randomly drawn sample and a poll of the entire population

tracking polls
polls that measure changes in public opinion over the course of days, weeks, or months by repeatedly asking respondents the same questions and measuring changes in their responses

push polls
a special type of poll that both attempts to skew public opinion about a candidate and provides information to campaigns about candidate strengths and weaknesses

Types of Political Polls

The process of measuring political opinions has evolved drastically from the days of the *Literary Digest's* straw poll or even George Gallup's first successful predictions of the results of presidential elections.[26] Today, political candidates, parties, and news organizations rely on several types of polls, depending on their goals and objectives. These include tracking polls, push polls, and exit polls.

- **Tracking polls** measure changes in public opinion over the course of days, weeks, or months by repeatedly asking respondents the same questions and measuring changes in opinion. Since the 1992 presidential election, tracking polls have been an important tool, particularly for presidential candidates seeking to glean information about how campaign strategy has affected public opinion. Tracking polls are useful in indicating the effectiveness of the media strategy, the success of a day's worth of campaigning, or whether the campaign has gotten its message across in the most recent news cycle.
- **Push polls** are a special type of poll that both attempts to skew public opinion about a candidate and provides information to campaigns about candidate strengths and weaknesses. Sometimes this is done by presenting survey respondents with a hypothetical situation and then asking them to gauge the importance of the hypothetical issue in determining their vote. For example, a push-pollster might ask: "If you knew that Congressman Fitzgerald lives outside the district, how would that affect your vote?" At their

best, push polls help gauge voter priorities so that a campaign can better target its message. The campaign can then determine whether to accentuate that message. But push polls have an unsavory reputation, because some campaigns and organizations have used them to smear an opponent, using hypothetical scenarios to make baseless accusations against an opponent without having to substantiate the charges.

• **Exit polls** are conducted at polling places on Election Day to project the winner of an election before the polls close. News organizations frequently sponsor exit polls, which help them predict the outcome of gubernatorial, congressional, and presidential elections. Because of exit polls, news organizations can frequently predict the outcome of a given election shortly after the polls have closed. Exit polls also provide the media, candidates, and political parties with information about why voters voted the way they did.

exit polls
polls conducted at polling places on Election Day to project the winner of an election before the polls close

What Americans Think About Politics

Public opinion research is the means by which individuals can convey their opinions and priorities to policy makers. Consequently, polls connect Americans to their government.[27] Through public opinion polls, whether conducted by campaigns or media organizations, government officials come to know and understand the opinions of the masses.[28] Through polls, leaders learn what issues are important to people, which policy solutions they prefer, and whether they approve of the way government officials are doing their jobs.[29] The role of opinion polls in shaping citizens' involvement with their government is also circular: Polls play a pivotal role in shaping public opinion, and the results of polls, frequently reported by the media, provide an important source of information for the American public.

The Most Important Problem

Several polling organizations routinely ask respondents to identify (either from a list or in their own words) what they view as "the most important problem" facing the country. In 2014, Americans identified a diversity of concerns as the most important issues, including the Ebola virus, dissatisfaction with government, the issue of immigration (which increased in importance when thousands of children crossed the Southwest border), and the economy[30] (which had been the top concern since April 2008). From 2003 through 2007, the war in Iraq was the top issue, with 34 percent of Americans citing it as the most important problem. The percentage of Americans concerned about the Iraq war was not as high as it has been for other wars. For example, 56 percent of respondents identified the Korean War as the most important problem in September 1951, and 62 percent named the Vietnam War as the top problem in January 1967.[31] In general, other problems Americans identify as important include gas prices, health care, and terrorism.

Public Opinion About Government

Analysts of public opinion, government officials, and scholars of civic engagement are all concerned with public opinion about the government at all levels, in particular about the institutions of the federal government. For decades, public opinion researchers have measured the public's trust in government by asking survey respondents to rate their level of trust in the federal government's ability to handle domestic and international policy matters and to gauge their amount of trust and confidence in the executive, legislative, and judicial branches of government.

The responses to these questions are important for several reasons. First, although these measures indicate public opinion about institutions rather than individuals, individual officeholders nonetheless can use the data as a measure of how well they are performing their jobs. Lower levels of confidence in the institution of the presidency, for example, tend to parallel lower approval ratings of specific presidents.[32] Second, trust in government is one measure of the public's sense of efficacy, their belief that the government works for people like them, as discussed in Chapter 1. If people trust their government, they are more likely to believe that it is responsive to the needs of citizens.

As indicated by the results of a Gallup poll, the public's trust in the ability of the federal government to handle both international affairs and domestic problems has in general declined over

FIGURE 6.7 ■ TRUST IN GOVERNMENT TO HANDLE INTERNATIONAL PROBLEMS Public trust in the government's ability to deal with international problems has decreased since 2012. Why do you think this is the case? Why was public trust comparatively low from 2003 through 2008?

SOURCE: Jeffrey M. Jones, "Trust in Government," www.gallup.com/poll/5392/Trust-Government.aspx.

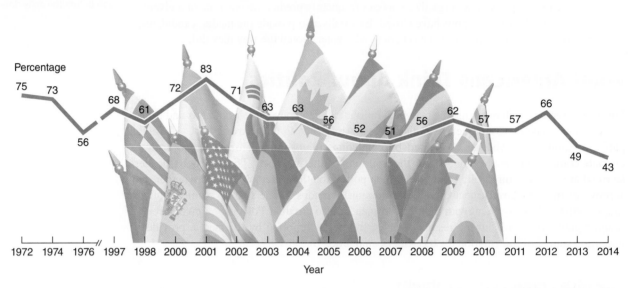

the years after rebounding slightly between 2009 and 2012. Many analysts attribute the decline to widespread dissatisfaction with the war in Iraq and the economic downturn during the George W. Bush administration, the temporary rebound caused by optimism during President Obama's first term, and then frustration with many of Obama's policies, particularly concerning the terror group ISIS.

As shown in Figure 6.7, the public's trust in government to handle international problems reached a record high immediately after the September 11, 2001, terror attacks, with 83 percent of those surveyed indicating a great deal or a fair amount of trust. The public's trust in government to handle international problems then declined steadily from 2004 through 2007, reaching a nadir of 51 percent in 2007, as the war in Iraq dragged on. The effect of President George W. Bush's "surge strategy" in Iraq and then the optimism generated by the election of President Obama accounted for a temporary increase in optimism, but as the war in Afghanistan dragged on, trust declined again, hitting 57 percent in late 2011. Faith in Obama's ability to handle international problems increased to 66 percent leading up to the 2012 election, but then declined to record lows after the administration's early bungled response to the ISIS terror threat.

The public's trust in the government's ability to handle domestic matters also peaked in 2001, as shown in Figure 6.8, which indicates the percentage of people who trust the government to handle domestic problems. Notably, a significant dip in the assessment of the government's ability to handle domestic matters occurred in 2005, immediately after Hurricane Katrina devastated parts of Louisiana, Mississippi, and other southern states. The drop in confidence that began in 2005 reflected the widely perceived inability of the government to manage this crisis. By 2007, worries about the economy dominated the public's thinking, and trust in government to handle domestic problems dropped to 47 percent, a figure that rivals the record-low confidence levels of 51 percent to 49 percent seen in the period between 1974 and 1976, following the Watergate scandal. An uptick registered in 2009, coinciding with Barack Obama's assuming the presidency. But that trust declined to 43 percent in 2011, rebounded to 51 percent in 2012, and then continued in a downward spiral to 42 percent reaching a record-low of 40 percent in 2013 and 2014, respectively. This decline in trust was viewed by many analysts as a repudiation of the president's handling of the economy, his health care plan, and the fractured nature of the relationship between Democrats and Republicans in Congress, which resulted in widespread dissatisfaction with government.

The public's trust in specific institutions has also been affected by the September 11, 2001, terror attacks; the subsequent weariness with the war in Iraq; the optimism following Barack Obama's

FIGURE 6.8 ■ TRUST IN GOVERNMENT TO HANDLE DOMESTIC PROBLEMS What impact does the state of the economy have on the public's trust in the government's ability to handle domestic problems? What can you infer about the state of the economy in May 1972? In September 2004? In September 2012?

SOURCE: Jeffrey M. Jones, "Trust in Government," www.gallup.com/poll/5392/Trust-Government.aspx.

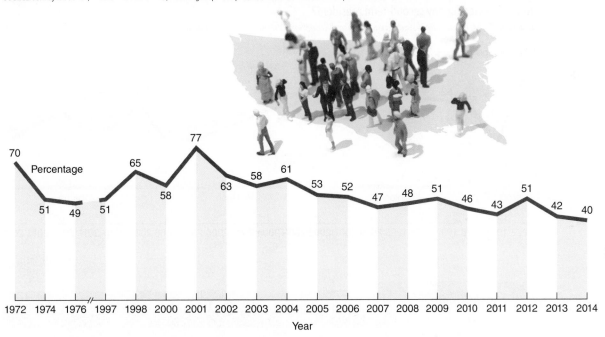

election as president, and the ultimate disappointment in his administration. As Figure 6.9 shows, for example, trust in the executive branch hit a near-record-high mark in 2002, when fully 72 percent of Americans voiced a great deal or a fair amount of trust. But then, in 2007, as this figure shows, public trust in the executive branch dropped to 43 percent, marking a 9-percentage-point decline from 2005. As noted previously, the decline in trust in the institution of the presidency is closely related to public approval of individual presidents: In 2007, only 36 percent of those surveyed approved of the way President Bush was handling his job. Similarly, in 2009, trust in the executive branch spiked up to 61 percent, mirroring Barack Obama's higher approval ratings during that time. By 2011, public trust in the executive branch declined to 47 percent, but rebounded to 56 percent in 2012, reflecting the effectiveness of the Obama reelection campaign before plummeting to a record low rating of 40 percent in 2014, marking the lowest level of public trust in the executive branch ever measured, including trust in the executive before Richard Nixon resigned the presidency.[33]

Sometimes, Americans view the president and Congress as competitors for approval. For example, in 2009, 61 percent of those surveyed expressed trust in the executive branch, but only 45 percent expressed trust in the legislative branch. But this is not always the case. Take 2007, for example. As shown in Figure 6.10, trust in the legislative branch also declined to 50 percent from 62 percent in 2005. Before 2006, part of this decline of trust could be attributed to the public's dissatisfaction with the Republican Congress's consent to Bush administration policies concerning Iraq. From 2006 through 2010, increasing dissatisfaction with the Democrats in Congress was apparent, culminating in the Republican takeover of the House of Representatives in 2010. Public dissatisfaction could be attributed to the economic downturn. Since 2010, though, Congress has not fared any better, as the level of trust in Congress has declined to a record low of 28 percent reflecting the widespread dissatisfaction with partisan bickering in the legisature.

The judicial branch of government consistently scores higher in levels of public trust than do the other two branches. Figure 6.11 shows that confidence in the judiciary typically hovers between 65 percent and 75 percent, sometimes climbing into the high 70s (or even 80 percent in 1999). The judiciary's lowest rating came in 1976, when there was widespread dissatisfaction with government as a whole in the aftermath of the Watergate scandal. But overall, opinion of the judiciary tends to be the most consistent and the most positive of all branches of government.

FIGURE 6.9 ■ TRUST IN THE EXECUTIVE BRANCH OF GOVERNMENT The public's trust in the executive branch declined steeply (from 73 percent to 40 percent in two years) during the Nixon presidency as a result of the Watergate scandal. The decline during George W. Bush's and Barack Obama's presidencies were more gradual, from 72 percent to 42 percent and 61 to 43 percent, respectively, in six years. Was this decline partly to be expected for any second-term president?

SOURCE: Jeffrey M. Jones, "Trust in Government," www.gallup.com/poll/5392/Trust-Government.aspx.

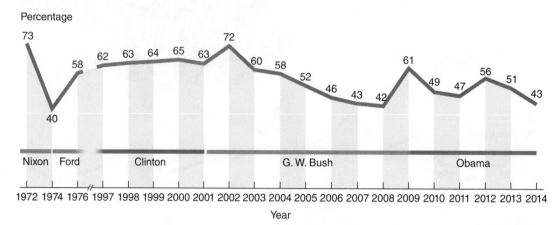

Percentage

73 · 40 · 58 · 62 · 63 · 64 · 65 · 63 · 72 · 60 · 58 · 52 · 46 · 43 · 42 · 61 · 49 · 47 · 56 · 51 · 43

Nixon Ford Clinton G. W. Bush Obama

1972 1974 1976 1997 1998 1999 2000 2001 2002 2003 2004 2005 2006 2007 2008 2009 2010 2011 2012 2013 2014

Year

FIGURE 6.10 ■ TRUST IN THE LEGISLATIVE BRANCH OF GOVERNMENT Trust in the legislative branch plummeted from 62 percent in 2005 to 28 percent in 2014. What factors can explain that trend? Why do you believe that trust in both the executive branch and the legislative branch was low from 2006 to 2008, even though those branches were controlled by different political parties?

SOURCE: Jeffrey M. Jones, "Trust in Government," www.gallup.com/poll/5392/Trust-Government.aspx.

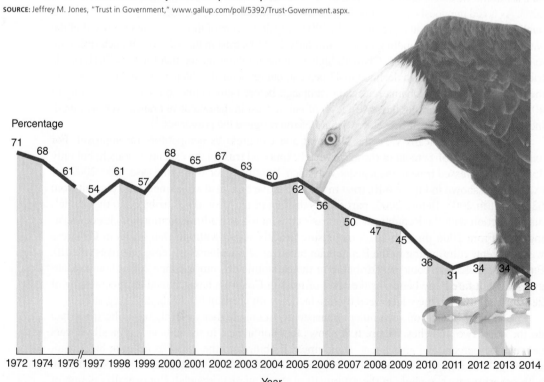

Percentage

71 · 68 · 61 · 54 · 61 · 57 · 68 · 65 · 67 · 63 · 60 · 62 · 56 · 50 · 47 · 45 · 36 · 31 · 34 · 34 · 28

1972 1974 1976 1997 1998 1999 2000 2001 2002 2003 2004 2005 2006 2007 2008 2009 2010 2011 2012 2013 2014

Year

FIGURE 6.11 ▦ TRUST IN THE JUDICIAL BRANCH OF GOVERNMENT Trust in the judicial branch is consistently high, but it climbed in 2009 after a period of steady decline. What could account for this change in public trust?

SOURCE: Jeffrey M. Jones, "Trust in Government," www.gallup.com/poll/5392/Trust-Government.aspx.

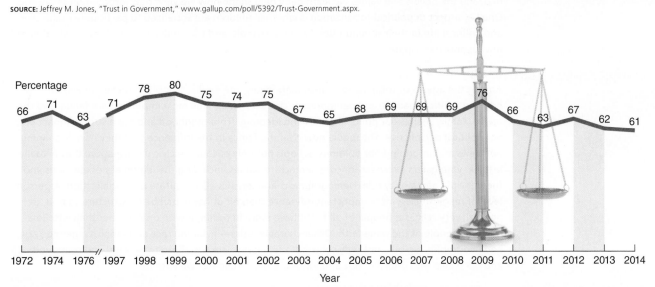

Conclusion

Thinking Critically About What's Next in Public Opinion

The process of political socialization is quite different from what it was even a generation ago. Although some agents of socialization such as families, peers, and churches remain important, other agents, particularly the media, are more pervasive and influential than ever before. Although television and radio have played a part in socializing the average 40-year-old in 2015, today's young people are almost constantly bombarded by various forms of media, which may influence their viewpoints, priorities, behaviors, and opinions.

Technology has also drastically changed the way public opinion is measured. The advent of the computer alone—from powerful mainframes to personal computers—has revolutionized the data-collection process; today, computers facilitate near-instant access to polling data. They also provide the means to generate and survey increasingly representative samples to gauge the public's views with a high degree of accuracy.

The catch-22, however, has been the pervasiveness of public opinion polls. People's opinions are solicited by every kind of survey from cheesy Internet polls to reputable polling organizations. As a result, the public has become poll weary, dubious of the value of the pollster's next set of questions. Will increasing weariness with Internet polling result in less representative samples? How might pollsters overcome this challenge? How will the universality of cell phones revolutionize the process of public opinion polling?

Technology has provided—and will continue to provide—ways to solve the problems that technology itself has generated in accurately measuring public opinion. Stratified samples and other increasingly sophisticated microsampling techniques have improved the ability of reputable pollsters to gauge public opinion. And pollsters are incorporating new technologies, including text messaging and cell phone surveys, as they work to develop new ways to accurately measure and convey the public's views to candidates, to policy makers, and, through the media, to the public itself.

Summary

1. Political Socialization and Civic Participation

Political socialization begins at home in very early childhood, when our political ideology, our beliefs about people of different races and sexes, and even our party identification can be firmly embedded, and the beliefs and values we learn early help shape how we view new information as we age. One key aspect of political socialization is whether children are socialized to participate in the civic and political life of their communities. Families, schools, and the media all contribute to whether and how people participate.

2. Agents of Socialization

Among the agents of socialization—including family, the media, schools, churches, peers, community and political leaders, and demographic characteristics—the most important are family and the media. Family shapes our political values and ideology from childhood and has a strong impact on our political perspective. The media now rival the family in the influence that they have in shaping our views and informing our opinions. Schools not only encourage civic participation, they actually instill in youngsters a respect for core democratic values, including the legitimacy of elections and the principle of majority rule. Demographic characteristics also facilitate our socialization: A person's level of religiosity is a more important influence than his or her actual belief structure so that, in general, very religious people of all faiths have more in common with one another than with less religious people of the same faith. Other characteristics—including race and ethnicity, gender, age, and geographic region—not only contribute to how we are socialized to political and community life and our values and priorities but also influence the candidates we vote for.

3. Measuring Public Opinion

The measurement of public opinion has evolved and become increasingly complex and reliable when done scientifically, though the proliferation of questionable straw polls on the Internet, similar to the initial attempts to predict presidential elections in the early 20th century, still offers dubious results to the gullible. In measuring public opinion, reputable pollsters identify the target population, design an accurate measure, select a sample, and administer the poll. Through various methods of sampling, pollsters attempt to select a subset of the population that is representative of the population's views. Different types of polls, including tracking polls, push polls, and exit polls, are used for different purposes in political campaigns.

4. What Americans Think About Politics

Americans identify the economy and dissatisfaction with government as the "most important problem." Polls also indicate that their overall satisfaction with the direction the country is headed in is low. Among the three branches of government, people's trust in both the presidency and Congress is at record lows, while trust in the judiciary remains relatively stable.

Key Terms

agents of socialization 192
exit polls 207
gender gap 198
generational effect 199
political socialization 190
population 203

public opinion 201
public opinion poll 201
push polls 206
quota sample 204
random sampling 204

sampling error
  (margin of error) 206
stratified sampling 204
straw poll 201
tracking polls 206

For Review

1. How are political socialization and civic participation linked?

2. Explain in detail the agents of socialization. How does each agent influence an individual's political views over a lifetime?

3. What demographic characteristics contribute to how individuals view politics?

4. How did public opinion polls evolve historically?

5. Explain how public opinion polls are conducted.

6. What factors influence what Americans perceive as the "most important problem"?

7. Describe the most recent trend regarding Americans' trust in government.

For Critical Thinking and Discussion

1. Were you brought up in a family in which joining groups was important? Do your parents belong to any interest groups? Do you? If not, why do you think that is the case?

2. How have your demographic characteristics—your age, the area of the country in which you were raised, for example—contributed to the formation of your political views? How relevant are the generalities described in the chapter to your own experience and beliefs?

3. What do you think is the "most important problem" facing the United States? Is it a problem discussed in this book? Is it one shared by your classmates?

4. What factors influence how satisfied you feel about the direction of the country?

5. Which branch of government do you trust the most? Why?

MULTIPLE CHOICE: Choose the lettered item that answers the question correctly.

1. The public's expressed views about an issue at a specific point in time are called
   a. public opinion.
   b. time frame analysis.
   c. time tracked sample.
   d. stratified sample.

2. Agents of socialization *do not* include
   a. pets.
   b. peers.
   c. churches.
   d. the media.

3. A majority of which of the following demographic groups did not support Barack Obama's candidacy for the presidency?
   a. Latinos
   b. women
   c. whites
   d. Asians

4. The influence of an important external event in shaping the views of a generation is called
   a. the age-cohort effect.
   b. the generational effect.
   c. the lifetime effect.
   d. both (a) and (b).

5. A poll conducted in an unscientific manner, used to predict election outcomes, is called
   a. an exit poll.
   b. a tracking poll.
   c. a push poll.
   d. a straw poll.

6. In a poll, the group of people whose opinions are of interest and/or about whom information is desired is called the
   a. quota sample.
   b. target sample.
   c. population.
   d. bull's-eye group.

7. A method by which pollsters structure a sample so that it is representative of the characteristics of the target population is called a
   a. quota sample.
   b. target sample.
   c. population.
   d. bull's-eye group.

8. Polls that measure changes in public opinion over the course of days, weeks, or months by repeatedly asking respondents the same questions and measuring changes in their responses are called
   a. exit polls.
   b. tracking polls.
   c. push polls.
   d. straw polls.

9. A special type of poll that both provides information to campaigns about candidate strengths and weaknesses and attempts to skew public opinion about a candidate is called
   a. an exit poll.
   b. a tracking poll.
   c. a push poll.
   d. a straw poll.

10. Polls conducted at polling places on Election Day to determine the winner of an election before the polls close are called
    a. exit polls.
    b. tracking polls.
    c. push polls.
    d. straw polls.

FILL IN THE BLANKS

11. The process by which we develop our political values and opinions throughout our lives is called _____.

12. The measurable difference in the way women and men vote for candidates and in the way they view political issues is called the _____.

13. A survey of a given population's opinion on an issue or a candidate at a particular point in time is called a _____.

14. A scientific method of selection for a poll in which each member of the population has an equal chance at being included in the sample is called _____.

15. A process of random sampling in which the national population is divided into fourths and certain areas within these regions are selected as representative of the national population is called _____.

Answers: 1. a, 2.a, 3. c, 4. d, 5. d, 6. c, 7. a, 8. b, 9. c, 10 a, 11. political socialization, 12. gender gap, 13. public opinion poll, 14. random sampling, 15. stratified sampling.

Internet Resources

Annenberg National Election Studies
www.electionstudies.org The ANES website contains information on American public opinion as well as a valuable user guide that can help acquaint you with using the data.

The Gallup Organization
www.gallup.com You will find both national and international polls and analysis on this site.

Polling Report
www.pollingreport.com This independent, nonpartisan website offers a clearinghouse for a wide range of polls on both elections and public policy issues.

The Roper Center
www.ropercenter.uconn.edu This website features the University of Connecticut's Roper Center polls, the General Social Survey, presidential approval ratings, and poll analysis.

Recommended Readings

Bishop, George F., and Stephen T. Mockabee. *Taking the Pulse of Public Opinion: Leading and Misleading Indicators of the State of the Nation.* New York: Springer, 2010. This analytical work examines how psychology and the media influence well-established public opinion indicators.

Fiorina, Morris P. *Culture War: The Myth of a Polarized America.* New York: Pearson Longman, 2006. A critical view of the notion that the United States is divided along ideological lines. Fiorina asserts that Americans are generally moderate and tolerant of a wide variety of viewpoints.

Jamieson, Kathleen Hall. *Electing the President, 2008.* Philadelphia: University of Pennsylvania Press, 2008. A fascinating "insider's view"

of how public opinion shaped the 2008 presidential campaigns by the director of the Annenberg National Election Studies.

Page, Benjamin I., and Robert Y. Shapiro. *The Rational Public: Fifty Years of Trends in Americans' Policy Preferences.* Chicago: University of Chicago Press, 1992. An analysis of the policy preferences of the American public from the 1930s until 1990. The authors describe opinion on both domestic and foreign policy.

Traugott, Michael W., and Paul J. Lavrakas. *The Voter's Guide to Election Polls,* 4th ed. New York: Chatham House, 2008. A user-friendly approach, written in question-and-answer format, that helps beginners understand the polling process and how to interpret public opinion data.

Welch, Susan, Lee Sigelman, Timothy Bledsoe, and Michael Combs. *Race and Place: Race Relations in an American City* (Cambridge Studies in Public Opinion and Political Psychology). Cambridge: Cambridge University Press, 2001. An analysis of the effect of residential changes on the attitudes and behavior of African Americans and whites.

Movies of Interest

Lions for Lambs (2007)
Directed by Robert Redford and starring Redford, Meryl Streep, and Tom Cruise, this film about a platoon of U.S. soldiers in Afghanistan demonstrates the influence that educational socialization can have on individuals.

Wag the Dog (1997)
A classic Barry Levinson film featuring a spin-doctor (Robert De Niro) and a Hollywood producer (Dustin Hoffman) who team up 11 days before an election to "fabricate" a war to cover up a presidential sex scandal.

CHAPTER 7

Interest Groups

 THEN

Individuals joined voluntary organizations to achieve goals of value to their members and to influence the direction of society and government.

 NOW

Interest groups continue to be an important vehicle for citizens to persuade government to act in their interest, as evidenced by the efforts of the gay rights and immigrant rights movements.

 NEXT

Will digital fund-raising, organizing, and communicating strengthen the clout and efficacy of interest groups?

Will expanding Web-based activism change the face of who participates in interest groups?

Will digital group activism have unintended negative consequences?

This chapter surveys the composition, power, and strategies of interest groups in the United States. We explore the development of interest groups over time and analyze what makes an interest group successful.

FIRST, we examine the value of interest groups as tools of citizen participation.

SECOND, we consider the questions of who joins interest groups and why.

THIRD, we examine how interest groups succeed.

FOURTH, we look at various types of interest groups.

FIFTH, we focus on interest group strategies.

SIXTH, we probe the intersection of interest groups, politics, and money: specifically, the influence of political action committees.

Organizations that seek to

achieve their goals by influencing government decision making are called interest groups. Also called *special interests,* interest groups differ from political parties in that interest groups do not seek to control the government, as parties do. Interest groups simply want to influence policy making on specific issues. Interest groups are more important in the political process of the United States than anywhere else in the world.[1] Their strong role is due partly to the number of interest groups that attempt to influence U.S. policy.

Take just one issue—the environment, say—and chances are that you or someone in your class is a member of one of the almost 200 organizations concerned with the environment, conservation, or ecology in the United States.[2] The multitude of interest groups focused on any given issue is an important component of how government policy is formulated.

Interest groups shape the policy process by helping determine which issues policy makers will act on and which options they will consider in addressing a problem.

When we think of interest groups, the typical images that come to mind are of wealthy lobbyists "schmoozing" with easily corrupted politicians. Although that may sometimes be the case, interest groups do not require the leadership of the rich and well connected to be effective. But today, using new technologies such as Twitter and Facebook, the organized effort of people from all walks of life can influence policy making. Although moneyed interests may dominate politics, interest groups play a crucial role in leveling the political playing field by providing access for organized "average" people.

The Value of Interest Groups

The 19th-century French historian and writer Alexis de Tocqueville, author of the influential work *Democracy in America,* dubbed Americans "a nation of joiners" in 1835, and his analysis still rings true today.[3] Indeed, estimates indicate that about 80 percent of all Americans belong to some kind of voluntary group or association, although not every group is an **interest group.**[4] The key role that interest groups would play in politics was foreseen by the founders—James Madison acknowledged the idea that people with similar interests would form and join groups to prompt government action. He believed that the only way to cure "the mischiefs of faction" was by enabling groups to proliferate and compete with one another.[5]

Yet despite this heritage, some contemporary scholars argue that Americans today are increasingly staying at home. Political scientist Robert Putnam, author of *Bowling Alone: The Collapse and Revival of American Community,* found a marked decrease in the number of people who belong to interest groups and other types of clubs and organizations. These organizations, Putnam argues, are essential sources of **social capital,** the relationships that improve our lives by giving us social connections with which to solve common problems. Putnam demonstrates that social capital improves individual lives in very concrete ways: People with a greater number of social ties live longer, happier, and healthier lives. But social capital also improves communities, and even larger polities, because it stimulates individuals to communicate and interact with their governments. Efficacy increases, because when people are engaged and communicate with government officials, government responds by meeting their needs more effectively. This response in turn creates the feeling among individuals that government listens to people like them. And when government responds, it becomes more likely that those affected will try to influence government decisions again.[6]

interest group
organization that seeks to achieve goals by influencing government decision making

social capital
the many ways in which our lives are improved by social connections

Critics of Putnam's work have noted that although the number of people belonging to the kinds of groups Putnam analyzed may be declining, people are engaged in other types of groups and clubs and enjoy various forms of group recreation.[7] For example, it is unlikely that you are a member of a gardening club such as those that Putnam researched. (But if you are, good for you!) Yet it is likely that you belong to an online community such as Facebook. Such communities facilitate social relationships and may even provide the opportunity for participants to solve community problems. And although people may be less likely to entertain friends and relatives in their homes today (another activity Putnam measured), they are more likely to socialize

>Can a conversation over a skim latte create social capital? People may not be joining gardening clubs, but are they really less connected than in the past? Or are their connections just different?

with friends and relatives over meals in restaurants. So even if Putnam is correct in his analysis that we are no longer socially engaged the way Americans used to be, we may still be engaged—but through different channels and in different settings.

Political scientist E. E. Schattschneider has written: "Democracy is a competitive political system in which competing leaders and organizations define the alternatives of public policy in such a way that the public can participate in the decision-making process."[8] One of the key types of competitive organizations Schattschneider was describing is interest groups. Schattschneider and other political scientists study and assess the value that interest groups provide in American democracy. This value centrally includes interest groups' usefulness in channeling civic participation—serving as a point of access and a mechanism by which people can connect with their governments. Political scientists also explore interest groups, on the one hand, as valuable avenues by which people can influence the policy process and, on the other hand, as resources for policy makers. In this section, we consider various perspectives on the role of interest groups in a democracy, the diverse value that interest groups confer, and the drawbacks of interest groups.

Interest Groups and Civic Participation

Scholars who study civic engagement acknowledge the significant ways in which interest groups channel civic participation. Interest groups afford a way for people to band together to influence government as a *collective force*. Interest groups also seek to involve *individuals* more actively in the political process by encouraging them to vote and to communicate their views one-on-one to their elected officials. In addition, interest groups assist in the engagement of *communities* by providing a forum through which people can come together and form an association. Importantly, too, interest groups offer an alternative means of participation to individuals who are disenchanted with the two-party system. By taking part in interest groups, individuals, acting together, perform important roles in the polity not only by communicating their viewpoints to policy makers but also by providing a medium that other people can use to express their opinions.

Pluralist Theory versus Elite Theory

An interest group can represent a wide variety of interests, as in the case of a community Chamber of Commerce that serves as an umbrella organization for local businesses. Alternatively, an interest group can restrict itself to a narrower focus, as does the Society for the Preservation and

How Group Participation Has Changed in the United States

Then (1960s)	Now
Individuals joined bowling leagues, civic associations, and community service organizations.	People join virtual communities and use social networking sites to keep in touch with others who share their personal and public interests.
Many people entertained and socialized a great deal at home.	People are more likely to visit with friends and relatives in restaurants, cafés, and other public settings, as well as online through "virtual visits," like Skyping and Snapchatting.
Groups used traditional activities to communicate their interests to policy makers, including letter writing and lobbying.	Groups rely on traditional activities but also increasingly use new technologies, including Twitter, to communicate with members, to fundraise, and to lobby policy makers.

WHAT'S NEXT?

> What new media technologies and strategies might shape how interest groups organize and mobilize members in the future?

> Are there *negative* consequences to relying on the Internet as an organizing tool? What obstacles will some Internet-based organizations face in mobilizing their supporters around a given issue?

> In what ways will technology change how policy makers are influenced in the future?

pluralist theory
a theory that holds that policy making is a competition among diverse interest groups that ensure the representation of individual interests

elite theory
a theory that holds that a group of wealthy, educated individuals wields most political power

Encouragement of Barbershop Quartet Singing. Scholars who support **pluralist theory** emphasize how important it is for a democracy to have large numbers of diverse interest groups representing a wide variety of views.[9] Indeed, pluralists view the policy-making process as a crucial competition among diverse groups whose members attempt to influence policy in numerous settings, including agencies in the executive branch of government, Congress, and the courts.[10] Pluralists believe that interest groups are essential players in democracy because they ensure that individual interests are represented in the political arena even if some individuals opt not to participate. Like some of the founders, pluralists argue that individuals' liberties can be protected only through a proliferation of groups representing diverse competing interests, so that no one group dominates.

Pluralists believe, moreover, that interest groups provide a structure for political participation and help ensure that individuals follow the rules in participating in civic society. Following the rules means using positive channels for government action rather than extreme tactics such as assassinations, coups, and other forms of violence. Pluralists also stress that groups' varying assets tend to counterbalance one another. Pluralists contend that this is frequently the case with many policy debates. And so although an industry association such as the American Petroleum Institute, an interest group for the oil and natural gas industry, may have a lot of money at its disposal, an environmental group opposing the industry, such as Greenpeace, may have a large membership base from which to launch grassroots activism.

Proponents of elite theory dispute some claims of pluralist theory. In particular, elite theorists point to the overwhelming presence of elites as political decision makers. According to **elite theory,** a ruling class composed of wealthy, educated individuals wields most of the power in government and also within the top universities, corporations, the military, and media outlets. Elite theorists claim that despite appearances that the political system is accessible to all, elites hold disproportionate power in the United States. They also emphasize that elites commonly use that power to protect their own economic interests, frequently by ensuring the continuation of the status quo. And so, although non-elites represented by interest groups may occasionally win political victories, elites control the direction of major policies. But elite theorists posit that there is mobility into the elite structure; they emphasize that (in contrast to the situation in aristocracies) talented and industrious individuals from non-elite backgrounds can attain elite status in a democracy, often through education. This mobility, they say, gives the political system an even greater façade of accessibility.

Although these theories offer competing explanations for the role and motivation of interest groups in the United States, many political scientists agree that aspects of both theories are true: elites do have disproportionate influence in policy making, but that power is checked by interest groups. Undisputed is that interest groups are an essential feature of American democracy and provide an important medium through which individuals can exercise some control over their government.

Key Functions of Interest Groups

Many Americans join interest groups, and yet interest groups have a generally negative reputation. For example, it has been said of many a politician that he or she is "in the pockets of the special interests." This statement suggests that the politician is not making decisions based on conscience or the public interest but instead has been "bought." This notion is closely linked to the ideas held by elite theorists, who argue that elites' disproportionate share of influence negatively affects the ability of the average person to get the government to do what she or he wants it to. Yet despite the criticisms frequently leveled by politicians, pundits, and the populace about interest groups' efforts to influence government, these groups serve several vital functions in the policy-making process in the United States:

- *Interest groups educate the public about policy issues.* Messages from interest groups abound. For example, thanks to organizations such as Mothers Against Drunk Drivers (MADD), most people are aware of the dangers of drinking and driving. In educating the public, interest groups often provide a vehicle for civic discourse, so that genuine dialogue about policy problems and potential solutions is part of the national agenda.

- *Interest groups provide average citizens with an avenue of access to activism.* Anyone can join or form an interest group. Although wealthy and well-educated people are most likely to do so, interest groups can speak for all kinds of people on all kinds of issues. Historically in the United States, groups have been significant forces for advocates of civil rights for African Americans[11] as well as for supporters of equal rights for women,[12] gays and lesbians, and ethnic minorities. Even you and your fellow students can form an interest group. One example of students undertaking such an effort is the group ReEnergize Texas, a coalition of students from more than 20 universities and high schools in Texas. ReEnergize Texas focuses on environmental advocacy, and students from colleges in El Paso, College Station, San Antonio, McAllen, and Houston contact members of the state legislature and voice their views on environmental legislation under consideration.

- *Interest groups mobilize citizens and stimulate them to participate in civic and political affairs.* Some people are "turned off" by politics because they feel that neither the Democratic nor the Republican Party represents their views. In these cases, interest groups, with their typically narrower area of focus, can sometimes fill the void. Moreover, interest groups nurture community involvement by encouraging the formation of local chapters of larger interest groups.

- *Interest groups perform electoral functions.* By endorsing and rating candidates and advertising their positions, interest groups provide voters with cues as to which candidates best represent their views. Interest groups also mobilize campaign volunteers and voters. These activities facilitate informed civic participation. For example, before the congressional midterm elections of 2014, the Republican-oriented interest group the American Conservative Union rated members of Congress, enabling voters to learn which members are the most conservative; at the same time, Democratically aligned groups, including Democracy for America, used sophisticated get-out-the-vote software to turn Democratic voters out for Democratic candidate slates.

- *Interest groups provide information and expertise to policy makers.* The private sector often has greater resources than the public sector and can be a source of meaningful data and information for policy makers on pressing social issues. Sometimes, interest group "experts" might include celebrities, who, through their status, not only provide information to legislators but also increase public awareness of their issue. Such was the case in 2014 when actor Seth Rogen testified before a U.S. senate subcommittee about the toll that Alzheimer's disease takes on families. Rogen's mother-in-law was diagnosed with the disease at age 55.

- *Interest groups can protect the common good.* The federal government is structured so that only one individual (the president) is elected from a national constituency. Interest groups can work to protect the nation's interest as a whole rather than just the needs of a specific constituency. For example, Clean Water Action, with more than a million members nationally, advocates for clean, safe, and affordable water for all Americans.

- *Interest groups are an integral part of the government's system of checks and balances.* Interest groups often "check" one another's influence with competing interests, and they can similarly check the actions of policy makers. For example, in 2012 the Recording Industry

> Celebrity "experts" frequently offer testimony before Congress on many issues. Seth Rogen, whose mother-in-law suffers from Alzheimer's disease, testified before a U.S. senate subcommittee about the toll that Alzheimer's disease takes on families. His celebrity helped to focus attention on the economic and psychological plight of families living with the disease.

political action committee (PAC) entity whose specific goal is to raise and spend money to influence the outcome of elections

Association of America and Motion Picture Association of America lobbied Congress to pass a law that would crack down on Internet piracy (the Stop Online Piracy Act, known as SOPA). But many technological corporations opposed the policy because they believed that it squelched innovation and violated principles of free speech. Using the Internet, the tech companies mobilized the public to lobby against the act, which was defeated, demonstrating the ability of one set of organized interests to check another.

The Downside of Interest Groups

Despite the valuable functions of interest groups, certain criticisms of these organizations are valid. Interest groups do contribute to the appearance of (and sometimes the reality of) corruption in the political system. Indeed, there are various criticisms of the "interest group state." Former president Jimmy Carter (1977–1981) bemoaned the influence of special interests, saying that they are "the single greatest threat to the proper functioning of our democratic system," and former president Ronald Reagan charged that interest groups are "placing out of focus our constitutional balance."[13]

Another criticism is that interest groups and their **political action committees (PACs),** entities whose specific goal is to raise and spend money to influence the outcome of elections, make money a vital force in American politics. (See Chapter 9 for a detailed discussion of PACs.) By contributing large sums of money to political campaigns, interest groups' PACs make campaigns expensive and often lopsided; candidates without well-stuffed campaign war chests have a difficult, if not impossible, task in challenging those who receive large PAC contributions. Money also changes the nature of campaigns, making them less engaging for citizens on a grassroots level and more reliant on the mass media. These concerns have been exacerbated by a 2010 U.S. Supreme Court ruling that enables corporations and labor unions to spend money freely on political ads supporting or targeting candidates for federal office and allows corporations and unions to buy advertisements even in the last days of political campaigns. Critics, including President Barack Obama, say these rule changes will increase the importance of money in political campaigns and will enable corporations to exert greater influence over the electoral process.

Interest groups, moreover, are faulted with strengthening the advantages enjoyed by incumbents. Most interest groups want access to policy makers, regardless of these elected officials' party identification. Realizing that the people already in office are likely to be reelected, interest groups use their resources disproportionately to support incumbent candidates. Doing so increases incumbency advantage even further by improving the odds against a challenger.

Finally, although the option to form an interest group is open to any and all activists and would-be activists, elites are more likely to establish and to dominate interest groups than are non-elites. This fact skews the policy process in favor of elites. Interest group activism is much more prominent among the wealthy, the white, the upper middle class, and the educated than among the poor, the nonwhite, the working class, and the less educated. Although Internet-based interest groups have been particularly effective in attracting young people and others not traditionally drawn to such organizations, many of the most effective national interest groups remain dominated by traditional interest group populations.

Who Joins Interest Groups, and Why?

People are not all equally likely to join or form interest groups, and this reality has serious consequences for the ability of interest groups to represent everyone's views. Political scientists agree that income and education tend to be the best predictors of interest group membership. That said, enormous diversity exists in the types of people who choose to join or form interest groups.

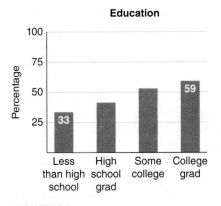
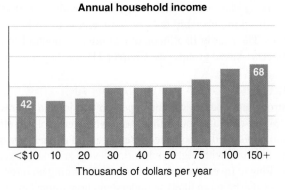
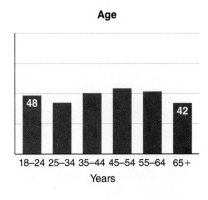

FIGURE 7.1

Participation in Online Groups by Education, Income, and Age

SOURCE: Pew Internet Research Project, "Civic Engagement," 2013, www.pewinternet.org/2013/04/25/civic-engagement/.

Patterns of Membership

Interest group participation is related to three demographic characteristics: income, social class, and education. People with higher incomes are more likely to participate in interest groups than those with lower incomes. Also, many surveys show that those who identify themselves as upper-middle or middle class are more likely to join interest groups than those who self-identify as lower-middle or working class. Similarly, higher education levels are a strong predictor of interest group participation. But interest group participation also frequently reflects one's occupation: People tend to belong to associations related to their work. Interestingly, as shown in Figure 7.1, these patterns of membership hold true even for online activities. The affluent and the well educated are more likely to participate in online groups and civic activities.

INTEREST GROUP PARTICIPATION BASED ON OCCUPATION   There are several reasons for interest group membership patterns, some of which, as we shall see, are interconnected. For example, people with higher incomes have more disposable income to spend on membership dues for organizations. They are also likely to have occupations in which interest group activity is useful (or even required, as in some professional fields such as the law).

Doctors and lawyers, for example, are likely to be members of professional associations such as the American Medical Association and the American Bar Association. These organizations give incentives for membership, such as accreditation of qualified professionals, and also attempt to influence government policy on members' behalf. Workers such as teachers and tradespeople are likely to belong to labor unions, while executives in business and industry are likely to be members of industry-specific and general business organizations that advocate on behalf of their members.[14] All of these professional associations, labor unions, and business organizations are types of interest groups.

INTEREST GROUP PARTICIPATION AND SOCIAL CLASS   Differentiating the influence of income from that of class can be difficult when examining the impact of social class on the likelihood of joining an interest group. But in general, people who identify themselves as working class are less likely to have been socialized to participate in interest groups, with the important exception of labor unions, which historically have been most likely to organize working-class occupations. As we considered in Chapter 6, an important predictor of political participation (and interest group participation, specifically) is whether a person learns to take part and join from a young age. If your mother participated in your town's historical preservation society, and your father attended meetings of the local Amnesty International chapter, you are likely to view those behaviors as "what people do" and do them yourself. If you come from a working-class family, you are generally less likely to see your parents engage in these participatory behaviors, rendering you similarly less likely to participate. Although scholars trace much of the lack of participation of working-class people to how they are socialized, the overlapping occurrence of working-class status and lower income is also a factor.[15] Working-class people may not be able to afford membership dues or have access to child care that would allow them to attend meetings. Their lower likelihood of owning a computer limits their chances of taking an active role in Internet-based groups (see Chapter 11). Or they may simply lack the leisure time to participate.

INTEREST GROUP PARTICIPATION AND EDUCATION Educational attainment also has a strong influence on whether a person will join an interest group. One recent study surveyed 19- to 23-year-olds and found that those who were college students were more than twice as likely to join a politically motivated interest group as their age-group peers who did not attend college.[16] Individuals with higher education levels are more likely to be informed about issues and more willing to invest the time and energy in joining an interest group that represents their views. They may also be more likely to understand how important interest groups are in shaping public policy.

College students are among the most avid participants in Internet-based activist groups. But "belonging" to these groups varies a great deal (not unlike the situation in "real-world" interest groups). A member of an Internet-based interest group may play a highly active role—communicating with other members regularly, attending rallies and other campus events, and taking concrete actions such as signing an Internet petition and participating in a protest (see "Global Context"). Or members may be more passive. They may limit their activity to reading the regular e-mails from the group that inform them of issues and events, and may only occasionally participate. Or they may be members of a group in name only. But this phenomenon is not unique to Internet-based groups. Many interest groups are dominated by a cadre of committed activists supported by "sometimes-activists." And nearly every group has a contingent of "members" who signed up mainly for the free T-shirt, tote bag, or umbrella.

Motivations for Joining Interest Groups

Some people may join an interest group for the benefits they can gain. Others may gravitate to a group sponsoring a particular cause. Still others may become members of a group for the simple reason that they want to meet new people. Recognizing that individuals have various motivations for joining, interest groups typically provide a menu of incentives for membership.

solidary incentive

motivation to join an interest group based on the companionship and the satisfaction derived from socializing with others that it offers

SOLIDARY INCENTIVES Some people join interest groups because they offer **solidary incentives**—the feeling of belonging, companionship, friendship, and the satisfaction derived from socializing with others. Solidary incentives are closely linked to Robert Putnam's idea of social capital: Both solidary incentives and social capital are related to the psychological satisfaction derived from civic participation. For example, a person might join the Sierra Club because she wants to participate in activities with other people who enjoy hiking or care deeply about wilderness protection. Your uncle might join the National Rifle Association because he likes to compete in shooting contests and wants to get to know others who do the same.

purposive incentive

motivation to join an interest group based on the belief in the group's cause from an ideological or a moral standpoint

PURPOSIVE INCENTIVES People also join interest groups because of **purposive incentives,** that is, because they believe in the group's cause from an ideological or a moral standpoint. Interest groups pave the way for people to take action with like-minded people. And so you might join People for the Ethical Treatment of Animals (PETA) because you strongly object to animal abuse and want to work with others to prevent cruelty to animals. A friend who is passionately pro-life might join the National Right to Life Committee, whereas your pro-choice cousin might join NARAL Pro-Choice America (formerly the National Abortion Reproductive Rights Action League).

The Internet is a particularly effective forum for attracting membership through purposive incentives. Accessible anyplace and anytime, the Internet provides resources for you to join an interest group even during a bout of insomnia at 3 a.m. Suppose a conversation earlier in the day got you thinking anew about the plight of South Sudanese refugees in Uganda. In those dark predawn hours, you can Google "Sudanese refugees" and within seconds have a variety of access points for becoming civically engaged by participating in an interest group. Some interest groups may ask you to contribute money; others may urge you to sign an online petition or to call the White House to make your opinions known. You may follow other interest groups on Twitter,

USING THE INTERNET FOR CHANGE.ORG

Change.org is an international petition platform that enables users to pressure governments, corporations, and other organizations to undertake actions that petitioners advocate. Today Change.org boasts 45 million users in 196 countries.

According to Change.org's website, "we live in an amazing time, when the opportunity to make a difference is greater than ever before. Gathering people behind a cause used to be difficult, requiring lots of time, money, and a complex infrastructure. But technology has made us more connected than ever. It's now possible for anyone to start a campaign and immediately mobilize hundreds of others locally or hundreds of thousands around the world, making governments and companies more responsive and accountable."

Change.org's effectiveness can be seen in many instances, including a 2014 petition started by Great Britain's Emma Pooley and Chrissie Wellington, Kathryn Bertine of St. Kitts and Nevis, and Marianne Vos of the Netherlands. All four women are champion cyclists, and through Change.org, they petitioned for women to be allowed to race in the Tour de France, a famed three-week bike race through France with a hundred-year-old tradition in which only men can participate. With 97,000 signatures on their petition, the women cyclists successfully pressured race

organizers into creating "La Course by Le Tour de France." Though not the parallel race that the cyclists sought, there is satisfaction in "this huge step forward" that offers women cyclists "the opportunity to showcase our talents to the world and grow the sport."

SOURCE: Change.org, "ASO (Amaury Sports Organization): Allow Female Professional Cycling Teams to Race the Tour de France," 2014, www.change.org/petitions/aso-amaury-sports-organization-allow-female-professional-cycling-teams-to-race-the-tour-de-france.

enabling you to learn about demonstrations sponsored by other groups right on your college campus and in your community. You may even find out about state and national demonstrations. The media contacts provided by online interest groups make it easy for you to write a letter to an editor, attempting to convince others of the correctness of your views. Just learning about the wide variety of activities available can make you feel that you are "doing something" about a cause you believe in.

ECONOMIC INCENTIVES Many people join interest groups because of material or **economic incentives;** that is, they want to support groups that work for policies that will provide them with economic benefits. Sometimes these groups advocate for tangible, concrete items. For example, the National Association of Police Organizations lobbies Congress concerning many appropriations measures that could affect its membership, including bills that would provide or increase funding for Community Oriented Policing Services (COPS) programs, bulletproof vests, and overtime pay for first responders to disasters.

Nearly all corporate and labor interest groups offer economic incentives to their members. They sometimes do so by advocating for policies that support business or labor in general, such

economic incentive
motivation to join an interest group because the group works for policies that will provide members with material benefits

as policies focused on the minimum wage, regulations concerning workplace conditions, and laws governing family leave or health coverage.

Other interest groups offer smaller-scale economic benefits to members. Many Americans over age 50 join the American Association of Retired Persons (AARP) because of the discounts members receive on hotels, airfares, and car rentals. Other organizations provide discounts on health insurance, special deals from merchants, or low-interest credit cards. Most people join and remain in interest groups for a combination of reasons, purposive incentive, economic benefits, or even social connections.

> Interest groups pave the way for people to take action with like-minded people. When people join interest groups because of purposive incentives, they take action because they believe in the group's cause from an ideological or a moral standpoint. Among the most passionate interest group joiners are animal rights activists.

How Interest Groups Succeed

Given that interest groups attempt to influence all kinds of policies, why are some interest groups better than others at getting what they want? Political scientists agree on various factors that influence whether an interest group will succeed. These factors include the interest group's *organizational resources,* the tools it has at its disposal to help achieve its goals, and its *organizational environment,* the setting in which it attempts to achieve those goals.

Organizational Resources

The effectiveness of interest groups in influencing government policy often depends on the resources these groups use to sway policy makers.[17] Interest groups rely on two key types of resources: membership, the people who belong to a given group, and financial resources, the money the group can spend to exert influence.

HOW MEMBERSHIP AFFECTS SUCCESS   A large membership enhances an interest group's influence because policy makers are more likely to take note of the group's position. The age-old concept of "strength in numbers" applies when it comes to interest groups. The sheer number of a group's membership is often an important factor in forcing policy makers, the media, and the public to pay attention to an issue. Among the largest U.S. interest groups is the American Association of Retired Persons (AARP), which boasts a membership of more than 40 million people. This vast size gives the organization incredible clout and historically has made policy makers unwilling to take on any issue that would unleash the wrath of AARP's formidable membership. For example, for years many economic analysts have suggested increasing the age at which people become eligible to receive Social Security. They reason that the average life span has risen significantly since the eligibility age was set and that people are working longer because they remain healthier longer. But this potential policy solution has long simmered on the back burner. The reason? Politicians in Congress and the White House have not wanted to incur the disapproval of the AARP's members, who would widely oppose increasing the eligibility age and might respond by voting unsympathetic officials out of office.

But size is not the only important aspect of an interest group's membership. The *cohesion* of a group, or how strongly unified it is, also matters to participants and to policy makers.[18] For example, the Human Rights Campaign (HRC) lobbies for federal legislation to end discrimination on the basis of sexual orientation and provides research to elected officials and policy makers on issues of importance to people who are gay, lesbian, bisexual, or transgender. The HRC has a membership of about 1.5 million people, but because the organization limits its advocacy to issues affecting gay, lesbian, bisexual, and transgender people, it is an extremely cohesive association.

Another significant aspect of an interest group's membership is its *intensity*. Intensity is a measure of how strongly members feel about the issues they are targeting. Some organizations may reach an intense crescendo of activism but may find it difficult to sustain that level of intensity. But certain kinds of organizations, including pro-life interest groups such as the National Right to Life Committee, environmental groups such as the Sierra Club and Greenpeace, and animal rights groups such as People for the Ethical Treatment of Animals (PETA), are known for sustaining high levels of intensity. These organizations are more adept at attracting new members and younger members than are older, more entrenched kinds of groups. These newer, youthful members are a significant force behind the persistence and intensity of these groups.

The *demographics* of a group's membership also may increase its success. Members who know policy makers personally and have access to them mean greater influence for the group.[19] Other demographic attributes also matter. Members who are well educated or affluent tend to have more influence. Policy makers perceive these attributes as important because the group's membership is more likely to lobby and to contribute financial resources on behalf of the organization's cause. But today geographically dispersed members are becoming an increasingly important interest group demographic, as technology enables individuals around the country to have quick input in the policy process. Increasingly, this use of technology in lobbying policy makers means younger citizens are becoming more effective at articulating their concerns to them.

> Intensity is a measure of how strongly members feel about the issues they are targeting. The Washington Area Bicyclist Association holds a National Bike Summit each year to lobby policy makers on pro-bicyclist agenda items. Nelle Pierson rallies cyclists who are participating in the Congressional Bike Ride, one tactic used to draw attention to the group's priorities.

HOW FINANCIAL RESOURCES AFFECT SUCCESS For an interest group, money can buy power.[20] Money fuels the hiring of experienced and effective staff and lobbyists, who communicate directly with policy makers, as well as the undertaking of initiatives that will increase the group's membership. Money also funds the raising of more money.[21] For example, the Business Roundtable represents the interests of 150 chief executive officers of the largest U.S. companies, including American Express, General Electric, IBM, and Verizon. In 2013, it spent over $12 million lobbying the president, Congress, and several cabinet departments for policies that would benefit its member corporations, their shareholders, and their member corporations' 10 million employees.[22] Issues of concern to the Business Roundtable include policies such as Securities and Exchange Commission rules, laws concerning corporate ethics, and reform to the nation's class action lawsuit regulations. Many critics believe that the financial resources of an organization will play an even greater role in determining the group's success in the future because of new campaign finance rules that allow unlimited expenditures by business and labor.

Sometimes interest groups form a political action committee (PAC) to shape the composition of government; that is, they contribute money to the campaigns of favored candidates, particularly incumbents who are likely to be reelected.[23] Interest groups representing the economic concerns of members—business, industry, and union groups—generally tend to have the greatest financial resources for all these activities.[24]

Organizational Environment

The setting in which an interest group attempts to achieve its goals is the *organizational environment*. Key factors in the organizational environment include its leadership and the presence or absence of opposition from other groups.[25]

LEADERSHIP Strong, charismatic leaders contribute to the influence of an interest group by raising public awareness of the group and its activities, by enhancing its reputation, and by making the organization attractive to new members and contributors. Stephanie Schriock, the president of EMILY's List, is recognized as a talented and inspirational leader who is expanding the influence and membership of the organization, which is dedicated to getting Democratic women who are pro-choice and support the passage of the Equal Right Amendment elected to Congress.

OPPOSITION   The presence of opposing interest groups can also have an impact on an interest group's success. When an interest group is "the only game in town" on a particular issue, policy makers are more likely to rely on that group's views. But if groups with opposing views are also attempting to influence policy, getting policy makers to act strongly in any one group's favor is more difficult. Consider this example: Hotel Employees and the Restaurant Employees International Union supported increasing the minimum wage, but the National Restaurant Association, which advocates for restaurant owners, opposed a minimum wage hike, arguing that the higher wage would cut into restaurant owners' profits or limit its members' ability to hire as many employees as before. In the face of such opposing interests, policy makers are often more likely to compromise than to give any one group exactly what it wants.

Although each of these factors—organizational resources and the organizational environment—influences how powerful an interest group will be, no single formula determines an interest group's clout. Sometimes an interest group has powerful advocates in Congress who support its cause. Other times, a single factor can prove essential to an interest group's success.

Types of Interest Groups

A wide variety of political interest groups try to exert influence on virtually every type of policy question, from those concerning birth (such as the minimum hospital stay an insurance company must cover after a woman gives birth) to matters related to death (such as what funeral home practices should be banned by the government). Despite the broad range of issues around which interest groups coalesce, political scientists generally categorize interest groups by what kinds of issues concern them and who benefits from the groups' activities.

Economic Interest Groups

When economic interest groups lobby government, the benefits for their members can be direct or indirect. In some cases, the economic benefits flow directly from the government to the interest group members, as when an agricultural interest group successfully presses for *subsidies,* monies given by the government to the producers of a particular crop or product, often to influence the volume of production of that commodity. In other instances, economic interest groups lobby for or against policies that, though not directly benefiting their members, have an indirect impact on the interest group's membership.

CORPORATE AND BUSINESS INTERESTS   Large corporate and smaller business interest groups are among the most successful U.S. pressure groups with respect to their influence on government. These groups typically seek policies that benefit a particular company or industry. For example, the Motion Picture Association of America (MPAA) lobbies policy makers (often by hosting prerelease screenings of films and lavish dinner receptions) with the goal of securing the passage of antipiracy laws, described earlier.

Certain industries' associations are stand-alone organizations, such as the National Beer Wholesalers Association. But industry and business groups also commonly advocate for policies using **umbrella organizations,** which are interest groups representing groups of industries or corporations. Examples of umbrella business organizations include the Business Roundtable and the U.S. Chamber of Commerce. But increasingly, other types of organizations are mimicking this model. For example, in 2014, ten organizations, including the Council on American-Islamic Relations (CAIR), Islamic Circle of North American, Muslim Legal Fund of America, Muslim Alliance in North America, and the other groups that advocate on behalf of Muslim Americans, formed U.S. Council of Muslim Organizations. This new umbrella organization seeks to help Muslim Americans to better communicate with one another, and with the American public. Their first tasks are to conduct a census of American Muslims to create a database that will be used to mobilize Muslim American voters in elections.

umbrella organizations
interest groups that represent collective groups of industries or corporations

A relatively new trend that has emerged among business interests is the role that hedge funds—investment groups consisting of pooled money administered by a professional management firm—are now playing in shaping policy. In 2014, for example, *The New York Times* reported on the activities of William Ackman, whose hedge fund stood to make an enormous profit if the stock of Herbalife, a company that provides a nutritional supplement, dropped. Ackman undertook a sophisticated campaign to undermine Herbalife's value, which included lobbying a member of Congress, Representative Linda Sanchez (D-Calif.), to call on the Federal Trade Commission to investigate the company. Although the incident was unscrupulous, this trend indicates the strong influence that those lobbying the government can have on policy decisions.[26]

>Labor interest groups, including the AFL-CIO, an umbrella organization made up of more than 50 labor unions, are among the nation's most powerful interest groups. Today about 11 percent of all U.S. workers belong to unions.

LABOR INTERESTS Like corporate interest groups, labor interest groups include both national labor unions and umbrella organizations of unions. The AFL-CIO, an umbrella organization made up of more than 50 labor unions, is among the nation's most powerful interest groups, although its influence has waned over the past several decades, as union membership has declined generally. During the 1950s and 1960s, nearly 35 percent of all U.S. workers were union members. By 1983, membership had decreased to about 20 percent, and today about 11 percent of all U.S. workers belong to unions. In part, this decline stems from changes in the U.S. economy, with many highly unionized manufacturing jobs being replaced by less unionized service sector jobs. Given the drop in union membership, labor interest groups' influence has also waned, although the unions' reduced clout is also due to a lack of cohesion among labor union members.

Recently, **public employee unions**—comprising federal, state, and municipal workers, have wrestled with governors who have challenged the terms of the public employee contracts, including salaries, pensions, and benefits. Republican governor of Wisconsin Scott Walker succeeded in limiting public employees' collective bargaining rights, but some observers have argued that these strategies may have resulted in a backlash that is serving to energize union employees.[27] Public employees are among the most unionized workforces, with 35 percent of all governmental employees belonging to a labor union.[28]

public employee unions
labor organizations comprising federal, state, and municipal workers, including police officers and teachers

AGRICULTURAL INTERESTS Of all types of U.S. interest groups, agricultural interest groups probably have the most disproportionate amount of influence, given the small number of farmers and farm workers in the country relative to the general population. And because agricultural producers in the United States are also very diverse, ranging from small farmers to huge multinational agribusinesses, it is not surprising to see divergent opinions among people employed in the agricultural sector.

The largest agricultural interest group today is the American Farm Bureau Federation (AFBF), which grew out of the network of county farm bureaus formed in the 1920s. With more than 5 million farming members, the AFBF is one of the most influential interest groups in the United States, primarily because of its close relations with key agricultural policy makers. It takes stands on a wide variety of issues that have an impact on farmers, including subsidies, budget and tax policies, immigration policies that affect farm workers, energy policies, trade policies, and environmental policies. For example, when President Obama sought to end direct subsidies to farmers with sales of over $500,000 as part of his 2010 budget proposal, the opposition by agricultural interest groups, including the AFBF, killed the proposal in Congress.

In addition to large-scale, general agricultural interest groups such as the AFBF, there is an industry-specific interest group representing producers for nearly every crop or commodity produced in the agricultural sector. Table 7.1 shows that corn producers are among the most

TABLE 7.1

Top 10 Recipients of Federal Subsidies as Direct Payments to Farmers

	PROGRAM	SUBSIDY TOTAL 2012
1	Corn Subsidies	$2,702,462,268
2	Conservation Reserve Program	$1,749,656,753
3	Soybean Subsidies	$1,469,484,005
4	Wheat Subsidies	$1,109,821,903
5	Disaster Payments	$ 795,259,247
6	Cotton Subsidies	$ 560,924,418
7	Dairy Program Subsidies	$ 447,081,952
8	Tobacco Subsidies	$ 188,776,927
9	Sorghum Subsidies	$ 141,933,892
10	Livestock Subsidies	$ 58,653,613

SOURCE: Environmental Working Group, "The United States Summary Information," 2012, http://farm.ewg.org/region.php?fips=00000&progcode=total&yr=2012.

effective groups in securing subsidies for their growers. In 2012, corn farmers across the United States received nearly $3 billion in government subsidies. Table 7.1 reveals as well that the producers of several other crops—wheat, cotton, soybeans, and tobacco—have managed to secure billions of dollars in subsidies.

TRADE AND PROFESSIONAL INTERESTS Nearly every professional occupation—doctor, lawyer, engineer, chiropractor, dentist, accountant, and even video game developer—has a trade or professional group that focuses on its interests. These interest groups take stands on a variety of policy matters, many of which indirectly affect their membership.

Public and Ideological Interest Groups

Public interest groups typically are concerned with a broad range of issues that affect the populace at large. These include social issues such as the environmental causes of clean air and clean water, as well as economic issues such as Social Security reform and revision of the federal tax structure. Examples of public interest groups include National Taxpayers Union, Common Cause, and Sierra Club. Usually, the results of the efforts of a particular public interest group's advocacy cannot be limited to the group's members; rather, these results are **collective goods** (sometimes called *public goods*)—outcomes that are shared by the general public. For example, if Sierra Club succeeds in winning passage of an environmental bill that improves water and air quality, everyone shares in the benefits. Specifically, it is impossible to make pure drinking water and clean air a privilege restricted to Sierra Club members.

The nature of collective goods—the fact that they cannot be limited to those who worked to achieve them—creates a **free rider problem,** the situation whereby someone derives a benefit from the actions of others. You are probably familiar with the free rider problem. Suppose, for example, that you form a study group to prepare for an exam, and four of the five members of the group come to a study session having prepared responses to essay questions. The fifth member shows up but is unprepared. The unprepared group member then copies the others' responses, memorizes them, and does just as well on the exam. The same thing happens to interest groups that advocate for a collective good. The group may work hard to improve the quality of life, but the benefits of its work are enjoyed by many who do not contribute to the effort.

Economist Mancur Olson asserted in his **rational choice theory** that from an economic perspective it is not rational for people to participate in a collective action designed

collective goods
outcomes shared by the general public; also called *public goods*

free rider problem
the phenomenon of someone deriving benefit from others' actions

rational choice theory
the idea that from an economic perspective it is not rational for people to participate in collective action when they can secure the collective good without participating

to achieve a collective good when they can secure that good without participating. So, in the study group example, from Olson's perspective, it is not economically rational to spend your time preparing for an exam when you can get the benefits of preparation without the work. Of course, taking this idea to the extreme, one might conclude that if no one advocated for collective goods, they would not exist, and thus free riders could not derive their benefit.

CONSUMER INTERESTS   Well before attorney and activist Ralph Nader gained nationwide attention as a Green Party candidate for the presidency in 2000, he founded numerous organizations to promote the rights of consumers. In the 1970s and 1980s, these organizations lobbied primarily—and successfully—for changes in automotive design that would make cars safer. One result was the mandatory installation of harness safety belts in rear seats, which then typically had only lap belts. In 1971 Nader founded the interest group Public Citizen, which lobbies Congress, the executive branch, and the courts for openness in government and consumer issues, including auto safety, the safety of prescription drugs, and energy policy. Public Citizen paved the way for the formation of other consumer interest groups.

ENVIRONMENTAL INTERESTS   Many groups that advocate for the protection of the environment and wildlife and for the conservation of natural resources came about as a result of a broader environmental movement in the 1970s. Some environmental groups, such as Greenpeace and Save the Whales, use confrontational tactics, such as zip-lining into the Cincinnati headquarters of Procter and Gamble in 2014 to unfurl a banner protesting the company's practices in Indonesia. Greenpeace alleges that Procter and Gamble's products that use palm oil come from companies that destroy tropical forests including endangered orangutan habitats. In addition to stalling the undesired action, the confrontational protest tactic also has the advantage of attracting media attention, which serves to increase public awareness.[29] Other groups, such as Environmental Defense Fund, forge partnerships with corporations to research solutions to environmental problems and then persuade the government to provide market incentives for these solutions.

> Environmental interest groups include groups like Greenpeace, which often relies on confrontational tactics such as zip-lining into the Cincinnati headquarters of Procter and Gamble in 2014 to unfurl a banner protesting the company's practices in Indonesia. Greenpeace alleges that Procter and Gamble's products that use palm oil come from companies that destroy tropical forests, including endangered orangutan habitats. Such tactics result in media coverage, which generates public awareness that may pressure governments and corporations to change their practices.

RELIGIOUS INTERESTS   For a long time, organized religions in the United States were essentially uninvolved in politics, partly because they were afraid of losing their tax-exempt status by becoming political entities. But formal religions increasingly have sought to make their voices heard, usually by forming political organizations separate from the actual religious organizations. Today, religious interests are among the most influential interest groups in U.S. politics.

In the early stages of their activism, Christian organizations typically were most politically effective in the Republican presidential nomination process, when the mobilization of their members could alter the outcome in low-turnout primaries. During the 1970s, several conservative Christian organizations, most notably the Moral Majority, became a force in national politics. The Moral Majority helped to elect Ronald Reagan, a Republican, to the presidency in 1980 and was instrumental in shaping the national agenda of the Reagan years, particularly regarding domestic policy. In 1989, another conservative Christian organization, the Christian Coalition, took shape, emphasizing "pro-family" values[30] and becoming a pivotal player in presidential elections. During the 2000 election, the organization was an important supporter of George W. Bush's candidacy for the presidency, and with his election, the group's influence grew considerably. These groups also play a role in Republican primaries, as in 2012, when they threw their support behind former U.S. senator Rick Santorum (R-Pa.) at the expense of eventual nominee, former Massachusetts governor Mitt Romney. And in the 2014 midterm congressional elections, Christian organizations threw their weight behind candidates who opposed gay marriage and supported repealing the Affordable Health Act.

The Christian Coalition and other religious groups—including Pax Christi USA (the national Catholic peace movement), B'nai B'rith (an interest group dedicated to Jewish interests), and the Council on American-Islamic Relations (CAIR, a Muslim interest group)—also advocate for the faith-based priorities of their members. Many of these organizations have become increasingly active in state and local politics in recent years, by running slates of candidates for local school boards, for example, or by spearheading efforts in state legislatures to pass polarizing bills that allow business owners to refuse service to gays and members of other groups, if the business owners claim that doing so violates their religious beliefs, as has occurred in Arizona, Ohio, Mississippi, Idaho, Kansas, South Dakota, Tennessee, and Oklahoma. These bills, which supporters claim facilitate religious freedom and detractors argue facilitate discrimination, have been the subject of national furor since 2014.

Foreign Policy Interests

In the United States, interest groups advocate for specific foreign policies and foreign governments, as well as international corporations based abroad, vigorously pressing for U.S. policies beneficial to them. Often a foreign government benefits from the efforts of an interest group made up of U.S. citizens of the foreign nation's heritage. Indeed, one of the more influential interest groups lobbying for foreign concerns is the U.S.-based American Israel Public Affairs Committee (AIPAC), which has 100,000 members. AIPAC lobbies the U.S. government for pro-Israel foreign policies such as the grant of $3 billion in economic and military aid for Israel in 2014.[31] Sometimes interest groups of ex-patriots advocate for policies that they feel will improve the conditions in their country of origin. The Cuban American National Foundation, made up largely of Cuban Americans, works to influence Congress to adopt measures that it believes will promote democracy in Cuba.

Although foreign nationals cannot contribute money to political campaigns, foreign entities do lobby the U.S. government—especially for favorable trade policies. One foreign government with increasing political influence on Capitol Hill is China, which has spent millions of dollars trying to influence trade and other U.S. policies to its advantage.[32] It has enjoyed particular success with the 60-member congressional U.S.-China Working Group, which has strengthened diplomatic ties and was instrumental in killing a measure that would have penalized China with tariffs if it continued to manipulate its currency, making its exports cheaper and more competitive internationally. Many members of the working group represent congressional districts that are dependent on China for trade.[33]

Sometimes it is readily apparent when foreign interests are lobbying for their own causes—as, for example, when a trading partner wants better terms. But in other cases, particularly when international corporations are lobbying, it is difficult to discern where their "American" interest ends and their "foreign" interest begins. So when BP (British Petroleum) spends $8 million annually lobbying Congress, it may be benefiting its thousands of U.S.-based employees. However, Europe's second largest oil company may also be attempting to secure policies that serve the international corporation's interest, such as lessening harsh penalties in the aftermath of the oil spill in the Gulf of Mexico. Americans living along the coast suffered tremendous economic hardship when the oil spill decimated the fishing and tourism industries. Did BP adequately compensate these individuals? Or did it avoid doing so by expending monies on lobbying efforts? Although only U.S. citizens and legal immigrants can contribute to federal PACs, American employees of foreign companies do form and contribute to PACs. But because many subsidiaries of these corporations are important American businesses, their lobbying activities are not necessarily a foreign encroachment on U.S. politics. Yet the results of their lobbying efforts may not always be in the best interests of U.S. citizens affected by their policy.

Interest Group Strategies

Interest groups use two kinds of strategies to advance their causes. *Direct strategies* involve actual contact between representatives of the interest group and policy makers. *Indirect strategies* use intermediaries to advocate for a cause or generally to attempt to persuade the public, including policy makers, to embrace the group's position.

Direct Strategies to Advance Interests

Groups often opt for direct strategies when they seek to secure passage or defeat of a specific piece of legislation. These strategies include lobbying, entering into litigation to change a law, and providing information or expert testimony to decision makers.

LOBBYING, ISSUE NETWORKS, AND IRON TRIANGLES

Interest groups hire professionals to **lobby,** or to communicate directly with, policy makers on the interest groups' behalf. President Ulysses S. Grant (1869–1877) coined the term *lobbyist* when he walked through the lobby of the Willard Hotel in Washington, D.C., and commented on the presence of "lobbyists" waiting to speak to members of Congress.

Today, lobbying is among the most common strategies that interest groups use, and the practice may include scheduled face-to-face meetings, "buttonholing" members of Congress as they walk through the Capitol, telephone calls, and receptions and special events hosted by the interest groups. The professional lobbyists whom interest groups hire are almost always lawyers, and their job is to cultivate ongoing relationships with members of Congress (and their staff) who have influence in a specific policy area. In many situations, lobbyists help navigate access to these policy makers for industry and interest group members.

Interest groups have learned that one of the most effective ways of influencing government is to hire as lobbyists former government officials, including cabinet officials, members of Congress, and congressional staffers (see Table 7.2). Because these ex-officials often enjoy good relationships with their former colleagues and have an intimate knowledge of the policy-making process, they are particularly effective in influencing government. Frequently, this practice creates an **issue network,** the fluid web of connections among those concerned about a policy and those who create and administer the policy.

Similarly, an interest group's effectiveness often depends on its having close relationships with the policy makers involved in decisions related to the group's causes. During the rough-and-tumble policy-making process, the interaction of mutual interests among a "trio" comprising (1) members of Congress, (2) executive departments and agencies (such as the Department of Agriculture or the Federal Emergency Management Agency), and (3) organized interest groups is sometimes referred to as an **iron triangle,** with each of the three players being one side of the triangle (see Figure 7.2).

Although each side in an iron triangle is expected to fight on behalf of its own interests, constituents, or governmental department, the triangle often seeks a policy outcome that

TABLE 7.2

Top 10 Lobbying Interests, 2013

U.S. Chamber of Commerce	$74,470,000
National Association of Realtors	$38,584,580
Blue Cross/Blue Shield	$22,510,280
Northrop Grumman	$20,590,000
National Cable & Telecommunications Association	$19,870,000
American Hospital Association	$19,143,813
Comcast Corp.	$18,810,000
American Medical Association	$18,160,000
Pharmaceutical Research and Manufacturers of America	$17,882,500

SOURCE: Center for Responsive Politics, "Top Spenders," 2013, www.opensecrets.org/lobby/top.php?indexType=s&showYear=2013.

lobby
to communicate directly with policy makers on an interest group's behalf

issue network
the fluid web of connections among those concerned about a policy and those who create and administer the policy

POLITICAL Inquiry

FIGURE 7.2 ■ IRON TRIANGLE Who are the players in an iron triangle? How do interest groups benefit from their iron triangle relationships? Why do you think the triangular relationship has been described as "iron"?

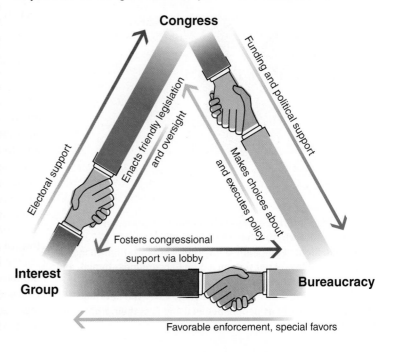

Congress

Funding and political support

Enacts friendly legislation and oversight

Electoral support

Makes choices about and executes policy

Fosters congressional support via lobby

Interest Group

Bureaucracy

Favorable enforcement, special favors

benefits all parts of the triangle. Often this outcome occurs because of close personal and professional relationships that develop as a result of the interactions among the sides in an issue-based triangle. (See Chapter 14 for further discussion of the role of iron triangles in policy making.)

LITIGATION BY INTEREST GROUPS Sometimes interest groups challenge a policy in the courts. For example, the 2010 U.S. Supreme Court case that resulted in a drastically altered political landscape for campaign funding came as the result of a lawsuit filed by an interest group. In *Citizens United v. Federal Election Commission,* the interest group Citizens United argued that federal bans on corporate and union expenditures to promote or target candidates for federal office violated the organizations' right to free speech. A 5–4 majority of Supreme Court justices agreed with the interest group and lifted the ban.[34]

By litigating, interest groups can ensure that laws passed by legislatures and signed by executives are in keeping with current constitutional interpretation. By bringing their causes before the courts, they also can shape policy and encourage enforcement by executive agencies.

PROVIDING INFORMATION AND EXPERT TESTIMONY Interest groups are one of the chief sources of information for policy makers. Interest groups have the resources to investigate the impact of policies. They have access to data, technological know-how, and a bevy of experts with extensive knowledge of the issues. Most interest groups provide information to policy makers, and policy makers understand that the information received is slanted toward the group's interest. But if competing interest groups supply information to policy makers, then policy makers can weigh the merits of the various sets of information.

Sometimes interest groups use celebrities as "experts" to testify, knowing that they will attract greater attention than most policy experts—for example, actor George Clooney testified before the U.S. Senate Committee on Foreign Relations concerning findings from his Satellite Sentinel Project, an organization he founded that uses satellites to monitor conflict and human rights abuses in the Sudan.

Indirect Strategies to Advance Interests

Reaching out to persuade the public that their position is right, interest groups deploy citizens as grassroots lobbyists, and they engage in electioneering. These two activities are examples of indirect strategies that interest groups use to pursue their public policy agendas. Indirect tactics are likely to be ongoing rather than targeted at a specific piece of legislation, although that is not always the case.

PUBLIC OUTREACH Interest groups work hard—and use a variety of strategies—to make the public, government officials, their own members, and potential members aware of issues of concern and to educate people about their positions on the issues. Some interest groups focus solely on educating the public and hope that through their efforts people will be concerned enough to take steps to have a particular policy established or changed. Thus the groups promote civic engagement by informing individuals about important policy concerns, even if the information they provide is skewed toward the group's views. The groups also encourage civic discourse by bringing issues into the public arena. Often they do so by mounting advertising campaigns to alert the public about an issue. Consider, for example, the use of the Human Rights Campaign logo (an equal sign) in red and pink, which went viral and became used widely as a Facebook and Twitter profile picture during the

> Sometimes interest groups rely on indirect strategies, including public outreach, to advance their group's interest. In 2013, the Human Rights Campaign, a gay rights organization, changed its logo—a yellow equal sign on a blue background—to pink and red to build awareness and show support of gay marriage as the U.S. Supreme Court heard a gay marriage case. The new logo went viral overnight as people began using it as their profile picture on Facebook.

U.S. Supreme Court hearings on the issue of gay marriage. Human Rights Campaign's new logo reached more than 9 million people and was shared directly from HRC's Facebook page 77,000 times, including by actor George Takei, Maryland governor Martin O'Malley, and at least 13 members of Congress.

Sometimes interest groups and corporations engage in **climate control,** the practice of using public outreach to build favorable public opinion of the organization or company. The logic behind climate control is simple: If a corporation or an organization has the goodwill of the public on its side, enacting its legislative agenda or getting its policy priorities passed will be easier, because government will know of, and may even share, the public's positive opinion of the organization. For example, when Walmart encountered opposition to the construction of its superstores in communities across the country, it relied on public relations techniques, particularly advertising, to convince people that Walmart is a good corporate citizen. As critics complained about Walmart's harmful effects on smaller, local merchants, the firm's ads touted Walmart's positive contributions to its host communities. When opponents publicized the company's low-wage jobs, Walmart countered with ads featuring employees who had started in entry-level positions and risen through the ranks to managerial posts. These ads were viewed both by policy makers (municipal planning board members, for example) and by citizens, whose opinions matter to those policy makers.

Other groups, especially those without a great deal of access to policy makers, may engage in protests and civil disobedience to be heard. Sometimes leaders calculate that media attention to their actions will increase public awareness and spark widespread support for their cause.

climate control
the practice of using public outreach to build favorable public opinion of an organization

electioneering
working to influence the elections of candidates who support the organization's issues

ELECTIONEERING Interest groups often engage in the indirect strategy of **electioneering**—working to influence the election of candidates who support their issues. All the tactics of electioneering are active methods of civic participation. These techniques include endorsing particular candidates or positions and conducting voter-registration and get-out-the-vote drives. Grassroots campaign efforts often put interest groups with large memberships, including labor unions, at an advantage.

Campaign contributions are considered a key element of electioneering. The importance of contributions puts wealthier interest groups, including corporate and business groups, at an advantage. Figure 7.3 shows the breakdown of contributions by incumbency status. From this figure, we see that incumbent candidates have a significant edge in raising money from political action committees. The data indicate that most PACs recognize that incumbents—who are most likely to win reelection—are best situated to look after their interests following the election.

The issue of party affiliation also matters to PACs. Business PACs and individuals with business interests make up the largest sources of revenue for political candidates and tend to favor Republicans over Democrats. Labor groups and individuals associated with them give overwhelmingly to Democratic candidates, but they contribute a great deal less money than do business PACs. Ideologically driven PACs and individuals are nearly evenly divided between Democrats and Republicans.

Interest groups also commonly use the tactics of endorsements and ratings to attract support for the candidates whom they favor and to reduce the electoral chances of those whom they do not (see "Analyzing the Sources"). Through endorsements, an interest group formally supports specific candidates and typically notifies its members and the media of that support. An endorsement may also involve financial support from the interest group's PAC. With the technique of rating candidates, the interest group examines candidates' responses to a questionnaire issued by the group. Sometimes a group rates members of Congress on the basis of how they voted on measures important to the group. The ratings of a liberal interest group such as Americans for Democratic Action (ADA) or a conservative interest group such as American Conservative Union (ACU) can serve as an ideological benchmark.

POLITICAL **Inquiry**

FIGURE 7.3 ▨ INCUMBENTS AND CHALLENGERS In 2014, 454 incumbents, 793 challengers, and 414 candidates for open seats ran for the House or Senate, but incumbents received more than 60 percent of all contributions. What are some of the reasons PACs are more likely to contribute to incumbents? What might be the effect of contributing to challengers?

SOURCE: Center for Responsive Politics, "2014 Election Overview," 2014, www.opensecrets.org/overview/.

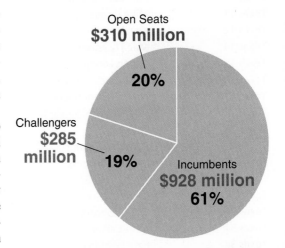

Open Seats
$310 million
20%

Challengers
$285 million
19%

Incumbents
$928 million
61%

Contributions to 2014 Congressional Candidates by Political Action Committees

RATING TEXAS'S CONGRESS MEMBERS ON IMMIGRATION

Project Vote Smart is a nonpartisan organization that collects the ratings of many interest groups so that they are available in a single website (projectvotesmart.org). Below are the ratings for members of the House of Representatives from Texas from two interest groups, both concerned with the issue of immigration.

Americans for Better Immigration is a nonpartisan organization that lobbies Congress for reductions in immigration numbers. It "believes the problem with immigration today is not the individual immigrant but the numbers." The William C. Velásquez Institute is a nonpartisan public policy analysis organization. Its purpose is to "conduct research aimed at improving the level of political and economic participation in Latino and other underrepresented communities; To provide information to Latino leaders relevant to the needs of their constituents; To inform the Latino leadership and public about the impact of public policies on Latinos; To inform the Latino leadership and public about political opinions and behavior of Latinos."

Evaluating the Evidence

1. Compare how each group rates the same individual. In general, what pattern can you observe?

2. Given these patterns, what can you conclude about the policy goals of these two organizations?

3. Though both organizations are nonpartisan, is there a pattern in terms of party affiliation and a representative's rating?

DISTRICT	MEMBER U.S HOUSE OF REPRESENTATIVES	PARTY	RATING William C. Velásquez Institute	RATING Americans for Better Immigration
Texas 1	Louie Gohmert	Republican	0%	86%
Texas 2	Ted Poe	Republican	0%	93%
Texas 3	Sam Johnson	Republican	0%	93%
Texas 4	Ralph Hall	Republican	0%	79%
Texas 5	Jeb Hensarling	Republican	0%	71%
Texas 6	Joe Barton	Republican	17%	57%
Texas 7	John Culberson	Republican	0%	71%
Texas 8	Kevin Brady	Republican	0%	71%
Texas 9	Al Green	Democratic	86%	21%
Texas 10	Michael McCaul	Republican	14%	71%
Texas 11	Mike Conaway	Republican	13%	79%
Texas 12	Kay Granger	Republican	14%	64%
Texas 13	Mac Thornberry	Republican	20%	57%
Texas 15	Rubén Hinojosa, Sr.	Democratic	88%	7%
Texas 18	Sheila Jackson Lee	Democratic	100%	7%
Texas 19	Randy Neugebauer	Republican	11%	71%
Texas 21	Lamar Smith	Republican	0%	93%
Texas 22	Pete Olson	Republican	0%	64%
Texas 24	Kenny Marchant	Republican	0%	100%
Texas 26	Michael Burgess	Republican	0%	71%
Texas 28	Henry Cuellar	Democratic	57%	35%
Texas 29	Gene Green	Democratic	86%	7%
Texas 30	Eddie Johnson	Democratic	88%	21%
Texas 31	John Carter	Republican	13%	100%
Texas 32	Pete Sessions	Republican	0%	86%

SOURCES: Project Vote Smart, "National Latino Congreso/William C. Velásquez Institute," 2014, http://votesmart.org/interest-group/1934/national-latino-congresowilliam-c-velasquez-institute#.Ux5P_nrD-Uk; and "Americans for Better Immigration," http://votesmart.org/interest-group/118/rating/6864#.Uz3UfVfLLOd.

Interest Groups, Politics, and Money: The Influence of Political Action Committees

The influence of money on politics is not a recent phenomenon. Louise Overacker, one of the first political scientists to do research on campaign finance, wrote in 1932: "Any effective program of control must make it possible to bring into the light the sources and amounts of all funds used in political campaigns, and the way in which those funds are expended."[35] Years later, Congress saw the wisdom of Overacker's analysis and enacted regulations stipulating that a group that contributes to any candidate's campaign must register as a political action committee (PAC). For that reason, most interest groups form PACs as one arm of their organization, although federal law now permits corporations and labor unions to use their financial resources to purchase advertisements for federal campaigns directly.

Whereas an interest group pursues a group's broad goals by engaging in a variety of activities, its PAC raises and spends money to influence the outcome of an election. Typically it will do so by contributing to candidates' campaigns. Funding campaigns helps an interest group in various ways. For one thing, it establishes the interest group as a formal supporter of one or more candidates. And, importantly, campaign contributions are a door opener for an interest group's lobbyists. For a lobbyist, access to policy makers is crucial, and campaign contributions provide a means of contact and help to ensure that a phone call will be returned or an invitation responded to, even if the policy maker does not support the group's position on every issue.

Table 7.3 lists the PACs that contribute the most money to U.S. campaigns and highlights the party their contributions favor. As the table illustrates, labor groups tend to support Democrats,

TABLE 7.3

Top 20 PAC Contributors to Candidates, 2013–2014

PAC NAME	TOTAL AMOUNT	PERCENTAGE OF FUNDS TO DEMOCRATS	PERCENTAGE OF FUNDS TO REPUBLICANS
Every Republican Is Crucial PAC	$1,390,000	0%	100%
Lockheed Martin	$1,388,500	39%	61%
Operating Engineers Union	$1,387,458	79%	21%
Honeywell International	$1,382,687	42%	58%
AT&T Inc.	$1,351,500	41%	59%
Northrop Grumman	$1,351,250	39%	61%
International Brotherhood of Electrical Workers	$1,336,174	97%	3%
National Beer Wholesalers Association	$1,306,000	42%	58%
Credit Union National Association	$1,187,500	50%	50%
American Crystal Sugar	$1,148,499	62%	38%
Carpenters & Joiners Union	$1,083,000	78%	22%
Boeing Co.	$1,062,500	37%	63%
National Association of Realtors	$1,036,876	47%	52%
American Bankers Association	$1,028,500	24%	76%
American Association for Justice	$1,019,500	95%	5%
National Auto Dealers Association	$1,011,200	29%	71%
General Electric	$978,000	40%	60%
Deloitte LLP	$977,500	37%	63%
National Rural Electric Cooperative Association	$916,455	28%	72%
Comcast Corp.	$916,000	53%	47%

NOTE: Totals include subsidiaries and affiliated PACs, if any.
SOURCE: Center for Responsive Politics, "Heavy Hitters: Top All-Time Donors, 1989–2014," 2014, www.opensecrets.org/orgs/list.php.

Democracy

Should Super PACs Enjoy Unlimited Free Speech?

The Issue: Super PACs emerged as an important factor in the 2012 elections, and remained so in the 2014 midterm congressional races. Super PACs are a special, relatively new form of PAC that raise unlimited amounts of money from individuals and then spend unlimited amounts in political races. Unlike traditional PACs, they may not contribute directly to the candidates they are supporting, and they must report their independent expenditures to the Federal Election Commission (FEC). The legal path for the creation of Super PACs was paved in the 2010 D.C. District Court of Appeals decision *SpeechNow.org v. Federal Election Commission*. The question has thus become whether Super PACs represent an important tool of free speech or whether they constitute merely another avenue for the wealthy to dominate the electoral process.

Yes: Some free speech proponents argue that the ruling has increased the amount of information available to voters. Under previous regulations, free speech advocates argue, the contribution limitations to PACs restricted "the individuals' freedom of speech by limiting the amount that an individual can contribute to Speech-Now and thus the amount the organization may spend."[*] Brad Smith, former chairman of the FEC and founder and chair of the Center for Competitive Politics, argued in favor of the decision: "The rise of independent expenditure groups made possible by the *SpeechNow* ruling has increased the information available to voters and increased the number of competitive races."[**] Many conservatives also argue that organizations consist of individuals who form associations and that the Constitution protects not only free speech but also freedom of association.

No: Critics of the decision argue that it facilitates unmitigated corporate influence in political campaigns. Giving organizations protected rights that individuals enjoy, like free speech, detracts from the protection of individual human rights. Some critics argue that enabling these organizations to spend freely to influence campaigns has a detrimental effect on campaigns, because the wealthy have a disproportionate say in campaigns through their ability to spend unlimited sums.

Other Approaches: In light of the *SpeechNow* ruling, voters need to be increasingly skeptical of claims made by organizations about political candidates. In effect, these Super PACs are only as powerful as average Americans enable them to be, and their influence can be countered through the formation of opposing groups comprising individuals who share a viewpoint. The availability of technology provides a medium for average citizens both to get information and to form groups with like-minded people, thus potentially mitigating the effect of the influence of Super PACs.

[*]Federal Election Commission, "*Speechnow.org v. FEC* Case Summary," 2010, www.fec.gov/law/litigation/speechnow.shtml#summary.

[**]Center for Competitive Politics, "*SpeechNow.org v. FEC*—Protecting Free Speech for the Last 2 Years," 2012, www.campaignfreedom.org/2012/03/23/speechnow-org-v-fec-protecting-free-speech-for-the-last-2-years/.

What do you think?

1. Do you believe that enabling Super PACs to purchase unlimited independent expenditure ads is a protected right?

2. What will be the effect of this decision, in your view?

3. How can average Americans get their opinions about candidates heard? How can they find out whether allegations made by Super PACs are accurate?

whereas many business and corporate PACs favor Republicans. At the top, traditional PACs tend to contribute more heavily to Democrats than to Republicans. (See "Thinking Critically About Democracy" for more information on Super PACs.) In addition, PACs, particularly those formed by economic interest groups, overwhelmingly favor incumbents. PACs' powers-that-be know that incumbent candidates are likely to be reelected, and thus the PACs support their reelection bids. As we examine further in Chapter 9, interest groups rely on PACs to channel their support to candidates that espouse their views.

Conclusion

Thinking Critically About What's Next for Interest Groups

Interest groups are a powerful vehicle by which individuals can join forces and collectively persuade policy makers to take legislative action on their goals. As such, interest groups play a strong role in the policy-making process. Throughout U.S. history and continuing today, the prevalence of interest groups is testimony to people's desire to influence the pathways of their society and government.

Interest groups are one of the great leveling devices in U.S. politics. They are organizations that enable ordinary people to influence policy through collective action and organization. Although not all Americans are equally likely to join and form interest groups, these groups represent an avenue of participation open to all, and with enough variety in tactics and strategies to offer appealing means of civic participation to a broad spectrum of the population. Particularly today, with the Internet providing a highly accessible medium for participation, interest groups give individuals the opportunity to increase their own social capital—to improve their lives and the life of their community by making government more responsive to their needs and concerns and by increasing the effectiveness of the public policy-making process.

Although opinions differ about the role and the value of interest groups in U.S. politics, their influence in policy making is unquestioned. Thus interest groups offer enormous potential for people who wish to become civically engaged. The abundance of groups for virtually every cause (and the ability of anyone to form his or her own group) means that like-minded individuals can work together to ensure that government policy represents their views. How does the number of groups available today differ from decades past? What is the result of that difference in terms of potential members?

Today, through the Internet and other digital technology, interest groups can provide individuals with instantly accessed information and organizational tools. Advances in computing, telephone communications, and television have opened the doors to participation in politics and government in ways that were undreamed of a few decades ago. Thanks to technology, the potential exists for interest groups to reach new and ever-widening audiences. As we have seen, however, the potential audience, at least in the present day, excludes many members of the working class, who may not have been socialized to take part in groups and who may lack the time and means to access computer technology. This lack of access poses a challenge to interest groups, because they rely ever more heavily on digital recruiting, communicating, organizing, and fund-raising. How will new technologies continue to alter the landscape for interest groups?

In becoming increasingly dependent on relatively low-cost technological tools, interest groups also have to deal with the challenges of paying for the expertise needed to design, build, and maintain their websites and blogs. Once such issues are resolved, and once access is opened to people not currently wired, digital strategies will further strengthen the clout and efficacy of interest groups, and these groups will speak for larger and more diverse numbers of Americans.

Summary

1. The Value of Interest Groups

Interest groups offer individuals a vehicle for engaging in civic actions and improving their communities and the nation as a whole. The positive effects of improved social capital are reciprocal: As participation benefits individuals, it also benefits communities and larger governments, which in turn provide benefits to individuals, and so on. Interest groups also have some downsides: They can allow well-organized minority views to dominate less well-organized majority viewpoints; they emphasize the role of money in politics; they strengthen the incumbency advantage of elected officeholders; and they tend to draw participants disproportionately from among society's elites.

2. Who Joins Interest Groups, and Why?

Although interest groups serve as an accessible channel for citizen participation, not everyone is equally likely to join or form an interest group. In general, people with high incomes, individuals who are upper-middle and middle class, and those with high levels of education are more likely to join interest groups than are people with low incomes, those who are lower-middle and working class, and those who have less education. In addition, some people join interest groups related to their occupations. People typically join interest groups for a variety of reasons that can be categorized as solidary incentives, purposive incentives, and economic incentives.

3. How Interest Groups Succeed

Interest groups succeed by using their organizational resources and maximizing the effectiveness of their organizational environment. Organizational resources consist of groups' membership and financial resources. The organizational environment comprises the group's leadership and the presence of opposing or competitive interest groups in the policy-making environment.

4. Types of Interest Groups

Interest groups typically fall into one of three categories. (1) Economic interest groups, such as business, agricultural, and labor union groups, advocate for financial benefits for their members—for example, in the form of subsidies or wage policies. (2) Public and ideological interest groups lobby for policies that affect public, or collective, goods and include, for instance, abortion-rights groups and environmental groups. (3) Foreign governments and corporations also use interest groups to influence a wide variety of policies, especially trade and military policy.

5. Interest Group Strategies

Interest groups usually combine direct and indirect strategies in their attempts to influence the policy process. Direct strategies typically involve lobbying a policy maker, and indirect strategies may include public outreach, using campaign contributions to build favorable public opinion of an organization, electioneering to influence who will be making policy, and educating the public so that they share a group's position and can convey that view to policy makers.

6. Interest Groups, Politics, and Money: The Influence of Political Action Committees

PACs are the tool by which interest groups contribute to electoral campaigns. Some PACs are partisan, but in general PACs tend to support incumbent candidates, making it difficult for nonincumbents effectively to challenge those already in office.

Key Terms

climate control 235
collective goods 230
economic incentive 225
electioneering 235
elite theory 220
free rider problem 230
interest group 218

iron triangle 233
issue network 233
lobby 233
pluralist theory 220
political action committee (PAC) 222
public employee unions 229

purposive incentive 224
rational choice theory 230
social capital 218
solidary incentive 224
umbrella organizations 228

For Review

1. Explain in detail how the pluralist and elite theories differ in their views of interest groups in U.S. democracy.

2. Why do people join interest groups? Who is most likely to join an interest group? Why?

3. What kinds of interest groups exist in the United States? Which types are the most influential? Why are they most influential?

4. What resources help determine how powerful an interest group is?

5. How do political action committees attempt to influence government action?

For Critical Thinking and Discussion

1. Were you brought up in a family in which joining groups was important? Do your parents belong to any interest groups? Do you? If not, why do you think that is the case?

2. What kinds of interest groups are you and your friends most likely to be involved in (even if you are not)? Why are the issues these groups advocate important to you? How are you most likely to act on the issues that you care about?

3. How has the Internet changed how interest groups operate? What kinds of groups has it made more effective? Has it made any groups less effective?

4. Select a controversial issue such as abortion or gun control, and use the Internet to search for and learn about the interest groups that represent opposing views. What tactics does each group use? Is one strategy more effective than the other?

5. The Supreme Court has ruled that political expenditures constitute a form of free speech. Do you agree? Can you think of any other ways in which "money talks"?

MULTIPLE CHOICE: Choose the lettered item that answers the question correctly.

1. The idea that a group of wealthy, educated individuals wields most political power is called
   a. pluralist theory.
   b. elite theory.
   c. rational choice theory.
   d. democratic theory.

2. The motivation to join an interest group based on a belief in the group's cause from an ideological standpoint is called a(n)
   a. solidary incentive.
   b. purposive incentive.
   c. economic incentive.
   d. organizational incentive.

3. A restaurant owner who joins a trade association interest group because it advocates for wage policies that would benefit the business is an example of someone motivated by
   a. solidary incentives.
   b. purposive incentives.
   c. economic incentives.
   d. organizational incentives.

4. A group that raises and spends money to influence the outcome of an election is called
   a. an interest group.
   b. a bundling organization.
   c. a political action committee.
   d. a social compact.

5. The phenomenon of someone deriving benefit from others' actions is called
   a. the problem of collective action.
   b. the bundling problem.
   c. the free rider problem.
   d. the slacker problem.

6. A direct strategy to advance the interest of an interest group is
   a. lobbying.
   b. public outreach.
   c. electioneering.
   d. contributing to political parties.

7. The fluid web of connections among those concerned about a policy and those who create and administer the policy is called
   a. a political action committee.
   b. a congressional quorum.
   c. an issue network.
   d. a social network.

8. The interaction of mutual interests among members of Congress, executive agencies, and organized interests during policy making is called
   a. a social network.
   b. an iron triangle.
   c. a square cube.
   d. an issue network.

9. The practice of using public outreach to build a favorable public opinion of the organization is called
   a. climate control.
   c. agenda setting.
   b. interest outreach.
   d. maximizing spin.

10. Working to influence the election of candidates who support the organization's issues is called
    a. interest group bias.
    b. incumbency advantage.
    c. agenda setting.
    d. electioneering.

FILL IN THE BLANKS

11. To social scientists, the ways in which our lives are improved by social connections is called _____.

12. The motivation to join an interest group based on the companionship and the satisfaction derived from socializing with others is called _____.

13. A group that represents collective groups of industries or corporations is called a(n) _____.

14. Outcomes shared by the general public are called _____.

15. The idea that it is not economically rational for people to participate in collective action when the resultant collective good could be realized without participating is the essence of _____.

Answers: 1. b; 2. b; 3. c; 4. c; 5. c; 6. a; 7. c; 8. b; 9. a; 10. d; 11. social capital; 12. solidary incentives; 13. umbrella organization; 14. collective goods; 15. rational choice theory.

242   CHAPTER 7 | Interest Groups

Internet Resources

Center for Responsive Politics
www.opensecrets.org This nonpartisan website provides information on the campaign financing of candidates for federal office.

Common Cause
www.commoncause.org This website features a special section on money and politics and provides links to sites related to its endorsed reform measures.

Federal Election Commission
www.fec.org Here you'll find a multitude of information about campaign financing, including regulations, contributions and expenditures, specific candidates, individual donors, political action committees, and political parties.

Recommended Readings

Alexander, Robert M. *Rolling the Dice with State Initiatives: Interest Group Involvement in Ballot Campaigns.* Westport, CT: Praeger, 2001. A probing analysis of the impact of interest groups on gambling initiatives in California and Missouri that, unlike most treatments of interest group activity, focuses on interest group initiatives within states and on lobbying in a nonlegislative arena.

Berry, Jeffrey M. *The Interest Group Society,* 5th ed. New York: Longman, 2009. Analyzes the proliferation of various types of interest groups in the United States, as well as the strategies interest groups use to sway policy makers.

Cigler, Alan J., and Burnett A. Loomis. *Interest Group Politics,* 8th ed. Washington, D.C.: CQ Press, 2011. A classic analysis, first published in 1983, detailing the effects of interest groups in modern American politics.

Franz, Michael M. *Choices and Changes: Interest Groups in the Electoral Process.* Philadelphia: Temple University Press, 2008. A comprehensive examination of interest groups' use of electioneering tactics, especially campaign contributions, and how electioneering strategies are shaped by the campaign regulatory environment.

Hays, Richard A. *Who Speaks for the Poor: National Interest Groups and Social Policy.* New York: Routledge, 2001. An examination of how the poor gain political representation in the policy process through the efforts of interest groups.

Herrnson, Paul S., Ronald G. Shaiko, and Clyde J. Wilcox. *The Interest Group Connection: Electioneering, Lobbying, and Policymaking in Washington,* 2nd ed. Washington, D.C.: CQ Press, 2004. A collection of essays describing the role of interest groups on the federal level. The essays focus on elections, Congress, the president, and the judiciary.

Holyoke, Thomas T. *Interest Groups and Lobbying.* Boulder, CO: Westview Press, 2014. Examines why interest groups form and how they are able to gain influence, as well as why their adversarial nature often makes voters uncomfortable with their role in the political process.

Loomis, Burdett A. (ed.) *Guide to Interest Groups and Lobbying in the United States.* Washington, D.C.: CQ Press, 2011. Examines how interest groups have grown in scope and size and which tactics they have relied on that have made them an essential part of the U.S. political system.

Wright, John. *Interest Groups and Congress (Longman Classics Edition).* New York: Longman, 2002. A study of the influence of both historical and modern interest groups; it asserts that interest groups' practice of providing specialized information to members of Congress increases their influence there, has an impact on the resultant policy, and shapes opinion.

Movies of Interest

Casino Jack (2010)
Kevin Spacey stars as a K-Street lobbyist (the character was based loosely on Jack Abramoff, a lobbyist who was convicted on multiple federal charges) whose unethical tactics lead to murder.

Thank You for Smoking (2005)
Aaron Eckhart stars as a lobbyist in this satirical comedy about the big tobacco lobby.

Erin Brockovich (2000)
Starring Julia Roberts, this film is based on the true story of Erin Brockovich, an activist fighting for the rights of a community whose water supply has been contaminated.

The Pelican Brief (1993)
Based on the John Grisham novel of the same name, this film, starring Julia Roberts and Denzel Washington, spotlights competition between big business and the environmental movement and illuminates how interested parties can use the courts to make policy.

Paths of Glory (1957)
This Stanley Kubrick film delves into the realities of trench warfare during World War I, but through it we see how organizations may succeed or fail at motivating individuals.

CHAPTER 8

Political Parties

THEN

Political parties relied on patronage and voter loyalty to become powerful entities in American politics.

NOW

Voter loyalty has declined, and many voters are dissatisfied with the two dominant political parties.

NEXT

Will the dominance of the Democratic and Republican Parties continue?

Can a viable third party emerge that will satisfy a sizeable bloc of voters?

How will digital technologies further shape parties' strategies and expand their reach—and change the membership of parties?

political party
an organization that recruits, nominates, and elects party members to office in order to control the government

Tea Party movement
a grassroots, conservative protest movement that opposed recent government actions, including economic stimulus spending and health care reform

Political parties have been

essential channels for the realization of American democracy. Political parties serve the American system in many crucial capacities, from recruiting candidates, to conducting elections, to distributing information to voters, to participating in governance. One of their essential functions is to provide an open arena for participation by civic-minded individuals while reaching out to involve those who do not participate.

Because Americans place high value on independent thought and action, some citizens view political parties with suspicion. For such observers, the collective activity of parties brings worries about corruption and control by elite decision makers. And in contemporary times, many Americans across the ideological spectrum are disgruntled with the two dominant political parties. Despite these criticisms and dissatisfaction, parties remain one of the most accessible forums for citizens' participation in democracy. Indeed, political scientist E. E. Schattschneider, who believed that parties represented the foremost means for citizens to communicate with political decision makers—and in this way to retain control over their government—wrote that "modern democracy is unthinkable save in terms of political parties."[1]

Are Political Parties Today in Crisis?

In the United States today, two major political parties—the Democratic and the Republican Parties—dominate the political landscape. Generally speaking, a **political party** is an organization of ideologically similar people that nominates and elects its members to office in order to run the government and shape public policy. Parties identify potential candidates, nominate them to run for office, campaign for them, organize elections, and govern.

Historically, political parties have performed important functions, discussed later in this chapter. Since the founding of the United States, it has not been uncommon for one political party to dominate the political landscape temporarily, such as when Democrats controlled national politics during the tenure of Franklin D. Roosevelt, or when Republicans did the same during the Reagan years. The popularity of one or the other major political parties ebbs and flows over the decades. However, in recent years, both political parties have struggled to win the approval of the American people. In fact, a majority of Americans today believe that the Democrats and the Republicans are not doing an adequate job representing the American people, as shown in Figure 8.1.

Part of the reason for this decline in popularity stems from the increasing polarization of political parties nationally. This growing schism is particularly evident among members of Congress, who in general tend to be more ideologically extreme than in decades past. This is a consequence of the process of congressional elections (discussed in greater detail in Chapter 12), which relies on increasingly sophisticated technology to create congressional districts dominated by one political party. This one-party dominance in districts facilitates the election of more extreme ideological members of Congress, who do not have to appeal to moderate constituents, or those of the opposing party. Thus in Congress, there is little incentive to moderate one's views, work with the other party, or compromise.

The Republican Party in particular has struggled with the increasing levels of conservatism espoused by some members of their congressional delegation. Members of the **Tea Party movement**—a grassroots, conservative protest movement that opposed recent government actions, including economic stimulus spending and health care reform—argue that smaller government should be the main goal of the modern Republican Party. They have flexed considerable muscle to prevent the more moderate members of their political party from compromising.

FIGURE 8.1 ■ THE PEOPLE'S OPINION OF DEMOCRATS AND REPUBLICANS The figure shows the percentage of survey respondents who have a favorable view of the Republican and Democratic parties at selected dates between September 1993 and October 2013. What is the general trend with regard to party favorability ratings? Look at particular high and low points for each political party. What events may have caused people's favorable opinions of the parties to increase or decline?

SOURCE: Gallup, "Party Images," 2013, www.gallup.com/poll/24655/Party-Images.aspx#1.

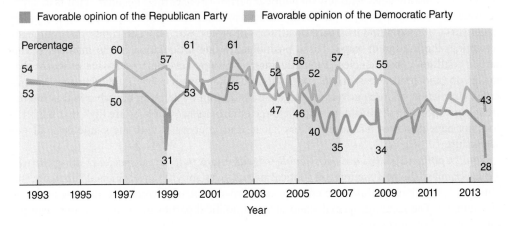

These efforts reached a climax in October 2013 when the Tea Party Caucus forced a 16-day government shutdown. The shutdown was the result of a failure of the U.S. Congress to pass a budget, which it is required to do by October 1 of each year in order to fund government agencies. In the House of Representatives, members of the Tea Party Caucus refused to vote for a budget or a temporary budget, known as a continuing resolution, unless Congress passed a series of measures and defunded President Barack Obama's health care reform law, the Patient Protection and Affordable Care Act of 2010, also called Obamacare. Many conservatives, especially among the Tea Party, oppose the act, arguing that the federal government is overstepping its function in mandating and providing mechanisms for health care coverage, while many liberals assert that it is the responsibility of the federal government to ensure what they claim is a basic right. To appease the Tea Party Caucus, Speaker of the House John Boehner, a moderate Republican himself, introduced a series of continuing resolutions peppered with Tea Party demands. These resolutions passed in the Republican-controlled House, but were not even brought up for votes in the Democrat-controlled Senate. Without a budget or a continuing resolution, the government shut down. Meanwhile, the pressing issue of the debt ceiling arose—with Tea Party members threatening to let the U.S. government default on its debt obligation, a move that could send the world into a recession. Moderate Republicans, worried more about the impact on the economy than about appeasing Tea Party activists, crossed over and joined the Democrats in supporting a compromise measure. After a 16-day standoff, the Tea Party Caucus won a single concession: the delay of a medical device tax. Most Americans blamed the Republican Party (rather than the Democratic president) for the fiasco. Figure 8.1 shows, in particular, the blow that the Republican Party's reputation took in the aftermath of the shutdown. The crisis raised questions about whether the two major American parties would be able to compromise sufficiently in the future to pass legislation to address the needs of the American people.

Parties Today and Their Functions

Political scientists agree that parties can be distinguished from other political organizations, such as interest groups and political action committees, through four defining characteristics.

First, political parties run candidates under their own label, or affiliation. Most candidates who run for office are identified by their party affiliation. Running a candidate under the party label requires party functions such as recruiting candidates, organizing elections, and campaigning.[2] And political parties typically are the only organizations that regularly run candidates for political office under the party label on a ballot.

Second, unlike interest groups, which hope to have individuals sympathetic to their cause elected but which typically do not want to govern, *political parties seek to govern.* Political parties run candidates hoping that they will win a majority of the seats in a legislature or control the executive branch. Such victories enable the party to enact a broad partisan agenda.

A *third* defining characteristic is that *political parties have broad concerns, focused on many issues.* The major parties in the United States are made up of coalitions of different groups and constituencies who rely on political parties to enact their agendas. That is to say, if we were to look at a party's **platform**—the formal statement of its principles and policy objectives—we would find its stance on all sorts of issues: war, abortion rights, environmental protection, the minimum wage. These positions are one articulation of the interests of that party's coalition constituencies. Typically, interest groups have narrower issue concerns than parties do, and some focus on only a single issue. For example, we know that the National Rifle Association opposes governmental controls on gun ownership, but what is this interest group's position on the minimum wage? On the environment? Chances are high that the NRA does not have positions on those matters because its concern is with the single issue of gun ownership.

Finally, political parties are quasi-public organizations that have a special relationship with the government. Some functions of political parties overlap with governmental functions, and some party functions facilitate the creation and perpetuation of government (running elections, for example). The resulting special status subjects political parties to greater scrutiny than private clubs and organizations.

platform
the formal statement of a party's principles and policy objectives

>In recent years, political parties have increasingly embraced and championed diversity. In 2012, the Democratic Party included a plank supporting gay marriage in its platform. Here, Rick Stafford, LGBT caucus chair and activist, addresses the LGBT caucus during the 2012 Democratic National Convention in Charlotte, North Carolina.

How Parties Engage Individuals

Political scientists who study the nature of Americans' civic engagement recognize that political parties represent one of the main channels through which citizens can make their voices heard. A fixture in the politics of American communities large and small, parties today are accessible to virtually everyone.

Historically, political parties excluded various groups from participating. For example, in many states, women were shut out of party meetings until the mid-20th century.[3] African Americans were formally excluded from voting in Democratic primaries in the South until the U.S. Supreme Court banned the practice in 1944, though it took decades before the party complied with that decision.[4] But in recent times, political parties have increasingly embraced and championed diversity. They have encouraged various groups beyond the traditional white European American male party establishment to get involved formally in the party organization, to participate in campaign activities, and to vote. Evidence of outreach to diverse constituencies can be seen today as Republicans court Latino voters as the 2016 presidential election approaches. And both parties today are much more inclusive of women, ethnic and racial minorities, and students, providing an important avenue for those traditionally excluded from political life to gain valuable experience as party activists, campaign volunteers, and informed voters. This increasingly diverse participation has also contributed to the parties' health, because it has caused them to recognize that to be successful, candidates must reflect the diverse identities and interests of voters.

What Political Parties Do

As we have seen, by promoting political activity, political parties encourage civic engagement and citizen participation and in that way foster democracy. Parties provide a structure for people to participate in grassroots organizing—that is, engaging in tasks that involve direct contact with potential voters, including volunteering on and contributing to party-run campaigns, volunteering in party headquarters, and running for office. During the 2014 congressional elections, Democratic and Republican activists registered, canvassed, and mobilized voters. Both parties focused their efforts on competitive congressional districts—districts where either party had a chance at winning.

For example, some Republican incumbents who had supported the government shutdown suffered a loss of support, while some Democrats who had supported the Affordable Care Act also faced competitive elections. In this way, parties allow citizens to express their preferences and influence government by choosing candidates running under the party label they support. Despite the small amount of competition fostered by these issues in the 2014 campaigns, increasingly, one characteristic of congressional elections is an overall lack of competition.

On the local level, a political party's ability to promote citizen participation varies with its relative influence within the community. Viable political parties—those that effectively contest and win some elections—are more effective at promoting citizen participation than weak political parties. A party that typically is in the minority in a local government—on the town council, in the county legislature—will find it more difficult to attract volunteers, to bring people out to fund-raisers, and to recruit candidates. It follows naturally that parties that are better at attracting public participation are more likely to win elections.

Political parties also grease the wheels of government and ensure its smooth running. Nearly all legislatures, from town councils to Congress, consist of a majority party, the party to which more than 50 percent of the elected legislators belong, and the minority party, to which less than 50 percent of the elected legislators belong. Thus, if five of the nine members of your town council are Republicans and four are Democrats, the Republicans are the majority party and the Democrats are the minority party. The majority party elects the legislature's leaders, makes committee assignments, and holds a majority on those committees.

By serving as a training ground for members, political parties also foster effective government. This role of parties is particularly important for groups that traditionally have not been among the power brokers in the government. Historically, African Americans, Latinos, and women have gained valuable knowledge and leadership experience in party organizations—by volunteering on party-run campaigns, assisting with candidate recruitment, or helping with fund-raising endeavors—before running for office.[5] Party credentials established by serving the party in these ways can act as a leveling device that can help make a newcomer's candidacy more viable.

Perhaps most important, political parties promote civic responsibility among elected officials and give voters an important "check" on those elected officials. There is no doubt that the 2014 congressional elections were partially a mandate on President Obama's second term, even though the president's name was not on the ballot. When an elected leader, particularly a chief executive, is the crucial player in enacting an important policy, the existence of political parties enables voters to hold party members responsible even if that particular elected official is not running for reelection. The system thus provides a check on the power of elected officials, because it makes them aware that the policy or position they are taking may be unpopular.

Historically, political parties also have fostered cooperation between divided interests and factions, building coalitions even in the most divisive of times, though this task is proving increasingly difficult given the growing polarization of political parties, especially in Congress. Civic engagement researchers point out that political parties' work in building coalitions and promoting cooperation among diverse groups often occurs away from the bright lights of the media-saturated public arena, where the parties' differences, rather than their common causes, often are in the spotlight.

Historically, according to one theory, political parties have also made government more effective and have provided important cues for voters. The **responsible party model,** developed by E. E. Schattschneider, posits that a party tries to give voters a clear choice by establishing priorities or policy stances different from those of the rival party or parties. Because a party's elected officials tend to be loyal to their party's stances, voters can readily anticipate how a candidate will vote on a given set of issues if elected and can thus cast their vote according to their preferences on those issues.

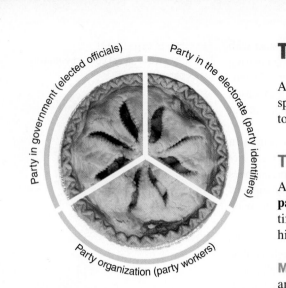

Party in government (elected officials)

Party in the electorate (party identifiers)

Party organization (party workers)

FIGURE 8.2

The Three Faces of Parties

The Three Faces of Parties

American political parties perform their various functions through three "faces," or spheres of operation.[6] The three components of the party include the party in the electorate, the party organization, and the party in government (see Figure 8.2).

The Party in the Electorate

All the individuals who identify with or tend to support a particular party make up the **party in the electorate.** Several factors influence which party an individual will identify with, including personal circumstances, race, and religion, as well as the party's history, ideology, position on issues of importance to the voter, and candidates.[7]

MEASURING THE PARTY IN THE ELECTORATE   The term **party identifier** refers to an individual who identifies himself or herself as a member of one party or the other; party identifiers typically are measured by party registration. In most states, party registration is a legal process in which a voter formally selects affiliation with one political party. This declaration of affiliation often occurs when a person registers to vote; the prospective voter selects his or her party identification by filling out a voter registration form or party declaration form. Depending on the state, a voter may select the Democratic or the Republican Party, a variety of third parties, or no party. When a voter does not select a party, he or she is technically an unaffiliated voter, but often analysts refer to such a voter as an **independent.**

People's party identification sometimes does not match their actual voting preferences. When we refer to the party in the electorate, we also consider those individuals who express a tendency to vote for one party or a preference for that party.

DETERMINING WHO BELONGS TO EACH POLITICAL PARTY
Although we commonly speak in terms of which groups affiliate with and "belong to" each of the political parties, those are just generalizations, with many exceptions. In general, each political party counts specific demographic groups as part of its base of support. A party will often draw party activists and leaders from the ranks of this bloc of individuals who can be counted on for support.

Although whites, men, and people with some college education are naturally found in both parties, they are more likely to be Republicans. For the Democrats, key voting blocs include African Americans, women, and people with no college education. Hispanics, a demographic group that is increasing in importance, has traditionally leaned Democratic, though some Hispanics—particularly Cuban Americans and deeply religious Hispanics—are more likely to identify with Republicans, and both political parties are actively courting this group. Individuals with a college degree or more are divided evenly between the two parties. Social class also plays a role in party preference. The working class is largely Democratic; the upper-middle class is largely Republican; and the middle class, by far the largest class in the United States, is divided between the two parties. But the best predictor of a person's party identification is his or her ideology. People who identify themselves as conservative are much more likely to be Republicans; people who identify themselves as liberal are much more likely to be Democrats. (See the discussion of ideology in Chapter 1.)

Voter Registration Application
Before completing this form, review the General, Application, and State specific instructions.

Are you a citizen of the United States of America? ☐ Yes ☐ No
Will you be 18 years old on or before election day? ☐ Yes ☐ No
If you checked "No" in response to either of these questions, do not complete form.
(Please see state-specific instructions for rules regarding eligibility to register prior to age 18.)

This space for office use only.

| 1 | (Circle one) Mr. Mrs. Miss Ms. | Last Name | First Name | | Middle Name(s) | | (Circle one) Jr Sr II III IV |

| 2 | Home Address | | Apt. or Lot # | City/Town | State | Zip Code |

| 3 | Address Where You Get Your Mail If Different From Above | City/Town | State | Zip Code |

| 4 | Date of Birth — Month / Day / Year | 5 | Telephone Number (optional) | 6 | ID Number - (See Item 6 in the instructions for your state) |

| 7 | Choice of Party (see item 7 in the instructions for your State) | 8 | Race or Ethnic Group (see item 8 in the instructions for your State) |

9
I have reviewed my state's instructions and I swear/affirm that:
■ I am a United States citizen
■ I meet the eligibility requirements of my state and subscribe to any oath required.
■ The information I have provided is true to the best of my knowledge under penalty of perjury. If I have provided false information, I may be fined, imprisoned, or (if not a U.S. citizen) deported from or refused entry to the United States.

Please sign full name (or put mark) ▲

Date: ___ Month ___ Day ___ Year

If you are registering to vote for the first time: please refer to the application instructions for information on submitting copies of valid identification documents with this form.

Please fill out the sections below if they apply to you.

If this application is for a **change of name**, what was your name before you changed it?

| A | Mr. Mrs. Miss Ms. | Last Name | First Name | | Middle Name(s) | | (Circle one) Jr Sr II III IV |

If you were registered before but this is the first time you are registering from the address in Box 2, what was your address where you were registered before?

| B | Street (or route and box number) | Apt. or Lot # | City/Town/County | State | Zip Code |

If you live in a rural area but do not have a street number, or if you have no address, please show on the map where you live.

C
■ Write in the names of the crossroads (or streets) nearest to where you live.
■ Draw an X to show where you live.
■ Use a dot to show any schools, churches, stores, or other landmarks near where you live, and write the name of the landmark.

NORTH ▲

Example
Route #2
● Grocery Store
Woodchuck Road
Public School ●
X

If the applicant is unable to sign, who helped the applicant fill out this application? Give name, address and phone number (phone number optional).

D

Mail this application to the address provided for your State.

Revised 10/29/2003

> Most states offer voters the opportunity to declare their party affiliation when registering to vote. Affiliated voters are the party in the electorate.

DIFFERENCES BETWEEN DEMOCRATS AND REPUBLICANS

We can trace to the 1930s some of the differences—in both ideologies and core constituencies—between today's Democrats and Republicans. That was the era of the Great Depression, a time of devastating economic collapse and personal misery for people around the world. President Franklin D. Roosevelt's drive to expand the role of government by providing a safety net for the most vulnerable in society has remained part of the Democratic agenda to this day. In the past several decades, this agenda has centered on pressing for civil rights for African Americans and for the expansion of social welfare programs. Evidence of Democrats' continued commitment to a government-provided safety net can be seen in the passage of Obamacare, which reformed the nation's health care system. Today, key components of the Democratic agenda include gay rights (including a plank advocating gay marriage), environmental protection, and freedom of choice with respect to abortion.

Traditionally, Republicans have countered the Democratic agenda by advocating a smaller government that performs fewer social welfare functions. But a major priority for the Republican Party today is advocacy of a stronger governmental role in regulating traditional moral values. Because of this stance, a solid voting bloc within the Republican Party comprises conservative Christians, sometimes called the Christian Right or the Religious Right, who agree with the Republicans' pro-life position on abortion (which includes support for increased regulation of abortion) and appeals for a consti-

>Hispanics are an increasingly important demographic group, as both the number of eligible Hispanic voters grows and their participation rates increase. While many Hispanics are staunchly Democratic, the traditional moral values espoused by the Republican party often resonate with many religious Latinos. Here New Jersey governor Chris Christie, a possible GOP presidential candidate, courts young Latino voters.

tutional amendment banning gay marriage. Republicans also support measures that protect business and business owners. They generally support a decreased role for the federal government, particularly with respect to the economy and social welfare issues, including staunch opposition to Obamacare, and a corresponding larger role for state governments.

It is not surprising that the base constituencies of the parties are drawn from the groups that each party's platform favors. The base of the Democratic Party prominently includes women, the majority of whom, since 1980, have voted for the Democratic presidential nominee. Since Franklin D. Roosevelt's New Deal social welfare policy during the 1930s, African Americans have been an important voting bloc within the Democratic Party, and this support for the Democratic Party among African Americans was shored up during Obama's presidency. Other ethnic minorities, including Latinos and Asian Americans, also tend to support the Democratic Party (as described in Chapter 6), as do many working-class voters. The base of the Republican Party prominently includes many small-business owners, citizens who identify themselves as being very religious, and upper-middle-class voters.[8]

Today, there are a few similarities between the two political parties. For instance, economic recovery remained a focal point for both Democratic and Republican candidates during the period leading up to the 2014 midterm congressional elections. Both parties are perceived as equally adept at keeping the country prosperous. Nonetheless, some differences exist between Democrats and Republicans. Democrats are much more likely to see the difference between the rich and the poor as a central problem, and Republicans are more likely to identify the federal budget deficit as an important issue.[9]

The Party Organization

Thomas P. "Tip" O'Neill (D-Mass.), Speaker of the House of Representatives from 1977 until 1987, is often quoted as having said, "All politics is local." In no case is that statement truer than it is for American political parties.

Party organization refers to the formal party apparatus, including committees, headquarters, conventions, party leaders, staff, and volunteer workers. In the United States, the party organization is most visible at the local level. Yet county and local parties tend to be loosely organized—centered predominantly on elections—and may be dormant after election season passes.[10] Except during presidential elections, state and local political parties typically function

party in the electorate
individuals who identify with or tend to support a party

party identifiers
individuals who identify themselves as a member of one party or the other

independent
a voter who does not belong to any organized political party; often used as a synonym for an unaffiliated voter

party organization
the formal party apparatus, including committees, party leaders, conventions, and workers

FIGURE 8.3

Theoretical Structure of Political Parties: A Hierarchical Model of Party Organizations

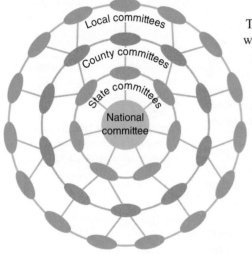

FIGURE 8.4

Modern Structure of Political Parties: Power Diffused Through Many Party Organizations

loyal opposition
a role that the party out of power plays, highlighting its objections to policies and priorities of the government in power

soft money loophole
Supreme Court interpretation of campaign finance law that enabled political parties to raise unlimited funds for party-building activities such as voter registration drives and get-out-the-vote (GOTV) efforts

quite separately from the national party. Although the number of individuals who actually participate in the party organization is quite small when compared with the party in the electorate, on the local level, political parties offer one of the most accessible means for individuals to participate in politics.

With respect to political power, county and local parties are the most important components of a party organization. Theoretically, political parties' organization resembles a pyramid (see Figure 8.3), with a broad base of support at the bottom and power flowing up to a smaller group at the state level and then to an even smaller, more exclusive group at the national level.[11] In reality, the national committees of both major U.S. political parties exist separately from the committees of the state and local parties (see Figure 8.4), and real political power can usually be found at the local or county party level, as we will see in the following discussion.

NATIONAL PARTIES Every four years, political party activists meet at a national convention to determine their party's nominee for the presidency. Here the delegates also adopt rules and develop a party platform that describes the party's policy priorities and positions on issues.

The national party committees (the Democratic National Committee, or DNC, and the Republican National Committee, or RNC) are the national party organizations charged with conducting the conventions and overseeing the operation of the national party during the interim between conventions. The national committee elects a national chair, who is often informally selected by the party's presidential nominee. The national chair, along with the paid staff of the national committee, oversees the day-to-day operations of the political party.

The role of the national chair depends to a large extent on whether the party's nominee wins the presidency. If the party's nominee is victorious, the national chair has a less prominent role because the president serves as the most public representative of the party. If the party's nominee loses, however, the national chair may take on a more public persona, serving as the spokesperson for the **loyal opposition**—the out-of-power party's objections to the policies and priorities of the government in power. In recent years, regardless of whether the party's nominee has won or lost, one of the most important roles of the national chair has been to raise funds. Money donated to the national parties is often redirected to the state and local parties, which use it to help contest elections and mobilize voters.

STATE PARTIES Both national parties have committees in each state (the Illinois State Democratic Committee, for example) that effectively *are* the party in that state. State committees act as intermediaries between the national committees and county committees. Typically, state committees are made up of a few members from each county or other geographic subdivision of a given state.

Historically, state parties were important because of their role in the election of U.S. senators, who until 1913 were elected by their states' legislatures. Since the ratification of the Seventeenth Amendment in that year, the voters of each state have directly elected their senators by popular election.

Later in the 20th century, state political parties began a rebound of power, partly because of the U.S. Supreme Court's decision in *Buckley v. Valeo* (1976). In this case, the Court ruled that political parties are entities with special status because their functions of educating and mobilizing voters and contesting elections help to ensure democracy.[12] This ruling created the so-called **soft money loophole,** through which the political parties could raise unlimited funds for party-building activities such as voter registration drives and get-out-the-vote (GOTV) efforts, although contributions to specific candidates were limited. The Court's decision strengthened the influence of the state parties, which the national parties often relied on to coordinate these efforts. The Bipartisan Campaign Reform Act of 2002 eliminated the soft money loophole, but until that time state parties were strengthened by their ability to channel those contributions to political parties. (See Chapter 9 for further discussion of soft money.)

COUNTY AND LOCAL PARTIES County committees consist of members of municipal, ward, and precinct party committees. The foot soldiers of the political parties, county committees help recruit candidates for office, raise campaign funds, and mobilize voters. The importance of a given county committee's role depends largely on whether its candidates are elected and whether its party controls the government. Party success tends to promote competition for candidates' slots and for seats on the county committee.

In most major cities, ward committees and precinct committees dominate party politics. Because city council members are often elected to represent a ward, ward committees are a powerful force in city politics, providing the grassroots organization that turns voters out in city elections. Precinct committees (a precinct is usually a subdivision of a ward) also help elect city council members.

Besides fund-raising, county and local political parties still play key roles in shaping both community engagement and individual participation in the political process, as they have done historically. During election season (in most places, from the end of August through the first week in November), county and local parties recruit and rely on volunteers to perform a host of functions, including answering phones in party headquarters, registering voters, coordinating mailings, doing advance work for candidates, compiling lists for GOTV efforts, supervising door-knocking campaigns, and staffing phone banks to remind voters to vote on Election Day.

The Party in Government

When candidates run for local, state, or national office, their party affiliation usually appears next to their names on the ballot. After an elected official takes the oath of office, many people do not think about the official's party affiliation. But in fact, the **party in government**—the partisan identifications of elected leaders in local, county, state, and federal government— significantly influences the organization and running of the government at these various levels.

party in government
the partisan identifications of elected leaders in local, county, state, and federal government

In most towns, the party identification of the majority of the members of the legislative branch (often called the *city council* or *town council*) determines who will serve as the head of the legislature (sometimes called the *president of city council*). And in most towns, the president of city council hails from the majority party. In addition, paid professional positions such as city solicitor (the town's lawyer), town planner, and city engineer are often awarded on the basis of the support of the majority of council. Even though the entire council votes on appointments, the minority party members often defer to the majority, since appointments typically are viewed as a privilege of winning a majority. Other appointments might include positions on voluntary boards such as a town planning or zoning board.

On the state level, the party in government plays a similarly prominent role in organizing government work. Typically, state legislatures are organized around political party.

Seating assignments and committee assignments are made by the majority party leadership and are based on a legislator's party affiliation. Figure 8.5 illustrates the partisan breakdown of state legislatures. In each state, the party with a majority in the legislature (shown in the figure) also has a majority on the legislature's committees, which decide the outcome of proposed legislation. Parties moreover are important in the executive branch of state government, since state governors typically appoint party loyalists to key positions in their administrations. Depending on the appointment powers of the governor, which vary from state to state, a governor may also appoint party members to plum assignments on state regulatory boards. In states where the governor appoints the judiciary, the governor also frequently selects judicial nominees from his or her own political party.

Parties perform a similar role in the federal government. Presidents draw from party loyalists to fill cabinet and sub-cabinet appointments and typically appoint federal judges from their own political parties. Congress is organized

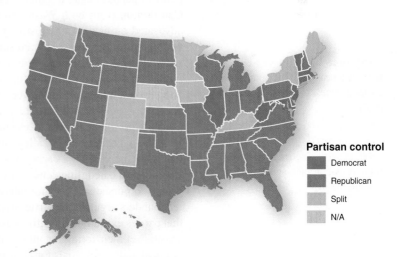

Partisan control
- ■ Democrat
- ■ Republican
- ■ Split
- ■ N/A

FIGURE 8.5

Partisan Control of State Legislatures, 2014

SOURCE: The National Conference of State Legislatures, www.ncsl.org/documents/statevote/ 2010_Legis_and_State_post.pdf.

> Congressional leadership is part of the party in government. Senate Majority Leader Mitch McConnell (R-Ky.), right, and House Speaker John Boehner (R-Ohio) work to further the GOP's priorities in Congress.

divided government
the situation that exists when Congress is controlled by one party and the presidency by the other

truncated government
the situation that exists when one chamber of Congress is controlled by the same party that controls the White House, while the other chamber is controlled by the other party

party system
the categorization of the number and competitiveness of political parties in a polity

realignment
a shift in party allegiances or electoral support that propels a political party to majority status

based on the party affiliation of its members. When representatives or senators refer to a colleague "on the other side of the aisle," they are referring to a member of the other political party, since congressional Democrats and Republicans sit across the aisle from one another. As in state legislatures, the party with the majority in Congress essentially runs the legislative branch. From its ranks comes the congressional leadership, including the Senate majority leader, the Speaker of the House of Representatives, and the House majority leader (see Chapter 11).

DIVIDED GOVERNMENT   There are limits to a party's power. Probably the most important check comes from the opposition party, which can openly criticize the party in power and sometimes succeed in obstructing policy initiatives. During some of their years in office, Presidents Barack Obama, Bill Clinton, and George W. Bush faced **divided government,** the situation in which one party controls both houses of Congress and the other party holds the presidency.[13] Before Republicans took control of the Senate in 2015, President Obama also faced **truncated government,** when one chamber of Congress is controlled by the same party that controls the White House, while the other chamber is controlled by the other party. The power that the Republicans wielded was particularly notable in the fall of 2013, when Republicans shut down the government for 16 days. To strengthen its position, the opposing party has also aggressively investigated alleged misconduct on the part of an elected leader, a common occurrence during the presidencies of both Clinton and George W. Bush.

Political Parties in U.S. History

Modern Americans' divided opinions of political parties would not be surprising to the founders, who viewed political parties with suspicion.[14] Thomas Jefferson said, "If I could not go to heaven but with a party, I would not go there at all." That sentiment was shared by George Washington, who warned of "the baneful effects of the spirit of party."[15] Despite those reservations, political parties began to emerge in the United States during the debate over ratification of the Constitution (with both Washington and Jefferson instrumental in their creation). Those who advocated ratification and a strong central government were called Federalists, and those who opposed ratification and favored states' rights were called Anti-Federalists. Thus began the first party system in the United States. **Party system** refers to the number and competitiveness of political parties in a polity[16]—for example, a government may have a two-party system in which one party is ascending in power. As we will see, the demarcation of party systems typically occurs in hindsight, when social scientists recognize points where there has been **realignment,** a shift in party allegiances or electoral support.[17]

Although these shifting allegiances have played a pivotal role in shaping the context of politics since the country's early days, the founders generally believed that parties threatened the stability of the fledgling democracy.[18] Most thought that political parties enabled individuals and groups to pursue self-serving interests that were often contrary to the common good. Some of the founders argued that parties discouraged independence in thought and action. Some thought that parties exacerbated conflicts and disagreements among the people rather than building consensus. Yet their formation and continued evolution testifies to their important role in achieving political and policy goals for their members.[19]

The First Party System: The Development of Parties, 1789–1828

In 1788, George Washington was elected president, but the consensus surrounding his election proved short-lived. Washington deeply opposed the idea of political parties and ruled during an era without formal parties. But he recognized that despite his popularity, he needed legislators who would push his initiatives through Congress. Washington's secretary of the treasury and close ally, Alexander Hamilton, gathered legislators into a loosely knit party, the Federalists, that favored a strong national government.

Thomas Jefferson, secretary of state during Washington's first term (1789–1793), feared a strong central government, and he and his backers opposed Hamilton's Federalists. But Jefferson's primary concern was that the new government should succeed, and so, despite his opposition, he remained in Washington's cabinet during the president's first term. When Jefferson later resigned his secretarial post, in 1793, many of those who shared his apprehensions about a strong central government remained in Congress.

Although Jefferson lost to Federalist John Adams in the 1796 presidential election, he paved the way for his future electoral success by building a base of support—including partisan groups in the states and newly established political newspapers—that allowed him to get his message out.[20] This direct communication with voters marked a significant step in the civic development of the U.S. electorate. The strategy was effective: Jefferson won election to the presidency in 1800 over Adams, and Adams's defeat marked the end of the Federalist Party. Jefferson was reelected in 1804, and both of his elections demonstrated the important function that political parties would play in elections.[21] His supporters became known as Jeffersonian Republicans; later, Democratic-Republicans. The modern descendants of the Democratic-Republicans today are called Democrats.

The Jeffersonian Republicans' effective campaign tactics of communicating with voters, along with the absence of well-organized opposition, resulted in their continued dominance from 1815 to 1828. Historians call those years the Era of Good Feelings, largely because of the widespread popular support for Democratic-Republican presidents James Madison (1809–1817), James Monroe (1817–1825), and John Quincy Adams (1825–1829).

The Second Party System: The Democrats' Rise to Power, 1828–1860

By 1828, some dissension among the Jeffersonian Republicans was becoming apparent. Members of the party, including the charismatic military general and politician Andrew Jackson (1829–1837) of Tennessee, chafed at the elitism of the party and the era. The Jacksonian Democrats—the name for the new coalition that Jackson formed—emphasized leadership through merit rather than birth.[22] They espoused **populism,** a philosophy supporting the rights and empowerment of the masses, particularly in the area of political participation, and the **spoils system,** in which political supporters were rewarded with jobs (from the phrase "to the victor go the spoils"). The Jacksonian Democrats succeeded in mobilizing the masses, sweeping Jackson to victory in the presidential election of 1828.[23] Political parties had become the medium through which many Americans were politicized, and in 1828, for the first time, more than one million Americans cast their ballots in the presidential contest.

Jackson's populism marked a critical step in opening up the civic life of the polity to many new groups of citizens who had not been involved in politics previously.[24] It redefined not only who was eligible to succeed as political leaders but also who should be eligible to participate in the selection of those leaders. Historian Richard P. McCormick noted that the Jacksonian Democrats extended voting rights to all white adult males, changed the mechanism for selecting presidential electors to popular elections by voters instead of by the state legislatures, and increased the importance of the party convention, in effect giving party members more say in candidates' selection. And although women would not gain the right to vote until 1920, the Jacksonian era saw the formal beginnings of the women's suffrage movement with the formation of the two major women's suffrage organizations and the advent of the Seneca Falls Convention (1848) in support of expanded rights for women.[25]

During the 1830s, southern plantation owners and northern industrialists became concerned about the impact the Democrats' populism would have on economic elites.[26] Their mutual interests crystallized in the formation of the Whig Party in 1836, which succeeded in electing William Henry Harrison (1841) as president. Upon Harrison's death, he was succeeded by his vice president and fellow member of the Whig party, John Tyler (1841–1845).[27] But the era of the Second Party System ultimately was defined by the long-standing effects that Jacksonian principles would have on U.S. politics—namely, through the politicization of a previously excluded mass of citizens—many of whom had been initiated into the rites of full citizenship and others of whom had begun the struggle to win their own status as full citizens.[28]

populism
a philosophy supporting the rights and empowerment of the masses as opposed to elites

spoils system
the practice of rewarding political supporters with jobs

> President Abraham Lincoln with African Americans expressing gratitude for the Emancipation Proclamation, in 1863. For decades after his presidency, African Americans would remain an important Republican party constituency, loyal to "the party of Lincoln."

political machine
big-city party organization that exerted control over many aspects of life and lavishly rewarded supporters

patronage
system in which a party leader rewarded political supporters with jobs or government contracts in exchange for their support of the party

The Third Party System: The Republicans' Rise to Power, 1860–1896

In the 1850s, slavery became the primary concern for both the Whigs and the Democrats.[29] This highly charged issue divided the Whig Party into proslavery and abolitionist factions, and the party consequently faded away.[30] In its place, a new antislavery party, the Republicans (also called the Grand Old Party, or GOP), took shape in 1854 and gained the support of abolitionist Whigs and northern Democrats.[31] The victory of the Republican presidential nominee, Abraham Lincoln, in the election of 1860 marked the beginning of a period of dominance of the antislavery Republicans, which continued even after the Civil War.[32] During this time, the Republican Party enjoyed strong support from newly franchised African American voters. Although many African Americans in the South were prevented from exercising their right to vote through threats, intimidation, and tactics such as the white primary (see Chapter 5), African Americans in the North widely voted Republican. They would remain strong supporters of the "party of Lincoln" for decades.

During this time, political parties grew very strong, and political machines came to dominate the political landscape. A **political machine** was both a corrupt and a useful organization that dominated politics around the turn of the 20th century, particularly in cities. Each political machine was headed by a "boss," whose power rested on a system of patronage. A party leader used **patronage** as a device to reward political supporters—rather than individuals who might demonstrate greater merit or particular competence—with jobs or government contracts. In exchange, those receiving patronage would vote for the party and might be expected to volunteer on a campaign or kick back some of their wages to the party.

Although political machines were known for corruption, they did accomplish some good. Richard Croker was political boss of Tammany Hall, New York City's Democratic Party political machine from 1886 until 1902. He explained: "Think of what New York is and what the people of New York are. One half are of foreign birth. . . . They do not speak our language, they do not know our laws. . . . There is no denying the service which Tammany has rendered to the Republic, there is no such organization for taking hold of the untrained, friendless man and converting him into a citizen. Who else would do it if we did not?"[33]

On that score, Croker was right. At the time, political machines provided the vital service of socializing a generation of immigrants to democracy and to the American way of political life. Some machines, including Tammany Hall, generated widespread political participation, and some allowed the participation of women.[34] Political machines helped integrate immigrants into the social, economic, and political fabric of the United States, usually by awarding jobs for loyalty to the party. And in an era when the federal government had not yet become a large-scale provider of social services, urban political machines also provided a safety net for the injured, the elderly, and widows.

The Fourth Party System: Republican Dominance, 1896–1932

The 1896 presidential election between populist Democrat William Jennings Bryan and Republican William McKinley (1897–1901) marked the beginning of a new era in party politics. Bryan appealed widely to Protestants, southerners, midwesterners, and rural dwellers who were suspicious of Catholic, ethnic, working-class immigrants in the urban Northeast. McKinley emphasized economic growth and development and garnered support from industrialists, bankers, and even working-class factory workers, who saw his backing of business as being good for the economy. McKinley won the election handily, his victory ushering in an era of Republican dominance in presidential politics that would last until the election of 1912.

That year, Theodore Roosevelt (1901–1909), who had succeeded McKinley as president in 1901 after the latter's assassination, and who had been elected president as a Republican in 1904, ran in the presidential election as a Progressive. The Progressive Party advocated widespread governmental reform and sought to limit the power of political bosses. The Republicans' split between William Howard Taft's regular Republicans and Roosevelt's Progressives powered Democrat Woodrow Wilson to the presidency with only 42 percent of the popular vote.

As Wilson's Democratic administration ended up enacting many of the Progressive Party's proposals, the power of the urban political machines declined. For example, recorded voter registration and secret ballot laws were passed, the direct party primary was established, and civil service reform was expanded. The national leaders who spearheaded those measures designed them to take political power out of the bosses' hands and give it to the electorate.

After Wilson's two terms, the Republicans continued to enjoy the support of business elites and the industrial working class. They also benefited from the backing of the many African Americans in the northern cities who continued to support the party of Lincoln, and of women voters, many of whom had been activists in the Progressive movement. With this widespread and diverse support, the Republicans retained control of the presidency throughout the 1920s.

The Fifth Party System: Democratic Dominance, 1932–1968

When the stock market crashed in 1929, the economy entered the deep downturn that history remembers as the Great Depression. In the election of 1932, a broad constituency responded to the calls of the Democratic candidate, Franklin D. Roosevelt, for an increased governmental role in promoting the public welfare. Roosevelt pressed tirelessly for a **New Deal** for all Americans, a broad program in which the government would bear the responsibility of providing a safety net to protect the most disadvantaged members of society.

A new alignment among American voters swept "FDR" into presidential office. In fact, the **New Deal coalition**—the name for the voting bloc comprising traditional southern Democrats, northern city dwellers (especially immigrants and the poor), Catholics, unionized and blue-collar workers, African Americans, and women—would give Roosevelt the presidency an unprecedented four times.[35]

The era of the Fifth Party System significantly opened up party politics and civic activity to a widening spectrum of Americans. Notably for African Americans and women, Roosevelt's elections marked the first time that they had been actively courted by political parties, and their new political activism—particularly in the form of voting and political party activities—left them feeling they had a voice in their government.

Vice President Harry Truman assumed the presidency on Roosevelt's death in 1945 and was elected in his own right in 1948, but subsequent Democrats were unable to keep Roosevelt's coalition together. Republican Dwight Eisenhower won the White House in 1952 and again in 1956. And although Democrats John F. Kennedy and Lyndon Johnson held the presidency through most of the 1960s, the events of that decade wreaked havoc on the Democratic Party, with deep divisions opening up over the Vietnam War and civil rights for African Americans.[36]

A New Party System?

Barack Obama's election in 2008 and reelection in 2012, particularly his strong support among young and first-time voters, points to a continuation of the trend of Democratic dominance established in the Fifth Party System. But political scientists are seeking to determine whether the era that began when Richard Nixon was elected president in 1968 can be considered a separate party system. Republican dominance of the presidency since 1968, including the presidencies of presidents Nixon, Ford, Reagan, George H. W. Bush, and George W. Bush, coupled with increasing

In this cartoon by the famous 19th-century caricaturist and cartoonist Thomas Nast, what does the tiger represent? What point is the cartoonist making about the "clean linen" the tiger is wearing?

THE CURIOUS EFFECT OF CLEAN LINEN UPON THE DEMOCRATIC PARTY

New Deal
Franklin D. Roosevelt's broad social welfare program in which the government would bear the responsibility of providing a safety net to protect the most disadvantaged members of society

New Deal coalition
the group composed of southern Democrats, northern city dwellers, immigrants, the poor, Catholics, labor union members, blue-collar workers, African Americans, and women that elected Franklin D. Roosevelt to the presidency four times

Party Politics in Flux

Then (1889)	Now
Powerful political parties were in their heyday, and party bosses ruled the cities with an iron fist.	The era of party politics in the United States is over, according to some scholars.
The patronage system was in high gear, and political parties derived enormous power and loyalty from the recipients of jobs and lucrative contracts.	A merit-based civil service system has largely replaced patronage, and parties are weakened because of a decline in the number of loyal members.
Elected officials toed the party line, because they depended on the party for their office.	Elected officials pride themselves on their "independence" and sometimes owe very little to their political parties, particularly since the *Citizens United* decision.

WHAT'S NEXT?

> How are advancing technologies likely to change political parties and their operations in the future? Will these weaken or strengthen the parties? Explain.

> How do parties today help voters evaluate candidates? Will they still perform this function in the future? Will the nature of this process change? Explain.

> Are there any problems with "independent" elected officials? Will political parties be able to ensure voters that candidates will act consistently with their stated principles in the future?

support of the Republican Party by southern whites and the increasing activism of conservative Christians in the party, gives support to the claim that a new party system has emerged.

Additional characteristics of this new party system, according to scholars, include *intense party competition,* in which the two major U.S. political parties have been nearly evenly matched and neither one has dominated; and *divided government,* where a president of one party has to deal with a Congress of the other. This fierce partisan competitiveness is clearly apparent in the outcomes of recent national elections. In particular, the 2000 presidential campaign demonstrated the ferocious rivalry of the two parties, with a presidential election so close that the outcome was in question for weeks after the voting had ended. That year, voters also evenly divided the Senate, electing 50 Democrats and 50 Republicans.

The Party System Today: In Decline, in Resurgence, or a Post-Party Era?

Given the various historical changes to the U.S. political party system that we have examined, many political scientists have inquired into what the impact of those changes will be. Do the changes signify an end to party control in American politics? Or can political parties adapt to the altered environment and find new sources of power?

The Party's Over

Some scholars argue that changes in the political environment have rendered today's political parties essentially impotent to fulfill the functions that parties performed during stronger party systems. In 1982, political scientist Gary Orren wrote: "In a world in which political scientists disagree on almost everything, there is remarkable agreement among the political science profession that the strength of American political parties has declined significantly over the past several decades."[37] Although some political scientists would subsequently challenge Orren's perspective, many agreed with him at the time.

These theorists note several key factors that have contributed to party decline. Some argue that the elimination of political patronage through the requirement of civil service qualifications for government employees has significantly hurt parties' ability to reward loyal followers with government jobs. Patronage jobs still exist, but most government positions are now awarded upon an applicant's successful performance on a civil service exam that is designed to measure qualifications based on objective criteria. Whereas the recipients of patronage jobs were among the most loyal party members in previous decades, party loyalty has decreased as political parties have lost a significant amount of control in the awarding of jobs.

Other political scientists emphasize the government's increased role over time in providing social welfare benefits as a contributor to the decline of political parties. Because of President Franklin D. Roosevelt's New Deal and further expansion of the government's role as the key provider of social services, the parties typically no longer perform that function. Thus changing times have brought the elimination of another source of party loyalty.

Primary elections—elections in which voters choose the party's candidates who will run in the later general election—also have decreased parties' power by taking the control of nominations from party leaders and handing it to voters. In the past, when a party machine anointed nominees at nominating conventions, those nominees became indebted to the party and typically responded with loyalty if they got elected. But today's candidates are less likely to owe their nomination to the party: Instead, in many cases they have fought for and won the nomination by taking their campaign directly to primary voters.

Changes in the mass media have also meant a drastically decreased role for political parties. In their heyday, political parties were one of the most important providers of news. Parties published so-called penny papers that reported information to the public. Today, political parties may still provide some information to voters at election time, but most voters rely on other, independent media outlets—newspapers, television, radio, and Internet news sources—rather than exclusively partisan sources.

The rise in candidate-centered campaigns has also weakened political parties. **Candidate-centered campaigns,** in which an individual seeking election, rather than an entire party slate, is the focus, have come about because of changes in the parties' functions, the advent of direct primaries, trends in the mass media that have shifted the focus to individual office-seekers, and the 2010 U.S. Supreme Court decision *Citizens United v. Federal Election Commission*,[38] which paved the way for the explosion of campaign spending by independent groups. Candidate-centered campaigns also must rely more heavily on paid professional campaign workers (instead of party volunteers), making it necessary for contributors to support individual candidates rather than political parties.

These changes in the nature of political parties and in their ability to perform their traditional functions have led some political scientists to conclude that the era of party rule is ending. Other players, they say—including interest groups, candidate-based organizations, and the media—will come to assume the roles traditionally performed by political parties.

The Party's Just Begun

Pointing to the pervasiveness of political discourse, as well as heightened interest and turnout in several recent presidential primaries and general elections, other political scientists strongly disagree that U.S. parties' prime has passed.[39] While conceding that political parties' functions have changed, these theorists observe that parties have proved themselves remarkably adaptable. When the political environment has changed in the past, political parties have responded by assuming different functions or finding new avenues by which to seed party loyalty. According to this view, the parties' ability to rebound is alive and well.

These scholars also argue that the continued dominance in the United States of two political parties—through decades of threats to their survival—has demonstrated a strength and a resilience that are likely to prevail. Today's Republicans, the party of Lincoln, have endured the assassinations of party leaders, the Great Depression, the four-term presidency of popular Democrat Franklin D. Roosevelt, and the Watergate scandal during the Nixon presidency. Today's Democrats are the same party that opposed suffrage for African Americans in the aftermath of the Civil War, and that survived internal divisions over civil rights through the 1960s, to become strong supporters of African American rights in recent decades. The Democrats too have endured assassinations and scandals and have weathered Republican control of the White House for all but 19 years since 1968. Both political parties have remained remarkably competitive despite the challenges to their success.

Scholars who argue that the two main U.S. political parties are once again rebounding cite the lack of viable alternatives to the two-party system. Yes, third parties have made a mark in recent presidential elections. But the present-day party system has not seen the emergence of a strong, viable third party with a cohesive ideology that has attracted a significant portion of the vote in more than one election. And civic education scholars agree that third parties have served an important function by encouraging the political participation of people who are disenchanted with the current two-party system. They also acknowledge, however, the continued dominance of the two main parties in creating opportunities for civic engagement within communities.

primary election
an election in which voters choose the party's candidates who will run in the later general election

candidate-centered campaign
a campaign in which an individual seeking election, rather than an entire party slate, is the focus

A Post-Party Era?

Whether one views U.S. political parties as in decline or rebounding, the evidence demonstrates that the responsible party model (discussed earlier) is not as strong as it once was. Some scholars argue that, as a nation, we are entering a post-partisan era in which political parties are continually decreasing in their importance in national politics, but retain a role as loose organizing structures in government. These scholars see **dealignment,** the phenomenon in which fewer voters support the two major political parties and instead self-identify as independent, as a notable characteristic of this post-partisan era.[40] Others view the increasing trend toward supporting candidates from both parties (**ticket splitting**) or from other parties as evidence of this phenomenon.

One characteristic that lends credence to the assertion of a post-partisan era is the growing importance of candidate-centered politics. The rise of **candidate committees,** organizations that candidates form to support their individual election as opposed to the party's slate of candidates, is one reflection of how politics has become increasingly candidate centered. Candidate committees compete with political parties in many arenas. They raise and spend money, organize campaigns, and attempt to mobilize voters. One effect of their enhanced influence has been that elected officials, particularly members of Congress, are less indebted to their parties than in previous eras and thus sometimes demonstrate less party loyalty when voting on bills in the legislature.

Whether or not the United States is entering a post-partisan era, we do know that the rise of candidate committees and the increase in ticket splitting mean that parties are less useful to voters as they assess candidates, because the differences between Republican and Democratic candidates may dissipate in the face of constituent opinion. Yet most Americans disagree: A recent Gallup poll indicated that nearly two-thirds of those surveyed believe that there are important differences between the Democratic and the Republican Parties.[41] And the research of some scholars, including David Karol, Hans Noel, John Zaller, and Marty Cohen, indicates that party elites, including elected officials and former elected officials, have increased their control in selecting party presidential nominees, suggesting a potential revival of the importance of parties as players in politics today.[42]

Two-Party Domination in U.S. Politics

Since the ratification of the Constitution in 1787, the United States has had a two-party system for all but about 30 years in total. This historical record stands in marked contrast to the experience of the many nations that have third parties.[43] A **third party** is a political party organized as opposition or an alternative to the existing parties in a two-party system. Many countries even have multiparty systems.

The United States' two-party system has had two contradictory influences on people's civic engagement. On the one hand, the dominance of only two strong political parties through most of American history has made it easy for individuals to find avenues for becoming civically engaged. Further, at various historical points, political parties have worked for the outright extension of political rights to groups that were excluded, although often with the foremost aim of bolstering their core supporters. On the other hand, the dominance of just two political parties that tend to be ideologically moderate discourages the political participation of some people, particularly those who hold more extreme ideological positions.

Although the grip of the United States' two-party system is frustrating to people who support a greater diversity of parties, the reasons for the two-party system are numerous and difficult to change.

The Dualist Nature of Most Conflicts

Historically, many issues in the United States have been dualist, or "two-sided." For example, the debate over ratification of the U.S. Constitution found people with two basic opinions. On one side, the Federalists supported ratification of the Constitution, which created a federal government that separated powers among three branches and shared power with state governments. They

" IT JUST WOULDN'T WORK OUT, DEREK. I'M FROM A RED STATE, AND YOU'RE FROM A BLUE STATE."

dealignment
the situation in which fewer voters support the two major political parties, instead identifying themselves as independent, or splitting their tickets between candidates from more than one party

ticket splitting
the situation in which voters vote for candidates from more than one party

candidate committees
organizations that candidates form to support their individual election

third party
a party organized as opposition or an alternative to the existing parties in a two-party system

were opposed by the Anti-Federalists, who campaigned against ratification of the Constitution, supported stronger states' rights, and wanted to see states and individuals enjoy greater protections. This split provided the initial structure for the two-party system, and a multitude of issues followed that format.

Political scientists Seymour Martin Lipset and Stein Rokkan asserted that the dualist nature of voter alignments or cleavages shapes how political parties form. In particular, these alignments or cleavages concern the character of the national fabric (for example, whether religious ideals or secular notions should prevail), and they are determined by function (business versus agrarian interests, for example).[44] These cleavages shaped party formation during the 19th century, when the dualist nature of conflict continued to be in evidence in public affairs. Some states wanted slavery; other states opposed "the peculiar institution" of human bondage. In some states, commercial and industrial interests dominated; in other states, agricultural interests held the reins of power. Immigrants, often Catholics, controlled the politics of some states, whereas native-born Protestants held sway in others.

By the 20th century, the dualist conflict had become more ideological. Some Americans agreed with President Franklin D. Roosevelt's plan to help lift the country out of the Great Depression by significantly increasing the role of government in people's everyday lives. Others opposed this unprecedented expansion of the federal government's power. In later decades, debates over civil rights and women's rights demonstrated the continued dualist nature of conflict in American society and culture. And today, the great dualist ideological issue of our time centers around the Patient Protection and Affordable Care Act of 2010, or Obamacare, with many conservatives arguing that the federal government is overstepping its function in mandating and providing mechanisms for health care coverage, while many liberals assert that it is the federal government's responsibility to ensure what they claim is a basic right.

The Winner-Take-All Electoral System

In almost all U.S. elections, the person with the most votes wins. If a competitor gets just one vote fewer than the victor, he or she wins nothing. If a third party garners a significant proportion of the vote in congressional elections nationwide but does not win the most votes in any given district, the party will not win any seats in Congress.

Compare the **winner-take-all system** with the proportional representation system found in many nations. In a **proportional representation system,** political parties win the number of parliamentary seats equal to the percentage of the vote each party receives. So, for example, if the Green Party were to capture 9 percent of the vote in a country's election, it would get nine seats in a 100-member parliament. In a proportional representation system, the 19 percent of the vote that Reform Party candidate Ross Perot won in the 1992 U.S. presidential election would have given the Reform Party about 85 seats in the House of Representatives!

In nations with proportional representation, third parties (which we consider in more detail later in the chapter) are encouraged, because such parties can win a few seats in the legislature and use them to further their cause and broaden their support.[45] In addition, in proportional representation systems, third parties sometimes form a *coalition,* or working union, with a larger party so that the two together can control a majority of a legislature. And so, for example, the Green Party that won nine seats in Parliament in the preceding example might form a coalition with another party that had received 42 percent of the vote, together forming a majority government. In this way, a third party can get members appointed to key positions as a reward for forming the coalition (see "Global Context"). Consequently, societies with proportional representation systems can sometimes be more inclusive of differing points of view, because even those winning a small proportion of the vote achieve representation, and that representation can be pivotal in the formation of coalitions.

winner-take-all system
an electoral system in which the candidate who receives the most votes wins that office, even if that total is not a majority

proportional representation system
an electoral structure in which political parties win the number of parliamentary seats equal to the percentage of the vote the party receives

Continued Socialization to the Two-Party System

Another reason the two-party system dominates in the United States is that party identification—like ideology, values, and religious beliefs—is an attribute that often passes down from one generation to the next. Hence many an individual is likely to be a Democrat or a Republican because his or her parents were one or the other. Many people first learn about government and politics at

THE RISE OF EUROSCEPTIC PARTIES IN EUROPE

The European Union (EU) is an alliance of European states that has evolved into a single market with supranational political institutions. Since 2002, many of the EU states adopted a shared currency, the euro. Yet euroscepticism, opposition to the political integration and the EU in general, has increased significantly in the wake of the economic recession that occurred in 2007, and which is still being felt in drastic ways in parts of the EU. This decline has coincided with a decrease in global prestige for the EU. And anti-EU sentiment has been compounded by the expansion of the EU, which encompasses 28 member states today.

Should members of parliament participate in a government they would like to abolish?

A common theme among these parties is that the EU is undemocratic, bureaucratic, and nonresponsive to its member states and their citizens. Across Europe, eurosceptic parties can be found in every nation and across the ideological spectrum. Some wish to reform the EU or to change certain EU policies. Many oppose the federalization of Europe, which created a unified sovereignty.

Many eurosceptic parties are right wing, accentuating sentiments of nationalism—or pride in one's country—that many perceive as lost when nations join the EU. Among the most influential is the Europe of Freedom and Democracy group (EFD) in the European Parliament. The EFD is comprised of 35 members of the 766-member European Parliament. Although this is a small proportion, the EU's multiparty proportional representation system offers smaller parties the opportunity to form coalitions with larger parties, which can increase their influence considerably as they are able to parlay a small number of seats into an alliance forming a majority.

Members of the EFD hail from 13 political parties, including Belgium's Vlaams Beland party; Bulgaria's People for Real, Open and United Democracy; the Danish People's Party; Finland's Finns Party; the Movement for France; Greece's Popular Orthodox Rally; Italy's Northern League and I Love Italy parties; Lithuania's Order and Justice Party; the Reformed Political Party of the Netherlands; United Poland; Slovakia's Slovak National Party; and the United Kingdom's Independence Party. Among the most important of these are Italy's Northern League, which has 8 members of the European Parliament, and the United Kingdom's Independence Party, which has 10. Of course, the irony is that members of these political parties are part of the government of the EU, the very entity they would like to abolish.

home. Around the dinner table, a child may have heard her parents rail against Barack Obama's health care reform law or criticize the Tea Party. Having become socialized to their household's political culture, children are likely to mimic their parents' views.

Even children who do not share their parents' political outlook or who grow apart from it over time (as commonly occurs during the college years) have been socialized to the legitimacy of the two-party system—unless, of course, their parents routinely criticized both Democrats and Republicans or voiced dissatisfaction with the two-party system.

Election Laws That Favor the Two-Party System

At both the federal and the state levels in the United States, election laws benefit the two major parties because they are usually written by members of one of those parties. Although some local governments mandate nonpartisan elections, in most cities and towns, getting on the ballot typically means simply winning the party's nomination and collecting a state-specified number of signatures of registered party members on a nominating petition. Usually, the party organization circulates this petition for a candidate. Third parties have a much steeper climb to get their candidates in office—sometimes, just getting a candidate's name on the ballot is a serious challenge. Scholars of civic engagement point to the structural impediments to the formation of third parties as key to the low level of civic engagement on the part of individuals who are dissatisfied with the two-party system. Facing seemingly insurmountable structural obstacles to the formation of successful third parties, some Americans shy away from political engagement.

Third Parties in the United States

As we have seen, the absence of viable U.S. political parties beyond the Democrats and the Republicans is a source of frustration for some Americans, and many Americans feel that the Democratic and Republican political parties do not do an adequate job of representing the American people. At different times, the proportions of conservatives, liberals, and moderates vary in their likelihood of agreeing that a third party is needed. According to pollsters, this difference may reflect the respondents' opinions of the effectiveness of their party at representing their views. For example, at high points in the George W. Bush presidency, conservatives would have been less likely to say a third party was needed, and the same would hold true for liberals during high points in Barack Obama's presidency (see "Analyzing the Sources").

Because of the differing ideological viewpoints of those who agree a third party is needed, third parties have had little success in contesting elections. Ralph Nader was an influential candidate in 2000, not because he netted a sizeable proportion of votes but because the 3 percent that he did win was enough to change the outcome of that razor-close election. Other third-party candidacies have proved influential because of their role in focusing attention—particularly the attention of the victorious candidate—on an issue that might not otherwise have been addressed.[46] Such was the case in 1912 when Progressive Party candidate Theodore Roosevelt ran against Woodrow Wilson. Although he lost the election, Roosevelt succeeded in shaping public opinion so that Wilson felt compelled to enact part of the Progressives' national agenda, including sweeping changes to the nation's child labor laws.

One of the most significant obstacles to the formation of a viable third party is that people who are dissatisfied with the two dominant parties fall across the ideological spectrum. As shown in Figure 8.6, some are very liberal, others are quite conservative, and still others are moderate. In fact, the Gallup organization has found that roughly 50 percent of all Americans *across all ideologies* support the idea of a third party. Thus, although many Americans are dissatisfied with the current parties, a third party would have difficulty attracting enough support from among these diversely dissatisfied party members.

Nonetheless, third parties have played, and continue to play, an influential role in American electoral politics. Third parties are particularly effective at encouraging the civic engagement of people who feel that the two dominant parties do not represent their views or do not listen to them. In recent years, we have seen this role played by the Tea Party, which has channeled the participation of many conservatives frustrated with the two major political parties. Third parties give such citizens a voice. And even though third parties often do not succeed electorally, their mere presence in the political arena enlivens civic discourse and frequently encourages debate about urgent policy issues that the two major parties ignore or slight.

Types of Third Parties

Third parties have existed in the United States since the early 19th century. Over the nation's history, third parties typically have fallen into one of three general categories: issue advocacy parties, ideologically oriented parties, and splinter parties.

ISSUE ADVOCACY PARTIES   Formed to promote a stance on a particular issue, many issue advocacy parties are short-lived. Once the issue is dealt with or fades from popular concern, the mobilizing force behind the party disintegrates. An example is today's United States Marijuana Party, which advocates the legalization of marijuana as well as libertarian views on most issues. The difficulty faced by such parties are exemplified by the struggle of the Green Party, which promotes environmental protection as a primary issue, to become a mainstream party: In the 2000 presidential election, the Green Party sought to win 5 percent of the vote in order to automatically qualify for federal matching funds in the 2004 campaign. It fell short, however, capturing only 3 percent of the vote, and then faded from the national electoral arena.

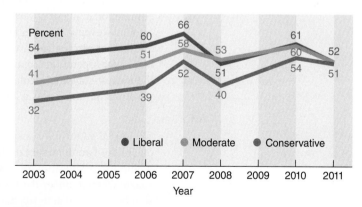

FIGURE 8.6

Majorities Support a Third Major Party Across the Ideological Spectrum
SOURCE: Gallup, "Support for Third U.S. Party Dips, but Is Still Majority View," 2012, www.gallup.com/poll/147461/Support-Third-Party-Dips-Majority-View.aspx.

IS A THIRD PARTY NEEDED?

Support for a third party has fluctuated since October 2003, when Gallup first asked this question, but it increased drastically after the government shut down in the fall of 2013. Today a sizeable majority of Americans believe a third party is needed.

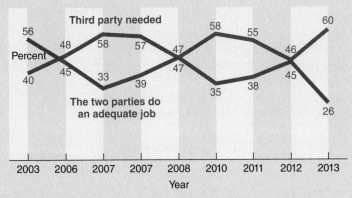

SOURCE: Jeffrey M. Jones, "In U.S., Perceived Need for Third Party Reaches New High," 2013, www.gallup.com/poll/165392/perceived-need-third-party-reaches-new-high.aspx.

Evaluating the Evidence

1. What long-term trend do the polling data in this figure show?

2. What factors in the political and social environments might explain this trend?

IDEOLOGICALLY ORIENTED PARTIES   The agenda of an ideologically oriented party is typically broader than that of an issue-oriented party. Ideologically oriented parties are structured around an *ideology*—a highly organized and coherent framework concerning the nature and role of government in society (see Chapter 6). Such parties have broad views about many different aspects of government. For example, the Libertarian Party, which holds the ideological position that government should not interfere with individuals' social, political, and economic rights, advocates a very limited role for government: no guarantees of minimum wages or other forms of governmental regulation of the economy, including environmental regulation; no governmental interference in individuals' privacy; the legalization of prostitution and drugs; and the elimination of major governmental bureaucracies, including the Central Intelligence Agency, the Internal Revenue Service, and the Federal Bureau of Investigation.

Another ideologically oriented party is the Socialist Party, which lies at the other end of the ideological spectrum from the Libertarian Party. The Socialist Party, formed in 1901, is one of the longest-standing ideologically oriented parties in the United States. Socialists believe that government should play a large role in ensuring economic equality for all people.

SPLINTER PARTIES   A splinter party is a political party that breaks off, or "splinters," from one of the two dominant parties. Often a group splinters off because of intraparty (internal, or within the party) disagreement on a particular issue. Though many Tea Party candidates have sought election under the Republican Party label since 2010, the sometimes-fractured relationship between the activists and more moderate Republicans caused many to view the Tea Party as a splinter from the Republican Party. In 1948, a group of southern Democrats who opposed the Democratic Party's support of civil rights for African Americans splintered from the Democratic Party to form the States' Rights Party, which quickly became known as the Dixiecrat Party. The party called itself the States' Rights Party because it claimed that Congress had no power to interfere with the administration of laws made by the states. It used that claim to retain the policies that created a system of racial segregation in the South. Although the States' Rights Party was a separate, formal organization, many southern Democratic elected officials and party leaders who agreed with the States' Rights Party's platform supported its views from within the Democratic Party.

The Impact of Third Parties

Despite the difficulties associated with sustaining support in American electoral politics, third parties have important effects in the political arena. First, third parties provide a release valve for dissatisfied voters. People who are disgruntled with the two major parties can join or form another political party. This has been the case with the Tea Party, which has channeled the energy of staunch conservatives who view the mainstream Republican Party as too moderate. And while a third party's chances of electoral success are not great, such parties provide a mechanism for like-minded people to come together to try to effect change. At the national level, third parties were a release valve for discontented voters in several elections, as shown in Figure 8.7.

Second, although U.S. third parties usually do not win elections, they can influence electoral outcomes. For example, given the closeness of the 2000 presidential race, many Democrats believe that Green Party candidate Ralph Nader caused Democrat Al Gore to lose the election. They reason that Nader voters would have been more likely to vote for the liberal Gore than for the conservative George W. Bush if Nader had not been a candidate. In a state such as Florida, where the electorate was divided evenly, Nader's candidacy in fact could have changed the outcome of that state's balloting and thus the results of the national election as well. Of course, many third-party advocates claim that supporters of a third-party candidate may not have voted at all if their party had not been on the ballot. (See "Thinking Critically About Democracy.")

In U.S. history, third-party presidential candidates have won more than 10 percent of the vote seven times, the latest being in 1992, when Independent Party candidate H. Ross Perot captured 19 percent of the vote. As Figure 8.7 illustrates, in five of those seven cases, the incumbent party's presidential nominee lost the presidency. Thus, third parties tend to help the major out-of-power party win election.

Finally, third parties put a variety of issues on the national political agenda. When a third party, especially an issue-oriented third party, draws attention to an issue of concern, sometimes government officials respond to that concern even if the third party fails in its election bid. In some such cases, the issue has not previously been given priority, and the attention the third party draws to it creates a groundswell of political pressure that forces action. In other cases, policy makers might act to address the issue in order to woo the supporters of the third party who have expressed that particular issue concern.

Historically, the two major parties' cooption of issues that were first promoted by third parties has sometimes contributed to the demise of third parties. For example, as we have seen, the Progressives' presidential candidate, Theodore Roosevelt, lost to Democrat Woodrow Wilson in 1912, but Wilson enacted many elements of the Progressive Party's platform, including antitrust regulations, corporate law reforms, and banking regulations. Lacking a unique platform, and with comparatively little electoral success, the Progressives faded away.

New Ideologies, New Technologies: The Parties in the Twenty-First Century

American political parties have changed dramatically in recent years. Global events such as the end of the Cold War, the rise of international and domestic terrorism and multifront wars, and the impact of the Internet and cellular technologies have partly driven the changes. Within the Republican and Democratic Parties, the changes have reflected an ideological shift from an era when a party's defining position was its position on social welfare policy, to a time when foreign policy issues were central, and back again. Today, much emphasis is placed on the differences between the Democrats and the Republicans, but for many citizens there are shades of "purple" between the reds and the blues (see Figure 8.8).

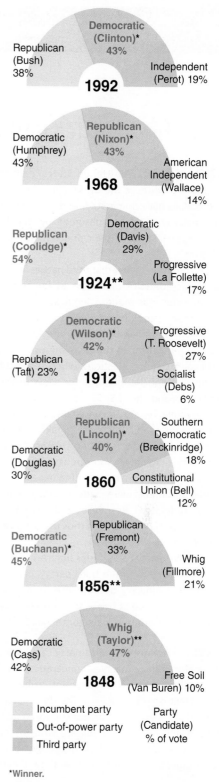

*Winner.

**Denotes election in which incumbent party retained power in face of a strong third-party challenge.

FIGURE 8.7

Third Parties Help the Out-of-Power Party

Democracy

Are Third Parties Bad for the United States?

The Issue: The United States' political culture and electoral structure predispose the country to a two-party system. Historically, two parties have dominated, and when third parties have emerged, they have either been subsumed by the dominant parties or simply disappeared when their primary issue of concern was no longer relevant.

The question of whether third parties are bad or good for American democracy dates back almost as far as the democracy itself. But the question has modern implications. Third-party candidates are often seen as spoilers who siphon off votes from the majority's top candidate and thereby enable the less-favored candidate to win. Many pundits argued that was the case during the 2010, 2012, and 2014 congressional elections, when Tea Party candidates challenged Democrats and Republicans for seats in the U.S. House of Representatives and the U.S. Senate. In some races, critics charged that conservative Tea Party candidates who had won primaries against mainstream candidates were weaker general election candidates, and paved the way for some Democratic victories. In other races, Tea Party candidates who ran as independents may have siphoned votes from Republicans, resulting in a stronger Democratic showing. Similar arguments were made in 1992, when pundits charged Reform Party candidate H. Ross Perot with taking votes away from Republican George H. W. Bush and thus ushering Democrat Bill Clinton into the White House.

Do third-party candidacies hurt American democracy by skewing elections away from the third party's major party rival? Or are they good for democracy because they bring out voters who otherwise would have stayed at home and because they help ensure that issues of crucial concern to the electorate get on the national agenda?

Yes: The presence of third-party candidates on a ballot means that the major political party—Democratic or Republican—that is closest to the third party in ideology and in base of support will be hurt. This effect occurs because if the third-party candidate were not on the ballot, many of his or her supporters would vote for the candidate (Democratic or Republican) who is ideologically closest to the third-party candidate. Thus, that major party candidate is at a disadvantage, because the third-party candidate essentially siphons off

or splits the vote for the major party candidate. Democracy is subverted, because often a candidate wins who is least appealing to the majority of voters (that is, those who voted for the losing major party candidate and those who voted for the third-party candidate). As a result, people are highly dissatisfied with both the political process and elected officials.

No: Only through third parties and third-party candidacies can voters get the national agenda they desire. Leading up to the 2012 election, Tea Party candidates were successful at framing the national political agenda, and their prioritization of their key values—including a limited role of government—attracted many voters who previously had been apathetic to the two-party system. Without third parties to spearhead such conversations of democracy, many more people will be turned off by and disaffected from the political process.

Other Approaches: Third parties are a mixed blessing for the United States. Proponents of third parties are correct in asserting that they provide a safety valve for participation by those dissatisfied with the status quo. Third parties have been effective at getting specific policy concerns on the national agenda, even though frequently that has occurred because one of the major parties co-opts a third party's key issue. But supporters of third parties should realize that the electoral politics in the United States is structured to ensure the perpetuation of the two-party system and that, by supporting a third-party candidate, they run the risk of spoiling the chances of their preferred major party candidate.

What do you think?

1. Do you think third parties help or hurt American democracy? Why?

2. What kind of third party do you think would be successful in winning elections?

3. What role might third parties play in the 2016 presidential election? Which political party has the most to lose from a third-party candidate?

A Battle for the Soul of the Republican Party Today

The Republican Party today faces a watershed moment in its history. Throughout the country, a battle for the soul of the party is taking place between staunchly conservative activists and more moderate members of the party. In the wake of the inauguration of Barack Obama in January 2009, a grassroots movement began growing in communities across the United States. Outraged by what they saw as excessive spending by the administration and the Democrats in Congress, and particularly incensed during the debates concerning health care reform, conservative activists formed the Tea Party movement. The moniker is a reference to the colonial era, when colonists dumped tea into Boston Harbor to protest taxes imposed by the British Crown, an action that contributed to the American Revolution.

Although plagued with the growing pains characteristic of virtually any large-scale political movement, Tea Partiers have identified five key principles in which they believe:

- Less government
- Fiscal responsibility
- Lower taxes
- States' rights
- National security

Activism centering on these principles has involved a variety of tactics. Some, such as the formation of a political action committee that contributes donations to endorsed candidates who espouse the Tea Party's views, are standard for such movements. Other strategies have proven more controversial: From the outset, moderate Republicans have feared the electoral threat that Tea Party activists pose. For example, the first candidate endorsed by the Tea Party movement was Speaker of the Florida House of Representatives Marco Rubio, who challenged Florida's then–Republican governor, Charlie Crist, for the GOP nomination for the U.S. Senate. Faced with Rubio's strong challenge and eventually trailing in the polls, Crist effectively conceded the nomination to Rubio and announced his intention to run for the Senate as an Independent candidate, a bid that he lost to Rubio in 2010.

Also controversial has been the Tea Party's ability to drive moderate Republican candidates to the ideological right to placate Tea Party activists. Although helpful in the primary election, this shift to the right has wound up hurting the candidates during general election campaigns. During the 2012 presidential election, many Republicans believed that Tea Party activists weakened Republican nominee Mitt Romney's presidential candidacy by backing a series of candidates—former Alaska governor Sarah Palin, Representative Michele Bachmann of Minnesota, businessman Herman Cain, and former U.S. senator Rick Santorum of Pennsylvania, all of whom were more conservative than Romney—throughout the primary election process. In an effort to bring staunch conservatives into the fold, Romney moved many of his positions to the right, a strategy that hurt his electoral chances against President Obama.

But among the most controversial tactics was the effort undertaken by members of the Tea Party Caucus in Congress to defund health care reform by refusing to authorize spending, which resulted in the 16-day shutdown of the federal government in 2013. In the aftermath of this event, moderate Republicans sought ways to limit the influence of the Tea Party and other conservatives. One method to curb this influence was efforts to change nomination systems within states that had caucuses or conventions, rather than primary elections. Moderate Republicans argue that opening up the nomination system to broader bases of voters within states will lead to greater support for their candidates. Tea Party members and more extreme conservatives argue that the convention system ensures that candidates will espouse the party position, and loyal party members' support will not be diluted.

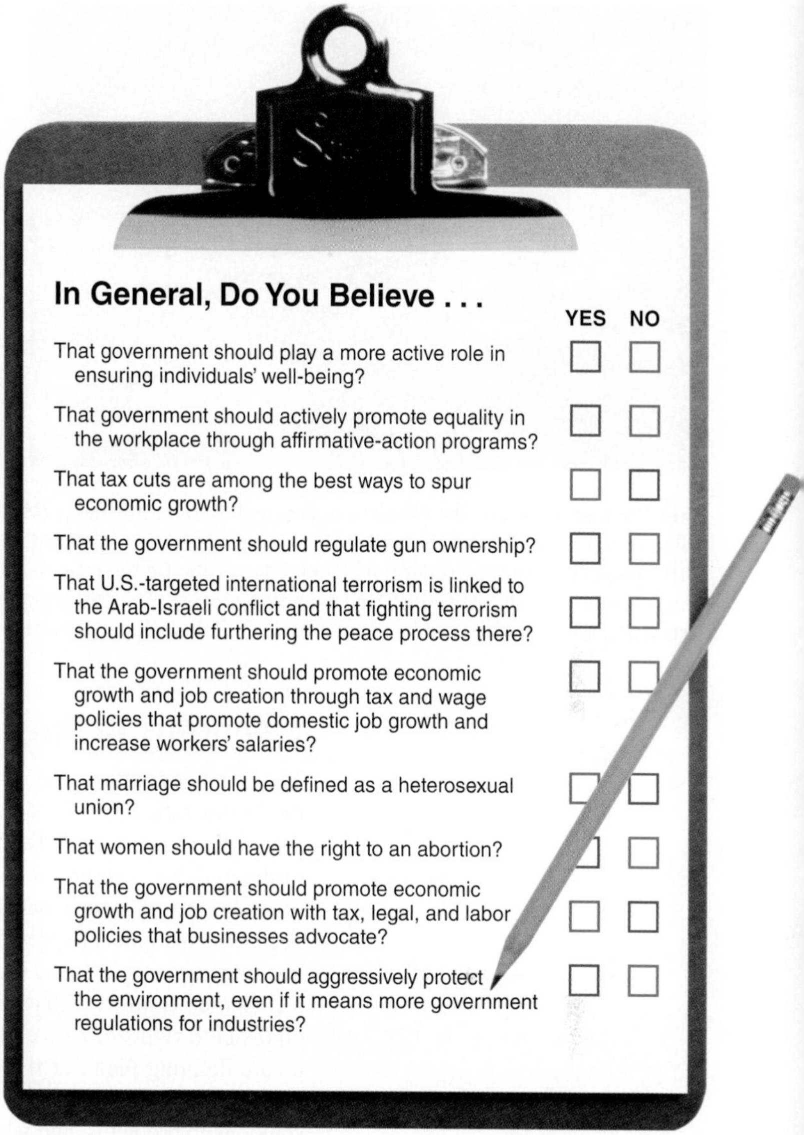

In General, Do You Believe . . .

	YES	NO
That government should play a more active role in ensuring individuals' well-being?	☐	☐
That government should actively promote equality in the workplace through affirmative-action programs?	☐	☐
That tax cuts are among the best ways to spur economic growth?	☐	☐
That the government should regulate gun ownership?	☐	☐
That U.S.-targeted international terrorism is linked to the Arab-Israeli conflict and that fighting terrorism should include furthering the peace process there?	☐	☐
That the government should promote economic growth and job creation through tax and wage policies that promote domestic job growth and increase workers' salaries?	☐	☐
That marriage should be defined as a heterosexual union?	☐	☐
That women should have the right to an abortion?	☐	☐
That the government should promote economic growth and job creation with tax, legal, and labor policies that businesses advocate?	☐	☐
That the government should aggressively protect the environment, even if it means more government regulations for industries?	☐	☐

FIGURE 8.8

Are You Red, Blue, or Purple? News commentators use red and blue to refer to Republicans and Democrats, respectively. Although the basis for an individual's political ideology is complex (see Chapter 1), party identification in the United States often reflects differences in viewpoint on several key issues. Do you know what each party stands for? Do you know which party best represents your views? Take this brief quiz to find out which party you lean toward. Of course, before voting for candidates of that party or even counting yourself as a party identifier, you should further investigate the positions of the parties. The websites listed at the end of the chapter are a good place to start.

Then   Now

> In 1964, members of the Mississippi Freedom Democratic Party (MFDP) challenged the right of the regular Mississippi Democratic Party's delegation to take part in the national party convention in Atlantic City, New Jersey. Aaron Henry, chair of the MFDP delegation (shown left), speaks before the Credentials Committee at the Democratic National Convention, arguing that the state's regular delegation had been chosen in an illegal segregated selection process. The national party sat the all-white regular party delegation but offered the MFDP two seats, which it refused to accept. Today, the Mississippi delegation, like that of every other state's, is quite diverse.

Democrats Today

The Democratic Party today—the party of Barack Obama—is a markedly different party from the Democratic Party President Bill Clinton molded in the 1990s. When it comes to issues and policy priorities, today's Democrats, under Obama's leadership, more resemble the Democrats of the mid-20th century: a party that emphasized a strong role for government and the support of civil rights of groups marginalized in society. In particular, today's Democrats emphasize the need for government to provide a safety net for its most disadvantaged citizens, particularly during tough economic times. President Obama's priority of reforming health care demonstrates the Democrats' comfort with expanding the role of the federal government. And today we see focus on the civil rights of gays and lesbians—particularly centered on the issue of gay marriage—as a core defining plank of the Democratic Party. This is contrasted with Democrats during the Clinton era, sometimes called New Democrats, who were less likely to emphasize government solutions to problems, and who, during a healthy economic era, recognized that *globalization*— the continuing integration of world markets for goods, services, and financial capital—was the most significant factor in framing public policy problems and their solutions.

But coupled with the Democratic Party's emphasis today on its traditional values, there also is an emphasis and a sophistication when it comes to maximizing the use of new technologies in politics, particularly in appealing to younger Millennial voters. Indeed, part of President Obama's success has stemmed from the savvy use of technology—from being among the first political candidates to tap into the resource of social networking by relying on Facebook to mobilize student primary voters in 2008 to raising millions online for his general election campaign in 2012. And so, although the values of today's Democrats resemble those of presidents Franklin D. Roosevelt and Lyndon Johnson more closely than those of Bill Clinton, the means by which these values and priorities are communicated is decidedly modern and technologically sophisticated.

Changing Both Parties: New Technologies

The ways in which party members and voters give and get information, as well as the methods by which parties campaign, have changed drastically in recent years. These changes are discussed in greater detail in Chapter 11, but today more and more people in the electorate are finding information about issues on the Internet and via their cell phones. For their part, the parties are increasingly using new technologies as tools for reaching loyalists and communicating with potential supporters. Take, for example, the way the president now communicates with the electorate. Using a medium unheard of only a decade ago, President Obama regularly relies on YouTube not just as a means of disseminating information but also as a two-way tool of communicating with Americans. And throughout the 2014 congressional campaigns, we saw an ever-expanding use of technology by candidates who Instagram supporters, tweet their staff, text volunteers, organize through Facebook, and raise money online.

During the 2012 campaign, both the Romney and the Obama campaigns used their websites to plug their supporters into assorted outlets for their interest and activism. Both offered downloadable apps that allowed supporters to link their social networking pages and to raise funds by linking the campaign site to their own websites, and this availability has democratized the party process. Partisan activism is no longer limited to individuals who can attend meetings. Whole new forms of Internet activism have emerged. People with access to the Internet can chat, organize, plan, lobby, raise funds, contribute, and mobilize without leaving their desks.

Increasingly, too, we see that the ability of the candidates and the political parties to master the use of technology is paramount in determining the outcome of elections. In 2011, Representative Anthony Weiner (D-N.Y.) resigned his seat in the House of Representatives after media outlets released photographs he had sexted to women. Weiner's comeback effort—a bid for mayor of New York City—was thwarted when new images emerged that Weiner had sent after resignation.

On a less lascivious note, the failure of the Republican Party's ORCA web app, created to help the Romney campaign get out the vote in the 2012 election, will go down as one of the more notorious failures by a political party to use technology. The gaffes—forcing volunteers to print out more than 60 pages of voter registration information the night before the election, failing to forward web searches from the "http" default site to the secure "https" secure site, problems with passwords and log-ins, and the crash of the system at 4 p.m. on Election Day—demonstrate one potential problem with political parties' reliance on technology to mobilize voters: It must be created to be user-friendly to be effective.

Conclusion
Thinking Critically About What's Next in American Political Parties

Despite the cynicism with which people often view them, political parties are a vital institution for the civic engagement of Americans and are essential to democracy. For many citizens, political parties are the gateway to political participation. For others, they provide cues that guide decisions at the ballot box. The role of parties in teaching individuals essential skills that may lead to elective office, in recruiting candidates, in contesting elections, and in governing—all these valuable functions often do not get the recognition they deserve.

Despite the comparative low esteem in which the two major U.S. political parties are currently held, they both have demonstrated enormous adaptability over time. The ability to change in response to constituent demands is a consistent trait of these two dominant parties, and we can see the Republican Party today struggling to adapt to the intraparty wrangling that has occurred between conservative members of the Tea Party and more moderate Republicans. But the cultural and structural forces that perpetuate the two-party system show little sign of relenting. And although groups such as the Tea Party movement provide rich fodder for political pundits who speculate about their importance, in electoral terms third parties have demonstrated very little ability to win elections. Instead, third parties commonly advocate issues that eventually are co-opted by one or both of the major parties, and they sometimes play the role of spoiler in elections.

In the future, the parties will be challenged to adapt. In particular, they will need to adjust continually to new circumstances, as technology changes how the party organizations identify, organize, mobilize, and communicate with the party in the electorate, as well as how the party in government governs. The contemporary faces of the two major parties demonstrate their continuing evolution and responsiveness to their identifiers and constituents.

Summary

1. Are Political Parties Today in Crisis?

Many Americans today do not believe that the Democratic and Republican Parties do an adequate job representing their views. Part of this dissatisfaction stems from the fact that the parties are becoming more polarized, as was evidenced during the 2013 government shutdown.

2. Parties Today and Their Functions

Political parties run candidates in elections in an effort to control government. They advance the cause of civic engagement by facilitating citizens' participation, providing unity and cohesiveness, encouraging civic discourse, and communicating important cues to voters.

3. The Three Faces of Parties

Three spheres of operation of parties are the party in the electorate (the individuals who tend to support a particular party), the party organization (the formal party apparatus), and the party in government (the partisan identification of elected leaders).

4. Political Parties in U.S. History

Political scientists have identified five U.S. party systems. Stretching back to the 18th century, these systems describe the evolution of party competition and dominance. Through these party systems, we see the ideological roots and political foundations of the two dominant political parties today.

5. The Party System Today: In Decline, in Resurgence or a Post-Party Era?

Some political scientists argue that recent times show a decline in the influence of the two major U.S. parties. As factors, they cite waning constituent loyalty to parties, caused by decreases in patronage, and the advent of direct primaries and candidate-centered campaigns. Other scholars assert that parties are rebounding, and they note parties' adaptability, as well as the lack of viable alternatives to the two major parties.

6. Two-Party Domination in U.S. Politics

Explanations of why two political parties dominate include the ideas that parties reflect the dualist nature of conflict in the United States, that the winner-take-all election system creates a two-party structure, that people are socialized to the two-party system, and that election laws strengthen and perpetuate that structure.

7. Third Parties in the United States

Third parties, which include issue advocacy parties, ideologically oriented parties, and splinter parties, sometimes act as a spoiler for one of the two major parties. Although third-party candidates typically lose elections, they do succeed in getting various issues on the national agenda.

8. New Ideologies, New Technologies: The Parties in the Twenty-First Century

Today, the Republican Party is struggling to define itself, trying to balance the demands of staunch conservatives within the party with the desire to win national elections. While New Democrats shy away from the traditional liberal advocacy of government as the chief solution to social problems and focus on globalization as a determining factor shaping public policy dilemmas and their solutions, more traditional Democratic values currently dominate the Democratic Party. Today, both political parties rely on increasingly sophisticated technological advances to communicate with and mobilize voters.

Key Terms

candidate-centered
  campaign 259
candidate committees 260
dealignment 260
divided government 254
grassroots organizing 249

independent 250
loyal opposition 252
New Deal 257
New Deal coalition 257
party identifiers 250
party in government 253

party in the electorate 250
party organization 251
party system 254
patronage 256
platform 248
political machine 256

For Review

1. Why do some political scientists assert that political parties are in crisis today?

2. What functions do political parties perform? How do these functions encourage the civic engagement of Americans?

3. What are the three faces of political parties?

4. Explain the development of the five party systems in U.S. history. Why, historically, does the majority change from one party to another?

5. Why do two parties dominate in politics and government in the United States?

6. Which arguments state that political parties are in decline? What do opponents of these arguments contend?

7. How have third parties influenced recent elections?

8. Describe the struggle today's Republican Party is grappling with, and describe the philosophy of the Democratic Party today.

For Critical Thinking and Discussion

1. How were you socialized to the two-party system? Do your views reflect your parents' views? Were third parties even mentioned in your house when you were growing up?

2. What factors explain the demographic bases of the two major parties? How could each party expand its base of support?

3. What evidence is there that a new party system is emerging? Do the 2014 election results support the claim that a new party system is taking shape?

4. In your view, how should the Republican Party balance the staunchly conservative agenda of the Tea Party faction with the desire to win national elections?

5. In what ways beyond those discussed in the chapter might the Internet and other new technologies be used as means of communication between voters and parties? In your view, what are the most important uses for new technologies in partisan politics?

MULTIPLE CHOICE: Choose the lettered item that answers the question correctly.

1. The formal statement of a party's principles and policy objectives is called a
   a. policy memo.
   b. policy manifesto.
   c. platform.
   d. mission statement.

2. Individuals who identify with or tend to support a party are called the
   a. the party in the electorate.
   b. the party organization.
   c. the party in government.
   d. responsible party members.

3. The formal party apparatus, including committees, party leaders, conventions, and workers, is called
   a. the party in the electorate.
   b. the party organization.
   c. the party in government.
   d. responsible party members.

4. The situation that exists when Congress is controlled by one party and the presidency by the other is called
   a. party disorganization.
   b. bipartisan camaraderie.
   c. divided government.
   d. executive/legislative split.

5. A philosophy supporting the rights and empowerment of the masses as opposed to elites is called
   a. libertarianism.
   b. conservatism.
   c. New Deal philosophy.
   d. populism.

6. A significant shift in party allegiances or electoral support is called
   a. populism.
   b. dealignment.
   c. realignment.
   d. disalignment.

7. Franklin D. Roosevelt's broad social welfare program in which the government would bear the responsibility of providing a safety net to protect the weakest members of society was called
   a. the New Deal.
   b. the Grand Formula.
   c. the War on Poverty.
   d. the Social Contract.

8. The situation in which voters vote for candidates from more than one party is called
   a. populism.
   b. dealignment.
   c. realignment.
   d. ticket splitting.

9. An election structure in which political parties win the number of parliamentary seats equal to the percentage of the vote the party receives is called
   a. a first-past-the-post system.
   b. a winner-take-all system.
   c. a proportional representation system.
   d. a two-party system.

10. An election in which voters choose the party's candidates who will run in the later general election is called a
    a. primary election.
    b. recall election.
    c. general election.
    d. referendum election.

FILL IN THE BLANKS

11. A new, grassroots, conservative protest movement that opposed recent government actions, including economic stimulus spending and health care reform, is called the _____.

12. Political scientists' view that a function of a party is to offer a clear choice to voters by establishing priorities or policy stances that differ from those of rival parties is called the _____.

13. The role that the party out of power plays, highlighting its objections to policies and priorities of the government in power, is called the _____.

14. Organizations that candidates form to support their individual election are called _____.

15. A campaign in which an individual seeking election, rather than an entire party slate, is the focus in a _____.

Answers: 1. c, 2. a, 3. b, 4. c, 5. d, 6. c, 7. a, 8. d, 9. c, 10. a, 11. Tea Party movement, 12. responsible party model, 13. loyal opposition, 14. candidate committees, 15. candidate-centered campaign.

Internet Resources

The American Presidency Project
www.presidency.ucsb.edu/platforms.php The American Presidency Project website at the University of California–Santa Barbara provides the party platforms of every party whose presidential candidate received electoral votes.

Democratic National Committee
www.democrats.org The Democrats' website contains hotlinks for state and local party websites and opportunities for volunteering, internships, and employment, as well as party position papers and platforms and candidate information.

Project Vote Smart
www.vote-smart.org This nonpartisan site provides independent, factual information on candidates and elected officials of all political parties.

Republican National Committee
www.gop.com The Republicans' site also has links for state and local party sites and opportunities for volunteering, internships, and employment, as well as party position papers and platforms and candidate information.

Recommended Readings

Berlatsky, Noah. *Does the U.S. Two-Party System Still Work?* Belmont, CA: Greenhaven Press, 2010. Part of the At Issue series, this work examines the effectiveness of the U.S. party system.

Flammang, Janet. *Women's Political Voice.* Philadelphia: Temple University Press, 1997. A well-researched account of women's political participation in general and women's participation in political parties in particular.

Hershey, Marjorie Random. *Party Politics in America,* 15th ed. New York: Longman, 2012. A classic work on American political parties, analyzing the changing roles of parties in the 20th century and the impact of the campaign finance system on political parties.

Lijphart, Arend. *Electoral Systems and Party Systems: A Study of Twenty-Seven Democracies 1945–1990.* New York: Oxford University Press, 1994. An exploration of the nature of party systems in many industrialized democracies, both historically and in modern times.

Pimlott, Jamie Pamelia. *Women and the Democratic Party: The Evolution of EMILY's List.* Amherst, NY: Cambria Press, 2010. Consists of both descriptive and quantitative analysis of the growth and impact of EMILY's List, the leading fund-raising organization that supports Democratic women candidates.

Schattschneider, E. E. *Party Government.* New York: Rinehart, 1942. A classic work that explains the nature of political parties and their influence on party government.

Skocpol, Theda, and Vanessa Williamson. *The Tea Party and the Remaking of Republican Conservatism.* New York: Oxford University Press, 2012. An examination of the underlying values of Tea Party activists combined with an analysis of the larger movement, its impact on the American political realm, and the movement's future.

Movies of Interest

Game Change (2012)
This film is based on John Heilemann and Mark Halperin's account of Sarah Palin's entry into the 2008 presidential race as U.S. senator John McCain's vice-presidential running mate.

Primary Colors (1998)
Starring John Travolta, and based on the anonymously written book of the same name, this popular movie—a fictionalized account of Bill Clinton's 1992 campaign—provides insight into the primary election season of a presidential nominee.

Chicago 1968 (1996)
This is an episode of *The American Experience,* an award-winning PBS documentary, which examines the chaotic events of the 1968 Democratic National Convention in Chicago using interviews with historians, convention participants, and protestors along with actual news footage of the events.

City Hall (1996)
This film, starring Al Pacino and John Cusack, shows the workings of a corrupt political machine—and the consequences of that corruption.

The War Room (1993)
This movie is a behind-the-scenes look at Bill Clinton's 1992 presidential campaign from the first primaries and caucuses, through to the national convention and his ultimate election win.

CHAPTER 9

ELECTION NIGHT

Elections, Campaigns, and Voting

THEN

Political party–dominated campaigns and grassroots activism were deciding factors in how people voted.

NOW

Candidate-centered campaigns rely on paid professionals to shape and spin candidates' messages—and on costly media buys to disseminate them.

NEXT

How will new technologies drive how people vote and how campaigns are run?

How will changes in the campaign finance system, including the advent of super PACs, affect how campaigns are waged?

How will the new campaign environment affect the diversity of candidates willing to seek public office?

PREVIEW

In this chapter, we explore opportunities for—and the value of—citizens' participation in electoral politics; the processes of voting and running for office; and the elements of modern campaigns and elections. We also analyze the factors that determine whether an individual will vote, how voters decide among candidates, and why some people do not vote.

FIRST, we examine political participation in the electoral process.

SECOND, we consider the various kinds of elections in the United States.

THIRD, we focus on the act of voting, including how the changing voting environment, especially mail-in balloting, is changing participation in elections, as well as the effect that the type of ballot used can have on election outcomes.

FOURTH, we examine the requirements of running for office as well as how candidates make the choice to run.

FIFTH, we look at the nature of political campaigns today, paying particular attention to campaigns' extensive use of professional consultants and deep reliance on electronic media and the Internet.

SIXTH, we survey legislators' efforts at regulating federal campaign contributions, and the aftermath of the *Citizens United* Supreme Court decision.

SEVENTH, we probe the long duration and various stages of presidential campaigns.

EIGHTH, we look at who votes—the factors influencing voter participation.

NINTH, we delve into the question of how voters decide on the candidates whom they will endorse at the ballot box.

TENTH, we investigate the many reasons why some people do not vote, including factors such as lack of efficacy, voter fatigue, and negative campaigns.

grassroots organizing
tasks that involve direct contact with voters or potential voters

When Americans think about

politics, their first thought is often about elections, campaigns, and voting. In the eyes of many of us, these activities are the essence of political participation, because it is through the electoral process that we feel we participate most directly and meaningfully in our democracy. Often viewed as the pinnacle of the democratic experience, the act of voting is the culmination of a wide range of forms of political engagement. In the discussion that follows, we see the interconnectedness of many aspects of political campaigns and elections, including fund-raising, **grassroots organizing,** candidate selection, and voter mobilization. These opportunities for civic participation in the democratic process are present in such a broad variety of forms that they are accessible to everyone who wants to be engaged.

Political Participation: Engaging Individuals, Shaping Politics

Elections, campaigns, and voting are fundamental aspects of the civic engagement of Americans and people in other democracies. These activities represent concentrated forms of civic engagement and are important both for the polity as a whole and for the individuals who participate.[1] But intensive political engagement—working on a campaign or running for office, say—rarely represents an individual's first foray into a civically engaged life. Rather, people who are engaged in the political process usually are initiated through smaller, less intensive steps. Perhaps a group of classmates who especially enjoy the political discussions in your American government class might continue their conversations of democracy over a cup of Starbucks after class. Those same classmates might begin regularly reading political blogs and daily newspapers to become better informed about candidates and issues. Some members of the informal group might decide to hear a candidate who is giving a speech on campus—and wind up volunteering on his or her campaign. Political engagement often begins with small steps such as these, but the cumulative results are large: They help to ensure that the government is representative of the people and responsive to their needs. Representative governments, which are the product of individuals' political engagement, tend to be more stable and to make decisions that best reflect the needs and the will of the people who elect them.

Direct forms of political participation such as voting, volunteering on a campaign, and running for office are of keen interest to political scientists and scholars of civic engagement. Many scholarly analysts have noticed an overall decrease in levels of political participation. As discussed in Chapter 7, political scientist Robert Putnam argues that the United States is seeing a decline in its social capital, the social networks and reciprocal relationships characteristic of a community or a society. Some scholars have challenged Putnam's assertion that social capital has declined. They point out that new forms of social capital have arisen in the form of online social networks, instant messaging, and Internet activism to replace the traditional social networks that Putnam studied. Despite these differing views, there is consensus that civic participation is essential and that among its most important forms is electoral political participation.

Indeed, elections offer a wealth of opportunities for citizen involvement:

- Members of political parties recruit candidates to run for election.
- Cadres of volunteers organize campaign events, including fund-raisers, rallies, and neighborhood leafleting.
- Phone bank volunteers try to persuade other people to participate in the electoral process—for instance, by giving a campaign contribution, putting a candidate's sign on their lawn, or simply voting for the candidate.

- Other volunteers focus exclusively on **GOTV**—that is, they work to get out the vote. They register voters for both primary and general elections, and they provide absentee ballots to people who are ill or who will be out of town on Election Day. Then on Election Day, they remind people to vote by phoning them or knocking on their doors and asking if they need a ride to the polls.[2]
- Others (who may be paid) volunteer to work at the polls on Election Day.

Although each volunteer effort plays a part in ensuring the success of a democracy, a key form of political participation is running for office. Electoral contests in which more than one candidate seeks to win office are a fundamental component of a democracy.

Elections in the United States

Every state holds at least two types of elections. A *primary election* comes first and determines the party's nominees—those who will run for office. For most political offices, there is little or no competition in the primary election. But in presidential and gubernatorial primary elections, vigorous contention is often the rule, particularly within the out-of-power party. House and Senate primary elections that lack an incumbent candidate (that is, one who has been elected to that office before) are also often highly competitive as many candidates attempt to win their party's nomination.

> Are more people really "Bowling Alone"? Political scientist Robert Putnam has argued that the United States is experiencing a decline in social capital because its citizens are participating less in civic life. But perhaps Americans are engaged in civic life in ways very different from those of previous generations. Here, a group of Wii bowling enthusiasts compete in a friendly match in an Illinois restaurant.

GOTV
get out the vote

In a **general election,** the parties' respective nominees run against each other, and voters decide who should hold office, since the person with the most votes wins. For example, in the 2014 U.S. Senate elections, South Carolina's incumbent Republican senator Lindsey Graham won his party's primary, as did his Democratic challenger Brad Hutto (Presidential elections, discussed later in this chapter, are a notable exception.) The degree of competition in general elections depends on a number of factors, including the presence of and the strength of incumbency, the degree of party competition, and the level of the office. In recent times, presidential elections have been brutally competitive, as have been certain gubernatorial races and many congressional contests in which no incumbent is seeking reelection. Some communities, particularly big cities, may also experience intense competition for office in general elections.

general election
an election that determines which candidates win the offices being sought

Nominations and Primary Elections

In a primary election, voters decide which nominees the political parties should run in the general election. But *which* voters decide varies greatly from state to state. In some states, only registered party members are eligible to vote in primary elections, whereas in other states, any registered voter can vote in any party's primary, and in North Dakota, voters are not even required to register.

In U.S. presidential primaries, voters do not vote directly for the candidate whom they would like their party to nominate. Instead, the popular vote determines which candidate's delegates will attend the party's nominating convention and vote for that party's nominee. This system of selecting delegates through primary voting is different from the earlier system, when party leaders selected the presidential nominee with little or no input from the rank-and-file party members.

>Chicago police restrained protesters during the 1968 Democratic National Convention by using tear gas, among other methods. As a result of the riots during this convention, sparked by dissatisfaction over the selection of Hubert Humphrey as the nominee by party insiders, the two major U.S. parties made major reforms to the delegate-selection process.

caucus
meeting of party members held to select delegates to the national convention

open primary
a type of primary in which both parties' ballots are available in the voting booth, and voters select one on which to register their preferences

closed primary
a type of primary in which voting in a party's primary is limited to members of that party

Super Tuesday
the Tuesday in early March on which the most primary elections are held, many of them in southern states

The two major U.S. parties made reforms to the earlier delegate-selection process after the 1968 Democratic National Convention in Chicago. Anti–Vietnam War activists outside the convention protested the presumed nomination of Vice President Hubert Humphrey as the Democratic Party's presidential candidate. Humphrey had not won any primaries but was favored among the convention's delegates who had been hand-picked by party leaders. The activists instead supported the candidacy of Senator Eugene McCarthy (D-Minn.), an outspoken war opponent. The demonstrations turned into riots when Chicago police beat the protesters. The Democratic National Committee, in an attempt to address the concerns of those complaining that they had been excluded from the nomination process, appointed the McGovern-Fraser Commission (named after its co-chairs), which recommended a series of reforms to the delegate-selection process.

The reforms, many of which both the Democratic Party and the Republican Party adopted, significantly increased the influence of party voters. Voters could now select delegates to the national conventions, a power previously restricted to the party elite. Party voters today select the delegates at statewide conventions or through primary elections or **caucuses**—meetings of party members held to select delegates to the national convention. The reforms also included provisions that would ensure the selection of a more representative body of delegates, with certain delegate slots set aside for women, minorities, union members, and young party voters. These slots roughly correspond with the proportion of support the party receives from those groups.

When an individual is elected to be a delegate at the national convention, often that delegate has pledged to vote for a specific candidate. That pledge is nonbinding, however, since delegates of a losing candidate often switch their support to the apparent victor.

TYPES OF PRIMARY ELECTIONS   In an **open primary** election, any registered voter can vote in any party's primary, as can independent voters not registered with a party. In the 17 states with an open presidential primary, parties' ballots are available in the voting booth, and the voter simply selects privately or publicly one on which to register his or her preferences.

In a **closed primary** election, voting in a party's primary is limited to members of that party. In some states, voters must declare their party affiliation well in advance of the primary election—sometimes as many as 60 days before. In other states, voters can declare their party preference at the polling place on the day of the election. Such restrictions on who can vote in a party's primary originated in the parties' maneuvering to have the strongest candidate nominated. For example, if a popular incumbent president were running unopposed in a primary election, members of the president's party might choose to vote in the other party's primary as a way of scheming to get a weak candidate nominated. A closed primary aims to thwart that strategy.

PRESIDENTIAL PRIMARIES   The states determine the timing of primary elections. Historically, states that held their presidential primaries earlier in the year had a greater say in determining the nominee than did states with later primaries. The reason is that candidates tended to drop out if they did not win primaries, did not meet media expectations, or ran out of funds. (See "Thinking Critically About Democracy.") In general, past presidential primaries gave great sway to the agricultural states, because many of the more urban states' primaries fell later in the season.

Super Tuesday is the day in early March (March 6 in 2012) on which the most presidential primary elections take place, many of them in southern states. Super Tuesday had been the fruit of a successful effort in 1988 by several southern and rural states to hold their primaries

Democracy

Should the United States Have a National Primary?

The Issue: The party primary process that selects each party's nominee for president was a hot-button issue in the 2008 presidential race. Historically, the primary system focused enormous attention on the states of Iowa, where the first caucus is held, and New Hampshire, where the first party primary takes place. In these states, voters have had the opportunity to gain a deep familiarity with all the candidates seeking the parties' nominations. But critics of the system have charged that these two states' political cultures do not reflect that of the vast majority of Americans. As a result, many of the most populous states moved their primaries to the earliest day allowed by the political parties—in 2008, that day was February 5. Other states, including Pennsylvania, Texas, West Virginia, and Kentucky, held off having their primaries in the hopes that one state could find itself in the position of kingmaker by bringing one of the party candidates over the top in the needed delegate count. Given this structure, many citizens have asked: "Is this any way to begin electing a president?"

Should states matter when it comes to selecting the parties' nominees? One potential solution to the skewed emphasis on various states is to hold a national primary so that party members throughout the country can choose their nominees on the same day. People have voiced arguments for and against the idea of a national primary.

Yes: Having a national primary will help the parties, because it will ensure that the nominee chosen in each case is the best candidate for the party. With the shift to a national primary, states that currently have late primaries will no longer be forced to accept a nominee chosen by party members who might be very different from themselves. Furthermore, if more people have a say in choosing their party's nominee, voter turnout might rise in both the primary and the general election. Holding a national primary also will shorten the election season, so that voters will be less fatigued by the length of the campaign.

No: The primary system ensures that small, agricultural states have a voice in national politics. In the general election, smaller states are overshadowed because the Electoral College, which is based on state population, determines the winner. The current primary and caucus system enables voters in those states to analyze the candidates thoroughly, without the noise and distraction that would come with a large-scale, media-saturated national primary. And because the voters in states such as Iowa and New Hampshire are, after all, party members, they naturally understand that a large part of their responsibility is to select the nominee best equipped to win the general election.

Other Approaches: Some have suggested the idea of holding regional primaries instead of one national primary, with a different region holding its primary election first in each presidential election year so that no region would have the influence that Iowa and New Hampshire now enjoy. Each region would include a mix of large and small states and urban and rural areas. Candidates would need to campaign throughout each region in turn rather than the entire country, thus allowing them to focus their efforts more than they would be able to with one national primary, and with three or four regional primaries, the campaign season would still be shortened significantly, thus eliminating voter fatigue.

What do you think?

1. Do you believe that we should have a national primary? Explain.

2. What impact would a national primary have on your home state's say in the nomination process? How will small states fare compared with large states? Rural compared with urban?

3. What influence do you think a national primary or regional primaries would have on voter turnout? What effect might either type of primary have on how presidential campaigns are waged? Would money be more or less important? Why?

on the same day so as to increase their political importance and allow expression of southern voters' political will.[3] In 2007, the Super Tuesday strategy was challenged by state legislators in some of the most populous states, including California, New York, Illinois, and New Jersey, who sought to have their presidential primaries on the earliest day that national political party rules allowed. In 2008, that day, dubbed "Super-Duper Tuesday" by the media, was February 5. In all, 20 other states jumped on the early-primary bandwagon, with the result that 24 states held their primaries and caucuses on February 5, 2008. But because of the reapportionment and redistricting process that reconfigured congressional districts in 2011–2012, the majority of the most populous states did not seek to have early primaries in 2012, fearing that their congressional maps might not be complete in time. There is, however, the expectation that many of the most populous states will again seek to move their primaries forward during the 2016 presidential race.

General Elections

In a general election, voters decide who should hold office from among the candidates determined in the primary election. Most general elections, including presidential elections, are held on the first Tuesday after the first Monday in November. But because the states schedule and oversee elections, you might find that your gubernatorial election, state legislative election, or town council election occurs at a different time of the year.

General elections for Congress and most state legislatures feature a winner-take-all system. That is, the candidate who receives the most votes wins that office (even if that total is not a majority, or even if an opponent receives only one vote fewer than the victor). Thus, a member of the U.S. House of Representatives or Senate can be elected with less than a majority of the votes in his or her district, particularly when three or more candidates are seeking that seat.

Because electoral law varies from state to state, and counties and municipalities within those states have their own structures of governance, less common kinds of elections are possible and are used in some locales. For example, some states require a runoff election when no candidate receives the majority of the votes cast. In a **runoff election,** if no candidate receives more than 50 percent of the vote, several of the top vote-getters (usually the top two) run in another, subsequent election. Typically, the field of candidates is winnowed down until one candidate receives the requisite 50 percent plus one vote. Runoff elections often occur in *nonpartisan* municipal elections, in which candidates do not run on a party label.

Owing to advances in technology, runoff elections can occur immediately in some states when needed. In an **instant runoff election,** a computerized voting machine simulates the elimination of last-place vote-getters. How does this system work? In an instant runoff, voters rank candidates in order of preference (first choice, second choice, and so on). If any candidate garners more than 50 percent of all the first-choice votes, that candidate wins. But if no candidate gets a majority of first-choice votes, the candidate in last place is eliminated electronically. The voting machine computer then recalculates the ballots, using the second-choice vote for those voters who voted for the eliminated last-place finisher; in effect, every voter gets to choose among the candidates remaining on the ballot. This process is repeated until a candidate who receives more than 50 percent of the votes emerges. Today's voting machines allow this process to take place instantly.

runoff election

a follow-up election held when no candidate receives the majority of votes cast in the original election

instant runoff election

a special runoff election in which the computerized voting machine simulates the elimination of last-place vote-getters

referendum

an election in which voters in a state can vote for or against a measure proposed by the state legislature

initiative

a citizen-sponsored proposal that can result in new or amended legislation or a state constitutional amendment

proposition

a proposed measure placed on the ballot in an initiative election

> A referendum is an election in which voters in a state can vote for or against a measure proposed by the state legislature. Here, opponents of an amendment that defined marriage solely as a union between a man and a woman rally in 2012, though the amendment passed.

Referendum, Initiative, and Recall

Whereas primary elections and general elections select an individual to run for and serve in office, other kinds of elections are held for the purpose of deciding public policy questions. Although no national mechanism allows all Americans to vote for or against a given policy proposal, citizens can directly decide policy questions in their states by referendum or initiative.[4]

A **referendum** is an election in which voters in a state can vote for or against a measure proposed by the state legislature. Frequently, referenda concern matters such as state bond issues, state constitutional amendments, and controversial pieces of legislation. An **initiative,** sometimes called an initiative petition, is a citizen-sponsored proposal that can result in new or amended legislation or a state constitutional amendment. Initiatives differ from referenda in that they are typically propelled to public vote through the efforts of citizens and interest groups.[5] The initiative process usually requires that 10 percent of the number of the voters in the previous election in that state sign a petition agreeing that the **proposition,** or proposed measure, should be placed on the ballot. An example of an initiative is the 64th amendment to Colorado's constitution, an initiative that Colorado voters passed in 2012, which reformed the state's policy regarding the criminalization of the possession, sale, and distribution of cannabis. The state law currently allows for adults 21 years and older to grow up to three mature and three immature plants in a locked space, to possess the harvest of these plants, to distribute up to one ounce of marijuana produced by these plants to another adult, and to travel (within the state) with one ounce in possession. In addition, the use of marijuana is legal in a manner consistent with the state's liquor consumption laws.[6]

A third type of special election, the recall, differs from referenda and initiatives in that it is not concerned with policy-related issues. Rather, the **recall** election allows voters to cut an officeholder's term of office short. Recall elections are typically citizen-sponsored efforts that demonstrate serious dissatisfaction with a particular officeholder. Concerned citizens circulate a petition, and, after they gather the required number of signatures, an election is held to determine whether the official should be thrown out of office. For example, in 2012, Wisconsin voters succeeded in getting a recall vote to oust Republican governor Scott Walker from office, but they failed in their efforts, when 53 percent of voters voted to keep the conservative in office.

> An initiative is a citizen-sponsored proposal that can result in new or amended legislation or a state constitutional amendment, as was the case in Colorado, when activists initiated an amendment to the state constitution that legalized the growing and use of marijuana.

The Act of Voting

The process of voting begins when a voter registers to vote. Voting registration requirements vary greatly from state to state. Some states require registration months in advance of an election; others allow voters to register on the day of voting. In the United States, the voters use an **Australian ballot,** a secret ballot prepared by the government, distributed to all eligible voters, and, when balloting is completed, counted by government officials in an unbiased fashion, without corruption or regard to individual preferences. Because the U.S. Constitution guarantees the states the right to conduct elections, the mechanics and methods of voting vary widely from state to state. Some states use touch-screen technology; others employ computer-based ballots or punch cards that are counted by computers. Still other states use traditional lever ballots, in which voters pull a lever to register their vote for a particular candidate. Despite those differences, all ballots are secret ballots.

Although secret ballots are the norm today, that was not always the case. From the days of the early republic through the 19th century, many citizens exercised their right to vote using oral votes cast in public or written votes witnessed by others; some made their electoral choices on color-coded ballots prepared by the political parties, which indicated which party the voter was supporting.

recall
a special election in which voters can remove an officeholder before his or her term is over

Australian ballot
a secret ballot prepared by the government, distributed to all eligible voters, and, when balloting is completed, counted by government officials in an unbiased fashion, without corruption or regard to individual preferences

The 2000 Election and Its Impact

In the 2000 presidential election between Democrat Al Gore and Republican George W. Bush, an enormous controversy erupted over the voting in Florida. Because of the closeness of the electoral vote, the outcome of the Florida election turned out to be pivotal. But the tallies in that state's election were in question, not only because of the narrow difference in the number of votes won by each candidate, but also because of the voting process itself. Florida citizens cast their vote on a punch card by poking through a **chad,** a ready-made perforation, near the name of their candidate of choice. Officials then counted the punch card ballots using a computer program that calculated votes by counting the absence of chads. But in the case of the 2000 election, thousands of ballots could not be read by the computer and needed to be counted by hand. This unexpected development put election officials in the difficult, and ultimately deeply controversial, position of gauging "voter intent." If a chad was hanging by one perforation only, did the voter intend to vote for that candidate? What if the chad was "pregnant" (that is, sticking out but not removed; see the photo)? What if the chad was dimpled, and the voter had cast his or her entire ballot by only dimpling the chads?

chad
a ready-made perforation on a punch card ballot

> The problems with chads: A hanging chad . . . and a pregnant chad.

In the end, the U.S. Supreme Court had the final say. On December 12, 2000, the Court halted the hand counting of ballots in Florida, with the Court's majority ruling that the differing standards of hand counting ballots from one county to the next and the absence of a single judicial officer charged with overseeing the hand counts violated the equal protection clause of the Fourteenth Amendment to the U.S. Constitution. The ruling meant that George W. Bush, who was leading in the count, was certified the winner of the Florida race, thus securing that state's 25 Electoral College votes and the presidency of the United States.

Indignation surrounding the 2000 election resulted in federal policy changes to the conduct of elections by the states. The key policy revision came through the passage of the Help America Vote Act of 2002 (HAVA). HAVA allocated $650 million to assist states in changing from punch card ballots to electronic voting systems and set a deadline of 2005 for states to comply. To date, most states have implemented the election reforms required by HAVA, though voters in four counties in Idaho still rely on punch card ballots.[7]

Types of Ballots

Two types of ballots are most commonly used in general elections in the states today. The first, the **party-column ballot,** organizes the candidates by party, so that all of a given party's candidates for every office are arranged in one column. The opposing party's candidates appear in a different column.

The impact of a party-column ballot is twofold: First, party-column ballots increase voters' tendency to vote the "party line," that is, to vote for every candidate of a given party for every office. In fact, some states provide a party lever, which allows a voter to vote for all of a given party's candidates simply by one pull of a lever or one press of a "vote party" button. Second, because they increase the tendency to vote the party line, party-column ballots also increase the **coattail effect,** the phenomenon whereby *down-ballot candidates* (candidates who are running for lower-level offices, such as city council) benefit from the popularity of a top-of-ticket nominee. Often, the composition of city councils, county legislatures, and even state legislatures changes because of a coattail effect from a popular presidential or gubernatorial candidate. Because party-column ballots strengthen political parties, parties tend to favor this type of ballot, which is the most commonly used ballot in the United States.

Another type of general election ballot is the **office-block ballot,** which arranges all candidates for a particular office under the name of that office. Office-block ballots are more likely to encourage ticket splitting, where voters "split their ticket"—that is, divide their votes—between candidates from different parties.[8] Because office-block ballots deemphasize political parties by breaking up the party line, the parties do not tend to favor them.

Why Ballot Design Matters

The 2000 presidential election voting in Florida provides evidence that not only the voting process but also the design of ballots can make a difference in outcomes. Specifically, with respect to the vote in Florida's Palm Beach County, where voters push a button on their voting machine ballot to register their vote, critics charge that the ballot in use, the *butterfly ballot* (so called because candidates are listed on two "wings" with a common "spine"), was particularly confusing to voters.

Because of the lack of ballot clarity, many Democrats complained that this ballot layout put the Gore/Lieberman ticket at a disadvantage. Although supporters of Reform Party candidate Pat Buchanan in Palm Beach County projected that he should have received at best 1,000 votes there, Buchanan received over 3,400 votes. Many people, including Buchanan *himself,* believed that these votes were mistakenly cast for him and intended for Al Gore.[9]

In fact, an additional 19,000 votes were nullified in the Palm Beach County election because voters cast *two* votes for president, presumably with balloters realizing too late that they had pushed the wrong button. Buchanan himself addressed this issue, saying: "If the two candidates

party-column ballot
a ballot that organizes the candidates by political party

coattail effect
the phenomenon by which candidates running for lower-level offices such as city council benefit in an election from the popularity of a top-of-ticket nominee

office-block ballot
a type of ballot that arranges all the candidates for a particular office under the name of that office

they pushed were Buchanan and Gore, almost certainly those are Al Gore's votes and not mine. I cannot believe someone would vote for Gore and say 'I made a mistake, I should have voted for Buchanan.' Maybe a small minority of them would have done that. But I—I've got to think that the vast majority of those [votes] would naturally belong to Al Gore and not to me."[10]

Voting by Mail

A relatively recent development is the advent of statewide voting by mail, a practice that states have adopted in an attempt to increase voter participation by making voting more convenient. Traditionally, **absentee voting,** in which voters cast their ballots in advance by mail, was allowed only when disability, illness, school, work, service in the armed forces, or travel prevented voters from casting a ballot in their voting precincts. Every state has a provision that allows some voters—the elderly, the infirmed, or those traveling—to vote via absentee ballot. To cast a traditional absentee ballot, an individual must typically apply (before a specific state-designated deadline) to vote by absentee in the county where he or she usually votes and is then mailed a ballot. The voter then votes and mails back the ballot. The absentee ballots are counted and added to the votes cast in the voting precincts. Requirements for absentee ballots vary from state to state.

absentee voting
casting a ballot in advance by mail in situations where illness, travel, or other circumstances prevent voters from voting in their precincts

Increasingly, many states accept mail-in ballot applications simply because absentee voting is more convenient for the voter. The first experiment with statewide vote by mail occurred in Oregon in 1996. In a special election there, where officials had predicted a turnout of less than 50 percent, more than 66 percent of voters cast their ballots. This experiment brought another benefit: It saved taxpayers more than $1 million. Oregon decided to continue the practice in the presidential elections and has regularly seen voter turnout at 85 percent in those elections. Oregon has now taken the drastic step of abandoning voting in polling places on Election Day.

Since that time, the practice of enabling citizens to cast their ballots by mail—often before Election Day—has become much more widespread, as indicated in Figure 9.1. In Oregon and now in Washington State, all voters are sent mail ballots automatically. In 32 states plus the District of Columbia, any registered voter can cast a ballot in person during a designated period before Election Day. States vary in how long they allow early voting, with some states holding balloting for 4 days, others up to 45 days. Most states with early voting require that polling places—usually government offices—be open at least one weekend day, enabling those who work long hours to cast their ballots.

There are obvious advantages to voting by mail. When voting becomes easier, more people participate. Further, increased participation may bring to office candidates who are more representative of the will of the people because more people had a say in their election.

Some scholars, however, have criticized both the vote-by-mail and early voting trends. One important criticism is that early voting means that people vote before the final days of the campaign, thus casting their ballots before some additional last-minute information might be revealed about a candidate. Voting by mail also increases the chances of vote fraud. Even though states take measures to ensure the principle of "one person, one vote," voting by mail presents opportunities for corruption. Voting at the polls requires a face-to-face encounter, but voting by mail does not, so ballots could be stolen from individuals' mailboxes or intercepted after having been mailed by a voter.

Voting by mail also may eliminate the privacy associated with voting in recent times. With mail

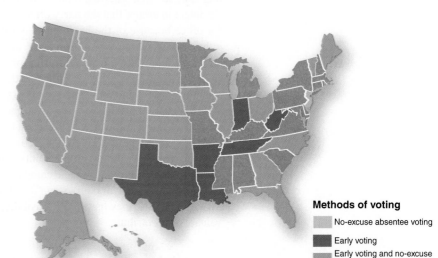

Methods of voting
No-excuse absentee voting
Early voting
Early voting and no-excuse absentee voting
All-mail voting
No early voting: excuse required for absentee

FIGURE 9.1

Methods of Voting in the States

SOURCE: National Conference of State Legislatures, "Absentee and Early Voting," 2014, www.ncsl.org/research/elections-and-campaigns/absentee-and-early-voting.aspx.

balloting, the vote occurs in a less controlled setting, and the voter might feel pressured by others to select a particular candidate. In contrast, booth voting affords privacy and secrecy that go far toward ensuring that the votes cast behind the curtain reflect the individual voter's will.

Finally, voting by mail may undermine feelings of civic engagement by eliminating a source of psychological rewards for voters. Going to a polling place, signing the voting registry, entering the voting booth, and casting your vote can elicit feelings of patriotism, civic pride, and fulfillment of civic responsibility—the sense that you are doing your duty to help ensure the election of the best-qualified candidates. Although the results may be the same with voting by mail, some evidence suggests that voting by mail does not bring with it the same sense of civic satisfaction that voting at a polling place confers.

Running for Office: The Choice to Run

The reasons that individuals become political candidates vary almost as much as the individuals do. Yet four types of motivation are generally in play when a person decides to declare a candidacy:

- Sense of civic responsibility—the feeling on the candidate's part that he or she bears an obligation to govern
- Sense of party loyalty—of filling the need for parties to run viable candidates
- Interest in increasing the candidate's name recognition and stature in the community, often for business reasons
- Personal goals, and in particular, interest in electoral politics and officeholding as a career

Some people believe they have an obligation to put their experience, knowledge, and skills to work for the greater good of the community or country. Often these civically motivated people become politically involved out of concerns about specific issues. For example, Representative Carolyn McCarthy (D-N.Y.) ran for and won a seat in the House of Representatives after her husband was killed and her son was injured in a mass shooting on the Long Island Railroad. While nursing her adult son's injuries after the senseless tragedy, McCarthy decided to run when her congressman voted to repeal a ban on assault weapons.

Sometimes an individual may choose to run for office out of a sense of party duty. The candidate may run as a "sacrificial lamb" for a seat he or she has little chance of winning, mainly with the intent to ensure that the party offers an alternative to the favored candidate. Some people run for office because of the heightened stature that a candidacy brings to their "regular" careers, either through name recognition or networking opportunities.

Other people are motivated to run for a particular office because of personal goals. Many of these individuals seek elected office as their career. Whereas presidents and governors typically serve no more than eight years, members of Congress, state legislators, county commissioners, and council members often serve for decades. Holding office is what they do—and because of the advantages of incumbency, once elected, many remain in office for years. Other candidates run for office because of political ambitions. For example, a town council member who aspires to serve in the state legislature might run for county commissioner even if she thinks she will not win because she realizes that running a viable campaign might help her in a later bid for the statehouse.

Many candidates, of course, run for office for a combination of reasons. They might believe, for example, that they have a responsibility to serve their country *and* that they have something valuable to contribute.

Formal Eligibility Requirements

Article I of the U.S. Constitution specifies some minimum criteria for those seeking election to federal office:

- **President.** A candidate for the presidency must be a natural-born citizen. Naturalized citizens, who are born citizens of another country and then choose to become American citizens such as Ileana Ros-Lehtinen (R-Fla.), a member of the House of Representatives and a native of Cuba, cannot run for president. Presidential candidates also must be at least 35 years old. The youngest person elected president was the 43-year-old John F. Kennedy, but Theodore Roosevelt, who assumed the presidency after William McKinley's assassination, was the youngest to hold the office, at age 42. A presidential candidate also must have been a resident of the United States for 14 years by the time of inauguration.

- **Vice president.** A vice-presidential candidate, like a contender for the presidency, must be a natural-born citizen and must be at least 35 years old; he or she must not be a resident of the same state as the candidate for president with whom he or she will serve. John Breckinridge, elected vice president in 1856 at age 35, was the youngest person to win the office.
- **U.S. senator.** A candidate for the Senate must have citizen status of at least 9 years, must be at least 30 years old when taking office, and must be a resident of the state from which he or she is elected. Currently the youngest person serving in the Senate is Chris Murphy (D-Conn.), born in 1973 and sworn into the Senate at age 39 in 2013.
- **U.S. representative.** A candidate for the House of Representatives must be a citizen for at least 7 years, must be at least 25 years old when taking office, and must be a resident of the state from which he or she is elected. Representative Patrick Murphy (D-Fla.), born in 1983, was elected to the House in 2012 and was sworn into office at age 29.

>Informal qualifications for Congress vary according to the political culture in the district. Openly gay members of Congress are a rarity. U.S. Senator Tammy Baldwin (D-Wisc.) is the only openly lesbian member of Congress. Before being elected to the Senate in 2012, Baldwin had served seven terms in the U.S. House of Representatives.

Typically, a state's constitution determines the minimal qualifications for the governorship and the state legislature, and these vary from state to state. In general, state requirements address the same issues as federal guidelines—citizenship, age, and residency.

Informal Eligibility Requirements

In addition to the legal eligibility requirements prescribed by the federal and state constitutions, informal eligibility criteria—that is, the characteristics that voters expect officeholders to have—help to determine who is qualified to run for a particular office. By and large, the eligibility pool for elected office depends on the office—and so although your car mechanic might be considered a good candidate for your town council, he would not likely meet the informal eligibility criteria to be elected president of the United States.

Generally speaking, the higher and more prestigious the political office, the greater the informal eligibility requirements are. On the local level, particularly in smaller communities, an individual would be considered eligible to run for town council if he or she was liked and respected in the community, had lived in the community long enough to know the voters, and was gainfully employed, a homemaker, or retired.

Farther up the political office ladder, state legislative candidates in most states are expected to have some kind of professional career. Still, there is a great deal of variation from state to state, and certainly nonprofessionals occupy many state legislative seats. State legislatures tend to be dominated by lawyers and business professionals, occupations that offer the prestige to be considered part of the informal eligibility pool and that allow enough flexibility to facilitate campaigning and legislative work.

The informal eligibility requirements for federal office are even more stringent. Voters expect candidates for the House of Representatives, the U.S. Senate, and the presidency to have higher qualifications than candidates for state and local offices. Among most congressional constituencies, candidates for federal office would be viewed as "qualified" to hold office if they had a college degree, considerable professional and leadership experience, and strong communication skills. But informal qualifications vary according to the political culture in a district, with some districts favoring a particular religious affiliation, ethnicity, or other characteristic. In races for the U.S. Senate and the presidency, the popular press examines the minutest details of candidates' professional and educational backgrounds. For example, sometimes it is not enough that candidates are college graduates; where they went to college, whose university is more prestigious, and who had the higher grade point average are all fodder for the media and political pundits.

The Nature of Political Campaigns Today

Campaigns today are different from the campaigns of the 1980s or even the early 1990s. The main reasons for the changes are the professionalization of campaign staffs; the dramatically expanded role of the media, the Internet, and digital technologies; and the changing nature of campaign finance driven by candidates' ever-rising need for funding to keep pace with the unprecedented demands of contemporary campaigning.[11]

The Professionalization of Political Campaigns

campaign consultant
paid professional who specializes in the overall management of political campaigns or an aspect of campaigns

One of the most significant changes in the conduct of campaigns is the rise in prominence of **campaign consultants,** paid professionals who specialize in the overall management of political campaigns or an aspect of campaigns, such as fund-raising or advertising. Previously, volunteers who believed in the party's ideals and in the candidate ran most campaigns. Although some volunteers may have been motivated by the expectation that they would personally benefit from the election of their candidate, their efforts focused largely on the election itself—of a single candidate or a slate of candidates.

> In 1960, campaigns, even those for the presidency, relied primarily on political party organizations and cadres of volunteers, including celebrities like famed author Kurt Vonnegut, who tells then-senator Kennedy, "On occasion, I write pretty well." Now, campaigns are highly professional, with the labors of a campaign divided among many hired consultants, and technology driving participation among voters. Here, Senator Claire McCaskill's website directs individuals on how to donate, keep informed, or volunteer on the campaign.

In contrast, professional consultants dominate modern campaigns for federal offices, many state offices, and some municipal offices. Typically, these advisors receive generous compensation for their services. Although professional consultants may not be as dedicated to a single candidate as earlier grassroots volunteers were, these strategists are typically committed to seeing their candidate elected and often are quite partisan, usually working only for candidates of one party throughout their careers. For example, during the 2012 presidential campaign, President Barack Obama relied on Democratic strategist David Axelrod as his senior campaign advisor. Axelrod had managed Obama's 2008 campaign and then served as senior advisor to the president before resuming his campaign position in the president's reelection bid. Similarly, Matt Rhoads, who managed Mitt Romney's presidential campaign, works exclusively for Republican candidates.

One of the top jobs in a political campaign is that of **campaign manager,** a professional whose duties include a variety of strategic and managerial tasks. Among these responsibilities may be the development of the overall **campaign strategy,** the blueprint for the campaign, which includes a budget and fund-raising plan, an advertising strategy, and staffing objectives. Once the campaign strategy is set, the campaign manager often hires and manages the office staff; selects the campaign's theme, colors, and slogan; and shapes the candidate's image. Another crucial campaign professional is the pollster, who conducts focus groups and polls that help develop the campaign strategy by identifying the candidate's strengths and weaknesses and by revealing what voters care about.

Other professionals round out the candidate's team. A **fund-raising consultant** works with the candidate to identify likely contributors and arranges fund-raising events and meetings with donors. Policy directors and public relations consultants help to develop the candidate's stance on crucial issues and to get the candidate's positions out to the voters, and a **media consultant** brings the campaign message to voters by creating handouts and brochures, as well as newspaper, radio, and television promotions. And now campaigns increasing rely on social media consultants to bring the campaign to voters through YouTube, Facebook, Twitter, e-mail campaigns, Web-based advertising, and blogs (see Chapter 11).[12]

campaign manager
a professional whose duties include a variety of strategic and managerial tasks, from fund-raising to staffing a campaign

campaign strategy
blueprint for the campaign, including a budget and fund-raising plan, advertising strategy, and staffing plan

fund-raising consultant
a professional who works with candidates to identify likely contributors to the campaign and arranges events and meetings with donors

media consultant
a professional who brings the campaign message to voters by creating handouts and all forms of media ads

Media and New Technologies: Transforming Political Campaigns

Today, with the presence everywhere of the media in all its forms—television, Internet news sites, blogs, Twitter, radio, podcasts, newspapers, magazines—citizens' access to information is unprecedented. Whereas our ancestors had far fewer sources of news—word of mouth and the printed newspaper dominated for most of American history—people today can choose from a wide range of information sources and a bounty of information. Today, 24-hour news channels such as Fox News, CNN, and MSNBC compete with Internet news outlets, satellite radio programming, and news text messages to grab audience attention, while candidates attempt to spin coverage through the creation of videos available on their YouTube channels. But not all of this bombardment of information is accurate.

Given the abundance of information disseminated today, and in light of its diverse and sometimes questionable sources, engaged citizens have a greater responsibility to be discerning consumers of the news, including coverage of campaigns, voting, and elections. They cannot be passive listeners and spoon-fed watchers of news as it is dished out on blogs or Facebook, or by daily newspapers, nightly newscasts, and the occasional weekly or monthly periodical. Vivé Griffith, at the University of Texas at Austin's Think Democracy Project, writes: "The challenge for the contemporary citizen is to be more than an audience member. Voters have unprecedented opportunities to access information and, at the same time, myriad ways to see issues obscured. An informed polity is essential to a democracy, and it can be difficult to sort through whether our media-saturated world ultimately serves to make us more or less informed."[13] We consider media coverage of elections, campaigns, and voting in detail in Chapter 10.

Revolutionizing the Campaign: New Technologies

New technologies have dramatically changed the conduct of political campaigns in recent years, and further developments promise to force campaigns to continue to evolve and adapt as

How Political Campaigns Have Changed in the Past 30 Years

Then (1980s)	Now
Many campaigns were managed and staffed by volunteers.	Campaigns are increasingly managed professionally by "guns for hire" and often have an extensive staff dedicated to strategy setting, fund-raising, and media relations.
Grassroots activism was the norm in all but the largest campaigns.	Netroots activism—political activism driven by candidates' websites, tweets, blogs, and social networking sites—uses the Internet as a complement to traditional grassroots campaign efforts.
Money was a crucial consideration in campaigns, but grassroots activism demanded fewer financial resources.	Money rules the day in most campaigns, but technology has the potential to level the campaign playing field.

WHAT'S NEXT?

> How can the Internet change the need for money in political campaigns?

> Given the extent of technologically driven activism during the 2014 campaigns, is there still a role for grassroots activism in future campaigns? Explain.

> Will campaigns continue to be dominated by professional staffers? Why or why not?

technology generates new and faster ways to communicate and interact. Through texting, tweeting, Instagram, YouTube, and webchatting, candidates can use technologies to communicate with voters, mobilize supporters, and interact with the media. The Internet is among the most valuable and powerful new tools used by candidates. It serves as an efficient means by which office seekers can communicate with potential supporters, contributors, and the media. Candidates' websites provide a readily available forum where the electorate can find out about candidates' experiences, policy positions, and priorities. Voters can use this information to make more informed decisions in the voting booth. In addition, the Internet is a powerful fund-raising tool. In discussing the growth of campaign fund-raising on the Internet, Eli Pariser, founder of MoveOn.org's Peace Campaign, noted that "candidates are wasting their time with rubber-chicken donors,"[14] an allusion to donors who contribute to candidates by paying to attend campaign dinners.

Using e-mail and instant messaging, campaigns can communicate quickly with the media, both informing them of positive campaign developments and spinning negative developments in the best possible light for the candidate. Through campaign blogs, candidates can also supplement the information available in more traditional news media outlets. Internet communities and social networking sites such as Facebook and Twitter also provide a powerful tool for campaigns and an important mechanism for political engagement for individuals. Some Internet communities may be dedicated to advancing the electoral chances of a candidate for a particular office—and may or may not be sponsored by that candidate. But Internet communities and social networking sites also provide a forum for average citizens to engage in political discourse, become informed about candidates and issues, and get information that facilitates activism in their communities.

Citizens United v. Federal Election Commission
Supreme Court ruling stating that corporations and labor unions are entitled to the same First Amendment protections that individuals enjoy, resulting in drastically increased spending through superPACs by corporations and labor organizations

super PACs
political organizations that use contributions from individuals, corporations, and labor unions to spend unlimited sums independent from the campaigns, yet influencing the outcomes of elections

Money and Politics

Money—lots of it—is essential in electoral races today. Money and the modern campaign are inextricably linked because of the importance of costly media advertising in modern campaigns.[15] Federal regulations require any group that contributes to candidates' campaigns to register as a political action committee (PAC), and these organizations are subject to constraints in the amount of money that they can contribute to candidate campaigns. But today, in the wake of the Supreme Court ruling *Citizens United v. Federal Election Commission* in 2010, these regulation are being circumvented through the increasing use of a new class of **super PACs,** political organizations that use contributions from individuals, corporations, and labor unions to spend unlimited sums independent of the campaigns, yet influencing the outcomes of elections. Although super PACs are a relatively recent phenomenon, the influence of money in electoral politics goes back a long time, as do the efforts to regulate it.[16] Reformers have attempted to limit the influence of money on political campaigns for almost as long as campaigns have existed.

Early Efforts to Regulate Campaign Finance

Efforts to limit the influence of money started after a scandal that erupted during the administration of President Warren Harding (1921–1923). In 1921, the president transferred oil reserves at Teapot Dome, Wyoming, from the Department of the Navy to the Department of the Interior. The following year, Harding's secretary of the interior leased the oil fields without competitive bidding. A Senate investigation into the deal revealed that the lessee of the fields had "loaned" the interior secretary more than $100,000 in order to win political influence. The interior secretary was convicted and sentenced to a year in prison and a $100,000 fine. Dubbed the Teapot Dome scandal, this sordid affair led Congress to try to limit the influence of money on politics through legislation.

The Federal Corrupt Practices Act of 1925 sought to prevent future wrongdoing. This act aimed to regulate campaign finance by limiting campaign contributions and requiring public disclosure of campaign expenditures, and it was one of the first attempts at campaign finance regulation. But because the act did not include an enforcement mechanism, it was a weak attempt to fight corruption, and candidates found numerous loopholes in the law.

The Political Activities Act of 1939, also known as the Hatch Act, marked another congressional attempt to eliminate political corruption. With the growth of the federal bureaucracy as a result of the New Deal programs of President Franklin D. Roosevelt, several scandals had emerged, demonstrating the problems that could arise when government employees took an active role in politics. The Hatch Act banned partisan political activities by all federal government employees except the president, the vice president, and Senate-confirmed political appointees. The act also sought to regulate the campaign finance system by limiting the amount of money a group could spend on an election and placing a $5,000 cap on contributions from an individual to a campaign committee. Although the Hatch Act was more effective than the Federal Corrupt Practices Act of 1925, it also contained a significant loophole: Groups that wanted to spend more than the legislated limit of $3 million simply formed additional groups.

© N. Y. "Tribune."

> A *New York Tribune* cartoon titled "The First Good Laugh They've Had in Years" depicts the Democrats' jubilation over the Teapot Dome Scandal of 1921, which saddled Republicans with a reputation for corruption. The scandal led Congress to try to limit the influence of money on politics.

In 1971, Congress passed the Federal Election Campaign Act (FECA), the most significant attempt at overhauling the nation's campaign finance system. The law was sponsored by Democrats in Congress who were concerned about the enormous fund-raising advantage the Republicans had had during the 1968 presidential election. This law placed considerable limitations on both campaign expenditures and campaign contributions, and it provided for a voluntary tax-return check-off for qualified presidential candidates. This provision enables you, when filling out your federal income tax return, to contribute three dollars, which will go toward the matching funds that qualified presidential candidates receive.

In 1974, FECA was amended to place more stringent limitations on individual contributions and to limit expenditures by PACs, and it revamped the presidential election process by restricting spending and providing public financing for qualified candidates who abided by the limits. The act also required public disclosure of contributions and expenditures by all candidates for federal office. Most important, the act created an enforcement mechanism in the Federal Election Commission (FEC), the agency charged with enforcing federal campaign finance laws.

The Court Weighs In: Money = Speech

In the subsequent, highly significant Supreme Court case *Buckley v. Valeo* (1976), however, the plaintiffs contended that placing limitations on the amount an individual candidate could spend on his or her own campaign violated First Amendment protections of free speech. The Court agreed, ruling that "the candidate . . . has a First Amendment right to engage in the discussion of public issues and vigorously and tirelessly to advocate his own election."[17] This ruling paved the way for the subsequent explosion in the formation of PACs by recognizing political expenditures as a protected form of speech and removing limits on overall campaign spending, on personal expenditures by an individual candidate, and on expenditures not coordinated with a candidate's campaign and made by independent interest groups. In its *Buckley* ruling, the Court boldly overturned the limitations on expenditures that to that point had been written into law.

The Growth of PACs

After the ruling, the number of political action committees shot up dramatically, as Figure 9.2 demonstrates, and since the *Citizens United* decision in 2010, the number of PACs has again risen dramatically. Today, nearly 5,700 organizations raise and spend money to influence

POLITICAL **Inquiry**

FIGURE 9.2 ■ PAC COUNT, 1974 TO PRESENT What trends does the figure show with respect to the number of political action committees since 1977? For which groups has the growth in PACs risen most steeply?

SOURCE: Federal Election Commission, "PAC Count: 1974 to Present," 2014, www.fec.gov/press/summaries/2011/2011paccount.shtml.

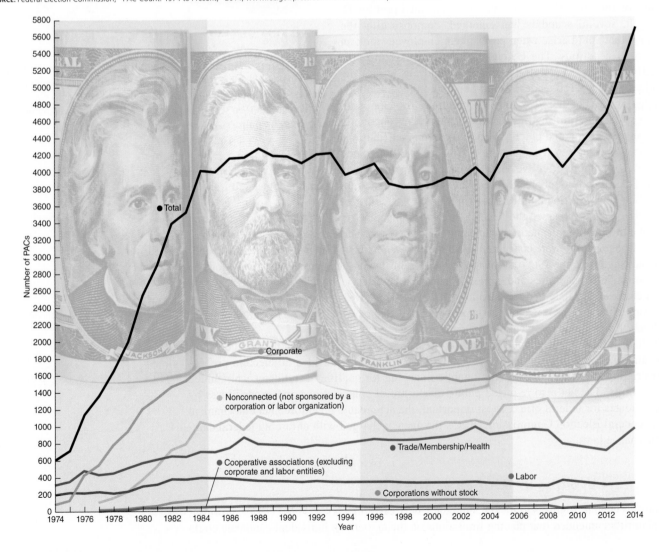

federal elections. The figure shows that the number of corporate PACs alone nearly doubled between 1977 and 1980. Many of those PACs were formed by corporations that do business with the federal government and by associations whose members' livelihoods are significantly affected by federal regulations, including defense contractors, agricultural producers, and government employee unions. The ballooning of the number of PACs over time is indicative of the increased power that PACs have wielded in campaigns for federal office since 1980.

Independent Expenditures

Because expenditures are protected from limitations, many PACs now use independent expenditures to spend unlimited sums for or against political candidates.[18] **Independent expenditures** are outlays, typically for advertising supporting or opposing a candidate, that are uncoordinated with a candidate's campaign. Although PAC contributions to a candidate are limited, a PAC can spend as much as it wants on advertisements and mailings, supporting (or working against) candidates for federal office. This tactic is legal if these expenditures are not coordinated with the candidates' campaigns. Until the Court's ruling in the 2010 *Citizens United* decision, these ads could not "expressly advocate" a candidate by using terms such as "Vote for . . ." or "Elect . . . ,"[19] but the Court's decision eliminated those restrictions.

independent expenditures outlays by PACs and others, typically for advertising for or against a candidate, but uncoordinated with a candidate's campaign

The Bipartisan Campaign Finance Reform Act of 2002

Throughout the 1980s and 1990s, campaign finance reform was a perennial topic in presidential campaigns, and candidates roundly criticized the role of "special interests" in politics. But members of Congress had little to gain from reforming the system that had brought them to office. Although various campaign finance proposals were considered, only one passed both the Senate and the House, in 1992, and President George H. W. Bush vetoed it.

Then in 2002, the world's largest energy-trading company and one of the nation's biggest corporations, Enron, collapsed after an internal accounting scandal, leaving in its wake furious stockholders, employees, and retirees whose financial health depended on the company. Investigations revealed extensive corporate fraud, including accounting improprieties that had enabled corporate leaders to lie about profits and debt. Investigations also revealed that Enron had contributed nearly $4 million to state and federal political parties in soft money contributions for "party-building activities," such as voter registration drives and later generic campaign advertising. Public indignation at the scandal flared, leading to the passage of the McCain-Feingold Act. This bipartisan campaign reform proposal, named after its two sponsors, Senator John McCain (R-Ariz.) and Senator Russell Feingold (D-Wisc.), had been making its way at a snail's pace through committees before the Enron scandal broke.

The McCain-Feingold Act, formally known as the Bipartisan Campaign Finance Reform Act (BCRA) of 2002, banned nearly all soft money contributions, although PACs can contribute up to a total of $10,000 to state, county, or local parties for voter registration and GOTV drives. Table 9.1 shows that the law also increased individual contribution limitations and regulated some independent expenditure advertising. Although BCRA sought to fix many of the system's problems, some of the remedies remain in dispute.

One aspect of the McCain-Feingold Act that became the subject of a series of legal challenges was a ban on independent issue ads that aired close to elections. In many campaigns, groups would target candidates with advertisements critical of their issue positions. In 2003, Senator Mitch McConnell (R-Ky.), an opponent of the act, and a variety of groups affected by the new law (including the National Rifle Association and the California State Democratic Party) filed *McConnell v. the Federal Election Commission*.[20] The suit alleged that McCain-Feingold was a violation of the plaintiffs' First Amendment rights because the act prohibited airing these

>Before the 2007 Supreme Court decision that limited the McCain-Feingold Act, this ad would not have been legal if it had run less than 60 days before the general election.

Campaign Finance Rules under the Bipartisan Campaign Finance Reform Act, 2014 Cycle

TABLE 9.1

	TO EACH CANDIDATE OR CANDIDATE COMMITTEE PER ELECTION	TO NATIONAL PARTY COMMITTEE PER CALENDAR YEAR	TO STATE, DISTRICT, AND LOCAL PARTY COMMITTEE PER CALENDAR YEAR	TO ANY OTHER POLITICAL COMMITTEE PER CALENDAR YEAR**	SPECIAL LIMITS
INDIVIDUAL MAY GIVE	$2,600*	$32,400*	$10,000 (combined limit)	$5,000	$123,200* overall biennial limit: $48,600* to all candidates; $74,600* to all PACs and parties[†]
NATIONAL PARTY COMMITTEE MAY GIVE	$5,000	No limit	No limit	$5,000	$45,400* to Senate candidate per campaign[‡]
STATE, DISTRICT, AND LOCAL PARTY COMMITTEE MAY GIVE	$5,000 (combined limit)	No limit	No limit	$5,000 (combined limit)	No limit
PAC (MULTI CANDIDATE) [§]MAY GIVE	$5,000	$15,000	$5,000 (combined limit)	$5,000	No limit
PAC (NOT MULTI CANDIDATE) MAY GIVE	$2,600*	$32,400*	$10,000 (combined limit)	$5,000	No limit
AUTHORIZED CAMPAIGN COMMITTEE MAY GIVE	$2,000[§§]	No limit	No limit	$5,000	No limit

*These contribution limits are increased for inflation in odd-numbered years.

**A contribution earmarked for a candidate through a political committee counts against the original contributor's limit for that candidate. In certain circumstances, the contribution may also count against the contributor's limit to the PAC; 11 CFR 110.6. See also 11 CFR 110.1(h).

[†]No more than $46,200 of this amount may be contributed to state and local party committees and PACs.

[‡]This limit is shared by the national committee and the Senate campaign committee.

[§]A multicandidate committee is a political committee with more than 50 contributors that has been registered for at least 6 months and, with the exception of state party committees, has made contributions to five or more candidates for federal office; 11 CFR 100.5(e)(3).

[§§]A federal candidate's authorized committee(s) may contribute no more than $2,000 per election to another federal candidate's authorized committee(s); 2 U.S.C. 432(e)(3)(B).

SOURCE: Federal Election Commission, "Contribution Limits for 2013–2014, 2013, www.fec.gov/info/contriblimitschart1314.pdf.

ads 30 days before a primary election and 60 days before a general election. The Supreme Court at first upheld the ban, but then reversed itself in another 5-4 decision. In 2007's *Federal Election Commission v. Wisconsin Right to Life, Inc.*,[21] the justices held that advertising within the 30- and 60-day windows could not be prohibited, thus paving the way for its extensive use in the 2008 presidential race.

Circumventing the Rules: 527s and 501(c)4s

501(c)4s
nonprofit organizations operated exclusively for the promotion of social welfare, including lobbying or engaging in political campaigning

Loopholes in the campaign finance law became apparent with the emergence of new forms of political groups, so-called 527s and 501(c)4s. **501(c)4s** are nonprofit organizations operated exclusively for the promotion of social welfare, including lobbying or engaging in political campaigning. 501(c)4s go largely unregulated by the FEC, and their activities are not subject to the transparency requirements that interest groups and campaign organizations are. Named after the section of the IRS tax code that regulates such organizations, a **527** is a tax-exempt group that raises money for political activities. If a 527 engages only in activities such as voter registration, voter mobilization, and issue advocacy, it has to report its activities only to the government of the state in which it is located or to the IRS. Disclosure to the FEC is required only if a 527 engages in activities expressly advocating for the election or defeat of a federal candidate, or if it participates in electioneering communications.

In 2004, two 527s—Swift Boat Veterans and POWs for Truth, which opposed the presidential bid of Senator John Kerry (D-Mass.), and MoveOn.org, which opposed President George W. Bush's candidacy—grabbed national attention as each ran television "issue advocacy" advertisements across the country targeting the opposing candidate. Many observers viewed the emergence of these and other 527s as attempts to get around the ban on unlimited soft money contributions to political parties. Campaign finance reform advocates note that several 527s have been partially funded by large contributions from a few wealthy individuals, bolstering the charge that 527s are a way to evade the soft money ban. In 2012, 527s spent about $200 million to influence the outcome of federal elections through voter registration and mobilization efforts and through ads that, though purportedly issue-based, typically criticized a candidate's record. Like 527s, 501(c)4s are used by their often-wealthy organizers as a means of channeling money to influence political campaigns. For example, Americans for Prosperity, a libertarian group that spent nearly $35 million for negative advertisements opposing many of President Obama's policies, has been financed by billionaire brothers David H. and Charles Koch.

527

a tax-exempt group that raises money for political activities

The Court Weighs In (Again): The Birth of Super PACs

The 1976 Supreme Court ruling in *Buckley v. Valeo* eventually would be the basis of the ruling in *Citizens United* that paved the way for super PACs. The year 2010 saw one of the most dramatic episodes in U.S. campaign finance history, with the Supreme Court's decision in the *Citizens United* case. According to this ruling, corporations and labor unions are entitled to the same First Amendment protections that individuals enjoy. The impact of the *Citizens United* decision has enormously increased the importance of money in politics, as corporations and labor unions now recognize the uncontestable influence that they may have in federal elections. The controversial 5-4 decision was hailed by conservatives as a victory for free speech rights and was decried by liberals as an avenue by which corporations could increase their stranglehold on politics and the policy process.

The impact of the *Citizens United* decision could be seen both in the 2012 presidential campaign and in the 2014 midterm congressional elections, as candidates courted wealthy donors who might fund a super PAC to advocate for their candidacy. For example, after Newt Gingrich's failed effort to win the Republican nomination in 2012, Mitt Romney swayed billionaire conservative casino mogul Sheldon Adelson to donate more than $10 million to the super PAC Restore Our Future, which supported Romney. By 2014, nearly 1,000 groups had organized as super PACs, having raised almost $600 million and spending more than $330 million to influence federal elections in the 2013–2014 election cycle.[22]

Presidential Campaigns

To many Americans, presidential campaigns epitomize the democratic process. In presidential election years, nonstop campaigning affords ample opportunities for the public to learn about the candidates and their positions. Campaigns also provide avenues for participation by the people—for example, by volunteering in or contributing to candidates' campaigns or even just by debating candidates' views on Twitter. Although these opportunities for citizen engagement are especially abundant during a presidential election, they arise well before that time, because potential candidates typically position themselves years in advance of a presidential election to secure their party's nomination and to win the general election.

Party Conventions and the General Election Campaign

As Figure 9.3 illustrates, political parties hold conventions in presidential election years to select their party's nominee for president of the United States. As discussed in Chapter 8 and as reviewed earlier in this chapter, the delegates to the national conventions are chosen by citizens in each state who vote in their parties' primary elections. After the conventions are over and the nominees have been decided (typically by late August or early September of the election year), the nominees and their vice-presidential running mates begin their general election campaigns. Usually, the parties' choice of nominee is a foregone conclusion by the time of the convention. Eligible incumbent presidents (who have served only one term) are nearly always nominated again, and the nominee of the opposing party is often determined by the primary results.

The Electoral College

The votes tallied on Election Day determine which presidential candidate's slate of electors will cast their ballots, in accordance with state law. There are 538 electors in the Electoral College because the number of electors is based on the number of members of Congress—435 in the House of Representatives, 100 in the Senate—plus 3 electors who represent the District of Columbia. A presidential candidate needs a simple majority of votes (270) to win. Figure 9.4 shows the electoral votes of each state from the 2012 election.

On the Monday following the second Wednesday of December, the slates of electors chosen in each state meet in the state capitals and casts their electoral votes. The results are then

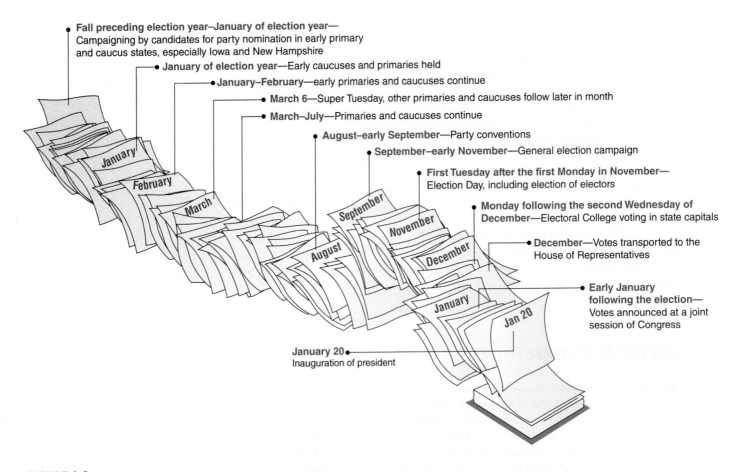

- **Fall preceding election year–January of election year—**Campaigning by candidates for party nomination in early primary and caucus states, especially Iowa and New Hampshire
- **January of election year—**Early caucuses and primaries held
- **January–February—**early primaries and caucuses continue
- **March 6—**Super Tuesday, other primaries and caucuses follow later in month
- **March–July—**Primaries and caucuses continue
- **August–early September—**Party conventions
- **September–early November—**General election campaign
- **First Tuesday after the first Monday in November—**Election Day, including election of electors
- **Monday following the second Wednesday of December—**Electoral College voting in state capitals
- **December—**Votes transported to the House of Representatives
- **Early January following the election—**Votes announced at a joint session of Congress
- **January 20**Inauguration of president

FIGURE 9.3

TIMELINE OF PRESIDENTIAL ELECTIONS U.S. presidential elections occur every four years; the next one will take place in November 2016.

announced in a joint session of Congress in early January. In most presidential elections, however, the winner is known on election night, because analysts tabulate the outcome in each state and predict the electoral vote. The winner takes the oath of office as president in inaugural ceremonies on January 20.

Who Votes? Factors in Voter Participation

Not all people are equally likely to participate in the process of voting for the president or other government officials. Yet of all the forms of political participation, the act of voting has been analyzed perhaps more than any other.[23] Scholars such as Angus Campbell, Philip E. Converse, Warren Miller, and Donald Stokes have examined what factors influence who votes and how voters decide.[24] They and others have analyzed how characteristics such as education level, income, age, race, and the degree of party competitiveness in a given election influence whether a person will vote.[25] Of course, in considering demographic characteristics such as voter age and income level, we must remember that these are merely generalizations.

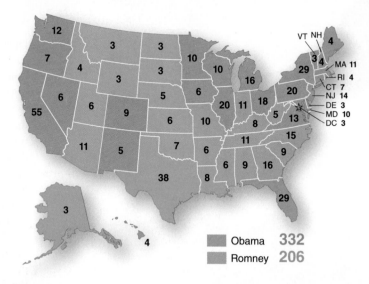

Obama **332**
Romney **206**

FIGURE 9.4

THE 2012 ELECTORAL COLLEGE VOTE In what areas of the country did President Obama get much of his support? Where did Mitt Romney win? Which candidate won the most populous states?

Education Level—the Number One Predictor of Voting

An individual's level of education is the best predictor of whether that person will vote. Table 9.2 shows that in 2012 less than a third of U.S. citizens with less than a ninth-grade education were registered to vote, and only 22 percent actually voted. As education increases, so, too, does the likelihood of voting, with measurable differences even among those who have only attended college and those who have graduated. Among those with a college or an advanced degree, about 80 percent are registered and three-quarters voted in 2012's presidential election.

TABLE 9.2

U.S. Voters' Rates of Registering and Voting by Educational Attainment, 2012

EDUCATIONAL ATTAINMENT	REGISTERED (%)	VOTED (%)
Total	65	56
Less than 9th grade	29	22
9th to 12th grade, no diploma	43	32
High school graduate	59	49
Some college or Associate's degree	71	61
Bachelor's degree	76	70
Advanced degree	79	75

SOURCE: U.S. Census Bureau, Current Population Survey, "Voting and Registration in the Election of November 2012," 2012, www.census.gov/hhes/www/socdemo/voting/publications/p20/2012/tables.html.

The Age Factor

During any presidential campaign, you will hear much about age as a factor in the likelihood of voting. Despite efforts by organizations such as MTV's Rock the Vote, and despite campus-focused initiatives by presidential campaigns, young adults are less likely to vote than are Americans who are middle aged and older, though that figure has increased in recent years.[26] In the 2012 election, the turnout rate among young Americans—those aged 18 to 29—had dropped slightly from the 2008 rates, which had seen the highest turnout rate for voters of that age group since 18-year-olds were first granted the right to vote in 1972. Although the 2012 turnout rate may not have broken records, the youth vote was key in President Obama's election: 62 percent of young voters favored Obama. In 2012, young people's comparatively high participation rendered them a political force to be reckoned with. But Figure 9.5, which plots the percentage of people in various age groups who voted in the 2008 presidential election, shows a historic trend: As Americans age, they are more likely to vote. There are numerous reasons why young people do not vote. Among 18- to 24-year-olds, the reason most often cited is that they were too busy or had a schedule conflict, but members of this age group are also more likely to report that they forgot to vote or were out of town. Age also is related to mobility—young people might move when they leave for college or to start a new job, and mobility depresses voter turnout.

FIGURE 9.5

AGE AND VOTING IN THE 2012 PRESIDENTIAL ELECTION For which age group was the percentage of people voting highest? For which age group was the voting percentage lowest? What overall pattern does the graph show? How do you explain it? In 2012, about 38 percent of individuals aged 18 to 24 voted, compared with a national average of 56 percent. Why did the youth vote matter in 2012? Do you think it will be as important in 2016?

SOURCE: U.S. Census Bureau, "Voting and Registration in the Election of November 2012," www.census.gov/hhes/www/socdemo/voting/publications/p20/2012/tables.html.

Race and Voter Participation

As the 2012 presidential contest demonstrated, race plays a significant role in voter turnout. For decades after the Voting Rights Act of 1965 ensured that African Americans could freely exercise the right to vote, turnout rates among African Americans lagged substantially behind those of non-Hispanic white Americans. In the 2012 presidential election, however, voter participation among African Americans surpassed that of whites (see "Analyzing the Sources"). This increase in participation by African Americans has been a steady trend that was bolstered significantly by the candidacy of Barack Obama in 2008 and 2012. Importantly, in addition to increased turnout by African Americans, Barack Obama's candidacy netted him 95 percent of all votes cast by African Americans, a performance consistent with his 2012 election.

Voting participation among Hispanics and Asian Americans continues to lag behind that of whites and African Americans. Nonetheless, the percentage of non-Hispanic whites who reported they voted in the 2012 presidential election marked a significant increase over previous years, and came in the wake of the 2008 election, which saw increases in the turnout rate among all racial and ethnic groups. Today, Hispanics are viewed as an increasingly important constituency because they are an expanding proportion of the population.

Income—A Reliable Predictor of Voting

Besides education, income is one of the best predictors of whether an American will vote.[27] Typically in recent presidential election years, U.S. citizens with the lowest income level have had voter turnout levels of 50–60 percent, whereas those with the highest income level have had turnout levels above 85 percent.[28] As income increases, so too does the likelihood of voting.

EXPLORING RACE AND VOTING

Voter turnout rates in presidential elections, 1988–2012

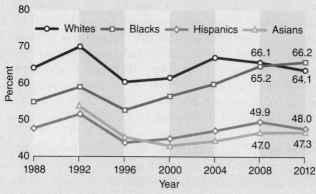

NOTE: Hispanics are of any race. For the years 1988 through 2008, whites, blacks, and Asians include only non-Hispanics. For 2012, blacks and Asians include Hispanics. Data for non-Hispanic Asians were not available in 1988.

SOURCE: P. Taylor, and M. H. Lopez, "Six Take-Aways from the Census Bureau Voting Report," 2013, www.pewresearch.org/fact-tank/2013/05/08/six-take-aways-from-the-census-bureaus-voting-report/.

Evaluating the Evidence

1. In general, what has been the trend with regard to voter turnout among blacks and whites over time?

2. What has been the trend among Hispanics and Asian Americans? In your view, why has participation by members of these groups differed from that of blacks and whites?

3. From these data, we see a significant occurrence in 2012. Can you identify this event? Why might this have occurred?

The reasons for the close correlation between income and likelihood of voting are complex.[29] One possibility is that people with lower incomes may have less belief than higher-income earners that the government listens to people like them. Another factor may be that individuals with lower incomes have less leisure time in which to learn about candidates and issues and even to vote. Further, in contrast to American voters, European voters are often mobilized—by class-based trade unions and by the parties themselves—to vote on the basis of their economic interests. In the United States, the lowest-income workers are less likely to be members of organized labor unions and thus are less likely to be mobilized to vote on the basis of their own economic interests.

Party Competitiveness and Voter Turnout

Finally, researchers have found that party competitiveness in elections also influences voter turnout.[30] In tight contests, in which either party has a viable chance of winning, voter turnout typically is high because the race generates more voter interest than an election in which the winner is a foregone conclusion. Sometimes turnout is high in competitive elections because voter efficacy is higher—a voter may believe that her vote "counts" more in a close election than in a less competitive race. Voter turnout also runs high in competitive elections because the parties and other campaign organizations work harder to get out the vote when they think they have a chance at winning but know that victory is not guaranteed.

Competitive races also draw increased media attention. A tightly competitive local mayoral race might get greater than usual regional news attention, and a close race for the White House brings nearly nonstop media reports and candidate advertisements. The barrage of media coverage increases public awareness and may also boost voter efficacy by conveying the message that every vote counts.

The impact of this competitiveness can be seen in recent presidential elections. In 2012, about 120 million Americans voted, fewer than the 130 million who voted in 2008, but about 5 million more than the 126 million who voted in 2004. In both elections, the **turnout rate,** the proportion of eligible voters who actually voted, was 64 percent.[31] The 2012 election saw higher turnout rates among those in competitive battleground states, where intense party competition generated turnout. Turnout also was higher among African Americans, Hispanics, and young voters, but lower or flat turnout among other demographic groups offset those increases.

turnout rate
the proportion of eligible voters who actually voted

How Voters Decide

When deciding for whom they will vote, some voters evaluate candidates on the basis of their positions on issues and then cast their ballots for those who best represent their views. Called **prospective voting,** this method of candidate evaluation focuses on what the candidates will do in the future. A more common form of candidate evaluation is **retrospective voting,** in which a voter evaluates an incumbent candidate on the basis of whether the incumbent's past decisions and actions are satisfactory to the voter.[32] If they are satisfactory, the voter will likely support the incumbent. If not, the voter will be disposed to support the incumbent's opponent. The prevalence of an incumbency advantage in election outcomes indicates that many voters have a favorable view of the decisions and actions of incumbent candidates for most offices.[33]

prospective voting
a method of evaluating candidates in which voters focus on candidates' positions on issues important to them and vote for the candidates who best represent their views

retrospective voting
a method of evaluating candidates in which voters evaluate incumbent candidates and decide whether to support them based on their past performance

The most important factor that plays into how a voter decides on a candidate and perceives specific candidates, however, is the voter's party identification. Other influential determinants include those specific to a given election, such as candidates' attributes and the effectiveness of the candidates' campaigns.

The strongest bearing on voter preference is party identification, with about half of all voters basing their candidate choice on the party with which they identify. Table 9.3 shows that in the 2012 presidential election, party identification was a potent influence on how voters decided among candidates. Among voters who identified themselves as either Democrats or Republicans, loyalty to their party's candidate was high, with 90 percent of both Democrats and Republicans voting for their party's nominee for president. President Obama's victory came in part because of his support among the nation's independent or unaffiliated voters—those who do not identify themselves as either Democrats or Republicans.

Major Factors in Voter Decision Making

Often a significant determinant in why people vote the way they do, policy priorities are to a certain extent aligned with party identification (or, even more generally, with ideology), because the political parties usually embrace differing viewpoints on issues. National issues that top the list of concerns among voters have remained consistent over many years and include several domestic policy matters, such as the health of the economy, education, crime, health care, and Social Security.

But how do voters decide which party and which candidate to support at the polls, based on the issues? First and foremost, an issue must be **salient** to voters—that is, it must resonate with them and reflect something that they care deeply about, an issue they are willing to base their

salient
in relation to a voting issue—having resonance, being significant, causing intense interest

TABLE 9.3 **Party Loyalty in the 2012 Presidential Election**

	VOTED FOR ROMNEY (%)	VOTED FOR OBAMA (%)
Democrats	8	92
Independents	50	50
Republicans	93	7

298   CHAPTER 9 | Elections, Campaigns, and Voting

vote on.[34] The ability of voters to cast an issue-based vote increases when candidates differ in their positions on an issue. For example, in 2008, one of the most salient issues for voters—the issue they cared about the most—was the wars in Iraq and Afghanistan. Barack Obama, who opposed the war in Iraq, waged a successful campaign centered on this salient issue, and he contrasted his position to the position held by the Bush administration and his opponent, Senator John McCain (R-Ariz.).

Incumbency, the situation of already holding an office or an official position, as we've seen, is also a key factor influencing how people vote. Because an incumbent is a "known commodity" with demonstrated experience to serve in office, voters are much more likely to vote for incumbents than for their challengers. Thus, for most offices, incumbents are much more likely to be reelected than their challengers are to be elected. Indeed, in congressional elections, generally more than 88 percent of incumbent U.S. senators and 95 percent of incumbent members of the House of Representatives win reelection. But incumbency is also an influence in presidential elections, gubernatorial and state legislative elections, and probably even your local city council elections. Incumbents have notable advantages over challengers, namely, greater name recognition, a track record that voters can evaluate, and access to campaign contributions that help them to get their message out.

incumbency
the situation of already holding the office that is up for reelection

Campaign Influences on Voter Choice

As we have seen, parties and candidates conduct campaigns to influence voters' choices at the polls. Campaigns today vary a great deal in how they are waged. Whereas a candidate for a small town's board of selectmen might knock on the door of every voter in the community, a U.S. Senate or gubernatorial candidate might spend most of his or her time raising money to pay for expensive television and radio advertisements. Generally, the lower the level of office, the greater the likelihood that the candidate will rely on grassroots activism.

Trends in modern campaigns, including a far deeper reliance on paid professional staffers and the prevalence of the media as a tool for communicating with voters, are catapulting the costs of campaigns sky-high. Voter choices are also affected by increasingly negative campaigns, one outcome of the modern political campaigns' reliance on paid professionals. Outside consultants typically have far fewer qualms about "going negative" than do activists in the all-community volunteer-run campaigns that were more typical of earlier times.

Consultants use negative campaign tactics for a simple reason: Research shows that the approach sways voter opinion.[35] Although the candidates themselves often prefer to accentuate a positive message that highlights their background, experience, and qualifications, paid campaign consultants generally do not hesitate to sling the mud. Once a candidate establishes name recognition and credibility with voters, many consultants believe highlighting the opponent's negative qualities and actions is an effective campaign strategy.

But the effect of negative campaigning is not limited merely to swaying voters from one candidate to another. Research by political scientists shows that negative campaigning can suppress voter turnout in several ways. For example, Shanto Iyengar and Jennifer A. McGrady note that negative advertising may suppress voter turnout among the attacked candidate's supporters.[36] Other political scientists' research shows that negative campaigning undermines the democratic process by decreasing civic engagement among all voters. According to these findings, the electorate becomes disenchanted with the candidates (about whom voters get a barrage of negative information), with the campaigns (because campaigns serve as the primary messengers for delivering negative information about opponents), or with the entire electoral process that facilitates this negativity. Some voters view negative campaigning as being completely at odds with their idealized conception of the democratic process, and this belief may discourage them from voting.

Why Some People Do Not Vote

Negative campaigning is one reason why some people do not vote, but political scientists have proposed several others. Lack of civic engagement on the part of voters underlies many of these ideas. Other reasons have to do with the nature of campaigns and the structure of elections.

Lack of Efficacy

Some voters do not vote because they do not participate in civic affairs, either locally or at the national level. Many of these nonvoters lack efficacy.[37] They do not believe that the government listens to people like them or that their vote actually matters in determining the outcome of elections and the business of government.[38]

Scholars have determined that individuals who lack efficacy exist across the social and economic spectrums but that poorer people are more likely than better-off individuals to feel that the government does not listen to people like them. Yet although it is a common notion that people are alienated from politics or think that the government does not listen to their concerns, a recent study estimated that only about 9 percent of the U.S. population feels that way.[39] This same survey indicated that people lacking efficacy—a group that the study called the "disaffecteds"—typically had a low level of educational attainment and were less likely to follow current events than more engaged citizens.

Voter Fatigue and Negative Campaigns

Another explanation for why some Americans do not vote stems from the nature of political campaigns. In the United States, campaigns tend to be long-drawn-out affairs. For example, presidential campaigns typically last for more than a year, with some candidates positioning themselves three or four years in advance of an election. Contrast that with many parliamentary systems, including Germany's, in which an election must be held within 60 days of the dissolution of parliament because of a "no confidence" vote of the chancellor (similar to a prime minister). Some scholars say that the lengthiness of the campaigns leads to **voter fatigue,** the condition in which voters simply grow tired of all candidates by the time Election Day arrives, and may thus be less likely to vote.

voter fatigue
the condition in which voters grow tired of all candidates by the time Election Day arrives, and may thus be less likely to vote

American journalist and humorist Franklin Adams commented that "elections are won by men and women chiefly because most people vote against somebody rather than for somebody."[40] The prevalence of negative campaigning compounds the phenomenon of voter fatigue. Even the most enthusiastic supporters of a candidate may feel their advocacy withering under the unceasing mudslinging that occurs in many high-level campaigns. And so, although evidence shows that negative advertising is effective in swaying voters' opinions, sometimes such advertising also succeeds in suppressing voter turnout by making voters less enthusiastic about voting.

The Structure of Elections

Political scientists also cite the structure of U.S. elections as a reason why more Americans do not vote. For years, voting rights activists claimed that the registration requirements in many states were too complicated and discouraged people from voting by making it too difficult to register. In 1993, Congress sought to remedy that situation by passing the National Voter Registration Act, frequently called the "Motor Voter" Act, which allows eligible people to register to vote when they apply for a driver's license or enroll in a public assistance program or when they submit the necessary information by mail. Although there was enormous anticipation that the motor voter law would significantly boost voter registration and turnout, in fact its impact has been negligible.

Critics of the structure of elections also point to their frequency. In the United States, the number of elections varies from municipality to municipality, and local government charters may call for more than four elections for municipal offices alone. Although most federal offices require only two elections (a primary and a general), these elections are not always held in conjunction with state, county, and municipal elections.

The timing of elections also affects voter participation. Most general elections are held on a weekday—the first Tuesday after the first Monday in November. Moreover, although states decide when to hold primary elections, state legislative elections, and municipal and school board elections, these elections, too, typically occur on a weekday. Critics say that holding elections on weekends or over a two-day period instead, or establishing a national voting holiday, would increase voter turnout by ensuring that voters had ample opportunity to cast their ballots. (See "Global Context.")

ELECTIONS IN SOUTH AFRICA

The year 1994 marked the end of apartheid in South Africa, the practice of segregation between the races in that nation, which also prohibited blacks from voting. Since that time, South Africa has had five elections held under the practice of universal suffrage, in which all adults are afforded the right to vote. The most recent balloting, which saw the election of a new National Assembly and provincial legislatures, occurred between April and July of 2014.

South Africa's National Assembly has 400 members, who are elected through a system of proportional representation, in which a political party's representation in the assembly is based on the proportion of the vote the party receives. Half of the members of the assembly are elected at-large, the other half are elected specifically from each of the country's nine provinces. The at-large members of the National Assembly elect the president of South Africa, while majority parties in the provinces select the provincial premiers, comparable to governors in the United States.

In 1994, the ruling African National Congress party formed an alliance with two other parties—the Congress of South African Trade Unions and the South African Communist Party. In 2013, however, the National Union of Metalworkers of South Africa, which is an important voting bloc within the Congress of South African Trade Unions, announced that it would not support the African National Congress in the 2014 elections, instead hoping to lay the groundwork for a viable socialist party that will contest the 2019 elections. But the ANC expelled ANC Youth League leader Julius Malema, who then formed his own political party, attracting young people with an anti-ANC platform that endorsed socialist principles. As a result, the ANC's vote share decreased from 66 percent in 2009 to 62 percent in 2014, while Malema's Economic Freedom Fighters received over 6 percent of the vote. ANC's traditional rival, the Democratic Alliance, also increased its vote share from nearly 17 percent in 2009 to over 22 percent in 2014.

The Rational Abstention Thesis

A final explanation as to why some people do not vote is that they make a conscious choice that not voting is a rational, logical action. Called the **rational abstention thesis,** this theory states that some individuals decide that the "costs" of voting—in terms of the time, energy, and inconvenience required to register to vote, to become informed about candidates and elections, and actually to vote—are not worth the effort when compared with the expected "benefits," or what the voters could derive from voting.

In light of these cumulative "costs," it is perhaps surprising that so many people choose to vote.[41] One explanation for why they do is that most voters report that they derive psychological rewards from exercising this citizens' right—feelings of being civically engaged, satisfied, and patriotic. But when the costs associated with voting increase too much, turnout drops; more people choose not to vote when voting becomes too inconvenient. This drop-off occurs, for example, when municipalities shorten voting hours and during inclement weather.

rational abstention thesis
a theory that some individuals decide the costs of voting are not worth the effort when compared to the benefits

The Consequences of Nonvoting

From a civic engagement perspective, nonvoting is both a symptom and a result of a lack of civic involvement on the part of individuals.[42] Your roommate might not vote because she is not civically engaged—because she feels that she has little to contribute and that the government does not listen to "people like her" anyway. But by not voting, she perpetuates this lack of efficacy by remaining outside the process rather than staking a claim to what is rightfully hers: the idea that every individual has the right to a voice in the composition and priorities of the government. Only by becoming civically engaged—learning about the candidates, discussing issues, and voting—can she break the cycle of inefficacy. Voting will make her pay more attention to campaigns, candidates, and issues.

Beyond the effects of nonvoting on individuals, low voter turnout affects the polity (Chapter 1). When relatively few people vote in a given election, the outcome is likely to represent the will of only that subset of the electorate who voted. Consider that polls indicate that the outcomes of the 2000 and 2004 presidential elections would have been different if voter turnout had been higher. In each of those elections, the Democratic nominee (Al Gore and John Kerry, respectively) was the favored candidate among several groups whose turnout falls below average, including voters under age 24, African American voters, and voters with lower incomes. The process becomes cyclical: These nonvoters who disagree with the outcome conclude that the government does not represent them, they feel less efficacious, and they are less inclined to vote in the future.

Moreover, some scholars assert that democracies with low voter turnout are more likely to generate threats to their own well-being.[43] In democracies with low turnout, these scholars say, charismatic, popular political figures may rise to power and become authoritarian leaders. Corruption, too, can be a problem in low-turnout democracies where government officials might feel relatively unconcerned about the disapproval of disgruntled constituents.

Other researchers, however, contend that nonvoting is not a big problem, especially in cases where large numbers in the electorate are relatively uninformed about candidates and issues.[44] A number of scholars in this camp argue that participation by the uninformed is undesirable, because it may lead to drastic changes in government. Opponents of this view counter that because of political parties' role in selecting candidates, the menu for voter choice is actually quite limited in most elections. Those who argue that nonvoting does not matter also ignore the fact that voting tends to produce more engaged citizens who, because they vote, feel a duty to be informed and involved.

Other scholars who claim that low voter turnout is not a problem argue that low voting rates are simply a function of people's satisfaction with the status quo: Their nonvoting simply means that they do not seek change in government. This argument, however, does not explain why lower turnout is most likely to occur in populations that are least likely to be satisfied with their situation. For example, people with lower incomes are much less likely to vote than those with higher incomes. Whatever the reason—a lack of efficacy as argued by some, satisfaction as argued by others—nonvoters' best chances of having their views reflected in the policy process is to articulate them through voting.

Conclusion | Thinking Critically About What's Next in Elections, Campaigns, and Voting

The nature of political campaigns in the United States has continuously evolved, but the changes in recent decades have been especially dramatic. An era in which political parties and grassroots activism dominated campaigns has given way to the present-day realities where money, media, and mavens of strategy are key forces in shaping campaigns, which have grown increasingly candidate and technology centered. Prominently driving the changes are the simultaneous *decrease* in political party clout and *increase* in the need for money—money to pay for the small army of professional staffers that run the campaigns; and money to cover the expensive media buys that candidates, especially those running for national and state office, heavily depend on for communicating with the electorate. Increasingly, this money is being raised outside the regulated campaign finance system, with wealthy donors circumventing federal election reporting requirements by contributing to 527s, 501(c)4s, or super PACs, whose influence in federal campaigns is growing.

But today technology offers the potential to bring the politics of electoral campaigns back to the grassroots—now perhaps more appropriately called the netroots. Although campaigns' use of technology certainly is not free, digital communication is cost-effective and rapid. The options that campaigns and candidates have to communicate with voters through media such as social networking sites, YouTube, e-mail, and instant messaging present an exciting alternative to high-priced "campaigning-as-usual."

Through the new media of communication, there is great potential, too, for the inclusion of a variety of new voices in the political campaigning process. Groups that want to influence campaigns and voters have at their disposal a vast arsenal of new technology that makes such influence possible.

Summary

1. Political Participation: Engaging Individuals, Shaping Politics

Active political engagement benefits both the individual and the polity. When it comes to elections, campaigns, and voting, the opportunities for civic engagement are numerous. Although some civic activities, such as working full time on a campaign, might represent enormous commitments, others, including casting a ballot and engaging in political discourse, are less time-consuming and are manageable for even the busiest people.

2. Elections in the United States

U.S. elections include the primary election, in which a party's nominee to run in the general election is selected; the general election, in which the winning candidate attains the office being sought; and special-purpose elections such as the initiative, the referendum, and the recall, which enable citizens to have a greater say in the political process.

3. The Act of Voting

Although all the states rely on the Australian (secret) ballot, the types of ballots used vary significantly among states, and increasingly states allow mail-in, early, and no-justification absentee balloting. The type of ballot can have an effect on election outcomes, as can the election process.

4. Running for Office: The Choice to Run

Most offices have formal eligibility requirements, but there are also more subjective requirements by which voters view candidates as qualified to hold a given office. Often these characteristics have to do with occupation, education, and experience.

5. The Nature of Political Campaigns Today

Today's political campaigns hire a wide variety of professionals who perform the tasks that were once accomplished by volunteer staffs. Office seekers' increasing reliance on electronic media, in particular television, has drastically changed both the ways in which campaigns are conducted and the costs of those campaigns. The widespread use of the Internet, too, continues to alter the nature of campaigns.

6. Money and Politics

Government efforts over the years to regulate campaign contributions have led to laws with numerous loopholes. The latest attempt to curtail the influence of money on politics is the Bipartisan Campaign Finance Reform Act of 2002. The current campaign system is becoming increasingly dominated by super PACs, whose development was made possible by the U.S. Supreme Court's *Citizens United* decision.

7. Presidential Campaigns

Presidential campaigns are increasing in duration. They begin with the primary process, continue through the national party conventions, proceed to the general election campaign and voting, and end with the Electoral College vote.

8. Who Votes? Factors in Voter Participation

Influences on voter participation include education, age, race, income, and party competitiveness.

9. How Voters Decide

Party identification, policy priorities, incumbency, and campaigns are factors influencing how voters decide for whom to vote.

10. Why Some People Do Not Vote

The many reasons why people don't vote include a lack of efficacy, voter fatigue and negative campaigns, the structure of elections, and the rational abstention thesis. Whatever the reason, nonvoting has a harmful effect on individuals and the government.

Key Terms

absentee voting 283
Australian ballot 281
campaign consultant 286
campaign manager 287
campaign strategy 287
caucus 278
chad 281
Citizens United v. Federal Election Commission 288
closed primary 278
coattail effect 282
501(c)4s 292
527 293

fund-raising consultant 287
general election 277
GOTV 277
grassroots organizing 276
incumbency 299
independent expenditures 291
initiative 280
instant runoff election 280
media consultant 287
office-block ballot 282
open primary 278
party-column ballot 282

proposition 280
prospective voting 298
rational abstention thesis 301
recall 281
referendum 280
retrospective voting 298
runoff election 280
salient 298
super PACs 288
Super Tuesday 278
turnout rate 298
voter fatigue 300

For Review

1. What are some opportunities for civic engagement related to elections, campaigns, and voting?

2. What are the different kinds of elections in the United States? What is the difference between a primary election and a general election?

3. How do states vary in how elections are conducted?

4. What is the difference between formal and informal eligibility requirements for political office?

5. Why is regulating campaign finance so difficult? Explain the various efforts to limit the impact of money on campaigns.

6. What factors influence whether a person will vote or not?

7. What factors influence how or for whom an individual will vote?

8. What is the rational abstention thesis? Is it rational? What factors might not be calculated into the costs and benefits of voting?

For Critical Thinking and Discussion

1. Why do formal and informal eligibility requirements for office differ? What are the informal eligibility requirements to run for the state legislature where you live? What are the requirements for the city or town council in your hometown or the community where your school is located? How do these differences reflect the nature of the constituency for the office being sought?

2. How has the increasing cost of political campaigns changed the nature of American politics? Why have costs escalated?

3. What have been the effects of the increasing negativity in American political campaigns?

4. Using the text discussion of factors influencing whether a person votes, assess a classmate's likelihood of voting based solely on those factors. Then ask the person if he or she votes. Was your assessment accurate?

5. In your view, what are the consequences of nonvoting?

MULTIPLE CHOICE: Choose the lettered item that answers the question correctly.

1. An election that determines which candidates win the offices being sought is called a(n)
   a. blanket primary.
   b. open primary.
   c. caucus.
   d. general election.

2. A meeting of party members held to select delegates to the national convention is called a(n)
   a. blanket primary.
   b. open primary.
   c. caucus.
   d. general election.

3. A special election in which voters can remove officeholders before their term is over is called a(n)
   a. referendum.
   b. initiative.
   c. recall.
   d. proposition.

4. An election in which voters in a state can vote for or against a measure proposed by the state legislature is called a(n)
   a. referendum.
   b. initiative.
   c. recall.
   d. proposition.

5. The phenomenon by which candidates running for lower-level office such as city council benefit in an election from the popularity of a top-of-ticket nominee is called
   a. the petticoat effect.
   b. the bustle effect.
   c. the coattail effect.
   d. the bolster effect.

6. A professional who brings the campaign message to voters by creating all forms of media ads is called a(n)
   a. campaign manager.
   b. fund-raising consultant.
   c. outreach manager.
   d. media consultant.

7. The proportion of voters who actually voted is called
   a. the turnout rate.
   b. the electoral rate.

c. the eligibility factor.
d. the voter sample.

8. An outlay by PACs and others, typically for advertising for or against a candidate but uncoordinated with a candidate's campaign, is called
   a. a soft money expenditure.
   b. an independent expenditure.
   c. a 527 expenditure.
   d. a 626 expenditure.

9. An issue that has resonance and intense interest among voters is said to be
   a. a divide issue.
   b. a fence-sitting issue.
   c. a salient issue.
   d. a litmus-test issue.

10. The condition in which voters grow tired of all candidates by the time Election Day arrives, making them possibly less likely to vote, is called
    a. rational abstention.
    b. absentee voting.
    c. voter ennui.
    d. voter fatigue.

FILL IN THE BLANKS

11. A follow-up election held when no candidate receives the majority of votes cast in the original election is called a(n) _____.

12. A special election in which the computerized voter machine simulates the elimination of last-place vote-getters to eventually decide a winner is called a(n) _____.

13. A measure proposed by voters and placed on the ballot for their approval is called a(n) _____ election.

14. A ballot that organizes the candidates by political party is called a(n) _____.

15. A(n) _____ is the blueprint for an election campaign, including a budget and fund-raising plan, an advertising strategy, and a staffing plan.

Answers: 1. d, **2.** c, **3.** c, **4.** a, **5.** c, **6.** d, **7.** a, **8.** b, **9.** c, **10.** d, **11.** runoff election, **12.** instant runoff, **13.** initiative, **14.** party-column ballot, **15.** campaign strategy.

Research AND Action

Internet Resources

The Living Room Candidate

www.livingroomcandidate.org This site, maintained by the Museum of the Moving Image, provides videos of television commercials run by presidential campaigns from 1956 to 2012.

Project Vote Smart

www.votesmart.org This nonpartisan website provides independent, factual information on election procedures in each state.

Ready To Run

www.cawp.rutgers.edu/education_training/ReadytoRun/ This nonpartisan campaign training program encourages and trains women to run for elective office, position themselves for appointive office, or work on a campaign.

Rock the Vote

www.rockthevote.org This nonprofit, nonpartisan organization encourages political participation by young people and provides resources on policies of interest, as well as voting information.

Vote, Run, Lead

www.voterunlead.org This is the website for an organization that encourages the civic engagement of young women as voters, activists, and candidates for political office.

Recommended Readings

Abramson, Paul R., John H. Aldrich, and David W. Rohde. *Change and Continuity in the 2008 and 2010 Elections.* Washington, D.C.: CQ Press, 2012. The latest in this series of election analyses examines the tactics employed in the 2008 presidential and 2010 congressional elections.

Burns, Nancy, Kay Lehman Schlozman, and Sidney Verba. *The Private Roots of Public Action: Gender Equality, and Public Action.* Cambridge, MA: Harvard University Press, 2003. Explores the differences in political participation between men and women.

Faucheux, Ron. *Campaigns and Elections: Winning Elections.* New York: M. Evans and Company, 2003. A collection of the "best of the best" articles from *Campaigns and Elections* magazine; a practical guide to conducting campaigns.

Gainous, Jason, and Kevin M. Wagner. *Tweeting to Power: The Social Media Revolution in American Politics.* New York: Oxford University Press, 2014. Describes the rise of social media in campaigns and elections.

Herrnson, Paul S., Richard G. Niemi, Michael J. Hanmer, Benjamin B. Bederson, and Frederick C. Conrad. *Voting Technology: The Not-So-Simple Act of Casting a Ballot.* Washington, D.C.: Brookings Institution Press, 2008. Explains the intricacies of voting technology, including the electoral implications of how votes are cast.

Jacobson, Gary C. *The Politics of Congressional Elections.* New York: Longman, 2012. A classic work explaining the process of congressional elections and demonstrating how electoral politics reflects and shapes other basic components of American democracy.

Nelson, Michael. *The Elections of 2012.* Washington, D.C.: CQ Press, 2014. Examines the 2012 elections through a historical perspective, while seeking to explain the implications of events that occurred.

Plouffe, David. *The Audacity to Win: The Inside Story and Lessons of Barack Obama's Historic Victory.* New York: Viking Press, 2009. A captivating political memoir of the 2008 campaign, written by Barack Obama's campaign manager.

Zukin, Cliff, Scott Keeter, Molly Andolina, Krista Jenkins, and Michael X. Delli Carpini. *A New Engagement? Political Participation, Civic Life, and the Changing American Citizen.* New York: Oxford University Press, 2006. Describes the changing ways in which Americans are participating in the political life of their country and communities.

Movies of Interest

Swing Vote (2008)
Kevin Costner stars in this film in which one man—an average apolitical American—determines the outcome of a presidential election.

Bulworth (1999)
Warren Beatty stars in this offbeat skewering of the influence of money on political campaigns in the United States.

The Candidate (1972)
Robert Redford's character is convinced to run for the Senate on the premise that, with no chance at success, he can say whatever he wants. But success changes him, and his values shift as the prospect of winning becomes apparent.

CHAPTER 10

The Media

THEN

The relationship between the media and consumers was one-way.

NOW

Technology has created a two-way relationship between the media and consumers, involving the exchange of a seemingly limitless amount of information of varying quality.

NEXT

Will the abundance and the reach of the media overload people with information?

Will people select media sources that serve only to confirm their views?

Will new technologies continue to change the nature of the news business?

This chapter focuses on the role of the contemporary U.S. media as both an information source and a conduit through which individuals convey information and opinions to others, and it explores the growing, shifting influence of the media on politics and civic life over time.

FIRST, we examine what the modern media are.

SECOND, we consider the political functions of the media.

THIRD, we explore the press and politics, taking a historical view.

FOURTH, we analyze how the advent of the first electronic media, radio and television revolutions, transformed political communication, campaigns, and elections.

FIFTH, we examine how media convergence and consolidation—when various forms of media are provided by fewer and fewer corporate entities—is effecting the type of news Americans consume.

SIXTH, we ponder charges that the U.S. media are biased. Do most people believe that the media are too liberal or too conservative? Are they right?

SEVENTH, we consider the government's regulation of the media and examine how the media's rapidly continuing transformation affects government's ability to regulate new communication formats.

If you are like most Americans

and indeed like multitudes of people across the globe—the media are a fixture in your daily life. You may wake and check Instagram, Twitter, or Facebook before you even get out of bed. You may read a newspaper over breakfast and listen to a radio show each morning when driving to school or work. In the evening, you may watch YouTube videos of televised news stories concerning the latest international crisis. You may receive real-time news updates on your cell phone, visit Internet news sites and blogs regularly, or tune in to the 24-hour news channels available virtually everywhere. As a citizen of the 21st century, you are bathed in a sea of news and information. Some of what the media offer you is meant to entertain, some is meant to inform, but increasingly the lines between the two have blurred.

No one can dispute that the sheer amount of information and entertainment available courtesy of the media has increased immeasurably over the past few decades. Within a generation, the modern media have transformed American life. Where once people had to seek out news and information, today they are inundated with it, and they must develop the skills needed to distinguish the reliable from the unreliable.

Although this abundance of information at times may rise to the level of a blitz, information is empowering. It serves as the basis on which people shape well-founded opinions. Those opinions are the building blocks for meaningful civic engagement and political participation. In the discussion that follows, we see how the media continuously shape the ways we receive information and the ways we exercise the rights and privileges of our American democracy.

The Modern Media

When faced with the challenge of meeting his goal of enrolling 7 million Americans in the nation's new health insurance program in 2013, President Barack Obama turned to an unlikely accomplice. Zach Galifianakis is best known for playing the character Alan Garner in the *Hangover* movies and for hosting a video series, *Between Two Ferns with Zach Galifianakis,* on the website Funny or Die. In the series, Galifianakis "interviews" celebrities (while seated between two potted ferns) and often goes off on bizarre tangents or asks guests impertinent questions about their sex lives. Obama's appearance on *Between Two Ferns* had 33 million views on the website.

President Obama agreed to appear on the video series to encourage young people to sign up for health insurance under the Affordable Care Act using the HealthCare.gov website. Months prior, the nonpartisan Congressional Budget Office created a target to enroll 7 million Americans between the program's rollout in October 2013 and the end of its first open-enrollment period on March 31, 2014. The Obama administration agreed to the target, but the rollout was plagued with website problems that continued through 2013. Once the website issues were resolved, enrollment began to increase. Despite the administration's full court press to increase enrollments, it did not appear that the target would be hit.

So the president arranged to appear on *Between Two Ferns.* Between Galifianakis's funny, if snarky, questions ("Is it going to be hard in two years when you're no longer president and people will stop letting you win in basketball?"), the president interjected drolly, "If I ran a third time, it would sort of be like doing a third *Hangover* movie. It didn't really work out very well, did it?" The appearance gave the president an opportunity to make his pitch on the health insurance program. Obama described the benefits of coverage: "most young Americans, right now, they're not covered. The truth, is that they can get coverage all for what it costs to pay your cell phone bill." Some critics bashed Obama's appearance on *Between Two Ferns* as "unpresidential" or "undignified," but it

created a significant "Galifianakis bump," attracting large numbers of young, healthy uninsured Americans—the administration's target audience—to enroll in the health insurance program. The Obama administration surpassed its target, enrolling 7.1 million Americans by March 31, 2014.

Traditionally, it was easy to recognize the media: newspapers, television news, and cable news networks, to name a few. But defining the media today is trickier: Do tweets from your mayor, Instagrams from your roommate, or Facebook posts from your mom count as media? Although many observers regard the **media** simply as tools used to store and deliver information or data (in which case, all the preceding communications would be considered media), we must differentiate between media outlets that distribute unverifiable or opinion-based information and those that disseminate verifiable information.

The media exist in various forms today, including print media such as newspapers and magazines; electronic media, which traditionally means radio and television; and **new media,** sources of information including Internet websites, blogs, social networking sites such as Facebook and Twitter, photo- and video-sharing platforms such as Instagram and YouTube, apps, and the cellular and satellite technologies that facilitate their use. In previous eras, media consumers often accepted what was broadcast or printed as fact, but today one must be a critical consumer of information. Just because information appears on a blog, or even hundreds of blogs, it is not necessarily true. How can today's media consumers be certain the information they are receiving is accurate? One good method is by relying on media outlets with a track record of providing solid information and adhering to journalistic standards. Another is to check sources independently: Today, the Internet has made it possible to verify some information simply by clicking on a hotlink to the original sources. More and more, news organizations will come to rely on citizen "journalists," increasing the probability that unscrupulous individuals will distribute false information widely. Thus today's media consumers must exercise a high level of caution when reading, listening, and viewing.

media
tools used to store and deliver information or data

new media
sources of information including Internet websites, blogs, social networking sites such as Facebook and Twitter, photo- and video-sharing platforms such as Instagram and YouTube, apps, and the cellular and satellite technologies that facilitate their use

The Political Functions of the Media

In the United States today, the media in all forms—including print, television, radio, and new media—fulfill several key functions. Much of what the media do revolves around entertaining us, whether that means playing *Grand Theft Auto,* watching *Modern Family,* or reading the Sunday comics. But the media perform important political functions as well and are a vital element of our democracy. Specifically, the media perform these political functions:

- Provide political information
- Help us to interpret events and policies and influence agenda setting in the national political arena
- Provide a forum for political conversations
- Socialize children to the political culture

Context

BASSEM YOUSSEF: EGYPT'S JON STEWART

Bassem Youssef is a cardiothoracic surgeon who treated some of the Tahrir Square protesters who were wounded in Egypt's Jasmine Spring uprising in 2011, which forced Egyptian leader Hosni Mubarek from power. In the midst of the political and cultural revolution that was defining the future in Egypt and the Arab world, Youssef launched a political satire program called *The B1 Show.* When the show went viral on YouTube, Youssef, who has been characterized as "Egypt's Jon Stewart," gained an international reputation. "In Egypt and the Arab world in general, you had these really serious talk shows or the slapstick, farce, ha-ha stuff," Youssef said. "I can't be placed in either category. Our aim is to inform but also to entertain people." One of Egypt's television networks, ONTV, then offered Youssef the opportunity to create and host a regularly scheduled program, *El-Bernameg,* which was launched in August 2011.

In June 2012, Youssef appeared as a guest on Jon Stewart's *The Daily Show.* The host asked Youssef: "How difficult is it to do a show like you're doing—a comedy show—when the political stability of the country is still in question? Because it's difficult for me, and we're pretty stable." Youssef described the changes that television is undergoing throughout the Arab world and the positive responses that informative, entertaining programming is

receiving: "What we do is, actually we have broke ground in the television programming because now people say, 'wow! He actually says what we want to say!'"*

But Stewart's observation was dead-on. The Egyptian satellite channel CBC canceled Youssef's show after he faced several charges from Egypt's general prosecution that he had ridiculed supporters of former army chief Abdel Fattah al Sisi, who went on to win Egypt's presidential election in a landslide after a crackdown on dissent, as well as the Egyptian military, and that he had threatened the safety and stability of the country by insulting the symbols of Egypt and its government. In 2013, Youssef was awarded the International Press Freedom Award by the Committee to Protect Journalists, but he announced in June 2014 that he was canceling his show, alluding to the harassment he and his network faced.

*http://thedailyshow.cc.com/episodes/xbkxlz/june-21--2012---bassem-youssef.

Providing Information

One long-standing function of the mass media is to serve up a steady diet of news and information to readers, viewers, and listeners. Indeed, the media, particularly the electronic media, are the primary source of information for most individuals. And today the quantity of information available—on blogs, websites, and cable television stations—surpasses the volume available at any other time in history. Coverage includes everything from weather watches, to sports scores, to the latest legislative developments on Capitol Hill, to serious analysis of top domestic policy issues and international problems. From this steady diet arises the problem of information overload—the constant availability of news information to the point of excess, which may cause media consumers to ignore, dismiss, or fail to see the significance of particular events. Media critics especially fault the television networks for injecting entertainment into news shows. They dub this combination **infotainment** (a hybrid of the words *information* and *entertainment*). More recent is the trend of uniting comedy with political content, as in *Saturday Night Live*'s "Weekend Update," and Jon Stewart's *The Daily Show,* both of which interpret news events with a comedic slant (see "Global Context").

infotainment

a hybrid of the words *information* and *entertainment;* news shows that combine entertainment and news

Interpreting Matters of Public Interest and Setting the Public Agenda

Besides reporting information, the media help people to comprehend and interpret matters of public interest and to make informed decisions about public policies (see Analyzing the Sources). Political scientist Shanto Iyengar asserts that this process often begins with the media **framing**—setting a context that helps people to understand important events and matters of shared interest. For example, in 2014 when Russia annexed Crimea, the international media contextualized the situation. They reminded readers and viewers that, while a majority of Crimeans supported annexation, Russia's actions were cause for concern because of Russia's previous aggressive takeover of Balkan nations and the installation of puppet regimes in Eastern Europe in the aftermath of World War II.

Political scientist Pippa Norris has analyzed the process of framing as it relates to gender. She asserts that gender has become a common frame through which journalists provide context for different kinds of political stories.[1] Norris explains that voters, candidates, public opinion, and issues all may be viewed from a gender-based perspective. For example, in the early stages of the 2016 presidential race, the media initially covered the race for the Democratic nomination by accentuating the gender of Senator Hillary Clinton (D-N.Y.) and playing up Clinton's potential to be the first woman president of the United States, including speculating on the possibility of a two-woman ticket if Clinton were to run and choose a female running mate, and the impact that being a grandmother would have on Clinton's decision to run.

The media also help to shape the **public agenda**—public issues that most demand the attention of government officials. Such has been the case with the issue of same-sex marriage in the United States, which has generated significant media coverage in recent years, both nationally and within states. In doing so, the media have engaged in **priming**—using their coverage to bring particular policies on issues to the public agenda, a common tactic used in shaping the public agenda.

framing
the process by which the media set a context that helps people to understand important events and matters of shared interest

public agenda
the public issues that most demand the attention of government officials

priming
bringing certain policies on issues to the public agenda through media coverage

Providing a Forum for Conversations About Politics

Although the media have provided an often lively forum for conversations about politics, the prominence of this role has reached new heights in the Internet era. Historically, information flowed from the media—which through the years have included everything from the political broadsides and leaflets of colonial times to modern newspapers, radio news, and television programming—to the people. The people then formed opinions based on what they read, heard, and saw. This historical one-way tradition typically featured little give-and-take between media sources and their consumers. A notable exception has been the **letter to the editor,** in which a reader responds to a newspaper story, knowing that the letter might be published in that paper. The advent of talk radio gave listeners one of their first regular opportunities to express their views publicly. Television took note, and call-in shows became common fare on cable television stations.

letter to the editor
a letter in which a reader responds to a story in a newspaper, knowing that the letter might be published in that paper

But no other medium has expanded the ability of people to communicate their views to the degree that the Internet has. Today, blogs provide an ideal forum for online conversations about issues, inviting an ongoing dialogue between blog hosts and posters. Discussion boards (even those that are "nonpolitical") are filled with political discussion and opinions. The comment section following an online newspaper article has become the new water cooler around which opinions are voiced. And social networking sites such as Facebook and Twitter provide an easily accessible means by which people can communicate facts, eyewitness accounts, and opinions. David Weinberger, a Democratic marketing consultant and Internet adviser, describes this phenomenon: "Think of it as conversation space. Conversation is the opposite of marketing. It's talking in our own voices about things we want to hear about."[2]

Socializing Children to Political Culture

The media also socialize new generations to the political culture. For young children, television remains a dominant medium for both entertainment and socialization, though iPad apps are increasingly playing these roles in the lives of today's small children. TV-viewing toddlers receive regular messages about important cultural values. Shows such as *Sesame Street* and *Sanjay and Craig* send powerful messages about the value of diversity in society. Young children's shows also subtly instruct watchers on the value of patriotism and of specific

CONFIDENCE IN THE MEDIA

The Gallup Organization has asked the following question in surveys since 1972: "In general, how much trust and confidence do you have in the mass media—such as newspapers, TV, and radio—when it comes to reporting the news fully, accurately, and fairly: a great deal, a fair amount, not very much, or none at all?"

The line graph illustrates survey respondents' views on that question, showing survey data at various times between May 1972 and September 2014. You can see that considerable changes have occurred in people's assessment of news organizations in this period.

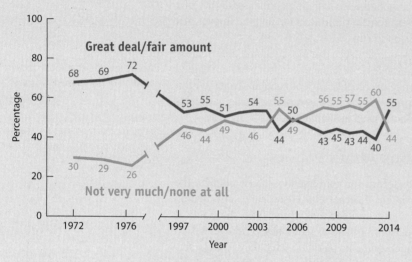

SOURCE: Gallup Poll, "In U.S., Trust in Media Recovers Slightly From All-Time Low," www.gallup.com/poll/164459/trust-media-recovers-slightly-time-low.aspx.

Evaluating the Evidence

1. Describe trends during the 1970s in people's confidence in the media, citing specific data from the graph.

2. Describe trends since 2001 in people's confidence in the media, citing specific data.

3. What do the latest surveys indicate about respondents' opinions on the issue of confidence in the media?

4. What do the data say about the overall trends with regard to people's confidence in the media?

5. What factors could have contributed to the changes in people's assessment of the media over time? Explain.

> Television shows such as *The Voice* that we often think of as pure entertainment frequently reinforce and legitimize dominant American political values.

civic behaviors. TV programming for older children similarly takes on political issues. A series of episodes of *SpongeBob SquarePants* depicts Bikini Bottom's first presidential election, in which SpongeBob's best friend, Patrick Starfish, runs against Crustacean Party candidate Larry the Lobster.

Even television and radio programs not specifically aimed at youth often reinforce democratic principles and practices. What is *The Voice* if not a televised election? And when the tribe speaks on *Survivor*, they do so through the process of voting. Talk radio and television call-in programs rest on the assumption that individuals' opinions matter and that they have the right to voice them. These kinds of programming may not directly spur a particular political behavior on the part of viewers. Nonetheless, television and other forms of media that we often think of as pure entertainment frequently reinforce and legitimize dominant American political values.

The Press and Politics: A Historical View

The sheer volume of information available through the media today makes the media's influence in our times beyond dispute. Historically, too, the media have played an essential role in setting the political agenda and shaping public policy. The power of the media was evident even in pre-Revolutionary times, when, for example, newspaper owners and readers rallied against the Stamp Act's (1765) imposition of taxes on newspapers and other kinds of legal documents. Newspaper publishers sympathetic to the colonists' cause of ejecting Great Britain from American shores used their "power of the pen" to arouse public opinion, and they strongly supported the patriot cause throughout the Revolution. Taking sides in an internal conflict was a new role for the press, one that would sow the seeds of future media influence on the country's domestic and foreign policy. The early history of media development also raised issues that continue to create conflict about the media's role in society.

The Early Role of the Press

Great leaders learned early how intimately their careers were linked to favorable press coverage and influence. From the 1790s to the 1830s, the press served primarily as a vehicle for the leaders of political parties, who expressed their opinions through newspapers known to reflect their particular viewpoints in reporting the news. The circulation of these newspapers was small, but so was their audience; most people could not read and write and did not vote.

By the 1830s, the environment had changed. For openers, the average American was now able to read. New technology made possible the **penny press**—newspapers that sold for a penny. The field of **journalism,** the practice of gathering and reporting events, flourished. Circulation increased, and the working class became interested in what the newspapers had to offer. Another reason newspapers reduced their price was the advent of advertising; newspaper owners figured out that if they sold advertising, they could increase both their profits and their papers' circulation. The 1830s was the first time advertising became part and parcel of the newspaper business, and although pressures from advertisers sometimes affected coverage and editorial opinion, few readers noticed that practice, and even fewer challenged it.

Over time, the influence of advertising grew exponentially. Although today's major newspapers do not openly change their editorial opinions to please their advertisers, occasionally advertisers flex their muscles, as General Motors did when it withdrew its advertising from the *Los Angeles Times* after the newspaper recommended the firing of the company's CEO.[3]

penny press
newspapers that sold for a penny in the 1830s

journalism
the practice of gathering and reporting events

Yellow Journalism and Muckraking

Throughout the last part of the 19th century, newspapers competed vigorously with one another for ever-greater shares of readership. Publishers found that stories about sex, gore, violence, and government corruption sold papers faster than reports about garbage collection and school budgets. Well-known publishers William Randolph Hearst and Joseph Pulitzer established their reputations and their fortunes at that time, Hearst with the *New York Journal American* and Pulitzer with the *New York World*. Along with Hearst and Pulitzer at the beginning of the 20th century came the practice of yellow journalism, so named after the yellow ink used in the "Yellow Kid" cartoons in the *New York World*. The term **yellow journalism** has come to signify an irresponsible, sensationalist approach to news reporting and is used to this day to criticize certain elements of the press.

The most famous example of the impact of yellow journalism came with both Hearst's and Pulitzer's support of the United States' entry into the Spanish-American War (1898). This conflict is sometimes referred to as "the newspaper war" because of the major role of the press in President William McKinley's decision to invade Cuba and later the Philippines. Influenced by reports of Spanish cruelty toward the Cubans during and after the Cuban independence movement, public sentiment in the United States strongly favored Cuba. Hearst and Pulitzer, followed by other newspapers across the country, fanned the flames of war with sensational and lurid anti-Spanish stories, dwelling on the brutality of the Spanish toward Cuban rebels.

yellow journalism
irresponsible, sensationalist approach to news reporting, so named after the yellow ink used in the "Yellow Kid" cartoons in the *New York World*

> Yellow journalism can influence the national policy agenda. When the battleship *Maine* exploded in Havana harbor in February 1898, newspaper coverage significantly molded public opinion, and in turn Congress declared war on Spain. Can you think of examples of recent media coverage of events that have influenced public opinion?

The precipitating event, the explosion of the U.S. battleship *Maine* in Havana harbor in February 1898, may or may not have been due to a Spanish torpedo, according to recent evidence. But press reports, accompanied by the cry "Remember the *Maine,*" galvanized the public and Congress. The president responded to the intensifying pressures, and Congress declared war on Spain in April. The press and the public had guided public policy.

Hard on the heels of the Spanish-American "newspaper war" came the era of **muckraking,** an about-face that placed journalists in the heroic role of exposing the dark underbelly of government and industry. The most famous of the muckrakers included Ida Tarbell, who exposed the oil industry in a series of articles running from 1902 to 1904 in *McClure's* magazine; Lincoln Steffens, who published *The Shame of the Cities* in 1904; and Upton Sinclair, whose novel *The Jungle* (1906) revealed the horrors of the meat-processing industry, leading to passage of the Pure Food and Drug Act and later to the establishment of the Food and Drug Administration.[4]

muckraking
criticism and exposés of corruption in government and industry by journalists at the turn of the 20th century

A Widening War for Readership

Yellow journalism died down after World War I, and newspapers entered a period that at least on the surface valued objectivity. Newspapers increasingly found themselves competing with the new media that were just coming into being: radio stations from 1920 to 1950; television from the 1940s to 1980; and from then on, the explosion of the new media—including the Internet websites and social networking sites such as Facebook and Twitter, photo- and video-sharing platforms such as Instagram and YouTube, and cellular and satellite technology. This increased competition has had several effects on the newspaper industry. First, for over a decade, newspaper readership had steadily declined, particularly the audience for printed local newspapers, before stabilizing in recent years This decline is reflected in Figure 10.1, which shows the decline in

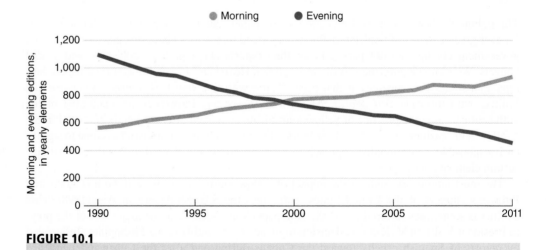

FIGURE 10.1

Number of Newspapers Continues to Decline

SOURCE: Pew Research Center, "Number of Newspapers Continues to Decline," State of the News Media 2013, www.journalism.org/media-indicators/number-of-newspapers/.

the number of newspapers published. Of particular note is the strong decline in the number of evening editions—a role presumably now filled by the Internet, as more people rely on newspapers' digital formats. Indeed, some media analysts suggest that in the next several years, some newspapers will resort to digital-only formats, or publish printed editions only on Sundays. For much of the past decade, this trend, along with increased competition from native online news sites like Slate, Salon, and Huffington Post, decimated many local newspapers whose subscriptions and advertising revenue plummeted as more and more people relied on free Internet content—often provided by the newspapers' online sites—to get their information.

To date, newspapers have not solved the challenge faced by declining print ad revenue that has not been replaced by online ad revenue. But increasingly today, newspapers are starting to profit by providing information to readers via the Internet using a **digital paywall**—the practice of limiting access to a website unless users pay a fee or purchase a subscription. *The New York Times* has—after many false starts—successfully implemented a digital paywall for online content, and many other newspapers and weekly magazines are now generating revenue by forcing readers to pay for content or use online subscriptions. Other news outlets have joined forces with Apple to create fee-based subscription apps in which e-editions of publications are available on Apple products. Others have attempted to go it alone (thus avoiding the 30 percent fee that Apple charges) by creating apps accessible on non-Apple smartphones and tablets.

Beyond changing platforms, sources of revenue, and readership the newspaper industry has changed as society has changed. Gone are the grand urban headquarters that housed newspapers—and anchor entire downtown areas—of days gone by. Today, many city newspapers have relocated to the cheaper real estate of the suburbs, with smaller newsrooms that rely on telecommuting reporters. Large cities are now likely to have smaller weekly publications targeted to specific demographic audiences—gays, women, African Americans, for example—and to publish foreign-language newspapers appealing to diverse newcomers to the United States, such as Mexican, Brazilian, Vietnamese, Iranian, Nigerian, and Russian immigrants.

As the industry has changed, so too has the human face of the newsroom. First, there are fewer faces in the newsroom, as the long-term trend of declining revenue led many newspapers to reduce its reporting staff. Second, Figure 10.2 shows that, in 2012, more than one-third of all newsroom supervisors were women, as were more than 40 percent of all layout and copy editors and reporters. Those figures reflect societal changes from the times when "newsmen" were in fact news*men*. Among all positions measured in the annual newsroom census, women were least likely to hold jobs in the visual arts, such as photographer and artist.

Table 10.1 shows another measure of how modern newsrooms have changed along with American society. The table illustrates the proportion of minority journalists working at newspapers in eight circulation categories. We can see that minority journalists are much more likely to be employed at larger-circulation newspapers, with minorities constituting nearly one-fifth of the journalists at papers having a circulation of 250,000 to 500,000. That proportion is nearly identical at the largest-circulation newspapers and steadily tapers off among newspapers with a circulation of less than 250,000.

POLITICAL Inquiry

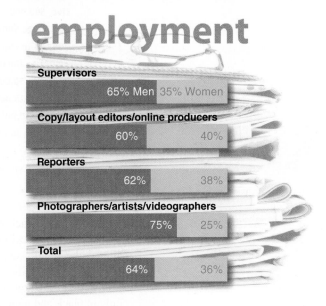

FIGURE 10.2 ▦ NEWSROOM EMPLOYMENT BY GENDER
In the past, "newsmen" were in fact news*men.* What does the graph indicate about women's employment in today's newsrooms?

employment

Supervisors
65% Men | 35% Women

Copy/layout editors/online producers
60% | 40%

Reporters
62% | 38%

Photographers/artists/videographers
75% | 25%

Total
64% | 36%

digital paywall
the practice of limiting access to a website unless users pay a fee or purchase a subscription.

The Media Go Electronic: The Radio and Television Revolutions

It is impossible to overemphasize the transformative impact of the early electronic media. From the time of the first U.S. radio broadcasts in the early 1920s, radio allowed listeners to hear news in real time. That immediacy marked a drastic change from the standard, delayed method of

TABLE 10.1

Minority Journalists as a Percentage of the Professional Workforce of Newspapers in Eight Circulation Categories

NEWSPAPER CIRCULATION	1980	1992	YEAR 2000	2005	2013
Over 500,000	7	16	18	18	18
250,001 to 500,000	6	13	18	21	19
100,001 to 250,000	6	10	14	16	15
50,001 to 100,000	6	9	10	12	12
25,001 to 50,000	4	6	8	10	8
10,001 to 25,000	3	6	7	8	8
5,001 to 10,000	2	5	6	6	6
5,000 and Under	3	5	6	7	6

SOURCE: The American Society of Newspaper Editors, "Newsroom Employment Census," http://asne.org/content.asp?pl=140&sl=134&contentid=134. Copyright © 2013 The American Society of Newspaper Editors.

receiving news, which was by reading the morning and evening editions of newspapers, plus the occasional "extra edition" published when important breaking news warranted it. Radio also altered the relationship between politicians—particularly presidents—and their constituents, because it enabled listeners to hear the voices of their elected leaders. Television further revolutionized that relationship by making it possible for people to see their leaders (though initially only in black and white).

How Radio Opened Up Political Communication

Radio was the first electronic medium that brought people into direct contact with their leaders. Beginning in the 1920s, radios became a fixture in American living rooms, and families who could not afford a radio of their own would often spend evenings at the homes of friends or neighbors who could.

FDR'S FIRESIDE CHATS   Franklin D. Roosevelt was the first politician to realize the value of radio as a device for political communication—and to exploit that value. As governor of New York (1928–1932), Roosevelt faced a Republican state legislature hostile to many of his liberal social welfare programs. To overcome the opposition, Roosevelt used radio addresses to appeal directly to his constituents, who would then lobby the legislators for his policies. Indeed, after some of Roosevelt's radio addresses, legislative offices were flooded with letters from constituents asking lawmakers to support a particular policy.

fireside chats
President Franklin D. Roosevelt's radio addresses to the country

By the time Roosevelt became president in 1933, he had grasped the importance of radio as a tool for communicating directly with the people. FDR often began his radio addresses to the country—his **fireside chats**—with the greeting, "Good evening, friends," highlighting the personal relationship he wished to cultivate between himself and his listeners. (You can listen to many of Roosevelt's fireside chats in MP3 format from the Vincent Voice Library at Michigan State University.) Through the folksy fireside chats, Americans learned about presidential initiatives on the banking crisis, New Deal social welfare programs, the declaration of war on Japan after that nation's attack on Pearl Harbor, and the progress of U.S. forces during World War II. In all, Roosevelt had 30 fireside chats with Americans over his 12 years as president.

During the golden age of radio—the period from the early 1920s through the early 1960s—radio was the dominant form of electronic entertainment. Radio programming included a wide array of shows, from newscasts, to serial dramas, to comedies, to variety shows. Although political and news radio programming remained popular during the 1950s and 1960s, radio generally took a backseat to television during that era.

>President Franklin D. Roosevelt was recognized as a master political communicator. Roosevelt relied on a folksy, conversational tone and the medium of radio to bring his message to the people. While President Barack Obama often uses lofty rhetoric, he also has been adept at using new technologies and the mass media to reach younger Americans, including his slow jamming of the news with Jimmy Fallon. How does a politician's ability to communicate successfully with the people influence his or her governing?

TALK RADIO: TALKING THE POLITICAL TALK Radio began to emerge from the shadows of television in the 1970s and 1980s. Those decades brought a renaissance of sorts for radio, as the medium saw tremendous growth in **talk radio**—a format featuring conversations and interviews about topics of interest, along with call-ins from listeners. As many AM station owners switched to an all-talk format in those years, music programming migrated to the FM band.

In 1987, the Federal Communications Commission (FCC), the U.S. government agency that regulates interstate and international communications by radio, television, wire, satellite and cable, repealed the **fairness doctrine,** which had required stations holding broadcast licenses to present controversial issues of public importance and to do so in a manner that was honest, fair and balanced. Since the law's repeal, partisan radio programming has grown dramatically. Today, listeners tend to tune in to radio hosts who share—many say, reinforce—their opinions and they interact with them through call-in opportunities. Although the number of listeners has dwindled since talk radio's heyday between 2002 and 2004 (when about one-third of all Americans listened to a talk radio program at least several times per week), today roughly 10 percent of all Americans remain faithful talk-radio listeners. Talk radio features numerous well-known personalities, including Rush Limbaugh and Sean Hannity, whose shows are also available via the Internet and through podcasts, thus potentially reaching a significantly expanded number of listeners.

Talk radio was one of the first forums that allowed media consumers to "talk back" to the host. At its best, talk radio allows for a natural, real-time exchange of information between the host and the audience; at its worst, it has given rise to loud, angry rants and arguments. Scholars widely agree that talk radio programs promote citizen engagement in the form of civic discourse. Recall from earlier chapters that civic discourse means the sharing of viewpoints and the articulation of personal positions on public issues (along with the information gathering and reflective thinking that must accompany that expression). This information sharing is fundamental to a civic society. That is, without informed and shared opinions, people cannot be responsible, politically engaged citizens.

talk radio
a format featuring conversations and interviews about topics of interest, along with call-ins from listeners

fairness doctrine
the requirement that stations holding broadcast licenses present controversial issues of public importance and to do so in a manner that was honest, fair, and balanced

Television and the Transformation of Campaigns and Elections

Although radio predates television, TV nonetheless has been the centerpiece of U.S. home entertainment for a long time. Television began to make a mark on the American scene in the 1940s, when small TV sets—their screens flecked with static snowflakes—hit the market. Its effect on the world of politics cannot be overstated. Suddenly, being **telegenic,** or looking good on TV, became almost mandatory for serious political candidates. It is unlikely that President

telegenic
the quality of looking good on TV

William Howard Taft (1909–1913), who weighed over 300 pounds, would ever have been elected if he had been forced to appear on television. Nor would Abraham Lincoln, whose handlers would have marched him straight to a cosmetic surgeon to have the giant mole on his cheek removed. Richard Nixon might have won the presidency in 1960 had it not been for his nervous demeanor and the "five o'clock shadow" on his face that made him look sinister in the first-ever televised presidential candidate debates that year. In appearance and demeanor, his opponent, the handsome, relaxed, and articulate John F. Kennedy, won the debate hands down, even though in hindsight most analysts agree that Nixon "won" the debate on its verbal merits. Since that election, the effective use of television has been a necessity for high-ranking elected office. Today, the images we view are crystal clear, as high-definition big-screen TVs increasingly dominate households, but the networks that once dominated the United States' national political life—ABC, CBS, and NBC—play a less significant role than in years past.

Today, people are as likely to watch cable television as the original three networks, and they are less likely to watch television at all than Americans two or three decades ago. Figure 10.3 shows one measure of the nature of these changes, as viewership of nightly network news broadcasts on ABC, CBS, and NBC plummeted between 1992 and 2012. Significantly, nightly news network viewership strongly correlates with age, with the youngest Americans being least likely to watch the news. But even among the oldest Americans, viewership has steeply declined: Whereas 75 percent of older Americans (aged 65 and over) watched the news in 1992, only 45 percent did so in 2012. Part of this decline is the result of the skyrocketing number of cable channels that provide tough competition for the networks.

As cable news channels such as CNN and FOX News have increased their viewing audience, it is no wonder the word *broadcasting* has spawned the term **narrowcasting:** the practice of aiming political media content at specific segments of the public, divided according to political ideology, party affiliation, or economic interests. This winnowing of audiences has led to **media segmentation,** the breaking down of the media in general according to the specific audiences they target. Examples of segmented media include Black Entertainment Television (BET); the U.S.-based Spanish-language television network Telemundo; and the Lifestyle Network, which includes the Food Network and HGTV. Through media segmentation, advertisers can hone their advertising to the tastes of their targeted markets.

But media segmentation is only partially responsible for the decline of television networks. Figure 10.4 shows that there are other causes as well. Specifically, since 2006, Americans are

narrowcasting
the practice of aiming media content at specific segments of the public

media segmentation
the breaking down of the media according to the specific audiences they target

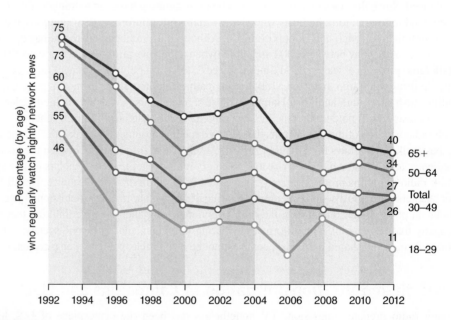

FIGURE 10.3

Network News Viewership Declines

SOURCE: Pew Research Center, "Who Is This Man? Many Americans Don't Recognize Top News Anchor," State of the News Media 2013, http://stateofthemedia.org/2013/digital-as-mobile-grows-rapidly-the-pressures-on-news-intensify/18-digital-grows-again-as-a-source-for-news/.

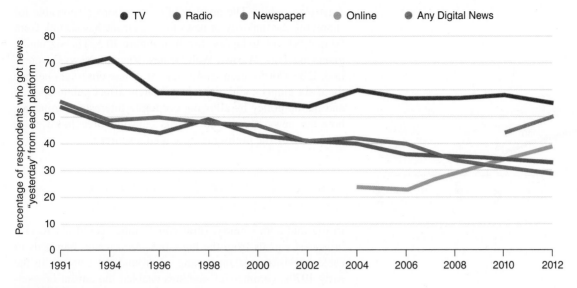

FIGURE 10.4

Digital Grows as a Source for News

SOURCE: Pew Research Center, "Digital Grows Again as a Source for News," State of the News Media 2013, http://stateofthemedia.org/2013/digital-as-mobile-grows-rapidly-the-pressures-on-news-intensify/18-digital-grows-again-as-a-source-for-news/.

increasingly likely to rely on online sources for their news, and since 2010, the number of people relying only on digital sources has increased while the number of people accessing traditional news outlets has declined.

Convergence and Consolidation

Technology has changed the business of news. Today, our expectations of news outlets have increased. No longer will the afternoon paper delivered to your doorstep by a bicycle-riding paperboy suffice. Today's "newspapers" are media outlets: We expect them to Tweet us updates, and we "like" them on Facebook. We are increasingly likely to read them on a tablet rather than in print form. And as our expectations of the role of the media have changed, so too have the businesses that are the media.

Increasingly, we are likely to see **convergence**—the merging of various forms of media (newspapers, television stations, radio networks, and blogs) that share resources or perform the same task. An example of this concept is the emergence of multimedia startup Politico. When the *Washington Star*, a newspaper owned by Capital News Corporation, folded in 2007, Capital News moved the enterprise online with many of the same political staff and rebranded it as Politico. Politico's mission is to report on daily politics on Capitol Hill and in the White House.

Today, corporations are increasingly likely to be universal providers of all our digital needs. Thus **consolidation** occurs—the phenomenon of large corporations buying smaller ones so that there are fewer and fewer companies' products available. Apple is notoriously committed to controlling the user experience from start to finish and so has created partnerships with various media outlets that distribute their content via Apple's product. In doing so, it has gobbled up several smaller companies, including the voice-recognition platform Siri. Facebook, too, has entered into agreements with technology corporations, such as the messaging service WhatsApp and the photo-sharing platform Instagram, and with media outlets, including News Corporation's *The Wall Street Journal* and also *The Washington Post* and *The Guardian*.

Consolidation has also occurred among entertainment and news media outlets. Consolidation centralizes the control of the media into the hands of a few large corporations. Some critics fear this will stifle the number of alternative viewpoints that are presented to the

convergence
the merging of various forms of media, including newspapers, television stations, radio networks, and blogs, under one corporate roof and one set of business and editorial leaders

consolidation
the phenomenon of large corporations buying smaller ones so that there are fewer and fewer companies' products available

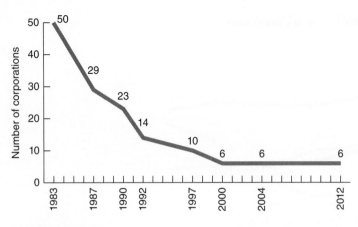

FIGURE 10.5

Media Consolidation

American public. The number of corporations responsible for supplying the majority of news to Americans has shrunk from 50 in 1983 to 6 today, as shown in Figure 10.5. The six media giants are Time Warner, Walt Disney, Viacom, News Corporation, CBS Corporation, and Comcast. Some observers believe these six giants could disproportionately affect public opinion and public policy by allowing corporate interests to influence how the news is reported. Media consolidation, however, is countered by the proliferation of media sources.

The Proliferation of News Sources and Greater Scrutiny

In the mid-20th century, rural communities could not receive broadcast signals from the big cities. As a result, hundreds of cable television systems sprang up around the country. In the early 1970s, commercial satellites enabled the advent of satellite networks. Media entrepreneurs established many new, non-broadcast networks—Home Box Office (HBO) in 1975, followed by others in the 1980s, such as CNN, ESPN, and MTV. Then in the 1990s, another technological revolution created profoundly more diverse sources of news and information—the Internet.

The rise of cable stations and the Internet have fundamentally changed politics by increasing the number of sources from which Americans can get their news. This trend results not only in narrowcasting but also in greater scrutiny of government officials and public policy. Things happen now in the time it takes to swipe a phone, and politicians guard against ever-present cell phone video cameras chronicling their every move for YouTube posterity. Such was the case in 2010, when Vice President Joseph Biden used an expletive caught on an open microphone. After introducing President Barack Obama, who had just succeeded in shepherding health care reform through Congress, the vice president turned to the president and said, "This is a big [expletive] deal." Video footage of the gaffe spread like wildfire on the Internet, and more than 1 million people watched a YouTube video of the blunder. In response (and in an effort to control damage), Robert Gibbs, the White House press secretary, tweeted, "And yes Mr. Vice President, you're right" (see Chapter 11 for more on Twitter's impact on politics).

The portability of cellular technology has also contributed to Americans' consumption of news. Using our smartphones, we always have access to news outlets, and this access has increased our consumption of news, including "long form" news—not just the 140-character Tweet or a brief Facebook posting but real news coverage, analysis, debate, and discussion. In fact, one study found that smartphones and tablets increased traffic on major newspaper websites by 9 percent.[6] Simultaneously, the timeframe of "news" also has changed. The adage that a "week is an eternity in politics" has become an understatement in the age of the Internet and the 24-hour news cycle.

Blogs: The New Penny Papers?

Technology also has changed the format of news. Today blogs have become an important component of how individuals communicate and convey information, and how media outlets keep us informed. And like the penny papers of early American times, blogs offer the opportunity for political viewpoints to infiltrate a medium whose holy grail was once neutrality. Blogging has increased enormously in the past five years, a trend that is likely to continue. Today, three blogging platforms dominate: Blogger, with 46 million unique visitors; WordPress.com, with 20 million; and Tumblr (the fastest-growing platform), with 14 million. Blogs are playing an increasingly important role not just in providing a platform for citizen journalists but also in shaping the agenda of the traditional media establishment. It is not uncommon for bloggers to "break" a story that then becomes a traditional media firestorm. Chapter 11 offers further discussion of the increasingly important role that blogs are playing in the American political arena.

Biased Media?

A recent joke about how the media will cover the end of the world stereotyped the nation's major newspapers while also emphasizing their importance in reporting world events. As the story goes, *The New York Times* headline would be: "World Ends; Third World Hit Worst." *The Washington Post*'s front page would blare: "World Ends; Unnamed Source Says White House Had Prior Knowledge." In *USA Today,* a newspaper with a huge national and international circulation, the story would be titled "We're Dead; State-by-State Analysis, page 4A; Sports, page 6C." And *The Wall Street Journal?* "World Ends; Stock Market Goes Down."

Media critics today are everywhere. All of them claim that both print and electronic media exhibit bias in their reporting, in their selection of what issues to cover, and in favoring one side of an issue (or one politician) over another. One of the most common complaints is that the media have an ideological bias.

THE QUESTION OF IDEOLOGICAL BIAS A long-standing complaint is that the media—particularly big-city newspapers—evidence a liberal bias. For example, in 2014, New Jersey governor Chris Christie attacked the "liberal media" after MSNBC—a network that had previously hosted the governor frequently on its *Morning Joe* talk show—aired reports alleging that members of Christie's administration had participated in a politically motivated scheme to shut down the George Washington Bridge into Manhattan, and had awarded municipalities federal Hurricane Sandy relief funds based on politics.

Christie's criticism of the national media is not a new charge—the notion that the media have a liberal bias is an often-heard criticism. In 1964, former president Dwight D. Eisenhower, in his address to the Republican National Convention, condemned a liberal media bias: "My friends, we are Republicans. If there is any finer word in the field of partisan politics, I have not heard it. So let us particularly [scorn] the divisive efforts of those outside our family, including sensation-seeking columnists and commentators, who couldn't care less about the good of our party."[7] Many conservatives point to studies indicating that a majority of newsroom reporters identify themselves as liberal or Democrat. Conservatives charge that the ideological bent of journalists carries through to the topics covered and to the perspectives of the stories. But studies conducted by various political scientists, including C. Richard Hofstetter, Michael J. Robinson, and Margaret A. Sheehan, refute the idea that journalists' personal viewpoints tinge the content of the news in a liberal way.[8] Indeed, studies suggest that most news stories take the form of a debate, with the journalist presenting the various sides of an issue and leaving the conclusion to the reader's interpretation.

Changes in the nature of the mass media have led to increasingly vocal charges, especially by Democratic elected officials, that newer media outlets, particularly talk radio and the blogosphere, are dominated by conservatives.

Then Now Next

How Technology Has Changed How We Get Information

Then (1960s)	Now
Three television networks—ABC, NBC, and CBS—provided all the nightly news.	Americans are increasingly likely to get their news from digital sources, including websites, podcasts, and social networking sites.
Network television programming matured and revolutionized how the media entertained and provided information.	Digital cable technology and new delivery methods—including Internet television sites such as Hulu, Internet music streaming sites like Pandora, and apps like the news app Swell—are revolutionizing entertainment and information-getting.
Television accentuated a new set of candidate qualities—including being telegenic—that had not mattered much in earlier political campaigns.	Omnipresent cell phone cameras mean that candidates must consistently display the qualities that make them appealing to voters, lest their mistakes be caught in a YouTube moment.

WHAT'S NEXT?

> How will the content of television change in the next several years? What factors might influence how television content is changing?

> Is there a downside to the new pervasiveness of television and other electronic media for candidates? For voters? If so, what?

> What new media technologies will shape the evolution of television in the future?

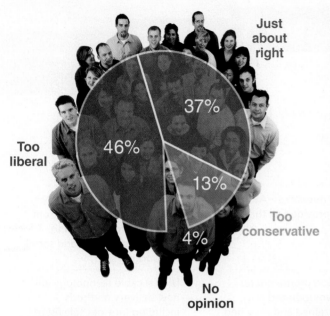

Just about right

Too liberal

37%

46%

13%

4%

Too conservative

No opinion

FIGURE 10.6

Public Opinion of Ideological Media Bias

SOURCE: Gallup Poll, "In U.S., Trust in Media Recovers Slightly From All-Time Low," www.gallup.com/poll/164459/trust-media-recovers-slightly-time-low.aspx.

THE PUBLIC'S VIEW ON MEDIA BIAS   What does the public think about partisan bias? Figure 10.6 shows that when asked the question "In general, do you think the news media are _____?" (the survey rotated the potential responses: "too liberal," "just about right," and "too conservative"), 46 percent responded that they thought the news media were too liberal. Thirty-seven percent said they thought the media were "just about right" ideologically, and 13 percent said they believed the news media were too conservative.

Thus more than half (59 percent) of those surveyed believed that the media are biased (either liberally or conservatively). Yet research by William P. Eveland, Jr., and Dhavan V. Shah into people's perception of media bias concluded that it is often linked to whether people have conversations with others whose views differ from theirs. When they do not have such dialogues, they are more likely to believe that the media are biased against their views.[9]

THE ISSUE OF CORPORATE BIAS   Most professional journalists hold journalistic objectivity to be important, and that principle well serves the interests of the large corporations that dominate the U.S. media industry today. Within the giant media conglomerates, motivated as they are by the drive for profits, there is strong disincentive for ideological bias on the part of their reporters. Newspapers and television stations rely on advertisers, and advertisers want not only to attract the largest number of readers or viewers but also to avoid offending the largest numbers. Thus, given the corporate nature of today's media, neutrality is generally a guiding principle.

Critics on the left, however, argue that these corporate structures create their own bias and that this bias has altered what is considered news and how that news is covered.[10] Corporate bias—and the desire to attract, keep, and please an audience—produces skewed programming. Will corporate conglomerates be willing to report on situations that may put themselves and their advertisers in a negative light? How does the drive for profits influence what is in the news? Are viewers being fed "news" that is not particularly newsworthy? There is no doubt that profits influence the media to cover the kinds of stories that viewers and readers want. In particular, violence dominates most local news programming, so much so that the principle of "if it bleeds, it leads" now extends into the first 15 minutes of many local news broadcasts. Fires; political, sports, and sex scandals; and celebrity-heavy news are also powerful audience attractors.

"Why don't the media report good news?" is an oft-repeated question from those who feel scarred by bad publicity. Are the media biased in favor of the negative? If the sun comes up in the morning, is that news? In fact, although many individuals bemoan the emphasis on the negative, good news typically does not attract the audience that bad news does.

Regulation of the Media: Is It Necessary?

The government regulates and controls the ownership of radio and television stations through the independent regulatory agency known as the Federal Communications Commission (FCC), founded in 1934 by Congress to regulate interstate and international communications by radio, television, wire, satellite, and cable throughout the United States. Most of the FCC's rules have concerned ownership, such as the number of outlets a network may own. Some regulations, however, govern the content of radio and television programming, attempting to ensure that "decent" content—an ambiguous term, according to many broadcasters—is on the airwaves (see "Thinking Critically About Democracy"). Although the FCC was not hypervigilant in its enforcement of the indecency ruling, it began cracking down on broadcasters after fielding many complaints from viewers of several awards programs in which celebrities, including Cher, Paris Hilton, Bono, and others, used foul language. Networks that violate the indecency policy

Democracy

Should Television Be Subject to Stricter Regulations Than Other Media Are?

The Issue: In 1978, the U.S. Supreme Court ruled that the Federal Communications Commission should have the power to regulate the content that broadcasters provide. In *Federal Communications Commission v. Pacifica Foundation,** the Supreme Court asserted that regulating content served to protect children from indecent material, since broadcasted content in television and radio had become permanent fixtures in most homes in the United States. The Court also justified regulation, because the networks relied on public airwaves to broadcast their content, and that giving the FCC broad authority would protect individuals from unwanted speech in their private homes.

The case initially stemmed from a lawsuit filed by a father whose son had heard comedian George Carlin's routine called "Filthy Words" (also known as the "seven words you can never say on television"). He complained to the FCC, which fined Pacifica Foundation, the entity that owned the radio station that broadcast the comedy bit. After the ruling, content deemed indecent by the FCC (including Carlin's filthy words) was bleeped out or edited from broadcasts. In 2012, the Supreme Court ruled in *Federal Communications Commission v. Television Stations, Inc.* concerning fines issued by the FCC for the "single use of vulgar words," on the FOX television network. During the 2002 and 2003 Billboard Music Awards, Cher and Nicole Richie used obscene words and the network was fined by the FCC. FOX challenged the fines in court. The Court invalidated the fines and ruled that while the regulations at the time did not cover "fleeting expletives," the FCC's regulations do not violate the First Amendment because the FCC is regulating on behalf of the public interest. The FCC has since amended broadcasting rules to encompass fleeting expletives.

Yes: The FCC should continue to have broad authority over the regulation of television content, since the same circumstances that held true in 1978 remain a reality for many Americans today. Television networks provide a "safe haven" for children and other individuals who do not wish to be bombarded with indecency that is prevalent in cable television. Removing regulations or failing to penalize violators will mean a degeneration of the quality of the content available on network television. In addition, the public nature of the airwaves means that the content provided by broadcasters should meet common standards of decency that would be acceptable to most Americans.

No: Current FCC regulations impinge on the First Amendment free speech rights guaranteed by the Constitution and create a tiered structure in which cable television programming, the Internet, and newspapers are not held to the same standards as radio and television. This differential creates an unfair playing field and stymies free speech by individuals communicating through regulated media. In addition, the standards enforced by the FCC reflect the values of a bygone era. Moreover, technological changes in American homes allow for parental control. Nearly all televisions have V-chips, which allow for parents to control content, and most cable subscribers have parental control capability.

Other Approaches: The FCC's current policy is ambiguous, because it does not provide broadcasters with concrete guidelines as to what is indecent and what is permissible. The creation of such guidelines would enable broadcasters to create compliant programming and work within a predictable framework. In addition, broadcasters operate without a reliable guide as to what the commission would find offensive.

*438 U.S. 726 (1978).

What do you think?

1. Do you believe that the Federal Communications Commission should regulate decency on broadcast television? Why or why not?

2. Do such regulations stifle free speech? Do the same criteria the Court cited in 1978 apply today? Why or why not?

3. Do you think that the Supreme Court has an obligation to voice an opinion on the matter of indecency rules? Why or why not?

have received fines of up to $325,000. But in the wake of these increasing fines levied by the FCC, several broadcasters sued, arguing that the FCC's enforcement of indecency regulations violates the First and Fifth Amendments' guarantees of free speech. In 2012, the Supreme Court ruled that broadcasters were not sufficiently notified of more stringent enforcement of indecency rules but declined to address whether the FCC's enforcement of these rules is constitutional.

Media also are regulated by the Telecommunications Act of 1996, which opened the communications markets to telephone companies. This sweeping law allowed competition in the communications industry. It presented new (often confusing) options for consumers, as individual companies began to offer a suite of services, from local and long-distance telephone service, to Internet access, to cable and satellite television.

With the combination of all of these services provided by single companies, large corporate conglomerates have increasingly gained control of the media. These firms exert a powerful influence over what news the average American sees and reads on a given day. The advent of these media titans has given rise to concerns about whether this type of control will deter balanced reporting of the news and unbiased presentations of issues. In addition, public conversations about our democracy are questioning whether the relative lack of competition (because there are so few competitors) means that a valuable check on what the media do and how they do it has been lost.

Conclusion
Thinking Critically About What's Next for the Media

The surge in the number and the variety of media outlets—along with the changes in the nature of the media and in people's interactions with them—have affected politics and government in many ways. Once defined as a one-way relationship, the relationship between the media and consumers has evolved in unforeseen ways. Even the nature of the "old media" has changed, although many people would ask whether the change has been for the better. On the one hand, narrowcasting and the resulting segmentation of media markets, a central feature of media growth, might raise the comfort level of many people, who no longer have to throw soft objects at their television sets in protest but can instead pick and choose what they watch. On the other hand, media segmentation also limits the exposure of many people to new ideas. Like gated communities, segmented media are also segregated media, detached environments that expose people only to viewpoints with which they agree, thus cordoning them off from society and from many of its problems. Segmented media also confuse genuine political participation with mere ranting. After all, sounding off on a radio talk show is much easier and more entertaining than attending a zoning board meeting to fight urban congestion or becoming civically engaged in other ways.

While the number of media sources and platforms available to consumers continue to proliferate, we know that convergence and consolidation are now characteristic of the business of media. So, although we may rely on an ever-increasing number of different news outlets, these outlets are owned and operated by a shrinking number of global media conglomerates, giving those corporations nearly unprecedented power in controlling the information available to consumers. This consolidation of the business of media is offset by the proliferation of other new technologies, including the advent of citizen journalism and blogging, that have diversified the sources of information available to media consumers. Nonetheless, we can anticipate even greater levels of consolidation and convergence in the future.

Can we predict the future of the media by examining the past and the present? Certainly we can foretell increasing transparency because of the pervasive nature of today's media and the steady trend in that direction, but we cannot predict the forms media will take. What we can guarantee is continued change in the forms and usage of media and steadily increasing access to information. Will this expanding access overload people with information? It appears that many of us are developing new skills to cope with the abundance of information, much in the way that our grandparents may have developed the skill of skimming a newspaper, selecting only those stories that mattered to them. The question remains as to whether we will select only information that confirms what we already think. One trend is clear: The ever-increasing volume of information and the speed of its delivery will yield an abundance of both poor-quality and high-quality information that media consumers will need to evaluate in their efforts to get accurate information.

Summary

1. The Modern Media

Changing technology has meant an overabundance of information, which varies greatly in quality. The modern media are also increasingly reliant on citizen journalists. Both trends mean that consumers of the media must be cautious and consider the sources of information.

2. The Political Functions of the Media

The media perform several key political functions, including disseminating information, helping to interpret matters of public interest and to set the national policy agenda, providing a forum for political conversations, and socializing children to the political culture.

3. The Press and Politics: A Historical View

Since early in American history, the press has played a vital role in shaping the political context. As the format of the media has evolved over the centuries, so has the media's impact on politics and policy making.

4. The Media Go Electronic: The Radio and Television Revolutions

The advent of the electronic media marked a revolutionary change with respect to the influence of media on politics. Television has altered the nature of politics and campaigning, affecting everything from how campaigns for office are conducted to how candidates look and dress. Talk radio, too, has had a significant impact on politics and government by providing a forum for political discourse that is open to participation by virtually everyone.

5. Convergence and Consolidation

In recent years, the merging of various forms of media, including newspapers, television stations, radio networks, and blogs under fewer and fewer corporate roofs has changed the nature of news and has serious implications for the ability of many Americans to receive news from a variety of sources.

6. Biased Media?

In considering the question of media bias, we must consider the issues of content bias and ideological bias. A frequent complaint is that the media—particularly big-city newspapers—have a liberal bias. However, studies by various political scientists conclude that journalists' personal views do not color news content in a liberal way. This research stresses, rather, that most news stories take the form of a debate that presents the various sides of an issue and leaves the conclusion to the reader's interpretation.

7. Regulation of the Media: Is It Necessary?

The Federal Communications Commission is the government agency charged with regulating radio and TV stations and controlling their ownership. The Telecommunications Act of 1996 allowed competition in the communications industry and presented new options for consumers, as individual companies began to offer a suite of services. With the combination of these services under single companies, large corporate conglomerates increasingly have gained control of the media. Thus, in an era of new media technologies, the FCC's job has become more complex.

Key Terms

consolidation 321
convergence 321
digital paywall 317
fairness doctrine 319
fireside chats 318
framing 313
infotainment 312

journalism 315
letter to the editor 313
media 311
media segmentation 320
muckraking 316
narrowcasting 320
new media 311

penny press 315
priming 313
public agenda 313
talk radio 319
telegenic 319
yellow journalism 315

For Review

1. How have changing technologies affected the type of information available to media consumers?

2. What political functions do the media perform? How have these functions changed over time?

3. Describe the evolution of the press in the United States. How do newspapers today differ from newspapers in earlier centuries?

4. How did television affect how people get information? How did television change how political campaigns are waged?

5. How have changes in technology changed the media? What changes do you expect to see in years to come?

6. What evidence is there to support claims of media bias? Is all bias ideological?

7. In what specific ways does the government regulate media? What aspects of the media and their coverage does the government not regulate?

For Critical Thinking and Discussion

1. Has the Internet changed how you personally participate in politics? Does virtual activism make real-world activism less likely or more likely? Explain.

2. What do you think are the most important functions the media perform? Why? Does the diversity of media outlets hinder the media's ability to serve some of their more traditional functions? Explain.

3. Compare and contrast the penny papers of the 19th century with today's blogs. What are the similarities and differences between the two? How will blogs evolve given the evolution of other media forms?

4. Discuss the dangers of the unchecked Internet in the political world. Can these dangers be combated? If so, how?

5. What difficulties are associated with government regulation of the media in an era of cable television, the Internet, and satellite radio?

MULTIPLE CHOICE: Choose the lettered item that answers the question correctly.

1. New media does not include
   a. television.
   b. Instagram.
   c. the Internet.
   d. blogs.

2. When it comes to content on the Internet,
   a. all information posted must be verifiable.
   b. all information posted must be opinion.
   c. consumers must exercise caution and consider the source of the information.
   d. citizen journalists do not play a role in providing information.

3. What media source do more Americans rely on than any other to get their news?
   a. newspapers
   b. radio
   c. the Internet
   d. television

4. President Franklin D. Roosevelt's radio addresses to the country were called
   a. great communications.
   b. White House communiqués.
   c. roundtable conversations.
   d. fireside chats.

5. The federal law that had required stations to provide equal time to all sides regarding important public issues and equal access to airtime to all candidates for public office was called the
   a. equality provision.
   b. fairness doctrine.
   c. access clause.
   d. public issue rule.

6. The practice of aiming media messages at specific segments of the public is called
   a. limited media.
   b. media messaging.
   c. narrowcasting.
   d. information limitation.

7. *Saturday Night Live*'s "Weekend Update," and Jon Stewart's *The Daily Show* are examples of
   a. Net neutrality.
   b. infotainment.
   c. convergence.
   d. new media.

8. The breaking down of the media according to specific audiences they target is called
   a. media segmentation.
   b. media messaging.
   c. narrowcasting.
   d. media categorization.

9. The merging of various forms of media—including newspapers, television stations, radio networks, and blogs—that share resources or perform the same task target is called
   a. convergence.
   b. media micromanagement.
   c. media specialization.
   d. cross-media content.

10. The phenomenon of large corporations buying smaller ones so that there are fewer and fewer companies' products available is called
    a. media segmentation.
    b. consolidation.
    c. convergence.
    d. media categorization.

FILL IN THE BLANKS

11. Public issues that most demand the attention of government officials are called the _____.

12. The process of bringing certain policies on issues to the public agenda through media coverage is called _____.

13. The journalists who criticized and exposed corruption in government and industry at the turn of the 20th century were called _____.

14. The government agency that regulates and controls the ownership of radio and television stations is called _____.

15. A person who looks good on TV is called _____.

Internet Resources

State of the Media
www.stateofthemedia.org Run by the Project for Excellence in Journalism, this site features an annual report on the media and tracks trends in media usage and confidence in the media.

The Pew Research Center for People and the Press
http://people-press.org This site provides independent research, surveys, data sets, and commentary on the media and issues of media interest.

Media Watch
www.mediawatch.com Visit this site to learn about the initiatives of an activist group that monitors media content and seeks to combat stereotypes and violence in the media.

Recommended Readings

Arnold, R. Douglas. *Congress, the Press, and Political Accountability.* Princeton, NJ: Princeton University Press, 2004. Analyzes how local newspapers cover members of Congress in their districts throughout a legislative session.

Bennett, W. Lance. *News: The Politics of Illusion,* 7th ed. New York: Longman, 2006. Offers a behind-the-scenes tour of the media in politics while grappling with this question: How well does the news, as the core of the national political information system, serve the needs of democracy?

Berry, Jeffrey M., and Sarah Sobieraj. *The Outrage Industry: Political Opinion Media and the New Incivility.* New York: Oxford University Press. The book examines "outrage rhetoric," the incendiary talk common on many talk radio and cable news programs, and evaluates its impact.

Cook, Timothy E. *Governing with the News: The News Media as a Political Institution.* Chicago: University of Chicago Press, 1998. Examines the media as the "fourth branch" of government and how the media shape public policy and how policy makers respond to the media's agenda setting.

Crouse, Timothy. *The Boys on the Bus.* New York: Random House, 1973. A classic tale of the presidential campaign press corps.

Graber, Doris. *Media Power and Politics.* Washington, D.C.: CQ Press, 2010. Analyzes the influence of the media on opinions, elections, and policies, as well as efforts to shape the content and impact of media coverage.

Iyengar, Shanto. *Media Politics: A Citizen's Guide,* 2nd ed. New York: Norton, 2011. Surveys how politicians use the media to get elected, wield power in office, and achieve policy goals.

Jamieson, Kathleen Hall, and Paul Waldman. *The Press Effect: Politicians, Journalists, and the Stories That Shape the Political*

World. Oxford: Oxford University Press, 2003. Demonstrates how the national press molds the news through its reporting, using the examples of the 2000 presidential election, the Supreme Court's decision on the Florida vote that year, and the press's response to national politics after September 11.

Plissner, Martin. *The Control Room: How Television Calls the Shots in Presidential Elections.* New York: Free Press, 1999. Describes the effect of television news and advertising on presidential elections.

Wolfsfeld, Gadi. *Making Sense of Media and Politics: Five Principles in Political Communication.* New York: Taylor and Francis, 2014. Describes the relationship between the impact of politics on the news media and how the media influence politics.

Movies of Interest

Good Night and Good Luck (2005)
Directed by George Clooney, this film tells the story of famed CBS newsman Edward R. Murrow, who takes on Senator Joseph McCarthy and the House Un-American Activities Committee's communist witch hunt during the 1950s despite pressure from corporate sponsors and from McCarthy himself.

Shattered Glass (2003)
Stephen Glass was a staff writer for the *New Republic* and was also freelancing for other prominent publications when it was discovered that he had fabricated stories. This film depicts his career and his downfall.

Veronica Guerin (2003)
Starring Cate Blanchett, this film is based on the true story of Veronica Guerin, a crime reporter for the *Dublin Sunday Independent,* who was murdered in 1996.

Live from Baghdad (2002)
This movie demonstrates the differences in tactics between 24-hour news channels and network news shows, telling the story of CNN's coverage of the U.S. invasion of Iraq in 1990.

All the President's Men (1976)
Starring Dustin Hoffman and Robert Redford, this film, based on Bob Woodward and Carl Bernstein's best-selling book of the same title, tells the saga of the two *Washington Post* reporters' investigation of the Watergate scandal that rocked the Nixon White House.

Network (1976)
Faye Dunaway, Peter Finch, William Holden, and Robert Duvall star in this classic satirizing the nature of newscasting in the 1970s.

Citizen Kane (1941)
This classic, directed by and starring Orson Welles, is Welles's fictionalized version of newspaper scion William Randolph Hearst, who purportedly attempted to halt release of the film.

CHAPTER 11

Politics and Technology

 ## THEN

Technology had little influence on politics.

 ## NOW

Technology is the most important tool that determines how people participate in democracies—shaping how campaigns are run, how candidates behave, and how governments provide services.

 ## NEXT

Will people use technology as the great equalizer to facilitate participation in our democratic system?

Will campaigns use increasingly sophisticated microtargeting mechanisms to deliver better information to voters?

Will the ever-increasing speed, portability, and volume of information affect its quality?

This chapter focuses on the role technology plays as a force in contemporary U.S. politics, investigating how technology has transformed the ways the individual, groups and organizations, and government engage in politics. In this chapter, we learn how technology is changing political communication, and we discover and evaluate new technologies that will change how we participate in the life of our democracy in the future.

FIRST, we examine the modern technological revolution and explore who uses new technology.

SECOND, we analyze how technology is changing the political arena through accessibility on-demand and how it has changed the nature of political communication, citizen participation, community activism, political participation, and campaigning.

THIRD, we assess how technology is transforming how governments govern.

FOURTH, we examine the positive impact of new technologies on politics and how they will transform political life in the future.

FIFTH, we explore the potential negative consequences of new technologies on politics.

SIXTH, we evaluate whether regulation of the Internet is necessary.

social networking sites
platforms that enable users to construct a profile, specify other users with whom they share a connection, and view others' connections

We turn to Twitter when

discussing the latest tiff between Real Housewives or what Kim and Kanye did over the weekend, but Twitter is increasingly entering the fray when politicians are embroiled in controversy, sometimes, even, when countries are at odds. Witness the war of tweets that ensued in 2014 when Russia annexed Ukraine's Crimean peninsula into the Russian Federation. The British embassy tweeted: "Russian armed forces installed pro-Russian puppet administration and rail-roaded through referendum vote illegal. #Crimea #Ukraine." Russia, fortunately, did not whip out the heavy artillery and aim at Great Britain. Instead, it took aim with its smartphones, replying, "@ukinrussia The people of Crimea think otherwise, dear colleagues! Will of people comes first, does it not?" That nations would communicate using social networking in public view over such a heated issue demonstrates how central technology in general and social media in particular have become in our daily lives and in our politics. Technology shapes modern political life. Governments use technology to communicate with their citizens and to administer policies. Citizens use technology to convey their views to elected leaders and to organize groups that influence policy making. Candidates and political organizations, including political parties and interest groups, rely on technology to both inform and mobilize their members.

A half century ago, the advent of television changed the nature of political life in the United States in many ways—it changed the characteristics essential for candidates to be successful. It changed how campaigns were run and how voters were kept informed of issues. From the start, some Internet innovators hoped new technologies might usher in an age of better democratic governance. The founder of the World Wide Web, Tim Berners-Lee (who created the first successful communication between a hypertext transfer protocol [http] client and a server using the Internet), stated that "greater openness, accountability, and transparency in government will give people greater choice and make it easier for individuals to get more directly involved in issues that matter to them."[1] Or, as influential communication expert Howard Rheingold of Stanford University wrote, "learning to use blogs, wikis, podcasts, and digital video as media of self-expression, with an emphasis on 'public voice,' should be considered a pillar—not just a component—of twenty-first-century civic [education]."[2]

Today, the hardware of modern technology—the Internet, smartphones, and other cellular devices—is revolutionizing how politics is done in the United States. This transformation is being facilitated not just by the devices we use, but also by the platforms, software, and apps that these devices use. Of particular importance in politics is the use of **social networking sites,** which enable users to construct a profile, specify other users with whom they share a connection, and view others' connections.[3] Technology is transforming how campaigns operate—from raising a candidate's first campaign contribution to getting the last voter to the polls on election night. For voters, new technology means that an abundance of information is available instantaneously, but the sheer volume of information and the dubious nature of much of it mean that voters must work harder to get accurate facts about candidates and organizations. Even after the campaigns are over, technology is also helping the government communicate with and provide services to its citizens, and helping those citizens to convey their needs to government officials.

The Modern Technological Revolution: The Internet and Cellular Technology

The modern media revolution began with the birth of the Internet. As a medium of communication, a source of news and information, and a tool for political engagement and organizing at the grassroots, the Internet has had an incalculable—and a global—impact on the way people interact. Figure 11.1 shows that today 87 percent of American adults now use the Internet. Among certain populations, including members of the Millennial generation, those with a household income over $75,000, and those with a college degree, usage is essentially universal (with 97 percent, 99 percent, and 97 percent of those populations, respectively, using the Internet).[4] In addition, more than two-thirds of adult Americans (68 percent) use mobile devices like iPads or smartphones to connect to the Internet, and the average user spends more than two hours per day using a smartphone or tablet.[5]

The modern media revolution continues today as cellular technology makes the Internet portable and constantly available. Thus, we spend so much time on the Internet because we can—using cellular technology, we can Facebook while waiting for the bus, check e-mail in line at the grocery store, blog while eating lunch in the cafeteria (but of course we would *never* text in class . . .). The convenience and power of the combination of these technologies have enormous implications for how politics takes place now and how politics will happen in the future as access to cell phones continues to increase. Today, over half (58 percent) of all American adults own a smartphone.[6] Since 90 percent of Americans own some kind of mobile phone, the number of smartphone owners is likely to increase as contracts on standard phones expire and prices of smartphones drop.

The Digital Divide

But not everyone has equal access to the Internet. Even today there remain differences between groups concerning who uses technology and who doesn't. The term for this unequal access to computer technology is the **digital divide.** Historically, one of the largest sources of the digital divide has been income: Poorer people were less likely to have access to new technologies. Today, however, the chief condition fueling the digital divide is age: Whereas 98 percent of Millennials own cell phones, only 74 percent of those over age 65 do**.** Today's technology means

digital divide
unequal access to computer technology

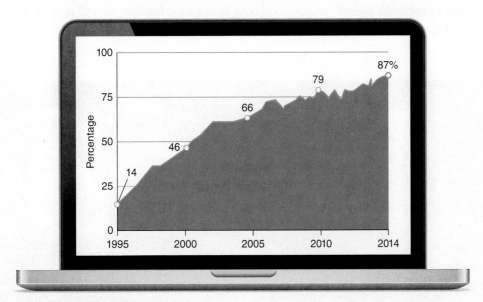

FIGURE 11.1

Percentage of Adult Americans Who Use the Internet

SOURCE: Susannah Fox and Lee Rainie, "The Web at 25 in the U.S.," February 27, 2014, Pew Research Internet Project, www.pewinternet.org/2014/02/27/summary-of-findings-3/.

that those with smartphones have access to the Internet, and with the expansion of free Wi-Fi access, the ability to use the Internet increases even among those who cannot afford large data plans or high-speed Internet access at home.

Nonetheless, even today, affluent individuals are more likely to have smartphones, unlimited data plans, computers, and high-speed Internet connections than are other people. Ninety-eight percent of those with incomes over $70,000 have cell phones, whereas 84 percent of those earning less than $30,000 do. Access to high-speed Internet service even in the world's most affluent democracies can be expensive,[7] and in the developing world, access to technology is nearly always limited. Where information technology is relatively broadly available, as in the United States, several political scientists, including Matthew Hindman[8] and Laura McKenna, argue that access to the Internet produces unequal benefits politically. McKenna notes that "those with lower levels of political capital are lost in a sea of facts, distracted by online poker and joke e-mails, and may be simply not interested in reading political content . . . [while] those who avail themselves of superior political resources on the Internet accelerate their political skills."[9] But evidence indicates that as the use of cellular technology increases (and becomes cheaper) and free Wi-Fi service becomes more widely available, the income-based digital divide will shrink even further. The geographic digital divide, by which residents of rural areas lack access to wired broadband technology, also is changing because of greater availability of Internet access through cellular technology, even in many remote regions.

Disabilities can also contribute to a kind of digital divide. Today, about 81 percent of Americans use the Internet, but Internet use shrinks to 54 percent among adults living with a disability that interferes with daily life, a group that constitutes about 25 percent of the U.S. population.[10]

Who Uses the Internet?

Demographic factors, including region, income, education, race, and age, certainly play a role in predicting whether an individual will use technology, as shown in Table 11.1. A gap in Internet usage exists between those with household incomes of less than $30,000 and those earning more than $30,000. Internet usage is also highly correlated with educational attainment, with three-quarters of those without a high school diploma using the Internet and nearly all of those (99 percent) with college degrees using it. Community type also matters, although to a lesser extent: People living in rural areas (where access to high-speed Internet connections is more limited) are slightly less likely to use the Internet than are suburbanites and urban dwellers. Also, the younger a person, the greater the likelihood he or she uses the Internet, with 97 percent of those between ages 18 and 29 using the Internet, compared to only 57 percent of those over age 65.

>Demographic factors, including income, education, race, and age, play a role in predicting whether an individual will use technology. But because of the propensity for young people to use the Internet, and because of the increasing use of smartphones, Internet usage is likely to be nearly universal in the future.

Internet usage today is skewed toward highly educated, high-income earners. But because of the propensity for young people to use the Internet, and because of the increasing use of smartphones, Internet usage is likely to be nearly universal in the future.

Yet, despite the fact that some Americans do not own computers or have online access, the Internet has broadly transformed life in the United States in general and political life specifically. Technology has changed the structure of how information is communicated, how political participation occurs, and how governments govern. As political scientist Michael Cornfield noted: "I can't think of anything except kissing babies that you can't do online."[11] (Today, candidates probably do that on the video web-chatting service Skype.) In any case, the influence of the Internet has been both positive and negative, and it continues to evolve.

New Forms of Community

Internet technology also facilitates the formation of virtual communities. These networks of interested participants, although different from their IRL (in-real-life) counterparts, share features with those real-world groups.[12] Many blogs, for example, have community leaders, regular contributors, expert commentators, and participants with established roles. Blogs promote civic engagement and participation by disseminating information, exposing readers to the viewpoints of others, providing a forum allowing bloggers to share their own views, serving as a venue for the formation of online communities that can foster feelings of efficacy among participants, and channeling activism, both virtual and real.

Facebook, Instagram, and other social networking sites also create **virtual communities,** online networks—of friends, of fans, and groups—where individuals perform as leaders, information and opinions can be shared, and strategies can be planned, priorities organized, and roles assigned. Clay Skirky's *Here Comes Everybody* chronicles why some online entities—including flashmobs and Wikipedia—effectively create organizational structure and channel participation, while others flounder.[13] And the success that individuals enjoy in virtual roles may spill over into real-life behaviors in political organizations. For example, much research indicates that the use of social media sources including Facebook increases civic engagement and participation in the real world,[14] although some social network users are no more likely to participate in politics than are users of other media.[15] Furthermore, online groups perform many of the same positive civic functions as offline groups, specifically in terms of mobilizing political participation (although not in terms of increasing political knowledge).[16] In many ways, social networking sites undertaking political work closely resemble the in-real-life groups that preceded them and also spur activism that may not have been possible through offline groups.

The Internet has also facilitated the formation of communities by enabling people in disparate places to communicate and work toward shared goals or share information. Consider, for example, the Facebook group Ethiopia Community, where Ethiopian diaspora can communicate with each other, share news items, and discuss current events and history about corruption, crime, and civic problems.

But communities need not be nationalistic in nature. For example, the Gay Rights cause on Facebook has over 1.2 million members from all over the world. The group is an arm of the advocacy group Change.org, which provides a community-building tool for the lesbian, bisexual, gay, and transgender (LBGT) communities to start campaigns to fight for gay rights. According the Gay Rights' Cause Facebook page, they "empower millions of people to start, join, and win campaigns for equality in their community, city, and country." The platform enables communities to form around a wide array of issues affecting the LGBT community, including supporting anti-bullying policies in states and communities and pressuring corporations to condemn anti-gay government policies abroad. The group facilitates the replication of effective strategies by enabling local communities to rely on the tried-and-true methods that have worked in other locales.

Virtual communities have been particularly important for people with disabilities, as new technologies enable them to circumvent the physical obstacles they may face in networking with

POLITICAL Inquiry

TABLE 11.1 ■ WHO USES THE INTERNET?
In general, what demographic groups are most likely to be Internet users? What factors might prevent less likely populations from using the Internet?

SOURCE: Susannah Fox and Lee Rainie, "The Web at 25 in the U.S.," February 27, 2014, Pew Research Center Internet Project Survey, www.pewinternet.org/files/2014/02/PIP_25th-anniversary-of-the-Web_0227141.pdf.

	USE INTERNET
ALL ADULTS	87%
SEX	
Men	87
Women	86
RACE/ETHNICITY	
White	85
African American	81
Hispanic	83
AGE GROUP	
18–29	97
30–49	93
50–64	88
65 +	57
EDUCATION LEVEL	
High school grad or less	76
Some college	91
College +	97
HOUSEHOLD INCOME	
Less than $30,000	77
$30,000–$49,999	85
$50,000–$74,999	93
$75,000+	99
COMMUNITY TYPE	
Urban	88
Suburban	87
Rural	83

virtual communities

online networks where individuals perform as leaders, information and opinions can be shared, and strategies can be planned, priorities organized, and roles assigned

> Shrinking the digital divide for visually impaired: A Ray smartphone enables users who are visually impaired to navigate all smartphone features with eyes-free operation, thus enabling the user to communicate with friends, family, and colleagues. Technology is increasingly making it easier for people who are physically challenged to participate in the civic life of their communities.

people with similar disabilities. For example, using the Siri voice recognition tool on an iPhone or Ray—a smartphone created specifically for individuals who are visually impaired, which allows eyes-free operation—a nonseeing person can communicate in real time to anyone, including members of the Visually Impaired Support Group on Facebook, which connects people with vision impairment in numerous countries.

Technology Now: Changing How Candidates Campaign and Citizens Participate

The 2008 presidential campaign—dubbed the Web 2.0 election—was a watershed event in terms of technology. Although both campaigns relied on a groundbreaking technological innovation on many campaign fronts, then-Senator Barack Obama consistently had the advantage. A Pew Research Center study found that, when compared to John McCain's website, Barack Obama's website made it easier for users to actively participate in the campaign. Users could opt to receive up-to-the-minute campaign news (including links to stories about the candidate and campaign in the popular media), review talking points, download campaign posters and flyers, make computer-assisted phone calls to undecided voters in swing states, and map out door-to-door canvassing operations in their area.[17]

Obama's campaign relied on social networking sites to familiarize voters—particularly young voters—with his campaign's message. Obama had more Facebook friends than McCain by a 5-to-1 margin, and the campaign and its supporters posted twice as many videos to his official YouTube channel.[18] Obama's YouTube channel bested McCain's in the number of subscribers by an 11-to-1 margin.[19] As the campaign heated up, this vast social network helped to spin news and deflate opposition messages. Finally, new cellular technologies and software platforms provided for a sophisticated get-out-the-vote effort on Election Day, with many "armchair activists" relying on their computers and telephones to encourage turnout. Obama's success made campaign organizers, political candidates, and the media realize how crucial it is to leverage emerging technology to create strategic advantages.

Since that game-changing campaign, technology has continued to transform how American politics happen. Technology has changed not only how campaigns are run, but also how we receive information and how governments provide services. Perhaps most important is technology's promise: Cellular technology and the Internet hold the potential of serving as a mean by which people can exercise control over their democracy. And because of the differences in how generations use technology, it holds the greatest promise for younger people. Communications scholar Howard Rheingold argues that the digital media in particular serve as a key avenue through which young people can use their "public voice" to consume and share information.[20] This information is available immediately at any time of the day or night. Since the information superhighway is no longer a one-way street, it provides greater opportunities for political conversations, debates, and reactions. It is also increasingly serving as a platform through which communities that influence political life come together and exert influence.

Politics on Demand

Immediate, on-demand access to political information is a recent phenomenon. Whereas political party members in a given town might have had to wait for a monthly newsletter to learn information or find out about events, today they can simply visit a local party's website, subscribe to an e-mail listserv, or sign up for text messaging alerts to get on-the-spot updates. Governments, too, can provide information in real time: from Facebook updates about the status of pending legislation to the use of text messaging as part of the Emergency Alert System, citizens can receive information as soon as it's available.

Nightly newscasts—once the main method by which Americans got their news—now seem quaint, as information is transmitted instantaneously to our cell phones via the Internet. News websites—including those of all the network and cable news stations, plus sites maintained by Internet service providers—give Internet users access to news stories when they want them instead of at predetermined times. And **news aggregators,** services such as Google News, the

news aggregators
services that compile in one location news we want from various outlets

Huffington Post, and the Drudge Report, compile all the news we want from various outlets, including news headlines, blogs, and podcasts, in one location so that we can consume information quickly. As shown in Figure 11.2, Americans get their news from a variety of devices, including television (87 percent), laptops/computers (69 percent), radio (65 percent), and print newspapers or magazines (61 percent). Most Americans report that they follow the news using, on average, four different devices or technologies[21] and a variety of ways to connect to the Internet. These users can selectively search for specific information or sign up for alerts to keep informed about public issues that matter to them, building their knowledge base at a finger's click. Moreover, many contemporary news outlets, such as magazines and radio programs, make available downloadable podcasts that give individuals even greater access to reports on social issues, policy initiatives, and politics.

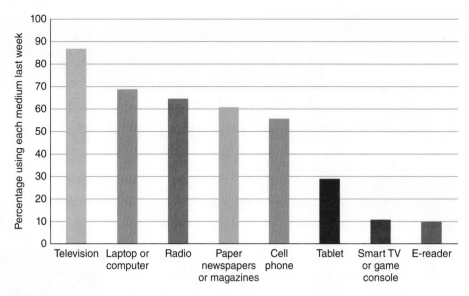

FIGURE 11.2

Where Americans Get Their News

SOURCE: American Press Institute, "How Americans Get Their News," www.americanpressinstitute.org/publications/reports/survey-research/how-americans-get-news/.

YouTube provides a compelling example of how the evolving Internet has worked to provide on-demand and real-time information. This website, which debuted in February 2005 and is now owned by Google, allows individuals to post and watch original videos. The success of the YouTube experiment would have been inconceivable in a world of dial-up Internet connections that was the norm just a few years ago. Today, 100 hours of video are uploaded to YouTube every minute by its one billion unique users. More video is uploaded to YouTube in one month than has been broadcast by the three television networks in the past 60 years, and three billion hours of video are viewed each month.[22]

One way the behemoth of YouTube is affecting political life in the United States is by furnishing an unprecedented amount and variety of on-demand data concerning candidates and elections. Consider, for example, PoliticsTV, which is an online network of YouTube members who uploaded political videos related to presidential and congressional campaigns so that others may view them. PoliticsTV is modeled on the pivotal YouChoose '08 YouTube channel, which enabled viewers to watch videos posted by the Obama and McCain campaigns and the news media, as well as YouTube's own sponsored presidential debate. The channel was so successful in 2008 that it was expanded in 2012 and has continued to experience heavy traffic. If you want to watch a political advertisement, check out a Jon Stewart clip, or watch John Green's **vlog**—or video weblog—*Crash Course in History: the Constitution, the Articles, and the Federalism,* you can do so in seconds.

vlog
video weblog

But the political impact of the Internet is not limited to the United States, or even to democracies. The interactivity embodied in viewing, commenting, posting, and vlogging has revolutionized civic discourse globally. Indeed, the Internet has made the world smaller, enabling the global spread of news and information and exerting an influence on national politics that was unheard of before (see "Global Context").

Technological Tools: Paving the Two-Way Communication Street

In its early years, the Internet functioned in much the same way that traditional media formats, such as newspapers and periodicals, functioned: It provided a convenient but "one-way" means for people to get information at times determined by the publishers. As **bandwidth**—the amount of data that can travel through a transmission medium in a given time period—has increased, so, too, has the sophistication of Web content, as well as the venues and formats that serve as information sources. In the early 1990s, when Tim Berners-Lee invented hypertext and researchers

bandwidth
the amount of data that can travel through a transmission medium in a given time period

BLOGGING FOR REFORM IN UKRAINE

Ukrainian blogger Tetyana Chornovol was driving to her home outside of Kiev when a Porsche Cayenne SUV cut her off and blocked her car's path in the early morning hours of Christmas 2013. "People came out of it and began beating me. I tried to bypass it, but it was impossible. The jeep hit me. It tried to kill me. They broke my window. I jumped out, tried to run. I was caught and they began beating me."

The assault on Chornovol came just hours after she had written a blog post describing the new construction of a villa being built in the village of Pidhirtsi by Vitaly Zakharchenko, who then served as the country's interior minister and headed up the national police service, the Militsiya.

Ukraine, facing serious budgetary difficulties and monumental decisions concerning whether it should link its economic future to Russia or Europe, saw serious antigovernment protests from November 2013 through the spring of 2014, leading up to the May elections. The protest movement spread through social networking sites and blogs, as the government controlled many traditional news outlets. The protestors sought significant government reforms, and a Ukrainian alliance with Europe.

Chornovol had long documented abuses by Zakharchenko in her blog. In 2012, she scaled the walls of Zakharchenko's compound, which he had characterized as a modest residence, to reveal astounding grandeur, including elaborate gardens, a pen for Zakharchenko's pet ostriches, and a helipad. Other bloggers had documented how Zakharchenko came to own the residence

illegally, after having companies illegally privatize the property and then turn it over to him. After Chornovol's beating, she became a *cause célèbre* among antigovernment protestors, including many calling for Zakharchenko's ouster.

Zakharchenko was suspended by the Ukrainian parliament on February 21, 2014. On May 25, 2014, Petro Poroshenko, a politician who had supported the protests, was elected president of the Ukraine with 54 percent of the vote. Tetyana Chornovol currently leads the government's anticorruption bureau.

at the University of Illinois introduced the first graphic Web browser, Mosaic, Internet users could e-mail, post, and access text files and even communicate via rudimentary bulletin boards. Yet accessing a single page with graphics or photos could take well over a minute. By the mid-1990s, however, businesses and venture capitalists recognized the commercial potential of the World Wide Web. Cable supplanted dial-up modem-driven access and thus expanded bandwidth. Start-up companies and IT giants raced to develop hardware and software products that allowed for the exchange of text, voice, images, and videos in new ways. Cell phone towers sprang up around the world as these devices evolved to provide laptop functionalities. Within just a few years, instant messaging, voicemailing, and posting images, audio, videos, and text had become built in to the pattern of 21st-century communication.

As a result, communication is a two-way street, no longer mediated by media outlets. Governments, candidates, their organizations, grassroots organizations, interest groups, and political parties use technology to communicate directly with individuals, and vice versa. Civic participation has been facilitated by the rise of these new forms of communication, which enable conversations about information, rather than just information reception. The Internet has also created a hybrid between producers and consumers of news, as many individuals simultaneously consume and produce information in the forms of videos, postings, and websites.

One of the key means by which individuals now communicate with government leaders and others is through Facebook and other (more specific) social networking sites. These sites enable direct two-way communication between groups or individuals and "friends" or supporters in both the social and the political realms. One unique platform for voters to determine their position on issues and communicate these opinions to elected representatives is the website VoteTocracy. Here, visitors can uncover information about bills under consideration by the U.S. Congress. Visitors can also select an issue, learn about it, determine their position on the issue, and then prompt VoteTocracy to communicate that position to their representatives in Congress.

Facebook also provides an invaluable mechanism by which those sharing a political viewpoint can organize, communicate, and mobilize successfully, efficiently, and cost-effectively. For example, during the 2012 election, Facebook partnered with CNN to create America's Choice 2102, an interactive social networking platform for CNN's on-air, mobile, and online audiences and Facebook's users. America's Choice 2012 sought to "amplify the voices of the social site's users as they share their thoughts and feelings on candidates and critical issues facing the country ahead of Election Day." By using the "I'm Voting" Facebook app, Facebook surveys, and a metric to gauge "Facebook buzz," the collaboration sought to provide both information and an interactive mechanism for political participation.

Candidates, too, rely on social networking to inform voters. For example, during the 2014 congressional elections, Senator Cory Booker's (D-N.J.) organization used Facebook effectively to keep supporters informed, to grow Booker's base of support, and to mobilize voters during primary elections. Indeed, during the campaign, nearly 300,000 people had "liked" his Facebook page. Booker's message resonated particularly with some young voters, who are more likely to use technology as a medium for their political participation. Just a decade ago, this kind of structure did not exist.

Another tool that establishes a new "two-way street" of political communication is the blog. Today, new language has sprouted up to incorporate this development, beginning with **blogosphere**—the community, or social network, of bloggers. Increasing numbers of people are as likely to subscribe to popular blogs such as *Daily Kos, ThinkProgress,* and *RedState* as they are to

blogosphere
the community of bloggers

> VoteTocracy enables users to easily learn about legislation pending in Congress. After users formulate their opinion, then can then use the website to communicate their views to their members of Congress.

POSTING AND TWEETING ABOUT POLITICS

The graph shows the proportion within each age group who engage in different civic or political behaviors.

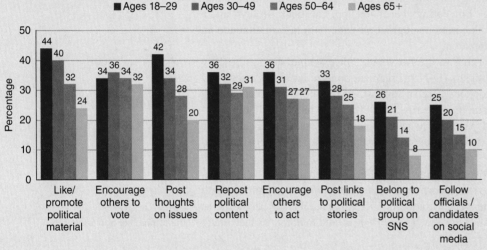

Percentage of social networking site and Twitter users who engage in these activities

■ Ages 18–29   ■ Ages 30–49   ■ Ages 50–64   ■ Ages 65+

SOURCE: Pew Research Center's Internet & American Life Project Civic Engagement Survey, conducted July 16–August 7, 2012, on landline and cell phones and in English and Spanish. *N* for social media users ages 18–29=323. *N* for social media users ages 30–49=388. *N* for social media users ages 50–64=323. *N* for social media users ages 65+=167.

Evaluating the Evidence

1. What is the most common way in which each age group participates in politics online?

2. Generally, describe the trend with regard to age and political activities online. What is the implication of this trend?

3. Are there any political activities in which Millennials are not the most likely group to participate? Why do you think this might be the case?

---

local or national newspapers. Using the blog platforms WordPress, Tumblr, Blogger, or many others, anyone can blog, and the number of blogs increases enormously each year, with some observers estimating that one million blogposts are posted each day.[23] As the number has multiplied, their variety and credibility have increased. Research indicates that there is enormous crossover between the blogosphere and traditional media outlets, with many traditional media outlets increasingly providing blogs written by professional journalists. For example, the *Washington Post*'s Chris Cillizza's blog, *The Fix*, is a must-read for many D.C.-based political insiders.

Grassroots is a term that describes political efforts that start at the local level and eventually grow to reach higher levels, including the state and national levels. The blog's rise as a tool of grassroots organizing has given birth to the term **netroots** to describe Net-centered political efforts on behalf of candidates and causes. The blog provides immediate distribution of information to large numbers of users, spreading news and energizing supporters more rapidly than any other medium. Blogs, like the partisan penny papers that were a specialized medium of information in early American times, also enable people to select sources of information that mimic and confirm their own views.[24] And those who participate online tend to be among the most active citizens in offline forms of engagement as well (see "Analyzing the Sources").

One of the most effective means by which blogs provide immediate distribution of information to large numbers of people is through **micro-blogs.** Sites, including Twitter and other micro-blogs that enable short communication, often target specifically on-the-move audiences or empower individuals to collect information at opposition events. Although Twitter enjoys comparatively fewer users than do social networking sites like Facebook, Twitter is enormously important among political operatives and many activists.

netroots
the Internet-centered political efforts on behalf of candidates and causes

micro-blog
sites, including Twitter, that enable short communication, often targeted specifically at on-the-move audiences

New Campaign Strategies and Modes of Political Participation

Technology has changed the nature of political participation and of political campaigns through the introduction of new strategies that give candidates advantages and enable new modes of political participation.

E-CAMPAIGNING Among the first to understand the value that information technology held for political campaigns was Jesse Ventura, a professional wrestler who served as the governor of Minnesota from 1999 to 2003. He represented the Reform Party, founded in 1995 and supported by people who were disillusioned with what they saw as the corruption and ineffectiveness of the two major parties. Ventura credited the Internet with opening up the political process by enabling grassroots mobilization through **e-campaigning,** the practice of mobilizing voters using the Internet, which allowed an outsider like him to be elected governor. Winning half of the under-30 vote, Ventura conducted the first stage of his campaign without any physical headquarters. Armed with a large e-mail list, he collected pledges of support that short-circuited the traditional doorbell ringing and telephone calls that go with the territory when running for office. His tactics gave him the final surge of voters that he needed to win. Ventura's victory foreshadowed the power of the Internet as a political campaign tool.

The potential of the Internet as a force in political campaigns came into sharp focus again in 2004, when liberal Democrat Governor Howard Dean of Vermont used the Internet extensively for recruiting volunteers and raising money. Dean's efforts proved so successful that other candidates quickly followed his strategy. By the 2008 campaign, every major presidential candidate had a staff of website designers, Internet campaign managers, and blog managers.

The Internet has also opened up the process of political organizing to party rank and file or outsiders. On the day that Senator Obama announced his bid for the presidency, Farouk Olu Aregbe, a student government adviser at the University of Missouri, logged on to Facebook and announced the formation of a group called "One Million Strong for Barack." Within a month, Aregbe's Facebook group had over a quarter of a million members, and other Facebook users had formed more than 500 groups supporting the candidate.

Today, Facebook plays a key role in political campaigns. The site's Government and Politics page (www.facebook.com/GovtPolitics) highlights how elected leaders, candidates, and campaigns are using Facebook to reach constituents. The page also showcases best practices for Facebook campaigns, and provides tips for developing social networking tools in campaigns.

But the rapid expansion of Internet technology also has made it more difficult for presidential campaigns (and administrations) to manage the news.[25] Regarding the phenomenon of videos going viral, Patrick Healy of *The New York Times* wrote: a "video clip may have been trivial, but the brief episode surrounding it illustrated how visual and audio technologies like video streaming have the potential to drive political news in unexpected directions, and how White House candidates are aggressively monitoring and trying to master them."[26] As a case in point, when President Obama attended the funeral of legendary South African leader Nelson Mandela, Obama caught flak for posing for a selfie with Danish prime minister Helle Thorning-Schmidt and British prime minister David Cameron. (It didn't help matters that first lady Michelle Obama sat respectfully nearby and appeared annoyed.) Photos of the incident went viral, making President Obama appear as if he had detracted from the solemnity of the occasion.

Then Now Next

The Future of FB

Then (2004)	Now
It was called "The Facebook"	It's just Facebook
It had 1 million users	It has over 1 billion active monthly users around the world
Users posted on a Facebook wall	Users post on a Timeline
Fewer than 800 college networks were part of the Facebook	750 million people use Facebook on their cell phones or tablets

WHAT'S NEXT?

> How might governments use Facebook in the future?

> How might Facebook be used as political tool by activists and campaigns in the future?

> What does Facebook's potential expansion internationally mean for its political utility?

e-campaigning
the practice of mobilizing voters using the Internet

> The rapid expansion of Internet technology also has made it more difficult for presidential campaigns and administrations to manage the news. President Obama was chastised in the media and on the Internet (and, from the look of the first lady, probably at home) for posing for a selfie with Danish prime minister Helle Thorning-Schmidt and British prime minister David Cameron. Critics charged that Obama's actions, which took place at the funeral of South African leader Nelson Mandela, were disrespectful.

promoted tweets
targeted advertising found on a Twitter page that targets Twitterers based on whom they follow and who follows them

remarketing
targeting political Google ads based on the cookies that a user drops on other websites

microtarget
data-mining techniques that facilitate the tracking of individual voter preferences so that tailored messages in various forms can be used to generate support, contributions, and votes

The same technology that is used to target potential consumers of products is now being used to target votes. Twitter currently boasts 241 million users who tweet over 500 million messages of 140 or fewer characters. Research indicates that in addition to the important role Twitter plays among political consultants and activists, it also plays a significant role in shaping public opinion. Researchers Fei Xiong and Yun Liu ran six million tweets through a computer algorithm and discovered that the diffusiveness that characterizes initial public opinion on an issue evolves and consolidates quickly, often through endorsements of large groups, which are most effective at swaying opinions. Despite the evolved consensus, small segments of Twitter users who hold minority views may not change, but for candidates and elected officials, it is crucial to act early in order to forge the consensus view, as once public opinion solidifies around an issue on Twitter, it is difficult to change. Thus, **promoted tweets**—that is, targeted advertising—found on a Twitter page that target Twitter users based on whom they follow and who follows them, may be an effective tool for candidates and elected officials to shape opinion.

Increasingly, Google is **"remarketing"**—that is, targeting political Google ads based on the cookies that a user dropped on other websites. So, for example, if you visited the Ready for Hillary website and then read *The New York Times* online, a Google ad soliciting support for Hillary Clinton might appear on your screen, because, when selling ads to campaigns and other organizations, Google recognizes that, based on your Internet behavior, you're more likely to contribute to or support causes that you have demonstrated an interest in through your online behavior.

MICROTARGETING   One of the hallmarks of today's technology is that it allows candidates and other organizations to **microtarget**—that is, to use data-mining techniques to facilitate the tracking of individual voter preferences so that tailored messages in various forms can be used

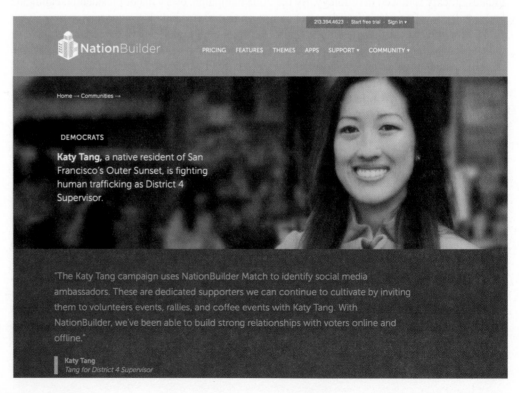

> NationBuilder is one platform that enables candidates, interest groups, community organizations, and businesses to microtarget individuals and then communicate with, organize, and mobilize their supporters.

to generate support, contributions, and votes. For example, NationBuilder is a software package that mines Internet data, and enables a candidate organization, political party, interest group, or other organization to use that mined data to create lists of potential supporters based on their online profiles. Using social networking platforms, organizations can then target these individuals and try to garner their support.

Other programs use surveys to determine voter priorities and preferences and then, based on the potential supporters' responses, campaign canvassers can access already-prescribed talking points to convince potential supporters to vote for their candidate or join their cause. They can even access compelling videos targeted at the respondents on a smartphone or an iPad. Using the smartphone, a canvasser can immediately sign up residents for text or e-mail subscriptions. Once back at headquarters, the canvasser will sync the phone with databases that will track the voter for years, and update his or her preferences and concerns.

E-MAIL CAMPAIGNS AND E-PETITION DRIVES Campaigns can also benefit or suffer from e-mail campaigns. With one click, you can influence how someone you know thinks about a political leader. Consider, for example, the case of the "money photograph" e-mail: During Republican Mitt Romney's 2012 campaign for president, a widely circulated e-mail contained an image of Romney posing with five children, whose T-shirts spelled out the word *money*. Critics asserted that this image demonstrated Romney's crassness and inability to understand the economic woes facing most Americans. This charge was particularly damaging because Romney's net worth was estimated at between $150 and $200 million. The image became part of a **cyber cascade**—which occurs when an electronic document "goes viral" or becomes widely distributed digitally through e-mail, social networking, or video sharing.[27] But, in fact, the image was a digitally edited version of a campaign photo in which the children's shirts' spelled out *Romney*. Today, people who are unsure about the accuracy of claims made in e-mails (or on the Internet) can be assisted by such fact-checking websites as snopes.com and politifact.com, but many people pass on hoax e-mails without checking.

cyber cascade
when an electronic document becomes widely distributed digitally through e-mail, social networking, or video sharing

But e-mail campaigns are not always damaging, or inaccurate.[28] Sometimes e-mail provides a quick means by which those with a common interest, from the environment to school funding, can keep informed about issues and be advised when action is necessary. Groups will often e-mail "action alert" messages asking members to contact government officials to pass a particular piece of legislation or to join a protest against a government official or another organization.

From the early days of the Internet, individuals used chain e-mails to garner support and communicate with policy makers. You would receive a petition within an e-mail, add your name to the list, and forward it on. The 50th or 100th person to receive the petition would then e-mail the petition to a government official, a corporation, or another organization. Later, as technology advanced, Web-based petition hosts sprang up. Then services arose that integrate e-petitions into social network platforms. Using the Internet site Change.org, for example, any individual can create an **e-petition,** an online petition used as a tool to garner support for a position or cause. Today, the White House runs a website "We the People," in which individuals can submit or sign a petition, and if any petition makes the 100,000 signatures threshold, it will be considered and responded to by the president or a member of the administration.

e-petition
an online petition used as a tool to garner support for a position or cause

MACRO-PROTESTING Companies and organizations have also used their Internet sites to call attention to and protest what they feel is harmful legislation. If you tried to log on to Wikipedia on January 18, 2012, you were out of luck. Visitors to that website and dozens of others went dark to protest antipiracy bills being considered in Congress. On some sites, visitors were provided with information about the bills—Stop Online Piracy Act (SOPA) and the Protect IP Act (PIPA)—and asked to contact lawmakers to urge them to reject the measures. This macro-protesting generated enormous media coverage in traditional news outlets and in online news sites and blogs and created a groundswell of Internet information-sharing and activism through Facebook and Twitter. By influencing public opinion, within two days the macro-protests caused the defeat of the measures in Congress.

E-MOBILIZATION Some organizations have been particularly effective at advocating for candidates and policy changes, or compelling individual actions, by using the Internet to mobilize like-minded individuals. One of the earliest, most influential groups was MoveOn.org, a liberal organization spawned by two Silicon Valley tech entrepreneurs who were frustrated with the partisan bickering surrounding President Bill Clinton's impeachment hearings. On September 18,

1998, the two started an e-petition to "Censure President Clinton and Move On to Pressing Issues Facing the Nation." The petition netted hundreds of thousands of signatures.[29] Today, MoveOn.org has 5 million members, and nearly 600,000 people "like" it on Facebook. The organization circulates electronic petitions, endorses candidates, and uses traditional advertising to sway public opinion and generate support for candidates.

hacktivism
the authorized or unauthorized use of or destruction of electronic files in pursuit of a political or social goal

HACKTIVISM   In an era in which everything from our photos of Grandma's last visit to our bank accounts is stored electronically, hackers hold considerable power. **Hacktivism** is the authorized or unauthorized use of or destruction of electronic files in pursuit of a political or social goal. One of the best-known hacktivist groups is a loosely organized collection of individuals called Anonymous. These unidentified individuals collaborate, often in denial-of-service attacks, which prevent targeted servers from functioning by overloading them. For example, members of Anonymous crippled the mail servers and websites of Monsanto, a biotech giant that supplied Agent Orange to the U.S. government during the Vietnam War and currently produces genetically modified seeds. And they took down over 40 child pornography sites and published the names of hundreds of individuals associated with these sites. Anonymous supported WikiLeaks, a website that released millions of secret government documents, and attacked corporate and government entities working against WikiLeaks, including MasterCard and Visa, which cut off payments to WikiLeaks. Also, U.S. federal law enforcement officials feared that people linked with the hacker collective would target, in a form of cyber-retaliation, federal agents and prosecutors who had been investigating Megaupload.com, a file-sharing service, for violating piracy laws. Law enforcement officials declined to release the names of those working on the Megaupload investigation after a federal prosecutor investigating the WikiLeaks website (which disseminated volumes of classified U.S. government documents online) was targeted by Anonymous: The prosecutor's home address was distributed online, and his e-mail account was used to subscribe to a pornographic website. As hackers join forces, they resemble social movements undertaking protests in the real world, yet they have a much wider reach as they wreak havoc or work for the betterment of society.

Technology Now: Revolutionizing How Governments Work

Governments use technology more broadly than any other entity. Indeed, the roots of most technological innovation stem from government needs, particularly in the defense and national security arenas. For example, the Internet was developed by the Defense Advanced Research Projects Agency in late 1969 so that researchers from the U.S. Department of Defense could share information with one another and with defense researchers and scientists in other

Then   Now

>In 1976, Apple Computer was founded by Steve Jobs (left), Steve Wozniak (right), and Ronald Wayne (not pictured) in the garage of Jobs's parents. Today, Apple has revolutionized how we communicate, work, and play.

government agencies and in academia. But today, this technology has grown from its cloak-and-dagger past to represent the most important mechanism by which governments are communicating with and serving their citizens. This phenomenon, known as **e-Government,** is defined as "the employment of the Internet . . . for delivering government information and services to the citizens."[30] By using e-Government, practitioners hope that technology will enable governments to offer their services to citizens efficiently and cost-effectively. E-Government also should increase **transparency,** meaning that citizens will have more and better information about governmental processes as well as services.

Governments at all levels are using cutting-edge technology to transform the way they operate. Such practices may sometimes help governments rein in spending. For example, the Alabama Department of Conservation and Natural Resources implemented a program that enabled hunters and fishermen to obtain their licenses through an online licensing process, at an estimated cost savings of $200,000 annually.[31] But there also is evidence that technological innovation can be costly, as governments attempt to integrate **legacy systems**—that is, the old way of doing things, either in paper form or using outdated computer systems—using new, more efficient technologies.[32]

Increasingly, local governments also are using technology to improve the quality of services to residents through smartphone apps. For instance, the geolocation app **Foursquare** uses the iPhone's built-in GPS, or global positioning system (which determines your position using satellite-based radio navigation), to display civic attractions in your area as well as to broadcast your location to your friends. You can even use Foursquare to report a pothole in New York City. Soon governments will also use such programs to provide direct services to residents and visitors. For example, you may be able search nearby restaurants by health-department grade, enabling you to pass up the sushi restaurant with a C grade in favor of walking the four blocks to its A-rated competitor. In the future, many cities will rely on this and other geolocation services to provide services, especially in times of emergency.

Governments also rely on technology to increase direct communication among government officials and between officials and constituents. For example, the town of Virginia Beach relies on **wiki,** an Internet-based editing tool that allows documents to be created and edited online by multiple individuals, to eliminate the need for cumbersome streams of e-mails containing revised versions of documents. Nicole McGee, the town's librarian, believes that wikis enable governments to be more efficient: "When comparing wikis to the traditional e-mail chain of editing/collaboration, wikis can greatly reduce inbox clutter and allow the participants in the wiki to always be working from the most up-to-date version of the document/project, since there is no need to exchange documents back and forth."[33]

In Westerville, Ohio, municipal employees rely on Google Apps as a communication tool for government workers; by using this cloud-based service, they have reduced costs by over 40 percent and increased efficiency.[34] The city uses apps such as GTalk (Google Talk) to enable city workers to instant message one another; Google Docs to create, share, and edit documents; Google Videos for training purposes; Google Sites for collaboration on city projects; and Google Calendar for scheduling meetings. Says Todd Jackson, the city's chief information officer: "We delivered the budget to City Council for review two weeks early. That extra time for careful evaluation is an important part of getting the budget right, which is vital for both those who work for the city and the people we serve."[35]

Government leaders, too, are relying on technology to help them better communicate with their residents. For example, the Federal Election Commission (as well as the campaign finance oversight boards of most states) makes campaign finance information available online, so constituents can easily learn who is contributing to a politician's campaign (see Chapter 9, "Elections, Campaigns, and Voting," for more discussion of campaign finance). Governments also use the Internet to post Open Public Meetings Act notifications; bid alerts for public contracts; minutes of public meetings; video streams of state legislative meetings or city council meetings; texts of adopted laws, policies, or regulations; and even job openings.

In addition, political leaders increasingly rely on new technologies to form relationships with their constituents. For example, Senator Claire McCaskill (D-Mo.) reads and personally responds to tweets she receives. (She relies on staff to update her Facebook page, which is written in the third person to alert constituents that she is not doing the posting.)

e-Government
employment of the Internet for delivering government information and services to the citizens

transparency
ability of citizens to have more and better information about governmental processes as well as services

legacy systems
the old way of doing things, either in paper form or using outdated computer systems

Foursquare
geolocation app that uses an iPhone's built-in GPS to display attractions in your area

wiki
Internet-based editing tool that allows documents to be created and edited online by multiple individuals

CIA ✓
@CIA

+ Follow

We can neither confirm nor deny that this is our first tweet.

↩ Reply ↻ Retweet ★ Favorite ••• More

RETWEETS FAVORITES
302,266 188,572

10:49 AM - 6 Jun 2014

What Is the Impact of Technology on Political Life?

We know that technology is changing how we participate in the political life of our communities, states, nation, and world. On the whole, these changes signify greater access to information and influence by everyday people. Nonetheless, technology affects political life negatively as well.

Technology Is a Powerful Tool for Protestors and Activists

Technology has put the power to communicate into the hands of the masses and, in many circumstances, outside the reach of government control or manipulation. Such was the case during the Jasmine Revolution throughout the Middle East in 2011, when antigovernment protestors took to the streets, relying on social networking sites as a key medium of communication. And in 2014, as ISIS insurgents in Iraq battled their way toward Baghdad, the government attempted to thwart the rebels' use of social media sites by denying access to Twitter and Facebook, which the rebels were using to communicate. But one characteristic of modern technology is that it is becoming increasingly difficult for governments to control access. In Iraq, insurgents relied on fiber-optic lines and satellite links from Turkish, Jordanian, and Iranian telecommunications companies. Whether antigovernment protestors or Islamic insurgents, technology provides an enormous tool for the masses, and increasingly this tool is outside the reach of government. The implication for this is twofold: Technology in the hands of some may foster the development of democracies; in the hands of others, it can be used by those seeking to overturn democratic governments.

In democratic societies, technology can also be an equalizer for candidates and for political and community groups. Before information technology, the cost of running a campaign or organizing a group could be prohibitive. Campaign mailers, lawn signs, or informational brochures might be out of reach for some candidates or groups. But for many candidates and organizations, new technology means that mobilizing can become much more affordable. For some candidates seeking local or state office, technology has revolutionized campaign costs, in some places eliminating the need for prohibitively expensive network television advertising. Though some forms of technology can be pricey for campaigns, civic organizations, interest groups, and the like, networking through social media can provide a cost-effective and efficient means of reaching out to like-minded citizens.

Technology Increases the Amount of Political Information Available

Earlier in this chapter, we discussed the phenomenon of the on-demand news cycle. This innovation has shrunk the news cycle, and candidates and organizations need to be constantly at the ready to spin events to their favor. So although officials may still attempt to manipulate the cycle (by timing announcements to garner more or less news coverage, depending on whether it is good or bad news), the reality is that today elected officials and government agencies are less capable of manipulating the news cycle. In addition, the advent of blogs, YouTube, and social networking means that relatively obscure events—gaffes or poignant moments—may go viral at any turn and create a whirlwind of unanticipated media coverage (positive or negative) for an official or a candidate.

Finally, as a result of new technology, individuals, and particularly young people, are more interested in political news, even though they may generally lack a depth of knowledge about current events, given the nature of the information they receive. This is particularly true of our shrinking global environment: Not so long ago, it would take time for news reports to emerge from hotspots around the world. Today, we are able to watch governments being overthrown live on our iPhones. Individuals may be glued to minute-by-minute coverage of an international crisis, yet these reports often do not explain the context of those events or provide in-depth analysis as to why these situations are unfolding.

What's Next: How Technology Will Continue to Transform the Political Landscape

The effect that today's technology has had on political life was unimaginable a generation ago. We know that nearly all aspects of the political landscape are being transformed, including how we register to vote, how we contribute to candidates, how we are mobilized by campaigns, and how grassroots organizing and fundraising take place. So, although we can barely speculate about some of the ways that technology will transform political life in the generation to come, there are some very clear trends that we can say with certainty will prove to be political game-changers.

One of the most important transformative tools for politics is in the palm of your hand. Smartphone apps will continue to facilitate increasingly sophisticated targeting operations and to help candidates and other organizations to create voter profiles that track voter concerns and opinions of candidates, thus facilitating enormously strategic get-out-the-vote efforts. In the future, it is likely that smaller, wearable (even implantable) devices will transform our political, social, and economic lives by altering our real-life perceptions. Imagine, for example, the experience of going on a blind date 25 years from now: Will our glasses perform facial recognition on our date, and immediately scour the Internet for his or her social networking profile, work history, past purchases, and so on?

Decades ago, campaigns were transformed by television advertising. Suddenly a new set of candidate characteristics became mandatory, including the ability to present well on television, and campaigns had to develop expertise in media strategy. Campaign television advertising also increased negativity in campaigns, and negative charges could be spread to wider audiences than through older means of reaching voters. In the future, new strategies will emerge as paramount, as video advertisements on such outlets as YouTube and Hulu increasingly replace television ads. With fewer people watching television, and fewer still watching television in real time (a necessity for ad viewing), greater numbers of political advertisements will be seen on new IT venues. Because the length of a YouTube user session is just 15 minutes,[36] in all likelihood campaign ads will shrink to become mini sound bites that appear before videos. Decades ago, many television ads were 60 seconds long. Then 30-second ads became more common. In the future, 15-second video ads will appear before feature videos that have been targeted by campaigns as having viewers who will likely be sympathetic to the candidate's or group's message.

But also changing the nature of political advertising will be data-driven Internet advertising that capitalizes on technology to build better databases for campaigns. By collecting cookies from sites that constituents use, companies such as CampaignGrid can strategically target their candidate- and issue-based advertising, as shown in the example in Figure 11.3. Increasingly, these will be nonstatic ads: By asking viewers to click through to the campaign's website, campaigns can drop cookies to examine viewership and can offer opportunities to sign up for e-mail lists, follow on Twitter, friend on Facebook, or otherwise collect identifying information about viewers.

Another area of politics that will be affected by technological change is in absentee balloting. Although election policy expert Roy Saltman asserts that American history is replete with examples of our perception of technology as a natural way to expand the participating franchise in the United States,[37] evidence shows that, in the future, new technologies will transform how military service members and citizens living abroad will be enfranchised. This will prove increasingly important for countries with high numbers of educated citizens living abroad, including India and Turkey and other diaspora.

The Downside of Technology in Politics

The positive effects of information technology are undeniable, but the technology also presents a series of challenges both to users and to society. As technology grows more sophisticated, privacy issues are becoming critical.[38] And with such an abundance of information readily available, one key challenge for those who rely on the Internet is the problem of accuracy of information. Finally, balancing free speech rights while protecting the rights of individuals who face physical threats or threats to their reputations is another issue with which modern societies are struggling.

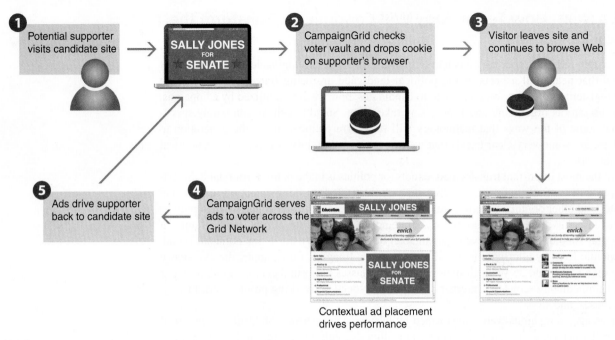

FIGURE 11.3

How Grid Retargeting Works

Domestic Surveillance and Other Privacy Issues

Today, we see that the roots of technological innovation continue to shape how governments use technology. In June 2013, a series of newspaper articles around the world described a domestic surveillance operation being conducted by the U.S. National Security Agency (NSA). A former CIA employee, Edward Snowden, leaked information that revealed that the NSA had been monitoring the actions of Americans on U.S. soil, including collecting metadata of phone communications, e-mail traffic, and other Internet communications. The NSA's domestic surveillance program began under the George W. Bush administration, and Snowden held off on whistleblowing in the hopes that President Obama would end the program after being elected. Snowden was disappointed when Obama continued and then expanded the program, and leaked documents revealing the extent of the United States' domestic surveillance program in 2013. Among the revelations was the fact that the NSA and 16 other spying agencies, working with a $56 billion "black budget,"[39] conducted a multitude of operations, including:

- Compelling U.S. telecommunications corporations, including Verizon, to provide information on a daily basis concerning telephone calls both within the United States and between the United States and other nations.[40]
- Monitoring the location of cell phones and tracking five billion records each day.[41]
- Using cookies acquired by Google to identify and locate targets for government hacking.[42]
- Monitoring foreign communications traffic occurring over Microsoft, Google, Yahoo!, Facebook, PalTalk, YouTube, Skype, AOL, and Apple through a secret NSA program named PRISM,[43] while copying metadata flowing from Yahoo! and Google across fiber-optic cables[44] through a program called MUSCULAR.
- Searching e-mails, online chats, and "nearly everything a typical user does on the Internet" using XKeyscore,[45] a top-secret data-mining analytical tool.
- Infiltrating multiplayer video games, including Xbox Live, World of Warcraft, and Second Life, in collaboration with its British counterpart, Government Communications Headquarters (CGCH), in an effort to catch real-life terrorists.[46]

Snowden, who was both hailed as a hero whistleblower and reviled as a traitor to his country, feared for his own life as well as the lives of the journalists with whom he entrusted his information. He currently lives in Russia, where he has temporary asylum.

Technological innovation poses a host of unknown potentialities in terms of privacy, particularly for individuals who dwell in the technologically connected world. Today, government surveillance of our use of technology means that not just our communications can be monitored but also our whereabouts, our physical appearance, our habits, our associations with others, and even—to the extent that our Google search history indicates our interests—our thoughts. We live in an era in which society is attempting to balance the value that technology brings with the protection of individuals' rights. Today, privacy concerns center on the tools that law enforcement and other government officials have at their disposal to monitor individuals and their locations. But corporations also can access an enormous volume of material—from our grocery shopping habits to the kinds of apps we buy for our phones—and the challenges that our society faces will escalate with new technological innovations. Most people concerned with the issue of government surveillance agree that increased technological developments—through encryption and other surveillance-blocking mechanisms—hold the greatest promise in the potential to protect our privacy.

>Edward Snowden, a computer specialist who worked for the Central Intelligence Agency and the National Security Agency, released classified documents in 2013 that revealed that the NSA had engaged in a vast array of domestic surveillance tactics.

The NSA was granted broad powers by the Foreign Intelligence Surveillance Act (FISA) Amendments passed in 2008, which force U.S. telecommunications companies to provide information to the NSA as part of its domestic surveillance program. But unlike traditional law enforcement agencies, which have been overseen by the courts (which, for example, might produce a warrant if there is probable cause), NSA's domestic surveillance program lacks oversight. The NSA asserts that such oversight—whether by Congress or the courts—would render the program less effective. This argument has resonated when discussing foreign targets abroad, but after Edward Snowden's revelation that the NSA was spying on U.S. citizens in the United States, there has been significant resistance to these practices, which many Americans perceive as a violation of their Fourth Amendment rights.

Striking a balance between security and privacy is a daunting task. Consider, for example, the use of video surveillance using facial recognition biometrics (essentially a geometrical means of recognizing an individual face). Many Americans would not object to law enforcement officers using facial recognition biometrics to identify known terrorists in line at airport security checkpoints. But should this technology be used in public places—sporting events, parades, or concerts—to identify criminals in the crowd? What if law enforcement wanted to use the technology to monitor individuals participating in protests who had not performed illegal acts and had not consented to be monitored? These kinds of issues characterize the new waters being charted concerning the use of technology today.

Cellular technology—combined with GPS and tower triangulation (which enables a specific cell phone signal to be geographically targeted using directional data from cell towers)—provides an invaluable service when tracking lost hikers or kidnapping victims. In 2011, 29-year-old Nathan Parsons kidnapped a college student, forcing her into the back of his pickup truck. She called 911, and the dispatcher advised her to leave her cell phone's GPS on and hide her phone. Ohio police tracked down the truck within 21 minutes, and the college student emerged unharmed. Similar incidents have proven that law enforcement agencies can use GPS devices to save lives. But at what point could GPS tracking violate an individual's privacy? Should law enforcement and other government agencies be permitted to track our whereabouts, even if we haven't been convicted of a crime? Should retailers have access to our locations so that they can text us coupons for lattes as we pass by Starbucks? Should our employers be able to track our locations after hours?

>Edward Snowden revealed that the National Security Agency, headquartered in Fort Meade, Maryland, has engaged in extensive efforts to monitor the activities, communications, and whereabouts of Americans living in the United States.

The increasing prevalence of cloud computing, whereby files are stored on remote servers rather than on users' personal hard drives, means that our information may be more vulnerable to misuse by corporations, government officials, and hackers than if we stored our data privately. For example, Web-based e-mail services (Gmail, Outlook, Yahoo!, and so on), certain word processing and spreadsheet programs (such as those stored on SkyDrive), and photo storage applications (Picasa, Snapfish) hold our information "in the cloud." Although these sites strive to protect users' privacy, the sheer volume of information available may lead to vulnerabilities as a result of both intentional damage through hacking and unintentional potential damage through technological glitches.

The Issue of Accuracy

The explosion of the Internet into politics has also opened up a Pandora's box of misinformation. Unlike newspapers, magazines, and television networks, where editors and fact checkers are responsible for ensuring accuracy, the Internet is almost entirely unmonitored. A humorous example of the problem with accuracy was apparent when late-night talk show host Jimmy Kimmel pulled a prank in which he posted, through American luger Kate Hansen's Twitter account, a video that shows a wolf walking in a hallway outside a dorm room in the Olympic Village in Sochi, Russia. Kimmel shot the video in Los Angeles with a rented wolf on a set built to look exactly like the hallway in the Olympic dorm, but did not reveal the prank for more than 24 hours. By that time, many media outlets, including CNN and FOX News, had reported the wolf's appearance as fact.

In political campaigns, misinformation can be devastating, and once a damaging charge is sounded, it is often almost impossible to unring that bell, even if the allegations are false. One example of this problem is the coverage on several Internet sites, including the Drudge Report,[47] that questioned President Obama's U.S. citizenship. The allegations followed the president from the early days of his 2008 presidential campaign until he released the long-form copy of his birth certificate in April 2011.

The sheer volume of information available online can in itself create a problem. To become and remain accurately informed, voters and other individuals must develop the critical thinking skills needed to discern what information is valuable. Consumers of information need to assess the validity of claims made on the Internet; they need to consider the sources of information and determine the sources' biases or perspectives. In short, devoid of a trusted source of information, we should treat many claims made on the Internet with a healthy dose of skepticism.[48]

>The wolf that wasn't at the Olympics. The American media widely reported the presence of a wolf in the Olympic Village in Sochi, Russia, in 2014, based on a tweet from Jimmy Kimmel through American Olympic luger Kate Hansen's Twitter account, emphasizing the problem with accuracy in a digital age.

Fomenting Polarized Partisanship and Extremism

The Internet has also contributed to the decline in civility in political discourse. In describing the political climate regarding threats to presidential candidates, Secret Service director Mark Sullivan noted that "historically, it's the same issues we've always had and the same things people are upset about. There are just a lot more venues for people to put it out there, including the Internet."[49] The Secret Service established an Internet Threat desk to monitor chatter concerning protected individuals in 2000. In 2012, a group of Arizona men (including a Peoria, Arizona, police sergeant) appeared in a photo posted on Facebook that showed the men armed with weapons and what appeared to be a bullet-riddled President Obama. The Secret Service conducted an investigation into the matter.

Some bloggers and anonymous message-board posters seek to destroy their opponents' reputations. The nature of the Internet means that lies and slanderous accusations can often be leveled with no consequence to the poster. Sometimes the claims—made via e-mail messages, Facebook postings, and/or tweets—are quite sophisticated and seem believable.

Information technology also helps to foment increased extremism, both domestically and internationally. The Internet makes selective exposure—the phenomenon of individuals choosing to read or view information that enforces their already-held beliefs while rejecting sources that provide contradictory views—quite easy. This lack of exposure to contradictory sources of information means that peoples' views—even the most extreme—will only be confirmed and reinforced. The lack of contradictory information may steer people to more polarized ideological viewpoints, as the moderate, compromising views are eschewed by those relying on partisan information. Some research indicates that this scenario has served to increase political polarization in the United States and has fostered the adoption of more extremist political viewpoints.[50]

The Internet and Free Speech

Part of the political conundrum faced by Americans is the desire to balance free speech rights with the ability of government to protect those whose person or reputation may be threatened by someone's speech. The rise of the Internet has overwhelmed our guarantees of free speech, with the volume and content of speech growing faster than society's ability to digest their impact. In parts of Europe, for example, hate speech on the Internet is forbidden and carefully regulated; in the United States, it is not. As a result, a large number of hate sites register their domains in the United States, where they can operate freely and spew their venom throughout the world without fear of government interference.

The danger is that some of these activities can lead to acts of violence, including even murder. In the spring of 2005, U.S. District Court judge Joan Humphrey Lefkow returned home from work to find the murdered bodies of her husband and mother in the basement of her home on Chicago's North Side. The killer, an unemployed electrician, had found Judge Lefkow's name and address posted on several hate websites, where readers were encouraged to take justice into their own hands. The day after the murders, Bill White, editor of one of the hate sites, posted his approval: "Everyone associated with the Matt Hale trial [over which Judge Lefkow had presided] has deserved assassination for a long time. I don't feel bad that Judge Lefkow's family was murdered. . . . In fact . . . I laughed."[51]

The availability of cheap worldwide communications technology makes the Internet an ideal tool for terrorists and other haters who hide among the world's 2.2 billion users, including about 245 million Americans.[52] The murder of Judge Lefkow's husband and mother introduced a new dimension to the nation's debate over the limits of free speech. The Internet has allowed extremists to seize on new technologies to spread their messages far more effectively than did the soapboxes of olden days; it also enhances their ability to promote and recruit like-minded bigots to support their causes.

The United States is deeply wedded to the principle of freedom of speech, refusing to regulate the Internet or any other vehicle of free speech. Throughout the nation's history, speech of all kinds has been protected, with periodic exceptions for sedition in wartime, as well as for child pornography and hate speech in peacetime. Americans have great tolerance for language and believe that fringe groups can flourish freely in a democracy without risking tears in the fabric of society. But the world has changed since September 11, 2001, and as the threat of terrorism grows, many citizens expect lawmakers to do whatever is necessary—including setting limits on free speech—to curb violence spawned by the prevalence of hate on the Internet.[53]

Regulation of the Internet: Is It Necessary?

When Noah Kravitz left his job as an editor and videoblogger at PhoneDog, a company that reviews cell phones and other electronics, he took his Twitter account and his 17,000 followers with him. The U.S. District Court in Northern California must decide whether the account and the followers are in fact Kravitz's or whether they are legally comparable to a customer list and thus the possession of PhoneDog. The case offers another example of how technology has presented an abundance of disputes with which the law has yet to keep up. The Internet raises issues that could not have been foreseen by the framers of the U.S. Constitution. Some issues concern contract law; others, privacy rights; yet others, freedom of speech, the press, and assembly. Take, for example, freedom of the press: The framers had to be concerned only with print media when they guaranteed this freedom, one of the fundamental liberties they ensured in the Bill of Rights. As media evolved into formats such as radio and television, government created a regulatory structure to govern them as well. But technology has outpaced the government's ability to regulate certain forms of electronic media, including the Internet and cellular technology. In 2012, a battle raged between two titan industries in the United States—the entertainment industry and the technology industry. The entertainment industry, led by the Motion Picture Association of America, had successfully lobbied for a series of reforms aimed at reining in Internet piracy. Specifically, the Stop Online Piracy Act (SOPA) and the Protect IP Act (PIPA) were introduced in Congress to enable U.S. authorities to crack down on foreign-based Internet sites that pirated copyrighted music, movies, books, and other products. If passed, the laws would have prevented U.S. companies from advertising on such sites and could have enabled the U.S. Justice Department to force U.S. Internet service providers to block access to foreign pirating sites. The battle over the bills turned into a showdown between the Hollywood entertainment industry and Northern California's Silicon Valley tech companies. Through the efforts of e-campaigning and macro-protesting, the tech companies won, and the legislation was pulled from consideration amid a storm of Internet-spawned public protests.

Democracy

Should Congress Regulate the Internet Infrastructure?

The Issue: The technological revolution has brought ongoing, exponential growth in Internet traffic. As rising numbers of people turn to the Internet for more and more uses—from viewing videos online to sending pictures to Grandma, and from buying gifts and personal items to calling friends and relatives—the volume of information that the Internet's broadband infrastructure must transmit is becoming overwhelming. The owners of that infrastructure—corporate giants such as AT&T, Verizon, and Comcast—are seeking legislation and pursuing lawsuits that would allow them to charge companies that produce high volumes of traffic. In effect, this legislation would set up a two-tiered system of broadband access, in which one tier is an "express lane" with tolls and the other is an older, slower lane with free access. One problem is that many of today's services (video streaming, for example) require the faster access to make them effective.

Yes: Congress should regulate the Internet infrastructure. We need a two-tiered system of broadband access. The telecommunications titans in command of the Internet infrastructure argue that in order to keep up with the increasing demand for broadband space, they will continually have to expand and improve the system. These improvements cost money, and companies should be able to pass the costs and benefits on to their customers. Corporate advocates of a two-tiered system of broadband access also are interested in providing premium-quality broadband service to their own clientele. Thus, for example, Verizon wants to ensure that its Internet subscribers (rather than the subscribers of its competitors) have high-quality access to the broadband infrastructure technology that Verizon owns, so that its subscribers do not get caught in an Internet traffic jam.

No: "Fast Lane" services would hurt both businesses and consumers. In 2011, the FCC released its final rules for Preserving a Free and Open Internet, stating that providers must have transparency of network management practices, not block lawful content, and not unreasonably discriminate in transmitting lawful network traffic. The owners of the broadband infrastructure should comply with this ruling. In fact, a broad coalition of businesses and interest groups, including savetheinternet.com, oppose measures that would enable broadband providers to charge for their services. These entities also include such firms as Microsoft, Google, eBay, and Yahoo! and powerful citizen organizations such as the American Association of Retired Persons (AARP).

It is the very accessibility of the Internet that has fostered strong business growth. Startups such as YouTube and Vonage Internet phone service are examples of ventures that may not have been able to compete and survive in a tiered broadband system. A paying system could prevent future Internet business development.

Other Approaches: Tax dollars should be used to expand the Internet infrastructure. Without essential maintenance and expansion, the Internet infrastructure will be incapable of keeping up with soaring demand. In addition, the security of the infrastructure is crucial to continued business activity and corporate financial growth, as well as to national economic health. Broadband availability is a national security issue, because if law enforcers, airports, hospitals, nuclear power plants, and first responders do not have adequate or immediate access to the information they need to perform their jobs, human lives are at risk. Because of these critical financial and security implications, a tax or user fee could be instituted that would pay for Internet infrastructure improvements.

What do you think?

1. Do you believe that Congress should reject proposals to create a for-fee fast lane for Internet traffic? If so, why? Or do you think that the marketplace should determine which services get faster access to broadband lines? If so, why would the latter be preferable?

2. What effect would the creation of a two-tiered Internet structure have on Internet business development? On national security?

3. Should the federal government help to defray the costs of improvements to the Internet infrastructure? Why or why not?

Net neutrality
the idea that Internet traffic should flow through the Internet pipeline without interference or discrimination by those who own or are running the pipeline

Congress is currently considering the question of control over the business of the media (see "Thinking Critically About Democracy"). The issue, a controversial one, centers on **Net neutrality:** the idea that Internet traffic—e-mail, websites, videos, and phone calls—should flow through the Internet pipeline without interference or discrimination by those who own or are running the pipeline. *Should* these broadband behemoths be able to use their market power to control information or to favor certain clients online? Critics charge that congressional passage of legislation supporting the service providers would destroy the neutrality and openness of the Internet. Tim Berners-Lee, the inventor of the World Wide Web, says: "The neutral communications medium is essential to our society. . . . It is the basis of democracy, by which a community should decide what to do."[54] Do you agree with Berners-Lee? In what ways would you say that neutral media are the basis of a democracy?

Conclusion

Thinking Critically About What's Next in Politics and Technology

Technology has revolutionized how politics happens in the United States, and it is revolutionizing political life throughout the world. One of the most remarkable characteristics of the technological revolution has been the swiftness of the transformation it has propelled. Though the Internet is only 25 years old, it has spawned earth-shattering changes in our political lives and indeed throughout society. And although there remains a digital divide both within and outside the United States, that divide is shrinking domestically. Because of cellular technology and increasing access to the Internet, information technology represents one of the most powerful tools in helping people communicate with government officials, secure political information, and participate in the political life of their communities, states, and country.

Whether through traditional websites, blogging, Facebook, Twitter, or politically specific technological platforms, technology has transformed political life by making information more easily available. But the sheer volume of information means that consumers must be wary of the information they receive. Political communication has become a two-way street, where individuals' opinions matter and can be more easily measured by campaign and other groups.

In particular, social networking has opened up a host of opportunities for political communication and participation. These and other technologies are providing avenues of communication between constituents and elected officials, among candidate or issue supporters, and between governments and the people they serve. Although there are negative effects of technology, much of technology's impact has been positive. And increasingly, technology is providing more efficient and cost-effective means by which governments can provide services. In the future, technology will become a more integrated and essential part of our lives, having sweeping implications for how campaigns, governments, and citizens use technology in political life.

Summary

1. The Modern Technological Revolution: The Internet and Cellular Technology

The modern media revolution began with the birth of the Internet. As a medium of communication, a source of news and information, and a tool for political engagement and organizing at the grassroots, the Internet and cellular technology are having an unprecedented influence on the way people interact and how politics is conducted. Although disparities exist in who uses new technologies as political tools—in terms of age, education, and income—evidence points to these technologies as transforming how individuals act as political beings, and increasing the potentiality of equality by providing an important medium of participation. Technologies also have spawned virtual communities that break down national and physical boundaries and facilitate the cohesive formation of virtual communities of interest.

2. Technology Now: Changing How Candidates Campaign and Citizens Participate

Over the past decade, technology has transformed how American politics happens, including how candidates campaign and how citizens participate in politics. Technology has created a two-way street for political communication, so that candidates and officials can listen to constituents as well as be heard by them. Campaigns have been transformed by new forms of participation and new means of tracking supporters. In the future, campaigns will continue to facilitate increasingly better voter-targeting operations. In addition, more sophisticated uses of technology, including data-driven Internet advertising, will prevail.

3. Technology Now: Revolutionizing How Governments Work

Cellular technology combined with the Internet are the most important transformative tools for governments. Technology has changed how we get services and receive information from governments, and how we communicate with them. The Internet also has opened up new avenues for citizens to voice their concerns. In the future, the use of geolocation applications and cloud platforms for politics will transform political life.

4. What Is the Impact of Technology on Political Life?

Technology has proven a game-changer in terms of political participation—for example, information technology has the potential of leveling the playing field for average citizens. It has become an important tool for protestors throughout the world and for citizen activists in our own democracy. And technology has drastically altered the amount of information available to citizens.

5. The Downside of Technology in Politics

Technology presents a series of challenges, including concerns generated by the U.S. government's domestic surveillance operation and other privacy issues, the problem of accuracy of information, and balancing free speech rights while protecting the rights of individuals who face physical threats or threats to their reputations.

6. Regulation of the Internet: Is It Necessary?

Technology has outpaced the government's ability to regulate certain forms of electronic media, including the Internet and cellular technology. But state legislatures, Congress, and the courts are continuing to consider several policies that could change the technological environment, including policies concerning Internet privacy. Given the rapid pace of technological development, policy makers will continue to be challenged by technological innovations and their implications.

Key Terms

bandwidth 339
blogosphere 341
cyber cascade 345
digital divide 335
e-campaigning 343
e-Government 347
e-petition 345
Foursquare 347

hacktivism 346
legacy systems 347
micro-blog 342
microtarget 344
Net neutrality 354
netroots 342
news aggregators 338

promoted tweets 344
remarketing 344
social networking sites 334
transparency 347
virtual communities 337
vlog 339
wiki 347

For Review

1. How is cellular technology likely to affect politics in the decade to come?

2. What are differences among various demographic groups regarding the use of technology?

3. What is microtargeting, and how is it being used politically?

4. What are some of the drawbacks of technological evolution?

5. What are the arguments for regulation of the Internet?

For Critical Thinking and Discussion

1. Should the National Security Agency be able to monitor the actions of Americans living in the United States?

2. Do you believe Anonymous was justified in its attack on Monsanto and WikiLeaks? Why or why not?

3. Do you believe that information technology has the potential to be the "great equalizer" in U.S. politics? Why or why not?

4. Do you support the idea of Net neutrality? Why or why not?

5. What action should the U.S. government take to protect individuals' privacy online?

MULTIPLE CHOICE: Choose the lettered item that answers the question correctly.

1. What fraction of Americans do *not* use the Internet?
   a. less than one-fifth
   b. about one-fourth
   c. a little more than one-third
   d. approximately one-half

2. What demographic factors influence who uses the Internet?
   a. income and age
   b. population density and race
   c. age and gender
   d. age, gender, and education

3. Which campaign served as a watershed in leveraging new media?
   a. Barack Obama's 2008 presidential bid
   b. Nancy Pelosi's 2008 congressional race
   c. John Boehner's 2010 congressional race
   d. Mitt Romney's 2012 presidential bid

4. Which of the following technological developments has contributed the most to the emergence of two-way political communication?
   a. introduction of the microcomputer
   b. increased bandwidth
   c. the digital divide
   d. Net neutrality

5. According to information leaked by Edward Snowden, the National Security Agency monitors
   a. phone calls within the United States.
   b. phone calls from within the United States to outside the United States.
   c. video game players who play World of Warcraft and Xbox Live.
   d. all of the above.

6. Which of the following sites could campaign organizers use to develop new media campaign strategies?
   a. Match.com
   b. The Huffington Post
   c. NationBuilder
   d. all of the above

7. Who supports the idea of Net neutrality?
   a. The Republican Party
   b. AT&T
   c. Tim Berners-Lee, inventor of the World Wide Web
   d. all of the above

8. The idea that Internet traffic—e-mails, website content, videos, and phone calls—can be transmitted through the Internet pipeline without interference or discrimination by those who own or run the pipeline is called
   a. Net neutrality.
   b. Internet objectivity.
   c. the neutral frontier.
   d. absolute Web domain.

9. Who launched an online awareness campaign to derail the Stop Online Piracy Act, which was under consideration in Congress?
   a. the hacktivist group Anonymous
   b. foreign-based Internet sites
   c. the entertainment industry
   d. the technology industry

10. How are governments using new technology?
    a. to monitor the activities of citizens
    b. to provide services to residents
    c. to post documents to increase transparency
    d. all of the above

FILL IN THE BLANKS

11. A potential negative effect of technology on politics is that it helps foment _____.

12. A potential positive effect of technology is that it can increase the level of _____.

13. The inequality of access to computers and Internet connections is called _____.

14. A _____ is a video weblog.

15. Services that compile news we want from various outlets in one location are called _____.

Answers: 1. a, 2. a, 3. a, 4. b, 5. d, 6. c, 7. c, 8. a, 9. d, 10. d, 11. extremism, 12. political participation, 13. the digital divide, 14. vlog, 15. news aggregators.

Resources for Research AND Action

Internet Resources

YouTube Nation's News
**www.youtube.com/playlist?list=PLHidivwwcWAhmvaAF3Rqc64O
0Hbho6mF7** This site provides viewers with information about current events around the world.

The Guardian's NSA Files
www.theguardian.com/world/the-nsa-files This site provides a trove of documents and analyses of the NSA documents that Edward Snowden leaked, which reveal the extent of the United States' and Britain's Internet surveillance operations.

VoteTocracy
www.votetocracy.com This website enables user to learn about pieces of pending congressional legislation, determine their opinions, and communicate their opinions to their legislators.

Recommended Readings

Coleman, Stephen, and Jay G. Blumler. 2009. *The Internet and Democratic Citizenship: Theory, Practice, and Policy.* Cambridge, MA: Cambridge University Press. An examination of the theoretical foundations for renewing democratic citizenship using practical case studies of e-democracy, in the context of contemporary political communication. This book concludes by proposing an online civic commons: "a trusted public space where the dispersed energies, self-articulations and aspirations of citizens can be rehearsed, in public, within a process of on-going feedback to the various levels and centers of governance: local, national and transnational."

Cook, Timothy E. 2005. *Governing with the News: The News Media as a Political Institution.* Chicago: University of Chicago Press, 2nd ed. This work contends that the press is in fact a political institution that shares in governances, and it examines the increasing fragmentation of the media caused by technological changes.

David, Richard. 2009. *Typing Politics: The Role of Blogs in American Politics.* New York: Oxford University Press. This volume assesses the increasing importance of political blogs in the American political arena and evaluates their relationship with traditional media outlets.

Deibert, Ronald, John Palfrey, Rafal Rohozinski, and Jonathan Zittrain, Eds. 2010. *Access Controlled: The Shaping of Power, Rights, and Rule in Cyberspace.* Cambridge, MA: MIT Press. An analysis of new technologies and what they mean for relationships between citizens and states, and evaluation of how new technologies will shape civic interaction in the future.

Greenwald, Glenn. 2014. *No Place to Hide: Edward Snowden, the NSA, and the U.S. Surveillance State.* New York: Macmillan. Greenwald was one of the reporters to whom Edward Snowden leaked some of the most explosive and consequential news concerning the actions of the National Security Agency in monitoring the activities of citizens. This book tells that story and considers various reforms to how governments monitor their citizens.

Hindman, Matthew. 2009. *The Myth of Digital Democracy.* Princeton, NJ: Princeton University Press. This volume asserts that the Internet empowers a small set of elites, rather than broadening political discourse among the masses.

Howard, Philip N. 2010. *The Digital Origins of Dictatorship and Democracy: Information Technology and Political Islam.* New York: Oxford University Press. Drawing from data from 74 Muslim nations, this book examines how digital technologies, instrumental for a nation's development, are being used by young people—in particular, in creating civil society, communicating, and circumventing state and religious organizations' controls.

Karpf, David. 2012. *The MoveOn Effect: The Unexpected Transformation of American Political Advocacy.* New York: Oxford University Press. This book examines the structure of netroots political organizations, including MoveOn.org. Using interviews, content analysis, and direct observation, it examines changes in membership and fundraising systems.

Rheingold, Howard. 2000. *The Virtual Community: Homesteading on the Electronic Frontier.* Cambridge, MA: MIT Press. This classic work written by the "first citizen of the Internet" examines the nexus between virtual and real-life communities and argues that a distinction between the two is not totally valid.

Rigby, Ben. 2008. *Mobilizing Generation 2.0.* Hoboken, NJ: Jossey-Bass. A guidebook for individuals who want to use technology to maximize their political behaviors, as well for campaigns, government officials, and organizations that would like to use new media tools to recruit, engage, and mobilize young people.

Sunstein, Cass R. 2006. *Infotopia: How Many Minds Produce Knowledge.* New York: Oxford University Press. This work grapples with the question of how leaders and ordinary people can challenge insular decision making and gain access to the sum of human knowledge.

Tewksbury, David, and Jason Rittenberg. 2012. *News on the Internet: Information and Citizenship in the 21st Century.* New York: Oxford University Press. This work considers the Internet as both a source of authoritative news and as a vehicle for citizens in contemporary democracies to create and share political information; it also examines the tension between these two functions in terms of increased citizen participation in a polarized climate of fragmented knowledge.

Movies of Interest

The Social Network (2010)
This Oscar-winning film traces the creation of Facebook by Harvard student Mark Zuckerberg and demonstrates the speed with which communication was revolutionized.

Minority Report (2002)
Tom Cruise stars in this futuristic saga in which criminals are caught before they commit crimes. It raises questions about how technology should be used by government officials.

CHAPTER 12

Congress

 ## THEN

The framers granted to Congress both explicit powers and implied powers, by which the national government strengthened and broadened its authority.

 ## NOW

A much more demographically diverse but ideologically polarized Congress exercises wide powers, its decision making influenced by shifting constituencies in a changing nation.

 ## NEXT

Will increased polarization of Republicans and Democrats in Congress continue to define the congressional agenda?

Will the composition and policy making of Congress more broadly reflect the changing face of the United States?

Will technology significantly affect the ability of "average" citizens to influence Congress?

PREVIEW

This chapter provides a foundation for your study of Congress.

FIRST, we examine the origins of Congress.

SECOND, we explore the process of congressional elections.

THIRD, we consider the powers of Congress.

FOURTH, we survey the functions of Congress, including representation, policy making, oversight, agenda setting and civic engagement, and management of societal conflict.

FIFTH, we take stock of the similarities and differences between the two chambers of the national legislature as we compare the House and the Senate.

SIXTH, we focus on how a bill becomes a law by examining the legislative process.

SEVENTH, we analyze how the congressional leadership affects the legislature's ability to perform its functions.

EIGHTH, we consider decision making in Congress, with a particular eye to the legislative context.

NINTH, we examine the similarities and differences between the people and their elected representatives.

by the people elected to serve there, men and women acting as the trusted representatives of the constituents who voted them into office. Congress and the policies it sets are molded by the times; laws passed in one generation may seem antiquated to the next. And Congress and the policies it creates are influenced by many other factors, including the legislative body's institutional history, the lawmaking process, and the internal and external actors—congressional leaders, political parties, interest groups, the president, staff members, ordinary citizens, and the media—who seek to influence congressional actions.

The Constitution's framers structured the government so that Congress—more so than the two other institutions of the federal government—would be responsive to the needs and the will of the people. In representing their constituents, members of Congress provide an easily accessed point of contact for people to connect with their government and to have their voices heard.

Citizens today have countless opportunities to participate in shaping Congress's agenda and influencing how the members of Congress vote. Individuals and groups of constituents communicate through Twitter, Instagram, Facebook, e-mail, and telephone, and they meet face-to-face with members of Congress on issues that concern them. Constituents meet with congressional staff members for help in understanding how to deal with government bureaucracy. Through congressional campaigns and elections, citizens learn about issues of national importance and can participate in a variety of ways, such as volunteering in support of a candidate's run for office, contributing to the individual's campaign, becoming informed about the candidates and the issues, and casting a ballot on Election Day.

Throughout this chapter, we view Congress through the lens of civic engagement, seeing that Congress—the people's branch of the federal government—though imperfect, is structured to empower citizens to play a role in determining public policy priorities. And ultimately it is the people, through their choices at the ballot box, who decide who the creators of those policies will be.

The Origins of Congress

For the United States' founders, creating the Congress was a crucially important task. Fearful of a powerful executive, but having endured the problems stemming from the weak confederal government under the Articles of Confederation, the framers of the Constitution believed that the legislature should be the key branch of the newly formed confederal government. In their vision, the Congress would be the institution responsible for making laws that would create effective public policy. In structuring the Congress, the framers strove to create a legislative branch that was at once powerful enough to govern and to check the power of the president and yet not so powerful that the legislature itself would exercise tyrannical rule.

As they debated the shape of the Congress, the Constitution's framers had to balance the desires of representation of two opposing groups. The Constitution created a bicameral, or two-house, legislature in which one house, the House of Representatives, would be based on population, and the other chamber, the Senate, would be based on state representation.[1] The constitutionally specified duties of each house of Congress reflect the framers' views of the essential nature of the two chambers and the people who would serve in them.

The House of Representatives, with the smallest constituencies of any federal office (currently about 711,000 people reside in each congressional district), is the chamber closer to

Context

INDIA'S SANSAD

India's Sansad, or Parliament, is the equivalent of the U.S. Congress. Like the United States, India has a bicameral legislature consisting of the upper house, or Rajya Sabha, and the lower house, or Lok Sabha. Members of the Rajya Sabha and Lok Sabha are called members of parliament, or MPs. The Indian Parliament is composed of 790 members, compared with the 535 members of the U.S. House and Senate.

The Indian Parliament strongly resembles the U.S. Congress as originally designed by the founders. Like the U.S. House of Representatives, the Lok Sabha is elected by popular election. Constitutionally, it can consist of 552 members who serve 5-year terms. Of the 552 members, 530 members represent districts within states, 20 members represent the Union Territories, and the president of India may appoint up to two members to represent the Anglo-Indian constituency if that constituency is not sufficiently represented.

Like the U.S. Senate prior to the ratification of the Seventeenth Amendment to the Constitution in 1913, the members of the Rajya Sabha, or Council of States, are chosen by the state legislative assemblies. Unlike U.S. senators prior to 1913, members of the Rajya Sabha are elected according to the principle of proportional representation, in which a party is awarded a number of seats in the legislature in proportion to the percentage of votes that party received. In practice, proportional representation facilitates a wide diversity of political parties in the governing body. Each member serves a 6-year term, and one-third of the members retire every 2 years. Of the 250 members, 238 are elected from geographic territories, and 12 are nominated by the president of India and have expertise in matters of science, art, literature, or social service.

The 790 MPs serving in the Lok Sabha and the Rajya Sabha represent nearly 715 million registered voters in India, compared with the 146 million registered voters in the United States.

the people. As such, the framers intended the House to closely represent the people's views. The Constitution thus requires, for example, that all revenue bills (bills that would impose taxes) must originate in the House of Representatives. In the framers' eyes, unwarranted taxation was an egregious offense. By placing the power to tax in the hands of the members of the House of Representatives—the officials who face more frequent federal elections—the framers sought to avoid the types of unpopular, unfair taxes that had sparked the American Revolution. A short electoral cycle, they reasoned, would allow disfavored politicians to be voted out of office. Like all other bills, revenue bills must be passed in identical form by both the House and the Senate to become law, but requiring revenue bills to originate in the House reflected a victory by the large states at the Constitutional Convention. (Smaller states wanted taxation power to reside with the Senate.)

The framers viewed the House of Representatives as the "people's chamber," and they conceived the Senate to be a more elite, more deliberative institution, one not subject to the whims of mass politics like its lower-house counterpart (see "Global Context" for a comparison with India's Sansad). Today, because of its smaller size and because its members face elections less frequently than do House members, the Senate remains a more deliberative body than the House. In addition, because of the specific constitutional duties mandated to the upper house, particularly the requirement that treaties must be ratified in the Senate, many U.S. senators have specialized in U.S. foreign policy issues. (See "The House and the Senate Compared" later in this chapter for further discussion of differences between the two chambers.)

The framers' vision was to structure the Congress to embody republican principles, ensuring that in its central policy-making responsibilities, the national legislature would be responsive to the needs and the will of the people. Both historically and continuing in the present day, civically engaged citizens have exerted a strong influence on the outcome of the policy-making process. One important avenue by which individuals influence Congress and its acts is through congressional elections, a topic we now consider.

Congressional Elections

The timetable for congressional elections reflects the framers' views of the differing nature of the House of Representatives and the Senate. House members, as public servants in the legislative body that the framers conceived as closer to the people, are elected every 2 years, in even-numbered years (2014, 2016, and so on). But the framers also sought to check the power of the people, who they believed could be irrational and unruly, and so members of the Senate originally were chosen by state legislators. Ratification of the Seventeenth Amendment to the Constitution in 1913 shifted the election of senators to popular election within the states. Senators serve 6-year terms, which are staggered so that one-third of the Senate is elected every 2 years. Thus, in any given congressional election year, 33 or 34 members of the Senate are up for election. Usually, the two senators from a given state will not be elected in the same cycle, unless the death or resignation of a sitting senator requires a special election. As we saw in Chapter 2, the Constitution requires that the number of seats in the House of Representatives awarded to each state be based on that state's population and that each state have two U.S. senators. On average, a successful campaign for a seat in the House of Representatives cost about $1.7 million in 2012. That is a veritable bargain compared with the price tag for a successful bid for the U.S. Senate, which averaged about $10.5 million that year. Compare this with the annual salary of $174,000 that rank-and-file members of the House and the Senate collect.

Incumbency

The status of already holding office—known as *incumbency*—strongly influences a candidate's ability to raise money and is probably the most important factor in determining success in a congressional campaign. Indeed, in any election year, about 90 percent of incumbent members of the House of Representatives running for reelection win, and about 91 percent of their Senate counterparts do. These outcomes may indicate what *individual* members of Congress are doing right: representing their own constituencies effectively, engaging with their constituents, and listening to and addressing their needs. But voters typically think about Congress in terms of *a whole,* rather than individuals, viewing it as a body that is overwhelmingly composed of "other people's" representatives, who do not reflect their views.[2] Thus the voting public frequently attacks Congress as a collective entity.

Why do incumbents so often win reelection? Several factors make it more likely that someone already in office will be returned to that office in a reelection bid:

- **Stronger name recognition.** Having run for election before and served in government, incumbents tend to be better known than challengers are.
- **Easier access to media coverage.** Media outlets routinely publicize the activities of elected congressional officials, rationalizing that they are covering the institution of Congress rather than the individuals. Nonincumbent challengers face an uphill battle in trying to get coverage of their campaigns.
- **Redistricting that favors the incumbent party.** Often, after reapportionment, district lines are drawn to benefit the incumbent officeholder's political party, thus making it likely that the incumbent will retain the seat.
- **Campaign contributions.** Political action committees and individuals are interested in supporting candidates who will be in a position to help them once the election is over. Because donors are aware of the high reelection rates of incumbent candidates, incumbents garner an enormous proportion of contributions, sometimes as much as 80 percent in any given congressional election year.
- **Casework.** When an incumbent personally helps constituents solve problems with the federal bureaucracy, the resulting loyalty and good word-of-mouth reputation help to attract support for that candidate during a run for reelection.

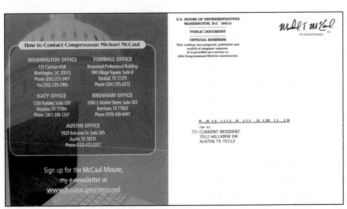

▶A piece of franked mail from a congressional office. Note the signature of the sending member of Congress, which serves as a postage stamp.

- **Franking.** The privilege of sending mail free of charge is known as *franking*. Federal law allows members of Congress free mailings to every household in their state or congressional district. These mailings make it easy for members of Congress to stay in touch with their constituencies throughout their tenure in office.

Thus incumbency is a powerful obstacle for outsiders who seek to unseat an elected member of Congress. Despite the incumbency advantage, in each congressional election, many individuals challenge incumbent members of Congress, often doing so knowing that the odds are stacked against them but believing in giving voters a ballot choice. Others run because they seek to bring attention to a particular issue or to shape the policy agenda—or sometimes because they simply underestimate the power of incumbency.

Reapportionment and Redistricting

Sometimes the advantages of incumbency can be diminished, as in election years after reapportionment and redistricting. **Reapportionment** is the reallocation of seats in the House of Representatives on the basis of changes in a state's population since the last census. Every 10 years, in years ending in zero (2010, 2020, and so on), the federal government counts the number of people in the country as a whole. If the census indicates that a state's population has changed significantly, that state may gain or lose seats in the House of Representatives (see "Analyzing the Sources"). **Redistricting,** the redrawing of congressional district boundaries within a state, is based on the reapportionment from the census.

Because the composition of a given congressional district can change as a result of reapportionment and redistricting, this process can mitigate the influence of incumbency. Frequently, the greatest shifts in the composition of the House of Representatives occur in election years ending in 2 (2002, 2012, and so on), when the first elections take place that incorporate the changes from reapportionment and redistricting. When a state loses a seat, the result is that an incumbent member of Congress is likely to lose a seat. When a state gains a seat, a new member of Congress can be elected to the open seat.

reapportionment
reallocation of seats in the House of Representatives to each state based on changes in the state's population since the last census

redistricting
redrawing of congressional district boundaries within each state, based on the reapportionment from the census

In some states, the goal of congressional redistricting is to protect House incumbents. The redrawing of congressional boundaries for the purpose of political advantage is a form of **gerrymandering,** the

gerrymandering
the drawing of legislative district boundaries to benefit an incumbent, a political party, or another group

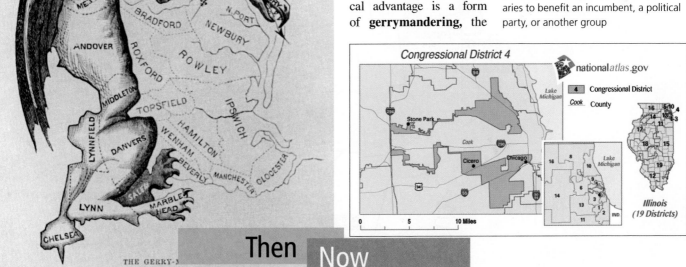

Then Now

> The term *gerrymander* originated from this Gilbert Stuart cartoon of a Massachusetts electoral district. To Stuart, the district looked like a salamander. A friend christened it a "Gerry-mander," after Massachusetts governor Elbridge Gerry, a signer of the Declaration of Independence and the politician who approved redrawing district lines for political advantage. What point does this famous historical cartoon of 1812, representing Massachusetts legislative districts, make about the nature of a gerrymander? Gerrymandering remains a practice today, as seen in Illinois's fourth congressional district. What are your own views on the practice?

practice of drawing legislative district boundaries to benefit an incumbent, a political party, or some other group. The term was coined in reference to Massachusetts governor Elbridge Gerry after a district shaped like a salamander was created to favor his party in 1811. The illustration shows the first gerrymander.

Most forms of gerrymandering are legal. The U.S. Supreme Court ruled in 1986 that a gerrymandering plan is unconstitutional only when it eliminates the minority party's influence statewide.[3] Because of the strict standards, only one partisan gerrymandering plan filed after the 1990 census was successfully challenged.

Scholars believe that this ruling, along with changes in how congressional district maps are drawn, explains increased partisan voting in the House of Representatives. In earlier times, redistricting occurred through a simple redrawing of the lines of a congressional district to accommodate population changes. But today, with the widespread use of computer-driven map-making technology, congressional seats can be configured to ensure a "safe seat"—one in which the party identification of the majority of a district's voters makes it likely that a candidate from a given party will win election. Sometimes, for example, more than 60 percent of a district's population identifies with one political party. A House member holding a safe seat generally can be partisan with immunity because his or her constituency often agrees with the representative's partisan stance. In contrast, when congressional districts were more competitive, a House member typically would have to temper partisan impulses to placate the sizeable proportion of his or her constituency that identified with the opposing party. Today, that is no longer the case, and it

FIGURE 12.1 ■ MAJORITY-MINORITY DISTRICTS IN CONGRESS TODAY

SOURCE: P. Bell and D. Wasserman, "Since 1982, Minority Congressional Districts Have Tripled," *National Journal,* April 13, 2012, www.nationaljournal.com/congress/since-1982-minority-congressional-districts-have-tripled-graphic-2012041.

appears that Republicans in the House of Representatives have become more conservative and their Democratic counterparts have become increasingly liberal. Consequently, House members are less likely to compromise or to be moderate in their positions in negotiating issues with the opposition.

While partisan gerrymandering tends to protect the status quo, another form of gerrymandering is sometimes relied upon to help ensure that a diversity of voices are elected to the House of Representatives. State legislatures have attempted to address the issue of racial imbalance in the House of Representatives by constructing a kind of gerrymander called a majority-minority district. A **majority-minority district** is composed of a majority of a given minority community—say, African Americans—and the creators' intent is to make it likely that a member of that minority will be elected to Congress. The Supreme Court has ruled that such racial gerrymandering is legal unless the state legislature redrawing the district lines creates majority-minority districts at the expense of other redistricting concerns. Typically, those concerns include preserving the geographic contiguity of districts, keeping communities within one legislative district, and reelecting incumbents. The number of majority-minority districts in the United States has grown significantly in recent years. Figure 12.1 shows that today, there are 106 districts in 26 states in which an ethnic or a racial minority is in the majority.

majority-minority district
a legislative district composed of a majority of a given minority community—say, African Americans—the intent of which is to make it likely that a member of that minority will be elected to Congress

Powers of Congress

The primary source of congressional authority is the U.S. Constitution. As shown in Table 12.1, the Constitution enumerates to Congress a number of different powers. The nature of these responsibilities reveals that the Constitution is both very specific in describing congressional powers (as in punishing illegal acts on the high seas) and at the same time quite vague (as in its language establishing the federal court system). Many of the specific duties of Congress reflect Americans' bitter experience in the colonial era, in that the framers granted powers to Congress that they did not want to place in the hands of a strong executive. For example, the economic powers granted to Congress, including the ability to tax and spend, to establish tariffs, and to borrow money, all limit the power of the president.

Powers specifically granted to Congress still have a distinct impact on our everyday lives. For example, Congress regulates currency, establishes weights and measures, and administers post offices. As we have seen, the connection between Congress, particularly the House, and the people was crucial to the framers, and so the Constitution requires that all taxation and spending measures originate in the House, because the framers believed this chamber would be nearer to the people—and that House members would therefore ensure that the people's will was done.

The Constitution moreover imbues the Congress with an additional source of power, one that has proved important in the expansion of legislative authority over time. As discussed in Chapter 2, the necessary and proper—or elastic—clause states that the Congress shall have the power to "make all Laws which shall be necessary and proper for carrying into Execution the foregoing powers, and all other Powers vested by this Constitution in the Government of the United States, or in a Department or Officer thereof." This clause has been responsible for Congress's ability to legislate in many matters not described in the enumerated powers. Reforming our nation's health care system, determining the powers of law enforcement in investigating terrorism, and overhauling our

TABLE 12.1

Enumerated Powers of the Congress

JUDICIAL POWERS
Establish the federal court system
Punish counterfeiters
Punish illegal acts on the high seas

ECONOMIC POWERS
Impose taxes
Establish import tariffs
Borrow money
Regulate interstate commerce
Coin and print money, determine the value of currency

NATIONAL SECURITY POWERS
Declare war
Raise and regulate national armed forces
Call up and regulate state national guard
Suppress insurrections
Repel invasions

REGULATORY POWERS
Establish standards of weights and measures
Regulate copyrights and patents

ADMINISTRATIVE POWERS
Establish procedures for naturalizing citizens
Establish post offices
Govern the District of Columbia

CONGRESSIONAL APPORTIONMENT

Article I Section 2 of the U.S. Constitution requires that "Representatives . . . shall be apportioned among the several states which may be included in this Union according to their respective numbers. . . ." How this requirement has been put into practice has been that after every census, the seats in the House of Representatives are apportioned to ensure that each congressional district has approximately the same number of people. In 2012, that meant that each House district had about 711,000 members. Because the Constitution guarantees that each state has at least one House delegate, states whose populations may not reach that threshold are nonetheless ensured a seat. (These include Alaska, Delaware, Montana, North Dakota, South Dakota, Vermont, and Wyoming.)

Evaluating the Evidence

1. In general, where are states that lost congressional seats in 2010's apportionment located? Why do you think these states lost population?

2. Which states gained seats after apportionment? Why do you think they gained population?

3. In your view, what might be the impact of states losing representatives? Of gaining them?

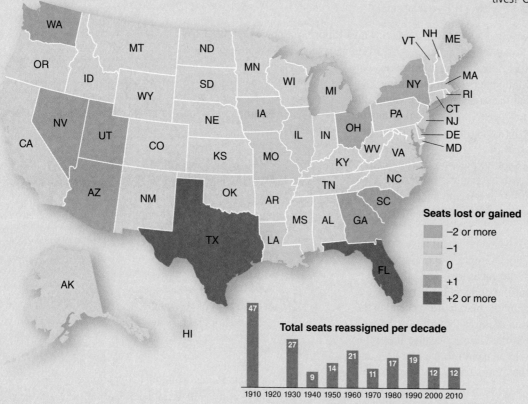

Seats lost or gained

- −2 or more
- −1
- 0
- +1
- +2 or more

Total seats reassigned per decade

1910: 47 | 1920: — | 1930: 27 | 1940: 9 | 1950: 14 | 1960: 21 | 1970: 11 | 1980: 17 | 1990: 19 | 2000: 12 | 2010: 12

SOURCE: U.S. Census Bureau, www.census.gov/2010census/.

system of immigration are all examples of powers not enumerated in the Constitution but that Congress exercises because of the broad scope of authority provided by the necessary and proper clause.

In addition to the Constitution, Congress derives power from Supreme Court decisions, the media, and the people. Supreme Court decisions often uphold the constitutionality of a law, in a sense verifying Congress's ability to create policy on a given subject. The media grant Congress power by providing members with a forum in which to communicate with constituents, sway public opinion, and create a favorable climate for the passage of legislation. The people are a key source of congressional power through civic participation in the electoral and legislative processes. Citizens communicate their views and priorities to their representatives, who then can claim public support in their endeavors to enact policy.

Functions of Congress

The Constitution is far more explicit in defining the responsibilities of the national legislature than it is in describing the function of the other branches of the government.[4] In its shaping of congressional functions, the Constitution's concerns with limited government, checks and balances, the separation of powers, and the creation of a federal system are all readily apparent. Today, Congress has a number of functions beyond lawmaking, including representation, oversight, agenda setting, and managing social conflict.

Representation Comes in Many Forms

In delineating the composition of the federal legislature and the procedures for electing its members, the Constitution shapes the congressional function of representation in several ways. Representation traditionally involves a House or Senate member's articulating and voting for the position that best represents the views of his or her constituents.[5] But sometimes a member of Congress may speak for other constituencies as well. For example, a feminist legislator might "represent" feminists nationwide,[6] just as a gay legislator might "represent" the collective interests of gays across the United States.

Often, Congress's policy-making function is at odds with its representation function. A legislator may be pressured—by his or her political party or own conscience—to vote for a policy that clashes with constituents' interests or views. In representing constituents, legislators frequently follow one of two models of representative behavior.

MODELS OF REPRESENTATION   According to the **trustee model** of representation, a member of the House or the Senate follows his or her own conscience when deciding issue positions and determining how to vote. Sometimes a legislator relying on the trustee model will act contrary to the views of his or her constituents. This model was espoused by British political theorist Edmund Burke (1729–1797), who served in Parliament as a representative of Bristol, England. Explaining his conception of representation, Burke emphasized to his constituents, however, that a member of Parliament "is not a member of Bristol, he is a member of Parliament."[7] Burke accordingly argued that a member of Parliament should follow his conscience when making decisions in the legislature: "Your representative owes you, not his industry only, but his judgment; and he betrays, instead of serving you, if he sacrifices it to your opinion."[8] In this trustee view, a legislator may act in opposition to the clear wishes of his or her constituents, such as in cases where an action is "for their own good" or the good of society.

Another model of representation is the **instructed delegate model,** the idea that a legislator, as a representative of his or her constituents, should vote in keeping with the constituents' views, *even if those views contradict the legislator's personal views.* This model of representation conceives of legislators as the agents of their constituents. A legislator hewing to the instructed delegate model faces a dilemma when his or her constituency is evenly divided on an issue.

Given these two different models of representation, which one do legislators typically follow? Most analyses of representation indicate that legislators are likely to combine the approaches. Specifically, with regard to many important or high-profile issues, legislators act as instructed delegates, whereas for more mundane matters about which their constituents are less likely to be aware or to hold a strong position, they rely on the trustee model.

PORK BARREL AND EARMARKS   Members of Congress also represent their constituencies through pork barrel politics. **Pork barrel** (also called simply *pork*) refers to legislators' appropriations of funds for special projects located within their congressional districts. Because pork

trustee model
a model of representation in which a member of the House or Senate follows his or her own conscience when deciding issue positions

instructed delegate model
a model of representation in which legislators, as representatives of their constituents, should vote in keeping with the constituents' views, even if those views contradict the legislator's personal views

pork barrel
legislators' appropriations of funds for special projects located within their congressional districts

> Senators Pat Toomey (R-Pa.) and Claire McCaskill (D-Mo.) are among the chief advocates of permanently banning earmarks—a designation within a spending bill that provides for a specific expenditure. In your view, should earmarks be banned permanently?

brings money and jobs to a particular district, legislators who are seeking reelection work aggressively to secure monies for their states or districts—to "bring home the bacon."[9] Traditionally, members have used transportation bills as a means of creating pork barrel projects for their districts.[10] Members of Congress also use **earmarks**—designations within spending bills that provide for specific expenditures—as a means of representing constituent interests. In 2010, Republicans in Congress sought to eliminate earmarks as part of a larger effort to reign in government spending, and Republicans in both chambers endorsed a 2-year moratorium on earmarks (see "Thinking Critically About Democracy"). That year, Congress appropriated about $16.5 billion for earmarked projects. Hawaii received the most per capita, at $259.78. Wyoming took home the least, $12.28 per capita. Senate Democrats followed suit in 2011, and the moratorium largely held for about a year, with essentially no earmarks included in appropriations measures. In 2012, the number of earmarked projects increased slightly—to about $3.3 billion. This expenditure funded 152 projects—but this reflects an 80 percent decrease in the costs of projects and a 98 percent decrease in the number of projects funded since the ban was enacted in 2011.[11]

earmark
a designation within a spending bill that provides for a specific expenditure

casework
personal work by a member of Congress on behalf of a constituent or a group of constituents, typically aimed at getting the government to do something the constituent wants done

ombudsperson
a role in which an elected or appointed leader acts as an advocate for citizens by listening to and investigating complaints against a government agency

CASEWORK   A special form of representation called **casework** refers to providing representation in the form of personal aid to a constituent or a group of constituents, typically by getting the government to do something the constituent wants done. Members of Congress and their staffs commonly assist constituents in dealing with bureaucratic agencies. In doing so, they serve in the capacity of an **ombudsperson,** an elected or appointed representative who acts as a citizens' advocate by listening to their needs and investigating their complaints with respect to a particular government agency. For example, a member of Congress might intervene with U.S. Citizenship and Immigration Services to request that a constituent's relative in a foreign country be granted a visa to travel to the United States.

According to political scientist Morris Fiorina, casework is a valuable tool for legislators. Fiorina points out that serving constituents is relatively easy for members of Congress, because bureaucrats—who depend on Congress for their funding—typically respond quickly to the requests of legislators.[12] The loyalty derived from assisting constituents is one aspect of the incumbency advantage that makes current members of Congress more likely to be elected than their challengers, who do not enjoy that source of constituent loyalty.

Casework benefits constituents when, for example, a member of Congress's staff works with a local branch of a Veterans' Administration clinic to secure services for a retired veteran, whose family members derive a sense of efficacy—a feeling that they can get things done and that the government works for people like them. They perceive that their individual member of Congress genuinely represents them and protects their interests, with the result that these constituents not only feel engaged but also are likely to advocate for their member's reelection bid.

But casework is not without its costs, as noted by Walter F. Mondale. Mondale, who served as a member of both the House and the Senate, as well as vice president of the United States, warns that casework can take a legislator's time away from his or her legislative responsibilities:

> Good constituent service is, of course, necessary—and honorable—work for any member of Congress and his [sic] staff. Citizens must have somewhere to turn for help when they become victims of government bureaucracy. But constituent service can also be a bottomless pit. The danger is that a member of Congress will end up as little more than an ombudsman between citizens and government agencies. As important as this work is, it takes precious time away from Congress's central responsibilities as both a deliberative and a law-making body.[13]

In describing the constituent service dilemma, Mondale raises questions worthy of citizens' reflection. For example: Is the national interest served when a congressional staff member has to track down your grandma's Social Security check? Does doing so result in a missed opportunity for government officials to create policy with broad, significant implications? And is the use of congressional staff members as ombudspeople a prudent use of taxpayers' money?

Policy Making: A Central Responsibility

Each year, Congress passes laws determining everything from the minimum wage, to what restrictions should govern gun purchases, to what law enforcers can do when they suspect someone of being a terrorist. The Constitution invests Congress with other policy-making powers as well, including the authority to tax and spend, to declare war, to establish courts, and to regulate the armed forces. This policy-making function is the central responsibility that the Congress carries out, and nearly all its other functions are related to its policy-making role. Congressional policy-making power also extends to the operations and priorities of governmental departments and agencies.

Oversight: A Check on the Executive Branch

In creating a system of checks and balances in the Constitution, the framers established the key congressional function of oversight.[14] **Oversight** is the process by which Congress "checks" the executive branch to ensure that the laws Congress passes are being administered in keeping with legislators' intentions. Congressional oversight is a check on the executive branch because the federal bureaucracy that implements laws is part of the executive branch. For example, in early 2014 members of Congress proposed a bill that would limit the Obama administration's ability to negotiate free-trade agreements with other nations, and would allow any member of Congress to sit in on trade negotiating sessions. Sponsors of the measure argue that scaling back the president's ability to negotiate free-trade agreements would enable them to protect jobs in their congressional districts.

In carrying out their oversight function, members of Congress use a variety of tools, some of which are listed here:

- Congressional hearings, in which government officials, bureaucrats, and interest groups testify as to how a law or a policy is being implemented and examine the impact of its implementation
- Confirmation hearings on presidential appointees to oversee executive departments or governmental agencies
- Investigations to determine whether a law or a policy is being implemented the way Congress intended it to be, and inquiries into allegations of wrongdoing by government officials or bureaucrats
- Budgetary appropriations that determine funding of an executive department or a government agency

These tools ensure that Congress has some say in how the executive branch administers the laws that Congress creates. Members of Congress increasingly have viewed their role of checking the executive branch as crucially important.

oversight
the process by which the legislative branch "checks" the executive branch to ensure that the laws Congress has passed are being administered in keeping with legislators' intent

Agenda Setting and Civic Engagement

Congress engages continuously in **agenda setting:** determining which public policy issues the federal legislature should consider.[15] Indeed, political scientists such as Gary Cox and Mathew McCubbins assert that agenda setting relieves the pressure that parties face in getting their members to vote with the party.[16] At the beginning of a congressional term, House and Senate leaders announce their goals for the coming session. Those goals reflect the issues and positions that predominated during the electoral campaign and that congressional leaders perceive to represent the people's priorities.

In setting the national agenda, Congress serves as a key agent in molding the scope of civic engagement and discourse, as people learn about, discuss, and form positions about issues. Frequently, agenda setting is itself influenced by public discourse, as when constituents complain to a member of Congress about a problem that needs to be solved or when an interest group contacts a legislator about a policy its membership would like to see implemented. For example, in 2010, pressure from gay rights activists led Congress to eliminate the "Don't Ask, Don't Tell" policy on gays in the military as part of a defense spending measure. The repeal was signed by President Obama and was implemented in September 2011, demonstrating how the public shapes the congressional agenda.

agenda setting
the determination by Congress of which public issues the government should consider for legislation

Managing Societal Conflict

Congress also has a significant influence in managing the societal conflict inherent in a divided society such as the United States. Americans are divided in many ways, and in the past several years, ideological divisions have become greatly apparent as congressional district maps facilitate the election of staunchly ideological candidates, as discussed earlier. Issues also divide Americans: Some citizens want policies benefiting rural areas, and others give higher priority to urban areas. Some want more money for programs for senior citizens; others seek funding for children's programs. With respect to abortion policy, some people are pro-life, and others are pro-choice. In addition, there are divisions related to social class, race, geography, gender, sexual orientation, religion, and so on. Congress manages these conflicts by representing a wide range of views and interests, by taking stands on these positions, and then finally by compromising and negotiating on these issues.

The House and the Senate Compared

Although the House of Representatives and the Senate share numerous functions, the two chambers of Congress differ in significant ways. As President Woodrow Wilson remarked, the "House and Senate are naturally unalike."[17] Constitutionally, the two houses are conceived as unique organizations, and the framers designated their duties to match the strengths and expertise of the people who would come to hold office in each chamber. Table 12.2 highlights these major differences. As discussed earlier in this chapter, the Constitution empowers the House of Representatives, as the legislative body closer to the people, with initiating any bills that result in taxes; whereas it empowers the Senate, as the more deliberative house, to give the president advice and consent on appointments and the ratification of treaties. The differences between the House and the Senate are not limited merely to their functions, however. The electoral and legislative structures are also sources of differences between the two houses.

Each of the 435 current members of the House of Representatives represents a legislative district determined by the reapportionment and redistricting process that occurs every 10 years, as described earlier in this chapter. In more populated areas, these congressional districts are often homogeneous, cohesive units in which a House member's constituency is likely to have fairly unified positions on many issues.[18] Senators, however, are elected by the population of an entire state, and although the political culture in some states is somewhat cohesive (for example, Vermont voters are more liberal on most issues than are Kansas voters), in many states there are notable differences in constituents' views, ideologies, and policy priorities. For instance, senators Barbara Boxer and Dianne Feinstein both represent the entire state of California, and both are Democrats. Although California is generally viewed as having a very liberal political

>The U.S. senators representing California are Barbara Boxer and Dianne Feinstein (both Democrats). Boxer and Feinstein must balance a wide variety of interests, including the concerns of liberal urban coastal dwellers and the more conservative views of those who live in the state's heartland to the east, including the state's considerable agricultural interests that often lobby for support from federal government programs.

TABLE 12.2

Differences between the House and the Senate

House	Senate
Larger (435 members)	Smaller (100 members)
Shorter electoral cycle (2-year term)	Longer electoral cycle (6-year term)
Narrow constituency (congressional districts)	Broad constituency (states)
Less prestigious	More prestigious
Originates all revenue bills	Ratifies treaties; confirms presidential nominees
Less reliant on staff	More reliant on staff
Power vested in leaders and committee chairs	Power distributed more evenly

culture, Boxer and Feinstein must represent the interests of both liberal voters in the western coastal areas of the state and more conservative voters inland to the east. At times, moreover, the interests of a senator's constituents divide over a given issue: In California, for example, environmental activists and fishers have argued against programs that divert water from lakes and streams so that it can be used for irrigation on commercial farms, whereas affluent agribusinesses advocate water diversion. A U.S. senator must balance such conflicting positions when making policy decisions.

The differing lengths of representatives' and senators' terms of service affect how members of each chamber of Congress relate to their constituents. Given their short 2-year terms, members of the House of Representatives naturally are reluctant to defy the will of the electorate on a given issue because of the likelihood that their opposition will be used against them during their reelection campaign. As the framers structured it, the House remains "the people's house," the chamber in which civically engaged individuals can effectively have their interests represented. And although U.S. senators naturally also want to please their constituents, they recognize that voting against their constituents' will on a particular issue might be less significant than such an action would be for a House member, especially if the issue arises early in their term and is not important enough for people to hold against them 6 years down the road.

The size of the chambers and the length of terms also affect the relative prestige of each chamber. In general, the smaller Senate is considered more prestigious than the House of Representatives, although some individual House members may enjoy more prestige than some senators.

Although the House and the Senate differ in their constitutionally determined duties, both must pass any piece of legislation before it can become law. But the way in which legislation is considered and voted on differs in each house of Congress.

The larger size of the House of Representatives, with its 435 members, necessitates a more formal legislative structure to prevent unruliness. The House, for example, generally has more, and more formal, rules guiding debate than the Senate. Despite the differences between the two chambers, the legislative process is remarkably similar in both.

The Legislative Process

Article I, Section 1, of the Constitution states, "All Legislative Powers herein granted shall be vested in a Congress of the United States, which shall consist of a Senate and House of Representatives." A **bill** is a proposed piece of legislation. As shown in Figure 12.2, every bill must be approved by *both houses* (the House and the Senate) *in identical form*. In general, bills must pass through five steps to become law:

FIGURE 12.2 ■ THE LEGISLATIVE PROCESS Where are there similarities between the House and the Senate in the legislative process? How do the Senate and the House resolve differences in versions of a bill passed in each chamber? What outcomes are possible once a bill goes to the president for approval?

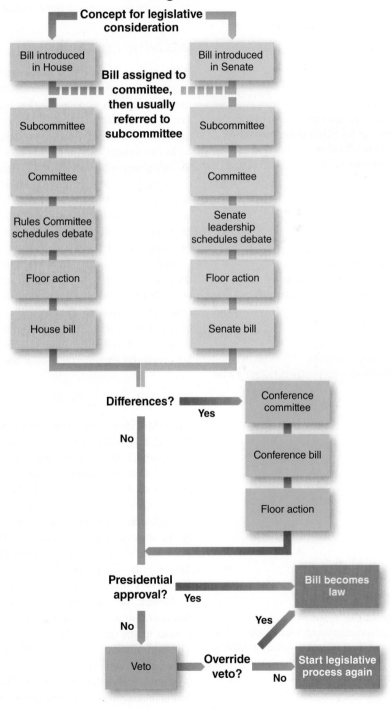

bill

a proposed piece of legislation

1. **Introduction.** A member of the House of Representatives or the Senate formally proposes the bill.

2. **Committee review.** Subgroups within the House and the Senate, composed of legislators who have expertise in the bill's subject matter, review the bill.

3. **House and Senate approval.** If the bill makes it out of committee, a majority of members in the House and the Senate must approve it.

4. **Conference committee reconciliation.** The conference committee reconciles the bill when different versions have passed in the House and the Senate.

5. **Presidential approval.** If the president signs the bill, it becomes law. But even after this arduous process, a presidential veto can kill the bill.

Introducing a Bill

Bills are introduced differently in each chamber of Congress. In the House of Representatives, a member of a legislator's staff drafts the proposed legislation, and the House member puts the bill into the **hopper,** a wooden box that sits on a desk at the front of the House chamber. Upon introduction, a bill is referred to as "H. R.," meaning House of Representatives, followed by a number that indicates the order in which it was introduced in a given legislative session, for example, "H. R. 207."

In the Senate, the process is less formal. Here, senators can announce proposed legislation to colleagues in a speech on the Senate floor. Alternatively, a senator can submit a written draft of the proposed legislation to an official known as the Senate clerk, or sometimes a senator will propose legislation simply by offering it as an amendment to an already pending piece of legislation. Once a bill is introduced in the Senate, it is referred to as "S.," or "Senate," followed by its number reflecting the order in which it was introduced in a given legislative session—for example, "S. 711."

Before 1995, a bill introduced in the House of Representatives could be subject to **joint referral,** the practice of referring the bill simultaneously to two different House committees for consideration. But the 104th Congress abolished joint committee referrals. Today, bills introduced in the House are referred to one committee, called the **lead committee.** Occasionally, when the substance of a bill warrants additional referrals to other committees that also have jurisdiction over the subject of the bill, the bill might be subsequently referred to a second committee.[19] In the Senate, bills typically are referred to only one committee.

The Bill in Committee

After introduction by a member of the House or the Senate, a bill is read into the *Congressional Record,* a formal record of all actions taken by Congress. Because of the large number of bills introduced, both chambers rely on an extensive committee structure that facilitates the consideration of so high a volume of bills.[20] Most bills that are introduced "die" in committee. That is, a committee does not consider the bill (sometimes because the committee does not have the time in a legislative session to take up the measure) or declines to forward the bill to the full chamber.

Each congressional committee and subcommittee is composed of a majority of members of the majority party in that chamber. For example, if 218 or more members (a majority in the House) elected to the House of Representatives are Republicans, then every committee and subcommittee in the House has a majority of Republicans. The parties in each chamber decide members' committee and subcommittee assignments.

Though the selection of committee chairs varies between chambers and parties, committee chairs are often chosen using the **seniority system,** by which the member with the longest continuous tenure on a standing committee receives preference when the committee chooses its chair. The committee chairs run committee meetings and control the flow of work in each committee. Although the seniority system is an institution in Congress, it is an informal system, and seniority does not always determine who will be the committee chair.[21] Chairs are chosen by a secret ballot, and in recent years junior members sometimes have won out over senior committee members.

Standing committees are permanent committees with a defined legislative jurisdiction. The House has 21 standing committees, and the Senate has 20. The House Committee on Homeland Security and the Senate Armed Services Committee are examples of standing committees.

hopper
a wooden box that sits on a desk at the front of the House of Representatives, into which House members place bills they want to introduce

joint referral
the practice, abolished in the 104th Congress, by which a bill could be referred to two different committees for consideration

lead committee
the primary committee considering a bill

seniority system
the system in which the member with the longest continuous tenure on a standing committee is given preference when the committee chooses its chair

standing committee
a permanent committee in Congress, with a defined legislative jurisdiction

Select committees are specially created to consider a specific policy issue or to address a particular concern. In 2007, the House formed a select committee, the Select Committee on Energy Independence and Global Warming, an advisory committee that held hearings on the issue of climate change. The committee was eliminated by the Republican majority in 2011. Other select committees have focused on issues such as the response to Hurricane Katrina, homeland security and terrorism, aging, and transportation.

Joint committees are bicameral committees composed of members of both chambers of Congress. Currently there are four joint committees; one is concerned with issues of taxation, another with economic issues, yet another deals with printing. Sometimes these committees offer administrative or managerial guidance of various kinds. For example, one joint committee supervises the administration of the Library of Congress.

In addition to the congressional committees, the House has more than 90 subcommittees, and the Senate has 68. **Subcommittees** typically handle specific areas of the committees' jurisdiction. For example, the House Committee on Foreign Affairs is a standing committee. Within the committee there are six subcommittees: Subcommittee on Africa, Global Health, Global Human Rights, and International Organizations; the Subcommittee on Asia and the Pacific; the Subcommittee on Europe, Eurasia, and Emerging Threats; the Subcommittee on the Middle East and North Africa; the Subcommittee on Terrorism, Nonproliferation, and Trade; and the Subcommittee on the Western Hemisphere. Each subcommittee handles bills relevant to its specified jurisdiction.

When a committee or a subcommittee favors a measure, it usually takes four actions:

1. **Agency review.** During **agency review,** the committee or subcommittee asks the executive agencies that would administer the law for written comments on the measure.

2. **Hearings.** Next the committee or subcommittee holds **hearings** to gather information and views from experts, including interest groups, concerned citizens, and policy experts involved with the issue.

3. **Markup.** During **markup,** the committee "marks up" the bill with suggested language changes and amendments. The committee does not actually alter the bill; rather, members recommend changes to the full chamber. In a typical bill markup, the committee may eliminate a component of the proposal or amend the proposal in some way.

4. **Report.** After agreeing to the wording of the bill, the committee issues a **report** to the full chamber, explaining the bill and its intent. The bill may then be considered by the full chamber.

select committee
a congressional committee created to consider specific policy issues or address a specific concern

joint committee
a committee composed of members of both chambers of Congress

subcommittee
a subordinate committee in Congress that typically handles specific areas of a standing committee's jurisdiction

agency review
part of the committee or subcommittee process of considering a bill, in which committee members ask executive agencies that would administer the law for written comments on the measure

hearings
sessions held by committees or subcommittees to gather information and views from experts

markup
the process by which members of legislative committees "mark up" a bill with suggested language for changes and amendments

report
a legislative committee's explanation to the full chamber of a bill and its intent

> As part of the legislative process, committee members hold hearings to gather information and views from experts, including interest groups, and concerned citizens, such as Neil Heslin. During his 2013 testimony before the Senate Judiciary Committee, Heslin holds a photograph of himself and his 6-year-old son, Jesse Lewis, who was killed during the Sandy Hook Elementary School rampage in Newtown, Connecticut, in December 2012. Despite the pleas of Heslin and others affected by the mass shooting, the Judiciary Committee rejected gun control measures advocated for by the victims and their families.

In the House of Representatives, a special measure known as a **discharge petition** is used to extract a bill from a committee to have it considered by the entire House. A discharge petition requires the signature of a majority (218) of the members of the House.

Debate on the House and Senate Floor

Table 12.3 compares the legislative process in the House and the Senate. For example, if a House bill is "discharged," or makes it out of committee, it then goes to the **Rules Committee,** one of the most important committees in the House, which decides on the length of debate and the scope of amendments that will be allowed on a bill. The Rules Committee sets the structure for the debate that ensues in the full House. For important bills, the Rules Committee tends to set strict limits on the types of amendments that can be attached to a bill. In general, the Rules Committee also establishes limits to floor debate in the House.

The Senate does not have a committee to do the work of the Rules Committee, but the Senate's small size allows members to agree to the terms of debate through **unanimous consent** agreements. Unanimous consent must be just that: Every senator needs to agree to the terms of debate (including time limits on debate), and if even one senator objects, unanimous consent does not take effect. Senators do not look favorably on objections to unanimous consent, and so such objections are rare. Objecting to unanimous consent agreements can potentially undermine a senator's ability to get legislation passed by provoking the ire of other senators.

If the Senate does not reach unanimous consent, the possibility of a **filibuster** arises—a procedural move that attempts to halt passage of the bill.[22] Sometimes the mere threat of a filibuster is enough to compel a bill's supporters to alter a bill's content. During a filibuster, a senator can speak for an unlimited time on the Senate floor. Filibustering senators do not need to restrict themselves to speaking only on the subject of the bill—they just need to keep talking. Some senators have read the Bible, cookbooks, and even the Nynex Yellow Pages into the *Congressional Record.* In the 1930s, Senator Huey P. Long (D-La.) filibustered many bills, once speaking for 15 hours to block one that he viewed as "helping the rich get richer and the poor get poorer." Long, viewed as a character by many of his Senate colleagues, was a favorite among visitors to the Senate galleries, where he would entertain onlookers with New Orleans recipes for "pot-likkers" and with his articulations of Shakespeare in a Louisiana drawl. Former senator Strom Thurmond (R-S.C.) holds the Senate record for the longest filibuster. In an attempt to block passage of the Civil Rights Act of 1957, Thurmond filibustered for 24 hours and 18 minutes. A filibuster can end by a vote of **cloture,** in which a supermajority of 60 senators agrees to invoke cloture and end debate. Cloture is initiated if 16 senators sign a cloture petition. In 2010, when Senator Scott Brown (R-Mass.) was elected in a special election to replace the late Democratic senator Edward M. Kennedy, the specter of filibusters in the Senate became more likely, because Brown's election as the 41st Republican in the Senate meant that Democrats had lost the 60-member filibuster-proof majority they had held.

Differences in the Legislative Process in the House and Senate

TABLE 12.3

House	Senate
Bill introduced by member placing bill in hopper	Bill introduced by member
Relies on Rules Committee to schedule debate on House floor and to establish rules for amendments	Relies on unanimous consent agreements to determine rules for debate and amendments
Has a rule barring nongermane amendments	No rule banning nongermane amendments
Does not allow filibusters	Allows filibusters
Discharge petition can be used to extract a bill from a committee	Does not allow discharge petitions

In November 2013, Senate Democrats exercised the so-called **nuclear option,** a maneuver eliminating the possibility of filibusters on federal judicial nominations (excluding those to the U.S. Supreme Court) and appointments to the executive branch. This tactic was based on a 1957 opinion drafted by then–vice president Richard M. Nixon, who asserted that the Constitution grants the presiding officer of the Senate the power to override Senate rules. The Democrats in charge of the Senate declared that filibusters on appointments and nominations could be subjected to a simple majority vote, requiring 51 votes rather than the 60 votes that would be necessary to end a filibuster. This 60-vote minimum had prevented President Obama—and Presidents Bill Clinton and George W. Bush before him—from getting many of their executive and judicial appointments confirmed in the Senate. Then-Senate majority leader Harry Reid (D-Nev.) argued that a backlog of appointments to the Obama administration and the federal courts was a result of Republican opposition to President Obama's administration overall rather than a reflection of the qualifications of individuals nominated to various positions. At the time the Senate voted to use the nuclear option, 59 executive branch nominees and 17 judicial nominees were awaiting confirmation. Weeks later, the Senate voted, by a 56-38 vote margin, to confirm Patricia Millett's nomination to the D.C. Circuit Court of Appeals. The tight margin of Millett's confirmation vote demonstrated the effect that exercising the nuclear option has, as the path then became clear for other Obama appointees.

After a bill is debated by the full chamber, the members vote on it. Before a bill can become law, identical versions of the bill must pass in both the House and the Senate. If only one chamber passes a bill during a congressional term, the bill dies. If both the House and the Senate pass bills on the same topic but with differences between the bills, the bills are then sent to a **conference committee,** a bicameral, bipartisan committee composed of legislators whose job is to reconcile the two versions of the bill. After the committee develops a compromise version of the bill, the bill then goes back to both chambers for another vote. If the bill does not pass in both chambers during a congressional term, the bill is dead, although it can be reintroduced in the next session. If both chambers approve the bill, it then goes to the president for signature or veto.

Presidential Action

When both the House and the Senate manage to pass a bill in identical form, it proceeds to the president, who may take one of three actions. First, the president may sign it, in which case the bill becomes a law. Second, the president may choose to do nothing. If the president does nothing and Congress is in session, the bill becomes law after 10 days without the president's signature. A president may take this route if he or she does not support the bill but knows that Congress would override a veto. If, however, the Congress has adjourned (that is, the bill was passed at the end of a legislative session), then the president may exercise a pocket veto. A **pocket veto** occurs when Congress has adjourned and the president waits 10 days without signing the bill; the president effectively "puts the bill in his pocket," and the bill dies. Finally, a president may exercise the executive power of a *veto:* rejecting the bill and returning it to Congress with a message explaining why the bill should not become law. Congress can vote to override the veto by a two-thirds vote in both houses, in which case the bill becomes law. But overriding a presidential veto is a difficult and rare achievement.

Congressional Leadership

The House and the Senate alike choose the majority and minority leaders for their adept negotiating skills, their finely honed abilities to guide compromise, and their skills of persuasion. A majority leader nurtures compromise in the legislative process by knowing the members' positions on legislation well enough to recognize which issues are negotiable and which are deal-breakers; by engineering trade-offs between players; and by convincing committee chairs that a negotiated compromise is the best outcome they can expect.

> As the population of the United States becomes increasingly diverse, so too does Congress, and as the proportion of Latinos in the population grows, so too does their political clout. Here, U.S. Senator Robert Menendez (D-N.J.), one of three Hispanic senators, joins in a celebration of Hispanic Heritage Month. Both Democrats and Republicans are courting Latino voters in the lead up to the 2016 presidential election.

nuclear option
a maneuver exercised by the presiding officer in the Senate that eliminates the possibility of filibusters by subjecting votes on certain matters to a simple majority vote

conference committee
a bicameral, bipartisan committee composed of legislators whose job is to reconcile two versions of a bill

pocket veto
a special presidential veto of a bill passed at the conclusion of a legislative session, whereby the president waits 10 days without signing the bill, and the bill dies

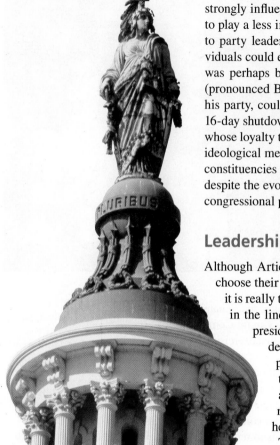

Speaker of the House
the leader of the House of Representatives, chosen by the majority party

House majority leader
the leader of the majority party, who helps the Speaker to develop and implement strategy and who works with other members of the House of Representatives

majority whip
a go-between with the majority leadership and party members in the House of Representatives

In earlier eras, forceful leaders rose to the position of majority leader in both houses and strongly influenced congressional priorities and legislation.[23] But as political parties have come to play a less important role in the election of members of the House and the Senate, allegiance to party leaders in these institutions has dwindled.[24] The era has long passed in which individuals could essentially control what Congress did through their assertive personalities.[25] This was perhaps best illustrated in 2013 by the struggle of Speaker of the House John Boehner (pronounced BAY-ner) (R-Ohio), who, because of pressure put on him by conservatives within his party, could not come to a compromise with Democrats on the budget. The result was the 16-day shutdown of the federal government. Today's congressional power brokers face members whose loyalty to the party and the leadership is tempered by the increase in the number of highly ideological members hailing from safe congressional districts and the increasing need to please constituencies that themselves are less loyal to the parties than in bygone times.[26] Nonetheless, despite the evolution in the role of congressional leader, partisanship remains a strong aspect of congressional politics, particularly since 1994.

Leadership in the House of Representatives

Although Article I, Section 2, of the Constitution states, "The House of Representatives shall choose their Speaker and other Officers," and all members of the House vote for the Speaker, it is really the members of the majority party who select their **Speaker of the House.** Second in the line of presidential succession (after the vice president), the Speaker serves as the presiding officer and manager of the House. In this capacity, the Speaker chairs floor debates, makes majority party committee assignments, assigns members to the powerful Rules Committee, negotiates with members of the minority party and the White House, and guides legislation through the House.[27] But the Speaker is also the leader of his or her party in the House, and a key duty associated with this role is helping party members to get reelected. Finally, the Speaker is himself or herself an elected member of the House.

The House leadership—which, in addition to the Speaker, includes the majority leader, the minority leader, and the party whips—is chosen at the beginning of each session of Congress through a conference also known as a *caucus*. During a caucus, all the members of the political party meet and elect their chamber leaders, approve committee assignments, and elect committee chairpersons. Party leaders also may call a party caucus during a legislative session to shore up support on an issue being voted upon or to formulate the party's position on an issue on the agenda.[28]

The 2010 elections in which the Republicans took control of the House paved the way for the election of John Boehner as Speaker of the House. As Speaker, Boehner's priority has been repealing the Affordable Care Act, President Obama's health care reform package that was passed in 2009 while the Democrats controlled both houses of Congress and Representative Nancy Pelosi (D-Calif.) served as Speaker (see "Thinking Critically About Democracy"). Boehner, who had enjoyed respect and loyalty among his colleagues, struggled in the year before the 2014 congressional election. Moderate Republicans in the House became concerned with the decline in approval of Congress and Boehner's inability to rein in conservative Tea Party members within his caucus, and conservatives became frustrated with Boehner's sometimes willingness to compromise with Senate Democrats and the Obama administration. Historically, however, Boehner has been a vocal critic of the Obama administration, much in the way that Pelosi opposed the Bush administration during her tenure. As speaker, it is Boehner's responsibility to herd the various elements of the Republican Party in the House, including those members ascribing the Tea Party positions, to a cohesive position. He must unify liberal, moderate, and conservative Republicans, building coalitions composed of representatives from different districts, generations, ethnicities, and sexes. These skills are essential attributes for the Speaker of the House.

The Speaker relies on the **House majority leader** to help develop and implement the majority party's legislative strategy, to work with the minority party leadership, and to encourage unity among majority party legislators. In this last task, the Speaker and the House majority leader are assisted by the **majority whip,** who acts as a go-between with the leadership and the party members

Democracy

Should Congress Repeal the Affordable Care Act?

The Issue: In the spring of 2010, Congress passed the Patient Protection and Affordable Care Act, which became known as Obamacare. The Affordable Care Act represents the most significant reform of our nation's health care system since Congress created Medicaid and Medicare in 1965. The Affordable Care Act seeks to increase the quality, affordability, and accessibility of health insurance using mandates, subsidies, and insurance exchanges within states. Through these mechanisms, the number of uninsured individuals should decrease, as should future federal spending on Medicare and health care in general.

Yes: The Affordable Care Act should be repealed because it represents an unauthorized and unnecessary expansion of the role of the federal government. It is unfair that individuals are being forced to purchase health insurance. The law also violates the First Amendment right to freedom of religion by mandating that health insurance cover birth control. Some religious entities, such as the Roman Catholic Church, oppose birth control. Individuals, private companies, and organizations that espouse these beliefs should not have to pay for medical procedures and products that violate their principles.

No: Duly elected representatives passed the Affordable Care Act, and it was signed by a president who went on to win reelection. Obamacare does expand the role of the federal government, but this expansion is necessary because the costs associated with health care were dragging down the U.S. economy, slowing growth, and contributing to the federal deficit. To fix the economy, health care had to be fixed. In addition, access to health care is a basic human right. Sweeping reforms, including Medicare and Medicaid, have faced strong opposition before, eventually garnering widespread support.

Other Approaches: The federal government did have to address the rising cost of health care and the lack of coverage, but Congress and the president overstepped their boundaries, particularly in mandating that individuals carry health insurance. The solution needs to address the concerns of individuals whose premiums have increased and organizations, like religious orders, that are being forced to purchase health insurance that covers treatments or procedures that violate their teachings.

What do you think?

1. Is it the duty of the federal government to provide health care for its citizens?

2. If governments should not meddle in health care policy, how can they address the large economic impacts that health care has on the economy and on government spending (for example, through Medicare)?

3. Should religious organizations be forced to purchase insurance coverage for treatments to which they object, or should this be a decision made by the individual who is insured?

---

in the House. The term *whip* comes from the English hunting term *whipper-in,* a hunter whose job is to keep the foxhounds in the pack and to prevent them from straying during a fox hunt. Similarly, the job of the party whip is to keep party members together, encouraging them to vote with the party on issues and preventing them from straying off into their own positions. The minority party in the House also elects leaders, the **House minority leader** and the **minority whip,** whose jobs mirror those of their majority-party colleagues but without the power that comes from holding a majority in the House.

Leadership in the Senate

In the Senate, the vice president of the United States serves as the president of that body, according to the Constitution. But in actual practice, vice presidents preside over the Senate only rarely. Vice presidents, however, have one power in the Senate that, although rarely exercised, is enormously important. If a vote in the upper house of Congress is tied, the vice president breaks the

House minority leader
the leader of the minority party, whose job mirrors that of the majority leader but without the power that comes from holding a majority in the House of Representatives

minority whip
a go-between with the minority leadership whose job mirrors that of the majority whip but without the power that comes from holding a majority in the House of Representatives

tie. Such a situation occurred in 2005 when Vice President Dick Cheney cast the tie-breaking vote on a major budget bill that slashed federal spending by nearly $40 billion by allowing states to impose new fees on Medicaid recipients, cutting federal funds that enforce child-support regulations, and imposing new federal work requirements on state welfare recipients. Since 1789, vice presidents have broken 244 ties in the Senate.

The majority party in the Senate elects a Senate leader called the **president pro tempore.** Meaning "president for the time," this position is often referred to as "president pro tem." The job of the president pro tem is to chair the Senate in the vice president's absence. Historically, this position has been honorary, with the majority-party senator who has the longest record of continuous Senate service being elected to the office. Although the position is honorary, the Senate's president pro tem is third in the line of presidential succession (following the vice president and the Speaker of the House). Senator Patrick Leahy (D-Vt.), who was first elected to the Senate in 1974, has served as the president pro tem since 2012.

The real power in the U.S. Senate is held and wielded by the **Senate majority leader,** whose job is to manage the legislative process so that favored bills are passed; to schedule debate on legislation in consultation with his or her counterpart in the minority party, the **Senate minority leader;** and to act as the spokesperson for the majority party in the Senate. The majority and the minority leaders both play crucial roles in ushering bills through the Senate, and the majority leader facilitates the numerous negotiations that arise when senators bargain over the content of a given piece of proposed legislation.[29]

Senate majority leader Mitch McConnell (R-Ky.) was elected after the Republicans won a majority of seats in the 2014 Senate elections. McConnell was elected after serving as minority leader and has a reputation as a skillful and tough-minded politician. As majority leader, McConnell faces pressure from more conservative members of his party to dismantle Obamacare and to block proposed reforms to the nation's immigration laws. McConnell succeeded Harry Reid (D-Nev.), who had served as speaker since 2006, and who evoked the ire of Senate Republicans who have criticized his use of the nuclear option on executive branch and judicial appointments as a "power grab."

Decision Making in Congress: The Legislative Context

When deciding whether to "toe the party line" on a legislative vote, members of Congress do not operate independently and in isolation. Throughout the legislative process, they face a variety of external pressures that influence their views. Some of these pressures are subtle; others are more pronounced. Moreover, the effectiveness of the pressure varies according to the timing and type of legislation being considered. For example, political scientist Barry C. Burden has noted that the personal experiences of legislators sometimes have a bearing on their policy stances on issues.[30] Among the most important influences on members of Congress with respect to the legislative process are political parties, members' colleagues and staff, interest groups, the president, and of course their constituents—the people who elected them to serve as their representatives in our system of republican government.

Political Parties and Partisanship in Decision Making

Figure 12.3 shows the party breakdown in Congress since 1985. The data show that 1994 was a pivotal year, ending Democratic control in the House and the Senate. For nearly all of the next 12 years, Republicans retained control over both the House and the Senate. (Republicans lost their narrow majority in the Senate in 2001 when one Republican senator switched parties, but they regained control in the 2002 elections.) But in 2006 the balance of power shifted back to the Democrats, who won majorities in both houses, squeaking out a majority in the Senate with a one-member lead. That year, Democratic candidates benefited from President George W. Bush's unpopularity and public weariness with the war in Iraq. As shown in Figure 12.4, in 2008 the Democrats continued to increase their majorities in both

president pro tempore
(also called *president pro tem*) theoretically, the chair of the Senate in the vice president's absence; in reality, an honorary title, with the senator of the majority party having the longest record of continuous service being elected to the position

Senate minority leader
the leader of the minority party in the Senate, who works with the majority leader in negotiating legislation

Senate majority leader
the most powerful position in the Senate; the majority leader manages the legislative process and schedules debate on legislation

FIGURE 12.3 ■ PARTY REPRESENTATION TRENDS What trends does this graph show with respect to party representation in the House of Representatives since 1987? What trends does it indicate for the Senate? Generally speaking, do the patterns for the House resemble those for the Senate?

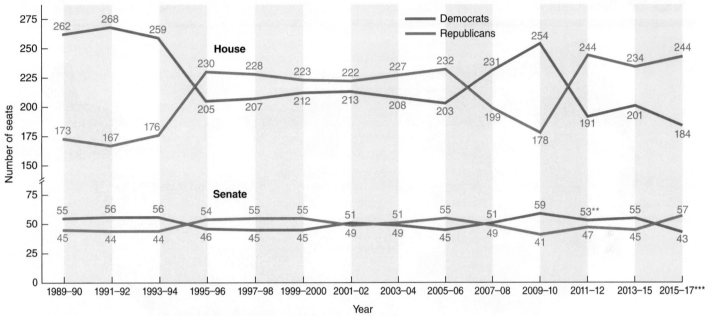

Party Breakdowns in the House and Senate, 1989–2017*

*Races in seven House districts and Louisiana's U.S. Senate election had not been decided at time of publication.
**Two Independent members of the Senate typically voted Democrat.
***One Independent member of the Senate typically votes Democrat.

houses, as a result of voters' continuing dislike of Bush's policies, and—for some Democratic congressional candidates—from Barack Obama's coattails. But this trend was reversed in 2010, with Republicans winning a majority of seats in the House of Representatives and increasing their numbers in the U.S. Senate. In the 2012 elections, in which President Obama topped the Democratic ticket, Democrats increased their margins slightly in both the House and the Senate.

The partisan breakdown of Congress is important because most major legislative votes cast are "party votes," meaning that most members of one political party vote one way, and most members of the other party vote the other way. In some cases, this divide is due to the differing ideologies. In other instances, party voting is simply pure partisanship: Democrats vote against something because Republicans vote for it and vice versa. For example, in 2009, when Congress voted to overhaul the nation's health care system, all 60 Democrats in the Senate voted for the bill, and all 39 Republicans voted against it (Senator Jim Bunning, a Republican, did not vote). Similarly, in the House of Representatives, only 1 of 216 Republicans supported the measure, whereas all 219 Democrats voted for it.

Partisan voting increased after the Watergate scandal in the 1970s, rose again after the 1994 congressional elections, in which Republicans took control of Congress, and again when the conservative Tea Party members of Congress began flexing their political muscle after the 2010 elections. Partisan voting tends to be particularly acrimonious immediately before congressional and presidential elections. It occurs more often when members are voting on domestic policy issues, such as environmental or economic regulatory policy and entitlement programs, that tend to crystallize ideological differences between the parties, as the health care bill did.

FIGURE 12.4 ■ PARTY REPRESENTATION IN THE HOUSE OF REPRESENTATIVES, 2015 How many seats in the House do the Republicans have as a result of the 2014 election? How many seats do the Democrats have? Which party has the majority? Given the party of the president, how do you think the new House composition might affect lawmaking?

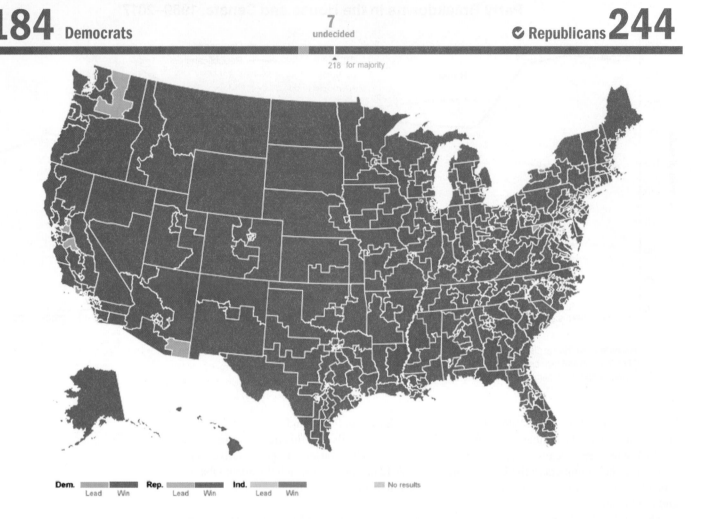

184 Democrats   **7** undecided   ✓ **Republicans 244**

218 for majority

Dem. ▭ Lead ▬ Win   Rep. ▭ Lead ▬ Win   Ind. ▭ Lead ▬ Win   ▨ No results

But often, partisan votes are politically motivated, plain and simple. One of the most partisan votes on record in Congress was the 1998 vote on whether President Bill Clinton should be impeached. In that vote, 98 percent of all members of Congress voted the party line—Republicans for impeachment, Democrats against. And as previously mentioned, majorities of both parties have often refused to consider the appointments and nominations made by presidents of the opposite party.

As previously discussed, the increasingly sophisticated ability of mapmakers to draw congressional districts that offer partisan advantage to one party means that partisanship has increased in the House of Representatives. Few members have to placate moderate or competitively bipartisan constituents in their districts, and the many members whose seats are assured by partisan gerrymandering have become among the more firmly partisan members in recent years. But many scholars assert that a similar bifurcation of political ideology has not occurred in the Senate.

They claim that, because state populations as a whole tend to be more ideologically diverse and less homogeneous than House districts, U.S. senators often must temper their views to reflect the wider range of their constituents' perspectives. Thus senators tend to be more willing than their House counterparts are to compromise and to take a more moderate stance in negotiating with the opposing party. Nonetheless, on some issues, other scholars note that the Senate is increasingly dividing along strongly partisan lines.[31]

Colleagues and Staff: Trading Votes and Information

Congressional colleagues provide cues for members of the House and the Senate in their decision making over whether to vote for a pending piece of legislation. Members may seek the opinions of like-minded colleagues in determining how to vote on a proposed bill. In addition, legislators may consult with peers who are policy experts.

Members of Congress also engage in **logrolling,** the practice of trading votes between members. Logrolling is a reciprocal tactic by which a member agrees to vote on one piece of legislation in exchange for a colleague's vote on another. For example, a representative from an urban area might agree to vote for a farm aid bill that has little effect on her constituents in exchange for a colleague's vote for increased funds for community policing in cities.

In addition, House and Senate members rely on their staffs to inform their decision making on legislation.[32] Staff members frequently have policy expertise that can guide a legislator's decision on an upcoming vote. They also figure in the legislative voting process by communicating with legislators about the desires of constituents and interest groups with respect to a pending piece of legislation.

Then Now Next

Partisanship in Congress

Then (1980s)	Now
Congress was divided; Democrats controlled the House of Representatives, and Republicans controlled the Senate.	Republicans control both the House and Senate.
Although incumbents enjoyed a considerable advantage, many congressional districts were a mix of constituents of both major parties.	Fewer congressional districts are competitive. Many districts are more homogeneous because district boundaries can be drawn with sophisticated computer programs.
Partisan voting was evident, but legislators were often forced to base their positions on constituent preferences in addition to their own party loyalty.	With the advent of less competitive districts, legislators are more partisan than their predecessors.

WHAT'S NEXT?

> Has the outcome of the 2014 elections increased or decreased party tensions, in your view? Why?

> In recent years, partisanship has increased when there has been a president of one party and a Congress of another. Does such a scenario exist today? What implications does that have for the future of partisanship in Congress for the next several years?

> Increases in technological sophistication could make redistricting an even more exact science. What effect would this change have on partisanship in Congress?

logrolling
the practice in which members of Congress agree to vote for a bill in exchange for their colleague's vote on another bill

Interest Groups: Influence Through Organization

In various ways, interest groups also influence congressional elections. They can affect electoral outcomes, for example, through an endorsement process by which a group notifies its members that it backs a certain candidate in the hope that members get on the bandwagon and express their support at the polls. In addition, through their political action committees, interest groups make financial contributions to congressional campaigns. And interest groups whose memberships are mobilized to support or oppose a candidate often provide grassroots activists to political campaigns.[33]

As we considered in Chapter 7, interest groups also shape the legislative process. They make their mark by influencing congressional campaigns, by providing information to members of Congress as they try to decide whether to vote for a particular piece of legislation, and by lobbying members of Congress to support or oppose legislation.[34]

The President's Effect on Decision Making

As we have seen, the president determines whether to sign or to veto legislation that reaches his desk. But often, before a bill reaches the signing stage, the president's position on it carries enough influence to sway members of Congress, particularly members of his political party, to vote for or against the proposed legislation.

The president can compel congressional action on an issue. Consider, for example, the issue of health care. President Obama challenged the Congress in 2012 to reform the nation's tax structure, specifically to increase taxes on the highest income earners, stirring congressional debate, and prioritizing the issue for many Democrats in the legislature.

Constituents: The Last Word

Of all the players with a voice in the legislative process, congressional constituents—the people whom the members of Congress represent—wield perhaps the strongest, if indirect, influence with respect to congressional decision making. Most members of Congress want to be reelected, and representing constituents' views (and being able to convince voters that their views are represented well) is a major avenue to reelection to Congress. Thus constituents influence the legislative process by ensuring that their representatives in Congress work hard to represent their perspectives and policy interests, whether those concerns are over environmental pollution, crime, or the soaring cost of higher education.

attentive public
the segment of voters who pay careful attention to political issues

In fact, some research shows that the public's "potential preferences" can motivate legislators to espouse a policy position likely to be embraced by constituents.[35] But other research shows that most voters are not especially vigilant when it comes to monitoring their elected officials in Congress. In fact, only a very small percentage of voters, sometimes called the **attentive public,** pay careful attention to the public policies being debated by Congress and to the votes cast by their representatives and senators. But the fact that the attentive public is a relatively small minority does not mean that votes taken in Congress are insignificant as far as constituents' opinions go. Indeed, if a member of Congress should disregard constituents' views in voting on a major issue, it is quite likely that an opposing candidate or political party will bring this misstep to the public's attention during the individual's next congressional campaign.

The People and Their Elected Representatives

Although members of Congress may make it a priority to represent the viewpoints and interests of their constituents, demographically speaking, they do not represent the American public at large. As Table 12.4 shows, Congress, especially the Senate, is older, whiter, more educated, and more likely to be male than the population as a whole. That said, Congress is not designed to be a perfect sampling of American demographics.[36] It is logical that the leaders of government would more closely

TABLE 12.4

Demographic Characteristics of the 113th Congress Compared to the U.S. Population

	House (%)	Senate (%)	Population (%)
PARTY			
Democrat	46	54	34
Republican	54	45	29
Independent Unaffiliated	0	1	37
AVERAGE AGE	57 years	62 years	37 years
SEX			
Male	82	80	49
Female	18	20	51
RACE			
White	85	95	81
Black	10	1	13
Hispanic (any race)	7	3	16
Asian/Pacific Islands	2	1	3.5
Native American	.22	0	0.7
EDUCATION			
Bachelor's degree	92	99	27
Master's degree	19	16	7
Law degree	38	55	1
Ph.D.	4	0	1
M.D.	5	4	2

SOURCES: Jennifer E. Manning, *Membership in the 112th Congress: A Profile* (Washington, DC: Congressional Research Service), www.senate.gov/reference/resources/pdf/R41647.pdf; U.S. Census Bureau, *Statistical Abstract of the United States.*

Woman in congressional delegation—current and past

Woman in congressional delegation—past only

No woman to date in congressional delegation

* As of publication date, the run-off for the Louisiana U.S. Senate had not taken place.

FIGURE 12.5

States Represented by Women in the U.S. Congress

SOURCE: Center for American Women and Politics, Eagleton Institute of Politics, Rutgers, The State University of New Jersey, www.cawp.rutgers.edu/fast_facts/levels_of_office/documents/cong.pdf, and authors' calculations.

resemble individuals who have achieved leadership positions in other realms, such as the corporate world and academia.

Yet Congress is more diverse today than at any other point in history. Figure 12.5 shows that most states have women as part of their congressional delegations. But the proportion of women in Congress is not nearly equal to their proportion in the national population. In 2014, at least 82 women were elected to the House of Representatives, constituting 19 percent of the 435 members. In addition, 20 women (or 20 percent of the 100 members) serve in the Senate. Despite this upward trend, the United States lags behind many industrialized democracies with respect to the proportion of women serving in the national legislature.

Similarly, African Americans have historically been underrepresented in Congress. To date, only eight African Americans have served in the Senate, including two, Hiram Revels and Blanche Bruce, who served during the Reconstruction era that followed the Civil War. After Bruce left the Senate in 1881, no other African American would be elected to that chamber until 1967, when Senator Edward Brooke (R-Mass.) was elected for one term. More recently, Senator Carol Moseley Braun (D-Ill.) was elected in 1992 and served for one term, and Barack Obama was elected from the state of Illinois in 2004. Upon Obama's election to the presidency, then–Illinois governor Rod Blagojevich appointed Ronald Burris to the seat amid controversy. Blagojevich was subsequently convicted on corruption charges. Burris held the seat until November 2011, when his successor was elected. From 2011 through 2013, no African Americans served in the U.S. Senate, but in October 2013, Cory Booker (D-N.J.) was elected to fill the remainder of the term vacated when Senator Frank Lautenberg passed away. Booker was reelected to a full 6-year term in 2014, and was joined in the Senate by Tim Scott (R-S.C.), the first African American to be elected to the Senate from the South since the Reconstruction era.

FIGURE 12.6 ▨ AFRICAN AMERICANS ELECTED TO THE HOUSE What explains the rise in African American representation in the House from 1871 through 1887? Why did blacks' representation fall after 1877? What pattern do you see since the late 1960s, and what political and social changes explain it?

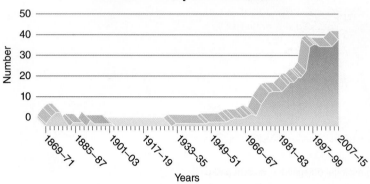

African Americans in the House of Representatives

Figure 12.6 traces the increasing success of African Americans in getting elected to the House of Representatives. The figure shows that, as in the Senate, African Americans' initial service in the House came about in the Reconstruction period. But the successes of that era were short lived, and the numbers of African Americans in Congress would not match those of the immediate post-Reconstruction period until after the civil rights movement of the 1960s. Today, as is the case for women, more African Americans serve in Congress than at any other point in U.S. history, and with each election history continues to be made. In 2014, for example, Mia Love (R-Utah) made history by becoming the first Republican African-Amercan woman elected to the House of Representatives.

Latinos' success at winning election to Congress still lags drastically behind their proportion of the population, with Latinos constituting nearly 16 percent of the population but just 7 percent of the members of the House of Representatives (or 31 members) and 3 percent of the Senate (Senators Robert Menendez, D-N.J.; Marco Rubio, R-Fla.; and Ted Cruz, R-Tex., are Hispanic). But many states, including New Mexico, California, Texas, and Arizona, are seeing rising numbers of Latinos elected to state legislatures, providing a pool of candidates who could move on to run for Congress. As women, African Americans, and ethnic minorities take up an increasing proportion of the eligibility pool—the group of people deemed qualified for office—diversity in Congress is sure to grow.

Thinking Critically About What's Next in Congress

Congress is an ever-evolving institution. The national legislature is shaped by the framers' vision that created it; by the groups and individuals that seek to, and do, influence it; and by the broader electorate who vote for the representatives who serve in it. The Constitution's framers ingeniously created a strong legislative system designed to dominate the national government. In doing so, they simultaneously—and significantly—checked the power of the executive.

The framers ensured that the legislative branch of the federal government would be responsive to changing times. Today, Congress is more demographically diverse than ever before in history. It has also responded to modern challenges by exercising a wider scope of powers, concerned with issues that were unimaginable even two decades ago, let alone more than two centuries ago. Congressional decision making today is influenced by shifting constituencies in a country that is rapidly growing more diverse. How will continued increasing diversity affect congressional decision making in the future?

With Congress well-structured to respond to constituents' needs, ongoing technological advances and the spread of cheap technology to more and more citizens mean that members of Congress and their staffs should be increasingly accessible to the people. And representatives' district offices will continue to provide constituents another easily accessed channel through which to convey their needs and interests to their representatives—and through which their representatives, in turn, can monitor the opinions of their constituents so that they may better represent them. But technology also has driven the process of congressional redistricting, rendering more highly partisan districts and creating a more polemic legislature that is often prioritized over party issues, sometimes at the expense of the national interest.

Congress has proved itself to be a remarkably flexible institution, responding to changes in society, shifting constituencies, and increasingly diverse members, particularly in recent times. That Congress will become even more diverse is relatively ensured.

Summary

1. The Origins of Congress

The Constitution's framers intended Congress to be the strongest and most important branch of the federal government, a body both representative and deliberative. They structured the national legislature in such a way as to ensure both a check on the power of the executive and a voice for the people. The Constitution provided a flexible framework for the evolution of Congress to meet changing times. That framework continues to this day to shape the structural and procedural differences between the House of Representatives and the Senate, including the two houses' respective sizes, rules, and processes.

2. Congressional Elections

One of the most important factors shaping congressional elections is incumbency, which confers numerous advantages to those already serving in elective office. Congressional elections are also shaped by the processes of reapportionment and redistricting, which occur every 10 years.

3. Powers of Congress

The Constitution enumerates certain powers for Congress, including judicial, economic, national security, regulatory, and administrative powers. Other powers of the federal legislature have evolved through national legislators' interpretation of the Constitution's necessary and proper clause, which has been a mechanism for the expansion of congressional authority.

4. Functions of Congress

The primary functions of Congress are public policy making, popular representation, oversight of the executive branch to ensure the proper administration of laws, civic education, and management of societal conflict. In their representation function, members of Congress may follow the instructed delegate model or the trustee model of representation.

5. The House and the Senate Compared

Members of the House of Representatives and the Senate serve different constituencies for different terms of office. House members are elected for a 2-year term from a congressional district, and senators serve for a 6-year term and represent an entire state. With respect to the legislative structure and environment, the House, with its larger size (435 members today), is more formal, and the Senate (100 members) is less formal.

6. The Legislative Process

A member of the House or the Senate can introduce a bill, the precursor to a law. Once proposed, the bill is then referred to a committee, where it is debated, reviewed, and amended. If it passes out of committee, it is debated by the full chamber; if it passes in both the House and the Senate, the president may sign the bill, veto it, or take no action. By far, most bills introduced do not become law.

7. Congressional Leadership

House leadership consists of the Speaker of the House of Representatives and the House majority and minority leaders, plus the majority and minority whips. In practice, the Senate majority leader wields the power in the upper chamber of the national legislature. Frequently, the skills demonstrated by various leaders in Congress reflect the needs of their chambers—quiet fortitude in some circumstances, adept partisanship in others.

8. Decision Making in Congress: The Legislative Context

Political parties, congressional colleagues, interest groups, the president, and constituent viewpoints all influence members of Congress. In recent years, partisanship has increased in Congress, making legislators' debates more rancorous and divisive.

9. The People and Their Elected Representatives

Although Congress is not demographically representative of the United States, it is more demographically diverse than the leadership structure of other institutions. Nonetheless, Congress is becoming increasingly diverse, with higher proportions of women, African Americans, and Latinos serving today than ever before.

Key Terms

agency review 375
agenda setting 371
attentive public 384
bill 373
casework 370
cloture 376
conference committee 377
discharge petition 376
earmark 370
filibuster 376
gerrymandering 365
hearings 375
hopper 374
House majority leader 378
House minority leader 379

instructed delegate
    model 369
joint committee 375
joint referral 374
lead committee 374
logrolling 383
majority whip 378
majority-minority
    district 367
markup 375
minority whip 379
nuclear option 377
ombudsperson 370
oversight 371
pocket veto 377

pork barrel 369
president pro tempore 380
reapportionment 365
redistricting 365
report 375
Rules Committee 376
select committee 375
Senate majority leader 380
Senate minority leader 380
seniority system 374
Speaker of the House 378
standing committee 374
subcommittee 375
trustee model 369
unanimous consent 376

For Review

1. Why was Congress created in the way it was?

2. How does incumbency affect congressional elections?

3. What is the difference between reapportionment and redistricting?

4. How has technology changed the process of congressional redistricting?

5. Historically, what has been the impact of the necessary and proper (elastic) clause?

6. Describe the two types of congressional powers.

7. What influence do the constitutionally enumerated duties of the House and the Senate have on the expertise of each chamber?

8. Outline the basic steps of the legislative process.

9. How do the qualities of congressional leaders differ today from those needed in earlier eras?

10. Why has party-line voting increased in Congress in recent years?

For Critical Thinking and Discussion

1. If you were serving in Congress, would you tend to follow the instructed delegate model of representation or the trustee model? Why? What might be the likely outcome of your choice?

2. How does the legislative process differ in the House and the Senate? In which chamber is the process more streamlined? More deliberative? Why?

3. What do you and the people you know think about the work and contributions of Congress? Would you give Congress high or low approval ratings as an institution, or something in between? Who is your own congressional representative, and what rating would you give her or him? Why?

4. Log on to the Library of Congress website (www.loc.gov) and read about issues currently on the floor of the House of Representatives. Can you identify any of the external influences mentioned in this chapter on the legislative process? Describe these influences, and discuss how they are shaping the process.

5. Why do you think so few women and racial and ethnic minorities have been elected to Congress? Why is this situation changing? What do you imagine that Congress will look like, demographically, in the year 2050?

Practice Quiz

MULTIPLE CHOICE: Choose the lettered item that answers the question correctly.

1. Reallocation of seats in the House of Representatives to each state based on changes in the state's population since the last census is called
   a. logrolling.
   b. reapportionment.
   c. gerrymandering.
   d. redistricting.

2. Redrawing congressional district boundaries within each state is called
   a. earmarking.
   b. reapportionment.
   c. gerrymandering.
   d. redistricting.

3. A model of representation that says that a member of Congress should vote for the position that best represents his or her constituents' view even if the legislator does not share those views is called
   a. the instructed delegate model.
   b. the hopper model.
   c. the trustee model.
   d. the pork barrel model.

4. The process by which the legislative branch checks the executive branch to ensure that the laws Congress passed are being administered in keeping with the legislature's intent is called
   a. oversight.
   b. earmarking.
   c. gerrymandering.
   d. agenda setting.

5. Differences between the House and the Senate do not include
   a. the Senate's being more prestigious than the House.
   b. the Senate's being larger than the House.
   c. the Senate's being more reliant on staff than the House.
   d. the Senate's having broader constituencies than the House.

6. A primary committee considering a bill is called
   a. a standing committee.
   b. a subcommittee.
   c. a select committee.
   d. a lead committee.

7. The system in which the member with the longest continuous tenure on a standing committee is given preference when the committee chooses its chair is called
   a. the spoils system.
   b. the patronage system.
   c. the seniority system.
   d. the last man standing principle.

8. A congressional committee created to consider specific policy issues or address a specific concern is called
   a. a standing committee.
   b. a subcommittee.
   c. a select committee.
   d. a joint committee.

9. A special tactic used to extract a bill from a committee to have it considered by the entire House is called
   a. a report.
   b. a markup.
   c. a filibuster.
   d. a discharge petition.

10. A procedural move in which a supermajority of 60 senators agrees to end a filibuster is called
    a. cloture.
    b. unanimous consent.
    c. a discharge petition.
    d. senatorial courtesy.

FILL IN THE BLANKS

11. A designation within a spending bill that provides for a specific expenditure is called a(n) _____.

12. A role in which an elected or appointed leader acts as an advocate for citizens by listening to and investigating complaints about a government agency is called a(n) _____.

13. A proposed piece of legislation is called a _____.

14. A legislative committee's explanation to the full chamber of a bill and its intent is called a _____.

15. _____ is an agreement by every senator to the terms of debate on a given piece of legislation.

Answers: 1. b, 2. d, 3. a, 4. a, 5. b, 6. d, 7. c, 8. c, 9. d, 10. a, 11. earmark, 12. ombudsperson, 13. bill, 14. report, 15. Unanimous consent.

Research AND Action

Internet Resources

C-Span

www.c-span.org The cable television network C-Span provides a large amount of information on Congress, including Internet video, audio, and podcast programs of congressional hearings, committee meetings, C-Span video series, and a variety of public affairs information.

Library of Congress

www.loc.gov The website for the Library of Congress, the most important clearinghouse for information about Congress, legislation, hearings, votes, and other federal matters.

Roll Call

www.rollcall.com This website for *Roll Call,* the "source for news on Capitol Hill since 1955," offers an insider's look at the world of Capitol Hill, including issue analysis, politics, and opinions.

U.S. Senate and U.S. House of Representatives

www.senate.gov and **www.house.gov** These websites for the Senate and the House provide information about members of Congress, votes, pending legislation, committees, and session schedules, plus information about the Capitol and information for visitors.

Recommended Readings

Ahuja, Sunil. *Congress Behaving Badly: The Rise of Partisanship and Incivility and the Death of Public Trust.* Santa Barbara, CA: Praeger, 2008. This analysis examines the causes and the results of increased party cleavages in Congress.

Dodd, Lawrence C., and Bruce J. Oppenheimer. *Congress Reconsidered,* 10th ed. Washington, D.C.: CQ Press, 2012. The most recent edition of a classic series providing comprehensive coverage of the evolution of the American Congress.

Fenno, Richard F., Jr. *Home Style: House Members in Their Districts.* New York: Longman, 2009. Fenno traveled the United States observing members of Congress at home in their districts and explains how constituent interaction affects congressional decision making.

Forman, Sean D., Robert Dewhirst, Peter Bergerson, and Margaret Banyan. *The Roads to Congress 2012.* Lanham, MD: Lexington Books, 2013. This work examines the processes and issues associated with key congressional races in 2012.

Loomis, Burdett, and Wendy J. Schiller. *The Contemporary Congress.* Belmont, CA: Wadsworth, 2005. A concise yet comprehensive analysis of Congress, particularly the legislative context that influences the legislative process.

O'Neill, Thomas P. *Man of the House: The Life and Political Memoirs of Speaker Tip O'Neill.* New York: Random House, 1987. The political memoir of a long-term Speaker of the House of Representatives provides a fascinating glimpse into the "real world" of Capitol Hill politics from the 1960s through the 1980s.

Thomas, Sue. *How Women Legislate.* New York: Oxford University Press, 1994. Groundbreaking analysis of the differences and similarities between how men and women approach the task of legislating.

Movies of Interest

The Congress (1988)

This Ken Burns documentary provides a fine introduction to the U.S. Congress (both the institution and the Capitol building). Burns traces the history of the institution and the people who have served in it, including 19th-century statesmen Henry Clay and Daniel Webster and continuing to Congress's modern leaders.

The Ugly American (1963)

This drama stars Marlon Brando as Harrison Carter MacWhite, who, after surviving an acrimonious Senate confirmation hearing, becomes ambassador to a Southeast Asian nation on the brink of civil war.

Mr. Smith Goes to Washington (1939)

This classic Frank Capra movie features Jimmy Stewart as Jefferson Smith, who, after the death of a senator, is appointed to serve in the U.S. Senate despite his political naiveté. Stewart's depiction of a filibuster informs most Americans' perception of this political maneuver.

CHAPTER 13

The Presidency

THEN

Presidential power grew over the centuries to "imperial" proportions and then ebbed in the late 20th century in the wake of scandals.

NOW

In recent years, a new era of presidential imperialism appears to have emerged.

NEXT

Will future presidents continue down the path of an imperial presidency?

What checks will constrain future presidents' exercise of power?

How will the relationship between presidents and the people change in the future?

In this chapter, we survey the election, functions, and powers of American presidents and analyze the complex relationship between presidents and the people. We also examine the evolution of presidential powers over time, including the idea of an "imperial presidency."

FIRST, we look at the process of presidential elections.

SECOND, we focus on presidential roles in the domestic sphere.

THIRD, we study presidential roles in the foreign policy sphere.

FOURTH, we consider points of overlap in the president's domestic and foreign policy roles.

FIFTH, we turn attention to the president and the executive branch and consider the key offices that influence the president in making and carrying out public policy.

SIXTH, we review the formal procedures in place for presidential succession.

SEVENTH, we explore the sources of presidential power, including constitutional, statutory, and emergency powers; executive privilege; and the power to issue executive orders.

EIGHTH, we examine the people as a source of presidential power.

NINTH, we trace the evolution of presidential power from the administration of George Washington to the present day, analyzing in particular the development of what some analysts have called the imperial presidency.

TENTH, we probe the various roles of women in the White House and anticipate the likelihood that a woman will be elected president in the future.

Each presidency is shaped not

only by the person who holds the office but also by the support of constituencies within the public, the support of Congress for presidential policy priorities, and the societal context of the day. Each presidential term can be molded and manipulated in many ways, with the result that one president may appear strong, and the next, weak—or a president may be both effective and ineffectual during the course of just one term. In looking at the roles presidents play in conducting their office, as well as the sources of their power, we consider in this chapter why some presidents are more effective than others.

The presidency is constantly evolving. The institution of the presidency that Barack Obama has is not the one that George Washington left behind. In the discussion that follows, we examine the development of the presidency to gain historical perspective on how the individuals who have served as president have changed the nature of the institution over time and what the impacts of those changes are for presidents today.

The presidency has changed in part because of the way this institution—which for many Americans embodies their government—has evolved.[1] We consider that even within this most "imperial" of the American institutions of government, the people play a vital part in determining not only who serves as president but also how effective and successful the president is in exercising the executive power.[2]

Presidential Elections

The relationship between Americans and their president begins well before a president takes the oath of office. In presidential election years, nonstop campaigning provides ample opportunities for the public to learn about presidential candidates and their positions on issues. Campaigns also present many avenues for participation by the people—for example, by volunteering in or contributing to candidates' campaigns or even just by debating candidates' views around the water cooler. Although these opportunities for citizen engagement are especially abundant during a presidential election year, similar chances to get involved arise well before, because potential candidates typically position themselves years in advance of Election Day to secure their party's nomination and to win the general election.

As discussed in Chapter 8, citizens in each state who vote in their party's primary election choose the delegates to the national conventions, where the parties' nominees are officially decided upon. After the nominees have been decided, typically by late August, they and their vice-presidential running mates begin their general election campaign. Usually, the parties' choice of nominee is a foregone conclusion by the time of the convention. The votes tallied on Election Day determine which presidential candidate's slate of electors will cast their ballots, in accordance with state law. There are 538 electors in the Electoral College because the number of electors is based on the number of members of Congress—435 in the House of Representatives, 100 in the Senate—plus 3 electors who represent the people of the District of Columbia. (See "Thinking Critically About Democracy.") A presidential candidate today needs a simple majority of votes (270) to win the presidency. On the Monday following the second Wednesday of December, the slate of electors chosen in each state meets in their respective state capitals and casts their electoral votes. The results are then announced in a joint session of Congress in early January. In most presidential elections, however, the winner is known on election night because analysts tabulate the outcome in each state and predict the electoral vote. The winner takes the oath of office as president in inaugural ceremonies on January 20.

Should We Abolish the Electoral College?

The Issue: In the world's oldest democracy, the idea that the president of the United States might not be the choice of the majority of the voting population is a distinct reality. Such was the case in the 2000 presidential election: The candidate with the most popular votes, Democrat Al Gore, lost the presidential election to his opponent, Republican George W. Bush. In every other election for federal office, the candidate with the most popular votes wins that seat. But instead of the direct election of the president, the Constitution requires that the president be elected by the Electoral College. Essentially, the winner is determined by the cumulative results of 51 separate elections, one conducted in each state plus the District of Columbia, with the number of electoral votes determined in proportion to the size of the state's congressional delegation. Is the Electoral College system unfair? Should we abolish it?

Yes: The Electoral College is exclusive and undemocratic. The Electoral College system demands that candidates focus nearly exclusively on key swing states that will be pivotal to their election and on populous states that carry the most electoral votes. The system is undemocratic because of its reliance on plurality elections within the states. In a plurality, the candidate with the most votes wins, even if that candidate does not receive a majority of the votes. The ultimate victory in the 2000 presidential election by the candidate whom the most people did not prefer (George W. Bush), highlights the undemocratic nature of the Electoral College. The Electoral College should be abolished.

No: The constitutionally mandated Electoral College system provides a crucial check on what would otherwise be the unchecked will of the people. In structuring the Electoral College as they did, the Constitution's framers devised a way of representing the views of both the *people* who elect the electors and the *states* because of the state-based nature of the elections. Other checks on the will of the people include staggered senatorial elections (in which one-third of that body is elected every two years) and appointed Supreme Court justices, and these are evidence of the framers' view that the will of the people needed to be tempered. If the Electoral College were abolished, the most populous geographical regions would dominate in presidential elections. Urban areas would have tremendous clout in presidential elections, and less densely populated rural areas would be virtually ignored. The current structure strengthens the power of the states and in this way ensures that our federal system remains strong.

Other Approaches: Because of the difficulty of abolishing the Electoral College, various schemes have been proposed that would make it almost impossible for the loser of the popular vote to win the presidency, including awarding a state's electoral votes proportionally instead of on a winner-take-all basis, dividing electoral votes by congressional district (currently done in Maine and Nebraska), and awarding extra electoral votes to the winner of the popular vote. Legislation recently passed in Maryland, Hawaii, Illinois, and New Jersey would commit those states' electors to vote for the winner of the popular vote if states representing a 270-vote majority in the Electoral College enact similar legislation.

What do you think?

1. Do you think that the Electoral College should be abolished, should remain the same, or should be reformed? Why? If your answer is "should be reformed," what changes would you implement?

2. If the Electoral College were abolished, what impact would the change likely have on voters in your home state? Does that scenario influence your view?

3. Americans revere the Constitution as a near-sacred document. Typically, citizens are reluctant to advocate amending the "supreme law of the land." What is your view concerning amending the Constitution?

Presidential Roles in the Domestic Sphere

A newly elected president quickly discovers that the presidential office requires a variety of functions to be performed each day. Many of these roles involve leadership in domestic policy issues,[3] whether it was Barack Obama's desire to overhaul health care, George W. Bush's priority of reforming schools, or all presidents' need to keep the economy sound and growing strongly. As leaders in the domestic sphere, presidents must interact with Congress, manage the economy, and serve as the leader of their party.[4]

Chief Legislator

Although the separation of powers precludes the president from actually creating laws, presidents nonetheless have significant legislative power.[5] Presidents can influence Congress by lobbying its members to support or oppose pending legislation and by defining the congressional agenda in the annual presidential State of the Union message, a constitutionally required address to Congress. Presidents also "legislate" when they submit the budget for the entire federal government to Congress annually, although Congress ultimately passes the spending plan.

Today, one of the most important legislative tools at a president's disposal is the authority either to sign legislation into law or to veto it,[6] as described in Chapter 2. Although a veto allows the president to check the power of Congress, it also provides Congress with the opportunity to check presidential power by overriding the veto with a two-thirds majority vote.[7] In giving the president the right to veto laws, the Constitution essentially integrates the executive into the legislative process.[8]

As discussed in Chapter 12, there are several variations on the veto. During a regular legislative session, if the president does not sign or veto a bill within 10 days after receiving it from Congress, the bill becomes law even without the president's consent. But if the president receives a congressional bill for his signature and Congress is scheduled to adjourn within 10 days, the president can exercise a pocket veto, in which the bill is vetoed if the president takes no action at all. Further, during the presidency of Bill Clinton, Congress statutorily equipped the president with a new kind of veto power: the **line-item veto** allowed the president to strike out specific line items on an appropriations bill while allowing the rest of the bill to become law. In 1997, however, the Supreme Court declared the line-item veto unconstitutional, asserting that it violated separation of powers because the Constitution grants Congress the inherent power to tax and to spend.

Figure 13.1 shows that the use of the veto varies widely from president to president. Modern presidents are generally much more likely to veto legislation than their predecessors were. A primary determinant of whether a president will regularly exercise veto power is whether the president's party has a majority in Congress. For example, President Obama has issued only two vetoes thus far, neither of which was controversial. One vetoed a stop-gap spending measure because the spending had already been rolled into another bill; the other vetoed a measure concerning the notarization of legal documents. His predecessor, George W. Bush, also vetoed few pieces of legislation during his two terms, but nearly all of his vetoes occurred after Democrats took control of Congress in 2006.

An exception to this trend was the presidency of Franklin D. Roosevelt. As Figure 13.1 shows, during Roosevelt's 12-year term in the White House, he issued 372 vetoes, or 12 percent of all presidential vetoes. Roosevelt chalked up this exceptional record despite having strong Democratic majorities in Congress throughout his tenure. But Roosevelt used the veto much differently than most presidents do. Because he was such a strong president, he exercised his veto power to prevent the passage of even small pieces of legislation with which he disagreed. Most presidents save the veto for important legislative matters, because they are unwilling to offend members of Congress over smaller laws that they do not favor.

But presidents today use a different tactic—the signing statement—to influence how policies are to be administered during their tenure in office. A presidential **signing statement** is a written message that the president issues upon signing a bill into law. A presidential signing statement may, for example, direct executive departments in how they should implement a law, taking into account constitutional or political considerations. Controversy arose during the administrations of George W. Bush over the perception that, by using the tool widely, he was modifying the intent of the laws by asserting unconstitutional legislative authority.[9] Nonetheless, the use of signing statements was continued by President Obama, who actually increased his use of signing statements in the wake of the 2012 presidential election, One signing statement, for example, announced his intention to ignore parts of the National Defense Authorization Act, including provisions that bar the United States from sharing certain sensitive missile defense systems data.

line-item veto
the power of the president to strike out specific line items on an appropriations bill while allowing the rest of the bill to become law; declared unconstitutional by the Supreme Court in 1997

signing statement
a written message that the president issues upon signing a bill into law

FIGURE 13.1 ■ PRESIDENTIAL VETOES, 1789–2014 What does this graph generally indicate about the use of the presidential veto over time? What trend is evident in presidents' use of the veto from the administration of Franklin D. Roosevelt to the present? Why do you think a president is more likely to veto legislation when one party controls Congress and the other controls the presidency?

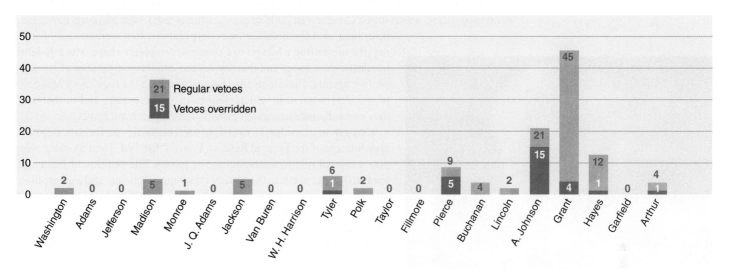

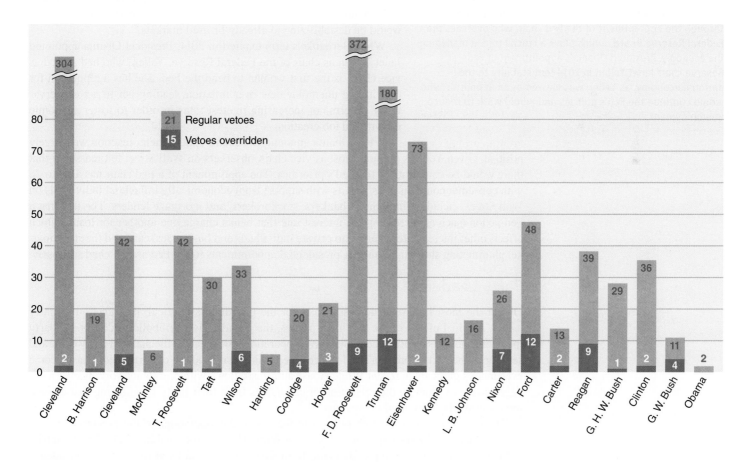

Chief Economist

Although the Constitution makes no mention of presidential responsibilities with respect to the economy, submitting a budget to Congress reflects what has become another key presidential role: the manager of the economy. Of course, the president does not exert a great deal of control over the enormous national economy, but presidents have numerous tools at their disposal that powerfully influence the country's economic performance. This power has been quite apparent in the past decade with President Obama persuading Congress to pass a $787 billion program intended to stimulate the U.S. economy in 2009. Obama's plan came on the heels of Bush administration policies, which urged Congress in 2008 to allocate funds to bail out banking, mortgage, insurance, and financial services corporations that were at risk of failing. By submitting a budget to Congress, presidents shape where federal tax dollars are spent and thereby set the economic priorities of the legislative agenda. Presidents also help to establish the regulatory and economic environment in which businesses must operate, and in that way they can influence economic growth and employment levels.

>One way presidents try to affect the nation's economy is through the appointment of the Fed chair, who oversees the Federal Reserve Board, which plays a crucial role in managing the economy. President Obama's appointment of Federal Reserve chair Janet Yellen in 2014 lent stability to the national economy, as Yellen was viewed as an appointee who would continue the Fed's policies and would work to reduce unemployment.

Central in presidents' oversight of economic performance is the appointment of the Federal Reserve Board ("the Fed") and its chair, who play a crucial role in managing the economy. The position of Fed chair tends to be less partisan than many other appointments, and a given chair often serves under presidents of both political parties. In 2005, President Bush named Ben Bernanke as Fed chair, replacing Alan Greenspan, who had served for 18 years under both Democrats and Republicans. President Obama reappointed Bernanke to a second four-year term in 2009, despite criticism that Bernanke was slow to recognize the severity of the economic crisis.[10] But many lauded Obama's reappointment of Bernanke, arguing that appointing a new, inexperienced Fed chair would be destabilizing to already-bruised markets.

When Bernanke's term expired in 2014, President Obama appointed Janet Yellen as chair of the Federal Reserve. Yellen, who had served as vice chair, is the first woman to head the Fed. She has a reputation for prioritizing unemployment over inflation, leading her to act conservatively in terms of increasing interest rates in order to foster economic growth and job creation.

When Obama announced Yellen's appointment, reaction was largely positive. Given Yellen's previous post as vice chair, observers on Wall Street felt reassured that there would be continuity in the Fed's priorities. The appointment of a Fed chair has a lot to do with consumer confidence, as well as with support from economically influential individuals on Wall Street, including investment bankers, stockbrokers, and mortgage lenders. The fact that a Fed action (such as increasing the interest rate that banks charge one another for loans, which affects other interest rates charged to private individuals and businesses) can send the stock market plummeting sheds light on why presidential appointments to the Fed are watched so closely.

Party Leader

One of the most important domestic roles for the president is political: the function of party leader. As chief of one of the two main parties, the president is a symbolic leader for the party members and asserts influence in the party's operations by selecting the national party chair and serving as the party's premier fund-raiser. The presidential function of party leader has become even more significant in recent White House administrations, with presidents working ever more aggressively to promote the reelection of candidates from their party by ensuring that enough money is available for their campaigns.

The president also acts as party head in the day-to-day operations of the executive branch, because many of the staff appointments to the White House Office, cabinet, subcabinet, ambassadorships, and judiciary typically come from party ranks. Finally, at the end of a president's term, he likely campaigns on behalf of his party's presidential nominee.

Presidential Roles in the Foreign Policy Sphere

Presidential responsibilities also extend to setting and executing foreign policy. The president's foreign policy powers are for the most part constitutionally derived.[11] Specifically, the Constitution gives the president the authority with which to carry out the roles of chief diplomat and commander in chief of the U.S. armed forces.

Chief Diplomat

Serving in the capacity of chief diplomat, the president (along with advisers) shapes and administers the nation's foreign policy. Supported by a wide array of foreign policy resources, including the State Department, the National Security Council, the Central Intelligence Agency, and the various branches of the U.S. military, the president creates and administers foreign policy (see "Global Context"). In setting foreign policy, the president can act more unilaterally than with most domestic policies. Members of Congress, who, in reflection of their constituents' main interests, tend to be concerned primarily with domestic policy issues, are much less likely to challenge presidents in the foreign policy arena.

As chief diplomat, the president, in conjunction with his or her staff, negotiates treaties and other international agreements with foreign nations and represents the United States at international summits. The president also has the authority to enter into an **executive agreement,** a kind of international agreement. Executive agreements are based on the constitutional authority vested in the president, and, unlike treaties, they may not be binding on future presidents nor do they require Senate approval.

The Constitution also empowers the president to appoint ambassadors to other nations. As high-ranking diplomats, ambassadors are the official representatives of the United States in their host nation. Ambassadors' duties vary widely, depending on the locale of their appointment. Some ambassadors play an influential, highly visible role in carrying out U.S. foreign policy, but others remain in the background.

The president, acting in the role of chief diplomat, is the leader of the diplomatic corps. In the capacity of chief diplomat, the president also hosts state dinners at the White House and formally receives the ambassadors of other nations.

executive agreement
an international agreement between the United States and other nations, not subject to Senate approval and in effect only during the administration of the president who negotiates the agreement

Commander in Chief

As commander in chief, the president is the supreme military commander of the U.S. Army, Navy, Air Force, Marines, and Coast Guard. Counseled by advisers, the president decides when to send troops into battle (although only Congress can formally declare war) and sets military strategy in times of both peace and war.[12]

During President Obama's first term, he exercised his role as commander in chief in withdrawing troops from Iraq and also in initially increasing the number of troops in Afghanistan and then decreasing American presence as the Afghanis assumed greater control. During his second term, President Obama has seemed reluctant to commit American forces in the world's global hotspots, recognizing that the American public is weary after more than a decade of war. But this war-weariness does not preclude the president from exercising his role as commander in chief in other ways. For example, during his second term President Obama authorized the use of drones targeting terror cells in Pakistan as well as air strikes against ISIS targets in Iraq and Syria in 2014.

President Obama also was acting as commander in chief when he voiced his position on the "Don't Ask, Don't Tell" policy regarding gays in the military. Obama urged Congress to repeal the 17-year-old policy so that gays might serve openly in the military, and in July 2011, he succeeded in having the policy repealed.

The role of commander in chief is often a difficult one for presidents. President Obama identified his 2009 order to send an additional 34,000 troops into Afghanistan as the most difficult decision of his presidency. He hoped to secure the nation so that Afghani forces could retain control of the nation after U.S. forces leave. Obama explained, "There is a sobriety that comes

EXAMINING WORLD OPINION OF U.S. LEADERSHIP

While President Barack Obama's approval rating has been mediocre throughout much of his tenure in office, he fares much better globally and when being compared with other world leaders. The Gallup organization has polled residents of 137 countries and asked them whether they approve or disapprove of the leaders of the five global powers—the United States, China, the European Union, Germany, and Russia. As has been the trend since being elected, President Obama has polled higher than most other world leaders.

Obama's approval typically has fallen in the high 40s, though it dipped considerably in 2012 as people worldwide held the United States as partially responsible for the financial crises that ripped through Europe in 2012.

While U.S. leadership appears to have rebounded, the 2013 data do not reflect any of the fallout from the Edward Snowden affair, in which a former National Security Administration employee leaked documents that indicate that the United States engages in a far-reaching global surveillance program, including revelations that the United States had monitored the phone calls of world leaders, including German Chancellor Angela Merkel. In the wake of these disclosures, it is likely that world opinion of U.S. leadership has declined.

But that decline would have to be significant to rival Russia's, which has consistently held the bottom spot in world approval, typically hovering in the 20–30 percent range.

But does global approval of leadership matter? After all, citizens of Senegal or Vietnam cannot cast votes for president of the United States. Researchers Benjamin Goldsmith and Yusaku Horiuchi argue that "public opinion about U.S. foreign policy in foreign countries does affect their policies toward the U.S., but this effect is conditional on the salience of an issue for the mass publics."* That is to say, for a president's foreign policy to be effective, it is helpful to have support for that policy abroad.

Global Opinion of World Leaders: Do you approve or disapprove of the job performance of the leadership of . . .?

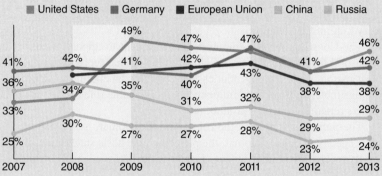

*Benjamin E. Goldsmith and Yusaku Horiuchi, Crawford School Research Paper No. 8: "In Search of Soft Power: Does Foreign Public Opinion Matter for U.S. Foreign Policy?" *World Politics:* January 24, 2012.

SOURCE: Jon Clifton, "U.S. Tops Other Global Leaders in Approval," The Gallup Organization, April 11, 2014, www.gallup.com/poll/168467/tops-global-leaders-approval.aspx?utm_source=tagrss&utm_medium=rss&utm_campaign=syndication/.

with a decision like that because you have to expect that some of those young men and women are going to be harmed in the theater of war."[13]

Overlap in the Domestic and Foreign Policy Roles: Chief Executive and Chief of State

Some presidential functions overlap the domestic and foreign policy spheres. This spillover notably exists in the president's role as chief executive—in which the president, as head of the executive branch, appoints advisers and staff—and the role of chief of state, the ceremonial function of the president.

Chief Executive

As the nation's leader in domestic and foreign policy initiatives, the president serves as chief executive. In this capacity, the president appoints the *secretaries* (top administrators) of the cabinet—the 15 departments of the federal government—as well as the heads of other federal government agencies charged with developing and implementing the administration's policy. As chief executive, the president also appoints other staff members and numerous advisers, including staff in the Executive Office of the President. In the capacity of chief executive, the president determines how the bureaucracy will implement the laws Congress has passed and which policies—those concerning education, crime, social welfare, and so on—will be emphasized.[14]

Chief of State

The president's role as chief of state reflects the chief executive's embodiment of the values and ideals of the nation, both within the United States and abroad. The function of chief of state is similar to the ceremonial role played by the constitutional monarch in parliamentary systems such as Great Britain's. In the United States, the role of symbolic leader of the nation enhances the president's image and authority and promotes national unity. We may experience this sense that we are one indivisible nation when, for example, the president, as chief of state, makes a formal state visit to another nation, hosts Olympic medalists at the White House, or visits Fort Hood to console survivors of the attack by an armed gunman at the Killeen, Texas, military base.

>As chief of state, the president embodies the symbolic role of leader of the nation. Often, this role enhances the president's image and authority and promotes national unity, as when President Obama and the first lady traveled to the military base at Fort Hood in Texas to console family members of victims and survivors of the attack by an armed gunman.

The President and the Executive Branch

Because daily news reports so often showcase the president acting as head of state and chief diplomat, it is easy to overlook one of the president's primary responsibilities—administering the federal government. As chief executive, the president is constitutionally charged with ensuring that the "laws be faithfully executed." Today, this responsibility means that the president oversees a bureaucracy of more than four million government employees, including the members of the military, while presiding over an astonishing annual federal budget of nearly *$4 trillion*. In addition, as we now consider, the president is the leader of the executive branch of government, which includes the vice president, the cabinet, the offices within the White House, and the entire federal bureaucracy.

The Vice President's Role

John Nance Garner, Franklin D. Roosevelt's vice president from 1933 to 1941, vulgarly commented that "the vice presidency isn't worth a pitcher of warm piss."[15] This insider's observation on the vice-presidential office matches the perceptions of many Americans fairly well. But although the media and the public tend to ignore the vice presidency and to marginalize the responsibilities of the second-in-command, vice presidents have an enormously important function. They are first in the line of succession to the presidency if the president should die or become incapacitated. Only eight presidents have died while in office, and although presidential succession may not be the foremost consideration in selecting a running mate for many presidential candidates, it can be an issue. Bill Clinton, in describing his selection of Tennessee senator Al Gore as his running mate, explained that his choice of Gore in part reflected Clinton's belief that Gore would make a good president "if something happened to me."[16]

> Presidential candidates often choose a running mate who complements their attributes. Vice President Joe Biden, who served 36 years in the U.S. Senate, brought foreign policy experience to Democratic president Barack Obama's ticket when he first sought the presidency in 2008, whereas Representative Paul Ryan of Wisconsin brought federal budget experience to Republican Mitt's Romney's campaign in 2012.

THE VICE PRESIDENT'S JOB Many vice presidents serve a largely ceremonial function, performing such activities as attending state dinners, visiting foreign nations, and attending the funerals of foreign dignitaries. But vice presidents may have more substantive responsibilities, depending on their skills and the needs of the administration. Sometimes, for example, a vice president acts as legislative liaison with Congress, particularly if the vice president has more experience in dealing with the legislative branch than the president. Such was the case with Al Gore, who had served eight years in the House of Representatives and eight years in the Senate, whereas the president under whom he served, Bill Clinton, lacked Washington experience. In other instances, vice presidents' policy expertise is a crucial resource for the administration. In the case of Vice President Dick Cheney, experience in foreign policy and national security determined the pivotal role he played in developing the foreign policy of George W. Bush's administration.

Although vice presidents are only "a heartbeat away" from the presidency, their own election to the presidency (should they decide to run) is not ensured when their term as second-in-command has ended. It is true that several vice presidents—among them, George H. W. Bush and Lyndon B. Johnson—have won election to the presidency in their own right; but many other former vice presidents have failed.[17] Notably, Al Gore, Walter Mondale, and Gerald Ford (the vice presidents of Bill Clinton, Jimmy Carter, and Richard Nixon, respectively) all went down to defeat at the polls in their bids for the White House.

CHOOSING A VICE PRESIDENT In selecting a vice-presidential running mate, presidential candidates weigh several considerations. Would-be presidents strive for a **balanced ticket;** that is, to broaden their appeal to the electorate and increase their chances of getting elected, they select a running mate who brings diversity of ideology, geographic region, age, gender, race, or ethnicity to the slate.

balanced ticket
the selection of a running mate who brings diversity of ideology, geographic region, age, gender, race, or ethnicity to the slate

Or they may base their vice-presidential selection on their own shortcomings, whether in policy expertise or in governing experience. For example, as a candidate vying for the presidency against Senator John McCain of Arizona, an older and respected member of the U.S. Senate, Barack Obama chose Senator Joe Biden of Delaware, who was thought to complement Obama in terms of age (Biden was 65 years old, compared with Obama's 47); experience (Biden had served in the Senate since 1972, Obama since 2000); and expertise (Biden was chair of the Senate Foreign Relations Committee, Obama had faced media criticism about his lack of foreign policy experience). Similarly, Mitt Romney, who had served as governor of Massachusetts, squashed criticism that he lacked "inside the Beltway" experience and that he was too liberal for conservative GOP voters when he selected Representative Paul Ryan, the conservative congressman from Wisconsin, who chairs the House Budget Committee.

The Cabinet

cabinet
the group of experts chosen by the president to serve as advisers on running the country

Since George Washington's presidency, every president has depended on the advice of a **cabinet,** the group of experts chosen by the president to serve as advisers on running the country. These advisers serve as the heads of each of the executive departments. Figure 13.2 shows the 15 departments of the cabinet and their respective websites. Each cabinet member except the head of the Department of Justice is called the *secretary* of that department. The head of the Department of Justice is called the attorney general.

President George W. Bush created the newest department, the Department of Homeland Security, in 2002. This department is charged with increasing the nation's preparedness, particularly

Department of Agriculture
Secretary Thomas J. Vilsack
www.usda.gov

Department of Commerce
Secretary Penny Pritzker
www.commerce.gov

Department of Defense
Secretary Chuck Hagel
www.defense.gov

Department of Education
Secretary Arne Duncan
www.ed.gov

Department of the Interior
Secretary Sally Jewell
www.doi.gov

Department of Justice
Attorney General
Loretta Lynch*
www.justice.gov

Department of Labor
Secretary Thomas E. Perez
www.dol.gov

Department of State
Secretary John Kerry
www.state.gov

Department of Energy
Secretary Ernest Moniz
www.energy.gov

Department of Health
& Human Services
Secretary Sylvia Mathews Burwell
www.hhs.gov

Department of
Homeland Security
Secretary Jeh Johnson
www.dhs.gov

Department of Housing
& Urban Development
Secretary Julián Castro
www.hud.gov

Department of Transportation
Secretary Anthony Foxx
www.dot.gov

Department of the Treasury
Secretary Jack Lew
www.treasury.gov

Department of Veterans Affairs
Secretary Robert McDonald
www.va.gov

*Lynch was nominated as Attorney General by President Obama in November 2014, but had not been confirmed by the Senate at time of publication.

FIGURE 13.2

THE DEPARTMENTS OF THE PRESIDENT'S CABINET The presidential cabinet consists of the heads of the 15 departments shown in the figure. Which department is concerned with finding alternatives to the use of fossil fuels? Which one addresses the problems of the dedicated service men and women who served in Afghanistan and Iraq? Which department arose as a result of the September 11, 2001, terrorist strikes?

with respect to catastrophic events such as terrorist attacks and natural disasters. George Washington's cabinet consisted of the heads of only four departments—justice, state, treasury, and war. (The last is now called the Department of Defense.) Subsequent presidents added other departments.

Each president may also designate cabinet rank to other advisers whose agencies are not permanent cabinet departments. Typically, presidents have specified that their national security adviser, director of the Office of Management and Budget, and administrator of the Environmental Protection Agency be included in their administration's cabinet.

Today, presidents and the public scrutinize presidential cabinet appointments to determine whether, in the words of Bill Clinton, they "look like America." As the data in Table 13.1 confirm, this is a relatively new gauge, since only three women and two members of ethnic minority groups had served in presidential cabinets until the Carter administration. Increasingly, however, as the table shows, presidential cabinets have become more diverse, with significant strides made during the Clinton administration.[18] President Clinton became the first president to appoint a woman to any of the "big four" posts when he named Janet Reno attorney general and Madeleine Albright secretary of state. George W. Bush named Colin Powell the first black secretary of state, and when Powell resigned, Bush replaced him with Condoleezza Rice, an African American woman who had served previously as national security adviser.

The Obama administration has continued the trend of increasing diversity. Female members who served in President Obama's cabinet during his first term included Hillary Rodham Clinton, who served as secretary of state; Labor Secretary Hilda Solis, who is Latina; Secretary of Homeland Security Janet Napolitano; Secretary of Health and Human Services Kathleen Sebelius; head of the Small Business Administration Karen Mills; as well as Environmental Protection Agency Administrator Lisa Jackson and United Nations Ambassador Susan Rice, both of whom are African American. Other African Americans to serve in Obama's first cabinet

Women and Minorities Appointed to Presidential Cabinets

TABLE 13.1

President	Number of Women* Cabinet Members	Number of Minority** Cabinet Members	Tenure
Obama	13	12	2009–2017
G. W. Bush	7	10	2001–2009
Clinton	13	11	1993–2001
G. H. W. Bush	4	3	1989–1993
Reagan	4	2	1981–1989
Carter	4	1	1977–1981
Ford	1	1	1974–1977
Nixon	0	0	1969–1974
Johnson	0	1	1963–1969
Kennedy	0	0	1961–1963
Eisenhower	1	0	1953–1961
Truman	0	0	1945–1953
F. Roosevelt	1	0	1933–1945

*Includes cabinet and cabinet-level appointments.
**Includes African Americans, Latinos/as, and Asian Americans.

SOURCES: Brigid C. Harrison, *Women in American Politics: An Introduction* (Belmont, CA: Wadsworth Publishing, 2003); the Center for the American Woman and Politics, National Information Bank on Women in Public Office, Eagleton Institute of Politics, Rutgers University; www.whitehouse.gov, and various presidential library websites.

included U.S. Trade Representative Ron Kirk and Attorney General Eric Holder. President Obama's first-term cabinet also included Interior Secretary Ken Salazar, who is Latino, as well as two Asian Americans, Energy Secretary Steven Chu, and Secretary of Veterans Affairs Eric Shinseki.

Today, female members of the president's cabinet include Interior Secretary Sally Jewell and Commerce Secretary Penny Pritzker. In addition, Environmental Protection Agency Administrator Gina McCarthy, UN Ambassador Samantha Power, Small Business Administration head Maria Contreras-Sweet, and Office of Management and Budget director Sylvia Mathews Burwell hold cabinet-level posts in the Obama administration. In addition, Transportation Secretary Anthony Foxx and Secretary of Homeland Security Jeh (pronounced "Jay") Johnson are African American. Second term Latino cabinet members include Contreras-Sweet, Labor Secretary Thomas Perez, and HUD Secretary Julián Castro.

The Executive Office of the President

Whereas the cabinet usually functions as an advisory board for the president, the **Executive Office of the President (EOP)** typically is the launch pad for the implementation of policy. The offices, councils, and boards that compose the EOP help the president to carry out the day-to-day responsibilities of the presidency and similarly assist the first lady and the vice president in their official activities. The EOP also coordinates policies among different agencies and departments.

Among the EOP offices, several are particularly important, including the White House Office, the National Security Council, the Office of Management and Budget, and the Council of Economic Advisers. These offices are crucial not only because of the prominent issues with which they deal but also because of their strong role in developing and implementing policy in these issue areas.[19]

THE WHITE HOUSE OFFICE   Playing a pivotal role in most presidential administrations, **White House Office (WHO)** staff members develop policies favored by the presidential administration and protect the president's legal and political interests. They research policy and keep the president informed about policy issues on the horizon. WHO staffers also regularly interact with members of Congress, their primary goal being to get presidential policy priorities enacted into law. They strive to ensure that those policies, once passed into law, are administered in keeping with the president's expectations.

Because of the enormous influence of staff members in the White House Office, presidents take pains to ensure their loyalty and trustworthiness. Among the top staff members of the White House Office is the **chief of staff,** who serves as both an adviser to the president and the manager of the WHO. Other staff members with clout include the **press secretary,** the president's spokesperson to the media, and the **White House counsel,** the president's lawyer. The president's secretary and appointments secretary are also influential WHO employees; they act as gatekeepers by controlling access to the president by other staffers and by members of Congress and the cabinet.

NATIONAL SECURITY COUNCIL   The president consults members of the **National Security Council (NSC)** on domestic and foreign matters related to national security. Since its creation in 1947 during the Truman administration,[20] the NSC has advised presidents on key national security and foreign policy decisions and assisted in the implementation of those decisions by coordinating policy administration among different agencies. For example, once the president has decided on a specific policy, the NSC might coordinate its implementation among the Department of State, the Central Intelligence Agency, various branches of the military, and diplomatic officials.

The president officially chairs the National Security Council. Its other regular members include the vice president, the secretary of defense, the secretary of state, the secretary of the treasury, and the assistant to the president for national security affairs, who is responsible for

Executive Office of the President (EOP)
offices, councils, and boards that help the president to carry out the day-to-day responsibilities of the office

White House Office (WHO)
the office that develops policies and protects the president's legal and political interests

chief of staff
among the most important staff members of the WHO; serves as both an adviser to the president and manager of the WHO

press secretary
the president's spokesperson to the media

White House counsel
the president's lawyer

National Security Council (NSC)
consisting of top foreign policy advisers and relevant cabinet officials, this is an arm of the EOP that the president consults on matters of foreign policy and national security

administering the day-to-day operations of the NSC and its staff. Other administration officials serve the NSC in advisory capacities or are invited to meetings when matters concerning their area of expertise are being decided.

Office of Management and Budget (OMB)
office that creates the president's annual budget

OFFICE OF MANAGEMENT AND BUDGET   Once part of the Department of the Treasury, the **Office of Management and Budget (OMB**—originally called the Bureau of the Budget) has been a separate office within the EOP since 1939. Its chief responsibility is to create the president's annual budget, which the president submits to Congress each January. The budget outlines all of the anticipated revenue that the government will receive in the next year, usually from taxes and fees paid by businesses and individuals. The budget also lists the anticipated expenditures for the coming year, detailing how much money the various departments and agencies in the federal government will have available to spend on salaries, administrative costs, and programs. The OMB is among the president's most important agencies for policy making and policy implementation.

The director of the Office of Management and Budget (OMB), a presidential appointee confirmed by the Senate, has a staff of about six hundred career civil servants. In recent decades, the OMB director has figured prominently in presidential administrations and typically has been designated a member of the cabinet. The director's job is complex. He or she interacts intensively with Congress, trying to ensure that the budget that passes resembles the president's proposed budget as closely as possible. The director also lobbies members of Congress with the goal of ensuring that the key provisions of the budget that are important to the president remain intact in the congressionally approved version.

Once Congress approves the budget, the director of the OMB turns attention to its implementation, since it is the job of the OMB staff to manage the budget's execution by federal departments and agencies—to ensure that monies are spent on their designated purposes and that fraud and financial abuse do not occur. This managerial responsibility of the OMB was the reasoning behind the change in the office's name (from the Bureau of the Budget) in 1970.

Presidential Succession

No examination of the executive branch would be complete without considering the question, What happens if the president dies? Presidential succession is determined by the Presidential Succession Law of 1947. But sometimes incapacitation other than death prevents presidents from fulfilling their duties. In such cases, the Twenty-Fifth Amendment, ratified in 1967, determines the course of action.

When the President Dies in Office

When the president dies, the course of action is clear in most cases: The vice president assumes the presidency. Such was the situation when Harry S. Truman became president upon Franklin D. Roosevelt's death from natural causes in 1945 and when Lyndon B. Johnson was sworn in as president after the assassination of John F. Kennedy in 1963. Vice presidents sometimes fill the unexpired term of their president for reasons other than the president's death, as when Gerald Ford acceded to the presidency upon the resignation of Richard Nixon after the Watergate scandal.

The Presidential Succession Law of 1947 determines presidential succession if the vice president also dies or is unable to govern. Table 13.2 shows that after the vice president, the next in line for the presidency is the Speaker of the House of Representatives, then the president pro tem of the Senate, followed by a specified order of the members of the cabinet. Notice that as new cabinet departments have been established, their secretaries have been added to the bottom of the line of succession. As a precaution, at the State of the Union address each year, one cabinet member

> When a president dies in office, the line of presidential succession is clear. Crowds watched the funeral procession for President Franklin D. Roosevelt, who died in office in 1945 and was succeeded by his vice president, Harry S. Truman (1945–1953).

is chosen not to attend the president's speech before Congress but, rather, to stay behind at the White House. This measure ensures that if a catastrophe should occur in Congress during the address, someone in the line of succession will be able to assume the duties of the president.

When the President Cannot Serve: The Twenty-Fifth Amendment

What happens when a president is alive but unable to carry out the responsibilities of the office? Until the ratification of the Twenty-Fifth Amendment in 1967, the course of action was not clear. Such was the case in 1881, when an assassin shot President James Garfield, and Garfield lived two and a half months before succumbing to his injuries. In another such instance, President Woodrow Wilson was so ill during his last months in office that he was incapacitated. First Lady Edith Wilson assumed some of his responsibilities and decision making. Questions about presidential health also arose toward the end of Franklin D. Roosevelt's tenure; and during Dwight D. Eisenhower's administration, the president authorized Vice President Richard Nixon to determine whether Eisenhower, who was battling a series of illnesses, was competent to govern. President John F. Kennedy, who suffered from a host of physical ailments including severe, chronic back pain and Addison's disease, similarly empowered Vice President Lyndon B. Johnson: In an informal agreement, the men arranged that if Kennedy was physically unable to communicate with Johnson, Johnson was authorized to assume the presidency.

TABLE 13.2

The Line of Presidential Succession

1. Vice president
2. Speaker of the House of Representatives
3. President pro tem of the Senate
4. Secretary of state
5. Secretary of the treasury
6. Secretary of defense
7. Attorney general
8. Secretary of the interior
9. Secretary of agriculture
10. Secretary of commerce
11. Secretary of labor
12. Secretary of health and human services
13. Secretary of housing and urban development
14. Secretary of transportation
15. Secretary of energy
16. Secretary of education
17. Secretary of veterans affairs
18. Secretary of homeland security

After Kennedy's assassination, the ratification of the Twenty-Fifth Amendment (1967) finally put codified procedures in place for dealing with an incapacitated president. According to the Twenty-Fifth Amendment, if a president believes he or she is unable to carry out the duties of the office, the president must notify Congress, and the vice president becomes the acting president until the president can resume authority. The amendment would apply in the case when a president is anesthetized for surgery, for example, or perhaps recuperating from a debilitating illness.

In other situations, a president might be incapable of carrying out the duties of office and incapable of notifying Congress. In such a case, the Twenty-Fifth Amendment requires that the vice president and a majority of the cabinet notify Congress, and the vice president becomes the acting president. If a question arises as to whether the president is fit to reassume the duties of office, a two-thirds vote of Congress is required for the acting president to remain.

Sources of Presidential Power

The presidency that Barack Obama assumed on January 20, 2009, scarcely resembled George Washington's presidency in the 1790s. From the late 18th century to today, the powers of the president have evolved, reflecting the expansion of the federal government, changes in public attitudes about the proper role of government, and the personalities and will of those who have served as president.

In describing the powers that would guide presidents for centuries to come, the framers of the Constitution created a unique office. These visionary authors had lived through a repressive era in which an authoritarian monarch had exercised absolute power. They subsequently had witnessed the new American nation's struggles under the ineffectual Articles of Confederation, in which the federal government had too little power and the states too much. Thus the framers sought to establish an office that would balance the exercise of authority with the preservation of the rights and the will of the people.

Given their colonial experience, it was no surprise that the framers granted the presidents both *expressed powers* and *inherent powers* in the Constitution. Congress grants presidents additional powers, called *statutory powers,* through congressional action. We consider these various powers in this section.

Additional presidential powers have emerged over time. These newer authorities reflect both changes in the institution of the presidency and shifts in popular views on the appropriate role of government and the president. These powers include emergency powers granted in Supreme Court decisions and powers that, though not formalized, are given to presidents by the public through election mandates, presidential popularity, or unified public opinion on a particular issue or course of action.

The Constitution: Expressed Powers

expressed powers
presidential powers enumerated in the Constitution

The primary source of presidential power comes from the Constitution in the form of the **expressed powers,** which are those enumerated in the Constitution. Article II, Sections 2 and 3, list the following powers:

- Serve as commander in chief of the armed forces
- Appoint heads of the executive departments, ambassadors, Supreme Court justices, people to fill vacancies that occur during the recess of the Senate, and other positions
- Pardon crimes, except in cases of impeachment
- Enter into treaties, with two-thirds consent of the Senate
- Give the State of the Union address to Congress
- Convene the Congress
- Receive ambassadors of other nations
- Commission all officers of the United States

The expressed powers outlined in the Constitution provide a framework for presidential responsibilities and an outline of presidential power. They also shape how presidents themselves develop their authority.

The Constitution: Inherent Powers

take care clause
the constitutional basis for inherent powers, which states that the president "shall take Care that the Laws be faithfully executed"

inherent powers
presidential powers that are implied in the Constitution

One of the principal ways by which the Constitution provides for presidents themselves to assert additional powers, beyond those expressed in the Constitution, is the **take care clause,** which states that "the executive Power shall be vested in a President of the United States of America" and that "he shall take Care that the Laws be faithfully executed." On the basis of that clause, presidents throughout U.S. history have asserted various **inherent powers,** which are powers that are not expressly granted by the Constitution but are inferred.

President Thomas Jefferson exercised inherent powers in his far-reaching Louisiana Purchase in 1803. Jefferson authorized this $15 million purchase of 800,000 square miles of land, even though the Constitution did not authorize any such action on the part of a president. Interestingly, in the civic discourse over the Constitution, Jefferson, an Anti-Federalist, had argued for states' rights and against a strong central government and a powerful presidency. Jefferson had believed that the powers enumerated in the Constitution defined the powers of the government. But Jefferson thought that the purchase of the Louisiana Territory was of crucial strategic and economic importance. He believed that the deal was key to the United States' averting war with France and to securing the port of New Orleans, which was essential for the new American republic's fortunes in trade. Jefferson could not wait for a constitutional amendment to authorize the transaction, and so he forged ahead with the purchase. Congress and many Americans of the day agreed with his actions, and so there were no negative consequences to them.

President Franklin D. Roosevelt also drew on the inherent powers when he expanded the size of the federal government in the 1930s to administer his New Deal programs, designed to relieve the economic and human distress of the Great Depression. Beginning in 2002, President George W. Bush used the inherent powers when he suspended the civil liberties of foreign nationals being held in a military prison at the U.S. naval base at Guantánamo Bay, Cuba, as part of the administration's war on terror. The individuals at Guantánamo Bay have been detained indefinitely for questioning about their possible terrorist activities. These instances of presidents' exercise of inherent powers generated varying degrees of controversy among Americans of the times.

More recently, President Obama exercised his inherent powers by again expanding the scope of the federal government through passage of the Patient Protection and Affordable Care Act of 2010, also known as Obamacare. This health care reform act, which was approved by the Democratically controlled Congress at President Obama's behest, expands Medicaid, subsidizes health insurance premiums for middle-income families, offers incentives for employers to provide health care to their employees, and mandates that uninsured individuals purchase government-approved health insurance.

Statutory Powers

The Constitution's expressed and inherent powers provided a foundation for presidential power that has evolved over time. Those powers have been supplemented by additional powers, including **statutory powers,** which are explicitly granted to presidents by congressional action.

An example of such a grant of statutory powers is the 1996 Line Item Veto Act, discussed earlier, which gave the president the power to strike down specific line items on an appropriations bill while allowing the rest of the bill to become law. As noted, in 1997 the Supreme Court declared the line-item veto unconstitutional on the grounds that the congressional action violated the separation of powers.

statutory powers
powers explicitly granted to presidents by congressional action

Special Presidential Powers

Presidents also have special powers that have evolved from various sources, including the Constitution and Supreme Court decisions. These powers, which numerous presidents have exercised, have come to be regarded as accepted powers and privileges of the presidency. They include *executive orders, emergency powers,* and *executive privilege.*

EXECUTIVE ORDERS The president has the power to issue **executive orders** that have the force of law. Executive orders carry the same weight as congressional statutes and have been used in a variety of circumstances to guide the executive branch's administrative functions.[21] In general, executive orders:

executive order
power of the president to issue orders that carry the force of law

- Direct the enforcement of congressional statutes or Supreme Court rulings
- Enforce specific provisions of the Constitution
- Guide the administration of treaties with foreign governments
- Create or change the regulatory guidelines or practices of an executive department or agency

Executive orders can be an important strategic tool, because they convey the president's priorities to the bureaucracy that implements the laws. For example, in 1948 President Harry Truman signed Executive Order 9981, which states, "It is hereby declared to be the policy of the President that there shall be equality of treatment and opportunity for all persons in the armed services without regard to race, color, religion, or national origin."[22] This executive order effectively banned segregation in the U.S. military. Why would Truman issue an executive order instead of working for congressional passage of a statute that would desegregate the military? Many analysts think that Truman, who ardently believed that the military should be desegregated, not only doubted that Congress would pass such a measure but also faced pressure from early civil rights activists who had pledged an African American boycott of military service if the military was not desegregated.

Executive orders have very few limitations and stipulations. One limitation is that presidents cannot use them to create new taxes or appropriate funds, because the Constitution reserves those powers for Congress. But although there are few limitations on executive orders, an order itself is sometimes not sufficient to ensure that the president's will is followed. Take the case of President Obama, who two days into his tenure as president issued an executive order declaring

Evolution of the Modern Presidency

Then (1970s)	Now
The presidency had become an increasingly powerful institution, shaped by the predecessors of Richard Nixon, who assumed office in 1969.	Congress continues to attempt to "check" the power of modern presidents, and presidents rely on increasingly bold tactics to act as unilateral actors.
The presidency supplanted Congress as the epicenter of power in the federal government.	Presidential exercise of authority in the foreign policy realm serves to limit Congress's ability to rein in presidential power.
Backlash against abuses of executive power in the Nixon administration paved the way for the election of Jimmy Carter, a comparatively weak president.	Barack Obama is reelected in 2012, but his presidency is constrained by Republican majorities controlling the House and Senate.

WHAT'S NEXT?

> In what direction do you believe the imperial presidency will go after the 2016 election?

> What public policy issues will likely dominate in the months and years to come? How will these issues influence the ways presidential power is exercised?

> What conditions facilitate the creation of "imperial" presidencies? Do these conditions exist now?

emergency powers
broad powers exercised by the president during times of national crisis

executive privilege
the right of the chief executive and members of the administration to withhold information from Congress or the courts, or the right to refuse to appear before legislative or judicial bodies

that the detention facilities at Guantánamo Naval Base in Cuba be closed by January 2010. Because of the complexity of the Guantánamo situation—the need to determine the status of all prisoners and to relocate them—the detention facility remains open.

EMERGENCY POWERS Broad powers that a president exercises during times of national crisis have been invoked by presidents since Abraham Lincoln's claim to **emergency powers** during the Civil War. Lincoln used emergency powers during the war to suspend the civil liberties of alleged agitators, to draft state militia units into national service, and to federalize the governance of southern states after the war.

In 1936, the U.S. Supreme Court acknowledged the existence of presidential emergency powers in *United States v. Curtiss-Wright Export Corp.*[23] In this case, the U.S. government charged the Curtiss-Wright Corporation with conspiring to sell 15 machine guns to Bolivia, in violation of a joint resolution of Congress and a presidential proclamation. Without congressional approval, President Franklin D. Roosevelt had ordered an embargo on the machine gun shipment. The Court supported Roosevelt's order, ruling that the president's powers, particularly in foreign affairs, are not limited to those powers expressly stated in the Constitution. The justices also stated that the federal government is the primary actor in foreign affairs and that the president in particular has inherent powers related to his constitutional duties in foreign relations.

EXECUTIVE PRIVILEGE Presidents also can exercise **executive privilege,** the authority of the president and other executive officials to refuse to disclose information concerning confidential conversations or national security to Congress or the courts. In invoking executive privilege, presidents draw on the idea that the Constitution's framework of separation of powers justifies the withholding of certain information from Congress or the judiciary,[24] a claim initially asserted when George Washington refused to grant Congress access to all documents pertaining to treaty negotiations. Typically, presidents claim executive privilege so that they can get advice from aides without fear that such conversations might be made public or scrutinized by members of Congress or the judiciary. Presidents also have invoked executive privilege when negotiating foreign policies with other heads of state, to shield these leaders from having sensitive negotiations examined by the other branches of the federal government.

On occasion, the judicial branch of the federal government has successfully challenged executive privilege. For example, when President Richard Nixon refused to turn over tapes of Oval Office conversations to a special prosecutor investigating the Watergate scandal in 1974, the Supreme Court intervened. In *United States v. Richard M. Nixon,* the Court asserted that although executive privilege does exist, it was not applicable regarding the tapes because President Nixon's claim of executive privilege concerning the tapes was too broad.[25] (See page 416 for more on Watergate.)

More recent cases in which a president has invoked executive privilege are notable. President Bill Clinton attempted to do so to prevent White House aides from testifying before special prosecutor Kenneth Starr during the Monica Lewinsky scandal. (Clinton was accused of having extramarital relations with Lewinsky, a White House intern.) Clinton's maneuver failed, and his aides were compelled to testify. In general, the courts have allowed executive privilege in cases where a clear issue of separation of powers exists—as with respect to international negotiations and conversations regarding matters of policy or national security. The courts have tended to limit the use of executive privilege when presidents have exercised it in an effort to prevent the revelation of misdeeds by members of the executive branch.

The People as a Source of Presidential Power

One of the most important sources of presidential power today comes from the people. Although one president generally will have the same formal powers as the next, presidents' ability to wield their power, to control the political agenda, and to get things done typically is a function of political skill, charisma, and what political scientist Richard Neustadt has called "the power to persuade."[26]

> Presidents use their bully pulpits to persuade the public. Here, basketball superstar LeBron James was one of many celebrities President Obama relied on to convince seven million Americans to enroll in health insurance plans under the Affordable Care Act.

The President and the Bully Pulpit

Modern presidents work to persuade the public on a virtually continuous basis. They know that if they win popular support for their views and political agenda, they will have an easier time getting their policy priorities through Congress. In their efforts to persuade the people, they exploit the power of their office, using the presidency as a forum from which to speak out on any matter—and to have their views listened to. This ready access to the public ear and broad power of the president to communicate led President Theodore Roosevelt to exclaim, "I have got such a bully pulpit!"[27]

In using their bully pulpit, presidents seek to communicate that their stances on important issues are the right choices and that their actions, particularly controversial decisions, should be supported. Presidents also strive to persuade the public that they are doing a good job on key policy fronts such as economic and foreign policy. Sometimes presidents seek to mobilize the public to take specific actions or to adopt certain beliefs. For example, in 2014, President Obama led his administration's effort to enroll seven million people in health insurance plans under the Affordable Care Act, which he succeeded in doing by appearing on online comedy shows, using celebrities such as NBA star LeBron James, comedienne Amy Poehler, singer and actress Jennifer Hudson, and pop star Lady Gaga to urge people to enroll.

The reason why presidents work so tirelessly to win public support for their agenda is that they understand that getting Congress to act on policy priorities, to approve budgets, and to pass favored legislation depends heavily on the perception that the public supports presidential initiatives. Indeed, political scientist Richard Neustadt argues that the modern institution of the presidency is weak and that presidents in fact must rely on public and congressional support in order to enact their agendas.[28] Getting Congress to do what the president wants is more difficult when a president faces divided government, the situation in which the president belongs to one political party and Congress is controlled by a majority of members of the other party, or when the president must deal with a truncated government in which the president and one house of Congress is controlled by one party, but the other house of Congress is controlled by the other, as discussed in Chapter 8. Truncated government occurred in 2010, when Republicans won control of the House of Representatives during President Obama's administration. Since that time, the Republicans have succeeded in blocking several of the president's priorities, including increasing the ceiling on federal debt in 2011 in order to secure budget cuts and increasing the minimum wage in 2014. When a frustrated President Obama received the debt ceiling bill only one day before the federal government's ability to borrow was about to end, he commented, "Voters may have chosen divided government, but they sure didn't vote for dysfunctional government."[29]

FIGURE 13.3 ▪ GEORGE W. BUSH'S APPROVAL RATINGS (2001–2009) COMPARED TO BARACK OBAMA'S APPROVAL RATINGS (2009–2014) How do President Bush's approval ratings compare to President Obama's? What circumstances influenced each president's approval levels? How important is the economy in determining the president's approval ratings? What other issues or circumstances might have an impact on presidential approval ratings in the future?

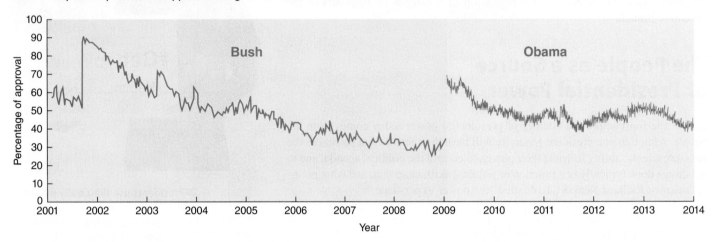

But beyond partisan differences, presidents' ability to get things done in Congress also is a function of their popularity with the people. A popular president can use that clout to persuade members of Congress that his positions are the right ones; an unpopular president, or one distracted by issues not related to policy, will face greater obstacles to having his legislative agenda enacted.

The President and Public Approval

honeymoon period

a time early in a new president's administration characterized by optimistic approval by the public

approval ratings

the percentage of survey respondents who say that they "approve" or "strongly approve" of the way the president is doing his job

When Barack Obama was sworn in as president in 2009, fully 67 percent of the American people approved of the way he was handling his job as president. He enjoyed a strong **honeymoon period,** a time early in a new president's administration characterized by optimistic approval by the public. As his presidency progressed, however, the president's **approval rating**—the percentage of survey respondents who say that they "approve" or "strongly approve" of the way the president is doing his job—steadily declined, reaching a low point of 43 percent in August 2010. It then began rebounding, reaching a peak of 52 percent during his 2012 reelection campaign, but problems with implementation of the Affordable Care Act, including the glitch-plagued Health-Care.gov website, caused his popularity to plummet once again, bottoming out at 41 percent in late 2013. Since that time, the president's approval rating has rebounded slightly as shown in Figure 13.3, though the partisan gridlock that has characterized relations between the president and Republicans who control the House of Representatives has clearly taken a toll on President Obama's popularity.

The flow and ebb of presidential popularity during the administration of George W. Bush illustrates how essential the people's support is to the success of a chief executive's initiatives. After the September 11, 2001, terrorist attacks and President Bush's rapid and dignified response to them, Bush enjoyed record high approval ratings. Immediately after September 11, President Bush's approval ratings hovered in the high 80s, occasionally reaching 90 percent, meaning that 90 percent of those surveyed indicated that they approved of the way the president was handling his job. (In contrast, the average presidential approval rating since the Franklin D. Roosevelt administration was 56 percent.) During this time, Bush had enormous legislative successes. These included the passage of the USA PATRIOT Act of 2001, which gave law enforcement

Analyzing the Sources

RANKING THE PRESIDENTS

From time to time, historians and political scientists have rated the U.S. presidents, as have average Americans. The ratings given the presidents by scholars have been remarkably consistent. Abraham Lincoln, George Washington, Franklin D. Roosevelt, Woodrow Wilson, and Thomas Jefferson are universally recognized as the greatest American presidents. Ulysses S. Grant and Warren G. Harding both dominate on the bottom of most rating lists as the least successful presidents. But historians have more difficulty rating recent presidents, because the views of historians are influenced by current political controversies. Often the passage of time allows scholars to make more objective evaluations. Conversely, average Americans are much more likely to name recent presidents as the greatest. They may lack historical knowledge about presidents who held office long ago, or their attitudes may be skewed by sentiments favoring recent officeholders.

Evaluating the Evidence

1. List your ranking of the top five presidents, and the worst five. Were most of your selections recent presidents? If so, why do you think this was the case?

2. Do you think that political party plays a role in determining which presidents Americans define as great? Do the rankings bear your opinion out?

3. Modern presidents that scholars have evaluated positively include Clinton (#13) and Obama (#15), while George W. Bush was ranked among the worse at #39. Why do you think this was the case?

Average Americans' Evaluation of Presidential Greatness
RESPONSES TO: "WHO DO YOU REGARD AS THE GREATEST UNITED STATES PRESIDENT?"

PRESIDENT	PERCENT
Ronald Reagan	19
Abraham Lincoln	14
Bill Clinton	13
John Kennedy	11
George Washington	10
Franklin Roosevelt	8
Barack Obama	5
Theodore Roosevelt	3
Harry Truman	3
George W. Bush	2
Thomas Jefferson	2
Jimmy Carter	1
Dwight Eisenhower	1
George H. W. Bush	1
Andrew Jackson	*
Lyndon Johnson	*
Richard Nixon	*

*Less than 0.5 percent.
SOURCE: Gallup Organization, "Americans Say Reagan Is the Greatest President," www.gallup.com/poll/146183/americans-say-reagan-greatest-president.aspx.

Presidential Scholars' Evaluation of Presidential Greatness

RANKINGS	RANKINGS
1. Franklin Roosevelt	23. Martin Van Buren
2. Theodore Roosevelt	24. William Howard Taft
3. Abraham Lincoln	25. Chester Arthur
4. George Washington	26. Ulysses S. Grant
5. Thomas Jefferson	27. James Garfield
6. James Madison	28. Gerald Ford
7. James Monroe	29. Calvin Coolidge
8. Woodrow Wilson	30. Richard Nixon
9. Harry Truman	31. Rutherford B. Hayes
10. Dwight Eisenhower	32. Jimmy Carter
11. John Kennedy	33. Zachary Taylor
12. James Polk	34. Benjamin Harrison
13. Bill Clinton	35. William Henry Harrison
14. Andrew Jackson	36. Herbert Hoover
15. Barack Obama	37. John Tyler
16. Lyndon Johnson	38. Millard Fillmore
17. John Adams	39. George W. Bush
18. Ronald Reagan	40. Franklin Pierce
19. John Quincy Adams	41. Warren Harding
20. Grover Cleveland	42. James Buchanan
21. William McKinley	43. Andrew Johnson
22. George H. W. Bush	

SOURCE: Siena College Research Institute, www2.siena.edu/uploadedfiles/home/parents_and_community/community_page/sri/independent_research/Presidents%202010%20Rank%20by%20Category.pdf.

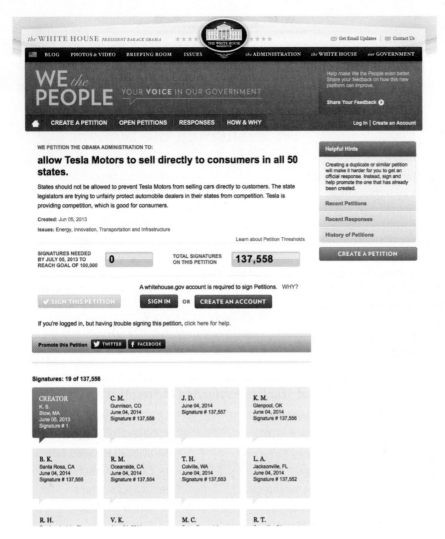

WE PETITION THE OBAMA ADMINISTRATION TO:

allow Tesla Motors to sell directly to consumers in all 50 states.

States should not be allowed to prevent Tesla Motors from selling cars directly to customers. The state legislators are trying to unfairly protect automobile dealers in their states from competition. Tesla is providing competition, which is good for consumers.

Created: Jun 05, 2013

Issues: Energy, Innovation, Transportation and Infrastructure

> Today, the president relies on technology, including Facebook, Twitter, and YouTube to communicate directly with voters, and voters can use the Internet to communicate directly with the president. One effective way is the We the People web page on the White House website, which enables people to sign petitions about various issues. If a petition receives 100,000 signatures, someone in the president's administration will consider the policy recommendation.

rally 'round the flag effect
peaks in presidential approval ratings during short-term military action

officers greater authority in handling suspected terrorist acts, and the congressional declaration of a "war on terror." When Bush's popularity subsequently waned because of the people's dissatisfaction with the rate of progress in the war in Iraq, the high number of casualties in the war, and continued weakness in the American economy, so, too, did support decrease for the continuation of the war, the president's economic policies, and a proposed extension of the USA PATRIOT Act.

In general, presidential approval ratings reveal that some presidents are simply more popular than others (see "Analyzing the Sources"). For example, presidents Reagan and Clinton tended to enjoy high approval ratings, with President Clinton's second-term ratings running particularly high, especially in light of the Monica Lewinsky scandal and the subsequent impeachment proceedings against him. When the United States engages in a short-term military action or is the subject of an attack by terrorists, we see similar peaks in approval ratings, sometimes referred to as the **rally 'round the flag effect.** A president rarely sustains high public approval continuously. Once achieved, however, high ratings help the chief executive to achieve his goals by demonstrating the people's support of the presidential agenda.[30]

Technology and the Media as a Tool of Presidential Influence

Modern presidents rely heavily on technology and the mass media to convey their message to the people. In the 1930s, Franklin D. Roosevelt transformed the nature of the presidency by using radio to communicate directly with the American people. President Kennedy would replicate this transformation using the medium of television in the 1960s. Today, President Obama has again revolutionized how presidents communicate with their constituents by using social networking, the Internet, and cellular technology to forge a new type of relationship with voters (see Chapter 11 for further discussion of the president's use of technology).

For every president, technology and the media can be used as a tool of influence as the expertise of the White House communications office can "spin" news in a favorable light for the administration. In particular, the White House can manage direct communication using new technologies by releasing videos on the President's Facebook page or YouTube channel, or by holding "office hours" on Twitter. Relying on traditional media, the communication director forges relationships with the most prominent media outlets by providing access, exclusive interviews, and scoops on breaking stories to reporters considered friendly to the administration. And today, the president relies on YouTube, Facebook, and Twitter to communicate directly with the American people.

Although the nature of presidential press conferences and other media forums has evolved over time, the mass media have served as a key avenue by which modern presidents have communicated directly to the population at large. Because the nature of the president's relationship with his constituency is constantly evolving, so, too, is presidential power.

The Evolution of Presidential Power

Although the constitutional powers of the presidency have changed little over time, the power of the presidency has evolved a great deal.[31] This development stems in part from some presidents' skillful use of powers not granted by the Constitution, such as the powers to persuade and to assert more authority. But the political environment within which presidents have governed has also contributed to the evolution of presidential power.[32]

The history of the early republic saw an incremental expansion of the power of the presidency, whereas the Great Depression of the 1930s and the election of Franklin D. Roosevelt in 1932 spawned an enormous growth in presidential authority.[33] As successor presidents inherited the large bureaucracy that Roosevelt built, presidential powers have expanded further—gradually creating what historian Arthur Schlesinger, Jr., has called the "imperial presidency."

Early Presidents and the Scope of Presidential Power

Thomas Jefferson's election to the presidency in 1801 marked one of the earliest expansions of presidential power. Jefferson broadened the powers of the office despite his Anti-Federalist reluctance to delegate too much power to the national government. Jefferson increased presidential power in two significant ways. First, as we have seen, Jefferson established the principle of inherent powers of the presidency by undertaking the Louisiana Purchase. Second, Jefferson's tenure in office witnessed the first time that a president had to act as party leader. Jefferson had no choice but to assume this role: If he had not, he would not have been elected president, given the dominance of the Federalist Party during this era (see Chapter 8).

Twenty-five years later, Andrew Jackson would also adopt the role of president-as-party-leader, but he would add a new twist. Jackson's emphasis on *populism,* a political philosophy that emphasizes the needs of the common person, spawned a new source of presidential power, because Jackson was the first president to derive real and significant power from the people. Whereas earlier politics had mostly emphasized the needs of the elite, Jackson's populism mobilized the masses of common people who traditionally had not been civically engaged. This populism augmented the power of the presidency by increasing the popularity of the president and investing him with power that came from the people's goodwill.

In the 20th century, the nature and scope of presidential power changed as a consequence of the prevailing political environment. One of the most extraordinary shifts in the nature of the presidency occurred during Franklin D. Roosevelt's administration, which lasted from 1932 until his death in 1945. (Roosevelt was elected to an unprecedented four terms; the Twenty-Second Amendment to the Constitution, which allows only two elected presidential terms, was ratified six years after his death.)

Having come to power during the Great Depression, Roosevelt engineered a significant change in the function of the federal government. He called for a New Deal for the American people, a series of social welfare programs that would provide employment for many of the nation's unemployed workers. Roosevelt's New Deal was based on the ideas of economist John Maynard Keynes, who argued for temporary deficit spending by the government (that is, going into debt) to spur the economy during economic downturns.

Roosevelt's primary weapon in his New Deal arsenal was the **Works Progress Administration (WPA),** a federal government program that employed 8.5 million people at a cost of more than $11 million between 1935 and 1943. The idea was that government-funded employment would create economic growth in the private sector because those employed by the government would have the money to buy goods and services, thus creating spiraling demand. The rising demand for goods and services would mean that the private sector could then employ more people, and the cycle of recovery and growth would continue. For example, if during the 1930s the government employed your great-great-grandfather to work on a road-building project in his town, he might have put his paycheck toward buying more bread and other baked goods than he previously could have afforded. If enough people in town could have similarly patronized the bakery, then the baker might have had to hire an assistant to keep up with demand, and consequently the assistant would have had money to spend on, say, new shoes for his children. In that way, the increased demand for products and services would continue, creating additional economic growth.

Works Progress Administration (WPA)
a New Deal program that employed 8.5 million people at a cost of more than $11 million between 1935 and 1943

Roosevelt's New Deal was important to the presidency for two reasons. First, it dramatically changed people's views of the role of the federal government. Many people now tend to think of the federal government as the provider of a "safety net" that protects the most vulnerable citizens—a safeguard that did not exist before the New Deal, when those needing assistance had to rely on the help of family, friends, churches, and private charities. Second, this popular perception and the programs that emerged—the WPA, unemployment insurance, Social Security—meant that the federal government would have to grow larger in order to administer these programs. As a result, the president's role as chief executive of a large federal bureaucracy would become much more important to modern presidents than it had been to those who served before Roosevelt.[34]

The Watershed 1970s: The *Pentagon Papers,* Watergate, and the "Imperial Presidency"

Americans' penchant for strong presidents modeled after Roosevelt diminished drastically in the 1970s. In 1971, an employee of the Department of Defense named Daniel Ellsberg leaked a classified, top-secret 7,000-page history of the nation's involvement in and thinking on Vietnam dating from the Truman administration in 1945 to the Nixon administration then installed in the White House. Called the *Pentagon Papers,* the work first appeared as a series of articles in *The New York Times.* When the Nixon administration in 1971 successfully petitioned the Department of Justice to prevent the publication of the remainder of the articles, the *Washington Post* assumed publication of them. When the Department of Justice sued the *Post,* the *Boston Globe* resumed their publication. Two weeks later, in an expedited appeals process, the U.S. Supreme Court ruled in *The New York Times Co. v. The United States* that the government "carries a heavy burden of showing justification for the imposition of such a restraint" and that the government had failed to meet that burden, thus allowing the continued publication of the papers.[35]

The *Pentagon Papers* tainted the public's view of the presidency. The published work revealed miscalculations by policy makers in presidential administrations from Truman's to Nixon's, as well as arrogance and deception on the part of policy makers, cabinet members, and presidents. Specifically, the *Pentagon Papers* revealed that the federal government had repeatedly lied about or misrepresented the fact of increasing U.S. military involvement in Southeast Asia. In particular, the analysis in the *Pentagon Papers* indicated not only that U.S. marines had conducted offensive military maneuvers well before the public was informed but also that the U.S. military had engaged in other actions, including air strikes over Laos and military raids throughout the North Vietnamese coastal regions. The Nixon administration's legal wrangling to prevent release of the *Pentagon Papers* cast a dark cloud over the public's perception of the presidency.

Cynicism about the presidency continued to grow in light of the **Watergate** scandal that took place a year later. In 1972, men affiliated with President Nixon's reelection campaign broke into the headquarters of the Democratic National Committee (located in the Watergate Hotel in Washington, D.C.) to retrieve wiretaps that they had previously installed to monitor their opponents. *Washington Post* reporters Bob Woodward and Carl Bernstein, in a groundbreaking series of stories, traced the burglaries and the subsequent cover-up to high-level officials in the Nixon administration. This crime and the Nixon administration's attempts at cover-ups became known as the Watergate scandal. A Senate investigation revealed that President Nixon had secretly taped conversations in the Oval Office that would shed light on "what the president knew [about the break-in] and when he knew it."[36] Nixon claimed executive privilege and refused to turn over the tapes to a special prosecutor who had been appointed to investigate the scandal. When the U.S. Supreme Court ruled in *United States v. Richard Nixon* that Nixon must provide the tapes to the special prosecutor, one key tape was found to have a gap of almost 20 minutes where someone, reportedly his secretary, Rosemary Woods, had erased part of the recording.

Meanwhile, all the Watergate burglars had pleaded guilty and been sentenced, and only one refused to name the superiors who had orchestrated the break-in. But the testimony of burglar James W. McCord, Jr., linked the crime to the Committee to Re-Elect the President (CREEP), Nixon's campaign organization, and to high-ranking Nixon White House officials. The

Watergate
during the Nixon administration, a scandal involving burglaries and the subsequent cover-up by high-level administration officials

 William Frazee, the chief of the presses for the *Washington Post*, makes the victory sign after learning of the Supreme Court's decision allowing newspapers to publish the *Pentagon Papers.* Applause broke out in the press room as the first print run began rolling.

disclosure prompted John Dean, Nixon's White House counsel, to remark: "We have a cancer within, close to the presidency, that is growing."[37] With indictments handed down for many of Nixon's top aides, and with a Senate investigation and a special prosecutor's investigation in progress, the House Judiciary Committee took up the matter of impeachment. The committee handed down three articles of impeachment against Nixon—one for obstruction of justice, a second for abuse of power, and a third for contempt of Congress. When a newly released tape documented that Nixon had planned to block the investigations by having the Federal Bureau of Investigation and the Central Intelligence Agency falsely claim that matters of national security were involved, the tape was referred to as a "smoking gun."[38] Nixon lost the support of his few loyalists in Congress and on August 8, 1974, announced that he would resign from office the following day.

Watergate might seem like a relatively insignificant event in the history of the American presidency, but the impact of the Watergate scandal on the presidency has been enormous. Watergate badly wounded the trust that many Americans held for their president and for their government. Combined with the unpopularity of the Vietnam War and the release of the *Pentagon Papers,* it created a deep cynicism that pervades many Americans' perception of their government even today—a pessimistic attitude that has passed from generation to generation.

Watergate also dramatically demonstrated how enormously the presidency had changed. Modern presidents had supplanted Congress as the center of federal power and in so doing had become too powerful. Historian Arthur Schlesinger, Jr., and other presidential scholars have decried the problem of the growth of the executive branch and, in particular, the imperial "courts"—the rising number of Executive Office of the President staff members, many of whom are not subject to Senate confirmation and share a deep loyalty to the person who is president rather than to the institution of the presidency. In juxtaposition with an attitude like that expressed by Richard Nixon in his comment that "when the president does it, that means it is not illegal,"[39] the imperial presidency left much room for abuse.

The Post-Watergate Presidency

With the election of Jimmy Carter to the White House in 1976, many observers believed that the era of the imperial presidency had passed. Carter, the mild-mannered governor of Georgia and thus a Washington outsider, seemed to be the antidote the nation needed after the display of power-run-amok during Nixon's tenure. But given the significant challenges Carter faced during his term, many people believed that he did not exercise *enough* authority—that he acted weakly when faced with various crises. Ronald Reagan's election in 1980 in some ways represented a return to a more powerful, "imperial" presidency. Reagan, a former actor, was Hollywood swagger personified, speaking tough talk that many Americans found appealing. His administration was not unlike an imperial court, featuring a group of advisers with deep loyalties to Reagan. Although the era of unchecked presidential power was gone for good, many would argue that the George W. Bush administration was best at re-creating a form of an imperial presidency. Bush was able to exercise strong authority because of the fear created both among the citizenry and in Congress after the September 11, 2001, terror attacks. And given President Bush's activist foreign policy, he exercised great authority in that realm, with Congress having little ability to check him. Ironically, many critics of the Bush administration would assert that he was assisted in creating a modern imperial presidency by many of the same staff members who were part of the Nixon administration. But administration supporters would note that a strong presidency was necessary at this critical juncture in the nation's history.

Many Democrats were frustrated by President Obama's comparative lack of assertiveness when exercising presidential power in the early years of his first term. Many analysts faulted his conciliatory, consensus-building nature as an impediment to exercising strong authority, and many thought his powers increasingly dissipated after the 2010 congressional elections, in which a Republican majority was elected in the House and served as a heavy check on the latter portion of Obama's first term. But after the government shutdown in 2013, President Obama seemed more willing to exert stronger authority in exercising presidential duties, oftentimes while circumventing Congress. In 2014, for example, the president issued an executive order that increased the minimum wage paid by the government to federal contractors from $7.25 to $10.10 an hour. The action was designed to generate momentum and heighten awareness of the

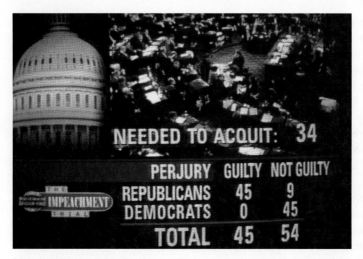

>On the basis of an investigation by special prosecutor Kenneth Starr, the House impeached President Bill Clinton for committing perjury by lying to a grand jury about his relationship with White House intern Monica Lewinsky and for obstructing justice. The Senate voted to acquit Clinton on those perjury charges.

impeachment
the power of the House of Representatives to formally accuse the president (and other high-ranking officials, including the vice president and federal judges) of crimes

articles of impeachment
charges against the president during an impeachment

minimum wage issue. Other critics point to his continuation and expansion of the National Security Administration domestic surveillance program as evidence that President Obama is, perhaps, a more imperial president that many observers initially believed.

Impeachment: A Check on Abuses of Presidential Power

Although presidential powers are flexible and can be shaped by the individuals holding the office, these powers do not go unchecked. One crucial check on presidential power is **impeachment,** the power of the House of Representatives to formally accuse the president (and other high-ranking officials, including the vice president and federal judges) of crimes. The Constitution specifically refers to charges of "Treason, Bribery, or other high Crimes and Misdemeanors," an appropriately vague description of the potential offenses a president could commit. An impeachment can be thought of as an indictment: If a majority of the members of the House of Representatives vote to impeach the president, they forward the charges against the president, called the **articles of impeachment,** to the Senate. The Senate then tries the president and, in the event of conviction for the offenses, determines the penalty. In convicting a president, the Senate has the authority to punish the president by removing him from office.

Although the Senate can force a president to step down, it has never done so in practice, and only two presidents have been impeached by the House of Representatives. The first was Andrew Johnson, who succeeded Abraham Lincoln as president in 1865 upon the latter's assassination. When he assumed the presidency, Johnson faced not only a divided nation but also a government in turmoil. The 11 articles of impeachment against him had to do primarily with his removal of the secretary of war, Edwin Stanton, who was working with Johnson's congressional opponents to undermine Johnson's reconstruction policies in the South. The so-called Radical Republicans in the House believed that Johnson's policies were too moderate, and they sought to treat the Confederate states as conquered territories and to confiscate the land of slaveholders. Those same House members wanted to protect their ally Stanton and prevent him from being removed from office. The Senate ultimately recognized the politically motivated nature of the articles of impeachment against Johnson and acquitted him on all counts.

The most recent occurrence of the impeachment of a president was in 1998, when the House of Representatives approved two articles of impeachment against President Bill Clinton. On the basis of an investigation by a special prosecutor, the House impeached Clinton for lying to a grand jury about his relationship with White House intern Monica Lewinsky and for obstructing justice. The Senate acquitted Clinton on both counts.

During the Watergate scandal that rocked Richard Nixon's presidency, the House Judiciary Committee approved articles of impeachment against the president and sent them to the full House for a vote. Republican members of Congress convinced Nixon that the House would vote to impeach him and that the Senate would convict him and remove him from office. Faced with the inevitable, Nixon became the first president to resign from office before the House could vote to impeach him.

Women in the White House

Of the three branches of government, the executive branch has been the most challenging for women to gain entry into as formal participants. As we saw earlier in this chapter, no woman served as a cabinet member until the 20th century, and to date, a woman has not been elected president. Yet cabinet positions are not the only place where women's influence in the executive branch has been felt. Historically, the women who have served as first lady have influenced both presidents and policy.

> Virginia "Bess" Truman, Edith Wilson, and Eleanor Roosevelt were modern first ladies of their era. Wilson assumed some presidential responsibilities and decision making while her husband, Woodrow, was ill. Truman was recognized as a strong campaign asset, and Roosevelt is widely regarded as being the first modern feminist first lady. Today, the role of first lady is still defined by the woman who holds that position, with Michelle Obama, Laura Bush, Hillary Rodham Clinton, Barbara Bush, and Rosalyn Carter each embracing different priorities during her tenure.

Some recent first ladies, among them Nancy Reagan and Hillary Rodham Clinton, have exercised undisguised public power. Following President Obama's election, many Americans wondered whether First Lady Michelle Obama would take up the reigns as policy leader, but that has not been the case. And with women becoming an increasing proportion of the pool of candidates deemed eligible to be president, a woman's election to the presidency in the near future becomes almost assured. As President Richard Nixon remarked: "Certainly in the next 50 years we shall see a woman president, perhaps sooner than you think. A woman can and should be able to do any political job that a man can do."[40]

The First Lady

Much like the presidency itself, the office of the first lady has been defined by the individuals who have occupied it. That women as different as Barbara Bush, the wife of President George H. W. Bush, and Hillary Rodham Clinton, the wife of President Bill Clinton, could consecutively and successfully serve as first lady demonstrates the open-mindedness with which the American people view the role. First Lady Michelle Obama has shunned the policy-oriented role that Hillary Rodham Clinton forged, though she has prioritized the issue of childhood obesity, using her status to bring attention to the issue and to shape policy impacting it. By and large, though, Obama has instead preferred to focus on raising the Obamas' young daughters, Malia and Sasha, and on the more ceremonial aspect of serving as first lady.

Other first ladies have used their proximity to the chief executive to influence policy concerns more broadly and more forcefully. Some have acted "behind the scenes," as was the case with Edith Wilson, the wife of Woodrow Wilson. Others have taken a more public role. Eleanor Roosevelt, the wife of Franklin D. Roosevelt, fought for many causes during her husband's administration, including human rights and civil rights for African Americans. Hillary Clinton transformed the office of first lady by serving, at her husband's appointment, as the chair of a presidential task force on health care reform. Her role in the task force, and indeed throughout the Clinton administration, proved to be a lightning rod for critics who thought that a first lady should not be so prominent. Laura Bush, the wife of President George W. Bush, by contrast was a more reserved and less public first lady.

When a Woman Is Elected President

As first lady, Barbara Bush speculated about the election of a woman president. She wryly commented, "Somewhere out in this audience may even be someone who will one day follow my footsteps and preside over the White House as the president's spouse. I wish him well!"[41]

FIGURE 13.4 ■ AMERICA'S WILLINGNESS TO VOTE FOR A WOMAN PRESIDENT What has been the trend since the late 1930s in the American electorate's willingness to vote for a woman president? What factors do you think explain this shift?

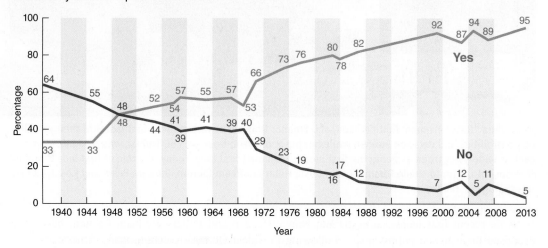

Over a period of time, pollsters have explored the possibility that Americans would vote for a qualified woman for president. Figure 13.4 shows that since 1937, when only 33 percent of Americans said they would cast their presidential ballot for a qualified woman, that figure has risen steadily. By 1999, 92 percent of respondents said they would vote for a female presidential candidate. In 2005, that number declined to 89 percent. One explanation for this drop could be that Senator Hillary Clinton was frequently mentioned at the time of the poll as a likely 2008 presidential candidate and respondents unwilling to support her candidacy responded that they were unwilling to vote for a woman for president. By 2013, though, the number had risen again, and 95 percent of Americans said they were willing to vote for a women for president.

Inevitably, the United States will have to face the issue of the role of the first gentleman. We can wonder about the dilemmas that might arise for the men who pioneer this new role. Will the ceremonial functions of the first spouse remain the same? Will the first gentleman choose the White House china; will he assist in the organization of state dinners and other social functions? Will he work in a private-sector job outside the White House? Will he have a voice in influencing administration policy?

We will learn the answers only when a married woman becomes president. In all likelihood, people's fascination with the role of first gentleman will wane when the novelty of the office wears off. And similarly to the various interpretations of the role that first ladies have created, it is likely that the role of first gentleman will be flexible and adaptable, responding to the inclinations and the personalities of the men who occupy it, as well as to public preferences.

Thinking Critically About What's Next in the Presidency

The American presidency is a dynamic institution, one that is molded by the individuals who serve as president and by the American people—by their changing interests, viewpoints, struggles, and needs. The presidency has a symbiotic relationship with the larger culture in which it exists; it is at once shaped by, and shapes, the culture.

The executive branch of the federal government is also flexible, incorporating the needs of diverse constituencies and participants, particularly in recent times. The continued evolution of the presidency as a more diverse institution is relatively ensured. How will this evolution take place in the next several decades? In your view, what is the likelihood of a woman being elected president in the next 20 years?

The presidency is a product of both the design of the framers and the desires of the citizenry. As the country's need for stronger presidents has increased, the resources and authorities of presidents have grown to accommodate new powers. But at what point does the presidency become, in the minds of Americans, *too* powerful?

Since the activist administration of Franklin D. Roosevelt, the characterization of the presidency as an "imperial" institution has dogged numerous presidents, most recently former president George W. Bush. Looking ahead, how will the citizens of the future view the scope of presidential power? The answer will depend in large part on the people themselves, particularly those who vote. It will depend on whom citizens elect to the highest office in the land; on how the people's opinions shape (or, in some cases, fail to shape) presidential actions; and on how the people's relationship with their presidents develops. Although the Constitution created a system in which presidential powers can be checked institutionally, the framers did not foresee the most significant checks on modern presidents: the will of the people and a ruthlessly investigatory media, both of which ensure that presidential power is not unrestrained.[42]

Summary

1. Presidential Elections

Campaigns are the primary mechanism by which candidates for the presidency outline their priorities and their positions on issues. It is during campaigns that the people forge their relationship with the president. Campaigns are key avenues by which individuals can become involved in the electoral process, such as through participating in nominating conventions, voting on Election Day, and voicing their opinions about the formal selection of the president through the Electoral College system.

2. Presidential Roles in the Domestic Sphere

As chief legislator, the president helps to define Congress's agenda through the annual State of the Union address and influences congressional legislation, particularly concerning the federal budget. Presidents also "legislate" when they veto legislation. As chief economist, the president uses a variety of tools, including the federal budget and the appointment of the chair of the Federal Reserve, to shape economic policy. As party leader, the president helps party members get elected to federal, state, and local offices.

3. Presidential Roles in the Foreign Policy Sphere

As chief diplomat, the president and the administration shape the foreign policy of the United States. As commander in chief, the president is the leader of all branches of the armed forces.

4. Overlap in the President's Domestic and Foreign Policy Roles

The president's roles of chief executive and chief of state encompass both domestic and foreign policy spheres. The responsibility as chief executive includes the job of chief administrator of the entire executive branch of government, including the cabinet departments. As chief of state, the president is the ceremonial head of state, a function that is carried out by a separate officeholder in many other nations.

5. The President and the Executive Branch

Leading the executive branch of the federal government is among the president's top responsibilities. Key executive branch offices are the vice president, the cabinet, and the Executive Office of the President (EOP). The EOP includes the White House Office, the Office of Management and Budget, the National Security Council, and the Council of Economic Advisers. Each office assists the president in devising and implementing policy.

6. Presidential Succession

A president who dies in office is succeeded by the vice president, the Speaker of the House, the president pro tem of the Senate, and then by a specified order of cabinet officials, according to the Presidential Succession Act of 1947. When a president becomes incapacitated in office, the Twenty-Fifth Amendment to the Constitution prescribes the course of action.

7. Sources of Presidential Power

Article II, Sections 2 and 3, of the U.S. Constitution enumerate the expressed powers of the president. Inherent powers emanate from the "take care" clause of the Constitution and have been asserted by presidents as constitutionally implied. Statutory powers include powers that Congress grants presidents, and special presidential powers include emergency powers, executive privilege, and the power to issue executive orders.

8. The People as a Source of Presidential Power

Because the people are a major source of presidential power, presidents continuously seek to secure public support. To that end, presidents exploit their easy access to the "bully pulpit" and the media. High public approval ratings can be an important source of presidential power and are of particular help in getting Congress to enact popular presidential proposals.

9. The Evolution of Presidential Power

The presidential powers of George Washington contrast strikingly with the powers of contemporary presidents. Presidential power first expanded during the administration of Thomas Jefferson, and this authority continued to grow through Andrew Jackson's tenure of office. Franklin D. Roosevelt's administration witnessed the greatest expansion in executive power to date, to the point that modern presidencies have been characterized as "imperial presidencies." The Watergate scandal in 1973 significantly damaged the notion of the imperial presidency. Since then, presidents have fought hard to secure the public trust while often facing media that are skeptical of their integrity and motivations.

10. Women in the White House

Traditionally, the most prominent role for women in the White House has been that of first lady. Some first ladies, among them Eleanor Roosevelt and Hillary Rodham Clinton, have been much more powerful and visible public figures than others. As the pool of potential female presidential candidates increases, there is a growing likelihood that a woman will be elected president.

Key Terms

approval ratings 412

articles of impeachment 418

balanced ticket 402

cabinet 402

chief of staff 405

emergency powers 410

executive agreement 399

Executive Office of the President (EOP) 405

executive order 409

executive privilege 410

expressed powers 408

honeymoon period 412

impeachment 418

inherent powers 408

line-item veto 396

National Security Council (NSC) 405

Office of Management and Budget (OMB) 406

press secretary 405

rally 'round the flag effect 414

signing statement 396

statutory powers 409

take care clause 408

Watergate 416

White House counsel 405

White House Office (WHO) 405

Works Progress Administration (WPA) 415

For Review

1. Explain the process of presidential elections. What role do states play in the process?
2. List the various roles of the president, and provide an example of each.
3. What are the sources of presidential power?
4. How has presidential power evolved over time?
5. Explain the organization and the functions of the Executive Office of the President.
6. Discuss Americans' willingness to vote for a qualified woman for president.

For Critical Thinking and Discussion

1. What do you think are the most important roles for presidents today? Why do these roles matter more than others?
2. Who do you think has been the greatest president in U.S. history? What characteristics do you admire about the president you chose?
3. What factors affect how frequently a president vetoes legislation? Does vetoing legislation signify presidential strength or weakness? Explain.
4. How did Watergate affect people's perception of the presidency and of government? Have there been lasting effects from this scandal? Explain.
5. Would people you know vote for a woman for president? Which demographic groups do you think would be more willing? Which groups would be less willing? Why?

Practice Quiz

MULTIPLE CHOICE: Choose the lettered item that answers the question correctly.

1. A written message that the president issues upon signing a bill into law is called
   a. a veto message.
   b. a presidential resolution.
   c. a signing statement.
   d. an executive decree.

2. Appointing the Fed chair and submitting a budget to Congress are part of the president's responsibilities as
   a. party leader.
   b. chief economist.
   c. chief legislator.
   d. chief diplomat.

3. Appointing the cabinet and determining how the bureaucracy will implement the laws are part of the president's responsibilities as
   a. chief executive.
   b. chief economist.
   c. chief legislator.
   d. chief diplomat.

4. The office that develops policies and protects the president's legal and political interests is
   a. the Executive Office of the President.
   b. the Chief Executive's Office.
   c. the Office of Management and Budget.
   d. the White House Office.

5. The office that creates the president's annual budget is
   a. the Executive Office of the President.
   b. the Chief Executive's Office.
   c. the Office of Management and Budget.
   d. the White House Office.

6. Presidential powers that are implied in the Constitution are called
   a. enumerated powers.
   b. inherent powers.
   c. expressed powers.
   d. statutory powers.

7. Presidential powers granted to presidents by congressional action are called
   a. enumerated powers.
   b. inherent powers.
   c. expressed powers.
   d. statutory powers.

8. The right of the president to withhold information from Congress or the courts is called
   a. emergency powers.
   b. executive privilege.
   c. expressed powers.
   d. statutory powers.

9. A time early in a new president's administration characterized by optimistic approval by the public is called
   a. the rose-colored-glasses period.
   b. the honeymoon period.
   c. the benefit-of-the-doubt period.
   d. the goodwill period.

10. During the Nixon administration, a scandal involving burglaries and the subsequent cover-up by high-level administration officials was called
    a. Watergate.
    b. Iran-Contra.
    c. Whitewater.
    d. Newport.

FILL IN THE BLANKS

11. The _____ is the group of experts chosen by the president to serve as advisers on running the country.

12. The executive staff member who serves as both an adviser to the president and manager of the White House Office is the _____.

13. The _____ consists of the top foreign policy advisers and relevant cabinet officials who advise the president on matters of foreign policy and national security.

14. The constitutional basis for inherent powers is the _____.

15. A(n) _____ is the power of the president to issue orders that carry the force of law.

Research AND Action

Internet Resources

270 to Win

www.270towin.com This interactive website demonstrates how the Electoral College outcome is determined; users can experiment with altering the results of elections. It also contains past voting information for all states.

Center for the Study of the Presidency

www.thepresidency.org This research center analyzes presidential leadership and offers seminars and symposia for presidential researchers, including the Center Fellows program for undergraduate students.

Presidential Libraries

You can find the websites of the libraries of recent presidents, which typically include a wealth of information about individual presidencies and archival resources, by searching "[President's name] Presidential Library."

The White House

www.whitehouse.gov You can visit the White House website for information about current issues and news, the text of presidential speeches, links to cabinet departments, the EOP, and information about the first lady and the vice president.

Recommended Readings

Borrelli, MaryAnne. *The President's Cabinet: Gender, Power, and Representation.* Boulder, CO: Lynne Rienner, 2002. Analysis of the evolution of presidential cabinets in terms of gender representation.

Ehrenhalt, Alan. *The United States of Ambition: Politicians, Power and the Pursuit of Office.* New York: Times Books, 1991. Interesting account of the importance of personal drive and ambition in catapulting would-be presidents to the White House.

Halberstam, David. *The Best and the Brightest.* New York: Fawcett Books, 1993. Riveting analysis of how the Kennedy and Johnson administrations entrenched the United States in the war in Vietnam.

Milkis, Sidney M. *The American Presidency: Origins and Development, 1776–2011.* Washington, D.C.: CQ Press, 2011. This volume describes the constitutional foundations as well as the social, economic, political, and international factors that have shaped the Constitution's expansion through its origins to the Obama presidency.

Neustadt, Richard E. *Presidential Power and the Modern President.* New York: The Free Press, 1990. Update of the author's classic 1960 volumes, explaining the evolution of power in the modern presidency and probing, in particular, presidents' ability to persuade.

Schlesinger, Arthur M., Jr. *The Imperial Presidency.* Boston: Houghton Mifflin, 1973. Classic volume describing how the presidency has become a rarely checked, "imperial" institution (introduction updated in the 2004 edition).

Woodward, Bob, and Carl Bernstein. *All the President's Men,* 2nd ed. New York: Simon & Schuster, 1994. Classic work that launched investigative journalism, particularly concerning the presidency, in which the authors describe their investigation of the Watergate scandal that led to President Richard Nixon's resignation.

Movies of Interest

John Adams (2008)

This television mini-series stars Paul Giamatti and Stephen Dillane in a chronicle of the first 50 years of the U.S. presidency.

Recount (2008)

This movie chronicles the 2000 presidential election, focusing on the controversy surrounding ballot counting in Florida that culminated in the U.S. Supreme Court case *Bush v. Gore*.

Air Force One (1997)

In this suspense thriller, the president of the United States, played by Harrison Ford, is forced to do battle with terrorist hijackers aboard Air Force One.

The American President (1995)

Rob Reiner directed this comedic drama about an unmarried male president (portrayed by Michael Douglas) and a lobbyist (Annette Bening), who fall in love.

All the President's Men (1976)

In this 1976 film adaptation of the book by the same name, Robert Redford and Dustin Hoffman star as *Washington Post* reporters Bob Woodward and Carl Bernstein (respectively), who uncover the details of the Watergate scandal that led to President Nixon's resignation.

In addition, there are numerous biographical movies of American presidents, including many that air on the A&E network's *Biography* series. You can find these programs at www.biography.com.

CHAPTER 14

The Bureaucracy

THEN

The federal bureaucracy under President George Washington had three departments and two offices staffed with public servants engaged in mostly clerical work, serving a national population of 4 million.

NOW

Almost 3 million civilian federal bureaucrats—plus close to 28 million state, local, private for-profit, and nonprofit bureaucrats—engaged in every occupation imaginable, serve a national population of over 310 million.

NEXT

Will the use of e-government boost citizen satisfaction with the bureaucracy?

Will the best and the brightest respond to the call to serve, as a large proportion of federal employees retire in the next decade?

Will the volume of public service outsourced to private organizations continue to increase?

Public servants in the executive

branch of government are truly the key to citizens' satisfaction with their government. Citizens turn to the government to solve their problems and provide services. Through policy-making processes, Congress and the president determine which problems the national government will address and what services it will provide. After Congress and the president approve policies and the funding to pay for their implementation, millions of public servants put them into action. It is the daily implementation of public policy by millions of bureaucrats that citizens focus on when they are evaluating government performance.

In October 2013, the daily implementation of many federal public policies stopped for 16 days. Congress and the president did not approve the funding necessary to pay for policy implementation and so the government did not have authority to spend money at the start of the 2014 fiscal year, which began on October 1, 2013. Without money to pay the bills, including wages, federal agencies had to send nonessential bureaucrats home. With about 40 percent of the civilian workforce on furlough (forced days off), millions of Americans were affected by eliminated or reduced services and delays in government assistance payments.[1] In addition to the citizens who were harmed, many observers in government feared that the partial government shutdown would discourage workers from taking government jobs at a time when record numbers of government workers are resigning and retiring from government service.

Despite this wave of departures, almost 3 million national civilian bureaucrats and 1.5 million military personnel provide public services. Beyond the legions of federal public servants, millions of state and local bureaucrats assist in implementing national public policies. In addition, through grants and contracts with the national government, millions of employees in private for-profit businesses and in nonprofit organizations help to do the work of the national government. President Barack Obama estimated the cost of providing national public services in his proposed 2015 budget to be $3.9 trillion.[2] This staggering sum amounts to $10.7 billion per day, $446 million per hour, or $7.4 million per minute.

For their trillions of tax dollars, Americans expect the millions of government and nongovernment employees to provide public services and benefits efficiently and effectively. In our democracy, citizens also expect accountability. But accountability is difficult when the services bureaucrats provide often involve complex procedures and include ensuring justice and domestic tranquility, defending the nation, and promoting the general welfare.

Bureaucrats and Bureaucracy

bureaucrats
people employed in a government executive branch unit to implement public policy; public administrators; public servants

bureaucracy
the collection of all national executive branch organizations

What do you want to be when you grow up? How many times have you been asked that question? Chances are that whatever your career aspiration, you can do it as a **bureaucrat**—that is, a government employee working in the executive branch implementing public policies. The federal government employs more people than any other single employer in the nation in over 900 occupational categories. Currently, the federal **bureaucracy,** the collection of all national executive branch organizations, is experiencing a "retirement wave, with nearly twice as many executive branch employees leaving in the past fiscal year than did in 2009."[3] To ensure that

≫From A (air traffic controller) to Z (zookeeper), and every occupation in between, whatever your dream job, you can do it as a bureaucrat. As a matter of fact, some occupations are available only as government jobs. Can you think of one or two occupations for which only governments hire? Can you think of a (legal) occupation for which the government does not hire?

the best and the brightest are hired for public service, the Obama administration is bringing a 21st-century approach to the federal hiring process, making the process faster and more candidate friendly.

Even with an improved hiring process, the federal bureaucracy must deal with the perpetual criticism leveled against it. Unfortunately, for most people the word *bureaucracy* conjures up the image of a large government organization with inefficient, dehumanizing procedures that require tedious paperwork. They visualize long lines at the Department of Motor Vehicles as uncaring workers, who they believe the government cannot fire, slowly process mounds of forms. Taxpayers are not the only people who think and speak negatively of the bureaucracy. Even our presidents and congressional members—who rely on bureaucrats to implement their policy promises—historically have not hesitated to criticize bureaucrats. Are the negative images and the criticisms of bureaucrats and bureaucracies fair? Before we can answer, we must understand who the bureaucrats are, what they are hired to do, and how they are expected to accomplish their work.

Who Are the Bureaucrats?

Because elected officials and ordinary citizens perpetually criticize bureaucrats and bureaucracies, individuals working in the national bureaucracy do not take being called a bureaucrat as a compliment. Bureaucrats prefer the term *public servant,* because that phrase captures how they see themselves and their essential job goal.[4] Charles Goodsell, a respected scholar of public administration and public policy, notes that studies show government employees to be very hard workers who are motivated by the recognition of the importance of public service. This motivation is key because private-sector employees historically have received higher salaries and worked shorter hours.[5] Compared with private-sector employees, public servants have higher levels of formal education, must comply with more stringent codes of behavior, and express a greater concern for serving the public.[6] In addition, government bureaucrats tend to report somewhat higher levels of job satisfaction than do their private-sector counterparts.[7]

Very few children say that they want to be bureaucrats. Yet millions do aspire to careers as public servants, including teachers, police officers, lawyers, and health care professionals. National, state, and local governments hire professionals such as these to implement public

The Bureaucratic Structure

shadow bureaucrats
people hired and paid by private for-profit and nonprofit organizations that implement public policy through a government contract

contracting-out
also called *outsourcing* or *privatizing;* a process by which the government contracts with a private for-profit or nonprofit organization to provide public services, such as disaster relief, or resources needed by the government, such as fighter planes

bureaucratic structure
a large organization with the following features: a division of labor, specialization of job tasks, hiring systems based on worker competency, hierarchy with a vertical chain of command, and standard operating procedures

policy—to do the business of government. Chances are, whatever your major in college, you can get a job as a public servant. In fact, approximately 40 percent of federal civilian public servants and almost 50 percent of both state and local public servants have at least a bachelor's degree. In comparison, only about 25 percent of private-sector workers have at least a bachelor's degree.[8]

Joining the approximately 23 million national, state, and local bureaucrats are the so-called **shadow bureaucrats**—employees on the payroll of private for-profit businesses and private nonprofit organizations who have received government contracts and grants. Through a process of **contracting-out** (also called *outsourcing* or *privatizing*), the government signs work contracts with these organizations to assist in the implementation of national policy. In other words, shadow bureaucrats do the work of government, but they do not receive a government paycheck.

Today, a mix of national, state, and local bureaucrats, as well as shadow bureaucrats, deliver national public services and share a similar work environment. That is, they all work in bureaucratic organizations.

The Bureaucratic Structure

Max Weber (1864–1920), the "father of sociology," is famous for creating an ideal model of a bureaucracy. As shown in Figure 14.1, Weber's **bureaucratic structure** had the following features: a division of labor, specialization of job tasks, hiring systems based on worker competency, hierarchy with a vertical chain of command, and standard operating procedures. Today, government agencies as well as large, nongovernmental organizations typically conform to this bureaucratic structure.

Colleges and universities (public and private) are good examples of bureaucratic organizations. They have a division of labor with specialization of tasks. (Consider the various academic departments, each specializing in a different discipline.) They hire employees (such as professors, computer technicians, and student affairs staff) with the knowledge, skills, and abilities essential to doing their jobs well. Colleges and universities also have a hierarchy with a chain of command (faculty members report to chairpersons, who report to a dean, who reports to the vice president for academic affairs, who reports to the president, who makes final decisions). University employees implement standardized procedures to register students for classes, determine financial aid eligibility, and punish violations of the conduct code.

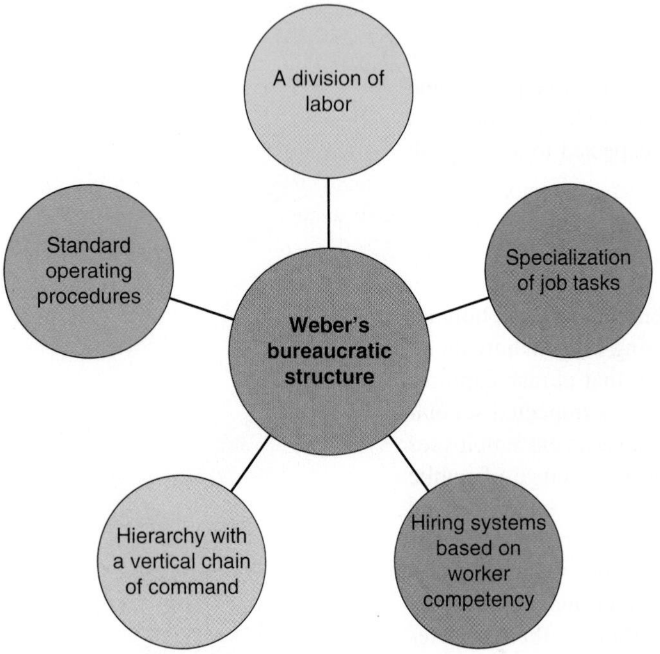

Although most people think of government when they hear the word *bureaucracy,* a bureaucracy is *any* organization with Weber's bureaucratic structure. Yet in this chapter, as is appropriate to our study of American national government, we focus on the departments and agencies that compose the national government bureaucracy. And even though most people think of government employees when they hear the term *bureaucrat,* nongovernment employees, as we have seen, may also be paid with taxpayer money to serve the public, and so it is appropriate that we consider these shadow bureaucrats, too.

Federal Bureaucrats

Political scientists distinguish among national bureaucrats according to several factors, including the processes by which they are hired, the procedures by which they can be fired, and the grounds for which they can be fired. On the basis of these factors, we can differentiate among three categories of national civilian bureaucrats: political appointees, Senior Executive Service appointees, and civil servants.

FIGURE 14.1

Weber's Model of Bureaucracy

Political Appointees

In 1863, President Abraham Lincoln, suffering from small-pox, told his secretary to "send all the office seekers in here. I finally have something I can give to them all." Indeed, before the creation of the federal civil service system in 1883, presidents had the authority to hire bureaucrats, selecting whomever they wanted and establishing whatever qualifications they desired, through the **patronage system** of hiring. Under the patronage system, hordes of men seeking government jobs presented themselves to the president after each election.

Now, after each presidential election, the federal government publishes the **plum book,** which lists thousands of top jobs in the federal bureaucracy to which the president will appoint people through the patronage system. There is no standard process for assessing the knowledge, skills, and abilities needed for appointive positions, nor is there open competition for these patronage jobs. Further, because citizens expect presidents to be responsive and accountable to them, and presidents rely on their political appointees to meet those expectations, presidents tend to appoint people who support their policy preferences. Patronage positions come with a downside for the appointees: no job security. The president not only hires but also can fire political appointees at his pleasure.

Today, presidents are able to hire approximately 3,000 political appointees through the patronage system. These appointees serve under the president, in the top several layers in the federal executive branch's hierarchy (vertical chain of command). Below the layers of political appointees are members of the Senior Executive Service (SES), and below them are the civil servants.

>This engraving depicts President James Garfield's assassination. Shot in July 1881, Garfield died two and a half months later of a fatal heart attack brought on by his doctors' attempts to find the assassin's bullet in his body. What was his assassin's motivation? How did the tragedy spark proposals to change the process of choosing civil servants?

patronage system
a personnel system in which the chief executive officer (CEO) can appoint whomever he or she wants to top bureaucratic positions, without the need for open competition for applicants; those hired through patronage typically serve at the pleasure of the CEO who hired them

plum book
a publication that lists the top jobs in the bureaucracy to which the president will appoint people through the patronage system

Senior Executive Service (SES)
a unique personnel system for top managerial, supervisory, and policy positions offering less job security but higher pay than the merit-based civil service system

Senior Executives

The keystone of the Civil Service Reform Act of 1978, was the creation of the **Senior Executive Service (SES)** to improve public service.[9] The SES is comprised of the top managerial, supervisory, and policy positions that link the political appointees to the rest of the federal bureaucracy.

The SES bureaucrat is a hybrid of the political appointee and the civil servant. At least 90 percent of SES bureaucrats are career appointees hired based on merit through an open, competitive process. These employees can be moved from job to job and from agency to agency, as can political appointees. However, unlike political appointees, they cannot be fired at the discretion of the president. To fire a SES career appointee, the government must prove that the employee is not performing the job, is performing it poorly, or is performing it in a manner that violates agency rules or the law.

The remaining SES bureaucrats are noncareer and temporary appointees hired without open, competitive procedures. The noncareer and temporary SES bureaucrats are appointed with approval of the Office of Personnel Management (the federal government's central personnel office) and the White House Office of Presidential Personnel, and they can be removed at the pleasure of the president.[10]

Civil Servants

During the first century of U.S. history, all federal bureaucrats were hired through the patronage system. Then in 1883, after the assassination of President James Garfield by an unsuccessful seeker of a patronage position, Congress and President Chester Arthur (1881–1885) approved the

Education Requirements* and Salary Ranges for White-Collar Federal Civil Servants (2010–2015)**

TABLE 14.1

LEVEL	SALARY RANGE	QUALIFYING EDUCATION
GS-1	$17,803–$22,269	No high school diploma required
GS-2	$20,017–$25,191	High school graduation or equivalent
GS-3	$21,840–$28,392	One academic year above high school
GS-4	$24,518–$31,871	Two academic years above high school, or associate's degree
GS-5	$27,431–$28,345	Four academic years above high school leading to a bachelor's degree, or a bachelor's degree
GS-6	$30,577–$39,748	
GS-7	$33,979–$44,176	Bachelor's degree with superior academic achievement or one academic year of graduate education or law school
GS-8	$37,631–$48,917	
GS-9	$41,563–$54,028	Master's (or equivalent graduate degree) or two academic years of progressively higher level graduate education
GS-10	$45,771–$59,505	
GS-11	$50,287–$65,371	PhD or equivalent degree or three academic years of progressively higher level graduate education
GS-12	$60,274–$78,355	Completion of all requirements for a doctoral or equivalent degree (for research positions only)
GS-13	$71,674–$93,175	Appropriate specialized experience
GS-14	$84,697–$110,104	Appropriate specialized experience
GS-15	$99,628–$129,517	Appropriate specialized experience

*Table shows the amount and level of education typically required for each grade for which education alone can be qualifying.

**Congress froze salaries for white-collar federal civil servants at the 2010 rates through 2015.

SOURCES: U.S. Office of Personnel Management, "Salary Table, 2012 GS," www.opm.gov/flsa/oca/12tables/html/gs.asp; GovCentral, "What Determines Where You Stand on the GS Scale?," http://govcentral.monster.com/benefits/articles/1757-what-determines-where-you-stand-on-the-gs-scale.

merit-based civil service

a personnel system in which bureaucrats are hired on the basis of the principles of competence, equal opportunity (open competition), and political neutrality; once hired, these civil servants have job protection

civil servants

bureaucrats hired through a merit-based personnel system and who have job protection

Pendleton Civil Service Act. This law introduced a merit-based civil service system to the national government. The hiring principles of the **merit-based civil service** system are open competition, competence, and political neutrality. The goal of the Pendleton Act was to eliminate the expectation that government jobs were the spoils of an electoral victory, distributed by the winning candidate. Those calling for the reform of the patronage system argued it was corrupt. **Civil servants** are bureaucrats hired through the merit-based personnel system established by the Pendleton Act and reinforced by the 1978 Civil Service Reform Act.

OPEN COMPETITION AND COMPETENCE Today, merit-based civil service jobs, which compose close to 90 percent of the federal bureaucracy, are open and accessible to all who wish to compete for a position. The competition requires that candidates prove their competence to do the job (their merit). Jobs covered by the merit-based civil service system are analyzed and ranked on the basis of the knowledge, skills, and abilities needed to do the job competently. A job's rank determines its salary. The pay scales offer equal pay for jobs of equal worth. (See Table 14.1 for the pay scales and education requirements for white-collar federal government jobs.)

Several national laws have helped to make today's civil servants, as a group, look more like the U.S. population at large than they did in the past. Title VII of the 1964 Civil Rights Act, as amended, prohibits employers, including the government, from making personnel decisions based on factors irrelevant to job competence, such as sex, race, color, ethnicity, age, and disabilities that can be reasonably accommodated. The merit principles of the 1978 Civil Service Reform Act (CSRA) reiterate this prohibition against discrimination in personnel practices. The bans against discrimination in Title VII and the CSRA do not apply to the positions of elected officials or political appointees.

Title VI of the 1964 Civil Rights Act prohibits discrimination based on race, color, religion, and ethnicity in educational opportunities offered by institutions receiving federal funding. Title IX, which was added to the act in 1972, extended this prohibition to sex-based

Then   Now

> As the educational opportunities for women and minority men expanded and became comparable to those of white men, due to the implementation of Title VI of the Civil Rights Act of 1964 and Title IX (enacted in 1972), elected officials have become more aware of the benefits of and citizen expectations for a representative bureaucracy. From political appointees, such as the members of the president's cabinet, down to civil servants, today's federal bureaucracy is more diverse and therefore more representative of the population than in the past. Increased diversity is evident when comparing President Kennedy's cabinet with President Obama's cabinet. With women earning the majority of bachelor's and master's degrees today, do you think a cabinet dominated by women will exist in the not-too-distant future?

discrimination. Enforcement of these laws has increased the diversity of people who are able to gain the education and experience needed to do government jobs competently. The interaction of Titles VI, VII, and IX, combined with the merit principles of the Pendleton Act and the CSRA of 1978, has fostered the movement toward **representative bureaucracy,** which means that the bureaucrats, as a group, resemble the larger population whom they serve in demographic characteristics such as race, age, ethnicity, sex, religion, and economic status.

representative bureaucracy
a bureaucracy in which the people serving resemble the larger population whom they serve in demographic characteristics such as race, age, ethnicity, sex, religion, and economic status

POLITICAL NEUTRALITY   Merit-based civil servants cannot be fired merely because someone with different political beliefs is elected or appointed to supervise them. They can be fired for poor quality of work (misfeasance), or for nonperformance of their work (nonfeasance), or for violating the law or the rules and regulations that guide their work (malfeasance). The merit-based civil service system thus gives competent civil servants job protection and does not require them to adhere to the president's policy preferences (unlike political appointees). Hence, the civil service system supports political neutrality.

CIVIL SERVICE REFORM ACT (1978)   "There is widespread criticism of federal government performance. The public suspects that there are too many government workers, that they are underworked, overpaid, and insulated from the consequences of incompetence."[11] With those words, President Jimmy Carter (1977–1981) announced proposed civil service reforms in 1978. The resulting Civil Service Reform Act of 1978 reaffirmed and expanded the merit principles established by the Pendleton Act, established the SES, and reorganized the management of the national civil service.

Three new independent administrative agencies—the Office of Personnel Management (OPM), the Merit System Protection Board (MSPB), and the Federal Labor Relations Authority (FLRA)—replaced the old Civil Service Commission, the central personnel office created by the Pendleton Act. Today, the OPM, as the central personnel office, is responsible for developing and implementing merit-based civil service personnel policies and procedures. The MSPB ensures proper implementation of the merit system. The CSRA also legislated for the collective bargaining rights (unionization rights) of national civil servants and created the FLRA to monitor relations between unionized bureaucrats and the federal government.

UNIONIZED CIVIL SERVANTS   Twenty-seven percent of U.S. federal civil servants belong to labor unions. By comparison, the percentage of unionized workers among private-sector employees is 7 percent.[12] Whereas about 90 percent of U.S. Postal Service employees are union

Then Now Next

Civil Service Hiring Reform Progress

Then (2009)	Now (2012)
President Obama announces reforms to bring federal hiring into the 21st century.	The Office of Personnel Management has a website providing the latest news and changes in federal hiring.
Approximately 50 percent of job opportunity announcements (JOA) are in written plain language, as opposed to bureaucratic jargon.	Approximately 85 percent of JOAs are written in plain language, as opposed to bureaucratic jargon.
Approximately 35 percent of JOAs require only the uploading of a resume and cover letter.	Approximately 90 percent of JOAs require only the uploading of a resume and cover letter.
Approximately 35 percent of JOAs do not require specialized questionnaires or essays.	Approximately 99 percent of JOAs do not require specialized questionnaires or essays.
After the hiring manager validates the need for the job, the average number of days to hire is 122.	After the hiring manager validates the need for the job, the average number of days to hire is 87.
Many applicants experience a "black hole," never receiving a response to their application.	Applicants are notified in a timely manner at several stages of the hiring process, eliminating the black hole.

SOURCES: U.S. Office of Personnel Management, "2013 Annual Performance Report," www.opmgov/about-us/budget-performance/performance; U.S. Office of Personnel Management, "Measures Cut Previous Red Tape Clogging the Federal Hiring System," May 11, 2010, www.opm.gov/news/opm-omb-announce-unpresedented-hiring-reforms,1562.apx.

WHAT'S NEXT?

> The U.S. Government Accountability Office estimates that 30 percent of the federal workforce will be eligible to retire in the next 3 years. Will the salary freeze that began in 2010 make it hard to replace retiring bureaucrats?

> Will partisan politics and the fear of a future government shutdown affect federal hiring?

> Will the new, improved hiring process help to bring the best and the brightest to federal civil service?

members, the level of union membership among bureaucrats in the State Department is close to zero. Part of the explanation for the range of unionization levels across national agencies is the percentage of each agency's workers that is composed of blue-collar workers. In general, blue-collar workers are likelier to be union members than are white-collar workers.

Unionized civil servants have leverage to negotiate certain conditions of work. For example, they may bargain for improved training opportunities and enhanced due process protections in disciplinary matters. Federal civil service employee unions cannot negotiate salaries or work hours, however. And unlike private-sector unions, federal civil servant unions do not have the legal right to strike. The prohibition of strikes by federal civil servants is typically justified by the fact that these workers provide essential services that are vital to public safety. A strike by these workers would therefore threaten public safety and health.

BRINGING A 21ST-CENTURY APPROACH TO FEDERAL HIRING "Federal workers fill crucial roles that defend Americans from terrorism, infectious diseases, food-borne pathogens, forest fires and countless other threats. . . . [Therefore,] we must cut the red tape clogging the federal hiring process in order to bring aboard outstanding applicants quickly," declared then–OPM director John Berry as he introduced reforms to the federal merit-based hiring process in May 2010. The reforms attempt to speed up the process and reinforce the core merit principles by simplifying the application process, taking advantage of digital technology, enhancing communications with applicants throughout the hiring process, and supporting more proactive recruitment on college campuses.[13] (See the "Then, Now, Next" feature for some of the reforms.)

Unfortunately, at the same time that the federal hiring process was made more efficient and effective, Congress and the president enacted a pay freeze for federal bureaucrats and raised the pension contributions required of future civil servants. By 2012, congressional Republicans had proposed no less than 20 bills that would negatively affect the federal workforce, according to federal employee unions. The proposals included imposing mandatory 2-week, unpaid furloughs; extending the pay freeze through at least 2015; limiting the number of replacement hires (such as allowing only one new hire for every three employees who leave government service); and increasing pension contributions while cutting back on pension payments.[14] These proposals (several of which have become law), intended to help balance the federal budget, come at a time when the number of students who claim they want to work in the public sector is dropping precipitously, according to the National Association of Colleges. Meanwhile, federal retirements are increasing.[15] Add to this combination of events the threat of government shutdowns caused by partisan politics in the annual budget process and you can understand why people worry about the federal government's ability to hire the best and the brightest to serve the nation. These realities help account for the growth in the contracting-out of government work.

State, Local, and Shadow Bureaucrats

Today, the overwhelming majority of the almost 20 million state and local bureaucrats, and at least 7 million shadow bureaucrats,[16] provide various national public services. Through devolution and contracting-out, the federal government relies on these nonfederal bureaucrats to serve the people's daily needs. Federal bureaucrats are responsible for monitoring these state, local, and shadow bureaucrats' compliance with the rules and regulations that come with devolution and outsourcing.

As you may recall from Chapter 3, devolution is the federal government's shifting of greater responsibility for financing and administering public policies to state and local governments, putting the implementation of national policy in the hands of state and local bureaucrats. Mandates in federal laws require state and local governments to implement national policies. In cases where federal law preempts (takes precedence over) state and local law, state and local bureaucrats have to implement federal policy instead of state or local programs. Preemption is common, for example, in the area of environmental protection, where state and local officials must ensure private- and public-sector compliance with federal air, water, and landfill standards.

As we've seen, the national government also contracts with shadow bureaucracies—private for-profit and nonprofit organizations—to provide vital services as well as to produce certain resources needed to serve the public. Outsourcing, for example, includes the federal government's contracting-out with Lockheed Martin and Boeing for the production of defense resources such as helmets, fighter planes, and laser-guided missiles. As part of the Affordable Care Act of 2010 (also known as Obamacare), the government contracted out the bulk of the work to develop the website through which citizens can purchase health insurance. Traditionally, too, the government undertakes large capital projects such as the construction of roads and government buildings through contracts with private businesses. Further, the federal government outsources medical as well as social research to cure disease and address the ills of society. And through government contracts, the Red Cross has dispensed disaster relief for decades. The federal government's contracts totaled more than $520 billion in 2012.[17]

The federal government expects that contracting-out will reduce the expense of government by eliminating the overhead costs (including employee benefits and basic operating costs) of producing public goods and services. Outsourcing also provides a means by which the government can hire experts and specialists only when they are needed and keep them off the payroll at other times. Some observers also believe that private- and nonprofit-sector employees and organizations will be more efficient and effective than government bureaucracies. However, as we discuss later in this chapter, the benefits of contracting out are debatable.

Even with the increased use of state, local, and shadow bureaucrats, the federal bureaucracy itself is neither small nor streamlined. It is composed of thousands of bodies with a variety of names and organizational structures. The federal bureaucracy, an evolving organism, continues to grow in complexity even as it privatizes and devolves more of its work.

The Evolution of the Federal Bureaucracy

Four million people resided in the United States in 1789, the year George Washington was sworn in as the first president. Most of them lived off the land and were self-sufficient; they expected few services from the federal government. The federal bureaucracy consisted of the Department of War, Department of Foreign Affairs, Treasury Department, Attorney General's Office, and Postal Services Office. Those three departments and two offices handled the core functions demanded of the national government at that time: respectively, providing defense, managing foreign affairs, collecting revenues and paying bills, resolving lawsuits and legal questions, and delivering mail. With the exception of defense, the work of public servants was mostly clerical in nature.

FIGURE 14.2 ■ GROWTH IN CIVILIAN BUREAUCRATS What has been the trend in the growth of the national civilian bureaucracy since 1965? What has been the pattern for the growth of state and local bureaucracies over the same period? What explains the patterns?

SOURCES: News Release, USDL-12-040, Bureau of Labor Statistics, March 9, 2012, www.bls.gov/news.release/pdf/empsit.pdf; Deirdre Baker, "Annual Survey of Public Employment & Payroll Summary Report: 2011," August 22, 2013, www2.census.gov/govs/apes/2011_summary_report.pdf.

FIGURE 14.3 ■ GROWTH IN FEDERAL EXPENDITURES What has been the overall trend in the growth of federal government spending since 1940? What would you say about the pattern since 2000? What political factors—domestic and international—explain the trend in federal spending over the past decade?

SOURCE: White House Office of Management and Budget, "Table 4.1: Outlays by Agency, 1962–2019," www.whitehouse.gov/omb/budget/Historicals.

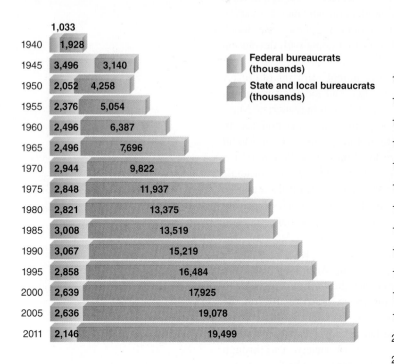

1,033

Year	Federal bureaucrats (thousands)	State and local bureaucrats (thousands)
1940	1,928	
1945	3,496	3,140
1950	2,052	4,258
1955	2,376	5,054
1960	2,496	6,387
1965	2,496	7,696
1970	2,944	9,822
1975	2,848	11,937
1980	2,821	13,375
1985	3,008	13,519
1990	3,067	15,219
1995	2,858	16,484
2000	2,639	17,925
2005	2,636	19,078
2011	2,146	19,499

Year	Budget
1940	$10
1945	$93
1950	$43
1955	$68
1960	$92
1965	$118
1970	$196
1975	$332
1980	$591
1985	$946
1990	$1,253
1995	$1,516
2000	$1,789
2005	$2,472
2011	$3,603

Budget in billions of current dollars (rounded to nearest billion)

Since the nation's founding, congresses and presidents have enacted laws creating thousands of executive branch bureaucracies. The size, scope, and complexity of today's federal bureaucracy are products of elected officials' efforts to respond to the needs and demands of U.S. citizens. Elected policy makers rely on the federal bureaucracy to faithfully execute the laws they enact, providing a range of services and benefits that would shock George Washington.

Today, as the U.S. population tops 310 million, approximately 2,000 executive branch units, employing more than 4 million bureaucrats (2.7 million civilian bureaucrats and about 1.5 million military personnel), implement volumes of national policies. The number of bureaucrats is comparable to the nation's population in 1789. Figures 14.2 and 14.3 show the growth in size and cost of the national bureaucracy since 1940.

Political scientists distinguish among five categories of executive branch organizations based on their structure and the type of work they perform: (1) departments, (2) independent administrative agencies, (3) independent regulatory commissions, (4) government corporations, and (5) agencies in the Executive Office of the President. Within each category there is much variation in size, structure, and function. When Congress and the president authorize a new policy, they must decide whether they will assign its implementation to an existing agency or create a new agency. If they choose the latter option, they must determine which type of agency to create.

Sources

EVOLUTION OF FEDERAL GOVERNMENT DEPARTMENTS

In 1789, there were three cabinet departments. Today, there are 15 cabinet departments, which, according to the Congressional Research Service, employ more than 90 percent of federal civilian employees. A review of the establishment of new departments since 1789 offers some insight into the expanding scope of federal activity over the nation's history.

	NUMBER OF CIVILIAN EMPLOYEES (2012)	BUDGET OUTLAY (2012) IN BILLIONS OF DOLLARS
State, 1789	41,438	$ 27.0
Treasury, 1789	112,461	$464.7
Interior, 1849	76,827	$ 12.9
Justice, 1870 (attorney general's office 1789; department status 1870)	117,016	$ 31.2
Agriculture, 1889	99,503	$139.7
Commerce, 1913 (separated from Department of Commerce and Labor, which was created in 1903)	44,317	$ 10.8
Labor, 1913 (separated from Department of Commerce and Labor, which was created in 1903)	17,752	$104.6
Defense, 1947 (previously Department of War, created 1789; Army Department and Navy Department created 1798)	729,559	$650.9
Housing & Urban Development, 1965	8,655	$ 49.6
Transportation, 1966	57,036	$ 75.2
Energy, 1977	15,632	$ 32.5
Health & Human Services, 1979 (created from Department of Health, Education and Welfare, established 1953)	74,017	$848.1
Education, 1979 (created from Department of Health, Education and Welfare, established 1953)	4,250	$ 57.5
Veterans Affairs, 1988	323,208	$124.1
Homeland Security, 2003	191,326	$ 47.4

SOURCES: U.S. Office of Personnel Management, "Employment and Trends—September 2012," www.opm.gov/policy-data-oversight/data-analysis-documentation/federal-employment-reports/employment-trends-data/2012/september/table-2/; White House Office of Management and Budget, "Table 4.1: Outlays by Agency, 1962–2019," www.whitehouse.gov/omb/budget/Historicals; Curtis W. Copeland, *The Federal Workforce: Characteristics and Trends* (Washington, D.C.: Congressional Research Service, 2011).

Evaluating the Evidence

1. Which department employs the most federal bureaucrats? Which employs the fewest?

2. For taxpayers, which is the most expensive department? Which is the least expensive?

3. What do the names of the departments indicate about the concerns and interests that have won federal policy makers' attention over the nation's history? What mobilized Congress and President George W. Bush to establish the Department of Homeland Security? Is there an area of national concern for which you would advocate Congress and the president establish a new department to address?

4. Seven departments have been created since 1965; however, the total number of federal civilian employees today is comparable to the number in 1965. What helps to explain this apparent paradox?

> In 1958, President Dwight D. Eisenhower signed into law the National Aeronautics and Space Act, which created NASA (the National Aeronautics and Space Administration). Congress viewed the Soviet Union's October 1957 launch of Sputnik 1, the first artificial satellite, as a threat to the national security of the United States and a challenge to U.S. technological leadership. NASA is responsible for the U.S. civilian space program. In October 2012, NASA's Curiosity rover created this self-portrait at Rocknest in Gale Crater on Mars. Like many government programs, many people are critical of the federal government's spending some of its limited resources on space programs and aerospace research; NASA's budget for fiscal year 2014 was about $17 billion. How does space exploration help fulfill the mission of the federal government?

department
one of fifteen executive branch units responsible for a broadly defined policy area and whose top administrator (secretary) is appointed by the president, is confirmed by the Senate, and serves at the discretion of the president

independent administrative agency
an executive branch unit created by Congress and the president that is responsible for a narrowly defined function and whose structure is intended to protect it from partisan politics

independent regulatory commission
an executive branch unit outside of cabinet departments responsible for developing standards of behavior within specific industries and businesses, monitoring compliance with these standards, and imposing sanctions on violators

Departments

The Department of Homeland Security, established in 2002, is the newest of 15 federal **departments,** each responsible for one broadly defined policy area. The president holds the 15 departments accountable through the appointment of a head official. *Secretary* is the title of this top political appointee in all departments except the Department of Justice, where the head is the attorney general. Although the Senate must confirm them, these top appointees serve at the president's pleasure. In addition to appointing the department secretaries, the president names bureaucrats to positions in several levels of the hierarchy below the secretaries. These political appointees have titles such as *deputy secretary, assistant deputy secretary, agency director,* and *deputy director.* "Analyzing the Sources" lists the 15 departments, from oldest to newest, and gives the number of employees and budget outlay for each in 2012.

Independent Administrative Agencies

Whereas each executive branch department has authority for a broadly defined policy area, a host of **independent administrative agencies** are each responsible for a more narrowly defined function of the national government. Congress and the president create these agencies to fulfill one of several purposes. Some of them, such as the Smithsonian Institution, were established to handle new governmental functions that did not easily fall within the scope of responsibilities of existing departments. Other independent administrative agencies support the work of existing departments and agencies, including recruiting and training employees (Office of Personnel Management) and managing government properties and records (General Services Administration). Still others, such as the National Science Foundation and the National Aeronautics and Space Administration, focus on research and preservation of national resources.

These agencies are "independent" because Congresses and presidents place them outside of the cabinet departments. In addition, some independent administrative agency heads serve fixed terms, making their agencies independent from the president. In other agencies, the heads serve at the pleasure of the president, but the president must have a cause (such as misconduct) to remove them. In yet other agencies, the president can remove the head without specifying a cause. Although the structures of independent administrative agencies are expected to make them "independent" of partisan politics, ultimately such agencies still need to earn the support of those who authorize the spending of money and who have authority to restructure the agency or its mission—Congress and the president.

Independent Regulatory Commissions

Over time, Congress and presidents have recognized the need for expertise in regulating the country's diverse economic activities and in evaluating their impact on the overall economy, workers, consumers, and the environment. Acknowledging their own lack of such expertise, they have created numerous **independent regulatory commissions,** bureaucracies outside of the cabinet departments with the authority to develop standards of behavior for specific industries and businesses, to monitor compliance with these standards, and to impose sanctions on those it finds guilty of violating the standards.

Initially, such government regulation centered on *economic regulation*—matters such as setting the prices of goods and services and ensuring competition in the marketplace.

The first independent regulatory commission, the Interstate Commerce Commission, was set up in 1887 to oversee the prices and services of the railroad industry. Beginning in the 1960s, Congress turned more in the direction of *social regulation,* establishing regulatory commissions that focused on how business practices affected the environment, and the health and safety of consumers and workers. For example, legislation created the Consumer Product Safety Commission in 1972.

Independent regulatory agencies are under the direction of bipartisan boards whose members do not need to be loyal to the president's preferences. Typically, the president nominates and the Senate confirms an odd number of board members. Board members serve staggered fixed terms. This structure allows the agency to make decisions based on the expertise of its board members, not on the preferences of the president or Congress. Still, the agencies need both presidential and congressional support to survive.

Government Corporations

Like private businesses, **government corporations** sell a service or a product; but unlike private businesses, they are government owned. Congress and the president create government corporations when they believe it is in the public interest for the federal government to engage in a commercial activity, such as selling stamps to pay for the cost of delivering mail. Unlike the other categories of bureaucracies, government corporations, such as the U.S. Postal Service, are expected to make enough money to cover their costs, instead of being funded by tax dollars.

government corporation
an executive branch unit that sells a service and is expected to be financially self-sufficient

A bipartisan board typically directs each government corporation. The president appoints the board members to serve for staggered fixed terms. Typically, the Senate is not required to confirm the board members. Like regulatory commissions and administrative agencies, government corporations are independent of cabinet departments.

Executive Office of the President

By 1939, the federal bureaucracy had grown tremendously in size and diversity. Acknowledging that the president, who serves as the chief executive of the bureaucracy, needed help to manage this constellation of departments, independent administrative agencies, independent regulatory commissions, and government corporations, President Franklin Roosevelt and the Congress created the Executive Office of the President (EOP).

The EOP is composed of dozens of offices and councils that assist the president in managing the complex and sprawling executive branch of the bureaucracy. The president appoints the top-level bureaucrats in EOP agencies, and the majority of these appointments are not subject to Senate confirmation. The president has the authority to fire these appointees at his pleasure. Therefore, the EOP serves the president; it is in fact the presidential bureaucracy. (See Chapter 13 for a detailed discussion of the EOP.)

As the U.S. government organizational chart (Figure 14.4) indicates, the legislative branch has several offices supporting its work (including the Government Accountability Office, the Government Printing Office, and the Library of Congress). In addition, there are offices in the judicial branch supporting the work of the courts (the Administrative Office of the United States Courts, the Federal Judicial Center, and the United States Sentencing Commission). Federal bureaucrats employed in these legislative and judicial bodies support the formulation, implementation, and evaluation of public policies.

Federal Bureaucrats' Roles in Public Policy

Although the primary work of bureaucrats is policy implementation—putting public policy into action—bureaucrats play an active, vital role in all six stages of the public policy cycle. These stages are (1) agenda setting, (2) policy formulation, (3) policy approval, (4) appropriation approval, (5) policy implementation, and (6) policy evaluation. (Figure 14.5 presents an example of how the Affordable Care Act of 2010 is working through the six-stage policy cycle.)

FIGURE 14.4 ■ U.S. GOVERNMENT ORGANIZATIONAL CHART How is the federal bureaucracy's division of labor evident in the national government organizational chart? How is the vertical chain of command evident in the chart?

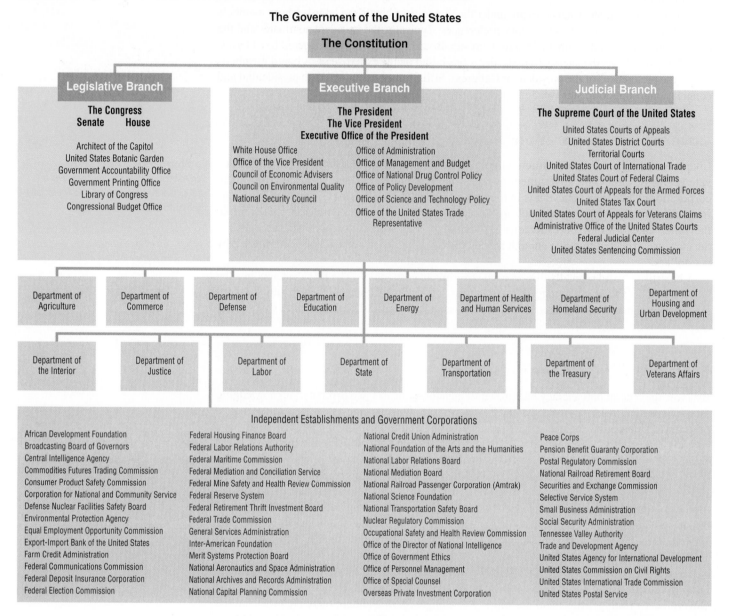

politics-administration
dichotomy
the concept that elected government officials, who are accountable to the voters, create and approve public policy, and then competent, politically neutral bureaucrats implement the public policy

According to the **politics-administration dichotomy,** there is a clear line between *politics* (deciding what government should accomplish, enacting those goals into laws, and allocating money to pay to execute laws) and the *administration* of public policy (the real work of putting the laws into action). The dichotomy says that elected officials (whom citizens hold accountable through the ballot box) have authority for politics and that competent bureaucrats (hired through merit-based civil service) have authority for policy administration. Theoretically, this arrangement fosters not only government by and for the people (responsive government) but also efficient and effective public services.

The politics-administration dichotomy may sound good, but the reality of public policy processes does not allow for such a clean separation between those who "do politics" and those who administer policy. Although bureaucrats are hired to implement policy made by elected

FIGURE 14.5 ▨ STAGES OF THE POLICY PROCESS This flowchart shows how the Affordable Care Act continues to work through the policy cycle. In reality, the stages of the policy cycle often overlap. Today, additional rules and regulations are being established as the policy is being implemented. At the same time critics and supporters are evaluating the policy, as are government agencies. Calls for reforms to the act may force it back to the agenda setting stage, which could lead to the formulation of new legislation revising the ACA.

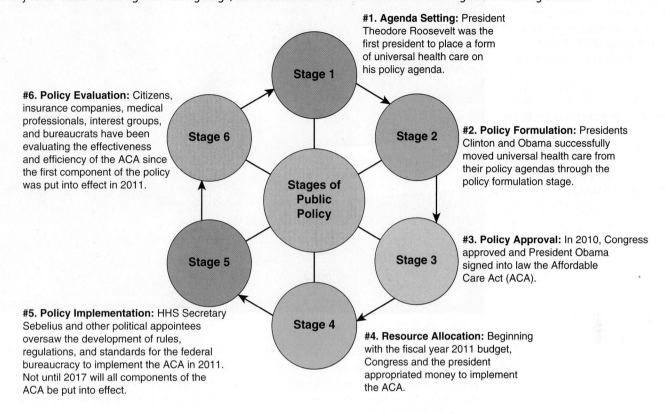

#1. Agenda Setting: President Theodore Roosevelt was the first president to place a form of universal health care on his policy agenda.

#2. Policy Formulation: Presidents Clinton and Obama successfully moved universal health care from their policy agendas through the policy formulation stage.

#3. Policy Approval: In 2010, Congress approved and President Obama signed into law the Affordable Care Act (ACA).

#4. Resource Allocation: Beginning with the fiscal year 2011 budget, Congress and the president appropriated money to implement the ACA.

#5. Policy Implementation: HHS Secretary Sebelius and other political appointees oversaw the development of rules, regulations, and standards for the federal bureaucracy to implement the ACA in 2011. Not until 2017 will all components of the ACA be put into effect.

#6. Policy Evaluation: Citizens, insurance companies, medical professionals, interest groups, and bureaucrats have been evaluating the effectiveness and efficiency of the ACA since the first component of the policy was put into effect in 2011.

officials, elected officials tap the expertise of bureaucrats throughout the other five stages of the policy process, allowing bureaucrats to influence and even make policies themselves, as we now shall see.

Agenda Setting

In the first stage of the public policy cycle, elected officials decide what issues they want to discuss and possibly address by placing them on their lists of items to work on, their policy agendas. Bureaucrats play an instrumental role in setting the policy agenda. Because their focus is to implement public policy at the street level, bureaucrats have a clear view of the societal problems that citizens expect the government to address and strong views on how best to address those problems. Political scientists use the term *iron triangle* to describe long-term collaborative efforts among bureaucrats in a government agency, the members of an interest group, and the members of a legislative committee to get their mutual concerns on the agenda and then addressed through approved public policies. *Issue networks,* which are temporary collaborations among bureaucrats, elected officials, and the members of numerous interest groups, work to set the agenda, as well as to influence policy formulation and approval. Bureaucrats who want to get their concerns and proposed programs on the agenda may work to create issue networks as well as iron triangles. For more about iron triangles and issue networks, see Chapter 7.

Policy Formulation

The second stage of the policy process, policy formulation, involves defining a problem that has made it to the agenda and developing a plan of action (a policy) to address the problem. Many issues that reach an elected official's agenda—or even the agendas of numerous elected officials—do not make it to the policy formulation stage. Although anyone can formulate a

> After tackling the initial implementation of the Affordable Care Act (ACA), particularly the problematic launching of HealthCare.gov, Kathleen Sebelius resigned her position as Secretary of Health and Human Services (HHS). President Obama immediately nominated Sylvia Mathews Burwell, his director of the Office of Management and Budget, to replace Sebelius. The Obama administration was pleased with her quick confirmation by the Senate because there were still details for the ACA implementation that needed to be worked out under the direction of the HHS secretary.

public policy, only elected officials can officially introduce policy proposals into the lawmaking process. Thus individuals and groups outside government, as well as bureaucrats, must identify members of Congress to introduce policy proposals for legislative action. The president can also make policy by issuing an executive order, a lawmaking authority that lies outside the legislative process (see Chapter 13).

Because bureaucrats are the people who actually provide public service daily, they often have specialized knowledge of societal problems. Recognizing their expertise, elected officials rely on bureaucrats when formulating policies. House and Senate committees frequently call on bureaucrats to review and comment on bills that, if approved, the bureaucrats will implement. Bureaucrats often testify at the hearings congressional members hold to investigate and study problems. Thus bureaucrats regularly take part in policy formulation, whether at their own impetus or at the request of elected officials.

In recognition of bureaucrats' expertise, Congress often includes vague or ambiguous language in bills and relies on bureaucrats to fill in the program details after it approves a bill, as they implement the policy. Vague legislative language may also reflect the congressional sponsors' need to win majority votes in both the House and the Senate and to secure presidential approval of the policy. Fuzzy language means that if the bill becomes law, bureaucrats will need to discern what the policy is directing them to do before they can implement it.

Policy Approval

Policy approval, the third stage of the policy cycle, occurs when Congress and the president vote to approve or reject a bill that presents the policy formulated to address a societal problem. When Congress and the president, or Congress alone over a president's veto, approves such bills, the laws thus created authorize government action. These **authorization laws** provide the plan of action to address a given societal concern and identify the executive branch unit that will put the plan into effect. The law may authorize an existing executive unit to carry out the policy, or it may establish a new unit to do the job. Although some authorization laws mandate the spending of money every year to achieve the law's goals, such as the law that created Social Security, most authorization laws do not authorize the spending of money. Instead, the majority of public policies rely on the approval of annual spending bills for their funding.

authorization law
a law that provides the plan of action to address a given societal concern and identifies the executive branch unit that will put the plan into effect

Appropriation Approval

In the next phase of the policy process, appropriation, Congress and the president specify how much money each bureaucracy is authorized to spend during the budget year. Through the budget process (see Chapter 16), Congress and the president formulate appropriation bills, which are plans for the distribution of government revenue to government entities, including bureaucracies, legislative bodies, and judicial bodies. Approved appropriation bills—**appropriation laws**—give bureaucracies the legal authority to spend money during a specific fiscal year.

Bureaucrats play three key roles in the budget process. First, at the request of the president, bureaucrats develop an annual budget request for their agencies. Second, Congress calls on bureaucrats to justify their budget requests. In turn, bureaucrats lobby members of Congress to allocate to their agencies the funds they requested. With limited money available, bureaucracies typically do not receive all the funding they request. Therefore, bureaucracies compete with one another for their piece of the limited budget pie. Once Congress and the president approve the appropriation bills, bureaucrats take on another role in the budget process; they spend money to put public policy into action.

appropriation law
a law that gives bureaucracies and other government entities the legal authority to spend money

Policy Implementation

Policy implementation, the second-to-last stage of the policy cycle, is the main work of bureaucrats. To put policy into action, bureaucrats must first interpret the authorization law and then carry it out. Congress and the president delegate to bureaucrats the authority to determine the best way to implement the policy; this authority is called **administrative discretion.** Applying administrative discretion, bureaucrats use their expertise and best judgment to interpret vague laws, establish programs and procedures aimed at achieving the policy goals, and make the day-to-day decisions necessary to execute public policy. Elected officials risk the loss of control over the content of public policy when they delegate administrative discretion to bureaucrats. However, they have numerous tools to limit this risk, which we discuss later in this chapter.

administrative discretion
the authority delegated to bureaucrats to use their expertise and judgment when determining how to implement public policy

Bureaucrats, specifically those in independent agencies, use administrative discretion to establish programs, rules, regulations, and standards necessary for the effective and efficient implementation of policy. **Administrative rule making** is the process by which upper-level bureaucrats use their administrative discretion and their expertise in the policy area to create rules, regulations, and standards that the bureaucracy will then enforce. For example, recognizing its lack of expertise in the specifics of how to prevent air and water pollution, Congress delegated to the Environmental Protection Agency (EPA) the authority to establish policy. The EPA sets specific pollution emissions standards to implement the Clean Water and Clean Air Acts. Although Congress does not approve these EPA administrative standards, the standards have the force of law.

administrative rule making
the process by which an independent commission or agency fills in the details of a vague law by formulating, proposing, and approving rules, regulations, and standards that will be enforced to implement the policy

Agencies involved in administrative rule making also engage in **administrative adjudication;** they have the authority to determine if their rules are violated and to impose penalties on the violators. Citizens who disagree with an agency's application of its administrative rules or those whom an agency finds guilty of violating its rules may challenge the agency's decisions through a lawsuit. Indeed, claiming that the EPA was not properly implementing the Clean Air Act of 1970 because it was not regulating carbon dioxide as a pollutant, Massachusetts attorney general Martha Coakley, along with the attorneys general of 17 other states, as well as two cities and 11 environmental interest groups, sued the EPA in April 2008. The Court ruled against the EPA; the EPA's claim that the law did not give it the legal authority to regulate carbon dioxide as a pollutant was determined to be an incorrect interpretation of the Clean Air Act.[18]

administrative adjudication
the process by which agencies resolve disputes over the implementation of their administrative rules

Policy Evaluation

The last stage of the policy process is policy evaluation—the assessment of the intended and unintended effects of policy implementation. People do not assess government success by the number of laws their elected officials pass or by the promises made in the language of the laws. Rather, the effectiveness and the efficiency of the delivery of public services are what matter to the public. The implementation of policy by bureaucrats, that is, bureaucratic performance, is thus the key to citizens' satisfaction with government—and the key to government success.

In 1973, political scientists Jeffrey L. Pressman and Aaron B. Wildavsky published their study of a federally funded economic development program, which concluded that it is "amazing that federal programs work at all" given the hurdles that policy implementers encounter.[19] Their landmark research fueled outcries for increased transparency and evaluations of public policies. As a result, policy evaluation has become a larger component of the workload of legislators and bureaucrats. Because elected officials and citizens want proof of the efficiency and the effectiveness of implemented policies, agencies must document what they do and the impact of their work. Because citizens do not elect bureaucrats, they do not have the opportunity to fire public servants whose performance is unsatisfactory. Therefore, citizens defer the responsibility for bureaucratic accountability to members of Congress, the president, and the judges who preside over the courts because these elected and appointed government officials have legal means to monitor bureaucrats' work and to hold them accountable.

Federal Bureaucratic Accountability

When it comes to public service, everyone is watching. The courts, through the mechanism of lawsuits, review the actions of the executive and legislative branches to ensure that they are constitutional and legal. Congress and the president, as the creators and funders of bureaucracies, can threaten to revamp or eliminate any bureaucratic organization, or to decrease its funding, if its performance falls short of expectations. Congress and the president not only structure bureaucracies to foster efficient, effective, and accountable public service but also pass laws to increase self-policing by bureaucrats.

People outside government, including many ordinary citizens, also keep a close eye on bureaucracies. National **sunshine laws** open up government activities and documents to the public, fostering transparency and supporting the public's right to know about government actions and decision making. However, these laws are effective only if citizens know about them and take advantage of them.

sunshine laws
legislation that opens up government activities and documents to the public

Accountability to the People

One of the first national sunshine laws was the Administrative Procedure Act (APA) of 1946. The APA responded to citizens' and interest groups' concerns about the fast growth in the number of agencies involved in administrative rule making and the lack of transparency and accountability of the bureaucratic rule makers. The APA, with which all federal agencies except those specifically excluded by their authorization legislation must comply, standardized rule-making procedures and requires bureaucracies to publicize their proposed rules in the *Federal Register*, a daily national government publication. They also must publish an invitation for people to offer comments on the agency's proposals.

To facilitate this open process, the national government website www.regulations.gov posts proposed administrative rules and accepts electronically submitted comments on the rules. In this way, people can have a voice in administrative rule making. Such citizen input is essential to democracy, because bureaucrats propose and approve more administrative rules each year than Congress proposes and approves pieces of legislation. Once the agency collects and reviews the comments that people have submitted, it must publish its approved rules in the *Federal Register*.

The Freedom of Information Act (FOIA) is a 1966 amendment to the APA. The FOIA requires national agencies to give citizens access to government documents upon request and at a reasonable cost. Today, the act, as amended, also requires all federal departments and executive units to proactively post on their websites information of interest to the public, without the need for a FOIA request. In the last decade, countries throughout the world have enacted FOIA laws, commonly known as right-to-know laws. (See "Global Context" for an assessment of such laws.)

Another law that aims to make the federal bureaucracy accountable to the people is the Government in the Sunshine Act of 1976. This act of Congress requires all multi-headed national agencies, except those in the Executive Office of the President, to conduct open, public meetings

Context

FREEDOM-OF-INFORMATION LAWS WORLDWIDE

Over the past decade, laws have spread from one country to another, giving citizens the right to discover what their governments are doing behind closed doors. Today, over 5.3 billion people in over 100 countries have this right—at least in theory, and in practice, these laws are a powerful mechanism to empower citizens and expose corruption.

However, an Associated Press (AP) report found that in more than half the countries with right-to-know, or freedom-of-information, laws, the governments do not follow these laws. In response to AP requests for information from the European Union and 105 countries, less than half of the governing bodies released any information, and about 30 percent never even acknowledged the AP request for information.

India was one of the 14 countries that responded to the AP request, in full, within 1 month. Mexico responded within 2 months. After 10 months, the U.S. Justice and Homeland Security Departments responded with very limited, partial information. Governments on the African continent had the poorest

response rate, with only 4 out of 15 countries eventually providing requested information.

In the last decade, dozens of countries passed right-to-know laws to meet conditions tied to financial support from donors such as the International Monetary Fund (IMF) or as a condition for membership in international organizations such as the World Trade Organization (WTO). However, governments with right-to-know laws adopted as a condition for financial support or organization membership ignore such laws more often than do governments that developed and adopted right-to-know laws in response to citizens' pressure to make their governments more transparent.

Acceptance—on paper—of the principle of open, transparent government continues to grow throughout the world. However, the first-ever worldwide assessment of right-to-know laws highlights a significant gap between citizens' rights on paper and citizens' rights in the real world.

SOURCE: Martha Mendoza, Associated Press, "Tough to Tame a Paper Tiger," *Scranton Sunday Times*, November 20, 2011.

where citizens can testify and present their concerns about these agencies' procedures and past, current, and potential actions.

As discussed in Chapter 11, all levels of government are using the Internet to offer services to citizens more efficiently and cost effectively, and to foster accountability. In September 2000, the General Services Administration (GSA) of the national government launched its FirstGov website, the national government's one-stop portal to national, state, local, and tribal government agency websites. In 2007, the GSA renamed the website USA.gov (www.usa.gov) in response to feedback from users who wanted a name that was easier to remember. This portal puts government information and services at your fingertips.

Strongly supporting the use of the Internet as a means to enhance citizen access to government information and services, Congress approved and President George W. Bush signed into law the E-Government Act of 2002. This law established a federal chief information officer in the newly created Office of Electronic Government, within the Office of Management and Budget (OMB). Moreover, it requires federal agencies to use Internet-based information technology.

Within his first week in office, President Obama called for "an unprecedented level of openness in government" that would "strengthen our democracy" and "promote efficiency and effectiveness in government."[20] He also created a new position, chief technology officer, to focus on improving the government's efficiency, effectiveness, and transparency through expanded use of Internet technology.

In a democracy, bureaucrats, like elected officials, operate in a fishbowl. Working face to face, or computer screen to computer screen, with the people whom they serve, they are in full view of anyone interested in monitoring them. Sunshine laws and e-government provide citizens with the means to find out what is going on in the bureaucracy. When citizens or watchdog groups identify a problem with bureaucratic operations, they frequently turn to the media to bring public attention to the issue, because the media are always ready to report on bureaucratic inefficiency and impropriety. A more expensive option for citizen and interest group action against bureaucratic waste and misconduct is the filing of a lawsuit.

Accountability to the Courts

Through the litigation process, the U.S. judicial system seeks to ensure that bureaucrats and bureaucracies comply with the law (including constitutional protections, the Administrative Procedures Act, and sunshine laws). If an individual or group believes that a bureaucrat or bureaucracy has violated the law, they can file a lawsuit. For example, people or organizations can file lawsuits against the National Security Administration if they believe NSA employees violated the Fourth Amendment's protection against unreasonable search and seizure. If the Social Security Administration denies an individual Social Security benefits, that person can file a lawsuit challenging the denial (after exhausting all appeal processes offered by the Social Security Administration). Moreover, all bureaucratic agencies must follow the laws that create and fund them, and any additional laws Congress applies to them. As discussed earlier in this chapter, 18 states' attorneys general, two cities, and 11 environmental interest groups successfully sued the EPA in April 2008, claiming it was not properly implementing its authorization legislation because it was not regulating carbon dioxide as a pollutant.

Accountability to Congress

Bureaucrats must always keep in mind the preferences of Congress if they want to survive, for Congress approves the legislation that creates (and eliminates), regulates, and funds bureaucracies. The Senate has an additional mechanism for promoting bureaucratic accountability, in that more than one-quarter of the president's appointees are subject to Senate confirmation. The confirmation process for top bureaucrats gives senators a degree of influence over the leadership and direction of executive departments and agencies.

Another means by which Congress encourages bureaucratic accountability is through the monitoring of bureaucracies' policy implementation, a form of legislative oversight. When the media, citizens, or interest groups bring concerns about a bureaucracy's policy implementation to the attention of legislators, Congress might launch an investigation. If, consequently, Congress and the president are dissatisfied with that bureaucracy's performance or behavior, they can cut its budget, modify its legal authority, or even eliminate the agency.

In most cases, legislative oversight does not occur unless citizens, interest groups, and the media push for congressional action, as occurred after a tainted drug caused a meningitis outbreak killing 64 people and sickening 751 others across the country in 2012. The tainted drug was tailor-mixed at a compounding pharmacy, a type of pharmacy that was not at the time regulated by the federal government. Within months of the meningitis outbreak, and in response to the demands of citizens and interest groups that media reports fueled, Congress drafted legislation delegating to the Food and Drug Administration new authority to police compounding pharmacies. Congress sent the bill to President Obama, who signed it in late 2013.[21]

Congress can force itself to evaluate a bureaucracy's performance by including a **sunset clause** in the authorization law that establishes an agency or a program. A sunset clause creates an expiration date for a program or policy, meaning the program or policy will end unless Congress and the president reauthorizes it through new legislation.

sunset clause
a clause in legislation that sets an expiration date for an authorized program or policy unless Congress reauthorizes it

Accountability to the President

The president also has several tools for holding bureaucracies accountable. Like Congress, the president can use the legislative process to ensure accountability by approving or vetoing authorization and appropriation bills. In addition, because most top political appointees serve at the president's pleasure, they are responsive to the president's policy preferences—and in this way, they and their agencies are accountable to the president.

Today, the Office of Management and Budget (OMB), an EOP agency, is the key lever in the president's efforts to hold the bureaucracy accountable. The OMB evaluates bureaucratic performance for the president. To enhance this OMB function, President Obama established the new position of chief performance officer (CPO) within the OMB. The CPO focuses on government performance and reforms to improve it.

Based on OMB performance assessments, the president proposes budget increases or decreases, agency growth or elimination, or even a reorganization of the executive branch. In addition to overseeing performance evaluations of bureaucratic agencies, the OMB spearheads the development of the president's budget, controls the implementation of appropriation laws, and regulates administrative rule making. Through its Office of Information and Regulatory Affairs, the OMB ensures that regulations created by executive branch agencies are not "unnecessarily costly"[22] and that they support the president's policy preferences.

Internal Accountability

The president, Congress, the courts, and ordinary citizens have multiple means by which to hold bureaucrats accountable. But bureaucrats, who themselves are taxpayers, also worry about inefficiency and waste in public service. Legislated codes of behavior, whistleblower protections, and inspectors general help foster accountability from within bureaucracies.

>In this photo, released by the Air Force in response to a Freedom of Information Act (FOIA) request, we see coffins of fallen service members coming home to Dover Air Force Base in Maryland. In 2009, William Zwicharowski and two colleagues became pariahs after they raised concerns about the mishandling of remains of fallen military service members and September 11 victims at the Dover Air Force Mortuary. The Defense Department investigation that followed the whistleblowing found that gross mismanagement and insufficient training led to remains being mistakenly sent to a landfill. The Office of Special Counsel stated that the courageous whistleblowers' actions led to significant improvements at the mortuary.

CODES OF BEHAVIOR AND THE ETHICS IN GOVERNMENT ACT   To ensure the best public service, bureaucracies have codes of behavior. These codes specify guidelines for ethical, efficient, and effective behavior on the part of bureaucrats. Each government agency has its own such code. In addition, in 1992, the Office of Government Ethics published a comprehensive set of ethical standards for federal bureaucrats. Moreover, many of the professions in which bureaucrats are members (lawyers, doctors, nurses, accountants, engineers, and so on) also have established codes of behavior. Importantly, however, codes of behavior are just guidelines. They do not stipulate what a bureaucrat should do in a given situation. Thus bureaucrats must use discretion when applying such codes to their daily work of providing public service.

The Ethics in Government Act of 1978 established the U.S. Office of Government Ethics, which is charged with preventing conflicts of interest by bureaucrats (political appointees, SES bureaucrats, and civil servants). A **conflict of interest** arises when a public servant is in a position to make a decision or take an action from which he or she can personally benefit. In such a situation, the public servant's private interest is in conflict with his or her responsibility to serve the public interest.

WHISTLEBLOWER PROTECTIONS AND INSPECTORS GENERAL   Whistleblower laws offer an additional means of internal accountability in the federal bureaucracy. The 1978 Civil Service Reform Act provided some protections to civil servant **whistleblowers**—employees who disclose government misconduct, waste, mismanagement, abuse of authority, or a threat to public health or safety. The CSRA established the Office of Special Counsel to protect whistleblowers' job security. Then in 1986 Congress approved the False Claims Act. This law allows for a monetary reward for government whistleblowers who expose fraud that harms the U.S. government.

In another attempt to improve internal accountability, Congress approved the Inspector General Act in 1978. This law aims to ensure the integrity of public service by creating government watchdogs, called **inspectors general,** appointed by the president and embedded in government agencies to monitor policy implementation and investigate alleged misconduct. The law requires the appointment of the inspectors general without regard to their political affiliation and strictly based on their abilities in accounting, auditing, or investigation. "We're supposed to check our politics at the door and call things as we see them. If we uncover things that reflect badly on the government, we're legally and morally obliged to report it. We're obliged to do that for the good of the country." So explained Clark Ervin, who held the position of inspector general at the Departments of State and Homeland Security.[23]

conflict of interest
in the case of public servants, the situation in which they can personally benefit from a decision they make or an action they take in the process of doing their jobs

whistleblower
a civil servant who discloses to the government mismanagement, fraud, waste, corruption, or threats to public health and safety

inspectors general
political appointees who work within a government agency to ensure the integrity of public service by investigating allegations of misconduct by bureaucrats

In summary, whistleblower protection laws and inspectors general enhance the ability of the bureaucrats themselves to police the agencies in which they work, and sunshine laws give government outsiders various instruments for monitoring the bureaucracy. But many citizens and government officials believe that more needs to be done to improve bureaucrats' record of performance.

Can Bureaucratic Performance Be Improved?

In the United States, bureaucrats perform every job imaginable. They generally do their jobs so well that we rarely think about how their work positively affects us around the clock. We and our elected officials are nevertheless quick to bash the bureaucracy at the slightest hint of inefficiency. Similarly, the media seize upon any opportunity to report on problems with bureaucrats and bureaucracies. Our public discourse infrequently covers bureaucrats' *good* performance. When was the last time you heard a news report or were a party to a friendly conversation that praised a public servant?

Yet the U.S. Postal Service delivers hundreds of millions of pieces of mail 6 days a week, and rarely is a letter or a package lost. Thousands of planes safely take off from and land at U.S. airports every hour, guided by federal bureaucrats in the person of air traffic controllers. Millions of senior citizens receive a monthly Social Security benefit on time every month. Even more people travel the interstate highway systems without incident each day.

Public administration and policy scholar Charles Goodsell has found that two-thirds to three-fourths of Americans report their encounters with government bureaucrats and bureaucracy as "satisfactory."[24] However, research consistently shows that some federal agencies perform better than do others.

The Best-Performing Bureaucracies

Political scientists William T. Gormley and Steven Balla reviewed national performance data and summarized the characteristics of federal agencies that perform well.[25] They found several characteristics common among better-performing bureaucracies. They include language in the agency's authorization legislation that clearly states what the agency is expected to accomplish and that delegates high levels of administrative discretion, allowing bureaucrats to determine the best way to achieve the goal. Better-performing bureaucracies tend to be those with easily measured goals, especially goals that include providing resources to citizens (such as Social Security benefits) as opposed to taking resources (tax collection). Another factor correlated with good performance is high levels of support for the agency's mission from elected officials, the media, and diverse groups of citizens. High levels of support typically result in an agency's receiving the funding it needs to accomplish its goals. Effective agency leaders who develop and maintain high levels of support from government officials and interested citizens and groups also are important to well-performing bureaucracies.

Does Contracting-Out Improve Performance?

In addition to analyzing citizen satisfaction with public bureaucracies, Charles Goodsell has analyzed the body of research that assesses the efficiency of public policy implementation by government bureaucrats compared with the efficiency of private organizations. He has found that "the assumption that business always does better than government is not upheld."[26] In fact, Goodsell reports that "despite antigovernment rhetoric to the contrary, the federal government achieves essentially the same degree of satisfaction for its services as corporate America does for its products."[27] Nevertheless, many commentators and elected officials argue that private businesses are more efficient than are governments and therefore that more public service should be outsourced to private businesses. (See "Thinking Critically About Democracy.")

Contracting-out to private businesses certainly decreases the number of bureaucrats on the national payroll. But does outsourcing foster more efficient and effective public service? Does it save taxpayer dollars? For-profit organizations must make a profit to survive, so how can

Democracy

Does Contracting-Out Save Taxpayer Dollars?

The Issue: Over the past half century, governments throughout the world have increasingly turned to networks of public, private, and nonprofit organizations to deliver services. The theory behind contracting-out, or outsourcing, government work is that the government can save taxpayer money by contracting work to private organizations that can do it cheaper and quicker. As government budgets get tighter, the calls to outsource government work have increased. Are these calls justified? Does contracting-out save taxpayer dollars?

Yes: If a private organization is willing to fix roads, build planes, or provide health care for veterans for less money, the government can save taxpayers money. When the government opens up a bidding process, private organizations compete with one another to do the work for less money than the competitors, thereby pushing down the costs. In addition, private organizations are more efficient in their operations than are government organizations, because they need to be to make a profit to survive. Government bureaucracies do not have to worry about making a profit, and so they are less efficient. Efficiency is also improved when the government pays for expertise only when needed, by contracting out instead of hiring federal bureaucrats.

No: Much contracting-out is done without a competitive bidding process either because of an emergency situation, which does not allow time for a bidding process, or because one private company has a monopoly on the expertise needed to do the job. Without a competitive bidding process, there is no reason to expect costs to be pushed down. In addition, if the price looks too good, it probably is. Either the contractor has failed to include an important deliverable for the project, or the contractor has underestimated costs, which will begin to run over. Private companies exist to make a profit, not to provide for the common good. Public servants, in government bureaucracies, are motivated to serve the public good.

Other Approaches: Research suggests that there is fraud, waste, and abuse in government-contracted work because of disorganization in the government's contractor auditing processes. Governments that have created permanent, professional, centralized units to monitor and manage projects, from the initial ideas through the contracting process and implementation, have prevented these problems. Several federal agencies have also begun to "insource" government work to save money.

What do you think?

1. In times of tight budgets, which option do you think taxpayers will find more reasonable: shrinking the size of the government bureaucracy by outsourcing or increasing the size of the bureaucracy by bringing work inside the government through insourcing? Explain.

2. Contractors that have committed fraud, waste, and other inefficiencies are often rehired because government-contracting officers cannot find performance information. How can the government use new technology to solve this problem?

they accomplish public service at a lower cost? Paul Light, a renowned political scientist who studies public service and contracting-out notes that although the salaries of shadow bureaucrats are about the same as government bureaucrats doing similar work, the full cost to the government for contracted work includes administrative costs and profit. Therefore, in many cases, the government pays more for work contracted out to shadow bureaucrats. In addition, Light notes that the federal bureaucracy does not have enough bureaucrats to monitor government contractors.[28] As the number of contracts continues to increase, the federal government will be less able to monitor contractors. Holding contractors accountable for delays, cost overruns, and quality issues is complicated when policy implementation occurs through the shadow bureaucracy, which is outside the government's vertical chain of command.[29] Unlike government bodies, private businesses can legally function behind closed doors—unless and until concerned citizens, watchdog groups, the media, and government officials force the doors open through congressional investigations or lawsuits.

The government's efforts in the fall of 2013 to implement HealthCare.gov (the website through which people could sign up online for health insurance provided through the Affordable Care Act) provides a good case study of the problems of contracting-out. The federal government

> President Obama, then–secretary of the Department of Health and Human Services Kathleen Sebelius, and the federal bureaucracy experienced a tsunami of criticism when the HealthCare.gov website went live in October 2013. Citizens connecting to the site more often than not found that it was not functioning. Therefore, the government's forecasts for the number of citizens purchasing health insurance through the site by the end of 2013 were not met and the media reported on the problems daily. Is HealthCare.gov still making headlines today?

contracted with numerous companies with the expertise needed to develop the online market for health insurance. However, the government did not have sufficient staff (quantity or expertise) to oversee the development process. In addition, because of lack of financial investment, the government's information technology systems caused problems when the site went live. President Obama commented on the government's inadequate contracting processes and oversight when addressing criticism of the health care roll-out. On top of all the glitches with HealthCare.gov, many citizens were not fully aware of their opportunities and obligations under the Affordable Care Act, which also hampered the program's efficiency and effectiveness.

Citizens' Role in Bureaucratic Performance

Citizens turn to the government to provide services and solve problems. As we have discussed, the government's success in serving the people well depends on many factors. Ultimately, even if all other factors correlated with a well-performing bureaucracy are in place, the bureaucracy will fail without the participation and compliance of the people it serves. The effectiveness of public policies depends on people's knowledge of and compliance with the law. It depends on their applying for the government programs for which they qualify. It depends on their conformity to the rules, regulations, standards, and directions of bureaucrats. This symbiotic relationship is essential to the success of government. Governments are tapping into new media technologies to enhance citizens' knowledge of and ability to apply for government services and benefits. Governments are also using new media technologies to increase transparency and, hence, accountability.

Thinking Critically About What's Next in the Bureaucracy

Candidates, elected officials, and the media perpetually criticize government bureaucrats and bureaucracies. Citizens take for granted the overwhelming majority of public services because they are provided day-in and day-out without problem. And although citizens typically use the terms *bureaucrat* and *bureaucracy* to insult public servants and government agencies, surveys consistently report that the majority of citizens are satisfied with their interactions with bureaucrats.

Will contemporary personnel challenges in the federal government threaten citizen satisfaction with bureaucratic performance? Growing numbers of federal bureaucrats are retiring, possibly in response to pay freezes and changes to pension plans. In addition, a shrinking proportion of college graduates plan on working in public service. At the same time, Congress is deliberating numerous proposals to cut the federal workforce through attrition (not hiring people to replace retiring bureaucrats).

Although governments throughout the world have turned to contracting-out to deliver public goods and services, questions have been raised about the efficiency and effectiveness of the practice. Research overwhelming indicates that it does not save money. Research also challenges the notion that private-sector organizations are more effective than government agencies in providing for the common good. However, elected officials continue to try to shrink the size of the federal bureaucracy in response to complaints about waste and fraud. At the same time, citizens expect government to provide more and better services at the same or lower costs.

To boost citizen satisfaction and decrease their costs, governments are increasing their use of new technology. E-government and one-stop web portals are proliferating. In addition, enhanced reporting requirements for federal contractors and grant recipients, and the posting of much of this information on government websites is fostering greater transparency and accountability. In the long term, these changes should also improve efficiency and effectiveness. However, if the government does not employ bureaucrats (including shadow bureaucrats) with the essential expertise or spend the money to upgrade its electronic technology, citizens will criticize e-government, too. We need to learn from the government's efforts to implement the online health care marketplace associated with the Affordable Care Act of 2010.

Summary

1. Bureaucrats and Bureaucracy

Traditionally, bureaucrats are defined as employees in the executive branch of government who are hired to deliver public services. Today, however, many private-sector employees—the so-called shadow bureaucrats—also implement public policy. Although most people think of government agencies when they hear the word *bureaucracy,* a bureaucracy is any large, hierarchical organization featuring a division of labor, specialization of tasks, standard operating procedures, and a chain of command.

2. Federal Bureaucrats

The national government hires almost 3 million civilians into the executive branch to administer public policies. The president appoints a small percentage of these bureaucrats. The government hires the overwhelming majority of national bureaucrats on the basis of merit, using a hiring process that includes open competition and equal opportunity. As a result, the national bureaucracy features a more diverse representation of the people than do the elective institutions of the federal government.

3. State, Local, and Shadow Bureaucrats

The overall number of national bureaucrats has been stable over the past few decades. However, the number of state, local, and shadow bureaucrats has grown significantly because of devolution and the practice of contracting-out more and more public services.

4. The Evolution of the Federal Bureaucracy

The federal bureaucracy has grown tremendously in size, scope, and complexity since 1789. Political scientists typically put government agencies in one of five categories—departments, independent administrative agencies, independent regulatory commissions, government corporations, and Executive Office of the President agencies. But this categorization oversimplifies the diversity of structure, size, and function of the thousands of national bureaucracies.

5. Federal Bureaucrats' Roles in Public Policy

Federal bureaucrats do much more than implement policy. Bureaucrats lobby elected officials in all stages of the policy cycle to get their concerns, and the concerns of the citizens who are their clients, addressed. Elected officials frequently defer to the expertise of bureaucrats when it comes to determining the detailed programs, rules, and standards that are needed to serve the people. Citizen satisfaction with government is deeply dependent on the efficient and effective work of bureaucrats.

6. Federal Bureaucratic Accountability

Elected officials delegate administrative discretion to bureaucrats. Interested parties inside and outside government closely scrutinize bureaucrats' use of this discretion. Taxpayers, clients, the media, and interest groups, as well as the president, Congress, and the courts, hold bureaucrats accountable. In addition to sunshine laws and ethics codes, the structure of national bureaucracies lends itself to accountability.

7. Can Bureaucratic Performance Be Improved?

All those who scrutinize bureaucracies are quick to find fault and slow to offer praise. Certainly, not every agency is evaluated as performing well, but for the most part, citizens report that their interactions with government bureaucrats are satisfactory.

Key Terms

administrative adjudication 443

administrative discretion 443

administrative rule making 443

appropriation law 443

authorization law 442

bureaucracy 428

bureaucratic structure 430

bureaucrats 428

civil servants 432

conflict of interest 447

contracting-out (privatizing, outsourcing) 430

department 438

government corporation 439

independent administrative agency 438

independent regulatory commission 438

inspectors general 447

merit-based civil service 432

patronage system 431

plum book 431

politics-administration dichotomy 440

representative bureaucracy 433

Senior Executive Service (SES) 431

shadow bureaucrats 430

sunset clause 446

sunshine laws 444

whistleblower 447

For Review

1. Compare and contrast the characteristics of national bureaucrats to those of private-sector employees. List and describe the structural characteristics of bureaucratic organizations.

2. Compare and contrast the following categories of bureaucrats: political appointees, civil servants, Senior Executive Service bureaucrats, and shadow bureaucrats.

3. What accounts for the fact that the national budget and the scope of its responsibilities have continued to grow in recent decades, yet the number of its civilian employees has remained stable?

4. Differentiate the five categories of national bureaucracies by discussing differences in their structures and the type of services they provide.

5. Describe the role that bureaucrats play at each of the six stages of the policy process.

6. List the many people, groups, and government officials to whom bureaucrats are accountable and give some examples of how they hold bureaucrats accountable. Describe some mechanisms internal to bureaucracies that foster bureaucratic accountability.

7. According to Gormley and Balla, what are three or four characteristics of bureaucracies that perform well?

For Critical Thinking and Discussion

1. Do citizens expect too much from government and hence from bureaucrats and bureaucracies? Explain your answer.

2. Does the profit motive of private businesses threaten the efficient use of taxpayer money when public services are contracted out? Why or why not?

3. Identify at least one public service that you believe the national government should not contract out to private-sector organizations, and defend your choice(s).

4. How often do you interact with national bureaucrats? What about state bureaucrats? Local bureaucrats? Give some recent examples of each interaction. Can you identify some shadow bureaucrats that have provided you with public services?

5. Compose a list of public services provided to you since you woke up this morning. Were you satisfied with the services? Which of those services do people generally take for granted?

Practice Quiz

MULTIPLE CHOICE: Choose the lettered item that answers the question correctly.

1. The number of federal civilian bureaucrats is
   a. almost 3 million.
   b. almost 5 million.
   c. almost 13 million.
   d. almost 20 million.

2. The youngest department in the national bureaucracy is the Department of
   a. Energy.
   b. Homeland Security.
   c. State.
   d. Veterans Affairs.

3. The demographics of what category of federal employee are most comparable to those of the population as a whole?
   a. elected officials
   b. civil servants
   c. political appointees
   d. Senior Executive Service employees

4. The legislation that created the federal merit-based civil service system was the
   a. Civil Rights Act (1964).
   b. Civil Service Reform Act (1978).
   c. Pendleton Act (1883).
   d. Title IX (1972).

5. The independent administrative agency that is the central personnel office for the federal bureaucracy today is the
   a. EOP.
   b. FLRA.
   c. MSPB.
   d. OPM.

6. In what category of federal bureaucracies are secretaries the top appointed officials?
   a. department
   b. independent administrative agency
   c. independent regulatory commission
   d. government corporation

7. Bureaucracies in which category are expected to make enough money to cover their costs?
   a. department
   b. independent administrative agency
   c. independent regulatory commission
   d. government corporation

8. Bureaucrats make policy, using the administrative discretion that Congress delegates to them, at the stage of the policy process that is called
   a. policy formulation.
   b. policy approval.
   c. policy implementation.
   d. policy evaluation.

9. All of the following are merit principles except
   a. competence.
   b. open competition.
   c. political neutrality.
   d. Senate confirmation.

10. Political appointees who work within a government agency to ensure the integrity of public service by investigating allegations of misconduct by bureaucrats are
    a. inspectors general.
    b. shadow bureaucrats.
    c. watchdogs.
    d. whistleblowers.

FILL IN THE BLANKS

11. An organization with a _____ structure has the following characteristics: a division of labor; workers hired based on competence to do a specialized task; standard operating procedures; and a vertical chain of command.

12. The hiring system initially used by the federal government, which allowed the president to hire anyone he wanted based on whatever qualifications he decided on, is the _____ system.

13. People hired and paid by private for-profit and nonprofit organizations that implement public policy through a government contract are _____.

14. _____ is the authority delegated to bureaucrats to use their expertise and judgment when determining how to implement public policy.

15. Laws that force the government to be transparent by holding open meetings and providing citizens with requested information at a reasonable cost are collectively known as _____.

Answers: 1. a, 2. b, 3. b, 4. c, 5. d, 6. a, 7. d, 8. c, 9. d, 10. a, 11. bureaucratic, 12. patronage, 13. shadow bureaucrats, 14. administrative discretion, 15. sunshine laws.

Resources for Research AND Action

Internet Resources

Office of Management and Budget
www.whitehouse.gov.omb This website provides access to the current and previous federal budget documents and historical budget tables.

Office of Personnel Management
www.usajobs.gov To find out about government job opportunities as well as apprenticeships, fellowships, and internships, visit this Office of Personnel Management website.

Partnership for Public Service
www.ourpublicservice.org/OPS/ This nonprofit, nonpartisan organization is working to revitalize the federal government by inspiring a new generation of public servants.

Regulations.gov
www.regulations.gov You can review proposed and approved rules, regulations, and standards of federal executive agencies and submit your comments about them.

U.S. Government Printing Office
www.gpoaccess.gov/gmanual/browse This website allows you to view the most current *United States Government Manual* as well as several older editions of the manual.

USA.gov
www.usa.gov Use this site as a one-stop portal to national, state, and local government officials, agencies, and documents.

Recommended Readings

Goodsell, Charles T. *The Case for Bureaucracy: A Public Administration Polemic,* 4th ed. Washington, D.C.: CQ Press, 2004. A review of the common myths and criticisms of bureaucracy, with evidence to show that they are indeed unsupported.

Gormley, William T., Jr., and Steven J. Balla. *Bureaucracy and Democracy: Accountability and Performance.* Washington, D.C.: CQ Press, 2004. Uses case studies and examples to illustrate what the national bureaucracy does and why it is important, and draws on social science theories to describe how bureaucracy works and the complex and conflicting demands put on it.

Kettl, Donald F. *System Under Stress: Homeland Security and American Politics.* Washington, D.C.: CQ Press, 2004. Analysis of the environmental factors that led to the creation of the newest cabinet-level department, the Department of Homeland Security, with an examination of the intergovernmental nature of the endeavor to protect homeland security.

Light, Paul. *A Government Ill Executed: The Decline of the Federal Service and How to Reverse It.* Boston: Harvard University Press, 2008. Claiming that the federal government is no longer able to "faithfully execute the laws," Light offers an agenda for reform to reverse the decline in federal service, which includes decreasing the size of the bureaucracy and reducing federal outsourcing.

Stillman, Richard. *The American Bureaucracy: The Core of Modern Government.* Chicago: Nelson-Hall Publishers, 1996. A comprehensive introductory textbook in public administration, with excellent description and analysis of bureaucracies (national, state, and local) in the United States.

Movies of Interest

Argo (2012)
Based on real events, this movie tells the story of a collaboration between the U.S. State Department, the CIA, Hollywood moviemakers, and the Canadian government to smuggle American officials out of Iran after the 1979 invasion of the U.S. embassy there. The plan to save 6 U.S. officials hiding in the Canadian Embassy in Iran, while Iranians hold 56 other U.S. officials hostage, revolves around the claim that the U.S. officials are part of a Canadian movie crew searching for a location for their movie.

Pentagon Papers (2003)
In this made-for-TV movie, a Department of Defense bureaucrat, Daniel Ellsberg, has access to classified documents that he decides should be brought to the public's attention. The documents detail the secret history of U.S. involvement in Vietnam, which includes bureaucrats misinforming decision makers and the public. Ellsberg risks his career and his freedom to try to get the truth to the public. Based on a true story.

Mississippi Burning (1989)
Two committed FBI agents, with very different personal styles, investigate the disappearance of three civil rights workers during the 1960s. Based on a true story.

Serpico (1973)
The story of a New York City police officer who is living his dream of being a cop. His dream job turns life threatening when he blows the whistle on corruption in the police force, the existence of which shows that not all of Serpico's coworkers are as committed to public service as he is. Based on a true story.

CHAPTER 15

The Judiciary

 THEN

The federal judiciary did not have a great effect on the daily lives of citizens due to its limited jurisdiction as established by the Judiciary Act of 1789.

 NOW

All major policy issues—social, economic, and political—eventually end up in the courts; therefore, courts make policies that affect the daily lives of citizens.

 NEXT

Will the nuclear option, which limits the use of the Senate filibuster, change the politics of judicial appointments?

Will the ideological makeup of the Supreme Court continue to come under scrutiny as both conservative and liberal justices engage in judicial activism?

Will the judicial branch retain its status as the most trusted branch of government?

In this chapter, we survey the foundations, structure, and workings of the contemporary U.S. judiciary. We examine how the courts make policy as they resolve legal disputes that affect social, economic, and political aspects of the polity. We also explore constraints on judicial policy making.

FIRST, we answer the question, what do courts do.

SECOND, we focus on the sources of U.S. law, including constitutions, statutes, judicial decisions, executive orders, and administrative law.

THIRD, we consider different types of lawsuits.

FOURTH, we examine the structure of the federal court system.

FIFTH, we look at the criteria and process for appointing federal judges.

SIXTH, we survey how the U.S. Supreme Court functions today.

SEVENTH, we examine judges as policy makers, including the constraints on judicial policy making.

EIGHTH, we review the work of the Roberts Court.

adversarial judicial system
a judicial system in which two parties in a legal dispute each present its case and the court must determine which side wins the dispute and which loses

jurisdiction
the legal authority of a court to resolve a case, established by either a constitution or a statute

Courts resolve legal disputes,

conflicts over the law, and in the process, judges and jurors must determine the facts of the case. At the same time, judges must interpret relevant laws and then apply them to the facts of the case while protecting the due process rights of defendants. Why do judges have to interpret laws before applying them? As discussed throughout this textbook, laws—whether found in constitutions, legislation, executive orders, or administrative rules and regulations—are often vague, ambiguous, and even contradictory. Therefore judges, through their interpretation and application of laws in the context of a lawsuit, play an important role in lawmaking.

In *Federalist* No. 78, Alexander Hamilton explains that the Constitution intentionally structures the federal judiciary to be the weakest branch of government. Several characteristics of the courts highlight the weakness of the judiciary in relation to the other branches. Unlike the executive and legislative branches, which are proactive in making policies that address societal concerns as they arise, courts must wait for people to bring conflicts to them through lawsuits. Courts are reactive. In addition, once courts have resolved a conflict, they must rely on the other branches of government to implement their decisions. Unlike Congress and the president, judges do not approve federal budgets nor do they supervise bureaucrats who put policy into effect.

Eventually, all major policy questions (stemming from conflicts over what the law means) end up in front of the courts. Frequently, court decisions spark changes in how the executive branch implements existing or new laws. Because of the constitutionally created system of checks and balances, the elected officials in the executive and legislative branches have several means to check judicial authority. Therefore, the three branches engage in ongoing dialogue over the foundational principles of U.S. democracy, found in the Constitution, and the laws enacted by elected and appointed officials that regulate individual, group, and governmental behavior. According to Supreme Court justice Ruth Bader Ginsburg, "In so many instances, the court and Congress have been having conversations with each other, particularly recently in the civil rights area."[1] In our democracy, citizens engage in these ongoing conversations as they try to influence all three branches.

What Do Courts Do?

Unlike the legislative and executive branches that proactively respond to citizens' needs and demands by formulating, approving, funding, and implementing laws, judges (and the courts in which they work) are reactive. Judges must wait for someone to file a lawsuit (a legal dispute) before they can do their work. In addition, while elected legislators and executives must represent their constituents, judges do not have constituents to represent. Judges are responsible for upholding constitutions. Therefore, in our democracy we expect elected legislators and executives to be partial to the majority of their constituents; majority rule. At the same time, we expect judges to be impartial to individuals or groups and partial to constitutions.

To resolve legal disputes, courts in the United States implement an **adversarial judicial system,** with each of the two parties in a legal dispute presenting its set of facts. At the end of a lawsuit, one party will win and the other party will lose. (See the "Global Context" to learn of Mexico's recent adoption of an adversarial judicial system.) The ability of a court to hear a case depends on whether that court has **jurisdiction**—the legal authority of a court to resolve a case, which is established by either a constitution or a statute.

Context

MEXICAN COURTS TRANSITIONING TO THE ADVERSARIAL SYSTEM OF JUSTICE

Under its traditional, written-based inquisitorial judicial system, Mexican judges conduct trials behind closed doors. The two parties to the dispute submit written reports, documents, and briefs to a judge. The judge reviews the documents in private and issues a verdict typically without comment or explanation. This closed justice system fosters a lack of trust in the system, with worries about possible bribery, corruption, and violation of the rights of the accused.*

In 2008, Mexico amended its constitution, radically overhauling its court system. Every state and federal judicial system in Mexico must transition to an adversarial system by 2016. The Mexican constitutional mandate to overhaul the judicial systems will allow both parties in a legal dispute to present their facts, evidence, and witnesses in open-to-the public courtrooms. Both parties will have the opportunity to question all witnesses and object to the questions posed and evidence presented by the opposing party. Judges, lawyers, and citizens at-large believe that open, adversarial trials are more transparent, better protect due process and the rights

of the accused, and bolster the presumption of innocence until proven guilty.**

Mexican federal prosecutor Catalina Leon believes that Mexico's transition from its current written-based inquisitorial justice system to an oral-based adversarial system, similar to the system U.S. courts use, is "going to help us a lot [because] it guarantees better justice." Victor Romero, a Mexico City federal judge, tells of his initial resistance to the change to an adversarial system. However, after learning about the U.S. court system during a U.S. Department of Justice–sponsored institute, he noted, "This experience has impacted me favorably because I have been able to see its benefits."*

Mexican officials believe that if the transition to an adversarial system is successful, it will improve the public's trust of judges and the legitimacy of court procedures and verdicts.

SOURCES: *Karla Zabludovsky, "In Mexico, Rehearsing to Inject Drama into the Courtroom," *The New York Times*, August 28, 2012, A7. **Jose Antonio Caballero, "Judiciary: The Courts in Mexico," *Americas Quarterly* (Spring 2013), www.americasquarterly.org/judiciary-courts-mexico.

There are two generic legal disputes brought to courts. The first dispute is over the facts of a case, and the second dispute is over the proper interpretation and application of the law to the case. **Trial courts** have **original jurisdiction,** which means they are the first courts to hear a case and try to resolve it based on determining the truth of what occurred—the facts of the case. Trial courts must decide if the party accused of harming an individual, group, or society at-large by violating law (the defendant) is guilty (in criminal cases) or liable (in civil cases). If the court finds the defendant guilty or liable, then it will levy a punishment or sanction.

Appellate courts with **appellate jurisdiction** are responsible for correcting errors made by other courts when they interpret and apply law in a specific case. Therefore, courts with appellate jurisdiction review the procedures used and decisions made by judges in cases already decided by another court. Often, appellate courts must clarify laws to determine if the judge(s) in the previous legal dispute properly interpreted and applied the relevant laws in the specific case. At other times, appellate courts must choose between laws that conflict. In the process of clarifying laws and choosing between conflicting laws, appellate courts determine what the law is; they make law.

In resolving disputes, courts are responsible for ensuring that the U.S. Constitution is not violated. In the landmark case *Marbury v. Madison* (1803), the Supreme Court, led by Chief Justice John Marshall, grabbed for itself the power of judicial review.[2] **Judicial review** is the Court's authority to determine that an action taken by any government official or governing body violates the Constitution (see Chapter 2). In the *Marbury* case, the Supreme Court ruled that a section of the Judiciary Act of 1789 that gave new authority to the Supreme Court was

trial court
courts with original jurisdiction in a legal dispute that decides guilt or liability based on its understanding of the facts presented by the two disputing parties

original jurisdiction
judicial authority to hear cases for the first time and to determine guilt or liability by applying the law to the facts presented

appellate courts
courts with authority to review cases heard by other courts to correct errors in the interpretation or application of law

appellate jurisdiction
judicial authority to review the interpretation and application of the law in previous decisions reached by another court in a case

Marbury v. Madison
the 1803 Supreme Court case that established the power of judicial review

judicial review

the court's authority to determine that an action taken by any government official or governing body violates the Constitution

U.S. Supreme Court

serves as the court of last resort for conflicts over the U.S. Constitution and national laws; in addition to its appellate jurisdiction, the Court also has limited original jurisdiction

dual court system

the existence of 50 independently functioning state judicial systems, each responsible for resolving legal disputes over its state laws, and one national judicial system, responsible for resolving legal disputes over national laws

law

a body of rules established by government officials that bind governments, individuals, and nongovernment organizations

common law

judge-made law grounded in tradition and previous judicial decisions, instead of in written law

doctrine of *stare decisis*

from the Latin for "let the decision stand," a common-law doctrine that directs judges to identify previously decided cases with similar facts and then apply to the current case the rule of law used by the courts in the earlier cases

precedent cases

previous cases with similar facts that judges identify for use in a new case they are deciding; judges apply the legal principles used in the precedent cases to decide the legal dispute they are currently resolving

unconstitutional. In its ruling, the **U.S. Supreme Court** argued something that it had never argued before: that it had the power not only to review acts of Congress and the president, but also to decide whether those laws were consistent with the Constitution, and to strike down laws that conflicted with constitutional principles.

Legal scholar Joel B. Grossman observes that in *Marbury,* "[John] Marshall made it abundantly clear that the meaning of the Constitution was rarely self-contained and obvious and that those who interpreted it—a role he staked out for the federal courts but one that did not reach its full flowering until the mid-twentieth century—made a difference."[3] Judicial review is the most significant power the Supreme Court exercises. Over time, the Court has extended this power to apply not only to acts of Congress, the president, and federal bureaucrats but also to laws passed by state legislatures and executives, as well as to state court rulings and acts of state and local bureaucrats. Today, all courts in the United States, federal and state, have judicial review authority.

In our federal system of government, with dual sovereignty, both the national government and the state governments are sovereign, each having its own authority to make laws, execute laws, and resolve conflicts over its laws (as explained in Chapters 2 and 3). One characteristic of this dual sovereignty is that the national government establishes national law and each state government establishes state laws. A second characteristic of dual sovereignty is the **dual court system,** in which each state has a judicial system that is responsible for resolving legal disputes over the state's laws and the federal judicial system is responsible for resolving legal disputes over national laws.

Sources of Laws in the United States

Law is a body of rules established by government officials that bind governments, individuals, and nongovernment organizations. A goal of law is to create a peaceful, stable society by establishing rules of behavior that government enforces, with punishments imposed on those who the government finds guilty of violating the law. Another goal of law is to create processes by which conflicts about the rules and expected behaviors can be resolved. There is a variety of sources of law in the United States, including constitutions, pieces of legislation, executive orders, rules and regulations made by administrative bodies, and judicial decisions. From these sources come different types of law.

Judicial Decisions: Common Law

Common law is judge-made law grounded in tradition and previous judicial decisions, instead of in written laws. When there was no written law for judges to apply when resolving legal disputes, the judges used their understanding of the societal norms of justice and fairness to resolve conflicts. The legal principle established by the judge (common law) became binding on judges when resolving later cases with similar facts. This common-law **doctrine of *stare decisis*** (Latin for "let the decision stand") directs judges to identify previously decided cases with similar facts and then apply to the current case the rule of law used by the courts in the earlier cases. The previous cases with similar facts identified by judges are **precedent cases.**

The United States inherited, and then built on, a system of common law from England. When there was not written law to which the U.S. courts could turn, the newly established courts in the United States used British common law, and then eventually U.S. common law. Common law was the predominant form of law in the United States in the 19th century, before the volume of state and national legislation, rules, and regulations expanded. Eventually, many of the legal rules and principles developed by judges to resolve legal disputes over property, contracts, and harm caused by another person's negligent behavior were enacted in written laws.

Although the doctrine of *stare decisis* directs judges to ground their decisions in precedents, judges do have the discretion to step away from precedent if there are contradictory precedents, or if they believe the earlier decision was wrong (that is, if it misinterpreted or misapplied the law). Ultimately, common law gives judges the responsibility for interpreting law, especially if there are few precedents to guide them.[4]

In her book *The Majesty of the Law: Reflections of a Supreme Court Justice*, Sandra Day O'Connor notes, "The United States is a common-law country, not a civil-law country, and so in the United States a single case can be of great importance."[5] According to O'Connor, "the genius of the common law in the United States has been its capacity to evolve over time—case by case and issue by issue—as the courts apply basic legal principles developed over the past to resolve the challenges posed by new situations."[6]

Constitutions: Constitutional Law

Constitutions regulate the behavior of governments and the interactions of governments with their citizens. The body of law that comes out of the courts in cases involving constitutional interpretation is known as **constitutional law.** In cases concerning the Constitution, the highest court is the U.S. Supreme Court, and its decisions bind all Americans, including Congress and the president.

constitutional law
the body of law that comes out of the courts in cases involving the interpretation of the Constitution

In the United States, the U.S. Constitution is the supreme law of the land. All other laws must comply with the U.S. Constitution. National laws and treaties cannot violate the U.S. Constitution. State constitutions and laws cannot violate the U.S. Constitution. Throughout U.S history, courts have had to resolve disputes over the meaning of the U.S. Constitution.

For example, conflicts over the constitutional distribution of authority among the branches of the national government (the separation of powers) have landed in the courts. In its 2013 term, the U.S. Supreme Court was asked to determine the constitutionality of making presidential appointments while the Senate is in recess, which bypasses the Senate's authority to advise and consent (*National Labor Relations Board v. Noel Canning*).[7] The Court found that the president's authority to make recess appointments is limited to Senate recesses lasting no fewer than 10 days. During shorter recesses, the president cannot make recess appointments.

Disputes over the distribution of sovereignty between the national and state governments (federalism) also continue to end up in the courts. For example, in the summer of 2012, in the *National Federation of Independent Businesses v. Sebelius* case,[8] the U.S. Supreme Court found that the national government could not mandate that state governments extend Medicaid coverage as a requirement of its Affordable Care Act (2010).

The courts regularly have to resolve disputes over the proper balance between the common good and individual civil rights and liberties. To resolve these disputes, courts have to interpret language in the U.S. Constitution. In one recent case the Supreme Court had to determine the constitutionality of overall limits on contributions from individuals to political candidates and political parties (*McCutcheon v. Federal Election Commission*).[9] Do such limits infringe on First Amendment free speech rights? The Supreme Court ruled the limits unconstitutional.

Legislation

By the early 20th century, rapid changes in society and the economy forced legislators in Congress and the states to create laws to regulate the behavior of individuals and organizations to further the public good and protect individual liberties and rights. Laws written by legislatures are called legislation, acts, and statutes. Governments often compile legislative law in one document. All legislation may be in one consolidated document, such as is found in the **U.S. Code,** which is a compilation of all the laws ever passed by the U.S. Congress. The U.S. Code has 50 sections spanning a range of issues including agriculture, bankruptcy, highways, the postal service, and war and defense. At the state level, each state has a **penal code,** which is the compilation of all its criminal law.

U.S. Code
a compilation of all the laws passed by the U.S. Congress

penal code
the compilation of a state's criminal law—legislation that defines crime—into one document

National legislation and state legislation must comply with the U.S. Constitution. State legislation also must comply with the state constitution, which must comply with the U.S. Constitution.

Executive Orders

Article II, Section 1, of the U.S. Constitution states that "the executive power shall be vested in [the] president of the United States." This power allows the president to issue orders that create and guide the bureaucracy in implementing policy. A president can enact an executive order

>In 2013, President Obama signed an executive order to establish the White House Council on Native Americans. In 2011, Obama established the White House Council on Women and Girls through an executive order. What might explain why Obama utilized executive orders to create these councils instead of relying on Congress to create them through legislation?

without input from the other branches of government, though executive orders are subject to judicial review and depend on the legislature for funding. Because executive orders have the force and effect of law, they represent a crucial tool in the president's lawmaking toolbox.

A review of President Barack Obama's executive orders shows a range of public matters addressed in laws created by executive order. Obama's first executive order as president established new policies and procedures governing the use of executive privilege by past presidents to prevent the release of presidential records held by the National Archives and Records Administration (Executive Order 13489). Obama used executive orders to establish the White House Council on Native Americans in 2013.[10] Today, presidents enact numerous laws through executive orders during their presidencies, laws that can be challenged in the federal courts.

Administrative Rules and Regulations: Administrative Law

As we saw in Chapter 14, legislation that creates policies and programs also delegates discretion to the bureaucrats in the executive branch whose job it is to implement them. Applying their administrative discretion, bureaucrats determine the best means to achieve the goals of the policies they execute. In the lawmaking process known as administrative rule making, bureaucrats use their administrative discretion to establish specific rules, regulations, and standards necessary for the effective and efficient implementation of policy. The rules, regulations, and standards made by bureaucrats through administrative rule making have the force of law.

Examples of administrative law include the standards established by the Social Security Administration to determine eligibility for Social Security disability benefits. Once established, bureaucrats in the Social Security Administration offices apply the standards case-by-case in their review of medical documentation to determine which applicants are qualified to receive disability benefits. An applicant denied benefits by the bureaucrat can appeal the decision to the Social Security Administration's Office of Disability Adjudication and Review, where an administrative law judge (another employee of the Social Security Administration, a bureaucrat, not a judicial branch employee) reviews the case. The administrative law judge can overturn the denial of benefits or uphold it. If the administrative law judge upholds the denial of benefits, the claim goes to the Appeals Council within Social Security (a multimember body of bureaucrats). The applicant can appeal a denial of benefits from this council in the federal judicial branch. At that point, judicial branch judges will resolve the dispute over the implementation of administrative law.

Types of Lawsuits

Trial courts resolve disputes over the facts in a case. The dispute in a trial court may involve the claim that a defendant harmed society by violating criminal law, or it may involve the claim that a defendant caused harm to an individual, a group, or an organization by violating civil law. Verdicts in criminal trials and civil trials may be appealed for review to correct errors in the interpretation or application of law made by the judge presiding over the trial. We now turn to differentiating criminal and civil law, the procedures of criminal and civil trials, and trial procedures from appellate procedures.

Criminal Law and Trials

criminal law
the body of law dealing with conduct so harmful to society as a whole that it is prohibited by statute and is prosecuted and punished by the government

Criminal law is the body of law dealing with conduct considered harmful to the peace and safety of society as a whole, even when directed against an individual. Each state establishes its own criminal law, compiled in its penal code. Congress has established national criminal law, however, the vast majority of crimes are defined by state legislation, not national legislation.

Therefore, state courts resolve the overwhelming majority of criminal lawsuits. The government whose criminal statute was violated, either the national government or a state government, files the lawsuit, as the prosecutor against the defendant. For example, when a government arrests and accuses a person of setting a house on fire (arson), or sexually assaulting someone, or stealing and using someone's credit cards, it is the state in whose territory the crime occurred that has the authority to bring a lawsuit, charging the person with violating its criminal law.

In a criminal case, the government as prosecutor has the burden to prove its case against the defendant **beyond a reasonable doubt,** which means there is no doubt in the mind of the judge or the jury (depending on the type of trial it is, as discussed later) that the defendant is guilty of violating the criminal law as charged. When a court finds a criminal defendant guilty, typically the judge (even where there is a jury) determines the punishment. However, because the overwhelming majority of defendants charged with criminal offenses plead guilty prior to trial, most criminal cases never go through a trial.

As discussed in Chapter 4, criminal defendants who go to trial have a variety of constitutional rights to guarantee due process. Some of these rights include the right to a speedy trial; exclusion of evidence that law enforcement gained through an unreasonable search or seizure; assistance of counsel, including counsel paid for by the government for indigent defendants accused of serious crimes; and protection from cruel and unusual punishment. Defendants found guilty have the legal right to an appeal, although the overwhelming majority do not appeal guilty verdicts. Because the Constitution protects people from double jeopardy, which is the trying of a person again for the same crime that he or she has been cleared of in court, the government does not have the right to appeal not-guilty verdicts.

State and federal courts resolve criminal cases; however, they spend much more time resolving the larger volume of civil cases brought to them. Unlike criminal defendants, neither party in a civil lawsuit has a constitutional right to a speedy trail, and so it may take years before a civil lawsuit makes it to the courtroom.

Civil Law and Trials

Civil law is the body of law dealing with private rights and obligations that are established by voluntary agreements (written and oral contracts), legislation, constitutions (which establish civil rights and liberties), administrative rules and regulations, or common law.[11] Civil lawsuits involve disputes between individuals, between an individual and a corporation, between corporations, and between individuals and their governments. In civil law disputes, one party (the complainant) alleges that some action or inaction by the other party (the respondent) has caused harm to his or her body, property, psychological well-being, reputation, or civil rights or liberties.

When the harm is to a person's body or property and is caused by another person's negligence or other wrongful act, other than the violation of a contract, it is known as a **tort.** Well-publicized tort lawsuits include medical malpractice suits (disputes over claims that negligence of medical professionals caused harm) and product liability lawsuits (disputes over claims that a product, from toys to make up to medicine, caused harm). Until the recent writing of tort law into legislation, tort law was common law. The most common civil lawsuits stem from traffic accidents. Divorce and other family conflicts are also resolved in civil lawsuits because these disputes deal with obligations and rights created by a marriage contract.

Courts use different procedures for the variety of civil lawsuits. However, some common practices are found in the majority of civil suits. For example, the complainant who files the lawsuit has the burden to prove that the respondent caused the harm. The burden of proof used in civil lawsuits is lower than that used in criminal trials. In civil trials, the complainant must prove that the **preponderance of evidence** is on his or her side; the evidence indicates that it is more likely than not that the accused caused the harm and is therefore liable.

Unlike criminal defendants, the respondents in civil suits do not have a constitutional right to the assistance of counsel. Nor do the complainants. This may explain why so few people who are harmed by the action or inaction of another, and have grounds to file a civil lawsuit, do not do so; they often cannot afford a lawyer. In addition, the overwhelming majority of civil lawsuits are settled (resolved) prior to trial. Respondents found liable for causing harm are not punished like those found guilty in criminal cases, but instead are required to remedy the harm, which often means paying monetary damages to the complainant.

beyond a reasonable doubt
the standard of proof the government must meet in criminal cases; the government must convince the judge or the jury that there is no reasonable doubt that the defendant committed the crime

civil law
the body of law dealing with disputes between individuals, between an individual and corporations, between corporations, and between individuals and their governments over harms caused by a party's actions or inactions

tort
situation when a person's body or property is harmed by another person's negligence or other wrongful act, other than the violation of a contract

preponderance of evidence
the standard of proof used in civil cases; the evidence must show that it is more likely than not that the accused caused the harm claimed by the complainant

Democracy

Should Jury Trials Be Eliminated?

The Issue: Article III, Section 2, of the Constitution, as well as the Sixth Amendment for criminal cases (interpreted by the Supreme Court to mean serious, "nonpetty" cases) and the Seventh Amendment for civil cases (if a dispute exceeds 20 dollars), establish the right to a trial by an impartial jury in federal courts. The framers established the jury system as a safeguard of constitutional liberties, to protect citizens from oppressive government. However, after sensational trials in which juries have acquitted accused murders, such as the 2011 Florida case acquitting Casey Anthony of murdering her 5-year-old daughter, the public and some legal experts have called for the elimination of jury trials. Is it time to eliminate jury trials?

Yes: Jury trials are much more expensive and time-consuming than bench trials. In addition, jury service is so onerous that most people try to get out of it. In fact, juries are not representative of the community. Therefore, it is not possible to receive an "impartial" jury of peers, since juries are comprised of those not smart enough to get out of jury duty. In civil cases, in which the issues are often very complicated and technical—such as medical malpractice lawsuits—jurors do not have the knowledge required to make the correct judgment.

No: Jurors—listening to the facts as presented in the courtroom and the instructions of a learned judge in the application of the law to the facts and using common sense grounded in societal norms—are a protection against government inquisitions and oppression. The government must prove its case beyond a reasonable doubt before it can abridge the defendant's life, liberty, or pursuit of happiness. In this era of government wiretapping and eavesdropping, citizens need as much protection as they can get from government. Furthermore, it is each citizen's responsibility to participate in this duty in order to uphold our democratic system.

Other Approaches: There are reforms that would increase the likelihood that citizens would embrace jury service, improving the quality of jurors and justice. For example, the federal government pays its employees their salary during their jury service. If jurors did not lose their pay, then they would be more willing to serve. Permitting jurors to take notes during the trial and requiring the judge to use plain English when instructing jurors would enhance the jurors' understanding of complex issues and the jury's deliberations.

What do you think?

1. Would justice be enhanced if jurors with expertise and knowledge related to the issues being disputed were called to serve, instead of a random selection of citizens? Explain.

2. When a person agrees to plead guilty to a lesser offense (known as plea bargaining), he or she gives up the constitutional rights that protect due process. Is the fact that so few cases go to trial, either a bench or a jury trial, due to plea bargaining, a threat to protecting constitutional rights and liberties? Explain.

3. It would take an amendment to the U.S. Constitution to eliminate the right to have an impartial jury hear your case. How likely do you think it is that two-thirds of the members of the House and the Senate would agree to propose and three-quarters of the states would agree to ratify such a constitutional amendment?

4. Would U.S. citizens be willing to give up their constitutional right to an impartial jury? Explain.

Trials versus Appeals

Television shows often feature cases in a trial court, not an appellate court. That is because the procedures used in trial courts, which differ from those used in appellate courts, are much more interesting to observe.

Criminal and civil trials include the questioning of witnesses by lawyers for both parties, presentation of evidence, and the right to a jury trial for those accused of more serious crimes or more extensive (and expensive) harm in a civil suit. In more serious criminal trials, the defendant usually has the choice between a bench trial or a jury trial. In civil trials with more extensive and expensive harm, the norm is to have a jury trial unless both parties agree to a bench trial. In a **jury trial,** a group of citizens selected to hear the evidence makes the determination of guilt or liability. Each juror (member of the jury) is expected to be impartial and neutral and

jury trial
a trial in which a group of people selected to hear the evidence presented decides on guilt or liability

base her or his decision on the facts presented in the courtroom. In federal trial courts, there must be unanimous agreement among the jurors on the verdict. In a **bench trial,** the judge who presides over the court proceedings decides guilt or liability. There is an ongoing conservation about whether jury trials should be replaced with bench trials (see "Thinking Critically About Democracy").

Appellate court cases do not include the questioning of witnesses, nor do they use juries. Instead, each party to the legal dispute submits legal briefs that present the facts as it sees them and legal material, including what they see as relevant law and favorable legal findings in similar, previously decided legal disputes (precedents). The goal of each party's legal brief is to persuade the court to rule in its favor. A panel of judges reviews the legal briefs as well as transcripts from the trial court and any previous appellate court hearings on the same case. The judges may allow each party to make a brief oral argument, typically about 20 minutes per side. The panel of judges decides the case (with a simple majority vote) based on the review of this paperwork, oral arguments when they are allowed, and conversations among themselves and their law clerks. Appellate courts often write, announce, and publish opinions that provide the legal rationale for the court's decision.

In the dual court system, as presented in Figure 15.1, each state's court system resolves criminal and civil lawsuits stemming from disputes over the state's laws. At the same time, the federal court system resolves criminal and civil lawsuits stemming from disputes over federal law. One twist to the independent functioning of state and federal courts is that a lawsuit that began in a state court system can end up in the federal court system. Specifically, if a state court case raises

>Juries are an option for the defendant in trial courts. Jurors in federal trial courts must be unanimous in their verdicts. The presiding judge can declare a hung jury if all jurors cannot agree on the verdict. Then the government (or complainant, in civil cases) must decide if it will try the case again, with a new trial and jury, or drop the case. How does this help explain the preference for jury trials among defendants?

bench trial
a trial in which the judge who presides over the trial decides on guilt or liability

POLITICAL

Inquiry

FIGURE 15.1 ▦ JURISDICTION IN THE DUAL COURT SYSTEM In the dual court system, the cases that state courts have authority to hear differ from those that the federal courts have authority to hear. What cases are within the jurisdiction of a state's court system? What cases are within the jurisdiction of the federal court system? When can a case that began in a state court system move into the federal court system?

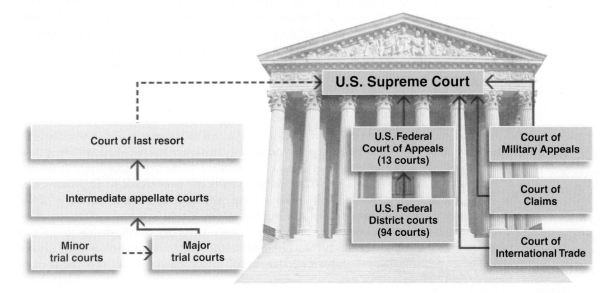

>A panel of judges presides over appellate cases, and the majority of judges must agree on the verdict. Unlike during trials, witnesses do not take the stand to be questioned during an appellate hearing. Moreover, the panel of judges may decide that no oral argument is necessary, in which case the judges decide the case based on legal briefs and transcripts from previous trials and appeals in the case. How does this help to explain why television shows do not present appellate case courtroom scenes?

court of last resort
the highest court in a court system

questions about federal laws (typically about U.S. constitutional rights on appeal), then the case may be brought to a federal appeals court after the state **court of last resort,** the highest court in the state's court system, has an opportunity to hear the case. We now turn to an examination of the federal judicial system.

The Federal Court System

Under the Articles of Confederation, there was no national judiciary. The state courts handled all lawsuits, including suits to resolve disputes over state laws and suits to resolve disputes over national laws. State courts had original jurisdiction in all lawsuits.

During the Constitutional Convention, delegates agreed on the need for a national judiciary, but they sparred over the appropriate structure and powers of a national judiciary. The debate was not resolved at the Constitutional Convention. Instead, Article III of the Constitution established that "Judicial power of the United States shall be vested in one supreme Court and in such inferior Courts as the Congress may from time to time ordain and establish." Article III also stated that the power of the national judiciary extended to all disputes over the U.S. Constitution, national laws, and treaties. While the Constitution provided for the basic structure of the U.S. Supreme Court and power of the national judiciary, it is through legislation that Congress established inferior courts and special courts with distinctive jurisdiction. In addition, through legislation and judicial decision making, the authority of the federal courts has evolved.

Jurisdiction of Federal Courts

federal question
a question of law based on interpretation of the U.S. Constitution, federal laws, or treaties

diversity of citizenship
the circumstance in which the parties in a legal case are from different states or the case involves a U.S. citizen and a foreign government

The ability of a court to hear a case depends on whether that court has jurisdiction—the authority of a court to hear and decide a case. Article III, Section 2, of the Constitution strictly defines federal court jurisdiction. In this passage, federal courts are empowered to hear only cases involving a federal question or diversity of citizenship. A **federal question** is a question of law based on interpretation of the U.S. Constitution, federal laws (including common law, statutory law, administrative law, and executive orders), or treaties. **Diversity of citizenship** means that the parties in the case are individuals from different states or that the case involves a U.S. citizen and a foreign government. It may also mean that the suit centers on the complaint of one or more states against another state or states.

The Structure of the Federal Courts

The federal court system is a three-tiered hierarchical system. At the bottom, in the first tier, are the U.S. district courts, which are the federal trial courts with original jurisdiction over a case. In the middle tier of the federal system are the U.S. courts of appeals, which have appellate jurisdiction. At the top of the federal court hierarchy, in the top tier, is the U.S. Supreme Court. The U.S. Supreme Court has appellate jurisdiction and rarely used, very limited original jurisdiction. The U.S. Supreme Court is the federal court of last resort.

Congress has complemented the three-tiered system of Article III courts (district courts, courts of appeals, and the U.S. Supreme Court) with specialized courts. Congress established the specialized courts through legislation grounded in its authority under Article I of the Constitution to "constitute tribunals inferior to the Supreme Court," and so the specialized courts are known as Article I courts.

U.S. SPECIAL COURTS   In 2013, media coverage highlighted the activities of the Foreign Intelligence Surveillance Act (FISA) court. Congress established the FISA court in a 1978 act that spells out the procedures for the collection of human and electronic intelligence.[12] In June 2013, Britain's *Guardian* newspaper reported that the U.S. National Security Agency (NSA) was collecting telephone records of millions of Verizon customers. Then, *The Washington Post* reported that the NSA was wiretapping servers of nine companies, including Google and Facebook. The FISA court approved the national government's applications for this electronic surveillance. This government infringement on their privacy startled American citizens, but was quickly defended by President Obama and members of Congress as necessary to national security.

The FISA court is one example of an Article I court, or U.S. special court. Other special courts include the U.S. Bankruptcy Court, the U.S. Court of Military Appeals, the U.S. Tax Court, and the U.S. Court of Veterans' Appeals. Congress establishes Article I courts to help administer specific federal laws; therefore, these courts have administrative as well as judicial responsibilities.[13] Unlike the judges sitting on the benches in the Article III courts, who are appointed to life terms, the judges who preside over these special Article I courts are appointed to serve for fixed terms.

U.S. DISTRICT COURTS   There are 94 federal district courts with 677 judgeships. Each state has between 1 and 4 district courts, and Washington, D.C., and Puerto Rico each have a district court. These trial courts do the bulk of the work of the federal judiciary because the courts have original, **mandatory jurisdiction,** which means they must hear every case filed with them. A judge presides over the trial court, and the judge, or a jury if the defendant chooses the jury option, decides what happened in the case, based on the application of the law to the facts presented in the courtroom. It is in the trial court that two parties to the lawsuit present evidence and witnesses testify. Federal district courts operate throughout the United States; every state has at least one. Congress, through legislation, can modify the jurisdiction of district courts as well as change the number of district court judgeships.

mandatory jurisdiction
the requirement that a court hear all cases filed with it

Defendants who lose in the district courts have the right to appeal their cases to a federal court of appeals if they believe the presiding judge misinterpreted or misapplied the law. However, the majority of cases decided by the district courts are not appealed. Therefore, the overwhelming majority of federal lawsuits are resolved in the district courts.

U.S. COURTS OF APPEALS   At the middle level of the federal judicial hierarchy are 13 courts of appeals. Figure 15.2 shows the 12 courts of appeal that cover specific geographic regions (circuits), including the District of Columbia (D.C.) Circuit, plus the Federal Circuit. Each of the 12 circuit courts with geographically based jurisdiction hears appeals from the U.S. district courts within its region. D.C. Circuit also handles appeals stemming from conflicts over administrative law for the many federal agencies located in Washington, D.C. Confirmation battles for President Obama's nominees to three seats on this court led to changes in the Senate's filibuster rules in 2013, as discussed later in this chapter. The Federal Circuit has issue-based jurisdiction (as opposed to geographically based jurisdiction, as in the other circuits), covering specific kinds of cases, involving such matters as international trade, government contracts, and patents. Congress has authorized 179 judgeships for these courts.

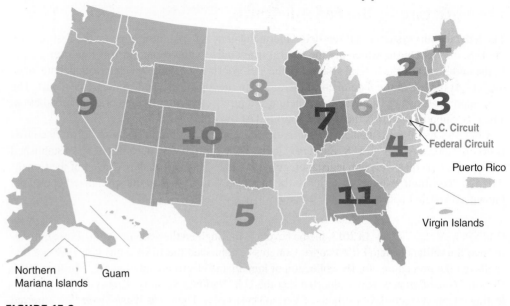

FIGURE 15.2

THE U.S. COURTS OF APPEALS

SOURCE: www.judicialnominations.org.

Judges on the courts of appeals work in panels of three to review cases. Similar to the U.S. district courts, the U.S. courts of appeals have mandatory jurisdiction, therefore they hear all cases that are filed with their court. The U.S. courts of appeals are considered intermediate appellate courts, because they are not constitutionally the court of last resort. Losing parties can appeal to the U.S. Supreme Court; however, only a very small percentage do. Therefore, the courts of appeals are in fact the court of last resort for the overwhelming majority of appealed cases.

THE U.S. SUPREME COURT At the top of the federal judicial hierarchy sits the U.S. Supreme Court. Although this court has a very limited original jurisdiction, it hears appeals from both the federal courts and the state courts when cases decided there concern a conflict over federal law, or a federal question. The framers limited the Supreme Court's original jurisdiction to those cases that concern ambassadors, public ministers, and consuls, and those involving two or more states. But over time, Congress, in cooperation with the Court, has decided that the Court should retain original jurisdiction only in cases involving suits between two or more states.

The U.S. Supreme Court's appellate jurisdiction is **discretionary jurisdiction,** which means the justices choose the cases they will hear from among all the cases appealed to the Court. Ultimately, the justices select to hear only a fraction of the cases appealed to the Supreme Court.

Since 1869, nine judges, called justices, sit on the Supreme Court. One of these justices has been specially selected by a president to serve as the **chief justice,** the judge who provides both organizational and intellectual leadership on the Court. Each of the remaining eight justices is an **associate justice.** Political scientists distinguish periods of court activity by changes in the chief justices; therefore, Supreme Courts are named for the chief justice. Today, we have the Roberts Court, named for the current chief justice, John Roberts, whom President George W. Bush nominated and the Senate confirmed in 2005.

Appointing Federal Judges

The framers wanted to ensure **judicial independence** so that federal judges could make impartial decisions based on the law, protected from the need to win the votes of citizens or support from elected officials to keep their job. To foster judicial independence, Article II of the Constitution establishes the president's authority to appoint, with the advice and consent of the Senate,

discretionary jurisdiction
the authority of a court to select the cases it will hear from among all the cases appealed to it

chief justice
the leading justice on the Supreme Court, who provides both organizational and intellectual leadership

associate justice
title of the eight Supreme Court justices who are not the chief justice

judicial independence
insulating judges from the need to be accountable to voters or elected officials so that they can make impartial decisions based on the law

Then Now

> Before Thurgood Marshall joined the U.S. Supreme Court as its 96th justice in 1967, all Supreme Court justices had been white men. Marshall, the first African American to sit on the Court, replaced Justice Tom Clark on the Court led by Chief Justice Earl Warren. The "Then" photo shows the all-male, all-white Warren Court (1953–1969) in a 1957 photo. Today, the Supreme Court has a record high of three women justices, including the first justice (male or female) of Hispanic descent, and the second African American to serve on the Supreme Court. While women (Caucasian and one Latina) and African American men have served on the Court as justices, only white men have served as chief justice of the Supreme Court. Should the Supreme Court offer descriptive representation, that is, look like the population in terms of demographic characteristics such as sex, race, and ethnicity, even if only for symbolic reasons?

Supreme Court and other federal judges. In addition, Article III states that U.S. Supreme Court justices and the judges of the inferior courts Congress creates "shall hold their offices during good behavior, and shall at stated times, receive for their services, a compensation, which shall not be diminished during their continuance in office." Therefore, the term of office for Article III judges extends until they resign, retire, or pass away, or until Congress removes them through the impeachment process. Because of the life term of Article III judges, the selection of federal judges for the district courts, the courts of appeal, and the U.S. Supreme Court is very important. Unfortunately, growing partisanship has increased the challenges presidents confront when identifying judicial nominees and winning Senate confirmation.

According to the Brennan Center for Justice, the number of judicial vacancies in federal district courts averaged 60 in each of the first 5 years of President Obama's administration; the 10 percent vacancy rate is a historic high in district court vacancies.[14] At the end of 2013, there were 18 vacancies in the federal courts of appeals, which is 10 percent of the judgeships in those courts.[15] In December 2013, there were 10 court of appeals nominees pending and 42 district court nominees pending.[16]

In both 2009 and 2010, President Obama faced one of the most important decisions of his presidency—filling a vacancy on the U.S. Supreme Court. His nominations, if confirmed, would have implications for policy decades after his presidency had ended. In May 2009, Obama announced Sonia Sotomayor as his nominee for the seat that had been occupied by Supreme Court justice David Souter, who had retired at the end of the Court's 2008–2009 term. The following year, he selected Elena Kagan as his nominee to replace retiring associate justice John Paul Stevens. Obama's selections of Sotomayor and Kagan illustrate the differing characteristics presidents might emphasize when selecting judges for the federal bench.

Selection Criteria

In selecting Sonia Sotomayor, President Obama sought a competent individual who would win Senate confirmation. Sotomayor had sat on the second circuit of the U.S. Court of Appeals since 1998. Obama also wanted to appoint a justice who promoted his ideology. Finally, following his election, Obama wanted to increase the diversity of the bench. Sotomayor was the Court's first Latino member.

Obama's selection of Elena Kagan was perhaps more surprising. Kagan, who served as the dean of the Harvard Law School, had never served as a judge. Though there was precedent for nonjudges being appointed to the Court, that career path was not the usual one. But in Kagan, many analysts believe that Obama saw traits that far outweighed her lack of experience on the bench. Throughout her career, Kagan had gained a reputation as a conciliator—a peacemaker who could bring divergent ideological sides together, a characteristic that could prove important, given the often-divided nature of the Court. In addition to Kagan's impeccable academic credentials, because she had not served as a judge, Kagan was not saddled with an enormous record of judicial opinions that could have been used against her during the confirmation process.

In Obama's two Supreme Court nominations, we clearly see several of the criteria presidents consider when nominating federal judges and justices: judicial competence, political ideology, representativeness of the population, and political considerations. These are the most common criteria presidents considered.

JUDICIAL COMPETENCE   Competence is of central concern for nominees to the federal bench. First and foremost, judges must be qualified, and some nominees in recent decades have been rejected because of senatorial doubts about their qualifications. For example, when President George W. Bush nominated his White House counsel Harriet Miers as an associate Supreme Court justice in 2005, he was forced to withdraw his nomination because of concerns about Miers's lack of qualifications. Those objections indicated strongly that Miers would face a steep uphill climb in achieving Senate confirmation.[17]

POLITICAL IDEOLOGY   Mindful that federal judges typically serve far beyond their own tenure, presidents often regard these nominations as a way of cementing their own legacies. They give the nod to judges, and more significantly, to Supreme Court justices, with whom they are ideologically compatible: liberal presidents nominate liberal judges, and conservative presidents nominate conservative judges. When George W. Bush nominated Chief Justice John Roberts, he chose an individual who shared the president's own policy views, particularly with regard to issues such as abortion, church and state relations, and criminal due process protections. In nominating Sonia Sotomayor, President Obama chose a person who held liberal views consistent with his own.

Using party affiliation and previous decisions as a measure of a nominee's political ideology, presidents tend to nominate judges with their own party affiliation. However, a judge's ideology can shift over time. For example, President George W. Bush nominated David Souter, expecting him to be a solid conservative vote on the Court. Instead, Souter became a solid member of the Court's liberal bloc, voting often with the more liberal justices. Then Justice Souter resigned from the Supreme Court just months after President Obama took office, allowing a Democratic president to replace the Republican-nominated Souter.[18]

REPRESENTATION OF DEMOGRAPHIC GROUPS   The impulse to diversify the Court's membership serves the goal of **descriptive representation,** which is representation on governing bodies, including the Court, of the country's leading demographic groups in proportion to their representation in the population at large. There is an implicit assumption that a justice occupying one of these seats will best serve the concerns of the racial, ethnic, gender, or other group to which he or she belongs, thereby offering **substantive representation.** That is, the Latino justice will take the perspective of Latinos, the female justice will consider the policy preferences of women, and so on. However, the representation may be more symbolic than real because not all women have the same views, nor do all men, even if they are of the same race or ethnicity. Therefore, one female or Latino judge cannot represent the diversity of views of the people they look like. Nevertheless, many public figures and citizens say that the Court should mirror as closely as possible the main contours of the national demographic profile, offering **symbolic representation,** which indicates that our democracy, our government by and for the people, is functioning appropriately by offering equal opportunity to influence government as a government official.

Some presidents appear more concerned than others with enhancing diversity on the federal bench. Table 15.1 suggests that, compared to Republican presidents, Democratic presidents have been more concerned about descriptive representation.

descriptive representation
the attempt to ensure that governing bodies include representatives of major demographic groups—such as women, African Americans, Latinas, Jews, and Catholics—in proportions similar to their representation in the population at large

substantive representation
the assumption that a government official will best serve the concerns of the racial, ethnic, gender, or other group to which he or she belongs

symbolic representation
diversity among government officials is a symbol, an indication, that our democracy, our government by and for the people, is functioning appropriately by offering equal opportunity to influence government by becoming a government official

POLITICAL CONSIDERATIONS Clearly, the nomination and confirmation of federal judges by the Senate does not take place in a vacuum. Beyond presidents' and senators' concerns about judicial qualifications, political ideology, and demographic representation, these players are acutely aware of what their constituencies will think of any nominee and of what might happen at the confirmation hearings. For that reason, they continuously gauge public opinion throughout the nomination and confirmation process. In addition to being mindful of the voters, the president and the senators calculate how interest groups, particularly those that helped to put them in office, will view the nominee.

Demographics of Federal Judges as a Percentage of Those Confirmed (1993–2013)

CHARACTERISTIC	BILL CLINTON	GEORGE W. BUSH	BARACK OBAMA
Asian	1%	1%	7%
Hispanic	7%	9%	13%
Black	17%	8%	18%
White	75%	82%	62%
Female	29%	22%	42%
Male	71%	78%	58%

SOURCE: American Constitution Society for Law and Policy, www.judicialnominations.org.

Interest groups often have a significant voice in the confirmation hearings. Some groups almost always participate in the hearings, among them the American Bar Association, labor and civil rights organizations, law enforcement groups, and business interests. These groups let the members of the Senate know clearly whether they support or oppose a given candidate.

senatorial courtesy
a custom that allows senators from the president's political party to veto the president's choice of federal district court judge in the senator's state

The Senate's Role: Judicial Confirmation

Article II of the Constitution gives the president the authority, with the advice and consent of the Senate, to appoint federal judges. This sharing of power, with the president nominating judges and the Senate confirming them, operates in accordance with our system of checks and balances. In the case of the federal district court judges, a custom known as **senatorial courtesy** gives senators—although only those who are of the same political party as the president—a powerful voice in who the president nominates to serve as district court judges in their state. Under this tradition, a senator from the same political party as the president can block the president's nomination of a federal district court judge in the senator's state.

Because courts of appeals judges and Supreme Court justices serve more than one state, the individual senators from any one state play a far less powerful role in the appointment of these judges. Rather, the Senate Judiciary Committee takes the lead. Committee members are charged with gathering information about each nominee and providing it to the full Senate. The Senate Judiciary Committee votes on nominees to the federal bench, and the full Senate uses this vote to signal whether the nominee is acceptable. Sometimes the judiciary committee does not make a recommendation about a nominee, as when members split their vote 7-7 on the nomination of Clarence Thomas to the U.S. Supreme Court in 1991.

President Obama, like Presidents Bill Clinton and George W. Bush before him, ran into problems with many of his judicial nominees, particularly those nominated to the courts of appeals. Sparked by partisanship, senators from both political parties have used the filibuster to block votes on judicial nominees to promote partisan bias on specific courts. In November 2013, after repeated filibustering of President Obama's nominees, the Democratic majority in the U.S. Senate argued that the Republican minority had gone too far in its efforts to thwart the president. Without one vote from the Republican minority, the Democratic majority approved a filibuster rule change, called the nuclear option, prohibiting the use of the filibuster to block votes on presidential nominees to executive branch positions and all judicial positions except those for the U.S. Supreme Court. This rule change will force the Senate to provide its advice and consent on all presidential nominees.

>Among the criteria President George H. W. Bush considered when he nominated Clarence Thomas to the U.S. Supreme Court in 1991 were Thomas's competence and political ideology, public concern for demographic representation, and political considerations. Thomas's conservative ideology, experience on the U.S. Court of Appeals—combined with public interest in replacing retiring Justice Thurgood Marshall, the first black Supreme Court justice, with another black justice—made Thomas a good choice for President Bush. However, liberal organizations raised concerns about Thomas, including the fact that he had served only two years as a federal judge. Here we see nominee Thomas, with his wife behind him, during the Senate Judiciary Committee confirmation hearings. The Judiciary Committee's 7–7 split vote was followed by the Senate's 52–48 vote to confirm. Today, Thomas remains the lone black justice on the U.S. Supreme Court.

Once Supreme Court justices and other Article III judges are confirmed by the Senate, they serve for life, as long as they do not commit any impeachable offense. Although lifetime tenure is controversial, it also means that such appointees often are the longest-lasting legacies of the presidents who appoint them.

How the U.S. Supreme Court Functions

collegial court

a court made up of a group of judges who must evaluate a case together and decide on the outcome; compromise and negotiation take place as members try to build a majority coalition

As a **collegial court,** the Supreme Court is made up of a panel of justices who must work closely together to evaluate a case and decide, with a majority vote, the outcome. Collegially, they decide what cases to hear, resolve each case heard, and develop the legal reasoning that, as presented in the Court's written opinion, will persuade the public that the Court's decision is correct. The *correct decision* means the justices upheld the legal principles found in the Constitution. Today's reality is that it is common for Supreme Court cases to be decided by a 5–4 vote, which indicates that the justices do not all agree on the same interpretation of constitutional language and its legal principles.

The overwhelming majority of cases decided by the U.S. Supreme Court are appeals. Therefore, we focus on how the Court processes the appeals that are filed with it.

Choosing Cases for Review

certiorari petition

a petition submitted to the Supreme Court requesting review of a case already decided

Approximately 7,000 *certiorari* **petitions** are filed with the Court each year, each asking for the review of a case already decided. Ultimately, the justices agree to review less than 100 cases in each annual term that begins in October and typically runs through the following June or July. For the thousands of cases the Court decides not to hear, the decision made by the last court to hear the case stands. How do the justices decide which cases to hear? Like the other stages of the decision-making process, "deciding to decide," as Supreme Court scholar H. W. Perry puts it, is a joint activity.[19]

cert memo

description of the facts of a case filed with the Court, the pertinent legal arguments, and a recommendation as to whether the case should be taken, written by one of the justices' law clerks and reviewed by all justices participating in the pool process

The decision to place a case on the Supreme Court's docket (schedule of cases it will review) is a collaborative one, with the nine justices and their law clerks (four clerks per associate justice, and five for the chief justice) working together. The Supreme Court justices pool their law clerks so that only one clerk reviews a *certiorari* petition and writes a **cert memo,** which includes a description of the facts of the case, the pertinent legal arguments, and a recommendation as to whether the Court should hear the case. The clerk's cert memo is shared with all the justices. After reviewing the cert memos, the chief justice distributes a list of possible cases, the discuss list. The associate justices may add cases to the discuss list based on their own reviews of cert memos.

writ of certiorari

Latin for "a request to make certain"; issued by a higher court, this is an order for a lower court to make available the records of a past case it decided so that the higher court can review the case

On Fridays throughout the Court's term, the justices meet in conference to discuss the cases on the discuss list.[20] At this point, they vote on whether to issue a writ of *certiorari*—a Latin term roughly translated as "a request to make certain"—for specific cases. The **writ of certiorari** is a higher court's order to a lower court to make available the records of a past case so that the higher court can review the case.[21] A writ of *certiorari* is sent when the justices, using their discretionary jurisdiction, agree to hear a case. The justices determine which cases to hear according to a practice known as the **Rule of Four,** under which the justices will hear a case if four or more of the nine justices decide they want to hear it. They do not need to give reasons for wanting or not wanting to hear a case—they simply must vote.

Rule of Four

practice by which the Supreme Court justices determine if they will hear a case if four or more justices want to hear it

Considering Legal Briefs and Oral Arguments

When the justices agree to put a case on the docket, the parties in the litigation shift into high gear (see Figure 15.3). The petitioner (the party that sought the Court's review) files with the Court a brief—a document detailing the legal argument for the desired outcome. After the filing of this brief, the opposing party files its own brief with the Court.

amicus curiae brief ("friend of the court" brief)

a legal brief, filed by an individual or a group that is not a party in the case, written to influence the Court's decision

Today, *amicus curiae* briefs are a common part of Supreme Court litigation. Filed by a person or group that is not a party to the lawsuit, an ***amicus curiae* brief, or "friend of the court" brief,** is written to influence the Court's decision in a specific case. Controversial cases with the potential to affect public policy trigger the filing of many *amicus* briefs.

In comparison with the legal briefs filed by the two parties involved in the legal dispute, *amicus curiae* briefs typically put forth new legal arguments, and discuss broader societal effects of potential Court decisions (not just the effect on the litigants). Jurists do not legally have to consider the information provided in *amicus curiae* briefs. However, research indicates that judges often use the information or the legal arguments contained in *amicus curiae* briefs to help them decide cases.[22] Judicial scholar Paul Collins found that no type of interest group dominated *amicus* activity, but instead "*amicus* participation in the Court is pluralistic."[23] Associate Supreme Court justice Stephen Breyer argues that the participation of organized interests in the judicial decision-making process provides an avenue for citizen engagement and civic discourse, which support a healthy democracy.[24]

In addition to reviewing legal briefs, justices listen to oral arguments—attorneys' formal spoken arguments that lay out why the Court should rule in their client's favor. Heard in the Supreme Court's public gallery, oral arguments give the justices the opportunity to ask the parties and their lawyers specific questions about the arguments in their briefs. To assist in their preparation for oral argument, justices typically have their clerks prepare **bench memos,** which summarize the case and outline relevant facts and issues presented in the case documents and the legal briefs. The bench memos may also suggest questions for the justices to ask during oral arguments.[25]

In typical cases, each side's lawyers have 30 minutes to make a statement to the Court and to answer the justices' questions. However, the justices can provide more time for oral argument, as they did in 2012 when they scheduled six hours of oral argument, over the course of three days, for the case challenging the constitutionality of the Patient Protection and Affordable Care Act (2010). The justices frequently interrupt the attorneys during their oral arguments by asking questions and sometimes seem to ignore the lawyers entirely, instead talking with one another. Chief Justice Roberts points out that the justices do not discuss the cases before oral argument. "When we get out on the bench, it's really the first time we start to get some clues about what our colleagues think. So we are often using questions to bring out points that we think our colleagues ought to know about."[26] Associate Justice Kagan notes that "part of what oral argument is about is a little bit of the justices talking to each other with some helpless person standing at the podium who you're talking through."[27] This discourse takes place entirely in public view, and transcripts (and sometimes even tapes) are readily available to the public.

After the oral arguments, the justices meet in a private, justice-only conference to deliberate; no law clerks are present, and no information is shared with the public. The justices take a nonbinding vote on the case. If the chief justice votes with the majority, he chooses whether he wants to write the opinion that will provide the legal reasoning for the Court's decision or if he will assign the task to one of the other justices in the likely majority. If the chief justice is not with the majority, the senior member of the majority decides whether to write the opinion or assign the opinion to another justice. The assignment of the majority opinion is crucial to the resolution of the case because, in writing the opinion, the justice may persuade some justices to change their votes, making for a larger majority or possibly turning the majority into the minority, turning the losing party (based on the nonbinding conference vote) into the winning party. So let's consider how judges decide cases.

Resolving the Legal Dispute: Deciding How to Vote

How does each justice decide how to vote in a particular case? Judicial scholars offer several judicial decision-making models. The **legal model** focuses on legal norms and principles as the guiding force in judicial decision making. Specifically, according to the legal model, judges consider existing precedents, relevant constitutional and statutory law, and the intent of those who wrote the relevant laws, when deciding cases. Law schools train lawyers, and therefore judges, to follow the legal model. The **attitudinal model** indicates that judges allow their policy and ideological preferences to influence their decisions. In fact, evidence suggests that Supreme Court justices are for the most part ideologically consistent in their own decision making.[28] Constitutional law professor Dale Carpenter notes, "There's evidence that the justices do vote against their policy preferences from time to time, enough to disrupt the general narrative that they just vote their ideological preferences. But that doesn't stop the general story from being true."[29]

FIGURE 15.3 ■ DECISION MAKING ON THE SUPREME COURT What is the Rule of Four? At what stages of the process do law clerks have the potential to influence the decisions of the Court?

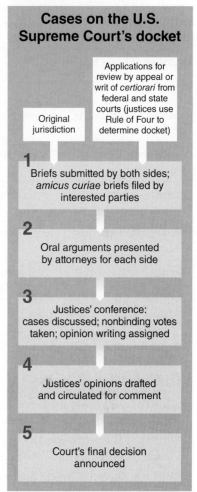

Cases on the U.S. Supreme Court's docket

Applications for review by appeal or writ of *certiorari* from federal and state courts (justices use Rule of Four to determine docket)

Original jurisdiction

1 Briefs submitted by both sides; *amicus curiae* briefs filed by interested parties

2 Oral arguments presented by attorneys for each side

3 Justices' conference: cases discussed; nonbinding votes taken; opinion writing assigned

4 Justices' opinions drafted and circulated for comment

5 Court's final decision announced

bench memo
written by a justice's law clerk, a summary of the case, outlining relevant facts and issues presented in the case documents and briefs, that may also suggest questions to be asked during oral arguments

legal model
judicial decision-making model that focuses on legal norms and principles as the guiding force in judicial decision making, including existing precedents, relevant constitutional and statutory law, and the lawmakers' intent

attitudinal model
judicial decision-making model that claims judicial decision making is guided by policy and ideological preferences of individual judges

Changes in the Supreme Court

	Then (1801–1835)	Now*
Number of Justices	5	9
Number of Law Clerks	0	37 (4 per associate justice, and 5 for the chief justice)
Authors of First Drafts of Most Opinions	Chief Justice	Law clerks
Occurrence of Unanimous Decisions	Most cases	Rare
Average Percentage of Dissenting Opinions	6 percent**	60 percent**
Average Percentage of Concurring Opinions	2 percent**	40 percent**
Amicus Brief Activity	First adversarial amicus filed in 1823 case[+]	At least one brief filed in 90 percent of cases[++]

*The Rehnquist Court is the most recent court for which data are readily available.
**Paul M. Collins, Jr., Friends of the Supreme Court: Interest Groups and Judicial Decision Making (New York: Oxford University Press, 2008): 143.
[+]Collins, p. 39.
[++]Collins, p. 46.

WHAT'S NEXT?

> Will Congress enact legislation to decrease the role of law clerks (who individual judges hire with no checks) in opinion writing?

> Will the pattern of dissent among the justices, as evidenced by the increase in the proportion of dissenting and concurring opinions, continue?

> Will the volume of amicus brief activity continue as the partisan nature of politics grows even more divisive?

strategic model
judicial decision-making model that states that the primary guide for judges is their individual policy preferences; however, their preferences are tempered by their consideration of institutional factors, as well as concern over the legitimacy of the court system

concurring opinion
judicial opinion agreeing with how the majority decides the case but disagreeing with at least some of the legal interpretations or conclusions reached by the majority

dissenting opinion
judicial opinion disagreeing both with the majority's disposition of a case and with their legal interpretations and conclusions

According to the **strategic model,** "while justices' decisions are primarily motivated by policy concerns (thus accepting the attitudinal model), institutional constraints exist that limit the ability of the justices to vote in a manner that is compatible with their attitudes and values in every case."[30] The institutional constraints identified by proponents of the strategic model include the preferences of Congress, the president, and other justices sitting on the collegial court, as well as concern for maintaining the legitimacy of the court system. If the Court makes decisions that are too far afield from societal norms, the public might begin to question the legitimacy of the Court in our democracy.

Research on the decision making of the Supreme Court justices suggests that none of these models explains every aspect of judicial decision making. Indeed, the three models must be combined to better understand these decision makers. Judicial scholars Bryan W. Marshall, Richard L. Pacelle, Jr., and Christine Ludowise argue that "the behavior of the Supreme Court is governed by the personal preferences of the justices, but that is tempered by the need to attend to precedent as well as the institution's sense of duty and obligation to the law and the Constitution."[31]

Legal Reasoning: Writing the Opinions

After the conference at which the nonbinding vote to decide a case occurs, justices and their law clerks begin writing opinions. The justices' law clerks often write the first draft of their opinions and frequently take the lead in communicating with the other justices through their law clerks. In fact, judicial scholar Artemus Ward states: "Modern justices now see themselves and their clerks as comprising an opinion writing team."[32]

When the justices disagree about a decision, it is likely that several draft opinions circulate. The justice assigned the majority opinion will circulate a draft and revise it based on input from the other justices. Revisions are made to strengthen the legal reasoning, to win new votes from justices who were in the minority, or to keep the votes of justices in the majority. Other justices, with their clerks, will draft and circulate opinions with their legal reasoning. Some of these drafts may become concurring opinions; others may become dissenting opinions. **Concurring opinions** agree with how the majority opinion decides the case but disagree with at least some of the legal reasoning or conclusions reached in this majority opinion. **Dissenting opinions** not only disagree with the legal reasoning but also reject the underlying decision in the case.

After the opinions are written and signed off on, the Court announces the decision by publishing it. On rare occasions, the justices read their opinions from the bench. In 2007, Justice Ginsburg read her dissenting opinion in the *Ledbetter v. Goodyear Tire & Rubber*[33] case to bring immediate attention to a decision that she believed would have great, negative consequences, especially on women. Ginsburg's reading was a catalyst for Congress to formulate and enact the Lilly Ledbetter Fair Pay Act in 2009, which was the first bill President Obama signed into law. The Fair Pay Act overruled the Court's interpretation of a piece of the 1964

Civil Rights Act (in the 2007 *Ledbetter* case). In the *Ledbetter* case, the Court decided that when Ledbetter finally found out about her discriminatory pay, 19 years after her first discriminatory paycheck, it was too late for her to sue because she had only 180 days after the first discriminatory paycheck was issued in which to sue, according to the majority of justices' interpretation of the 1964 law. The Fair Pay Act of 2009 states that the 180-day statute of limitation to file an equal pay lawsuit (created in the 1964 law) resets after each new discriminatory paycheck. The Fair Pay Act is now the law that the Supreme Court must apply to pay discrimination cases.

Although the U.S. Supreme Court is the court of last resort, it does not always have the final word. As in the *Ledbetter* case, Congress can write new legislation to overrule the Court's interpretation of law. In this way, the U.S. Supreme Court is part of an ongoing dialogue, with officials in the other branches and levels of government, on laws and policies.

Judges as Policy Makers

Courts make law—common law—by deciding cases and establishing legal principles that guide future litigants and judges. The lawmaking function of courts ensures that judges have a powerful role as public policy makers, because the decisions they make profoundly affect not only the parties in the case but also society, the economy, and politics.

Law professor Tom Ginsburg, who compares constitutions from across the globe adopted since 1787, notes that the U.S. Constitution is briefer and covers fewer topics than do more recently approved constitutions. It also does not cover contemporary issues and topics because it was ratified over 200 years ago and has been amended only 27 times. This means that the U.S. Constitution leaves more room for courts to fill in gaps. According to Ginsburg, "all of these factors perversely empower the Supreme Court and makes the court much more likely to engage in public policy."[34]

From Judicial Review to Judicial Policy Making

The Court's decision in *Marbury v. Madison* (1803) claimed the power of judicial review for the courts, making the courts a major policy maker. The courts determine what policies are constitutional. In 1896, the Supreme Court decided in *Plessy v. Ferguson*[35] that the Fourteenth Amendment did not prohibit segregation of people based on race and color in public accommodations, specifically train cars. The Court in *Plessy* established the common-law legal principle of separate but equal. That decision allowed state and local governments to enact laws that permitted, and in some cases even required, segregation by race in a variety of venues, from movie theaters to housing developments to public schools. Then the Court struck a blow to segregation policies with its decision in *Brown v. Board of Education of Topeka, Kansas* (1954).[36] In *Brown,* using the common-law principle of judicial review, the Court reinterpreted the Fourteenth Amendment's equal protection clause, ruling the legal principle of separate but equal unconstitutional, and found segregation laws unconstitutional. The Court took its decision further, calling for integration of public schools with all deliberate speed. Clearly, the Court was engaged in policy making, and the policy has had a tremendous effect on society, the economy, and politics.

Supreme Court Justice Sandra Day O'Connor argues that the *Brown* case was a catalyst for lawsuits in which litigants claim violations of their constitutional rights to equal protection of the law and due process. O'Connor notes that prior to the *Brown* case, conflicts over the separation of powers within the national government and the distribution of powers between the national and state governments dominated the Supreme Court's docket. However, since the *Brown* case, "the Supreme Court's decisions on individual rights have recognized for the first time many of the freedoms that most Americans today assume as our birthrights. Among them are the right to speak freely and advocate for change, the right to worship as we please, and the privilege of political participation."[37] Therefore, judicial policy making includes defending and creating individual rights.

POLITICAL Inquiry

> Standing behind President Barack Obama as he signs his first bill into law is Lilly Ledbetter, whose loss in the Supreme Court (with a divided 5-4 vote) mobilized Congress to approve the Lilly Ledbetter Fair Pay Act in 2009. How did Justice Ruth Bader Ginsburg, the lone woman on the Supreme Court at the time, vote on this sexual discrimination case? What did Justice Ginsburg do to light the spark that mobilized congressional action to enact a law to "correct" the Court's (mis)interpretation of the 1964 Civil Rights Act?

>In a May 1954 landmark decision in the case of *Brown v. the Board of Education of Topeka, Kansas* (discussed in Chapter 5), the U.S. Supreme Court ruled *de jure* segregation in American public schools unconstitutional. Today, *de facto* segregation exists in many public schools. What is *de jure* segregation? What is *de facto* segregation? What causes *de facto* segregation?

Judicial Activism versus Judicial Restraint

judicial activism
an approach to judicial decision making whereby judges are willing to strike down laws made by elected officials as well as step away from precedents

When considering the courts' role as policy makers, legal analysts often categorize judges and justices as exercising either judicial activism or judicial restraint. **Judicial activism** refers to the courts' willingness to strike down laws made by elected officials as well as to step away from past precedents, thereby creating new laws and policies. It reflects the notion that the role of the courts is to check the power of the federal and state executive and legislative branches when those governmental entities exceed their authority or violate the Constitution.

During the Warren Court (the tenure of Chief Justice Earl Warren, 1953–1969), using the common-law doctrine of judicial review, the Supreme Court took an activist stance, most notably in rejecting the constitutionality of racial segregation. By barring southern states from segregation in a variety of contexts—including schools and other public facilities—the activist Warren Court powerfully bolstered the efforts of civil rights activists. The activism of the Warren Court was also instrumental in shaping the modern rights of the accused and the modern definitions of the privacy rights of individuals, which would later form the framework for the Court's thinking about abortion rights. Supported by presidents who enforced its rulings, the Warren Court took on a leadership role in changing the nature of U.S. society.

Although many people connect judicial activism with liberal-leaning court decisions, such as those made by the Warren Court, the reality is that judicial activism is also used to further conservative causes. The Burger Court (1969–1986) and the Rehnquist Court (1986–2005) were both conservative and activist. In fact, judicial scholar Thomas Keck labeled the Rehnquist

Court "the most activist Supreme Court in history."[38] The Rehnquist Court's conservative-leaning activism is evident in *Planned Parenthood of Southeastern Pennsylvania v. Casey* (1992). In this case, the Court checked the authority of the state of Pennsylvania to implement a state law that limits access to abortion. In its decision, the Court laid the framework for the tightening of abortion laws in many states by clarifying what measures the states could take in restricting abortions.

Today, political scientists argue that "judicial activism simply means that the courts make public policy when the elected branches cannot or will not, often by declaring the actions of other political actors to be unconstitutional."[39] In addition, judicial activism means that the judges view the Constitution as a living, evolving document. However, the term *judicial activism* is often used by people to criticize judges when they do not agree with a court's decision.

Some judges reject the idea that the courts' role is to actively check legislative and executive authority. Noting that people elect officials to those branches to carry out the people's will, these judges observe **judicial restraint**—the limiting of their own power as judges. Practitioners of judicial restraint believe that the judiciary, as the least democratic branch of government, should not check the power of the democratically elected executive and legislative branches unless their actions clearly violate the Constitution.[40]

Although the policy making of judges, particularly U.S. Supreme Court justices, is an acknowledged reality today, justices do not have the last word. Associate Justice Sandra Day O'Connor notes, "the Constitution is interpreted first and last by people other than judges. The judicial branch is only an intermediate step in the continuing process of making our Constitution work."[41]

judicial restraint
an approach to judicial decision making whereby judges defer to the democratically elected legislative and executive branches of government

Constraints on Judicial Policy Making

The U.S. judiciary is a powerful institution. Nonetheless, judges and justices face checks and constraints that limit how they decide cases, make law, and act as policy makers. Among the most important checks on the judiciary's power are the other branches of government. But lawyers, interest groups, and individual citizens also check the courts and constrain their activism. Moreover, judges and justices are trained to, and actively attempt to, make good law by correctly interpreting the Constitution.

CHECKS AND BALANCES Formidable checks on the judiciary come from the legislative and executive branches. Article II of the Constitution explicitly gives the legislative and executive branches crucial checks on the structure of the courts. It grants Congress the power to create all federal courts other than the Supreme Court and gives both the president and the U.S. Senate important powers in determining who sits on all federal courts. Indeed, the procedures for choosing the judges who will serve on the federal bench afford the legislative and executive branches significant control over the judiciary.

Beyond giving the president a check on the judiciary through the power to nominate judges, the Constitution also empowers the president and the executive branch due to the courts' reliance on them for the enforcement of its decisions. Specifically, if presidents fail to direct the bureaucracy to carry out judicial decisions, those decisions carry little weight. Frequently, it is executive implementation that gives teeth to the judiciary's decisions.

The Constitution also creates a legislative check on the judiciary because the framers established only the Supreme Court and left it up to Congress to create the lower federal courts. In addition, the Constitution allows Congress to control the Supreme Court's jurisdiction. Congress also can control, through legislation, the number of judges or justices who serve in the federal judiciary. Historically, Congress has been willing to increase the number of judges only when its majority is of the same party affiliation as the incumbent president, who will have the authority to nominate judges to the newly created judgeships. In 2013, Republicans in the Senate used the filibuster to prevent President Obama from filling three vacancies on the D.C. Circuit Court, claiming the Court did not have a sufficient workload for its eleven judgeships and therefore there was no need to fill the three vacancies. However, they did not propose legislation to reduce the number of judgeships on the D.C. Circuit Court. This conflict resulted in the nuclear option discussed earlier.

The two houses of Congress moreover have a central role in deciding whether to impeach federal judges. The House issues the articles of impeachment, and the Senate conducts the impeachment trial. Finally, Congress initiates the process of constitutional amendment and can attempt to change the Constitution to overrule a court decision with which it disagrees. In fact, in several cases Congress has embarked on constitutional amendment procedures in direct response to a Court decision with which members of Congress or their constituencies have disagreed. For example, the Twenty-Sixth Amendment (1971), which standardized the voting age to 18 years, came about after the Supreme Court ruled that states could set their own age limits for state elections.[42]

Although the courts can check the lawmaking (and hence policy-making) power of the legislative and executive branches by exercising judicial review, the legislature and the executive can check the courts' power of judicial review through the creation of new laws. For example, as discussed earlier in this chapter, in response to the Supreme Court's interpretation of the law in the *Ledbetter v. Goodyear Tire & Rubber* in 2007, Congress approved and President Obama signed the Lilly Ledbetter Fair Pay Act in 2009, which overruled the Court's interpretation of a piece of the 1964 Civil Rights Act.

PUBLIC ACCOUNTABILITY Public opinion seems to have a distinct influence on what the courts do, especially appellate courts such as the U.S. Supreme Court. The Court rarely issues a decision that is completely out of step with the thinking of the majority of the population. In fact, most cases seem to follow public opinion. When the Court does break with public opinion, it opens itself up to harsh criticism by the president, Congress, interest groups, and/or the general public.

But sometimes in the case of a landmark decision that is out of touch with public sentiment, the Court's ruling and people's opinions align over time. This shift can occur either because later courts adjust the original, controversial decision or, less commonly, because the Supreme Court's decision changes public opinion. One example of the interplay between public opinion and judicial decisions can be seen in the *Brown v. Board of Education* Court ruling. Initially, many southern state legislatures and even judges in federal district and appellate courts in the South did not comply with the Court's call to integrate schools. Not only did some school districts continue to segregate, but more than 100 southern legislators signed the "Southern Manifesto," a document that claimed the U.S. Supreme Court had overstepped its authority. By the 1970s, progress in integrating schools had been made. However, there are still legal conflicts over segregation and integration today.

Citizens can also constrain the courts by threatening to ignore their rulings. When members of the public disagree with judicial decisions, or with any law for that matter, they can engage in civil disobedience. In acts of civil disobedience, individuals or groups flout the law to make a larger point about its underlying unfairness. Keep in mind that the courts have little ability to enforce their decisions, and if people refuse to recognize those decisions and the other branches of the government fail to enforce them, the courts risk losing their authority and power. Fear of losing authority may explain in part why judicial decisions rarely fall out of step with the larger public stance on an issue. Like legislators, executives, and their colleagues sitting on the bench, citizens can impose significant constraints on courts and probably limit how judges handle cases and interpret laws. These constraints may not be written into the U.S. Constitution as the checks by the other branches are, but they are nonetheless very powerful and have a significant impact on how judges decide cases.

INTERNAL CONSTRAINTS Judges and justices also face powerful internal constraints on their judicial actions. Law schools train lawyers, and hence judges, to focus on the facts of the case and the relevant legal principles (found in law and precedent cases) when deciding cases. For lower-court judges, precedents from higher courts, as well as earlier decisions made by the court itself, impose limitations through the common-law doctrine of *stare decisis*. In addition, federal district court and appeals court judges do not diverge far from Supreme Court precedent because if they did so, they would risk having their decisions overturned. According to judicial scholar Paul Collins, "judges are concerned with making good law: attempting to determine the *most* legally appropriate answer to the controversy."[43]

Analyzing the Sources

THE ROBERTS COURT

JUSTICE	YEAR APPOINTED	NOMINATING PRESIDENT	CONFIRMATION VOTE	YEAR OF BIRTH
Antonin Scalia	1986	Ronald Reagan (R)	98-0	1936
Anthony M. Kennedy	1988	Ronald Reagan (R)	97-0	1936
Clarence Thomas	1991	George H. W. Bush (R)	52-48	1948
Ruth Bader Ginsburg	1993	Bill Clinton (D)	96-3	1933
Stephen G. Breyer	1994	Bill Clinton (D)	87-9	1938
John G. Roberts	2005	George W. Bush (R)	78-22	1955
Samuel Anthony Alito	2006	George W. Bush (R)	58-42	1950
Sonia Sotomayor	2009	Barack Obama (D)	68-31	1954
Elena Kagan	2010	Barack Obama (D)	63-37	1960

SOURCE: www.supremecourt.gov/about/biographies.aspx.

Evaluating the Evidence

1. Considering the party affiliation of the president who nominated each justice, what is the expected ideological bias of the Supreme Court today?

2. Considering the age of the Supreme Court justices nominated by President George W. Bush, what do you think is President Bush's long-term effect on the decision making of the Court?

3. Considering age and party affiliation of the president who nominated them, which, if any, Supreme Court justices do you believe might consider resigning during President Obama's second term? Explain your answer.

4. What would happen to the ideological bias of the Supreme Court if President Obama has the opportunity to appoint at least one more justice to the Court? What would be the effect if he has the opportunity to appoint two justices to the Court? Explain.

5. What might explain the pattern of change in confirmation votes?

The Supreme Court Today: The Roberts Court

John G. Roberts became chief justice of the Supreme Court in 2005. President George W. Bush initially nominated Roberts to replace Associate Justice Sandra Day O'Connor, who announced her retirement in the summer of 2005. Before the Senate had the opportunity to vote on Roberts's nomination for associate justice, Chief Justice William Rehnquist died. President Bush withdrew his nomination of Roberts for the associate justice position and nominated him instead for the vacant chief justice position. The Senate confirmed Roberts, and he began his term as chief justice in September 2005. O'Connor agreed to stay on the bench until the Senate confirmed her replacement. In January 2006, the Senate confirmed Samuel Alito to replace O'Connor on the bench. "Analyzing the Sources" presents information about the justices currently serving on the Roberts Court.

The ideological distribution of the Supreme Court today tilts slightly toward the conservative side, with Justices Clarence Thomas, Antonin Scalia, and Samuel Alito, as well as Chief Justice Roberts, reflecting a conservative viewpoint and Justices Sonia Sotomayor and Ruth Bader Ginsburg taking a more liberal stance on many issues. In the center are Justice Anthony Kennedy (the swing-voter), a moderate conservative, and Justices Stephen Breyer and Elena Kagan, moderate liberals. Judicial scholars Lee Epstein and Andrew D. Martin summarize the ideological nature of the Roberts Court, commenting that "Unlike the other Roberts justices, no underlying ideological pattern seems to exist to [Associate Justice] Kennedy's votes."[44] That is, unlike the other justices whose ideological biases are often evident, Kennedy's votes swing between decisions supported by liberals and those supported by conservatives.

Court watcher Adam Liptak noted in the summer of 2012 that Chief Justice Roberts "has worked hard to insulate his institution from the charge that it has political motivations, an accusation that it is especially vulnerable to because the court's five more conservative members were appointed by Republican presidents and its four more liberal ones by Democrats."[45] Roberts's vote to uphold the Affordable Care Act (2010), a key legislative initiative of the Democrats, supports Liptak's assessment. According to Gallup polls, 4 in 10 Americans believe that the Supreme Court is ideologically balanced (not too liberal, not too conservative), 3 in 10 believe the Court is too liberal, and 2 in 10 believe the Court is too conservative.[46]

Associate Justice Ruth Bader Ginsburg, the most senior member of the liberal-leaning justices, claimed in the summer of 2013 that the Court "is one of the most activist in history." However, if judicial activism is measured by the number of laws struck down by the Court, the Roberts Court is the least activist in the past 60 years. The liberal Warren Court, the more conservative Burger Court, and the conservative Rehnquist Court each overturned federal, state, and local laws at a higher rate than has the Roberts Court.[47]

There seems to be agreement among the justices that their questioning of attorneys has dominated oral arguments. Justice Roberts is concerned that he has had to "act as an umpire in terms of the competition among my colleagues to get questions out. . . . I do think the lawyers feel cheated sometimes . . . it also would be nice for them to have a chance to present their argument."[48]

According to Gallup polls, the public's approval of the Roberts Court has been dropping since its height in 2009 (61 percent approval).[49] Before the Court's 2013–2014 term began on October 7, 2013, 46 percent of Americans approved, whereas 45 percent disapproved of the way the Supreme Court was handling its job. Chief Justice Roberts is faring better than the Court. Just prior to the beginning of the term, Roberts enjoyed a 55 percent approval rating. Interestingly, Roberts's approval rating among Democrats was 61 percent, whereas it was only 46 percent among Republicans. Prior to Roberts's 2012 vote to uphold the Affordable Care Act, his approval was higher among Republicans than Democrats.

Gallup polls also show that Americans trust the judicial branch of the federal government more than the other two branches: 6 in 10 Americans report having a "great deal" or a "fair amount" of trust in the federal courts.[50] Although many people criticize appellate courts for judicial activism when they disagree with a court decision, citizens trust the nonelected policy makers (judges and justices) of the federal judicial branch more than they trust their elected federal representatives in the executive and legislative branches. This trust is a challenge to those who believe that in a representative democracy only elected government officials should make policy. Because of the vague and ambiguous language in laws that courts have to apply to resolve conflicts, judicial policy making is inevitable.

Conclusion

Thinking Critically About What's Next For the Judiciary

Rooted in a common-law tradition and framed by the Constitution, the American judiciary in its early form strongly reflected its English heritage, with its emphasis on law made by judges. Over the past two-plus centuries, the judiciary has evolved powerfully to accommodate a broad spectrum of societal changes in a continuously developing country. Today the policy-making role of the courts is acknowledged, if not appreciated, by political scientists, government officials, and most citizens.

French philosopher Alexis de Tocqueville noted the uniqueness and political consequences of the U.S. courts' power of judicial review in his famous 1835 book *Democracy in America*. He wrote: "The Americans have given their judges the right to base their decisions on the Constitution rather than on laws. In other words, they allow them not to apply laws which they consider unconstitutional."[51] Moreover, Tocqueville stated, "there is hardly a political question in the United States which does not sooner or later turn into a judicial one."[52] Politics have always been a part of the federal court system, and still are.

The judicial activism practiced by liberal and conservative justices, as they apply the common-law doctrine of judicial review, feeds concerns that the courts are engaged in partisan policy making, just like the other two branches of government. Although judges strive to make decisions that are legally correct, grounded in the fundamental rights found in the U.S. Constitution, the reality of 5–4 Supreme Court decisions indicates that not everyone agrees on what the Constitution means. The Senate's adoption of the nuclear option to limit the power of the partisan minority in the judicial appointment process speaks volumes to the partisan battles to control the direction of court decisions about the meaning of laws—constitutional law, legislation, executive orders, administrative law, and common law.

Whatever the future holds, the courts will remain a bastion in defense of individual liberties and rights. And public opinion of the judiciary will likely continue to run high, particularly when this institution is compared with the other branches of the government.

Summary

1. What Do Courts Do?

The primary responsibility of courts is to resolve legal disputes over the facts of a case and the proper interpretation and application of law. Through the common-law doctrine of judicial review, the courts determine when acts of government bodies or officials are unconstitutional.

2. Sources of Laws in the United States

There are five sources of law in the American system: judicial decisions, constitutions, legislation, executive orders, and administrative law. Ultimately, courts resolve conflicts over these laws.

3. Types of Lawsuits

Trial courts resolve disputes over the violations of criminal laws and civil laws. The procedures used in criminal trials differ from those used in civil trials. Courts of appeals review cases to determine if errors were made in the interpretation or the application of law during the previous court hearing(s) of a legal dispute.

4. The Federal Court System

The Constitution expressly established only the Supreme Court, and, in a series of laws, beginning in 1789, Congress created the U.S. district courts, U.S. courts of appeals, and U.S. special courts. The district courts, special courts, and Supreme Court have original jurisdiction, although the Supreme Court rarely uses this jurisdiction. The courts of appeal and the Supreme Court have appellate jurisdiction.

5. Appointing Federal Judges

The president nominates and the Senate must confirm federal judges and justices. In selecting and evaluating nominees, the president and senators examine the nominee's competence and political ideology, consider how the nominee's demographic characteristics might represent the population at large, and may be influenced by the political support for nominees.

6. How the U.S. Supreme Court Functions

The Supreme Court has limited original jurisdiction. The overwhelming majority of cases the Court hears are appeals, and the justices choose to hear only a fraction of cases that come before them. Through a collegial process, justices decide what cases to hear, review legal briefs, listen to oral arguments, decide cases, and support their decisions with legal reasoning described in written opinions. The justices take many factors into consideration when deciding cases, including legal norms, their own policy preferences, and the preferences of their peers and the public.

7. Judges as Policy Makers

Since establishing the power of judicial review, the Supreme Court has become a key player in policy making. Although constrained by laws, checks and balances, and public opinion, judges interpret law and they make law as they determine what vague and conflicting laws should mean in light of the U.S. Constitution's fundamental principles.

8. The Supreme Court Today: The Roberts Court

Today, under the leadership of Chief Justice Roberts, the Supreme Court leans in a conservative direction. However, the public views the court as ideologically balanced and trusts the judicial branch more than the other two branches of the federal government.

Key Terms

adversarial judicial system 458

amicus curiae brief ("friend of the court" brief) 472

appellate courts 459

appellate jurisdiction 459

associate justice 468

attitudinal model 473

bench memo 473

bench trial 465

beyond a reasonable doubt 463

cert memo 472

certiorari petition 472

chief justice 468

civil law 463

collegial court 472

common law 460

concurring opinion 474

constitutional law 461

court of last resort 466

criminal law 462

descriptive representation 470

For Review

1. What legal disputes do trial courts resolve? What disputes do appellate courts resolve? What does the power of judicial review allow the courts to decide?

2. What are the five sources of law in the U.S. legal system, and for each source, who has the authority to create law?

3. What differentiates criminal law from civil law?

4. What is the structure of the federal court system? Which courts have original jurisdiction and which have appellate jurisdiction? How can a state lawsuit end up in a federal appellate court?

5. What criteria do presidents use when selecting judicial nominees? What role does the Senate play in the judicial selection process?

6. Outline the stages by which the Supreme Court decides cases. Explain the three judicial decision-making models.

7. In what ways do federal judges participate in civic discourse as policy makers? How is judicial policy making constrained?

8. What are the characteristics (mix of sex, political ideology, and level of activism) of the Roberts Court?

For Critical Thinking and Discussion

1. Explain judicial activism and judicial restraint. Which judicial behavior do you believe best serves the country? Why?

2. The Supreme Court has the power of judicial review, that is, the power to strike down federal and state laws that it views to be in conflict with the U.S. Constitution. In a representative democracy, what argument can be made against allowing the Court to overturn laws passed by the democratically elected branches? In a government founded on the principle of protecting rights of all people, even those in the minority, what argument can be made in support of allowing the Court to overturn laws passed by democratically elected branches?

3. When a president nominates a prospective federal judge, a number of factors are at play, and the nominee's qualifications are only one of these. What are the other factors? Should they be in play? Why or why not? In what ways do these factors reinforce or undermine democratic principles?

4. Which do you think impose greater limitations on policy making by federal courts: legal norms, the system of checks and balances, or public opinion? Explain your answer.

5. Unlike in the federal court system, in many states, judges are elected by the voters. Which system of judicial selection do you think best protects civil rights and liberties for all citizens, popular election or appointment (nomination by the chief executive and confirmation by a senate)? Explain.

6. Did the framers believe that judges should be accountable to the people or independent of the people and public opinion? Do you think Americans expect judicial accountability or judicial independence? What is your preference? Explain.

MULTIPLE CHOICE: Choose the lettered item that answers the question correctly.

1. The notion that it is the role of the Court to check the power of the federal and state executive and legislative branches when those governmental entities exceed their authority is called
   a. judicial review.
   b. judicial constraint.
   c. judicial restraint.
   d. writ of *certiorari.*

2. The federal court of last resort with a limited original jurisdiction whose decision may not be appealed is called
   a. the U.S. Court of Appeals.
   b. the U.S. Supreme Court.
   c. federal District Court.
   d. the U.S. Superior Court.

3. The middle level of the federal court structure includes
   a. district courts.
   b. courts of appeals.
   c. special courts.
   d. the U.S. Supreme Court.

4. Judges who identify previously decided cases with similar facts and then apply the legal principles used in the earlier case to decide the current case
   a. are applying the common-law doctrine of judicial review.
   b. are applying the common-law doctrine of *stare decisis.*
   c. are engaging in policy making.
   d. are practicing judicial activism.

5. Law created by legislators that identifies conduct so harmful to society as a whole that it is prohibited is called
   a. administrative law.
   b. civil law.
   c. constitutional law.
   d. criminal law.

6. What type of jurisdiction authorizes a court to review the interpretation and application of law from a previous trial?
   a. appellate jurisdiction
   b. discretionary jurisdiction
   c. mandatory jurisdiction
   d. original jurisdiction

7. Legal principles established by earlier cases are referred to as
   a. precedent.
   b. statutory law.
   c. tort law.
   d. oral law.

8. A wrongful act involving personal injury or harm to one's property or reputation is called
   a. administrative law.
   b. statutory law.
   c. tort law.
   d. oral law.

9. The practice by which the Supreme Court justices determine if they will hear a case is called
   a. the Rule of Two.
   b. the Rule of Four.
   c. the Rule of Six.
   d. the Rule of Eight.

10. The document written by a law clerk that identifies the facts of a case filed with the Court, the pertinent legal arguments, and a recommendation as to whether the Court should hear the case is called
    a. an *amicus curiae* brief.
    b. a bench memo.
    c. a cert memo.
    d. an opinion.

FILL IN THE BLANKS

11. The type of brief an individual or a group that is not a party to a lawsuit can file to influence the justices' decisions in a lawsuit is _____.

12. Judges who focus on legal norms and principles as the guiding force in their judicial decision making are following the judicial decision-making model known as the _____.

13. A judicial opinion agreeing with how the majority decides the case but disagreeing with at least some of the legal interpretations or conclusions reached by the majority is called a _____.

14. A custom that allows senators from the president's political party to veto the president's choice of federal district court judges in the senator's home state is called _____.

15. Judge-made law grounded in tradition and previous judicial decisions instead of written law is called _____.

Answers: 1. a, 2. b, 3. b, 4. b, 5. d, 6. a, 7. a, 8. c, 9. b, 10. c, 11. *amicus curiae* brief, 12. legal model, 13. concurring opinion, 14. senatorial courtesy, 15. common law.

Internet Resources

FindLaw

www.findlaw.com This website provides a wealth of information about lawmaking in the federal and state judiciaries, as well as ongoing cases in the news. It allows users easy access to federal and state code law, case law, and regulatory law. It also helps prelaw and law students stay connected to helpful information about legal education and practice.

Legal Information Institute (LII)

www.law.cornell.edu This is a valuable resource for information not only on the U.S. Supreme Court but also on the other courts in the federal and state judiciaries. The site provides an excellent catalog of statutory, regulatory, and administrative laws, as well as executive orders. It also allows you to search for all sources of law in a particular area of the law, including federal and state court decisions as well as laws coming out of the other branches.

Oyez

www.oyez.org/oyez/frontpage This interactive website allows you to access recordings of the oral arguments in a select group of cases. You can also visit the site to take a virtual tour of the Supreme Court building and to learn interesting trivia about the Court, including a list of the most active lawyers before the Court.

U.S. Supreme Court

www.supremecourtus.gov The official website of the U.S. Supreme Court is an excellent resource for information on the Court. You can access the briefs and oral argument transcripts for cases currently before the Court, as well as for cases decided recently. The site also allows easy access to nearly all cases that the Court has decided, including historical decisions.

Recommended Readings

Collins, Paul M., Jr. *Friends of the Supreme Court: Interest Groups and Judicial Decision Making.* New York: Oxford University Press, 2008. A study of the influence *amicus curiae* briefs have on judicial decision making, including an explanation for the increased occurrence of split decisions, concurring opinions, and dissenting opinions.

Miller, Mark C. *Exploring Judicial Politics.* New York: Oxford University Press, 2009. An edited volume offering studies by political scientists on the role of the courts as both legal institutions and political institutions.

O'Connor, Sandra Day. *The Majesty of the Law: Reflections of a Supreme Court Justice.* New York: Random House, 2003. In her reflections, O'Connor offers a history of the Supreme Court and discusses the important influence of several justices on the shape of the Court, the effect the Court has had on public policy, and the role of the Court in the 21st century.

Samuels, Suzanne U. *Law, Politics, and Society: An Introduction to American Law.* Boston: Houghton Mifflin, 2006. A comprehensive survey of the foundations of the American legal system, lawmaking by institutions and groups, and law and public policy.

Savage, David G. *Guide to the U.S. Supreme Court.* Washington, D.C.: Congressional Quarterly, 2010. Contains a thorough description of the U.S. Supreme Court, including its origins, its functions, and its influence.

Movies of Interest

The Runaway Jury (2003)

This film provides critical examination of the role of the jury in the American judicial system.

Monster's Ball (2001)

Probing the issues of capital punishment and racism in a personal way, this film explores the relationships among a white executioner, his African American prisoner, and their families.

A Civil Action (1998)

Based on a real-life story, this engrossing film takes the viewer through the pitfalls of civil litigation in a series of cases involving the pollution of a Massachusetts town's water supply by several corporations and businesses.

Gideon's Trumpet (1980)

This classic film starring Henry Fonda traces the true story of Clarence Gideon's fight to have a counsel appointed to his case at the expense of the state. *Gideon v. Wainwright* was the 1963 Supreme Court decision that extended state-appointed attorneys to all criminal defendants.

12 Angry Men (1957)

Henry Fonda starred in and produced this classic drama depicting the acrimonious deliberations of a jury in a death penalty case.

CHAPTER 16

What American Dream?!
I just keep having
NIGHTMARES
education budget cuts
NO jobs
50,000 student loan debt
uNequal rights
Unjust WAR
corporate greed
Corrupt government

Economic Policy

THEN

The federal government played a limited role in the economy, and there was consensus about the need for a balanced federal budget.

NOW

The federal government makes taxing, spending, regulatory, and monetary policies that affect the health of the economy, and it persistently borrows money to balance the federal budget.

NEXT

Will partisan battles continue to bring the federal government to the brink of government shutdowns and debt defaults?

Will the national government enact major taxation and spending reforms to shrink annual deficits and eventually the federal debt?

Will your generation and future generations achieve the American dream?

"America was built on the idea

that anyone who is willing to work hard and play by the rules can make it if they try—no matter where they started out," declared President Barack Obama in the first sentence of the budget message that accompanied his proposed 2013 budget.[1] Then in his 2015 budget message, Obama acknowledged that this idea "has suffered some serious blows" in the past few decades and said that "We need to return to an America where our success depends not on accident of birth, but on the strength of our work ethic and the scope of our dreams. That is what drew our forebears here. Opportunity is who we are. And the defining project of our generation is to restore that promise."[2] Republicans in Congress, such as Wisconsin representative Paul Ryan (chair of the House Budget Committee at the time), agreed that "we should be focusing on equality of opportunity."[3] However, Democrats and Republicans typically do not agree on what actions the government should take to enhance equal opportunity that fosters the American dream—which in President Obama's words is "the simple, profound belief in opportunity for all—the notion that if you work hard and take responsibility you can get ahead."[4]

According to a 2014 Pew Research Center poll, the majority of Republicans (76%) believed that "most people who want to get ahead can make it if they're willing to work hard," while a minority (49%) of Democrats believed this to be true. In addition, Pew found that although the majority of Americans (60%), including the majority of Democrats (75%), believed that the U.S. economic system "unfairly favors the wealthy," the majority of Republicans (53%) believed that the U.S. economic system is "generally fair to most Americans."[5]

Today, Congress and the president battle over enacting a variety of laws that will affect the U.S. economic system with the goal of ensuring economic prosperity and the American dream. These laws include tax laws, laws that regulate economic activity in the domestic and international marketplaces, laws that protect the health and safety of workers and consumers, and spending policies that encourage economic growth as well as provide for the public good. In addition, the Federal Reserve—the United States' central banking system—makes policy decisions that affect the amount of money in circulation, which in turn impact consumer prices and employment rates, hence the economy.

Debates among elected and appointed officials at the national and state levels, economists, business leaders, and taxpayers about the proper role for the national government in creating and maintaining a healthy economy have been ongoing since the birth of the American republic. This chapter explores how national policies affect the U.S. economic system and the reality of the American dream. In the exploration, we consider economic theories, various measures of economic health, fiscal policy, monetary policy, regulatory policy, and trade policy.

Economic Health and the American Dream

The American national government seeks a healthy economy so that it can raise the revenue it needs to serve the people in compliance with the mission laid out in the Preamble to the Constitution: to establish justice, ensure domestic tranquility, provide for the common defense, promote the general welfare, and secure the blessings of liberty today and in the future. On a more personal level, many U.S. citizens desire a healthy economy so that they can achieve the **American dream**—a financially secure, happy, and healthy life, with upward mobility, attained through an individual's hard work and persistence.

The desire for enough money to buy not only what we require to meet our basic needs (food, shelter, and clothing) but also what many people would consider luxuries seems natural to most Americans. In developed countries such as the United States, "luxuries" typically include owning a home instead of renting, owning a car or two, dining at a nice restaurant now and then, taking vacations, and sending children to good schools. The American dream includes sustaining this middle-class lifestyle through retirement and expecting our children's lives to be even better than our own.

Clearly, it takes money to live the American dream. For some, being born into a wealthy family or just dumb luck (winning the lottery!) may provide the means to live the American dream. For most individuals, however, the ability to earn enough money to attain the American dream is the product of several factors, including their education level, their work ethic, and the availability of well-paying jobs.

Why are you attending college? Are you taking classes to develop your intellectual capacities? To better understand yourself and the world around you? To get a better-paying job so you can live the American dream? If you read your college's mission statement, you will find that your institution hopes to facilitate all those accomplishments. Probably the easiest accomplishment to assess is gaining a well-paying job, and personal income is a logical measure of a well-paying job. Figure 16.1 shows that personal income correlates positively with educational attainment; generally, the more education you acquire, the higher your personal income will be. In addition, Figure 16.1 shows that sex and race/ethnicity—factors that you cannot control—also correlate with personal income. So earning a college degree is the best step you can take in your quest to live the American dream. However, for women and nonwhite men, the income benefits of a college education are muted.

Although you may be able to increase your level of education, and you have some control over your work ethic, the availability of well-paying jobs commensurate with your level of education is not within your control. The health of the national economy determines the availability of jobs and their compensation (pay and benefits). So, although achieving the American dream depends on individual attributes and opportunities to develop those attributes, the health of the national economy also plays a major role.

A healthy national economy supports a nation's ability to raise sufficient revenue to serve its people. The better the economy's performance, the greater the **tax base:** the overall wealth (income and assets, such as property) of citizens and corporations that governments tax to raise revenue to pay its bills.

The American Economy

In the United States and other countries, national government policies influence the **economy**—the system for producing, selling, buying, and using goods and services. **Economic policy** is a collection of public policies that affect the health of the economy, which includes taxing and spending policies (fiscal policy), monetary policy, regulatory policy, and trade policy. Economists view a healthy economy as one in which unemployment is low, the prices of consumer

Inquiry

FIGURE 16.1 ■ EDUCATION, RACE/ETHNICITY, SEX, AND MEDIAN WEEKLY EARNINGS OF FULL-TIME WAGE AND SALARY WORKERS (2013) On average, do women or men make more money? Does this pattern hold for blacks, Hispanics, and whites? On average, people of which racial/ethnic background earn the most money? Which group earns the least? Do these patterns hold for all levels of education? What are some of the possible explanations for these patterns?

SOURCE: Current Population Survey, reported in U.S. Department of Labor, U.S. Bureau of Labor Statistics, *Usual Weekly Earnings Summary Economic New Release,* USDL-14-0094, January 22, 2014.

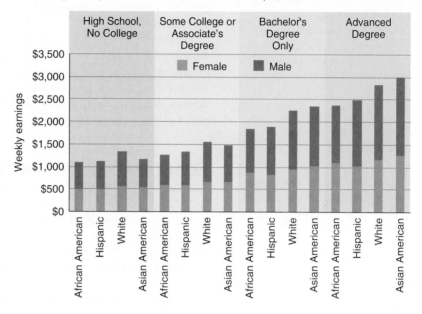

American dream
the belief that in the United States hard work and persistence will reap a financially secure, happy, and healthy life, with upward mobility

tax base
the overall wealth (income and assets of citizens and corporations) that the government can tax to raise revenue

economy
a system for producing, selling, buying, and using goods and services

economic policy
a collection of public policies that affect the health of the economy, which includes taxing and spending policies (fiscal policy), monetary policy, regulatory policy, and trade policy

goods are relatively stable, and the productivity of individual workers and of the economy as a whole are increasing.

Although labeled as a capitalist economy, the U.S. economy is not an example of pure capitalism. In a **pure capitalist economy,** private individuals and companies own the modes of producing goods and services, and the government does *not* enact laws aimed at influencing the marketplace transactions that distribute those goods and services. In other words, a pure capitalist economy has a government-free marketplace. Although private ownership of the modes of production dominates the U.S. marketplace, it is not a government-free marketplace. National government policies in some cases encourage, and in other cases mandate, certain business practices that the government deems essential to sustain a healthy economy, as well as a clean environment and a safe and productive citizenry. Because of the many national policies enacted to influence the economy, the U.S. economy is an example of a **regulated capitalist economy (mixed economy),** not a pure capitalist economy.

People around the world want their governments to engage in actions that ensure a healthy economy. Yet the actions a government takes to ensure a healthy economy depend on the economic theories its lawmakers follow. In the United States, Democrats and Republicans traditionally disagree on economic policies, each justifying their policy preferences with different economic theories. Next, we survey several economic theories that have influenced U.S. national economic policy in various historical periods.

Economic Theories That Shape Economic Policy

Today's debates about the proper role of the national government in the economy are nothing new. It was the lack of an economic role for the national government and the poor health of the economy under the Articles of Confederation that sparked the call for a constitutional convention in 1787. The framers of the new system of government established by the Constitution envisioned a national government more involved in the economy. So, citizens initially supported a limited role for the government in the economy—a *laissez-faire* economic policy. However, as the national economy evolved and experienced ups and downs, citizens and corporations sought greater government involvement in creating and maintaining a healthy economy. In addition, economists developed new theories about the proper role for governments in the economy: Keynesian economics, supply-side economics, and monetarism.

Laissez-Faire Economics: An Unrealized Policy

Until the late 1800s, a majority of the American people believed that the national government should take a relatively **laissez-faire,** or "hands-off," stance with regard to the marketplace. That is, they thought that the government should neither encourage nor discourage (through its laws) business practices that affected economic health. In his *Wealth of Nations* (1776), economist Adam Smith described the principles underlying the theory of laissez-faire economics. Smith's classical capitalist argument emphasized that the most effective means of supporting a strong and stable economy in the long term is to allow unregulated competition in the marketplace. According to Smith, people's pursuit of their self-interest in an unregulated marketplace would yield a healthy economy. Although it supported a hands-off approach in general, the national government became involved in economic activity as early as 1789, when Congress approved and President George Washington signed the first import tariff (tax on imported goods).

As a manufacturing economy replaced the farming-dominated economy during the 19th century, the general laissez-faire stance of the national government disappeared. Technological advances fueled industrialization and the movement of workers from farms to manufacturing jobs in the cities. As immigrants flocked to the United States in search of the American dream, the supply of cheap labor ballooned. Giant corporations formed, and individuals with money to invest accumulated great wealth. Monopolies and trusts also developed, limiting competition in a variety of industries. Although the economy grew (with increased productivity) and unemployment was low, "a huge gap between rich and poor defined the Gilded Age" (1870–1900) when 80 percent of workers "who toiled twelve to sixteen hours a day, stayed poor."[6] The quality

> In the late 19th and early 20th centuries, very low wages forced many American families to rely on the income brought home by their children who worked in mines, glass factories, textiles, agriculture, canneries, and home industries such as cigar making. Child labor is illegal today in the United States and in most other countries. However, due to low wages and poverty, child labor is a reality throughout the world, as witnessed in a carpet factory in Kathmandu, Nepal. Estimates of the number of children ages 5–17 working in dangerous, illegal, or exploitative situations range from 200 million to 250 million. What is the long-term effect on a nation's economy of children working instead of attending school? What is the effect on the children's future quality of life?

of life for most working-class citizens deteriorated as additional family members, including children, needed to work to pay for life's basic necessities. As fewer and fewer people achieved the American dream, even with all family members working, many Americans began to look to the federal government to improve working and living conditions.

In the late 19th century, the federal government began to respond to workers' demands for better wages and working conditions and to business owners' calls for uniform (national) rules for business practices. Moreover, by the early 20th century, the national government took steps to protect public health by passing laws regulating the processing of foods and drugs, and the cleanliness and safety of manufacturing plants. Though not directed at the health of the economy, such regulations increased the costs of doing business and, hence, affected the economy.

Clearly, the national government never fully implemented a laissez-faire economic policy. Moreover, as the national economy grew with industrialization, Americans accepted and even called for a mixed economy featuring regulated capitalism. Today, consensus exists on the need for some level of government involvement in the marketplace to ensure a healthy and sustainable economy, environment, and standard of living. But, debate continues over how much government involvement is appropriate and what specific policies the government should enact.

Keynesian Economics

Before the Great Depression of the 1930s, government officials and economists believed that a **balanced budget** was important for a healthy economy. When the budget is balanced, the government's expenditures (costs of doing business) are equal to or less than its revenues (money raised from taxes and other sources excluding borrowing). Yet officials and economists recognized that during wartime the government might need to engage in **deficit spending,** spending more than is raised during the budget year, to pay for the military effort.

During the Great Depression, when unemployment rates soared to 25 percent, President Franklin D. Roosevelt and Congress supported deficit spending to address the severe economic depression that engulfed the nation. The Roosevelt administration implemented numerous economic regulations and a number of innovative work and public assistance programs. Those policies drove up government spending at a time of shrinking government revenues. A key objective of the government's increased spending was to trigger economic growth by lowering unemployment rates, thereby increasing demand for goods (because more employed people means more

balanced budget
a budget in which the government's expenditures are equal to or less than its revenues

deficit spending
government expenditures costing more than is raised in taxes during the budget year, leading to borrowing and debt

people with money to spend), thus boosting the national economy. Deficit spending, Roosevelt said, would provide the solution to the American people's economic woes.

The new economic theory of John Maynard Keynes supported Roosevelt's unprecedented peacetime deficit spending. **Keynesian economics** recommends that during a **recession**—an economic downturn during which unemployment is high and the production of goods and services is low—the national government should increase its spending (to create jobs) and decrease taxes (so that people have more money to spend) to stimulate the economy. Based on this theory, during a **depression,** which is a long-term and severe recession, deficit spending is justified. During times of rapid economic growth—an **economic boom,** which is the opposite of a recession/depression—Keynesian theory recommends cutting government spending and possibly increasing taxes. In the long term, deficit spending during recessions and collecting a surplus when the economy is booming should lead to a balanced budget. Hence Keynesian economic theory advocates using **fiscal policy,** the combination of tax policy and spending policy, to ensure a healthy economy. So, fiscal policy is one type of economic policy.

In response to the Great Recession (2007–2009), President George W. Bush adopted a Keynesian policy. In February 2008, Congress and President Bush approved tax refunds for citizens totaling $168 billion along with tax cuts for select businesses. Later the same year, Congress and the president pledged to spend $300 billion to rescue three giant mortgage, insurance, and financial services companies from financial disaster and $700 billion to bail out faltering Wall Street financial institutions.

President Barack Obama and Congress continued to stimulate the sagging economy by enacting the American Recovery and Reinvestment Act (ARRA), which authorized $787 billion in combined tax cuts and federal spending, in February 2009. The goals of the ARRA, better known as the "stimulus package," were to create and save jobs, jump-start the nation's economy, and build the foundation for long-term economic growth. Although the success of the stimulus package continues to be debated due to the slow pace of recovery from the Great Recession, most economists agree that the recession would have been even worse without the ARRA.[7]

Supply-Side Economics

Not all administrations have embraced Keynesian economics. President Ronald Reagan (1981–1989) stepped away from Keynesian theory and introduced the nation to **supply-side economics,** which advocates tax cuts and a decrease in government regulation to stimulate the economy in times of recession. Supply-siders argue that the government collects so much money in income taxes from workers that they are discouraged from working more than they absolutely need to (because any extra effort will just mean they pay more in taxes). In addition, supply-siders argue that high taxes drain the economy because they diminish people's ability to save and corporations' ability to invest to increase productivity. Therefore, the theory goes, if the government cuts taxes, workers will be more productive and people will have more money to save and invest, thus stimulating economic growth. Supply-siders also argue that, because government regulation increases the cost of producing goods, **deregulation**—reduction or elimination of government rules that businesses must follow—will reduce production costs.

Monetarism

Economist Milton Friedman, a onetime supporter of Keynesian economics, is today best known for yet another economic theory, **monetarism,** which advocates that the government's proper role in promoting a healthy economy is through its regulation of the amount of money circulating in the economy (including coin, currency, and bank deposits). By controlling the amount of money in the economy, the government tries to ensure that the rate of inflation remains low. **Inflation** refers to rising prices of consumer goods, which decreases the purchasing power of money. The Bureau of Labor Statistics provides an inflation calculator that allows you to determine what yesterday's dollar is worth today because of inflation. For example, according to the calculator, you had to pay $1.24 in 2014 for something that cost you $1.00 in 2004.[8]

Monetarists believe that *too much* money in circulation leads to a high inflation rate, which slows economic growth as people spend less because of higher prices. In addition, as the rate of

Keynesian economics
theory that recommends that, during a recession, the national government should increase its spending and decrease taxes and, during a boom, it should cut spending and increase taxes

recession
an economic downturn during which unemployment is high and the production of goods and services is low

depression
a long-term and severe recession

economic boom
rapid economic growth

fiscal policy
government spending and taxing and their effect on the economy

supply-side economics
theory that advocates cutting taxes and deregulating business to stimulate the economy

deregulation
reduction or elimination of government rules and regulations (laws) that businesses and industries must follow

monetarism
theory that says the government's proper economic role is to control the rate of inflation by controlling the amount of money in circulation

inflation
the decreased value of money as evidenced by increased prices

inflation increases, investors begin to worry about the health of the economy, and investments may decline as a result, ultimately limiting economic growth. On the flip side, the monetarists say, *too little* money in circulation means there is not enough for new investments and that consequently new jobs are not created; this situation, too, retards economic growth. Today, monetarists target an inflation rate of 1–3 percent per year to ensure an adequate money supply for a healthy economy. They believe that the national government must use its **monetary policy,** which is the body of Federal Reserve actions (discussed later in this chapter) aimed at adjusting the amount of money in the economy to maintain a stable, low level of inflation.

monetary policy
the body of Federal Reserve actions aimed at adjusting the amount of money (coin, currency, and bank deposits) in the economy to maintain a stable, low level of inflation

Should One Economic Theory Predominate?

Although economists, government officials, and citizens broadly agree that the government should act to ensure a healthy economy, there is perpetual debate over the proper level of government involvement in the economy and what specific policy actions it should take. Where people stand in this debate depends on which economic theory they advocate. Each theory supports the use of different government policies to promote a healthy economy. Before we discuss the various policies that theoretically promote economic health, we consider how governments measure economic health. Once we know what a healthy economy looks like, we can then consider the effects that various policies have on the performance of the economy.

Measuring Economic Health

Economists and government officials describe a healthy economy as one that has these characteristics: expanding gross domestic product (GDP), low unemployment rate, and low inflation rate. These traditional measures of economic health together provide a useful snapshot of how the national economy is doing. Other measures of economic health focus on the general well-being of the people by accounting for factors such as rates of poverty and literacy and the financial situation of households. These less traditional measures include the United Nations Human Development Index, real median household income, income inequality, and the poverty rate.

Traditional Measures of Economic Health

Most economists assume that growth in the gross domestic product translates into a prosperous nation with improving living standards—hence progress toward living the American dream. **Gross domestic product (GDP)** is the total market value of all goods and services produced within a country's borders. Rising GDP is a sign of an expanding economy, which means the production of more goods and services—and thus the availability of more goods and services for consumers. The "Analyzing the Sources" feature presents the change in GDP and other measures of economic health from 2007 through 2013.

gross domestic product (GDP)
the total value of all goods and services produced within a country's borders

Economists also expect a healthy economy to correlate with a low level of inflation. When inflation rises, consumers' purchasing power falls and they cannot buy as much this year with the same amount of money they spent last year. The government agency known as the Bureau of Labor Statistics publishes the **consumer price index (CPI),** which measures the average change in prices over time of a "market basket" of goods and services, including food, clothing, shelter, fuel, transportation costs, and selected medical costs. The CPI is the most commonly used measure of the impact of inflation on people. According to economists, when the economy is healthy, the inflation rate (measured by the change in CPI) ranges between 1 and 3 percent.

consumer price index (CPI)
the most common measure of inflation, it gauges the average change in prices over time of a "market basket" of goods and services including food, clothing, shelter, fuels, transportation costs, and selected medical costs

A low unemployment rate, 5 percent or less, is also characteristic of a healthy economy, according to economists. When more people are working, the financial situation of families overall should improve. In addition, in a growing economy with falling unemployment, government revenues should increase (since there is more corporate and personal income to tax), and government spending for social welfare programs should decrease (because fewer people should need public assistance). These trends create a healthier financial situation for government.

In sum, a high or rising GDP, low inflation rate, and low unemployment rate suggest a healthy national economy. Yet as the U.S. Department of Commerce's Bureau of Economic Analysis

HOW IS THE U.S. ECONOMY DOING?

According to the U.S. Census Bureau, the Great Recession began in 2007 and ended in June 2009. Considering the measures of economic health presented below, how was the U.S. economy doing 4 years after the end of the Great Recession?

	2007	2008	2009	2010	2011	2012	2013
Annual change in U.S. GDP	4.5%	1.7%	−2.1%	3.7%	3.8%	4.6%	3.4%
Average annual inflation rate	2.8	3.8	−0.4	1.6	3.2	2.1	1.5
Average annual unemployment rate	4.6	5.8	9.3	9.6	8.9	8.1	7.4
Poverty rate	12.5	13.2	14.3	15.1	15.0	15.0	N/A
Real median household income in 2012 dollars	$55,627	$53,644	$53,285	$51,892	$51,100	$51,017	N/A

N/A = not available.

SOURCES: U.S. Bureau of Economic Analysis, "Gross Domestic Product; Percent Change From Preceding Period," www.bea.gov/national/xls/gdpchg.xls; U.S. Inflation Calculator, "Historical Inflation Rates: 1914–2014," www.usinflationcalculator.com/inflation/historical-inflation-rates/; U.S. Bureau of Labor Statistics, "Labor Force Statistics From the Current Population Survey," http://data.bls.gov/timeseries/LNU04000000?years_option=all_years&periods_option=specific_periods&periods=Annual+Data; U.S. Census Bureau, "Historical Poverty Tables—People," Table 23, www.census.gov/hhes/www/poverty/data/historical/people.html; U.S. Census Bureau, "Historical Income Tables—Households," Table H9, www.census.gov/hhes/www/income/data/historical/household/.

Evaluating the Evidence

1. Referencing the data presented above, how do you think the U.S. economy is doing? Explain.

2. Does the fact that the unemployment rate does not account for people who have given up hope and stopped looking for a job call into question the rate's accuracy? Justify your answer.

3. The GDP takes into account the total amount of consumer spending, government spending, business investment in new capital resources (such as equipment, computers, and facilities), and the total net exports (the difference between the value of all the nation's exports and the value of all its imports). The GDP does not include the value of unpaid work done in the home, such as home-cooked meals, child care, adult care, house cleaning, and laundry. Should it include the costs of those services? Why or why not?

4. What measure, or combination of measures, would you argue provides citizens with the most accurate picture of the health of the nation's economy? Explain.

points out, "While the GDP is used as an indicator of economic progress, it is not a measure of well-being."[9] Therefore, we next describe other measures that attempt to assess the well-being of individuals and households, which most people expect is a product of a healthy economy and is correlated with achieving the American dream.

Other Measures of Economic Health

Human Development Index (HDI)
UN-created measure to determine how well a country's economy is providing for a long and healthy life, educational opportunities, and a decent standard of living

The United Nations (UN) created the **Human Development Index (HDI)** to measure the standard of living of the people of various nations. The HDI assesses three components of human development that people in prosperous nations should be able to enjoy: a long and healthy life, educational opportunities, and a decent standard of daily living. These measures of economic health shed light on the ability of individuals and households to earn enough to *enjoy a decent quality of life.* Thus, they are probing into something quite different from the traditional measures of national economic health that we have just discussed.

TABLE 16.1

2013 Human Development Index Rankings

TOP FIVE COUNTRIES	BOTTOM FIVE COUNTRIES
1. Norway (.955)	183. Burkina Faso (.343)
2. Australia (.938)	184. Chad (.340)
3. United States (.937)	185. Mozambique (.327)
4. Netherlands (.921)	186. Democratic Republic of Congo (.304)
5. Germany (.920)	186. Niger (.304)

SOURCE: United Nations Development Programme, "Table 1: Human Development Index and Its Components," https://data.undp.org/dataset/Table-1-Human-Development-Index-and-its-components/wxub-qc5k.

FIGURE 16.2 ■ Income Inequality

SOURCE: Carmen DeNavas-Walt, Bernadette D. Proctor, and Jessica C. Smith, U.S. Census Bureau, Current Population Reports, P60-245, *Income, Poverty, and Health Insurance Coverage in the United States: 2012* (Washington, D.C.: U.S. Government Printing Office, 2013), 10; www.census.gov/hhes/www/poverty/data/incpovhlth/2012/index.html.

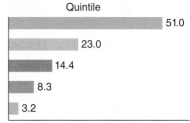

Quintile

Percentage of aggregate money income

With an HDI score of .937 (1.0 is the highest score possible), the United States ranked third out of 187 countries in the Human Development Report of 2013. Table 16.1 presents the countries with the five highest HDI scores and those with the five lowest HDI scores in the 2013 report.[10] How do we know what this rank means to American households and their ability to live the American dream? Additional measures—looking at household income, income inequality, and the level of poverty within the population—can help us answer this question.

Real median household income is an important measure of the financial well-being of American households. **Real income** is income adjusted for inflation so that it can be compared across years. **Household income** is the total pretax earnings of all residents over the age of 15 living in a home. **Median household income** is the income level in the middle of all household incomes; 50 percent of the households have incomes less than the median and 50 percent have incomes greater than the median. An increase in real median household income should characterize a healthy, expanding economy if we assume that increases in workers' productivity will translate into increases in workers' incomes. The table in the "Analyzing the Sources" feature shows that in 2012, the real median household income was $51,017, which is 8.3% lower than the real median household income in 2007.[11]

To determine whether people at all income levels are benefiting from a healthy economy, the government measures changes in **income inequality,** which is the gap in the proportion of national income held by the richest compared to that held by everyone else. Governments and economists use several measures to assess income inequality. One measure calculates the percentage of the total national income possessed by households in five income groups, five *quintiles,* each comprised of 20 percent of the households in the nation, based on total household income. The bottom quintile comprises the 20 percent of households with the lowest incomes, and the top quintile comprises the 20 percent of households with the highest incomes. In 2012, the lowest quintile held 3 percent of the money income while the highest quintile held 51 percent of the total money income. Changes in the percentage of the total income held by each quintile over time indicate whether income inequality is growing or shrinking (see Figure 16.2). The ideal is to see a shrinking of income inequality as the national economy expands.

The ideal healthy economy would ensure that all workers earn enough to stay out of **poverty**—the condition of lacking sufficient income to purchase the necessities for an adequate living standard. The **poverty rate** is the percentage of the population with income below the nationally designated poverty level. In 2012, the poverty rate was 15 percent, or 46.5 million people living in poverty.[12] (The "Analyzing the Sources" feature presents the poverty rates for 2007 through 2013.) The U.S. Census Bureau calculates the poverty rate by using its **poverty thresholds**—an annually updated set of income measures (adjusted for family size) that define who is living in poverty. According to the poverty thresholds for 2013,[13] a family of four, with two children under the age of 18 years, earning less than $23,624 was living in poverty. In 2013, one person under 65 years of age earning less than $12,119 was living in poverty, according to the federal government. What quality of life would you have earning $12,120, just $1 over the poverty threshold?

real income
earned income adjusted for inflation

household income
total pretax earnings of all residents over the age of 15 living in a home

median household income
the middle of all household incomes—50 percent of households have incomes less than the median and 50 percent have incomes greater than the median

income inequality
the gap in the proportion of national income held by the richest compared to that held by the poorest

poverty
the condition of lacking sufficient income to purchase the necessities for an adequate living standard

poverty rate
proportion of the population living below the poverty line as established by the national government

poverty thresholds
the U.S. Census Bureau's annually updated set of income measures (adjusted for family size) that defines who is living in poverty

We have seen that not only traditional economic measures such as GDP, inflation, and employment serve as indicators of national economic health, but also other measures shed light on the quality of life of people in the United States. With this context in mind, we next explore the way the national government uses fiscal policy to promote a healthy national economy that provides benefits to individuals and households.

Fiscal Policy and Economic Health

As noted earlier, fiscal policy comprises a government's spending and tax policies. The national government, through its budget process, annually approves a 12-month plan for raising revenue and spending revenue. The 12-month accounting period for revenue raising and spending is a **fiscal year (FY).** The national government's fiscal year runs from October 1 through September 30 of the following calendar year, and is named for the calendar year in which it ends. Therefore, the federal FY 2015 began on October 1, 2014, and ends on September 30, 2015.

National government expenditures accounted for 21 percent of the GDP of the United States in 2013—unquestionably, a substantial percentage of national economic output.[14] Although government spending certainly can create jobs, its primary goal is to provide the services necessary to fulfill the Constitution's mission. The other side of the coin, tax policy, raises revenue needed by the national government to serve the people. Although the main goal of tax policy is to collect revenue, taxation also decreases the amount of money taxpayers have to spend in the marketplace and corporations have to invest. Hence, taxation may reduce consumer demand for goods and services, with possible effects on the unemployment rate as well as company profits. It may also affect investment, which contributes to economic growth. Thus tax policy, like spending policy, powerfully affects the economy.

To understand fiscal policy, we look next at the sources of the funds the federal government uses to run the nation, as well as the spending decisions that Congress and the president must make.

fiscal year (FY)
the 12-month accounting period for revenue raising and spending, which for the national government begins on October 1 and ends on September 30 of the following year

POLITICAL Inquiry

FIGURE 16.3 ■ FISCAL YEAR 2015 EXECUTIVE BUDGET What does President Obama estimate will be the top source of revenue in FY 2015? Do you project that the revenue from this source will remain high in future budgets? Why or why not? What are the other two main sources of national revenue? How do you think they may change in future budgets? To determine how accurate President Obama's estimates were, you can visit the historical budget documents on the White House website (see the source for this figure for the website address).

SOURCE: "Table 2.2—Percentage Composition of Receipts by Source: 1934–2019," www.whitehouse.gov/omb/budget/Historicals.

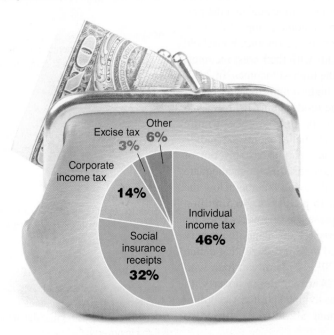

Tax Policy

The Constitution delegates the power of the purse to Congress. By the authority of the Constitution, Congress formulates and approves (and then sends to the president for his approval or rejection) *tax laws* to raise money along with *appropriations laws*—legislation that authorizes the spending of government money for a fiscal year. The Constitution specifies that the House must introduce revenue-raising bills before the Senate can consider them. The House Ways and Means Committee and the Senate Finance Committee are the congressional standing committees from which tax bills emerge.

Figure 16.3 presents the tax mix for the FY 2015 budget. Today, the national tax on individual income is the largest revenue source for the national government. The federal individual income tax is imposed on each individual's *earned income* (salaries and wages) and *unearned income* (profits made from investments).

The second-largest revenue category, social insurance receipts, includes taxes collected for Social Security and

Context

A NEW TAX IN MEXICO: 16 PERCENT SALES TAX ON PET FOOD

In its search to raise more revenue, the federal government in Mexico began taxing processed pet food on January 1, 2014. Since 1981, processed pet food had been tax-exempt. With half of Mexican homes caring for pets, the government sees the sales tax on pet food as a good revenue source. The estimated total sales of major brands of pet food in Mexico in 2013 was $2.2 billion, the 10th largest market in the world. (The United States had the largest market for major pet food sales in 2013, worth an estimated $21.4 billion.)

The new tax law labels pet ownership a "recreational activity" instead of a "basic need." Opponents of the new tax argued that a pet is part of the family, not a recreational activity. Critics of the tax also say that, like all sales taxes, it will have a regressive effect, hitting the country's low-income households the hardest. Moreover, animal welfare advocates and animal shelter employees worry that the tax will increase the number of homeless pets as low-income families find they are no longer able to afford pet food because of the tax.

Although pet food is taxed now, feed for horses (a common pet of the Mexican elite) will continue to be tax-exempt because it is considered livestock feed. The government does not tax livestock feed as a means to support the agricultural sector of the Mexican economy.

In the United States, there is no national sales tax. Each state determines if it will impose a sales tax and to what goods and services the sales tax will apply. Across the United States, processed pet food is taxed. In both the United States and Mexico, if a household feeds its pet table scraps, it will not pay the tax on pet food. As Mexico imposes the new 16 percent sales tax on pet food, pet owners, particularly lower-income owners, may turn to feeding their pets table scraps, which means the tax will not raise as much revenue as predicted.

SOURCE: Amy Guthrie, "Pet Food to Be Taxed at 16% in Mexico," *The Wall Street Journal,* December 28, 2013.

Medicare. Because employers deduct from workers' paychecks the amount they owe for social insurance taxes, these taxes are referred to as *payroll taxes.* The federal government's third-largest revenue source is corporate income taxes. The national government also collects *excise taxes,* which are taxes levied against a specific item such as gasoline or liquor, *estate and gift taxes,* and *customs duties* (import taxes).

Taxes levied by the federal government do not affect the income of all taxpayers in the same way. The national income tax is a **progressive tax** because it takes a larger percentage of the income of wealthier taxpayers and a smaller percentage of the income of less-well-off taxpayers. Most taxpayers view a progressive tax as fair. However, some people believe that a **proportional tax (flat tax),** which takes the same percentage of each taxpayer's income, is fairer than a progressive tax. A flat tax of 10 percent would equal $3,500 for a person earning $35,000 and $13,500 for a person earning $135,000. Although these two taxpayers pay a different amount of money in taxes, the *proportion* of their income collected is the same—hence the name proportional tax. Taxes can also be regressive. A **regressive tax** takes a greater percentage of the income of lower-income earners than of higher-income earners. States' sales taxes are the prime example of a regressive tax because lower-income households spend a larger proportion of their income to pay for sales taxes than do wealthier households, when the two are purchasing the same items. The "Global Context" feature highlights a new sales tax in Mexico and concerns about its regressive effect.

Taxes may also affect various taxpayers differently because the government grants **tax expenditures** (better known as *tax breaks* or *tax loopholes*). These are government financial incentives that encourage individuals and corporations to behave in a way that promotes the public good. For example, to encourage home ownership, the government gives tax breaks to individuals paying interest on a home mortgage. The government also offers tax breaks to businesses for job creation and worker retraining.

progressive tax
a tax that takes a larger percentage of the income of wealthier taxpayers and a smaller percentage of the income of lower-income taxpayers

proportional tax (flat tax)
a tax that takes the same percentage of each taxpayer's income

regressive tax
a tax that takes a greater percentage of the income of lower-income earners than of higher-income earners

tax expenditures
also called *tax breaks* or *loopholes;* government financial supports that allow individuals and corporations to pay reduced taxes, to encourage behaviors that foster the public good

State and local governments, as well as nonprofit organizations that provide a public service, pay no federal taxes. Thus we say that they are exempt from federal taxes. Included in this group of tax-exempt organizations are the overwhelming majority of colleges and universities, which are public or nonprofit institutions. They are tax exempt because they provide the public good of higher education without making a profit; they must invest any surplus money back into the institution.

Tax expenditures and tax cuts would not be such a big concern if the government raised enough money to balance its budget. Unfortunately, the national government spends more than it raises in annual revenues. How is the government spending all this money?

Spending Policy

Decisions the federal government makes about spending significantly affect both the national economy and the ability of individuals to achieve the American dream. Although setting the budget is an annual process, with Congress and the president approving a spending plan one fiscal year at a time, not all national government spending is approved annually.

For the government to spend money, Congress and the president must enact laws that establish **budget authority,** which is the legal authority for agencies to spend federal money. Programs granted budget authority each year are **discretionary spending** programs. There are two categories of discretionary spending programs: defense programs and nondefense programs. As Figure 16.4 indicates, defense spending is a bigger piece of the budget pie than is nondefense spending. Nondefense spending covers an array of activities and programs, including the administration of justice, agriculture, education, energy, environment, health, housing, income security for those who are poor and disabled, and transportation.

Annual appropriations acts are pieces of legislation that define how much money to spend each year. Congress and the president deliberate each year over how much budget authority to include in these acts for discretionary spending programs. Typically, Democrats and Republicans differ on their priorities for such programs.

The share of the budget spent on discretionary spending has been shrinking, though, because the growing share goes to **mandatory spending,** spending mandated by the authorization legislation that created a government program (see Figure 16.4), Social Security (income security for retired Americans and people with certain disabilities), Medicare (health insurance for elderly individuals), and Medicaid (health insurance for low-income individuals) are prime examples of mandatory spending programs. The government is obligated to pay for the program every year, whatever the cost may be, as long as the program exists. Because the government is legally obligated to pay back money it borrows, payments for the national debt also fall within the category of mandatory spending.

In the annual budget process, Congress and the president do not make annual decisions about most of the money spent by the national government because most expenditures are mandatory. Other than interest payments on the debt, mandatory spending could be controlled by Congress and the president by rewriting the legislation that established these open-ended budget obligations. Recent attempts to rewrite the legislation that created the Social Security retirement program have shown that many mandatory programs are difficult to change. This is partly because elected officials fear the impact such changes would have on their reelection prospects, and partly because of partisanship. Therefore, most mandatory spending is considered **politically uncontrollable spending.** Not only do Democrats and Republicans disagree on the proper reforms, but also members of each party disagree among themselves on specific reforms. Without major reforms to programs like Social Security and Medicare, mandatory spending continues to grow as a percentage of the federal budget.

Creating Fiscal Policy Through the National Budget Process

The federal government creates its policies and programs through authorization legislation that specifies policy goals and establishes whether the policy will be funded through budget authority obligated for the life of the program (mandatory spending) or budget authority that must be set annually (discretionary spending). In an annual appropriations process, Congress and the

budget authority
authority provided by law for agencies to spend government funds

discretionary spending
payment on programs for which Congress and the president must approve budget authority each year in appropriations legislation

mandatory spending
government spending for debt and programs whose budget authority is provided in legislation other than annual appropriations acts; this budget authority is open ended, obligating the government to pay for the program whatever the cost, every year

politically uncontrollable spending
spending on programs that are so popular that elected officials are not willing to change the laws that authorize the programs for fear of the effect on their reelection prospects

POLITICAL Inquiry

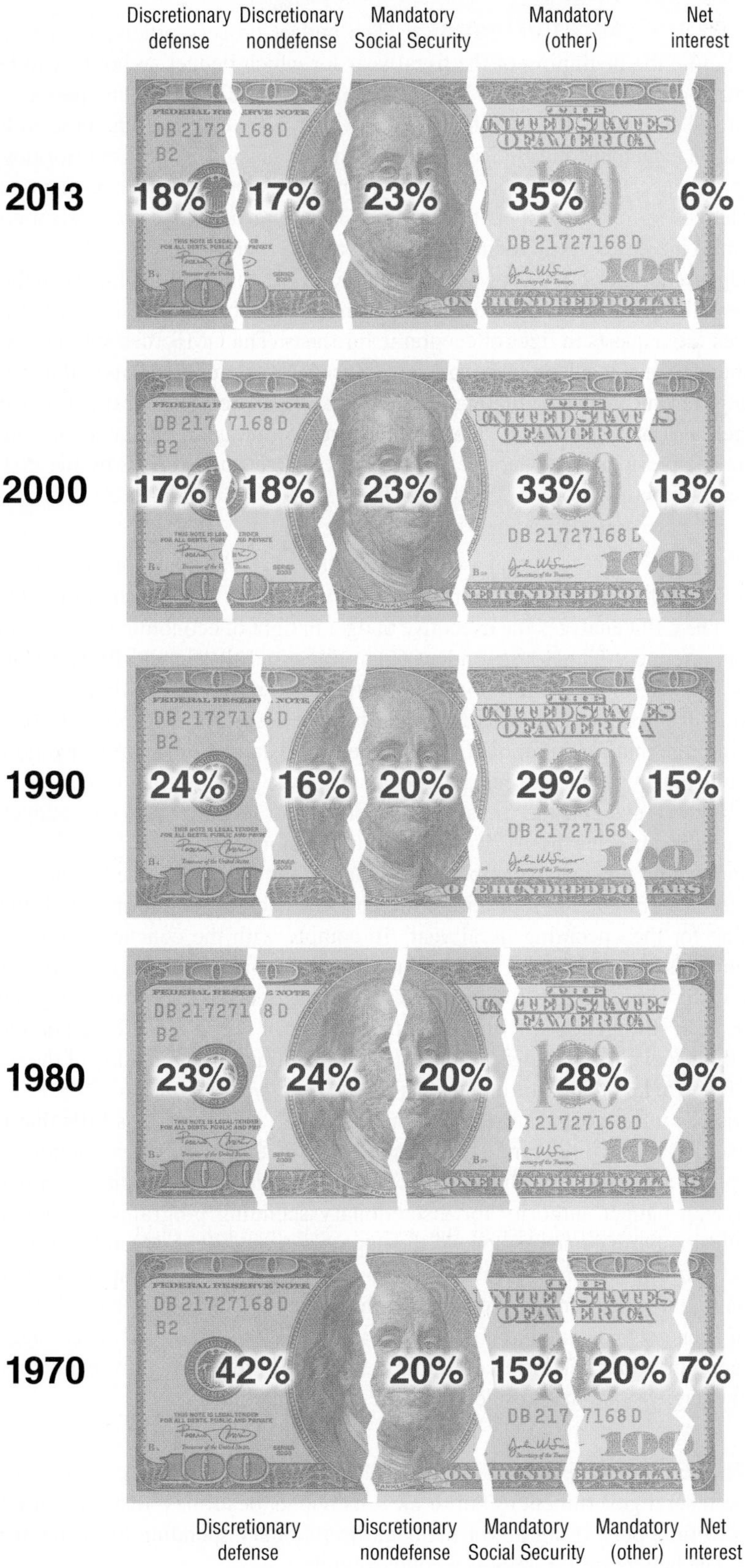

Discretionary defense
Discretionary nondefense
Mandatory Social Security
Mandatory (other)
Net interest
2013
18%
17%
23%
35%
6%
2000
17%
18%
23%
33%
13%
1990
24%
16%
20%
29%
15%
1980
23%
24%
20%
28%
9%
1970
42%
20%
15%
20%
7%
Discretionary defense
Discretionary nondefense
Mandatory Social Security
Mandatory (other)
Net interest

FIGURE 16.4 FEDERAL EXPENDITURES BY BUDGET CATEGORIES (AS A PERCENTAGE OF TOTAL) The figures present the proportion of actual budget outlays by budget category for select years since 1970. What category of spending has experienced the largest increase as a proportion of total federal spending? What category of spending has experienced the largest decrease as a proportion of total spending? What is the most expensive mandatory spending program? What are some of the programs in the "other" mandatory spending category? What proportion of the federal budget was "politically uncontrollable" in 2013?

NOTE: Annual total percentages may be more than 100% due to undistributed, offsetting receipts.

SOURCE: "Table 8.3—Percentage Distribution of Outlays by Budget Enforcement Act Category: 1962–2019," www.whitehouse.gov/omb/budget/Historicals.

president establish yearly funding for discretionary spending programs and possibly change tax policy to increase revenue raised—to pay the bills—or to cut taxes in an effort to stimulate the economy. This process begins in the executive branch.

THE PRESIDENT'S EXECUTIVE BUDGET   The budget process officially starts about a year and a half before the beginning of the fiscal year for which budget authority will be obligated. For example, work on the budget for FY 2015 (which covered the spending period of October 1, 2014, through September 30, 2015) began during the spring of 2013. The process begins when the Office of Management and Budget (OMB) sends the president's budget priorities (policy and financing preferences) to the executive branch agencies. Executive branch agencies use the president's guidelines to formulate their funding requests. Typically, these requests are incremental changes (small increases) to their current fiscal year's budget authority.

The budget requests work their way back up the executive branch hierarchy to the OMB. The OMB reviews the budget requests, conducts hearings in which the agencies justify their requests, and analyzes the requests in light of economic forecasts. The OMB then submits its budget recommendations to the president, who works with the OMB to create a proposed fiscal plan for the entire national government for the upcoming fiscal year. The OMB drafts a budget document and a budget message, collectively labeled the **executive budget,** which explains the president's fiscal plan. The president is to submit the executive budget to Congress by the first Monday in February, eight months before the fiscal year begins.

CONGRESSIONAL ACTION   Once Congress receives the president's executive budget, the Congressional Budget Office (CBO), the legislative branch's counterpart to the OMB, swings into action. The CBO analyzes the executive budget in light of economic forecasts and predicted government revenues. The House Budget Committee and the Senate Budget Committee use the CBO's analysis, along with reports from other congressional committees, to develop the concurrent budget resolution. The **concurrent budget resolution** establishes a binding expenditure ceiling (the maximum amount that can be spent) and a binding revenue floor (the minimum amount that must be raised) as well as proposed expenditure levels for major policy categories. The House and the Senate must both agree to the concurrent budget resolution. This agreement is to occur by April 15, less than six months before the fiscal year begins.

After approval of the concurrent budget resolution, the House and the Senate Appropriations Committees each draft 12 appropriations bills to provide budget authority for all the discretionary spending for the upcoming fiscal year. To comply with the concurrent budget resolution, Congress may also need to revise the legislation that authorized selected government programs to stay below the expenditure ceiling, or it may have to agree to changes in tax legislation to meet the revenue floor. **Budget reconciliation** is the process of rewriting authorization legislation to comply with the concurrent budget resolution. The deadline for completion of the reconciliation process is June 15, less than four months before the fiscal year begins.

Congress has until the end of June to approve the 12 appropriations bills that fund discretionary spending for the upcoming fiscal year. This timetable leaves two months for the president to approve all 12 bills so that by October 1 the national government can begin the new fiscal year with budget authority for discretionary spending programs. If Congress and the president fail to approve one or more of the appropriations bills by October 1, Congress must approve a **continuing resolution** to authorize agencies not covered by approved appropriations laws to continue to spend money typically within their previous budget year's levels. If a program or an agency is not extended budget authority before the next fiscal year begins, through either an appropriations bill or a continuing resolution, then it cannot operate and must shut down until Congress and the president approve its budget authority.

THE PARTIAL GOVERNMENT SHUTDOWN IN FY 2014   By the 21st century, it became common for the federal government to fail to meet its budget deadlines. Instead, it used continuing resolutions to fund part, if not all, of national discretionary spending for some, if not all, of a fiscal year. The budget for FY 2014 is a good example.

By October 1, 2013 (the first day of FY 2014), Congress had not approved a budget resolution (due April 2013) nor had it approved any of the 12 appropriations bills required to

executive budget
the budget document and budget message that explains the president's fiscal plan

concurrent budget resolution
document approved by the House and the Senate at the beginning of their budget processes that establishes a binding expenditure ceiling and a binding revenue floor as well as proposed expenditure levels for major policy categories

budget reconciliation
the annual process of rewriting authorization legislation to comply with the expenditure ceiling and revenue floor of the concurrent budget resolution for the upcoming fiscal year

continuing resolution
an agreement of the House and the Senate that authorizes agencies not covered by approved appropriations laws to continue to spend money within their previous budget year's levels

fund the discretionary spending of the national government for FY 2014. Therefore, the national government had to shut down all nonessential functions until Congress enacted a continuing resolution allowing the government to spend money, which it did 16 days later. Then in December 2013 (8 months late), the House and the Senate agreed to a budget resolution drafted by Senate Budget Committee chairperson Patty Murray (D-Wash.) and House Budget Committee chairperson Paul Ryan (R-Wisc.). Next, a few members of the Senate and House Appropriations Committees, not the full membership of the committees as prescribed by law, negotiated one omnibus budget bill that included all 12 appropriations bills needed to fund discretionary spending for FY 2014. The omnibus budget bill, which met the spending ceilings and revenue floors established in the Murray-Ryan budget resolution, was sent to the House and the Senate for enactment. To prevent another government shutdown at the expiration of the continuing resolution, the president needed to sign the omnibus bill into law by January 18, 2014. Congress approved and President Obama signed into law the Consolidated Appropriations Act of 2014 (the proper name for the omnibus budget law) on January 17, 2014, almost four months after the fiscal year had begun.

After the Consolidated Appropriations Act of 2014 became law, House Appropriations Committee chairperson Harold Rogers (R-Ky.) and Senate Appropriations Committee chairperson Barbara Mikulski (D-Md.) talked publicly about the need for Congress to get back to meeting the budget process deadlines, including House and Senate approval of all 12 appropriations bills, drafted by the appropriations committees, by the end of each June.[15] In March 2014, President Obama delivered to Congress his executive budget for FY 2015 (October 1, 2014, through September 30, 2015); his FY 2015 Executive Budget had been due to Congress by the first week of February 2014.

The nature of the annual budget process is such that, at any given time, some government body in the executive or legislative branch is preparing a future budget, even as the executive branch is implementing the current budget. At the same time, the Government Accountability Office (GAO) is evaluating the implementation of the previous fiscal year's budget. Thus budgeting is a perpetual government activity, one that takes up a great deal of national officials' time.

Deficit Spending and Debt

Most Americans highly value the ideal of a balanced budget, in which the government spends no more than the revenues that it raises. Although the nation had a **budget surplus** (money left over when all expenses are paid) for several years at the end of the 1990s, **budget deficits** (more money spent than collected through revenues) recurred as the first decade of the 21st century unfolded. Indeed, deficit spending has become the norm, not the exception (see Figure 16.5).

A government that engages in deficit spending borrows money and hence goes into debt. The **national debt** is the total amount of money the national government owes to all the creditors (individuals and groups) that loaned it money. The long-term impact of debt is the legal obligation to pay back not only the money initially borrowed (the *principal*) but also *interest,* an additional amount of money equal to a percentage of the amount initially borrowed. In the case of government borrowing, future generations must pay back the debt of their parents and grandparents. Today, to pay off the $17.5 trillion national debt, each citizen would have to chip in about $55,126.[16] Even as politicians, some economists, and many concerned citizens call for a balanced budget (see "Thinking Critically About Democracy"), deficit spending continues, and so the national debt grows.

Democrats and Republicans battle annually over what taxing and/or spending policies they should change to decrease annual deficits, moving the government toward a balanced budget. These battles grow more intense and bitter as the proportion of the budget that goes to mandatory spending grows (particularly due to the ever-expanding costs of Social Security and Medicare). Failed attempts to rein in deficit spending, as required by law, resulted in across-the-board, automatic spending cuts—called **sequestration**—in FY 2013. Across-the-board cuts force agencies to cut their spending by a set percentage during the fiscal year.

To pay its annual financial obligations, including debt already incurred, Congress and the president have to regularly increase the **debt ceiling,** the legal borrowing limit for the national government.

> On December 10, 2013, Senate Budget Committee chairperson Patty Murray (D-Wash.) and House Budget Committee chairperson Paul Ryan (R-Wisc.) announced agreement on a budget resolution that set the overall discretionary spending for FY 2014 at $1.012 trillion. Defense discretionary spending would be set at $520.5 billion, and nondefense discretionary spending would be set at $491.8 billion. Murray stated that the resolution was "a good step in the right direction that can hopefully rebuild some trust and serve as a foundation for continued bipartisan work." Ryan said he was proud of the agreement. Did this bipartisan budget resolution serve as a foundation for bipartisan work? Have the Democrats and the Republicans been working together on budget issues, or is lack of cooperation and gridlock still the norm?

budget surplus
money left over after all expenses are paid

budget deficit
more money spent than collected through revenues

national debt
the total amount of money the national government owes to all the individuals and groups that loaned it money

sequestration
automatic spending cuts during the fiscal year

debt ceiling
the legal borrowing limit for the national government

FIGURE 16.5 ■ FEDERAL DEFICIT SPENDING SINCE 1945 IN CONSTANT 2009 DOLLARS What is a budget deficit? What is a budget surplus? What is a debt? In what recent years has there been a surplus rather than a deficit? Explain how the health of the economy might explain the budget surplus in these years.

SOURCE: "Table 1.3—Summary of Receipts, Outlays, and Surpluses or Deficits (−) in Current Dollars, Constant (FY 2009) Dollars, and as Percentages of GDP: 1940–2019," www.whitehouse.gov/omb/budget/Historicals.

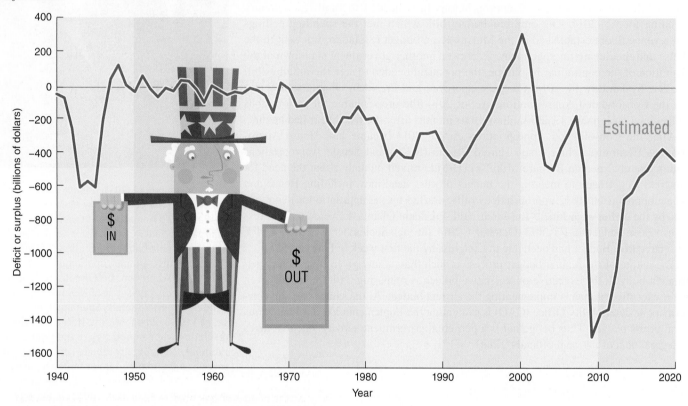

> The digital national debt clock outside the Internal Revenue Service (IRS) offices in Times Square, in New York City, constantly updates the total national debt and each family's share of the debt. To find out what the national debt is right now, go to www.usdebtclock.org/. Did you know that anyone can make a contribution to reduce the debt? If you want to contribute to reducing the debt, visit www.treasurydirect.gov/govt/resources/faq/faq_publicdebt.htm#DebtOwner.

Congresses and presidents have raised the debt ceiling almost 100 times since it was first established in 1917.[17] Democrats and Republicans battle regularly about raising the debt ceiling, even though a decision not to raise the debt ceiling would leave the national government unable to pay all its financial obligations—a *default*. Countries around the globe worry that a U.S. government default on its debt would spark a global financial and economic disaster.

Elected officials fear that citizens harmed by spending cuts and tax increases will not vote for them on Election Day; therefore, attempts to shrink annual deficits often fail. While elected officials struggle with budget decisions and their impact on reelection hopes, appointed officials, whom citizens cannot hold accountable through the ballot box, make monetary policy that like fiscal policy, affects the national economy.

Monetary Policy and the Federal Reserve System

The federal government seeks to influence the value of money by controlling its availability. When more money is in circulation, it is lower in value; consequently, consumers need to spend more

Should We Demand a Balanced National Budget?

Issue: Prior to the Great Depression, there was national consensus on the need for a balanced national budget. Since the Great Depression, the norm has been for the national government to engage in deficit spending each fiscal year. Decades worth of deficit spending has created today's national debt of more than $17.5 trillion. Should we demand a balanced national budget?

Yes: Without a balanced budget, the government must borrow money. When the government has to borrow more than $600 billion in a fiscal year, as it did in FY 2014, to cover its costs, then the amount of money available for others to borrow is limited. There is less money available for corporations to borrow to invest in job creation. There is less money available for individuals to borrow to achieve the American Dream. Moreover, today's decision to borrow obligates tomorrow's taxpayers (our children, grandchildren, and their children and grandchildren) to pay off our debts. Deficit spending harms the national economy and the financial status of American families. It threatens the American dream

No: The ups and downs of the economy cannot be ignored. During recessions, the national government needs to engage in deficit spending because more people are unemployed and need assistance, and tax collections are decreasing. The national government has a constitutional obligation to provide for the general welfare. Moreover, to demand a balanced budget will mean radical cuts in spending (for Social Security, Medicare, and Medicaid) if the Republicans are in charge, or radical increases in taxes if the Democrats are in charge—or both. The short-term harm is not worth the long-term benefit of a lower national debt. Economists generally agree that shrinking the

deficit is important to the economic health of the nation and families, but it is a long-term goal, not an immediate necessity.

Other Approaches: We should demand that Congress take the time to formulate fundamental reforms to tax policies (making the tax system more efficient and fair) and open-ended mandatory spending programs (making them more efficient and sustainable) so that deficits are cut rationally over the long term. It serves no one well to balance the budget in this time of a very slow economic recovery, for it would reap severe economic hardship. One long-term approach to controlling deficit spending would be to require an expiration date for all government spending programs, which means Congress would have to actively review and reauthorize programs regularly. Most economists agree that the really important thing is to ensure that the debt does not grow faster than the GDP.

What do you think?

1. Can Congress stop its pattern of deficit spending without a legal requirement to balance the budget? Explain.

2. Can the budget be balanced without raising more revenue through reforming the tax system? Explain.

3. Can the budget be balanced without legislative reforms that will cut some mandatory spending? Explain.

4. The handful of balanced budgets that we witnessed in the past few decades were the result of a strong economy, not merely because of tax increases and spending cuts. What can the national government do to grow the economy?

money to keep buying the same goods and services. Inflation is at work. The costs of running a business also increase with inflation. As a result of increased costs and decreased sales (because fewer people can maintain their levels of spending), businesses may choose to lay off workers. To avert these potential problems, the Federal Reserve, the nation's central banking system, works to maximize employment, ensure stable prices (keep inflation low), and moderate long-term interest rates.

Congress and President Woodrow Wilson established the Federal Reserve System (the Fed) in 1913. The Fed is composed of the Board of Governors (a government agency whose seven members the president nominates and the Senate must confirm), 12 Federal Reserve banks, and the Federal Open Market Committee (FOMC). The Board of Governors, the president of the Federal Reserve Bank of New York, and the presidents of four other Federal Reserve banks, who serve on a rotating basis, make up the FOMC. Today, the Fed's responsibilities include (1) setting *monetary policy*—the body of government policies aimed at maintaining price stability; (2) supervising and regulating banking institutions; (3) maintaining the stability of financial markets; and (4) providing financial services to depository institutions, the national government, and foreign official institutions—central banks of other nations, and international organizations such as the International Monetary Fund.

The Fed has three primary tools for setting monetary policy. It can raise or lower the *reserve requirement*—the amount of money that financial institutions must keep out of circulation. In times of high inflation, the Fed may raise the reserve requirement to decrease the amount of money available through credit, hence, decreasing the money supply. The Fed can also raise or lower the *discount rate*—the interest charged to financial institutions that borrow money from the Federal Reserve bank—and thereby make it more or less costly to borrow money. The Fed action that most influences the money supply, however, is its decision to buy or sell Treasury Securities (bills, notes, and bonds, which represent loans of money to the government). The Fed sells Treasury Securities when it wants to decrease the money supply and buys them to increase the supply.

Beyond its authority to set monetary policy, the Fed exerts supervisory and some regulatory authority over about 3,000 banks that are members of the Federal Reserve System (including all commercial banks chartered by the national government and those state-chartered banks that choose to join the Federal Reserve System), companies that control banks, and the U.S. activities of foreign banks. However, the Fed is not the only federal agency supervising and regulating the banking and financial industries.

Since the mid-1800s, the national government has created numerous regulatory agencies charged with ensuring the safety and soundness of the nation's banking and financial industries and systems, with the ultimate goal of promoting a healthy national economy. For example, the Office of the Comptroller of the Currency (OCC)—created in 1863 as a bureau within the Treasury Department—also charters, supervises, and regulates national banks. The Federal Deposit Insurance Corporation (FDIC)—an independent agency established in 1933—supervises state-chartered banks that are not members of the Federal Reserve System. Today, the national government regulates much more than just the banking and financial industries.

Regulatory Policy

Marketplace competition among private entities, each trying to make a profit, may threaten economic health as well as public safety, people's health, and the environment. Consider, for example, the unsafe products, including dangerous food and drugs, which may be manufactured and sold to make a profit. Think about production and manufacturing processes that may pollute the air, water, and land, creating conditions that are injurious to public health. Competition may also lead firms to cut salaries and benefits to ensure their profits, or their very survival. Such cuts decrease workers' ability to earn wages and benefits that keep them in the middle class, or even out of poverty. Unsafe and unhealthful working conditions may be another "cost" that workers "pay" so that firms can hold down or reduce production expenses. Moreover, if marketplace competition results in a few firms driving out their competition, they then have the power to raise prices or produce goods of lower quality, harming consumers.

In the U.S. economy today, the government regulates marketplace practices to protect the public and the economy. This regulation occurs in two broad categories: business regulation and social regulation. **Business regulation** includes government policies that aim to preserve competition in the marketplace. **Social regulation** refers to government policies directed at protecting workers, consumers, and the environment from the harm caused by marketplace competition. In Chapter 14, we surveyed the administrative rule-making process by which executive branch agencies establish business and social regulations. In this discussion, we trace the evolution of these two types of regulatory policy.

Business Regulation

The federal government created the first agency for the purpose of regulating business, the Interstate Commerce Commission (ICC), in 1887. The ICC initially regulated the prices of and services provided by the railroad industry to ensure that farmers could transport their goods to distant markets. Next, in 1914, the federal government established regulations to prevent large

business regulation
government rules, regulations, and standards directed at protecting competition in the marketplace

social regulation
government rules, regulations, and standards aimed at protecting workers, consumers, and the environment from market failure

corporations from engaging in business practices that harmed marketplace competition and established the Federal Trade Commission (FTC) to oversee these regulations.[18] In 1934, during the Great Depression, the government created the Securities and Exchange Commission (SEC) to regulate and make transparent the nation's stock markets and financial markets.

More recently, the United States experienced a failure in the financial market because of risky decisions by numerous financial and banking institutions. Loans and credit lines were extended to people without the means to repay the borrowed money. Ultimately, this sparked an increase in the number of people who could not pay their mortgages and therefore lost their homes. Hundreds of billions of dollars' worth of mortgages could not be repaid by the fall of 2008, and several large, prominent financial and banking companies collapsed. President Bush and Congress began discussions about the need for new regulations for the banking and financial industries to prevent similar market failures in the future. Congress and President Obama's administration continued those discussions, focusing on protecting consumers of the banking and financial industries. In the summer of 2010, President Obama signed legislation establishing the Consumer Financial Protection Bureau (CFPB), an independent unit within the Fed. The CFPB has the authority to regulate a wide range of financial products, including mortgages and credit cards, and to collect and monitor consumer complaints about the financial and banking industries. The CFPB also has a responsibility to educate consumers about financial products and services. Thus, within 50 years of the creation of the first regulatory agency, the ICC, the national government had put in place a full range of business regulations and regulatory agencies to maintain a healthy economy and protect consumers.

>In 2007, Harvard Law School professor Elizabeth Warren (left) proposed the creation of what would become the Consumer Financial Protection Board. Warren argued that a government agency that protected consumers as they interacted with the financial industry was needed. President Obama embraced Warren's idea in 2009, as he worked to overhaul the financial industry in response to its failings that sparked the Great Recession. Although Obama tapped Warren to set up the CFPB in 2010, he nominated Richard Cordray (right) as the first CFPB head, fearing that the Senate would not confirm Warren as the bureau's head. After blocking Cordray's confirmation for two years, during which Cordray headed the CFPB as an unconfirmed recess appointment, Senate Republicans dropped their challenges and the Senate confirmed Cordray in 2013. In the meantime, Warren ran for and won a seat in the U.S. Senate in 2012, representing the state of Massachusetts.

Social Regulation

The national government also uses social regulatory policy—which aims to protect the public's health and safety—to safeguard workers, consumers, and the environment from the potential harm created by the competitive quest for profits in the marketplace. Like business regulation, social regulation has an economic impact because it increases the costs of doing business.

The federal government first established social regulation when it passed two 1906 laws that protected *public* health—the Pure Food and Drug Act and the Meat Inspection Act. Upton Sinclair's descriptions of the dangerous and unsanitary conditions in the Chicago meatpacking industry in his novel *The Jungle* motivated President Theodore Roosevelt (1901–1909) to sign those two laws. The Pure Food and Drug Act created the Food and Drug Administration (FDA) and charged it with testing all foods and drugs produced for human consumption. It also requires individuals to present prescriptions from licensed physicians to purchase certain drugs and mandates the use of warning labels on habit-forming drugs. The Meat Inspection Act requires government inspection of animals that are slaughtered and processed for human consumption and establishes standards of cleanliness for slaughterhouses and meat processing plants.

The federal government first addressed working conditions that jeopardized *workers'* health and general welfare when it enacted the Fair Labor Standards Act (FLSA) in 1938. The FLSA established standards for a legal workweek, overtime pay for those working more than the standard workweek, minimum wages, record keeping of workers' hours, and limits on child labor. President Franklin D. Roosevelt characterized the law as the "most far-reaching, far-sighted program to the benefit of workers ever adopted."[19]

The Public's Top Priorities for the President and Congress

Percentage of Respondents Saying the Issue Is a "Top Priority"

	Then (2006)	Now
Defending against terrorism	80%	73%
Improving education	67	69
Strengthening nation's economy	66	80
Improving job situation	65	74
Securing Social Security	64	66
Reducing budget deficit	55	63
Securing Medicare	62	61
Reducing crime	62	55
Reforming the tax system	N/A	55

SOURCE: Pew Research Center for the People and the Press, "Thirteen Years of the Public's Top Priorities," www.people-press.org/interactives/top-priorities/.

WHAT'S NEXT?

> Will President Obama and Congress enact policies that strengthen the nation's economy by improving the job situation?

> Will the Federal Reserve, under new chair Janet Yellin, modify monetary policy to strengthen the nation's economy?

> Will the proportion of Americans listing "reforming the tax system" as a top priority continue to grow?

> Will global issues encourage more Americans to view "defending against terrorism" as a top priority?

In the 1960s, the government focused anew on growing concerns about product quality and safety. In his 1965 book *Unsafe at Any Speed,* attorney and consumer advocate Ralph Nader warned that "a great problem of contemporary life is how to control the power of economic interests which ignore the harmful effects of their applied science and technology."[20] Although Nader's book targeted the unsafe cars rolling off the assembly lines of the U.S. auto industry, his warning was equally relevant to the countless American industries that were discharging chemicals and toxins into the environment. Nader's book helped ignite an environmental movement (discussed in Chapter 17) and a consumer safety movement.

Lobbying by concerned citizens and interest groups led to passage of the Consumer Product Safety Act (CPSA) of 1973. The federal Consumer Product Safety Commission (CPSC), created through the CPSA, is charged with protecting the public from unreasonable risk of injury associated with more than 15,000 consumer products, including toys, products for children, products for inside and outside the home, and products made for sports and recreation. The CPSC can recall such products if it deems them unsafe, just as the FDA can recall food and prescription medicines it judges to be unsafe. To better serve the public, six federal agencies joined together to create a website, www. recall.gov, that provides the latest information on recalls. The agencies include the FDA, the CPSC, the National Highway Traffic Safety Administration (NHTSA), the U.S. Coast Guard (USCG), the U.S. Environmental Protection Agency (EPA), and the U.S. Department of Agriculture.

The Costs of Regulation

Business and social regulation has unquestionably lowered the risk of harm to citizens and the environment caused by marketplace competition. It also has cushioned economic downfalls. But the burden of government regulations has driven up the cost of doing business and of government expenditures, and in the end, consumers pay for this cost. In many industries, this increased cost poses greater problems for smaller firms than for larger ones. The higher costs caused by compliance with government regulations may also put U.S. industries and firms at a competitive disadvantage in the global marketplace, because many other countries do not have business or social regulations. Therefore, the production costs of firms in other countries are often lower than those in the United States.

The lack of regulations imposed by governments in other nations is a growing concern in the United States. The number of recalls of products manufactured in foreign countries, and even some products manufactured in the United States that use ingredients or components from foreign sources, is growing as the proportion of foreign products purchased in the United States increases: from Mexican mangoes to Canadian beef to toys, pet food, and drywall from China. Because of these concerns, trade policy and the interdependence of the global economy are prominent contemporary issues.

Trade Policy in the Global Economy

The next time you are shopping, try to purchase only American-made products. Is it possible? Stores in the United States offer products that are domestic (that is, American made) as well as imported (made overseas by American or foreign companies). Moreover, many American-made products have imported components and ingredients. For example, U.S. International Trade Commission data show that ingredients for food products are imported from more than 100 countries.[21] Today, marketplaces in every country offer products grown and produced in countries from throughout the world. Hence, national economies are integrated and interdependent—holistically forming the **global economy.**

To navigate in this global economy, each nation has its own **trade policy**—a collection of tax laws and regulations that support the country's international commerce. In addition, international organizations whose mission is to establish trade rules for all nations to follow have created a global trade policy. The goal of trade policy, like the other economic policies we have discussed, is ostensibly to promote prosperous economies.

Trade Policy: Protectionist or Free Trade?

A government's trade policy takes one of two basic forms: free trade or protectionism. **Protectionist trade policy** aims at protecting domestic producers and businesses from foreign competition through tariffs and nontariff trade barriers. A **tariff** is a special tax on imported goods. **Nontariff trade barriers** include government social and business regulations as well as government **subsidies**—tax breaks or another kind of financial support that encourages behaviors the government deems beneficial to the public good. Most subsidies are given to producers or distributors of goods to promote economic growth. Proponents of national government subsidies to U.S. farmers argue that to decrease these subsidies would place the farmers at a competitive disadvantage because European farmers receive even larger subsidies from their governments. Regulations include restrictions such as limits on the number of imports allowed into the country and bans on the sale of imports that a government deems unsafe.

From the 1790s until the 1930s, protectionism was the aim of U.S. trade policy. The first secretary of the Treasury, Alexander Hamilton, argued successfully that taxes on imported goods could be set high enough to protect American-made products in the domestic marketplace. In 1930, even as the American economy was failing, Congress hiked tariffs 20 percent—so high that it set off an international tariff war. This tariff hike fueled the Great Depression, whose economic toll was global in scope.

After World War II, the United States and its international partners gradually shifted toward a **free trade policy,** which aims at lowering or eliminating tariffs and nontariff barriers to trade. Free trade policies decrease the costs of bringing products to markets throughout the world and, in this way, open markets to a greater diversity of products and brisker competition. When other nations eliminate tariffs, American companies can participate in the global marketplace at a lower cost. These opportunities encourage an increase in the supply of U.S. goods and thus lead to an expansion of the U.S. economy. By the same token, when the United States eliminates its tariffs, more foreign products make their way into the American marketplace, increasing the diversity of consumer goods and producer competition and decreasing consumer prices in the United States.

International Trade Agreements

In 1947, the United States and 23 other nations signed the General Agreement on Tariffs and Trade (GATT). This multilateral agreement on guidelines for conducting international trade had three basic objectives. First, the signatory countries would not discriminate against one another in trade matters. Second, the signatory countries would work toward eliminating all tariff and regulatory barriers to trade among their countries. Third, the signatory countries would consult and negotiate with one another to resolve any trade conflicts or damages caused by trading activities of another signatory country. Through multilateral negotiations, the GATT established the guidelines for international trade and resolved trade disputes from 1947 to 1995.

global economy
the worldwide economy created by the integration and interdependence of national economies

trade policy
a collection of tax laws and regulations that support the country's international commerce

protectionist trade policy
establishment of trade barriers to protect domestic goods from foreign competition

tariff
a special tax on imported goods

nontariff trade barriers
business and social regulations as well as subsidies aimed at creating a competitive advantage in trade

subsidy
a tax break or another kind of financial support that encourages behaviors the government deems beneficial to the public good

free trade policy
elimination of tariffs and nontariff trade barriers so that international trade is expanded

>The 9th WTO Ministerial Conference was held in Bali, Indonesia, in December 2013. Running one day longer than planned, the conference produced the Bali Package, which was applauded by conference attendees as the first major agreement among WTO members since it was formed in 1995. The Bali Package is designed to make international trade more efficient, to bolster trade in the least developed countries, and to create more options for ensuring food security in developing countries.

Then in 1995, the World Trade Organization (WTO) came into being. The WTO continues the GATT's advocacy of free trade and punishment of protectionism. Specifically, the WTO monitors adherence to international trade rules and resolves charges of rule violations raised by any of its over 130 member countries. The WTO Ministerial Conference meets every two years to discuss and deliberate on international trade rules. The meetings have become magnets for massive and sometimes violent demonstrations by protesters from around the world who believe that free trade is harming the environment, impeding human development in developing countries, and hurting the poor in all countries. Opponents of free trade argue that the deregulation of nontrade barriers has exacerbated deplorable working conditions, child labor problems (see Table 16.2), and poverty.

Activists throughout the world are advocating policies to limit some of the harms they ascribe to free trade. Environmental groups fight for environmental protections to be included in international trade agreements. The International Labor Organization—a United Nations agency that promotes internationally recognized human and worker rights—advocates for bans on forced labor and child labor, prohibitions against discrimination in personnel decisions and policies, and safeguards for the rights of workers to organize and bargain collectively with employers, all of which are forms of social regulation. Groups concerned about human development worry that free trade agreements ignore the economic status of small family farmers, artisans whose goods are sold in local markets, and poor people in general. In addition to these global concerns, American activists look closer to home, concerned about the impact of free trade and the global economy on American living standards.

TABLE 16.2

Where Child Labor Is Most Prevalent in the World Today

Eritrea

Somalia

Democratic Republic of the Congo

Myanmar

Sudan

Afghanistan

Pakistan

Zimbabwe

Yemen

Burundi

Nigeria

SOURCE: Katie Hunt, "The 10 Worst Countries for Child Labor," October 15, 2013, www.cnn.com/2013/10/15/world/child-labor-index-2014/.

The U.S. Economy and the American Dream Today

In 2007, the Great Recession hit the U.S. economy and economies throughout the world. In the United States, the Fed used monetary policy to try to stimulate the economy, cutting interest rates six times between September 2007 and March 2008. However, consumer prices increased at the same time that economic growth (as measured by change in the GDP) was stagnating.[22] As discussed earlier, President Bush and Congress attempted to use fiscal policy to address this economic situation. In 2009, President Obama and Congress passed the American Recovery and Reinvestment Act (ARRA), which created jobs by investing federal money in clean energy, education, health care, and infrastructure (such as roads, bridges, schools, and broadband lines). Most economists agree that the U.S. economy would have declined even further without the 2009 ARRA.[23]

As the U.S. economy has been improving slowly since the end of the Great Recession in 2009, many citizens have focused on income inequality and the increasing poverty rate. The top 10 percent of Americans used to hold a third of the national income; today the top 10 percent hold about half of the national income. The typical corporate chief executive officer (CEO) used to make 30 times as much as the average worker; today the typical corporate CEO makes about 270 times as much as the average worker.[24] A larger concern is that people at the bottom of the income ladder seem to lack the opportunities essential to moving up the ladder. Some economists argue that economic recessions are more frequent in countries where income inequality is severe and the opportunities for upward economic mobility are limited or nonexistent.[25]

According to a 2014 Pew Research Center poll, the majority of Americans (65%)—including a majority of Democrats (68%), Republicans (61%), and independents (67%)—agree that income inequality has grown in the past 10 years. However, although a majority of Democrats (90%) and independents (69%) believe that the government should take some actions or do a lot to reduce the income gap, a minority of Republicans (45%) hold the same belief. Some 48 percent of Republicans believe that the government should do "not much" or "nothing" to reduce the gap.[26]

▶In his efforts to address the growing U.S. unemployment rate during the Great Recession (2007–2009), President Obama signed into law the American Recovery and Reinvestment Act (ARRA), which decreased taxes and increased spending with the goal of creating 3.5 million jobs. Across the country, construction work on roads and bridges was the most visible sign of the ARRA's effects on employment and the economy. What president was the first to turn to fiscal policy to address a long-lasting, deep recession?

At the same time, the majority of Republicans (64%), Democrats (94%), and independents (83%) believe the government should do "some" or "a lot" to reduce poverty.[27] Partisan disagreement exists, however, over what actions the national government should take to reduce poverty. This disagreement leads to congressional battles over fiscal policy. The majority of Democrats (75%) and independents (51%) support raising taxes on the wealthy and corporations, so that the government can expand programs to assist the poor. On the other hand, the majority of Republicans (59%) support lowering taxes on the wealthy and corporations, which they argue will encourage investment and economic growth.[28]

Conversations about income inequality are evolving into debates over inequality of opportunity. Democrats and Republicans are focusing on inequality of opportunity to achieve the American dream. It was during the Great Depression that historian James Truslow Adams coined the term "American dream." In his book *The Epic of America* (1931), Adams argued that what made America a unique nation was its inhabitants' "dream of a better, richer, and happier life" for all citizens based on equal "opportunity for each according to his [or her] ability or achievement."[29] Is the American dream to do better economically than your parents? Is it to be rich? Or is the American dream to live in a nation that has a stable, healthy economy and an equal opportunity to achieve (measured by home ownership, high levels of education, and comfortable retirement) according to your ability and effort? If the American dream is the last, can government policies—fiscal, monetary, regulatory, and trade—ensure a healthy national economy in today's interdependent global economy? In addition, can government domestic policies—which we discuss in Chapter 17—ensure equal opportunity for citizens to achieve according to their ability and effort? A recent Pew poll found that most Americans (60%) believe that "people who want to get ahead can make it if they are willing to work hard." At the same time, most Americans (60%) say the U.S. economic system unfairly favors the wealthy.[30]

Conclusion

Thinking Critically About What's Next in Economic Policy

Governments throughout the world seek to maintain healthy economies using economic policy. U.S. economic policy comprises taxing and spending policies (fiscal policy), monetary policy, regulatory policy, and trade policy. Today, the economic decisions made by the president, Congress, and the Fed are influenced by the realities of the global economy. Partisan battles over fiscal policy and shrinking the deficit have shut down the national government and brought it to the brink of debt defaults. Will the partisan battles continue or will Congress and the president be able to agree on a combination of tax policy reforms (such as eliminating tax expenditures) and spending policy reforms (such as changing the authorization law that established Social Security and Medicare as open-ended mandatory spending programs) to shrink the budget and eventually the federal debt?

The viability of the American dream depends on a healthy national economy. Even before the current recession began, income inequality was growing. The gap between those who have the largest share of the nation's wealth and everyone else has expanded in the past few decades. The American dream is in jeopardy for today's young people and future generations. Will Congress and the president agree on economic policies that bolster the opportunities essential to achieving the American dream for your generation and posterity, or will your generation be left with the tough policy choices?

Summary

1. Economic Health and the American Dream

Though work ethic and education level influence personal income, a healthy national economy is essential to the ability of people to live a financially secure, happy, and healthy life—to realize the American dream. The health of the economy influences the availability of jobs with adequate levels of compensation (salaries and benefits).

2. The American Economy

The national government's economic policy aims at establishing and maintaining a healthy economy so that it can raise the money necessary to fulfill its mission of serving the people. Because the government implements many policies that encourage, and sometimes mandate, certain business practices in the interest of creating and maintaining a healthy economy, the United States has what is known as a regulated capitalist economy.

3. Economic Theories That Shape Economic Policy

The national government's efforts to achieve and maintain a healthy economy have expanded as lawmakers have embraced various economic theories, among them Keynesian economics, supply-side economics, and monetarism. The specific policies implemented by the government depend on the particular economic theories government officials adopt.

4. Measuring Economic Health

Traditional measures of economic health include GDP, rate of inflation, and rate of unemployment. Other measures include the Human Development Index, real median household income, income inequality, and the poverty rate. Together, these measures can be used to assess how well a prosperous national economy enables its citizens to live the American dream.

5. Fiscal Policy and Economic Health

Taxing and spending decisions by the president and Congress influence how much money consumers have to spend, save, and invest; how much profit firms make and how much they have to invest in expanding business; and how much the government has to spend in order to serve the people. Deficit spending is a persistent reality of U.S. fiscal policy, creating economic problems in the long term.

6. Monetary Policy and the Federal Reserve System

The Fed, directed by a group of appointed officials, works to keep inflation and unemployment low by regulating the amount of money in circulation in the economy.

7. Regulatory Policy

Today, business regulation (to ensure competition) and social regulation (to protect workers, consumers, and the environment) are pervasive components of the U.S. economy, despite ongoing calls by business, some economists, and politicians (more apt to be Republicans than Democrats) to deregulate.

8. Trade Policy in the Global Economy

Protectionist trade policy dominated the United States until after World War II. Then free trade policy became the goal of international agreements and U.S. trade policy. Today, debate continues over the domestic and global effects (positive and negative) of free trade policy in the global economy.

9. The U.S. Economy and the American Dream Today

The recent global recession, the worst since the Great Depression of the 1930s, has sparked conversations about the nature of the American dream and whether or not it is achievable.

Key Terms

American dream 489
balanced budget 491
budget authority 498
budget deficit 501
budget reconciliation 500
budget surplus 501
business regulation 504
concurrent budget
    resolution 500
consumer price index (CPI)
    493
continuing resolution 500
debt ceiling 501
deficit spending 491
depression 492
deregulation 492
discretionary spending 498
economic boom 492
economic policy 489
economy 489
executive budget 500
fiscal policy 492

fiscal year (FY) 496
free trade policy 507
global economy 507
gross domestic product
    (GDP) 493
household income 495
Human Development Index
    (HDI) 494
income inequality 495
inflation 492
Keynesian economics 492
laissez-faire 490
mandatory spending 498
median household income
    495
monetarism 492
monetary policy 493
national debt 501
nontariff trade barriers 507
politically uncontrollable
    spending 498
poverty 495

poverty rate 495
poverty thresholds 495
progressive tax 497
proportional tax (flat tax)
    497
protectionist trade policy
    507
pure capitalist economy 490
real income 495
recession 492
regressive tax 497
regulated capitalist
    economy (mixed
    economy) 490
sequestration 501
social regulation 504
subsidy 507
supply-side economics 492
tariff 507
tax base 489
tax expenditures 497
trade policy 507

For Review

1. What is the American dream? Describe one effect that each of the following national policies can have on the American dream: tax policy, spending policy, business regulation, social regulation, monetary policy, trade policy.

2. What distinguishes a pure capitalist economy from a regulated capitalist economy?

3. Differentiate among Keynesian economics, supply-side economics, and monetarism.

4. Explain at least four measures of economic health.

5. What is fiscal policy and who makes it?

6. What is monetary policy and who makes it?

7. Distinguish between business regulation and social regulation. Indicate how each type of regulation affects the economy.

8. Differentiate between the goals as well as the techniques of free trade policy and protectionist trade policy.

9. What is the health of the U.S. economy as well as the American dream at the beginning of the twenty-first century?

For Critical Thinking and Discussion

1. If you were president of the United States and wanted to balance the annual budget, what programs' cost cuts do you think you could get partisans in the other political party to support? What tax increases or new taxes do you think you could get partisans in the other political party to support? Explain your choices.

2. Consider your family's financial situation. What economic policy would you propose the national government implement to improve your family's financial situation? Explain.

3. Which type of tax do you think is the most fair: progressive, proportional, or regressive? Explain your choice.

4. If the national government deregulates with regard to environmental protection, product safety, and/or working conditions, would there be negative consequences? Give some examples, or explain why there would not be negative consequences.

5. Some politicians have suggested that a flat income tax of about 17 percent could raise about the same amount of revenue for the national government as the current progressive income tax and should replace it. Politically speaking, who would support such a proposal, and who would oppose it?

6. Do you think Democrats and Republicans can agree on a plan to stop deficit spending through reform of tax policies and spending policies?

MULTIPLE CHOICE: Choose the lettered item that answers the question correctly.

1. The economic theory that advocates the use of fiscal policy to create and maintain a healthy economy is called
   a. Keynesian economics.
   b. laissez-faire economics.
   c. monetarism.
   d. supply-side economics.

2. Which of the following is *not* included in the mandatory spending category of the national government?
   a. debt payments
   b. defense
   c. Medicare
   d. Social Security

3. The officials that approve fiscal policy are
   a. Congress (on its own).
   b. Congress and the president.
   c. Congress, the president, and the Fed.
   d. the Fed (on its own).

4. The officials that approve monetary policy are
   a. Congress (on its own).
   b. Congress and the president.
   c. Congress, the president, and the Fed.
   d. the Fed (on its own).

5. The policy that decreases the costs of bringing products to markets throughout the world by lowering or eliminating tariffs and deregulating is
   a. free trade policy.
   b. monetary policy.
   c. protectionist trade policy.
   d. regulatory policy.

6. The policy in which the national government engages to protect consumers, workers, and the environment from the harm of marketplace competition is
   a. business regulation.
   b. deregulation.
   c. protectionist trade policy.
   d. social regulation.

7. The collection of national tax policies and spending policies is referred to as
   a. fiscal policy.
   b. monetary policy.

c. protectionist policy.
d. regulatory policy.

8. The largest revenue source for the national government is
   a. corporate income taxes.
   b. import taxes.
   c. individual income taxes.
   d. social insurance taxes.

9. During what president's administrations did the national government first adopt Keynesian economic principles to create and maintain a healthy national economy?
   a. George Washington
   b. Franklin D. Roosevelt
   c. Ronald Reagan
   d. George W. Bush

10. During what presidential administration did battles among the president, the House, and the Senate lead to sequestration, a partial 16-day government shutdown, and the brink of a debt default?
    a. Franklin D. Roosevelt
    b. Ronald Reagan
    c. George W. Bush
    d. Barack Obama

FILL IN THE BLANKS

11. When it spends more money than it collects in taxes, the government is engaging in _____.

12. _____ refers to the rising prices of consumer goods, which means the value of the dollar has decreased.

13. The date on which the national 2015 fiscal year (FY 2015) began is _____.

14. The _____ is an international, nongovernmental organization that advocates for free trade policy, monitors adherence to international trade rules, and resolves charges of trade rule violation raised by its member countries.

15. _____ is automatic spending cuts that occur when other legislated spending or revenue requirements are not accomplished by a legislated deadline.

Answers: 1. a, **2.** b, **3.** b, **4.** d, **5.** a, **6.** d, **7.** a, **8.** c, **9.** b, **10.** d, **11.** deficit spending, **12.** inflation, **13.** October 1, 2014, **14.** World Trade Organization (WTO), **15.** Sequestration.

Resources for Research AND Action

Internet Resources

American Enterprise Institute (AEI)
www.aei.org The AEI sponsors research on government policy and economic policy and advocates limited government involvement in the marketplace.

American Institute for Economic Research
www.aier.org This nonprofit research and educational organization provides studies and information on economic and financial issues.

Bureau of Economic Analysis (BEA)
www.bea.gov The BEA, an agency in the Department of Commerce, produces and disseminates data on regional, national, and international economies.

Economic Policy Institute
www.epi.org This nonprofit organization aims to broaden public debate on strategies to achieve a prosperous and fair economy.

Office of Management and Budget (OMB)
www.whitehouse.gov/omb The OMB's site has links to the most recent executive budget and historical budget documents.

U.S. Census Bureau
www.census.gov The Census Bureau, a bureau in the Department of Commerce, collects and disseminates data about the people and economy of the nation.

Recommended Readings

Bittle, Scott, and Jean Johnson. *Where Does the Money Go? Your Guided Tour to the Federal Budget Crisis.* Revised Edition. New York: Harper, 2011. This easy-to-understand book guides the reader through the jargon and essentials of the nation's fiscal problems with a nonpartisan perspective. It is informative and entertaining.

Derber, Charles. *People Before Profit.* New York: Picador, 2003. A disturbing analysis of globalization to date with a blueprint for a new form of globalization that will lead to a more stable and just global community.

Schick, Allen. *The Federal Budget.* Washington, D.C.: Brookings Institute, 2000. A comprehensive, in-depth consideration of the national budget process.

Sinclair, Upton. *The Jungle.* New York: Doubleday, Jabber & Company, 1906; and New York: Signet Classics, 2001. Sinclair's gruesome descriptions of work life and family life in Chicago at the beginning of the 20th century brought attention to income inequality, poverty, and deplorable and dangerous living and working conditions. The novel sparked enactment of national policies to protect public health and safety through regulation of the meat processing and packaging industries. The effect of this novel on government regulatory policy is immeasurable.

Woodward, Bob. *Maestro: Greenspan's Fed and the American Boom.* New York: Simon & Schuster, 2000. A probing look into how the Fed operated under the leadership of Alan Greenspan from 1987 to 2000. The effect of the evolving global economy on the economic health of the United States is an intriguing part of Woodward's account.

Movies of Interest

Too Big to Fail (2011)
A docudrama, this film shows federal government officials from the Treasury Department, the Federal Reserve, and the Securities and Exchange Commission working between late March and mid-October 2008 to prevent a national financial meltdown as banks and financial institutions move toward the brink of bankruptcy.

Inside Job (2010)
Narrated by Matt Damon, this is the first film to explore the global financial crisis that began in 2008. This sober, comprehensive analysis, based on extensive research, including interviews with politicians, financial professionals, journalists and academics, indicates that the meltdown was predictable and preventable.

Cinderella Man (2005)
Based on the life of prizefighter Jim Braddock, this film movingly depicts the common person's struggle to survive the Great Depression and the hopes and inspiration that one person's rise from the bottom can evoke in the population at large.

Enron: The Smartest Guys in the Room (2005)
Based on the best-selling book of the same title, this documentary spotlights the human drama of Enron's fall—the biggest corporate scandal in American history—including the company's collapse, the elimination of thousands of jobs, and the loss of $60 billion in market value and $2 billion in pension plans.

Commanding Heights: The Battle for the World Economy (2002)
This documentary exploration of the political side of today's global economy looks at the people, ideas, and events that fostered the liberalization of trade policies around the globe.

CHAPTER 17

Domestic Policy

THEN

In the 1930s, radical new federal government policies created a safety net that enabled economically distressed citizens to provide for their basic needs.

NOW

The federal government faces a host of domestic policy issues, from the high cost of maintaining the safety net to environmental degradation, homeland security threats, and calls for immigration reform.

NEXT

Will U.S. energy policy address the environmental challenges of dependence on fossil fuels while fostering economic development?

Will health care reform foster universal coverage and shrink the annual increases in health care costs?

Will national, state, and local governments continue to enhance intergovernmental communication and cooperation to address threats to homeland security?

PREVIEW

In this chapter, we survey national domestic policies that are most directly related to the basic needs of a sustainable, safe country where citizens can live healthy lives in pursuit of their happiness.

FIRST, we review the role of citizen engagement in establishing domestic policy.

SECOND, we consider the tools of domestic policy, the array of public programs by which the government provides for citizens' basic needs.

THIRD, we look at environmental policy, the government's efforts to preserve the environment, conserve scarce resources, and control pollution.

FOURTH, we examine energy policy, looking specifically at the problems of rising energy consumption and Americans' reliance on nonrenewable fossil fuels.

FIFTH, we consider income security programs—in particular, safety-net policies for citizens in financial need.

SIXTH, we probe health care policy, where soaring costs are prompting ongoing research and experimentation with new models.

SEVENTH, we discuss homeland security policy, which is directed at preventing and responding to natural and human-made disasters.

EIGHTH, we examine national and state government efforts to use immigration policy to address citizens' concerns about unauthorized immigrants.

NIMBY ("not in my backyard") syndrome
a pattern of citizens' behavior in which people decline to participate in politics until a government action or inaction threatens them directly

According to the Declaration

of Independence and the U.S. Constitution, American governments must ensure a just and safe society in which citizens can live their lives freely, in pursuit of their happiness. Essential to the achievement of these goals are the preservation and protection of the natural environment so that future generations can enjoy a quality of life comparable to today's. Since the Great Depression, the national government has tried to ensure that people who work hard have the opportunity to achieve the American dream. In addition, the national government has enacted a collection of public policies that create a safety net for the disadvantaged in American society, which includes programs providing income, food, and housing security as well as health insurance. Since 2001, homeland security has become an area of growing societal concern. Immigration policy is also the target of societal concern and conflicting reform efforts. Collectively, these policies aim to establish justice, ensure domestic tranquility, promote the general welfare, and secure the blessings of liberty to ourselves and our posterity (future generations).

In our federal system, when citizens bring societal problems to the attention of government officials, the ensuing legislative and public debates typically revolve around several key questions. First, government officials must decide whether the problem is one that government should address. If the answer to that fundamental question is yes, then additional questions follow. What level of government has legal authority to address the problem? What level of government has the financial resources? What is the most cost-effective means to deal with the problem? Beyond the expected positive effects of a policy's implementation, what unexpected costs and negative consequences might occur?

Today, multiple governments—at the national, state, and local levels—often must work together to implement domestic policy in the United States. Chapter 3 highlighted the intergovernmental nature of education policy. In this chapter, we focus on additional domestic policies formulated by the national government and implemented in collaboration with state and local governments.

Citizen Engagement and Domestic Policy

The Constitution established a government that is by and for the people. Previous chapters have explored the many ways in which individuals and groups engage with government officials and political processes to influence what government does and does not do. Yet a widespread national affliction is the **NIMBY,** or **"not-in-my-backyard," syndrome.** People with the NIMBY syndrome decline to participate in politics until a government action or inaction threatens them directly. Lobbying government officials is a common first step in citizen engagement, and it may be as basic as making a phone call, sending an e-mail, or writing a letter. Additional modes of participation include public protests and demonstrations, attendance at open government meetings, and testifying at government hearings. Citizens may also use lawsuits to press government officials to focus on issues of concern and to address them through policy making.

Complicating the work of U.S. policy makers, the diversity of citizens' needs and expectations for government action means that almost every call for government action sparks a call for either a different action or no action. The plurality of citizens' needs and priorities, the constantly changing priorities of citizens, and the range of political ideologies among citizens make for ongoing public conversations and legislative debates over which policies warrant government spending and who will pay the taxes to cover the bills. Democrats and Republicans frequently

DIFFERENCES IN TOP POLICY PRIORITIES OF U.S. CITIZENS YIELD POLICY DEBATES

Citizens in representative democracies expect their elected officials to listen to their concerns and priorities and then enact policies that address them. However, citizens do not speak with one voice. The policy priorities of citizens affiliated with the two major political parties as well as independents, those of the growing proportion of citizens not affiliated with either major party, all differ from each other. The result is that Democratic and Republican elected representatives frequently disagree on what policies government should enact and how bureaucrats should implement policies.

Evaluating the Evidence

1. According to Gallup Politics, in 2013 on average, 42 percent of Americans identified as independents, 31 percent as Democrats, and 25 percent as Republicans.** Explain how this distribution of affiliations and nonaffiliations coupled with the different priorities of the three groups noted in the table might help to explain today's stiff partisanship and gridlock in national policy making.

2. What five policies would you prioritize if you were an elected representative? Explain your selections.

3. Review the discussion on measuring public opinion in Chapter 6. What do you need to know about the Pew Research Center methodology to have confidence in the survey results presented in the table?

4. Review the discussion of political parties in Chapter 8. Do the policy priorities of the Democrats, Republicans, and independents presented in the table support the notion that America may be ready for a third party in national politics?

Top 10 Priorities of Democrats, Republicans, and Independents*

PARENTHETICAL VALUES REPRESENT THE PERCENTAGE OF SURVEY RESPONDENTS WHO INDICATED THE POLICY IS A TOP PRIORITY.

DEMOCRATS	REPUBLICANS	INDEPENDENTS
Strengthening the economy (85%)	Defending the country from terrorism (81%)	Strengthening the economy (81%)
Improving the job situation (81%)	Reducing the budget deficit (80%)	Improving the job situation (75%)
Improving the educational system (80%)	Strengthening the economy (76%)	Defending the country from terrorism (70%)
Defending the country from terrorism (70%)	Making the Social Security system sound (72%)	Improving the educational system (68%)
Reducing health care costs (67%)	Improving the job situation (66%)	Reducing the budget deficit (66%)
Protecting the environment (65%)	Strengthening the military (61%)	Making the Social Security system sound (65%)
Making the Medicare system sound (65%)	Reforming the tax system (57%)	Making the Medicare system sound (61%)
Dealing with the problems of the poor and needy (64%)	Improving the educational system (55%)	Reducing health care costs (56%)
Reducing crime (60%)	Reducing health care costs (55%)	Reforming the tax system (54%)
Reforming the tax system (56%)	Making the Medicare system sound (54%)	Reducing crime (52%)

*Pew Research Center for the People & the Press, "Deficit Reduction Declines as Policy Priority," January 27, 2014, www.people-press.org/2014/01/27/deficit-reduction-declines-as-policy-priority/.
**Jeffrey M. Jones, "Record-High 42% of Americans Identify as Independents," January 8, 2014, www.gallup.com/poll/166763/record-high-americans-identify-independents.aspx.

disagree on these matters. Democrats typically are liberal in inclination and tend to support **safety nets**—programs ensuring that every citizen's basic physiological needs (food, water, shelter, health care, and a clean environment) are met. Republicans more commonly have a conservative ideology and focus more on public safety and national security issues. A growing proportion of citizens do not affiliate with either major party and their collective views sometimes mirror Democratic tendencies, sometimes mirror Republican tendencies, and at still other times are distinct from both major parties. (The "Analyzing the Sources" feature focuses on variations in citizens' policy priorities.) Ultimately, elected officials—who typically want to get reelected—find it much easier to add new policies and programs, and consequently to drive up government expenses, than to eliminate programs or to decrease program costs. (Chapter 16 explored the pattern of deficit spending this leads to and its effect on the national economy.)

As we have seen in preceding chapters, the government makes policy in several ways. For one, Congress and the president set policy by approving *authorization bills,* which establish a policy and identify who will implement it, and *appropriations bills,* which authorize the spending of national revenue to pay for the authorized policies. Federal, state, local, and shadow bureaucrats also make policy, through both the administrative rule-making process and their daily use of administrative discretion as they implement policies. In addition, the presidential power of the executive order amounts to making policy, because it gives the president the authority to tell bureaucrats how to carry out a national policy. Finally, the federal courts resolve conflicts over the meaning and proper implementation of laws and, in doing so, make policy. In summary, each of the three branches of the national government has policy-making authority that it uses to fulfill the government's constitutionally established mission to serve present generations and their posterity.

Since 1789, the national government's scope of responsibility for addressing domestic matters has expanded gradually as individuals and groups have lobbied to press for their interests. Federal authority now covers a diverse collection of public policies. Today's national budget lists 17 superfunctions of the federal government (see Table 17.1). The numbers in the table show that most federal government functions are directed at (and most government spending goes toward) **domestic policies,** which are policies addressing the problems, needs, and relations of people residing within the country's borders, as opposed to matters involving relations with other countries and nations. In 2013, 74 percent of federal expenditures paid for domestic policies and 20 percent paid for international affairs and defense policies. The remaining expenditures paid for interest on the national debt incurred by past borrowing to cover deficit spending.

Because it would be impossible for us to examine every domestic policy program, we limit our focus in this chapter to a subset of national domestic policies. Specifically, we concentrate on national policies that address the most basic of human needs and are essential to sustaining life, liberty, and opportunities to pursue happiness: environmental, energy, income security, health care, and homeland security policies. We also look at the controversial policy area of immigration, defined by some as a national security concern, by others as an economic issue, and by still others as a humanitarian cause reflecting the United States' roots and highest ideals.

Tools of Domestic Policy

The national government attempts to address citizens' problems and to provide benefits and services to the people by using various policy tools. Domestic policy tools include laws and regulations, direct provision of public goods, cash transfer payments, loans, loan guarantees, insurance, grants-in-aid to state and local governments, and contracting-out the provision of public goods to nongovernmental entities (shadow bureaucracies and bureaucrats).

Laws and Regulations

At the federal, state, and local levels alike, governments strive to accomplish their domestic policy goals by creating laws with which individuals and organizations must comply. These include tax laws, environmental laws, and laws to ensure public health and safety. Many laws assign administrative agencies the authority to establish the specific rules, regulations, and standards

TABLE 17.1

National Budget Superfunctions and Expenditures:
Total Actual National Budget Outlays, 2013, $3.5 Trillion

Defense and International Affairs ($679,803 million; 19.6% of budget outlays)*	National defense ($633,385 million; 18.3%)
	International affairs ($46,418 million; 1.3%)
Domestic Policies ($2,553,917 million; 73.9%)	Social Security ($813,551 million; 23.6%)
	Income security ($536,511 million; 15.5%)
	Medicare ($497,826 million; 14.4%)
	Health ($358,315 million; 10.7%)
	Veterans benefits and services ($139,938; 4.1%)
	Transportation ($91,673 million; 2.7%)
	Education, training, employment, and social services ($72,808 million; 2.1%)
	Administration of justice ($52,601 million; 1.5%)
	Natural resources and environment ($38,145 million; 1.1%)
	Community and regional development ($32,336 million; 0.9%)
	Agriculture ($29,492 million; 0.9%)
	General science, space, and technology ($28,908 million; 0.9%)
	General government ($27,755 million; 0.8%)
	Energy ($11,042 million; 0.3%)
Net Interest ($220,885 million; 6.4%)	

*Numbers in parentheses represent total outlay for the function; percentage of total budget outlay (rounded to the nearest tenth of a percent).

SOURCE: Office of Management and Budget, "Table 3.1: Outlays by Superfunction and Function," *Historical Tables,* www.whitehouse.gov/omb.budget/Historicals.

that are essential to effective implementation of the laws (as discussed in Chapter 14). For example, the Internal Revenue Service establishes rules and regulations to administer tax law.

The overwhelming majority of people and organizations comply with most laws and regulations. But because some individuals and organizations fail to do so, the government must monitor compliance. For example, the government hires inspectors to ensure that meat, poultry, and eggs are processed safely, are wholesome, and are labeled correctly. The government counts on citizens, interest groups, and the media to assist in overseeing compliance by identifying violators.

Direct Provision of Public Goods

In addition to creating rules of behavior through laws and regulations, governments provide services and benefits. Using the domestic policy tool of **direct provision,** governments hire public servants—bureaucrats who receive a government paycheck—to dispense the services. For example, veterans hospitals hire doctors, nurses, and physical therapists to administer health care to veterans; the U.S. Postal Service hires mail carriers, postal clerks, and postal processing machine operators to deliver billions of pieces of mail each week. The workers hired by the national government to provide these services directly are on the payroll of the national government.

direct provision
the policy tool whereby the government that creates a policy hires public servants to provide the service

Cash Transfers

Another instrument of government policy is the **cash transfer**—the direct provision of cash (in various forms) to eligible individuals or to the providers of goods or services to eligible individuals. **In-kind assistance** is a form of a cash transfer in which the government pays cash

cash transfer
the direct provision of cash (in forms including checks, debit cards, and tax breaks) to eligible individuals or to providers of goods or services to eligible individuals

in-kind assistance
a cash transfer in which the government pays cash to those who provide goods or services to eligible individuals

>The Food Safety and Inspection Service (FSIS), an agency within the Department of Agriculture (USDA), hires food inspectors to ensure that the supply of commercial meat, poultry, and egg products is safe, wholesome, and correctly labeled and packaged. In 2014, food safety groups and officials of food inspector unions warned that a shortage of inspectors raised the possibility that contaminated products would make their way to markets. The claim that there is an inspector shortage comes as the USDA implements a new program that increases the number of lower-paid, temporary inspector positions and decreases the number of full-time permanent inspectors. The FSIS is having a difficult time filling the temporary positions, resulting in a large number of vacancies. How concerned should you be about the food inspector shortage?

noncontributory program

a benefit provided to a targeted population, paid for by a proportion of the money collected from all taxpayers

contributory program (social insurance program)

a benefit provided only to those who paid the specific tax created to fund the benefit

entitlement program

a government benefit guaranteed to all who meet the eligibility requirements

direct subsidy

a cash transfer from general revenues to particular persons or private companies engaged in activities that the national government believes support the public good

to those who provide goods or services to eligible individuals. Approximately 70 percent of the money spent by the national government goes toward cash transfers to citizens.[1] Nearly half of the American population lives in a household that receives a cash transfer.[2]

Examples of cash transfers include unemployment and Social Security checks, Pell grants to college students, grants-in-aid to state and local governments for payments to individuals, and tax breaks and subsidies to individuals and corporations (see Chapter 16). Medicaid, the government program that provides health care for the poor, is an example of an in-kind assistance, cash transfer program. The Medicaid recipient receives medical care at no cost or at a reduced cost because the government pays health care providers for their services. The Supplemental Nutrition Assistance Program (SNAP; better known to most by its old name, the food stamp program), was created in 1964 and is another example of in-kind assistance. The government provides cash to the stores that accept SNAP debit cards for food purchases.

The main cash transfer programs are of two kinds, depending upon their sources of revenue. For **noncontributory programs,** the general revenues collected by the government pay for the program. This means that a proportion of the money collected from all taxpayers funds the cash transfer. Temporary Assistance for Needy Families, the income security program for families who have children and no or very low income, is an example of a noncontributory cash-transfer program. In contrast, **contributory programs,** or **social insurance programs,** are funded by revenue collected specifically for these programs, and they benefit only those who have paid into the programs. Social insurance programs are **entitlement programs,** meaning the government guarantees the programs' benefits to all who meet the eligibility criteria. Thus workers who pay the payroll tax for Social Security will receive Social Security checks when they retire.

With a **direct subsidy,** another type of cash transfer, the government provides financial support to specific persons or organizations that engage in activities that the government believes benefit the public good. Individual farmers and agricultural corporations, for example, receive money from the government to grow specified crops or to limit how much they grow. College students receiving Pell grants, which students do not need to pay back, are also recipients of direct subsidies funded through the federal government's general revenues.

Loans, Loan Guarantees, and Insurance

In addition to using tax breaks and grants to encourage behaviors that accomplish its goals, the national government lends money to individuals and organizations, and it guarantees loans made by private businesses. Some examples are government loan programs to assist individuals in purchasing homes, reflecting the widespread belief that home ownership promotes the general welfare and domestic tranquility, and Stafford and Perkins loans, which pay some of the college expenses of students. In addition, the government guarantees banks that it will repay the loans they provide to college students if the students cannot repay the loans themselves. If the government did not guarantee them, it is unlikely that banks, which are profit-making organizations, would lend thousands of dollars to unemployed young people to pay for college costs.

The national government is also in the insurance business. The Federal Deposit Insurance Corporation (FDIC) is one example of a national insurance program. The FDIC insures bank deposits up to $250,000 in member banks to encourage people to save money not only for their own sake but also for the good of the national economy.

Grants-in-Aid and Contracting Out

State and local governments and private-sector organizations implement a growing proportion of national government policies. Through funded and unfunded mandates as well as grants-in-aid (explored in Chapter 3), the federal government requires and encourages state and local governments to carry out national policies. We see these forms of intergovernmental relations in policies as diverse as homeland security, primary and secondary education, and transportation.

The government also contracts with private and nonprofit organizations to produce essential resources or to deliver services. One example of contracting-out, or outsourcing (see Chapter 14), is the government's contracts with corporations such as Lockheed Martin and Boeing to build the planes and missiles it needs to defend the country. Another example is medical research funded by the government and conducted by private companies and institutions of higher education.

By means of contracting-out and the other various tools we have surveyed, the government delivers goods and services to its citizens now and in the future. In the rest of this chapter, we examine how government uses these tools to implement overall policy in several domestic policy areas, including the environment, energy, income security, health care, homeland security, and immigration.

Environmental Policy

At the most basic level, providing for the general welfare means ensuring that people have the basic necessities for sustaining life. These needs include clean and drinkable water, breathable air, and unpolluted land on which to grow food that is safe for consumption. No one argues against a clean environment. Yet there is no consensus on how to achieve and maintain one. In addition, appeals for environmental protection often conflict with demands for ample supplies of energy and for economic development, specifically the creation of jobs. For example, the extraction of coal and oil from the earth, as well as the development of nuclear energy, pose immediate as well as long-term threats to the environment. But these activities also create jobs. However, by the 1970s, several environmental crises had brought into stark view the harm that humans had caused to the natural environment, plants, animals, and people.

Environmental Degradation

Since the 1940s, farmers have used chemicals to destroy insects, weeds, fungi, and other living organisms that harm their crops. The threats such pesticides pose to air, water, and land became the focus of public concern and political debate after the publication of Rachel Carson's eye-opening best seller *Silent Spring* in 1962. Carson's book documented how pesticides were contaminating the environment and getting into human food. The use of chemicals, she warned, threatened the existence not only of birds—whose extinction would mean a silent spring—but of humankind itself.

Then, in 1969, those growing apprehensions became a spectacular reality when the heavily polluted Cuyahoga River in northeastern Ohio caught fire (again!). Around the same time, arsenic was found in the Kansas River, and millions of fish went belly-up in major waterways such as Lake Superior, killed by the chemicals and untreated waste emitted by industrial plants and local sewage systems. In response, state and local governments banned fishing in many waterways, including Lake Erie, because of their excessive pollution.

The mounting environmental crises and additional governmental studies brought amplified calls to action from both citizens' groups and elected officials during the 1960s and 1970s. Cleaning up air and water had become a top priority for a majority of Americans. In 1965, 17 percent of citizens listed this as one of their top three political priorities; by 1970, 53 percent of citizens listed it as one of their top three priorities.[3] U.S. senator Gaylord Nelson (D-Wisc.) responded to citizens' growing environmental concerns by proposing a national teach-in, organized at the grassroots level of community groups and college students. He hoped the national day of teach-ins would mobilize the national government to establish an environmental protection agenda. Nelson's

> Founded by U.S. senator Gaylord Nelson in 1970, Earth Day has evolved from a day of grassroots organized events across the United States to an international event with over a billion people participating in educational events in more than 190 countries. The Earth Day Network is the global organizer of the event and offers resources and tools for those interested in creating a local event. College campuses across the United States host Earth Day events each year. What events did your campus or a local community group host for the last Earth Day?

vision of a day of educational rallies became a reality on April 22, 1970. More than 200,000 people gathered on the National Mall in Washington, D.C. It is estimated that 20 million more congregated across the country to draw attention to environmental concerns.[4] Earth Day 1970 was so successful at bringing attention to the environmental cause that many consider it the beginning of the environmental movement. Celebrated every year and involving millions of people worldwide, Earth Day keeps concerns about environmental degradation on the public policy agenda.

Environmental Protection

The Environmental Protection Act of 1969 established the Environmental Protection Agency (EPA) to oversee the implementation of laws protecting the quality of air, water, and land. Then, a cascade of groundbreaking national legislation followed the first Earth Day.

CLEAN AIR The landmark Clean Air Act of 1970 delegates authority to the EPA to set air quality standards while giving state governments enforcement responsibility. Today, states in turn typically delegate some of their enforcement responsibilities to local governments. If states and their local governments do not enforce compliance with the national standards, the EPA can take over.

To bolster compliance with the Clean Air Act, the law gives citizens the right to sue those who are violating the standards. Citizens also have the right to sue the EPA if it does not enforce the Clean Air Act. Citizens and environmental interest groups have availed themselves of their right to sue, pushing the government and industries to comply with the law. For example, in 2007, Massachusetts and 11 other states, 3 cities, and several environmental groups successfully challenged the EPA and President George W. Bush's interpretation of the law, when the U.S. Supreme Court determined that carbon dioxide is a pollutant that the EPA has the authority to regulate.[5] Scientists and governments throughout the world have been raising concerns about air pollution, particularly emissions of carbon dioxide, for decades. Mounting evidence indicates that air pollution caused by burning fossil fuels produces a **greenhouse effect,** which is the heating of the earth's atmosphere as a result of the buildup of carbon dioxide and other gases. The climate change, particularly global warming, caused by the greenhouse effect is a growing concern internationally and a target of international treaties as discussed in this chapter's section on energy policy.

greenhouse effect

the heating of the earth's atmosphere as a result of humans' burning of fossil fuels and the resultant buildup of carbon dioxide and other gases

CLEAN WATER The Clean Water Act is actually the 1972 Federal Water Pollution Control Act as amended over the years. This law, which has the goal of making waterways clean enough to swim in and to eat fish from, authorizes the EPA to set water quality standards and to require permits for anyone discharging contaminants into any waterway. Under the Clean Water Act, state and local governments must monitor water quality, issue permits to those discharging waste into waterways, and enforce the national standards. If states and localities fail to carry out these mandated responsibilities, the EPA can step in and do the job. The law also provides for federal loans to local governments, funneled through state governments, for building wastewater treatment plants.

The Safe Drinking Water Act of 1974 authorizes the EPA to establish purity standards for drinking water. Because states or localities typically operate water systems, this act effectively requires the EPA to regulate state and local governments. The act provides for national grants to state and local governments for research and for improving their water systems.

Then Now

>Between 1942 and 1947, Hooker Electrochemical Company legally dumped 20,000 tons of toxic waste in the never-completed Love Canal near Niagara Falls, New York. Then homes and a school were built atop the toxic waste dumpsite. In 1978, a series of news articles exposed health problems suffered by residents of the area, who turned to their local, state, and eventually the national government for relief. After protests and national media attention, the governments relocated close to 900 residents from the contaminated area. After clean-up efforts, developers and residents returned to the area. However, in 2013, a half-dozen families filed several lawsuits claiming that the toxic waste was sickening a new generation of Love Canal—now known as Black Creek—residents.

CLEAN LAND   The United States produces more solid waste—from household garbage to toxic by-products of manufacturing—per person than any other country. If not properly disposed of or treated, all waste has the potential to harm the environment, as well as plants, animals, and people. Some toxic by-products, such as the radioactive nuclear wastes produced in manufacturing nuclear weapons and generating nuclear power, cannot be treated or disposed of, but they dissipate over time—from one hundred years for low-level radioactive waste to hundreds of thousands of years for high-level radioactive waste. Citizens with resources, including money and the time to organize or to join an existing organization, are able to fight the location of undesirable land uses in their communities. Lower-income communities are more likely than more affluent communities to bear the burden of land uses with negative environmental impacts such as landfills, industrial plants, and toxic waste sites. **Environmental racism** is the term used to describe the higher incidence of environmental threats and subsequent health problems in lower-income communities, which frequently are also communities dominated by people of color.[6]

The Resource Conservation and Recovery Act of 1976, administered by the EPA, regulates the disposal of solid and hazardous wastes and encourages recycling. Although this act authorized the cleanup of toxic waste sites, and the government identified thousands of such sites in the 1970s, no national funding was made available for the cleanup. Then in 1980, just as Congress was focused on the crisis at Love Canal, New York, where 833 families had to be relocated because of health problems tied to the toxic waste buried below their homes and school, an abandoned site for the storage, treatment, and disposal of hazardous waste in Elizabeth, New Jersey, exploded. Shortly thereafter, Congress approved the Comprehensive Environmental Response, Compensation and Liability Act of 1980 (known as the Superfund law) to pay for cleanup of the nation's most toxic waste dumps.

ENVIRONMENTAL PROTECTION, ENERGY PRODUCTION, AND JOBS   Although no one argues against a clean environment, tensions persist between the need for environmental protection and other policy areas. The environmental threats and damage created by energy production; accidents during the extraction and transportation of energy sources such as

environmental racism
the term used to describe the higher incidence of environmental threats and subsequent health problems in lower-income communities, which frequently are also communities dominated by people of color

>Demonstrators carry a replica of a pipeline during a February 2013 march against the Keystone XL pipeline in Washington. Tension between environmental policy, energy policy, and economic development (job creation) is evident in debates and protests over the proposed Keystone XL pipeline, and in the numerous extensions for review and revision of the proposal granted by President Obama. Environmentalists oppose the pipeline, fearing that potential leaks would harm humans, land, and water quality. Supporters of the pipeline include people who argue that importing oil from Canada, a friendly neighbor, will improve U.S. energy security and unions representing construction workers. What is the current status of the Keystone XL pipeline proposal?

coal, natural gas, and oil; and energy consumption are evident worldwide. Those tensions came into focus in February 2012, when President Barack Obama's administration rejected the proposed 1,700-mile Keystone XL pipeline. TransCanada, a Canadian firm, had applied to build the pipeline to transport oil sands from Alberta, Canada, through the United States to Texas. Because the proposed pipeline crosses an international border, the State Department had to issue a federal permit allowing the pipeline's construction, which it refused to do. In April 2014, Obama extended the ongoing review of a revised proposal for the Keystone XL pipeline.

Environmentalists adamantly oppose the pipeline for several reasons, including the potential for leaks that would endanger animals, land, water, and humans. Unions representing construction workers and congressional Republicans argue the pipeline means job creation, which should be a priority during a stagnant economy. Other pipeline supporters argue that by increasing the amount of crude oil the United States imports from Canada, a friendly neighbor and already the largest source of U.S. crude oil imports, we improve energy security. Others point out that these concerns could be addressed if the United States was less dependent on nonrenewable energy sources. Indeed the United States' dependence on imported nonrenewable energy sources is declining as the extraction of domestic fossil fuels increases and the use of renewable energy sources expands.

Energy Policy

Energy creation—the production of electricity and heat, as well as fuels to power automobiles, trucks, planes, trains, and other transport vehicles—is essential to the prosperity of the U.S. economy and to the American way of life. The United States uses more energy than any other country in the world. What underlies this demand? Industrial and commercial expansion, the construction of larger houses, and soaring computer use all have contributed to the high demand for electricity. Robust sales of trucks for personal use, as well as of gas-guzzling sport utility vehicles (SUVs), have driven up consumers' demand for gasoline. Moreover, the transportation system in the United States relies more heavily on passenger cars than is the case in other countries, where public transportation links cities to one another and to suburbs more effectively. The high energy demands of the U.S. economy and the lifestyle of U.S. residents are problematic for several reasons, as we shall see.

Evolution of U.S. Energy Policy

Before the 1973 refusal of the Organization of Petroleum Exporting Countries (OPEC) to sell oil to the United States and Western European nations, the United States did not have an identifiable energy strategy in place. However, when the Arab members of OPEC imposed the oil embargo in response to U.S. support of Israel in the Yom Kippur War, oil prices in the United States skyrocketed, and people quickly found themselves stuck in hours-long waits at gas stations. OPEC's actions served as a catalyst for the development of U.S. energy policy. U.S. dependence on foreign oil came into focus as an economic, quality of life, and national security concern. In response, the national government began to develop energy policy aimed at reducing the nation's dependence on foreign oil.

In 1975, the national government established the Strategic Petroleum Reserve, a store of crude oil to mitigate the security consequences of any future interruption in the supply of imported oil. The government enacted legislation also encouraging energy conservation and providing funding for research and development of alternative energy sources (such as solar, wind, and geothermal). Legislation created fuel efficiency standards for passenger cars and light trucks, the Corporate Average Fuel Economy (CAFE) standards. Then in 1976, the federal government created the Department of Energy to develop and oversee a comprehensive national energy plan. In 1977, President Jimmy Carter declared an "energy crisis" and called for energy conservation and for research and development into alternative energy. Toward that end, the United States established a national speed limit of 55 miles per hour, Daylight Saving Time, weatherization assistance programs, tax incentives to insulate homes, and building codes related to energy efficiency.

In 1980, oil prices were 10 times higher than they were in 1972, but by 1986, oil prices began to fall. With lower prices during the 1990s came reduced federal funding for research and development of alternative energy sources. Much of the public, too, lost interest in energy conservation.

Then, in 2001, Secretary of Energy Spencer Abraham sounded an alarm: "America faces a major energy-supply crisis over the next two decades. The failure to meet this challenge will threaten our nation's economic prosperity, compromise our national security, and literally alter the way we live our lives."[7] In response, President George W. Bush initially supported increased production of fossil fuels.

By 2006, however, President Bush, faced with concerns over the price and availability of both imported and domestic oil, called for an increase in funding for research in alternative renewable energy sources at the same time he recommended increased use of coal (a domestic fossil fuel resource). President Bush also called for expanded research in alternative means to power automobiles, including electricity, hydrogen, and ethanol.

Energy Policy Today

Today, U.S. energy policy highlights three main concerns: reducing carbon emissions, energy independence, and (therefore) development of renewable energy technologies. These concerns are related to national security; job creation; and the costs of environmental impacts caused by burning fossil fuels, such as global climate change.

CLIMATE CHANGE   Polls show that a majority of Americans are concerned about climate change, especially **global warming,** the rising temperature of the earth caused by pollution that traps solar heat, keeping the air warmer than it would otherwise be. The burning of fossil fuels (oil, coal, and natural gas), which results in a buildup of carbon dioxide and other gases in the air (greenhouse gases; see the earlier section in this chapter on clean air), is identified as one cause of global warming. People concerned about global warming often call for the development of alternative fuel sources to decrease carbon emissions.

global warming
the rising temperature of the earth caused by pollution that traps solar heat, keeping the air warmer than it would otherwise be

In 1997, international fears about global warming culminated in the Kyoto Protocol, which called on countries to work toward decreasing carbon emissions. By 2012, 191 countries had ratified the treaty, but the United States had not. Participants at the 2012 United Nations Climate Change Conference agreed to extend the Kyoto Protocol to 2020 and set 2015 as the deadline for the formulation of a new document that will eventually succeed the Kyoto Protocol.

Although the U.S. House and Senate have debated numerous clean energy bills during the past decade, no major reform in national regulation of carbon emissions has passed in Congress. At the same time, many state and local governments have been working collectively to meet the Kyoto Protocol provisions. For example, nine northeastern and mid-Atlantic states are involved in the Regional Greenhouse Gas Initiative (RGGI). The RGGI commits the states to capping emissions from power plants and to reducing emissions by at least 10 percent by 2018.

In late 2013, the EPA announced a proposal to limit carbon dioxide emissions from new coal-fired power plants. The EPA proposed the regulations so that it could better meet its obligations to implement the Clean Air Act. Immediately, congressional Republicans began efforts to thwart approval of the standards.[8] In addition, they have used the annual budget process to limit the EPA's ability to enforce existing regulations created to enforce the Clean Air Act.

A 2014 report by the Intergovernmental Panel on Climate Change, a United Nations group, concluded that "climate change is already having sweeping effects on every continent." The

Then Now Next

U.S. Energy Sources

	Then (2008)*	Now**
Nonrenewable	93%	91%
Crude oil	37	36
Natural gas	24	27
Coal	23	18
Nuclear	9	8
Renewable	7	9
Biomass	53	49
Hydropower	34	30
Wind	7	15
Geothermal	5	3
Solar	1	2
Net imported crude oil	57	40
Domestic production of crude oil	43	60

*Brigid Harrison and Jean Wahl Harris, *American Democracy Now,* 2nd ed. (New York: McGraw-Hill, 2011), 504.
** U.S. Energy Information Administration, "U.S. Energy Facts Explained," www.eia.gov/energyexplained/index .cfm?page=us_energy_home.

WHAT'S NEXT?

> Will growing concerns about climate change affect the velocity at which the proportion of energy produced from renewable sources increases in the United States and around the globe? Explain.

> How might the concerns about the environmental effects of hydraulic fracturing, or fracking (see the later section in this chapter on energy independence), affect the proportion of energy produced from domestic natural gas?

> How might tensions among environmental protection, economic development, and national security affect the ability of the United States to achieve energy independence in the near future?

report concluded that climate change is causing extremes in weather leading to floods, droughts, and other natural disasters. Moreover, coastal communities are affected by melting ice caps, water supplies are under stress, and the world's food supply is at "considerable risk."[9] President Obama welcomed the panel's report, hoping it would mobilize more support among congressional members for his efforts to impose new limits on the country's carbon dioxide and other greenhouse emissions.

ENERGY INDEPENDENCE The United States has come a long way since concerns about its dependence on foreign fossil fuels were raised in the 1970s. Between 2008 and 2013, the amount of crude oil produced in the United States increased by "40 percent, after declining every year for the previous 20."[10] By 2013, the United States had become the largest producer of natural gas in the world, and the International Energy Agency predicted that the United States would move ahead of Saudi Arabia by 2015 as the world's largest oil-producing country.[11]

The surge in natural gas production in the United States is the result of the hydraulic-fracturing drilling process, also known as fracking. Opponents of fracking raise concerns about the environmental and public health threats of the process, which infuses water, sand, and chemicals into rock formations deep in the earth to force out natural gas captured in the rock. They also argue that accidents during the transporting of natural gas through pipelines could threaten health and the environment. In addition, some research links fracking to an increased incidence of earthquakes. Proponents of fracking focus on the jobs created by the natural gas industry. According to the U.S. Energy Information Administration, employment in oil and gas increased by 40 percent between 2008 and 2013.[12] The production of steel pipes (for transporting natural gas) has created new jobs as well.

The surge in U.S. oil and gas production alarms people who are concerned about climate change. In particular, they are concerned that the increased production of energy via the burning of fossil fuels will perpetuate the world's dependence on fossil fuels and divert attention and resources from research and development on alternative, renewable energy sources. Democrats argue that we must do more to promote and develop alternative fuels. Republicans do not disagree, but they argue that, in the short term, there is no alternative to oil and gas and that, therefore, we need to increase our domestic production of oil and gas to ensure a stable supply of energy.

Increasing the fuel efficiency of cars is another strategy for reducing dependence on fossil fuels. In 2012, the Obama administration finalized new fuel economy standards for cars and light-duty trucks. The new standards increased the 35-miles-per-gallon fuel standard established in 2007 to 54.5-miles-per-gallon for model year 2025.

Today, the environmental impact of the continued use of fossil fuels threatens the quality of life for people in the United States and around the globe. Americans are looking to national and state governments for public policy solutions to these energy-related and environmental concerns. In a similar way, during the 1930s, Americans turned to the national government to address the economic downturn that prevented millions of Americans from enjoying a decent quality of life, as we consider next.

Income Security Programs

Before the Great Depression of the 1930s, Americans who could not provide for their basic needs relied on relief from family, friends, charities, and, in some cases, local or state government. During the Depression, however, the excessively weak economy left one-quarter of the U.S. labor force unemployed. Families lost jobs, savings, and homes. Charities were overwhelmed. State and local governments lacked the resources needed to assist the millions of people without incomes. Citizens, as well as state and local governments, looked to the federal government for assistance.

Within his first hundred days in office, President Franklin D. Roosevelt proposed a sequence of revolutionary bills to stimulate and regulate sectors of the depressed economy and to provide income to those in need. His administration's radical proposals placed the national government at the center of issues it had historically left to local and state governments. Those and the subsequent New Deal policies approved in Roosevelt's first few years in office provided income security for retired citizens and a safety net for people in financial need. Many of the New Deal programs are still in place today, though in modified form.

Social Security

The Social Security Act of 1935, a centerpiece of the New Deal, established a range of landmark income security programs. To this day, these programs, which represent the most expensive of the domestic policies, provide financial assistance to individuals who are elderly, disabled, dependent, and unemployed.

OLD-AGE AND SURVIVORS INSURANCE   The Social Security Act established the Old-Age and Survivors Insurance (OASI) Program, which initially provided income to individuals or families when a worker covered by the program retired. This contributory cash-transfer program is the traditional retirement insurance component of Social Security; most people are aware of it and anticipate benefiting from it in retirement. OASI is a social insurance entitlement program, funded by contributions that employees as well as employers make. Each year, the federal government establishes the amount of earnings subject to the Social Security tax, which is called the *covered income*. In 2014, income up to $117,100 was subject to the tax.[13]

A formula that accounts for how much individuals paid into Social Security over their years of employment determines the amount of each beneficiary's monthly Social Security check. The more money invested, the greater the check. Because OASI is an **indexed benefit,** the government makes regularly scheduled, automatic cost-of-living adjustments (COLAs), increasing the benefit based on the rate of inflation. The 1937 Federal Insurance Contribution Act (FICA) established the pay-as-you-go funding mechanism for OASI. Through FICA contributions, current workers and employers deposit money in the Social Security Trust Fund, and the government uses the money contributed today to pay today's beneficiaries. The money left over after today's payments are made is invested so that the trust fund will grow; income from investments will be combined with future FICA revenues to pay for future Social Security checks.

Most people collect more from Social Security than they pay into the fund, and the number of retirees is growing. With the increasing number of retirees and with those retirees living longer, the pay-as-you-go system will eventually reach the point of not covering the full costs of OASI. The surplus money in the Social Security Trust Fund is already shrinking. This situation generates intense public debate over what the national government should do to ensure that Social Security funds are available for workers who are currently contributing to the program.

indexed benefit
a government benefit with an automatic cost-of-living increase based on the rate of inflation

> On January 31, 1940, Ida Mae Fuller was the first person to receive an OASI check. Ms. Fuller paid a total of $22 into the Social Security insurance program from 1937 to her retirement in 1940. Her first check was for $22.54 and over the next 35 years, she collected a total of $22,000 (1,000 times what she paid into the system). Today, people paying into Social Security can visit the Social Security Administration website and create an account that allows them to review their earnings record and the government's estimate of their retirement, disability, and survivor's benefits. When you are ready to retire, you can apply for your OAIS benefits online. To create your own account, go to www.ssa.gov/myaccount/.

means-tested benefit
a benefit for which eligibility is based on having an income below a government-specified amount

AMENDMENTS TO THE SOCIAL SECURITY ACT Congress amended the Social Security Act in 1939 to provide benefits to the dependents and surviving spouse of a deceased worker. In 1956, the act was further amended to assist workers who, because of physical or mental disabilities, had to stop working after age 50 but before the OASI-designated retirement age. The new benefit program thus created, called Social Security Disability Insurance (SSDI), provides income to those covered by the Social Security program and to their families if they meet the guidelines for disability. Similar to OASI, SSDI is a contributory (social insurance) program.

In 1972, Congress again amended the Social Security Act by establishing the Supplemental Security Income (SSI) program, a noncontributory program. Recipients of SSI include low-income elderly people whose Social Security benefits are so low they cannot provide for themselves, individuals with disabilities, and blind people. Unlike other Social Security programs, SSI is a **means-tested benefit,** meaning that the eligibility criteria to receive the benefit include a government-specified income level, which is very low.

The Social Security Act of 1935 created other income security programs, including unemployment compensation and Aid to Dependent Children. Three years after passage of the Social Security Act, the Roosevelt administration also enacted a minimum wage, and several decades later, in 1975, Congress established an additional income security program known as the Earned Income Tax Credit. We now turn to these other income security programs.

Unemployment Compensation

The Federal-State Unemployment Insurance Program, created by the Social Security Act of 1935, requires each state government to administer its own unemployment insurance program within guidelines established by federal law. Through this program, employees who lose their jobs through no fault of their own, and meet other eligibility requirements established by their state, can collect unemployment compensation from the state for up to 26 weeks. Employees fired for cause (not doing the job, doing it poorly, or violating work rules or the law) cannot receive unemployment compensation. In general, the benefit received is based on a percentage of an individual's most recent earnings.

During economic recessions, the national government has sometimes extended the 26-week benefit period if the unemployment rate remains high for a long time. When the federal government extends the benefit period in times of high, long-term unemployment, it pays for the additional benefits. Since 2008, early in the Great Recession, the federal government has approved extensions in states with unemployment rates of at least 6 percent. In 2012 and then again in 2013, the federal government reauthorized these temporary extensions, which then expired on December 31, 2013.

Minimum Wage

We can thank Frances Perkins for the federal minimum wage. When President Franklin D. Roosevelt asked her to serve as his secretary of labor, Perkins told him she would join his cabinet only if he agreed to establish a minimum wage.[14] He agreed, she became the first woman to serve as a department secretary, and the minimum wage became law through the 1938 Fair Labor Standards Act.

living wage
a wage high enough to keep workers and their families out of poverty and to allow them to enjoy a basic living standard

The aim of the minimum wage was to guarantee most employed workers a **living wage**—a wage high enough to keep them out of poverty. Yet, there have always been some workers not guaranteed the federal minimum wage. Today these include full-time students, youths under 20 years of age for the first 90 days of their employment, workers who earn tips, commissioned sales employees, farm laborers, and seasonal and recreational workers. For workers guaranteed the minimum wage, employers must pay overtime (equal to one and a half times an employee's regular hourly rate) for all hours over 40 worked during a workweek.

In 1938, the government set the federal minimum wage at 25 cents per hour. Because the minimum wage is not an indexed benefit, battles to increase the minimum wage occur regularly. (See the "Thinking Critically About Democracy" feature for a debate on the federal minimum wage.) In 2009, Congress increased the minimum wage to $7.25. In December 2013, President Obama began calling on Congress to increase the minimum wage to $10.10, in three increments over two years. A November 2013 CBS News poll showed that two-thirds of Americans supported an increase in the minimum wage.[15] However, congressional Republicans argued that an increase in the minimum wage would force employers to cut their workforce at a time when the recovery from the Great Recession was anemic. By 2014, the $7.25 minimum wage was "in inflation-adjusted terms, more than $2 below where it stood 40 years ago."[16]

State and local governments can establish a minimum wage higher than the federal minimum for covered workers, and they can extend a minimum wage to workers not covered by the federal minimum wage. At the beginning of 2014, 21 states and the District of Columbia had minimum wages higher than the federal level. But even with these more generous benefits, many minimum wage workers are still living in poverty. Hence, today's minimum wage is not necessarily a living wage. To reduce the financial hardship on minimum and low-wage workers, the national government established the Earned Income Tax Credit program.

Earned Income Tax Credit

In addition to providing cash transfers and regulating wages, the government supports income security through programs offering tax breaks. One of these is the Earned Income Tax Credit (EITC) program, established in 1975. Citizens with low to moderate earned income from employment or from self-employment who file an income tax return are eligible for EITC benefits. Working parents are eligible for larger tax credits than are workers without children. The amount of the tax credit decreases (eventually reaching zero) as earned income increases. Because the EITC rewards work by supplementing the earnings of low-wage workers, there is broad bipartisan support for it. Since 2009, congressional Republicans and Democrats have supported enhancing the EITC for workers with and without children. According to the Center on Budget and Policy Priorities, a research organization concerned with the status of poor people, in 2011 the EITC kept an estimated 6.5 million people out of poverty, including 3.3 million children.[17]

Temporary Assistance for Needy Families

The Social Security Act established Aid to Dependent Children (ADC), which evolved into Aid to Families with Dependent Children (AFDC) and was then replaced by Temporary Assistance for Needy Families (TANF). Initially supporting stay-at-home single widows with children, the ADC program evolved into TANF, with its emphasis on assisting needy single-parent and two-parent families with children. The focus moreover has changed from one of encouraging women to stay home with their children to one of requiring recipients to work (those in single- and dual-parent households) and requiring fathers (particularly those not living with their children) to take on greater financial responsibilities for their children.

Federal grants and state funds paid for the ADC and AFDC noncontributory cash-transfer, entitlement programs, and a formula in the national law determined what percentage of each state's annual program costs the federal government would cover. The federal law also gave each state discretion to determine the level of benefits as well as the eligibility criteria for program recipients in that state. However, as mandated by federal law, eligibility criteria for AFDC in every state included the presence of children under the age of 18 and a means test indicating no or very low family income.

Democracy

Should There Be a Federal Minimum Wage?

The Issue: The federal government established the minimum wage to ensure that American workers did not live in poverty. A second goal of the minimum wage was to stimulate the economy by increasing the purchasing power of workers. The minimum wage is not indexed, which means that Congress must enact new legislation to raise the minimum wage to keep up with inflation. Every decade or so, there is a national debate on raising the minimum wage, which typically leads to a debate over whether there should even be a federal minimum wage.

Yes: Not only should there be a federal minimum wage, but it also should be indexed so that we can stop debating the issue every decade. Most people earning the minimum wage are adults, many of whom are financially responsible for children. A full-time worker paid the minimum wage ($15,080 per year) who has more than one other person in his or her household is living below the poverty level ($15,730 for a two-person family in 2014). Without a minimum wage, the income gap would grow even more as employers set wages lower than they currently are and more workers would find themselves living in poverty. Congressional members, millionaires who cannot agree on much of anything, should put themselves in the shoes of American workers to understand the stark reality of living on minimum wage. Having an indexed federal minimum wage would ensure that American workers and their posterity do not live in poverty.

No: Workers and employers should be allowed to negotiate whatever wages they want. That is part of what a free market is. The supply of and demand for workers should establish wages. A worker who is not worth hiring at the current minimum wage, because of a lack of education and skills (or maybe even a poor work ethic), would be hired at a lower wage, one based on his or her value as a worker. This step would provide businesses with more capital to hire additional workers, and thus decrease unemployment. Moreover, jobs that have been outsourced to countries that do not have a minimum wage would return to the United States.

Other Approaches: The wage necessary to have a decent standard of living depends on where you live and your family size. Housing, food, child care, transportation, energy, and health care costs vary across communities and regions. Instead of establishing a federal minimum wage, regional minimum wages should be established by local governments that cover areas in which employers compete for employees, based on the cost of living in the community. Currently, in some communities, local ordinances require employers who benefit from government contracts and economic development grants to pay wages higher than the federal minimum to ensure a decent standard of living based on local costs. Another option is to expand the Earned Income Tax Credit, which would not affect employment because it does not increase employers' costs.

What do you think?

1. Does the constitutional responsibility to provide for the general welfare obligate the government to ensure that all people have a decent standard of living? If so, what defines a "decent standard of living"?

2. Does the constitutional responsibility to provide for the general welfare require the establishment of a minimum wage that is indexed? Explain your answer.

3. If you believe there should be a legally established minimum wage, what level of government (national, state, or local) do you think should establish it? Explain your answer.

4. In 2014, a full-time worker working year-round, earning the federal minimum wage of $7.25 per hour, brought home $15,080 for the year. What standard of living would you have if you earned the minimum wage?

---

feminization of poverty
the phenomenon of increasing numbers of unmarried, divorced, and separated women with children living in poverty

Beginning in the late 1950s, the number of households headed by women with children living in poverty began to increase, a development referred to as the **feminization of poverty.** Although the overwhelming majority of AFDC beneficiaries were children, myths about a poor work ethic and irresponsible sexual practices on the part of their typically single mothers fueled many calls for reform. Although AFDC was modified several times over the next few decades, a major reform did not occur until the 1990s.

In 1996, President Bill Clinton signed the Personal Responsibility and Work Opportunity Reconciliation Act (PRWORA), which radically changed both the nature and the provision of income security for low-income families with children. PRWORA replaced the AFDC entitlement program and several other grant assistance programs for low-income families, including the Job Opportunities & Basic Skills Training Program and the Emergency Assistance Program with one grant, Temporary Assistance for Needy Families, or TANF.[18] Unlike AFDC, TANF is not an entitlement program.

TANF is designed to foster self-sufficiency among families with children by providing financial assistance for basic needs (like food, housing, and clothing), job training, child care, and transportation, among other needs. States receive block grants from the federal government that give them discretion to design programs that meet the purposes of the TANF program.

Although PRWORA gives state governments a great deal of flexibility in determining TANF eligibility, benefits, and programs, it comes with several very specific regulations. For example, a family can receive benefits only for two consecutive years and a lifetime maximum of five years. Moreover, program beneficiaries must work or be enrolled in an educational or a training program that prepares them for work. In addition, female TANF recipients must identify their children's father so that these men can be required to provide financial support for their children. Ultimately, the success of this radical approach to welfare reform depends on the availability of jobs that pay well and offer benefits; hence, its success depends on the overall health of the U.S. economy.

Government Definitions of Poverty

Despite the various income security programs we have considered, tens of millions of Americans, including millions who work full time, live in *poverty*—the condition of lacking sufficient income to purchase the necessities for an adequate living standard. Millions of others are one problem away from poverty, meaning that a health emergency, significant car repair, family relations issue, or job layoff could land them in poverty. The government defines poverty using two measures: *poverty thresholds* and *poverty guidelines*.

Since the 1960s, the U.S. Census Bureau has used the gauge of *poverty thresholds*—an annually updated set of income measures (adjusted for family size) that define who is living in poverty (see Chapter 16). The government uses these thresholds to collect data on how many families and individuals are living in poverty.

Using 100 percent of the poverty threshold as the definition of poverty, according to the Census Bureau, in 2012, 47 million individuals (15 percent of the U.S. population) were living in poverty. There were 16 million children below the age of 18 years (22 percent) living in poverty, and almost 4 million people over the age of 64 (9 percent) in the same situation. The poverty rate among blacks was 27 percent; Hispanics, 26 percent; Asians, 12 percent; and non-Hispanic whites, 10 percent.[19]

Government agencies that offer additional safety-net programs beyond those we have considered so far do not use the Census Bureau's poverty thresholds to determine eligibility. Instead, many use **poverty guidelines** established by the Department of Health and Human Services (HHS). These guidelines are a version of the poverty thresholds simplified for administrative use (see Table 17.2).

Most (in-kind assistance) safety-net programs allow families with incomes of a certain percentage above the HHS poverty guidelines (say, 185 percent) to receive benefits. Administrators recognize that families with even those income levels experience difficulties in meeting their basic needs. Programs that use the HHS poverty guidelines as the basis for determining eligibility include SNAP and the National School Lunch Program. These programs

poverty guidelines
a simplified version of the U.S. Census Bureau's poverty thresholds developed each year by the Department of Health and Human Services; used to set financial eligibility criteria for benefits

POLITICAL

Inquiry

What quality of life could you, as a single person, achieve at the income of 100 percent of the poverty guidelines? What quality of life could you, as a single person, achieve at the income of 185 percent of the poverty guidelines?

TABLE 17.2

Poverty Guidelines for the 48 Contiguous States and Washington, D.C., 2014 ($ per year)

Persons in Household	100 Percent of Poverty	185 Percent of Poverty*
1	$11,670	$21,590
2	15,730	29,101
3	19,790	36,612
4	23,850	44,123
5	27,910	51,634
6	31,970	59,145
7	36,030	66,656
8	40,090	74,167

*Calculated from the HSS poverty guidelines.

SOURCE: U.S. Department of Health and Human Services, "2014 Poverty Guidelines," http://aspe.hhs.gov/poverty/14poverty.cfm.

food insecurity

the situation in which people have limited or uncertain ability to obtain, in socially acceptable ways, enough nutritious food to live a healthy and active life

housing insecurity

situation in which people have limited or uncertain ability to obtain, in socially acceptable ways, affordable, safe, and decent-quality permanent housing

target the problem of **food insecurity,** the situation in which people have limited or uncertain ability to obtain, in socially acceptable ways, enough nutritious food to sustain a healthy and active life.

Housing insecurity—the condition in which people have limited or uncertain ability to obtain, in socially acceptable ways, housing that is affordable, safe, of decent quality, and permanent— is another problem for a growing proportion of the U.S. population. The U.S. Department of Housing and Urban Development reported that, in January 2013, there were 610,042 people homeless on a given night; "65 percent were living in emergency shelters or transitional housing and 35 percent were living in unsheltered locations."[20] Of the homeless, 23 percent were children under the age of 18 years. Advocates for the homeless question the one-night-in-January count and argue there are many uncounted homeless persons.[21]

Today, most federal revenue spent on housing assistance is in the form of tax breaks to homeowners, developers, and property owners who rent to low-income householders. But the programs that are most in the public eye are means-tested public housing and housing choice voucher (Section 8 rent subsidy) programs for which low-income households can apply. According to a 2013 report from the Joint Center for Housing Studies at Harvard University, the number of very low-income renters ballooned between 2007 and 2011, but less than a quarter received housing assistance.[22] In addition, the report noted that the availability of subsidized rental housing is steadily shrinking. Therefore, "policymakers must ensure that reform and expansion efforts are not lost in the federal budget debate."[23]

Health Care Policy

Lack of health insurance is an additional problem for low-income households, although the 2010 Patient Protection and Affordable Care Act attempted to ensure that everyone has health insurance by 2014. According to the U.S. Census Bureau, in 2012, 15 percent of the U.S. population was without health insurance. Among those uninsured, 9 percent were under 18 years of age. Of those with insurance, 64 percent had private insurance; 55 percent of people were covered by employer-provided insurance. Some 33 percent of the insured were covered by government health programs, 16 percent by Medicaid, and another 16 percent by Medicare.[24] These two programs were established in 1965 as part of President Lyndon B. Johnson's (1963–1969) Great Society plan, which included government programs to address the effects of poverty during a time of national economic prosperity. Medicare and Medicaid are part of today's safety net.

Medicaid

Title XIX, added to the Social Security Act in 1965, created Medicaid—a joint federal-state entitlement program providing health care to people meeting the means test. Because the national legislation delegates substantial discretion to state governments regarding eligibility and benefits, there are really 50 different Medicaid programs.

In this cash transfer program, state governments pay health care providers, and then the national government reimburses the states for a percentage of those bills. The national government's share of each state's cost is based on a formula that takes into account the state's wealth. The national government pays as little as 50 percent of the Medicaid bill in the 12 wealthiest states and as much as 74 percent in the poorest state, Mississippi.[25]

The State Children's Health Insurance Program (SCHIP), established in 1997, covers medical costs for low-income uninsured children under the age of 19 who are not eligible for Medicaid. In this joint federal-state cash transfer program, eligibility is based on a family income that is generally less than 200 percent of the HHS poverty guidelines. States participating in SCHIP can expand their current Medicaid program to cover these children, or they can create a new program that provides the standard coverage mandated by the national government.

The Affordable Care Act allows states to expand Medicaid and SCHIP eligibility for children, pregnant women, parents, and other adults who were excluded previously from the programs by decreasing the income requirements. Specifically, it allows states to extend Medicaid to low-income individuals and adults in families with incomes up to 133 percent of the federal poverty level.[26]

Traditionally, although most of those who benefit from Medicaid are women and children, the bulk of Medicaid spending covers the health care costs of the elderly. The largest percentage of Medicaid spending pays for nursing home and long-term care services, which Medicare does not cover.

Medicare

In 1965, President Lyndon Johnson signed legislation enacting Medicare, a program that provides health insurance to persons over age 65 and those under 65 who have been receiving SSDI for at least two years. Today, Medicare has four components.

Part A, Medicare's Hospital Insurance Program, is a social insurance program funded by a 1.45 percent tax paid by employees and employers that helps to pay for hospital stays. (This tax and the Social Security tax make up the "FICA" deduction from your paychecks.) All who pay into Medicare are eligible for Part A benefits when they reach the age of 65. Also eligible for Part A are persons under age 65 who have been receiving SSDI for at least two years. *Part B,* Medicare's Supplemental Medical Insurance, covers a percentage of physician costs and other outpatient health care expenses, such as laboratory fees and ambulance services. *Part C,* Medicare + Choice, allows Medicare beneficiaries to choose private health plans that provide them with the same coverage found in Medicare Parts A and B. *Part D* is a prescription drug plan that took effect in 2006.

The Affordable Care Act extended several preventive services to Medicare recipients at no cost, including cholesterol screening, mammograms, diabetes screening, and screening for colorectal, prostate, and cervical cancers. The act also filled in a prescription coverage gap in the Medicare Part D program.[27]

The Patient Protection and Affordable Care Act

On March 23, 2010, President Barack Obama signed into law the Patient Protection and Affordable Care Act (ACA). The ACA has several goals, including expanding consumers' protections in their dealings with health insurance companies, improving the quality and lowering the costs of health care, and increasing access to affordable health care. The ACA set several important precedents, including prohibiting insurance companies from denying coverage based on preexisting health conditions; prohibiting insurance companies from discontinuing coverage when a customer gets sick; eliminating lifetime limits on insurance coverage; providing preventive care services; and requiring insurance coverage to allow young adults to stay on their parents' health plan until they turn 26 years old. One provision that went into effect in 2011 requires that at least 80 to 85 percent of all premium dollars paid to health insurance companies be spent on benefits for the insured and quality improvements, thereby limiting the money that can be spent on administrative costs and that can go into the company's profits.

The law mandates that everyone (with some exceptions for low-income people) must purchase health insurance, if it is not provided through their employer or a government program, or they face an annual fine. The federal government makes subsidies available to individuals with incomes between 133 percent and 400 percent of the federal poverty level to help them purchase insurance. Moreover, employers with more than 50 employees must provide health insurance or pay annual fines for each of their employees who receive federal subsidies to purchase insurance.

In October 2013, online health insurance marketplaces opened so that individuals and small businesses could buy affordable health benefit

> On March 23, 2010, nearly a century after President Theodore Roosevelt first called for health care reform, President Barack Obama signed into law the Patient Protection and Affordable Care Act. Joining the president at the signing were Democratic congressional members and Vice President Joe Biden. Not present at the signing was even one Republican. The partisan battle over passage of this major health care reform did not end with its signing. The battle continued into the court system, all the way to the U.S. Supreme Court. Is the act still making headlines?

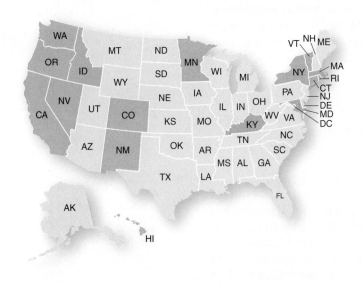

FIGURE 17.1

States That Established Online Health Insurance Exchanges

SOURCE: Obama Care Facts, "State Health Insurance Exchanges," http://obamacarefacts.com/state-health-insurance-exchange.php.

FIGURE 17.2

States That Have Expanded Medicaid

SOURCE: Families USA, "A 50-State Look at Medicaid Expansion," http://familiesusa.org/product/50-state-look-medicaid-expansion-2014.

plans in a transparent, competitive insurance market, which millions of Americans did on national and state websites (see Figure 17.1).

In addition to the ACA provision mandating that everyone, with a few exceptions, must have health insurance, another provision that went into effect in 2014 prohibits health insurance companies from refusing to sell coverage or renew coverage because of an individual's preexisting conditions. Insurance companies also can no longer charge higher rates due to sex or health status. Until 2014, insurance companies could and did charge women more than men for comparable health insurance plans.

Between March 2010 and January 2012, more than half of the state governments as well as numerous business associations filed lawsuits challenging various parts of the law. On June 28, 2012, the Supreme Court upheld the health insurance mandate, including the tax penalties (fines) that those who do not have health insurance will have to pay beginning in 2014. At the same time, the Court limited the law's expansion of Medicaid by finding that each state government had the option to expand or not to expand Medicaid to all families earning less than 133 percent of the federal poverty level. Figure 17.2 shows the Medicaid expansion decision made by each state. Implementation of the ACA has seen its ups and downs; however, the major provisions are now in place. Yet, debate over the law continues.

Homeland Security

The government's responsibility does not stop with ensuring basic necessities such as a clean environment; affordable energy; a secure income; and sufficient food, shelter, and health care. Federal, state, and local governments also cooperate to prevent threats to personal safety, home, and health. Such threats may come from natural disasters such as hurricanes and earthquakes or from human-made calamities such as terrorist attacks.

President George W. Bush and Congress established the Department of Homeland Security in 2002 in response to the September 11, 2001, terrorist attacks. The department's mission is to improve the coordination of efforts to prevent and respond to disasters, both human-made and natural, within U.S. borders. Homeland security is a central theme in contemporary U.S. domestic policy and an ever-present concern in Americans' daily lives. One of the main challenges for government officials is to ensure that national, state, and local bureaucrats, as well as other first responders, are able to coordinate their efforts to prevent and respond to homeland disasters. Communication, leadership, authority, and cooperation have all proven to be problematic during homeland disasters.

Hurricane Katrina and its aftermath in September 2005 presented the first real test of the response capacity of the Department of Homeland Security. The department failed the test, according to citizens living in the states damaged by the hurricane, along with local and state government officials, the media, and Bush administration investigators. According to the Bush administration's "Fact Sheet: The Federal Response to Hurricane Katrina: Lessons Learned," the hurricane and the subsequent flooding of New Orleans "exposed significant flaws in our national preparedness for catastrophic events and our capacity to respond to them."[28] The report highlighted the crucial need for the integration of homeland security plans across national, state, and local governments, as well as across organizations in the private and nonprofit sectors.

According to Donald Kettl, dean of the School of Public Policy at the University of Maryland and an expert on homeland security management, the response to the bombing at the 2013 Boston Marathon showed that governments learned important lessons after Katrina.[29] Immediately after the blast, Boston's first responders worked together well because they had practiced responding to disasters, developing working relationships. National law enforcement (agents from the Federal Bureau of Investigation, the Central Intelligence Agency, and the Bureau of Alcohol, Tobacco, Firearms, and Explosives) worked with state law enforcement, including the Massachusetts Bay Transportation Authority SWAT team, and local first responders (police, firefighters, ambulance companies). Unlike during Katrina, "unity of effort drove success in the federal-state-local-private-public-nonprofit-civilian response."[30]

According to Kettl, the following fundamental lessons were learned in the most recent homeland security challenges:

- Effective response begins with a strong, integrated, practiced-in-advance local response coupled with a nimble problem-solving ability.
- Homeland security is intergovernmental, interagency, and includes nongovernmental organizations as well as individual, ordinary Americans.
- The job of the leader is to identify the assets that are needed, who has them, and how to get them where they need to be; to coordinate, not command.

> The unity of effort by citizens and first responders from the public sector (local, state, and national governments) and the private sector (particularly nonprofit organizations) in response to the 2013 Boston Marathon bombing highlighted the lessons learned from the abysmal government response to Hurricane Katrina in 2005. In Boston, first responders had developed working relationships and communications networks through cooperative exercises that prepared them to respond to the catastrophic bombing. The response to the Boston Marathon bombing showed that homeland security is intergovernmental, interagency, and includes nongovernmental organizations as well as individual, ordinary Americans.

Another facet of the Department of Homeland Security's work is the implementation of immigration policy and border security. Continuing concerns about potential acts of terrorism on U.S. soil, as well as debates over the economic effects of immigrants coming to the United States, have placed immigration policy reform high on the agendas of state and local governments. Officials at these levels of government often complain that the national government is not fulfilling its responsibilities in this policy area.

Immigration Policy

The majority of immigrants to the United States are young people seeking two goals: reunification with family members residing here and work that will provide a better quality of life than they are able to achieve in their home countries. U.S. immigration policy, the collection of laws that specify which people the government will authorize to immigrate to the United States, allows approximately 1 million people to do so legally each year. Figure 17.3 shows that these legal immigrants come from around the globe. (See the "Global Context" feature to learn about U.S. citizens' emigration patterns.) In addition to the legal newcomers, about 500,000 unauthorized immigrants come into the United States annually.

Authorized and Unauthorized Immigration

Federal immigration policy determines who may immigrate to the United States as permanent residents and as temporary visitors (officially labeled nonimmigrant admissions, including tourists, students, diplomats, businessmen and businesswomen, and guest workers). Since the Immigration and Nationality Act of 1965, the largest category of immigrants authorized to

FIGURE 17.3 ■ GLOBAL SCOPE OF U.S. IMMIGRATION What world region is the source of most U.S. immigrants today? With respect to the Americas, what country or larger geographical unit is the source of most immigrants to the United States? From what area of the world do you think most Americans believe the largest proportion of immigrants come to the United States? Do you think these statistics would surprise most Americans?

SOURCE: U.S. Department of Homeland Security, "Table 2: Persons Obtaining Legal Permanent Resident Status by Region and Selected Country of Last Residence," *2012 Yearbook of Immigration Statistics*, www.dhs.gov/publication/yearbook-2012.

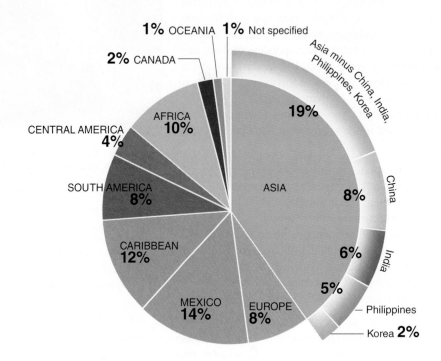

Types of Admissions

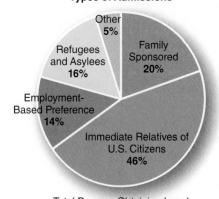

Total Persons Obtaining Legal Permanent Resident Status
1,031,631

FIGURE 17.4 ■ CLASSIFICATION OF IMMIGRANTS GRANTED PERMANENT RESIDENT STATUS, 2012

SOURCE: U.S. Department of Homeland Security, "Table 6: Persons Obtaining Legal Permanent Resident Status by Type and Major Class of Admission" *2012 Yearbook of Immigration Statistics*, www.dhs.gov/publication/yearbook-2012.

come to the United States permanently are those seeking to reunify with family members who are either U.S. citizens or authorized permanent residents. The second-largest category comprises individuals welcomed for their employment skills; this group includes highly skilled professionals and wealthy entrepreneurs expected to invest in job creation. Persons to whom the United States offers humanitarian protection from persecution (or likely persecution) because of race, religion, nationality, membership in a particular social group, or political views compose the third-largest category of authorized immigrants. Figure 17.4 presents the breakdown of 1 million people obtaining legal permanent resident status in 2012. The number of nonimmigrant admissions in 2012 totaled more than 165 million people.[31]

Who is *not* eligible for permanent authorized immigration to the United States? In addition to foreigners who do not fall within one of the categories described previously, foreign nationals perceived to be anarchists or political extremists have been excluded since 1901, when a Polish anarchist assassinated President William McKinley (1897–1901). More recently, in 2002, the USA PATRIOT Act established new criteria for denying entry to the United States. Today, the national government can deny authorized immigration to foreigners who it perceives as security or terrorist threats, who have a criminal history, who have previously been removed from the United States, or who present a health risk.[32]

Why do half a million immigrants enter the United States without authorization each year? There are several answers to that question. One is that economic opportunities may be better

Americans Immigrate Too!

While America is touted as a land of opportunity, with about 1 million immigrants from around the world gaining legal permanent resident status each year and another 500,000 entering the country each year without permission, U.S. citizens also leave the United States to take up residency in other countries throughout the world.

It is estimated that nearly 250,000 U.S. citizens leave the United States each year, and the State Department estimates that about 5 million Americans currently live abroad. About 32 percent of U.S. emigrants (people leaving a country) live in Latin American and Caribbean countries. Second on the list of destinations for U.S. emigrants is Europe (28 percent). Canada is another popular destination for citizens leaving the United States to take up residence in another country.*

The largest number of U.S. emigrants are living in Mexico. In fact, Mexico is increasingly an immigrant destination for people from around the globe. Its foreign-born population doubled between 2000 and 2010. With its economy growing more quickly than that of the United States, Canada, and Brazil in 2011 and 2012, Mexico's foreign-born population is booming.**

Not only are Americans emigrating, a growing number of U.S. citizens who are immigrants in other countries are renouncing their U.S. citizenship, according to the advocacy group American Citizens Abroad, often to eliminate U.S. tax obligations.***

Top Ten Countries for U.S. Emigrants**

COUNTRY	NUMBER OF U.S. EMIGRANTS IN 2013
Mexico	849,000
Canada	317,000
United Kingdom	222,000
Puerto Rico	189,000
Germany	111,000
Australia	90,000
Israel	80,000
South Korea	72,000
Japan	60,000
Italy	60,000

*Mark Rice, "Not Everyone Wants to Live in America," Forbes, June 4, 2010, www.forbes.com/2010/06/04/immigration-emigration-expats-opinions-contributors-mark-rice.html.

**Damien Cave, "For Migrants, New Land of Opportunity Is Mexico," The New York Times, September 22, 2013, www.nytimes.com/2013/09/22/world/americas/for-migrants-new-land-of-opportunity-is-mexico.html?pagewanted=all&_r=0.

***Brian Knowlton, "More American Expatriates Give Up Citizenship," The New York Times, April 26, 2010, www.nytimes.com/2010/04/26/us/26expat.html.

****Migration Policy Institute, "International Migrant Population by Country of Origin and Destination," www.migrationpolicy.org/programs/data-hub/charts/international-migrant-population-country-origin-and-destination.

here than those available in the home country. Yet unless an individual fits into one of the categories for authorized immigration, he or she has no basis on which to apply for permanent, legal entry into the United States. In addition, there are annual quotas for each admission category. The result is a backlog of more than 4 million applications that may mean up to a 20-year wait for authorized immigration.[33] Those are just some of the obstacles that explain why approximately 500,000 undocumented immigrants enter the United States each year.

Although undocumented immigrants are not eligible for safety-net benefits such as programs for income security and food security, all children born on U.S. soil—even those born to undocumented immigrants—are citizens and hence are eligible for these benefits. Moreover, the government guarantees a public education to all children, citizens and undocumented immigrants alike. State and local governments cover approximately 92 percent of the cost of public education, and the national government funds the remaining 8 percent. With respect to legal rights, the Fourteenth Amendment to the Constitution guarantees all people, not just citizens, due process before the government can infringe on their life, liberty, or pursuit of happiness, as well as equal protection of the law. Typically, the costs of these constitutional guarantees fall to state and local governments. Most undocumented immigrants *do* pay taxes and so are contributing to government revenues collected to pay these bills.

Proposed Immigration Policy Reforms

Discussions about immigration reform typically include four general questions. First, what can the government do about the more than 11 million immigrants living in the United States without legal permission? Second, how can the government tighten border security to decrease the number of undocumented immigrants? Third, how can the government prevent employers from hiring undocumented immigrants, thereby eliminating the jobs that lure so many people to come to the United States without legal permission? Finally, what must the government do to fix the current immigration system so that those following the rules to immigrate legally do not have to wait two decades to gain legal permanent resident status?

Immigration policy reform has been a topic of debate for the last two decades; however, due to the absence of agreement among national officials, and therefore lack of changes in national immigration policy, state and local governments have stepped in to the gap and enacted their own policies to address concerns about undocumented immigrants. Courts have had to resolve conflicts over the constitutionality of state and local policies, leading to a hodgepodge of local, state, and national immigration laws.

By early 2012, federal judges had struck down or prevented the implementation of portions of immigration laws in Alabama, Arizona, Georgia, Indiana, Pennsylvania, South Carolina, and Utah. While saying that states cannot enact laws that undermine federal immigration law, the Court in 2012 upheld a section of a 2010 Arizona law that requires police officers to check on the immigration status of persons they have stopped or arrested if they have reason to suspect the person is in the country illegally. At the same time, the court blocked the section of the law that made it a crime for undocumented immigrants to work or to try to find work.

Shortly before the Supreme Court handed down its decision in the Arizona immigration law case, the Obama administration said it would not move to deport undocumented immigrants under the age of 30 who came to the United States as children, if they met certain conditions. One condition is that they must have clean criminal records.

In June 2013, the U.S. Senate approved the Border Security, Economic Opportunity and Immigration Modernization Act. The senators intended this legislation to address all the key immigration questions "by finally committing the resources needed to secure the border, modernize and streamline our current legal immigration system, while creating a tough but fair legalization program for individuals who are currently here."[34] House Republicans quickly made it clear that they would not take up the Senate's immigration reform bill. Calls for tighter border security and increased deportations continued.

In 2013, the Obama administration's deportation efforts targeted criminals, serious immigration offenders, and people who crossed the borders recently without legal permission. By the end of 2013, close to 2 million deportations had occurred under the Obama administration; this was a record high for an American president. Republicans dismissed the high number of deportations, noting that long-term undocumented immigrants were not being deported. Immigrant advocates raised concerns about the large number of deportations and the negative effect on communities and families, including thousands of children in foster homes because one or both of their parents had been deported.[35] In 2014, President Obama ordered a review of the policies and procedures that the U.S. Immigration and Customs Enforcement (ICE) agency used to deport immigrants. Angela Kelley, the vice president for immigration policy at the Center for American Progress, noted that "We have reached a crisis point. The question is which end of Pennsylvania Avenue," the president in the White House or Congress at Capitol Hill, will address it.[36]

Conclusion
Thinking Critically About What's Next in Domestic Policy

A healthy environment is essential to human health, happiness, and survival. Reliance on non-renewable energy sources, specifically fossil fuels, as well as the volumes of waste produced by the world's growing population, harm the global environment. Today, there is consensus among environmentalists, as well as among Democrats and Republicans, that the United States must decrease its reliance on fossil fuels, which includes imported oil. However, debate on how to accomplish this while not harming economic development is ongoing.

Ensuring a healthy and safe society in which citizens can live their lives freely, in pursuit of their happiness, means more than protecting air, water, and land quality. Today, the ever-increasing costs of ensuring a just and safe society is forcing U.S. policy makers to take a hard look at Social Security and health care. Recently, the Affordable Care Act expanded access to affordable health care and increased the protections available to consumers in their dealings with health insurance companies. Although there is agreement among Democrats and Republicans that Congress must get these costs under control, the debate continues over the proper actions to take to accomplish this goal.

The national government regularly works with state and local governments to provide a phenomenal range of domestic policies, including almost every policy discussed in this chapter. However, which government has ultimate responsibility for specific policies is not always clear, as evidenced in immigration policy. This lack of clarity is a consequence of federalism, which the U.S. governments have been struggling with since 1789. Only through a unity of efforts, which requires clear communication and cooperation, can intergovernmental relations be successful, whether the goal is keeping our homeland secure, protecting the environment, establishing energy independence, or maintaining a safety net. Today, intergovernmental relations are key elements of effective and efficient national domestic policies.

Summary

1. Citizen Engagement and Domestic Policy

U.S. domestic policy addresses internal problems that threaten people's well-being, domestic tranquility, and civil liberties, as well as their ability to have a decent standard of living. The exponential growth in the number and range of domestic policies since 1789 is the product of the responses of elected representatives to citizens' and interest groups' lobbying efforts as well as national crises.

2. Tools of Domestic Policy

The national government uses various policy tools to accomplish its domestic goals. These include laws, regulations, direct provision of public goods, cash transfers, loans, loan guarantees, insurance plans, grants-in-aid, and contracting-out.

3. Environmental Policy

Through its regulatory policy, supplemented with grants-in-aid and loans, the national government has devolved the implementation of environmental protection to state and local governments. The tensions among the competing goals of protecting the environment, supporting economic development, and ensuring an ample supply of affordable energy are ongoing.

4. Energy Policy

Today, U.S. energy policy debates focus on combating global climate change and decreasing the country's reliance on fossil fuels by developing alternative, renewable energy sources in the long term and increasing conservation in the short term.

5. Income Security Programs

The idea that the government should provide a safety net for citizens in financial need took shape through key components of President Franklin D. Roosevelt's New Deal. The government expanded that safety net with President Lyndon B. Johnson's Great Society programs. The national government meets its responsibility to provide a safety net through income security, food security, and housing security policies.

6. Health Care Policy

The national government began guaranteeing health insurance to segments of the population in the 1960s, with Medicare and Medicaid. The 2010 Affordable Care Act's goal of ensuring that all citizens have health insurance is still controversial.

7. Homeland Security

The Department of Homeland Security's mission is to prevent terrorist attacks and to respond to domestic disasters (human-made and natural). To accomplish this mission, the national government uses the policy tools of direct provision and grants-in-aid, working in collaboration with state and local governments. Improvements in intergovernmental communication and cooperation have improved government responses to homeland disasters.

8. Immigration Policy

Approximately 1.5 million authorized and unauthorized immigrants come to the United States each year seeking family reunification, asylum from persecution, and a better quality of life. Debates about immigration policy reform continue at the national and state levels of government.

Key Terms

cash transfer 521

contributory program (social insurance program) 522

direct provision 521

direct subsidy 522

domestic policies 520

entitlement program 522

environmental racism 525

feminization of poverty 532

food insecurity 534

greenhouse effect 524

global warming 527

housing insecurity 534

indexed benefit 529

in-kind assistance 521

living wage 530

means-tested benefit 530

NIMBY ("not in my backyard") syndrome 518

noncontributory program 522

poverty guidelines 533

safety net 520

For Review

1. Explain the NIMBY syndrome.
2. Describe four or five of the domestic policy tools used by the federal government.
3. Discuss how the federal policy tools used for environmental protection make intergovernmental relations a key component of environmental policy.
4. Explain how the goals of environmental protection, economic development, and energy independence are in tension with each other.
5. Use the following terms to distinguish between OASI and TANF: contributory program, noncontributory program, means-tested program, and entitlement program.
6. Differentiate among Medicaid, Medicare, and the Affordable Care Act in terms of who benefits from each program.
7. What is the mission of the Department of Homeland Security and why are intergovernmental relations a key element of the department's success?
8. What are the major questions raised in conversations about reforming immigration policy?

For Critical Thinking and Discussion

1. Many critics of current environmental policy argue that government regulation of pollution amounts to ineffective policy. Some claim that using cash transfer tools, including tax expenditures, grants, and direct subsidies, would be more effective than setting caps on pollution. Explain how the government could use at least one of the cash transfer tools to protect the environment.
2. Which cash transfer programs (including tax expenditures) will the majority of Americans benefit from at some point in their lives? Explain.
3. A government concerned with sustainability makes policy decisions today that serve today's citizens without threatening the quality of life of future generations. Explain how at least two of the programs discussed in this chapter are important to a sustainable community that is safe and free.
4. What might explain why Social Security and Medicare are entitlements but TANF is not an entitlement? Keep in mind the nature of the programs (contributory or noncontributory) and the populations each program targets.
5. Frequently, a crisis or a disaster is the catalyst for revolutionary, new public policies. Discuss one or two crises or disasters that have occurred in your lifetime and that led to major changes in public policy.

MULTIPLE CHOICE: Choose the lettered item that answers the question correctly.

1. The largest national cash transfer program, which is also the most expensive domestic superfunction, is
   a. Old-Age and Survivors Insurance (OASI).
   b. Supplemental Nutrition Assistance Program (SNAP).
   c. Temporary Assistance for Needy Families (TANF).
   d. unemployment compensation.

2. Whose brainchild was Earth Day, which is considered the birth of the U.S. environmental movement?
   a. Rachel Carson
   b. Ida Mae Fuller
   c. John F. Kennedy
   d. Gaylord Nelson

3. Pell grants and financial support to farmers for growing or limiting the growth of crops are two examples of the policy tool of
   a. contributory cash transfer.
   b. direct subsidy.
   c. insurance.
   d. loan guarantee.

4. All of the following safety-net programs were created during President Franklin D. Roosevelt's administrations *except*
   a. Medicaid.
   b. the minimum wage.
   c. Social Security's Old Age and Survivors Insurance.
   d. unemployment compensation.

5. Whose refusal to sell oil to the United States in 1973 was a catalyst for the development of U.S. energy policy?
   a. CAFÉ
   b. Canada
   c. OPEC
   d. Venezuela

6. Which of the following income security program is the newest, established in 1975?
   a. AFDC
   b. EITC
   c. OASI
   d. TANF

7. The disaster that prompted the national government to establish the Department of Homeland Security is
   a. the Great Depression.
   b. Hurricane Katrina.

c. Love Canal.
d. the terrorist attacks on September 11, 2001.

8. The largest category of immigrants to the United States consists of
   a. authorized immigrants seeking family reunification.
   b. authorized immigrants with professional skills and/or wealth.
   c. authorized immigrants seeking humanitarian protection from persecution.
   d. unauthorized immigrants.

9. Which is the newest health care policy, enacted into law in 2010?
   a. ACA
   b. Medicaid
   c. Medicare
   d. SCHIP

10. The income security program that is indexed, and therefore is subject to a regular cost-of-living adjustment, is
    a. minimum wage.
    b. OASI.
    c. TANF.
    d. unemployment compensation.

FILL IN THE BLANKS

11. _____ is the national program that provides health insurance to the elderly.

12. _____ is the national program that provides health insurance to low-income citizens.

13. A (An) _____ program guarantees a benefit to all who meet the program's eligibility criteria, regardless of the total cost to the government.

14. An indexed benefit is one that increases automatically to keep up with inflation. The increase is a COLA, which stands for _____.

15. A (An) _____ benefit has a government-specified income level (typically based on the poverty guidelines) as one of its eligibility criteria.

Answers: 1. a, 2. d, 3. b, 4. a, 5. c, 6. b, 7. d, 8. a, 9. a, 10. b, 11. Medicare, 12. Medicaid, 13. entitlement, 14. cost-of-living adjustment, 15. means-tested.

Resources for Research AND Action

Internet Resources

Center for Budget and Policy Priorities
www.cbpp.org The center focuses on the impact of public policies on low-income households. On the website, you will find links to numerous reports elaborating on the effects of public policies on such households.

Environmental Protection Agency
www2.epa.gov/enforcement This section of the EPA's website provides information on its enforcement actions, efforts to clean up contaminated sites, and investigations of environmental law violations.

USA Government Information
www.usa.gov This easy-to-use first stop for government information offers links to government agencies and their programs.

Recommended Readings

Carson, Rachel. *Silent Spring*. New York: Houghton Mifflin, 1962. Thorough and alarming description of how the pesticide DDT harmed the food chain, caused cancer and genetic damage, and threatened the world as we know it.

Ehrenreich, Barbara. *Nickel and Dimed: On (Not) Getting By in America*. New York: Henry Holt, 2001. Documentation of the author's experiences when she joined the millions of Americans working full time, year-round, for wages higher than the minimum wage at the time ($6 to $7 per hour) in jobs with no benefits.

Gore, Al. *Earth in the Balance: Ecology and the Human Spirit*. Boston: Houghton Mifflin, 1992. Comprehensive assessment of the major post–Cold War threat to the United States and the world: planetary destruction due to overpopulation, deforestation, soil erosion, air pollution, and water pollution. Written before his more popularly known *An Inconvenient Truth*, Gore recommends far-reaching and specific governmental and corporate actions.

Kettl, Donald. *System Under Stress: Homeland Security and American Politics*, 2nd ed. Washington, D.C.: CQ Press, 2007. Comprehensive presentation of the massive bureaucratic reorganization that created the Department of Homeland Security. The effectiveness of this reorganization is assessed in light of the disastrous governmental response to Hurricane Katrina.

Movies of Interest

An Inconvenient Truth (2006)
A rallying cry for citizens and government to address the problem of global warming, this documentary presents the science of global warming as it follows Al Gore's environmental advocacy from his college years to today.

United 93 (2006)
An account of the fate of United Flight 93—the fourth plane hijacked on September 11, 2001—this fact-based film documents the plight of the passengers (who had become aware of the other hijackings) and their struggle to prevent another catastrophe. It also reveals the national government's lack of preparedness for the emergency.

A Civil Action (1998)
This movie highlights the enormous expense (financial and emotional) of proving in a court of law that a large corporation's chemical waste pollution caused the leukemia that killed children from eight families.

The Grapes of Wrath (1940)
The winner of two Academy Awards, this movie, set during the Great Depression, tells the story of the Joad family (and their acquaintances) as they struggle to meet their basic needs, first in the Oklahoma Dust Bowl and later in California.

CHAPTER 18

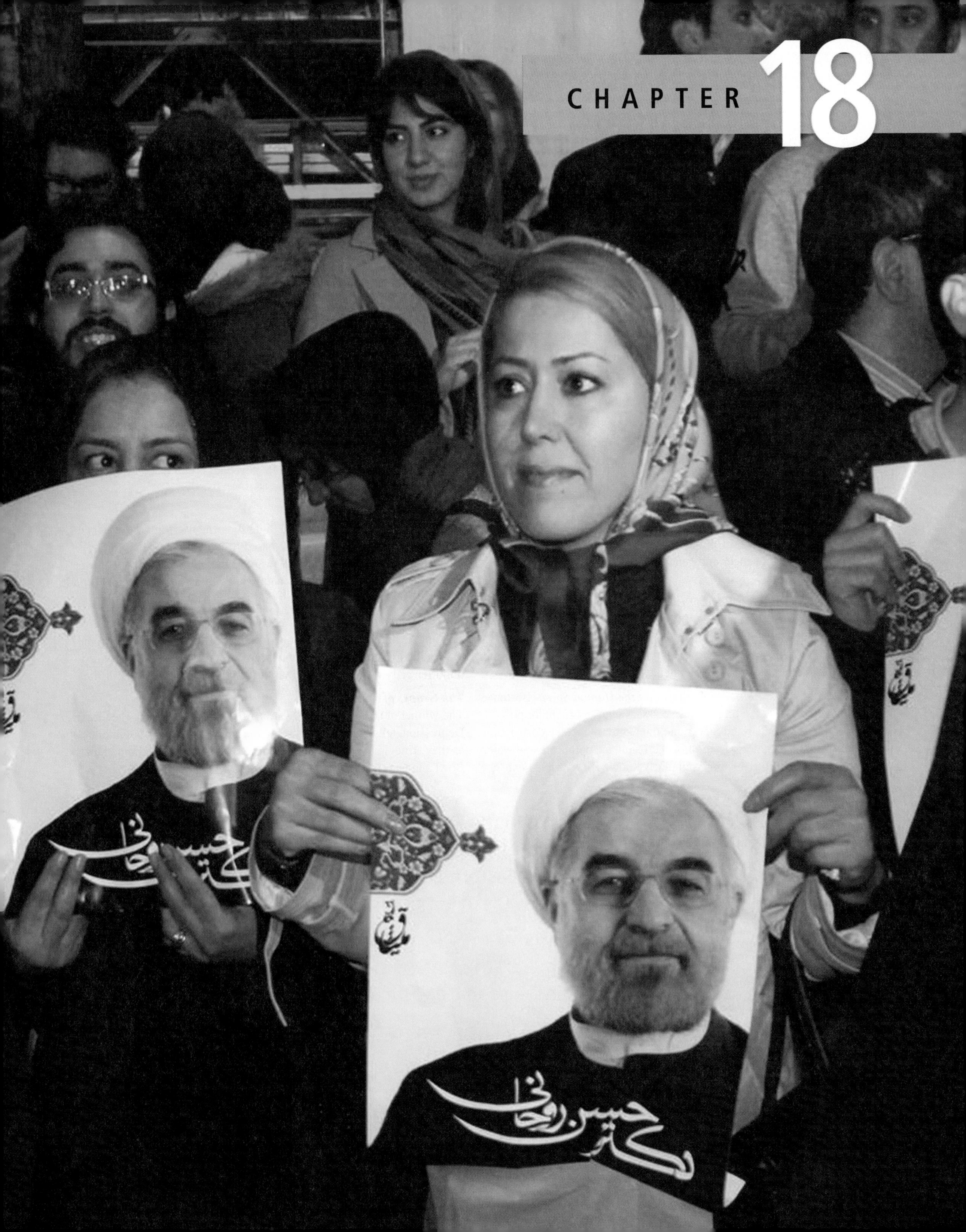

Foreign Policy
and National Security

THEN

The emergence of the United States as a superpower and the Cold War dominated U.S. foreign policy in the aftermath of World War II.

NOW

A rapidly changing global context defines U.S. foreign and national security policy.

NEXT

What long-term repercussions will tensions in current global hot spots, including the Middle East, Eastern Europe, and North Korea, have on the United States?

How will the continuing threat of terrorism against the United States influence foreign and national security policy in the future?

Will U.S. foreign policy in the coming years increasingly reflect a clash of civilizations between Western democracies and fundamentalist Islamic states?

diplomacy
the conduct of international relations, particularly involving the negotiation of treaties and other agreements between nations

foreign service officers
the diplomatic and consular staff at U.S. embassies abroad

normal trade relations (NTR) status
the international trade principle holding that the least restrictive trade conditions (best tariff rates) offered to any one national trading partner will be offered to every other nation in a trading network (also known as *most favored nations*)

The conventional view is that

foreign policy is all about wizened old statesmen negotiating treaties and about sophisticated ambassadors clinking wine glasses at chic cocktail parties. It is true that top government officials in Washington, D.C., formulate foreign policy—the politics and the programs by which the United States conducts its relations with other countries and furthers American interests around the globe. But the broader, everyday reality of U.S. foreign policy is that individual American citizens play an important part in shaping and implementing the programs decided on by foreign policy makers. Citizens play their part by staying informed about policy makers' decisions on war, peace, trade issues, and policies that ensure national security in the post-9/11 world, and by expressing their personal views to their representatives in government and through the ballot box.

Of all the country's policy arenas, the foreign policy arena is the most volatile. During the past 65 years, the goals of U.S. foreign policy have shifted significantly, from preventing the spread of communism in the post–World War II era, to redefining the national foreign policy agenda as the world's only superpower in the 1990s, to responding to the terrorist attacks of September 11, 2001, to waging and then ending a multifront war. As the objectives and the worldviews of policy makers have changed in concert with unprecedented world developments, so too have their priorities and the instruments available to them in implementing U.S. foreign policy.

The Tools of U.S. Foreign Policy

Government officials use a variety of instruments to shape foreign policy. That is, in creating foreign policy, policy makers rely on a variety of tactics to get foreign nations to bend to the will of the United States. Among these tools are diplomacy, trade and economic policies, and military options. Often, policy makers rely on more than one tool in their dealings with foreign nations.

Diplomacy

Covering a gamut of situations, diplomacy is often foreign policy makers' tool of choice. **Diplomacy** can generally be defined as the conduct of international relations, particularly involving the negotiation of treaties and other agreements between nations. It can include an occurrence as mundane as the communication between two embassies when a citizen of one country commits a crime in another. Or it can involve an event as significant as a major summit attended by world leaders. When diplomacy works, we typically do not hear about it.

Among the central figures in the diplomatic arena are **foreign service officers,** the diplomatic and consular staff at American embassies abroad. Foreign service officers, who are employees of the Department of State, conduct formal communications among nations. They are frequently responsible for negotiating many types of international agreements, including economic and trade policies.

Trade and Economic Policies

U.S. foreign policy makers rely on trade policies, economic aid (foreign aid), and economic penalties to compel foreign governments to conform to the United States' will. Consider the example of most favored nation status. In international trade, conferring **normal trade relations (NTR) status** means that a country grants to a particular trading partner the same, least restrictive trade conditions (that is, the lowest tariff rates) that the country offers to its other favored trading partners—its "most favored nations." U.S. foreign policy makers can bestow most favored nation status on a country to influence it to enact policies the United States prefers. Conversely, they can withhold this status to punish a nation that does not institute policies supportive of the United States' goals. Today, Cuba and North Korea are denied normal trade relations status by the United States, and the United States continues to put pressure on the regimes that rule those nations.

Governments also use trade agreements as a tool of foreign policy. Among the most important of these agreements in the United States is the North American Free Trade Agreement (NAFTA), whose members include the United States, Mexico, and Canada. NAFTA eliminated barriers to trade and financial investments across the economies of the three nations.

Beyond trade policy, American diplomats frequently use economic enticements in the form of foreign aid to pressure other countries into enacting and enforcing policies that the United States supports. Such was the case in the aftermath of the terrorist attacks of September 11, 2001, when the George W. Bush administration sought the cooperation of the Pakistani government in Operation Enduring Freedom, the U.S. military offensive in neighboring Afghanistan. The United States sought to overthrow the Islamic fundamentalist Taliban regime, which had harbored and provided training grounds for terrorists, and to capture 9/11 mastermind Osama bin Laden, who was believed to have been hiding in Afghanistan. Before the 9/11 terrorist strikes on domestic U.S. targets, Pakistan had received comparatively little aid from the United States. In fact, the United States had imposed sanctions on Pakistan because of its pursuit of nuclear weapons, its history of domestic coups, and its track record of defaulting on international loans. But after 9/11 and because of Pakistan's proximity to Afghanistan (they share a 1,500-mile-long border), Pakistan became a focal point of the U.S. war on terrorism. To encourage (and finance) the country's cooperation, the Bush administration waived the sanctions on Pakistan.[1] Moreover, whereas Pakistan had received only about $3.4 million in aid from the United States in the year before the terrorist attacks, in 2002 the country was the beneficiary of over $1 billion in U.S. aid. Although aid levels tapered off to between $400 million and $600 million annually between 2003 and 2007, the Bush administration requested $785 million for Pakistan in 2008.[2] Though the Barack Obama administration initially continued the policy of relying on economic enticements to compel Pakistani cooperation, those efforts soured in 2011 when it was discovered that Osama bin Laden had been hiding in the Pakistani city of Abbottabad. U.S. forces launched a surprise attack in May 2011, killing Bin Laden. Many U.S. foreign policy makers questioned whether the aid was an effective incentive to secure Pakistan's loyalty to the United States. Still, Congress awarded $1.2 billion in aid to Pakistan in 2014.[3]

American foreign policy makers also rely on other economic strategies to punish and reward countries. In February 2010, President Obama announced that the United States and its allies were developing a host of **sanctions**—penalties that halt economic exchanges (and that may include boycotts and a suspension of cultural exchanges)—on Iran (see "Global Context"). The Obama administration and its Western European allies object to Iran's pursuit of nuclear weapons. Obama's announcement came after Iranian state media reported that the nation had begun the uranium enrichment process. Iran stated that the uranium would be used for medical research, but the administration rejected that claim. However, as former senator Christopher Dodd (D-Conn.), who chaired the Banking, Housing, and Urban Affairs Committee, noted: "Economic sanctions are a critical element of U.S. policy toward Iran. But sanctions alone are not sufficient. They must be used as effective leverage, undertaken as part of a coherent, coordinated, comprehensive diplomatic and political strategy which firmly seeks to deter Iran's nuclear ambitions and other actions which pose a threat to regional stability."[4] The sanctions and other strategies appeared to have worked. Under economic pressure from the United States, Great Britain, China, Russia, Germany, and the member states of the European Union, Iran agreed to halt its uranium enrichment activities in a deal implemented in January 2014. In return, the United States and other nations agreed to lift some sanctions on Iran, allowing Iran to export petrochemicals and to imports goods and services for its automotive manufacturing and civilian aviation sector, and to trade in gold and other precious metals. The United States and other nations will also assist in developing financial channels to support humanitarian trade and facilitate tuition payments for Iranian students studying abroad. Almost a century ago, President Woodrow Wilson made this observation: "A nation that is boycotted is a nation that is in sight of surrender.

sanctions
penalties that halt economic relations

Context

THE UNITED STATES AND IRAN—A COMPLEX HISTORY

We can trace today's erratic and complex relations between the United States and Iran back to 1951. That year, the democratically elected prime minister of Iran, Mohammed Mossadegh, nationalized the country's oil reserves, and the Iranian government took over ownership of reserves that had been held by private corporations. Mossadegh's bold stroke set off a furious reaction by British and American leaders concerned about the increasing Soviet influence in Iran. The Central Intelligence Agency then orchestrated a coup to depose Mossadegh in 1953,* and Mohammad Reza Pahlavi, Iran's monarch (Shah), installed a prime minister favored by Great Britain and the United States.

Are Western democracies and fundamentalist Islamic states such as Iran destined to clash?

The 2013 election of Hassan Rouhani as president of Iran has brought about a thawing in relations between Iran and the United States.

With continued British and U.S. support, the Shah modernized Iran's infrastructure. His autocratic rule, however, opened him to criticism by Ayatollah Ruhollah Khomeini, an influential Islamic Iranian cleric. Khomeini was exiled from the country but remained a vocal critic of both the Shah and the United States, which he characterized as "the Great Satan."

In early 1978, individuals from a broad coalition of Iranians—including students, Marxists, and pro-democracy activists—took to the streets protesting the Shah's oppressive government and calling for Khomeini's return. The demonstrations evolved into what became known as the Iranian revolution and forced the Shah to flee Iran in January 1979. When a victorious Khomeini returned to Iran shortly after, many Iranians embraced the stern cleric. And although various groups had sought to depose the Shah, the Iranian people at large soon voted to make Iran an Islamic republic with Khomeini as its leader.

During the Iranian uprisings in 1979, students had seized control of the U.S. embassy in Tehran and taken its personnel as hostages. The students claimed that the diplomats were CIA agents plotting a coup against the Khomeini government, as indeed had occurred in 1953. During this time, tensions between the United States and Iran were sky-high, and 52 Americans were held hostage for 444 days. Khomeini supported the students' actions. Part of the American response was to freeze more than $12 billion in Iranian assets in the United States. Although the

United States later returned a sizeable portion of those assets, other parts remain frozen as the United States awaits the resolution of property disputes that arose out of the revolution. To the present day, this issue is a point of sharp contention between the two countries.

Over the next 15 years, relations between the United States and Iran remained contentious. The United States denounced Iran's support of terrorist organizations and its pursuit of nuclear weapons. In 1995, the Clinton administration imposed economic sanctions on Iran and penalized foreign corporations that invested in Iran's energy industry. This measure was a severe blow to the Iranian economy. In 1997, reformist Mohammad Khatami was elected president of Iran with a platform of strengthening democracy in Iran. For several years, the icy American-Iranian relations seemed to be thawing. When the terrorist attacks of September 11 occurred, young Iranians took to the streets in spontaneous demonstrations of support for the U.S. victims of the attacks.

That the goodwill had dissolved, however, was apparent when George W. Bush characterized Iran as part of an "axis of evil" in his 2002 State of the Union speech. Relations chilled primarily because of Iran's pursuit of nuclear weapons. After that time, the harsh rhetoric continued between the United States and Iran, and President Obama successfully sought sanctions against Iran in response to its continuing pursuit of nuclear weapons. Then, in June 2013,

Iranians elected a new president, Hassan Rouhani, a moderate cleric who had played a role in Iran's voluntary suspension of uranium enrichment in 2004, and who espoused a more concilia-tory approach to relations with the West. In September of that year, President Obama wrote Rouhani a letter saying that the crippling economic sanctions would be lifted if Rouhani's govern-ment cooperated with the international community's demands to end Iran's nuclear weapon program. On September 27, 2013, Presi-dent Obama and President Rouhani spoke by telephone, marking the first direct communication between leaders of these nations since the 1979 hostage crisis. By November, Iran had agreed to a temporary freeze of its nuclear program, which took effect on January 20, 2014, and later in the year it appeared that Iran and the United States would be cooperating in halting the efforts of the insurgent Islamist terror organization ISIS in Iraq and Syria.

*James Risen, "Secrets of History: The C.I.A. in Iran," www.nytimes.com/library/world/mideast/041600iran-cia-index.html.

Apply this economic, peaceful, silent, deadly remedy and there will be no need for force. It does not cost a life outside the nation boycotted, but it brings a pressure upon the nation which, in my judgment, no modern nation could resist."[5]

Economic strategies can also be used to reward countries whose behavior is improving. Take Myanmar (Burma), for example. When that nation held free elections and enacted a series of other democratic reforms after decades of military rule, the United States and other nations lifted sanctions on that country. However, critics argue that sanctions actually may worsen con-ditions, particularly for the poorest people in a sanctioned nation.[6] And given the high levels of **globalism,** or interconnectedness, among the world's countries today, a nation on which boy-cotts or sanctions are imposed often has recourse—sometimes in the form of aid from allies—to withstand the pressure of the economic penalty.

globalism
the interconnectedness between nations in contemporary times

The Military Option

The September 11 terrorist strikes and subsequent U.S. government actions demonstrate how the creators of foreign policy use the military option as an instrument of foreign policy. Hungry for an enemy after the deadly attacks on American soil, the United States targeted Afghanistan's Taliban regime. The Taliban had supported and harbored members of **al-Qaeda** ("The Base"), the radical international Islamic fundamentalist terrorist organization that took credit for the 9/11 bloodshed. Foreign intelligence had pointed to Osama bin Laden, a Saudi millionaire living in Afghanistan, as the engineer of the attacks. U.S. military presence in Afghanistan continued through 2014.

al-Qaeda
a radical international Islamic fundamen-talist terrorist organization

But the bases of world terrorist activity today transcend national borders. Like ISIS militants today, the September 11 terrorists themselves were not citizen-soldiers of any one country but were nationals from countries across the globe. They had trained in various nations, including Afghanistan, and had been supported by citizens of still other countries. Thus no single, clear nation-state was the enemy. Without a concrete enemy (over which a victory could be defined and declared), the Bush administration requested, and Congress passed, a formal declaration of a "war on terror."

Then–secretary of state Colin Powell subsequently made a case to the United Nations and to the American people alleging that U.S. intelligence indicated that the Saddam Hussein regime in Iraq was harboring **weapons of mass destruction (WMDs)**—nuclear, chemical, and biological weapons.[7] In response to what at the time appeared to be a credible threat, American troops invaded Iraq on March 20, 2003. The military strike toppled the Hussein regime, which the United States had supported for years through foreign aid.[8] Following the invasion, weapons inspectors conducted a thorough search of suspected weapons sites, but no WMDs were ever found, leaving many critics of the Bush administration to question the administration's motives and to ask whether the intelligence community had been pressured by administration officials to find intelli-gence rationalizing the war in Iraq.[9] From the time of the U.S. invasion until U.S. forces left Afghanistan in 2011, 4,486 U.S. troops died in Iraq, along with hundreds of other coalition forces and 100,000 Iraqi civilians. Today, we continue to see instability in Iraq, as the withdrawal of U.S. forces rendered it vulnerable to insurgent violence, including that undertaken by ISIS militants.

weapons of mass destruction (WMDs)
nuclear, chemical, and biological weapons

When they use the military as an instrument of foreign policy, policy makers send a strong signal. When military conflict occurs on a grand scale—for the United States, that would include the wars in Afghanistan and Iraq, as well as the Gulf War (1990–1991), the Vietnam War (1965–1975), the Korean War (1950–1953), and the two world wars (1914–1918 and 1939–1945), the goal often is **regime change,** the replacement of a country's government with another government by facilitating the deposing of its leader or leading political party. That is, rather than attempting to change another nation's policies, the wars are fought to end the reign of the enemy nations' leaders. On the other hand, most military action by the United States in the past century has occurred on a smaller scale, as policy makers have sought to change the policy in another country or perhaps to protect U.S. interests or allies. For example, in 1999 during the Clinton administration, the United States took military action in Kosovo in the former Yugoslavia to halt ethnic cleansing in that region. Other military actions—in Somalia (1992–1994), Bosnia (beginning in 1993), and Panama (1989)—have also been on a limited scale with specific and smaller goals than those of the major conflicts.

regime change
the replacement of a country's government with another government by facilitating the deposing of its leader or leading political party

Who Decides? The Creators and Shapers of Foreign Policy

In the United States, the executive and legislative branches are the primary foreign policy makers, with the president and the executive branch playing the dominant role. However, a variety of interests—from the media, to interest groups, to other nations, and even private individuals—provide the context of the foreign policy process and contribute to shaping the policy outcomes of that process.

The President and the Executive Branch

The president of the United States is the foremost foreign policy actor in the world. This vast power derives in part from the president's constitutionally prescribed duties, particularly the role of commander in chief of the U.S. armed forces. Presidents' foreign policy powers also have roots in the way the institution of the presidency has evolved and continues to evolve. Other government institutions, especially the U.S. Congress, have some ability to rein in the president's foreign policy authority. But U.S. presidents in the 21st century remain the central figures in the foreign policy arena, owing to presidential resources such as cabinet departments and the national intelligence community, as well as the executive prestige that supplements presidents' legal and administrative powers.

country desk
the official operation of the U.S. government in each country that has diplomatic ties to the United States

THE DEPARTMENTS OF STATE AND DEFENSE   In the executive branch, the Departments of State and Defense take the lead in advising the president about foreign and military policy issues. Specifically, the Department of State, headed by the secretary of state, has more than 30,000 employees located both within the United States and abroad. (State Department employees work at more than 300 U.S. consular offices around the world.) These staff members are organized according to topical specialty (trade policy, environmental policy, and so on) and geographic area specialty (the Middle East or Southeast Asia, for example). Political appointees hold many of the top ambassadorial posts. These ambassadors and the career members of the foreign service who staff each **country desk**—the official operation of the U.S. government in each country with diplomatic ties to the United States—help to shape and administer U.S. foreign policy in those countries.

The Department of Defense, often referred to as the Pentagon for its five-sided headquarters, is headed by the secretary of defense. The modern Department of Defense traces its history to the end of World War II, although it is the successor of the Department of War established at the nation's founding. The Defense

>Among the key foreign policy actors in the executive branch are the secretaries of state and defense and the national security adviser, all of whom advise the president about foreign and military policy issues. Here, Secretary of State John Kerry discusses U.S. foreign policy with Defense Secretary Chuck Hagel.

Department is the cabinet department that oversees all branches of the U.S. military. Thus, although the Army, Navy, Marines, Air Force, and Coast Guard operate independently, administratively they are part of the Department of Defense. The commanding officers of each branch of the military, plus a chairperson and a vice chairperson, make up the Joint Chiefs of Staff, important military advisers to the president. Increasingly, both the State and the Defense Departments rely on private contractors to perform some functions typically associated with these respective departments, particularly overseas.

> Every day, the president of the United States is briefed on the top U.S. foreign policy matters by staff members of the National Security Council. Here, President Obama uses an iPad during his briefing.

THE NATIONAL SECURITY COUNCIL AND THE INTELLIGENCE COMMUNITY

As discussed in Chapter 12, the National Security Council, consisting of the vice president, the secretary of state, the secretary of the treasury, the secretary of defense, and the national security adviser, advises and assists the president on national security and foreign policy.

Through the input of the National Security Council, the president's administration considers the country's top security matters. The National Security Council also coordinates foreign policy approaches among the various government agencies that will implement them. A recent addition to the foreign policy apparatus, the national security adviser has traditionally competed with the secretary of state for influence over foreign policy—and for influence over the president as well. The tension between the two advisers also stems from the differing approaches each agency takes in shaping foreign policy. Frequently, the State Department has a long-term view of world affairs and advocates for foreign policies in keeping with long-term goals. In contrast, the National Security Council focuses more on short-term crises and objectives.

A key resource in presidential foreign policy making is the intelligence community. Chief among the agencies in this community is the Central Intelligence Agency (CIA). This independent agency of the federal government is responsible for collecting, analyzing, evaluating, and disseminating foreign intelligence to the president and senior national policy makers. Like the National Security Council, the modern CIA was created by the National Security Act of 1947 at the dawn of the Cold War to monitor the actions of the expansionist Soviet Union. During the Cold War, the CIA expanded its mission, using agents to penetrate the governments of foreign countries, influence their politics, and foment insurrections when the president deemed such tactics necessary to promote American interests. But the clandestine nature of the CIA's activities has prompted some members of Congress to raise questions about the agency's operations. At times, critics have argued that the agency has engaged in illegal activities, and later—after the September 11 terrorist attacks—that they, along with the Federal Bureau of Investigation (FBI), had failed in their duty to avert the terrorist strikes. Congress scrutinized both agencies for lapses in intelligence and apprehension. Because the CIA and the FBI had been seriously understaffed in Arabic translators, neither agency had had the means to interpret intercepted messages that might have enabled them to prevent the tragedy.

Spurred by the 9/11 Commission's findings, President Bush announced in 2005 the appointment of a national intelligence czar, called the **director of national intelligence (DNI).** This individual is responsible for coordinating and overseeing all the intelligence agencies within the executive branch.

director of national intelligence (DNI)
the person responsible for coordinating and overseeing all the intelligence agencies within the executive branch

Congress

Along with the president, Congress enjoys significant constitutional authority in foreign policy making. The constitutional provisions that outline congressional authority with respect to foreign relations include, prominently, Congress's power to declare war. In modern times, however, presidential administrations have circumvented this congressional power by using U.S. troops without a formal congressional declaration of war. Such was the case in the Vietnam War, for example.

In response to this presidential tactic, Congress in 1973 passed the **War Powers Act.** This law limits presidential use of military forces to 60 days, with an automatic extension of 30 days if the president requests such an extension. But the nature of modern warfare has quickly made the War Powers Act less effective than in the days of traditional warfare, since most modern warfare is measured in weeks rather than months (the wars in Iraq and Afghanistan being exceptions).

War Powers Act
law that limits presidential use of military forces to 60 days, with an automatic extension of 30 days if the president requests such an extension

Thus it has been possible for modern presidents to wage full-scale wars without congressional involvement. Because of this reality, some critics have argued that designating war powers to the president is a cowardly decision. Representative Ron Paul (R-Texas), a conservative Republican presidential candidate in 2008 and 2012, observed that "Congress would rather give up its most important authorized power to the President and the [United Nations] than risk losing an election if the war goes badly."[10] Other critics contend that the war powers law itself violates the constitutional provision for the separation of powers by mitigating both the president's power as commander in chief and Congress's authority to declare war.

But Congress's ability to shape foreign policy does not rest merely with its authority to declare war. Congressional powers with respect to foreign relations also include the authority of the U.S. Senate to ratify treaties, as well as to confirm presidential appointees to ambassadorial posts and to cabinet positions (including those of the secretaries of defense and state). Furthermore, one of Congress's greatest powers is its control of the purse strings. This control means that although the president can order troops into action, the members of Congress must authorize spending for such an operation.

The Military-Industrial Complex

In his farewell address, President Dwight D. Eisenhower (1953–1961), Supreme Allied Commander of Europe during World War II, warned the nation of the influence of the expanding military-industrial complex. Eisenhower stressed that the American people and their representatives in government must "guard against the acquisition of unwarranted influence" and noted that "only an alert and knowledgeable citizenry can compel the proper meshing of the industrial and military machinery of defense with our peaceful methods and goals so that security and liberty may prosper together."[11]

Eisenhower was describing the mutually advantageous—and potentially corrupting—collusion among the U.S. armed forces, the defense industry, and Congress. These three entities have the potential to develop "unwarranted influence" over foreign policy in general and defense spending in particular, for several reasons. First, the goals of the military and the goals of the defense industry often intersect. Consider, for example, the military's need to supply soldiers with the appropriate equipment to fight wars. Both the military complex and the defense industry benefit from doing so: The military wants to protect its troops and help ensure their success on the battleground, and the defense industry seeks to sell such goods to the military—and reap a healthy profit.

A second reason that the military-industrial complex has the potential to be so highly influential is the close personal and professional relationships that flourish between the individuals in the military and their counterparts in the defense industry. These relationships are similar to the associations that develop in the case of iron triangles (see Chapter 15). Indeed, many retired military personnel often put their military expertise to work in "retirement jobs" with defense contractors or as congressional lobbyists.

For many congressional districts throughout the United States, spending by the federal government for military bases, personnel, and defense contracts represents an important infusion of money into the local economy. When this economic influence is combined with the clout members of the military, veterans, their interest groups, and their families can wield, we can see why many members of Congress support the military-industrial complex.

The Media and New Technologies

Because of the pervasiveness and reach of the media, foreign policy decisions provide prime fodder for news reporting. But the media go well beyond monitoring and reporting on foreign policy; they also frequently play a role in shaping the country's foreign policy and in influencing the conduct of that policy.

Since the beginning of the 20th century, the U.S. government has used the news media in an organized way to promote its foreign policy priorities. During World War I, newspapers ran ads calling on Americans to take all kinds of actions to help the war effort, from cleaning their plates and planting "victory gardens" (to conserve food supplies for soldiers) to buying war bonds to help finance the war. By World War II, filmmakers spurred Americans to action, from enlisting in the armed services to conserving food fats and saving scrap metal for the war effort. In those various wartime initiatives, the media worked hand in hand with the government and generally took a highly patriotic and supportive stance. By the era of the Vietnam War, however, journalists, particularly television reporters stationed among U.S. troops in the faraway Asian country, painted a grimmer, more realistic canvas, focusing on the ravages of war that most Americans had never before seen. Today, new technologies provide a check both on the government and on the media, as private citizens now have the ability to communicate directly with news and Internet platforms, and so enable the whole world to watch events across the globe unfold. And citizen activists rely on social media outlets to organize and mobilize across geographic borders.

The news media and technology influence the conduct and substance of foreign policy by increasing public awareness and thus by shaping the foreign policy agenda. Take, for example, the effect that media coverage of the beheadings of American journalists and a British journalist aid worker had on U.S. foreign policy in 2014: the horrific videos and images were widely disseminated, and a media-fanned public outrage forced the Obama administration into adopting a policy—military air strikes against ISIS targets—that clearly may not have occurred absent of the coverage. By focusing public attention on a certain area of the world or on a particular aspect of foreign policy, the media shape the priorities of, and the policies made by, the foreign policy apparatus. The media also play a powerful role by serving as a watchdog to ensure that the actions of men and women who implement foreign policy "in the trenches" are consistent with the intentions of policy makers who craft those policies.

Public Opinion

In general, public opinion tends to play a less influential role in shaping specific foreign policies than it does in the area of domestic issues. But in 2014 it was clear that public opinion influences foreign policy makers in one specific way. After two protracted wars in Afghanistan and Iraq, the American public was war-weary, and any politician who sought to use U.S. troops in a military action would have to work hard to convince the U.S. public that the action is necessary. To that point, the Syrian civil war had cost nearly 150,000 people their lives. But when the insurgent group ISIS uploaded video showing the beheading of two U.S. journalists and two British aid workers, public outcry demanded a response, forcing the Obama administration to undertake air strikes in Iraq and Syria designed to incapacitate the terrorist group. Without the incendiary videos, it is unlikely the United State would have intervened.[12]

Aside from the use of force, hot-button foreign policy issues may generate temporarily high levels of media coverage. The public might voice strong opinions on these issues in the wake of the saturated media reporting. Yet when it comes to foreign policy matters, public opinion is rarely the strong force that it can be in setting the domestic policy agenda. In general, people tend to be less concerned, less informed, and less interested in foreign policy matters than in domestic issues. Thus the public at large is likely to accept the views and actions of the individuals who make their country's foreign policy.

Public opinion plays a comparatively small role in shaping foreign policy for several reasons. First, foreign policy is made incrementally, over years and decades, and keeping up with international developments in different parts of the world is not something that many individuals or even news organizations do. Often, international issues must reach crisis proportions before media coverage becomes significant and exerts an impact on public opinion.

Many Americans also feel less connected to foreign policy decisions than they do to domestic policy issues. Individuals may feel empathetic toward North Korean citizens who endure human rights violations at the hands of their government or may express sympathy toward African child soldiers. Yet their compassion goes only so far, because those incidents have less bearing on their own lives than, say, whether their mortgage payments will increase because of Federal Reserve policy or whether more student loans will be available to pay their tuition. Despite the disconnect between most people's everyday lives and pressing issues in foreign policy, individuals nonetheless can and do influence foreign policy decisions, as we now consider.

> Public diplomats are individuals who promote their country's interests by shaping the host country's perception of their homeland, not only through educational but also through business or entertainment initiatives that advance mutual understanding. When Dennis Rodman traveled to North Korea and befriended the dictator Kim Jong-un, he was widely criticized in the United States, with some media outlets labeling him "Dennis the Menace."

Private Citizens

Individuals can have an impact on the foreign policy process. Consider the various educational exchange programs that arrange for students from one country to visit another. In effect, such visitors act as **public diplomats**—individuals who promote their country's interests by shaping the host country's perception of their homeland, not only through educational but also through business or entertainment initiatives that advance mutual understanding.

A world conflict can become an influence in American foreign policy, too, when individuals take personal causes that are related to their ethnic origins to the White House and Congress. The influence of domestic interests on foreign policy, called **intermestics,** plays a distinct part in foreign policy making.

Among the most powerful examples of intermestics is the importance of large numbers of Cuban immigrants in Florida, many of them refugees or descendants of refugees from the regime of Fidel Castro. This influential group has swayed U.S. policy toward the imposition of an embargo against the Castro government since 1962, as well as encouraged tightened travel and currency restrictions between the United States and Cuba.

U.S. Foreign Policy in Historical Context

As those who make and shape U.S. foreign policy continue to confront the challenges of a new century, they can look back on two broad historical traditions with respect to American foreign relations: isolationism and intervention. Historically, an initial policy of **isolationism,** a foreign policy characterized by a country's unwillingness to participate in international affairs, gave way to **interventionism,** the willingness of a country to take part and intervene in international situations, including another country's affairs.

The Constitutional Framework and Early Foreign Policy Making

In drafting the Constitution, the founders sought to remove the United States from international affairs. They reasoned that it was best for the new American republic to stay out of the deadly wars that had plagued Europe for centuries and because of which many Americans had left their native lands. Because of that isolationist outlook, the founders structured the Constitution so that responsibility for conducting foreign affairs rests exclusively with the national government rather than with the states.

THE CONSTITUTION AND FOREIGN POLICY POWERS   The Constitution provides for shared responsibility for foreign policy making in the national government between the executive and the legislative branches. The Constitution grants the president very specific powers. These include powers related to the role of commander in chief, to making treaties, and to appointing and receiving ambassadors. In comparison, Congress's powers in foreign policy making are broader. Moreover, the Constitution structures executive and legislative powers as complementary. Note that the Constitution provides for checks and balances: although the president is commander in chief, Congress declares war and raises and supports an army and navy. Political scientist Roger Davidson has termed the give-and-take between presidential and congressional power "an invitation to struggle," reflecting the founders' attempt to ensure that neither entity dominates the process.[13]

EARLY ISOLATIONISM   In keeping with the founders' emphasis on isolationism, President George Washington's Farewell Address in 1796 warned the young government against involving the United States in entangling alliances. Washington feared that membership in such international associations would draw a war-weary people and a war-weakened nation into further conflicts. He refused to accept the advice of either his secretary of state, Thomas Jefferson, who favored an alliance with France, or his treasury secretary, Alexander Hamilton, who wanted stronger ties to Great Britain. As a general who knew firsthand about the ravages of war and who also was the first American leader to connect foreign and defense policy, Washington set the tone for the United States' role in the world for the next 200 years.

public diplomat

an individual outside government who promotes his or her country's interests and thus helps to shape international perceptions of that nation

intermestics

the influence of domestic interests on foreign policy

isolationism

a foreign policy characterized by a nation's unwillingness to participate in international affairs

interventionism

a foreign policy characterized by a nation's willingness to participate and intervene in international situations, including another country's affairs

FOREIGN TRADE AND THE EROSION OF U.S. ISOLATIONISM During Washington's tenure as president and in the next several successive administrations, the United States' primary activity in the international arena was trade. Rich in natural resources and blessed with an industrious labor force, the United States sought to increase its wealth by selling raw materials and supplies to all sides in the Napoleonic Wars (1792–1815), the latest in the never-ending series of European conflicts. The French empire took exception to the United States' provision of supplies to its enemies, and when France captured ships that it alleged were bound for enemy ports, the United States was forced into an undeclared naval war with France in the 1790s.

Neutral international trade was a difficult feat to accomplish in the American republic's early years. American ships had to cross sea lanes where neutrality was not the governing principle; instead, pirates, warring nations, and the allies of warring nations controlled the seas, and nationality counted for little. When pirates off the Barbary Coast of Africa seized ships and their crews, which they held for ransom, the United States fought the Barbary Wars (1801–1805 and 1815) against the North African Barbary states (what are now Morocco, Algeria, Tunisia, and Libya).

Throughout the early part of the 19th century, the seas proved a difficult place for American sailors. During that time, the British Navy began the practice of **impressment,** or forcing merchant sailors off U.S. ships—in effect, kidnapping them—on the spurious grounds that American sailors were "deserters" from the British Navy. In protest of this policy, Congress passed the Embargo Act of 1807, which forced U.S. ships to obtain approval from the American government before departing for foreign ports. But the British continued impressments, and the Embargo Act seriously curtailed the amount of U.S. goods being exported. Overall, the Embargo Act harmed the U.S. economy, as the decline in trade spurred more economic woes.

impressment
the forcible removal of merchant sailors from U.S. ships on the spurious grounds that the sailors were deserters from the British Navy

The tensions between the United States and Great Britain escalated as the practice of impressment continued. When the United States sought to increase its territory northward into Canada (then still part of the British Empire), the United States and Great Britain fought the War of 1812 over the United States' desire to annex portions of Canada and to put a halt to the practice of impressments. The war was relatively short-lived, ending with the signing of the Treaty of Ghent in 1814, when the British decided that their military resources could be better used against France in the Napoleonic Wars.

Hegemony and National Expansion: From the Monroe Doctrine to the Roosevelt Corollary

After the conclusion of the War of 1812 in 1814 and of the Napoleonic Wars in 1815, peace settled over the United States and Europe. Still, some American politicians feared that European nations—especially France, Spain, and Russia—would attempt to assert or reassert their influence in the Western Hemisphere. Thus, the view arose in American foreign policy-making circles that the United States should establish **hegemony**—a form of imperial geographic dominance—over its own hemisphere. In 1823, President James Monroe declared that "the American continents by the free and independent condition which they have assumed and maintain, are henceforth not to be considered as subjects for future colonization by any European power." Known as the **Monroe Doctrine,** this policy attempted to prevent European nations from colonizing any nations in North or South America. Monroe's declaration, however, sounded more like bravado than policy, because the United States was still too weak militarily to chase a

hegemony
a form of imperial geographic dominance

Monroe Doctrine
President James Monroe's 1823 declaration that the Americas should not be considered subjects for future colonization by any European power

> The Panama Canal improved the flow of international trade by reducing the length of time ships took to travel between the Atlantic and Pacific Oceans. This is an aerial view of the Gatun Locks.

manifest destiny
the idea that it was the United States' destiny to spread throughout the North American continent; used to rationalize the expansion of U.S. territory

Roosevelt Corollary
the idea, advanced by President Theodore Roosevelt, that the United States had the right to act as an "international police power" in the Western Hemisphere to ensure stability in the region

European power away from South America, Central America, or the Caribbean. But the United States' interest in preventing the colonization of the Americas was consistent with the interest of the British, who did not want to see European rivals dominating in the Americas. Thus Monroe's doctrine had the backing of the still-formidable British fleet.

With the Americas out of play, European countries were expanding their colonial empires in Africa and the Middle East during the first half of the 19th century. Meanwhile, the United States also extended its territories westward and solidified its borders. Supporters of the theory of **manifest destiny**—the idea that it was the United States' destiny to expand throughout the North American continent—used this concept to rationalize the spread of U.S. territory. As the philosophy of manifest destiny took hold on the popular imagination, the United States expanded west to the Pacific Ocean, as well as south and southwest.

During this era, too, the United States became increasingly active in profitable international trade, particularly with China and Japan. To facilitate this Pacific trade—which was a primary goal of American policy makers—the United States acquired the islands of Hawaii, Wake, and Midway and part of Samoa in the 1890s. In 1898, on the pretext of ending Spanish abuses in Cuba and instigated by a jingoistic (extremely nationalistic and aggressive) President William McKinley and press, the United States decided to fight Spain, which by then was the weakest of the colonial powers. The United States won the Spanish-American War handily, and the victory increased the country's international prestige.

Theodore Roosevelt, who later became president, achieved enormous national popularity during the Spanish-American War for his leadership of the Rough Riders, a cavalry regiment. Their charge up San Juan Hill in Cuba in 1898 was the war's bloodiest and most famous battle. As spoils, the United States obtained the Philippines, Guam, Puerto Rico, and—temporarily—Cuba from Spain. Roosevelt supported the United States' entry into the war and later, as president (1901–1909), added his own famous dictum to the Monroe Doctrine: the **Roosevelt Corollary.** He announced that to ensure stability in the region, the United States had the right to act as an "international police power" and intervene in Latin America—and indeed, the entire Western Hemisphere—if the situation in any country warranted the intervention of a "civilized society."

After Roosevelt became president, the United States intervened in Panama, where U.S.-backed revolutionaries won independence from Colombia in 1903. The United States then immediately began construction on the Panama Canal in 1904. The canal improved the flow of trade by reducing the length of time ships took to travel between the Atlantic and Pacific Oceans. It also accomplished one of Roosevelt's more cherished dreams: to show off U.S. naval power. At one point, Roosevelt decided to send the navy around the world strictly for public relations reasons, as a "show of force." Congress protested the cost of this endeavor, however. To outsmart Congress, Roosevelt, who had enough funds in the treasury for half the trip, sent the troops as far as Tokyo Bay. To "bring the boys home," Congress had to ante up the rest of the money.

World War I and the End of U.S. Isolationism

Encouraged by its successful efforts at colonization and strong enough by this time to ignore George Washington's admonition about avoiding foreign entanglements, the nation became embroiled in two major European wars in the 20th century: World War I and World War II. The

United States' isolation from the world ended with these two wars, even though strong isolationist forces in Congress and the White House continued to play a role during the first half of the 20th century.

World War I came about primarily because of the balance of power system that dominated the world's foreign policy decisions from the end of the Napoleonic Wars in 1815 until the conclusion of World War I in 1918. The **balance of power system** was a system of international alliances that, in theory, would balance the power of one group of nations against the power of another group and thus discourage war. So, for example, when it was perceived that England was becoming too powerful in this European balance of power in the 1770s, France, Spain, and Holland assisted the colonial forces in the American Revolution in an effort to bring the British down a notch. For nearly a century, that attempt to bring order to international relations worked, and Europe enjoyed a long period of peace. But a flaw of the balance of power system was that a relatively small skirmish could escalate into a major international incident because of agreements for **collective defense**—the idea that allied nations agree to defend one another in the face of invasion—that were inherent in the system. Such was the case in 1914 in Sarajevo when a young Bosnian Serb student assassinated Archduke Ferdinand, heir to the Austro-Hungarian throne. The assassin was a member of a group seeking Bosnia's independence from the Austro-Hungarian empire. The empire demanded that Serbia respond to the assassination, and when it determined that Serbia had not responded, it declared war. Austria-Hungary's declaration of war led to a sweeping domino effect that had the European continent in full-scale war within weeks of that initial declaration because of those alliances and collective defense obligations between nations.

The United States entered World War I in 1917, three years after the conflict began and largely at the behest of Britain. U.S. participation led President Woodrow Wilson to formulate the first conceptual framework for world governance that had ever been articulated. The most effective way to maintain peace, Wilson believed, was through **collective security**—the idea that peace could be achieved if nations agreed to collectively oppose any nation that attacked another country. By using this approach, nations at peace could prevent war by working together to restrain the lawlessness inherent in more unstable parts of the world.

Internationalism and the League of Nations

In negotiating the end of World War I at the Paris Peace Conference, Wilson sought to organize a **League of Nations,** a representative body that would ensure the collective security of nations. Wilson was successful in convincing representatives at the Paris meetings of the need for such an organization. But he was less successful in convincing Congress of the merits of the League of Nations. In 1918, the Republican-controlled Senate (Wilson was a Democrat) refused to ratify the Treaty of Versailles, which included among the terms for ending World War I the formation of the League of Nations. Without the United States, the League died a natural death before being replaced near the end of World War II by the United Nations.

In the dawning days of World War I, the United States was still heeding George Washington's call to avoid entangling alliances. At the war's conclusion, isolationism remained a key tenet of U.S. foreign policy. In the years immediately following the war, trade reasserted itself as the key component of U.S. foreign policy. The Industrial Revolution was in full swing, and the United States depended on the import of raw materials and the export of manufactured goods to grease the wheels of its prosperous economy in the 1920s. During this time, however, Europe was healing from the ravages of World War I, and growth in its manufacturing sector meant serious competition for American industry.

The U.S. economy suffered another blow in 1929 when the stock market crashed, marking the beginning of the Great Depression. To protect American industry from international competition, Congress in 1930 passed the Smoot-Hawley Tariff, which imposed a significant tax on imported goods. Confronted with this measure, other nations responded in kind, placing tariffs on American goods imported into their countries. The result? International trade dropped dramatically, and the economies of various nations, burdened by lower demand for the goods they produced, faltered. Industrialists, as well as citizens who saw the economic impact of an isolated United States, began to question the isolationism that had characterized U.S. foreign policy to date—from the era of Washington to the era of Smoot-Hawley.

balance of power system
a system of international alliances that, in theory, would balance the power of one group of nations against the power of another group and thus discourage war

collective defense
the concept that allied nations agree to defend one another in the face of an invasion

collective security
the idea that peace could be achieved if nations agreed to collectively oppose any nation that attacked another country

League of Nations
a representative body founded in the aftermath of World War I to establish the collective security of nations

World War II: U.S. Foreign Policy at a Crossroads

World War I was supposed to be the "war to end all wars." In hindsight, however, many observers believed that the victors only sowed the seeds of World War II (1939–1945). By impoverishing the defeated Germany through the imposition of huge reparations (compensation paid by a defeated nation to the victors for war damages) and the loss of 13 percent of its territory, the Treaty of Versailles (1919) created the environment that gave Adolf Hitler, the fascist leader of Germany, the opportunity to succeed politically. With his aggressive foreign policy, Hitler aimed to expand the German homeland at the expense of non-Germanic populations.

Influenced by a strong isolationist group in Congress, the United States waited until two years after the official start of the war in 1939 to declare war. Following a deadly Japanese attack on the U.S. naval base at Pearl Harbor, Hawaii, in December 1941, the United States declared war first on Japan and then on the other Axis powers (Germany and Italy) after those countries declared war on the United States. Following years of fighting on multiple fronts, in August 1945 the United States dropped two atomic bombs on the Japanese cities of Hiroshima and Nagasaki. Those devastating attacks ended the war.

Holocaust
the genocide perpetrated by Adolf Hitler and the Nazis against six million Jews, along with political dissidents, Catholics, homosexuals, individuals with disabilities, and gypsies

The question remains whether the United States would have joined the efforts of the Allies (the United States, England, France, China, and the Soviet Union) sooner had policy makers known about the **Holocaust**—the murder by Hitler and his subordinates of six million Jews, along with political dissidents, Catholics, homosexuals, individuals with disabilities, and gypsies. Newspapers did not report the genocide until 1943, well after the war was under way. The experience of fighting World War II and dealing with its aftermath forced U.S. policy makers to reassess the country's role in the world, as well as the policies that governed its entire approach to foreign affairs.

The Postwar Era: The United States as Superpower

superpowers
leader nations with dominating influence in international affairs

multilateral
many-sided; having the support of numerous nations

The post–World War II era saw the emergence of two of the Allied victors, the United States and the Soviet Union, as **superpowers**—leader nations with dominating influence in international affairs. The United States' role as superpower in a new international system, and the relationship between these superpowers, would shape America's foreign policy for the remainder of the 20th century. Increasingly important in this new era was the role that **multilateral** (many-sided, or supported by numerous nations) organizations and agreements would play.

International Agreements and Organizations

In the aftermath of World War II, the United States was intent on avoiding the mistakes of the Treaty of Versailles, which many policy makers felt had led directly to the conditions that produced the war. They proceeded to address those mistakes one by one, often forming international organizations equipped to respond to the public policy challenges confronting the postwar world.

Marshall Plan
the U.S. government program that provided funds necessary for Western European countries to rebuild after World War II

A key component of the postwar recovery effort was the **Marshall Plan.** Named for Secretary of State George Marshall, the program provided the funds necessary for Western European countries—even the United States' enemies from World War II—to rebuild. War-ravaged nations, including defeated (West) Germany, soon became economic powerhouses, thanks to initial help from the Marshall Plan. Ironically, by forcing the Germans to demilitarize as a condition of their surrender, the Allies freed Germany from spending large amounts of its own tax money on defense, thus enabling the German people to devote more of its own resources to economic development. Other countries impoverished by war also benefited from the Marshall Plan (Figure 18.1), creating new markets for U.S. products. Eastern European nations, now securely under Soviet influence, were prevented from participating. Because of the plan's success in Western Europe, the United States recognized that economic development and peace were intertwined, that economic stability was critical if future wars were to be prevented, and that an international approach was preferable to isolationism in foreign policy.

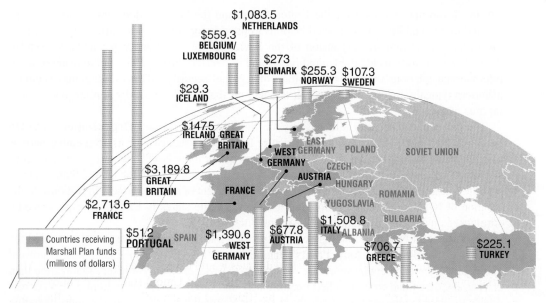

$1,083.5
NETHERLANDS

$559.3
BELGIUM/
LUXEMBOURG

$273
DENMARK

$255.3
NORWAY

$107.3
SWEDEN

$29.3
ICELAND

$147.5
IRELAND

GREAT
BRITAIN

EAST
GERMANY

POLAND

SOVIET UNION

WEST
GERMANY

CZECH

$3,189.8
GREAT
BRITAIN

AUSTRIA

HUNGARY

FRANCE

YUGOSLAVIA

ROMANIA

$2,713.6
FRANCE

BULGARIA

$1,508.8
ITALY

ALBANIA

Countries receiving
Marshall Plan funds
(millions of dollars)

$51.2
PORTUGAL

SPAIN

$1,390.6
WEST
GERMANY

$677.8
AUSTRIA

$706.7
GREECE

$225.1
TURKEY

FIGURE 18.1

Recipients of Marshall Plan Aid, 1948–1951

SOURCE: www.cnn.com/SPECIALS/cold.war/episodes/03/maps.

THE UNITED NATIONS   The Allied victors of World War II recognized the need for a structure to ensure collective security. In that spirit, U.S. officials organized a meeting in San Francisco in 1945 with 50 U.S. allies, all of whom agreed to create the **United Nations (UN).** Participants hoped that this international body, through collective security, would develop the capacity to prevent future wars. The charter of the United Nations created these components:

United Nations (UN)
an international body established in 1945 in order to prevent future wars by achieving collective security and peace

- *United Nations (UN):* established in 1945, an international body intended to prevent future wars by achieving collective security and peace.
- *Security Council:* 11 members, 5 of which—including the United States, the Soviet Union (now Russia), China, Great Britain, and France—are permanent members with the power to veto any action taken by the council. Today, the Security Council consists of 15 members, with the permanent members and their veto power remaining unchanged.
- *General Assembly:* consisting of all the member nations, each with a single vote (in 1945, there were 51 member nations; today there are 193).
- *Secretariat:* headed by a secretary-general with a staff at UN headquarters in New York City. The secretary-general in 2015 is Ban Ki-moon of South Korea.
- Several specialized organizations to handle specific policy challenges, including the Economic and Social Council, the Trusteeship Council, and the International Court at The Hague.

The United Nations' mission includes the promotion of economic and social development. Since its founding, it has added peacekeeping to its functions and has had some limited success in that endeavor in areas of the former Yugoslavia, the Middle East, and Africa. But in the immediate post–World War II era, the ability of the United Nations in general, and of the Security Council in particular, to provide for collective security was seriously undermined by the Soviet Union's presence on the Security Council. Because the Soviet Union was a permanent member with veto power, any attempt by the Security Council to thwart Soviet aggression was blocked by the Soviets' veto.

>Established on the eve of the end of World War II in 1945, the United Nations is an international body that seeks to prevent wars through collective security. Secretary-General Ban Ki-moon of South Korea met in 2013 with Nobel Peace Prize winner and pro-democracy leader Aung San Suu Kyi of Myanmar (Burma).

regional security alliance
an alliance typically between a superpower and nations that are ideologically similar in a particular region

North Atlantic Treaty Organization (NATO)
an international mutual defense alliance formed in 1949 that created a structure for regional security for its 15 member nations

Warsaw Pact
a regional security structure formed in 1955 by the Soviet Union and its seven satellite states in Eastern Europe in response to the creation of NATO

Southeast Asia Treaty Organization (SEATO)
a regional security agreement whose goal was to prevent communist encroachment in the countries of Southeast Asia

NATO   It did not take long for the United States and the Western democracies to be disappointed by the inability of the United Nations to provide for collective security. The UN's failure to halt the militaristic expansion of the Soviet sphere of influence particularly troubled them. Their frustrations led the United States and its Western allies to attempt to bring order to international relations through the creation of regional security alliances. **Regional security alliances** typically involve a superpower and nations that are ideologically similar in a particular area of the world.

The first regional security alliance was the **North Atlantic Treaty Organization (NATO).** Established in 1949, NATO created a structure for regional security for its 15 member nations through a declaration that "an armed attack against one or more NATO nations . . . shall be considered an attack against them all."[14] Through the formation of NATO, the United States made a specific commitment to defend Western Europe in the event of a Soviet attack. In response to the creation of NATO, the Soviet Union and its seven satellite states in Eastern Europe formed a similar regional security alliance, the **Warsaw Pact,** in 1955.

The success of NATO at holding Soviet expansion into Western Europe at bay motivated the creation of the **Southeast Asia Treaty Organization (SEATO),** whose goal was to prevent communist encroachment in Southeast Asia. SEATO was a decidedly weaker organization than NATO; decisions had to be reached unanimously and rarely were. For example, SEATO was unable to agree to intervene in Cambodia, Laos, or Vietnam because member nations, including France, Pakistan, and the Philippines, objected to intervention.

Both NATO and the Warsaw Pact reflected the tensions and the rivalry that existed between the United States and the Soviet Union. They also reflected the failure of the United Nations to provide for collective security, that is, the security of *all* nations. Instead, the regional security alliances more closely resembled the balance of power alliances established after the Napoleonic Wars.

NATO's role as a structure for regional security was highlighted in 2014, when Russia annexed Crimea, which had been part of the Ukraine. Stationing 40,000 troops along the border with Ukraine, Russia evoked fears that it intended to annex more of the Ukraine, or even parts of Eastern European and Baltic nations. In response to Russia's actions in Crimea, NATO ceased practical cooperation with Russia and drew up plans to reinforce NATO's defenses in NATO member states in the area.

INTERNATIONAL FINANCIAL ORGANIZATIONS   In addition to establishing the United Nations and NATO for the purposes of conflict management and security, the United States recognized the need to relinquish a great deal of its own economic power in exchange for the economic stability that would come from international financial institutions. Doing so would benefit the global economy in general but also the U.S. economy in particular.

International Monetary Fund (IMF)
institution charged with regulating monetary relationships among nations, including establishment of exchange rates for major world currencies; established in 1944 by the Bretton Woods Agreement

To that end, in 1944, an international agreement made in Bretton Woods, New Hampshire— the Bretton Woods Agreement—established the **International Monetary Fund (IMF).** The meeting delegates charged the newly created international financial institution with regulating monetary relationships among nations. One of the IMF's key purposes was to establish exchange rates for currencies, determining, for example, how many dollars a British pound or a Japanese yen was worth. To the present day, IMF member states provide the resources the IMF needs to operate through a formula by which nations pay amounts roughly proportional to the size of their economies. Based on these IMF contribution quotas, nations are allocated votes proportional to their contributions. Thus the IMF perpetuates the dominance of the high-contributing economic powerhouses. Today, the United States has nearly 17 percent of the IMF votes. The Bretton Woods agreement also established the institution that would become the **World Bank,** which initially focused on lending money to countries devastated in World War II. Today, the World Bank lends money to developing nations to help them become self-sufficient.

World Bank
international financial institution created by the Bretton Woods Agreement of 1944 and charged with lending money to nations in need

Still reeling from the effects of high tariffs on international trade during the Depression, the United States also encouraged an international agreement that would heal the economies of nations by lowering tariffs and promoting international trade. In 1948, 23 nations signed the General Agreement on Tariffs and Trade (GATT). The GATT is based on the most favored nation principle.

In 1995, the **World Trade Organization (WTO)** replaced the GATT. Whereas the GATT was a series of agreements among nations, the WTO is an actual organization that negotiates, implements, and enforces international trade agreements. Today, the WTO consists of 159 member nations. Although it has a one-nation, one-vote policy, this policy is moot because the largest economies have the greatest say. The organization's goal—to remove all types of trade barriers, including obstacles to investment—is more ambitious than that of the GATT.

World Trade Organization (WTO)
organization created in 1995 to negotiate, implement, and enforce international trade agreements

The Cold War: Superpowers in Collision

During World War II, the United States, Great Britain, and the Soviet Union were allies against the Nazis. But events at the wartime Yalta Conference in 1945 sowed the seeds of what would become known as the Cold War. The **Cold War** refers to the political, ideological, and military conflict that lasted from 1945 until 1990 between the Soviet Union and its allies, and the United States and its allies The causes of the Cold War include the competing desire to have dominant influence in Europe, as well as the fundamental dispute between communist versus capitalist economic systems.

Cold War
the political, ideological, and military conflict that lasted from 1945 until 1990 between communist nations led by the Soviet Union and Western democracies led by the United States

Each leader came to the Yalta Conference with an agenda. The United States' Franklin D. Roosevelt needed Soviet help in battling Japan in the naval wars of the Pacific. England's Winston Churchill sought democratic elections in Eastern Europe. And Soviet premier Joseph Stalin wanted Eastern Europe as a Soviet sphere of influence, arguing that the Soviet Union's national security depended on its hegemony in the region.

At the conference, Stalin agreed to allow free elections in the region, but he later broke that promise. In response, former British prime minister Churchill warned Americans in a 1946 speech that the Soviets were dividing Europe with an "Iron Curtain." Churchill's characterization was accurate, because Stalin's brutal dictatorship, combined with the force of the Soviet Red Army, would install a communist government in every Eastern European nation. When Stalin also refused to cooperate in the planned cooperative allied occupation of Germany, the result was the division of Germany into separate zones, one administered by the Soviet Union and the other three by the United States, Great Britain, and France. In 1948, when the Soviets backed communist guerillas who were attempting to take over Greece and Turkey, U.S. president Harry Truman (1945–1953) committed the United States to "support free people who are resisting attempted subjugation by armed minorities or by outside pressures."[15] This policy—the United States' foreign policy commitment to assist efforts to resist communism—was called the **Truman Doctrine.**

Truman Doctrine
articulated by President Harry Truman, a foreign policy commitment by the United States to assist countries' efforts to resist communism in the Cold War era

▶In 1945, British prime minister Winston Churchill, U.S. president Franklin Roosevelt, and Soviet premier Joseph Stalin each attended the Yalta Conference with an agenda. Today, presidents often have to balance an even greater number of demands from negotiating partners, as did Russian president Vladimir Putin, British prime minister David Cameron, and U.S. president Barack Obama at a G-8 meeting in Enniskillen, Northern Ireland, in 2013.

U.S. Efforts to Contain Communism: Korea, Cuba, and Vietnam

The Truman Doctrine reflected the ideas of George F. Kennan, the State Department's Soviet expert at the time. Specifically, Kennan advocated the principle of **containment,** the policy of preventing the spread of communism, mainly by providing military and economic aid as well as political advice to beleaguered countries that were vulnerable to communist takeover. Kennan argued: "It is clear that the main element of any United States policy toward the Soviet Union must be that of a long-term vigilant containment of Russian expansive tendencies."[16] The idea of containment would spur the United States to fight in two protracted wars, the Korean War and the Vietnam War, to contain communism.

THE KOREAN WAR, 1950–1953 The first military effort the United States engaged in to check the spread of communism occurred in 1950. In June of that year, North Korea, with the backing of Stalin and the Soviet Union, invaded South Korea in an attempt to reunify the Korean peninsula under communism. During that summer, the United States sent in forces as part of a UN force to help the South Koreans repel the attack. The defensive strategy quickly succeeded, but by October the United States changed military strategy. Instead of merely containing the spread of communism, the United States sought to reunify North and South Korea—and, in doing so, to depose the communists from North Korea. But as U.S. and South Korean forces edged north, they also came closer and closer to the North Korea–China border.

That October, China, wary of a potential invasion, came to the aid of fellow communists in North Korea. The two countries' combined forces repelled the UN forces back to the 38th parallel, the original border between North and South Korea. Over the next two years, U.S. forces (as part of the UN contingent), North and South Koreans, and Chinese soldiers would continue to do battle, with very little territory changing hands. When an armistice was reached in July 1953, the border established was the 38th parallel—exactly what it had been before the war—although a demilitarized zone (DMZ) was created. Today, U.S. and South Korean troops still patrol one side of the DMZ, while North Korean troops patrol the other.

The Korean War marked an escalation and expansion of the Cold War. Not only was the war the first occasion in which the two superpowers clashed militarily, but it also brought the Cold War outside the boundaries of Europe. Significantly, the outbreak of the Korean War also gave rise to the concept of **limited war**—a combatant country's self-imposed limitation on the tactics and strategy it uses, particularly its avoidance of the deployment of nuclear weapons. The idea of limited war would set the stage for subsequent conflicts.

THE CUBAN MISSILE CRISIS, 1962 Another tactic of U.S. foreign policy during the Cold War was brinkmanship, a term coined by John Foster Dulles, the secretary of state under President Dwight D. Eisenhower (1953–1961). In essence, **brinkmanship** meant fooling the enemy by going to the edge (the brink), even if the party employing brinkmanship had no intention of following through to its logical conclusion.

The Cuban Missile Crisis in October 1962 turned out to be a perfect example of brinkmanship, even though that was not the intention of President John F. Kennedy (1961–1963). Reacting to Soviet premier Nikita Khrushchev's decision to put ballistic missiles in Cuba, Kennedy imposed a naval blockade around that island nation 94 miles off the coast of Florida, and warned the Soviet Union to withdraw its missiles, or else—never specifying what he meant by "or else." Although this confrontation seemed like brinkmanship, it was no bluff; rather, it was an act of bravado that could easily have led to nuclear war. Luckily for the United States and the rest of the world, the Soviets backed down, withdrew their missiles, and entered a period of improved relations with the United States.[17]

THE VIETNAM CONFLICT, 1965–1975 The United States' involvement in the war in Vietnam was motivated in large part by policy makers' acceptance of the **domino theory,** the principle that if one nation fell to communism, other nations in its geographic vicinity would also succumb. As described by President Eisenhower, "You have broader considerations that might follow what you would call the 'falling domino' principle. You have a row of dominoes set up, you knock over the first one, and what will happen to the last one is the certainty that it will go over very quickly. So you could have a beginning of a disintegration that would have the most profound influences."[18]

And so the United States again sought to contain the spread of communism in Southeast Asia. Although Vietnam was not of particular strategic importance to the United States, it represented the second "domino" in the faraway region. U.S. involvement in Vietnam started in the late 1950s, and by 1963, the United States became enmeshed in an all-out ground, naval, and air war there. The United States supported the South Vietnamese against the North Vietnamese in the decade-long civil war that would take the lives of almost 60,000 U.S. soldiers and at least 3 million Vietnamese soldiers and civilians. On April 29, 1975, when the South Vietnamese capital, Saigon, fell to the North Vietnamese Vietcong forces, the event marked the first military failure by the United States in its efforts to contain communism.

> The United States supported the South Vietnamese against the North Vietnamese in the decade-long civil war that would take the lives of almost 60,000 U.S. soldiers who are memorialized on the Vietnam War Memorial in Washington, D.C. Three million Vietnamese soldiers and civilians also died in the conflict. Here, family members of a soldier killed in action find his name on the monument.

Détente: A Thaw in the Cold War Chill

Richard M. Nixon (1969–1974) was elected to the presidency in 1968, largely on his promise to conclude the war in Vietnam. Although several years would pass before the war ended, Nixon's approach to the top foreign policy issues of the day marked a departure from that of his predecessors. Specifically, the **Nixon Doctrine** emphasized the responsibility of U.S. allies to provide for their own national defense and security and sought to improve relations with the two communist world powers, the Soviet Union and China. As early as 1970, his administration sought **détente,** or the easing of tensions between the United States and its communist rivals. In keeping with this idea, the Nixon administration normalized diplomatic relations with China and began a series of nuclear arms control talks that would occur throughout the 1970s. Critics of the Nixon Doctrine argued that President Nixon's approach to foreign policy was accommodationist—that it sought the easy solution and ignored the moral and philosophical implications of improving relations between the Western democracies and their communist rivals.

Part of the motivation for détente was the recognition that any escalation of tensions between the superpowers would increase the probability of nuclear war. Since the early 1960s, the United States and the Soviet Union had engaged in a nuclear arms race in which each country attempted to surpass the other's nuclear capability. According to the doctrine of **mutual assured destruction (MAD),** if one nation attacked another with nuclear weapons, the other would be capable of retaliating, and *would* retaliate, with such force as to ensure mutual annihilation. The advent of intercontinental ballistic missiles (ICBMs) meant that both the United States and the Soviet Union were capable of sending nuclear warheads through space to targets in their rivals' homelands. The goal of the arms race (which would continue through the 1980s) was first-strike capability, meaning that each nation sought the ability to use nuclear weapons against another nation and to eliminate the possibility of that nation's retaliating in a second-strike attack.

Many foreign policy makers in both the United States and the Soviet Union believed in the power of **deterrence,** the idea that nations would be less likely to engage in nuclear war if the adversaries each had first-strike capability. But Nixon and his primary foreign policy adviser, Henry Kissinger (who served first as Nixon's national security adviser and then as his secretary of state), sought negotiations with the Soviets that would dampen the arms race.

SALT I AND SALT II   In 1972, the United States and the Soviet Union concluded two and a half years of **strategic arms limitation talks (SALT talks)** that focused on cooling the superheated nuclear arms race between the two superpowers. The resulting treaty, **SALT I,** limited the two countries' antiballistic missiles (ABMs) and froze the number of offensive missiles

Nixon Doctrine
policy emphasizing the responsibility of U.S. allies to provide for their own national defense and security, aimed at improving relations with the communist nations, including the Soviet Union and China

détente
easing of tensions between the United States and its communist rivals

mutual assured destruction (MAD)
the doctrine that if one nation attacked another with nuclear weapons, the other would be capable of retaliating and would retaliate with such force as to ensure mutual annihilation

deterrence
the idea that nations would be less likely to engage in nuclear war if adversaries each had first-strike capability

strategic arms limitation talks (SALT talks)
discussions between the United States and the Soviet Union in the 1970s that focused on cooling down the nuclear arms race between the two superpowers

SALT I
treaty signed in 1972 by the United States and the Soviet Union limiting the two countries' antiballistic missiles and freezing the number of offensive missiles that each nation could have at the number they already possessed, plus the number they had under construction

> In encouraging détente, President Nixon sent the U.S. table tennis team to China in 1971, marking the first visit to China by a U.S. delegation since China's communist revolution in 1949. The visit—dubbed ping pong diplomacy—as well as many back channel negotiations with China, paved the wave for a warming of relations between the two nations, including the United States' lifting of a trade embargo. In 1972 President Richard Nixon would visit China, the first U.S. president to do so.

SALT II
treaty signed in 1979 by the United States and the Soviet Union that set an overall limit on strategic nuclear launchers, limited the number of missiles that could carry multiple independently targeted reentry vehicles (MIRVs) with nuclear warheads, and limited each nation to the development of only one new type of intercontinental ballistic missile (ICBM)

defense conversion
President Jimmy Carter's attempt to convert the nation's vast military apparatus to peacetime functions

strategic arms reduction talks (START talks)
talks between the United States and the Soviet Union in which reductions in missiles and nuclear warheads, not merely a limitation on increases, were negotiated

strategic defense initiative (SDI, or "Star Wars")
a ballistic missile defense system advocated by President Ronald Reagan

that each nation could have at the number they already possessed, plus the number they had under construction.

The SALT II strategic arms limitation talks, begun during the Nixon administration and continuing through the Jimmy Carter presidency (1977–1981), resulted in the signing of the SALT II treaty in 1979. The **SALT II** treaty set an overall limit on all strategic nuclear launchers, including ICBMs, submarine-launched ballistic missiles (SLBMs), and cruise missiles. SALT II also limited the number of missiles that could carry multiple independently targeted reentry vehicles (MIRVs) with nuclear warheads, and limited each nation to the development of only one new type of ICBM.

Later in 1979, however, the Soviet Union invaded Afghanistan, sparking a new round of U.S-Soviet tensions. In response, President Jimmy Carter withdrew the SALT II treaty from consideration for ratification by the Senate. Nevertheless, Carter announced (as did his successor, Ronald Reagan) that the United States would abide by all the terms of SALT II as long as the Soviet Union complied as well. During his one term in office, Carter also sought to engage the world in a campaign for human rights, while at the same time attempting to convert the vast U.S. military apparatus to peacetime functions—a policy known as **defense conversion.**

The Reagan Years and Soviet Collapse

Ronald Reagan's presidency (1981–1989) marked a pivotal time in U.S.-Soviet relations. On the one hand, the Reagan administration pushed for a *reduction* in missiles and nuclear warheads, not merely a limitation on increases. Because of this new direction, Reagan named these arms reduction talks the **strategic arms reduction talks (START talks).** Despite this overture, the Reagan administration was passionate in the pursuit of a ballistic missile defense system, called the **strategic defense initiative (SDI, or "Star Wars").** In protest of the development of this system, the Soviet Union walked out of the START meeting in 1983. The two superpowers would return to the table in 1985, after Reagan won reelection with a resounding victory.

In 1987, the United States and the Soviet Union signed the Intermediate-Range Nuclear Forces Treaty (INF), the first agreement that resulted in the destruction of nuclear weapons. It eliminated an entire class of weapons—those with an intermediate range of between 300 and 3,800 miles. A pathbreaking treaty, the INF shaped future arms control talks. It provided for reductions in the number of nuclear weapons, established the principle of equality because both nations ended up with the same number of weapons (in this case, zero), and, through the establishment of on-site inspections, provided a means of verifying compliance.

In retrospect, many analysts credit the Soviet Union's eventual collapse to President Reagan. During his tenure, Reagan ratcheted up the rhetoric with his many speeches referring to the Soviet Union as "the Evil Empire." Under his administration, the U.S. defense budget also doubled, with much of the expenditure going toward the SDI. The Soviets reacted with fear and a surge in spending. These developments all came at a time when the Soviet Union was dealing with unrest in 15 republics that eventually would secede. The last straw, however, was the country's troubled economy, because to compete with the U.S. ballistic missile system, the Soviet Union had to increase its military budget to the point where its economy collapsed—and with it, the government.

Post-Soviet Times: The United States as Solo Superpower in an Era of Wars

The START talks, which had resumed in 1985, resulted in a long-awaited agreement that reduced the number of long-range strategic nuclear weapons to 3,000 for each side. In 1991, the agreement was signed by U.S. president George H. W. Bush and Soviet president Mikhail Gorbachev, whose tenure had ushered in the ideas of *glasnost* (openness) and *perestroika* (economic restructuring) in the Soviet Union. That same year, the Soviet Union broke apart, and Russia democratically elected its president, Boris Yeltsin. Upon Yeltsin's election, in another series of talks called START II, Yeltsin agreed to even deeper cuts in nuclear weapons. He also assented to the eventual elimination of all land-based missiles with multiple warheads (MIRVs). The START II agreement of 1992 between the superpowers was fully implemented in 2003 and significantly decreased the likelihood of a massive nuclear attack.

As a result of the breakup of the Soviet Union, a whole new order emerged in Eastern Europe, with the Balkan nations of Latvia, Lithuania, and Estonia reasserting their independence, and an additional 14 former Soviet republics establishing independent states. These sweeping changes meant a changed role for NATO, which in 1999 expanded to include Poland, Hungary, and the Czech Republic in the organization, over the objections of Russia. In 2004, another seven countries in central and Eastern Europe—Estonia, Latvia, Lithuania, Slovenia, Slovakia, Bulgaria, and Romania—joined NATO. Five years later, in 2009, Albania and Croatia also became members of the collective security alliance, in which each member nation pledges protection should any member of NATO be attacked.

The 1990s proved to be a watershed era in global relations in both Asia and Europe. In Asia, China emerged as a world power and has continued to increase its influence on the world stage. In Europe, the Maastricht Treaty, signed in 1992, paved the way for the formation of the European Union. The European Union is a political and economic alliance that prioritizes peace in Europe based on economic cooperation and stability. What started out as an economic union between six nations has grown into an enormous single market in which citizens of the 28 member states can move freely between states, and all members use a single currency, the euro.

This decade also proved to be a novel time in U.S. foreign relations. For the first time in over half a century, the United States was without an enemy, and it found itself the world's lone superpower. The tumult following the collapse of communism ushered in an era of wars—many of them fueled by long-standing ethnic rivalries or disputes—and the creation of new borders and new nations. By the start of the new century, 14 wars were going on around the globe. Some, such as the decades-long conflict in Northern Ireland, now seem to be resolved. Others seemed intractable, such as the conflict in the Middle East over the Palestinian question. Still others, such as the tribal wars in Africa, were all too often manipulated by foreign interests and by corrupt indigenous leaders who were reluctant to give up their power. And other events—such as fighting that erupted between UN and U.S. forces against Somali militia fighters loyal to warlord Mohamed Farrah Aidid in 1993; the 1998 attacks on U.S. embassies in Nairobi, Kenya, and Dar es Salaam, Tanzania; and the 2000 suicide bombing of the U.S. Navy guided missile destroyer USS *Cole* in the port of Aden, Yemen—were harbingers of clashes to come. It was as if a giant hand had lifted a rock at the end of the Cold War, freeing long-submerged problems to crawl out and presenting new challenges for U.S. foreign policy makers as the United States assumed its role as the world's leader.

Then Now Next

Defining U.S. Foreign Policy

Then (1984)	Now
The Cold War was the defining feature of U.S. foreign policy.	U.S. foreign policy is being reshaped after the withdrawal of U.S. forces from Afghanistan and as the nation deals with ongoing crises in the Middle East, Asia, Eastern Europe, and elsewhere.
The United States and the Soviet Union competed as the two world superpowers.	A rapidly changing global context means that the United States competes for its world power status, along with China, Russia, and the European Union.
The arms race resulted in unprecedented military spending.	Military spending decreases somewhat as multifront wars wind down, yet national security needs result in high spending levels.

WHAT'S NEXT?

> What new realities will shape U.S. foreign and national defense policy?

> Will the United States continue as the world's only superpower? How will a superpower be defined in the future? Will the term refer to military or economic might or a combination of these (and/or other) factors?

> What impact will continued spending have on the U.S. and global economy?

U.S. Foreign Policy After 9/11

U.S. foreign policy makers' challenges in the 1990s pale in comparison with those they have faced since the terrorist attacks of September 11, 2001. The incidents on that day have profoundly defined and determined recent American foreign policy.

The Bush Doctrine: A Clash of Civilizations

One prism for viewing the September 11 attacks is that posited by political scientist Samuel P. Huntington. He asserts that "the clash of civilizations will be the battle lines of the future."[19] Huntington's **clash of civilizations thesis** asserts that bitter cultural conflict will continue and escalate between modern Western democracies, whose culture emphasizes values rooted in democracy and capitalism, and fundamentalist Islamic states, where traditional values grounded in religious beliefs dominate. Huntington, whose thesis remains controversial, argues that the ideological divisions that characterized the 20th century—the clash between communism and democratic capitalism, for example—will be replaced by an older source of conflict: cultural and religious identity. Huntington initially posited his ideas in 1993, and his theories seemed particularly relevant during the 1990s when ethnic and religious warfare broke out in Bosnia and in parts of Africa. After 9/11, Huntington's neoconservative theory appeared to have significantly shaped the foreign policy of the George W. Bush administration.

Huntington's clash of civilizations thesis provides one explanation of *why* contemporary U.S. foreign policy has focused on the areas that it has. President George W. Bush himself articulated his views on the *how* of that policy's implementation. According to the **Bush Doctrine,** the United States has a responsibility to further the spread of democracy and create a global order that ensures the security of the United States and its allies, even if it means that the United States acts alone. This unilateral action, according to the Bush Doctrine, is both justifiable and feasible. The Bush Doctrine also asserted that the United States should use its role as the world's only remaining superpower to spread democracy and to create conditions of security that will benefit itself and its allies.

WAR IN AFGHANISTAN   The United States' first response to the 9/11 attacks was based on the connection of Osama bin Laden and the al-Qaeda terror network to the masterminding and execution of those attacks. For several years before 9/11, the fundamentalist Taliban regime in Afghanistan had allowed al-Qaeda training camps to operate in that country. In retaliation for the 9/11 strikes, in late 2001 the United States, a coalition of allies, and anti-Taliban rebels from within Afghanistan attacked the training camps and the Taliban government itself. Within weeks the Taliban government fell. By toppling the Taliban as the leaders of Afghanistan, the United States fulfilled the policy goal of regime change.

The multilateral forces worked to create first an interim government in Afghanistan and then, in 2004, a democratically elected government. Attacks from Taliban insurgents continue, though the U.S. presence in the nation has ended. Although the U.S. invasion of Afghanistan occurred largely in response to the Taliban's support of al-Qaeda, the invasion also demonstrated the potential consequences for nations that support terrorism against the United States.

WAR IN IRAQ   After the Taliban's fall, President Bush set his sights on changing another regime: that of Iraq's Saddam Hussein. During the presidency of Bush's father, George H. W. Bush (1989–1993), the United States had gone to war with Iraq when that country invaded Kuwait, an ally of the United States. During the younger Bush's 2003 State of the Union address, the president claimed that Iraq possessed weapons of mass destruction and said that the Iraqis were attempting to purchase the components of nuclear weapons. In the ensuing weeks, the Bush administration made a case for going to war with Hussein's regime to both the UN Security Council and the American people. In doing so, Bush introduced the concept of **preventive war,**

---

clash of civilizations thesis
Samuel Huntington's idea that bitter cultural conflict will continue and escalate between modern Western democracies and fundamentalist Islamic states

Bush Doctrine
the argument, articulated by President George W. Bush, that unilateral action directly targeted at an enemy is both justifiable and feasible

preventive war
the strategy of waging war on countries regarded as threatening in order to avoid future conflicts

the strategy of waging war on countries regarded as threatening to the United States in order to avoid future conflicts.

The concept of preventive war represents a shift in policy from responding to attacks to anticipating attacks. The idea of preventive war is in part an outgrowth of the drastically altered nature of warfare. The biological, chemical, and nuclear weapons of today can cross borders with far deadlier efficiency than troops, ships, or aircraft. In addition, U.S. enemies no longer declare themselves as openly as they did before. The national defense policy makers who advocate preventive war thus argue that the only way to defend the country against these various new threats is to invade *before* the fact, in hopes of deterring another attack.

The invasion of Iraq in March 2003 was initially successful in toppling Saddam Hussein's regime. Despite insurgency violence that prevented peace from taking root, elections were finally held in 2004 and 2005, and power officially passed to an elected government. In the face of continued violence, the Bush administration enacted a military surge policy, resulting in the addition of more than 20,000 troops in Baghdad and Al Anbar Province. Though not ending the conflict, the surge strategy was credited with quelling much of the insurgent violence in these areas.

> In the United States' crosshairs for over a decade, Osama bin Laden, mastermind of the September 11, 2001, terror attacks, was caught and killed in Abbottabad, Pakistan, in 2011. The terror attacks, and the U.S. response to them, have been the defining feature of U.S. foreign policy since they occurred.

In addition to the violence that has continued to plague Iraq, political turmoil has been characteristic of this nation. In March 2010, parliamentary elections were held—and large numbers of Iraqis defied the threat of violence and actual attacks to cast their ballots in one of the most open and competitive elections Iraq has had. The results were so close that only two seats separated the top two political parties, which then had to form a coalition with other parties to acquire the requisite number of seats to govern. Despite those challenges, the election was widely viewed as a success. U.S. troops left Iraq in 2011 and since that time, escalating insurgent attacks, including some by members of the terror group ISIS, have resulted in an all-out civil war.

Nation building in Iraq proved troublesome—far more so than the rebuilding of Japan after World War II, for example. There, U.S. general Douglas MacArthur undertook the task of reconstructing the nation and creating a system of democratic self-governance. It took four years, but when MacArthur left for duty in Korea, Japan was as close to democracy as any Far Eastern country. Japan's feudal aristocracy was abolished, the country had a new constitution that empowered the legislature to make laws, civil liberties and collective bargaining were guaranteed, the legal equality of the sexes was established, and citizens had been given the right of *habeas corpus* (a petition that allows a prisoner to go to a court where a judge will determine whether he or she is being held illegally). MacArthur also suspended banks that had financed the war, destroyed (at least temporarily) the giant monopolies, and refused to allow "war profiteers" to invade Japan at the expense of local businesses.

Fifty years later, as the United States sought to rebuild Iraq's war-torn infrastructure and feed its people after toppling Hussein's regime, a powerful insurgency thwarted American efforts. Unlike MacArthur, the U.S. military had allowed widespread looting in the early days of the occupation, including the looting of munitions warehouses. These munitions later helped to arm the insurgents, who continue to do battle in the absence of U.S. forces. Also unlike MacArthur, who had some familiarity with Japanese culture, few commanders knew either the Arabic language or Iraqi culture and rituals. Even fewer knew how to stem the war profiteering of the multinational corporations that had also "invaded" the country, making millions off the reconstruction of Iraq's infrastructure.

Democracy

Do the Geneva Conventions Apply When Terrorists Have So Drastically Altered the Rules of War?

The Issue: The Geneva Conventions are a set of four treaties signed in Geneva, Switzerland, in 1949, in the aftermath of World War II. The conventions established standards for the protection of humanitarian concerns under international law. They apply to injured or ill members of the armed forces, prisoners of war, and civilians. Article 13 of the Third Geneva Convention, which specifically guides the treatment of prisoners of war, states that "prisoners of war must at all times be humanely treated. Any unlawful act or omission by the Detaining Power causing death or seriously endangering the health of a prisoner of war in its custody is prohibited, and will be regarded as a serious breach of the present Convention. In particular, no prisoner of war may be subjected to physical mutilation or to medical or scientific experiments of any kind which are not justified by the medical, dental or hospital treatment of the prisoner concerned and carried out in his interest. Likewise, prisoners of war must at all times be protected, particularly against acts of violence or intimidation and against insults and public curiosity. Measures of reprisal against prisoners of war are prohibited."*

Beginning in 2002, military authorities at the U.S. naval base at Guantánamo Bay in Cuba have detained about 775 "enemy combatants." Captured primarily in Afghanistan, these individuals were transported to Guantánamo for questioning. Although authorities in the Bush and Obama administrations have released nearly two-thirds of the prisoners, over 200 remain. As designated enemy combatants, the prisoners have not enjoyed the legal rights granted to individuals charged with a crime in the United States. The detainees have no legal rights to a lawyer, a trial, or *habeas corpus*.

Yes: The Geneva Conventions clearly apply in this situation. As many human rights organizations, including Amnesty International, argue, the detention of prisoners at Guantánamo amounts to a violation of the Geneva Conventions. Specifically, as these critics cite, there have been emphatic allegations of torture by individuals who have been released. Furthermore, the indefinite nature of the detentions—combined with the captors' acknowledged practices of sleep deprivation and constant light exposure, plus the disrespect of the Muslim religion on the part of some—constitutes the abuse of their human rights in violation of the Geneva Conventions.

The moral high ground usually occupied by the United States is at stake, and if the United States does not grant these prisoners rights that are consistent with the Geneva Conventions, our own soldiers will be at risk of having their rights denied when they are captured by enemy forces.

No: The Geneva Conventions do not apply when the rules of engagement of war have changed so drastically. The Bush administration convincingly argued that the Geneva Conventions apply only to "prisoners of war" (POWs) and not to "unlawful combatants." Because the nature of the war on terror and of the tactics used by terrorists is in stark contrast to accepted international conventions of war, the treatment of combatants in that war should also vary. The Supreme Court has thus far agreed with the Bush administration's assessment that holding enemy combatants is legal.**

Other Approaches: The Geneva Conventions do not apply to detainees at Guantánamo because they are not conventional enemy combatants, but the detainees should be afforded their human rights. In times like these, when international terrorist organizations do not follow centuries-old rules of engagement in warfare, the United States cannot follow antiquated rules and expect to keep its citizens safe. Therefore, detention can prevent further terrorist attacks if potential terrorists are prevented from carrying them out. Nevertheless, the detainees are entitled to humane treatment and to a hearing before an impartial judge to determine if they are truly a threat.

*You can read the rules and explore other topics at this International Committee of the Red Cross site: www.icrc.org/ihl.nsf/7c4d08d9b287a42141256739003e636b/6fef854a3517b75ac125641e004a9e68.
**Hamdi v. Rumsfeld, 542 U.S. 507 (2004).

What do you think?

1. Are the prisoners held at Guantánamo different from the prisoners of war held in other wars? If so, how?

2. Are the Geneva Conventions, drafted soon after the conclusion of World War II, still applicable in the post-9/11 world, in which terrorism is such an urgent problem in international affairs?

The Obama Doctrine: A New Tone in U.S. Foreign Policy

With the election of President Barack Obama in 2008, it seemed that a new era in U.S. foreign policy had begun. As a candidate, Obama had called for an end to the U.S. presence in Iraq and a change in the tenor of U.S. foreign policy. Throughout his tenure both as a candidate and as president, Obama has used language that would seem to reject Huntington's clash of civilizations thesis, which was instrumental in shaping Bush administration policy. For example, in what was billed as an "address to the Muslim world," given in Egypt in 2009, Obama referred to the differences between his worldview and those of his predecessors:

> Violent extremists have exploited these tensions in a small but potent minority of Muslims. The attacks of September 11th, 2001, and the continued efforts of these extremists to engage in violence against civilians has led some in my country to view Islam as inevitably hostile not only to America and Western countries, but also to human rights. This has bred more fear and mistrust. . . .
>
> I have come here to seek a new beginning between the United States and Muslims around the world; one based upon mutual interest and mutual respect; and one based upon the truth that America and Islam are not exclusive, and need not be in competition. Instead, they overlap, and share common principles—principles of justice and progress; tolerance and the dignity of all human beings.

From his rhetoric, it appears that President Obama has rejected the idea that the United States and Islamic nations are destined to clash, instead seeking to build bridges between the United States and the Muslim nations. Nowhere is this in greater evidence that in Iran, where the Obama administration has negotiated a temporary halting of that country's nuclear program, with the promise that economic sanctions would be lifted if the nation complied with international demands to end the program.

Nonetheless, many observers are surprised at the similarities between the Obama and Bush administration policies, despite the change in rhetoric. For example, some analysts say that the success of President Bush's "surge strategy" in Iraq was the guiding principle behind President Obama's troop surge in Afghanistan, with Obama hoping that such a strategy would pave the way for a withdrawal of U.S. forces from Afghanistan. Others remark on President Obama's failure to close military prisons at Guantánamo Bay (see "Thinking Critically About Democracy"), and still others point to his continuation of drone attack programs, in which unmanned combat air vehicles carry out attacks abroad on people and other targets deemed a threat to the United States. President Obama has been criticized by some (and lauded by others) for his decision to enter the conflict in Libya only briefly after uprisings there, and for his decision to rely on air strikes rather than troops on the ground in assisting Syria's efforts to combat ISIS.

Future Challenges in American Foreign Policy

The volatility and the complexity of events in the global arena show no sign of abating. In the foreseeable future and beyond, U.S. foreign policy makers will undoubtedly continue to face a number of pressing issues. Certainly among the most urgent of these problems is the ongoing, acute threat of further terrorism directed at domestic and foreign targets. Issues such as the environment, human rights, and technology promise to remain a fixture on the U.S. foreign policy agenda in the years to come.

Russian Expansion

For decades, Russian expansionism seemed like a threat from the past. But in March 2014, Russian troops moved onto the Crimean Peninsula and annexed the area that had been under control of Ukraine. In the aftermath, large numbers of Russian troops moved onto the border with Ukraine, stirring fears that the nation, under the rule of Vladimir Putin, would continue its push. Fears were also raised in Eastern European nations, especially in the Balkan states of Latvia, Lithuania, and Estonia, which had been overtaken by the Soviets in the 1940s. The specter of Russian aggression is troublesome to foreign policy makers in the United States who recognize that the United States' role in NATO, the regional security organization, would necessitate the use of U.S. troops (likely as part of NATO forces) should a member of the NATO alliance be attacked (see "Analyzing the Sources").

AMERICANS' VIEWS ABOUT THE RETURN OF A COLD WAR

Do you think the United States and Russia are heading back toward a Cold War?

	YES	NO
February 1991	25%	64%
March 2014	50%	43%

In 2014, half of Americans believed that the United States and Russia are headed back to a Cold War, in large part spawned by Russia's annexation of Crimea. Gallup had asked Americans this question in 1991 as Cold War tensions were easing, and Americans expressed greater optimism then that the two nations were not headed back to a Cold War.

But Americans are not equally likely to believe that these recent tensions signify a real deterioration in relations, as demonstrated by the generational gap.

Do you think the United States and Russia are heading back toward a Cold War?

AGE	YES	NO
18–29	36%	58%
30–49	48%	48%
50–64	54%	37%
65+	64%	26%

SOURCE: Gallup Poll, "Half of Americans Say U.S. Headed Back to Cold War," March 27, 2014, www.gallup.com/poll/168116/half-americans-say-headed-back-cold-war.aspx.

Evaluating the Evidence

1. Which age group is most likely to believe that the United States and Russia are headed back toward a Cold War? Which age group is least likely to believe this is the case? Why do you think there are such differences among these groups?

2. In general, what is the trend with regard to age and the belief that the United States and Russia are headed back toward a Cold War?

Nuclear Proliferation

Not all challenges to come are new, however. The continued proliferation of nuclear weapons presents a serious problem to foreign policy makers throughout the world. Figure 18.2 shows that eight nations have a declared nuclear weapons capability, including India and Pakistan; another, Israel, has the undeclared potential; and yet another, Iran, is seeking such potential. Among the Obama administration's top foreign policy priorities has been to halt this proliferation, particularly in Iran. Nonetheless, the fact that dangerous weapons of mass destruction are in such wide distribution increases the likelihood of their use—either accidentally or intentionally.

The Ongoing Threat of Terrorism

As the terrorist attacks of 9/11 demonstrated tragically, foreign affairs can be unpredictable. Nonetheless, U.S. foreign policy makers are certain to confront some clear challenges in the years to come. First among these is the continued threat of terrorism. As a tactic, terrorism has proven enormously effective in accomplishing the goals of the attackers. Specifically, terrorism breeds terror—it has disrupted economies, created instability, and acted as a polarizing force.

FIGURE 18.2 ■ THE NUCLEAR CLUB What, if anything, do most or all of the countries that gave up or ended their nuclear programs have in common, either among themselves or with the countries that have nuclear capability? What do most or all of the countries that have nuclear capability—either declared or undeclared—have in common? What conclusions can you draw about these commonalities?

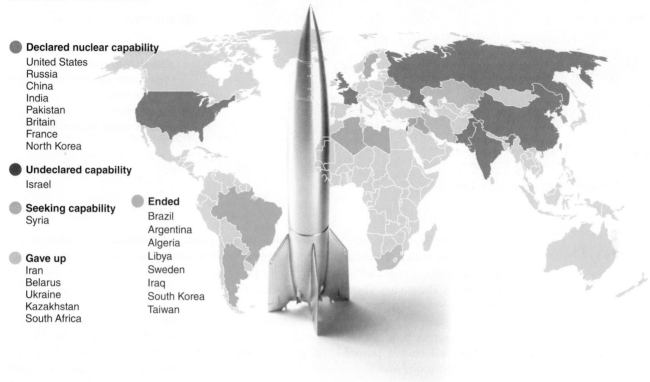

● **Declared nuclear capability**
United States
Russia
China
India
Pakistan
Britain
France
North Korea

● **Undeclared capability**
Israel

● **Seeking capability**
Syria

● **Gave up**
Iran
Belarus
Ukraine
Kazakhstan
South Africa

● **Ended**
Brazil
Argentina
Algeria
Libya
Sweden
Iraq
South Korea
Taiwan

The increasing availability of chemical and biological weapons to both nations and terror groups also promises to be a tough challenge for U.S. and other foreign policy makers. The potential, enormous damage of these weapons of mass destruction cannot be underestimated.

Environmental and Health Issues

Environmental concerns that by their very nature are worldwide challenges promise to remain on the United States' foreign policy agenda deep into the future. Environmental concerns that are sure to have a secure place in foreign policy makers' agendas for the future include the greenhouse gas emissions, enormous world consumption of fossil fuels, the deterioration of the oceans, worldwide deforestation, and ongoing air and water contamination. In 2014, the outbreak of the Ebola virus in Western Africa and its spread to Western nations demonstrated a keen vulnerability that increased globalism has created, and forced policy makers to grapple with difficult questions concerning global health issues.

Technology's Potential in Foreign Affairs

Although there are many uncertainties about what's next in the foreign policy arena, one certainty is that the impact of technology—as a tool in foreign policy and in citizens' efforts to influence the policies and institutions of government—will continue to increase. Today, we see that technology has transformed not only how nations communicate with each other but also

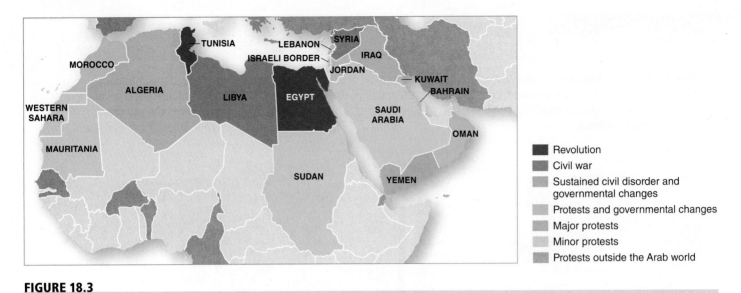

Revolution

Civil war

Sustained civil disorder and
governmental changes

Protests and governmental changes

Major protests

Minor protests

Protests outside the Arab world

FIGURE 18.3

Jasmine Spring Movements in the Middle East, 2011

how nonstate actors, including terrorists, can harness the power of social media to communicate directly with policy makers and private citizens. Video technologies increasingly enable nongovernmental organizations, cyberjournalists, and others to make compelling cases directly to individuals. Technology also is increasingly being relied on as a tool by private citizens, lobbying their governments for favored foreign policies.

Importantly, technology also is being used as a tool for those seeking to foster democracy. In 2014, protestors, many of them students, took to the streets of Hong Kong in an effort to pressure for democratic reforms. The protestors relied on technology to disseminate their message to the world. And also discussed in Chapter 11, the impact of new technologies could be seen in Jasmine Spring protest movements throughout the Middle East (Figure 18.3). In the spring of 2011, cellular and social networking technology provided the organizing tools that facilitated populist uprisings against oppressive regimes, toppling governments in Tunisia and Egypt. And in 2013, the hacker group Anonymous initiated a series of cyber-warfare attacks calling for the resignation of North Korea's leader Kim Jong-un, the abandonment of North Korea's nuclear weapon program, and the establishment of democracy in the totalitarian regime. The likelihood is great that technology will play an increasingly prevalent role in shaping new democracies, checking the authority and policies of governments, and providing a means for cross-national movements.

In retrospect, the development of the United States' foreign policy over time seems to have followed a natural progression as the nation itself grew and changed. The nation's initial isolationism, spawned by a healthy suspicion of foreign powers and their motives, gave way to international relations in the limited sphere of trade. Then, in both World War I and World War II, the importance of global alliances in helping to shape U.S. foreign policy became evident. With the end of World War II, the United States emerged as a superpower whose foreign policy came to be defined largely by its relations with its chief rival in the global arena, the Soviet Union. After the collapse of the Soviet empire in the 1990s, the foreign policy arena was murky as U.S. and world policy makers searched for a new prism through which to view the nations of the world. Could policy makers have anticipated the threat of terrorism that was to come?

On September 11, 2001, U.S. foreign policy instantly acquired a new focus. Their morning hardly going according to their daily planners, a shaken president and his aides scrambled to respond appropriately to the unforeseen and unprecedented terrorist attacks on U.S. soil. They asked the same question that the millions of Americans who watched the unbelievable events unfold on television asked: Why? Ultimately, the administration's responses to the terrorist strikes showed that significant cultural and political differences separate the United States and the other Western democracies on the one hand, and fundamentalist non-Western states that harbor terrorists on the other hand. The attacks crystallized perceptions both among U.S. policy makers and in the general public that no longer could the terrorist states be viewed simply as potential threats or as insignificant to the United States' interests. Do those perceptions remain widely held by the public and policy makers today?

When he became president in January 2009, President Obama signaled a departure from the tenor of the Bush administration. But it remains unclear whether Obama's more conciliatory approach will prove effective in building relations with Arab and Muslim nations. It also remains to be seen whether national security measures put in place by the Bush and Obama administrations will effectively deter future terror attacks on the United States.

Challenges facing U.S. foreign policy makers in the next several years are particularly acute, given their unpredictable nature. North Korean and Iranian leadership—and the threat of nuclear proliferation—are particularly perplexing issues. And given the distinctive nature of those who practice terrorism—their lack of geographic boundaries and their refusal to abide by the conventional rules of war—such a conflict surely would differ starkly from the last major clash of ideologies, the Cold War. In view of the unique qualities of terrorism, it is difficult to anticipate how the continued threat of terrorist acts will shape U.S. foreign policy. The randomness of terrorism confounds policy makers and other experts and prevents them from making accurate predictions and determining adequate modes of defense. Nonetheless, given the high stakes of another potential attack, the threat of terrorism—and the imperative to prevent it—clearly will remain a defining characteristic of U.S. foreign policy in the decades to come.

Summary

1. The Tools of U.S. Foreign Policy

The government officials who formulate U.S. foreign policy rely on diplomacy, by which nations conduct political negotiations with one another and settle disagreements. They also rely on economic policy to cajole other nations into enacting policies that the United States supports, and on military force, if needed, to force other countries to align with U.S. interests.

2. Who Decides? The Creators and Shapers of Foreign Policy

Because the Constitution grants important foreign policy-making powers to the president, the president along with the executive branch is the primary foreign policy maker in the United States. Congress also plays an important role in creating foreign policy, particularly through its decision making with respect to declaring war and appropriating funds. Interest groups, the media, and private individuals also influence the foreign policy process.

3. U.S. Foreign Policy in Historical Context

The conduct of foreign policy was at first influenced by a suspicion of foreign affairs. As the U.S. economy developed, government and business interests concentrated primarily on maximizing profits through international trade. In the 20th century, the balance of power system drew the United States into global conflict in World War I. Although the United States retreated into an isolationist position during the Great Depression, an alliance with the British and Japan's attack on the U.S. naval base at Pearl Harbor, Hawaii, precipitated U.S. entry into World War II.

4. The Postwar Era: The United States as Superpower

After the World War II, the United States and the Soviet Union emerged as competing superpowers locked in a Cold War of clashing ideologies. This rivalry defined U.S. foreign policy for half a century. During this period, international organizations were established that were charged with ensuring security and facilitating economic relations among nations. During the Cold War, the United States also attempted to curb the spread of communism on the Korean peninsula, in Cuba, and in Vietnam. President Richard Nixon initiated a period of détente; President Ronald Reagan outspent the Soviets and forced the collapse of the Soviet economy. The end of communism in the Soviet Union and Eastern Europe meant drastic changes in the context of international relations.

5. U.S. Foreign Policy after 9/11

With the terrorist attacks of September 11, 2001, a new era in U.S. foreign policy commenced, seeming to reflect acceptance of the theory that a clash of civilizations—warfare over cultural and religious differences—was inevitable. In espousing the tenets of the Bush Doctrine, administration officials promoted the strategy of preventive war. After 9/11, foreign policy officials pursued a program of regime change in both Afghanistan and Iraq, while also setting their sights on the regimes in Iran and North Korea. Though striking a different rhetorical tone, the Obama administration continued many of the Bush administration's foreign policy practices.

6. Future Challenges in American Foreign Policy

Among the greatest challenges for the United States in the foreign policy arena are the continued threats of terrorism and nuclear proliferation. Environmental challenges and the impact of technology will also serve as focal points in the future.

Key Terms

al-Qaeda 551
balance of power system 559
brinkmanship 564
Bush Doctrine 568
clash of civilizations thesis 568

Cold War 563
collective defense 559
collective security 559
containment 564
country desk 552
defense conversion 566
détente 565

deterrence 565
diplomacy 548
director of national intelligence (DNI) 553
domino theory 564
foreign service officers 548
globalism 551

For Review

1. What are the primary tools that policy makers use in the foreign policy process?

2. Why is the president the primary foreign policy maker in the United States? What tools do presidents have to assist them in creating foreign policy? Who are the other actors in foreign policy decision making?

3. How did the United States evolve from a nation that emphasized isolationism in its early years to internationalism in the post–World War II era? What factors spurred this transformation?

4. How did the Cold War between the United States and the Soviet Union affect U.S. foreign policy? How did it influence relations between the United States and other nations?

5. September 11, 2001, led to a significant shift in how the United States viewed itself and the world. What theories best explain how the United States now sees itself in the post-9/11 global context?

6. What specific, major challenges will U.S. foreign policy makers face in the years to come?

For Critical Thinking and Discussion

1. How have the 9/11 terrorist attacks changed the structure of the foreign policy-making apparatus in the executive branch?

2. How did World War II change the way the United States was perceived by other nations around the world? How did the war alter U.S. policy makers' perceptions of what the international order should look like?

3. In retrospect, was the theory of containment an accurate description of how the United States should have attempted to stem the tide of communism during the Cold War? Why or why not?

4. Does Samuel Huntington's clash of civilizations theory accurately reflect the current state of world affairs? Explain. What present-day realities are in keeping with Huntington's theory? What other realities defy it?

5. What additional challenges, beyond those we examined in the text, are likely to face the makers of U.S. foreign policy in the next decade?

MULTIPLE CHOICE: Choose the lettered item that answers the question correctly.

1. The conduct of international relations, particularly involving the negotiation of treaties and other agreements between countries, is called
   a. brinkmanship.
   b. diplomacy.
   c. counterintelligence.
   d. intermestics.

2. The policy emphasizing the responsibility of U.S. allies to provide for their own national defense and security, aimed at improving relations with the communist nations including the Soviet Union and China, is called
   a. the Kennedy Doctrine.
   b. the Nixon Doctrine.
   c. the Reagan Doctrine.
   d. the Clinton Doctrine.

3. The replacement of a country's government with another government by facilitating the deposing of its leader or leading political party is called
   a. regime change.
   b. bilateralism.
   c. brinkmanship.
   d. globalism.

4. The official operation of the U.S. government in each country that has diplomatic ties to the United States is called the
   a. American seat.
   b. nation's chair.
   c. country desk.
   d. capital consul.

5. Since 2005, the person responsible for coordinating and overseeing all the intelligence agencies within the executive branch has been
   a. the director of Homeland Security.
   b. the director of the Federal Bureau of Investigation.
   c. the director of the Central Intelligence Agency.
   d. the director of National Intelligence.

6. The law that limits presidential use of military forces to 60 days, with an automatic extension of 30 additional days if the president requests such an extension, is
   a. the Gulf of Tonkin Resolution.
   b. the War Powers Act.
   c. the Defense Authorization Act.
   d. the Executive Military Control Act.

7. An individual outside government who promotes his or her country's interests and thus helps to shape international perceptions of that nation is called a
   a. professional diplomat.
   b. public diplomat.
   c. foreign service officer.
   d. foreign advocate.

8. The influence of domestic interests on foreign policy is called
   a. globalism.
   b. domestic influence peddling.
   c. domestic engineering.
   d. intermestics.

9. A foreign policy characterized by a nation's unwillingness to participate in international affairs is called
   a. isolationism.
   b. interventionism.
   c. bilateralism.
   d. globalism.

10. A foreign policy characterized by a nation's willingness to participate and intervene in international situations, including another country's affairs, is called
    a. isolationism.
    b. interventionism.
    c. bilateralism.
    d. globalism.

FILL IN THE BLANKS

11. _____ are the diplomatic and consular staff at U.S. embassies abroad.

12. _____ is the international trade principle holding that the least restrictive trade conditions offered to any one national trading partner will be offered to every other nation in a trading network.

13. The interconnectedness between nations in contemporary times is called _____.

14. Nuclear, chemical, and biological weapons are known as _____.

15. The _____ is an organization created in 1995 to negotiate, implement, and enforce international trade agreements.

Answers: 1. b, 2. b, 3. a, 4. c, 5. d, 6. b, 7. b, 8. d, 9. a, 10. b, 11. Foreign service officers, 12. Normal trade relations status, 13. globalism, 14. weapons of mass destruction, or WMDs, 15. World Trade Organization.

Resources for Research AND Action

Internet Resources

Central Intelligence Agency
www.cia.gov This is the official website of the CIA. Its *World Factbook*, available online at this site, is an excellent resource for research on various nations. The site also hosts news and information, history, and career opportunities.

North Atlantic Treaty Organization
www.nato.int This site hosts an informative eLibrary as well as an impressive multimedia collection of documentation about NATO-related events and history.

State Department and Defense Department
www.state.gov and www.defense.gov These government sites offer a plethora of information from these two cabinet departments. Included are news and information, policy statements, career opportunities, virtual tours, and reports.

World Bank
www.worldbank.org This site explains the World Bank's policy priorities and offers data, research reports, and a wide variety of related international news.

Recommended Readings

Allison, Graham. *Nuclear Terrorism: The Ultimate Preventable Catastrophe.* New York: Times Books, 2004; and *The Essence of Decision: Explaining the Cuban Missile Crisis.* Boston: Little, Brown, 1971. This key scholar of U.S. foreign policy making uses the Cuban Missile Crisis as a model to explain foreign policy making. In his more recent work, he analyzes the foreign policy dilemma of nuclear terrorism.

Cameron, Fraser. *U.S. Foreign Policy after the Cold War.* New York: Routledge, 2002. This introduction to U.S. foreign policy looks at some aspects of U.S. foreign policy from the perspective of their domestic origins. Critical of the United States' unilateralism, Cameron also details relations between the United States and the European Union.

Coleman, Isobel, and Terra Lawson-Remer. New York: Council on Foreign Relations Press, 2013. *Pathways to Freedom.* This book offers a prescription on how the United States and other nations can foster the development of prosperous and stable democracies.

Huntington, Samuel P. *The Clash of Civilizations and the Remaking of World Order.* New York: Simon & Schuster, 1998. Huntington asserts that Western democracies are engaged in a clash of civilizations, particularly with Islamic societies.

Jervis, Robert. *American Foreign Policy in a New Era.* New York: Routledge, 2005. A noted foreign policy scholar explains the issues and influences on American foreign policy in today's international circumstances.

Keohane, Robert. *Neo-Realism and Its Critics.* New York: Columbia University Press, 1986. This classic work explains neorealism, a theory that emphasizes the power of state actors in international affairs.

Movies of Interest

Tinker Tailor Soldier Spy (2011)
Gary Oldman stars in this story of a Cold War veteran spy who is forced from semi-retirement to uncover a Soviet agent within MI6.

The Hurt Locker (2008)
This 2009 Oscar-winning film follows the story of a U.S. Army Explosive Ordnance Disposal (EOD) team during the war in Iraq.

The Good Shepherd (2006)
Directed by Robert De Niro and starring Matt Damon, Alec Baldwin, and Angelina Jolie, this film traces the creation of the CIA and its evolution through the Cold War.

The Killing Fields (1984)
Based on a true story, this film tells the story of an American journalist and his Cambodian guide during the vicious genocide by Cambodia's Khmer Rouge regime during the Vietnam War.

Dr. Strangelove or: How I Learned to Stop Worrying and Love the Bomb (1964)
This Stanley Kubrick film probes the dangers of the Cold War when an insane army general tries to start a nuclear war over the objections of political leaders and other generals.

The Mouse That Roared (1959)
This Peter Sellers comedy takes a satirical look at how the United States used foreign aid to ensure the support of allies. It features a fictional impoverished European nation that invades the United States with the goal of losing so that it can receive foreign aid.

The Declaration of Independence

In Congress, July 4, 1776

THE UNANIMOUS DECLARATION OF THE THIRTEEN UNITED STATES OF AMERICA

When in the Course of human Events, it becomes necessary for one People to dissolve the Political Bands which have connected them with another, and to assume, among the Powers of the Earth, the separate and equal Station to which the Laws of Nature and of Nature's God entitle them, a decent Respect to the Opinions of Mankind requires that they should declare the Causes which impel them to the Separation.

We hold these Truths to be self-evident, that all Men are created equal, that they are endowed, by their Creator, with certain unalienable Rights, that among these are Life, Liberty, and the Pursuit of Happiness.—That to secure these Rights, Governments are instituted among Men, deriving their just Powers from the Consent of the Governed, that whenever any Form of Government becomes destructive of these Ends, it is the Right of the People to alter or to abolish it, and to institute new Government, laying its Foundation on such Principles, and organizing its Powers in such Form, as to them shall seem most likely to effect their Safety and Happiness. Prudence, indeed, will dictate, that Governments long established, should not be changed for light and transient Causes; and accordingly all Experience hath shewn, that Mankind are more disposed to suffer, while Evils are sufferable, than to right themselves by abolishing the Forms to which they are accustomed. But when a long Train of Abuses and Usurpations, pursuing invariably the same Object, evinces a Design to reduce them under absolute Despotism, it is their Right, it is their Duty, to throw off such Government, and to provide new Guards for their future Security. Such has been the patient Sufferance of these Colonies; and such is now the Necessity which constrains them to alter their former Systems of Government. The History of the present King of Great-Britain is a History of repeated Injuries and Usurpations, all having in direct Object the Establishment of an absolute Tyranny over these States. To prove this, let Facts be submitted to a candid World.

He has refused his Assent to Laws, the most wholesome and necessary for the public Good.

He has forbidden his Governors to pass Laws of immediate and pressing Importance, unless suspended in their Operation till his Assent should be obtained; and when so suspended, he has utterly neglected to attend to them.

He has refused to pass other Laws for the Accommodation of large Districts of People, unless those People would relinquish the Right of Representation in the Legislature, a Right inestimable to them, and formidable to Tyranny only.

He has called together Legislative Bodies at Places unusual, uncomfortable, and distant from the Depository of their public Records, for the sole Purpose of fatiguing them into Compliance with his Measures.

He has dissolved Representative Houses repeatedly, for opposing with manly Firmness his Invasions on the Rights of the People.

He has refused for a long Time, after such Dissolutions, to cause others to be elected; whereby the Legislative Powers, incapable of Annihilation, have returned to the People at large for their exercise; the State remaining, in the mean Time, exposed to all the Dangers of Invasion from without, and Convulsions within.

He has endeavoured to prevent the Population of these States; for that Purpose obstructing the Laws for Naturalization of Foreigners; refusing to pass others to encourage their Migrations hither, and raising the Conditions of new Appropriations of Lands.

He has obstructed the Administration of Justice, by refusing his Assent to Laws for establishing Judiciary Powers.

He has made Judges dependent on his Will alone, for the Tenure of their Offices, and the Amount and Payment of their Salaries.

He has erected a Multitude of new Offices, and sent hither Swarms of Officers to harrass our People, and eat out their Substance.

He has kept among us, in Times of Peace, Standing Armies, without the Consent of our Legislatures.

He has affected to render the Military independent of and superior to the Civil Power.

He has combined with others to subject us to a Jurisdiction foreign to our Constitution, and unacknowledged by our Laws; giving his Assent to their Acts of pretended Legislation:

For quartering large Bodies of Armed Troops among us:

For protecting them, by a mock Trial, from Punishment for any Murders which they should commit on the Inhabitants of these States:

For cutting off our Trade with all Parts of the World:

For imposing Taxes on us without our Consent:

For depriving us, in many Cases, of the Benefits of Trial by Jury:

For transporting us beyond Seas to be tried for pretended Offences:

For abolishing the free System of English Laws in a neighbouring Province, establishing therein an arbitrary Government, and enlarging its Boundaries, so as to render it at once an Example and fit Instrument for introducing the same absolute Rule into these Colonies:

For taking away our Charters, abolishing our most valuable Laws, and altering fundamentally the Forms of our Governments:

For suspending our own Legislatures, and declaring themselves invested with Power to legislate for us in all Cases whatsoever.

He has abdicated Government here, by declaring us out of his Protection, and waging War against us.

He has plundered our Seas, ravaged our Coasts, burnt our Towns, and destroyed the Lives of our People.

He is, at this Time, transporting large Armies of foreign Mercenaries to complete the Works of Death, Desolation, and Tyranny, already begun with Circumstances of Cruelty and Perfidy, scarcely paralleled in the most barbarous Ages, and totally unworthy the Head of a civilized Nation.

He has constrained our fellow Citizens taken Captive on the high Seas to bear Arms against their Country, to become the Executioners of their Friends and Brethren, or to fall themselves by their Hands.

He has excited domestic Insurrections amongst us, and has endeavoured to bring on the Inhabitants of our Frontiers, the merciless Indian Savages, whose known Rule of Warfare, is an undistinguished Destruction, of all Ages, Sexes and Conditions.

In every Stage of these Oppressions we have Petitioned for Redress in the most humble Terms: Our repeated Petitions have been answered only by repeated Injury. A Prince, whose Character is thus marked by every Act which may define a Tyrant, is unfit to be the Ruler of a free People.

Nor have we been wanting in Attentions to our British Brethren. We have warned them, from Time to Time of Attempts by their Legislature to extend an unwarrantable Jurisdiction over us. We have reminded them of the Circumstances of our Emigration and Settlement here. We have appealed to their native Justice and Magnanimity, and we have conjured them by the Ties of our common Kindred to disavow these Usurpations, which would inevitably interrupt our Connections and Correspondence. They too have been deaf to the Voice of Justice and of Consanguinity. We must, therefore, acquiesce in the Necessity, which denounces our Separation, and hold them, as we hold the Rest of Mankind, Enemies in War, in Peace Friends.

We, therefore, the Representatives of the UNITED STATES OF AMERICA, in General Congress Assembled, appealing to the Supreme Judge of the World for the Rectitude of our Intentions, do, in the Name, and by Authority of the good People of these Colonies, solemnly Publish and Declare, That these United Colonies are, and of Right ought to be, Free and Independent States; that they are absolved from all Allegiance to the British Crown, and that all political Connection between them and the State of Great-Britain, is and ought to be totally dissolved; and that as Free and Independent States, they have full Power to levy War, conclude Peace, contract Alliances, establish Commerce, and to do all other Acts and Things which Independent States may of Right do. And for the Support of this Declaration, with a firm Reliance on the Protection of Divine Providence, we mutually pledge to each other our Lives, our Fortunes, and our sacred Honour.

John Hancock.

NEW-HAMPSHIRE
Josiah Bartlett
William Whipple
Matthew Thornton

MASSACHUSETTS BAY
Samuel Adams
John Adams
Robert Treat Paine
Elbridge Gerry

RHODE ISLAND
Stephen Hopkins
William Ellery

CONNECTICUT
Roger Sherman
Samuel Huntington
William Williams
Oliver Wolcott

NEW YORK
William Floyd
Philip Livingston
Francis Lewis
Lewis Morris

NEW JERSEY
Richard Stockton
John Witherspoon
Francis Hopkinson
John Hart
Abraham Clark

PENNSYLVANIA
Robert Morris
Benjamin Rush
Benjamin Franklin
John Morton
George Clymer
James Smith
George Taylor
James Wilson
George Ross

DELAWARE
Caesar Rodney
George Read
Thomas McKean

MARYLAND
Samuel Chase
William Paca
Thomas Stone
Charles Carroll

VIRGINIA
George Wythe
Richard Henry Lee
Thomas Jefferson
Benjamin Harrison
Thomas Nelson, Jr.
Francis Lightfoot Lee
Carter Braxton

NORTH CAROLINA
William Hooper
Joseph Hewes
John Penn

SOUTH CAROLINA
Edward Rutledge
Thomas Heyward, Jr.
Thomas Lynch, Jr.
Arthur Middleton

GEORGIA
Button Gwinnett
Lyman Hall
George Walton

Federalist No. 10

November 22, 1787

JAMES MADISON

TO THE PEOPLE OF THE STATE OF NEW YORK:

Among the numerous advantages promised by a well constructed Union, none deserves to be more accurately developed than its tendency to break and control the violence of faction. The friend of popular governments never finds himself so much alarmed for their character and fate, as when he contemplates their propensity to this dangerous vice. He will not fail, therefore, to set a due value on any plan which, without violating the principles to which he is attached, provides a proper cure for it. The instability, injustice, and confusion introduced into the public councils, have, in truth, been the mortal diseases under which popular governments have everywhere perished; as they continue to be the favorite and fruitful topics from which the adversaries to liberty derive their most specious declamations. The valuable improvements made by the American constitutions on the popular models, both ancient and modern, cannot certainly be too much admired; but it would be an unwarrantable partiality, to contend that they have as effectually obviated the danger on this side, as was wished and expected. Complaints are everywhere heard from our most considerate and virtuous citizens, equally the friends of public and private faith, and of public and personal liberty, that our governments are too unstable, that the public good is disregarded in the conflicts of rival parties, and that measures are too often decided, not according to the rules of justice and the rights of the minor party, but by the superior force of an interested and overbearing majority. However anxiously we may wish that these complaints had no foundation, the evidence, of known facts will not permit us to deny that they are in some degree true. It will be found, indeed, on a candid review of our situation, that some of the distresses under which we labor have been erroneously charged on the operation of our governments; but it will be found, at the same time, that other causes will not alone account for many of our heaviest misfortunes; and, particularly, for that prevailing and increasing distrust of public engagements, and alarm for private rights, which are echoed from one end of the continent to the other. These must be chiefly, if not wholly, effects of the unsteadiness and injustice with which a factious spirit has tainted our public administrations.

By a faction, I understand a number of citizens, whether amounting to a majority or a minority of the whole, who are united and actuated by some common impulse of passion, or of interest, adversed to the rights of other citizens, or to the permanent and aggregate interests of the community.

There are two methods of curing the mischiefs of faction: the one, by removing its causes; the other, by controlling its effects.

There are again two methods of removing the causes of faction: the one, by destroying the liberty which is essential to its existence; the other, by giving to every citizen the same opinions, the same passions, and the same interests.

It could never be more truly said than of the first remedy, that it was worse than the disease. Liberty is to faction what air is to fire, an aliment without which it instantly expires. But it could not be less folly to abolish liberty, which is essential to political life, because it nourishes faction, than it would be to wish the annihilation of air, which is essential to animal life, because it imparts to fire its destructive agency.

The second expedient is as impracticable as the first would be unwise. As long as the reason of man continues fallible, and he is at liberty to exercise it, different opinions will be formed. As long as the connection subsists between his reason and his self-love, his opinions and his passions will have a reciprocal influence on each other; and the former will be objects to which the latter will attach themselves. The diversity in the faculties of men, from which the rights of property originate, is not less an insuperable obstacle to a uniformity of interests. The protection of these faculties is the first object of government. From the protection of different and unequal faculties of acquiring property, the possession of different degrees and kinds of property immediately results; and from the influence of these on the sentiments and views of the respective proprietors, ensues a division of the society into different interests and parties.

The latent causes of faction are thus sown in the nature of man; and we see them everywhere brought into different degrees of activity, according to the different circumstances of civil society. A zeal for different opinions concerning religion, concerning government, and many other points, as well of speculation as of practice; an attachment to different leaders ambitiously contending for pre-eminence and power; or to persons of other descriptions whose fortunes have been interesting to the human passions, have, in turn, divided mankind into parties, inflamed them with mutual animosity, and rendered them much more disposed to vex and oppress each other than to co-operate for their common good. So strong is this propensity of mankind to fall into mutual animosities, that where no substantial occasion presents itself, the most frivolous and fanciful distinctions have been sufficient to kindle their unfriendly passions and excite their most violent conflicts. But the most common and durable source of factions has been the various and unequal distribution of property. Those who hold and those who are without property have ever formed distinct interests in society. Those who are creditors, and those who are debtors, fall under a like discrimination. A landed interest, a manufacturing interest, a mercantile interest, a moneyed interest, with many lesser interests, grow up of necessity in civilized nations, and divide them into different classes, actuated by different sentiments and views. The regulation of these various and interfering interests forms the principal task of modern legislation, and involves the spirit of party and faction in the necessary and ordinary operations of the government.

No man is allowed to be a judge in his own cause, because his interest would certainly bias his judgment, and, not improbably, corrupt his integrity. With equal, nay with greater reason, a body of men are unfit to be both judges and parties at the same time; yet what are many of the most important acts of legislation, but so many judicial determinations, not indeed concerning the rights of single persons, but concerning the rights of large bodies of citizens? And what are the different classes of legislators but advocates and parties to the causes which they determine? Is a law proposed concerning private debts? It is a question to which the creditors are parties on one side and the debtors on the other. Justice ought to hold the balance between them. Yet the parties are, and must be, themselves the judges; and the most numerous party, or, in other words, the most powerful faction must be expected to prevail. Shall domestic manufactures be encouraged, and in what degree, by restrictions on foreign manufactures? are questions which would be differently decided by the landed and the manufacturing classes, and probably by neither with a sole regard to justice and the public good. The apportionment of taxes on the various descriptions of property is an act which seems to require the most exact impartiality; yet there is, perhaps, no legislative act in which greater opportunity and temptation are given to a predominant party to trample on the rules of justice. Every shilling with which they overburden the inferior number, is a shilling saved to their own pockets.

It is in vain to say that enlightened statesmen will be able to adjust these clashing interests, and render them all subservient to the public good. Enlightened statesmen will not always be at the helm. Nor, in many cases, can such an adjustment be made at all without taking into view indirect and remote considerations, which will rarely prevail over the immediate interest which one party may find in disregarding the rights of another or the good of the whole.

The inference to which we are brought is, that the causes of faction cannot be removed, and that relief is only to be sought in the means of controlling its *effects*.

If a faction consists of less than a majority, relief is supplied by the republican principle, which enables the majority to defeat its sinister views by regular vote. It may clog the administration, it may convulse the society; but it will be unable to execute and mask its violence under the forms of the Constitution. When a majority is included in a faction, the form of popular government, on the other hand, enables it to sacrifice to its ruling passion or interest both the public good and the rights of other citizens. To secure the public good and private rights against the danger of such a faction, and at the same time to preserve the spirit and the form of popular government, is then the great object to which our inquiries are directed. Let me add that it is the great desideratum by which this form of government can be rescued from the opprobrium under which it has so long labored, and be recommended to the esteem and adoption of mankind.

By what means is this object attainable? Evidently by one of two only. Either the existence of the same passion or interest in a majority at the same time must be prevented, or the majority, having such coexistent passion or interest, must be rendered, by their number and local situation, unable to concert and carry into effect schemes of oppression. If the impulse and the opportunity be suffered to coincide, we well know

that neither moral nor religious motives can be relied on as an adequate control. They are not found to be such on the injustice and violence of individuals, and lose their efficacy in proportion to the number combined together, that is, in proportion as their efficacy becomes needful.

From this view of the subject it may be concluded that a pure democracy, by which I mean a society consisting of a small number of citizens, who assemble and administer the government in person, can admit of no cure for the mischiefs of faction. A common passion or interest will, in almost every case, be felt by a majority of the whole; a communication and concert result from the form of government itself; and there is nothing to check the inducements to sacrifice the weaker party or an obnoxious individual. Hence it is that such democracies have ever been spectacles of turbulence and contention; have ever been found incompatible with personal security or the rights of property; and have in general been as short in their lives as they have been violent in their deaths. Theoretic politicians, who have patronized this species of government, have erroneously supposed that by reducing mankind to a perfect equality in their political rights, they would, at the same time, be perfectly equalized and assimilated in their possessions, their opinions, and their passions.

A republic, by which I mean a government in which the scheme of representation takes place, opens a different prospect, and promises the cure for which we are seeking. Let us examine the points in which it varies from pure democracy, and we shall comprehend both the nature of the cure and the efficacy which it must derive from the Union.

The two great points of difference between a democracy and a republic are: first, the delegation of the government, in the latter, to a small number of citizens elected by the rest; secondly, the greater number of citizens, and greater sphere of country, over which the latter may be extended.

The effect of the first difference is, on the one hand, to refine and enlarge the public views, by passing them through the medium of a chosen body of citizens, whose wisdom may best discern the true interest of their country, and whose patriotism and love of justice will be least likely to sacrifice it to temporary or partial considerations. Under such a regulation, it may well happen that the public voice, pronounced by the representatives of the people, will be more consonant to the public good than if pronounced by the people themselves, convened for the purpose. On the other hand, the effect may be inverted. Men of factious tempers, of local prejudices, or of sinister designs, may, by intrigue, by corruption, or by other means, first obtain the suffrages, and then betray the interests, of the people. The question resulting is, whether small or extensive republics are more favorable to the election of proper guardians of the public weal; and it is clearly decided in favor of the latter by two obvious considerations:

In the first place, it is to be remarked that, however small the republic may be, the representatives must be raised to a certain number, in order to guard against the cabals of a few; and that, however large it may be, they must be limited to a certain number, in order to guard against the confusion of a multitude. Hence, the number of representatives in the two cases not being in proportion to that of the two constituents, and being proportionally greater in the small republic, it follows that, if the proportion of fit characters be not less in the large than in the small republic, the former will present a greater option, and consequently a greater probability of a fit choice.

In the next place, as each representative will be chosen by a greater number of citizens in the large than in the small republic, it will be more difficult for unworthy candidates to practice with success the vicious arts by which elections are too often carried; and the suffrages of the people being more free, will be more likely to centre in men who possess the most attractive merit and the most diffusive and established characters.

It must be confessed that in this, as in most other cases, there is a mean, on both sides of which inconveniences will be found to lie. By enlarging too much the number of electors, you render the representatives too little acquainted with all their local circumstances and lesser interests; as by reducing it too much, you render him unduly attached to these, and too little fit to comprehend and pursue great and national objects. The federal Constitution forms a happy combination in this respect; the great and aggregate interests being referred to the national, the local and particular to the State legislatures.

The other point of difference is, the greater number of citizens and extent of territory which may be brought within the compass of republican than of democratic government; and it is this circumstance principally which renders factious combinations less to be dreaded in the former than in the latter. The smaller the society, the fewer probably will be the distinct parties and interests composing it; the fewer the distinct parties and interests, the more frequently will a majority be found of the same party; and the smaller the number of individuals composing a majority, and the smaller the compass within which they are placed, the more easily will they concert and execute their plans of oppression. Extend the sphere, and you take in a greater variety of parties and interests; you make it less probable that a majority of the whole will have a common motive to invade the rights of other citizens; or if such a common motive exists, it will be more difficult for all who feel it to discover their own strength, and to act in unison with each other. Besides other impediments, it may be remarked that, where there is a consciousness of unjust or dishonorable purposes, communication is always checked by distrust in proportion to the number whose concurrence is necessary.

Hence, it clearly appears, that the same advantage which a republic has over a democracy, in controlling the effects of faction, is enjoyed by a large over a small republic,—is enjoyed by the Union over the States composing it. Does the advantage consist in the substitution of representatives whose enlightened views and virtuous sentiments render them superior to local prejudices and schemes of injustice? It will not be denied that the representation of the Union will be most likely to possess these requisite endowments. Does it consist in the greater security afforded by a greater variety of parties, against the event of any one party being able to outnumber and oppress the rest? In an equal degree does the increased variety of parties comprised within the Union, increase this security? Does it, in fine, consist in the greater obstacles opposed to the concert and accomplishment of the secret wishes of an unjust and interested majority? Here, again, the extent of the Union gives it the most palpable advantage.

The influence of factious leaders may kindle a flame within their particular States, but will be unable to spread a general conflagration through the other States. A religious sect may degenerate into a political faction in a part of the Confederacy; but the variety of sects dispersed over the entire face of it must secure the national councils against any danger from that source. A rage for paper money, for an abolition of debts, for an equal division of property, or for any other improper or wicked project, will be less apt to pervade the whole body of the Union than a particular member of it; in the same proportion as such a malady is more likely to taint a particular county or district, than an entire State.

In the extent and proper structure of the Union, therefore, we behold a republican remedy for the diseases most incident to republican government. And according to the degree of pleasure and pride we feel in being republicans, ought to be our zeal in cherishing the spirit and supporting the character of Federalists.

Publius

Federalist No. 51

February 6, 1788

JAMES MADISON

TO THE PEOPLE OF THE STATE OF NEW YORK:

To what expedient, then, shall we finally resort, for maintaining in practice the necessary partition of power among the several departments, as laid down in the Constitution? The only answer that can be given is, that as all these exterior provisions are found to be inadequate, the defect must be supplied, by so contriving the interior structure of the government as that its several constituent parts may, by their mutual relations, be the means of keeping each other in their proper places. Without presuming to undertake a full development of this important idea, I will hazard a few general observations, which may perhaps place it in a clearer light, and enable us to form a more correct judgment of the principles and structure of the government planned by the convention.

In order to lay a due foundation for that separate and distinct exercise of the different powers of government, which to a certain extent is admitted on all hands to be essential to the preservation of liberty, it is evident that each department should have a will of its own; and consequently should be so constituted that the members of each should have as little agency as possible in the appointment of the members of the others. Were this principle rigorously adhered to, it would require that all the appointments for the supreme executive, legislative, and judiciary magistracies should be drawn from the same fountain of authority, the people, through channels having no communication whatever with one another. Perhaps such a plan of constructing the several departments would be less difficult in practice than it may in contemplation appear. Some difficulties, however, and some additional expense would attend the execution of it. Some deviations, therefore, from the principle must be admitted. In the constitution of the judiciary department in particular, it might be inexpedient to insist rigorously on the principle: first, because peculiar qualifications being essential in the members, the primary consideration ought to be to select that mode of choice which best secures these qualifications; secondly, because the permanent tenure by which the appointments are held in that department, must soon destroy all sense of dependence on the authority conferring them.

It is equally evident, that the members of each department should be as little dependent as possible on those of the others, for the emoluments annexed to their offices. Were the executive magistrate, or the judges, not independent of the legislature in this particular, their independence in every other would be merely nominal.

But the great security against a gradual concentration of the several powers in the same department, consists in giving to those who administer each department the necessary constitutional means and personal motives to resist encroachments of the others. The provision for defense must in this, as in all other cases, be made commensurate to the danger of attack. Ambition must be made to counteract ambition. The interest of the man must be connected with the constitutional rights of the place. It may be a reflection on human nature, that such devices should be necessary to control the abuses of government. But what is government itself, but the greatest of all reflections on human nature? If men were angels, no government would be necessary. If angels were to govern men, neither external nor internal controls on government would be necessary. In framing a government which is to be administered by men over men, the great difficulty lies in this: you must first enable the government to control the governed; and in the next place oblige it to control itself. A dependence on the people is, no doubt, the primary control on the government; but experience has taught mankind the necessity of auxiliary precautions.

This policy of supplying, by opposite and rival interests, the defect of better motives, might be traced through the whole system of human affairs, private as well as public. We see it particularly displayed in all the subordinate distributions of power, where the constant aim is to divide and arrange the several offices in such a manner as that each may be a check on the other—that the private interest of every individual may be a sentinel over the public rights. These inventions of prudence cannot be less requisite in the distribution of the supreme powers of the State.

But it is not possible to give to each department an equal power of self-defense. In republican government, the legislative authority necessarily predominates. The remedy for this inconveniency is to divide the legislature into different branches; and to render them, by different modes of election and different principles of action, as little connected with each other as the nature of their common functions and their common dependence on the society will admit. It may even be necessary to guard against dangerous encroachments by still further precautions. As the weight of the legislative authority requires that it should be thus divided, the weakness of the executive may require, on the other hand, that it should be fortified. An absolute negative on the legislature appears, at first view, to be the natural defense with which the executive magistrate should be armed. But perhaps it would be neither altogether safe nor alone sufficient. On ordinary occasions it might not be exerted with the requisite firmness, and on extraordinary occasions it might be perfidiously abused. May not this defect of an absolute negative be supplied by some qualified connection between this weaker department and the weaker branch of the stronger department, by which the latter may be led to support the constitutional rights of the former, without being too much detached from the rights of its own department?

If the principles on which these observations are founded be just, as I persuade myself they are, and they be applied as a criterion to the several State constitutions, and to the federal Constitution it will be found that if the latter does not perfectly correspond with them, the former are infinitely less able to bear such a test.

There are, moreover, two considerations particularly applicable to the federal system of America, which place that system in a very interesting point of view.

First. In a single republic, all the power surrendered by the people is submitted to the administration of a single government; and the usurpations are guarded against by a division of the government into distinct and separate departments. In the compound republic of America, the power surrendered by the people is first divided between two distinct governments, and then the portion allotted to each subdivided among distinct and separate departments. Hence a double security arises to the rights of the people. The different governments will control each other, at the same time that each will be controlled by itself.

Second. It is of great importance in a republic not only to guard the society against the oppression of its rulers, but to guard one part of the society against the injustice of the other part. Different interests necessarily exist in different classes of citizens. If a majority be united by a common interest, the rights of the minority will be insecure. There are but two methods of providing against this evil: the one by creating a will in the community independent of the majority—that is, of the society itself; the other, by comprehending in the society so many separate descriptions of citizens as will render an unjust combination of a majority of the whole very improbable, if not impracticable. The first method prevails in all governments possessing an hereditary or self-appointed authority. This, at best, is but a precarious security; because a power independent of the society may as well espouse the unjust views of the major, as the rightful interests of the minor party, and may possibly be turned against both parties. The second method will be exemplified in the federal republic of the United States. Whilst all authority in it will be derived from and dependent on the society, the society itself will be broken into so many parts, interests, and classes of citizens, that the rights of individuals, or of the minority, will be in little danger from interested combinations of the majority. In a free government the security for civil rights must be the same as that for religious rights. It consists in the one case in the multiplicity of interests, and in the other in the multiplicity of sects. The degree of security in both cases will depend on the number of interests and sects; and this may be presumed to depend on the extent of country and number of people comprehended under the same government. This view of the subject must particularly recommend a proper federal system to all the sincere and considerate friends of republican government, since it shows that in exact proportion as the territory of the Union may be formed into more circumscribed Confederacies, or States oppressive combinations of a majority will be facilitated: the best security, under the republican forms, for the rights of every class of citizens, will be diminished: and consequently the stability and independence of some member of the government, the only other security, must be proportionately increased. Justice is the end of government. It is the end of civil society. It ever has been and ever will be pursued until it be obtained, or until liberty be lost in the pursuit. In a society under the forms of which the stronger faction can readily unite and oppress the weaker, anarchy may as truly be said to reign as in a state of nature, where the weaker individual is not secured against the violence of the stronger; and as, in the latter state, even the stronger individuals are prompted, by the uncertainty of their condition, to submit to a government which may protect the weak as well as themselves; so, in the former state, will the more powerful factions or parties be gradually induced, by a like motive, to wish for a government which will protect all parties, the weaker as well as the more powerful. It can be little doubted that if the State of Rhode Island was separated from the Confederacy and left to itself, the insecurity of rights under the popular form of government within such narrow limits would be displayed by such reiterated oppressions of factious majorities that some power altogether independent of the people would soon be called for by the voice of the very factions whose misrule had proved the necessity of it. In the extended republic of the United States, and among the great variety of interests, parties, and sects which it embraces, a coalition of a majority of the whole society could seldom take place on any other principles than those of justice and the general good; whilst there being thus less danger to a minor from the will of a major party, there must be less pretext, also, to provide for the security of the former, by introducing into the government a will not dependent on the latter, or, in other words, a will independent of the society itself. It is no less certain than it is important, notwithstanding the contrary opinions which have been entertained, that the larger the society, provided it lie within a practical sphere, the more duly capable it will be of self-government. And happily for the *republican cause,* the practicable sphere may be carried to a very great extent, by a judicious modification and mixture of the *federal principle.*

Publius

The Declaration of Sentiments

Seneca Falls Conference, 1848

When, in the course of human events, it becomes necessary for one portion of the family of man to assume among the people of the earth a position different from that which they have hitherto occupied, but one to which the laws of nature and of nature's God entitle them, a decent respect to the opinions of mankind requires that they should declare the causes that impel them to such a course.

We hold these truths to be self-evident: that all men and women are created equal; that they are endowed by their Creator with certain inalienable rights; that among these are life, liberty, and the pursuit of happiness; that to secure these rights governments are instituted, deriving their just powers from the consent of the governed. Whenever any form of government becomes destructive of these ends, it is the right of those who suffer from it to refuse allegiance to it, and to insist upon the institution of a new government, laying its foundation on such principles, and organizing its powers in such form, as to them shall seem most likely to effect their safety and happiness. Prudence, indeed, will dictate that governments long established should not be changed for light and transient causes; and accordingly all experience hath shown that mankind are more disposed to suffer, while evils are sufferable, than to right themselves by abolishing the forms to which they are accustomed. But when a long train of abuses and usurpations, pursuing invariably the same object, evinces a design to reduce them under absolute despotism, it is their duty to throw off such government, and to provide new guards for their future security. Such has been the patient sufferance of the women under this government, and such is now the necessity which constrains them to demand the equal station to which they are entitled.

The history of mankind is a history of repeated injuries and usurpations on the part of man toward woman, having in direct object the establishment of an absolute tyranny over her. To prove this, let facts be submitted to a candid world.

He has never permitted her to exercise her inalienable right to the elective franchise.

He has compelled her to submit to laws, in the formation of which she had no voice.

He has withheld from her rights which are given to the most ignorant and degraded men—both natives and foreigners.

Having deprived her of this first right of a citizen, the elective franchise, thereby leaving her without representation in the halls of legislation, he has oppressed her on all sides.

He has made her, if married, in the eye of the law, civilly dead.

He has taken from her all right in property, even to the wages she earns.

He has made her, morally, an irresponsible being, as she can commit many crimes with impunity, provided they be done in the presence of her husband. In the covenant of marriage, she is compelled to promise obedience to her husband, he becoming, to all intents and purposes, her master—the law giving him power to deprive her of her liberty, and to administer chastisement.

He has so framed the laws of divorce, as to what shall be the proper causes, and in case of separation, to whom the guardianship of the children shall be given, as to be wholly regardless of the happiness of women—the law, in all cases, going upon a false supposition of the supremacy of man, and giving all power into his hands.

After depriving her of all rights as a married woman, if single, and the owner of property, he has taxed her to support a government which recognizes her only when her property can be made profitable to it.

He has monopolized nearly all the profitable employments, and from those she is permitted to follow, she receives but a scanty remuneration. He closes against her all the avenues to wealth and distinction which he considers most honorable to himself. As a teacher of theology, medicine, or law, she is not known.

He has denied her the facilities for obtaining a thorough education, all colleges being closed against her.

He allows her in church, as well as state, but a subordinate position, claiming apostolic authority for her exclusion from the ministry, and, with some exceptions, from any public participation in the affairs of the church.

He has created a false public sentiment by giving to the world a different code of morals for men and women, by which moral delinquencies which exclude women from society, are not only tolerated, but deemed of little account in man.

He has usurped the prerogative of Jehovah himself, claiming it as his right to assign for her a sphere of action, when that belongs to her conscience and to her God.

He has endeavored, in every way that he could, to destroy her confidence in her own powers, to lessen her self-respect, and to make her willing to lead a dependent and abject life.

Now, in view of this entire disfranchisement of one-half the people of this country, their social and religious degradation—in view of the unjust laws above mentioned, and because women do feel themselves aggrieved, oppressed, and fraudulently deprived of their most sacred rights, we insist that they have immediate admission to all the rights and privileges which belong to them as citizens of the United States.

In entering upon the great work before us, we anticipate no small amount of misconception, misrepresentation, and ridicule; but we shall use every instrumentality within our power to effect our object. We shall employ agents, circulate tracts, petition the State and national Legislatures, and endeavor to enlist the pulpit and the press in our behalf. We hope this Convention will be followed by a series of Conventions, embracing every part of the country.

Firmly relying upon the final triumph of the Right and the True, we do this day affix our signatures to this declaration.

Harriet Cady Eaton	*Sarah R. Woods*	*Joel Bunker*
Elizabeth M'Clintock	*Lydia Gild*	*Isaac Van Tassel*
Mary M'Clintock	*Sarah Hoffman*	*Thomas Dell*
Margaret Pryor	*Elizabeth Leslie*	*E. W. Capron*
Eunice Newton Foote	*Martha Ridley*	*Stephen Shear*
Margaret Schooley	*Rachel D. Bonnel*	*Henry Hatley*
Catherine F. Stebbins	*Betsey Tewksbury*	*Amy Post*
Mary Ann Frink	*Rhoda Palmer*	*Frederick Douglass*
Lydia Mount	*Margaret Jenkins*	*Richard P. Hunt*
Delia Matthews	*Cynthia Fuller*	*Samuel D. Tillman*
Catharine C. Paine	*Mary Martin*	*Justin Williams*
Mary H. Hallowell	*P. A. Culvert*	*Elisha Foote*
Sarah Hallowell	*Susan R. Doty*	*Henry W. Seymour*
Catharine Shaw	*Rebecca Race*	*David Salding*
Deborah Scott	*Martha Coffin Wright*	*William G. Barker*
Mary Gilbert	*Jane C. Hunt*	*Elias J. Doty*
Sophrone Taylor	*Sarah A. Mosher*	*John Jones*
Cynthia Davis	*Mary E. Vail*	*William S. Dell*
Hannah Plant	*Lucy Spaulding*	*William Burroughs*
Lucy Jones	*Lavinia Latham*	*Azaliah Schooley*
Sarah Whitney	*Sarah Smith*	*Robert Smalldridge*
Elizabeth Conklin	*Eliza Martin*	*Jacob Matthews*
Lucretia Coffin Mott	*Maria E. Wilbur*	*Charles L. Hoskins*
Mary Ann M'Clintock	*Elizabeth D. Smith*	*Thomas M'Clintock*
Susan Quinn	*Caroline Barker*	*Saron Phillips*
Mary S. Mirror	*Ann Porter*	*Jacob Chamberlain*
Phebe King	*Experience Gibbs*	*Johnathan Metcalf*
Julia Ann Drake	*Antoinette E. Segur*	*Nathan J. Milliken*
Charlotte Woodard	*Hannah J. Latham*	*S. E. Woodworth*
Martha Underhill	*Sarah Sisson*	*Edward F. Underhill*
Dorothy Matthews	*Malvina Seymour*	*George W. Pryor*
Eunice Baker	*Phebe Mosher*	

A

absentee voting The casting of a ballot in advance by mail in situations where illness, travel, or other circumstances prevent voters from voting in their precincts.

administrative adjudication The process by which agencies resolve disputes over the implementation of their administrative rules.

administrative discretion The authority delegated to bureaucrats to use their expertise and judgment when determining how to implement public policy.

administrative rule making The process by which an independent commission or agency fills in the details of a vague law by formulating, proposing, and approving rules, regulations, and standards that will be enforced to implement the policy.

adversarial judicial system A judicial system in which two parties in a legal dispute each present its case and the court must determine which side wins the dispute and which loses.

advice and consent The Senate's authority to approve or reject the president's top appointments and negotiated treaties.

affirmative action In the employment arena, intentional efforts to recruit, hire, train, and promote underutilized categories of workers (women and minority men); in higher education, intentional efforts to diversify the student body.

agency review Part of the committee or subcommittee process of considering a bill, wherein committee members ask executive agencies that would administer the law for written comments on the measure.

agenda setting The determination by Congress of which public issues the government should consider for legislation.

agents of socialization The individuals, organizations, and institutions that facilitate the acquisition of political views.

al-Qaeda A radical international Islamic fundamentalist terror organization.

American dream The belief that in the United States hard work and persistence will reap a financially secure, happy, and healthy life, with upward mobility.

amicus curiae **brief ("friend of the court" brief)** A legal brief, filed by an individual or a group that is not a party in the case; it is written to influence the Court's decision.

Anti-Federalists Individuals who opposed ratification of the Constitution because they were deeply suspicious of the powers it gave to the national government and of the impact those powers would have on states' authority and individual freedoms.

appellate courts Courts with authority to review cases heard by other courts to correct errors in the interpretation or application of law.

appellate jurisdiction Judicial authority to review the interpretation and application of the law in previous decisions reached by another court in a case.

appropriation law A law that gives bureaucracies and other government entities the legal authority to spend money.

approval ratings The percentage of survey respondents who say that they "approve" or "strongly approve" of the way the president is doing his job.

articles of impeachment Charges against the president during an impeachment.

associate justice title of the eight Supreme Court justices who are not the chief justice.

attentive public The segment of voters who pay careful attention to political issues.

attitudinal model Judicial decision-making model that claims judicial decision making is guided by policy and ideological preferences of individual judges.

Australian ballot A secret ballot prepared by the government, distributed to all eligible voters, and, when balloting is completed, counted by government officials in an unbiased fashion, without corruption or regard to individual preferences.

authoritarianism System of government in which the government holds strong powers but is checked by some forces.

authorization law A law that provides the plan of action to address a given societal concern and identifies the executive branch unit that will put the plan into effect.

B

bad tendency test A standard extended in the 1925 case *Gitlow v. New York* whereby any speech that has the tendency to incite crime or disturb the public peace can be silenced.

balance of power system A system of international alliances that, in theory, would balance the power of one group of nations against the power of another group and thus discourage war.

balanced budget A budget in which the government's expenditures are equal to or less than its revenues.

balanced ticket The selection of a running mate who brings diversity of ideology, geographic region, age, gender, race, or ethnicity to the slate.

ballot measure A proposed piece of legislation, a constitutional amendment, or some other policy proposal placed on the Election Day ballot for voters to approve or reject.

bandwidth The amount of data that can travel through a network in a given time period.

bench memo Written by a justice's law clerk, a summary of the case, outlining relevant facts and issues presented in the case documents and briefs, that may also suggest questions to be asked during oral arguments.

bench trial A trial in which the judge who presides over the trial decides on guilt or liability.

beyond a reasonable doubt The standard of proof the government must meet in criminal cases; the government must convince the judge or the jury that there is no reasonable doubt that the defendant committed the crime.

bicameral legislature Legislature comprising two parts, called *chambers.*

bill A proposed piece of legislation.

Bill of Rights The first 10 amendments to the Constitution, which were ratified in 1791, constituting an enumeration of the individual liberties with which the government is forbidden to interfere.

Black Codes Laws passed immediately after the Civil War by the confederate states that limited the rights of "freemen" (people formerly enslaved).

block grant A grant-in-aid for a broadly defined policy area, whose funding amount is typically based on a formula.

blogosphere The community of bloggers.

brinkmanship The Cold War–era practice of fooling the enemy by going to the edge (the brink), even if the party using the brinkmanship strategy had no intention of following through.

Brown v. Board of Education of Topeka This 1954 Supreme Court decision ruled that segregated schools violated the equal protection clause of the Fourteenth Amendment.

budget authority The authority provided by law for agencies to spend government funds.

budget deficit More money spent than collected through revenues.

budget reconciliation The annual process of rewriting authorization legislation to comply with the expenditure ceiling and revenue floor of the concurrent budget resolution for the upcoming fiscal year.

budget surplus Money left over after all expenses are paid.

bureaucracy The collection of all national executive branch organizations.

bureaucratic structure A large organization with the following features: a division of labor, specialization of job tasks, hiring systems based on worker competency, hierarchy with a vertical chain of command, and standard operating procedures.

bureaucrats People employed in a government executive branch unit to implement public policy; public administrators; public servants.

Bush Doctrine The argument, articulated by President George W. Bush, that unilateral action directly targeted at an enemy is both justifiable and feasible.

business regulation Government rules, regulations, and standards directed at protecting competition in the marketplace.

C

cabinet The group of experts chosen by the president to serve as advisers on running the country.

campaign consultant A paid professional who specializes in the overall management of political campaigns or an aspect of campaigns.

campaign manager A professional whose duties comprise a variety of strategic and managerial tasks, from fund-raising to staffing a campaign.

campaign strategy The blueprint for the campaign, including a budget and fund-raising plan, an advertising strategy, and a staffing plan.

candidate committees Organizations that candidates form to support their individual election.

candidate-centered campaign A campaign in which the individual seeking election, rather than an entire party slate, is the focus.

capital budget A budget that accounts for the costs and revenues for expensive building and purchasing projects from which citizens will

benefit for many years and for which governments can borrow money.

capitalism An economic system in which the means of producing wealth are privately owned and operated to produce profits.

casework Personal work by a member of Congress on behalf of a constituent or group of constituents, typically aimed at getting the government to do something the constituent wants done.

cash transfer The direct provision of cash (in forms including checks, debit cards, and tax breaks) to eligible individuals or to providers of goods or services to eligible individuals.

categorical formula grant A grant-in-aid for a narrowly defined purpose, whose dollar value is based on a formula.

categorical project grant A grant-in-aid for a narrowly defined purpose for which governments compete with each other by proposing specific projects.

caucus A meeting of party members held to select delegates to the national convention.

centralized federalism Intergovernmental relations in which the national government imposes its policy preferences on state and local governments.

cert memo Description of the facts of a case filed with the Court, the pertinent legal arguments, and a recommendation as to whether the case should be taken, written by one of the justices' law clerks and reviewed by all justices participating in the pool process.

certiorari petition A petition submitted to the Supreme Court requesting review of a case already decided.

chad A ready-made perforation on a punch card ballot.

charter The constitution of a local government.

checks and balances A system in which each branch of government can monitor and limit the functions of the other branches.

chief justice The leading justice on the Supreme Court, who provides both organizational and intellectual leadership.

chief of staff Among the most important staff members of the White House Office (WHO); serves as both an adviser to the president and the manager of the WHO.

citizens Members of the polity who, through birth or naturalization, enjoy the rights, privileges, and responsibilities attached to membership in a given nation.

Citizens United v. Federal Election Commission Supreme Court ruling stating that corporations and labor unions are entitled to the same First Amendment protections that individuals enjoy, resulting in drastically increased spending through super PACs by corporations and labor organizations.

civic engagement Individual and collective actions designed to identify and address issues of public concern.

civil disobedience Active, but nonviolent, refusal to comply with laws or governmental policies that are morally objectionable.

civil law The body of law dealing with disputes between individuals, between an individual and corporations, between corporations, and between individuals and their governments over harms caused by a party's actions or inactions.

civil liberties Constitutionally established guarantees that protect citizens, opinions, and property against arbitrary government interference.

civil rights The rights and privileges guaranteed to all citizens under the equal protection and due process clauses of the Fifth and Fourteenth Amendments; the idea that individuals are protected from discrimination based on characteristics such as race, national origin, religion, and sex.

civil servants Bureaucrats hired through a merit-based personnel system and who have job protection.

clash of civilizations thesis Samuel Huntington's idea that bitter cultural conflict will continue and escalate between modern Western democracies and fundamentalist Islamic states.

clear and present danger test A standard established in the 1919 Supreme Court case *Schenck v. U.S.* whereby the government may silence speech or expression when there is a clear and present danger that this speech will bring about some harm that the government has the power to prevent.

clear and probable danger test A standard established in the 1951 case *Dennis v. U.S.* whereby the government could suppress speech to avoid grave danger, even if the probability of the dangerous result was relatively remote; replaced by the imminent lawless action (incitement) test in 1969.

climate control The practice of using public outreach to build favorable public opinion of an organization.

closed primary A type of primary in which voting in a party's primary is limited to members of that party.

cloture A procedural move in which a supermajority of 60 senators agrees to end a filibuster.

coattail effect The phenomenon by which candidates running for lower-level offices such as city council benefit in an election from the popularity of a top-of-ticket nominee.

Cold War The political, ideological, and military conflict that lasted from 1945 until 1990 between communist nations led by the Soviet Union and Western democracies led by the United States.

collective defense The concept that allied nations agree to defend one another in the face of an invasion.

collective goods Outcomes shared by the general public; also called *public goods*.

collective security The idea that peace could be achieved if nations agreed to collectively oppose any nation that attacked another country.

collegial court A court made up of a group of judges who must evaluate a case together and decide on the outcome; compromise and negotiation take place as members try to build a majority coalition.

commercial speech Advertising statements that describe products.

commission A form of local government that is more common in county and township governments than in other general-purpose governments and for which voters elect a body of officials who collectively hold legislative and executive powers.

common law Judge-made law grounded in tradition and previous judicial decisions, instead of in written law.

concurrent budget resolution A document approved by the House and the Senate at the beginning of their budget processes that establishes binding expenditure ceilings and a binding revenue floor as well as proposed expenditure levels for major policy categories.

concurrent powers Basic governing functions that are exercised by the national and state governments independently, and at the same time, including the power to make policy, raise revenue, implement policies, and establish courts.

concurring opinion A judicial opinion agreeing with how the majority decides the case but disagreeing with at least some of the legal interpretations or conclusions reached by the majority.

confederal system A government structure in which several independent sovereign states agree to cooperate on specified policy matters by creating a central governing body; each sovereign state retains ultimate authority over other governmental matters within its borders, so the central governing body is not a sovereign government.

confederation A union of independent states in which each state retains its sovereignty, that is, its ultimate power to govern, and agrees to work collaboratively on matters the states expressly agree to delegate to a central governing body.

conference committee A bicameral, bipartisan committee composed of legislators whose job is to reconcile two versions of a bill.

conflict of interest In the case of public servants, the situation in which they can personally benefit from a decision they make or an action they take in the process of doing their jobs.

conflicted federalism Intergovernmental relations in which elements of dual federalism, cooperative federalism, and centralized federalism are evident in the domestic policies implemented by state and local governments.

Connecticut Compromise (also known as the Great Compromise) The compromise between the Virginia Plan and the New Jersey Plan that created a bicameral legislature with one chamber's representation based on population and the other chamber having two members for each state.

consent of the governed The idea that, in a democracy, the government's power derives from the consent of the people.

conservatism An ideology that emphasizes preserving tradition and relying on community and family as mechanisms of continuity in society.

consolidation The phenomenon of large corporations buying smaller ones so that there are fewer and fewer companies products available.

constitution The fundamental principles of a government and the basic structure and procedures by which the government operates to fulfill those principles; may be written or unwritten.

constitutional law The body of law that comes out of the courts in cases involving the interpretation of the Constitution.

constitutionalism Government that is structured by law, and in which the power of government is limited.

consumer price index (CPI) The most common measure of inflation, it gauges the average change in prices over time of a "market basket" of goods and services including food, clothing, shelter, fuels, transportation costs, and selected medical costs.

containment The Cold War–era policy of preventing the spread of communism, mainly by providing military and economic aid as well as political advice to countries vulnerable to a communist takeover.

continuing resolution An agreement of the House and Senate that authorizes agencies not covered by approved appropriation laws to continue to spend money within their previous budget year's levels.

contracting-out Also called *outsourcing* or *privatizing;* a process by which the government contracts with a private for-profit or nonprofit organization to provide public services, such as disaster relief, or resources needed by the government, such as fighter planes.

contributory program (social insurance program) A benefit provided only to those who paid the specific tax created to fund the benefit.

convergence The merging of various forms of media, including newspapers, television stations, radio networks, and blogs, under one corporate roof and one set of business editorial leaders.

cooperative federalism Intergovernmental relations in which the national government supports state governments' efforts to address the domestic matters reserved to them.

Council of Governments (COG) A regional agency composed of representatives from several local governments who share resources to address one or more mutual problems.

council-manager (commission-administrator) A form of general-purpose local government found in many counties and the majority of cities; it is composed of an elected body with legislative and executive powers whose members hire a professional manager to oversee the government's day-to-day operations.

council-mayor (council-executive) A form of general-purpose local government comprising (1) a legislative body elected by voters and (2) an independently elected chief executive.

country desk The official operation of the U.S. government in each country that has diplomatic ties to the United States.

county government A general-purpose local government created by states to assist them in implementing policy in geographic subdivisions of the state.

court of last resort The highest court in a court system.

creationism A theory of the creation of the earth and humankind that is based on a literal interpretation of the biblical story of Genesis.

criminal due process rights Safeguards for those accused of crime; these rights constrain government conduct in investigating crimes, trying cases, and punishing offenders.

criminal law The body of law dealing with conduct so harmful to society as a whole that it is prohibited by statute, and is prosecuted and punished by the government.

cyber cascade When an electronic document becomes very widely distributed digitally through e-mail, social networking, or video sharing.

D

de facto segregation Segregation caused by the fact that people tend to live in neighborhoods with others of their own race, religion, or ethnic group.

de jure segregation Segregation mandated by law.

dealignment The situation in which fewer voters support the two major political parties, instead identifying themselves as independent, or splitting their ticket between candidates from more than one party.

debt ceiling The legal borrowing limit for the national government.

defense conversion President Jimmy Carter's attempt to convert the nation's vast military apparatus to peacetime functions.

deficit spending Government expenditures costing more than is raised in taxes, during the budget year, leading to borrowing and debt.

democracy Government in which supreme power of governance lies in the hands of its citizens.

department One of 15 executive branch units responsible for a broadly defined policy area and whose top administrator (secretary) is appointed by the president, is confirmed by the Senate, and serves at the discretion of the president.

depression A long-term and severe recession.

deregulation The reduction or elimination of government rules and regulations (laws) that businesses and industries must follow.

descriptive representation The attempt to ensure that governing bodies include representatives of major demographic groups—such as women, African Americans, Latinas, Jews, and Catholics—in proportions similar to their representation in the population at large.

détente The easing of tensions between the United States and its communist rivals.

deterrence The idea that nations would be less likely to engage in nuclear war if adversaries each had first-strike capability.

devolution The process whereby the national government returns policy responsibilities to state or local governments.

digital divide Unequal access to computer technology.

digital paywall The practice of limiting access to a website unless users pay a fee or purchase a subscription.

Dillon's rule The ruling articulated by Judge John Forrest Dillon in 1872 that local governments are creatures of the state that created them, and they have only the powers expressly mentioned in the charters written and approved by the state and those necessarily implied by the formally expressed powers.

diplomacy The conduct of international relations, particularly involving the negotiation of treaties and other agreements between nations.

direct democracy A structure of government in which citizens discuss and decide policy through majority rule.

direct provision A policy tool whereby the government that creates a policy hires public servants to provide the service.

direct subsidy A cash transfer from general revenues to particular persons or private companies engaged in activities that the national government believes support the public good.

director of national intelligence (DNI) The person responsible for coordinating and overseeing all the intelligence agencies within the executive branch.

discharge petition A special tactic used to extract a bill from a committee to have it considered by the entire House.

discretionary jurisdiction The authority of a court to select the cases it will hear from among all the cases appealed to it.

discretionary spending Payment on programs for which Congress and the president must approve budget authority each year in appropriation legislation.

dissenting opinion A judicial opinion disagreeing both with the majority's disposition of a case and with their legal interpretations and conclusions.

diversity of citizenship The circumstance in which the parties in a legal case are from different states or the case involves a U.S. citizen and a foreign government.

divided government The situation that exists when Congress is controlled by one party and the presidency by the other.

divine right of kings The assertion that monarchies, as a manifestation of God's will, could rule absolutely without regard to the will or well-being of their subjects.

doctrine of *stare decisis* From the Latin for "let the decision stand," a common-law doctrine that directs judges to identify previously decided cases with similar facts and then apply to the current case the rule of law used by the courts in the earlier cases.

domestic policies Policies addressing the problems, needs, and relations of people residing with the country's borders.

domino theory The principle that if one nation fell to communism, other nations in its geographic vicinity also would succumb.

double jeopardy The trying of a person again for the same crime that he or she has been cleared of in court; barred by the Fifth Amendment.

dual court system The existence of 50 independently functioning state judicial systems, each responsible for resolving legal disputes over its state laws, and one national judicial system, responsible for resolving legal disputes over national laws.

dual federalism The initial model of national and state relations in which the national government takes care of its enumerated powers while the state governments independently take care of their reserved powers.

dual sovereignty A system of government in which ultimate governing authority is divided between two levels of government, a central government and regional governments, with each level having ultimate authority over different policy matters.

due process The legal safeguards that prevent the government from arbitrarily depriving citizens of life, liberty, or property; guaranteed by the Fifth and Fourteenth Amendments.

E

e-campaigning The practice of mobilizing voters using the Internet.

e-Government Employment of the Internet for delivering government information and services to the citizens.

e-petition An online petition used as a tool to garner support for a position or cause.

earmark A designation within a spending bill that provides for a specific expenditure.

economic boom Rapid economic growth.

economic incentive Motivation to join an interest group because the group works for policies that will provide members with material benefits.

economic policy A collection of public policies that affect the health of the economy, which includes taxing and spending policies (fiscal policy), monetary policy, regulatory policy, and trade policy.

economy A system for producing, selling, buying, and using goods and services.

efficacy Citizens' belief that they have the ability to achieve something desirable and that the government listens to people like them.

electioneering Working to influence the election of candidates who support the organization's issues.

Electoral College The name given to the body of representatives elected by voters in each state to elect the president and the vice president.

elite theory A theory that holds that a group of wealthy, educated individuals wields most political power.

emergency powers Broad powers exercised by the president during times of national crisis.

entitlement program A government benefit guaranteed to all who meet the eligibility requirements.

enumerated powers The powers of the national government that are listed in the Constitution.

environmental racism The term used to describe the higher incidence of environmental threats and subsequent health problems in lower-income communities, which frequently are also communities dominated by people of color.

equal protection clause The Fourteenth Amendment clause stating that no state shall "deny to any person within its jurisdiction the equal protection of the laws."

essential services Public services provided by state and local governments on a daily basis to prevent chaos and hazardous conditions in society.

establishment clause The First Amendment clause that bars the government from passing any law "respecting an establishment of religion"; often interpreted as a separation of church and state but increasingly questioned.

exclusionary rule The criminal procedural rule stating that evidence obtained illegally cannot be used in a trial.

executive agreement An international agreement between the United States and other nations, not subject to Senate approval and in effect only during the administration of the president who negotiates the agreement.

executive budget The budget document and budget message that explains the president's fiscal plan.

Executive Office of the President (EOP) The offices, counsels, and boards that help the president to carry out his day-to-day responsibilities.

executive order The power of the president to issue orders that carry the force of law.

executive privilege The right of the chief executive and members of the administration to withhold information from Congress or the courts, or the right to refuse to appear before legislative or judicial bodies.

exit polls Polls conducted at polling places on Election Day to project the winner of an election before the polls close.

expressed powers Presidential powers enumerated in the Constitution.

extradition The return of individuals accused of a crime to the state in which the crime was committed upon the request of that state's governor.

F

fairness doctrine The requirement that stations holding broadcast licenses present controversial issues of public importance and to do so in a manner that was honest, fair, and balanced.

federal question A question of law based on interpretation of the U.S. Constitution, federal laws, or treaties.

federal system A governmental structure with two levels of government in which each level has sovereignty over different policy matters and geographic areas; a system of government with dual sovereignty.

The Federalist Papers A series of essays, written by James Madison, Alexander Hamilton, and John Jay, that argued for the ratification of the Constitution.

Federalists Individuals who supported the new Constitution as presented by the Constitutional Convention in 1787.

feminization of poverty The phenomenon of increasing numbers of unmarried, divorced, and separated women with children living in poverty.

fighting words Speech that is likely to bring about public disorder or chaos; the Supreme Court has held that this speech may be banned in public places to ensure the preservation of public order.

filibuster A procedural move by a member of the Senate to attempt to halt passage of a bill, during which the senator can speak for an unlimited time on the Senate floor.

fireside chats President Franklin D. Roosevelt's radio addresses to the country.

fiscal federalism The relationship between the national government and state and local governments whereby the national government provides grant money to state and local governments.

fiscal policy Government spending and taxing and their effect on the economy.

fiscal year (FY) The 12-month accounting period for revenue raising and spending, which for the national government begins on October 1 and ends on September 30 of the following year.

501(c)4s Nonprofit organizations operated exclusively for the promotion of social welfare, including lobbying or engaging in political campaigning.

527 A tax-exempt group that raises money for political activities, much like those allowed under the soft money loophole.

food insecurity The situation in which people have a limited or an uncertain ability to obtain, in socially acceptable ways, enough nutritious food to live a healthy and active life.

foreign service officers The diplomatic and consular staff at U.S. embassies abroad.

Foursquare Geolocation app that uses an iPhone's built-in GPS to display attractions in your area.

framing The process by which the media set a context that helps people understand important events and matters of shared interest.

free exercise clause The First Amendment clause prohibiting the government from enacting laws prohibiting an individual's practice of his or her religion; often in contention with the establishment clause.

free rider problem The phenomenon of someone deriving benefit from others' actions.

free trade policy The elimination of tariffs and nontariff trade barriers so that international trade is expanded.

full faith and credit clause The constitutional clause that requires states to comply with and uphold the public acts, records, and judicial decisions of other states.

fund-raising consultant A professional who works with candidates in identifying likely contributors to the campaign and arrange events and meetings with donors.

G

gender gap The measurable difference in the way women and men vote for candidates and in the way they view political issues.

general election An election that determines which candidates win the offices being sought.

general-purpose government A government providing services in numerous and diverse policy and functional areas to the residents living within its borders.

generational effect The impact of an important external event in shaping the views of a generation.

gerrymandering The drawing of legislative district boundaries to benefit an incumbent, a political party, or another group.

global economy The worldwide economy created by the integration and interdependence of national economies.

global warming The rising temperature of the earth as a result of pollution that traps solar heat, keeping the air warmer than it would otherwise be.

globalism The interconnectedness between nations in contemporary times.

GOTV Get out the vote.

government The institution that creates and implements policy and laws that guide the conduct of the nation and its citizens.

government corporation An executive branch unit that sells a service and is expected to be financially self-sufficient.

grandfather clause A clause exempting individuals from voting conditions such as poll taxes or literacy tests if they or their ancestors had voted before 1870, thus sparing most white voters.

grant-in-aid (intergovernmental transfer) The transfer of money from one government to another government that does not need to be paid back.

grassroots organizing Tasks that involve direct contact with voters or potential voters.

greenhouse effect The heating of the earth's atmosphere as a result of humans' burning of fossil fuels and the resultant buildup of carbon dioxide and other gases.

gross domestic product (GDP) The total value of all goods and services produced by labor and properties within a country's borders.

H

habeas corpus An ancient right that protects an individual in custody from being held without the right to be heard in a court of law.

hacktivism The authorized or unauthorized use of or destruction of electronic files in pursuit of a political or social goal.

hate crime A crime committed against a person, property, or society, in which the offender is motivated, in part or in whole, by his or her bias against the victim because of the victim's race, religion, disability, sexual orientation, or ethnicity.

hearings Sessions held by committees or subcommittees to gather information and views from experts.

hegemony A form of imperial geographic dominance.

heightened scrutiny test (intermediate scrutiny test) The guidelines used most frequently by the courts to determine the legality of sex-based discrimination; on the basis of this test, sex-based discrimination is legal if the government can prove that it is substantially related to the achievement of an important public interest.

Holocaust The genocide perpetrated by Adolf Hitler and the Nazis of six million Jews, along with political dissidents, Catholics, homosexuals, individuals with disabilities, and gypsies.

home rule Power delegated by a state government to its citizens to formulate and adopt their municipal and county government charters and to determine the extent of those governments' powers and responsibilities as long as they comply with state and national law.

home rule charter A local government constitution written and approved by citizens following state-mandated procedures, including a referendum.

honeymoon period A time early in a new president's administration characterized by optimistic approval by the public.

hopper A wooden box that sits on a desk at the front of the House of Representatives, into which House members place bills they want to introduce.

horizontal federalism The state-to-state relationships created by the U.S. Constitution.

House majority leader The leader of the majority party, who helps the Speaker to develop and implement strategy and who works with other members of the House of Representatives.

House minority leader The leader of the minority party, whose job mirrors that of the majority leader but without the power that comes from holding a majority in the House of Representatives.

household income The total pretax earnings of all residents over the age of 15 living in a home.

housing insecurity The situation in which people have limited or uncertain ability to obtain, in socially acceptable ways, affordable, safe, and decent-quality permanent housing.

Human Development Index (HDI) A UN-created measure to determine how well a country's economy is providing for a long and healthy life, educational opportunity, and a decent standard of living.

I

imminent lawless action test (incitement test) A standard established in the 1969 *Brandenburg v. Ohio* case, whereby speech is restricted only if it goes beyond mere advocacy, or words, to create a high likelihood of imminent disorder or lawlessness.

impeachment The power of the House of Representatives to formally accuse the president (and other high-ranking officials, including the vice president and federal judges) of crimes.

implied powers The powers of the national government that are not enumerated in the Constitution but that Congress claims are necessary and proper for the national government to fulfill its enumerated powers in accordance with the necessary and proper clause of the Constitution.

impressment The forcible removal of merchant sailors from U.S. ships on the spurious grounds that the sailors were deserters from the British Navy.

income inequality The gap in the proportion of national income held by the richest compared to that held by the poorest.

incumbency The situation of already holding the office that is up for reelection.

independent A voter who does not belong to any organized political party; often used as a synonym for an unaffiliated voter.

independent administrative agency An executive branch unit created by Congress and the president that is responsible for a narrowly defined function and whose structure is intended to be protected from partisan politics.

independent expenditures Outlays by PACs and others, typically for advertising for or against a candidate, but uncoordinated with a candidate's campaign.

independent regulatory commission An executive branch unit outside of cabinet departments, responsible for developing standards of behavior within specific industries and businesses, monitoring compliance with these standards, and imposing sanctions on violators.

indexed benefit A government benefit with an automatic cost of living increase based on the rate of inflation.

indirect democracy Sometimes called a *representative democracy,* a system in which citizens elect representatives who decide policies on behalf of their constituents.

individualistic political culture The view that the decision to take part in government is an individual choice and those who choose to participate determine the purpose of government and personally benefit from their participation.

inflation The decreased value of money as evidenced by increased prices.

information equilibrium The dissemination of information outside traditional channels of control.

infotainment A hybrid of the words *information* and *entertainment;* news shows that combine entertainment and news.

inherent characteristics Individual attributes such as race, national origin, religion, and sex.

inherent powers Presidential powers that are implied in the Constitution.

initiative A citizen-sponsored proposal that can result in new or amended legislation or a state constitutional amendment.

in-kind assistance A cash transfer in which the government pays cash to those who provide goods or services to eligible individuals.

inspectors general Political appointees who work within a government agency to ensure the integrity of public service by investigating allegations of misconduct by bureaucrats.

instant runoff election A special runoff election in which the computerized voting machine simulates the elimination of last-place vote-getters.

instructed delegate model A model of representation in which legislators, as representatives of their constituents, should vote in keeping with the constituents' views, even if those views contradict the legislator's personal views.

intelligent design The theory that the apparent design in the universe and in living things is the product of an intelligent cause rather than of an undirected process such as natural selection; its primary proponents believe that the designer is God and seek to redefine science to accept supernatural explanations.

interest group An organization that seeks to achieve goals by influencing government decision making.

intergovernmental relations (IGR) The collaborative efforts of two or more levels of government working to serve the public.

intermestics The influence of domestic interests on foreign policy.

International Monetary Fund (IMF) The institution charged with regulating monetary relationships among nations, including establishment of exchange rates for major world currencies; established in 1944 by the Bretton Woods Agreement.

intersectionality The experience of multiple forms of oppression (based on race, gender, class, and/or sexuality) simultaneously.

interstate compacts Agreements between states that Congress has the authority to review and reject.

interventionism A foreign policy characterized by a nation's willingness to participate and intervene in international situations, including another country's affairs.

iron triangle The interaction of mutual interests among members of Congress, executive agencies, and organized interests during policy making.

isolationism A foreign policy characterized by a nation's unwillingness to participate in international affairs.

issue network The fluid web of connections among those concerned about a policy and those who create and administer the policy.

J

Jim Crow laws Laws requiring the strict separation of racial groups, with whites and "non-whites" required to attend separate schools, work in different jobs, and use segregated public accommodations, such as transportation and restaurants.

joint committee A bicameral committee composed of members of both chambers of Congress.

joint referral The practice, abolished in the 104th Congress, by which a bill could be referred to two different committees for consideration.

journalism The practice of gathering and reporting events.

judicial activism An approach to judicial decision making whereby judges are willing to strike down laws made by elected officials as well as step away from precedents.

judicial federalism State courts' use of their state constitutions to determine citizens' rights, particularly when state constitutions guarantee greater protections than does the U.S. Constitution.

judicial independence Insulating judges from the need to be accountable to voters or elected officials so that they can make impartial decisions based on the law.

judicial restraint An approach to judicial decision making whereby judges defer to the democratically elected legislative and executive branches of government.

judicial review Court authority to determine that an action taken by any government official or governing body violates the Constitution; established by the Supreme Court in the 1803 *Marbury v. Madison* case.

judiciary The branch of government comprising the state and federal courts and the judges who preside over them.

jurisdiction The legal authority of a court to resolve a case, established by either a constitution or a statute.

jury trial A trial in which a group of people selected to hear the evidence presented decides on guilt or liability.

K

Keynesian economics The theory that recommends that during a recession the national government increase its spending and decrease taxes, and during a boom, cut spending and increase taxes.

L

laissez-faire The hands-off stance of a government in regard to the marketplace.

law A body of rules established by government officials that bind governments, individuals, and nongovernment organizations.

lead committee The primary committee considering a bill.

League of Nations A representative body founded in the aftermath of World War I to establish the collective security of nations.

legacy systems The old way of doing things, either in paper form or using outdated computer systems.

legal model Judicial decision-making model that focuses on legal norms and principles as the guiding force in judicial decision making, including existing precedents, relevant constitutional and statutory law, and the lawmakers' intent.

legislative referendum A ballot measure whereby voters approve or reject a law or an amendment *proposed* by state officials.

legitimacy A quality conferred on government by citizens who believe that its exercise of power is right and proper.

***Lemon* test** A three-part test established by the Supreme Court in the 1971 case *Lemon v. Kurtzman* to determine whether government aid to parochial schools is constitutional; the test is also applied to other cases involving the establishment clause.

letter to the editor A letter in which a reader responds to a story in a newspaper, knowing that the letter might be published in that paper.

libel False written statements about others that harm their reputation.

liberalism An ideology that advocates change in the social, political, and economic realms to better protect the well-being of individuals and to produce equality within society.

libertarianism An ideology whose advocates believe that government should take a "hands off" approach in most matters.

liberty The most essential quality of American democracy; it is both the freedom from governmental interference in citizens' lives and the freedom to pursue happiness.

limited government Government that is restricted in what it can do so that the rights of the people are protected.

limited war A combatant country's self-imposed limitation on the tactics and strategy it uses, particularly its avoidance of the use of nuclear weapons.

line-item veto The power of the president to strike out specific line items on an appropriation bill while allowing the rest of the bill to become law; declared unconstitutional by the Supreme Court in 1997.

literacy test A test to determine eligibility to vote; designed so that few African Americans would pass.

living wage A wage high enough to keep workers and their families out of poverty and to allow them to enjoy a basic living standard.

lobby To communicate directly with policy makers on an interest group's behalf.

logrolling The practice of members of Congress agreeing to vote for a bill in exchange for their colleague's vote on another bill.

loyal opposition A role that the party out of power plays, highlighting its objections to policies and priorities of the government in power.

M

majority rule The idea that in a democracy, only policies with 50 percent plus one vote are enacted, and only candidates that win 50 percent plus one vote are elected.

majority whip The go-between with the majority leadership and party members in the House of Representatives.

majority-minority district A legislative district composed of a majority of a given minority community—say, African Americans—the intent of which is to make it likely that a member of that minority will be elected to Congress.

mandates Clauses in legislation that direct state and local governments to comply with national legislation and national standards.

mandatory jurisdiction The requirement that a court hear all cases filed with it.

mandatory spending Government spending for debt and programs whose budget authority is provided in legislation other than annual appropriation acts; this budget authority is open ended, obligating the government to pay for the program whatever the cost, every year.

manifest destiny The idea that it was the United States' destiny to spread throughout the North American continent; used to rationalize the expansion of U.S. territory.

Marbury v. Madison The 1803 Supreme Court case that established the power of judicial review, which allows the Court to strike down laws passed by the other branches that it views to be in conflict with the Constitution.

marketplace of ideas A concept at the core of the freedoms of expression and press, based on the belief that true and free political discourse depends on a free and unrestrained discussion of ideas.

markup The process by which the members of legislative committees "mark up" a bill with suggested language for changes and amendments.

Marshall Plan The U.S. government program that provided funds necessary for Western European countries to rebuild after World War II.

matching funds requirement A grant requirement that obligates the government receiving the grant to spend some of its own money to match a specified percentage of the grant money provided.

McCulloch v. Maryland The 1819 case that established that the necessary and proper clause justifies broad understandings of enumerated powers.

means-tested benefit A benefit for which eligibility is based on having an income below a government-specified amount, typically based on a percentage of the poverty guideline.

media Tools used to store and deliver information or data.

media consultant A professional who brings the campaign message to voters by creating handouts and all forms of media ads.

media segmentation The breaking down of the media according to the specific audiences they target.

median household income The middle of all household incomes—50 percent of households have incomes less than the median and 50 percent have incomes greater than the median.

merit-based civil service A personnel system in which bureaucrats are hired on the basis of the principles of competence, equal opportunity (open competition), and political neutrality; once hired, these public servants have job protection.

merit selection process A process for selecting judges in which a nonpartisan committee nominates candidates, the governor or legislature appoints judges from among those candidates to a short term of service, and then the appointed judges face a retention election at the end of the short term.

micro-blog Sites, including Twitter, that enable short communication, often targeted specifically at on-the-move audiences.

microtarget Datamining techniques that facilitate the tracking of individual voter preferences so that tailored messages in various forms can be used to generate support, contributions, and votes.

minority whip The go-between with the minority leadership, whose job mirrors that of the majority whip but without the power that comes from holding a majority in the House of Representatives.

Miranda **rights** A criminal procedural rule, established in the 1966 case *Miranda v. Arizona,* requiring police to inform criminal suspects, on their arrest, of their legal rights, such as the right to remain silent and the right to counsel; these warnings must be read to suspects before interrogation.

monarchy Government in which a member of a royal family, usually a king or queen, has absolute authority over a territory and its government.

monetarism The theory that says the government's proper economic role is to control the rate of inflation by controlling the amount of money in circulation.

monetary policy The body of Federal Reserve actions aimed at adjusting the amount of money (coin, currency, and bank deposits) in the economy to maintain a stable, low level of inflation.

Monroe Doctrine President James Monroe's 1823 declaration that the Americas should not be considered subjects for future colonization by any European power.

moralistic political culture The view that the purpose of government is to serve the public good, including providing for those who are disadvantaged, and that all citizens should participate in government.

muckraking Criticism and exposés of corruption in government and industry by journalists at the turn of the 20th century.

multilateral Many-sided; having the support of numerous nations.

municipal government Self-governing general-purpose government—including city, borough, and town governments—created by states to provide goods and services within a densely populated area.

mutual assured destruction (MAD) The doctrine that if one nation attacked another with nuclear weapons, the other would be capable of retaliating and would retaliate with such force as to ensure mutual annihilation.

N

narrowcasting The practice of aiming media content at specific segments of the public.

national debt The total amount of money the government owes to all the individuals and groups that loaned it money.

National Security Council (NSC) Consisting of top foreign policy advisers and relevant cabinet officials, this is an arm of the Executive Office of the President that the president consults on matters of foreign policy and national security.

natural law The assertion that standards that govern human behavior are derived from the nature of humans themselves and can be applied universally.

natural rights (unalienable rights) The rights possessed by all humans as a gift from nature, or God, including the rights to life, liberty, and the pursuit of happiness.

naturalization The process of becoming a citizen by means other than birth, as in the case of immigrants.

necessary and proper clause (elastic clause) A clause in Article I, section 8, of the Constitution that gives Congress the power to do whatever it deems necessary and constitutional to meet its enumerated obligations; the basis for the implied powers.

Net neutrality The idea that Internet traffic should flow through the Internet pipeline without interference or discrimination by those who own or are running the pipeline.

netroots The Internet-centered political efforts on behalf of candidates and causes.

New Deal Franklin D. Roosevelt's broad social welfare program in which the government would bear the responsibility of providing a safety net to protect the most disadvantaged members of society.

New Deal coalition The group composed of southern Democrats, northern city dwellers, immigrants, the poor, Catholics, labor union members, blue-collar workers, African Americans, and women who elected Franklin D. Roosevelt to the presidency four times.

New Jersey Plan The proposal presented in response to the Virginia Plan by the less populous states at the Constitutional Convention, which called for a unicameral national legislature in which all states would have an equal voice (equal representation), an executive office composed of several people elected by Congress, and a Supreme Court whose members would be appointed by the executive office.

new media Sources of information—including Internet websites, blogs, social networking sites such as Facebook and Twitter, photo- and video-sharing platforms such as Instagram and YouTube, and apps—and the cellular and satellite technologies that facilitate their use.

news aggregators Services that compile in one location news we want from various outlets.

NIMBY ("not in my backyard") syndrome A pattern of citizens' behavior in which people decline to participate in politics until a government action or inaction threatens them directly.

Nixon Doctrine Policy emphasizing the responsibility of U.S. allies to provide for their own national defense and security, aimed at improving relations with the communist nations, including the Soviet Union and China.

noncontributory program A benefit provided to a targeted population, paid for by a proportion of the money collected from all taxpayers.

nonpartisan election An election in which the candidates are not nominated by political parties and the ballot does not include party affiliations.

nontariff trade barriers Business and social regulations as well as subsidies aimed at creating a competitive advantage in trade.

normal trade relations (NTR) status The international trade principle holding that the least restrictive trade conditions (best tariff rates) offered to any one national trading partner will be offered to every other nation in a trading network (also known as *most favored nations*).

North Atlantic Treaty Organization (NATO) An international mutual defense alliance formed in 1949 that created a structure for regional security for its 15 member nations.

nuclear option A maneuver exercised by the presiding officer in the Senate that eliminates the possibility of filibusters by subjecting votes on certain matters to a simple majority vote.

 O

obscenity Indecent or offensive speech or expression.

Office of Management and Budget (OMB) The office that creates the president's annual budget.

office-block ballot A type of ballot that arranges all the candidates for a particular office under the name of that office.

oligarchy Government in which an elite few hold power.

ombudsperson A role in which an elected or appointed leader acts as an advocate for citizens by listening to and investigating complaints against a government agency.

open meeting laws Laws requiring legislative bodies and executive agencies of government to conduct policy-making meetings in public.

open primary A type of primary in which both parties' ballots are available in the voting booth, and the voters simply select one on which to register their preferences.

operating budget A budget that accounts for all the costs of day-to-day government operations and covers such items as salaries and benefits, utilities, office supplies, and rent.

ordinary scrutiny test (rational basis test) On the basis of this test, sex-based discrimination is legal if it is a reasonable means by which the government can achieve a legitimate public interest.

original jurisdiction Judicial authority to hear cases for the first time and to determine guilt or liability by applying the law to the facts presented.

oversight The process by which the legislative branch "checks" the executive branch to ensure that the laws Congress has passed are being administered in keeping with legislators' intent.

 P

partisan election An election in which candidates are nominated by political parties and the ballot lists each candidate's political party affiliation.

party identifiers Individuals who identify themselves as a member of one party or the other.

party in government The partisan identifications of elected leaders in local, county, state, and federal government.

party in the electorate Individuals who identify with or tend to support a party.

party organization The formal party apparatus, including committees, party leaders, conventions, and workers.

party system The categorization of the number and competitiveness of political parties in a polity.

party-column ballot A ballot that organizes the candidates by political party.

patronage The system in which a party leader rewarded political supporters with jobs or

government contracts in exchange for their support of the party.

patronage system A personnel system in which the chief executive officer (CEO) can appoint whomever he or she wants to top bureaucratic positions, without the need for open competition for applicants; those hired through patronage typically serve at the pleasure of the CEO who hired them.

penal code The compilation of a state's criminal law—legislation that defines crime—into one document.

penny press Newspapers that sold for a penny in the 1830s.

platform The formal statement of a party's principles and policy objectives.

Plessy v. Ferguson 1896 Supreme Court ruling creating the separate but equal doctrine.

plum book A publication that lists the top jobs in the bureaucracy to which the president will appoint people through the patronage system.

plural executive system A state and local government structure in which the citizens elect more than two people to top positions in the executive branch of government.

pluralist theory A theory that holds that policy making is a competition among diverse interest groups that ensure the representation of individual interests.

pocket veto A special presidential veto of a bill passed at the conclusion of a legislative session, whereby the president waits 10 days without signing the bill, and the bill dies.

police powers The states' reserved powers to protect the health, safety, lives, and properties of residents in a state.

political action committee (PAC) An entity whose specific goal is to raise and spend money to influence the outcome of elections.

political culture The people's collective beliefs and attitudes about government and political processes.

political engagement Citizen actions that are intended to solve public problems through political means.

political ideology An integrated system of ideas or beliefs about political values in general and the role of government in particular.

political machines Big-city organizations that exerted control over many aspects of life and lavishly rewarded supporters.

political party An organization that recruits, nominates, and elects party members to office in order to control the government.

political socialization The process by which we develop our political values and opinions.

politically uncontrollable spending Spending on programs that are so popular that elected officials are not willing to change the laws that authorize the programs for fear of the effect on their reelection prospects,

politics The process of deciding who gets benefits in society and who does not.

politics-administration dichotomy The concept that elected government officials, who are accountable to the voters, create and approve public policy, and then competent, politically neutral bureaucrats implement the public policy.

poll tax A fee for voting; levied to prevent poor African Americans in the South from voting.

popular referendum A measure that allows citizens, by collecting signatures in a petition drive, to put before voters specific legislation that the legislature has *previously approved.*

popular sovereignty The theory that government is created by the people and depends on the people for the authority to rule.

population In a poll, the group of people whose opinions are of interest and/or about whom information is desired.

populism A philosophy supporting the rights and empowerment of the masses as opposed to elites.

pork barrel Legislators' appropriations of funds for special projects located within their congressional districts.

poverty The condition of lacking the income sufficient to purchase the necessities for an adequate living standard.

poverty guidelines A simplified version of the U.S. Census Bureau's poverty thresholds developed each year by the Department of Health and Human Services; used to set financial eligibility criteria for benefits.

poverty rate The proportion of the population living below the poverty line as established by the national government.

poverty thresholds The U.S. Census Bureau's annually updated set of income measures (adjusted for family size) that defines who is living in poverty.

precedent cases Previous cases with similar facts that judges identify for use in a new case they are deciding; judges apply the legal principles used in the precedent cases to decide the legal dispute they are currently resolving.

preemption The constitutionally based principle that allows a national law to supersede state or local laws.

preponderance of evidence The standard of proof used in civil cases; the evidence must show that it is more likely than not that the accused caused the harm claimed by the complainant.

president pro tempore Also called *president pro tem;* theoretically, the chair of the Senate

in the vice president's absence; in reality, an honorary title, with the senator of the majority party having the longest record of continuous service being elected to the position.

press secretary The president's spokesperson to the media.

preventive war The strategy of waging war on countries that are regarded as threatening in order to avoid future conflicts.

primary election An election in which voters choose the party's candidates who will run in the later general election.

priming Bringing certain policies on issues to the public agenda through media coverage.

prior restraint A form of censorship by the government whereby it blocks the publication of news stories viewed as libelous or harmful.

privileges and immunities clause The Constitution's requirement that a state extend to other states' citizens the privileges and immunities it provides for its citizens.

progressive tax A tax that takes a larger percentage of the income of wealthier taxpayers and a smaller percentage of the income of lower-income taxpayers.

promoted tweets Targeted advertising found on a Twitter page that targets Twitterers based on whom they follow and who follows them.

proportional representation system An electoral structure in which political parties win the number of parliamentary seats equal to the percentage of the vote the party receives.

proportional (flat) tax A tax that takes the same percentage of each taxpayer's income.

proposition A proposed measure placed on the ballot in an initiative election.

prospective voting A method of evaluating candidates in which voters focus on candidates' positions on issues important to them and vote for the candidates who best represent their views.

protectionist trade policy The establishment of trade barriers to protect domestic goods from foreign competition.

public agenda The public issues that most demand the attention of government officials.

public diplomat An individual outside government who promotes his or her country's interests and thus helps to shape international perceptions of the nation.

public goods Goods whose benefits cannot be limited and that are available to all.

public employee unions Labor organizations comprising federal, state, and municipal workers, including police officers and teachers.

public opinion The public's expressed views about an issue at a specific point in time.

public opinion poll A survey of a given population's opinion on an issue or a candidate at a particular point in time.

pure capitalist economy An economy in which private individuals and companies own the modes of producing goods and services, and the government does not enact laws aimed at influencing the marketplace transactions that distribute those goods and services.

purposive incentives Motivation to join an interest group based on the belief in the group's cause from an ideological or a moral standpoint.

push polls A special type of poll that both attempts to skew public opinion about a candidate and provides information to campaigns about candidate strengths and weaknesses.

Q

quota sample A method by which pollsters structure a sample so that it is representative of the characteristics of the target population.

R

rally 'round the flag effect The peaks in presidential approval ratings during short-term military action.

random sampling A scientific method of selection in which each member of the population has an equal chance of being included in the sample.

rational abstention thesis A theory that some individuals decide the costs of voting are not worth the effort when compared to the benefits.

rational choice theory The idea that from an economic perspective it is not rational for people to participate in collective action when they can secure the collective good without participating.

real income Earned income adjusted for inflation.

realignment A shift in party allegiances or electoral support that propels a political party to majority status.

reapportionment Reallocation of seats in the House of Representatives to each state based on changes in state populations since the last census.

recall A special election in which voters can remove an officeholder before his or her term is over.

recession An economic downturn during which unemployment is high and the production of goods and services is low.

Reconstruction era The time after the Civil War between 1866 and 1877 when the institutions and infrastructure of the South were rebuilt.

redistricting The redrawing of congressional district boundaries within each state, based on the reapportionment from the census.

referendum An election in which voters in a state can vote for or against a measure proposed by the state legislature.

regime change The replacement of a country's government with another government by facilitating the deposing of its leader or leading political party.

regional security alliance An alliance typically between a superpower and nations that are ideologically similar in a particular region.

regressive tax A tax that takes a greater percentage of the income of lower-income earners than of higher-income earners.

regulated capitalist economy (mixed economy) An economy in which private ownership of the modes of production dominate and the government enacts policies to influence the health of the economy.

remarketing Targeting political Google ads based on the cookies that a user drops on other websites.

rendition The transfer of suspected terrorists to other nations for imprisonment and interrogation; this practice circumvents U.S. law, which requires due process and prohibits torture.

report A legislative committee's explanation to the full chamber of a bill and its intent.

representative bureaucracy A bureaucracy in which the people serving resemble the larger population whom they serve in demographic characteristics such as race, age, ethnicity, sex, religion, and economic status.

republic A government that derives its authority from the people and in which citizens elect government officials to represent them in the processes by which laws are made; a representative democracy.

reserved powers The matters referred to in the Tenth Amendment over which states retain sovereignty.

responsible party model Political scientists' view that a function of a party is to offer a clear choice to voters by establishing priorities or policy stances different from those of rival parties.

retention election A noncompetitive election in which an incumbent judge's name is on the ballot and voters decide whether the judge should be retained.

retrospective voting A method of evaluating candidates in which voters evaluate incumbent candidates and decide whether to support them based on their past performance.

right to privacy The right of an individual to be left alone and to make decisions freely, without the interference of others.

Roosevelt Corollary The idea, advanced by President Theodore Roosevelt, that the United States had the right to act as an "international police power" in the Western Hemisphere to ensure stability in the region.

Rule of Four Practice by which the Supreme Court justices determine if they will hear a case if four or more justices want to hear it.

Rules Committee One of the most important committees in the House, which decides the length of debate and the scope of amendments that will be allowed on a bill.

runoff election A follow-up election that is held when no candidate receives the majority of votes cast in the original election.

S

safety net A collection of public policies ensuring that citizens' basic physiological needs are met.

salient In relation to a voting issue—having resonance, being significant, causing intense interest.

SALT I The treaty signed in 1972 by the United States and the Soviet Union limiting the two countries' antiballistic missiles and freezing the number of offensive missiles that each nation could have at the number they already possessed, plus the number they had under construction.

SALT II The treaty signed in 1979 by the United States and the Soviet Union that set an overall limit on strategic nuclear launchers, limited the number of missiles that could carry multiple independently targeted reentry vehicles (MIRVs) with nuclear warheads, and limited each nation to the development of only one new type of intercontinental ballistic missile (ICBM).

sampling error Also called *margin of error;* a statistical calculation of the difference in results between a poll of a randomly drawn sample and a poll of the entire population.

sanctions Penalties that halt economic relations.

select committee A congressional committee created to consider specific policy issues or address a specific concern.

selective incorporation The process by which, over time, the Supreme Court applied those freedoms that served *some* fundamental principle of liberty or justice to the states, thus rejecting total incorporation.

Senate majority leader The most powerful position in the Senate; the majority leader manages the legislative process and schedules debate on legislation.

Senate minority leader The leader of the minority party in the Senate, who works with the majority leader in negotiating legislation.

senatorial courtesy A custom that allows senators from the president's political party to veto the president's choice of federal district court judge in the senator's state.

senior executive service (SES) A unique personnel system for top managerial, supervisory, and policy positions offering less job security but higher pay than the merit-based civil service system.

seniority system The system in which the member with the longest continuous tenure on a standing committee is given preference when the committee chooses its chair.

separate but equal doctrine Established by the Supreme Court in *Plessy v. Ferguson,* it said that separate but equal facilities for whites and nonwhites do not violate the Fourteenth Amendment's equal protection clause.

separation of powers The Constitution's delegation of authority for the primary governing functions among three branches of government so that no one group of government officials controls all the governing functions.

sequestration Automatic spending cuts during the fiscal year.

shadow bureaucrats People hired and paid by private for-profit and nonprofit organizations that implement public policy through a government contract.

signing statement A written message that the president issues upon signing a bill into law.

slander False verbal statements about others that harm their reputation.

social capital The many ways in which our lives are improved in many ways by social connections.

social contract An agreement between people and their leaders in which the people agree to give up some liberties so that their other liberties are protected.

social contract theory The idea that individuals possess free will, and every individual is equally endowed with the God-given right of self-determination and the ability to consent to be governed.

social networking sites Platforms that enable users to construct a profile, specify other users with whom they share a connection, and view others' connections.

social regulation Government rules, regulations, and standards aimed at protecting workers, consumers, and the environment from market failure.

socialism An ideology that advocates economic equality, theoretically achieved by having the government or workers own the means of production (businesses and industry).

soft money loophole The Supreme Court's interpretation of campaign finance law that enabled political parties to raise unlimited funds for party-building activities such as voter registration drives and get-out-the-vote (GOTV) efforts.

solidary incentives The motivation to join an interest group based on the companionship and the satisfaction derived from socializing with others that it offers.

Southeast Asia Treaty Organization (SEATO) A regional security agreement whose goal was to prevent communist encroachment in the countries of Southeast Asia.

Speaker of the House The leader of the House of Representatives, chosen by the majority party.

special-purpose government A government providing one service or function for residents living within its borders.

spoils system The practice of rewarding political supporters with jobs.

standing committee A permanent committee in Congress, with a defined legislative jurisdiction.

standing to sue The legal right to bring lawsuits in court.

statutory powers Powers explicitly granted to presidents by congressional action.

strategic arms limitation talks (SALT talks) Discussions between the United States and the Soviet Union in the 1970s that focused on cooling down the nuclear arms race between the two superpowers.

strategic arms reduction talks (START talks) Talks between the United States and the Soviet Union in which reductions in missiles and nuclear warheads, not merely a limitation on increases, were negotiated.

strategic defense initiative (SDI, or "Star Wars") A ballistic missile defense system advocated by President Ronald Reagan.

strategic model Judicial decision-making model that states that the primary guide for judges is their individual policy preferences; however, their preferences are tempered by their consideration of institutional factors, as well as concern over the legitimacy of the court system.

stratified sampling A process of random sampling in which the national population is divided into fourths and certain areas within these regions are selected as representative of the national population.

straw poll A poll conducted in an unscientific manner, used to predict election outcomes.

strict scrutiny test Guidelines the courts use to determine the legality of suspect classification based discrimination; on the basis of this test, discrimination is legal if it is a necessary means by which the government can achieve a compelling public interest.

strong mayor An elected municipal government executive who holds the powers traditionally delegated to elected chief executives (veto power, power to formulate the budget, and power to appoint many executive branch officials).

subcommittee A subordinate committee in Congress that typically handles specific areas of a standing committee's jurisdiction.

subsidy A tax break or another kind of financial support that encourages behaviors the government deems beneficial to the public good.

substantive representation Assumption that a government official will best serve the concerns of the racial, ethnic, gender, or other group to which he or she belongs.

sunset clause A clause in legislation that sets an expiration date for an authorized program or policy unless Congress reauthorizes it.

sunshine laws Legislation that opens up government functions and documents to the public.

super PACs Political organizations that use contributions from individuals, corporations, and labor unions to spend unlimited sums independent from the campaigns, yet influencing the outcomes of elections.

Super Tuesday The Tuesday in early March on which the most primary elections are held, many of them in southern states.

superpowers Leader nations with dominating influence in international affairs.

supply-side economics The theory that advocates cutting taxes and deregulating business to stimulate the economy.

supremacy clause A clause in Article VI of the Constitution that states that the Constitution and the treaties and laws created by the national government in compliance with the Constitution are the supreme law of the land.

supreme law of the land The U.S. Constitution's description of its own authority, meaning that all laws made by governments within the United States must be in compliance with the Constitution.

suspect classifications Distinctions based on race, religion, and national origin, which are assumed to be illegitimate.

symbolic representation Diversity among government officials is a symbol, an indication, that our democracy, our government by and for the people, is functioning appropriately by offering equal opportunity to influence government by becoming a government official.

symbolic speech Nonverbal "speech" in the form of an action such as picketing, flag burning, or wearing an armband to signify a protest.

T

take care clause The constitutional basis for inherent powers, which states that the president "shall take Care that the Laws be faithfully executed."

talk radio A format featuring conversations and interviews about topics of interest, along with call-ins from listeners.

tariff A special tax on imported goods.

tax base The overall *wealth* (income and assets of citizens and corporations) that the government can tax to raise revenue.

tax expenditures (also, *tax breaks* or *loopholes*) Government financial supports that allow individuals and corporations to pay reduced taxes, to encourage behaviors that foster the public good.

Tea Party movement A grassroots, conservative protest movement that opposed recent government actions, including economic stimulus spending and health care reform.

telegenic The quality of looking good on TV.

third party A party organized in opposition or as an alternative to the existing parties in a two-party system.

Three-Fifths Compromise The negotiated agreement by the delegates to the Constitutional Convention to count each slave as three-fifths of a free man for the purpose of representation and taxes.

ticket splitting The situation in which voters vote for candidates from more than one party.

time, place, and manner restrictions Regulations regarding when, where, or how expression may occur; must be content neutral.

tort Situation when a person's body or property is harmed by another person's negligence or other wrongful act, other than the violation of a contract.

total incorporation The theory that the Fourteenth Amendment's due process clause requires the states to uphold *all* freedoms in the Bill of Rights; rejected by the Supreme Court in favor of selective incorporation.

totalitarianism System of government in which the government essentially controls every aspect of people's lives.

township A unit of government that serves people living outside municipalities, in rural areas where the population is more dispersed than in areas served by municipal governments.

tracking polls Polls that measure changes in public opinion over the course of days, weeks, or months by repeatedly asking respondents the same questions and measuring changes in their responses.

trade policy A collection of tax laws and regulations that support the country's international commerce.

traditionalistic political culture The view that the purpose of government is to maintain the status quo and that participants in government should come from the society's elite.

transparency Ability of citizens to have more and better information about governmental processes as well as services.

trial court Court with original jurisdiction in a legal dispute that decides guilt or liability based on its understanding of the facts presented by the two disputing parties.

Truman Doctrine Articulated by President Harry Truman, a foreign policy commitment by the United States to assist countries' efforts to resist communism in the Cold War era.

truncated government The situation that exists when one chamber of Congress is controlled by the same party that controls the White House, while the other chamber is controlled by the other party.

trustee model A model of representation in which a member of the House or the Senate follows his or her own conscience when deciding issue positions.

turnout rate The proportion of eligible voters who actually voted.

U

umbrella organizations Interest groups that represent collective groups of industries or corporations.

unanimous consent An agreement by every senator to the terms of debate on a given piece of legislation.

unicameral legislature A legislative body with a single chamber.

unitary system A governmental system in which one central government is *the* sovereign government and it creates other, regional governments to which it delegates some governing powers and responsibilities; however, the central government retains ultimate authority (sovereignty).

United Nations (UN) An international body established in 1945 in order to prevent future wars by achieving collective security and peace.

U.S. Code A compilation of all the laws passed by the U.S. Congress.

U.S. Supreme Court The court of last resort for conflicts over the U.S. Constitution and national laws; in addition to its appellate jurisdiction, the Court also has limited original jurisdiction.

V

veto The president's rejection of a bill, which is sent back to Congress with the president's objections noted.

Virginia Plan The new governmental structure proposed by the Virginia delegation to the Constitutional Convention, which consisted of a bicameral legislature (Congress), an executive elected by the legislature, and a separate national judiciary; state representation in Congress would be proportional, based on state population; the people would elect members to the lower house, and members of the lower house would elect the members of the upper house.

virtual communities Online networks where individuals perform as leaders, information and opinions can be shared, and strategies can be planned, priorities organized, and roles assigned.

vlog A video weblog.

voter fatigue The condition in which voters grow tired of all candidates by the time Election Day arrives, and may thus be less likely to vote.

W

War Powers Act A law that limits presidential use of military forces to 60 days, with an automatic extension of 30 additional days if the president requests such an extension.

Warsaw Pact A regional security structure formed in 1955 by the Soviet Union and its seven satellite states in Eastern Europe in response to the creation of the North Atlantic Treaty Organization (NATO).

Watergate During the Nixon administration, a scandal involving burglaries and the subsequent cover-up by high-level administration officials.

weak mayor An elected municipal government executive who holds few, if any, of the powers traditionally delegated to elected chief executives.

weapons of mass destruction (WMDs) Nuclear, chemical, and biological weapons.

whistleblower A civil servant who discloses to the government mismanagement, fraud, waste, corruption, or threats to public health and safety.

White House counsel The president's lawyer.

White House Office (WHO) The office that develops policies and protects the president's legal and political interests.

white primary A primary election in which a party's nominees for general election were chosen but in which only white people were allowed to vote.

wiki Internet-based editing tool that allows documents to be created and edited online by multiple individuals.

winner-take-all system An electoral system in which the candidate who receives the most votes wins that office, even if that total is not a majority.

Works Progress Administration (WPA) A New Deal program that employed 8.5 million people at a cost of more than $11 million between 1935 and 1943.

World Bank The international financial institution created by the Bretton Woods Agreement of 1944 and charged with lending money to nations in need.

World Trade Organization (WTO) The organization created in 1995 to negotiate, implement, and enforce international trade agreements.

writ of *certiorari* Latin for "a request to make certain"; issued by a higher court, this is an order for a lower court to make available the records of a past case it decided so that the higher court can review the case.

Y

yellow journalism An irresponsible, sensationalist approach to news reporting, so named after the yellow ink used in the "Yellow Kid" cartoons in the *New York World*.

REFERENCES

CHAPTER 1

1. Rogers Smith, *Civic Ideals: Conflicting Visions of Citizenship in U.S. History* (New Haven, CT: Yale University Press, 1997).
2. Robert A. Dahl, *Who Governs? Democracy and Power in an American City* (New Haven, CT: Yale University Press, 1961).
3. E. E. Schattschneider, *The Semi-Sovereign People* (New York: Holt, Rinehart, and Winston, 1960).
4. Institute of Politics at Harvard University, "Attitudes Towards Politics and Public Service: A National Survey of College Undergraduates," April 11–20, 2000, www.iop.harvard.edu/pdfs/survey/2000.pdf.
5. Ibid.
6. Ibid.
7. E. J. Dionne Jr., *Why Americans Hate Politics: The Death of the Democratic Process,* 2nd ed. (New York: Touchstone, 1992).
8. Gallup Poll, "Trust in Government," www.gallup.com/poll/5392/Trust-Government.aspx.
9. Institute of Politics at Harvard University, "Attitudes Towards Politics and Public Service: A National Survey of College Undergraduates," April 11–20, 2000, www.iop.harvard.edu/pdfs/survey/2000.pdf.
10. Barbara Roswell, "From Service-Learning to Service Politics: A Conversation With Rick Battistoni," http://reflectionsjournal.org/Articles/V3.N1.Battistoni.Rick.Roswell.Barbara.pdf.
11. Michael Delli Carpini, Director Pew Charitable Trusts, www.apa.org/ed/slce/civicengagement.html.
12. S. E. Finer, *The History of Government,* 3 vols. (London: Oxford University Press, 1997).
13. Martin A. Reddish, *The Constitution as Political Structure* (London: Oxford University Press, 1995).
14. Theodore Sky, *To Provide for the General Welfare: A History of the Federal Spending Power* (Newark: University of Delaware Press, 2003).
15. David Epstein, *The Political Theory of the Federalist* (Chicago: University of Chicago Press, 1984).
16. Thomas Hobbes, *Leviathan* (1651; New York: Oxford University Press, 1996), chap. 14.
17. *New York Times,* "America Enduring," September 11, 2002, http://query.nytimes.com/gst/fullpage.html?res=9A00E0DE1431F932A2575AC0A9649C8B63&scp=1&sq=america+enduring&st=nyt.
18. Oscar Handlin and Mary Handlin, *The Dimensions of Liberty* (Cambridge, MA: Harvard University Press, 1961).
19. Richard Labunski, *James Madison and the Struggle for the Bill of Rights* (London: Oxford University Press, 2006).
20. Jack N. Rakove, *Original Meanings: Politics and Ideas in the Making of the Constitution* (New York: Knopf, 1996).
21. Clyde W. Barrow, *Critical Theories of the State: Marxist, Neo-Marxist, Post-Marxist* (Madison: University of Wisconsin Press, 1993).
22. Seymour Martin Lipset and Gary Marks, *It Didn't Happen Here: Why Socialism Failed in the United States* (New York: W. W. Norton, 2001).
23. Giovanni Sartori and Peter Mair, *Parties and Party Systems: A Framework for Analysis* (Oxford, England: European Consortium for Political Research.
24. Ira Katznelson and Martin Shefter, eds., *Shaped by War and Trade: International Influences on American Political Development* (Princeton, NJ: Princeton University Press, 2002).
25. *Wing Hing v. City of Eureka* (Calif.), 1886.

CHAPTER 2

1. Adam Liptak, "'We the People' Loses Appeal With People Around the World," *New York Times,* February 6, 2012.
2. "Sugar Act of 1764," www.u-s-history.com/pages/h1211.html.
3. "Great Britain: Parliament—The Stamp Act, March 22, 1765," http://avalon.law.yale.edu/18th_century/stamp_act_1765.asp.
4. "Prelude to Revolution," www.historyplace.com/unitedstates/revolution/rev-prel.htm.
5. J. Alan Rogers, "Colonial Opposition to the Quartering of Troops During the French and Indian War," *Military Affairs* (1970): 7.
6. "Great Britain: Parliament—The Declaratory Act, March 18, 1766," http://avalon.law.yale.edu/18th_century/declaratory_act_1766.asp.
7. America's Homepage, "The Townshend Act," http://ahp.gatech.edu/townshend_act_1767.html.
8. Russell Bourne, *Cradle of Violence: How Boston's Waterfront Mobs Ignited the American Revolution* (Hoboken, NJ: Wiley, 2006).
9. "Committees of Correspondence," www.u-s-history.com/pages/h675.html.
10. Boston Tea Party Ships & Museums, www.bostonteapartyship.com/.
11. "The Intolerable Acts," www.ushistory.org/declaration/related/intolerable.htm.
12. "The Declaration of Rights and Grievances," www.usconstitution.net/intol.html#Rights.
13. "The Articles of Association," www.usconstitution.net/assocart.html.
14. For further discussion of the impact of *Common Sense* on colonial attitudes and beliefs, see Edmund S. Morgan, *The Birth of the Republic: 1763–89* (Chicago: University of Chicago Press, 1992), 71–76.
15. "Lee's Resolutions," http://avalon.law.yale.edu/18th_century/lee.asp.
16. You can find these constitutions at Yale Law School's Avalon Project, http://avalon.law.yale.edu/subject_menus/18th.asp.
17. Jack N. Rakove, "A Tradition Born of Strife," in *American Politics: Classic and Contemporary Readings,* 6th ed., ed. Allan J. Cigler and Burdett A. Loomis (Boston: Houghton Mifflin, 2005), 4–5.
18. For an excellent discussion of how the Articles benefited the states, see Keith L. Dougherty, *Collective Action Under the Articles of Confederation* (New York: Cambridge University Press, 2001), 76–82.
19. "Proceedings of Commissioners to Remedy Defects of the Federal Government: 1786," http://avalon.law.yale.edu/18th_century/annapoli.asp.
20. Charles Beard, *An Economic Interpretation of the Constitution of the United States* (New York: Macmillan, 1913).
21. "The Constitutional Convention," www.usconstitution.net/consttop_ccon.html.
22. Eddie Becker, "Chronology on the History of Slavery and Racisim," http://innercity.org/holt/chron_1790_1829.html.
23. Richard Beeman, *The Penguin Guide to the United States Constitution* (New York: Penguin Books, 2010): 161.
24. *Marbury v. Madison,* 5 U.S. 137 (1803).
25. Alexander Hamilton, "Federalist No. 84," *The Federalist Papers* (Cutchogue, NY: Buccaneer Books, 1992), 436–37.
26. Thomas Jefferson, Letter to James Madison on the Bill of Rights debate, March 15, 1789. Courtesy of Eigen's Political & Historical Quotations.
27. Larry M. Lane and Judith J. Lane, "The Columbian Patriot: Mercy Otis Warren and the Constitution," in *Women, Politics, and the Constitution,* ed. Naomi B. Lunn (New York: Harrington Park Press, 1990), 17–31.
28. John P. Roche, "The Founding Fathers: A Reform Caucus in Action," *American Political Science Review,* LV (1961).
29. Larry J. Sabato, *A More Perfect Constitution: Why the Constitution Must Be Revised—Ideas to Inspire a New Generation* (New York: Walker Publishing Company), fn4, 315.
30. Ibid., 218.
31. Ibid., 221.
32. Alexander Hamilton, "Federalist No. 78," *The Federalist Papers* (Cutchogue, NY: Buccaneer Books, 1992), 395–396.
33. "Charles Evans Hughes," http://c250.columbia.edu/c250_celebrates/remarkable_columbians/charles_hughes.

34. Richard Beeman, *The Penguin Guide to the United States Constitution* (New York: Penguin Books, 2010): 190.

35. *Plessey v. Ferguson*, 163 U.S. 537 (1896).

36. *Brown v. Board of Education*, 347 U.S. 483 (1954).

37. Thomas Marshall, "Representing Public Opinion: American Courts and the Appeals Process," *Politics and Policy*, 31 (December 2003): 726–739.

CHAPTER 3

1. Laurence J. O'Toole, Jr., *American Intergovernmental Relations*, 7th ed. (Washington, D.C.: CQ Press, 2000), 2.

2. Anna Fifield, "Kennesaw, Where Everyone Is Armed by Law," *Financial Times*, September 25, 2010, www.ft.com/cms/s/2/5c1b6a72-c5eb-11df-b53e-00144feab49a.html#slide0.

3. *Marbury v. Madison*, 5 U.S. 137 (1803).

4. National Conference of State Legislators, "Federal and State Recognized Tribes," www.ncsl.org/research/state-tribal-institute/list-of-federal-and-state-recognized-tribes.aspx#federal.

5. Dennis L. Dresang and James J. Gosling, *Politics and Policy in American States and Communities*, 4th ed. (New York: Pearson Longman, 2004).

6. *McCulloch v. Maryland*, 17 U.S. 316 (1819).

7. *Gibbons v. Ogden*, 22 U.S. 1 (1824).

8. *United States v. Lopez*, 514 U.S. 549 (1995).

9. "*United States v. Lopez*," www.oyez.org/cases/1990-1999/1994/1994_93_1260.

10. *Helvering v. Davis*, 301 U.S. 619 (1937).

11. Colby Itkowitz, "Gay Couple's Path to Marriage Dovetails with High Court Cases," *Sunday Times* (Scranton, PA), June 2, 2013.

12. *United States v. Windsor*, 570 U.S. _____ (2013).

13. *Pruneyard Shopping Center & Fred Sahadi v. Michael Robins et al.*, 447 U.S. 74, 100 S. Ct. 2035.

14. "Old Enough to Drive—And Vote?" *Governing* (October 2013): 9.

15. *San Antonio Independent School District v. Rodriguez*, 411 U.S. 1 (1973).

16. G. Alan Tarr, *Judicial Process and Judicial Policymaking*, 6th ed. (Boston, MA: Cengage Learning, 2014), 309.

17. David B. Walker, *The Rebirth of Federalism*, 2nd ed. (New York: Chatham House, 2000).

18. *National League of Cities v. Usery*, 426 U.S. 833 (1976).

19. *Garcia v. San Antonio Transportation Authority*, 469 U.S. 528 (1985).

20. *United States v. Oakland Cannabis Buyers' Cooperative*, 532 U.S., (2005).

21. *Raich v. Gonzales*, 545 U.S. 1 (2005).

22. Dylan Scott, "The United States of America: In the Absence of Strong Federal Policies, States Have Become More Active—and More Divergent—Than They've Been in Decades," *Governing* (June 2013): 45.

23. "Justice Department Announces Update to Marijuana Enforcement Policy," www.justice.gov/opa/pr/2013/August/13-opa-974.html.

24. *Bush v. Gore*, 531 U.S. 98 (2000).

25. Congressional Budget Office, *Federal Grants to State and Local Governments*, March 2013, www.cbo.gov/publication/43967.

26. See, for example, Walker, *Rebirth of Federalism*.

27. Office of Management and Budget, Historical Tables, FY 2013, Tables 12.1 and 12.2, www.whitehouse.gov/omb/budget/Historicals.

28. *Massachusetts v. Mellon*, 262 U.S. 447 (1923).

29. *South Dakota v. Dole*, 483 U.S. 208 (1987).

30. *National Federation of Independent Business v. Sebelius*, 567 U.S. _____ (2012).

31. Winnie Hu, "$5 Billion Offered to Revisit Teacher Policies," *The New York Times*, February 15, 2012.

32. Scott, "The United States of America: In the Absence of Strong Federal Policies, States Have Become More Active—and More Divergent—Than They've Been in Decades," *Governing*, (June 2013), 42–47.; Peter Harkness, "Shall We Overcome? After 50 Years, a New No-Holds Barred States' Rights Movement Has Emerged," *Governing* (November 2013): 18–19.

CHAPTER 4

1. Stephen L. Carter, *The Dissent of the Governed: Law, Religion, and Loyalty* (Cambridge, MA: Harvard University Press, 1998).

2. For an accessible and lively account of the central role of liberty in the American Revolution, see Thomas Fleming, *Liberty! The American Revolution* (New York: Viking, 1997).

3. For a history of civil liberties in wartime, see Geoffrey R. Stone, *Perilous Times: Free Speech in Wartime From the Sedition Act of 1798 to the War on Terrorism* (New York: W. W. Norton, 2004).

4. *Barron v. Baltimore*, 32 U.S. 243 (1833).

5. See *Hurtado v. California*, 110 U.S. 516 (1884) and *Turning v. New Jersey*, 211 U.S. 78 (1908) for a discussion of the standard the Court uses to determine whether a particular liberty should be incorporated into the Fourteenth Amendment.

6. *Gitlow v. New York*, 268 U.S. 652 (1925).

7. *Near v. Minnesota*, 283 U.S. 697 (1931).

8. *Palko v. Connecticut*, 302 U.S. 319 (1937).

9. For a detailed look at evolution of our constitutional understanding of the Second Amendment, see Michael Waldman, *The Second Amendment: A Biography*. (New York: Simon & Schuster, 2014).

10. *District of Columbia v. Heller*, 554 U.S. (2008).

11. *McDonald v. City of Chicago*, 561 U.S. 3025 (2010).

12. Pew Research, "Gun Homicide Rate Down 49% Since 1993 Peak," May 2013, www.pewsocialtrends.org/2013/05/07/gun-homicide-rate-down-49-since-1993-peak-public-unaware/.

13. Presidential Proclamation of September 24, 1862, by President Abraham Lincoln, suspending the writ of *habeas corpus*.

14. For two detailed accounts of the acts, see John C. Miller, *Crisis in Freedom: The Alien and Sedition Acts* (Boston: Little, Brown, 1951); and James Morton Smith, *Freedom's Fetters: The Alien and Sedition Laws and American Civil Liberties* (Ithaca, NY: Cornell University Press, 1956).

15. Ron Fournier, "Bush Orders Terrorist Trials by Military Tribunals," Associated Press, November 13, 2001. Executive order available at www.whitehouse.gov/news/releases/releases/2001/11/20011113-27.html.

16. Associated Press, "Obama Administration Considering DC Trial for Guantanamo Detainee Riduan Isamuddin, aka Hambali," January 15, 2010, www.nydailynews.com/news/national/2010/01/15/2010-01-15_administration_considering_dc_for_gitmo_detainee.html.

17. 112th Congress, 1st Session, H1540CR.HSE, §1021.

18. Niels Lesniewski, "Senate Bill Puts Guantanamo on Path to Close," *Roll Call*, May 22, 2014, www.blogs.rollcall.com/wgdb/senate-bill-puts-guantanamo-on-path-to-close/?dcz=.

19. President Barack Obama, "Statement by the President on H.R. 1540," The White House, Office of the Press Secretary, December 31, 2011, www.whitehouse.gov/the-press-office/2011/12/31/statement-president-hr-1540.

20. *Schenck v. United States*, 249 U.S. 47 (1919).

21. *Gitlow v. New York*, 268 U.S. 652 (1925).

22. *Dennis v. U.S.*, 341 U.S. 494 (1951).

23. *Brandenburg v. Ohio*, 395 U.S. 444 (1969).

24. *U.S. v. O'Brien*, 391 U.S. 367 (1968).

25. *Tinker et al. v. Des Moines Independent Community School District et al.*, 393 U.S. 503 (1969).

26. For a discussion of *Tinker* and similar cases, see Jamin B. Baskin, *We the Students: Supreme Court Cases for and About Students*, 3rd ed. (Washington, DC: CQ Press, 2008).

27. *Texas v. Johnson*, 491 U.S. 397 (1989).

28. *U.S. v. Eichman*, 496 U.S. 310 (1990).

29. *Citizens United v. Federal Election Commission*, 558 U.S. 310 (2010).

30. *Miller v. California*, 413 U.S. 15 (1973).

31. *Chaplinsky v. New Hampshire*, 315 U.S. 568 (1942).

32. *Virginia v. Black*, 538 U.S. 343 (2003).

33. *Reno v. ACLU*, 521 U.S. 844 (1997); *U.S. v. Playboy Entertainment Group*, 529 U.S. 803 (2000).

34. *Ashcroft v. Free Speech Coalition*, 535 U.S. 234 (2002).

35. James Risen and Eric Lightblau, "Bush Lets U.S. Spy on Callers Without Courts," *The New York Times*, December 16, 2005, www.nytimes.com/2005/12/16/politics/16program.html?pagewanted=all&_r=0.

36. Marc Ambinder, "Shut Up: It's Still a Secret," *The Atlantic*, April 7, 2009, www.theatlantic.com/politics/archive/2009/04/shut-up-its-still-a-secret/7304/.

37. *New York Times v. U.S.*, 403 U.S. 713 (1971).

38. Gallup poll, "Religion," www.gallup.com/poll/1690/Religion.aspx.

39. The phrase "wall of separation" first appeared in Thomas Jefferson's 1802 letter to the Danbury Baptist Association. This letter is available at the Library of Congress website: www.loc.gov/loc/lcib/9806/danpre.html.

40. For a discussion of the doctrine of accommodationism, see Kenneth D. Wald, *Religion and Politics in the United States*, 3rd ed. (Washington, DC: CQ Press, 1997). For a discussion of neutrality, see Robert Booth Fowler, Allen D. Hertzke, and Laura R. Olson, *Religion and Politics in America: Faith*,

Culture, & Strategic Choices, 2nd ed. (Boulder, CO: Westview Press, 1999).

41. *Everson v. Board of Education,* 330 U.S. 1 (1947).

42. *Lemon v. Kurtzman,* 403 U.S. 602 (1971).

43. *Zelman v. Simmons-Harris,* 539 U.S. 639 (2002).

44. *Engel v. Vitale,* 370 U.S. 421 (1962).

45. See, for example, the U.S. District Court ruling in *Tammy Kitzmiller et al. v. Dover Area School District et al.,* 400 F. Supp. 2d 707 (M.D. Pa. 2005).

46. *Prince v. Massachusetts,* 321 U.S. 158 (1944).

47. *Employment Division, Department of Human Resources of the State of Oregon et al. v. Smith,* 494 U.S. 872 (1990).

48. *Griswold v. Connecticut,* 381 U.S. 479 (1965).

49. *Roberts v. U.S. Jaycees,* 468 U.S. 609 (1984).

50. *Roe v. Wade,* 410 U.S. 113 (1973).

51. *Planned Parenthood v. Casey,* 505 U.S. 833 (1992).

52. *Cruzan v. Director, Missouri Department of Health,* 497 U.S. 261 (1990).

53. Ibid.

54. *Bowers v. Hardwick,* 478 U.S. 186 (1986).

55. *Lawrence v. Texas,* 539 U.S. 558 (2003).

56. This is a point of agreement among the Court's opinion, the concurring opinion, and the dissenting opinion issued in *Lawrence v. Texas,* 539 U.S. 558 (2003).

57. American Civil Liberties Union, "NSA Documents Released to the Public Since June 2013," www.aclu.org/nsa-documents-released-public-june-2013.

58. Global Government Surveillance Reform, www.reformgovernmentsurveillance.com/.

59. *Weeks v. U.S.,* 232 U.S. 383 (1914).

60. *Mapp v. Ohio,* 367 U.S. 643 (1961).

61. See Chief Justice Warren E. Burger's dissent in *Coolidge v. New Hampshire,* 403 U.S. 443.

62. *Segura v. U.S.,* 468 U.S. 796 (1984).

63. *U.S. v. Leon,* 468 U.S. 897 (1984).

64. *California v. Greenwood,* 486 U.S. 35 (1988).

65. *United States v. Jones,* 565 U.S. _____ (2012).

66. *Miranda v. Arizona,* 384 U.S. 436 (1966).

67. *Gideon v. Wainwright,* 312 U.S. 335 (1963).

68. *Furman v. Georgia,* 408 U.S. 238 (1972).

69. The de facto moratorium on the death penalty ended in 1976 in a series of cases starting with *Gregg v. Georgia,* 428 U.S. 153 (1976).

70. *Baze v. Rees,* 553 U.S. (2008).

71. *Wilkerson v. Utah,* 99 U.S. 130 (1878).

72. For a recent report, see ACLU, "History Repeated: The Dangers of Domestic Spying by Federal Law Enforcement," May 29, 2007, www.aclu.org/images/asset_upload_file893_29902.pdf.

73. *Amnesty et al. v. Clapper,* 09-4112-cv, 2011 WL 4381737 (2nd Cir. September 21, 2011).

74. Larry Siems, "Why We're Challenging the FAA," July 22, 2009, www.aclu.org/blog/national-security/why-were-challenging-FAA.

75. ACLU, "No Real Threat: The Pentagon's Secret Database on Peaceful Protest," January 17, 2007, available at www.aclu.org/safefree/spyfiles/27988pub20070117.html.

76. Jo Mannies, "Ashcroft Defends Bush on Spying," St. Louis *Post-Dispatch,* February 10, 2008.

77. The full title of the law (H.R. 3162) is the Uniting and Strengthening America by Providing Appropriate Tools Required to Intercept and Obstruct Terrorism (USA PATRIOT) Act of 2001.

78. Protect America Act of 2007 (Pub.L. 110-55, S. 1927) signed into law by George W. Bush on August 5, 2007.

79. Offices of Inspectors General of the Department of Defense, Department of Justice, the Central Intelligence Agency, the National Security Agency, and the Office of the Director of National Intelligence, "Unclassified Report on the President's Surveillance Program," Report No. 2009-0013-AS, July 10, 2009.

80. For an articulation of this argument, see Charles Krauthammer, "The Truth About Torture," *The Weekly Standard,* December 5, 2005.

81. For an articulation of this viewpoint, see Andrew Sullivan, "The Abolition of Torture," *New Republic,* December 19, 2005.

82. The full text of the Detainee Treatment Act of 2005 (H.R. 2863, Title X) is available at http://thomas.loc.gov/cgi-bin/query/R?r109:FLD001:S10909.

83. The full text of a statement delivered by Condoleezza Rice, the former U.S. secretary of state, at Andrews Air Force base in Maryland is available at www.timesonline.co.uk/tol/news/world/us_and_americas/article745995.ece.

84. European Parliament report, "Alleged Secret Detentions and Unlawful Inter-State Transfers Involving Council of Europe Member States," January 22, 2006.

85. United States Department of Justice, "Special Task Force on Interrogations and Transfer Politics Issues Its Recommendations to the President," August 24, 2009, www.justice.gov/opa/pr/2009/August/09-ag-835.html.

86. Jack Serle and Chris Woods, "Six-Month Update: US Covert Actions in Pakistan, Yemen, and Somalia," *The Bureau of Investigative Journalism,* July 1, 2013, www.thebureauinvestigates.com/2013/07/01/six-month-update-us-covert-actionsin-pakistan-yemen-and-somalia/.

87. Elliot C. McLaughlin, Jamie Crawford, and Joe Sterling, "Obama: U.S. Will Keep Deploying Drones—When They Are the Only Option," CNN Politics, May 23, 2013, www.cnn.com/2013/05/23/politics/obama-terror-speech/.

88. Allie Bohm, "The Year of the Drone: An Analysis of State Legislation Passed This Year," American Civil Liberties Union, November 7, 2013, www.aclu.org/blog/technology-andliberty/year-drone-roundup-legislation-passed-year.

CHAPTER 5

1. Rolan J. Pennock, "Rights, Natural Rights, and Human Rights—A General View," in *Human Rights,* ed. J. R. Pennock and J. W. Chapman (New York: New York University Press, 1981).

2. David Cole, "Are Foreign Nationals Entitled to the Same Constitutional Rights as Citizens?" *Thomas Jefferson Law Review* 25 (2003), 367–388.

3. *Loving v. Virginia,* 388 U.S. 1 (1967).

4. *United States v. Windsor,* 133 S. Ct. 2675, 2013.

5. *Bowers v. Hardwick,* 478 U.S. 186 (1986).

6. *Lawrence and Garner v. Texas,* 539 U.S. 558 (2003).

7. Jon W. Davidson, "Celebrating Recent LGBT Legislative Advances," www.lambdalegal.org/our-work/publications/facts-backgrounds/recent-lgbt-advances/html.

8. www.adl.org/learn/hate_crimes_laws/map_frameset.html.

9. Donald E. Lively, *The Constitution and Race* (New York: Praeger, 1992).

10. John Hope Franklin and Evelyn Higginbotham, *From Slavery to Freedom,* 9th ed. (New York: McGraw-Hill, 2010).

11. *Dred Scott v. Sandford,* 60 U.S. 393 (1857).

12. *Plessy v. Ferguson,* 163 U.S. 537 (1896).

13. George T. Blakey, *Hard Times and New Deal in Kentucky, 1929–1939* (Lexington: University of Kentucky Press, 1986).

14. Richard Kluger, *Simple Justice: The History of* Brown v. Board of Education *and Black America's Struggle for Equality* (New York: Knopf, 1976).

15. Jo Ann Robinson, *The Montgomery Bus Boycott and the Women Who Started It* (Knoxville: University of Tennessee Press, 1987).

16. Michael Klarman, *From Jim Crow to Civil Rights: The Supreme Court and the Struggle for Racial Equality* (New York: Oxford University Press, 2004).

17. Taylor Branch, *Parting the Waters: America during the King Years, 1954–1963* (New York: Simon & Schuster, 1988).

18. *Browder v. Gale,* 142 F. Supp. 707 (1956).

19. John Dittmer, *Local People: The Struggle for Civil Rights in Mississippi* (Champaign, IL: University of Illinois Press, 1995).

20. John Lewis, *Walking with the Wind: A Memoir of the Movement* (New York: Simon & Schuster, 1998).

21. David J. Garrow, *Protest at Selma: Martin Luther King, Jr., and the Voting Rights Act of 1965* (New Haven, CT: Yale University Press, 1978).

22. Michael Honey, *Going Down Jericho Road: The Memphis Strike, Martin Luther King's Last Campaign* (New York: W. W. Norton, 2008).

23. Steven Lawson, *Black Ballots: Voting Rights in the South, 1944–1969* (New York: Columbia University Press, 1976).

24. *Shelby County, Alabama v. Holder,* 570 U.S. _____ (2013).

25. U.S. Census Bureau, "Section 8: Elections" in *Statistical Abstract of the United States: 2000,* www.census.gov/prod/2001pubs/statab/sec08.pdf.

26. *Bradwell v. Illinois,* 83 U.S. 130 (1873).

27. *Minor v. Happersett,* 88 U.S. 162 (1875).

28. National Organization for Women, "The National Organization for Women's 1966 Statement of Purpose," www.now.org/history/purpos66.html.

29. *Reed v. Reed,* 404 U.S. 71 (1971).

30. *Craig v. Boren,* 429 U.S. 190 (1976).

31. *U.S. v. Virginia,* 518 U.S. 515 (1996).

32. Lisa Jervis. "The End of Feminism's Third Wave," *Ms. Magazine,* Winter 2004, www.msmagazine.com/winter2004/thirdwave.asp.

33. Joe R. Feagin and Clairece Booher Feagin, *Racial and Ethnic Relations* (Upper Saddle River, NJ: Prentice Hall, 2003): 135.

34. National Indian Gaming Commission, "2012 Indian Gaming Revenues Increase 2.7 Percent," July 23, 2013, www.nigc.gov/Media/Press_Releases/2013_Press_Releases.aspx.

35. Feagin and Feagin, *Racial and Ethnic Relations,* 135.

36. "Amicus Curiae Brief of the Navajo Nation in support of the respondents in *Shelby County v. Holder,*" 2013, www.naacpldf.org/files/case_issue/ShelbyBrief%20of%20Amici%20Curiae%20the%20Navajo%20Nation.pdf.

37. Jens Manuel Krogstad and Mark Hugo Lopez, "Hispanic Nativity Shift," April 29, 2014, www.pewhispanic.org/2014/04/29/hispanic-nativity-shift/.

38. Mark Hugo Lopez and Ana Gonzalez-Barrera, "Inside the 2012 Latino Electorate," June 3, 2013, www.pewhispanic.org/2013/06/03/inside-the-2012-latino-electorate/.

39. League of Latin American Citizens, "LULAC History—All for One and One for All," http://lulac.org/about/history/.

40. Ibid.

41. *Mendez v. Westminister,* 64 F. Supp. 544 (1946).

42. Feagin and Feagin, *Racial and Ethnic Relations,* 218.

43. *Corpus Christi Independent School District v. Cisneros,* 404 U.S. 1211 (1971).

44. Texas State Historical Association, "The Handbook of Texas Online," www.tshaonline.org/handbook/online/articles/CC/jrc2.html.

45. *Arizona v. United States,* 132 S. Ct. 2492 (2012).

46. Pew Research, "Demographics of Asian Americans," April 4, 2013, www.pewsocialtrends.org/2013/04/04/asian-groups-in-the-U-S/.

47. Feagin and Feagin, *Racial and Ethnic Relations,* 278, 310.

48. Ibid., 315.

49. Marisa Osorio, "New Edition of National Asian Pacific American Political Almanac Examines Group's Growing Impact," UCLA Newsroom, June 28, 2000, http://newsroom.ucla.edu/releases/New-Edition-Of-National-Asian-Pacific-1605.

50. U.S. Equal Employment Opportunity Commission, "The Americans with Disabilities Act Amendments Act of 2008," www.eeoc.gov/laws/statutes/adaaa_info.cfm.

51. *Regents of the University of California v. Bakke,* 438 U.S. 265 (1978).

52. *Grutter v. Bollinger,* 539 U.S. 306 (2003).

53. *Parents Involved in Community Schools v. Seattle School District No. 1 et al.,* and *Meredith v. Jefferson County Board of Education,* 551 U.S. 701 (2007).

54. *Fisher v. University of Texas,* 133 S. Ct. 2411 (2013).

CHAPTER 6

1. V. O. Key Jr., *Public Opinion and American Democracy* (New York: Knopf, 1961), 8.

2. J. Foster-Bey, *Do Race, Ethnicity, Citizenship and Socio-economic Status Determine Civic-Engagement?* (College Park, MD: CIRCLE: The Center for Information and Research on Civic Learning & Engagement, 2008), 4.

3. Mark Hugo Lopez, Peter Levine, Deborah Both, Abby Kiesa, Emily Kirby, and Karlo Marcelo, *The 2006 Civic and Political Health of the Nation: A Detailed Look at How Youth Participate in Politics and Communities* (College Park, MD: CIRCLE: The Center for Information and Research on Civic Learning and Engagement, 2006), 4.

4. Ibid.

5. Sidney Verba, Kay Lehman Schlozman, and Henry E. Brady, *Voice and Equality: Civic Voluntarism in American Politics* (Cambridge, MA: Harvard University Press, 1995), 439.

6. Frank Newport, "Religiousness a Key Factor for Romney and Obama Support," April 25, 2012, www.gallup.com/poll/154097/Religiousness-Key-Factor-Romney-Obama-Support.aspx.

7. David L. Leal, Matt A. Barreto, Jongho Lee, and Rodolfo O. de la Garza, "The Latino Vote in the 2004 Election," *PS: Political Science and Politics* (2005): 46.

8. Lopez et al., *The 2006 Civic and Political Health of the Nation,* 20–21.

9. David W. Moore, "Death Penalty Gets Less Support from Britons, Canadians Than Americans," Gallup News Service, February 20, 2006.

10. Karlo Barrios Marcelo, Mark Hugo Lopez, and Emily Hoban Kirby, *Civic Engagement Among Young Men and Women* (College Park, MD: CIRCLE: The Center for Information and Research on Civic Learning and Engagement, 2007), 12.

11. Elizabeth Noelle-Neumann, *The Spiral of Silence: Public Opinion—Our Social Skin,* 2nd ed. (Chicago: University of Chicago Press, 1993).

12. Susan Herbst, *Numbered Voices: How Opinion Polling Has Shaped American Politics* (Chicago: University of Chicago Press, 1993).

13. Robert S. Erikson, Gerald C. Wright, and John P. McIver, *Statehouse Democracy: Public Opinion and Policy in the American States* (New York: Cambridge University Press, 1994).

14. Walter Lippmann, *Public Opinion* (1929; repr. London: Free Press, 1997), 114.

15. "George Gallup, 1901–1984: Founder, The Gallup Organization," http://gallup.com/content/?ci=21364.

16. Herbert Asher, *Polling and the Public: What Every Citizen Should Know* (Washington, DC: CQ Press, 2001).

17. Ibid., 2.

18. Randolph Grossman and Douglas Weiland, "The Use of Telephone Directories as a Sample Frame: Patterns of Bias Revisited, *Journal of Advertising* 7 (1978): 31–36.

19. Stephen J. Blumberg and Julian V. Luke, "Coverage Bias in Traditional Telephone Surveys of Low-Income and Young Adults," *Public Opinion Quarterly* 71 (2007): 734–749.

20. "Wireless Solution: Early Release Estimates from the National Health Interview Survey, January–June, 2013," National Center for Health Statistics, Centers for Disease Control and Prevention, December 2013. www.cdc.gov/nchs/data/nhis/earlyrelease/wireless201312.pdf.

21. Blumberg and Luke, "Coverage Bias in Traditional Telephone Surveys of Low-Income and Young Adults," 734–749.

22. "Wireless Solution: Early Release Estimates From the National Health Interview Survey, January–June, 2013," National Center for Health Statistics, Centers for Disease Control and Prevention, December 2013.

23. Clyde Tucker, J. Michael Brick, and Brian Meekins, "Household Telephone Service and Usage Patterns in the United States in 2004: Implications for Telephone Samples," *Public Opinion Quarterly* 71 (2007): 3–22.

24. George Terhanian and John Bremer, "Confronting the Selection-Bias and Learning Effects Problems Associated with Internet Research," Harris Interactive white paper, August 16, 2000.

25. G. Terhanian, R. Smith, J. Bremer, and R. K. Thomas, "Exploiting Analytical Advances: Minimizing the Biases Associated with Internet-Based Surveys of Non-Random Samples," *ARF/ESOMAR: Worldwide Online Measurement* 248 (2001): 247–72.

26. Irving Crespi, *Pre-Election Polling: Sources of Accuracy & Error* (New York: Russell Sage Foundation, 1988).

27. Benjamin I. Page and Robert Y. Shapiro, *The Rational Public: Fifty Years of Trends in Americans' Policy Preferences* (Chicago: University of Chicago Press, 1992).

28. Frank Newport, *Polling Matters: Why Leaders Must Listen to the Wisdom of the People* (New York: Warner Books, 2004).

29. James A. Stimson, *Tides of Consent: How Public Opinion Shapes American Politics* (Cambridge: Cambridge University Press, 2004).

30. Lydia Saad, "One in Six Say Immigration Most Important Problem," July 16, 2014, www.gallup.com/poll/173306/one-six-say-immigration-important-problem.aspx.

31. Frank Newport and Joseph Carroll, "Iraq versus Vietnam: A Comparison of Public Opinion," August 24, 2005, www.galluppoll.com/content/default.aspx?ci=18097&pg=2.

32. Jeffrey M. Jones and Joseph Carroll, "National Satisfaction Level Dips to 25%, One of Lowest Since 1979," May 16, 2007.

33. David W. Moore, "Top Ten Gallup Presidential Approval Ratings," Gallup press release, September 24, 2001.

CHAPTER 7

1. Frank R. Baumgartner and Beth L. Leech, *Basic Interests: The Importance of Groups in Politics and in Political Science* (Princeton, NJ: Princeton University Press, 1998).

2. Peggy Daniels and Carol Schwartz, *Encyclopedia of Associations 1996* (Detroit, MI: Gale Research, 1995).

3. Alexis De Tocqueville, *Democracy in America: The Complete and Unabridged Volumes I and II* (1835–1840; New York: Bantam, 2000), 51.

4. Everett Carll Ladd, *The Ladd Report* (New York: Free Press, 1999).

5. Publius (James Madison), *Federalist #10,* 1787, www.ourdocuments.gov/doc.php?doc=10.

6. Robert D. Putnam, *Bowling Alone: The Collapse and Revival of American Community* (New York: Touchstone, 2000).

7. Claude S. Fischer, "Bowling Alone: What's the Score?" *Social Networks* 27 (May): 155–167.

8. E. E. Schattschneider, *The Semi-Sovereign People* (New York: Holt, Rinehart, and Winston, 1960), 132.

9. Earl Latham, *The Group Basis of Politics* (Ithaca, NY: Cornell University Press, 1952).

10. David B. Truman, *The Governmental Process* (New York: Knopf, 1951).

11. Hugh Davis Graham, *The Civil Rights Era: Origins and Development of National Policy, 1960–1972* (London: Oxford University Press, 1990).

12. Sidney Verba, Kay Schlozman, and Nancy Burns, *The Private Roots of Public Action: Gender, Equality, and Political Participation* (Cambridge, MA: Harvard University Press, 2001).

13. Quoted in Mark P. Petracca, *The Politics of Interests* (Boulder, CO: Westview, 1992), 347.

14. Julie Greene, *Pure and Simple Politics: The American Federation of Labor and Political Activism, 1881–1917* (New York: Cambridge University Press, 1998).

15. Elizabeth Sanders, *Roots of Reform: Farmers, Workers, and the American State, 1877–1917* (Chicago: University of Chicago Press, 1998).

16. Sharon E. Jarvis, Lisa Montoya, and Emily Mulvoy, *The Civic Participation of Working Youth and College Students: Working Paper 36* (Austin, TX: The Annette Strauss Institute for Civic Participation, and CIRCLE, the Center for Information and Research on Civic Learning and Engagement, 2005).

17. James Q. Wilson, *Political Organizations* (New York: Basic Books, 1973).

18. Jeffrey Berry, *The Interest Group Society,* 3rd ed. (New York: Longman, 1997).

19. Martin J. Smith, *Pressures, Power and Policy: Policy Networks and State Autonomy in Britain and the United States* (Pittsburgh, PA: University of Pittsburgh, 1994).

20. Herbert Alexander, *Money in Politics* (Washington, D.C.: Public Affairs Press, 1972).

21. Frank Sorauf, *Money in American Elections* (New York: Little, Brown, 1988).

22. OpenSecrets.org. www.opensecrets.org/lobby/clientsum.php?id=D000032202.

23. Frank Sorauf, *Inside Campaign Finance: Myths and Realities* (New Haven, CT: Yale University Press, 1992).

24. Gary C. Jacobson, *Money in Congressional Elections* (New Haven, CT: Yale University Press, 1980).

25. Allan J. Cigler and Burdett A. Loomis, *Interest Group Politics* (Washington, D.C.: CQ Press, 1991).

26. Michael S. Schmidt, Eric Lipton, and Alexandra Stevenson. "After Big Bet, Hedge Fund Pulls the Levers of Power," *The New York Times,* March 9, 2014. www.nytimes.com/2014/03/10/business/staking-1-billion-that-herbalife-will-fail-then-ackman-lobbying-to-bring-it-down.html?_r=0.

27. Tami Luhby, "Wisconsin's Walker: Union Man of the Year," March 11, 2011, http://money.cnn.com/2011/03/11/news/economy/wisconsin_unions_collective_bargaining/index.htm.

28. U.S. Bureau of Labor Statistics, "Union Members Summary, January 24, 2014, www.bls.gov/news.release/union2.nr0.htm.

29. Lucy G. Barber, *Marching on Washington: The Forging of an American Political Tradition* (Los Angeles: University of California Press, 2002).

30. Christian Coalition of America, "About Us," www.cc.org/about_us.

31. Jeremy M. Sharp, *U.S. Foreign Aid to Israel,* Congressional Research Service, April 11, 2013, www.fas.org/sgp/crs/mideast/RL33222.pdf.

32. John Pomfret, "China's Lobbying Efforts Yield New Influence, Openness on Capitol Hill," *The Washington Post,* January 9, 2010, www.washingtonpost.com/wp-dyn/content/article/2010/01/08/AR2010010803710.html?sid=ST2010010900293.

33. Ibid.

34. *Citizens United v. Federal Election Commission,* 558 U.S. 310 (2010).

35. Louise Overacker, *Money in Elections* (New York: Macmillan, 1932), 3.

CHAPTER 8

1. E. E. Schattschneider, *Party Government* (New York: Farrar & Rinehart, 1942), 1.

2. L. Sandy Maisel and Kara Z. Buckley, *Parties and Elections in America,* 4th ed. (Lanham, MD: Rowman & Littlefield, 2004).

3. Jo Freeman, *A Room at a Time: How Women Entered Party Politics* (New York: Rowman & Littlefield, 2000).

4. Ibid.

5. Melanie Gustafson, Kristie Miller, and Elisabeth Israels Perry, *We Have Come to Stay: American Women and Political Parties, 1880–1960* (Albuquerque: University of New Mexico Press, 1999).

6. V. O. Key, *Politics, Parties, and Pressure Groups* (New York: Thomas Y. Crowell, 1964).

7. Seymour Martin Lipset and Stein Rokkan, *Party Systems and Voter Alignments* (New York: Free Press, 1967).

8. Geoffrey Layman, *The Great Divide: Religious and Cultural Conflict in American Party Politics* (New York: Columbia University Press, 2002).

9. Jeffrey M. Jones, "Economy Is Paramount Issue to U.S. Voters," February 29, 2012, www.gallup.com/poll/153029/Economy-Paramount-Issue-Voters.aspx.

10. Walter Dean Burnham, *Critical Elections and the Mainsprings of American Politics* (New York: W. W. Norton, 1997).

11. John Aldrich, *Why Parties? The Origin and Transformation of Party Politics in America* (Chicago: University of Chicago Press, 1995).

12. *Buckley v. Valeo,* 424 U.S. 1 (1976).

13. Regina Dougherty, "Divided Government Defines the Era," in *America at the Polls: 1996,* ed. Regina Dougherty, Everett C. Ladd, David Wilber, and Lynn Zayachkiwsky (Storrs, CT: Roper Center for Public Opinion Research, 1997).

14. Richard Hofstadter, "A Constitution against Parties: Madisonian Pluralism and the Anti-Party Tradition," *Government and Opposition* 4 (1969), 345–366.

15. Jefferson and Washington, quoted in Richard Hofstadter, *The Idea of a Party System: The Rise of Legitimate Opposition in the United States, 1780–1840* (Berkeley and Los Angeles: University of California Press, 1969): 2, 123.

16. Richard Hofstadter, *The Idea of a Party System: The Rise of Legitimate Opposition in the United States 1780–1840* (Berkeley: University of California Press, 1970).

17. James L. Sundquist, *Dynamics of the Party System: Alignment and Realignment of Political Parties in the United States* (Washington, DC: Brookings, 1983).

18. Everett C. Ladd, *American Political Parties* (New York: W. W. Norton, 1970).

19. David R. Mayhew, *Electoral Realignments: A Critique of an American Genre* (New Haven, CT: Yale University Press, 2002).

20. William Nisbet Chambers, *Political Parties in a New Nation: The American Experience, 1776–1809* (New York: Oxford University Press, 1963).

21. Lance Banning, *The Jeffersonian Persuasion: Evolution of a Party Ideology* (Ithaca, NY: Cornell University Press, 1978).

22. Richard L. McCormick, *The Party Period and Public Policy: American Politics from the Age of Jackson to the Progressive Era* (New York: Oxford University Press, 1986).

23. Jules Witcover, *Party of the People: A History of the Democrats* (New York: Random House, 2003).

24. Lee Benson, *The Concept of Jacksonian Democracy* (Princeton, NJ: Princeton University Press, 1961).

25. Aileen Kraditor, *The Ideas of the Woman Suffrage Movement, 1890–1920* (New York: W. W. Norton, 1981).

26. Eric Foner, *Free Soil, Free Labor, Free Men: The Ideology of the Republican Party Before the Civil War* (New York: Oxford University Press, 1995).

27. William E. Gienapp, *The Origins of the Republican Party, 1852–1856* (New York: Oxford University Press, 1987).

28. Witcover, *Party of the People.*

29. McCormick, *The Party Period and Public Policy.*

30. Joel H. Silbey, *The Partisan Imperative: The Dynamics of American Politics Before the Civil War* (New York: Oxford University Press, 1985).

31. Lewis L. Gould, *Grand Old Party: A History of the Republicans* (New York: Random House, 2003).

32. Paul Kleppner, *The Third Electoral System, 1853–1892: Parties, Voters, and Political Cultures* (Chapel Hill: University of North Carolina Press, 1979).

33. Quoted in A. James Reichley, "Party Politics in a Federal Polity," in *Challenges to Party Government,* ed. John Kenneth White and Jerome M. Mileur (Carbondale: Southern Illinois University, 1992), 48.

34. Kristi Anderson, *After Suffrage* (Chicago: University of Chicago Press, 1996), 30.

35. John Petrocik, *Party Coalitions: Realignment and the Decline of the New Deal Party System* (Chicago: University of Chicago Press, 1981).

36. David G. Lawrence, *The Collapse of the Democratic Majority: Realignment, Dealignment, and Electoral Change from Franklin Roosevelt to Bill Clinton* (New York: Westview, 1997).

37. Gary Orren, "The Changing Styles of American Party Politics," in *The Future of American*

Political Parties: The Challenge of Governance, ed. Joel L. Fleishman (Englewood Cliffs, NJ: Prentice Hall, 1982), 31.

38. *Citizens United v. Federal Election Commission,* 558 U.S. _____ (2010).

39. The basis for this argument can be found in Larry J. Sabato and Bruce Larson, *The Party's Just Begun: Shaping Political Parties for America's Future,* 2nd ed. (New York: Longman, 2001).

40. Edward G. Carmines, John P. McIver, and James A. Stimson, "Unrealized Partisanship: A Theory of Dealignment," *Journal of Politics* 49 (1987): 376–400.

41. Jeffrey M. Jones, "Party Satisfaction on Healthcare, Foreign Affairs Varies Most," www .gallup.com/poll/163496/party-satisfaction-healthcare-foreign-affairs-varies.aspx.

42. David Karol, Hans Noel, John Zaller, and Marty Cohen, "Polls or Pols? The Real Driving Force behind Presidential Nominations," *Brookings Review* 21.3 (2003): 36–39.

43. Arend Lijphardt, *Electoral Systems and Party Systems: A Study of Twenty-Seven Democracies, 1945–1990* (New York: Oxford University Press, 1994).

44. Lipset and Rokkan, *Party Systems and Voter Alignments.*

45. Maurice Duverger, *Political Parties* (New York: Wiley, 1951).

46. Steven J. Rosenstone, Roy L. Behr, and Edward H. Lazarus, *Third Parties in America,* 2nd ed. (Princeton, NJ: Princeton University Press, 1996).

CHAPTER 9

1. V. O. Key, *The Responsible Electorate* (Cambridge, MA: Harvard University Press, 1966).

2. Samuel C. Patterson and Gregory A. Caldeira, "Getting Out the Vote: Participation in Gubernatorial Elections," *American Political Science Review* 77 (1983): 675–689.

3. Barbara Norrander, *Super Tuesday: Regional Politics and Presidential Primaries* (Lexington: University of Kentucky Press, 1992).

4. Thomas E. Cronin, *Direct Democracy: The Politics of Initiative, Referendum, and Recall* (Cambridge, MA: Harvard University Press, 1999).

5. David Broder, *Democracy Derailed: Initiative Campaigns and the Power of Money* (New York: Harvest Books, 2001).

6. Colorado State Constitution, Amendment 64: Use and Regulation of Marijuana.

7. The Pew Charitable Trusts, State and Consumer Initiatives, "Punch-Card Voting in Idaho," www.pewstates.org/research/analysis/punch-card-voting-in-idaho-85899399631.

8. John F. Bibby, *Politics, Parties, and Elections in America* (Belmont, CA: Wadsworth, 2000), 253.

9. Pat Buchanan on NBC's *Today Show,* "The American Presidency Project," November 9, 2000, www.presidency.ucsb.edu/showflorida2000.php?fileid=buchanan11-09.

10. Ibid.

11. Pippa Norris, ed., *Politics and the Press: The News Media and Their Influences* (Boulder, CO: Lynne Rienner Publishers, 1997).

12. See, for example, Matthew Dowd, "Campaign Organization and Strategy," in *Electing the President 2004: An Insider's View,* ed. Kathleen Hall Jamieson (Philadelphia: University of Pennsylvania Press, 2006).

13. Vivé Griffith, "The Influence of Media in Presidential Politics," Think Democracy Project, University of Texas at Austin, www.utexas.edu/features/archive/2004/election_media.html.

14. Dan Morain, "Small Democratic Donors Have an Online Pal," *Los Angeles Times,* http://articles.latimes.com/2007/mar/11/nation/na-actblue11.

15. Gary Jacobson, *Money and Congressional Elections* (New Haven, CT: Yale University Press, 1980).

16. David Adamany, "Money, Politics and Democracy," *American Political Science Review* 71 (1977): 289–304.

17. *Buckley v. Valeo,* 424 U.S. (1976).

18. See Anthony Corrado, Thomas E. Mann, Dan Ortiz, Trevor Potter, and Frank Sorauf, *Campaign Finance Reform: A Sourcebook* (Washington, D.C.: Brookings Institute, 1997).

19. *Federal Election Commission v. National Conservative PAC,* 470 U.S. 480 (1985).

20. *McConnell v. Federal Election Commission,* 540 U.S. 93 (2003).

21. *Federal Election Commission v. Wisconsin Right to Life, Inc.,* 551 U.S. (2007).

22. Center for Responsive Politics, "Super PACs," April 7, 2014, www.opensecrets.org/pacs/superpacs.php?cycle=2014.

23. Norman H. Nie, Sidney Verba, and John R. Petrocik, *The Changing American Voter* (Cambridge, MA: Harvard University Press, 1976).

24. Angus Campbell, Philip Converse, Warren Miller, and Donald Stokes, *The American Voter* (New York: Wiley, 1960).

25. Jan Leighley and Jonathan Nagler, "Who Votes Now? And Does It Matter?" (paper presented at the 2007 annual meeting of the Midwest Political Science Association, Chicago).

26. Norman H. Nie, Jane Junn, and Kenneth Stehlik-Barry, *Education and Democratic Citizenship in America* (Chicago: University of Chicago Press, 1996).

27. Jan E. Leighley and Jonathan Nagler, "Socioeconomic Class Bias in Turnout, 1964–1988: The Voters Remain the Same," *American Political Science Review* 86 (1992): 725–736.

28. The Annenberg National Election Study (ANES), "Voter Turnout 1948–2004," www.electionstudies.org/nesguide/2ndtable/t6a_2_2.htm.

29. Kim Nguyen and James Garand, "The Effects of Income Inequality on Political Attitudes and Behavior" (paper presented at the 2007 annual meeting of the Midwest Political Science Association, Chicago).

30. Richard A. Brody, "The Puzzle of Political Participation in America," in *The New American Political System,* ed. Anthony King (Washington, D.C.: American Enterprise Institute for Public Policy Research, 1978), 287–324.

31. Thom File, "The Diversifying Electorate—Voting Rates by Race and Hispanic Origin in 2012 (and Other Recent Elections)," U.S. Census Bureau, www.census.gov/Press-Release/www/releases /archives/voting/013995.html.

32. Pippa Norris, "Retrospective Voting in the 1984 Presidential Election: Peace, Prosperity, and Patriotism," *Political Studies* 35 (1987): 289–300.

33. Daniel M. Shea, *Campaign Craft: The Strategies, Tactics, and Art of Political Campaign Management* (Westport, CT: Praeger, 1996).

34. Nie, Verba, and Petrocik, *The Changing American Voter.*

35. Samuel Kernell, "Presidential Popularity and Negative Voting," *American Political Science Review* 71 (1977): 44–66.

36. Shanto Iyengar and Jennifer A. McGrady, *Media Politics: A Citizen's Guide* (New York: W. W. Norton, 2006).

37. Warren E. Miller, "Disinterest, Disaffection, and Participation," *Political Behavior* 2 (1980): 7–32.

38. E. E. Schattschneider, *The Semi-Sovereign People* (New York: Holt, Rinehart, and Winston, 1960).

39. Pew Research Center for People and the Press, "Beyond Red Versus Blue: Profiles of the Typology Groups," 2005, http://people-press.org/reports/display.php3?PageID=949.

40. Franklin Pierce Adams, *Nods and Becks* (New York: McGraw-Hill Publishers, 1944, p. 56).

41. Barbara Norrander and Bernard N. Grofman, "A Rational Choice Model of Citizen Participation in High and Low Commitment Electoral Activities," *Public Choice* 57 (1988): 187–192.

42. Sidney Verba and Norman H. Nie, *Participation in America: Political Democracy and Social Equality* (New York: Harper & Row, 1972).

43. Arend Lijphart, "Compulsory Voting Is the Best Way to Keep Democracy Strong," *The Chronicle of Higher Education,* October 18, 1996, B3–4.

44. Ruy A. Teixeira, "Just How Much Difference Does Turnout Really Make?" *The American Enterprise,* July/August 1992, 52–59.

CHAPTER 10

1. Pippa Norris, *Women, Media, and Politics* (New York: Oxford University Press, 1997).

2. David Weinberger, www.hillwatch.com/PPRC/Quotes/Internet_and_Politics.aspx.

3. On April 7, 2005, General Motors pulled its advertising from *The Los Angeles Times* after columnist Dan McNeil, who covers the automotive trade for the newspaper, published several columns critical of GM, including one that chastised the company for pushing gas-guzzling SUVs rather than pursuing hybrid technology and another that called for the "impeachment" of two of the company's top executives.

4. New editions of all of these works are available: Tarbell (New York: Norton, 1969); Steffens (New York: Sangamore Press, 1957); and Sinclair (Cambridge, MA: B. Bentley, 1971).

5. M. J. Lee, "Rush Limbaugh Loses 45 Advertisers," *Politico,* www.politico.com/news/stories/0312/73675.html.

6. Pew Research Center, *2012 State of the News Media,* http://stateofthemedia.org.

7. Dwight D. Eisenhower, Republican National Convention Speech, July 14, 1964, Eisenhower's Post-Presidential Speeches, www.eisenhower.archives.gov/speeches/Post-Presidential_speeches.pdf.

8. C. Richard Hofstetter, *Bias in the News: Network Television Coverage of the 1972 Election Campaign* (Columbus: Ohio State University Press, 1976); Michael J. Robinson and Margaret A. Sheehan, *Over the Wire and on TV: CBS and UPI in Campaign '80* (New York: Russell Sage Foundation, 1983).

9. William P. Eveland, Jr., and Dhavan V. Shah, "The Impact of Individual and Interpersonal Factors on Perceived News Media Bias," *Political Psychology* 24, no. 1 (2003): 101–117.

10. Michael Parenti, *Inventing Reality: The Politics of the Mass Media* (New York: St. Martin's Press, 1986).

CHAPTER 11

1. "Ordnance Survey Offers Free Data Access," BBC News, April 1, 2010, http://news.bbc.co.uk/2/hi/technology/8597779.stm.

2. Howard Rheingold, "Using Participatory Media and Public Voice to Encourage Civic Engagement," in *Civic Life Online: Learning How Digital Media Can Engage Youth,* ed. W. Lance Bennett, The John D. and Catherine T. MacArthur Foundation Series on Digital Media and Learning (Cambridge, MA: MIT Press, 2008), 97–118.

3. D. M. Boyd and N. B. Ellison, "Social Network Sites: Definition, History, and Scholarship," *Journal of Computer-Mediated Communication* 13 (2007), article 11, http://jcmc.indiana.edu/vol13/issue1/boyd.ellison.html.

4. Gallup Organization, "Computers and the Internet," www.gallup.com/poll/1591/Computers-Internet.aspx#1.

5. Ibid.

6. Susannah Fox and Lee Rainie, "Part 1: How the Internet Has Woven Itself into American Life," Pew Research Internet Project, February 27, 2104, www.pewinternet.org/2014/02/27/part-1-how-the-internet-has-woven-itself-into-american-life/.

7. Mark Wheeler, *Politics and the Mass Media* (Oxford: Blackwell, 1997), 228.

8. Matthew Hindman, *The Myth of Digital Democracy* (Princeton, NJ: Princeton University Press, 2009).

9. Laura McKenna, "The Internet and American Politics: Where the Politically Rich Get Richer and the Politically Poor Get Perez Hilton," presented at the annual meeting of the American Political Science Association, Toronto, Canada, 2009.

10. Susannah Fox, *Americans Living with Disability and Their Technology Profile,* Pew Internet and American Life Project, January 21, 2011, http://pewinternet.org/Reports/2011/Disability.aspx.

11. Michael Cornfield, *Politics Moves Online: Campaigning and the Internet* (New York: The Century Foundation, 2004).

12. Howard Rheingold, *The Virtual Community: Homesteading on the Electronic Frontier* (Cambridge, MA: MIT Press, 2000).

13. Clay Skirky, *Here Comes Everybody* (New York: Penguin, 2008).

14. See Josh Pasek, Eian More, and Daniel Romer, "Realizing the Social Internet: Online Social Networking Meets Offline Civic Engagement," *Journal of Information Technology and Politics* 6 (2009): 197–215.

15. See Jody C. Baumgartner and Jonathan S. Morris, "MyFaceTube Politics: Social Networking Websites and Political Engagement of Young Adults," *Social Science Computer Review* 28 (2009): 24–44; and Weiwu Zhang, Thomas J. Johnson, Trent Sletzer, and Shannon Bichard, "The Revolution Will Be Networked: The Influence of Social Networking Sites on Political Attitudes and Behaviors, *Social Science Computer Review* 28 (2010): 75–92.

16. Jessica T. Feezell, Meredith Conroy, and Mario Guerrero, "Facebook Is . . . Fostering Political Engagement: A Study of Online Social Networking Groups and Offline Participation," presented at the annual meeting of the American Political Science Association, Toronto, Canada, 2009.

17. Terri L. Towner and David A. Dulio, "The Web 2.0 Election: Voter Learning in the 2008 Presidential Campaign," in *Techno Politics in Presidential Campaigning: New Voices, New Technologies, and New Voters,* ed. John Hendricks and Lynda Lee Kaid (New York: Routledge, 2008).

18. Pew Research Center Journalism Project's Staff, "McCain vs. Obama on the Web," September 15, 2008, www.journalism.org/node/12772.

19. Ibid.

20. Howard Rheingold, "Using Participatory Media and Public Voice to Encourage Civic Engagement," in *Civic Life Online: Learning How Digital Media Can Engage Youth,* ed. Lance W. Bennett, The John D. and Catherine T. MacArthur Foundation Series on Digital Media and Learning (Cambridge, MA: MIT Press, 2008).

21. American Press Institute, "How Americans Get Their News," March 17, 2014, www.americanpressinstitute.org/publications/reports/survey-research/how-americans-get-news/.

22. Lev Grossman, "The Beast with a Billion Eyes," *Time,* January 30, 2012, www.time.com/time/magazine/article/0,9171,2104815,00.html#ixzz1mUAZdE8vYouTube.

23. Aaron Barlow, *The Rise of the Blogosphere* (New York: Praeger, 2007).

24. Christine Gibbs Springer, "Mastering Strategic Conversations," *PA Times* (September 2006).

25. See Howard Kurtz, *Spin Cycle—How the White House and the Media Manipulate the News* (New York: Simon & Schuster, 1998).

26. Patrick Healy, "To '08 Hopefuls, Media Technology Can Be Friend or Foe," *The New York Times,* January 31, 2007, A15.

27. Cass Sunstein, *Republic.com* (Princeton NJ: Princeton University Press, 2001), 83.

28. Andrew Paul Williams and Evan Serge, "Evaluating Candidate E-Mail Messages in the 2008 U.S. Presidential Campaign," in *Techno Politics in Presidential Campaigning: New Voices, New Technologies, and New Voters,* ed. John Hendricks and Lynda Lee Kaid (New York: Routledge, 2001).

29. David Karpf, *The MoveOn Effect: The Unexpected Transformation of American Political Advocacy* (New York: Oxford University Press, 2012).

30. United Nations Department of Economic and Social Affairs, "United Nations E-Government Survey 2010."

31. NIC Core Services, "Outdoor Licensing," www.egov.com/Solutions/CoreServices/Pages/Outdoor.aspx.

32. Dana Gardner, "Staying on Legacy Systems Ends Up Costing IT More," www.zdnet.com/blog/gardner/staying-on-legacy-systems-ends-up-costing-it-more/3231.

33. Jason Rollins, "Local Government Use of the Latest Technology," April 5, 2011, International City/County Management Association Alliance for Innovation, http://icma.org/en/Article/101091/Local_Government_Use_of_the_Latest_Technology_Webinar_Reflection.

34. Ibid.

35. "Government Transformers," www.govtransformers.com/todd-jackson.

36. Grossman, "The Beast with a Billion Eyes."

37. Roy Saltman, *The History and Politics of Voting Technology* (New York: Palgrave Macmillan, 2008).

38. Daniel Solove, *The Digital Person: Technology and Privacy in the Information Age* (New York: New York University Press, 2004).

39. Barton Gellman and Greg Miller, "'Black Budget' Summary Details U.S. Spy Network's Successes, Failures and Objectives," *The Washington Post,* August 29, 2013, www.washingtonpost.com/world/national-security/black-budget-summary-details-us-spy-networks-successes-failures-and-objectives/2013/08/29/7e57bb78-10ab-11e3-8cdd-bcdc09410972_story.html.

40. Glenn Greenwald, "NSA Collecting Phone Records of Millions of Verizon Customers Daily," *The Guardian,* June 5, 2013, www.theguardian.com/world/2013/jun/06/nsa-phone-records-verizon-court-order.

41. Barton Gellman and Ashkan Soltani, "NSA Tracking Cellphone Locations Worldwide, Snowden Documents Show," *The Washington Post,* December 4, 2013, www.washingtonpost.com/world/national-security/nsa-tracking-cellphone-locations-worldwide-snowden-documents-show/2013/12/04/5492873a-5cf2-11e3-bc56-c6ca94801fac_story.html.

42. "NSA Signal Surveillance Success Stories," *The Washington Post,* http://apps.washingtonpost.com/g/page/national/nsa-signal-surveillance-success-stories/647/.

43. Barton Gellman and Laura Poitras, "U.S., British Intelligence Mining Data from Nine U.S. Internet Companies in Broad Secret Program," *The Washington Post,* June 6, 2013, www.washingtonpost.com/investigations/us-intelligence-mining-data-from-nine-us-internet-companies-in-broad-secret-program/2013/06/06/3a0c0da8-cebf-11e2-8845-d970ccb04497_story.html.

44. Barton Gellman and Ashkan Soltani, "NSA Infiltrates Links to Yahoo, Google Data Centers Worldwide, Snowden Documents Say," *The*

Washington Post, October 30, 2013, www
.washingtonpost.com/world/national-security/
nsa-infiltrates-links-to-yahoo-google-data-
centers-worldwide-snowden-documents-say/
2013/10/30/e51d661e-4166-11e3-8b74-d89d
714ca4dd_story.html.

45. Glenn Freenwald, "XKeyscore: NSA Tool
Collects 'Nearly Everything a User Does on
the Internet,'" *The Guardian,* July 31, 2013,
www.theguardian.com/world/2013/jul/31/
nsa-top-secret-program-online-data.

46. James Ball, "Xbox Live Among Game Services Targeted by US and UK Spy Agencies,"
The Guardian, December 9, 2013, www.the
guardian.com/world/2013/dec/09/nsa-spies-
online-games-world-warcraft-second-life.

47. "Book to Reveal Obama's 'True' Identity?"
The Drudge Report, April 20, 2011, http://
drudgereport.com/flash7.htm.

48. Sunstein, *Republic.com 2.0.*

49. Donna Leinwand Leger, "Internet Creates
Wider Venue for Political Incivility, Threats,"
USA Today, February 2, 2012, p. 6A.

50. Thomas E. Mann and Norman J. Ornstein, *It's
Even Worse Than It Looks: How the American
Constitutional System Collided with the New
Politics of Extremism* (New York: Basic Books,
2012).

51. Jodi Wilgoren, "Shadowed by Threats, Judge
Finds New Horror, *The New York Times,* March 2,
2005, p. 1. See also Martin and Susan J. Tol-
chin, *A World Ignited: How Apostles of Ethnic,
Religious and Racial Hatred Torch the Globe*
(Lanham, MD: Rowman & Littlefield, 2006).

52. *The CIA World Fact Book: United States,*
https://www.cia.gov/library/publications/
the-world-factbook/geos/us.html.

53. Cass Sunstein, *Republic.com 2.0* (Princeton,
NJ: Princeton University Press, 2007).

54. Ibid.,

CHAPTER 12

1. See, for example, David E. Price, *The Congressional Experience: A View from the Hill*
(Boulder, CO: Westview, 1992).

2. Richard F. Fenno Jr., *Home Style: House
Members in Their Districts* (New York: Longman, 2002).

3. *Davis v. Bandemer,* 478 U.S. 109 (1986).

4. Samuel Kernell, ed., *James Madison: The Theory and Practice of Republican Government*
(Stanford, CA: Stanford University Press,
2003), 5.

5. Richard F. Fenno Jr., *Congressional Travels*
(New York: Pearson Longman, 2007).

6. Sue Thomas, *How Women Legislate* (New
York: Oxford University Press, 1994).

7. Edmund Burke, *Speeches at His Arrival at
Bristol,* November, 3, 1774, http://books.
google.com.

8. Ibid.

9. Diana Evans, *Greasing the Wheels: Using
Pork Barrel Projects to Build Majority Coali-
tions in Congress* (New York: Cambridge
University Press, 2004).

10. Bret Schulte, "A Bridge (Way) Too Far,"
U.S. News and World Report, August 8, 2005,
139:5, p. 26.

11. Citizens Against Government Waste, *2010
Congressional Pig Book Summary,* p. 63, http://
cagw.org/content/2010-pig-book-summary.

12. See, for example, Bruce Cain, John Ferejohn,
and Morris Fiorina, *The Personal Vote: Constituency Service and Electoral Independence*
(Cambridge, MA: Harvard University Press,
1987).

13. Walter F. Mondale, testimony in hearing
before the Joint Committee on the Organization of Congress, July 1, 1993, https://archive
.org/stream/testimonyofhonwa00unit/testimony
ofhonwa00unit_djvu.txt.

14. Walter J. Oleszek, *Congressional Procedures
and the Policy Process,* 7th ed. (Washington,
D.C.: CQ Press, 2007).

15. See Janet M. Martin, *Lessons from the Hill:
The Legislative Journey of an Education Program* (New York: St. Martin's, 1994).

16. Gary Cox and Mathew D. McCubbins, *Setting
the Agenda* (Cambridge: Cambridge University Press, 2004).

17. Woodrow Wilson, *Constitutional Government
in the United States* (New York: Columbia
University Press, 1911), 87.

18. David Butler and Bruce Cain, *Congressional
Redistricting: Comparative and Theoretical
Perspectives* (New York: Macmillan, 1992).

19. Christopher J. Deering and Steven S. Smith,
Committees in Congress, 3rd ed. (Washington,
D.C.: Congressional Quarterly, 1997).

20. Garrison Nelson, *Committees in the U.S. Congress, 1947–1992,* 2 vols. (Washington, D.C.:
CQ Press, 1993).

21. Steven S. Smith, Jason M. Roberts, and Ryan J.
VanderWielen, *The American Congress,* 5th ed.
(New York: Cambridge University Press, 2007).

22. Lawrence C. Dodd and Bruce I. Oppenheimer,
Congress Reconsidered, 8th ed. (Washington,
D.C.: CQ Press, 2004).

23. Sarah H. Binder, *Minority Rights, Majority
Rule: Partisanship and the Development of
Congress* (New York: Cambridge University
Press, 1997).

24. David W. Brady and Mathew D. McCubbins,
*Party, Process, and Political Change in Con-
gress: New Perspectives on the History of
Congress* (Stanford, CA: Stanford University
Press, 2002).

25. Joseph Martin Hernon, *Profiles in Character:
Hubris and Heroism in the U.S. Senate, 1789–1990*
(Armonk, NY: M. E. Sharpe, 1997).

26. Gary W. Cox, *Legislative Leviathan: Party
Government in the House* (Berkeley: University of California Press, 1993).

27. Ronald M. Peters Jr., *The American Speakership:
The Office in Historical Perspective,* 2nd ed. (Baltimore: Johns Hopkins University Press, 1997).

28. Susan Webb Hammond, *Congressional Caucuses in National Policy Making* (Baltimore:
Johns Hopkins University Press, 2001).

29. Barbara Sinclair, *Majority Leadership in the
US House and the Transformation of the US
Senate* (Baltimore: Johns Hopkins University
Press, 1990).

30. Barry C. Burden, *Personal Roots of Representation* (Princeton, NJ: Princeton University
Press, 2007).

31. Sean Theriault, "Party Polarization in Congress" (paper presented at the annual meeting
of the American Political Science Association,
Washington, D.C., September 1, 2005).

32. Michael J. Malbin, *Unelected Representa-
tives: Congressional Staff and the Future of
Representative Government* (New York: Basic
Books, 1980).

33. Burdett A. Loomis, *The Contemporary Congress,* 3rd ed. (Boston: Bedford/St. Martin's,
2000).

34. John R. Wright, *Interest Groups and Congress*
(New York: Allyn and Bacon, 1996).

35. R. Douglas Arnold, *The Logic of Congressional Action* (New Haven, CT: Yale University
Press, 1990).

36. For a discussion of the potential goals of
demographic representation, see, for example,
David T. Canon, "Representing Racial and
Ethnic Minorities," in *The Legislative Branch,*
eds. Paul J. Quirk and Sarah A. Binder (New
York: Oxford University Press, 2005).

CHAPTER 13

1. George C. Edwards III, John H. Kessel, and
Bert A. Rockman, eds., *Researching the
Presidency: Vital Questions, New Approaches*
(Pittsburgh, PA: University of Pittsburgh Press,
1993).

2. Theodore J. Lowi, *The Personal President*
(Ithaca, NY: Cornell University Press, 1985).

3. Jean Reith Schroedel, *Congress, the President, and Policymaking: A Historical Analysis*
(Armonk, NY: M. E. Sharpe, 1994).

4. William W. Lammers, *The Presidency and
Domestic Policy: Comparing Leadership
Styles, FDR to Clinton* (Washington, D.C.: CQ
Press, 2000).

5. Andrew Rudalevige, *Managing the Presi-
dent's Program: Presidential Leadership and
Legislative Policy Formulation* (Princeton, NJ:
Princeton University Press, 2002).

6. Richard A. Watson, *Presidential Vetoes and
Public Policy* (Lawrence: University of Kansas
Press, 1993).

7. Robert J. Spitzer, *The Presidential Veto: Touchstone of the American Presidency* (Albany:
SUNY Press, 1988).

8. Sidney M. Milkis and Michael Nelson, *The
American Presidency: Origins and Develop-
ment, 1776–1998,* 4th ed. (Washington, D.C.:
CQ Press, 2003).

9. American Bar Association Recommendation,
adopted by the House of Delegates August
7–8, 2006, www.americanbar.org/content/
dam/aba/migrated/leadership/2006/annual/
dailyjournal/20060823144113.authcheckdam.
pdf.

10. Jon Hilsenrath, David Wessel, and Sudeep
Reddy, "Obama to Reappoint Bernanke as
Fed Chief," *The Wall Street Journal,* August
25, 2009, http://online.wsj.com/article/SB125
116264837455591.html.

11. George C. Edwards III and Steven J. Wayne,
Studying the Presidency (Knoxville: University of Tennessee Press, 1983).

12. Louis Fisher, *Presidential War Power* (Lawrence: University of Kansas Press, 1995).

13. Jon Meacham, "A Highly Logical Approach," *Newsweek,* May 16, 2009, www.newsweek.com/id/197891.
14. Cornell G. Hooton, *Executive Governance: Presidential Administrations and Policy Change in the Federal Bureaucracy* (Armonk, NY: M. E. Sharpe, 1997).
15. O. C. Fisher, *Cactus Jack: A Biography of John Nance Garner* (Waco, TX: Texian Press), chap. 11.
16. Bill Clinton, *My Life* (New York: Knopf, 2004), 414.
17. Stephen Skowronek, *The Politics Presidents Make: Leadership from John Adams to George Bush* (Cambridge, MA: Belknap Press, 1997).
18. MaryAnne Borrelli, *The President's Cabinet: Gender, Power, and Representation* (Boulder, CO: Lynne Rienner, 2002).
19. Joel D. Aberbach and Mark A. Peterson, eds., *The Executive Branch* (New York: Oxford University Press, 2005).
20. William E. Leuchtenburg, *In the Shadow of FDR: From Harry Truman to Ronald Reagan* (Ithaca, NY: Cornell University Press, 1989).
21. Kenneth R. Mayer, *With the Stroke of a Pen: Executive Orders and Presidential Power* (Princeton, NJ: Princeton University Press, 2002).
22. Executive Order 9981, www.trumanlibrary.org/9981.htm.
23. *United States v. Curtiss-Wright Export Corp.,* 229 U.S. 304 (1936).
24. Mark J. Rozell, *Executive Privilege: Presidential Power, Secrecy, and Accountability,* 2nd ed. rev. (Lawrence: University of Kansas Press, 2002).
25. *United States v. Richard M. Nixon,* 418 U.S. 683 (1974).
26. Richard Neustadt, *The Power to Persuade* (New York: Wiley, 1960).
27. *Outlook,* February 27, 1909.
28. Richard E. Neustadt, *Presidential Power and the Modern President* (New York: The Free Press, 1990).
29. Jennifer Steinhauer, "Debt Bill Is Signed, Ending a Fractious Battle," *The New York Times,* August 3, 2011, www.nytimes.com/2011/08/03/us/politics/03fiscal.html?_r=1&ref=opinion.
30. George C. Edwards III with Alec M. Gallup, *Presidential Approval: A Sourcebook* [Eisenhower to Reagan] (Baltimore: Johns Hopkins University Press, 1990).
31. Harry A. Bailey, Jr., and Jay M. Shafritz, *The American Presidency: Historical and Contemporary Perspectives* (Pacific Grove, CA: Brooks/Cole, 1988).
32. Marc Landy and Sidney M. Milkis, *Presidential Greatness* (Lawrence: University of Kansas Press, 2000).
33. Harold J. Laski, *The American Presidency* (New York: Harper & Row, 1940).
34. William M. Goldsmith, *The Growth of Presidential Power: A Documented History,* 3 vols. (New York: Chelsea House, 1974).
35. *New York Times Co. v. United States,* 403 U.S. 713 (1971).
36. Statement of Senator Howard Baker (R-Tenn.) during the Senate Committee investigation.
37. John Dean, the Nixon presidential transcripts, March 21, 1973.
38. Watergate Special Prosecution Force (WSPF) conversations, Nixon Presidential Library and Museum, www.nixonlibrary.gov/forresearchers/find/tapes/watergate/wspf/transcripts.php.
39. David Frost, *I Gave Them a Sword* (New York: William Morrow, 1978).
40. *The Washington Post,* "The Days A Not-So-Grand Old Party," August 29, 2007, http://voices.washingtonpost.com/44/2007/08/a-party-in-disarray.html.
41. Barbara Bush, commencement address at Wellesley College, June 1, 1990.
42. Charles C. Thach, Jr., *The Creation of the Presidency, 1775–1789: A Study in Constitutional History* (Baltimore, MD: Johns Hopkins University Press, 1969).

CHAPTER 14

1. Annie Lowrey, "White House Puts Price on Government Shutdown," *The New York Times,* November 11, 2013, A20.
2. White House Office of Management and Budget, www.whitehouse.gov/omb/budget/Historicals.
3. Emily Wax-Thibodeaux, "Young Workers Souring on Federal Careers," *The Washington Post,* October 26, 2013.
4. For a review of the literature on public service motivation, see David J. Houston, "'Walking the Walk' of Public Service Motivation: Public Employees and Charitable Gifts of Time, Blood, and Money," *Journal of Public Administration Research and Theory* 16, no. 1 (2005): 67–86.
5. Charles T. Goodsell, *The Case for Bureaucracy: A Public Administration Polemic,* 4th ed. (Washington, D.C.: CQ Press, 2004), 104–106.
6. Norman J. Baldwin, "Public Versus Private Employees: Debunking Stereotypes," *Review of Public Personnel Administration* 12 (Winter 1991): 1–27.
7. Goodsell, *The Case for Bureaucracy,* 106.
8. Stuart Greenfield, "Public Sector Employment: The Current Situation" (Washington, D.C.: Center for State & Local Government Excellence).
9. Office of Personnel Management, "Senior Executive Service Overview and History," www.opm.gov/policy-data-oversight/senior-executive-service/overview-history/.
10. Ibid.
11. Jimmy Carter, "Federal Civil Service Reform Remarks Announcing the Administration's Proposals to the Congress: March 2, 1978," www.presidency.ucsb.edu/ws/?pid=30436.
12. Eric Katz, "Federal Employee Unions See Large Membership Boost Over Last Decade," January 28, 2013, www.govexec.com/management/2013/01/federal-employee-unions-see-large-membership-boost-over-last-decade/60959/.
13. "Measures Cut Previous Red Tape Clogging the Federal Hiring System," News Release, May 11, 2010, www.opm.gov/news/releases/2010/05/opm-omb-announce-unprecedented-hiring-reforms/.
14. Joe Davidson, "Union Lists GOP Initiatives to Make Federal Workers Pay," *The Washington Post,* February 28, 2012.
15. Max Stier, "No Respect for Federal Workers," March 25, 2012, www.politico.com/news/stories/0312/74440.html.
16. Paul C. Light. "Can't-Do Government," *The Washington Post,* June 25, 2008.
17. USASpending.gov, "Total Federal Spending," www.usaspending.gov/trends?trendreport=default&viewreport=yes&maj_contracting_agency_t=&pop_state_t=&pop_cd_t=&vendor_state_t=&vendor_cd_t=&psc_cat_t=&tab=Graph+View&Go.x=Go.
18. "States Sue EPA to Move on Global Warming," www.msnbc.msn.com/id/23919234.
19. Jeffrey L. Pressman and Aaron Wildavsky, *Implementation: How Great Expectations in Washington Are Dashed in Oakland: Or, Why It's Amazing That Federal Programs Work at All* (Berkeley and Los Angeles: University of California Press, 1973).
20. Barack Obama memo, "Transparency and Open Government," www.whitehouse.gov/the_press_office/TransparencyandOpenGovernment.
21. Sabrina Tavernise, "Bill on Drug Compounding Clears Congress a Year After a Meningitis Outbreak," *The New York Times,* November 19, 2013.
22. William T. Gormley Jr. and Steven J. Balla, *Bureaucracy and Democracy: Accountability and Performance* (Washington, D.C.: CQ Press, 2004), 67.
23. Matt Kelley, "Probes at NASA Plummet Under Its Current IG," *USA Today,* January 11, 2008.
24. Charles T. Goodsell, *The Case for Bureaucracy,* 139.
25. Gormley and Balla, *Bureaucracy and Democracy,* 164–178.
26. Goodsell, *The Case for Bureaucracy,* 54.
27. Ibid., 30.
28. Paul Light, "Contractors in Federal Workforce," November 12, 2013, www.c-spanvideo.org/program/CostofCo.
29. Richard Stillman, *The American Bureaucracy: The Core of Modern Government* (Chicago: Nelson Hall Publishers, 1996), 308.

CHAPTER 15

1. Adam Liptak. "Court Is 'One of Most Activist,' Ginsburg Says, Vowing to Stay," *The New York Times,* August 24, 2013.
2. Charles D. Shipan, *Designing Judicial Review* (Ann Arbor: University of Michigan Press, 1997).
3. Joel B. Grossman, "Paths to the Bench: Selecting Supreme Court Justices in a 'Juristocratic' World," in *The Judicial Branch,* ed. Kermit L. Hall and Kevin T. McGuire (Oxford: Oxford University Press, 2005), 143.
4. Brian L. Porto, *May It Please the Court: Judicial Processes and Politics in America* (New York: Longman, 2001), 4.
5. Sandra Day O'Connor, *The Majesty of the Law: Reflections of a Supreme Court Justice* (New York: Random House, 2003), 242.
6. Ibid., 271–272.
7. *National Labor Relations Board v. Noel Canning,* _____ U.S. _____ (2014).
8. *National Federation of Independent Businesses v. Sebelius,* 567 U.S. _____ (2012).

9. *McCutcheon v. Federal Election Commission,* _____ U.S. _____ (2014).

10. The White House, "Executive Orders," www.whitehouse.gov/briefing-room/presidential-actions/executive-orders.

11. G. Alan Tarr, *Judicial Process and Judicial Policymaking,* 5th ed. (Boston: Wadsworth/Cengage Learning, 2010), 209.

12. 50 U.S.C. §§1801–1811, 1821–29, 1841–46, and 1861–62.

13. Porto, *May It Please the Court,* 32.

14. Brennan Center for Justice. "Federal Judicial Nominations," www.brennancenter.org/analysis/federal-judicial-nominations.

15. U.S. Courts, "Judicial Vacancies," www.uscourts.gov/JudgesAndJudgeships/JudicialVacancies.aspx.

16. Ibid.

17. See, for example, Hugh Hewitt, "Why the Right Was Wrong," *The New York Times,* October 28, 2005.

18. Eric Black, "Something Changed: Picking a Supreme Court Justice Is Now a Partisan Battle," November 26, 2012, www.minnpost.com/eric-black-ink/2012/11/something-changed-picking-supreme-court-justice-now-partisan-battle.

19. H. W. Perry, Jr., *Deciding to Decide: Agenda Setting in the United States Supreme Court* (Cambridge, MA: Harvard University Press, 1994).

20. Bob Woodward, *The Brethren: Inside the Supreme Court* (New York: Simon & Schuster, 2005).

21. Henry J. Abraham, *The Judicial Process* (New York: Oxford University Press, 1998).

22. Benjamin N. Cardozo, *The Nature of the Judicial Process* (Mineola, NY: Dover, 2005); Paul Collins, Jr., *Friends of the Supreme Court: Interest Groups and Judicial Decision Making* (New York: Oxford University Press, 2008).

23. Paul Collins, Jr., *Friends of the Supreme Court: Interest Groups and Judicial Decision Making* (New York: Oxford University Press, 2008), 71–72.

24. Stephen Breyer, *Active Liberty: Interpreting Our Democratic Constitution* (New York: Vintage Books, 2006).

25. Artemus Ward, "Sorcerers' Apprentices: U.S. Supreme Court Law Clerks," in *Exploring Judicial Politics,* ed. Mark C. Miller (New York: Oxford University Press, 2009), 159.

26. Adam Liptak, "A Most Inquisitive Court? No Argument There," *The New York Times,* October 8, 2013.

27. Ibid.

28. Bryan W. Marshall, Richard L. Pacelle, Jr., and Christine Ludowise, "A Court of Laws or a Superlegislature? An Integrated Model of Supreme Court Decision Making," in *Exploring Judicial Politics,* ed. Mark C. Miller (New York: Oxford University Press, 2009), 194.

29. Black, "Something Changed."

30. Collins, *Friends of the Supreme Court,* 12.

31. Marshall, Pacelle, and Ludowise, "A Court of Laws or a Superlegislature?"

32. Ward, "Sorcerers' Apprentices," 168.

33. *Ledbetter v. Goodyear Tire & Rubber,* 550 U.S. 618 (2007).

34. Quoted in Eric Black, "How the Supreme Court Has Come to Play a Policymaking Role," November 20, 2012, www.minnpost.com/eric-black-ink/2012/11/how-supreme-court-has-come-play-policymaking-role.

35. *Plessy v. Ferguson,* 163 U.S. 537 (1896).

36. *Brown v. Board of Education of Topeka, Kansas,* 347 U.S. 483 (1954).

37. O'Connor, *The Majesty of the Law,* 266.

38. Thomas M. Keck, *The Most Activist Supreme Court in History: The Road to Modern Judicial Conservatism* (Chicago: University of Chicago Press, 2004).

39. Mark C. Miller, "The Interactions between the Federal Courts and the Other Branches," in *Exploring Judicial Politics,* ed. Mark C. Miller (New York: Oxford University Press, 2009), 278–279.

40. Antonin Scalia, *A Matter of Interpretation: Federal Courts and the Law* (Princeton, NJ: Princeton University Press, 1998).

41. O'Connor, *The Majesty of the Law,* 41.

42. *Oregon v. Mitchell,* 400 U.S. 112 (1970).

43. Collins, *Friends of the Supreme Court,* 175.

44. Adam Liptak, "How Activist Is the Supreme Court?" *The New York Times,* October 13, 2013, www.nytimes.com/2013/10/13/sunday-review/how-activist-is-the-supreme-court.html.

45. Adam Liptak, "Supreme Court Goes Beyond Old Divides," *The New York Times,* July 1, 2012.

46. Andrew Dugan, "Americans Still Divided on Approval of U.S. Supreme Court," October 4, 2013, www.gallup.com/poll/165248/americans-still-divided-approval-supreme-court.aspx.

47. Liptak, "Court Is 'One of Most Activist.'"

48. Liptak, "A Most Inquisitive Court?"

49. Dugan, "Americans Still Divided on Approval of U.S. Supreme Court."

50. Ibid.

51. Alexis de Tocqueville, *Democracy in America,* ed. J. P. Mayer (Garden City, NY: Doubleday, 1969), 99–102.

52. Ibid., 270.

CHAPTER 16

1. Barack Obama, "The Budget Message of the President," February 13, 2012, www.whitehouse.gov/sites/default/files/omb/budget/fy2013/assets/message.pdf.

2. Barack Obama, "The Budget Message of the President," March 4, 2014, www.whitehouse.gov/omb/budget/presidents-message.

3. Jackie Calmes, "Obama Moves to the Right in a Partisan War of Words," *The New York Times,* February 4, 2014, A11.

4. Obama, "The Budget Message of the President," March 4, 2014.

5. Pew Research Center for the People & the Press, "Most See Inequality Growing, but Partisans Differ over Solutions," January 23, 2014, www.people-press.org/2014/01/23/most-see-inequality-growing-but-partisans-differ-over-solutions/.

6. Charles Derber, *People Before Profit* (New York: Picador, 2002), 48.

7. David Leonhardt, "Judging Stimulus by Job Data Reveals Success," *The New York Times,* February 17, 2010.

8. U.S. Bureau of Labor Statistics, "CPI Inflation Calculator," www.bls.gov/data/inflation_calculator.htm.

9. U.S. Bureau of Economic Analysis, "Measuring the Economy: A Primer on GDP and the National Income and Product Accounts," September 2007, www.bea.gov/national/pdf/nipa_primer.pdf.

10. U.S. Development Programme, "Table 1: Human Development Index and Its Components," https://data.undp.org/dataset/Table-1-Human-Development-Index-and-its-components/wxub-qc5k.

11. Carmen DeNavas-Walt, Bernadette D. Proctor, and Jessica C. Smith, U.S. Census Bureau, Current Population Reports, P60-245, *Income, Poverty, and Health Insurance Coverage in the United States: 2012* (Washington, D.C.: U.S. Government Printing Office, 2013), 10; www.census.gov/hhes/www/poverty/data/incpovhlth/2012/index.html.

12. Ibid., Table 2, "Income Distribution Measures Using Money Income," 10.

13. U.S. Census Bureau, "Poverty Thresholds by Size of Family and Number of Children: 2013," www.census.gov/hhes/www/poverty/data/threshld/.

14. "Historical Tables," Table 1.2—Summary of Receipts, Outlays and Surpluses or Deficits," www.whitehouse.gov/omb/budget/Historicals.

15. Andrew Taylor, "Congress Aims to Fix Busted Budgeting," *The [Scranton] Sunday Times,* January 19, 2014, D6.

16. "U.S. National Debt Clock," www.brillig.com/debt_clock.

17. Ariana Eunjung Cha, "What's in the Debt Ceiling, and Why Is Everyone in Washington Talking About It?" *The Washington Post,* April 18, 2011.

18. Sherman Antitrust Act (1890); Clayton Antitrust Act (1914).

19. "United States History: Fair Labor Standards Act," www.u-s-history.com/pages/h1701.html.

20. Ralph Nader, *Unsafe at Any Speed: The Designed-in Dangers of American Automobiles* (New York: Grossman Publishing, 1965), ix.

21. Alexei Barrionuevo, "Globalization in Every Loaf," *The New York Times,* June 16, 2007.

22. Graham Bowley, "That 70's Look: Stagflation," *The New York Times,* February 21, 2008.

23. David Leonhardt, "Judging Stimulus by Job Data Reveals Success," *The New York Times,* February 17, 2010.

24. Bill Keller, "Inequality for Dummies," *The New York Times,* December 22, 2013.

25. Ibid.

26. Pew Research Center for the People & the Press, "Most See Inequality Growing, but Partisans Differ Over Solutions."

27. Ibid.

28. Ibid.

29. Quoted in David Kamp, "Rethinking the American Dream," *Vanity Fair*, April 2009.

30. Pew Research Center for the People & the Press, "Most See Inequality Growing."

CHAPTER 17

1. Office of Management and Budget, "Table 11.1: Summary of Outlays for Payments for Individuals," *Historical Tables*, www.whitehouse.gov/omb/budget/Historicals.

2. U.S. Census Bureau, "Measuring America," December 12, 2013, www.census.gov/how/infographics/government_benefits.html.

3. "Gaylord Nelson and Earth Day—Introduction: The Earth Day Story and Gaylord Nelson," nelsonearthday.net/earth-day/index.htm.

4. Ibid.

5. *Massachusetts v. EPA*, 549 U.S. 497 (2007).

6. David Hosansky, *The Environment A to Z* (Washington, D.C.: CQ Press, 2001), 80–81.

7. Spencer Abraham, "A National Report on America's Energy Crisis," March 19, 2001, www.ideasinactiontv.com/tcs_daily/2001/03/a-national-report-on-americas-energy-crisis.html.

8. Katie Weatherford, "Congress Continues Efforts to Thwart Climate Change Emissions Standards," www.foreffectivegov.org/congress-continues-efforts-thwart-climate-change-emissions-limits.

9. Justin Gillis, "Panel's Warning on Climate Risk: Worst Is Yet to Come," *The New York Times*, March 31, 2014.

10. Ibid.

11. Sean Cockerham, "U.S. Becoming 'Saudi America?': America Enjoying an Energy Revolution, But Some Wonder If It Will Last," *Scranton Times-Tribune*, November 28, 2013, A12.

12. Ibid.

13. Social Security Administration, "Update 2014," Publication No. 05-10003, www.ssa.gov/pubs/10003.html.

14. Jim Dwyer, "Exhausted Workers Recall Minimal Efforts to Enforce a Minimum Wage Law," *The New York Times*, November 7, 2013.

15. Jackie Calmes, "Obama Presses Case for Health Law and Wage Increase," *The New York Times*, December 5, 2013, A28.

16. John Harwood, "Missing Ingredient on Minimum Wage: A Motivated G.O.P.," *The New York Times*, April 11, 2014, A19.

17. Center on Budget and Policy Priorities, "Policy Basics: The Earned Income Tax Credit," www.cbpp.org/cms/index.cfm?fa=view&id2505#.

18. Office of Family Assistance, "TANF Final Rule—Executive Summary," www.acf.hhs.gov/programs/ofa/resource/exsumcl.

19. U.S. Census Bureau, "Income, Poverty & Health Insurance in U.S. 2012—Tables & Figures: People in Poverty by Select Characteristics 2011 and 2012," www.census.gov/hhes/www/poverty/data/incpovhlth/2012/tables.html.

20. U.S. Department of Housing and Urban Development, *The 2013 Annual Homeless Assessment Report (AHAR) to Congress*, www.onecpd.info/resources/documents/ahar-2013-part1.pdf.

21. Maria Foscarinis, "Homeless Problem Bigger Than Our Leaders Think: Report Misleads on Those Without Shelter," *USA Today*, January 16, 2014, http://usatoday.com/story/opinion/2014/01/16/homeless-problem-obama-america-recession-column/4539917/.

22. Joint Center for Housing Studies of Harvard University, "Rental Housing Assistance," *American's Rental Housing: Evolving Markets and Needs* 39, www.jchs.harvard.edu/americas-rental-housing.

23. Ibid., 34.

24. U.S. Census Bureau. "Income, Poverty and Health Insurance Coverage in the United States: 2012," www.census.gov/newsroom/releases/archives/income_wealth.cb13-165.html.

25. Henry J. Kaiser Family Foundation, "Federal and State Share of Medicaid Spending," http://kff.org/medicaid/state-indicator/federalstate-share-of-spending/.

26. Centers for Medicare and Medicaid, "Timeline: The Affordable Care Act Becomes Law," www.medicaid.gov/AffordableCareAct/Timeline/Timeline.html.

27. U.S. Department of Health and Human Services, "Key Features of the Affordable Care Act by Year," www.hhs.gov/healthcare/facts/timeline/timeline-text.html#Page_4.

28. "The Federal Response to Hurricane Katrina: Lessons Learned," http://georgewbush-whitehouse.archives.gov/reports/katrina-lessons-learned/.

29. Donald F. Kettl, "Boston's 'Unity of Effort,'" *Governing*, June 2013: 18–19.

30. Ibid.

31. U.S. Department of Homeland Security, "Table 25: Persons Obtaining Legal Permanent Resident Status by Region and Selected Country of Last Residence," *2012 Yearbook of Immigration Statistics*, www.dhs.gov/publication/yearbook-2012.

32. "Inadmissibility: When the U.S. Can Keep You Out," *NOLO Law for All*, www.nolo.com/legal-encyclopedia/us-deny-entry-inadmissibility-reasons-29715.html.

33. Julia Preston, "Legal Immigrants Seek Reward for Years of Following the Rules," *The New York Times*, July 15, 2013.

34. Immigration Policy Center, "A Guide to S.744: Understanding the 2013 Senate Immigration Bill," www.immigrationpolicy.org/special-reports/guide-s744-understanding-2013-senate-immigration-bill.

35. Michael D. Shear, "Obama Orders Review of Deportations, Citing a Concern for Families," *The New York Times*, March 14, 2014.

36. Ibid.

CHAPTER 18

1. Congressional Research Service Report to Congress, "U.S. Foreign Aid to East and Southeast Asia: Selected Recipients," August 22, 2007, www.fas.org/sgp/crs/row/RL31362.pdf, p. 31.

2. Ibid., 36.

3. "A Timeline of U.S. Aid to Pakistan," *Newsweek*, July 1, 2010, www.newsweek.com/timeline-us-aid-pakistan-81153.

4. "Dodd Assesses Efforts by U.S. to Increase Economic, Diplomatic, Political Pressure on Iran," March 21, 2007, http://dodd.senate.gov/index.php?q=node/3793.

5. Saul K. Padover, ed., *Wilson's Ideals* (Washington, D.C.: American Council on Public Affairs, 1942), 108.

6. UNICEF, "State of the World's Children," www.unicef.org/sowc97/.

7. Secretary of State Colin L. Powell, remarks to the United Nations Security Council, February 5, 2003, www.state.gov/secretary/former/powell/remarks/2003/17300.htm.

8. Alex Chadwick and Mike Shuster, "U.S. Links to Sadaam During Iran-Iraq War," September 22, 2005, www.npr.org/templates/story/story.php?storyId=4859238.

9. See, for example, James Risen, *State of War: The Secret History of the CIA and the Bush Administration* (New York: Free Press, 2006).

10. "Congress Abdicates War Powers," *The New American*, November 4, 2002: 5.

11. "President Dwight D. Eisenhower's Farewell Address (1961)," www.ourdocuments.gov/doc.php?flash=true&doc=90.

12. Roberta Rampton, "Obama Says U.S. Military Strikes Could Not Have Stopped Syria Misery," *Reuters*, www.reuters.com/article/2014/03/29/us-syria-crisis-obama-idUSBREA2R21O20140329.

13. Roger H. Davidson, "Invitation to Struggle: An Overview of Legislative-Executive Relations," *Annals of the American Academy of Political and Social Science* 499 (1988): 1, 9–21.

14. Article 5 of the North Atlantic Treaty, Washington, D.C., April 4, 1949, www.nato.int/docu/basictxt/treaty.htm.

15. President Harry S Truman's address before a joint session of Congress on March 12, 1947.

16. George F. Kennan, writing under the pseudonym "X," "Sources of Soviet Conduct," *Foreign Affairs*, July 1947: 25.

17. Graham T. Allison and Philip Zelikow, *Essence of Decision: Explaining the Cuban Missile Crisis*, 2nd ed. (New York: Longman, 1999).

18. President Eisenhower's News Conference, April 7, 1954, Public Papers of the Presidents, 1954, p. 382.

19. Samuel P. Huntington, "The Clash of Civilizations?" *Foreign Affairs* 72, no. 3 (Summer 1993): 22–49.

CHAPTER 19

1. Joel Lieske, "The Changing Regional Subcultures of the United States: A New Cultural Measure for Understanding Political Behavior" (paper presented at 2004 annual meeting of the Midwest Political Science Association, Chicago, April 15–18, 2004), p. 2.

2. Daniel Elazar, *American Federalist*, 3rd ed. (New York: Harper & Row, 1984).

3. Lieske, "The Changing Regional Subcultures of the United States," 5.

4. Ibid., 6.

5. Alemayehu Bishaw, "Table 1: Number and Percentage of People in Poverty in the Past 12 Months by State and Puerto Rico: 2011 and 2012," *Poverty: 2000 to 2012*, www.census.gov/prod/2013pubs/acsbr12-01.pdf.

6. Camille Ryan, "Table 4: Language Spoken at Home and English-Speaking Ability by State: 2011," *Language Use in the United States: 2011 (ACS-22),* www.census.gov/hhes/socdem/language/data/acs/index.html.

7. Ibid.

8. National Conference of State Legislatures, "State Severance Taxes," www.ncsl.org/research/fiscalpolicy/2011-state-severance-tax-collections.aspx.

9. U.S. Census Bureau, "2012 State Government Employment & Payroll Data," *Government Employment and Payroll,* www.census.gov/govs/apes/.

10. Ibid.

11. U.S. Census Bureau, "Table S1401: School Enrollment," American FactFinder, http://factfinder2.census.gov/faces/tableservices/jsf/pages/productview.xhtml?pid=ACS_12_1YR_S1401&prodType=table.

12. Calculated from U.S. Census Bureau, "State and County Quick Facts: USA," http://quickfacts.census.gov/qfd/states/00000.html; and U.S. Census Bureau, "Table S1401: School Enrollment," American FactFinder, http://factfinder2.census.gov/faces/tableservices/jsf/pages/productview.xhtml?pid=ACS_12_1YR_S1401&prodType=table.

13. Mike Maciag, "By the Numbers: Education Spending per Student Fell for First Time in 2011," *Governing,* May 21, 2013, www.governing.com/blogs/by-the-numbers/education-spending-per-pupil-declines-state-local-governments.html.

14. Calculated from U.S. Census Bureau, "2011 Data: State-Level Tables," *Public Elementary-Secondary Education Finance Data,* www.census.gov/govs/school/.

15. M. Stetser and R. Stillwell, *Public High School Four-Year On-Time Graduation Rates and Event Dropout Rates: School Years 2010–11 and 2011–12. First Look (NCES 2014-39)* (Washington, D.C.: U.S. Department of Education, National Center for Education Statistics, 2014).

16. Calculated from U.S. Census Bureau, *Statistical Abstract of the United States: 2012* (Washington, DC: U.S. Government Printing Office), Table 278.

17. Ibid., Table 278 and 280.

18. John Quinterno, "The Great Cost Shift: How Higher Education Cuts Undermine the Future Middle Class," April 3, 2012, www.demos.org/sites/default/files/publications/thegreatcostshift.pdf.

19. Patrick Temple-West, "Outlook for Online State Sales Tax Fix Dims in U.S. Congress," www.reutters.com/article/2014/03/12/us-usa-tax-internet-idUSBREA2B20120140312.

20. National Conference of State Legislatures, "Which States Rely on Which Tax," www.ncsl.org/documents/fiscal/WhichStatesRelyonWhichTax.pdf.

21. Nate Silver, "The Governors' Advantage in Presidential Races Is Bigger Than You Thought," http://fivethirtyeight.blogs.nytimes.com/2011/06/15/the-governors-advantage-in-presidential-races-is-bigger-than-you-thought/?_php=true&_type=blogs&_r=0.

22. Thad Beyle, ed., *State and Local Government: 2004–2005* (Washington, D.C.: CQ Press, 2004), 110.

23. Alternative Fuels Data Center, "State Laws and Incentives," www.afdc.energy.gov/laws/state.

24. Tom Arrandale, "A Bolder Boulder," *Governing* (February 2007): 56.

25. National Conference of State Legislatures, "Traumatic Brain Injury Legislation," www.ncsl.org/research/health/traumatic-brain-injury-legislation.aspx.

26. Craig Volden, "States as Policy Laboratories: Emulating Success in the Children's Health Insurance Program," *American Journal of Political Science* 50, No. 2, (April 2006): 294–312.

27. For information on women in elected and appointed government positions, see the Center for Women in Politics, www.cawp.rutgers.edu.

28. Data on the demographics of state legislators are available from the National Conference of State Legislatures, www.ncsl.org/research/about-state-legislatures/legislator-data.aspx. Data on the demographics of each state are available from the U.S. Census Bureau, http://quickfacts.census.gov/qfd/index.html.

29. Center for American Women and Politics, "Facts on Women in Statewide Executive Office 2014," www.cawp.rutgers.edu/fast_facts/levels_of_office/Statewide-CurrentFacts.php.

30. National Governors Association, "Current Governors," www.nga.org/cms/render/live/governors/bios.

31. Carma Hogue, "Government Organization Summary Report: 2012," *2012 Census of Governments,* September 26, 2013, www.census.gov/govs/cog/.

32. Ibid.

33. Theodore Roosevelt, "Charter of Democracy," speech to the 1912 Ohio Constitutional Convention.

34. M. Dane Waters, "The Initiative Industry: Its Impact on the Future of the Initiative Process," www.iandrinstitute.org.

35. Craig Gilbert, "Recall Drives Could Make History," *Journal Sentinel,* March 6, 2011, www.jsonline.com/news/statepolitics/117501513.html.

36. "A Case of Faulty Recall," *Governing* (December 2009): 12.

CREDITS

INDEX

National Defense Authorization Act of 2012, 126
National Farm Worker Association (NFWA), 177
National Federation of Independent Businesses v. Sebelius, 461
National Gay and Lesbian Task Force, 157
national government. *See* federal (national) government
National Guard, 9
National Indian Education Association (NIEA), 175
National Indian Gaming Commission, 175–176
National Labor Relations Board v. Noel Canning, 461
National Organization for Women (NOW), 173
national political parties, 252
National Restaurant Association, 228
National Rifle Association (NRA), 125, 248, 291
National Right to Life Committee, 227
national security
   civil liberties and, 120, 121, 121*f*, 144–146
   as government role, 9
National Security Act of 1947, 553
National Security Administration (NSA)
   Snowden case, 133, 350, 351*f*
   surveillance by, 15, 132, 140, 144, 467
National Security Council (NSC), 405–406, 553
National Taxpayers Union, 230
National Voter Registration Act ("Motor Voter" Act), 300
National Women's Party, 171
National Women's Suffrage Association (NWSA), 170–171
Nation Builder, 344, 344*f*
Native American Church, 137
Native Americans
   civil rights movement, 175–176, 175*f*
   population, 22, 24*f*
   treaties with, 91–92, 175
   White House Council on Native Americans, 462, 462*f*
NATO. *See* North Atlantic Treaty Organization
natural gas production, 528
naturalization, 9
natural law, 12
natural rights, 39, 41, 52
NAWSA. *See* National American Women's Suffrage Association
NBC Universal, 322
NCAPA. *See* National Council of Asian Pacific Americans
NCLB. *See* No Child Left Behind
Near, Jay, 132
Near v. Minnesota, 122, 123*t*, 132
necessary and proper clause (elastic clause), 91, 93, 94, 367

Nelson, Gaylord, 523–524
Netherlands, 100
net neutrality, 354
netroots, 342
Neustadt, Richard, 411
neutrality (preferential treatment standard), 134–136
New Deal
   as election mandate, 201
   income security in, 529
   intergovernmental relations, 98
   party affiliation and, 199, 257
   presidential power and, 415–416
New Deal coalition, 257
New Democrats, 268
new federalism, 98
New Jersey Plan, 46
news aggregators, 338–339
News Corporation, 322, 326
newspapers, 315–317, 316*f*, 317*f*. *See also specific newspapers*
"newspaper war" (Spanish-American War), 315–316, 316*f*, 558
news sources, 5, 320, 320*f*, 321, 321*f*, 322, 338–339, 339*f*
Newton, Isaac, 12, 12*f*
New York Journal American, 315
The New York Times
   on 9/11 anniversary, 14
   on Ackerman activities, 229
   on e-campaigns, 343
   online content, 317
   Pentagon Papers and, 132, 416
The New York Times Co. v. United States, 132, 416
New York Tribune cartoon, 289*f*
New York World, 315
NFWA. *See* National Farm Worker Association
NIEA. *See* National Indian Education Association
Nigerian kidnappings, 203
NIMBY. *See* not-in-my-backyard syndrome
Nineteenth Amendment, 47*f*, 54*t*, 79
95 Theses (Luther), 12
Ninth Amendment, 52, 75, 119*t*
Nixon, Richard
   on devolution, 98
   executive privilege, 410
   foreign policy, 565–566, 566*f*
   public opinion and, 209
   resignation, 6, 406, 417, 418
   telegenic quality, 320
   vice presidency, 407
   Watergate scandal, 416–417
   on women, 419
Nixon Doctrine, 565
No Child Left Behind (NCLB), 106
Noel, Hans, 260
Noelle-Neumann, Elizabeth, 201
nominations, in election process, 277–280, 294

noncontributory programs, 522
nonpartisan municipal elections, 280
nontariff trade barriers, 507
normal trade relations (NTR) status, 548–549
Norris, Pippa, 313
North American Free Trade Agreement (NAFTA), 549
North Atlantic Treaty Organization (NATO), 562, 567, 571
North Korea, 549, 555, 564, 574
not-in-my-backyard syndrome (NIMBY), 518
NOW. *See* National Organization for Women
NRA. *See* National Rifle Association
NSA. *See* National Security Administration
NSC. *See* National Security Council
NTR. *See* normal trade relations status
nuclear option (debate maneuver), 377, 471
nuclear weapons, 565–566, 572, 573*f*
NWSA. *See* National Women's Suffrage Association

O

OASI. *See* Old-Age and Survivors Insurance Program
Obama, Barack. *See also* Affordable Care Act of 2010
   approval ratings, 198*f*, 209, 400, 412, 412*f*
   birth certificate, 352
   birth control controversy, 14
   cabinet, 433*f*
   campaign advisor, 287
   on campaign funding, 222
   as chief of state, 401*f*
   as commander in chief, 399–400
   Consumer Financial Protection Board, 505, 505*f*
   on detainees, 126
   "Don't Ask, Don't Tell," 371, 399
   economic policy, 492, 509, 509*f*
   education projects, 107, 107*f*
   elections, 194, 196–197, 196*f*, 197*f*, 257, 295*f*, 296
   executive order, 409–410, 417–418, 462, 462*f*
   foreign policy, 571
   at G-8 meeting, 563*f*
   gender gap and, 198, 198*f*
   influence of, 196
   inherent powers, 409
   judicial nominations, 469, 470, 471, 477
   NSA surveillance, 132
   "One Million Strong for Barack," 343
   opposition to, 293, 377, 378
   power of, 417–418
   public opinions and, 208
   on same-sex marriage, 157, 157*f*
   selfie at Mandela funeral, 343, 344*f*
   senate term, 385

skepticism, of Internet, 352
Skirky, Clay, 337
slander, 130, 352
Slate, 317
slavery
    in Constitution, 158
    as Constitutional Convention issue, 47–48
    Madison on, 47
    modern, 162
    in United States, 158–161, 160*f*
smartphones and mobile phones, 335, 338*f*, 347, 349
Smeal, Eleanor, 198, 198*f*
Smith, Adam, 490
Smith Act of 1940, 128
Smoot-Hawley Tariff, 559
SNAP. *See* Supplemental Nutrition Assistance Program
SNCC. *See* Student Nonviolent Coordinating Committee
snopes.com, 345
Snowden, Edward, 133, 350, 351*f*
Snyder v. Phelps, 130*f*
social capital, 218–219, 219*f*, 276, 277*f*
social class
    interest group members, 223–224
    political party affiliation and, 250
social contract, 12, 13, 16
social contract theory, 13
social insurance programs, 522
social insurance taxes, 497
socialism, 17*t*, 18–19
Socialist Party, 264
socialization. *See* political socialization
social media. *See* social networking sites
social networking sites
    as activism tool, 348
    in civic discourse, 341, 342
    defined, 334
    as new media, 316
    online interest group membership, 223*f*, 224
    privacy rights and, 140
social regulation, 439, 504, 505–506
Social Security
    benefits, 529–530, 530*f*
    entitlement to, 522
    establishment of, 94–95
    revenue from, 497
    spending on, 501
Social Security Disability Insurance (SSDI), 530
societal conflict, 372, 372*t*
Society of American Indians, 175
soft money loophole, 252
solidary incentives, 224
Solis, Hilda, 404
Somalia, 552
Sons of Liberty, 37, 38
SOPA. *See* Stop Online Piracy Act
Sotomayor, Sonia, 469, 469*f*, 470, 479
Souter, David, 470

South African elections, 301
South Dakota v. Dole, 104, 104*f*
Southeast Asia Treaty Organization (SEATO), 562
Southern Christian Leadership Conference (SCLC), 165–166
"Southern Manifesto," 478
South Korea, 564
sovereign territory, 9
sovereignty, popular, 13
Soviet Union, 561–566
Spanish-American War ("newspaper war"), 315–316, 316*f*, 558
Speaker of the House, 378
special courts, 467
special interests. *See* interest groups
SpeechNow.org v. Federal Election Commission, 238
speedy trial, 123*t*, 142
spending policy, 498
splinter parties, 264–265
spoils system, 255
SpongeBob SquarePants, 314
SSDI. *See* Social Security Disability Insurance
SSI. *See* Supplemental Security Income
Stafford, Rick, 248*f*
Stalin, Joseph, 563, 563*f*
Stamp Act of 1765, 37, 315
standing committees, 374
standing to sue, 159
"Stand Your Ground" laws, 124*f*, 125
Stanton, Edwin, 418
Stanton, Elizabeth Cady, 169, 171
Starr, Kenneth, 418*f*
"Star Wars." *See* strategic defense initiative
State Children's Health Insurance Program (SCHIP), 534
State Department, 552–553. 552*f*
state governments
    Bill of Rights and, 52, 121–122, 123*t*
    concurrent powers, 90–91, 91*f*
    constitutions, 39–41, 89, 96–97
    federal grants to, 102–104, 102*f*, 108
    intergovernmental relations, 97–101
    judicial federalism, 96–97, 97*f*
    local governments within, 88, 89*f*
    national obligations to, 95*t*
    political parties in, 253
    preemption of, 105, 435
    reserved powers, 92, 93*f*
    sovereignty, 92–93
    state-to-state obligations, 95–96
    state-to-state relations, 49
state laws
    Bill of Rights incorporation, 121–122, 123*t*
    electoral law variations, 280, 281
    gun law variations, 124*f*
state political parties, 252
states' rights movement, 109
States' Rights Party, 264–265

statutory powers, 409
Steffens, Lincoln, 316
Stewart, John, 193, 312
Stewart, Potter, 143
stimulus package (ARRA), 492
stock market crash (1929), 559
Stone, Lucy, 170
Stone v. Graham, 136*t*
Stonewall Rebellion, 157
Stop Online Piracy Act (SOPA), 222, 345, 353
Stowe, Harriet Beecher, 159
strategic arms limitation talks (SALT I and II), 565–566
strategic defense initiative (SDI or "Star Wars"), 566
strategic model of decision making, 474
Strategic Petroleum Reserve, 527
stratified sampling, 204
straw poll, defined, 201
strict scrutiny test, 155, 173
Strong, Cecily, 311*f*
Stuart, Gilbert, 365*f*
student loans, 522
Student Nonviolent Coordinating Committee (SNCC), 165–166
subcommittees, 375
substantive representation, 470
suffrage, 169–171, 171*f*, 255
Sugar Act of 1764, 37
Sullivan, Mark, 352
Summer Project (1964), 166, 168*f*
sunset clause, 446
Sunshine Act of 1976, 444–445
sunshine laws, 444
Super-Duper Tuesday, 279–280
Superfund law, 525
super PACs, 238, 288. *See also* political action committees (PACs)
superpowers, defined, 560
Super Tuesday, 278–280
Supplemental Nutrition Assistance Program (SNAP), 522
Supplemental Security Income (SSI), 530
supply-side economics, 492
supremacy clause, 44, 50, 91, 94
Supreme Court. *See also* judges, federal; *specific cases; specific issues*
    Bill of Rights incorporation, 121–122, 123*t*
    constitutional interpretation, 49, 53, 55, 90, 93–95
    decision-making process, 472–474, 473*f*
    defined, 460
    establishment of, 49
    in federal court system, 468
    First Amendment rulings, 126–129
    justices, 468, 469*f*
    opinion writing, 474–475
    Roberts Court, 479–480
    role in congressional power, 368
    then and now, 469*f*, 474